THE OXFORD HANDBOOK OF

# THE GLOBAL
# STAGE MUSICAL

# THE OXFORD HANDBOOK OF

# THE GLOBAL STAGE MUSICAL

*Edited by*
ROBERT GORDON
*and*
OLAF JUBIN

OXFORD
UNIVERSITY PRESS

# OXFORD
UNIVERSITY PRESS

Oxford University Press is a department of the University of Oxford. It furthers
the University's objective of excellence in research, scholarship, and education
by publishing worldwide. Oxford is a registered trade mark of Oxford University
Press in the UK and certain other countries.

Published in the United States of America by Oxford University Press
198 Madison Avenue, New York, NY 10016, United States of America.

© Oxford University Press 2023

All rights reserved. No part of this publication may be reproduced, stored in
a retrieval system, or transmitted, in any form or by any means, without the
prior permission in writing of Oxford University Press, or as expressly permitted
by law, by license, or under terms agreed with the appropriate reproduction
rights organization. Inquiries concerning reproduction outside the scope of the
above should be sent to the Rights Department, Oxford University Press, at the
address above.

You must not circulate this work in any other form
and you must impose this same condition on any acquirer.

Library of Congress Cataloging-in-Publication Data
Names: Gordon, Robert, 1951 November 28– editor. | Jubin, Olaf, editor.
Title: The Oxford handbook of the global stage musical /
[edited by] Robert Gordon and Olaf Jubin.
Description: [1.] | New York : Oxford University Press, 2023. |
Includes bibliographical references and index.
Identifiers: LCCN 2023017616 (print) | LCCN 2023017617 (ebook) |
ISBN 9780190909734 (hardback) | ISBN 9780190909765 |
ISBN 9780190909758 (epub)
Subjects: LCSH: Musicals—History and criticism. | Musical theater—History
and criticism. | Music and globalization. | Theater and globalization.
Classification: LCC ML2054 .O94 2023 (print) | LCC ML2054 (ebook) |
DDC 782.1/4—dc23/eng/20230510
LC record available at https://lccn.loc.gov/2023017616
LC ebook record available at https://lccn.loc.gov/2023017617

DOI: 10.1093/oxfordhb/9780190909734.001.0001

Printed by Integrated Books International, United States of America

In loving memory of Naomi Lobbenberg (1945–2019), the best of friends

# CONTENTS

| | |
|---|---|
| *Acknowledgements* | xi |
| *Biographies* | xiii |

Introduction: The Stage Musical as Global Phenomenon      1
    ROBERT GORDON AND OLAF JUBIN

## PART I. THEORY AND PRAXIS

1. Theatre and Globalisation: Theoretical and Historical Dimensions      45
    CHRISTOPHER BALME

2. Musical Translation and Its Multiple Challenges      66
    EVA ESPASA

3. Training for Writers and Performers      89
    ZACHARY DUNBAR

## PART II. UNCHARTED TERRITORIES

4. 'Merrily She Waltzes Along': *Die lustige Witwe* (*The Merry Widow*)
    as Global Hit      119
    JOHN KOEGEL

5. Musical Travails in the British Empire: South Africa and Australia      158
    DAVID PEIMER

6. My Un-Fair Lady? Celebrity Producer Lars Schmidt and the
    Postwar International Success of Broadway Shows      190
    DIRK GINDT

## PART III. GLOBAL PRODUCTION ENTITIES

7. Paving the Way: Cameron Mackintosh and the Development and
    Impact of the Global Musical      217
    RICHARD M. SHANNON

viii    CONTENTS

8. Extending the Brand to the Stage: The Walt Disney Company       245
   SANNE THIERENS AND JEROEN VAN WIJHE

9. Going Dutch: Stage Entertainment       266
   JONAS MENZE

## PART IV. GOOD NEIGHBOURS?

10. Canadian Musicals and the Commercial Theatre of Broadway and
    the West End       291
    MEL ATKEY

11. Musicals in Mexico: Borders and Bridges       316
    EMILIO MÉNDEZ

12. Studies in Contrast: Chile and Brazil       345
    TIAGO MUNDIM

## PART V. POPULAR IN BRITAIN

13. That Special Relationship: Dolores Gray, Mary Martin, and
    Elaine Stritch on the Postwar London Stage       371
    ROBERT GORDON

14. The Most Beloved American Musical: *Guys and Dolls* in London       403
    JOHN SNELSON

15. Beloved in London, Ignored in New York: *Starlight Express* and
    *We Will Rock You*       429
    DAVID COTTIS

## PART VI. POPULAR IN GERMANY/AUSTRIA?

16. Kurt Weill's American Works in Twenty-First-Century Germany       451
    JUDITH WIEMERS

17. 'Ev'ry Hotsy Totsy Nazi Stand and Cheer': Cultural Sensitivity to
    Musicals about the Third Reich       478
    NILS GROSCH AND SUSANNE SCHEIBLHOFER

CONTENTS     ix

18. Between *Starlight Express* and *My Fair Lady*, Frank Wildhorn and Martin Lingnau: Musicals in Contemporary German-Language Theatre     507
    FRÉDÉRIC DÖHL

## PART VII.  POPULAR IN EAST ASIA

19. The Dream Machine: Takarazuka, Japan's All-Female Musical Theatre Extravaganza     553
    BUD COLEMAN

20. The Development Process and Characteristics of the South Korean Musical Market     570
    YONGMIN KWON, HYEYOUNG RA, AND KANGJOO CHO

21. The Path and Development of the Chinese Musical     594
    CAI FANGTIAN

## PART VIII.  SONDHEIM ABROAD

22. *A Little Night Music* in Sweden     613
    RENATE STRIDH

23. *Pacific Overtures*: Varied Perspectives     648
    GARY PERLMAN

24. From Fleet Street to Broadway and Back: Stages in the Career of Sweeney Todd     665
    ROBERT LAWSON-PEEBLES

## PART IX.  NATIONAL GENRES OF MUSICAL THEATRE IN WESTERN EUROPE

25. The French *spectacle musical*     701
    LUCA CERCHIARI

26. The German/Austrian 'Drama Musical', or 'I Sing Alone'     719
    OLAF JUBIN

27. The Swedish Folk Musical 758
MIKAEL STRÖMBERG

# PART X. NATIONAL TRADITIONS OF MUSICAL THEATRE IN EASTERN EUROPE

28. 'They Dated out of Pure Love': A Brief History of the
Czech Infatuation with the Musical 781
JAN ŠOTKOVSKÝ

29. Polish Musical Theatre since the 1960s 808
ALEKSANDRA ZAJAC-KIEDYSZ

30. Entertainment, Propaganda, and/or Resistance in Staging
Musicals in Hungary after World War II—*István, a király*
(*Stephen, the King*, 1983) and Beyond 825
ZOLTÁN IMRE

# PART XI. OUTLOOK, OR THE ROAD AHEAD

31. A *Bran Nue Dae*? Decolonising the Musical Theatre Curriculum 863
PAMELA KARANTONIS

32. 'Who Tells Your Story': A Reflection on Race-Conscious Casting
and the Musical 893
HANNAH THURAISINGAM ROBBINS

33. 'Superboy and the Invisible Girl': The Exclusion of the Female Voice
from Global Musical Theatre 914
GRACE BARNES

*Index* 933

# ACKNOWLEDGEMENTS

THIS is the second handbook on musical theatre we have jointly edited for the Oxford University Press series: many thanks to the commissioning editor, Norman Hirschy, for his far-sightedness in agreeing to work on what must at the time have seemed the most eccentric proposal, which recent world events have rendered a topic of surprising urgency, and to Oxford University Press's assistant editors Lauralee Yeary and Rachel Ruisart, who have once again ensured a most constructive collaboration.

We owe a great debt to the various contributors, as many of them helped find and secure the illustrations which enhance this volume. In a project as internationally situated as this, their assistance has been invaluable.

The many images in this volume were photographed by Akihito Abe, Massimo Barbaglia, Clive Barda, Peter Bischoff, Àgata Casanova, Rowena Chowdrey, Matt Crockett, Harry Croner, Tomasz Degórski, Alain Dejean, Marcos Delgado; Grzegorz Haremza, John Haynes, Petra Hellberg, Birgit Hupfelt, Béla Ilovszky, Thomas Jauk, Scott Kowalchyk, Jef Kratochvil, Franziska Krug, Brigitte Lacombe, Michael Le Poer Trench, Grzegorz Lewandowski, Manuel Litran, Joan Marcus, Leonel Martinez, Brendan McDermid, Brannäs Mikael, Luc Monsaert, Alastair Muir, Harry Naltchayan, Nigel Norrington, J. C. Parker, Johan Persson, John Phillips, Kylie Anee Picket, Cata Portin, Marty Reichenthal, Eric Roberts, David Ruano, Kevern Sandalls, Martin Skoog, Vilém Sochůrek, Pawel Sosnowski, Joakim Strömholm, Martha Swope, Deen van Meer, Robert Wallace, Masahiko Yako, and Georg Zimbel.

Our thanks goes to the following copyright holders, both individuals and companies, for permission to use photographs: Christopher Balme, Veronika Hypšová, Tino Kratochvil, and Tiago Mundim as well as Alamy Stock Photo; Allstar Picture Library Ltd.; ArenaPal; Cameron Mackintosh Ltd, Disney Enterprises; EMK Musical Company; Fortepan; Getty Images; Kanagawa Arts Theatre (KAAT); KTV; Kulturhuset Stadteaterns arkiv, Stockholm; Landesbühne Sachsen, Radebeul; Marmalade Ghent 2016; MTVA Archive; Nasjonalbiblioteket Norge; New National Theatre Tokyo; New York Public Library for the Performing Arts; Photostage; Shubert Archive; Shutterstock; and Ullstein Bild.

Special thanks must go to Gary Perlman, who graciously stepped in to analyse the first Japanese production of *Pacific Overtures* when the author we had originally contracted went incommunicado; we couldn't be happier with the replacement. We are also extremely grateful to Yongmin Kwon, Hyeyoung Ra, and Kangjoo Cho from the Arts Council Korea (ARKO), who took over at very short notice from a

xii   ACKNOWLEDGEMENTS

contributor who had fallen ill. It is a testament to their professionalism that they delivered a thoroughly researched essay in such a short time.

As always, our love and gratitude go to Janet, Britta, Susan, Oliver, Joshua, Amira, Helga, Godfrey, Jacqui, Kathy, Harry, and Fjara for their encouragement and support.

# BIOGRAPHIES

**Mel Atkey** (1958–2022) was a finalist in the Musical of the Year competition in Aarhus, Denmark, and his work has been short-listed for the Vivian Ellis Prize, the Quest for New Musicals, the Ken Hill Prize, and Musical Stairs. His first musical, *Shikara*, was produced on the radio in Canada. Mel was commissioned to write songs for CBC Radio and was a member of the Guild of Canadian Musical Theatre Writers' Lehman Engel Workshop. He made his New York debut in April 2001 with an off-off-Broadway showcase of *O Pioneers!*, with a book by Robert Sickinger. Their second musical, *A Little Princess*, was presented at Wings Theatre in New York in 2003, and his two-character musical *Perfect Timing*, for which he wrote the book as well as the music and lyrics, was showcased as part of Greenwich Theatre (London)'s Musical Futures series. It was produced as a film in 2021. His book *Broadway North: The Dream of a Canadian Musical Theatre* was published by Natural Heritage in 2006. His working follow-up, *A Million Miles from Broadway: Musical Theatre beyond New York and London* was first published in 2012, and in 2019 he published a greatly expanded revised edition. In 2016 he earned his master of arts degree in musical theatre from Goldsmiths, University of London.

**Christopher Balme** holds the chair in theatre studies at Ludwig-Maximilians-Universität, Munich. His publications include *Decolonizing the Stage: Theatrical Syncretism and Postcolonial Drama* (Clarendon Press, 1999); *Pacific Performances: Theatricality and Cross-Cultural Encounter in the South Seas* (Palgrave Macmillan, 2007); *Cambridge Introduction to Theatre Studies* (Cambridge University Press, 2008); *The Theatrical Public Sphere* (Cambridge University Press, 2014); and *The Globalization of Theatre 1870–1930: The Theatrical Networks of Maurice E. Bandmann* (Cambridge University Press, 2020). He is the principal investigator of the ERC Advanced Grant 'Developing Theatre: Building Expert Networks for Theatre in Emerging Countries after 1945'.

**Grace Barnes** is a lecturer in musical theatre at the University of Plymouth, UK. She obtained her master of science degree in gender studies from the University of Edinburgh as well as an master of arts in non-fiction writing and a doctorate from the University of Technology Sydney. During her doctoral studies she was awarded the Clare Burton Scholarship (2015) for research into gender equity. Grace was the associate director on the Australian productions of *War Horse*, *West Side Story*, *Guys and Dolls*, *Sunset Boulevard*, and *Fiddler on the Roof*, as well as on the West End premiere of *The Witches of Eastwick* and the national tour of *Martin Guerre*. She wrote the libretto for two new musicals, *Nevermore* (2007) and *Crossing* (2013), both of which premiered at Signature Theatre in Arlington, Virginia, USA. Grace is the author of *Her Turn on Stage:*

*The Role of Women in Musical Theatre* (McFarland, 2015) and *National Identity and the British Musical: From 'Blood Brothers' to 'Cinderella'* (Methuen Drama, 2022).

**Luca Cerchiari** has a PhD in ethnomusicology from the University of Graz. He teaches history of popular music at IULM University—Milan, where he also convenes the MA in music publishing and production. His main areas of research are African American music, discography, and popular music. Among his many publications are *Jazz and Europe* (Northeastern University Press, 2012; co-editor), *Miles Davis* (Feltrinelli, 2013), *On Record* (Odoya, 2014), *Around Jazz* (Bompiani, 2016), *A History of Musical Comedy* (Bompiani, 2017), *Jazz and Fascism* (Mimesis, 2019), *Mina* (Mondadori, 2020), and *Scott Joplin's 'Treemonisha'* (Mimesis 2020). For Mimesis, he edits the book series 'Contemporary Music'. www.lucacerchiari.it.

**Kangjoo Cho** majored in public administration at the Catholic University of Korea, where he also earned master's and doctorate degrees. He has served as a senior researcher at the Institute for Government Innovation and Productivity at the Catholic University and now works as an associate research fellow on the Arts Council Korea (ARKO) in the Policy and Evaluation Department. Cho has published a number of papers, including 'A Study on the Performance of Online Culture and Arts Platforms' (2019) as well as 'A Study on the Relationship between Fiscal Decentralization and Available Financial Resources in Korean Local Government (2018)'. kjcho@arko.or.kr.

**Bud Coleman** is the Roe Green Professor of Theatre and the Associate Dean of Faculty Success in the College of Arts and Sciences at the University of Colorado Boulder. A former dancer with Les Ballets Trockadero de Monte Carlo, Fort Worth Ballet, and Ballet Austin, Coleman has directed and choreographed many musicals. In 2008 he directed and choreographed the musical *Company* in Vladivostok, Russia (with the assistance of a US State Department grant), was selected to be a 2009–2010 Fulbright lecturer in Japan, and in the spring of 2017 directed the Thai premiere of *Fiddler on the Roof*. Recent publications include essays in *The Cambridge Companion to the Musical*, *The Great North American Stage Directors*, and *iBroadway: Musical Theatre in the Digital Age*. With Judith Sebesta he co-edited *Women in American Musical Theatre: Essays on Lyricists, Writers, Arrangers, Choreographers, Designers, Producers, and Performance Artists*. He is also the co-author (with Pamyla Stiehl) of *Backstage Pass: A Survey of American Musical Theater*.

**David Cottis** is senior lecturer in scriptwriting and programme leader for BA Film at Middlesex University. He received his PhD from Birkbeck College. He is also a theatre director, writer, lyricist, and dramaturge, most recently having worked with James Martin Charlton on the horror play *Black Stone* for Just Some Theatre Company. His five-actor adaptation of *Oliver Twist* was taken on national tour by the Love and Madness Company; his short plays *Cash* and *Semolina* were seen at the Royal Court Theatre, London; and his opera libretto *She Stops at Costa's* was short-listed for the English National Opera's 'New Voices' project. He has edited *A Dirty Broth* and *A Ladder of Words*, two anthologies of twentieth-century Welsh plays in English for the Parthian

Press, and wrote the chapter on Anthony Newley and Leslie Bricusse for *The Oxford Handbook of the British Musical*.

**Frédéric Döhl** holds PhDs in both musicology and law. He currently works as strategy consultant to the board of directors at the German National Library in Leipzig, Germany. As Privatdozent, he also teaches courses in musicology as well as dance, film, and theatre studies at the Free University Berlin, Germany. His main research interests are adaptation and borrowing, music journalism, genre history and theory, copyright law, and digital humanities. He has published six monographs: on barbershop harmony as an invented tradition (Franz Steiner Verlag, 2009); André Previn and musical versatility (Franz Steiner Verlag, 2012); mashup/digital musical borrowing and copyright law (Transkript, 2016); the sociology and aesthetics of the classical piano quintet (Transcript, 2019); the strategy of the German Government for the digitization of the public culture sector (Transkript, 2021); and the new copyright regime concerning adaptation (Transcript, 2022). He has also co-edited eight volumes on topics such as borrowing in the contemporary arts, contemporary American opera, music and narration, and genre theory. He regularly teaches and writes about contemporary American musical theatre and its reception in Germany.

**Zachary Dunbar** is associate professor of theatre and Performing Arts Research Convenor, Faculty of Fine Arts and Music, University of Melbourne. His research interests include performing arts training, musical theatre, classical reception and Greek tragedy, and practice-as-research methodologies. His most recent publication, co-authored with Stephe Harrop, is *Greek Tragedy and the Contemporary Actor* (Palgrave-Macmillan, 2018). As a freelance artist, he initially trained as a concert pianist in the United States (Rollins College, Yale University) before completing his studies as a Fulbright scholar at the Royal College of Music, London. Subsequently, he pursued an interdisciplinary career between theatre and music. In the United Kingdom, he created and directed original works across several genres, including radio drama (BBC Radio 4), Greek tragedy, musical theatre, Beijing opera, post-dramatic soundscape theatre, and dance theatre, with productions at the Pleasance Theatre, Bloomsbury Theatre, Brighton Underbelly, Embassy Theatre, Camden People's Theatre, several Edinburgh-fringe productions (Fringe-First nominated), and the prestigious Jungehunde festival (Denmark). He taught at the Royal Central School of Speech and Drama (London) and has given acting-through-song workshops in Australia, Chile, New York, and London. His recent original theatre works in Melbourne include *Florida* (La Mama) and *AntigoneX* (Theatreworks).

**Eva Espasa** is a professor at Universitat de Vic—Universitat Central de Catalunya (UVic-UCC), where she teaches audiovisual and theatre translation at the undergraduate and postgraduate levels. Her research focuses on theatre translation, audiovisual translation, and gender studies, areas in which she has lectured and published extensively. Espasa is the author of a monograph on theatre and musical translation in Catalonia (*La traducció dalt de l'escenari*, Eumo, 2001). She also co-edited the volume *Translating Audiovisuals* *in a Kaleidoscope of Languages* (Peter Lang, 2019). Her research on theatre and audiovisual translation has been published by international companies such as Routledge, John Benjamins, and Saint Jerome, and in academic journals such as *The Translator, The Interpreter and Translator Trainer*, and *Trans*. She is coordinator of the interdisciplinary research group TRACTE (Audiovisual Translation, Communication and Place) and has co-coordinated the TRAFILM research project on the translation of multilingual films. She has also organised research symposiums at UVic-UCC on translation and its connection with music (2014), accessibility (2011), film (2008), and theatre (2000). https://orcid.org/0000-0002-0463-9317.

**Cai Fangtian** is currently an associate professor in the School of Foreign Languages at Renmin University of China, where she teaches playwriting and English performance. She studied English literature and obtained her master of arts from Beijing Foreign Studies University; she then continued her doctoral studies in the Department of Dramatic Literature at the Central Academy of Drama. She has been a visiting scholar in the Department of Theatre and Performance at Goldsmiths, University of London, focusing on musical theatre studies. Her research interests include contemporary English drama, English musical theatre, Chinese drama, and traditional Chinese opera. She is a member of the International Association of Theatre Critics, China Section. She has published a number of scholarly articles in acclaimed national journals and is the author of the Chinese book *The Dramatic Art of Harold Pinter* (China Renmin University Press, 2016). She has participated in the Project for Disseminating Chinese Operatic Dramas Overseas and at present is working on the English translation and adaptation of the traditional Chinese opera *The Peony Pavilion*.

**Dirk Gindt** is a professor of theatre studies in the Department of Culture and Aesthetics at Stockholm University. He has published over twenty referred journal articles and book chapters on Swedish, Canadian, and French theatre. He is the co-editor of the volume *Viral Dramaturgies: HIV and AIDS in Performance in the Twenty-First Century* (Palgrave Macmillan, 2018), the author of the monograph *Tennessee Williams in Sweden and France, 1945–1965: Cultural Translations, Sexual Anxieties and Racial Fantasies* (Bloomsbury, 2019), and the co-editor of *Berätta, överleva, inte drunkna*, which explores anti-racism, decolonization, and migration in contemporary Swedish theatre (Atlas, 2022). Financed by a four-year grant from the Swedish Research Council, Gindt's latest project, analyses indigenous performance cultures in the Arctic and is conducted in consultation and close dialogue with Giron Sámi Teáhter in Kiruna/Giron, Sweden.

**Robert Gordon** is Professor of Theatre and the director of the Pinter Centre for Performance and Creative Writing at Goldsmiths, University of London, where in 2003 he introduced the first European masters degree in musical theatre for producers and writers. He is author of *The Purpose of Playing: Modern Acting Theory in Perspective* (University of Michigan Press, 2006), *Harold Pinter's Theatre of Power* (University of Michigan Press, 2012), and, with Olaf Jubin and Millie Taylor, *British Musical Theatre since 1950* (Bloomsbury, 2016). Edited collections include *The Oxford Handbook of*

*Sondheim Studies* (Oxford University Press, 2014) and, with Olaf Jubin, *The Oxford Handbook of the British Musical* (Oxford University Press, 2016). His monograph *The Theatre of Kander and Ebb* (Methuen) will be in print in March 2024. Robert has worked internationally as an actor, director, and playwright and is author of *Red Earth* (1985) and *Waterloo Road* (Young Vic Theatre, 1987). In 2012 he devised and co-directed *Pinter: In Other Rooms* for a tour of Eastern Europe and directed the European première of Kander and Ebb's *Steel Pier* at Na Zabradli in Brno, while his musical with Nick Hutson, *Five Children and It*, received a professional workshop performance in 2015. He is currently engaged as a writer and actor in *Shylock Speaks*, which premiered in February 2020, and in 2018 he introduced a bachelor of arts in musical theatre programme at Goldsmiths.

**Nils Grosch** holds the chair in musicology at the University of Salzburg, Austria, where he is also head of the Department of Art History, Musicology, and Dance Studies. He earned his doctorate at the University of Freiburg im Breisgau with a dissertation titled 'Die Musik der Neuen Sachlichkeit' and completed his habilitation at the University of Basel with a dissertation titled 'Lied und Medienwechsel im 16. Jahrhundert'. His major research interests are music and migration and the popular musical theatre. https:// orcid.org/0000-0002-7145-5315.

**Zoltán Imre** received his doctorate from Queen Mary College, University of London, in 2005 and is now an associate professor in the Department of Comparative Literature and Culture, Eötvös University, Budapest. His monographs include *Színház és teatralitás* (*Theatre and Theatricality*; Veszprémi Egyetemi Kiadó, 2003); *A színház színpadra állításai* (*Staging Theatre: Theories, Histories, and Alternatives*; Rácó, 2009); *A nemzet színpadra állításai* (*Staging the Nation: The Changing Concept of the Hungarian National Theatre from 1837 until Today*; Rácó, 2013); and *Az idegen színpadra állításai: A Magyar színház inter- és intrakulturális kapcsolatai* (*Staging the Other: The Inter- and Intracultural Connections of the Hungarian Theatre*; Rácó, 2018). He has edited *Átvilágítás: A magyar színház európai kontextusban* (*Transillumination: Hungarian Theatre in a European Context*, 2004) as well as *Alternatívok és alternatívák* (*Alternative Theatre Histories*, 2008) and was the co-editor of *Színház és szociológia határán* (*On the border of Theatre and Sociology*, 2005). In addition, he has published various articles on Hungarian and European theatre.

**Olaf Jubin** is currently the primary researcher on a four-year project funded by FWF (Austria) at the University of Salzburg on how musicals represent European history. He also is an associate lecturer in the bachelor's and master's of arts programmes in musical theatre at Goldsmiths, University of London. For seventeen years he worked at Regent's University London, where he was a professor of musical theatre and media studies. He earned his PhD from the Ruhr-Universität Bochum, Germany, and has written and co-edited several books on the mass media and musical theatre, including a study of the German dubbing and subtitling of Hollywood musicals and a comparative analysis of reviews of the musicals of Stephen Sondheim and Andrew Lloyd Webber. He

xviii    BIOGRAPHIES

is co-author of *British Musical Theatre since 1950* (Bloomsbury, 2016) and co-editor of *The Oxford Handbook of the British Musical* (Oxford University Press, 2016). In 2017 his monograph on *Into the Woods* appeared as part of the Routledge Fourth Wall series. He recently edited *Paris and the Musical: The City of Light on Stage and Screen* (Routledge, 2021) and is preparing a book on the dramaturgy and lyrics of Tim Rice. https://orcid.org/0000-0002-0200-9813.

**Pamela Karantonis** is Head of the Theatre and Performance Department (TaP) and a joint convenor of the musical theatre programme at Goldsmiths, University of London. She is also a member of the Royal Opera House's Engender Network and the UK's Musical Theatre Network. From 2010 to 2014 she jointly convened the Music Theatre Working Group of the International Federation for Theatre Research. Publications include editorships of and contributions to *Opera Indigene: Re/presenting First Nations and Indigenous Cultures* (2011) and *Cathy Berberian: Pioneer of Contemporary Vocality* (2014). Her most recent publication features in *The Female Voice in the Twentieth Century: Material, Symbolic and Aesthetic Dimensions* (Routledge, 2021). https://orcid.org/0000-0002-4171-1066.

**John Koegel** is a professor of musicology and the graduate advisor in the School of Music at California State University, Fullerton. He conducts research in American and Mexican musical topics, particularly musical theatre, and music in the context of ethnicity and immigration. Koegel is the recipient of a National Endowment for the Humanities research fellowship and of research grants from the American Council of Learned Societies and American Philosophical Society for his work on immigrant musical theater. His current in-progress books have the working titles 'Musical Theater in Immigrant America, 1840–1940' and 'Musical Theater in Mexican Los Angeles, 1840–1940'. His musical edition *Mexican-American Music from Southern California, circa 1830–1930: The Lummis Cylinder Collection and Other Sources* will be published as part of the Music of the United States of America series (A-R Editions). Koegel's previous book, *Music in German Immigrant Theater: New York City, 1840–1940* (University of Rochester Press, 2009) was given the 2011 Irving Lowens Book Award of the Society for American Music. His articles and reviews have appeared in journals such as the *Journal of the American Musicological Society, Journal of the Society for American Music, American Music, Latin-American Music Review, Journal of the Royal Musical Association, Historia Mexicana,* and *Heterofonía.*

**Yongmin Kwon** obtained a doctorate in public administration from Inha University in 2014. Since then, he has participated in research projects on various policy areas, including culture and the arts, information services, agriculture, social welfare, and public organizations. Since 2016 he has served as an associate research fellow in the Policy and Evaluation Department on the Arts Council Korea (ARKO) and has participated in various task forces to respond to ARKO's pending issues and to establish future strategies. In 2019 he participated in the establishment of ARKO Vision 2030, organising a seminar called 'The Fourth Industrial Revolution and Art' with experts from various fields to explore the direction future art-support policies should take, as well as a forum on how to appoint council members. Kwon recently created a web magazine that can quickly deliver the latest news on art-policy issues surrounding ARKO; its ultimate goal is to allow various stakeholders to participate in the discussion process on art-policy issues and to encourage new online discourse and criticism related to art. Kwon's current research focuses on social change and future art-support policies following the Fourth Industrial Revolution, and how the latter impacts technology, labour, employment, and leisure life. Another area of interest involves the project 'The Achievements, Problems and Future Strategies of the Council System', which was initiated in 2005; it focuses on the composition, role, and vision of councils, as well as on the relationship and role division between the Ministry of Culture, Sports, and Tourism and ARKO. Contact: yminarko@arko.or.kr.

**Robert Lawson-Peebles** has worked at Oxford University, Princeton University, the University of Aberdeen, and finally Exeter University, where he is now an honorary senior research fellow. He has been a Leverhulme emeritus fellow and was awarded a number of other fellowships, for instance from the Salzburg Seminar and the American Council of Learned Societies. He has published three books on the cultural history of the American environment, two on earlier writing about America, and articles on subjects ranging from Sir Walter Raleigh to the relationship of ideology and the arts. His interest in transatlantic music led to *Approaches to the American Musical* (University of Exeter Press, 1996) and contributions to the *Oxford Handbooks* on Stephen Sondheim (Oxford University Press, 2012) and the British musical (Oxford University Press, 2016). 'Paris and the Curse of Chicago', on Sondheim's *Sunday in the Park with George*, appeared in the collection edited by Olaf Jubin titled *Paris in the Musical: The City of Light on Stage and Screen* (Routledge, 2021). He has also recently written essays about twentieth-century versions of *The Beggar's Opera* and about the reception of jazz in Britain.

**Emilio Méndez** is an associate professor of theatre studies and dramaturgy at the National Autonomous University of Mexico (UNAM). He has worked as a director and a translator. His research interests include the reception, adaptation, and reterritorialization of musicals in Mexico, and the translation of lyrics into Spanish. He has published works on the history of theatre in Mexico and on Mexican training programmes for theatre. He presents regularly at the yearly Song, Stage, and Screen conference and received the 2015 National University Distinction for Young Academics in the field of artistic creation and cultural dissemination.

**Jonas Menze** studied media and music at the Hanover University of Music, Drama, and Media. Between 2008 and 2012 he joined a variety of musical theatre productions as production manager and production assistant. In 2017 he completed his doctoral degree in musicology at the University of Salzburg with a thesis on the framework conditions and production processes of German-language musicals, for which he had received a DOC fellowship from the Austrian Academy of Sciences (ÖAW). From 2016 to 2021 he worked as a scientific assistant at the Institute for Research on Musical Ability (IBFM) at Paderborn University. Since 2021 he has been employed by the Quality Assurance Department of the Westphalian University of Applied Sciences in Gelsenkirchen. Besides popular musical theatre, his research interests include empirical musicology, audience research and fan studies, the development of musical expertise, and lifelong learning in music as well as citizen science.

**Tiago Mundim** is a postdoctoral research fellow at Universidade de Brasília (UnB) and currently works in the performing arts department as a lecturer in acting and voice. In his dissertation he researched the influence of technologies on the teaching, learning, and performance processes of the actor-singer-dancer, and he spent two terms at Royal Central School of Speech and Drama (University of London) to complement his research. For ten years he studied musical theatre at the ETMB School of Musical Theatre in Brasília and was on the institution's faculty between 2014 and 2017. He has worked on more than fifty musical theatre productions both as performer and director. He directed the new Brazilian musicals *Domingo no parque* and *Quem um dia irá dizer*; as a performer he has starred in *Les Misérables* (as Jean Valjean) and *We Will Rock You* (as Galileo). https://linktr.ee/TiagoMundim.

**David Peimer** is a professor of theatre and creative writing at Edge Hill University, UK, where he also teaches musical theatre. Born in South Africa, he graduated from Columbia University, which he attended on a Fulbright scholarship. His publications include his edited book of plays *Armed Response: Plays from South Africa* (University of Chicago Press, 2009), which includes his play *Armed Response*, as well as chapters in Jonathan Pitches and Stefan Aquilina, eds., *Stanislavsky in the World: The System and Its Transformations across Continents* (Bloomsbury, 2017); Phillip B. Zarrilli, T. Sasitharan, and Anuradha Kapur, eds., *Intercultural Acting and Performer Training* (Routledge, 2019); Kim Wiltshire and Billy Cowan, eds., *Scenes from the Revolution: Making Political Theatre* (Pluto Press, 2018) ; and Tiziana Morosetti and Osita Okagbue, eds., *The Palgrave Handbook of Theatre and Race* (Palgrave Macmillan, 2021). He has written a theatrical adaptation of Elie Wiesel's *Night*, which was performed by Dame Janet Suzman, for Holocaust Memorial Day, UK; and a libretto, *Silver Spoon*, for the English National Opera board member and composer Lisa Logan. He is the co-author with Robert Gordon of the play *Shylock Speaks*, written for London's 2020 Jewish Book Week and is currently working on a project endorsed by the Nelson Mandela Foundation, *KwanSo gekle* (*Where the Old People Gather*), together with the University of Cape Town. He has directed in Vaclav Havel's Prague theatre and directed over forty productions in South Africa, the United Kingdom (for the Pinter Centre), the European Union, and New York.

**Gary Perlman** is a Tokyo-based translator, writer, and lyricist. His productions include *A Kabuki Christmas Carol* (Tokyo, original script); *The Fall Guy* (Off-Broadway, English script and producer); *I Got Merman* (Tokyo, English script); *When Gary Met Lily* (Fuji TV, original script and performer); Kabuki Online (English text) and the UK Royal Ballet's *A Soldier's Tale* (Tokyo New National Theatre, producer). He has contributed articles on theatre to the *Sondheim Review*, *Theatre Guide* (Japan) and other publications in Japan and the United States. He is also the author of an upcoming book on the wartime diplomat Chiune Sugihara and serves as advisor to the NPO Chiune Sugihara Visas for Life.

**Hyeyoung Ra** is an associate research fellow in the Policy and Evaluation Department of the Arts Council Korea (ARKO). She received her PhD from Inha University with a thesis titled 'Spatial Distribution and Local Factors of the Culture Contents Industry.' From 2011 to 2017 she was a lecturer at the Department of Public Administration at Inha University. She was also a postdoctoral researcher at the Public Performance Management Research Center in Seoul National University from 2018 until 2019. Her research interests are climate change and cultural policy, the cultural city and public sector performance management. Her publications include *Cultural Policy in the Age of Climate Change* (Arko, 2021), the essay 'The Study on Uneven Growth and Geographic Characters of Cultural Industries' (*Journal of Region and Culture*, 2017) as well as several other papers and articles. nhy3877@arko.or.kr.

**Hannah Thuraisingam Robbins** is an assistant professor of popular music and the director of Black Studies at the University of Nottingham, UK. Their research focuses on the interactions between 'identity'—race, especially Blackness, gender, and queerness— and the Anglophone stage and screen musical. Hannah has contributed chapters to *Adapting 'The Wizard of Oz': Musical Versions from Baum to MGM and Beyond* (Oxford University Press, 2018), *The Oxford Handbook of Musical Theatre Screen Adaptations* (Oxford University Press, 2019) and *Paris and the Musical: The City of Light on Stage and Screen* (Routledge, 2021) and has published essays in *Studies in Musical Theatre* and *Arts*. Their current projects explore how intersectionality and race are positioned in the stories we tell about musical theatre. https://orcid.org/0000-0001-8812-9615.

**Susanne Scheiblhofer** worked as a postdoc at the University of Salzburg until 2021, and she continues to teach courses there on music and media. Her research interests include musical theatre, film and television music, music and mobility and the interplay of music and politics in society. She graduated from the University of Vienna in 2006 and was awarded a Fulbright scholarship in 2007 to continue her studies in musicology and arts administration in the United States. In 2014 she earned her doctorate from the University of Oregon, writing about representations of National Socialism in Broadway musicals in her dissertation. She is co-editor of the upcoming handbook *Music and Migration* (Waxmann and Routledge) and currently working on musical theatre in postwar Vienna and musical hallucinations in television series. https://orcid.org/0000-0001-7083-8712.

**Richard M. Shannon** is the head of Radio (Department of Media, Communications and Cultural Studies) and module leader for the producer pathway of the MA in musical theatre at Goldsmiths, University of London. He set up the Myanmar Group in 2013 and has worked with the National University of Arts and Culture, Yangon. He is a fellow of the Royal Society of Arts and a senior fellow of the Higher Education Academy.

xxii    BIOGRAPHIES

Shannon is a published playwright, theatre director and radio drama producer. His play *The Lady of Burma* premiered at the Old Vic theatre in London in 2006. In 2012 the Dukes Theatre, Lancaster produced his play *Sabbat: The Story of the Pendle Witches*. He was a founding director of Independent Radio Drama Productions and has produced major series for LBC radio in London and National Public Radio in the United States. Richard is a judge for the British Podcasting Awards and the Audible Audio Production Awards. His theatre work includes productions at the Young Vic Studio, the Bristol Old Vic Studio and the Redgrave Theatre. He has also worked as a producer on major public events, including the royal opening of St. Pancras International.

**John Snelson** is a musicologist and cultural historian. He specialises in the lyric stage, especially twentieth-century British musical theatre and its relationship to national identity, the subject of his doctoral dissertation (2003). His publications include *Reviewing the Situation: The British Musical from Noël Coward to Lionel Bart* (Bloomsbury, 2023), *Andrew Lloyd Webber* (Yale University Press, 2004) and chapters in William A. Everitt and Paul R. Laird, eds., *The Cambridge Companion to the Musical* (Cambridge University Press, 2002; 3rd ed., 2017); Robert Gordon and Olaf Jubin, eds., *The Oxford Handbook of the British Musical* (Oxford University Press, 2016); and Michela Niccolai and Clair Rowden, eds., *Musical Theatre in Europe 1830–1945* (Brepols, 2017). He was a member of the three-year international research network 'Screen Adaptations of *Le Fantôme de l'Opéra*: Routes of Cultural Transfer', funded by the Leverhulme Trust, and contributed to the volume of *Opera Quarterly* (no. 34 [Spring–Summer 2018]) dedicated to the project. For twenty years he worked at the Royal Opera House, Covent Garden, where he was the head of publication and interpretation.

**Jan Šotkovský** graduated in 2005 with master of arts degree in theatre dramaturgy from the Janáček Academy of Performing Arts (JAMU), where he also completed his doctoral degree in 2012 with his thesis 'Narrative Techniques in Directorial and Dramaturgical Practice'. Since 2007 he has been a dramaturge at one of the leading Czech musical theatre venues, the Brno City Theatre, working on over twenty musical productions (mostly Czech premières or original works). He is the co-author of the lyrics and librettos for seven musicals directly commissioned by the City Theatre. At JAMU he teaches musical theatre theory and history, the theory and history of stage direction, and theatre history. Since 2005 he has been the resident dramaturge of Buranteatr, one of Brno's independent studio theatres. A translator from Polish and English, he has co-authored the Czech translations of *Jekyll and Hyde*, *Zorro*, and *Tick, Tick . . . Boom!* and has provided the Czech version of Polish musical *Painted on Glass*. He regularly publishes in-depth articles and book reviews in the Czech journals and magazines *Theatre Review*, *Theatralia*, and *Theatre News*.

**Renate Stridh** is a Swedish director and producer. She has a bachelor of arts in cinema history and theory and a master of arts in theatre history and theory from the University of Stockholm. Since 2009 she has lived in Norway, where she teaches musical theatre

BIOGRAPHIES    xxiii

and directs at Bårdarakademiet in Oslo. A member of the Norwegian Stage Directors' Union, she has directed the Scandinavian premières of *Bat Boy* (2009), *Parade* (2013), and *Dogfight* (2019). Other directing credits include *Ragtime* and *Fiddler on the Roof*, as well as several musicals by Stephen Sondheim (*Sunday in the Park with George, Company, Into the Woods*, and *A Funny Thing Happened on the Way to the Forum*) at Bårdarakademiet or Balettakademien in Gothenburg.

**Mikael Strömberg** earned his doctorate in theatre studies from Stockholm University. His primary areas of research are popular culture and popular entertainment. He has written on a variety of topics from outdoor theatre to operetta and has a special interest in entertainment 'for the people'. Strömberg is interested in historiography and the inclusion of previously excluded genres, not only to change how history is produced, but also to enhance our interpretation of the past. He has recently published a book on *buskis*, a Swedish entertainment phenomenon associated with sex, vulgarity, and a lack of quality. He is currently working in a project about entertainment as a form of infrastructure in Sweden from 1960 to 2000.

**Sanne Thierens** studied liberal arts and sciences at University College Roosevelt in Middelburg, the Netherlands. She subsequently obtained an master of arts in musicology from King's College London. Thierens has a PhD in musical theatre from the University of Winchester. Her research on the musicals of Annie M. G. Schmidt and Harry Bannink was published as *Mjoeziekul* (Nijgh & Van Ditmar, in 2021). She is a theatre critic and journalist for *Theaterkrant* and *Scènes theatermagazine* and works as a teacher and research supervisor at the Fontys Academy for Music Theatre and Musical Theatre in Tilburg, the Netherlands.

**Judith Wiemers** studied musicology and English at the University of Cologne and Queen's University Belfast. In her doctoral dissertation she investigated American cultural motifs in German film musicals of the Weimar Republic and Nazi Germany. She has published articles and book chapters on film operetta as well as on dance in film and has curated a photographic exhibition on the British film musical at the National Science and Media Museum, Bradford. Judith is a dramaturge for operettas, musicals, and opera at Staatsoperette Dresden. Previously she worked at Northern Ireland Opera, where she also led the Studio programme. Her other experience includes freelance positions and internships at Deutsche Oper Berlin, Staatsoper Hannover, and the Bavarian Radio Symphony Orchestra.

**Jeroen van Wijhe** studied educational psychology at Erasmus University Rotterdam and obtained a master of arts in theatre studies at Utrecht University. He is a theatre critic for Theaterkrant.nl, where he specialises in musical theatre and circus. He teaches courses in musical theatre history and circus dramaturgy at Fontys Academy for Music Theatre and Musical Theatre in Tilburg, the Lucia Marthas Institute for Performing Arts in Amsterdam and Codarts University for the Arts in Rotterdam. van Wijhe is a co-author, with Sanne Thierens and Sandra Verstappen, of *De Nederlandse Musical: Emancipatie van een fenomeen* (Uitgeverij Int. Theatre & Film Books, 2019), a treatise on the history

xxiv   BIOGRAPHIES

and practice of original Dutch musicals. For this book, he authored chapters on the state of education and critical discourse in Dutch musical theatre.

**Aleksandra Zajac-Kiedysz** is a graduate of the University of Gdansk and has a doctorate in literature studies. Her main research interests include Polish and worldwide musical theatre. In 2014 she won the Ministry of Culture and National Heritage of the Republic of Poland Scholarship (part of the Young Poland programme designed for artists under the age of thirty-five) for her research project on musical theater in Poland from 1989 to 2013. Three years later she received the Marshal of the Pomeranian Voivodship Scholarship for Creators of Culture. She publishes regularly in various periodicals, and her first book, *50 i pięć lat Teatru Muzycznego w Gdyni 1958–2013*, was published by in 2015 by University of Gdansk Press. She has presented at both Polish and international academic conferences, such as Popular Music Theatre under Socialism (University of Freiburg, 2017) and Song Stage and Screen XII (University of Surrey, 2017). She is also a lecturer at the Academy of Music in Gdansk and at the Vocal Training and Acting Studio in Gdynia, where she teaches courses on the history of the theatre and the history of musical theatre and also leads the graduate seminar. Currently she is working on a book on Polish musical theatre after 1989.

# PREAMBLE

## ROBERT GORDON AND OLAF JUBIN

THIS handbook was conceived before COVID-19 threw the global economy and its normal patterns of consumption into disarray; it has been completed in a time when most—but not all—performance spaces around the world are once again open to the public. It is still too early to say how theatre has changed; thousands of small production companies and venues have closed during the pandemic, drastically reducing the options for both audiences and creatives. On the other hand many stage musicals have been filmed for streaming services, creating more possibilities for disseminating musicals globally.

Yet whatever form stage productions take in a world living with COVID-19, there is no doubt that musical theatre will remain one of its most popular offerings. Thus, it is likely that it will continue to flourish globally.

## INTRODUCTION: THE STAGE MUSICAL AS GLOBAL PHENOMENON

Although musical theatre may not be an important cultural and economic force in all the 196 countries of the world, in the twentieth- and early twenty-first-century stage musicals have so proliferated as to constitute a major industry not just in English-speaking nations but in many other regions as well. Around the world—and increasingly in places where Western theatre forms have recently become a regular part of the commercial repertoire (e.g. South Korea, Japan, Singapore, and China)—the musical has become the predominant form of theatre and is often treated more seriously as an art form than in the major commercial centres of theatre internationally—Broadway and the West End.

Musicals continue to accrue increasing revenues in the United States and the United Kingdom; at the same time, other countries have established their own musical theatre industries, partly by importing hit shows from Broadway or the West End and partly by initiating or reviving local traditions of writing and staging. Such international developments make it feasible for a blockbuster production to open in New York or London and then be replicated in translation around the world; it is even possible for artists to earn a substantial income from foreign performance rights even if their musicals have never been performed in either centre of musical theatre production.

*The Oxford Handbook of the Global Stage Musical* intends to offer new conceptual approaches to comprehending the burgeoning of musical theatre as a global phenomenon, interrogating the various issues arising from the growth of new industries and markets rather than merely surveying the transcultural spread of musicals throughout the developing world. Thus, we have chosen contributors from various countries and cultures to reflect the diversity of the subject in order to avoid, as far as possible, an outsider's perspective.

To set the scene for the thirty-three chapters that follow, we wish to clarify the various terms that have dominated the discourse on the global stage musical for the last four decades, especially 'globalisation', 'McTheatre', 'deterritorialisation', and the 'megamusical'. In order to unravel the ways in which these concepts have affected the understanding of musical theatre which crosses national borders, they need to be not only explained but problematised.

# Globalisation and Its Discontents: The Musical as International Theatrical Form

The first chapter of this volume presents Christopher Balme's reflection on how the relationship between the global and the local in theatre has changed over the last half century:

> Today, theatre is a global artistic practice, a crucial cultural institution in many countries and a central part of transnational networks of artistic exchange. Often defying exact definition, its manifestations range from improvised street theatre in backyard slums to multimillion-dollar edifices purveying the latest performances of nineteenth-century opera to twenty-first-century cultural elites.

In his anthropologically oriented consideration of theatre around the world, Balme invokes the hierarchy of 'high art' paradigms of 'nineteenth-century opera' and 'twenty-first-century cultural elites' in contrast with the demotic register of popular forms such as 'improvised street theatre', thereby implicating questions of aesthetic value.

Despite its bewildering number of forms, which include puppet theatre, stand-up comedy, and abstract performance art, theatre makers and audiences are connected across cultures by mutual recognition of commonality in what they do. Yet, in the eyes of most theatre scholars, theatre remains a resolutely local, even parochial phenomenon in which the local perspective enjoys unconditional priority over other research paradigms, as some historians have begun critically to note.

Although the editors concur with this emphasis on the prime importance of the 'local perspective' as the determining context in the formation of any performance, the continuing success of musicals in global markets has tempted musical-theatre makers to produce work that might translate easily into a wide range of cultural contexts, prompting an increasingly complicated series of debates and theories that seek to explain the global popularity of the genre.

The debate about what globalisation means in cultural terms, especially for the theatre, gained additional traction in the mid-2000s. The theatre scholar Dan Rebellato opened his wide-ranging 2006 article 'Playwriting and Globalisation: Towards a Site-Unspecific Theatre' with a proposition that has by now become a cliché in the criticism and theorisation of postmodern musical theatre: 'Globalisation is in some ways a very new phenomenon and seems to require new cultural forms to express and resist it'.[1]

As an empirical assertion, this will not stand up in the context of European theatre history. While it is true that from the mid-nineteenth century musical theatre increasingly came to dominate global markets in a context of industrialisation, multinational business, and technological innovation,[2] it is nevertheless profoundly unhistorical to treat globalisation merely as a recent consequence of a postmodern economy—the bastard offspring of late consumer capitalism—because in some way or other cultural colonisation has existed throughout history. In fact, colonised people died resisting Roman ideology and—by extension—Roman culture in order to preserve their cultural identity. In subsequent centuries, the international spread of Shakespeare, Molière, Chekhov, and Brecht provides crucial examples of cultural globalisation at work.[3]

In response to the new possibilities of mass production and distribution, the Frankfurt School of cultural critics such as Theodor Adorno and Max Horkheimer employed the dialectical methods of critical social theory to reject and resist the fetishisation of the manufactured 'artistic' products when they critiqued the commodification of popular American culture (Hollywood movies, short stories, and jazz, the latter including songs from musical comedies) in their theorisation of the 'culture industry'. From this perspective, the capitalist logic of the mass entertainment industries (film, radio, comic strips, pulp fiction, television, and recorded music) creates the possibility for a culture of limitless repetition. Adorno and Horkheimer's theoretical concept remains a constant reference point for cultural critics in many countries, especially in continental Europe.

Yet in 2007 Yi Wang argued against extending their deterministic approach to cultural globalisation and against viewing it as an inevitable process of colonization of the weak by the powerful: 'Sometimes advocates of anti-globalisation overlook the power of people's subjectivity. [ . . . ] Globalisation is not simply homogenization'.[4]

Around the same time, Eric Swyngedouw explored the long history of globalisation:

> Capitalism has always been a decidedly geographical project and globalisation has been part of the capitalist enterprise from at least 1492, if not before. In fact, in many ways, the world economy and culture of the late 19th and early 20th century world were as globally interconnected as, and in some ways more so than, the present time.

[ ... ] Capitalist geographical dynamics are inherently tied up with processes of territorialisation, deterritorialisation and reterritorialisation and have been so for a long time.[5]

Yet Yi Wang believes that the impact of this is not necessarily negative:

In the new era of globalisation, people become much more concerned about the uniqueness and particularity of their own culture. Since people construct their identities through their cultures, they will defend them. Actually, globalisation brings much more awareness of cultural identity than before. [ ... ] Some people say globalisation and localisation are so much integrated that we have to coin a new word 'glocal', both global and local.

By 2005 the totalising model of globalisation was already becoming passé. In his long essay 'Globalisation Theory: A Post Mortem,' Justin Rosenberg had at this time declared the 'age of globalisation' to be over, a relic from the 1990s when many people

believed that the world was opening up to a new form of interconnectedness, that a multi-layered, multilateral system of 'global governance' was emerging, which was set to transform the very nature of international politics. The recent disappearance of this word from Anglo-American media and governmental commentaries has been almost as sudden as its meteoric rise a decade ago.[6]

Yet the concept of cultural globalisation persists, as do the fears and extreme reactions it triggers. The xenophobic political conflicts over migration and asylum-seeking in Europe and North America during the last few years have revealed yet one more sinister kind of counter-movement to such perceived loss of 'national culture'.[7] Those who fear the eventual destruction of live theatre as a result of the increasing success of recycled facsimile productions of Broadway and West End musical hits continue to perpetuate this outmoded model of cultural globalisation as well as another important concept it has produced—that of 'McTheatre'.

## 'McTheatre' and Its Myths

Up until the early 1980s, when people made fun of musicals as escapist kitsch, they used to refer to family shows like *The Sound of Music* (1959), *Oliver!* (1960), *Hello, Dolly!* (1964) or *Annie* (1977), accusing them of being either gratuitously sentimental or merely razzle-dazzle spectacle. Few would include Kander and Ebb's *Cabaret* (1966) or, from a later epoch, Sondheim's *Assassins* (1990) in this group—either because such sophisticated and hard-bitten musicals are regarded as the exception that proves the rule, or because they have never heard of them.

Over time, however, many of these have been revalued as classics in the field of popular culture,[8] so nowadays detractors of the form cite as a 'typical' musical they despise one of the ubiquitous hits from the 1980s or 1990s that they have heard of (but never seen on stage), such as *Cats* (1981), *Les Misérables* (1985), *The Phantom of the Opera* (1986), or *Mamma Mia!* (1999). For several decades reviewers have taught them to refer to these shows as 'megamusicals' or to denigrate them as instances of commercial McTheatre—the equivalent of fast food that is not intellectually nourishing and in the long term bad for your mental health. Supposedly, one defining feature of these works was that their commercial success was not confined to Anglophone cultures but that they had similar appeal around the globe, with no regard to national borders. Consequently, they began to be viewed as paradigmatic instances of the cultural globalisation discussed above.

In the train of those discussions of global consumerism as a postmodern phenomenon, which assumed prominence in the 1990s, came a number of studies of the so-called megamusical that assumed a link between the form and content of 1980s British musicals, and the exploitation of Fordist production and marketing systems that effect a 'McDonaldisation' of the musical. This in turn gave rise to the concept of 'McTheatre',[9] a notion originally popularised by a British television programme, *The Business: The McDonald's of Musicals*. Broadcast in 1995, it examined the work practices of Andrew Lloyd Webber's theatre company, the Really Useful Group.

The media scholar who first developed the McTheatre thesis in relation to the megamusical was Jonathan Burston, who in 1998 argued that with *Cats* (1981), Cameron Mackintosh introduced into live theatre a system of franchising in which productions were identically replicated throughout the world, reducing the live act of performance to a mechanical reproduction of the première staging around the world.[10] As with the McDonald's fast-food franchise, the averred aim is to standardise and preserve quality, but the underlying motive is to fix and control each show's brand identity:[11]

> We are witnessing a phenomenon that can only be described as the global-industrialisation of the musical theatre. [ ... ] With the arrival of megamusicals, we have witnessed the attainment of a level of standardisation in production regimes previously unknown in the field of live theatrical production. [ ... ] The megamusical's rationalising, industrial logic—including a quality-control model implemented and supervised outward from a single metropolitan centre—reproduces technical and artistic production detail with such rigour as to significantly delimit the interpretative agency of local musical performers. Hence the increasing use of terms like cloning, franchising, and McTheatre to describe the megamusical business.[12]

Ironically, Burston's most interesting insight may have been not his conceptualisation of the relationship between globalisation and artistic standardisation, but his understanding of the full implications of the technological innovations of modern stage sound,[13] observations that later proponents of the concept completely ignored. Without questioning its premises, Dan Rebellato picked up the 'McTheatre' idea in the mid-2000s and ran with it in different ways:

> The director of each 'new' production has no freedom to reinterpret the production; their role is to remount the original. [ ... ] These conditions are also deeply restrictive [ ... ] The actor is subordinate to the design. Try to make the part your own and you risk injury or singing in darkness. The effect of course is to automate the actor.[14]

It must however be stated that there is something fundamentally flawed about aspects of Rebellato's argument, first put forth by Burston, for this recording and reproduction of the première production is not necessarily inimical to live theatre. Ballet has functioned by means of such practices of creation and reproduction for almost two centuries, yet dancers do not complain of the lack of creative freedom when they spend years repeating precisely the same choreography in performances around the world. (The same has been true, though naturally for a shorter time, of modern dance.) Performers in Meyerhold's productions after 1917 did not balk at such repetition, nor do those in Robert Wilson's shows of the last fifty years resent repeating the same movements every time they perform his work.

Another flaw of the concept of McTheatre is that it doesn't specify when exactly a production moves from being an artwork which is simply restaged at another venue (or in another culture) to becoming a mere product, franchised and branded—is it the third, the tenth, the twenty-fifth staging? In other words, is it acceptable for directors to share their vision (but not their cast) via mass production from New York to London, Sydney or Toronto, but not once they have exhausted the English-speaking cultural centres?

The question also needs to be asked whether earlier luminaries of the Broadway stage such as Rodgers and Hammerstein, after all not just artists but also producers, would not have extended both their reach and their original stagings beyond the Anglophone market if they had had the opportunity. The songwriters, just as much a brand in their later career as Lloyd Webber or Disney, were adamant that their shows be staged in the West End in exactly the same way as in New York.[15] Jerome Robbins's masterful original 1964 staging of *Fiddler on the Roof*, for instance, was either copied or extensively referenced in subsequent productions in London, Amsterdam, Tel Aviv, Paris, Hamburg, and elsewhere.[16] Was every one of those foreign stagings still an artistic endeavour, or were some of them merely the result of production-line manufacturing procedures?

One could also ask why *A Chorus Line* isn't disparaged as McTheatre: ever since its 1975 New York première, the show has been restaged around the world (mostly by Baayork Lee) replicating its original set, costume, lighting, and sound designs while meticulously reproducing Michael Bennett's choreography and blocking. Lee may be a 'keeper of the flame' (or at least a perpetuator of the myth), but after nearly fifty years and dozens of remountings, how can any 'new' production of *A Chorus Line* be anything other than the copy of a copy of a copy?

Also unanswered is the thorny issue of quality control, another key factor when 'fabricating' consumer items: Beckett and Brecht famously took creatives to court when they changed their work, and Hammerstein's son James for a while forbade German theatres to produce *any* of his father's musicals, after witnessing a Berlin staging which

INTRODUCTION 7

he considered utterly amateurish.[17] So why is it that if Cameron Mackintosh and Andrew Lloyd Webber insist that their musicals be performed everywhere according to what they deem to be the highest standard, they are slavishly following a template instead of simply protecting their artistic vision?

# THE 'DETERRITORALISATION' OF THE BROADWAY MUSICAL

In 2017 David Savran formulated the thesis that the Broadway musical had become a deterritorialised form that 'has circumnavigated the globe countless times'.[18] However, Savran's concept is based on a series of misconceptions of theatre history as well as an outmoded notion of the global cultural economy. His identification of Lloyd Webber and Charles Hart's *The Phantom of the Opera* (1986) as to all intents and purposes a 'Broadway musical' initially reveals the problematic nature of Savran's argument, for it effaces the troubled history of Broadway in the 1980s after Lloyd Webber and Mackintosh triumphed there with the huge success of *Cats* in 1982. In the wake of what insiders called a 'British invasion', the New York theatre community—including reviewers and authors—rejected what they called the 'megamusical' as a meretricious *British* invention; it threatened their notion of the sacrosanct purity of the genre, which they believed to be inherently American in origin. To ignore this twentieth-century rivalry in musical theatre between Broadway and the West End by subsuming all shows playing on the Great White Way under the soubriquet 'Broadway musical' thus involves a profound historical misunderstanding. It constitutes an unspoken imperialistic deterritorialisation in its own right—that of musical theatre as a form—which has characterised American histories of the genre since the 1960s.

In fact, the deterritorialisation of musical theatre that interests Savran occurred a lot earlier. *The Beggar's Opera* (1728) initiated a craze for 'ballad opera' (not in fact an opera at all), which was imported by the American colonies from London and then imitated there until long after the declaration of American independence. Offenbach wrote proto-musicals that enchanted audiences far beyond the borders of France; Gilbert and Sullivan were a global British brand that stretched way beyond the British Empire and were particularly popular in the United States, while Lehár's *The Merry Widow* was an international hit that became a craze in all the ways that any British musical of the 1980s or Disney musical of the 1990s has done. It could also be pointed out that even the 'Princess musicals' of 1915–1918, often invoked as a milestone in the development of the American musical, were an international collaboration, since they were written by one Brit, one expatriate Brit, and an American composer who had learned his craft contributing to English musical comedies in the West End.

When it comes to exploiting international markets, Broadway actually came late to the party—and, oddly, through the Hollywood-based Disney corporation, at first much resented by Broadway insiders for transforming musicals into theme-park attractions.[19] A select few American musicals—like *My Fair Lady* (1956), *Fiddler on the Roof* (1964), *Cabaret* (1966), and, to some degree, *Hair* (1968)—were well received on several continents, but many of Broadway's most iconic works never became the kind of global phenomenon first pioneered by Tim Rice and Lloyd Webber's *Jesus Christ Superstar*, and later by Cameron Mackintosh and Disney. *A Chorus Line* (1975), the quintessential Broadway musical of the last fifty years has never fully succeeded outside the United States; neither have *Rent* (1996) or *The Producers* (2001); *Spamalot* (2005), and *The Book of Mormon* (2011) have been successful in London but nowhere else.[20] Of all the Broadway musicals, the Disney shows and *Chicago* (1975) are the only ones to have achieved the reach of *Cats* (1981), *Les Misérables*, *Phantom* or *Mamma Mia!*[21]—and the former were helped by their film versions.

Savran also projects his Broadway-centric view of musical theatre backwards onto German-language musical theatre.[22] His ignorance of popular German forms of theatrical entertainment permits him the misguided witticism that the 1936 US version of *Im weißen Rößl* (*The White Horse Inn*, 1930) 'so completely turns it into a musical comedy that it makes one realise that it must have been a Broadway musical from the start'.[23] In fact *Im weißen Rößl* was a huge hit partly because it combined operetta with distinctly German musical comedy and *Berliner Varieté* in its Austrian, German, and West End (1932) iterations, all directed by the legendary director-choreograper Eric Charell.[24] Yet the myth of Broadway as the be-all and end-all of twentieth- and twenty-first-century musical theatre continues to be perpetuated by the Broadway industry itself—a paradigmatic example of cultural imperialism.

## THE MEGAMUSICAL AND ITS DISCONTENTS: PROBLEMS OF CATEGORISATION

Ever since *Cats* threatened the pre-eminence of *A Chorus Line* as the longest-running show on Broadway, the New York theatre community, hotly pursued by reviewers and industry insiders, began to find reasons to belittle what they dubbed the megamusical. Originally the ubiquitous term was intended as a journalistic slur, and its condescending tenor became all-pervasive. John Kenrick in *Musicals 101* opines:

> The revolutionary thing about *Cats* was not the show itself—but the marketing. [ ... ] Like a theatrical cancer, *Cats* spread to places that had not seen professional theatre in years. From Vienna to Oslo to Topeka, dancers in furry spandex and garish make-up proved that 'Jellicles can and jellicles do' rake in a fortune [ ... ]*Cats* was that increasing rarity, a musical one can take children to [ ... ] The kids might die of vapidity poisoning but they would not be exposed to anything dangerous—like a coherent idea.[25]

FIG. 0.1 *Cats* may have won seven Tony Awards and run in New York for eighteen years, but it remains the most reviled of all British imports by the Broadway community. The image shows Calvin E. Ramsberg as Old Deuteronomy surrounded by the company in 1987. Photographer unknown; image provided by the editors.

Denny Martin Flynn summed up the views of the majority of Broadway professionals, unintentionally revealing the strong prejudice encountered by non-American musicals:

> *Cats* marked the beginning of the megamusical, wherein spectacle not only superseded but *replaced* drama. Its gargantuan environment by John Napier was a breathtaking achievement. [ ... ] Its lack of action, redundant songs, and pop-rock music caused many theatregoers (especially older ones) to walk out, but its awesome set, surround-sound, and energetic cast convinced people that they'd got their money's worth. With the success of *Jesus Christ Superstar*, *Evita* and *Cats*, English

poperetta travelled to every corner of the theatre world and began to influence local theatre.[26]

Flynn's critique of 'English poperetta'—why not 'British'?—becomes almost ludicrously exaggerated in his discussion of *Les Misérables*, a musical written by two Frenchmen which was first performed in Paris.

> But *Les Misérables*, for all its nobility, lacked musical theatre craft. [ ... ] Just when you get comfortable with the operatic milieu [ ... ] two supporting comedians enter and a little vaudeville is thrown in. The innkeeper and his wife burlesque their roles in a vaudeville style reminiscent of Rooster and Hannigan on 'Easy Street' in *Annie*. (Good American plays and musicals do not feature a hodgepodge of acting styles, devoted as they are to ensemble work, but this is accepted on the English stage.)[27]

The assumption that Trevor Nunn, the most successful artistic director of the Royal Shakespeare Company's sixty-year history, did not know how to achieve a coherent acting style for 'ensemble work' is laughable in its ignorance.[28] Also, if the comic relief provided by the Thénardiers has any theatrical roots, they are not in (American) vaudeville, but in the British music hall. But then, evidently, all forms of musical theatre must strive for American standards and conventions of musical theatre excellence; those that dare not to do so are found wanting or are ridiculed.

The term 'megamusical' was canonised in 2007 by Jessica Sternfeld's *The Megamusical*, the first major study of this subgenre, mostly made up of these and other British musicals, although Sternfeld also includes *Ragtime* (1996), *Titanic* (1997), and *Disney's Aida* (1998) as American examples of the form.[29] In her sympathetic and critically balanced overview, Sternfeld offers a helpful if not exhaustive catalogue of what are supposed to be the distinctive features of a megamusical:

> It features a grand plot from a historical era, high emotions, singing and music throughout, and impressive sets. It opens with massive publicity, which usually leads to millions of dollars in advance sales. Marketing strategies provide a recognizable logo or image, theme song and catch phrase. Audiences rave; critics are less thrilled. It runs for years, perhaps decades, becoming a fixture of our cultural landscape.[30]

However, very few of the so-called megamusicals evince all of these features, although most are almost completely through-sung and marketed by exploiting synergistic postmodern methods and media. But neither *Cats* nor *Starlight Express* (1984) has a grand plot from a historical era, while *Les Miz* actually has a minimal set, cunningly varied by complex hydraulic revolves but simply composed of chairs and tables. Other supposedly prime examples of the genre also do not fit the description: *Chess* (1986) took place in what was then the present, whereas *Time* (1986) and *Metropolis* (1989) were set in the future. *Sunset Boulevard* (1993) integrates musical numbers and lengthy dialogue scenes just like a classic book musical.

What distinguishes the ambitious *Sweeney Todd, the Demon Barber of Fleet Street* (1979) from megamusicals? To depict Victorian England as the backdrop of the show, the show's set designer, Boris Aronson, reassembled the whole of an actual factory on the enormous stage of the Uris (now Gershwin) Theatre, and the musical thriller has so much continuous music that it seems practically through-sung and has often been categorised as an opera. On the other hand, an earlier case of a highly publicised musical set in the past, full of high emotions and featuring impressive sets, is *Show Boat* (1927), which was produced by Florenz Ziegfeld, an impresario who certainly was very adept at creating massive publicity.

The crucial feature of megamusicals is that, in marked contrast to other subgenres of musical theatre such as the book/integrated musical or the concept musical, they cannot be clearly defined at the level of *content*—by their narrative or dramaturgical approach—as proved by the examples given above. All they have in common are similar *production circumstances*. It is therefore misleading to claim that megamusicals followed or replaced the artistically adventurous postmodern musicals of the 1970s and early 1980s (which in turn had taken over from the integrated shows of the 1940s, 1950s or 1960s). In fact, any musical that is regarded as part of the canon of 'classic' shows can be restaged and re-produced as a megamusical—the 1996 revival of *Chicago* is a case in

FIG. 0.2 No more than a massive set? The 1989 London production of *Metropolis*, which was directed by Jérôme Savary and starred (*left to right*) Graham Bickley, Judy Kuhn, and Brian Blessed. The impressive stage design was by Ralph Koltai. Photo: Alastair Muir, courtesy of the photographer.

point, since it uses exactly the same marketing, branding, and franchising mechanisms pioneered by *Cats, Miss Saigon* (1989), and others.

In short, globally successful blockbuster shows form a separate *production category*, and thus it would be more appropriate to set them against other production categories, such as 'fringe show' or 'amateur production'. It is their marketing savvy and their expansion into new markets such as continental Europe, Asia, and South America which was successfully emulated by Disney and other big-budget shows, like *Wicked* (2003). Nowadays every single big-budget show strives to follow in the footsteps of the megamusical, if the international roll-out of the Broadway hits *Kinky Boots* (2012), *Hamilton* (2015), and *Dear Evan Hansen* (2015) is any indication.[31]

## CULTURE WARS: HIGHBROW, MIDDLEBROW, AND LOWBROW

Ever since Broadway shows were labeled 'middle-brow' by Eric Bentley in the 1940s,[32] arguments have circulated about whether musicals should be loved and patronised as purely escapist 'lowbrow' diversions—as 'only entertainment', in Richard Dyer's words—or as highbrow art products, as in the case of many of the works of Stephen Sondheim (e.g. *Sweeney Todd* and *Sunday in the Park with George*).

Russell Lynes explained in a witty and provocative article in *Harper's* (1949) how the categories of post-war American cultural consumption underlie the hatred of the highbrow for middlebrow culture.[33] Serious promoters and theorists of musical theatre as popular or folk art are obliged to confront the conundrum that middlebrow attitudes to art are incompatible with the forms of mass or popular entertainment in which highbrows are content to indulge.[34] Yet musicals account for the highest proportion of attendance at theatres around the world, so they demand to be studied not only by musicologists and theatre scholars but also by sociologists of popular culture and, in their cinematic form, as a species of mass entertainment.

In 1953 Dwight Macdonald published 'A Theory of Mass Culture', in *Diogenes*.[35] Macdonald here cited, along with Clement Greenberg, critical works on mass culture by writers associated with the Frankfurt School, including Leo Löwenthal, Horkheimer, and Adorno, whose analysis of standardisation in popular music Macdonald called 'brilliant'. The Frankfurt School combined anticapitalist politics and modernist aesthetics. 'Folk Art was the people's own institution, their private little garden', Macdonald argued in his essay. 'But Mass Culture breaks down the wall, integrating the masses into a debased form of High Culture and thus becoming an instrument of political domination.'[36]

What Macdonald despised most was *l'avant-garde pompier*—fake avant-gardism: 'There is nothing more vulgar than sophisticated *kitsch*.'[37] Macdonald eventually categorised this pseudo avant-gardism as the culture of middlebrow aspiration—'Midcult'. True kitsch, he believed could be left to the masses. The real enemy was bourgeois high-mindedness in literature, music, theatre, art, and criticism, and over the next ten years he applied his critical acumen to the task of identifying this culture, exposing its calculated banalities and often persuading his readers of its meretriciousness. As first mooted by Bentley in his attack on Broadway theatre as 'middlebrow', the term 'Midcult' could most appropriately applied to the golden-age book musical.

While Adorno elevated the music of the great Western composers to an unmediated expression of genius beyond the determination of ideology, thereby consigning popular culture to the garbage heap of inauthentic kitsch, Walter Benjamin was the first Marxist cultural critic to view mass art as an expression of the culture of the proletariat, offering an inclusive prospectus of the new opportunities of the 'art-work in the age of mechanical reproduction'.[38] While analysing the 'aura' of an original artwork, he was nevertheless deeply sympathetic to the artistic ambitions of the fledgling film industry. In contrast, for instance, with the live stage production, which preeminently depended on the aura of its unrepeatable performance, the film drama could be copied and presented millions of times around the world.[39] For some, such reproducibility implied a loss of authenticity in the mechanically replicated work, an attitude echoed in the many excoriations of the megamusical for precipitating the death of the live art of performance. Yet for Benjamin, it inaugurated the possibility of a kind of mass art, whose reproducibility provided the opportunity for the proletariat to encounter and appreciate complex art objects, whose lack of aura was a sign of the democratic nature of their dissemination.

Ultimately the collapse of the highbrow-lowbrow distinction that is an aspect of postmodern conceptions of art can be traced to Benjamin's premonitory theorisations of film art and popular music. It was Vagelis Siropoulos who first elaborated a coherent theorisation of what Lloyd Webber's megamusicals represent as postmodern forms of musical theatre.[40] Rather than denigrating Lloyd Webber for dramaturgical incompetence, as so many US critics have done,[41] Siropoulos situates *Cats* and *Starlight Express* in the conceptual frame of Hans Thielman's post-dramatic theatre, indicating how a number of distinctive features of Lloyd Webber's work conform to the paradigm of the post-dramatic, deliberately avoiding the model of the golden-age book musical to reanimate the revue structures of early twentieth-century musical entertainment in order to revivify the form of the popular musical.'[42]

In '*Evita*, the Society of the Spectacle and the Advent of the Megamusical' Siropoulos points to the way 'spectatorship [is transformed] into an overwhelming immersive experience, to become emblematic of the socio-economic and phenomenological function of spectacle in postmodern culture—a fact that explains [these shows] immense commercial success'.[43] Far from trading crudely on spectacle, *Cats* is 'the prototypical megamusical' that functions in the context of the postmodern 'society of the spectacle'.[44] In Siropoulos's view the megamusical

> reconceives through the use of cutting-edge technology that revolutionizes set, light and sound design theatrical space as a hyperspace: [it promotes] new and

challenging aural and visual sensations. This hyperspatial anamorphosis of the theatrical environment must be seen as part of a larger process of hyperspatialisation, which [ . . . ] is one of the defining characteristics of postmodern culture.[45]

Rather than being the stepchild of the Broadway tradition, the megamusical thus proposes a new theatrical economy, an aesthetic which millions of non-English-speakers have found appealing because its music-and-spectacle-centred dramaturgy help overcome language barriers when such shows travel.

# SUMMARY OF CONTENTS

## Part I: 'Theory and Praxis'

The collection is constructed in eleven parts according to themes that the editors consider to represent major issues in the field of the international musical theatre industry, reflecting both its origin in the era of Western colonialism and the current tension between global and local interests in a postmodern economic and cultural context.

As the first step in encompassing the scope of musical theatre in a global perspective, the topic will be approached from both theoretical and empirical perspectives. Because the musical on the transnational stage is a phenomenon that exemplifies both globalisation and glocalisation, Part I will offer an explanation of the factors involved in exporting musical theatre and the problems which arise when cultural artefacts negotiate cultural boundaries and linguistic barriers.

In **Chapter 1** Christopher Balme explores the theoretical and historical dimensions of theatre and globalisation. Although theatre, in the eyes of most scholars, remains a resolutely local, even parochial phenomenon, it has in fact been subject to processes of globalisation for at least seventy years. As the author points out, these forces began affecting the art form with the rapid expansion of transportation, trading, and communication networks in the second half of the nineteenth century. After discussing some definitions of globalisation, especially its influential variant, glocalisation, the essay takes an in-depth look at the transfer of theatrical practices across different cultural environments before reformulating Peter L. Becker's influential theory of cultural globalisation under the heading 'the five faces of theatrical globalisation', i.e., marketisation, musicalisation, festivalisation, mediatisation, and musealisation. Balme demonstrates how these phenomena can be applied to current developments, especially but not solely in musical theatre.

Transporting any artefact from one culture to another necessarily involves a process of adaptation or translation into a new social, political, and artistic context. This applies first and foremost to its language. But because every culture comprises a variety of modalities, the challenge is to adapt the many characteristic cultural forms and mores to foreign frameworks without betraying the unique significance of the original artefact.

In **Chapter 2,** Eva Espasa analyses translated musical productions, where cultural, commercial, and theatrical forces are resituated in new musical and linguistic parameters. The author points out that the conjunction between music and words is an argument both for and against translation; this conjunction constitutes a major priority in singable translation, which treats articulation, rhythm, and rhyme as common but flexible requisites. The chapter shows how transposing a musical from its original language into a different one 'is affected by many challenges that, like intersecting concentric circles, sometimes clash but are often sources of creative solutions'. The collaborative nature of musical creation also applies to translation, because this task is undertaken by musical, theatrical, and translation professionals who often work in conjunction with one another and whose main priorities are exemplified by specific samples from musicals recently translated for and presented on the Barcelona stage.

As Zachary Dunbar underlines in 'Training for Writers and Performers', 'Musical theatre is a booming business the world over, and so is training in this complex art form'. The widespread growth of Broadway and West End musicals, especially after World War II, has produced a global market in need of industry-ready performers and writers, resulting in an exponential growth in training programmes. **Chapter 3** offers a global snapshot of the rise of systematic training. It looks at how innovations in the musical artform reinforce, in writing, *collaborative* training built primarily on the paradigm of close-knit, sophisticated dramaturgies of canonical exemplars, and in *integrative* performance training, a versatility characterised by a seamless fusion of singing, acting, and dancing (otherwise ubiquitously trademarked as the 'triple threat'). Summing up the status quo in an international context, the essay thus considers the vexed challenges of vocational training in the context of integration, industry-facing aims, and current social issues.

## Part II: 'Uncharted Territories'

Part II provides several case studies of early international success stories, identifying some of the earliest works of musical theatre to find enthusiastic audiences abroad. In what ways can their systems of production and reception in foreign countries be considered groundbreaking or paradigmatic of the global hits that came later?

After its enthusiastically received 1905 première in Vienna, the operetta masterpiece *Die lustige Witwe* (*The Merry Widow*), by Franz Lehár, Viktor Léon, and Leo Stein, went on to become the first truly global work of musical theatre: it was popular everywhere it was performed, in a multitude of languages and countries. As John Koegel explains, the success story of the wealthy widow Hanna Galwari and her noble suitor Count Danilo Danilovitsch not only sparked the 'silver age' of Viennese operetta, but was also one of the first productions to make extensive use of marketing, including the 'Merry Widow hat' and many other commercial tie-ins. **Chapter 4** charts the triumphant journey of *The Merry Widow* around the world and highlights how its enthusiastic reception and many revivals paved the way for numerous stage and film parodies, refunctionings, and film and television versions. More than a century after the *Widow*'s première, she 'continues to enchant audiences and to represent the practice of the globalisation of musical theatre that the work began a century ago and that continues unabated today'.

As part of the British Empire, South Africa and Australia were exposed early on to imported shows from the West End and—to a lesser degree—Broadway before beginning to conceive and perform homegrown works. In **Chapter 5** David Peimer explores the rich history of musical theatre of these two countries, by first briefly mapping their theatre industry under colonial rule in the first half of the twentieth century before discussing the indigenous postcolonial musicals created in both countries, some of which have been exported to the United Kingdom and, occasionally, New York. The contrasting trajectories of South African and Australian musical theatre, according to Peimer, 'distinctly reveal the dialectical process through which notions of colonial and postcolonial identity have developed and changed': starting with *King Kong* (1959), South African musicals offered new representations of black identity in contestation with or an embrace of the colonial/apartheid paradigm, whereas most Australian shows are comprehended by their exploration of different images of masculinity.

Although there has always been a lively cultural exchange between Broadway and the West End, even if at times the balance tilted from one side of the Atlantic to the other, it was only after World War II that Anglophone stage musicals succeeded in the non-English-speaking world. Lars Schmidt (1971–2010) is one of the unsung trailblazers in the business of exporting musical theatre to the European continent. In **Chapter 6**, Dirk Gindt outlines some of Schmidt's key artistic choices and financial strategies that paved the way for the transatlantic breakthrough of the book musical, using the 1959 production of *My Fair Lady* in Stockholm as a primary case study of how European audiences came to embrace the genre. As one of the most expensive theatrical productions in Sweden up until that point, it engendered significant anxieties about commercialisation and Americanisation and was accused of being 'prefabricated' theatre that seemingly valued profit over art. Gindt puts this criticism to the test by presenting various sides of the debate and teasing out the complexity of the (arguably very shrewd) business strategies Schmidt used to launch *My Fair Lady* as one of the defining cultural events of the postwar period in Northern and Western Europe, one that became a turning point for the financial and conceptual organisation of live theatre.

## Part III: 'Global Production Entities'

Although there are many businesses that operate in the international musical theatre industry, only three companies can truly be defined as global in their reach and seminal in their activities. In chronological order of their appearance on the scene, Part III will introduce these three corporations and analyse the impact and evolution of their business practices over the years.

Depending on one's point of view, über-producer Cameron Mackintosh is regularly credited with, or blamed for, the rise of the so-called 'megamusical', even if the impresario's more lasting achievement is arguably that he opened up the non-English-speaking world for musicals, initially from the West End and later from New York. Drawing extensively from interviews with key figures, Richard M. Shannon in **Chapter 7** seeks to establish Mackintosh's significance in the development of the global musical. Shannon proposes that *Cats* was the breakthrough production that set a template for developing large-scale musicals which could be reproduced globally. That template, including marketing and the importance of the show logo as well as the development and protection of a brand, is then analysed. The case is made that Mackintosh has established the importance of an interventionist producer and that other key global producers such as Disney and Little Star have made a conscious choice to follow his business methods. Shannon concludes that Mackintosh's productions are not simply commodified replications; rather, he has raised the bar for the whole industry by setting 'a standard for quality, always demanding that the audience, in no matter what country, should see the best possible version of his original works'.

It has sometimes been claimed that *The Lion King* is New York's answer to *Cats*: when the inhabitants of the African savannah replaced denizens of an English junkyard as Broadway's most successful felines, the unrivalled popularity of the screen-to-stage transfer seemingly proved that the American musical could beat the British productions at their own game—not just with regard to innovative scenography but, more important, in their ability to attract a family audience. Since first testing the waters in 1994 with *Beauty and the Beast*, Disney Theatrical Productions has over the last thirty years become a powerhouse in the world of musical theatre, amplifying one of the leading international brands into a multibillion-stage juggernaut.

Ever since the company started to export its Broadway musicals to Europe, changes have been made to adapt them to perceived requirements of local markets. Some of these changes have arguably made these productions more successful in continental Europe than they have been in New York, as Sanne Thierens and Jeroen van Wijhe explain: 'The staging, directing, casting and promotion of musicals such as *Tarzan, Beauty and the Beast* and *The Little Mermaid* have significantly changed when exported from Broadway to European theatres, which [ ... ] makes them all the more interesting to study and watch in their variety.' **Chapter 8** investigates the way in which Disney Theatrical Productions has, in collaboration with European producers, furthered the globalisation of the stage musical by turning stage adaptations that flopped in New York into unexpected regional hits, focusing on productions of Disney musicals the Netherlands and Belgium.

In **Chapter 9** Jonas Menze explores the development, business strategy, and challenges of the Dutch live entertainment company and musical producer Stage Entertainment, considering how it has moved from merely restaging Anglophone productions to initiating original material in several regions and cultures, always with an eye to international distribution. The company was established in 1999 by the Dutch media and theatre impresario Joop van den Ende, co-founder of the media company Endemol. After expanding into the German musical theatre market, Stage Entertainment evolved into the market leader for musical theatre production in continental Europe and turned into one of the major producers worldwide. The Amsterdam-based company became an important originator of local musicals and supporter of local musical theatre talent. Its portfolio of original productions includes musicals such as 3 *Musketiers* (2003), *Ciske de Rat* (2007), *Sister Act* (2009), and *Rocky* (2012).

## Part IV: 'Good Neighbours?'

The Broadway musical was met with a very mixed reception in other parts of the American continent: the genre completely dominates Canadian theatre to the point where there seems to be little reciprocity in the cultural exchange between the two nations, while Mexico has to this day remained reluctant to allow Anglophone musical theatre to monopolise its local theatres. Other countries, such as Chile and Brazil, have found their own particular ways of responding to shows coming from New York. Part IV of this handbook chronicles these various responses through tracing the creation and production of original musicals in both North and South America.

Canada is often in danger of being defined purely by how it relates to the larger nation with which it shares the longest undefended border in the world. The United States dominates both the economic and cultural exchange—which naturally includes musical theatre. On the other hand, as part of the Commonwealth, Canadian culture might be expected to fare better with British culture.

However, as Mel Atkey underlines, Canadian musical theatre writers hoped for decades to conquer New York and/or London, without much luck. These attempts have included such 'flops' as *Rockabye Hamlet*, *Billy Bishop Goes to War*, and *The Story of My Life*. **Chapter 10** discusses the general history of musicals originating in Canada and how they were exported. It also explores why, after many years of trying, two shows—*The Drowsy Chaperone* and *Come from Away*—were embraced by Broadway within a relatively short period of time. Atkey concludes that the popularity of the latter 'proves two things: firstly, each Canadian show [ ... ] has succeeded or failed for different reasons, closely linked to the individual work. Secondly, when it comes to musical theatre, Canada continues to forge its own path, gradually overcoming its former inferiority complex'.

In the second chapter of this part, Emilio Méndez explores how producers have attempted since 1956 to attract theatregoers in Mexico City with local productions of translated Anglophone musicals and how such attempts have prompted the Mexican theatre industry to build its own catalogue of original musicals. **Chapter 11** discusses how local audiences and critics have had to reconcile their experiences of the traditional Mexican revue or *revista* with the modern Broadway and West End musical. Alongside the production of *Ni fu ni fa* (1955), the essay considers the cases of *Rentas congeladas* (1960) and *Las fascinadoras* (1961)—early works that endeavoured to bridge the gap between *revista* and musical—as well as *Papacito piernas largas* (1977), ¡Qué plantón! (1989), and *Mentiras* (2009), long-running and successful Mexican shows. The chapter proposes four major stages of the assimilation process of Anglophone musical theatre

INTRODUCTION 19

as a foreign form and the development of indigenous Mexican musicals. Surveying the current status of the country's musical theatre, Méndez argues that local theatre makers in future need to 'force their traditionally complacent industry from its comfort zone in order that it might cultivate a national audience and compete for a global one'.

From 1933 onwards, the American government under Franklin Roosevelt followed a 'Good Neighbor' policy of non-intervention with regard to the countries south of its border. Not only was that foreign policy totally abandoned by later US presidents, but even in the 1930s and 1940s Latin America remained highly sceptical of Roosevelt's promise not to interfere with their national development, and so the hoped-for reciprocal trade agreements never materialised. What the United States has managed to export successfully to South America since then, however, is musicals, and **Chapter 12** charts how Anglophone musical theatre has been produced and received in two important foreign markets of very different sizes—small Chile, with its population of 18 million, and Brazil, with its 208 million people and fast-growing economy, today one of world's most powerful countries. Each of these nations has responded in its own distinctive way to the importation of Anglophone culture. The decentralised system of theatre productions in Chile uses a distinctive means of subsidised funding, staging, and development for musicals, while in Brazil there are federal tax incentives for sponsoring the performing arts and thus encouraging private investment in theatre. Presenting various case studies, Tiago Mundim contrasts the musical theatre industries in the two South American countries. He has observed in both of them 'an increase in the number of musicals that mix aspects of the Anglophone forms of the genre with local cultural features, [ ... ] , emphasising the unique culture of each respective Latin American country.'

## Part V: 'Popular in Britain'

Although their histories are closely linked, Broadway and the West End do not necessarily respond in the same way to the same offerings: there have always been artists (especially performers) and shows which were appreciated differently in the two centres. The three chapters in Part V will consider significant examples of shows and performers that for a variety of reasons have proved especially popular with British audiences, to a degree that might astonish readers not familiar with the reception of these musicals and stars outside their home country.

**Chapter 13** traces the development of the 'special relationship' between Britain and the United States between 1945 and 1982 in cultural terms by examining the career and reception of the three female American musical theatre stars who achieved the highest profile in the United Kingdom—Dolores Gray, Mary Martin, and Elaine Stritch. Analysing their performances, Robert Gordon perceives their reception as a function of changing post-war understandings of femininity, typifying for British audiences the modernity that the United States had come to represent. The particular affection with which these three stage stars were embraced manifested changes in British attitudes

FIG. 0.3 Not all performers connect with all audiences: Ethel Merman, the Broadway superstar whose appeal to theatre-goers abroad may have been limited. Photographer unknown; image provided by the editors.

to the repressiveness of the English class system as well as a desire for the consumerist aspirations celebrated in the popular culture of the United States: 'The intense affection for Gray and Martin immediately after the war exhibited the initial attraction to the freshness, classlessness, and glamour of all things American, while admiration for the ironic and more aggressive Stritch represented a more realistic embrace of the new dynamics of Cold War collaboration promoted between 1962 and 2002'.

It may seem surprising that a musical which deliberately marks itself as exotic by thoroughly exploiting Damon Runyon's brilliant stylization of mid-century New York street argot should have achieved iconic status in a culture seemingly so far removed from its peculiar milieu. Yet, paradoxically, *Guys and Dolls* has become the most often revived and critically acclaimed Broadway musical to play in the West End, even if the initial reception in London of its 1953 opening there was more equivocal than responses to its Broadway première. **Chapter 14** reveals where the world of Runyon and *Guys and Dolls* has parallels in London's Soho of a similar era. John Snelson locates a reason for the continued popularity of the Frank Loesser classic in the fact that 'the characters and their storylines arise from the deeper themes within the patterns and neuroses of aspects of city life that have proved especially recognizable and durable in London.' A detailed look at London productions from 1979 to 2018 illustrates how the show's more recent British reception as a classic of the musical comedy canon has prompted productions which prioritise nostalgia and theatricality as keys to the work's stage effectiveness.

In the era of social media, when everybody is a critic, the power of the all-important *New York Times* reviewer to close a Broadway show overnight with a single bad notice is a distant memory. Still, it is rare for a musical that has received predominantly bad reviews to remain a fixture on the Great White Way for years. This is not the case in London, where two productions—*Starlight Express* (1984) and *We Will Rock You* (2002)—achieved record-breaking runs in two of the city's largest theatres, despite being lambasted by the critics. Both shows also failed to reproduce their success in the United States: Andrew Lloyd Webber's roller-skate extravaganza ran two seasons as opposed to its eighteen in London, while the Queen jukebox show became the most successful British musical not to open on Broadway since *Salad Days* (1954). Thus they disprove the assumption, commonplace since the 1970s and the rise of the megamusical, that British and American audiences constitute a single market, with shows that triumph in the West End inevitably doing the same on Broadway and vice versa. **Chapter 15** examines the contrasting transatlantic fates of these two works and looks at what this tells us about national attitudes to rock music, spectacle, and musical theatre itself. Comparing one to the other, David Cottis deduces that both shows 'were deliberately lightweight concoctions, drawing on popular theatrical forms like the spectacle and pantomime, and taking an omnivorous attitude to musical styles. In Britain this is, for historical reasons, an aesthetic that has characterised much mainstream post-war popular music; in the United States, it is one that sits more comfortably in Vegas than on Broadway.'

## Part VI: 'Popular in Germany and Austria?'

After World War II Germany and Austria took a long time to warm to the Anglophone musical. In the 1950s touring productions of American shows (such as *Oklahoma!*, 1951, and later *South Pacific, Guys and Dolls,* and *West Side Story*) were met with incomprehension or disinterest, and there were very few attempts by local theatres to stage a Broadway musical themselves. Thus, in spite of the occasional hit (for instance, *My Fair Lady* in Berlin in 1961) it could be said that the genre only had its breakthrough in the mid-1980s. But once audiences succumbed to the lure of British and American imports, the German-language musical theatre industry quickly turned into a major market for the genre. Yet, like every region, it developed certain idiosyncrasies in respect to the reception of certain works and artists, setting Germany and Austria apart from other major musical theatre markets, partly as a consequence of these countries' particular histories. Part VI will explore some of the distinctive aspects of that response.

It is safe to say that the collaborations between Bertolt Brecht and Kurt Weill such as *Die Dreigroschenoper* (*The Threepenny Opera,* 1928), and *Der Aufstieg und Fall der Stadt Mahagonny* (*The Rise and Fall of the City of Mahagonny,* 1930) are nowadays regarded by German and Austrian critics as among the greatest of all stage works created in the twentieth century. This admiration of the composer's output, however, has never extended to the shows he wrote after he emigrated to the United States. In **Chapter 16** Judith Wiemers explores whether this attitude has changed by tracing the twenty-first-century German reception of Weill's works for the American musical stage, written between 1936 and the composer's death in 1950. Wiemers argues that certain prejudices associated with the evolving compositional style in Weill's Broadway shows and his affinity with the American theatre system continue to inform their reception in the country of the composer's birth, as do general reservations about the American entertainment industry on the one hand, and the genre of the stage musical on the other. Although Weill's American oeuvre, which often resists clear genre demarcations, still struggles to become firmly entrenched in the German repertory, the author sees 'cause for hope that eventually artistic directors and theatre critics will fully overcome the idea of the two Kurt Weills, one belonging to "us" and one belonging to "them".'

Germans took several decades to come to terms with what had happened in the country during the Third Reich. Especially in the first years after the Allied victory, any overt reference in popular culture to the time under Hitler was considered problematic. When distributors wanted to release foreign films in the newly founded Federal Republic, the films were either cut or had their dialogue changed in the German dubbing if they alluded to or directly addressed the Nazi regime. Serious public discussion of the years between 1933 and 1945 only started in the late 1960s, intensifying in the turbulent 1970s. Even today there is a perception abroad that the war and everything that led up to it is a sensitive topic, one best avoided in cross-cultural communication. (The most famous example of this attitude is the oft-quoted advice given in the BBC comedy series *Fawlty Towers*: 'Don't mention the war!') While this may be a misconception, it is true that most cultural critics in German-language countries still consider Nazism an unsuitable subject for entertainment and thus—by extension—for musicals.

**Chapter 17** discusses portrayals of National Socialism in popular musical theatre, focussing on such typical works as *Schweyk im Zweiten Weltkrieg* (*Schweyk in the Second World War,* 1957), *The Sound of Music* (1959), *Cabaret* (1966), *and The*

*Producers* (2001). It analyses their structural elements, such as the construction and musical depiction of Nazi representatives, as well as the dramaturgical forms that deal with them. Specifically, Nils Grosch and Susanne Scheiblhofer examine double-layer dramaturgy, alienation strategies and the use of caricature and irony. Their essay explores how the behaviour of Nazi figures is framed and sometimes de-demonised by the conventions and theatrical tools of both musical comedy and the musical play. The chapter also addresses the reception of these works in German-speaking countries and investigates their function in mirroring and developing processes regarding *Vergangenheitsbewältigung* ('coming to terms with the past'), politics of memory and denazification. The authors conclude that in 'a genre created predominantly by Jewish authors [ ... ], the question of whether it is legitimate to use Nazi protagonists and symbols in entertainment perhaps transforms into a vindication of the agency and empowerment entailed in laughing at one's enemies'.

**Chapter 18** investigates the repertoire of imported Anglo-American musicals post-reunification (1989–1990) as the core of contemporary popular musical theatre in German-speaking countries (Germany, Austria and northern Switzerland), in terms of gross income, audience attendance, productions and diversity, the third-biggest market for Anglophone popular musical theatre in the world. Frédéric Döhl pays particular attention to living composers and imported Anglo-American works that premiered after the mid-1990s, including comparative case studies of Stephen Sondheim and Frank Wildhorn. Additionally, Döhl focusses on the domestic production of new musicals, especially those by Martin Lingnau. After taking stock of the German-language musical theatre industry, Döhl reaches the conclusion that 'what is needed today is a work that does for the reputation of the genre at home and of the German-language musical abroad what *Cats* did nearly forty years ago for contemporary British and American musicals in continental Europe, namely to bring about a watershed moment which creates a new dynamic.' He is confident that 'the richness and strength especially of the public theatre sector here should be enough to provide a basis for such a development.'

## Part VII: 'Popular in East Asia'

What seemed unimaginable decades ago has now become a fact: Southeast Asia has opened up to Anglophone musical theatre. Today Japan and South Korea have turned into the two biggest foreign markets for British and American musicals after the German-speaking region. Both Asian countries also guarantee huge box office for film musicals—*Les Misérables* (2012), *Frozen* (2013), *Beauty and the Beast* (2017), and *Frozen II* (2019) all did exceptionally well in both countries. With its booming economy and huge population, China, on the other hand, constitutes the one market that every Western theatre writer and practitioner would like to conquer. Part VII of the volume surveys from a number of perspectives the ways musicals are produced and have been received in these three Asian countries.

Cross-gender casting has been a staple of British and American musical theatre for decades in shows as diverse as *Where's Charley?* (1948), *Privates on Parade* (1977), *La Cage aux Folles* (1983), *Hedwig and the Angry Inch* (1998), *Hairspray* (2002), and *Kinky Boots* (2012). All of these shows, however, focus on drag queens, not drag kings, the stage version of *Victor/Victoria* (1995) being one of the few exceptions. In contrast to this, Japanese theatre has traditionally relied on the art of both female and male impersonation. The Takarazuka Revue, for instance, features female performers in all of the roles. After a modest start in 1914 with a troupe of seventeen young Japanese women, the Takarazuka empire has grown into a large entertainment company which performs to 2.5 million fans every year. Now employing over four hundred women (divided into five troupes), the company owns two 2,000-seat theatres, and at least one troupe is touring at any given time.

As **Chapter 19** explains, the Takarazuka aesthetic is a Technicolor pastiche of many performing arts genres: Broadway musical, Vegas revue, Busby Berkeley extravaganza, and show choir. The most famous performers in the troupe are the women who perform the male characters and sing almost exclusively in the chest register. Yet their performance of masculinity is not conventional drag, where the intent is to pass, nor is it a camp performance, where the performer and audience share a knowing wink at the artifice. The *otokoyaku* simultaneously presents both traditional male and female visual codes. While they may thicken their eyebrows and add facial hair, they also don fake eyelashes and apply eyeshadow; the goal is not verisimilitude. With eighty to a hundred elaborately costumed performers on stage, the purpose of the company is clear: to manufacture dreams. As Bud Coleman witnessed himself, the Takarazuka fan culture is a major part of its allure and power in Japan: '[H]ere, the fans *made* the performance, not just with their applause and calling out the names of their beloved stars, but with their attention.'

Broadway has for decades been fixated on female stars to the degree that many of them are referred to by their first name alone (Ethel, Barbra, Liza, Bernadette, Patti, Idina, et al.); even today Hugh Jackman may be the only male performer to sell out any musical he appears in. South Korean audiences on the other hand are far more likely to be drawn to a production by its male lead. The Korean market is mostly driven by young female theatergoers in their teens, twenties, and thirties and has adapted the unusual practice of recruiting most of its performers from the country's music industry, also known as K-pop, which in recent years has become an international phenomenon, with many followers abroad.

**Chapter 20** provides an overview of the Korean musical market at large, examining in three sections its major characteristics, limitations, and prospects. The first delineates the history of Korean musicals in order to identify its unique characteristics. The second section inspects the current status of the Korean musical industry by assessing various recent statistics to determine which phenomena needed close attention in 2020. The last section focuses on Korean musicals' relationship to K-pop, considerably the most 'Korean' aspect of the market, highlighting phenomena derived from this relationship. Yongmin Kwon, Hyeyoung Ra, and Kangjoo Cho explain how the active involvement of large corporations which mainly invested in pretested licensed musicals starring high-profile celebrities restricted the creation of original musicals, which led to various problems related to celebrity casting, such as a rise in ticket prices and multiple casting. It also limited the popularisation of musicals and the acquisition of new audience pools, weakening the overall structure of the industry. The essay concludes that if the local market is to grow further, it 'is time for the Korean musical industry to reform its constitution and strengthen internal stability' by developing new works and a broader audience base.

Cai Fangtian begins **Chapter 21**: 'As one of the many imported products since China's "open and reform" policy, officially initiated in December 1978, musicals have appeared on Chinese stages for about three decades'. Her essay reviews the development of the Chinese musical theatre industry from the 1980s to the present day in order to examine the challenges and problems for musical theatre productions in China. The author also surveys the spread and influence of Western musicals since the Chinese translation of *The Music Man* made its debut in Beijing in 1987 and reviews three types of musicals in China: Western musicals, Chinese-language translations of Western musicals, and original Chinese musicals. Finally, the author examines musical theatre training in higher educational institutions in China, the cultivation of musical theatre talent and the future prospects for the Chinese musical theatre industry. Regarding the latter, Fangtian declares: 'The time has now surely arrived for Chinese musical practitioners [ ... ] to join their efforts towards the development of a musical theatre industry in the country in order to create more Chinese musicals with appealing stories and qualities that are entertaining in the current context of Chinese popular culture.'

## Part VIII: 'Sondheim Abroad'

The most important American musical theatre artist of the last fifty years, Stephen Sondheim, has written several shows that are set in other countries and/or use foreign source material. One is an original musical (*Pacific Overtures*, 1976) and the other two are adaptations. *Sweeney Todd, the Demon Barber of Fleet Street* (1979) is based on the English playwright Christopher Bond's 1973 drama of the same title, while *A Little Night Music* (1973) musicalises Ingmar Bergman's classic Swedish film comedy *Smiles of a Summer Night* (1955). Whenever an artist employs or refers to tropes, themes, and materials which are not part of his or her own culture, even if they are as scrupulous in their research as Sondheim and his collaborators, questions arise about cultural appropriation and cross-cultural misunderstanding. Part VIII will explore in chronological order the reception of these three musicals in the country in which each is set.

No other Swedish film director is as famous around the world as Ingmar Bergman: three of his movies won the Oscar for Best Foreign Language Film (*The Virgin Spring*, 1960; *Through a Glass Darkly*, 1961; and *Fanny and Alexander*, 1983) and his oeuvre has influenced filmmakers everywhere, most notably Woody Allen. However, Bergman's reputation as an artist who doesn't shy away from the darkest of subjects, be it war, death or despair, often overshadows the astonishing fact that he was in addition a brilliant writer and director of comedy, as attested by his masterwork *Smiles of a Summer Night*.

When the bittersweet romantic roundelay was adapted in the early 1970s by Sondheim, producer-director Harold Prince and librettist Hugh Wheeler, the musical version *A Little Night Music* not only won five Tony Awards and gave the composer-lyricist his biggest hit in the wistful ballad 'Send in the Clowns', but it also became one of the few Sondheim musicals to make a profit in its original Broadway production.

**Chapter 22** charts how critics and audiences reacted to the musical when it returned to the country where it is set, considering all seven productions of the show in various Swedish cities between 1974 and 2013. Renate Stridh relates the various ways in which the musical has been received and performed to both the changing attitudes towards the two artists associated in Sweden with this musical (Bergman and Sondheim) and to the general development of musical theatre there. At the end of her discussion, the author states that 'finding the perfect balance between the American and the Swedish artist proves difficult in the latter's home country', in spite of the fact that 'Bergman never saw them in any kind of competition.'

The 1975–1976 Broadway season saw the opening of three major musicals: *A Chorus Line*, *Chicago*, and *Pacific Overtures*. While the first two have entered record books for their long-running original production and revival, respectively, the Sondheim musical about the clash of Japanese and Western culture only lasted for 193 performances. Depicting the American-driven opening of isolationist Japan in the nineteenth century, the rarely produced show can be considered an oddity. In 2000, nearly a quarter of a century after its New York première, the musical finally received its first staging in the country where it takes place. Amon Miyamoto's Japanese-language production reflected a starkly different perception of events from the original version, yet won such high praise from the composer-lyricist that it was subsequently imported to Washington and then restaged in English in New York. As opposed to the daring kabuki-like format used on Broadway to highlight the exotic nature of the Japanese, the Japanese version is concerned less with the perils of progress than with its inevitability, a warning not against change but against a refusal to change. As Gary Perlman observes in **Chapter 23**: 'For Japanese audiences [ ... ] the show is a more timeless re-examination of their own past and present, notably whether it is desirable or possible forcibly to prevent the natural flow of history, even for the sake of apparent stability'.

Although *Sweeney Todd, the Demon Barber of Fleet Street* won nine Tony Awards and received glowing reviews in New York, the first London production in 1980 was a resounding flop and closed early. Since this memorable early failure, Sondheim's retelling has become one of the most frequently performed of all musicals in the British capital, in productions that run the full gamut from elaborate West End revivals with major stars to small-scale fringe stagings and a site-specific reimagining in a pie shop. (The 2007 film adaptation was also a huge hit in Britain.) In **Chapter 24** Robert Lawson-Peebles charts the journey the demon barber has taken from Fleet Street to Broadway and back to the British capital. His essay on *Sweeney Todd* is organised into two sections. The first discusses the criminal and unsanitary environment of Fleet Street, which prompted the serial publication *The String of Pearls* (1846–1847), with its protagonists, the murderous barber Sweeney Todd and his pie-shop accomplice Mrs Lovett. The metamorphosis of Todd from neighbourhood gangster to comic villain can be witnessed in a trio of melodramas, a British film, and a humorous monologue.

The second section of the essay shows how Stephen Sondheim and Hugh Wheeler restored Todd's status as a Fleet Street psychopath. The essay concludes with a survey of the productions, mainly in London, that established Todd as a demonic icon and the enterprise with Mrs Lovett as an urban myth.

## Part IX: 'National Genres of Musical Theatre in Western Europe'

In response to the transnational success of Anglophone musicals, various Western European countries began to create their own musicals, which in some cases has led to the gestation of homegrown paradigms that function differently from the American and the British models. Part IX of the collection will explore three of these national developments.

Although the composer Jacques Offenbach was one of the founders of international musical theatre, France's contribution to the genre since 1900 has, for various reasons, been comparatively minor. Inspired by the rock operas of Andrew Lloyd Webber and Tim Rice, a new generation of French writers in the 1970s began creating their own concept recordings which they later staged as big spectacles in huge venues, to great popular acclaim. This distinctively French form of musical may not be widely known in English-speaking countries, but it has been embraced by audiences across continental Europe as well as Asia. Claude-Michel Schönberg and Alain Boublil's *La Revolution française* (1973) and *Les Misérables* (in its original 1980 form) are two of these *spectacles musicaux*; the latter was picked up by British producer Cameron Mackintosh, who helped revise the Victor Hugo adaptation and then exported it globally, with tremendous success. In **Chapter 25** Luca Cerchiari deals in critical terms with these and other prominent examples of the subgenre, including shows by Luc Plamondon, Michel Berger, Riccardo 'Richard' Cocciante, and Gérard Presgurvic, such as *Starmania*, *Notre Dame de Paris*, and *Roméo et Juliette: De la haine à l'amour*, offering three reasons for the 'Anglophone resistance to practically all of these French shows [ . . . ]: (a) the traditional difficulties of translating the original text; (b) their limitations in theatrical and dramaturgical terms, and (c) the cultural differences between French and Anglophone musical theatre.'

Since 1992 there have been several internationally successful German and Austrian shows which claim to have introduced a new subgenre of musical theatre. The 'drama musical' was developed by the lyricist-librettist Michael Kunze, who first gained prominence as a lyricist for German *schlager* and other types of popular music. In 1975 the song 'Fly, Robin, Fly' reached number 1 on the US Billboard charts and won him a Grammy. Kunze later became the most in-demand translator of musicals for the German and

Austrian markets. In the 1990s Kunze started to create his own material, with great success; the long-running works for which he wrote both libretto and lyrics, most of which premiered in Vienna, include *Tanz der Vampire* (*Dance of the Vampires*, 1997, with music by Jim Steinman), *Elisabeth* (1992), *Mozart! The Musical* (1999), *Marie-Antoinette*, and *Rebecca: The Musical* (both 2006), the last four composed by his long-time collaborator, Sylvester Levay. All of these musicals have been produced abroad to enthusiastic response by the public in Japan, South Korea, Sweden, Hungary, Poland, France, and elsewhere.

In **Chapter 26** Olaf Jubin investigates the key elements of the 'drama musical' and explores the manner in which the storytelling techniques employed in these five shows differ from those of their British and American counterparts, not only interrogating how their dramaturgy functions but also tracing the influences detectable from the famous musicals Kunze has adapted into German and how he moves beyond their innovative forms. The author identifies 'at least one unique feature, and that concerns the way the score depicts the relationship between the protagonist and the ensemble', because 'in the drama musical the leading character is separated from the rest of society right from the start by birth, education, talent or morality, so that she or he can never join' the others in song.

Björn Ulvaeus and Benny Andersson's high-profile collaboration with the lyricist Tim Rice on the 1984 concept recording of *Chess* met with very mixed results once the show was transferred to the stage. The musical barely turned a profit in London and flopped badly in New York, so the Swedish songwriters subsequently turned their attention to material closer to home. Their next project was a musicalisation of a quartet of novels by the Swedish author Vilhelm Moberg published between 1949 and 1959. These were inspired by the historical fact that in the mid-nineteenth century more than one million Swedes emigrated to the United States. Premiering in Malmö in 1995, *Kristina från Duvemåla* follows the journey the eponymous character; her husband, Karl Oskar; and several of their friends and relatives take from Scandinavia to their new settlement in Minnesota. In the last twenty-five years the show has been staged six times around Sweden and has been seen by more than one million people—10 percent of the country's population. Although its creators have made several attempts to secure financing for an English-language staging of *Kristina*—including concert presentations in New York's Carnegie Hall and London's Royal Albert Hall—so far there has been no full production of the show outside Scandinavia. In **Chapter 27** Mikael Strömberg discusses *Kristina från Duvemåla* as a folk musical, exploring features of the lyrics, score, and staging while arguing that the original production's strong emphasis on themes and aspects familiar to Swedish theatregoers runs the risk of excluding a foreign audience. Recurrent references to Swedish traditions and the Swedish countryside explain why the musical has become such a huge success in Sweden yet so far has been unable to attract an international audience. As Strömberg emphasises: 'What has not yet been found is the perfect balance between the local elements which set the tone and offer a unique style and sound, and the musical's more general theme that will immediately chime with the concerns of a broader public.'

INTRODUCTION    29

# Part X: National Traditions of Musical Theatre in Eastern Europe

Since the dissolution of Soviet bloc, most former socialist countries have embraced Anglophone musical theatre. (In addition, some have become important markets for musicals originating in Germany, Austria, and France.) However, many of the formerly communist Eastern European countries also have a long history of homegrown musical theatre, which for a variety of reasons has seldom travelled beyond their borders. Part X of this handbook will survey the indigenous musicals of three states in Eastern Europe: the Czech Republic, Poland, and Hungary. Jan Šotkovsky summarises the main tendencies in the history of Czech musical theatre of the twentieth and twenty-first centuries in **Chapter 28**, which covers indigenous works as well as productions of foreign (especially British and American) musicals. As the author demonstrates, the Czech musical developed as a series of creative departures from the Broadway norm, even today tending towards looser cabaret and revue formats.

Discussing the pre-war period, the essay explores the Osvobozené divadlo (Liberated Theatre) and its political jazz revues, which took the form of historical parables and were innovative even by international standards. The chapter then emphasises the particular contribution of small and studio 'song theatres' during the communist regime of 1948–1989 and the difficulties state operetta theatres had adapting to the musical theatre repertoire, as well as some of the extraordinary achievements in the field of film musicals in the 1960s. When focusing on the democratic period after 1989, the essay covers the great boom of musical theatre as a business—often approached with naivety and without practical know-how—that has gradually led to the aim of a balance between the production models of the two Czech sectors, subsidised and commercial musical theatre. Šotkovsky explains that if the local musical theatre industry wants to progress, it needs to overcome certain weaknesses: 'its lack of local authors' with adequate theatre experience, and 'the absence of a domestic "Off-Broadway" scene that would allow artists to workshop drafts of musicals in small-scale performances.'

**Chapter 29** discusses Polish musical theatre after World War II. Since 1952 the Gdynia musical theatre has become the most remarkable native institution of its type, and its achievements are the focus of Aleksandra Zajac-Kiedysz's essay. She investigates the important role the seaside resort has played in establishing and fostering a Polish tradition of musical theatre production, both by performing works imported from the West and by creating a vibrant repertoire of homegrown shows, which spoke and continue to speak directly to the local audience. As a genre, 'musical theatre remains extremely popular in Poland and the country continues to stage both indigenous and international works,' to the point where this European republic, with its many excellent theatre companies, can be said to be going through a 'musical epidemic'.

Focusing on the 1983 historical musical *István, a király* (*Stephen, the King*), **Chapter 30** scrutinises the diverse roles art and theatre fulfilled in Hungary's socialist period after World War II. Before analysing *István*, Zoltán Imre briefly delineates the emergence of the musical as a genre in Hungary and its various functions in the socialist era before situating *István* within the Hungarian musical scene of the 1980s. The author explains how the rock opera managed to reuse an ancient historical tale to reflect the political and social conflicts of the Kádár regime and also analyses the process of its elevation to the status of a national classic. Finally, the chapter outlines the current situation of musical theatre in Hungary, which has become a flourishing market for all kinds of imported musicals, ranging from the French *spectacle musical* and screen-to-stage adaptations to the German and Austrian 'drama musicals'. Imre ends on a rather somber note when he decries the virtual disappearance from Hungary of 'socially engaged theatre, that is, theatre as public forum for society' under the current ultra-conservative/totalitarian government of Victor Orbán because 'musicals and operettas, which [ ... ] have recently focused on staging escapist stories, always with a happy ending, light music, and flashy sets and costumes, have played and continue to play a crucial role in that change.'

## Part XI: Outlook, or The Road Ahead

The three essays which form Part XI of the volume address current cultural discourses; they question the extent to which the musical theatre industry and musical theatre pedagogy have become more inclusive by looking closely at the representation of ethnicity and gender as well as by mapping the new challenges confronting universities and professional training schools.

If we want to decolonise musical theatre as a whole, the curricula of institutions within higher education seem a logical place to start; after all, this is where many professionals acquire the knowledge and skills they later bring to the industry. Yet, as Pamela Karantonis points out in **Chapter 31**, this endeavour is much more radical and comprehensive than merely exposing students to a greater volume of commercially celebrated work featuring Black, Indigenous, and Asian artists. The process of decolonisation begins by understanding how teachers and students could make universities accountable to the circumstances of the real artists who create the work. It also entails the problematisation of who curates and theorises the teaching material and who performs it as part of an educational programme. Methods of decolonising the training of skills are required for analysing and performing the genre as well as for choosing and staging student productions. After examining a number of Indigenous works, including *Bran Nue Dae* (1990), Karantonis suggests that if people in higher education want to share 'meaningful stories that identify and specify voices which have been silent', they should adopt a collaborative approach. This would entail 'identify[ing] a story' through discussion before students and staff 'share lived experiences, commit music to muscle memory, and embody choreography'.

In recent years, the theatre and film industries have made an effort to cast performers in musicals that come from the communities their characters represent—Ivo Van Howe's 2020 Broadway production and Steven Spielberg's 2021 remake of *West Side*

*Story* are cases in point. Still, staying true to an ethnic group's experience remains a complex and complicated issue.

In **Chapter 32** Hannah Thuraisingam Robbins interrogates a cluster of interconnected issues in the casting practice of the contemporary musical on stage and screen from the personal perspective of a queer woman of colour. Challenging the industry's supposedly progressive strategies of race-blind or racially inclusive casting in the high-profile musicals *Hamilton*, *In the Heights*, and *Moana*, they demonstrate the paradox that in order to promote the visibility of ethnic minorities in the utopian narratives of musicals, they must be falsely represented as 'belonging' to the (inevitably white) majority community. Consequently, performers of colour are often presented as the voices and faces of new musicals, while in reality they are excluded from the centres of power that actually determine what stories are being told and how. This in turn perpetuates the phenomenon that 'dialogues about race-conscious casting assume whiteness as the default identity and do not seek to address the absence of *our* stories and histories in the United Kingdom and the United States'.

While the arts in many countries have been at the forefront of promoting all kinds of inclusivity, there are far fewer female writers, composers, producers, and executives in all branches of the musical theatre industry than there are males. Probably the only two arenas where women outnumber men are in musical theatre training institutions and as audience members. This in turn exacerbates the problem of how the industry can make sure that women's experiences and interests are reflected in the works they have come to see and perform in.

In **Chapter 33** Grace Barnes offers a transnational survey of recent productions staged in the United Kingdom, Australia, and the United States, including *The Boy in the Dress* (2019), *SIX* (2017), and *Cinderella* (2021). The empirical evidence provided by these productions and the incisive, in-depth interpretation of their representation of gender does not leave much room for optimism. The title of Barnes's chapter, '"Superboy and the Invisible Girl": The Exclusion of the Female Voice from Global Musical Theatre', suggests her sobering conclusion: 'As it currently stands, diversity in musical theatre translates as stories about men who are not white and/or straight. What it categorically does not mean is stories about women, created, and directed by other women'. Barnes emphasises that the persistent refusal of both the industry and the media to acknowledge the chronic under-representation of women in key artistic positions 'will prevent the genre from developing its enormous potential to be a real and lasting instrument of change'.

## PROSPECTS FOR FURTHER RESEARCH

It was a conscious decision on the part of the editors to end the book with a fervent rallying cry to recognise and then to tackle a long-standing desideratum in global musical theatre. Yet the role women have played and are currently allowed to play in musical theatre is only one of various areas which warrant further examination in both industry and academic circles.

The thirty-three essays assembled in this collection not only approach the topic of the global stage musical in its various aspects and from a range of different angles; the book also engages the field of comparative theatre cultures by attempting for the first time a kind of trans-world snapshot of the genre. Although the volume aims for a complementary and multi-perspectival approach, it does not claim to be an exhaustive survey. Rather, the hope is to uncover trends, influences, differences, and commonalities that might demand further exploration by means of specialist studies. What follows is an indicative list of subjects addressed and issues highlighted by several of the contributors which warrant subsequent in-depth investigation. They have been subdivided into four main areas of research.

(1) The Anglophone Musical and Its Reception
- British and American musical theatre is often seen in other countries as 'the other', with all that entails—not as something indigenous that people respond to instinctively and immediately.
- The reception of Anglophone musical theatre has been coloured in most continental European countries (Germany, Austria, Sweden, and others) but also in Mexico by a deep-seated mistrust, not to say scorn, for American mass culture. Such a hostile reaction does not differentiate between the works of Rodgers and Hammerstein, Cole Porter, Stephen Sondheim, or even Andrew Lloyd Webber (who is British after all); it is the genre *as a whole* that is rejected. While other parts of American popular culture such as Hollywood movies and hip-hop have been able to move beyond discussions about their intrinsic worth, the musical has not. It is still seen as a threat to the 'genuine' art of theatre represented by straight plays, post-dramatic theatre, and opera. Musical theatre is often considered a core part of the 'culture industry' and thus of capitalism at its most degraded. This in turn deters some artists (directors, writers, composers, and performers alike) from working in the genre. Welfare states and others which subsidise theatre as a high or an educational form of cultural identity to this day see the Broadway musical as mindless 'escapism' designed to appeal to the lowest common denominator. This position by reviewers and other members of the cultural elite has been in evidence since the 1940s, and the discourse on the limited or non-existent qualities of the musical as a genre has raged for decades and recommences regularly at various stages of cultural change in different countries (for instance, Sweden in the 1950s and Germany and Austria in the 1980s).
- How musicals are defined in each respective country affects how the individual show is seen; musicals that cross genres and thus defy easy categorisation continue to have problematic receptions.
- In countries with a strong lineage of opera and operetta, the musical has had difficulties establishing itself, as it was not always clear to critics and audiences

what distinguished the genre. Thus, it has been seen as ersatz, especially when staged and performed by artists from the other two genres.

- The global reception histories of both the book musical and the so-called megamusical need to be written with more nuance and awareness of cultural differences. Anglophone musical theatre fans are often surprised that certain Broadway classics, like some works by Rodgers and Hammerstein, have failed to win over audiences and critics outside of English-speaking countries, whereas other integrated shows were far more influential: *Kiss Me, Kate, My Fair Lady,* and *Fiddler on the Roof* continue to be popular in places where *Oklahoma!* or *South Pacific* never made an impact.
- The global fame and title recognition of several American shows, such as *West Side Story, My Fair Lady,* and *The Sound of Music,* are closely linked to their film adaptations—in these cases, Hollywood opened up a pathway for Broadway.
- Many countries have developed their own kinds of musicals in response to the British musical of the 1970s and 1980s, such as the rock opera, the jukebox musical, and—to a lesser degree—the (American) concept musical, which in turn suggests that on a global scale the influence of the classic book musical has been surprisingly limited.
- *Jesus Christ Superstar* has proved far more influential, especially in Continental Europe, than *Hair* or any other concept musical.
- The triumphant spread of Cameron Mackintosh's productions needs also to be comprehended as a more checkered process than is usually assumed: in Austria and Germany *Cats* turned into a seismic event, whereas in South Korea it was *The Phantom of the Opera.* In China, the interest in Western musicals was kickstarted by *Les Misérables,* a show that failed in German-language countries.
- Many Anglophone musicals have been adapted or 'reterritorialised' in order to cross cultural barriers; these modifications were not necessarily intended by their creators.
- Even if a show flops on Broadway, it may have a long shelf life in other places; certain musicals (such as *Tarzan*) and artists (such as Frank Wildhorn) have become hugely popular elsewhere.
- In turn, just because a show earns praise, awards, and a dedicated following on Broadway does not mean it will travel; *A Chorus Line* and *Rent* have flopped repeatedly even in London, while the appeal of such hits as *Wicked* and *Kinky Boots* has proved finite.
- On the other hand, it would be worth studying how fantasies about American culture have often been a strong factor in the way audiences have read specific musicals (whether they were from the United States or not), for instance in the Jazz Age, the postwar era, the 1960s, etc.
- The role of amateur groups and societies, especially in the former British Empire and the Commonwealth, in promoting and distributing as well as in keeping certain works in the public eye deserves a lot more attention.

FIG. 0.4 The global spread of many musical theatre works was supported by countless amateur productions: the ensemble of *The Merry Widow* as performed in 1964 by the Cairo Amateur Dramatic and Musical Society (CADMS). Photographer unknown; image provided by the editors.

(2) The Non-Anglophone Musical
- Many national musical theatre industries and their artists still struggle to establish their own identity.
- The jukebox musical has become the only form that has seen local iterations everywhere—Mexico, Brazil, Chile, Spain, Germany, Austria, the Czech Republic, Korea, China. However, these musicals about local music heroes are very limited in their exportability.
- Some non-Anglophone musicals include elements of traditional indigenous theatre (such as the Mexican *revista*, the German *Varieté* or Chinese opera) and thus attempt to balance the 'old' and the 'new', the indigenous and the cosmopolitan.
- Often, local stage musicals have been strongly influenced by local film musicals.
- Broadway and to a lesser extent the West End remain the ultimate goal for musicals created elsewhere in the world; however, the Anglophone musical theatre industry is very rigid in its understanding of what constitutes

professionalism, craft or artistic value, which is only one of several hurdles foreign artists find impossible to overcome when trying to break into the English-speaking market.

- Just because a musical has never played successfully in New York or London does not mean that it cannot turn into a local or global smash; drama musicals such as *Elisabeth* and *spectacles musicaux* such as *Notre Dame de Paris* have become popular and influential far beyond their country of origin.

(3) Production Circumstances and Other Relevant Factors

- The history of musical theatre in authoritarian states (such as the countries of the former Soviet bloc and apartheid South Africa) shows that although there may be forms and pockets of resistance, political interference and censorship have severely restricted the spread and reception of musicals across borders.
  Today the threat to artistic endeavours, including those in musical theatre, remains prevalent, especially in countries with right-wing governments like (until recently) Brazil or Hungary, where freedom of expression is often curtailed.
- Although training for musical theatre performers has become more widespread and effective around the world, most nations still lack training facilities for musical theatre writers and producers.
- Performance schedules as well as funding mechanisms vary hugely from country to country; more detailed information about how these variables in basic parameters affect musical theatre would be welcome.
- Since the 1990s musical theatre around the world has attracted companies which belong to vertically integrated business empires. Producing is no longer dominated by the individual maverick impresario but by conglomerates that benefit from synergistic effects across their various (media) outlets.
- The availability of theatrical spaces is a huge factor in the reception of musical theatre.
- Celebrity casting is on the rise everywhere.
- Fandom takes many different forms; because musical theatre is popular theatre, the responses of its most ardent audiences are reflected in how the genre has evolved and continues to evolve.
- There have been forays into how social media influences musical theatre in the United States; however, there is not yet any detailed analysis of how the so-called prosumer culture is transforming the genre in other regions.
- Another worldwide phenomenon that takes many local forms is nostalgia.

(4) The Reach and Transferability of Musical Theatre

- The notion of a globalised musical means very different things in different cultures and contexts.
- In spite of what proponents of the Frankfurt School and other forms of *Kulturkritik* might claim, musical theatre remains a form that responds to and is received in relation to social needs and political circumstances, as is highlighted especially by examples from Eastern Europe.

- It is difficult to predict what people relate to and what they will accept in a musical; this leads to significant local variations in elements as basic as length, storytelling, and tone.
- Just as certain countries stubbornly resist the charm and lure of specific British or American musicals and artists, so too does the Anglophone market stubbornly reject others form of musical theatre. Commercial considerations clearly play a major part here—powerful players protecting their vested interests—but it is striking how especially American musicals nowadays are exported everywhere, while the US market has remained hostile to shows from abroad. To a certain extent, that also includes works from the United Kingdom and Canada. Countries as diverse as Italy, Austria, Japan, Hungary, and South Korea have been far more open to musicals which were conceived and premiered in non-English-speaking countries.
- In spite of assumptions that we are approaching one general and generalised 'global culture' heavily dominated by US products, the reactions to individual shows still vary widely from country to country.

This last point may give hope and solace to those who fear that we are moving towards a (musical) theatre culture where one size fits all. On the contrary, the global stage musical and its reception have far more layers than it is regularly given credit for. It will enrich all of us—fans, creatives, journalists, and academics—to take a closer look.

We hope that this volume provides some inspiration as to where to focus the attention.

## Notes

1. Dan Rebellato, 'Playwriting and Globalisation: Towards a Site-Unspecific Theatre', *Contemporary Theatre Review* 16, no. 1 (2006): 96–113, doi: 1080/10486800500451047, 96.
2. More recently, the history of music theatre evinces the popularisation and dissemination of baroque opera around Europe in the seventeenth and eighteenth centuries; a century later, the globalisation of *opéra comique* and operetta; a little later still, the repertoire of Gilbert and Sullivan; and in the twentieth century, Anglo-American musical comedy.
3. Globalisation of plays and performances from the Western world began as early as 330 BC, when Alexander the Great exported Athenian culture as far as Egypt, after which the new city of Alexandria began around 260 BC to build up an unparalleled library of ancient Greek texts, including of course, the plays of the great Athenian tragic and comic poets. The globalisation of theatre culture continued inexorably as the Romans assimilated Greek culture, in the process of translation transforming it and disseminating it across Europe and the Middle East. Not only was the transmission of play texts a major enterprise in what has become known as globalisation, but the building of Graeco-Roman and later Roman theatres throughout the countries of the Mediterranean introduced a uniform idea and material manifestation of performance throughout the Roman Empire.
4. Yi Wang claims: 'Culture does change in dialogue with changing economic and sociopolitical circumstances. A culture changes with other cultures with which it is brought into contact through commercial or political relations. However, cultures are constructed

by people. [ ... ] Creative persons can contribute to the change and development of a culture. People are not mere objects of cultural influences, but subjects who can sift various influences and reject or integrate them. Sometimes, advocates of anti-globalisation overlook the power of people's subjectivity[...]. Cultural identity provides the global significance of local knowledge and the sense of self, community, and nation. [ ... ] Globalisation is not simply homogenisation.' Yi Wang, 'Globalisation Enhances Cultural Identity', *Intercultural Communication Studies* 6, no. 1 (2007): 83–86; here: 84–85.

5. 'Globalisation' is invoked as shorthand to summarise these processes of deterritorialisation and reterritorialisation, but in such a way that makes them equally aspatial or ageographical and, as such, profoundly disempowering. As Hirst and Thompson, among others, have pointed out, the process of globalisation is perhaps not as pervasive and total as many make it out to be. They show how—at least until 1913—international interdependence in terms of global trade and foreign direct investment (FDI) was significantly higher compared with the subsequent period of national 'Fordist' development (1925–1973). Paul Hirst and Grahame Thompson, 'The Future of Globalisation', Cooperation and Conflict: *Journal of the Nordic International Studies Association* 37, no. 3 (2002): 247–265, eatonak.org/IPE501S2013/downloads/files/Hirst_and_Thompson.pdf, accessed 3 June 2020. According to Harvey, 'the adoption of the term "globalisation" signals a profound "natural" geographical unit within which capitalism's historical trajectory develops less and less meaningfully (if they ever were). We have to begin to see how the dynamics of capitalism are about the perpetual reconfiguration of space and spatial organisation in which space is a constitutive moment.' David Harvey, 'Globalisation in Question', Development Research Series, working paper no. 56, University of Aalborg, March 1997, 1–22; here: 6.

6. Justin Rosenberg, 'Globalisation Theory: A Post Mortem', *International Politics* 42, no. 1 (2012): 2–74; here: 3.

7. 'It is in this context not surprising, therefore, to find a great number of geographical tensions, conflicts and struggles arising in many parts of the world, many of which are not even remotely emancipatory, liberating or empowering, [ ... ] the rise of anti-internationalist and deeply regionalist struggles that bring out the profound spatial tensions and contradictions that arise out of the maelstrom of spatial transformations wrought from recent changes in the organisation of capital circulation processes, but also from the recent waves of plant closures, company restructuring and bank collapses'. Eric Swyngedouw, 'Globalisation or Glocalisation: Networks, Territories and Rescaling', *Cambridge Review of International Affairs* 17, no. 1 (2004): 25–48; here: 31.

8. Just compare the original reviews for the film version of *The Sound of Music* (1965) with more recent discussions of the Oscar winner.

9. According to George Ritzer, *The McDonaldisation of Society* (Thousand Oaks, CA: Sage, 2008), the domination of the world economy by consumer capitalism created the phenomenon of McDonaldisation. In the tradition of the sociologist Max Weber, Ritzer perceives McDonaldisation to comprise four factors:

   (1) efficiency: the optimum method of completing a task—no individuality;
   (2) calculability: quantifiable rather than subjectively assessed criteria (*Big* Mac, not *Good* Mac);
   (3) predictability: production process organised to guarantee uniformity of product; and
   (4) control: predictable non-human labor for human labor, through automation or the de-skilling of the workforce.

10. Jonathan Burston, *The Megamusical: New Forms and Relations in Global Cultural Production* (Ann Arbor, MI: UMI Disertations, 1998).

11. Disney was to embrace Mackintosh's example enthusiastically with *Beauty and the Beast* (1994), their first film-to-stage musical, and followed it even more triumphantly with *The Lion King* (1997).

12. Jonathan Burston, 'Enter, Stage Right: Neoconservatism, English Canada and the Megamusical', *Soundings* 5 (1997): 179–180.

13. Burston observed the achievement in theatre performances of a kind of CD sound by the mid-1980s, which mimics the customary levels and style of sound amplification heard at pop concerts, without regard for the natural acoustic properties of the auditoriums in which they are performed. He analyses this phenomenon as 'a chronic despatialisation—a kind of jettisoning into sonic limbo'. Jonathan Burston, 'Spectacle, Synergy and Megamusicals: The Global Industrialization of the Live-Entertainment Economy', in *Media Organisations in Society*, ed. James Curran (London: Arnold, 2000), 69–83; here: 78. This despatialisation in turn affects the relationship between actors' bodies onstage in relation to the various spectating positions of individual members of the audience, who all hear the same amplified sound from the set of speakers nearest them.

14. Dan Rebellato, 'Playwriting and Globalisation: Towards a Site-Unspecific Theatre', *Contemporary Theatre Review* 16, no. 1 (2006): 99–100.

15. Ethan Mordden. *Rodgers & Hammerstein* (New York: Harry N. Abrams, 1992), 167.

16. Richard Altman and Mervyn Kaufman, *The Making of a Musical: Fiddler on the Roof* (New York: Crown, 1971), vii.

17. 'Der Hammer von Hammerstein: US-Musicals wurden für den deutschen Markt gesperrt', *Die deutsche Bühne*, November 1982, 13.

18. David Savran, 'Trafficking in Transnational Brands: The New Broadway-Style Musical', *Theatre Survey* 55, no. 3 (2014): 318342; here: 318.

19. Steve Nelson, '*Broadway and the Beast*: Disney Comes to Times Square', *Drama Review* 2 (1995): 71–85; here: 79.

20. Certain Broadway musical comedies are hugely successful in the West End (e.g. *The Book of Mormon* and *Kinky Boots*), but many are untranslatable outside Anglophone contexts. Americans are often surprised that Rodgers and Hammerstein are virtually unknown in Germany, Austria, France, the Netherlands, Italy, Spain, and Scandinavian countries. *The Sound of Music* only became known in Austria when Salzburg realised the economic potential of a *Sound of Music* tour in the early 2000s.

21. *My Fair Lady*, *Fiddler on the Roof*, and *Cabaret* are among the few Broadway shows that are consistently revived in new productions around Europe.

22. David Savran, 'Broadway as Global Brand', *Journal of Contemporary Drama in English* 5, no. 1 (April 2017): 24–37; here: 29.

23. See Olaf Jubin, 'Horses for Courses oder mehr als "Zuschau'n kann i net": *White Horse Inn* als anglizierte bzw. amerikanische Version von *Im weißen Rößl*', in *Im weißen Rößl: Kulturgeschichtliche Perspektiven*, ed. Nils Grosch and Carolin Stahrenberg (Münster and New York: Waxmann, 2016), 157–178.

24. See Len Platt and Tobias Becker, '"A Happy Man Can Live in the Past": Musical Theatre Transfer in the 1920s and 1930s', in *Popular Musical Theatre in London and Berlin*, ed. Len Platt, Tobias Becker, and David Linton (Cambridge: Cambridge University Press, 2014), 118–132, for a brief discussion of the transfer of Eric Charell's legendary production of Ralph Benatzky's *Im weißen Rößl* to London's Coliseum Theatre.

25. *Musicals 101*, The 1980s: Part I, www.musicals101.com, accessed 15 April 2020.That the contempt for the T. S. Eliot adaptation—which is not limited to the New York theatre industry, but may be exceptionally prevalent there—has not abated over the last forty years was shown conclusively by two striking examples in 2019: 'Kimmy Is Rich', episode 11 of season 4 of *Unbreakable Kimmy Schmidt*, imagined *Cats* as an ever-evolving scam, while the much-maligned film adaptation (directed by Tom Hooper) finally allowed many people to express their deep-seated hatred of the musical, which they did gleefully, especially on social media.

26. Typical of the approach of Broadway insiders to the British musical is Denny Martin Flynn, *Musical! A Grand Tour* (New York: Schirmer, 1997), which includes a twenty-page diatribe (474–495) against the musicals of Lloyd Webber and of Boublil and Schönberg.

27. Ibid., 479–480.

28. At the time Nunn directed *Les Miz* for the Royal Shakepeare Company, the marketing department referenced the opinions of many contemporary reviewers in heralding the RSC as the greatest ensemble company in the world. The pinnacle of this reputation for ensemble acting was evinced in Nunn and Caird's epic nine-and-a-half-hour, two-part adaptation of Dickens's *Nickolas Nickleby*. A virtuoso feat of ensemble acting and storytelling, the legendary production provided a matrix for the crafting of *Les Miz*.

29. It should here be noted that *Disney's Aida*, although technically a Broadway show, has a score by two British songwriters, Elton John and Tim Rice.

30. Jessica Sternfeld, *The Megamusical* (Bloomington: Indiana University Press, 2006), 5.

31. Only time will tell whether the latter two will become as popular outside the English-speaking market as they have been in the United States and the United Kingdom.

32. The critic and scholar Eric Bentley had said that Broadway productions were 'middlebrow' at a time when highbrow and lowbrow were acceptable but middlebrow was viewed as bourgeois kitsch. Adopting Bernard Shaw's maxim that 'the theatre is always at a low ebb', Bentley in *The Playwright as Thinker* ironically positioned the much-touted 'integration' of *Oklahoma!* as the 'ebb' of a tradition of 'theatricalism', claiming that music drama was not in itself integrated but required the director to synthesise all the artistic components in order to achieve 'integration'. Eric Bentley, 'The Drama at Ebb', *Kenyon Review* 7, no. 2 (1945): 169–184. For a further exploration of the implication of Bentley's notion, see James O'Leary, '*Oklahoma!* "Lousy Publicity" and the Politics of Formal Integration in the American Musical Theater', *Journal of Musicology* 31, no. 1 (2014): 139–182.

33. Russell Lynes, 'Highbrow, Lowbrow, Middlebrow', *Harper's*, 11 April 1949, reprinted in *Wilson Quarterly* 1, no. 1 (Autumn 1976): 146–158, https://www.jstor.org/stable/40255171, accessed 3 June 2020.

34. This debate was concurrent with Benjamin and Adorno's influential argument about the aura of the high art object versus the worthlessness of mass art in the era of mechanical reproduction. For an interesting and succinct analysis of this debate, see Alex Ross, 'The Naysayers: Walter Benjamin, Theodor Adorno, and the Critique of Pop Culture', *New Yorker*, 15 September 2014, https://www.newyorker.com/magazine/2014/09/15/naysayers, accessed 3 June 2020.

35. Louis Menard, 'Browbeaten: Dwight Macdonald's War on Midcult', *New Yorker*, 12 August 2011, https://www.newyorker.com/magazine/2011/09/05/browbeaten, accessed 15 April 2020.

36. Dwight Macdonald, 'A Theory of Mass Culture', in *Mass Culture*, ed. Bernard Rosenberg and Manning White (New York: Free Press, 1957), 59–73; here: 60.

37. Ibid.
38. Walter Benjamin, 'The Work of Art in the Age of Mechanical Reproduction (1935)', trans. Harry Zohn, in *Illuminations*, 1–26 (New York: Schocken Books, 1969), https://web.mit. edu/allanmc/www/benjamin.pdf, accessed 15 April 2020.
39. 'Any thorough study proves that there is indeed no greater contrast than that of the stage play to a work of art that is completely subject to or, like the film, founded in, mechanical reproduction' (ibid.).
40. Vagelis Siropoulos, 'A Postdramatic Composer in Search of a Dramatic Aesthetic, or, The Apotheosis and Decline of Andrew Lloyd Webber', *Gramma: Journal of Theory and Criticism* 17 (2009): 145–162, www.enl.auth.gr/gramma/goulos.pdf, accessed 29 March 2020.
41. 'Despite his unprecedented financial success and the adoration of the audience, Lloyd Webber has been the subject of intense critical controversy. In Britain [ ... ] the critical response has been mostly divided, but, in the US, Lloyd Webber [ ... ] has been largely dismissed as an opportunist, in spite of his impressive output, the development of a personal aesthetic and the consistency of his success over the years. Led by Frank Rich, chief drama critic of the [ ... ] *New York Times* throughout the 1980s and early 1990s, [he received the most malicious reviews that a commercial composer/producer of his [ ... ] status has ever received' (ibid., 145–146).
42. Ibid., 149. While Sondheim's musicals are non-linear in their varied post-Brechtian explorations of form, Rice and Lloyd Webber pioneered a more populist dramaturgy based on instant recognition of an eclectic range of pastiche material and the fetishisation of music and spectacle as key components of dramaturgy rather than the carefully detailed narrative patterns that typify the Rodgers and Hammerstein model. Siropoulos notes a number of features in Rice and Lloyd Webber's early *Joseph and the Amazing Technicolor Dreamcoat* (1968), 'which [ ... ] employed [biblical narrative] in the most cartoonish and generic manner and becomes the excuse for the insertion of various straight-forward pastiches of recognizable musical styles: from rock 'n' roll to vaudeville two-step and calypso and from country and western to French chanson and disco' (ibid.).
43. Vagelis Siropoulos, '*Evita*, the Society of the Spectacle and the Advent of the Megamusical', *Image & Narrative: Online Magazine of the Visual Narrative* 2, no. 2 (2010): 165–176; here: 165, www.imageandnarrative.be/index.php/imagenarrative/article/view/84/60, accessed 15 April 2020.
44. Ibid., 165.
45. Ibid., 172.

## BIBLIOGRAPHY

Altman, Rick, and Mervyn Kaufman. *The Making of a Musical: Fiddler on the Roof*. New York: Crown, 1971.
Bentley, Eric. 'The Drama at Ebb'. *Kenyon Review* 7, no. 2 (1945): 169–184.
Benjamin, Walter. 'The Work of Art in the Age of Mechanical Reproduction (1935)'. Translated by Harry Zohn. In *Illuminations*, 1–26. New York: Schocken Books, 1969. https://web.mit. edu/allanmc/www/benjamin.pdf, accessed 15 April 2020.
Burston, Jonathan. *The Megamusical: New Forms and Relations in Global Cultural Production*. Ann Arbor, MI: UMI Dissertations, 1998.

Burston, Jonathan. 'Enter, Stage Right: Neoconservatism, English Canada and the Megamusical'. *Soundings* 5 (1997): 179–190.

Burston, Jonathan. 'Spectacle, Synergy and Megamusicals: The Global Industrialization of the Live-Entertainment Economy'. In *Media Organisations in Society*, edited by James Curran, 69–83. London: Arnold, 2000.

Flynn, Denny Martin. *Musical! A Grand Tour*. New York: Schirmer, 1997.

'Der Hammer von Hammerstein: US-Musicals wurden für den deutschen Markt gesperrt'. *Die deutsche Bühne* 11 (1982): 13.

Harvey, David. 'Globalisation in Question'. Development Research Series. Working paper no. 56, University of Aalborg, March 1997, 1–22.

Hirst, Paul, and Grahame Thompson. 'The Future of Globalisation'. In Cooperation and Conflict: *Journal of the Nordic International Studies Association* 37, no. 3 (2002): 247–265. eatonak.org/IPE501S2013/downloads/files/Hirst_and_Thompson.pdf, accessed 3 June 2020. doi: https://doi.org/10.1177/0010836702037003671.

Jubin, Olaf. 'Horses for Courses oder mehr als "Zuschau'n kann i net": *White Horse Inn* als anglizierte bzw. amerikanisierte Version von *Im weißen Rößl*. In *Im weißen Rößl: Kulturgeschichtlicke Perspektiven*, edited by Nils Grosch and Caroline Stahrenberg, 155–175. Münster and New York: Waxmann, 2016.

Kenrick, John. 'Musicals 101'. www.musicals101.com, accessed 20 March 2020.

Lamb, Andrew. *150 Years of Musical Theatre*. New Haven, CT: Yale University Press, 2000.

Lynes, Russell. 'Highbrow, Lowbrow, Middlebrow'. *Harper's*, 11 April 1949. Reprinted in *Wilson Quarterly* 1, no. 1 (1976): 146–158. https://www.jstor.org/stable/40255171, accessed 3 June 2020.

Macdonald, Dwight. 'A Theory of Mass Culture'. In *Mass Culture*, edited by Bernard Rosenberg and Manning White, 59–73. New York: Free Press, 1957.

Menard, Louis. 'Browbeaten: Dwight Macdonald's War on Midcult'. *New Yorker*, 12 August 2011. https://www.newyorker.com/magazine/2011/09/05/browbeaten, accessed 15 April 2020.

Mordden, Ethan. *Rodgers & Hammerstein*. New York: Harry N. Abrams, 1992.

Nelson, Steve. 'Broadway and the Beast: Disney Comes to Times Square'. *Drama Review* 2 (1995): 71–85.

O'Leary, James. '*Oklahoma!* "Lousy Publicity" and the Politics of Formal Integration in the American Musical Theater'. *Journal of Musicology* 31, no. 1 (2014): 139–182.

Platt, Len, and Tobias Becker. '"A Happy Man Can Live in the Past": Musical Theatre Transfer in the 1920s and 1930s'. In *Popular Musical Theatre in London and Berlin*, edited by Len Platt, Tobias Becker and David Linton, 118–132. Cambridge: Cambridge University Press, 2014.

Prece, Paul, and William Everett. 'The Megamusical: The Creation, Internationalisation and Impact of a Genre'. In *The Cambridge Companion to the Musical*, edited by William Everett and Paul Laird, 250–269. Cambridge: Cambridge University Press, 2008. doi:10.1017/CCOL9780521862387.015.

Rebellato, Dan. 'Playwriting and Globalisation: Towards a Site-Unspecific Theatre'. *Contemporary Theatre Review* 16, no. 1 (2006): 97–113. doi: 1080/10486800500451047.

Rebellato, Dan. *Theatre and Globalisation*. Basingstoke: Palgrave Macmillan, 2009.

Ritzer, George. *The McDonaldisation of Society*. Thousand Oaks, CA: Sage, 2008.

Rosenberg, Justin. 'Globalisation Theory: A Post Mortem'. *International Politics* 42, no. 1 (2012): 2–74.

Ross, Alex. 'The Naysayers: Walter Benjamin, Theodor Adorno, and the Critique of Pop Culture'. *New Yorker*, 15 September 2014. (https://www.newyorker.com/magazine/2014/09/15/naysayers), accessed 3 June 2020.

Savran, David. 'Broadway as Global Brand'. *Journal of Contemporary Drama in English* 5, no. 1 (April 2017): 24–37. doi: https://doi.org/10.1515/jcde-2017-0003.

Savran, David. 'Trafficking in Transnational Brands: The New Broadway-Style Musical'. *Theatre Survey* 55, no. 3 (2014): 318–342.

Siropoulos, Vagelis. '*Evita*, the Society of the Spectacle and the Advent of the Megamusical'. *Image & Narrative: Online Magazine of the Visual Narrative* 2, no. 2 (2010): 165–176. www.imageandnarrative.be/index.php/imagenarrative/article/view/84/60, accessed 15 April 2020.

Siropoulos, Vagelis. 'A Postdramatic Composer in Search of a Dramatic Aesthetic, or, The Apotheosis and Declineof Andrew Lloyd Webber'. *Gramma: Journal of Theory and Criticism* 17 (2009): 145–162. www.enl.auth.gr/gramma/gramma09/siropoulos.pdf, accessed 29 March 2020.

Sternfeld, Jessica. *The Megamusical*. Bloomington: Indiana University Press, 2006.

Swyngedouw, Eric. 'Globalisation or Glocalisation: Networks, Territories and Rescaling'. *Cambridge Review of International Affairs* 17, no. 1 (2004): 25–48.

Wang, Yi. 'Globalisation Enhances Cultural Identity'. *Intercultural Communication Studies* 6, no. 1 (2007): 83–86.

Wollman, Elizabeth. *The Theatre Will Rock: A History of the Rock Musical, from 'Hair' to 'Hedwig'*. Ann Arbor: University of Michigan Press, 2006.

# PART I

# THEORY AND PRAXIS

# CHAPTER 1

## THEATRE AND GLOBALISATION: THEORETICAL AND HISTORICAL DIMENSIONS

### CHRISTOPHER BALME

TODAY theatre is a global artistic practice, a crucial cultural institution in many countries and a central part of transnational networks of artistic exchange. Often defying exact definition, its manifestations range from improvised street theatre in backyard slums to multimillion-dollar edifices purveying the latest performances of nineteenth-century opera to twenty-first-century cultural elites. Despite its bewildering number of forms, which include puppet theatre, stand-up comedy, and abstract performance art, theatre makers and audiences are connected across cultures by mutual recognition of commonality in what they do. Yet in the eyes of most theatre scholars theatre remains a resolutely local, even parochial phenomenon in which the local perspective enjoys unconditional priority over other research paradigms, as some historians have begun to critically note.[1] Yet, in the 150 years stretching roughly between 1870 and 2023, the nature of theatre was transformed radically throughout the world as it changed from being for the most part locally defined, practiced, and experienced cultural form to one that had global reach. In the wake of colonialism, imperialism, and modernisation, processes that provided the political, economic, and cultural foundations of contemporary globalisation debates, Western concepts, practices, and institutions of theatre were exported to most territories around the globe.

But can one really speak of 'global theatre'? Is not theatre by definition restricted to the here and now, the short-lived community of spectators and performers who share a common space for a few hours and then go their separate ways? Is not globalisation something we associate with fast food, Gucci handbags, commercialisation, container shipping—in short, the homogenisation and not the diversity of culture? Today we certainly associate globalisation with dynamic processes leading to what some sociologists have termed the 'shrinking world'.[2] Despite the obvious trend towards globalisation in commerce and communication, the differences between Asian, African, and European theatre worlds still seem to be intact. The main division would still appear to be the association with a European theatre that established rigid generic and institutional distinctions between sung, danced, and spoken theatre, and non-European forms combining song and stylised movement, which in Asian contexts is often termed 'dance-drama'. This usually translates to a problematic dichotomy between non-European tradition and European or Western modernity. That this is no longer the case is now widely accepted. Spoken drama, opera, ballet, modern dance, and other forms of musical theatre on the Western model are performed throughout the world, and Western theatre has in turn absorbed aspects of non-European performance, especially in the area of corporeal practices. The current situation is one of multiple hybridisations of Western formats. To understand this situation, it is necessary to review both theoretical understandings of globalisation and place them in more precise historical contexts. The first section of the essay discusses some definitions of globalisation, especially its influential variant, glocalisation, and how we can use such terms in a theatrical context. The main part of the essay will revisit Peter L. Becker's influential theory of cultural globalisation and discuss how it can be applied to current developments, especially in but not restricted to musical theatre.

## Theatrical Globalisation: Standardisation through Diversity

Although globalisation is often spoken about in negative terms, especially in the arts and humanities, I would like to argue that it is (a) not a new phenomenon and (b) an enabling and productive process which, among other things, has led to increased cooperation and communication between artists, audiences, and scholars. I want to argue that this process in connection with theatre began much earlier than 1989 and the end of the Cold War. In fact, it can be traced back to the late nineteenth century, when there was a huge expansion of economic and cultural activity. Many historians speak therefore of the first age of globalisation, meaning roughly the years from 1870 to 1914. Niall Ferguson, for example, draws this comparison: 'a hundred years ago, globalisation was celebrated in not dissimilar ways (the earth is flat) as goods, capital and labour flowed freely from England to the ends of the earth. [ ... ] In 1914 the first age of globalisation ended with a spectacular bang'.[3] As early as the 1870s, John Darwin claims, 'it becomes possible to speak of a global economy in which improvements in transport and communication by telegraph had encouraged the integration of markets and the convergence of prices in ordinary foodstuffs—perhaps the best indicator that the world was becoming a single economic space'.[4]

The fact that today we can attend an opera production in Beijing, experimental media installations in Tokyo, and performing arts festivals in Bangkok owes a lot to the emergence of a concept and practice of theatre that we can all agree upon. Organisations such as the International Theatre Institute (ITI) and the International Federation for Theatre Research (IFTR) that bring together artists and scholars from many countries presuppose that we agree upon certain fundamental concepts and types of practice that we subsume under the rubric 'theatre'. This agreement is the result of exchanges that have taken place over the past one 150 years throughout the world, but particularly between Europe and Asia.[5]

Globalisation can mean many things. Most generally it refers to 'a widespread perception that the world is rapidly being moulded into a shared social space by economic and technological forces and that developments in one region of the world can have profound consequences for the life chances of individuals or communities on the other side of the globe.'[6] This broadly sociological definition highlights two central aspects of the term: economic and technological forces are pushing the world closer together—the 'shared social space'—which results in a growing interconnectedness of countries and regions with accelerated repercussions. This understanding tends to underplay the cultural dimensions of globalisation, which, despite Arjun Appadurai's formative essay from 1990, 'Disjuncture and Difference in the Global Cultural Economy', have received less scholarly attention than political, economic, and historical research.[7] If we narrow our focus even more, to the artistic dimension of globalisation, then the situation is even more pronounced. Artistic products, amongst which we can definitely count musical theatre, have remained largely outside the purview of globalisation research.

The 1990s were the heyday of globalisation studies and produced a plethora of standpoints, including Roland Robertson's famous reverse engineering of the concept under the term 'glocalisation' to designate the competing, heterogeneous effects of global consumption.[8] For Robertson, locally specific adaptations of global (especially) cultural products are just as characteristic as the more visibly homogeneous, 'the world is flat' tendencies that apologists such as Thomas Friedman have popularised.[9] Glocalisation is an attractive concept because it implies the possibility of 'a reverse flow of influence, in which local mutations of products influence the way they are consumed in the metropole.'[10] Glocalisation, with its emphasis on time-space relations and 'selective incorporation' of ideas and practices from other societies, is certainly a productive way to view globalisation processes in theatrical contexts.[11] At the risk of some simplification, theatre studies tend strongly to privilege the concept of locality and, under the influence of performance studies, have begun incorporating ethnographical concepts such as fieldwork and participant observation into its methodologies. Ethnology also has formulated responses to globalisation, perhaps most famously in George Marcus's concept of 'multi-sited ethnography', which responds in turn to Appadurai's challenge.[12] Theatre and performance studies have not, in general, followed this path, preferring instead to remain rooted in locality. If we are to formulate an approach to globalisation as a theatrical phenomenon and not just one pertaining to 'McWorld popular culture', then we need to integrate more nuanced theoretical models that recognise the homogenising tendencies of the 'flat world' while also accounting for heterogeneity and specific, 'glocal' responses.

A theorist of globalisation, David Singh Grewal, has argued in his book *Network Power: The Social Dynamics of Globalization* that as a social and cultural process globalisation is dependent on standardisation: 'In areas as diverse as trade, media, legal procedures, industrial control, and perhaps even forms of thought, we are witnessing the emergence of international standards that enable us to coordinate our actions on a global scale.[13] Grewal claims that the standards which enable such global coordination display what he calls 'network power':

> The notion of network power consists in the joining of two ideas: first, that coordinating standards are more valuable when greater numbers of people use them, and second, that this dynamic—which I describe as a form of power—can lead to the progressive elimination of the alternatives over which otherwise free choice can effectively be exercised. [ ... ] More precisely, certain versions of local practices, routines, and symbols are being catapulted onto a global stage and offered as a means by which we can gain access to one another.[14]

If we apply this insight to theatre, we find both agreement and disagreement. As already mentioned, the fact that we use a word such as 'theatre' all over the world suggests that standardisation has taken place. It does not mean, however, that standardisation results in homogenisation, that is, that only one form of performance is recognisable under this term. On the contrary: theatre today is remarkable for the degree of diversity that can be sustained within this concept. Historically speaking, however, the export of Western theatre did result in a certain degree of standardisation. In Grewal's terms, 'the local practices, routines, and symbols' of Western theatre were 'catapulted onto a global stage and offered as a means by which we can gain access to one another'. But how and under what conditions did this come about? A crucial role, I argue, was played by the openness of Western forms. To take an analogy from digital culture, we could say that Western theatre was open source; its forms and practices could be easily adapted to local conditions, and there was no particular dependency between software and hardware, although in practice the hardware (the proscenium theatre) was imported too. Many classical Asian forms, for example, could only be imported in their entirety and were often proprietary, the preserve of particular schools and families.

# INSTITUTIONS IN MOTION

If theatre on the generic level is characterised by diversity rather than standardisation, the latter comes into play on an institutional level. A central concern of transnational studies in general and global history in particular is how institutions relocate across geocultural space and intersect with new environments. How have they been adapted, resituated, hybridised, and transformed in processes of motion? If, as S. N. Eisenstadt argues, modernisation invariably led to a wide range of responses to the way 'societies interpret different symbolic premises of modernity and different modern institutional patterns and dynamics', then it is crucial that institutions be seen in terms of their cultural variability and not as monolithic entities.[15] In our context, theatre needs to be investigated as an institution in the sense of a complex of norms regulating social action; institutions invariably operate on the basis of law and impact on collectivities as much as on individuals. The introduction of pedagogical institutions for artistic training provides one way to understand the dynamics of institutional normativity in the performing arts. Whether privately organised or state-run, such institutions display by definition a degree of normativity and discursivity that permit us to examine precisely how local adaptations of mainly Western cultural practices were effected. By the same token, we need to ask how Western conceptions of training theatre artists institutionally—mainly actors, singers, and dancers. but also directors, designers and other professionals—were seen as a necessary part of cultural 'modernisation'. To use Grewal's concept of standardisation and network power, we could ask whether an approach such as Stanislavsky's acting system is an example of theatrical standardisation. To do this, it is necessary to trace as precisely as possible the paths of informational exchange, the migration of 'experts', the circulation of ideas, traditions, and aesthetic norms that gradually led to the implementation of globally comparable institutions such as theatre schools.[16]

The diffusion of Stanislavsky's 'method', although its first transplantation to the United States predates World War II, is closely imbricated in cold-war alliances. The more surprising aspect of this story is how it took root in Asia, especially China. This institutional transferral is surprising because Asian performance cultures proceed from quite different principles, mainly exhaustive physical training regimes than often begin in childhood. But perhaps it is not so surprising in the light of Soviet-Chinese relations in the immediate postwar period. Realist theatre, or rather socialist-realist theatre, the orthodox Soviet approach to the arts, was adopted by the communist Chinese state founded in 1949. 'Modernisation' was one of the watchwords of the revolution, and to this end China initially received direct support from the Soviet Union. The Central Academy of Drama in Beijing was founded in 1950, and while it continued to train performers in the traditional forms, modern drama, both foreign and homegrown, received as much if not more attention. In the early 1950s the Soviet Union sent several 'experts' to China to assist in establishing an acting school on Stanislavskian principles at both the Central Academy of Drama and the Shanghai Theatre Academy.[17] They were dispensed with after Sino-Soviet relations deteriorated in the late 1950s, but the long-term impact of Stanislavsky on acting in China is undeniable. Stanislavskian acting is, however, only one example of the diffusion of Western theatrical practices. At both the Central Academy and its rival, the Shanghai Theatre Academy, we find training programmes for opera singers, dancers—both classical ballet and modern—and, increasingly, musical theatre performers.

FIG. 1.1 Statue of Stanislavsky on the new campus of the Central Academy of Drama, Beijing. Photo: Christopher Balme.

## THE FIVE FACES OF THEATRICAL GLOBALISATION

The popularity of musical theatre in Asia and around the globe is undisputed. While the economic and political conditions are quite different—China is, for example, a leading geopolitical power with a penchant for building 'opera houses'—some of the dynamics, especially regarding standardisation, are still valid but need to be discussed under a new set of criteria. The sociologist Peter L. Berger proposed in 1997 a typology to explain cultural globalisation that he called 'the four faces of global culture'.

The first such face Berger calls *Davos culture*, after the famous annual meeting of politicians, economists, and businessmen and -women in the Swiss ski town of Davos. The cultural carrier is international business. This is a cultural elite who adopt similar behaviours: they dress alike, speak English, hold similar political views, and generally subscribe to neoliberal economic ideas and a commitment to free markets.

The second face is called *faculty club international*, a term that refers to the internationalisation of the values and ideologies of the Western intelligentsia. It is sustained by foundations, academic networks, non-governmental organisations, and some governmental and multinational agencies (such as development agencies with social and cultural missions). It internationalises local cultural debates and disputes such as anti-smoking, gay marriage, inalienable human rights, and climate change.

The face Berger calls *McWorld culture* refers to the popular consumer culture of fast food, blue jeans, and rock music but also *döner*, Chinese restaurants, Japanese manga, and Korean pop music.

The last face is *evangelical religion*. For Berger this meant mainly Protestantism, but today we would add Islam, especially the more radical forms.[18]

Berger understands the term 'culture' in its broadest anthropological or social scientific sense 'as the beliefs, values, and lifestyles of ordinary people'.[19] One can argue that theatre today evinces comparable but not identical 'faces', albeit in ways not immediately recognisable. They can be reformulated as: marketisation, musicalisation, festivalisation, mediatisation, and musealisation. The argument proposed here is that, like Berger's 'four faces', these categories provide comparative criteria that we find at work in many, even culturally diverse, countries, and regions.

*Marketisation* refers to the economic foundations of theatre. From a historical perspective, theatre has been funded in two main ways: directly supported through patronage, where performances were usually connected to festivals and often free of charge, or commercially, by selling tickets. Theatre supported by courtly or civic patronage was tied to a religious calendar and provided a few performances for invited guests or townspeople. In the late sixteenth century there was a move throughout Europe towards a market economy. Ferdinando Taviani has argued that the sixteenth century saw a significant transformation in theatrical organisation from an *economia di festa* to an *economia di mercato*, where, instead of providing theatre in the form of pre-financed, no-risk courtly festivals, itinerant troupes needed to sell their product on a fickle and open market of supply and demand.[20] Theatre became part of a growing entertainment industry but was still tightly regulated through licences. In London by 1700 there were only two theatres, Theatre Royal Drury Lane and Theatre Royal Haymarket, that were allowed to perform dramas; in Paris the situation before and after the French Revolution was very similar. Other theatres were, however, permitted to perform musical theatre, hence the emergence of genres such as vaudeville, singspiel, ballad opera, and pantomime, the forerunners of modern musicals.

Throughout the nineteenth century economic liberalisation took hold throughout Europe and North America, which saw the abolition of the licensing system. Operating a theatre was then legally no different to running any other kind of trade or company. A genuine capitalist entertainment industry emerged, with dozens of theatres and venues in the bigger cities and at least a handful in the smaller ones. These theatres offered everything from high art to variety shows. Countless touring companies emerged to cater to smaller centres and with them a system of agents, specialist magazines, and trade unions for performers. By the end of the nineteenth century an oversupply of theatre in the main cities and a high demand for it in the provinces and around the world generated a touring industry: hundreds of companies went east and west, and some Asian performers, circus acrobats but also actors, went west: the most famous were the Japanese actors Sada Yacco and Kawakami. This coincided with the first phase of theatrical globalisation.

Roughly parallel to the expansion and crisis of the entertainment industry, with its oversupply and high unemployment, calls for public financial support for theatre grew more urgent. Although state-supported theatres already existed in Germany and France, this was not the case in Great Britain or the United States. The first countries to heed the call were the new nations in Eastern Europe, where national theatres sprouted like mushrooms, sometimes even before full independence had been obtained.

The subsidisation debate drew on social democratic ideas that theatre should be seen as an integral part of the welfare state; that is, the provision of theatre was equivalent to that of other public amenities. The philosophy behind the welfare-state model was succinctly expressed in 1954 by Jean Vilar, director and founder of the National Popular Theatre in France: 'The Théâtre National Populaire is primarily a public service, just like gas, water, electricity.'[21] Vilar envisaged theatre as a public good that should enjoy the same status as basic necessities and services, free of the vagaries of the market. It was a vision with great prophetic foresight. By the late 1960s most of Western Europe and certainly all Eastern European and other socialist and communist countries, such as China, had publicly subsidised theatrical institutions including training schools.

In the neoliberal climate after 1989 we can observe a *convergence* of capitalist and socialist theatre systems. With the exception of Germany (almost a unique case), countries have seen a gradual reduction of direct state funding for theatre and increased pressure to open theatre to market forces. The global and local question facing theatre and cultural policy makers alike is how theatre can reconcile artistic performance with performance as a market player. Generally speaking, there is consensus across the developed world that cultural funding is necessary for theatre. The disagreement pertains to whether and how much public or private money should be dispensed to the theatres. Leaving aside the purely commercial theatre, there are at least four models that provide different answers to the question:

- the *American* model, where funding is secured through tax-deductible *private and corporate* donations and includes very little direct subvention, with a heavy reliance on the box office;

- the *British* model of mixed funding consisting of centralised, national arts council subvention plus sponsorship plus box office. This is found in many parts of the former British Empire such as Australia, New Zealand, Canada, and South Africa but also includes the Netherlands and Belgium. The British model has a proportionally low amount of direct institutional funding. Instead there is proportionally more support of independent groups according to ever-changing cultural policy incentives;
- the *German* model, which was widely adopted in former socialist and Scandinavian countries. It is characterised by a large amount of *institutional funding* of theatres and opera houses including semi-permanent ensembles and orchestras. In Germany institutionalised funding is decentralised: most comes from municipal and state sources, with little federal support for theatre. The German model results in a proportionally lower level of funding for independent groups; and
- the *Chinese* model, which uses state subvention for the building and running of venues but includes little support for ensembles. Although there are generous budgets for 'buying' both domestic and international productions, there is also a high expectation of performance at the box office and a relatively low level of funding for independent groups. Owing to China's economic predominance in Asia, it is reasonable to expect that this model in the future will find greater acceptance in neighbouring countries, if not further afield.

If globalisation is characterised by convergence and standardisation, then the question is whether there can be convergence of these models. Theatrical institutions are characterised by a high degree of path dependence, which means that their structures were established a long time ago, and it is normally difficult to depart from an established institutional trajectory.[22] This can happen, however, especially after radical political reform. In keeping with its overall policy of state control mixed with capitalist, market-driven economic policies, China shifted in the 1990s and 2000s from the German socialist model to its own mixed version. Similarly, South Africa departed from its quite heavily state-subsidised Performing Arts Councils, based on the German municipal theatres and employed during the apartheid years, to the neoliberal British model after 1992.

Convergence can be found in the area of *musical theatre*, our second 'face' of theatrical globalisation. In Jürgen Osterhammel's magisterial global history of the nineteenth century, *The Transformation of the World*, he argues that opera encapsulates a product that was circulated worldwide.[23] For centuries it was thought of as an Italian form, but after 1830 Paris became the nexus of the system for production and distribution, out of which stars were created who toured with successful repertoire in a network that reached to Moscow, Lisbon, London, the Ottoman Empire, the Brazilian rainforest, and the Australian coasts. By the 1860s opera was being produced on the banks of the Mississippi River and in Santiago, Chile. The example of opera reveals the importance of institutional frameworks (the financiers who built and sustained opera houses), social functions (the allure of a high-status form, especially with international singing stars), theatre environments (the significance of the architectural form linking widely distributed metropoles), circulation (of repertoire but also fandom), and highly expert communities of production involving multiple kinds of labour, artistry, and technical expertise. The genre of musical comedy also achieved remarkable diffusion from the 1890s onwards. Apart from Gilbert and Sullivan's comic operas, the Gaiety Theatre of George Edwardes produced a special combination of singing, dancing, and uncomplicated plots that resonated not just in Britain but wherever undemanding theatre audiences congregated. The global activities of Maurice E. Bandmann, owner of the exclusive rights to the Gaiety Theatre's output, which he toured in facsimile productions with his Bandmann Opera Company, underscore the wide appeal of musical theatrical forms.[24]

Today opera retains its status as a global form of theatre, and the term 'opera house' is used to designate iconic architecture, which does not necessarily mean that it hosts performances of Verdi or Wagner on a regular basis. Today opera houses stand for many things: conspicuous consumption and virtuosic performance, advanced modernity and a respect for tradition. Opera also faces different demographic challenges in different parts of the world, where audiences may appear to be either too old or perhaps too young.[25]

Apart from opera, the musical represents the other predominant face of musicalisation. As noted in the introduction, the term 'globalisation' is regularly used in a pejorative sense, in the sense that it often stands in for standardisation, loss of local identity, and the packaging and branding of products to make them saleable anywhere in the world: Berger's McWorld. Theatre, on the other hand, is traditionally framed in antithetical terms as being uncompromisingly local. It is produced and consumed in the here and now, and almost exclusively for local audiences. So can there be a theatrical Starbucks?

The global musical or megamusical, which the theatre scholar Dan Rebellato has termed 'McTheatre', is the theatrical equivalent of Berger's McWorld.[26] Rebellato is referring in particular to certain musicals produced in London or New York which are then exported in more or less identical versions to other global cities. The key element is standardisation to produce a homogeneous product, which is 'typical of the method of global capitalism'.[27] Although Rebellato is targeting mainly the London theatre producer Cameron Mackintosh and the entry of Disney into the musical theatre industry, the practice of standardisation goes back at least to the early twentieth century, when the practice of theatrical duplication had both an economic and an aesthetic dimension. Tracy C. Davis has examined how the major London producers organised ways to maximise the economic life cycle of their theatrical commodities. She draws parallels between the rise of retail chains such as Woolworths and Marks & Spencer, so-called multiples, and the practice of the 'Savoy's simultaneous operation of several touring companies with the same interchangeable repertoire'.[28]

Both then and now, similarity and standardisation had their own aesthetic dimension, albeit not one favoured by modernist aesthetics. Nevertheless, this dimension has significant economic potential. In 2013 the *Economist* published an article with an embedded short film that demonstrated, not surprisingly in the light of the magazine's neoliberal leanings, the economic potential of the musical as a global form.[29] The article points out that musicals are valuable intellectual property and that the most popular have grossed more than the most successful films. Such works can run for decades in multiple venues. Despite expensive tickets (a single seat might cost up to $1000 for a musical such as *Hamilton*), this does not deter consumers, and in fact, musicals defy economic downturns. Nevertheless, high risk remains the norm, with just one in ten returning a profit.[30] The article emphasises especially the potential for new markets outside the United States and Europe because, like luxury brands, musicals sell well in emerging markets.

Although the article notes that production is no longer limited to the United States and the United Kingdom, it still assumes that American and UK productions will be exported to the rest of the world. Recent research has shown that this is no longer the case. The American scholar David Savran refers to the 'transnationalised' musical, with South Korea and Germany becoming producers and exporters of musicals.[31] The production and consumption of musicals has greatly expanded beyond the English-speaking world. South Korea commands a rich reservoir of highly professionalised performers and dedicated spectators, including an extremely sophisticated fan culture. The Korean example shows how the combination of professional training, the existence of a theatrical district (the Daehangno area), and a fan culture interconnected with popular music (K-pop) can produce the conditions enabling a commercially viable, glocalised musical industry to flourish. There is also clear evidence that a musical industry is emerging in China as a response to the huge demand for this kind of theatrical entertainment amongst Chinese spectators.[32]

Large-scale international musicals are part of globalised commercial culture and have great economic potential. But how can artistically ambitious theatre flourish under the conditions of globality? One answer lies in area of festivals and festival networks. In 1920 there were only two theatre festivals in the whole of Europe: the Bayreuth Festival in Bavaria, devoted exclusively to the works of Wagner, and the newly founded Salzburg Festival. Today there are hundreds of theatre and arts festivals worldwide.

The history of modern theatre and music festivals began in 1919 with the Salzburg Festival, founded by Max Reinhardt and Hugo von Hofmannsthal. Salzburg is modern not only in terms of its concept of showcasing a variety of plays, operas, and orchestras, but also because of its economic model. In his application to the superintendent general of the Imperial Court Theatre in Vienna, Reinhardt stressed not just the artistic but also the economic advantages. Such a festival, Reinhardt argued, would be a drawcard for affluent tourists from home and abroad who would make a significant contribution to the economy of the region. This argument, known variously as referring to 'multiplier' or 'spillover' effects, is still used today to justify festivals.[33] Most festivals receive public money; they are seen as a means to attract tourists both national and foreign, and hence the public money is regarded as an investment.

FIG. 1.2 A performance of Hugo von Hofmannsthal's *Jedermann* (*Everyman*, 1911) at the Salzburg Festival. Postcard by Bergwelt Verlag, Salzburg.

Apart from the economic benefits for the host city or region, festivals are seen as contact zones between nations and cultures, a site of networking and connectivity on a cultural and artistic level. They also provide a key economic basis for many artistically ambitious groups that are often labelled 'experimental' or 'avant-garde'. One can speak of an economy of experimentation inasmuch as festivals often enable groups to make a living, especially in countries where there is little public money to support such work. Festivals are the theatrical equivalent of Berger's faculty club international: they cater to the values, ideologies, and tastes of the intelligentsia and cultural elite. Berger argues that this elite culture is disseminated by creating contacts between local artists and those from abroad. We could argue that festivals have played and continue to play a key role in establishing theatre as an art form independent of purely commercial considerations.

Festivals evince also a high degree of interconnectivity: their directors visit other festivals and learn from each other and thereby contribute to processes of artistic canonisation, that is, establishing particular artists and productions as important. This often leads to their being criticised for a certain uniformity of programming, as a limited number of productions often circulate around the world. While there is no doubt that festival favourites do gain currency, there is just as much evidence that the forces of glocalisation are equally at work. Most festivals include in addition to 'big names' a selection of local productions that thereby gain attention that they would normally not receive outside of a festival context. The most important aspect of festivals is the curatorial function. For the groups and companies invited, the invitations create prestige and lead to more invitations, which creates a festival economy that supports experimental work.

The French Canadian director Robert Lepage has been able productively to combine the artistic and economic aspects of the festival network. He can be considered the pre-eminent festival director of the 1990s. Not only do his works have global themes, often portraying different cultures, but his method of producing is based on networks of festivals that contribute to the costs. His beginnings were in experimental theatre in Quebec in the 1980s with a small theatre group known as Théâtre Repère. There he developed a method of collaborative or devised theatre-making. A low level of state subsidy—about 12 percent at the time—forced Lepage and his team to create a new business model: the multi-festival co-production, to which different festivals contribute. They share the risks and enable the artists to work with a great deal of autonomy. Lepage represents both an innovative artistic method that uses individual creative resources and a means of production that harnesses the financial resources of a globalised festival economy.[34]

Lepage's productions invariably use visual media in highly sophisticated ways, which merge live and digital representations. The use of media brings us to the fourth face of theatrical globalisation: *mediatisation*, which can be defined as theatre's imbrication with and distribution through other media. Nowadays it is possible to watch performances from the National Theatre in London in a Munich cinema. There are seven hundred such cinemas around the world. The Metropolitan Opera in New York now broadcasts to over two thousand cinemas in sixty-six countries. Livestreaming is also gaining in popularity, which means viewers can watch performances on their own computer at home. Such broadcasts are available as either live transmissions or as post-recorded versions of live performances of theatre productions. Because the live broadcasts, such as NT Live and The Met: Live in HD, require a satellite connection in a cinema, the quality is excellent. However, the costs are high; the technology is akin to that which enables sporting events to be broadcast around the world. Nevertheless, the expansion of opera's range has generated profits for both the Met and NT Live, although the latter still receives sponsorship. The On Demand In Schools programme makes NT Live productions available to every school in the United Kingdom free of charge. In 2017 1.2 million people watched NT Live broadcasts around the world in sixty-five countries.[35]

HD satellite is not, however, the only medium for broadcasting live theatre. In March 2017 a solo performance by Simon McBurney, director of the company Complicité, entitled *The Encounter* was livestreamed from the London Barbican. McBurney traces the journey of an American photographer, Loren McIntyre, into the depths of the Amazon rainforest in 1969. His experiences were recorded in a book, *Amazon Beaming*, by Petru Popescu. The performance was remarkable for several reasons. Firstly, it was a livestream transmitted on the internet without the need for a cinema. Secondly, the performance incorporated binaural technology to build a shifting world of 3-D sound for the listener. Its use of binaural sound required headphones to comprehend the performance. Spectators at the live performance in the Barbican also wore headphones, so the acoustic experience was the same whether you the viewer was in the theatre or at home in front of a computer.

We are standing on the threshold of new possibilities to distribute and receive theatre. This challenges many of our assumptions, but theatre as a medium has always been dependent on technology and has always adapted to it. The challenge for the future will be how we engage with this new technology in our training, our research, and our practice. The satellite technology used for cinematic live broadcasts is still Western-focused: London and New York transmit to the rest of the world. The next stage will be internet streaming, where any producer can make theatre accessible to anyone anywhere with a good broadband internet connection. We shall soon be seeing experimental avant-garde theatre like *The Encounter* in high-quality versions as well as opera and Shakespeare via satellite. This means that anyone anywhere can broadcast themselves and their productions.

The fifth face of theatrical globalisation is *musealisation*. Comparing theatre to a museum sounds contradictory. Museums exist to preserve and display the past; they preserve our cultural heritage. Theatre, on the other hand, is a medium of the present: live and immediate. Its relationship to history is problematic in many ways. Museums are, however, a cultural growth industry. Globally speaking, they are a success story, found even in the smallest and poorest countries. Museums are in fact inseparable from the nation-state.[36] The imagined community of the nation needs the museum to represent its narratives of historical legitimation.[37]

So, where do theatres and museums meet? Sometimes in the museum itself as a space for performance, but more frequently in the idea of cultural heritage as something worth preserving. Cultural heritage is itself a global discourse and an example of Berger's faculty club thinking. The most famous institution promoting this thinking is the UNESCO programme for cultural heritage, which refers mainly to buildings but also includes under the heading Intangible Cultural Heritage certain performance and theatre traditions. According to UNESCO, intangible cultural heritage refers to 'practices, representations, expressions, as well as the knowledge and skills, that communities, groups and, in some cases, individuals recognise as part of their cultural heritage'.[38] They enjoy a special protected status to ensure continued transmission from generation to generation. Amongst the many policy documents produced by and for the UNESCO Intangible Cultural Heritage programme we find explicit mention of globalisation: 'Culture has thus, for the first time in the history of international law, found its place on the political agenda, out of a desire to humanise globalisation.'[39] According to this thinking, globalisation can be 'humanised' by according certain buildings or traditions the status of cultural heritage and thereby declaring them sacrosanct and immutable. Examples from theatre include shadow puppetry as well as the Beijing Opera and Kunju and Yueju opera in China. In Japan the list includes Nô and Kabuki as well as bunraku puppet theatre. All these forms are

FIG. 1.3 A scene from the 1748 Bunraku play *Kanadehon Chūshingura* (*The Treasury of Loyal Retainers*). Bunraku puppet theatre is part of Japan's cultural heritage. Photographer unknown; image provided by the editors.

highly specific to a particular country, region, even town and are not transferable. In 2014 Germany registered its entire publicly funded 'theatre and orchestra landscape' as intangible cultural heritage, yet it has not registered any specific performance or cultural forms with UNESCO.

If intangible cultural heritage is considered to be a counter-measure to humanise or even oppose globalisation by declaring certain traditions off-limits to global forces, why should we even discuss musealisation in connection with the globalisation of theatre? Because, paradoxically, musealisation is a typical product of globalisation in Berger's sense of a set of shared ideas that function to connect disparate countries and to institutionalise a set of norms. This is a version of globalisation that emphasises difference and specificity, not similarity. It defines a set of practices that generally speaking appear to predate modernity and the first phase of globalisation and colonial expansion. Scholars will of course debate how 'unaltered' contemporary Beijing Opera really is, but that is an academic discussion which obscures the political argument underpinning cultural heritage thinking. Musealisation is a powerful global discourse that works to preserve and protect cultural difference by attaching value to specific theatrical traditions. This means that a certain group of performance forms is considered to be beyond the forces of continual innovation that characterise most theatre practice.

# CONCLUSION

This essay has argued that despite widespread scepticism about theatre's imbrication in globalisation processes on account of its local nature, it has been subject to these very forces. Two theoretical concepts can be usefully applied. The first is Roland Robertson's concept of glocalisation, which emphasises reciprocity and agency on the part of specific cultural locales and even argues for a two-way exchange of cultural products. At the same time, it is necessary to take account of undeniable processes of standardisation as outlined by David Singh Grewal, because without such dynamics there would be little communication and exchange. On the theatrical level, such exchange would remain within the frameworks of mutual exoticisation. I have argued that when it comes to theatrical training institutions and practices, a degree of standardisation has been attained that canonises Stanislavskian acting on the one hand and operatic singing on the other. The essay proposes a typology of five categories where comparative study is useful, especially in the area of musical theatre. These include the area of economic institutions and broadly speaking the tension between public funding and market forces, where several solutions have developed and been adopted around the world. Musical theatre itself is another area where we can speak of globalisation. This includes not just the popularity of identically packaged large-scale international musicals but also the growing evidence of non-Western centres of production and reception such as South Korea and China. Festivals provide an organisational form of global distribution which also enable more experimental forms to be sustained and fostered. They usually represent a balance of public funding, private sponsorship, and box-office receipts that synthesise the various funding models. The fourth category refers to the new possibilities afforded by new media to distribute theatrical productions globally. The most successful of these are the Metropolitan Opera's Live in HD programme and the British National Theatre's NT Live initiative. As well as these more mainstream offerings, livestreaming on the internet provides scope for more experimental work to reach niche audiences. Finally, the powerful discourse on cultural heritage, especially UNESCO's Intangible Cultural Heritage programme, has begun to place buildings and performance traditions within ideas of musealisation, which are antithetical to the 'open source' modernity of theatrical modernisation to date. In the light of such diverse forces, theatrical globalisation can be understood only in terms of multiplicity rather than just a single overarching notion of homogeneity. Nevertheless, this multiplicity is not infinite but a clustered a set of developments which act to bring geographically and culturally remote regions into dialogue with one another.

## Notes

1. See e.g. Marvin Carlson, 'Become Less Provincial', *Theatre Survey* 45, no. 2 (2004): 177–180; Jo Robinson, 'Becoming More Provincial? The Global and the Local in Theatre History', *New Theatre Quarterly* 23, no. 3 (2007): 229–240.
2. Mark Herkenrath, 'Shrinking World Concepts', in *Encyclopedia of Global Studies*, 4 vols., ed. Helmut K. Anheier and Mark Juergensmeyer, 1:1540–1540 (Thousand Oaks, CA: Sage).
3. Niall Ferguson, *The War of the World: Twentieth-Century Conflict and the Descent of the West* (New York: Penguin Press, 2006), 643.
4. John Darwin, *Unfinished Empire: The Global Expansion of Britain* (London: Penguin Press, 2012), esp. 179.
5. See for example Nicola Savarese, *Eurasian Theatre: Drama and Performance between East and West from Classical Antiquity to the Present*, trans. Richard Fowler and Vicki Ann Cremona (Holstebro: Icarus, 2010); originally published as *Teatro e spettacolo fra Occidente e Oriente* (Rome: Laterza, 1992).
6. David Held, Anthony McGrew, David Goldblatt, and Jonathan Perraton (eds.), *Global Transformations: Politics, Economics and Culture* (Cambridge: Polity Press, 1999), 1.
7. Arjun Appadurai, 'Disjuncture and Difference in the Global Cultural Economy', *Public Culture* 2, no. 2 (1990): 1–24.
8. Roland Robertson, 'Glocalization: Time-Space and Homogeneity-Heterogeneity', in *Global Modernities*, ed. Mike Featherstone, Scott Lash and Roland Robertson, 25–44 (London and Thousand Oaks, CA: Sage, 1995).
9. Thomas L. Friedman, *The World Is Flat: The Globalized World in the Twenty-First Century*, updated and expanded ed. (London: Penguin, 2006).
10. Petra Goedde, 'Global Cultures', in *Global Interdependence: The World after 1945*, ed. Akira Iriye, 537–680 (Cambridge, MA: Belknap Press of Harvard University Press, 2014); here: 579.
11. Robertson, 'Glocalization', 41.
12. George E. Marcus, 'Ethnography in/of the World System: The Emergence of Multi-Sited Ethnography', *Annual Review of Anthropology* 24 (1995): 95–117.
13. David Singh Grewal, *Network Power: The Social Dynamics of Globalization* (New Haven, CT and London: Yale University Press, 2008), 3.
14. Ibid., 4.
15. S. N. Eisenstadt, *Patterns of Modernity* (London: F. Pinter, 1987), 5.
16. See Jonathan Pitches and Stefan Aquilina (eds.), *Stanislavsky in the World: The System and Its Transformations across Continents* (London: Bloomsbury, 2017).
17. For a detailed discussion of Boris Kulnyov's teaching of the Stanislavsky system in China in the 1950s, see Jonathan Pitches and Ruru Li, 'Stanislavsky with Chinese Characteristics: How the System Was Introduced into China', in *Stanislavsky in the World: The System and Its Transformations across Continents*, ed. Jonathan Pitches and Stefan Aquilina (London: Bloomsbury, 2017), 66–195.
18. See Peter L. Berger, 'Four Faces of Global Culture', *National Interest* 49 (1997): 1–5. A more extended discussion is to be found in Peter L. Berger and Samuel P. Huntington (eds.), *Many Globalizations: Cultural Diversity in the Contemporary World* (Oxford and New York: Oxford University Press, 2002).
19. Berger, 'Four Faces of Global Culture', 2.

20. Ferdinando Taviani, 'L'ingresso della commedia dell'arte nella cultura del Cinquecento', in *Il teatro italiano nel Rinascimento*, ed. Fabrizio Cruciani and Daniele Seragnoli, 319–345 (Bologna: Il Mulino, 1987); here: 324.

21. 'Le T.N.P. est donc, au premier chef, un service public. Tout comme le gaz, l'eau, l'électricité' (my translation). Jean Vilar, 'Le T.N.P. service public,' in Jean Vilar, *Le théâtre service public et autres textes* (1954; Paris: Gallimard, 1974),; here: 173.

22. Path dependence refers to decision-making constellations in which the realm of possibility is curtailed by the unforeseen consequences of earlier decisions. Change and reform therefore are difficult but not impossible. Paths that have been entered on can only be deviated from at a very high cost or left at specific 'critical junctures'. See James Mahoney, 'Path Dependence in Historical Sociology', *Theory and Society* 29 (2000): 507–548.

23. Jürgen Osterhammel, *The Transformation of the World: A Global History of the Nineteenth Century*, trans. Patrick Camiller (Princeton, NJ: Princeton University Press, 2014), 5–6.

24. On the Edwardian musical comedy, see Ben Macpherson, *Cultural Identity in British Musical Theatre, 1890–1939: Knowing One's Place* (London: Palgrave Macmillan, 2018). On Bandmann, see Christopher Balme, *The Globalization of Theatre 1870–1930: The Theatrical Networks of Maurice E. Bandmann* (Cambridge: Cambridge University Press), 2020.

25. The average opera goer in Germany is fifty-six or older and female; see Karl-Heinz Reuband, 'Das Kulturpublikum im städtischen Kontext: Wie sich das Publikum der Oper von anderen Kulturpublika unterscheidet', in *Oper, Publikum und Gesellschaft*, ed. Karl-Heinz Reuband, 143–191 (Wiesbaden: Springer Fachmedien, 2018); here: 164. In China, however, opera productions, if they can be disambiguated from the musical audience, 'attract a predominantly young and educated audience who know clearly what they want.' Raymond Zhou, 'China's Theatre Bubble', *American Theatre*, 25 April 2017, n.p., https://www.americantheatre.org/2017/04/25/chinas-theatre-bubble/, accessed 27 August 2019.

26. The term 'McTheatre' was initially elaborated in an academic context in Jonathan Burston, 'Enter, Stage Right: Neoconservatism, English Canada and the Megamusical', *Soundings* 5 (1997): 179–190. Burston's article is subtitled 'Megamusicals and Global Culture: An International Diet of McTheatre for the Masses?' He traces the origin of the term in the Anglo-Canadian theatre community, 'invoking as much the new experience of working on what was perceived as a "theatrical assembly-line" as it did the (often only imagined) experience of attending a show that conformed to the expectations of a cultural McDonalds', 180.

27. Dan Rebellato, *Theatre and Globalization* (Basingstoke: Palgrave Macmillan, 2009), 39f.

28. Tracy C. Davis, *The Economics of the British Stage* (Cambridge: Cambridge University Press, 2007), 341.

29. 'The Tills Are Alive: The Musical Business Is Bigger, More Global and More Fabulous than Ever', May 4, 2013. http://www.economist.com/news/business/21577062-musicals-busin ess-bigger-more-global-and-more-fabulous-ever-tills-are-alive, accessed 25 August 2019.

30. Ibid.

31. David Savran, 'Trafficking in Transnational Brands: The New "Broadway-Style" Musical', *Theatre Survey* 55 (2014): 318–342.

32. See e.g. recent articles in the Chinese press: Xu Liuliu, 'Western Musicals to Find Larger Audience in China in 2019', *Global Times*, 28 January 2019, http://www.globaltimes.cn/content/1137307.html, accessed 25 August 2019; and Zhang Kun, 'A Hotbed for Musicals in China', *China Daily*, 22 February 2019, http://www.chinadaily.com.cn/a/201902/22/WS5c6 f3d9ca3106c65c34eab64_5.html, accessed 25 August 2019.

33. Max Reinhardt, 'Denkschrift Errichtung eines Festspielhaus in Hellbrunn' (1917), in *Max Reinhardt Schriften: Aufzeichnungen, Briefe, Reden*, ed. Hugo Fetting, 176–182 (Berlin: Henschel, 1974).

34. For discussions on this early phase, see Aleksandar Dundjerović, *The Theatricality of Robert Lepage* (Montreal and Ithaca: McGill-Queen's University Press, 2007), chap. 1.

35. https://review.nationaltheatre.org.uk/#2018/national-work/102, accessed 27 August 2019.

36. See the final chapter in Benedict Anderson, *Imagined Communities: Reflections on the Origin and Spread of Nationalism*. rev. ed. (London: Verso, 1991).

37. See for example Wan-Chen Chang, 'A Cross-Cultural Perspective on Musealization: The Museum's Reception by China and Japan in the Second Half of the Nineteenth Century', *Museum and Society* 10 (2012): 15–27.

38. UNESCO, 'Working Towards a Convention on Intangible Cultural Heritage', https://ich.unesco.org/doc/src/01854-EN.pdf, n.d., 2, accessed 27 August 2019.

39. Ibid., 12.

## BIBLIOGRAPHY

Anderson, Benedict. *Imagined Communities: Reflections on the Origin and Spread of Nationalism*. Revised ed. London: Verso, 1991.

Appadurai, Arjun. 'Disjuncture and Difference in the Global Cultural Economy.' *Public Culture* 2, no. 2 (1990): 1–24.

Balme, Christopher. *The Globalization of Theatre 1870–1930: The Theatrical Networks of Maurice E. Bandmann*. Cambridge: Cambridge University Press, 2020.

Berger, Peter L. 'Four Faces of Global Culture'. *National Interest* 49 (1997): 1–5.

Berger, Peter L., and Samuel P. Huntington, eds. *Many Globalizations: Cultural Diversity in the Contemporary World*. Oxford and New York: Oxford University Press, 2002.

Burston, Jonathan. 'Enter, Stage Right: Neoconservatism, English Canada and the Megamusical'. *Soundings* 5 (1997): 179–190.

Carlson, Marvin. 'Become Less Provincial'. *Theatre Survey* 45, no. 2 (2004): 177–180.

Chang, Wan-Chen. 'A Cross-Cultural Perspective on Musealization: The Museum's Reception by China and Japan in the Second Half of the Nineteenth Century'. *Museum and Society* 10 (2012): 15–27.

Darwin, John. *Unfinished Empire: The Global Expansion of Britain*. London: Penguin Press, 2012.

Davis, Tracy C. *The Economics of the British Stage*. Cambridge: Cambridge University Press, 2007.

Dundjerović, Aleksandar. *The Theatricality of Robert Lepage*. Montreal and Ithaca, NY: McGill-Queen's University Press, 2007.

Eisenstadt, S. N. *Patterns of Modernity*. London: F. Pinter, 1987.

Ferguson, Niall. *The War of the World: Twentieth-Century Conflict and the Descent of the West*. New York: Penguin Press, 2006.

Friedman, Thomas L. *The World Is Flat: The Globalized World in the Twenty-first Century*. Updated and expanded ed. London: Penguin, 2006.

Goedde, Petra. 'Global Cultures.' In *Global Interdependence: The World after 1945*, edited by Akira Iriye, 537–680. Cambridge, MA: Belknap Press of Harvard University Press, 2014.

Grewal, David Singh. *Network Power: The Social Dynamics of Globalization*. New Haven, CT: Yale University Press, 2008.

Held, David, Anthony McGrew, David Goldblatt, and Jonathan Perraton, eds. *Global Transformations: Politics, Economics and Culture*. Cambridge: Polity Press, 1999.

Herkenrath, Mark. 'Shrinking World Concepts'. In *Encyclopedia of Global Studies*, 4 vols. 1, edited by Helmut K. Anheier and Mark Juergensmeyer, 1:1540–1541. Thousand Oaks, CA: Sage, 2012. https://review.nationaltheatre.org.uk/#2018/national-work/102, accessed 27 August 2019.

Macpherson, Ben. *Cultural Identity in British Musical Theatre, 1890–1939: Knowing One's Place*. London: Palgrave Macmillan, 2018.

Mahoney, James. 'Path Dependence in Historical Sociology'. *Theory and Society* 29 (2000): 507–548.

Marcus, George E. 'Ethnography in/of the World System: The Emergence of Multi-Sited Ethnography'. *Annual Review of Anthropology* 24 (1995): 95–117.

Osterhammel, Jürgen. *The Transformation of the World: A Global History of the Nineteenth Century*. Translated by Patrick Camiller. Princeton, NJ: Princeton University Press, 2014.

Pitches, Jonathan, and Stefan Aquilina, eds. *Stanislavsky in the World: The System and Its Transformations across Continents*. London: Bloomsbury, 2017.

Pitches, Jonathan, and Ruru Li. 'Stanislavsky with Chinese Characteristics: How the System Was Introduced into China'. In *Stanislavsky in the World: The System and Its Transformations across Continents*, edited by Jonathan Pitches and Stefan Aquilino, 66–195. London: Bloomsbury, 2017.

Rebellato, Dan. *Theatre and Globalization*. Basingstoke: Palgrave Macmillan, 2009.

Reinhardt, Max. 'Denkschrift Errichtung eines Festspielhaus in Hellbrunn' (1917). In *Max Reinhardt Schriften: Aufzeichnungen, Briefe, Reden*, edited by Hugo Fetting, 176–182. Berlin: Henschel, 1974.

Reuband, Karl-Heinz. 'Das Kulturpublikum im städtischen Kontext: Wie sich das Publikum der Oper von anderen Kulturpublika unterscheidet'. In *Oper, Publikum und Gesellschaft*, edited by Karl-Heinz Reuband, 143–191. Wiesbaden: Springer Fachmedien, 2018.

Robertson, Roland. 'Glocalization: Time-Space and Homogeneity-Heterogeneity'. In *Global Modernities*, edited by Mike Featherstone, Scott Lash and Roland Robertson, 25–44. London and Thousand Oaks, CA: Sage, 1995.

Robinson, Jo. 'Becoming More Provincial? The Global and the Local in Theatre History'. *New Theatre Quarterly* 23, no. 3 (2007): 229–240.

Savarese, Nicole. *Eurasian Theatre: Drama and Performance between East and West from Classical Antiquity to the Present*. Translated by Richard Fowler and Vicki Ann Cremona. Holstebro: Icarus, 2010. Originally published as *Teatro e spettacolo fra Occidente e Oriente* (Rome: Laterza, 1992).

Savran, David. 'Trafficking in Transnational Brands: The New "Broadway-Style" Musical'. *Theatre Survey* 55 (2014): 318–342.

Taviani, Ferdinando. 'L'ingresso della commedia dell'arte nella cultura del Cinquecento.' In *Il teatro italiano nel Rinascimento*, edited by Fabrizio Cruciani and Daniele Seragnoli, 319–345. Bologna: Il Mulino, 1987.

'The Tills Are Alive: The Musical Business Is Bigger, More Global and More Fabulous than Ever' (2013). http://www.economist.com/news/business/21577062-musicals-business-bigger-more-global-and-more-fabulous-ever-tills-are-alive, accessed 25 August 2019.

UNESCO. 'Working Towards a Convention on Intangible Cultural Heritage', n.d. https://ich. unesco.org/doc/src/01854-EN.pdf, accessed 27 August 2019.

Vilar, Jean. 'Le T.N.P. service public.' In Jean Vilar, *Le théâtre service public et autres textes*. 1954; Paris: Gallimard, 1974.

Xu Liuliu. 'Western Musicals to Find Larger Audience in China in 2019'. *Global Times*, 28 January 2019. http://www.globaltimes.cn/content/1137307.html, accessed 25 August 2019.

Zhang, Kun. 'A Hotbed for Musicals in China'. *China Daily*, 22 February 2019. http://www. chinadaily.com.cn/a/201902/22/WS5c6f3d9ca3106c65c34eab64_5.html, accessed 25 August 2019.

Zhou, Raymond. 'China's Theatre Bubble'. *American Theatre*, 25 April 2017, n.p. https://www. americantheatre.org/2017/04/25/chinas-theatre-bubble/, accessed 27 August 2019.

CHAPTER 2

# MUSICAL TRANSLATION AND ITS MULTIPLE CHALLENGES

EVA ESPASA

## INTRODUCTION

> Think in concentric circles: in the centre is the play that must be translated, the source text. Through its linguistic elements it belongs to the source language, and through that source language it partakes of the whole of the source culture. It also belongs to the source literature which has a code all its own, a repertory of literary procedures.[1]

ANDRÉ Lefévere, a pioneering figure of translation studies, invited researchers to examine the contexts involved in the analysis of translated plays with this image of concentric circles in order to situate the source text to be translated at the core of the analysis but then consider its circumscription by the source language and its culture.

We can extrapolate this image to the analysis of translated and staged musicals. Here we have to consider two interrelated sets of concentric circles, in the source and target cultures, which intersect and sometimes clash. We include other circles in a complex, dynamic system like that of musicals, where commercial, theatrical, and musical aspects feature very prominently. In this chapter these will be studied as challenges, which consist of, from the outer circles to the inner ones, cultural, commercial, theatrical, musical, and linguistic challenges. These will be explored providing examples from translated musicals mainly in the Catalan context alongside references to other musicals translated worldwide.[2]

This chapter will focus on singable translation. However, it must be briefly mentioned here that there are several theoretical options for translating musical texts that pivot around the initial criterion of translating songs as text or as music, which has been researched by Lucile Desblache and Marta Mateo, among other scholars.[3] Text translation can include such diverse forms as interlingual summaries and audio introductions, translation of libretti as scripts and the use of subtitles or surtitles. These can be utilised to provide accessibility to musicals in their source context. Nevertheless, as singable translation is the norm for stage musicals in most target contexts, it will be the focus of this chapter.[4]

# CULTURAL CHALLENGES

The first question to consider is why musicals are translated at all. Why are *Rent* and *Les Misérables*, for example, the most often translated musicals (twenty-two languages)?[5] In other musical genres—opera, for example—translation and non-translation coexist, and there is discussion among supporters and detractors of translations, which has been extensively researched.[6] Apart from historical and sociological aspects, the main semiotic arguments for and against translation have been succinctly summarised by Peter Low.[7] The main argument against translating is that only in the source text do we have access to the 'actual words written by the songwriter and used by the composer' and all their phonic features.[8] However, a related argument is used in defence of translation. According to Harai Golomb, singable translation—or music-linked translation, in her terminology—is 'the only procedure that can possibly simulate the effect of synchronised verbal/music/rhetorical fusion, as it functions in the original, transmitted from a singer's mouth to a listener's ear as a melopoetic interaction realised in sound, sense and gesture'.[9] In short, the conjunction between music and words is an argument both for and against translation. In more classical genres such as opera, the current norm is either non-translation or the provision of surtitles.[10] A similar resistance towards translation can be observed in the case of jukebox musicals, when the power of the source text is important because the hits that form the show's score have become well known in their source language, usually English, given the dominant position of the United Kingdom and the United States in both global musical theatre and the global pop charts. Conversely, in musicals where understanding the words is important, translation is generally seen as necessary in order to maintain the immediate impact of the songs on the audience.

From a cultural perspective, musicals have been seen as filling a cultural gap and have fostered the autochthonous production of a genre which was apparently foreign to the musical tradition of countries such as Spain, where existing genres (for example, *zarzuelas*—Spanish popular light operas) were traditionally assigned different social and artistic functions.[11] Musicals have been considered to have social relevance in that they appeal to general audiences, affording light entertainment, an emotional experience, and a certain artistic pleasure.[12]

In Spain, for example, the turn of the twenty-first century witnessed a growing interest in musicals, and more shows opened in the first five years of the new millennium than throughout the entire twentieth century, which became cultural and tourist attractions in Spain's largest cities, such as Madrid.[13] Nearly twenty years later, the 2018–2019 season was a big one for musicals, either imported from Broadway and the West End or created anew. Many Spanish tourists (21 percent) travel to Madrid to see a musical, a city that has become the fourth capital of musicals and the first in Spanish.[14]

Translation generates both indigenous productions and those created abroad.[15] For example, the Catalan company Dagoll Dagom, founded in 1974 and specialising in musicals, combines both indigenous musicals such as *Mar i cel* (*Sea and Sky*, 1988) and imports such as *The Mikado* (1986); the company has been considered as a reference point for both the production and the importation of new musicals.[16] Likewise, successful imports of musicals such as *Mamma Mia!* led to the creation of Spanish jukebox musicals such as *Hoy no me puedo levantar* (*Today I Can't Get Up*, 2005), which was advertised as 'a musical in which you'll be able to sing all songs' and was then exported to Latin America, the United States, and Northern Europe, making it the first contemporary Spanish musical theatre production to be taken abroad.[17] Similarly, the popularity of large-scale translated musical productions at the turn of the millennium stimulated the production in Spain of original large-scale Korean musicals.[18]

The prestige of the source language and culture is important in the selection of musicals. It is the usual practice of theatre and musical programmers to travel to New York and London to select the pieces that they will then export to their target countries.[19] For example, Daniel Anglès, the Catalan director of the Barcelona production of *Fun Home* (2018), bought the rights to this musical after seeing it on Broadway.[20] Once the performance rights have been acquired, as in this case, the acculturation policy of the translation is decided. It is oriented towards either the source culture or the target culture, but there is no absolute dichotomy. Even when there are licensing restrictions requiring adherence to the source production of the musical (see the next section, 'Commercial Challenges'), there is always some acculturation on a textual level in order to adapt the musical to the time and place of the performance. For example, Catalan (1986, 2005) and Spanish productions (2005) of *The Mikado* included references to Catalan politics and the Franco dictatorship and omitted the racist and sexist elements in the original,[21] while in 2005 they made satirical comments on the Spanish ban on smoking, trashy television shows and Catalan politics.[22]

Some musicals are located in distant times or places for both cultural and commercial reasons. In these cases, licensing restrictions do not easily allow cultural transposition. Besides, maintaining the foreignness of certain elements which might be criticised by the public is also a safe decision. For example, *La Cage aux Folles* (1983) kept the location of the original play by Jean Poiret, the French Riviera, 'which gave audiences a foreign locus in which they could comfortably situate equally foreign behaviour such as homosexuality and female drag, thus reassuring themselves that if the location was un-American, so was the behavior.'[23] Its 2018 production in Barcelona kept this setting, but probably for different reasons: keeping the nostalgic atmosphere of the original 1973 play could more easily justify the rather clichéd plot. Besides, the translated musical libretto plays with stereotypical French phrases, in keeping with the humorous tone of the original musical.

Even if a musical keeps its original setting, decisions regarding acculturation have to be taken at a microtextual level, which will be discussed in the section 'Linguistic Challenges'.

# Commercial Challenges

A specific feature of musicals is the importance of extra-textual factors that intervene in the production and politics of their import and export. In this section we look at some of these under the general title 'Commercial Challenges', which is here used as an umbrella term for phenomena that include diverse and powerful economic factors, often involving aggressive marketing.

Musicals became especially popular globally during the 1980s, 'a decade of conspicuous consumption when musical theatre became part of the cultural zeitgeist'.[24] In the source cultures where musicals were produced, they started to generate enormous profits through tourism to New York and London,[25] especially after air travel began to be more affordable to the general public, which broadened the audiences to include international visitors.[26]

Musicals travelled abroad from their mainly Anglophone contexts courtesy of producers such as Cameron Mackintosh, who has been considered the progenitor of what critics began to refer to in the 1980s as the megamusical, a system of licensing that created a new generation of globally performed musicals.[27] This system has also been called 'McTheatre', 'a term used [ ... ] to draw a parallel between the McDonald's franchise model and Mackintosh's meticulous replication of productions around the globe'.[28] An important feature of megamusicals is their exportability, usually through full licensing, a practice that is becoming the norm in places as diverse as Spain and Korea,[29] and that controls all aspects of the production, including translation. The current international musical theatre landscape reflects how this system has opened up new markets across Europe and in Asia. For instance, translation has led to the popularisation of musicals in Korea:

> As of 2006, translated productions hold about 85% of the Korean musical market. [ ... ] The popularity of large-scale musical productions started from the fully licensed Korean production of *The Phantom of the Opera* in 2001 and since then the Korean musical market has grown by more than 300% and its market share has reached over 50% of all of the performing arts.[30]

In non-Anglophone contexts, this franchise model of licensing ensures that all aspects of a production—including the song translation—are controlled by the license owners, such as Music Theatre International, an important owner of secondary rights to musicals and now a company headed by Cameron Mackintosh, whose system of licensing has been summarised by Miranda Lundskaer-Nielsen:

For major productions, the licensee is required to replicate the original production exactly, with permission required for any changes. The production team credentials and theatres are rigorously examined and a Mackintosh team is sent out to work with the local producers throughout the casting and rehearsal process. With overseas productions, Mackintosh will himself attend the final stages of rehearsals or an early preview, make some changes, and then return to see the show again.[31]

Sung Hee Kirk details the multiple supervision processes connected specifically to the translation of a fully licensed production. Although he refers to the context of Korea, similar processes are used worldwide and involve:

1. a translation by a lyricist-translator;
2. supervision from the licensing production company;
3. provision of a back-translation from an independent translator, one not involved in the translation or the production company;
4. raising of questions or objections from the original producer;
5. justification from Korean translators; and
6. acceptance or requests for changes from the original producers.[32]

The purpose of such meticulous supervision, undertaken by companies such as Music Theatre International and Stage Entertainment, for example, is to offer the 'same' productions as London and New York and to bring 'West End quality musical productions to audiences who [cannot] travel to London and [present] them in the local language [ . . . ] in the confident belief that the *same* show can work in different markets and cultures.'[33]

This sameness can occasionally be negotiated. For example, the Barcelona production of *Guys and Dolls* for Teatre Nacional (1998) made changes that were explicitly indicated in the copyright pages of the translated libretto into Catalan:

[T]his production of *Guys and Dolls*, which takes place in a prison through a 'theatre within the theatre' format, reflects changes in the original libretto and lyrics which have been specifically approved by Music Theatre International, in representation of the authors of this musical, and only for the staging at Teatre Nacional de Catalunya. The authorisation for these modifications does not extend to any future production of the work.[34]

Such permission for adaptation is not always granted. The libretto of Andrew Lloyd Webber's *Cats* had been adapted in Finland in 1986 with culture-specific phraseology and concepts. Rehearsals had already begun when the T. S. Eliot Society rejected the translation on the grounds that it destroyed the 'spirit' of the original, and it had to be revised by Finnish and English specialists from a literary background before being accepted.[35]

Given the scrupulous attention to copyright, it is no surprise that published libretti offer much more detail and emphasis on licensing than published stage plays: for example, the acting edition of *La Cage aux Folles* contains four full pages of detailed credits, versus the one page (thirteen lines) of credits in the original play by Jean Poiret.[36]

Very often exported musicals are promoted in connection with their origin on Broadway or in the West End. For example, the Spanish productions of *Fun Home*, *La Cage aux Folles*, and *Rent* were all presented with reference to their Broadway originals, as was *The Addams Family* (*La familia Addams*), even though the producer and director insisted that it was not a franchise production.[37] Musicals are also promoted by exploiting those factors which gave the source materials prestige, such as awards. The importance that this prestige is given in the target cultures seems to be culturally specific to Spanish and Catalan contexts, for example. Thus, the playbill of *Rent* for its 2019 production in Barcelona devoted a whole page to the Broadway awards the musical has received: its four Tony Awards, six Drama Desk Awards, and the Pulitzer Prize for Best Drama. Similarly, the Barcelona production of *Fun Home* advertised it as the Broadway musical that received five Tony Awards, while the promotional material for *La Cage aux Folles* prominently featured its nine Tony and three Drama Desk Awards.[38]

Usually, the marketing of translated musicals highlights their previous international recognition with reference to earlier productions, to original sources or other derivations, be they cinema, theatre, opera classics or music hits.[39] *Rent*, for example, is based on Puccini's opera *La Bohème*, and this is mentioned in the playbill, even though opera audiences are very different from musical audiences.[40] Another resource is the use of an anniversary to produce a musical. Again, *Rent* was presented in Barcelona in 2016 to celebrate the twentieth anniversary of the musical's première in New York, while its first successful Spanish production in 1999 was followed by another revival exactly twenty years later, in 2019.

Proof of a certain reverence towards the source materials is the fact that the titles in the target productions are not translated,[41] a trend that one also finds in current film translation. For example, in the Madrid and Barcelona musical repertoires, *Fun Home*, *Rent*, *Guys and Dolls*, *Grease*, and *Company*, have all been presented under their English-language titles, even though in the case of *Company* the translator, Guillem-Jordi Graells, warned against this non-translation strategy, since 'company' can be pronounced as its Catalan homograph, meaning companion.[42] Elements of the target culture are also used as promotional factors, referencing, for instance, the prestige of certain companies, directors and actors.

An important commercial aspect is the high price of tickets, which can be related to many factors: the lack of institutional subsidies (since musicals are usually treated as commercial products), the need to recoup investment in copyright and the use of impressive stage sets (see the 'Theatrical Challenges' section below).[43] Another outstanding feature of musicals is that although audiences may love them, critics do not, necessarily.[44] Even though the success of musicals is regularly assessed by both box-office receipts and critical acclaim, in some countries these two seem to be at odds. Critical approval by theatre reviewers is generally not so significant a factor in establishing a musical's status as word of mouth and the big marketing campaigns and merchandising promoted by the international licensing systems.

FIG. 2.1 The cast of *Rent* in the 2019 Barcelona production, including Marc Gómez, lyricist, translator and actor, on the far right. Photo: David Ruano, provided by the author.

Finally, musical theatre productions can be initiated by fans in an age of *prosumer* power, that is, in a media era where users are both consumers and potential producers of media products.[45] Lucile Desblache has noted this phenomenon and how it involves translation: the Broadway musical *Newsies* (2012) was produced after the popularity with fans of its Disney film version. The action, which takes place in New York, is based on the newsboys' strike of 1899. However, it resonates with the economic difficulties young people all over the world are encountering in the early twenty-first century, and the film's cult status in the United States resulted in its adaptation for the stage through Disney and the global theatrical licensing agency MTI thanks to Disney's attention to US fan communities:

> Companies such as Disney [ . . . ] analyse [fans'] interest and engagement with musical/theatrical products in depth [ . . . ], on social networks and video-sharing websites. In this case [fans] drove a new production, internationally [and] the show was adapted beyond English-speaking countries. In some cases, such as for the Italian version, the adaptation was unusually target-culture-oriented for a Disney production.[46]

## THEATRICAL CHALLENGES

'[W]hat I know better than anyone is that a great set doesn't make a good show. I also know that in order to sound good it's got to look good.'[47] These words, of the producer Cameron Mackintosh, illustrate the relative importance of theatrical aspects, such as scenography, to a musical's success. On the one hand, impressive sets can distract attention from more profound meanings in musicals, or the lack thereof—an idea that has been graphically summarised by the phrase 'humming the scenery'.[48] On the other hand, it emphasises the close connection between a musical and the visual aspects of its production, which can be extrapolated to include more general theatrical aspects. Most theatrical challenges in musicals are common to other types of live performance events: their semiotic density, the multiplicity of agents involved in the productions, and the immediate reception and feedback from the audience.[49]

Licensing poses theatrical challenges. If copyright restrictions apply only to the libretto and music, translated musicals will usually have a new scenography in the target context which can be specifically attuned to its visual culture.[50] However, in fully licensed productions, it is more common to see the same stage design, a practice which is arguably defensible according to current globalisation trends, and to have supervision from the source production. Spectacular stage sets are also related to theatre capacity and large audiences, which has involved the adaptation or repurposing of theatres in Madrid and Barcelona.[51] Similar considerations extend to the presence of musicians on stage. Curiously, in the Barcelona production of *The Addams Family*, audiences knew that the musicians played below the stage, unseen by them, as a consequence of the size of the stage, through an audio announcement at the beginning of the performance. This is an example in which technical and stage requirements can affect touring. The requirements for touring can paradoxically also be considered an advantage. According to Esteve Ferrer, the director of *The Addams Family*, the original Broadway staging gained in focus through its stylisation on tour, which gave more importance to character and plot than to the (in his view) overly extravagant stage sets.[52] Conversely, according to a review, the stage set for *La Cage aux Folles* (2018) seemed a little small for the huge stage in Teatre Tívoli in Barcelona; it appeared to have been designed for future touring.[53]

Licensing and touring affect not only scenography but also acting. The Tokyo producer Mariko Kojima tells of an example of overzealous supervision when permission was required from Cameron Mackintosh for a specific body movement at the end of *Miss Saigon*. The character of Ellen stood still on-stage in the original production, which did not generate audience sympathy in Tokyo: '[I]n order to make the change they had to write a letter to Mackintosh asking whether she could extend her hand.'[54] Kojima also comments on the connections between translation and staging. The fact that the Japanese translation can accommodate only 30 to 50 percent of the original words can create problems with staging and choreography based on English words that cannot always be solved.[55]

The franchise model is often looked at with suspicion in the target cultures, where there is a parallel demand for more local productions. For example, in response to a decrease in audiences for big musicals in Barcelona in 2004, the Catalan playwright Sergi Belbel and director Joan Lluís Bozzo were in favour of reinventing the genre, of making it more Mediterranean.[56] Another question is the target language. In Barcelona, musicals in Catalan and Spanish coexist, but in spite of the success and tradition of musicals in Catalan, the current trend of imported global blockbuster musicals in Catalonia is for them to be translated into Spanish.[57] Anna Rosa Cisquella, the producer of successful musicals in Catalan such as *The Mikado* (1986), has recently denounced the decrease of big musicals in Catalan and praised the financial risk assumed by the

FIG. 2.2 The cast of *La Cage aux Folles* promoting the production in the city centre of Barcelona. Photo: Lab Creative Studio, provided by the author.

Catalan production of *Spring Awakening* (*El despertar de la primavera*) in the large Teatre Victòria in Barcelona in 2019.[58]

One specific theatrical challenge is the versatility demanded of the cast: actors must be capable of interpreting, singing, and dancing alike. Therefore, the 'incongruity' principle involved in characterisation, which is common in opera and prioritises musical qualities over actor adequacy, is much weaker in musicals.[59] This is probably why a 2018 review of *La Cage aux Folles* (2018) showed the critic's initial hesitation about the age appropriateness of the actors, who were in their early forties, playing the more mature characters Albin and George, a hesitation which was dispelled once the show began and he was immersed in enjoying the show.[60] Li Jin, in an analysis of translated musicals in China, also subordinates the different challenges posed by singable translations to the more general concept of enjoyability, which takes into account the need for recreational adjustments to foster interactivity with audiences from a theatrical perspective.[61]

## Musical Challenges

Some musicals alternate sung parts and spoken dialogue, while others are sung through. In this section we will focus on the specific challenges involved in singable translation, which have been characterised in the tongue-in-cheek words of the composer, director, and translator Jeremy Sams:[62] '[T]he difficulty is this; imagine recording some dialogue with people at a dinner party and then having to write different words for it but following exactly the same intonation.'[63]

Peter Low has summarised the challenges of musical translation through a less extreme image: the sporting metaphor of the pentathlon and its five components. In the case of musical translation, these are singability, sense, naturalness, rhythm, and rhyme. Low insists on flexibility and on the relative importance of each individual aspect: '[T]he objective is a *high aggregate score across all these five events*. Trade-offs are very likely to be required.'[64] Of these five elements, here we will focus on singability, rhythm, and rhyme, as these are more specific to musicals, whereas sense and naturalness are common prerequisites in many types of translation.

Singability, in Low's view, refers to the relative ease of vocalisation, which is 'achieved by meeting the demands of articulation, breath, dynamics and resonance in the physical action of singing'[65]—best evaluated by professional singers: 'The ideal translation [ ... ] will "have the same mouth-feel" as the original.'[66] Low has delineated the usual prescriptions applied to singable translations, especially into English. These involve, among others, being aware of pitch and avoiding hard-to-sing words on high notes, as well as avoiding short vowels and certain consonant clusters.[67] The specificity of translating into tonal languages such as Chinese has been considered by Low;[68] it has also been explored by Jin, who reminds us that translating songs into Chinese involves taking into account the tone system (rising and falling tones, which need to be compatible with pitch change).[69]

Regarding rhythm, guidelines on writing for musical theatre recommend 'making accented syllables coincide with strong beats or the stronger parts of a beat'.[70] Likewise, there are several ways to stress an important word: placing it on a strong beat, making it higher or lower than the rest of the phrase, or sustaining it.[71] The same applies to translation. Low recommends giving more emphasis to musical stress than exact syllable correspondence and to words which are rhythmically and melodically prominent, which ideally are translated at the same location.[72] In translating from English, translators often have to deal with longer words and more syllables, which is likely to involve omissions in the translation. This is common in many languages, and each finds resources to provide concise translations. For example, Korean does not require explicit subjects or objects if they are clear from the context, and this can help with syllable correspondence.[73]

Professional practice, as reported by Low, is pragmatic and defends 'tweaks', or small adjustments, regarding rhythm, the number of notes, or even the melody,[74] observing that those tricks must also be resorted to in the original. Low gives examples from classical music, but the situation also obtains for the lyrics in contemporary musicals. Tim Rice has been criticised for flouting the basic rules of lyric writing and using unclean rhymes, which he defends as common in rock music.[75] Some tweaking can also come from music directors: they may increase the tempo 'to compensate for loss of tension caused by words with more syllables and change in word order'.[76]

According to Allen Cohen and Steven L. Rosenhaus, rhyme is a challenge that needs to be considered functionally in the writing of musicals from the perspective of its purpose in the lyrics.[77] Similarly, translating rhyme can be less important that other factors, but if it is needed, it has to be anticipated: '[A]ny strategic decision to use rhyme needs to be made early in the process, so that some rhyming-words (the crucial ones) can be found early on.'[78] Therefore, flexible, imperfect rhyme schemes can be used when needed, as in rap music.[79] Rhyme is also a lower priority in the translation of Korean musicals.[80] In specific cases, however, rhyme can be all-important. In the 2010 Dutch production of *Mary Poppins*, the word 'supercalifragilisticexpialidocious' was modified because 'docious' is difficult to rhyme in Dutch, while the new ending 'dasties' rhymes with words that occur naturally in the context of the play, such as 'fantastisch'. This also involved changing the choreography, as dancers spelled out the word with their bodies.[81] Similarly, recent translations of musicals into Catalan and Spanish show a flexible, functional use of assonant rhyme.

So far, we have seen how musical translations are done. Let us now focus on who does them—on the agents involved in musical translation. What kind of expertise is most prominent in them: theatrical, musical or translation? As in theatre translation, the boundaries of these profiles are not clear and are connected to the perceived prestige or status of authors in the theatrical system. Kirk, in analysing translated musicals in Korea, outlines the basic kinds of translators of musicals: the content-translator, who has expertise in theatre translation, and the lyricist-translator, who has expertise in music (and is usually the musical director), and highlights that collaboration among them is the norm.[82] Collaboration is certainly common and combines different profiles. If we look at the credits of translated musicals in Barcelona in the 2018–2019 season, we can see the joint work of translators, usually involving successful long-term associations between teams of translators or of translators and directors with musical, theatrical, and translation expertise. (See the Appendix.)

Occasionally there are conflicts between translators and directors. For example, the Catalan playwright and translator Guillem-Jordi Graells, having already translated Stephen Sondheim's *Marry Me a Little* and other musical works into Catalan, undertook his translation of *Company* with the above-mentioned priorities of musical translation: singability, rhythm, and rhyme. To these he added the usual characteristics of Sondheim's libretti: abrupt changes in register and theatre conventions, as well as a strong connection between words and music. However, conflict arose with the well-known stage and opera director Calixto Bieito, who prioritised the harsh, sour perspective he read into Sondheim's libretto and introduced changes to Graells's translation. Since the translator disagreed with these changes on musical grounds, he withdrew his name from the credits for the songs and was credited as the translator, not the lyricist, of the Catalan version.[83]

Musical and translation priorities can be undertaken simultaneously when the translator has expertise in music, acting, singing, and translation. Such is the case in the

Barcelona musicals analysed. For example, Marc Gómez, together with Daniel Anglès, has translated *Fun Home* and *Rent*, as well as Jonathan Larson's previous work *Tick, Tick ... Boom*, which was staged posthumously in Barcelona (2017). In the prominent song 'Come to Your Senses', the translation of this phrase had to be powerful and render the initial impact of the song and its context. Therefore, Gómez prioritised the translated the long vowel 'e' in 'senses' and rendered the phrase as 'Sigues autèntic' (Be authentic), which allows the 'e' in 'autèntic' to be lengthened, as in the original.[84]

The above guidelines and experiences highlight the relative flexibility of different musical criteria. In the words of Low, '[L]ateral thinking is required—and lateral thinking requires elbow-room. The more margins of compromise are available, the greater the chance of a successful target text'.[85]

# Linguistic Challenges

The initial decision to import or export a musical can be attributed to several factors, as we have seen. However, the first linguistic challenge is to decide whether this musical will travel better in its source language or in a translation. This decision is connected, again, to both commercial and cultural criteria, including the prestige and world relevance of the source and target languages.

The next decision is whether to translate songs as text or as music. This has to do with the logocentric versus musicocentric orientation of the shows, that is, the relative importance of the text and the music.[86] A logocentric focus is important if intelligibility is paramount. In fact, Cohen and Rosenhaus list comprehensibility as an important principle for writing lyrics, as it involves matching lyrics and music,[87] whereas musicocentric orientation is a priority in well-known songs, which have become popular in their source language.

Even though in musicals singable translations tend to be the norm and have been the focus of this chapter, there is a growing trend to accompany the songs in the source language—usually English—with summary translations or surtitles, which can be connected to musical tourism as well as to a growing sensitivity towards the sensorial accessibility of shows.[88]

Another important choice is that of the target language in bilingual or multilingual settings, which is influenced by sociological, ideological, and financial factors: as we have mentioned, Spanish and Catalan coexist as target languages on Catalan stages. Similarly, translations will have to decide how to render other languages and linguistic varieties present in original musicals, such as the presence of French in *La Cage aux Folles* and *Beauty and the Beast*, in both source-language and target-language versions.[89]

Linguistic challenges often depend on the style of songwriters. We have already mentioned the attention to Sondheim's style in its Catalan translation. Another example is Tim Rice, whose lyrics include sarcasm and colloquialisms as well as a 'cheeky and effervescent, sometimes flippant turn of phrase [that] has become something of a trademark'.[90] Nowadays the phrase and homonymous song 'What's the Buzz' in *Jesus Christ Superstar* is topical, according to Rice,[91] but this was not an obstacle for the popularity of its Spanish translation, even though—or precisely because—it was devoid of colloquialisms and was rendered as 'Cuéntanos, dinos lo que va a pasar' (Speak to us, tell us what's going to happen) by Nacho Artime and Jaime Azpilicueta.[92]

The following examples from Jerry Herman's lyrics in *La Cage aux Folles* and their translation into Spanish by Roser Batalla and Roger Peña may serve as paradigms for the linguistic challenges of musical translation and their combination with all other challenges presented above.[93] I will focus on the Spanish translation of the well-known theme 'I Am What I Am', which was used in the promotion of the Barcelona production. For example, the opposition between 'give me the hook/or the ovation' has been kept and rendered as 'para silbar, para aplaudirme' (to whistle at [to boo] me/to applaud). The phonetic play, based on the original English unclean internal rhyme—'And so what/If I love each spar**kle** and each ban**gle**'—has been replaced by an alliteration: '¿Qué pasa/si me **p**irro **p**or la **p**urpurina?' (What happens/If I'm crazy about glitter?). We can also consider two translation options related to gender. Where the source text reads 'so it's time to open up your closet', the Spanish emphasises this reference: 'No hay más que salir del *puñetero* armario' (You've only got to come out of the *bloody* closet), probably for musical reasons (to gain syllables) but also in keeping with making explicit the gender politics in the Barcelona production, which were more covert at the time of *La Cage*'s opening, in 1983—during Ronald Reagan's presidency.[94] It is probably this context which gave rise to the following translation option: 'I bang my own drum/Some think it's noise/I think it's pretty' became 'Sí, esta es mi voz, / y os guste o no, / a mí me encanta' (Yes, this is my voice/And, whether you like it or not,/I love it). The reference to the character's own voice can be read as an assertive vindication of the voice of a male actor who sings in female dress.[95]

An opposite example comes from the Chinese translation of the song 'Dancing Queen' in *Mamma Mia!*, which tones down the sexual agency of women:

> In the lines 'You're a *teaser*, you *turn 'em on*/Leave 'em burning and then you're gone', the word 'teaser' and the expression 'turn 'em on' portray the image of a passionate girl. Nevertheless, according to the traditional Chinese values, young ladies must be elegant and shy and act passively in a relationship. Therefore, in the target text, the two lines are rendered as '你把他欲望开了头/放了一把火就想走' (which literally means 'You start his desire/Set a fire and then you want to leave') [ . . . ], avoiding possible cultural conflicts and ensuring the audience's acceptance of the show.[96]

Even when the overall presentation of a show is foreignising in that it tries to preserve is original cultural setting, it is common practice to adapt or generalise cultural referents. For example, Marc Gómez, the translator of Jonathan Larson's *Tick, Tick … Boom* (2001), refers to a specific adaptation he made when translating the song 'Sugar' for the 2017 Catalan production of the musical. This song refers to Twinkies, an American filled sponge cake generally unknown in Spain, which Gómez changed into Kinder Eggs; which was generally compatible with keeping the sense as in the original song, but involved replacing all references in the song to 'sugar' with 'chocolate'.[97]

Such microtextual acculturation was also common in the Barcelona musical productions of 2018–2019. For example, in the Catalan production of *Fun Home*, the emblematic song 'Telephone Wire' is translated as 'Línia continua ('Solid Line'), which emphasises the difficult father-daughter communication pervading the original song with a different image, compatible with the description of the short drive Alison and her father Bruce share during the song, when they miss the opportunity of openly talking about their homosexuality and instead resort to parallel monologues, separated, as it were, by solid lines. This context would explain the translation of the repeated phrase 'at the light' as 'som a prop' (we are close/near). Specific cultural references are generalised: 'There's a sign for Sugar Valley' becomes 'Veig l'antiga benzinera' (I can see the old petrol station), 'Junction 50' becomes 'cap cruïlla' (no crossing), and 'in Swanson's barn' is changed to 'De campaments' (in the summer camp). In the song 'Ring of Keys', where Alison as a girl becomes fascinated by the butch look of a delivery woman, some clothing references are changed to others that also have lesbian connotations, probably for rhythmic reasons—for instance, from 'your short hair and your dungarees' to 'la camisa a quadres i els cabells tan curts' (the checked shirt and your hair, so short).[98]

FIG. 2.3 The three Alisons in the Barcelona production of *Fun Home*. Photo: Àgata Casanovas, provided by the author.

With *The Addams Family*, the company promoted the fact that the translation was adapted to the Spanish context.[99] The production opened in Madrid, and there are references to Madrid cuisine and to bullfighting, which were not always appreciated by the Barcelona audiences where the production toured later.[100] However, there were topical references to Brexit and to social networks that did work, and in the song 'When You're an Addams', specific cultural referents were successfully adapted or generalised: Morticia's 'dress cut down to Venezuela' became 'escote suicida' (suicidal cleavage); on their first date Gómez took Morticia to see *La matanza de Texas* (*The Texas Chainsaw Massacre*) instead of *Death of a Salesman*, which can be understood in connection with the general public that attends musicals in Spain: they might not be familiar with Arthur Miller's classic work, since they do not necessarily attend straight plays. The references to dances were also adapted to Spanish equivalents, 'Line Dance' becoming 'La conga', 'Bunny Hop' morphing into 'La yenka' and 'Do the Twist' being replaced by 'Bailando el twist' (the chorus and title of a Spanish song by 1960s group Dúo Dinámico).

Finally, to mark the relative importance of linguistic challenges compared to others, Low has used the sea-transit metaphor, wherein

> a [source text] located in one country (one language) needs to travel to another, across an ocean with may be rough, and may seem to be affected by different gravitational fields. [ ... ] Fortunately the translator is not tasked with ensuring the survival of every single item of cargo, which would be impossible, but with preserving *all the most valuable items*, even at the expense of others.[101]

# CONCLUSION

In the previous pages we have tried to convey how the translation of musicals is affected by many challenges that, like intersecting concentric circles, sometimes clash but are often sources of creative solutions. The global versus local dynamics of cultural production, the coexistence of translation and indigenous musical production, the advantages and restrictions posed by licensing, the tensions between theatrical foreignising and domestic-oriented staging—all these are taken into account when tackling the musical and linguistic challenges of singable translations.

The different agents involved (licensing companies, producers, translators, directors, singers, and actors) ideally work collaboratively but are aware of one another's relative importance and status. From the perspective of cultures where translation is common, it is surprising to find resistance from licensing companies (usually from cultures where translation is less common) to specific translation and performance choices, which are part and parcel of the current creative practices of theatre and translation. Finally, examples from recently staged productions show how musical and linguistic criteria can be tackled simultaneously in successful translations.

## NOTES

1. André Lefévere, 'Translation: Changing the Code: Soyinka's Ironic Aetiology', in *The Languages of Theatre: Problems in the Translation and Transposition of Drama*, ed. Ortrun Zuber (London: Pergamon Press, 1980), 132–145; here: 132, doi: 10.1016/b978-0-08-025246-9.50017-0.
2. See the list of musicals in the Appendix.
3. See Lucile Desblache, *Music and Translation: New Mediations in the Digital Age* (London: Palgrave Macmillan, 2019), chap. 6, doi: 10.1057/978-1-137-54965-5; Marta Mateo, 'Music and Translation', in *Handbook of Translation Studies*, ed. Yves Gambier and Luc van Doorslaer (Amsterdam: John Benjamins, 2012), 115–121, 10.1075/hts.3.mus1; John Franzon, 'Choices in Song Translation: Singability in Print, Subtitles and Sung Performances', in 'Translation and Music', special issue, *Translator* 14, no. 2 (2008): 373–399, doi: 10.1080/13556509.2008.10799263.
4. Marta Mateo, 'Anglo-American Musicals in Spanish Theatres', in 'Translation and Music', special issue, *Translator* 14, no. 2 (2008): 319–342; here: 320, doi: 10.1080/13556509.2008.10799261
5. This information is prominently featured on the respective websites: the Barcelona production of *Rent* (https://www.teatrecondal.cat/ca/ex/1628/rent/, accessed 25 June 2019) and the new London production of *Les Misérables* (https://www.lesmis.com/london/about, accessed 17 November 2019).
6. Mateo, *Music and Translation*; Desblache, *Music and Translation: New Mediations*; Harai Golomb, 'Music-Linked Translation [MLT] and Mozart's Operas: Theoretical, Textual, and Practical Perspectives', in *Song and Significance: Virtues and Vices of Vocal Translation*, ed. Dinda Gorlée (Amsterdam: Rodopi, 2005), 121–162.
7. Peter Low, *Translating Song: Lyrics and Text* (London: Routledge, 2017), 72–75, doi:10.4324/9781315630281.
8. Ibid., 72.
9. Golomb, 'Music-Linked Translation', 14.
10. Mateo, 'Anglo-American Musicals', 320–321.
11. Ibid., 331–332.
12. Ibid., 332ff.
13. Alejandro Postigo, 'The Evolution of Musical Theatre in Spain Throughout the Twentieth and Twenty-first Centuries', in *Reframing the Musical: Race, Culture and Identity*, ed. Sarah Whitfield (London: Red Globe, 2019), 122.
14. Javier A. Fernández, 'Las mujeres que no dirigen ni producen musicales', *El País*, 9 June 2019, https://elpais.com/ccaa/2019/06/08/madrid/1560020733_827216.html, accessed 25 June 2019.
15. Sirkku Aaltonen, *Time Sharing on Stage: Drama Translation in Theatre and Society* (Clevedon: Multilingual Matters, 2000), 70.
16. Postigo, 'The Evolution of Musical Theatre', 120.
17. 'Por fin un musical en el que podrás cantar todas las canciones'. Santiago Fouz-Hernández, 'Me cuesta tanto olvidarte: Mecano and the Movida Remixed, Revisited and Repackaged', *Journal of Spanish Cultural Studies* 10, no. 2 (2009): 167–187; here: 173–174, doi: 10.1080/14636200902990695.
18. Sung Hee Kirk, 'Translated Musicals and Musical Translation in Korea', *The Journal of Translation Studies* 9, no. 1 (2008): 283–309; here: 304–305, doi: 10.15749/jts.2008.9.1.011.

19. Mateo, 'Anglo-American Musicals', 330.
20. Allwebber, 'Fun Home, Barcelona 2018', originally published 8 August 2017, revised November 2018, https://www.love4musicals.com/2017/08/08/fun-home-barcelona-2018-2/, accessed 25 June 2019.
21. Eva Espasa, *La traducció dalt de l'escenari* (Vic: Eumo, 2001), 165–168.
22. Mateo, 'Anglo-American Musicals', 335.
23. Norman Hart, 'The Selling of *La Cage aux Folles*: How Audiences Were Helped to Read Broadway's First Gay Musical', *Theatre History Studies* 23 (2003): 5–24; here: 8.
24. Nick Allott, quoted in Miranda Lundskaer-Nielsen, 'Cameron Mackintosh: Control, Collaboration, and the Creative Producer', in *The Oxford Handbook of the British Musical*, ed. Robert Gordon and Olaf Jubin (Oxford: Oxford University Press, 2016), 537–559; here: 542, doi: 10.1093/oxfordhb/9780199988747.013.22.
25. Robert Gordon and Olaf Jubin, 'Introduction', in *The Oxford Handbook of the British Musical*, ed. Robert Gordon and Olaf Jubin (Oxford: Oxford University Press, 2016), 1–228; here: 25, doi: 10.1093/oxfordhb/9780199988747.013.30.
26. Lundskaer-Nielsen, 'Cameron Mackintosh', 542.
27. Gordon and Jubin, 'Introduction', 10.
28. Lundskaer-Nielsen, 'Cameron Mackintosh', 538.
29. Spain: Mateo, 'Anglo-American Musicals', 336–337; Korea: Kirk, 'Translated Musicals', 285.
30. Kirk, 'Translated Musicals', 304–305.
31. Lundskaer-Nielsen, 'Cameron Mackintosh', 549–550.
32. Kirk, 'Translated Musicals', 291–292.
33. Lundskaer-Nielsen, 'Cameron Mackintosh', 551; my emphasis.
34. 'Aquesta producció de Guys & Dolls, que té lloc en una presó a través d'un format de «teatre dins del teatre», reflecteix canvis en el llibret i lletres originals que han estat específicament aprovats per Music Theatre International, en representació dels autors d'aquest musical, i només per a la posada en escena que es fa al Teatre Nacional de Catalunya. L'autorització d'aquestes modificacions no es fa extensiva a cap futura producció de l'obra'. Frank Loesser, Jo Swerling, and Abe Burrows, *Guys and Dolls* (Barcelona: Edicions del Teatre Nacional, 1998), 5.
35. Sirkku Aaltonen, *Acculturation of the Other: Irish Milieux in Finnish Drama Translation* (Joensuu: University of Joensuu Press, 1996), 55; Aaltonen, *Time-Sharing on Stage*, 80.
36. Jerry Herman and Harvey Fierstein, *La Cage aux Folles* (1983; New York: Samuel French, 2014); Jean Poiret, *La Cage aux folles* (1973; Paris: Presses Pocket).
37. Imma Barba and Miquel Gascón, 'Roda de premsa *La familia Addams* Teatre Coliseum 2018.10.03', *Voltar i voltar per les arts escèniques* [blog], https://voltarivoltar.com/2018/10/03/067-roda-de-premsa-la-familia-addams-teatre-coliseum-2018-10-03-temp-18-19-rdp-014/, accessed 25 June 2019. The blog includes the audio file of the press briefing.
38. https://www.funhome-elmusical.com/; https://www.lajauladelaslocas.es/la-historia-de-un-musical-que-ha-hecho-historia.html, accessed 25 June 2019.
39. Mateo, 'Anglo-American Musicals', 334. See the Appendix for the sources of recent Barcelona productions, all of which were highlighted in the respective promotional material and reviews of the musicals.
40. Mateo, 'Anglo-American Musicals', 333.
41. Ibid., 325 n. 15.
42. Guillem-Jordi Graells, 'Traduir musicals', *Quaderns Divulgatius* 10 (1998), 63–79; here: 68.
43. Mateo, 'Anglo-American Musicals', 335–336.

# MUSICAL TRANSLATION AND ITS MULTIPLE CHALLENGES  83

44. Jessica Sternfeld, *The Megamusical* (Bloomington: Indiana University Press 2006), 4.
45. The concept of *prosumer* in contemporary society was presented in Alvin Toffler, *The Third Wave* (New York: William Morrow, 1980): 265–288.
46. Ken Cerniglia, dramaturge and literary manager for the Disney Theatrical Group, quoted by Desblache, *New Mediations*, 84.
47. Lundskaer-Nielsen, 'Cameron Mackintosh', 544.
48. Christine White, '"Humming the Sets": Scenography and the Spectacular Musical from *Cats* to *The Lord of the Rings*', in *The Oxford Handbook of the British Musical*, ed. Robert Gordon and Olaf Jubin (Oxford: Oxford University Press, 2016), 408, doi: 10.1093/oxfordhb/9780199988747.013.17
49. Mateo, 'Anglo-American Musicals', 321.
50. Such was the case with the 2018–2019 Barcelona productions analysed here.
51. Mateo, 'Anglo-American Musicals', 336.
52. Barba and Gascón, 'Roda de premsa *La familia Addams*'.
53. Allwebber, '*La jaula de las locas* Barcelona 2018'. Originally published 11 December 2017, revised December 2018, https://www.love4musicals.com/2017/12/11/la-jaula-las-locas-esp ana-2018/, accessed 25 June 2019. The Madrid production, which opened in October 2019, adapted the set specifically for the smallerTeatro Rialto, according to set designer Enric Planas (https://www.lajauladelaslocas.es/la-escenografia--entrevista-a-enric-planas. html, accessed 10 November 2019).
54. Mariko Kojima, quoted in Lundskaer-Nielsen, 'Cameron Mackintosh', 550.
55. Quoted in ibid.
56. Jordi Subirana, 'Los musicales sufren una caída de público en BCN', *El Periódico* (14 February 2004).
57. Antoni Font Mir, 'El teatre musical a Catalunya', *Entreacte: revista d'arts escèniques i audiovisuals* (14 August 2016), http://entreacte.cat/entrades/perspectives/a-fons/el-tea tre-musical-a-catalunya-una-mirada-historica/, accessed 25 June 2019. Núria Juanico, 'El català, desterrat dels musicals de gran format', *Ara*, 23 September 2019, https://www.ara.cat/cultura/catala-desterrat-teatre-musical_0_2313368652.html, accessed 10 November 2019.
58. Jordi Bordes, 'El despertar dels actors de musicals', *El punt avui*, 19 March 2019, https://www.elpuntavui.cat/cultura/article/19-cultura/1573119-el-despertar-dels-actors-de-music als.html, accessed 25 June 2019.
59. Mateo, 'Anglo-American Musicals', 320.
60. Fernando Solla, 'Zaza Is Here to Stay', 10 October 2018, http://enplatea.com/?p=18484, accessed 25 June 2019.
61. Li Jin, 'A Three-Dimensional Framework of Acculturation in translation of Musicals', *Proceedings of the 2018 4th International Conference on Social Science and Higher Education (ICSSHE 2018)* (Paris: Atlantis Press: 2018), 88–91, doi: 10.2991/icsshe-18.2018.22
62. Jeremy Sams has been described as 'the ultimate polymath' for his prolific and acclaimed career as a director, composer, and translator of musicals, operas, and plays: https://www.mtishows.com/people/jeremy-sams,accessed 10 November 2019.
63. Jeremy Sams, 'Words and Music', in David Johnston (ed.) *Stages of Translation* (Bath: Absolute Press, 1996), 178.
64. Low, *Translating Song*, 80.
65. Ibid., 81.
66. Ibid.
67. Ibid., 85–87.

84    EVA ESPASA

68. Ibid., 87.
69. Jin, 'A Three-Dimensional Framework', 90.
70. Allen Cohen and Steven L. Rosenhaus, *Writing Musical Theater* (New York: Palgrave Macmillan, 2006), 127.
71. Ibid., 128.
72. Low, *Translating Song*, 97 and 99.
73. Kirk, 'Translated Musicals', 295.
74. Low, *Translating Song*, 100–102.
75. Olaf Jubin, 'Tim Rice: The Pop Star Scenario', in *The Oxford Handbook of the British Musical*, ed. Robert Gordon and Olaf Jubin (Oxford: Oxford University Press, 2016), 507–536; here: 514, doi: 10.1093/oxfordhb/9780199988747.013.21.
76. Kirk, 'Translated Musicals', 296.
77. Cohen and Rosenhaus, *Writing Musical Theater*, 108–109.
78. Low, *Translating Song*, 103.
79. A comparison drawn by both Cohen and Rosenhaus, *Writing Musical Theater*, and Low, *Translating Song*.
80. Kirk, 'Translated Musicals', 301.
81. Williem Metz, executive producer at Stage Entertainment in Holland; quoted in Lundskaer-Nielsen, 'Cameron Mackintosh', 551.
82. Kirk, 'Translated Musicals', 290–291.
83. Graells, 'Traduir musicals', 70–72.
84. Martí Figueras, 'Tick, tick … Boom: Una adaptació fidel a l'essència de Jonathan Larson', *Núvol: El digital de cultura*, 12 December 2017, https://www.nuvol.com/noticies/tick-tick-boom-una-adaptacio-fidel-a-lessencia-de-jonathan-larson/, accessed 25 June 2019.
85. Low, *Translating Song*, 109.
86. Ibid., 128–129.
87. Cohen and Rosenhaus, *Writing Musical Theater*, 114.
88. See Desblache, *New Mediations*, chap. 6.3, 'Music and Accessibility'. See also *New Paths in Theatre Translation and Surtitling*, ed. Vasiliki Misiou, and Loukia Kostopoulou (London: Routledge 2023).
89. For research on this, see Marta Mateo, 'Multilingualism in Stage and Film Musicals: Varying Choices in Various Translation Modes and Contexts', in *Translating Audiovisuals in a Kaleidoscope of Languages*, ed. Montse Corrius, Eva Espasa, and Patrick Zabalbeascoa (Berlin: Peter Lang, 2019).
90. Jubin, 'Tim Rice: The Pop Star Scenario', 511.
91. Ibid., 511–512.
92. See Mateo, 'Anglo-American Musicals', 321–322, for the introduction of *Jesucristo Superstar* in Spain.
93. Herman and Fierstein, *La Cage aux Folles*, 57–58.
94. Hart, 'The Selling'. Hart details the processes by which *La Cage aux Folles* was presented to mainstream American audiences in the early 1980s, during the conservatism of the Reagan era, and the generally homophobic atmosphere in the early days of AIDS. From the choice of creative team, of cast (with main characters' pedigree in previous masculine roles), to its publicity in the press (logos of the production and images of main characters emphasizing their masculinity) and the institutionalised critical attention it received. Hart details the deliberate decision 'to privilege commercial success over political content, by building a heterosexual narrative around homosexual characters and then by helping their audiences to read it as such' (21).

95. However, the gender dynamics of *La Cage aux Folles* and *The Addams Family* are much more traditional than those of the rest of the musicals analysed here. Specifically, the confusion of homosexuality with transvestitism and effeminacy in *La Cage* is completely different from, for instance, *Billy Elliot*, 'the first British musical to explore the connection between homophobic anxiety and the cultural implications of homosexual orientation within a society that prizes masculine strength as a heroic virtue'. Robert Gordon, '*Billy Elliot* and Its Lineage: The Politics of Class and Sexual Identity in British Musicals since 1953', in *The Oxford Handbook of the British Musical*, ed. Robert Gordon and Olaf Jubin (Oxford: Oxford University Press, 2016), 419–442; here: 421.
96. Li Jin, 'A Three-Dimensional Framework', 89–90.
97. Figueras, 'Tick, Tick . . . Boom'.
98. The effectiveness of the reference to the checked shirt in the target text can be assessed by its repeated mention in the reviews of the show.
99. Barba and Gascón, 'Roda de premsa *La familia Addams*'.
100. Imma Barba and Miquel Gascón, '116—Teatre Musical—*La familia Addams*—Teatre Coliseum—2018.12.12 (temp. 18/19—espectacle nº 088)', https://voltarivoltar.com/2018/12/15/116-teatre-musical-la-familia-addams-%f0%9f%90%8c%f0%9f%90%8c%f0%9f%90%8c%f0%9f%90%8c-teatre-coliseum-2018-12-12-temp-18-19-espectacle-no-088/, accessed 25 June 2019.
101. Low, *Translating Song*, 63.

## APPENDIX

## LIST OF ANALYSED MUSICALS IN BARCELONA, 2018–2019

| Original title | *Fun Home* | *La Cage aux Folles* | *The Addams Family* | *Rent* |
|---|---|---|---|---|
| Translated title | *Fun Home* | *La jaula de las locas* | *La familia Addams* | *Rent* |
| Dates | 13 September 2018–4 November 2018 | 27 September 2018–24 February 2019 | 19 October 2018–17 February 2019 | 2 April 2019–26 May 2019 |
| Language | Catalan | Spanish | Spanish | Spanish |
| Composer | Jeanine Tesori | Jerry Herman | Andrew Lippa | Jonathan Larson |
| Lyrics/book | Lisa Kron | Harvey Fierstein/Jerry Herman | Andrew Lippa/ Marshall Brickman and Rick Elice | Jonathan Larson |

| Translation | Daniel Anglès and Marc Gómez | Roser Batalla and Roger Peña | Esteve Ferrer and Silvia Montesinos | Daniel Anglès and Marc Gómez |
|---|---|---|---|---|
| Director | Daniel Anglès | Àngel Llàcer | Esteve Ferrer | Daniel Anglès |
| Production | No Day but Today | Nostromo | Let's Go | Focus and No Day but Today |
| Source material | Alison Bechdel's graphic novel *Fun Home: A Family Tragicomic* | Jean Poiret's play *La Cage aux Folles* | Charles Addams's comic strip *The Addams Family* | Giacomo Puccini's opera *La Bohème* |
| Web page | https://www.funhome-elmusical.com/ | https://www.lajauladelaslocas.es/ | https://lafamiliaaddams.com/ | http://www.rent-elmusical.com/ |

## BIBLIOGRAPHY

Aaltonen, Sirkku. *Acculturation of the Other: Irish Milieux in Finnish Drama Translation*. Joensuu: University of Joensuu Press, 1996.

Aaltonen, Sirkku. *Time Sharing on Stage: Drama Translation in Theatre and Society*. Clevedon: Multilingual Matters, 2000.

Allwebber. '*La jaula de las locas* Barcelona 2018'. Originally published 11 December 2018, revised December 2018. https://www.love4musicals.com/2017/12/11/la-jaula-las-locas-espana-2018/, accessed 25 June 2019.

Allwebber. 'Fun Home, Barcelona 2018'. Originally published 8 August 2017, revised November 2018. https://www.love4musicals.com/2017/08/08/fun-home-barcelona-2018-2/, accessed 25 June 2019.

Apter, Ronnie, and Mark Herman. *Translating for Singing: The Theory, Art and Craft of Translating Lyrics*. London and New York: Bloomsbury, 2016. doi: 10.5040/9781474219860.

Barba, Imma, and Miquel Gascón. 'Roda de premsa *La familia Addams* Teatre Coliseum 2018.10.03'. *Voltar i voltar per les arts escèniques* [blog]. https://voltarivoltar.com/2018/10/03/067-roda-de-premsa-la-familia-addams-teatre-coliseum-2018-10-03-temp-18-19-rdp-014/, accessed 25 June 2019.

Barba, Imma, and Miquel Gascón. '116—Teatre Musical—*La familia Addams*—Teatre Coliseum—2018.12.12 (temp. 18/19—espectacle nº 088)'. https://voltarivoltar.com/2018/12/15/116-teatre-musical-la-familia-addams-%f0%9f%90%8c%f0%9f%90%8c%f0%9f%90%8c%f0%9f%90%8c-teatre-coliseum-2018-12-12-temp-18-19-espectacle-no-088/, accessed 25 June 2019.

Bordes, Jordi. 'El despertar dels actors de musicals'. *El punt avui*, 19 March 2019. https://www.elpuntavui.cat/cultura/article/19-cultura/1573119-el-despertar-dels-actors-de-musicals.html, accessed 25 June 2019.

Cohen, Allen, and Steven L. Rosenhaus. *Writing Musical Theater*. New York: Palgrave Macmillan, 2006.

Desblache, Lucile. *Music and Translation: New Mediations in the Digital Age*. London: Palgrave Macmillan, 2019. doi: 10.1057/978-1-137-54965-5.

Espasa, Eva. *La traducció dalt de l'escenari*. Vic: Eumo, 2001.

Fernández, Javier A. 'Las mujeres que no dirigen ni producen musicales'. *El País*, 9 June 2019. https://elpais.com/ccaa/2019/06/08/madrid/1560020733_827216.html, accessed 25 June 2019.

Figueras, Martí. 'Tick, tick ... Boom: Una adaptació fidel a l'essència de Jonathan Larson'. *Núvol: El digital de cultura*,12 December 2017. https://www.nuvol.com/noticies/tick-tick-boom-una-adaptacio-fidel-a-lessencia-de-jonathan-larson/, accessed 25 June 2019.

Font Mir, Antoni. 'El teatre musical a Catalunya'. *Entreacte: Revista d'arts escèniques i audiovisuals*, 14 August 2016. http://entreacte.cat/entrades/perspectives/a-fons/el-teatre-musical-a-catalunya-una-mirada-historica/, accessed 25 June 2019.

Fouz-Hernández, Santiago. 'Me cuesta tanto olvidarte: Mecano and the Movida, Remixed, Revisited and Repackaged'. *Journal of Spanish Cultural Studies* 10, no. 2 (2009): 167–187. doi: 10.1080/14636200902990695.

Franzon, John. 'Choices in Song Translation: Singability in Print, Subtitles and Sung Performances'. In 'Translation and Music', special issue, *Translator* 14, no. 2 (2008): 373–399. doi: 10.1080/13556509.2008.10799263.

Golomb, Harai. 'Music-Linked Translation [MLT] and Mozart's Operas: Theoretical, Textual, and Practical Perspectives'. In *Song and Significance: Virtues and Vices of Vocal Translation*, edited by Dinda Gorlée, 121–162. Amsterdam: Rodopi, 2005.

Gordon, Robert. '*Billy Elliot* and Its Lineage: The Politics of Class and Sexual Identity in British Musicals since 1953'. In The Oxford Handbook *of the British Musical*, edited by Robert Gordon and Olaf Jubin, 419–442. Oxford: Oxford University Press, 2016.

Gordon, Robert, and Olaf Jubin, eds. *The Oxford Handbook of the British Musical*. Oxford: Oxford University Press, 2016. doi: 10.1093/oxfordhb/9780199988747.001.0001

Gorlée, Dinda L., ed. *Song and Significance: Virtues and Vices of Vocal Translation*. Amsterdam: Rodopi, 2005.

Graells, Guillem-Jordi. 'Traduir musicals'. *Quaderns Divulgatius* 10 (1998): 63–79.

Hart, Norman. 'The Selling of *La Cage aux Folles*: How Audiences Were Helped to Read Broadway's First Gay Musical'. *Theatre History Studies* 23 (2003): 5–24.

Herman, Jerry, and Harvey Fierstein. *La Cage aux Folles*. 1983; New York: Samuel French, 2014.

Jin, Li. 'A Three-Dimensional Framework of Acculturation in Translation of Musicals'. In *Proceedings of the 2018 4th International Conference on Social Science and Higher Education (ICSSHE 2018)*, 88–91. Paris: Atlantis Press: 2018. doi: 10.2991/icsshe-18.2018.22.

Juanico, Núria. 'El català, desterrat dels musicals de gran format'. *Ara*, 23 September 2019. [https://www.ara.cat/cultura/catala-desterrat-teatre-musical_0_2313368652.html, accessed 10 November 2019].

Jubin, Olaf. 'Tim Rice: The Pop Star Scenario'. In *The Oxford Handbook of the British Musical*, edited by Robert Gordon and Olaf Jubin, 507–536. Oxford: Oxford University Press, 2016. doi: 10.1093/oxfordhb/9780199988747.013.21.

Kaindl, Klaus. 'The Plurisemiotics of Pop Song Translation: Words, Music, Voice and Image'. In *Song and Significance: Virtues and Vices of Vocal Translation*, edited by Dinda Gorlée, 121–162. Amsterdam: Rodopi, 2005.

Kirk, Sung Hee, 'Translated Musicals and Musical Translation in Korea'. 번역학연구, 9, no. 1 (2008): 283–309. doi: 10.15749/jts.2008.9.1.011.

Lefévere, André. 'Translation: Changing the Code; Soyinka's Ironic Aetiology'. In *The Languages of Theatre: Problems in the Translation and Transposition of Drama*, edited by Ortrun Zuber, 132–145. London, Pergamon Press, 1980. doi: 10.1016/b978-0-08-025246-9.50017-0.

Loesser, Frank, Jo Swerling, and Abe Burrows. *Guys and Dolls* [Catalan translation by Salvador Oliva]. Barcelona: Edicions del Teatre Nacional, 1998.

Lundskaer-Nielsen, Miranda. 'Cameron Mackintosh: Control, Collaboration, and the Creative Producer'. In *The Oxford Handbook of the British Musical*, edited by Robert Gordon and Olaf Jubin, 537–560. Oxford: Oxford University Press, 2016. doi: 10.1093/oxfordhb/9780199988747.013.22.

Low, Peter. *Translating Song: Lyrics and Text*. London and New York: Routledge, 2017. doi:10.4324/9781315630281.

Mateo, Marta. 'Anglo-American Musicals in Spanish Theatres'. In 'Translation and Music'. special issue, *Translator* 14, no. 2 (2008): 319–342. doi: 10.1080/13556509.2008.10799261.

Mateo, Marta. 'Music and Translation'. In *Handbook of Translation Studies*, vol. 3, edited by Yves Gambier and Luc van Doorslaer, 115–121. Amsterdam: John Benjamins, 2012. doi: 10.1075/hts.3.mus1.

Mateo, Marta. 'Multilingualism in Stage and Film Musicals: Varying Choices in Various Translation Modes and Contexts'. In *Translating Audiovisuals in a Kaleidoscope of Language*, edited by Montse Corrius, Eva Espasa, and Patrick Zabalbeascoa, 23–46. Berlin: Peter Lang, 2019.

Minors, Helen Julia, ed. *Music, Text and Translation*. London: Bloomsbury, 2013. doi: 10.5040/9781472541994.

Poiret, Jean. *La Cage aux Folles*. 1973. Paris: Presses Pocket, 1979.

Postigo, Alejandro. 'The Evolution of Musical Theatre in Spain Throughout the Twentieth and Twenty-first Centuries'. In *Reframing the Musical: Race, Culture and Identity*, edited by Sarah Whitfield, 111–128. London: Red Globe, 2019.

Sams, Jeremy. 'Words and Music'. In *Stages of Translation*, edited by David Johnston, 171–178. Bath: Absolute Press, 1996.

Solla, Fernando. 'Zaza Is Here to Stay'. *En Platea*, 10 October 2018. http://enplatea.com/?p=18484, accessed 25 June 2019.

Sternfeld, Jessica. *The Megamusical*. Bloomington: Indiana University Press, 2006.

Subirana, Jordi. 'Los musicales sufren una caída de público en BCN'. *El Periódico*, 14 February 2004. http://www.gaudiclub.com/esp/e_links/ultimo/2004feb14.asp, accessed 10 November 2019.

Susam-Sarajeva, Şebnem, ed. Translation and Music. Special issue, *The* Translator 14, no. 2 (2008).

Susam-Saraeva, Şebnem. *Translation and Popular Music: Transcultural Intimacy in Turkish-Greek Relations*. Vienna: Peter Lang, 2015. doi: 10.3726/978-3-0353-0769-6.

Toffler, Alvin. *The Third Wave*. New York: William Morrow, 1980.

White, Christine. '"Humming the Sets": Scenography and the Spectacular Musical from *Cats* to *The Lord of the Rings*'. In *The Oxford Handbook of the British Musical*, edited by Robert Gordon and Olaf Jubin, 401–418. Oxford: Oxford University Press, 2016. doi: 10.1093/oxfordhb/9780199988747.013.17.

# CHAPTER 3

········································································································

# TRAINING FOR WRITERS
# AND PERFORMERS

········································································································

## ZACHARY DUNBAR

MUSICAL theatre is a booming business the world over, and so is training in this complex art form which has 'proved to be open and inclusive and now consists of many genres'.[1] And despite the worldwide industry meltdown brought about by the pandemic that began in 2020, musicals continue to be created and performers to be trained, with new opportunities emerging in virtual spaces and through pioneering technologies. In performance, the skills taught broadly stem from the allied though distinct practices of singing, acting, and dance; writing involves learning the collaborative craft of creating the book, lyrics, and music. Arguably, the widespread growth of Broadway and West End musicals, especially in the decades after World War II, has produced a global industry in need of such skills which serve industry-ready performers and writers proficient in repertoire representing everything from the 1950s 'golden age' canon through the experimentalist rock musicals, and dance spectacles of the 1970s and 1980s to the current abundance of contemporary and pop-influenced productions. The ensuing demand for the seamless multidisciplinary performer (the 'triple threat') has resulted in a rapid growth in training programmes currently offered by universities and conservatoires worldwide, including professional organisations that offer mentorships and development workshops, as well as training manuals and textbooks. Given this extensive history, surprisingly little research exists that captures the global picture, let alone provides some possible frameworks of how training developed alongside the worldwide growth of the musical theatre industry.

This chapter will initially examine modes of training through an historical lens.[2] I demarcate the advent of formal or systematic vocational training in the post–World War II era, when integrated pedagogy, which intended to balance the skills of acting, singing and dance, developed in parallel with the reputed integrated form of musical, which evidenced increasing dramaturgical and compositional convergence in the component arts. Yet, one can also assert that innovations in the art form reflected the perpetual recycling and renewing of methods and approaches, a process which in turn generated ad hoc training. Creatives, for instance, may have come together without necessarily drawing on formal musical training (a discussion I undertake in the section on glocal writing).

Despite these competing narratives, as Broadway and the West End musical productions fanned out regionally within the United States and United Kingdom, and across the world, so too did the value packaging of *integration* and *collaboration*. The majority of this chapter will therefore map out the reception of these two core values, reception here framed in a global-local nexus where exported values encounter local socio-economic and cultural realities. A summary of the global status quo covers the vexed problem of integration, industry-facing aims, and the social issues which currently shape the mindset of training. Throughout the chapter I assume that training encompasses a broad spectrum of activities including rehearsals, auditions, performance, and career transitions. Moreover, that integration, in context of performance training, refers to a physical amalgamation of various combinations of the three disciplines within musical theatre, without asserting a combined effect greater than the sum of its parts often talked about as synergistic, gestalt, holistic, or transdisciplinary.

# HISTORICAL LENS

The history of musical training, at least before World War I, is a construction of sepia-toned recollections mostly found in theatre trade publications and in the reportage of performers who were variously skilled in music hall, operetta, vaudeville, minstrelsy, melodrama, and other early forms of musical theatre. Anecdote, pearls of wisdom, and tricks of the trade often melded with classical training and formed the 'know-how' which travelled the byways from apprenticeship to stage, from teacher to student, and from port to port. It was the global transfer of early forms of music theatre that spurred and selected in-demand skills. For instance, Savoy operas, which travelled between London and New York, prompted the growth of opera societies which played a pivotal role in training amateurs to meet the performance standards demanded by this genre.[3] Such standards were less documented in the Asia-Pacific, where ships laden with European opera, zarzuela, and drama companies represented the thriving trade of 'migrant artists and entertainers' whose history of training fell 'between the cracks of archival and ideological boundaries'.[4]

The training conveyed by, or about, celebrated twentieth-century performing artists is often based on biographical narratives, the process of evolving from amateur to star status described more or less as assembling toolkits of the trade via autodidactic or mimetic means. In the United States, for instance, Gene Kelly optimised some homegrown breathing techniques by rehearsing in empty theatres, training his voice to hit the back wall without pulling an 'ugly face'.[5] Bernadette Peters, showed a precocious talent as a singer, took acting lessons at seventeen, and learned most of the rest on the job.[6] The distinguished brother-and-sister tap dance team Buddy and Vilma Ebsen learned by watching the dance routines of itinerant acting companies, such as the Honey Bunch Company. In Vilma Ebsen's words, 'Buddy and I learned to tap dance by doing what everybody did.'[7]

Similar to the performer, from the late nineteenth century to the early 1920s musical composers and writers forged their craft at the bustling crossroads of highbrow and lowbrow industries. In Broadway's Tin Pan Alley and London's West End music halls, tunesmiths learned the trade (what worked, what sold) in conveyor-belt fashion, often drawing on the fashions and sentiments of the times. Past (and current) writers and composers of the musical canon, on both sides of the Atlantic—Lionel Bart, Irving Berlin, Leonard Bernstein, Alain Boublil, Cy Coleman, Vivian Ellis and A. P. Herbert, Dorothy Fields, George Gershwin, Oscar Hammerstein II, Jerry Herman, Ivor Novello, Claude-Michel Schönberg, Stephen Sondheim, and Jule Styne—demonstrated a talent for creating popular forms of music or dramatic writing without formal institutional training in musical theatre.[8] Regarding stage writing alone, George Pierce Baker's *Dramatic Technique* (1916) is possibly the first bona fide playwriting book in the United States, as is the London-based theatre critic William Archer's *Play-Making: A Manual of Craftsmanship* (1912) in the United Kingdom. But on the writing craft of musical theatre, no such formal texts existed until the early 1960s, with the publication of Lehmann Engel's *Words with Music* and *American Musical Theatre: A Consideration*.

The shift from ad hoc training to a more systematic account of the musical craft may have coincided with two developments in musical theatre.

First, the emergent form of the integrated book musical, with its strong character-driven narratives and increasingly coherent dramaturgy, relied on exceptional song- and book-writing teams,[9] a new configuration in which writers were no longer enlisted in a supporting role for composers, nor as part of the conveyor-belt production system which sustained the Tin Pan Alley economy. Musicals such as *Oklahoma!* (1943), *Carousel* (1945), *Annie Get Your Gun* (1946), *West Side Story* (1957), and *Gypsy* (1959) are paradigmatic of creative collaborations, and in particular a quality of book writing which aspired to the literary heights of dramas created by T. S. Eliot, Thornton Wilder, and Arthur Miller (if not the overtly experimental works of Kurt Weill, Ira Gershwin, and Moss Hart).[10] Such aspirations aligned with the gradual cultivation of Broadway audiences, and resonated in the artistic ideals of the literary-minded New York Theatre Guild, who repeatedly commissioned, for instance, the collaborative musical team of Rodgers and Hammerstein.[11] The aim to understand, master, and possibly replicate the nuts and bolts of successful collaboration eventuated, in 1961, in the formation of the BMI Lehman Engel Musical Theatre Workshop in New York, whose sole aim was to provide professional collaborative training for composers, lyricists, and librettists. In the United Kingdom, a comparable writer-based organisation was not established until 1992, with the creation of Mercury Musical Developments.[12]

Second, the more tightly knit choreography, character development, dialogue, and music in such works as *West Side Story* and *Fiddler on the Roof* (1964) marked the

FIG. 3.1 Lehman Engel, author of several books on the craft of writing for musical theatre and founder of the BMI Lehman Engel Musical Theatre Workshop in New York. Photo: AP Newsfeatures.

demand for a musical theatre performer adept at characterisation through dance and singing. Similarly, the complex characters in a Stephen Sondheim musical such as *Company* (1970) or *A Little Night Music* (1973), as well as British vernacular musicals such as *Oliver!* (1960), called for an actor-singer equally competent in both skills. The creation of *A Chorus Line* (1975), *Chicago* (1975), and *Cats* (1981) demanded new virtuosic physical and singing stamina alongside the ability to convey a character role. The concomitant rise of choreographer-directors such as Jerome Robbins, Bob Fosse, and Michael Bennett, all to varying degrees inheritors of ballet traditions, and whose aesthetics also embraced contemporary movement and character-based storytelling, reinforced the demand for the holistic performer, technically expert in their ability to integrate the three disciplines.

# Global Transmission of Training:
## Integration and Collaboration

Out of these historical narratives, we might identify two cultural memes in musical theatre training that have spread globally: one is the notion of integration in performance training, and the other is collaboration within writing.

Hardly a musical theatre textbook or course description exists that does not promote the integration of the constituent disciplines as the sine qua non for performance training, implying (if not idealising) a seamless convergence of singing, acting, and dancing. At a baseline level, training begins with 'sufficient mastery of the skills independently' before live performance and production can weave those skills into a cohesive and useful craft.[13] Yet, there are different interpretations of the integrated performer. The worldwide export of the reputed megamusical by Disney, Cameron Mackintosh, or Andrew Lloyd Webber may call for a versatile performer, albeit one tailored to meet the exacting specifications of these highly franchised musicals.[14] The more sophisticated character-driven musical dramas, such as those exemplified in Stephen Sondheim's or Jeanine Tesori's oeuvre, demand acting as the core skill of the integrated performer (e.g., the actor-singer); on the other hand, innovative musicals with embodied instrumentalists in character, such as *Once* (2011), have generated a need to train the integrated actor-musician.[15]

In Anglophone cultures, the requisite dramaturgical principles for the making of a good musical are grounded in classical (and unacknowledged Aristotelian) paradigms of drama, effectively promulgating the concept of unity and coherence in aspects of character, song, dialogue, plot, and spectacle.[16] Such principles are enshrined in various books on musical theatre writing which have been in circulation since the 1960s.[17] The seminal work of many musical theatre directors, producers, choreographers, and writers such as Jerome Kern, Rodgers and Hammerstein, Lorenz Hart, Agnes de Mille, Jerome Robbins, Hal Prince, and Michael Bennett, from their particular discipline, have intentionally reinforced the principle of coherence between 'the spoken, musical, danced and scenic dimensions of a musical'.[18] British- and North American–based musical writing courses and workshops promote processes which reinforce the ethos of integration through collaborative creativity, eschewing the old-fashioned idea that writers and composers work in separate quarters and under their own steam.[19] Such values are currently imported around the world. Yet at the same time, innovations in the art form emerge from diverse encounters with local folk and indigenous song and drama, such as in South Korea, Japan, China, the Philippines, and countries in South America. These interactions have given rise to what could be described as 'glocalised' musical writing which takes place at the global nexus points where the fundamentals of Broadway- and West End-style productions are assimilated or possibly resisted by the distinct local culture and commercial forces.[20] I will return to this discussion later in the chapter when discussing the 'glocal' processes of writing.

# THE GLOBAL EMERGENCE OF THE 'TRIPLE THREAT' AND ITS COMMODIFICATION

The notion of a triple threat implies a performer who can easily switch between the technical proficiencies so that '[d]ancers sing and singers dance and actors have to move and dancers have to act'.[21] Yet, in the musical theatre canon, few works actually exist that call for a performer, at least in a lead role, to be equally adept in all three disciplines.[22] It is thus difficult to know when the notion of the triple-threat performer gained global currency or common usage. The musical theatre choreographer Liza Gennaro and historian Stacy Wolf describe how 'every musical choreographer, from George Balanchine to Andy Blankenbuehler, created movement materials' to dramatise the libretto.[23] Thus, as a catch-all descriptor for a multidisciplinary performer, the notion of a triple threat may coincide with the rise of the Broadway choreographer-director. It is also a label that describes a performer whose time-consuming mastery of the component disciplines can be summed up in *A Chorus Line*'s iconic opening number, 'I Really Need This Job', where the performers playing triple-threat characters are put through their triply difficult paces.

*Oklahoma!* (1943), arguably the first musical to transfer successfully to all Anglophone countries, heralded versatile performers who could, if they were the protagonists, sing and act (and move naturally in the 'world' of the drama), and, if part of the well-trained chorus of dancers, convey richer psychological detail in their actions than the drilled chorus lines of earlier musicals. Fourteen years later, *West Side Story*, a musical epitomising the fullest integration of dance, dramatic action, song, and character development yet seen on Broadway, marked the arrival of the American-brand triple-threat performer. The *West Side Story* performer distinctively and consummately embodied American dance and song that, upon the show's London transfer, caused its producer Harold Prince to insist that only an 'all-American cast' could do the show.[24] The notion of the triple threat was echoed in the reception of the British press: 'Dancer and singer alike unite to become the actor-singer-dancer, a total artist whose role is so conceived that only dancing (whether "dancing" or just "moving") is inseparable from singing and acting'.[25] These were fully integrated performers who were trained and rehearsed to this virtuoso level by the choreographer-director Jerome Robbins. Robbins was influenced by George Balanchine, who combined ballet technique with character-driven choreography.[26]

Robbins's earlier work in *On the Town* (1944) was influenced both by Agnes de Mille's psychologising dream ballet in *Oklahoma!* and the choreographer Gluck Sandor, who developed Stanislavski-based acting techniques with his dancers.[27] Robbins's signature directing style adhered rigorously 'to time, place, and the plausibility of dance', as demonstrated further in *Gypsy* and *Fiddler on the Roof*.[28] Such were Robbins's exacting demands on the integrated performer that upon *West Side Story*'s transfer to the Nissei Theatre in Tokyo in the summer of 1965, a full American cast travelled over and had to

FIG. 3.2 The birth of the triple-threat performer: Chita Rivera and other members of the cast in rehearsal for the original 1957 Broadway production of *West Side Story*. Photo: Fred Fehl © Harry Ransom Center, The University of Texas at Austin.

rehearse for two months in preparation for the performances, for two weeks of which Robbins himself flew over to get the cast into shape.[29]

Three other major musicals exemplified in their transfer abroad the need for the fully fledged triple threat. *Chicago* (1975), directed by the choreographer-director Bob Fosse, required the cast to combine contemporary and jazz dance elements in their singing character roles. Its transfer to London's West End in 1979, albeit as an entirely new production neither directed or choreographed by Fosse, drew on mainly British-trained performers, demonstrating an industry that was starting to respond to these imported highly choreographic musicals;[30] unlike in continental Europe, where the first German production in Hamburg (in 1977) highlighted the dearth of homegrown versatile talent, as the two leads (Velma and Roxy) were cast with singers who couldn't dance.

In *A Chorus Line* (1975), the choreographer-director Michael Bennett's self-referential use of Broadway dance styles brought to life the individual personal journeys of the triple threats in the eponymous musical chorus. In its first fifteen years on Broadway, the musical effectively projected in the American public's imagination (and eventually the world), through the iconography of the *Chorus Line* poster, the degree of training and commitment that the jobbing musical theatre performer, in their sweat-soaked leotards, needed to go through to make it on the Great White Way. Bennett devised the work from the real-life experiences of Broadway dancers, in a sense imbuing the fictional roles with the realistic demands of Broadway dance training. These were highly technical roles for which one couldn't simply rely on rehearsal time to 'get into character'. The message was clear: one had to train in a disciplined way, *and* in all three disciplines. Its transfer to London's Theatre Royal Drury Lane in 1976 featured in its first six months an American cast, which was eventually replaced by British performers who were unfazed by the singing and acting, but less skilful than their American counterparts in terms of dancing. By the mid-1970s the United Kingdom had established contemporary dance schools and companies that were influenced by the American postmodern dance schools as well as the British New Dance movement. However, without any conservatoires in London offering the sort of triple-threat training more readily available in New York, it became clear that modern dance training alone was not sufficient to threaten the virtuosic American musical theatre performer. The British cast easily excelled in acting and singing, perhaps even more than their American counterparts, but were not quite the 'one singular sensation' in terms of all three disciplines.[31]

During the 1980s, the emerging form of the dance-driven musical—or 'dancical'—such as *Cats* (1981) highlighted (still) a lag between Broadway-style dance training and the apparently less problematic alliance of singing and acting skills in the contemporary British musical performer. Yet, what *West Side Story* and *A Chorus Line* did to awaken the need to train the American triple threat, *Cats* (and possibly *Starlight Express*) achieved in London. The musical's completely sung-through score and danced-through anthropomorphic (feline) choreography might have easily called upon performers conversant with British music-hall style, light comedy, and mime. However, the innovative choreography and ability to sing *and* dance at virtuosic levels created challenges in casting. The British dancer-choreographer Gillian Lynne eventually found 'thirty [British] dancers who could also sing and act'. These exceptional few were trained up to serve the vocal and physical demands of this high-concept musical, showcasing British talent which was at least embraced by the critics as 'champions of the newfound British dance musical'.[32] *Cats* may have invaded Broadway in due course, but it certainly didn't displace the local ready-made talent. Auditioning in New York, Lloyd Webber, Lynne, and the other creatives were 'humbled' by the thousand-plus performers who queued up to audition and who unsurprisingly exhibited a level of dance training possibly unmatched in the United Kingdom.[33]

The advent of the global blockbuster musical—not just *Cats* but also *The Phantom of the Opera*, *Miss Saigon*, and *Les Misérables*—highlighted the demand for the actor-singer performer (who may not necessarily be a dancer). Such globetrotting musicals are to this day reproduced in playhouses around the world. Adopting the principles of free-market capitalism, they operate under strict levels of creative control and marketing[34] that monitor all aspects of production, branding, and franchising to ensure the musical is delivered, produced, and performed to the specifications of the original production template. Such McTheatre-style constraints on performers may conceivably stifle artistic freedom,[35] reducing acting or singing to mere imitations of the original. Yet such musicals have been a driving force, since the 1990s, in creating lucrative and long-term employment for performers aspiring to be the next Valjean of *Les Miz*, Christine of

*Phantom*, Kim of *Miss Saigon*, or Elphaba of *Wicked*, and with that, further inducement to bolster actor training in musical theatre.

Not-withstanding, training institutions globally have devised their own product-branding exercises, attracting students by claiming, often overtly, that their intensive three- or four-year programmes will transform the trainee into a dazzling triple threat, an elite Broadway-style performer. South Africa's Luitingh Alexander Musical Theatre Academy mentions how the 'triple threat performer' is perceived to be a 'a sought-after commodity', a kind of primary trading stock in the economics of musical theatre training: 'It is no wonder that most aspiring performers are looking towards a "triple threat" training in order to achieve success in a genre that requires an astonishing range of skills. A performer who wishes to pursue a career in musical theatre should, at the very least, be able to excel in singing, dancing and acting'.[36] A random selection of conservatoire-style training programmes from various parts of the world that adhere the same marketing strategy include Beijing's Central Academy of Drama, the American Musical and Dramatic Academy (AMDA, Los Angeles and New York City), the Western Australian Academy of Performing Arts (WAAPA), Griffith University (Brisbane), and LaSalle College of the Arts (Singapore).

During the 1980s and 1990s the impact of Anglophone Broadway and West End musicals in the major European capitals drove a demand for the integrated triple-threat performer.[37] In the post–World War II reconstruction, Western Europe's musical industry consumed American and British pop and rock culture, creating a generation of performers who learned how to move and sound like (if not re-invent) their pop idols. Yet, despite the regular transfer of popular musicals, Germany and Austria, which produced dance-heavy shows such as *Starlight Express*, predominantly cast US, British, or Australian performers, because they could not find German-language actors who had already developed the required skill set, a precedent which started in the late 1960s when the first Viennese production of *West Side Story* had most of its cast (including the opera-singer-to-be Julia Migenes) brought over from America. The foreign cast members then were taught how to sing and speak German phonetically, which is still the case today. By contrast, Komische Oper Berlin's production of *West Side Story* (2013) featured a fully versatile cast (although they still struggled with the show's ethnic dialect), an indication in Germany, if not across Europe, that musical theatre no longer needed to be 'in the hands of American actresses and performers' (as the Berlin University of the Arts musical theatre training website promotes in their program); nor do European performers need necessarily to travel to London or New York to train.

Sustained vocational training, responding to the cultural cachet and pervasive commercial impact of musicals in Europe's arts industry, can be accessed in such capital cities as Hannover, Berlin, Vienna, Madrid, and Copenhagen. Unsurprisingly, many of the instructors in these programmes are British- or American-trained instructors. Moreover, the management of bilingual issues (as in Vienna's Broadway Academy) and the product placement of the marketed triple threat (as in Copenhagen's Central Musical Theatre School) indicate a pragmatic response to a growing internationality of music theatre–going audiences (those who have seen their *Les Miz* or *Billy Elliot* in other countries). Such trainers and audiences alike participate in globalised product control and consumption fostered by the imported blockbuster musical.[38]

At the same time, the avant-garde impulses in the arts in Europe influenced musical theatre performance training within a more postmodern (or post-dramatic) understanding of music theatre making. Alongside the European-based 'schools' that teach and market the training of singing, dancing, and acting, tertiary courses encourage an interdisciplinary approach to training.[39] In the Netherlands' Fontys School of the Performing Arts and Germany's Folkwang University of the Arts,[40] training the actor-singer as an all-around theatre maker constitutes a practical pathway to success in the performing arts industry; dance, which may feature as an optional component, may define you specifically as a triple threat. In former Soviet-bloc states, where the megamusical phenomenon has had less of an effect on the arts economy, there has been concomitantly less evidence of programmes dedicated to musical theatre training.[41]

It is also worth noting that as countries develop their own local blockbuster musical, it may become less important to have a ready-made elite class of musical theatre performer waiting in the wings. For instance, the hugely successful *Hoy no me puedo levanter* (*Today I Can't Get Up*), Spain's response to the box-office success of *Mamma Mia!* (2004), generated a spate of similar Spanish-made jukebox musicals,[42] offering roles which local performers could fill without having to match the elite-trained performer of a Broadway or West End original. Nonetheless, the exacting performance demands of a big show, whether in singing, acting, dancing, or all three, can tax the existing talent in a host city. Early in its global transfer, the bilingual challenges of *Les Misèrables*, in the Japanese production by the Toho company, led to calls for a *Les Miz* school to be set up in order to teach performers singing, movement, acting, and French history.[43] The recent mounting of *Billy Elliot* (2019) in Chile required several months of rehearsals for the cast to achieve the required level of dance and singing skills.[44]

In Asia, booming economies have coincided with a modernised political will to adopt a more global cultural profile, and the musical represents one such product for the Chinese and South Korean global market. In South Korea, as early as 1962, the resounding cultural impact of *Porgy and Bess* fuelled the industry's need to emulate the trained American body and voice, a development which readied its performers for the later arrivals of *The Sound of Music* (1981), *Oliver!* (1983), *West Side Story* (1987), *Cats* (1990), and *The Phantom of the Opera* (2001).[45] In China, recent Mandarin translations of Anglophone musicals such as *Mamma Mia!* (2011) and *Cats* (2012), and auspiced by global-savvy producers such as United Asia Live Entertainment (UALE), have created a highly lucrative economy for the Western art form.[46] The professed aim to train up the Chinese population in (or through) the Anglophone musical had implications for Beijing's three traditionally separate 'schools' of drama, dance and music, where, since 2002, a musical theatre programme has developed, though conceivably not without the cultural and linguistic challenges that come with training through English-language musicals.

The problem of emulation leads down different paths, depending on what quality of versatility is being sought. At Taiwan-based Lan Creators, before any big shows, actors are expected to spend over forty hours a week intensively preparing themselves to serve the needs of the imported American musical. According to the director Lin Chia-yi, who is clearly aiming for a triple-threat, 'There doesn't seem to be enough co-ordination of the three essential elements: song, dance and acting. There also aren't enough performers that are good in all three respects'.[47] Elsewhere, for instance in Taiwan-based Dafeng Musical Theatre, they have accepted such training as only one of the options, which is to create (as has been similarly witnessed in South Korea and Japan) musicals from local traditions, tapping into embodied folkloric arts and contemporary pop practices.[48] In India, a popular version of Disney's *High School Musical* called *My School Rocks!* required performers who could exploit both the film's musical idioms and Bollywood song and dance, and this was effectively staged through interschool dance competitions.[49] The musical did not necessarily demand the training of American brand triple threats; instead, it developed virtuosic hybrid performers bilingual in their choreography and singing. In Singapore, the abundant musicals which feature Singaporean stories don't necessarily call upon triple threats. As a local musical theatre artist put it, '[T]he leads and supporting roles are quite often performed by people who have primarily been trained in acting and singing,' while the dance elements are filled by people who have 'specifically trained in dance'.[50] To some extent, this is also still usually the case on Broadway and London, and many regional theatres, where the choice of show, talent base, and the production budget dictate the versatile quality of a cast in a musical.

Situations where the local musical theatre industries are not perceived to be ethnically varied and/or appropriately skilled represent another challenge for the globe-hopping musical. Producers of *Miss Saigon* regularly continue to scout the Philippines to portray the show's Vietnamese characters. While much has been written about the controversial ethical issues surrounding the show's attempt at colour-blind casting (especially during the West End transfer of *Miss Saigon* to Broadway),[51] producers of the musical continue to see the Philippines as a source of ready-made musical theatre talent. Arguably, the unabashed Filipino performer derives self-assurance from the extroverted 'social dimension of performance' (or *palabas*) which is catered to in multicultural Filipino life.[52] When Cameron Mackintosh argued with the Actor's Equity stronghold in New York that he had auditioned twelve hundred women, among whom only Lea Salonga, from the Philippines, had the appropriate 'youth and range of talent',[53] he had in fact discovered talent which was a product of the country's enterprising entertainment culture and learn-as-you-go vocational training.

Salonga was a child star, singing 'professionally', while picking up training in school productions and participating in extension programmes offered by the University of the Philippines College of Music. A recent Filipina 'Kim', Aicelle Santos, also developed her pop-jazz voice early and embodied a performance craft that developed out of approximating the sound and intonations of her favourite (in this case, Disney) ingénues.[54] If Filipinos do train formally to Broadway or West End standards, the few that can afford it travel abroad. The existence abroad of such a ready-trained demographic supplied a casting call for Asian performers in the UK Royal National Theatre

FIG. 3.3 Filipina actor Lea Salonga in the 1991 Broadway production of *Miss Saigon*. Photo: Michael Le Poer Trench © Cameron Mackintosh Ltd.

production of *Here Lies Love* (2014), a spectacular, immersive dance musical based on the life of Imelda Marcos (and written by two non-Asian creatives, David Byrne and Fatboy Slim).[55]

## GLOCALISATION OF MUSICAL THEATRE WRITING

Dominant cultures that shaped the historical development of musicals also determined the quality of training of writers and composers. In the United States, the claim of national ownership over the art form of the musical implicates their oft-asserted proprietorship over rules and principles which govern the making of musicals,[56] and these are reflected in the country's formal higher education courses and industry-based training. They include the

BMI Workshop, created in 1961, as well as the two-year full-time graduate Master of Fine Arts degree in musical theatre writing at New York University's Tisch School of the Arts, both Manhattan-based programmes in which the craft skills of writing and composing in pairs are inculcated by professionally active teachers. The musical theatre industry across the country also supplies substantive and nationwide support in terms of incubation and development, historical archives, and professional mentorship.[57] The United Kingdom, having witnessed a proliferation of tertiary musical performance training programmes during the 1990s, has followed suit, albeit belatedly, with organisations that nurture and support book writers, lyricists, and composers such as Mercury Musical Developments (founded in 1992), or that promote partnerships between creatives and producers such as UK Perfect Pitch (established in 2005). More recently, Goldsmiths College (University of London) and the Royal Central School of Speech and Drama (University of London) have created tertiary courses in musical theatre production and writing.

If there is a set of values undergirding writing training taught on both sides of the Atlantic, these would include a strong sense of craft, storytelling, artistic coherence, and collaborative creation. Regionally and globally, there has been an explosion of new musical theatre writing. An argument could be made that writers who have received training in the United States or the United Kingdom and who have embraced the value systems of institutions such as Tisch/BMI or Mercury Musical Development significantly influence the predominant methods of writing training in other parts of the world. And often it is the classical and contemporary canon of Broadway or West End musicals, especially those that have been staged regularly around the world, that writers look to as the paradigms. Yet the musical is also perceived as a multidisciplinary art form, encompassing pedagogical approaches founded on traditional skills and free artistic exploration, where creatives yield as much to the necessities of the industry (what audiences or producers are perceived to *want*) as to the socio-cultural zeitgeist (what creatives sense their audiences might *need*). Glocalised writing is socially conditioned, 'characterized by tight global economic, political, cultural, and environmental interconnections'.[58] In glocalised settings, writers of musicals occupy a position that both resists and appropriates the Anglo-European canon, contributing to a need for training that is potentially transnational and intercultural.

In South Korea, musical theatre creatives can readily draw from a tradition of music-making that mixes body movement, song, and folk themes, represented in the musical storytelling art of *pansori* or its operatic formation in *ch'angguk*. A national effort to consolidate the American-style musical and Korean-style music theatre grew out of the politics of the 1960s, coinciding with the establishment of Korea as a modern nation and the government's desire to distinguish its arts and theatre from the large-scale populist spectacles of North Korea. A two-day conference in 1966 spearheaded a 'musical' manifesto to create the groundwork for modernising 'traditional performances' and exploring the 'feasibility of creating a Korean-style musical' that would resonate with Korean audiences.[59] Writers who study abroad return to Korea to foster new talent, such as in the Korea National University of the Arts (K-Arts) Musical Theatre Writing Program (established in 2009), where composers and lyricists are trained in a three-year curriculum which maximises 'genre-crossover'.[60] South Korea's 'heteroglossic' examples of new musical theatre,[61] such as the internationally award-winning comic instrumental piece *NANTA* (1997),[62] are influenced by distinctly Korean art forms, while at the same time glocal successes have launched transnational collaboration. For example, production groups such as Seoul-based EMK have created work involving American composers such as Frank Wildhorn, producing a musical based on a non-native theme, *Mata Hari*.[63] This, and the increasing collaboration between the Chinese musical market and the Korean technological know-how, potentially creates geopolitical centres for new musicals that challenge the global hegemony of Broadway and the West End.[64]

The commercially successful transfer of *Cats*, *Wicked*, *The Phantom of the Opera*, and *Chicago* in the Philippines quelled the trepidation felt by international companies when considering new Asian markets. Confident of itself as a global player in the blockbuster trade, Manila saw an opportunity in establishing entertainment centres, such as the Theatre at Solaire, which could navigate between scheduling the big-show draws and testing out homegrown musical entertainment. This has had the effect of generating during the past decade a renaissance of new musical theatre which taps into local Philippine culture.[65] A theatre arts organisation such as the Philippine Educational Theater Association (PETA), while not offering a formal degree programme, represents the type of Manila-based grassroots creative hub that provides training by bringing together writers, musicians, directors, and professional artists, all of whom are collectively invested in the musical theatre industry. The organisation's openness to take a chance on new material has fostered Filipino musical hits such as the rock comedy *Rak of Aegis* (2014) and the *Cyrano de Bergerac*–inspired romance *Mula sa Buwan* (2016). Glocal musical-making is defined by adherence to integrated dramaturgy, a globalised principle drawn from Broadway-style musicals, and local appeal to the Filipino television-style melodrama, comedy, and folklore.[66]

In Singapore, new kinds of writing are supported through production groups (often not-for-profit) such as Wild Rice. Their pantomimes, with original book, music, and lyrics are often based on social themes drawn from Singapore's multicultural society. Long-established training groups such as The Theatre Practice (TTP) produce rock musicals in the Mandarin vernacular, including the recent international success *Liao Zhai Rocks*.[67] In 2004 Musical Theatre Limited established a programme called 'Beat by Beat' that was intended to 'incubate' new musicals in a 'no-frills environment', with actors, producers, and collaborators involved in the works' earliest stages.[68]

Anglophone cultures outside Broadway and the West End try to tell local stories whilst building bridges between creative aspiration, incubation, and sustained industry development. The Canadian Music Theatre Project at Sheridan College,[69] formerly under the stewardship of Michael Rubinoff, represents a training programme with built-in periods of development. The multi-award-winning *Come from Away*, inspired by a local Newfoundland story, and their recent cross-cultural collaboration with Shanghai Dramatic Arts Centre, *Bethune*, evidence how incubating ideas locally (and carefully) can harness in due course global production forces.[70] In the early 2000s Australia started to address the lag in sustained development with sizeable investments by the Australian Council for Educational Research and Carnegie 18 (Melbourne) and, subsequently, short grants-based initiatives. Currently, grassroots initiatives such as Homegrown (Melbourne), regional development fostered by Hayes Theatre (Sydney), and short development residencies offered within universities all support training, albeit sporadically and with one-off masterclasses and brief mentorships.[71] Without sustained and structured writer training, such enterprising initiatives struggle, especially where invested efforts are coupled with unrealistic expectations to produce a country's next 'great musical'.

There are numerous examples throughout the world where successful musicals are created by individuals who haven't undergone years of intensive training in the craft, challenging the contingent links between formal training and commercial success. In Australia, two such successes include an aboriginal musical by Broome-based musician Jimmy Chi and his band Knuckles, called *Bran Nue Dae* (1990), and the sung-through musical based on the political career of former Australian prime minister Paul Keating, *Keating!* (2005), by polyglot writer-musician-performer Casey Bennetto. The Netherlands' multimedia spectacle *Soldier of Orange* (2010) was written by a composer-and-lyricist team who primarily attended ASCAP (American Society of Composers, Authors, and Publishers) workshops to learn the 'essential ins and outs of what works in musical theatre',[72] while the book writer developed his craft in television drama series. The hugely popular surreal docu-style musical *Stories from Norway* incorporates several musical genres and dramatic tropes lampooning the art form with great sophistication and knowledge. It was created and written by the Norwegian comedy duo of the brothers Vegard and Bård Ylvisåker (known as Ylvis), whose education involved primarily high school variety shows and working in the entertainment industry.

Accelerated economic wealth may also act as a barometer for new writing. From the early 2000s China has imported productions of blockbuster musicals, translating them into Mandarin and spawning a major musical industry, especially in Beijing and Shanghai. Such accelerated growth has fuelled sustained Sino-American collaborations, combining writing know-how from some of Broadway's leading creatives. Yet the ability of the Chinese to generate ready financial investment, which can speed project development, hasn't kept pace with 'Chinese artists versed in writing, directing, or designing for Western-styled musical theatre'.[73] Leading drama academies and music conservatoires have not yet provided comprehensive and structured courses in musical theatre dramaturgy or composition (as they have in performance training). In the post–Deng Xiaoping economic boom, the lead influencers of new writing are primarily industry-driven, where ad hoc training happens through 'cross-cultural education' initiatives. For example, Richard Fei, the seasoned programming director for the performing arts complex Shanghai Culture Square, has been running musical theatre development symposia since 2014.[74] The sharing of skills and best practice happens intranationally among Chinese artists. A case in point is when the composer Zou Hang began to write *Shi Jing Cai Wei*, a musical inspired by a collection of early Chinese poems. Hang was mentored by the songwriter Liang Mang, who was part of a successful creative team that developed the Broadway-bound Chinese musical *Shimmer* in 2017.[75]

## A Current Global Snapshot

Globally, terms such as 'integration' and 'collaboration' infiltrate the language of training, reinforced by dramaturgical and performance-based principles operating in the commercial musical industry. Yet musicals also represent an art form that intrinsically disaggregates training. Teachers continue to differentiate 'those who can sing more than dance, and act more than sing';[76] and trainees, based on their formative training, may self-identify automatically more as singer than actor, or more as dancer than singer. Moreover, a teacher may struggle to understand, let alone demonstrate, the distinct vocabulary and techniques of singing, acting, and dance. While institutes of training may attempt to correct this by creating uniformity or consistency in the use of terms or practices, there remain unresolved anomalies which accompany any amalgamated multidisciplinary process;[77] for instance, in acting courses, lyrics may be turned into a kind of monologue as an acting exercise to actuate plausible characterisation, a common practice for integrating personal imagination and character. Nonetheless there are also the vocal physiological requirements of the music, such as belting or lyrical classical singing, that may induce psychophysical responses in the performer at odds with their acting choices.[78] Likewise, choreographed dance sequences and gestures may not necessarily align with a performer's 'lived bodily experience' and their innate interpretation of a character's movements.

The multidisciplinary nature of musical theatre training raises the question of what may thus constitute a full, viable training cycle in all three arts.[79] In the UK/European-based three-year, or four-year tertiary training, introductory stages of learning breath control, pas de deux, and embodying character to a final-year professional showcase represent the standard tertiary degree–granting training cycle. Psychological studies, drawn from sports science and music performance, suggest that the amount of time necessary to acquire and embed expertise in any one performing-art skill is approximately 'ten thousand hours' of deliberate practice.[80] In musical theatre, these practice hours (and fees) are expressed exponentially causing universities and performing arts institutes to shrink-wrap multidisciplinary practice into budget-brand courses for larger cohorts. Yet despite these challenges, new teaching methods are arising that connect the seemingly separate disciplines. A notable trend in this global context is an approach to musical theatre education that increasingly envisages the student-performer or writer more broadly as an aspiring artist rather than a performer or creator prepared solely for the industry. This shift possibly coincides with changes in thinking around several related issues including, interrogating the need for skills integration, questioning whether there is such an entity as a musical industry, and sensitising local debates around inclusivity and diversity in the training environment.

First, skill integration as a training ideal calls into question, as previously discussed, the degree and frequency with which the three disciplines can be taught simultaneously when they are also taught separately and in different sequences.[81] Within multi-ethnic rehearsal spaces, performers may also question the perceived notion of integration as assimilation or homogeneity. Such cross-cultural negotiations within a training environment potentially contest the 'ableist, androcentric, Eurocentric, and heterocentric principles' of commercial-brand musicals. Contesting such sites engenders in students the values of critical thinking, adaptability, and longevity—perhaps the new triple threats in an ever-changing vocation.[82]

Globally, industry-facing training responds to the increasingly varied demands, needs, and forms of the musical theatre industry. Yet these industries are variegated across economies and cultures. One of the emerging core skills expected of trainees is simply being able to adapt to such rapidly shifting opportunities and repertoires in the entertainment industry at large. The complexity of training in musical theatre may in fact prepare the performer for a career across several specialities where, for instance, an embodied sense of musicality or multidisciplinarity is a valued skill set.

Localising factors also play a role in not only shaping training but how students see themselves and where they aim to develop their careers. The newly established BA Hons Musical Theatre at Leeds Conservatoire has networked its programme with local theatres such as Leeds Playhouse (formerly West Yorkshire Playhouse), rather than those in London. The aim is to grow an arts ecology with graduates from their programme. A sense of training in the neighbourhood can also determine how students see themselves entering the larger musical world. For instance, attending an elite institute of training may generate false expectations, even a sense of entitlement. Institutes that attract a more diverse cohort from less affluent areas may on the other hand 'engender a healthy sense of artistry', an attitude that may be more open to associated artistic paths or vocations.[83]

Musical theatre training worldwide is responding in different ways to the deepening social consciousness and debates around ethnicity, gender, sexuality, and indigeneity. In the United States, and to some extent the United Kingdom, this heightened awareness has led to new musical theatre writing that reflects historically absented voices, or challenges heteronormative dramaturgies.[84] Racist and misogynist representations in the musical canon have, for instance, sensitised training programmes, allowing debate in the current reception and historical context of these works, and informed casting 'outside the parameters of traditional casting patterns when the story supports this'.[85] The Canadian Music Theatre Project developed *Starlight Tours*, a musical which tells the stories of indigenous youth and police oppression.[86] In South Korea, which may see itself as a mono-ethnic nation, the issue of racial conflict may not have had the same kind of impact on writing or performance training as in other cultures. Yet, the ubiquity of social media and online discussions about gender has heightened the recognition of such diversity within its thriving musical industry.[87] A recent international conference at the VCA, Faculty of Fine Arts and Music (University of Melbourne), on what future training in musical theatre might look like, focused much-needed and belated attention on equity, inclusivity and diversity. It signalled freshly forged alliances across diverse communities and highlighted emerging brave spaces for reimagining musical theatre performance and writing.[88] It's also 'unfinished' business',[89] such as the art form itself, which continues to be shaped and reshaped by acts of local resistance and global conformity.

# LIST OF UNIVERSITY AND CONSERVATOIRE TRAINING COURSES

The university or conservatoire course websites listed here are referred to in the main text and in the endnotes, and do not represent an exhaustive survey.

American Musical and Dramatic Academy (US), https://www.amda.edu/about, accessed 03 July 2023.

Beijing Central Academy of Drama (China), http://web.zhongxi.cn/en/departments/8270.html, accessed 03 July 2023.

Copenhagen Central Musical Theatre School (Denmark), https://www.centralschool.dk/about, accessed 03 July 2023.

Folkwang University of the Arts (Germany), https://www.folkwang-uni.de/en/home/theater/, accessed 03 July 2023.

Fontys School of the Performing Arts (Netherlands), https://fontys.edu/About-us/Fontys-School-of-Fine-and-Performing-Arts/About-us/Theatre/Music-Theatre-and-Musical-Theatre.htm, accessed 03 July 2023.

Goldsmiths, University of London (UK), https://www.gold.ac.uk/ug/ba-drama-musical-theatre/, accessed 03 July 2023.

Goldsmiths, University of London (UK), https://www.gold.ac.uk/pg/ma-musical-theatre/, accessed 03 July 2023.

Griffith University (Australia), https://www.griffith.edu.au/study/music/musical-theatre, accessed 03 July 2023.

Korea National University of Arts (South Korea), http://www.karts.ac.kr/en/schools/dnp.do?CODE=02, accessed 03 July 2023.

Lasalle College of the Arts (Singapore), https://www.lasalle.edu.sg/programmes/ba-hons/musical-theatre, accessed 03 July 2023.

Leeds College of Music, Musical Theatre (UK), https://www.lcm.ac.uk/courses/undergraduate-study-18plus/undergraduate-courses/ba-hons-musical-theatre/, accessed 03 July 2023.

Luitingh Alexander Musical Theatre Academy (South Africa), https://www.lamta.co.za/why-triple-threat-training, accessed 01 July 2023.

Rose Bruford College (UK), https://www.bruford.ac.uk/courses/actor-musicianship-ba-hons/, accessed 01 July 2023.

Sheridan College (Canada), http://cmtp.sheridancollege.ca/, accessed 03 July 2023.

Victorian College of the Arts, Faculty of Fine Arts and Music, University of Melbourne (Australia), https://finearts-music.unimelb.edu.au/study-with-us/discipline-areas/music-theatre, accessed 03 July 2023.

Vienna Broadway Academy of Musical Theatre (Austria), https://www.musicalaus bildung.wien/, accessed 03 July 2023.

WAAPA, Edith Cowan University (Australia), https://www.waapa.ecu.edu.au/cour ses-and-admissions/our-courses/music-theatre, accessed 03 July 2023.

## ACKNOWLEDGMENTS

I am grateful to Sherrill Gow, Ethel Yap, Osvaldo A. Iturriaga Berríos, Joe Deer, Donna Dunmire, Chris Nolan, Adam Stadius, Marc Richards, Donna Soto-Morettini, and Jongyoon Choi.

## NOTES

1. See David Roesner, 'Challenges to the Mainstream Musical', in *The Oxford Handbook of the British Musical*, ed. Robert Gordon and Olaf Jubin (Oxford and New York: Oxford University Press, 2017), 651–671, n. 1. And despite the worldwide industry meltdown brought about by the pandemic that began in 2020, musicals continue to be created and performers to be trained, with new opportunities discovered in the globalising effects of virtual spaces and technologies, which spawn innovative practices, pedagogies, and forms.

2. For historical differentiations between music and musical theatre, see Zachary Dunbar, 'Music Theatre and Musical Theatre', in *The Cambridge Companion to Theatre History*, ed. David Wiles and Christine Dymkowski (Cambridge and New York: Cambridge University Press, 2012), 197–209. On the challenges of narrating a history of acting, see also Josette Féral, 'The Art of Acting', in ibid., 184–196.

3. See Ian Bradley, 'Amateur Tenors and Choruses in Public: The Amateur Scenes' in *The Cambridge Companion to Gilbert and Sullivan*, ed. David Eden and Meinhard Saremba (Cambridge and New York: Cambridge University Press, 2009), 177–189; here: 179–180.

4. meLê Yamomo, 'Global Currents, Musical Streams: European Opera in Colonial Southeast Asia', in *Nineteenth Century Theatre and Film* 44 (2017): 54–74; here: 57–58.

5. David Craig's interview with Gene Kelly, in David Craig, *On Performing: A Handbook for Actors, Dancers, Singers on the Musical Stage* (New York: McGraw-Hill, 1987), 269.

6. Craig's interview with Bernadette Peters, in ibid., 164, 167.

7. Vilma Ebsen's personal recollections, 1988, published in Rusty E. Frank, *Tap! The Greatest Tap Dance Stars and their Stories, 1900–1955* (New York: Da Capo Press, 1990), 137.

8. Both Bernstein and Sondheim had extensive classical training.

9. These included Ira and George Gershwin, Cole Porter, Irving Berlin, Jerome Kern, and Guy Bolton, alongside their British counterparts, including Noel Coward, Ivor Novello, and P. G. Wodehouse, who used the song as a vehicle for storytelling.

10. For a case-study discussion of literary aspirations vis-à-vis Oscar Hammerstein II, see Zachary Dunbar, '"How Do You Solve a Problem Like the Chorus?" Hammerstein's *Allegro* and the Reception of the Greek Chorus on Broadway', in *Choruses, Ancient and Modern*, ed. Joshua Billings, Felix Budelmann, and Fiona Macintosh (Oxford and New York: Oxford University Press, 2013), 243–258.

11. For the effect of the Theatre Guild on Broadway, see Claudia Wilsch Case, 'Refining the Tastes of Broadway Audiences: The Theatre Guild and American Musical Theatre', in *The Palgrave Handbook of Musical Theatre Producers*, ed. Laura MacDonald and William A. Everett (New York: Palgrave Macmillan, 2017), 153–161.

12. BMI, https://www.bmi.com/offices/new_york; MMD, http://www.mercurymusicals.com/, accessed 01 July 2023.

13. Joe Deer, email communication. Deer is also the co-author of the field's cornerstone textbook, which is now in its third edition and in worldwide circulation; see Joe Deer and Rocco Dal Vera, *Acting in Musical Theatre: A Comprehensive Course*, 3$^{rd}$ ed. (Abingdon and New York: Routledge, 2021).

14. Dan Rebellato, *Theatre and Globalization* (Basingstoke and New York: Palgrave Macmillan, 2009), 44–45.

15. An actor-musician training programme at Rose Bruford College (UK) represents the distinctive training: https://www.bruford.ac.uk/courses/actor-musicianship-ba-hons/, accessed 03 July 2023. See also Jeremy Harrison, *Actor-Musicianship* (London: Bloomsbury Methuen Drama, 2016).

16. Geoffrey Block, 'Integration', in *The Oxford Handbook of the American Musical*, ed. Raymond Knapp, Mitchell Morris, and Stacy Wolf (Oxford and New York: Oxford University Press, 2011), 97–110; here: 97.

17. On 'coherence', see Scott McMillin, *The Musical as Drama* (Princeton, NJ: Princeton University Press, 2006), 165, 170. The list of standard training books on writing musicals begins notably with the seminal work of Lehman Engel, *Words with Music* (New York: Schirmer, 1972); others in regular circulation include Richard Andrews, *Writing a Musical* (Wiltshire: Crowood Press, 1997); David Spencer, *The Musical Theatre Writer's Survival Guide* (Hanover, NH: Heinemann, 2005); Allen Cohen and Steven L. Rosenhaus, *Writing Musical Theater* (New York: Palgrave Macmillan, 2006); Julian Woolford, *How Musicals Work* (London: Nick Hern Books, 2012).

18. Block, 'Integration', 97.

19. This is a carryover from opera, which clearly distinguished between the art of the composer and that of the librettist.

20. For 'glocalisation', see Manfred Steger, *Globalization: A Short Introduction* (Oxford and New York: Oxford University Press, 2013), 2.

21. See Lyn Cramer's interview with the Broadway choreographer Kathleen Marshall in Lyn Cramer, *Creating Musical Theatre: Conversations with Broadway Directors and Choreographers* (London: Bloomsbury Methuen Drama, 2017), 131.

22. The published training guides in fact reflect this in their relative silence on the matter of acting *through* dance; only in recent years has research started to address physiological and psychological aspects of dancing *and* singing.

23. Liza Gennaro and Stacy Wolf, 'Dance in Musical Theater', in *The Oxford Handbook of Dance and Theatre*, ed. Nadine George-Graves (Oxford and New York: Oxford University Press, 2015), 148–168; here: 149. See also Liza Gennaro, 'Evolution of Dance in the Golden Age of the American "Book Musical"', in *The Oxford Handbook of the American Musical*, ed. Raymond Knapp, Mitchell Morris, and Stacy Wolf (Oxford and New York: Oxford University Press, 2011), 45–61.

24. Elizabeth A. Wells, *'West Side Story': Cultural Perspectives on an American Musical* (Lanham, MD: Scarecrow Press, 2011), 229. This was also true for the first German-language production (1968) in Vienna.

25. Peter Brinson, 'The New Kind of Dancer', *Sunday Times* (1958), cited in Wells, '*West Side Story*'.
26. See Zachary Dunbar, 'Dionysian Reflections upon *A Chorus Line*', in *Studies in Musical Theatre* 4, no. 2 (2010): 155–169; here: 158.
27. Deborah Jowitt, *Jerome Robbins: His Life, His Theater, His Dance* (New York: Simon & Schuster, 2004), 16.
28. Gennaro and Wolf, 'Dance in Musical Theater', 154.
29. Wells, '*West Side Story*', 236.
30. Most of the leads in the West End cast were UK-based performers, as were those in the ensemble.
31. At the time, London's drama schools covered the voice training, while the dance schools offered contemporary and classical technique. The eventual selected British cast, from a line-up of a hundred short-listed, represented the UK's top-league triple threats, for whom the London reviewers were rooting when they replaced the American cast. See 'A Chorus Line—the British Recasting of the Original Production', https://overtures.org.uk/?p=2691, accessed 03 July 2023.
32. Jessica Sternfeld, *The Megamusical* (Bloomington: University of Indiana Press, 2006), 119.
33. Ibid., 123. For current discussion about the required expertise of performers for *Cats*, see http://www.playbill.com/article/the-casting-of-cats-is-a-difficult-matter, accessed 03 July 2023.
34. See Miranda Lundskaer-Nielsen, 'Cameron Mackintosh: Control, Collaboration, and the Creative Producer', in *The Oxford Handbook of the British Musical*, ed. Robert Gordon and Olaf Jubin (Oxford and New York: Oxford University Press, 2017), 537–559.
35. Rebellato, *Theatre and Globalization*, 44.
36. For South Africa, see https://www.lamta.co.za/why-triple-threat-training. The musical theatre department in Beijing's Central School was founded in 1992, http://web.zhongxi.cn/en/departments/8270.html. Listings of musical theatre training courses that explicitly mention training the 'triple threat' include https://www.amda.edu/programs/music-theatre, https://www.griffith.edu.au/study/music/musical-theatre, https://www.waapa.ecu.edu.au/courses-and-admissions/our-courses/music-theatre, and https://www.lasalle.edu.sg/programmes/ba-hons/musical-theatre, all accessed 03 July 2023.
37. For an overview of musical transfers to Europe, see Judith Sebesta, 'The Marriage of the Musical in Europe', in *The Cambridge Companion to the Musical*, ed. William A. Everett and Paul R. Laird (Cambridge and New York: University of Cambridge Press, 2008), 270–283.
38. Hannover's Stage Perform, School for Musical and Performing Arts, https://www.stageperform.de; Berlin University of the Arts, https://www.udk-berlin.de/studium/musicalshow/; Vienna Broadway Academy, https://www.musicalausbildung.wien/ and Copenhagen Central Musical Theatre School, https://www.centralschool.dk/about, all accessed 03 July 2023.
39. Institute of the Arts in Barcelona, https://www.iabarcelona.com/musical-theatre/ba-hons-musical-theatre/; and Norwegian College of Musical Theatre, https://www.musikkteaterhoyskolen.no/english/about/, all accessed 03 July 2023.
40. See Folkwang University of the Arts, https://www.folkwang-uni.de/en/home/theater/; for Fontys School of the Performing Arts, see https://fontys.edu/About-us/Fontys-School-of-Fine-and-Performing-Arts/About-us/Theatre/Music-Theatre-and-Musical-Theatre.htm, both accessed 03 July 2023.

41. Hungary, however, has proven a successful market for the American and British block-buster musical, even though its academies haven't produced training programmes to match the popularity of the form.
42. Alejandro Postigo, 'The Evolution of Musical Theatre in Spain throughout the Twentieth and Twenty-first Centuries', in *Reframing the Musical: Race, Culture and Identity*, ed. Sarah Whitfield (London: Red Globe Press, 2019), 111–128.
43. Sternfeld, *The Megamusical*, 218.
44. Osvaldo A. Iturriaga Berrios, email communication.
45. Hyunjung Lee, 'Emulating Modern Bodies: The Korean Version of *Porgy and Bess* and American Popular Culture in the 1960s South Korea', in *Cultural Studies* 26, no. 5 (2012): 723–739.
46. This development has undoubtedly been fuelled by China's 'culture industry promotion plan' and the rise of a new, affluent middle-class consumer in post–Deng Xiaoping China. For an overview of recent developments in China's musical ventures, see Shin Dong Kim, 'The Industrialization and Globalization of China's Musical Theater', *Media Industries* 1, no. 3 (2015): 12–17; https://quod.lib.umich.edu/m/mij/15031809.0001.303/--industrializat ion-and-globalization-of-chinas-musical?rgn=main;view=fulltext, accessed 03 July 2023. For a helpful comprehensive account of Mandarin versions, see Qian Yu, 'The Challenges and Opportunities of Producing Mandarin Version of Western Musicals in China' (master's thesis, Faculty of Teachers College, Columbia University, 2013).
47. See https://taiwantoday.tw/news.php?unit=20,29,35,45&post=25000, accessed 03 July 2023.
48. See https://taiwantoday.tw/news.php?unit=20,29,35,45&post=25000, accessed 03 July 2023.
49. Kristen Rudisill, 'Localization: My School Rocks! Dancing Disney's *High School Musical* in India', *Studies in Musical Theatre* 3, no. 3 (2009): 253–271. See also, Mel Atkey, *A Million Miles from Broadway: Musical Theatre Beyond New York and London* (Vancouver: Friendlysong Books, 2012).
50. Ethel Yap, email communication.
51. Edward Behr and Mark Steyn, *The Story of 'Miss Saigon'* (New York: Arcade, 1991).
52. Broderick Chow, 'Seeing as a Filipino: *Here Lies Love* (2014) at the National Theatre', in *Reframing the Musical: Race, Culture and Identity*, ed. Sarah Whitfield (London: Red Globe Press, 2019), 17–34; here: 30.
53. Sternfeld, *The Megamusical*, 300.
54. Lea Salonga and Aicelle Santos have Wikipedia sites which profile their formative professional training.
55. Chow, 'Seeing as a Filipino'.
56. For an in-depth study of musicals and national identity, see Raymond Knapp, *The American Musical and the Formation of National Identity* (Princeton, NJ: Princeton University Press, 2004); and John Bush Jones, *Our Musicals, Ourselves* (Hanover, NH: University Press of New England, 2004).
57. Miranda Lundskaer-Nielsen, 'Musical Theatre Writer Training in Britain: Contexts, Developments and Opportunities', *Studies in Musical Theatre* 9, no. 2 (2015): 129–141.
58. Steger, *Globalization*, 9.
59. Ji Hyon Yuh, 'Korean Musical Theatre's Past: Yegrin and the Politics of 1960s Musical Theatre', in *The Palgrave Handbook of Musical Theatre Producers*, ed. Laura MacDonald and William A. Everett (New York: Palgrave Macmillan, 2017), 253–259; here: 253, 255.

60. Korea National University of Arts degree programme, see http://www.karts.ac.kr/en/scho ols/dnp.do?CODE=02, accessed 03 July 2023.

61. Hyewon Kim, 'Celebrating the Heteroglossic Hybridity: Ready-to-Assemble Broadway-Style Musicals in South Korea', *Studies in Musical Theatre* 10, no. 3 (2016): 343–354.

62. On the musical *Nanta*, see https://www.nanta.co.kr:452/Pages/En/About/Nanta.aspx, accessed 03 July 2023.

63. See Jae-yeon Woo, 'Musical "Mata Hari" eyes global audience from the onset', in https://en.yna.co.kr/view/AEN20160308006600315, accessed 04 July 2023.

64. Shin Dong Kim, 'The Industrialization and Globalization of China's Musical Theater', *Media Industries* 1, no. 3 (2015), https://quod.lib.umich.edu/m/mij/15031809.0001.303/--industrialization-and-globalization-of-chinas-musical?rgn=main;view=fulltext, accessed 03 July 2023. .

65. David Savran, 'Trafficking in Transnational Brands: The New "Broadway-Style" Musical', *Theatre Survey* 55, no. 3 (2014): 318–342.

66. Thomas Hill discusses the Filipino musical renaissance in https://www.broadwayworld.com/philippines/article/The-Renaissance-of-Musical-Theater-in-the-Philippines-Will-It-Last-20151007. For current Filipino musicals, see http://tarafrejas.com/5-filipino-music als/. Both links accessed 03 July 2023.

67. Wild Rice, https://www.wildrice.com.sg/; Theatre Practice (TTP), https://practice.org.sg/ both accessed 03 July 2023.

68. For an overview of Singapore's musical theatre, see Singapore-based Kenneth Lyen's website, https://kenlyen.wixsite.com/website, accessed 03 July 2023. 'The rise of musical theatre requires a democracy, and also economic well-being'; Lyen cited in Atkey, *A Million Miles from Broadway*, 215.

69. Sheridan College (Toronto), http://cmtp.sheridancollege.ca/, accessed 03 July 2023.

70. MacDonald, https://www.americantheatre.org/2017/04/25/the-sound-of-musicals-in-china/, accessed 03 July 2023.

71. Australian performing arts programmes at WAAPA, VCA, and Monash University host short musical theatre residencies; for Hayes Theatre (Sydney), see https://hayestheatre.com.au/create/; for grassroots initiative in Melbourne, see Homegrown, http://www.homegrownaus.com/; for a recent account of musical theatre development and writing in Australia, see David Spicer, 'Making Australian Musicals Great', http://www.stagewhisp ers.com.au/news/australian-musicals. All accessed 03 July 2023.

72. One of the creatives, Pamela Phillips Oland, talks about the development of the musical in Tim Hayes's interview, 'Pamela Phillips-Oland and Tom Harriman on *Soldier of Orange*', https://www.pamoland.com/soldier-of-orange-the-musical/, accessed 03 July 2023.

73. MacDonald, 'The Sound of Musicals in China', https://www.americantheatre.org/2017/04/25/the-sound-of-musicals-in-china/, accessed 03 July 2023.

74. MacDonald, https://www.americantheatre.org/2017/04/25/the-sound-of-musicals-in-china/, accessed 29 August 2023. Ibid.

75. For information about the making of the musical *Shimmer*, see http://www.playbill.com/article/shimmer-set-to-become-first-chinese-musical-to-play-broadway, accessed 03 July 2023. For information about the collaborative making of the musical *Shi Jing Cai Wei*, see Chen Nan's article in *China Daily*, http://www.chinadaily.com.cn/a/201810/13/WS5bc15 162a310eff303282257.html, accessed 03 July 2023.

76. UK-based educator and performance coach Donna Soto-Morettini, email communication. The vocal coach and researcher Joan Melton rightly argues that 'three worlds of voice

training are often separated and often pitted against each other: classical singing, musical theatre and voice for the actor'. See Joan Melton, *Singing in Musical Theatre: The Training of Singers and Actors* (New York: Allworth Press, 2007), 197.

77. On the problematic ontology of dance in musical theatre, see Joanna Dee Das and Ryan Donovan, 'Special Issue: Dance in Musical Theatre', *Studies in Musical Theatre* 13, no. 1 (2019), 3–7; here: 5; for reconsiderations of acting, see Phillip Zarrilli, ed., *Acting (Re) considered: Theories and Practices* (London and New York: Routledge, 1995). In recent years the discipline of performance studies has highlighted the porous boundaries and transcultural problematics of the voice, body, and actor. Nonetheless, research into integrated training and curricula forges ahead determined to resolve the disjunction in the three arts. Joan Melton, *One Voice: Integrating Singing and Theatre Voice Techniques* (Long Grove, IL: Waveland Press, 2012), considers combining the breathing techniques of the singer and dancer as a form of integrated training. In Leeds College of Music (UK), the acting coach and programme leader Adam Stadius suggests: 'Rather than learn a song, learn a dance and then put the two together, students are guided through appropriate and alternate breathing techniques whereby they can maintain efficient breath safely [even] whilst their mechanics are somewhat compromised by the nature of the dance-style'. Adam Stadius, email communication; https://www.lcm.ac.uk/courses/undergraduate-study-18plus/undergraduate-courses/ba-hons-musical-theatre/, accessed 03 July 2023..

78. On anomalies of acting through song, see Zachary Dunbar, 'Stanislavski's System in Musical Theatre Actor Training: Anomalies of Acting Song', *Stanislavski Studies* 4, no. 1 (2016): 63–74.

79. For the notion of acting and teachability, see Ross W. Prior, *Teaching Actors: Knowledge Transfer in Actor Training* (Bristol: Intellect, 2012).

80. See Laura Vorweg, 'Rehearsing (Inter)disciplinarity: Training, Production Practice and the 10,000-Hour Problem', in *Time and Performer Training*, ed. Mark Evans, Konstantinos Thomaidis, and Libby Worth (London: Routledge, 2019), 166–171. For further reading, see Malcolm Gladwell, *Outliers: The Story of Success* (Camberwell, Australia: Penguin Books, 2009).

81. For definitions of degree, frequency, and intensity of integrated research, see Zachary Dunbar, 'Practice-as-Research in Musical Theatre: Reviewing the Situation', *Studies in Musical Theatre* 8, no. 2 (2014): 57–75.

82. Sherril Gow, email communication. See also special issue, 'Against the Canon', in *Theatre, Dance and Performance Training* 11.3 (September 2020); http://theatredanceperformancet raining.org/2020/09/tdpt-11-3-against-the-canon/, accessed 05 July 2023.

83. Gow, email communication.

84. In the United States, the NAMT Thirtieth Annual Festival of New Musicals (2018) featured musicals which covered transgender, racism, and feminist narratives. BEAM (2018), an annual showcasing of new British musicals, also featured a similar spectrum of writing and themes.

85. Deer, email communication.

86. Marc Richards, email communication. See also Ben Macpherson, 'Some Yesterdays Always Remain: Black British and Anglo-Asian Musical Theatre', in *The Oxford Handbook of the British Musical*, ed. Robert Gordon and Olaf Jubin (Oxford and New York: Oxford University Press, 2017), 673–696, on how the global narratives of immigration infuse the conventional tropes of new musicals through the local ecology of the theatre (in this case, Stratford East, London).

87. Jongyoon Choi, email communication.
88. See https://blogs.unimelb.edu.au/music-theatre-futures/, accessed 03 July 2023.
89. A reference to the historiographical analysis of musicals in Bruce Kirle, *Unfinished Show Business: Broadway Musicals as Works-In-Process* (Carbondale: Southern Illinois University Press, 2005).

## BIBLIOGRAPHY

Atkey, Mel. *A Million Miles from Broadway: Musical Theatre Beyond New York and London*. Vancouver: Friendlysong Books, 2012.

Behr, Edward. *The Complete Book of 'Les Misérables'*. New York: Arcade Publishing, 1989.

Behr, Edward, and Mark Steyn. *The Story of 'Miss Saigon'*. New York: Arcade Publishing, 1991.

Berrios, Osvaldo A. Iturriaga. Email communication with the author, 27 June 2019.

Block, Geoffrey. 'Integration'. In *The Oxford Handbook of the American Musical*, edited by Raymond Knapp, Mitchell Morris, and Stacy Wolf, 97–110. Oxford and New York: Oxford University Press, 2011.

Case, Claudia Wilsch. 'Refining the Tastes of Broadway Audiences: The Theatre Guild and American Musical Theatre'. In *The Palgrave Handbook of Musical Theatre Producers*, edited by Laura MacDonald and William A. Everett, 153–161. New York: Palgrave Macmillan, 2017.

Choi, Jongyoon. Graduate Musical Theatre Writing Program, Korea National University of Arts. Email communication with the author, 14 May 2019.

Chow, Broderick. '*Here Lies Love* (2014) at the National Theatre'. In *Reframing the Musical: Race, Culture and Identity*, edited by Sarah Whitfield, 17–34. London: Red Globe Press, 2019.

Craig, David. *On Performing: A Handbook for Actors, Dancers, Singers on the Musical Stage*. New York: McGraw-Hill, 1987.

Cramer, Lyn. *Creating Musical Theatre: Conversations with Broadway Directors and Choreographers*. London and New York: Bloomsbury Methuen Drama, 2013.

Dee Das, Joanna, and Ryan Donovan. 'Special Issue: Dance in Musical Theatre'. *Studies in Musical Theatre* 13, no. 2 (2019): 3–7.

Deer, Joe. Wright State University, OH. Email communication with the author, 6 May 2019.

Deer, Joe, and Rocco Dal Vera. *Acting in Musical Theatre: A Comprehensive Course*. 3$^{rd}$ ed. Abingdon and New York: Routledge, 2021.

Dunbar, Zachary. 'Music Theatre and Musical Theatre'. In *The Cambridge Companion to Theatre History*, edited by David Wiles and Christine Dymkowski, 197–209. Cambridge and New York: Cambridge University Press, 2012.

Dunbar, Zachary. ' "How Do You Solve a Problem Like the Chorus?": Hammerstein's *Allegro* and the Reception of the Greek Chorus on Broadway'. In *Choruses, Ancient and Modern*, edited by Joshua Billings, Felix Budelmann, and Fiona Macintosh, 243–258. Oxford and New York: Oxford University Press, 2013.

Dunbar, Zachary. 'Practice-as-Research in Musical Theatre: Reviewing the Situation'. *Studies in Musical Theatre* 8, no. 2 (2014): 57–75.

Dunbar, Zachary. 'Stanislavski's System in Musical Theatre Actor Training: Anomalies of Acting Song'. *Stanislavski Studies* 4, no. 1 (2016): 63–74.

Eden, David, and Meinhard Saremba, eds. *The Cambridge Companion to Gilbert and Sullivan*. Cambridge and New York: Cambridge University Press, 2009.

Frank, Rusty E. *Tap! The Greatest Tap Dance Stars and their Stories, 1900–1955*. New York: Da Capo Press, 1990.

George-Graves, Nadine, ed. *The Oxford Handbook of Dance and Theatre*. Oxford and New York: Oxford University Press, 2015.

Gordon, Robert, and Olaf Jubin, eds. *The Oxford Handbook of the British Musical*. Oxford and New York: Oxford University Press, 2017.

Gow, Sherrill. Mountview, London. Email communication with the author, 6 April 2019.

Hayes, Tim. Interview, 'Pamela Phillips-Oland and Tom Harriman on *Soldier of Orange*'. N.d. https://www.pamoland.com/soldier-of-orange-the-musical/, accessed 03 July 2023.

Hill, Thomas. 'The Renaissance of Musical Theatre in the Philippines: Will It Last?' *Broadway World*, 7 October 2015. https://www.broadwayworld.com/philippines/article/The-Renaissance-of-Musical-Theater-in-the-Philippines-Will-It-Last-20151007, accessed 03 July 2023.

Jowitt, Deborah. *Jerome Robbins: His Life, His Theater, His Dance*. New York: Simon & Schuster, 2004.

Kim, Hyewon. 'Celebrating the Heteroglossic Hybridity: Ready-to-Assemble Broadway-Style Musicals in South Korea'. *Studies in Musical Theatre* 10, no. 3 (2016): 343–354.

Kim, Shin Dong. 'The Industrialization and Globalization of China's Musical Theater'. *Media Industries* 1, no. 3 (2015): 12–17. https://quod.lib.umich.edu/m/mij/15031809.0001.303/--industrialization-and-globalization-of-chinas-musical?rgn=main;view=fulltext, accessed 03 July 2023.

Kirle, Bruce. *Unfinished Show Business: Broadway Musicals as Works-In-Process*. Carbondale: Southern Illinois University Press, 2005.

Lee, Hyunjung. 'Emulating Modern Bodies: The Korean Version of *Porgy and Bess* and American Popular Culture in the 1960s South Korea'. *Cultural Studies* 26, no. 5 (2012): 723–739.

Lundskaer-Nielsen, Miranda. 'Cameron Mackintosh: Control, Collaboration, and the Creative Producer'. In *The Oxford Handbook of the British Musical*, edited by Robert Gordon and Olaf Jubin, 537–559. Oxford and New York: Oxford University Press, 2017.

Lundskaer-Nielsen, Miranda. 'Musical Theatre Writer Training in Britain: Contexts, Developments and Opportunities'. *Studies in Musical Theatre* 9, no. 2 (2015): 129–141.

Lyen, Kenneth. 'Musicals: A Singapore Perspective'. N.d. http://www.kenlyen.com/, accessed 15 June 2019. https://kenlyen.wixsite.com/website/the-singapore-musical

MacDonald, Laura. 'The Sound of Musicals in China'. *American Theatre*, 25 April 2017. https://www.americantheatre.org/2017/04/25/the-sound-of-musicals-in-china/, accessed 03 July 2023.

McMillin, Scott. *The Musical as Drama*. Princeton, NJ: Princeton University Press, 2006.

Melton, Joan. *One Voice: Integrating Singing and Theatre Voice Techniques*. Long Grove, IL: Waveland Press, 2012.

Melton, Joan. *Singing in Musical Theatre: The Training of Singers and Actors*. New York: Allworth Press, 2007.

Nan, Chen, 'Turning Poetry into Song'. *China Daily*, 13 October 2018. http://www.chinadaily.com.cn/a/201810/13/WS5bc15162a310eff303282257.html, accessed 03 July 2023.

Postigo, Alejandro. 'The Evolution of Musical Theatre in Spain throughout the Twentieth and Twenty-first Centuries'. In *Reframing the Musical: Race, Culture and Identity*, edited by Sarah Whitfield, 111–128. London: Red Globe Press, 2019.

Prior, Ross W. *Teaching Actors: Knowledge Transfer in Actor Training*. Bristol: Intellect, 2012.

Rebellato, Dan. *Theatre and Globalization*. Basingstoke: Palgrave Macmillan, 2009.

Richards, Marc. Sheridan College, Canada. Email communication with the author, 1 June 2019.

Rudisill, Kristen. 'Localization: My School Rocks! Dancing Disney's *High School Musical*'. *Studies in Musical Theatre* 3, no. 3 (2009): 253–271.

Savran, David. 'Trafficking in Transnational Brands: The New "Broadway-Style" Musical'. *Theatre Survey* 55, no. 3 (2014): 318–342.

Soto-Morettini, Donna. Edinburgh Napier University. Email communication with the author, 18 March 2019.

Spicer, David. 'Making Australian Musicals Great'. *Stage Whispers*, 2015, December 2015, http://www.stagewhispers.com.au/news/australian-musicals, accessed 03 July 2023.

Stadius, Adam. Leeds College of Music, UK. Email communication with the author, 26 March 2019.

Steger, Manfred. *Globalization: A Short Introduction*. Oxford and New York: Oxford University Press, 2013.

Stempel, Larry. *Showtime: A History of the Broadway Musical Theatre*. New York: W. W. Norton, 2010.

Sternfeld, Jessica. *The Megamusical*. Bloomington: University of Indiana Press, 2006.

Vorweg, Laura. 'Rehearsing (Inter)disciplinarity: Training, Production Practice and the 10,000-Hour Problem'. In *Time and Performer Training*, edited by Mark Evans, Konstantinos Thomaidis, and Libby Worth, 166–171. London: Routledge, 2019.

Wells, Elizabeth A. *'West Side Story': Cultural Perspectives on an American Musical*. Lanham, MD: Scarecrow Press, 2011.

Whitfield, Sarah. *Reframing the Musical: Race, Culture and Identity*. London: Red Globe Press, 2019.

Wolf, Stacy, and Liza Gennaro. 'Dance in Musical Theater'. In *The Oxford Handbook of Dance and Theater*, edited by Nadine George-Graves, 148–168. Oxford and New York: Oxford University Press, 2015.

Woo, Jae-yeon, https://en.yna.co.kr/view/AEN20160308006600315, accessed 04 July 2023.

Yamomo, meLê. 'Global Currents, Musical Streams: European Opera in Colonial Southeast Asia'. *Nineteenth Century Theatre and Film* 44 (2017): 54–74.

Yap, Ethel. Email communication with the author, 30 April 2019.

Yu, Qian. 'The Challenges and Opportunities of Producing Mandarin Version of Western Musicals in China'. Master's thesis, Faculty of Teachers College, Columbia University, 2013.

Yuh, Ji Hyon, 'Korean Musical Theatre's Past: Yegrin and the Politics of 1960s Musical Theatre'. In *The Palgrave Handbook of Musical Theatre Producers*, edited by Laura MacDonald and William A. Everett, 253–259. New York: Palgrave Macmillan, 2017.

# PART II

## UNCHARTED TERRITORIES

CHAPTER 4

# 'MERRILY SHE WALTZES ALONG'

## Die lustige Witwe (The Merry Widow) as Global Hit

JOHN KOEGEL

## INTRODUCTION: THE FIRST TRULY GLOBAL WORK OF MUSICAL THEATRE

BY October 1907 Franz Lehár's beloved operetta *Die lustige Witwe* (*The Merry Widow*), which had premiered at Vienna's famous Theater an der Wien on 30 December 1905, had played to rapturous responses in most German-speaking cities and triumphed in London, New York, and elsewhere.[1] As the American writer Henry T. Fink noted in his 1913 article 'Does Music Pay?', in one season alone early in its New York City run *The Merry Widow* reportedly earned more than one million dollars in profit, while three million sheet music copies of its great hit 'The Merry Widow Waltz' had been sold in Europe.[2] By 1909, when it finally reached Paris and Madrid, four years after its Viennese première, the operetta reportedly had been performed more than 18,000 times all around the world.[3] *The Merry Widow* sparked the silver age of Viennese operetta of Lehár, Emmerich Kálmán, Leo Fall, and Oscar Straus, following after the golden age of Johann Strauss, Franz von Suppé, Karl Millöcker, and other earlier Viennese operetta composers.

*The Merry Widow* was also probably the first hit musical to feature extensive international tie-in marketing and fashion trends, including the famous Merry Widow hat craze following the London première of the work, as well as the sale of merchandise such as Merry Widow chocolates, cigars, perfumes, liqueurs, salads, and a myriad of other Merry Widow-ized items, including the erotic, sexualized Merry Widow corset and Merry Widow condom.[4]

But the success story of the wealthy widow Hanna Glawari and her noble suitor Count Danilo Danilowitsch did not stop there. The operetta masterpiece can be seen as the first truly global work of musical theatre and was popular everywhere it was performed, in dozens of languages on all continents (except Antarctica), throughout Europe and the Americas, and in Australia,[5] New Zealand,[6] Vietnam,[7] China, Japan, India, Indonesia, the Philippines, Singapore,[8] Egypt,[9] and sub-Saharan Africa,[10] as well as in other European settler societies and colonies and in other locations. It was the direct predecessor of the modern megamusical that today plays simultaneously in different languages and theatres around the world.[11] As Tobias Becker tells us, 'for all its global success, [Andrew Lloyd Webber's very popular musical] *The Phantom of the Opera* has played in far fewer cities than *The Merry Widow*.'[12]

*The Merry Widow* was a success everywhere it was performed for several reasons. The principal attractions for global audiences included Lehár's lush and varied musical score, with its famous waltz, fine orchestration, and collage of Viennese, Slavic, and American musical influences, along with the libretto's rich comedic vein and romance tinged with irony. And since it was all the rage in Vienna, London and New York, audiences in major cities and small towns all across the globe wanted to see it. *The Merry Widow* was performed throughout the world for decades in the English-language translation and adaption created for the 1907 London première and later in other English-language versions. *The Merry Widow* was also translated into many different European and non-European languages for its stage, film, radio and television adaptations (see the tables below), and beginning in 1906 many recordings were released of the principal musical numbers.[13] Although these numerous versions change some of the details of the original operetta—locations and character names, orchestration style and size of orchestra and the length and arrangement of the work, to suit local taste, customs and circumstances—the essence of the musical romance between Hanna and Danilo, as well as the most memorable musical numbers, are usually retained. But *The Merry Widow* could not have conquered the world as it did without the growing global infrastructure that supported its triumphs: developments in global travel and communications; the growth of the music publishing, recording, radio and film industries; the increase in theatrical touring companies and routes; and the growth of newspapers and widespread publicity.

# THE WORK AND ITS COMPOSER

Franz Lehár's three-act operetta *Die lustige Witwe* (*The Merry Widow*), with a libretto by Viktor Léon and Leo Stein,[14] adapted from Henri Meilhac's French play *L'Attaché d'ambassade* (The Embassy Attaché, 1861),[15] opens in Paris at the embassy of the imaginary Balkan principality of Pontevedro, a stand-in for the real Balkan state of Montenegro (and the imaginary German principality of Birkenfeld in Meilhac's play). The extremely rich Pontevedrin widow Hanna Glawari (first played by Mitzi

Günther) arrives at a party in honor of the birthday of the prince who rules that small, impoverished imaginary country. Her compatriot, the envoy Baron Mirko Zeta, is determined that she marry the Pontevedrin legation secretary Count Danilo Danilowitsch (played by Louis Treumann)—a thinly veiled reference to the real-life Montenegrin Crown Prince Danilo Petrović-Njegoš.[16] Zeta needs Hanna to marry Danilo to save her fortune for Pontevedro, otherwise the country will be bankrupt. Hanna and Danilo had once been lovers, but their marriage was opposed by Danilo's aristocratic family. Instead, Hanna married a rich banker who subsequently died and left her extremely wealthy. Although Danilo still loves Hanna, and she him, he refuses to woo her, since it would place him in line with all the other men in Paris who are after her only for her money.

The operetta's many antics include the scheming of Baron Zeta and a subplot of a suggested affair between Zeta's beautiful, younger wife Valencienne and the French aristocrat Camille de Rosillon. Hanna assumes a disguised identity to avoid a scandal between Valencienne and her husband in act 2. The appearance of the Grisettes, the dancers Lolo, Dodo, Jou-Jou, Frou-Frou, Clo-Clo and Margot from the famous Parisian restaurant Maxim's, in act 3 adds a sparkling fizz to the story. *The Merry Widow* concludes after Hanna and Danilo's subtly eroticized singing and dancing to the famous 'Merry Widow Waltz' and their declaration of mutual love ('Lippen schweigen, s'flüstern Geigen: Hab mich lieb!' [Lips are silent, violins whisper: Love me!]). Danilo capitulates, since he is happy that Hanna will lose all her money once they marry, and he won't be marrying her for her fortune. But at the end he finds out that as her husband he will gain the millions she will lose. In their famous waltz, Danilo and Hanna sing sensuously to the accompaniment of solo violin and cello, whose musical lines symbolically intertwine, as do the two lovers.

Franz Lehár (1870–1948) was born in the city of Komárno (Komárom in Hungarian, Komorn in German) at the confluence of the Danube and Váh rivers, which was then in Hungary (and was part of the Austro-Hungarian Empire) and is now in Slovakia.[17] The son of a military band-master, he studied violin at the Prague Conservatory in the 1880s, a few years before Antonín Dvořák taught there. Dvorak examined the younger musician's scores and encouraged him to compose, telling him he should 'hang up his violin and dedicate himself to composition.'[18] Prior to his composition of *The Merry Widow*, and like his father before him, Lehár had served as a military band-master and conductor in numerous places throughout the Austro-Hungarian empire.[19] Since by the time of *Die lustige Witwe* he had been a resident of Vienna for several years, Lehár was able to follow new compositional and theatrical trends in person in the Austrian capital's many concert halls and theatres. He was also conversant with the major dramatic, operatic, and symphonic repertories of his day. Lehár was very familiar with developments on Vienna's operetta stages, then a dominant form of musical and theatrical entertainment, since he had written several stage works before *The Merry Widow*, including the successful operetta *Der Rastelbinder* (*The Tinker*) of 1902.

Lehár's score for *The Merry Widow* is fresh at every turn, and he captures the essence of the personality of his characters in his music. With *Die lustige Witwe* he hit his stride as a stage composer, remembering several years later that with his most famous work

FIG. 4.1 Composer Franz Lehár (*left*), with librettists Leo Stein (*middle*) and Viktor Léon (*right*), celebrating the five hundredth performance of *Die lustige Witwe* in Vienna in 1907. Source: Billy Rose Theatre Division, New York Public Library for the Performing Arts, *Merry Widow* File.

he found his true compositional style.[20] As writers such as Edward Michael Gold and Bernard Grun have noted, the music of *Die lustige Witwe*, especially its orchestration, reveals the composer's knowledge and use of stylistic techniques developed by Richard Strauss, Gustav Mahler and Claude Debussy, but adapted by Lehár to fit the popular stage, its audiences, and their expectations.[21]

The music to *Die lustige Witwe* includes a prominent use of low-register woodwind writing; the extensive employment of harp, playing more than the typical glissandi or arpeggiation; divided four-to-eight-part strings; and the use of brass at softer moments and not only in fortissimo sections. An onstage group (*Bühnenmusik*) is used, with a string ensemble and a *Tamburizza-Kapelle*, featuring the mandolin-like tamburizza (two tamburizzas and one bass tamburizza), guitar, tambourine, and bumbass (a 'devil's fiddle' or 'bladder and string' drone bass). Lehár's's *Bühnenmusik* suggests local ethnic Pontevedrin colour during the opening of act 2 as well as in Hanna's famous song 'Vilia' and its interspersed dances.

A greater use of independent contrapuntal lines than was usual for operetta at the time is a stylistic hallmark of Lehár's's musical approach in this and later works. One highlight of his musical style in *Die lustige Witwe* is his mixing of Viennese and Slavic musical elements, with the use of Central and Eastern European dances such as the waltz, polonaise, mazurka, and kolo, along with the American-derived cakewalk. As Michaela Baranello suggests, 'Austro-Hungarian Vienna was itself a collage, and *Witwe*'s mixture of ethnicities could be read as a plausible representation of its sound.'[22] She shows how the music dramatizes 'the libretto's duality between Paris and Pontevedro' and contrasts those numbers in Lehár's score representing the buffo Parisian musical style that 'stage the external outer plot' with those that 'portray the characters' internal psychological states' in a 'sentimental, romantic folksong-influenced style.' She also identifies those numbers that represent a mixed or ambiguous style.[23]

Lehár's biographer Stephan Czech emphasized the musical lightness and clarity of *Die lustige Witwe*, and that its 'harmonic fabric, with its rich nuances, has impressionistic luminosity.' He also noted that '[a]s in Puccini a glittering tremolo tissue hovers over the melodic invention.'[24] Bernard Grun believed that 'the complete novelty of *The Merry Widow* lies in the frankly erotic nature of its subject, and in the ingenious boldness with which the vibrant sensuality of the story is musically interpreted.'[25] Despite the countless changes and refashionings that *The Merry Widow* has undergone over more than a century in musical adaptation, libretto, staging, and varying performance approaches, it is the music that remains the operetta's main attraction. The strength of Lehár's musical score and the underlying eroticism of the story continue to make this work a perennial favorite. The success of the work is also due to its believable dramatic characterisations, representing real-life experiences of love, rejection, jealousy, comedy, and flirtation as well as political maneuvering for power and control.

Although Lehár tried his hand at composing opera, operetta and light music were truly his métier—one should not underestimate the talent it takes to write good, memorable light music. Mahler, who admired the music of *Die lustige Witwe*, considered commissioning Lehár to write a ballet score for the Wiener Hofoper (Viennese Court Opera) until it was pointed out to him that a Lehár ballet score would only have a few performances and would garner the composer small royalties in comparison to the tremendous artistic and financial success he was having with *Die lustige Witwe*—and later, with his operettas such as *Der Graf von Luxemburg* (*The Count of Luxembourg*) and numerous others.[26]

# DIE LUSTIGE WITWE AND THE STATUS OF OPERETTA

In the past, scholars often viewed operetta with misunderstanding or condescension, with some prominent exceptions such as Siegfried Kracauer and Richard Traubner.[27] Even in recent years, some leading writers have judged operetta as insignificant in the overall development of musical theatre—trivial, cheap, and/or banal in music and story[28]—or not even as part of the history of musical theatre at all. However, this misguided view has begun to change.[29] Music and theatre scholars as well as those from other humanistic disciplines now generally regard operetta as an important transnational and global form and as a product of commercial entertainment, with interlocking local, national, and international histories. They also see it as a direct predecessor of current musical theatre forms and works.[30]

A number of leading scholars have closely examined *Die lustige Witwe* and the history of the operetta in recent years, offering complementary readings of the work and the genre.[31] Michaela Baranello's important 2014 study of *The Merry Widow* is the most extensive article on Lehár's famous operetta to date.[32] She reminds us that even though *Die lustige Witwe* is set in the Pontevedrin embassy in Paris, its real location is 1905 Vienna, with its many ethnic and political tensions and social divisions. Kiril Tomoff, in his work on operetta in Soviet Russia, suggests that golden age and pre–World War I silver age Viennese operettas such as *Die lustige Witwe*, with their settings in mythic, imagined Balkan states such as Pontevedro, are examples of the 'self-orientalisation' inherent in theatrical works from the end of the Habsburg Austro-Hungarian empire.[33] Tobias Becker positions *The Merry Widow* in terms of cultural globalisation, 'cross-national mobility', and cosmopolitanism and demonstrates how operetta represented encounters with the foreign and was connected to growing urbanisation.[34] Stefan Schmidl explains that 'operetta played an essential part in the construction of national identities, of the Self and Other [ ... ]. Taking up everyday idioms and turning them into collective symbols, librettists and composers of operetta could praise, defame, integrate, or exclude nationalities.'[35] Derek Scott and contributors to the essay collection *Popular Musical Theatre in London and Berlin 1890 to 1939* demonstrate the centrality of operetta on the commercial stage in Britain and Germany and by extension, elsewhere in the world.[36]

Finally, Laurence Senelick examines what he calls the omni-local and transglobal in relation to musical theatre. The omni-local 'describes a work significant enough to be influential in a wide sphere but which undergoes local adaptation to ensure its reception.'[37] This is especially true of *The Merry Widow*, since, although societies throughout the world have taken what they wished from cultural imports such as Lehár's famous cosmopolitan operetta, its underlying structure generally survives, along with its most memorable melodies and songs: each culture adapts the *Widow* to its own purposes.

These scholars have added to our understanding of the work's success both within its time and local place and within its global context.

# THE TRAVELING *WIDOW*, TRANSLATED

The march of *The Merry Widow* across Europe began soon after its Viennese première at the Theater an der Wien on 30 December 1905. It opened at Hamburg's Neues Operetten-Theater on 3 March 1906, and the same company presented its Berlin première a few months later, on 1 May. Copenhagen likely saw the first non-German-language performance, given in Danish as *Den glade Enke*, on 18 August.[38] Warsaw followed with the Polish version, *Wesola wdówka*, on 16 October, and Budapest with *A víg özvegy*, in Hungarian, on 27 November. According to Kurt Gänzl, the operetta was also performed in Czech, Norwegian, Russian, Swedish, and Croatian before it received its first English-language performances.[39] Later it was performed in numerous other languages.

The British music publisher William Boosey, who attended performances of *Die lustige Witwe* in Vienna, encouraged the British impresario George Edwardes to purchase the English-language performance rights to the operetta from Adolf Sliwinski and Felix Bloch of the Berlin-based firm Felix Block Erben, the dramatic and musical agents and publisher.[40] Lehár and Léon and Stein had sold their rights to *Die lustige Witwe* to Felix Bloch Erben on 25 November 1905, a month before the Viennese première.[41] At Boosey's urging, Edwardes bought the rights on 27 February 1906 and commissioned an English translation and adaptation (book and lyrics) for his London première of *The Merry Widow* on 8 June 1907 at Daly's Theatre.[42]

Edwardes and his dramatic team of lyricist Adrian Ross and book authors Basil Hood and Edward Morton made changes for the English production: Pontevedro became Marsovia, Hanna's and Count Danilo's names were changed to Sonia and Prince Danilo, Baron Zeta became Baron Popoff, and Valencienne was called Natalie. Edwardes's version was mostly faithful to the original German operetta, and Ross's English lyrics captured the essence of *Die lustige Witwe*. However, the orchestra was reduced at Daly's Theatre (over Lehár's objections) because of the size of the theatre's orchestra pit. The comic role of Baron Popoff was expanded to capitalize on the personality of the very popular comedian George Graves. Edwardes removed a few numbers from the score, and Lehár composed several new songs for the London production. Edwardes hired the beautiful young singing actress Lily Elsie for the role of the widow Sonia (Hanna) and the American comedian Joseph Coyne for her Prince Danilo. Because he could not sing, Coyne recited the song lyrics in rhythm, as Rex Harrison did later in *My Fair Lady*. *The Merry Widow* was a smash hit in London, racking up 778 performances in its initial run.

Soon after he purchased the rights from Felix Bloch Erben on 27 February 1906, Edwardes sold the English-language performing rights for the United States and Canada on 16 March 1906 to American impresario Henry W. Savage, who reportedly was to pay

FIG. 4.2 An article celebrating '25 Merry Widows'. Source: Shubert Archive, New York, *Merry Widow* file.

him a deposit of five hundred pounds and no less than fifty pounds per week for each of Savage's several *Merry Widow* companies.[43] Savage used Edwardes's London adaptation for his own US and Canadian version, with some small changes. Although writers have always stated that Lehár's operetta received its US première at the New Amsterdam Theatre in New York City, it was actually first performed in the United States at the 2,100-seat Wieting Opera House in Syracuse, New York on 22 September 1907. Savage prepared his company very carefully and spared no expense with his production, and as a result the Syracuse première earned critical acclaim: 'So perfect was the performance [ ... ] not even the most experienced stage manager could have detected the marks of a first night.'[44] After Syracuse, Savage's *Merry Widow* company played in Ithaca, Rochester, and Buffalo, New York, and in Philadelphia, Pennsylvania, before its New York City opening night on 21 October 1907. As with the US première in Syracuse, the first performance in New York City at the New Amsterdam Theatre received high praise from critics and audience members and was an artistic and financial success, running for 416 performances until it closed in October 1908. Over the years it has been frequently revived in New York. The influential and highly opinionated music critic Henry Krehbiel published a positive but ironic review in the *New-York Tribune*.[45] He praised Lehár's orchestration, the gorgeous costumes and scenery, and the principal performers, especially Ethel Jackson as Sonia and Donald Brian as Danilo:

> At length a real operetta, one that does not filch the appellation, but fits it [ ... ].
> We shall have to walk and talk and read and smoke to the waltz rhythms that Franz
> Lehár has invented. [ ... ] Would that all operetta writers could appropriate familiar
> formulas as ingeniously as has Lehár and sprinkle over them the same dewy fresh-
> ness. The waltzes and marches bear the hallmark of Vienna, but some of the melodies
> also have a familiar lilt, showing that idioms racy of America have penetrated to the
> home of Strauss and Suppé.

Tables 4.1 and 4.2 list the currently known early premières of *The Merry Widow* in cities throughout the world and the various titles by which the operetta has been known. Table 4.1 highlights the operetta's truly international reach within four years of its Viennese opening night; that impressive global record has only continued to expand since 1909.

Because of the huge success of *The Merry Widow* in New York City, Henry W. Savage soon sent out the first of what would be his multiple *Merry Widow* road companies, and his *Widow* toured for several consecutive years non-stop throughout the United States and Canada. The first extended run of performances after the 21 October 1907 New York City première was at Chicago's Colonial Theatre, beginning on 2 December 1907. Savage advertised the well-received Chicago production, starring the soubrette Lina Abarbanell, a sometime Metropolitan opera singer and regular Broadway musical star, as Sonia/Hanna.[46] The Chicago production featured an 'Augmented Orchestra of 32 Pieces, [and a] Full Hungarian Band'.[47] Ever the master of the publicity campaign, Savage promoted his several *Merry Widow* road companies heavily through a barrage of

### Table 4.1 *The Merry Widow* Premières, 1905–1909

| | | | |
|---|---|---|---|
| 30 December 1905 | Vienna | April 1908 (?) | Rio de Janeiro |
| 3 March 1906 | Hamburg | April 1908 (?) | Shanghai |
| 1 May 1906 | Berlin | 4 May 1908 | Yokohama |
| 18 August 1906 | Copenhagen | May 1908 (?) | Colombo |
| 16 October 1906 | Warsaw | 16 May 1908 | Melbourne |
| 27 November 1906 | Budapest | June 1908 (?) | Singapore |
| 26 December 1906 | Oslo | September 1908 (?) | Jakarta |
| 29 December 1906 | St. Petersburg | September 1908 (?) | Havana |
| 7 April 1907 | Milan | September 1908 (?) | São Paulo |
| 8 June 1907 | London | 8 February 1909 | Madrid |
| 23 September 1907 | Syracuse | 10 April 1909 | Wellington |
| 21 October 1907 | New York | 28 April 1909 | Paris |
| 21 March 1908 | Buenos Aires | 19 June 1909 | Mexico City |
| March 1908 (?) | Hong Kong | 20 July 1909 | Montevideo |

FIG. 4.3 Norwegian version of *The Merry Widow*, as *Den glade Enke*, Trondheim, Norway, 1907. Source: Digital Collections, Nasjonalbiblioteket/National Library of Norway.

## Table 4.2 *Die lustige Witwe* Around the World

| Country | Title | Country | Title |
|---|---|---|---|
| Austria | *Die lustige Witwe* | [Latin America] | *La viuda alegre* |
| Brazil | *A viúva alegre* | Latvia | *Jautrā atraitne* |
| China | 风流寡妇 | Netherlands | *De vrolijke weduwe* |
| Denmark | *Den glade Enke* | Norway | *Den glade Enke* |
| Egypt | *Al-Armalah al-taroub* | Poland | *Wesola wdówka* |
| Finland | *Iloinen Leski* | Portugal | *A viúva alegre* |
| France | *La Veuve joyeuse* | Russia | веселая вдова |
| Germany | *Die lustige Witwe* | Slovakia | *Veselá vdova* |
| Hungary | *A víg özvegy* | Spain | *La viuda alegre* |
| Italy | *La vedova allegra* | Sweden | *Den glade Änkan* |
| Japan | メリー・ウィドウ | Taiwan | 风流寡妇 |
| Korea | 메리 과부 | United Kingdom/United States | *The Merry Widow* |

advertisements, puff pieces, and articles strategically placed in small-town and big-city newspapers throughout the United States and Canada. The (usually) positive reviews of performances given along these extensive tour circuits gave free publicity to Savage's productions; they also increased audience size and interest, as well as Savage's profits. *The Merry Widow* was the must-see show in New York City in the 1907–1908 season and after. With several companies simultaneously traversing much of North America north of Mexico, the number of performances of *The Merry Widow* mounted quickly. Savage extensively advertised the reported five thousandth performance of Lehár's operetta in his production, which took place at the Cort Theatre in San Francisco on 30 March 1913.[48]

Developments and improvements in steamship and railway travel, international postal delivery, telegraphic wire newspaper services, international commerce and global markets, recording technology, film and recording production and distribution, and other modes of fast communication facilitated the *Widow*'s quick spread throughout the world. Newspaper and magazine reportage of *The Merry Widow* and excerpts from the musical score in wind band, orchestra, piano, salon music, and popular sheet music arrangements, as well as recordings, music box discs, and player piano rolls, often preceded the famous operetta's arrival in towns and cities everywhere. People around the world often read about *The Merry Widow* and played and heard its music well before they actually saw it in person.

FIG. 4.4 Henry W. Savage's US production of *The Merry Widow*, with Lina Abarbanell as Hanna and Donald Brian as Count Danilo. Postcard provided by the author.

# The Maurice Bandmann Company and the Touring *Widow*

Among the most active impresarios in producing and promoting performances of *The Merry Widow* internationally was Maurice E. Bandmann (1872–1922). As Christopher Balme has expertly documented, the theatrical empire that Bandmann established and operated from the first years of the twentieth century until his death in 1922 stretched from Gibraltar and the Mediterranean, to Egypt, Japan, Burma (Myanmar), the Philippines, Indonesia, Hong Kong, China, Singapore, India, and Australasia, and was a truly global enterprise.[49] Bandmann was one of many theatrical impresarios who created extensive networks of theatres, resident and touring companies, and/or interconnected theatrical businesses: the Arcaraz Brothers (Hermanos Arcaraz) in Mexico, the Shubert Brothers and Henry W. Savage in the United States, Isidore Schlesinger in South Africa, George Edwardes in the United Kingdom, and J. C. Williamson in Australia and New Zealand, among many others. The organisation of theatrical touring companies was often centered on a dominant individual or pair who chose and licensed repertoire; hired stage directors, designers, composers, and performers; owned or controlled theatres; and managed regular touring routes over vast geographic regions. These manager-impresarios stressed a vertical integration of the various components of theatrical production and moved their touring companies along national, international, and global lines of performance transmission. Some, such as Bandmann, Williamson, and Savage, had direct connections to such London West End producers as Edwardes, from whom they licensed their productions of *The Merry Widow*. New York City's influential Shubert Brothers, who produced different versions of *The Merry Widow* over the years, were intimately familiar with theatrical developments in the United Kingdom and continental Europe through their own theatrical reconnaissance trips there and business and personal connections with European impresarios. They also received regular reports on European theatrical developments from their agent abroad, the former theatre owner and manager Gustav Amberg.[50]

Bandmann's touring companies performed live musical theatre and spoken drama for European colonial settlers and local peoples throughout his vast theatrical territory. Table 4.3 lists some of the cities in which Bandmann's various operetta troupes performed *The Merry Widow* in the four-year period between 1908 and 1911, usually to an enthusiastic and lucrative reception. Although a significant portion of his audiences was made up of European expatriates and individuals of European heritage, those groups never represented the totality of his target group. For example, his audiences in British colonial India—for some years he maintained his main theatrical headquarters in Calcutta—included both British and European expatriates and native Indians. Indeed, he often presented Shakespeare's comedies and tragedies for local Indian audiences. Tobias Becker has shown how companies such as Bandmann's also emphasized a sense of Britishness in colonial surroundings and circumstances. Musical theatre 'was an important social space where the British diaspora constituted itself as a community' and a 'lifeline to the home

## Table 4.3 The Bandmann Company's *Merry Widow* Performances, 1908–1911[a]

| Date | City |
| --- | --- |
| March 1908 | Hong Kong |
| April 1908 | Shanghai |
| May 1908 | Yokohama |
| June 1908 | Singapore |
| August 1908 | Colombo |
| September 1908 | Batavia (Jakarta) |
| September 1908 | Bandoeng (Bandung) |
| Early 1909 (14-week season) | Calcutta (Kolkata) |
| March 1909 | Colombo |
| April 1909 | Singapore |
| April 1909 | Rangoon (Yangon) |
| January 1910 | Singapore |
| March 1910 | Shanghai |
| May 1910 | Shanghai |
| September 1910 | Medan |
| May 1911 | Shanghai |
| July 1911 | Shanghai |
| June or July (?) 1911 | [Japan] |
| July 1911 | Hong Kong |

[a] Historical sources used include digitised editions of the following newspapers: *Bataviaasch Nieusblad* (Batavia/Jakarta, Dutch East Indies/Indonesia), *Ceylon Observer* (Colombo, Ceylon/Sri Lanka), *China Mail* (Hong Kong), *Japan Weekly Mail* (Yokohama), *North China Herald and Supreme Court and Consular Gazette* (Shanghai), *De Preanger-bode* (Bandoeng/Bandung, Dutch East Indies), *Shanghai Times, Singapore Free Press and Mercantile Advertiser, Straights Times* (Singapore), and *De Sumatra Post* (Medan, Dutch East Indies).

country'. It 'not only allowed colonial audiences to participate in the metropolitan culture; it inadvertently helped to unify the British empire'.[51]

Shanghai, with its foreign concessions and expatriates, international trading communities, famous Art Deco architecture, and large resident Chinese population, was also a major center for non-Chinese touring companies and European theatrical and musical performances.[52] Bandmann's companies, and many other troupes, appeared there regularly, and they frequently performed *The Merry Widow* in English in Shanghai for audiences made up of Europeans, Americans, Chinese, and individuals of other races and ethnicities.

Although Lehár's famous operetta was generally well received in Shanghai, not all reviews were entirely laudatory. For example, in 1911 the *North China Herald and Supreme Court and Consular Gazette* (27 May, 531) described the Bandmann Company's performance of *The Merry Widow* that concluded its three-week run in the International Settlement area of Shanghai (controlled by the United Kingdom and the United States). It noted that the voice of the prompter—in use because of the rapid change of different musicals—was audible to the audience. On 14 April 1917 this same expatriate newspaper reported that the company had a financial success and a full house for *The Merry Widow*, while at the same time noting that 'the company was scarcely strong enough to do justice to such a pretentious musical play as *The Merry Widow*' (77). Bandmann's Comic Opera Company also performed in several cities in the Dutch East Indies (Indonesia), giving *The Merry Widow* in English for Dutch expatriate and local Indonesian audiences. For example, on 8 August 1908 the *Bataviaasch Nieusblad* in Batavia (Jakarta) noted that the company had scheduled performances of a dozen operettas and musical comedies in Batavia in the second half of September.[53]

## *LA VIUDA ALEGRE/A VIÚVA ALEGRE/LA VEDOVA ALLEGRA* IN LATIN AMERICA

*The Merry Widow* was an audience favorite throughout Latin America.[54] It was also very popular with Spanish-speaking audiences in the United States, from Los Angeles, California, to San Antonio, Texas, Tampa, Florida, and New York City, wherever significant numbers of Latinos and Latinas resided. It was also very well-known in Brazil, in at least four different languages—Portuguese, Italian, Spanish, and German—and perhaps also in English and French. Spanish companies such as the famous Emilio Sagi-Barba operetta-zarzuela-opera troupe performed it in Spanish in Rio de Janeiro, São Paulo, and other Brazilian cities. Ettore Vitale's Italian Operetta Company appeared in Brazil on a number of occasions, as did the German-language Grande Companhia Allemã de Operetas, led by A. F. Papke. The José Ricado Company performed it in Portuguese in Brazilian cities as *A viúva alegre*. At the Teatro Solís in Montevideo, Uruguay, the operetta was performed in Italian (1909), German (1910), French (1913), and Spanish (1914).[55] As in Brazil and Uruguay, Lehár's operetta was frequently performed in multiple languages for Argentina's diverse immigrant audiences, especially in the polyglot, theatrically inclined capital city of Buenos Aires. *La viuda alegre* was also performed in Havana, Cuba, by the touring Adelaide Hermann Company in September 1908.[56]

In Mexico City *La viuda alegre* was first performed in 1909 in a reduced, approximately hour-long zarzuela version as part of the *tanda* or *teatro por horas* tradition, in which several fifty-to-sixty-minute musical theatre works such as zarzuelas and *revistas* were given as an afternoon's or evening's entertainment. The Mexican librettists José Castellanos Haaf and Alberto Michel adapted it for its 18 June 1909 Mexican première starring Amparo Romo at the famous Teatro Principal, the palace of the quickly changing *tanda*, managed by Hermanos Arcaraz.[57] On 21 June 1909 the Mexico City paper *El Diario* reported that on that same program were included dances by the company Las Argentinas and the Spanish zarzuela *Las bribonas* (1908) by Rafael Calleja Gómez (1). A few months later the English-language *Mexican Herald* commented on the benefit performance of this abbreviated one-hour version in Spanish of *La viuda alegre* given at the Teatro Principal for the victims of the recent earthquake in Acapulco and the floods in Monterrey and compared it to the full-length English-language version: 'Lehár's operetta, as rendered in Spanish, is as interesting as the English [version], although there are few points of resemblance' (18 August 1908). The Mexican president, Porfirio Díaz, attended the benefit to lend his support. In November 1908 *El Diario* noted that *La viuda alegre* was given its full-length, three-act première in Mexico City, also at the Teatro Principal, to great success (28 November, 7). This full-length production followed more closely the original three-act version of the operetta. The popularity of *The Merry Widow* in Mexico continued unabated for many years, and it is still performed there today.

# THE MERRY WIDOW IN IMMIGRANT NORTH AMERICA

Although *The Merry Widow* as presented throughout the United States and Canada during the first half of the twentieth century reached the largest audiences in the various English-language versions, countless numbers of performances in many of America's immigrant communities were also given in languages other than English. The greatest source of information about this aspect of *The Merry Widow*'s reception history resides in the very substantial non-English-language immigrant press of the period.[58]

The first US immigrant group to embrace *The Merry Widow* in a language other than English was New York City's very large German American community.[59] Soon after the impresario Henry Savage opened his English-language New York City production at the New Amsterdam Theatre in October 1907, local German companies began performing *Die lustige Witwe* in the original German-language version. One notable production was given at the intimate Orpheum Concert Garden beer hall–theatre at 134–136 East Thirteenth Street (Third Avenue and Thirteenth Street), at first without Savage's permission. It ran for all of 1908 and received extensive—and favorable—coverage in the English- and German-language press. Savage's legal position regarding the performance rights for *Die lustige Witwe* was shaky, especially in languages other than English, since at the time the United States had not yet signed the Berne Convention governing international copyright protection, and Austria-Hungary had no copyright agreement with the United States. Nonetheless, Savage threatened legal action against the managers of the Orpheum Concert Garden, even though his own agent admitted that he had no control over non-English-language performances of *Die lustige Witwe*.[60] The managers of the Orpheum reportedly settled with Savage.[61] Gustav Stickley's important turn-of-the-century

Arts and Crafts journal *The Craftsman* published a laudatory review of this company's performances that illuminates their theatrical approach and musical performance style.

> The Orpheum, on lower Third Avenue, has been giving a spirited presentation of *The Merry Widow* nearly all winter. [ ... ] The German production employs the original text, which is in a vein of comedy quite different from the peculiar brand of buffoonery and farce demanded on Broadway. [ ... ] In the American version the characters are all—with the exception of the two principals—the traditional wearisome comic opera abortions in which ambassador and prince and servant carouse on equal terms. [ ... ] Although the orchestra of the little German performance [ ... ] is composed of only six pieces besides the piano, the rendering of this fragrant midsummer night music shows a most delicate musical sense of its light rhythms. But the dancing is heavy and the women of the chorus are not pretty. They are selected for their vocal ability. [ ... ] Fräulein Thury [ ... ] [cross-dressed] takes the part of the prince [Count Danilo].[62]

Other New York German companies also put on *Die lustige Witwe*, or excerpts from the work, in German.[63] New York's huge German American population was spread out all around the city, with large concentrations in Harlem in upper Manhattan and in Yorkville on the Upper East Side, and in cities close to or part of the greater metropolitan New York City area. Lehár's operetta came to them where they lived, as it did when it was performed in the summer of 1908 at the Harlem Casino at 124th Street and Seventh Avenue on Manhattan's Upper West Side.[64] And Lehár's famous music was also used for many different occasions that stressed a sense of German *Gemütlichkeit* (warmth, coziness, good cheer) and German American pride and solidarity. In 1920 the German Volksbühne (People's Stage) of the White Rats Actors' Union, under the sponsorship of the New Jersey Gesangvereine (New Jersey German Singing Societies), performed a 'Musik Melange' of music from *Die lustige Witwe* at Becker's Atlantic Garden, in Union Hill, New Jersey.[65] The *New Yorker Volkszeitung* (25 May, 5), the long-lived socialist, pro-labor paper, announced the performance and proclaimed that '[e]very union man should support this troupe!'

Notices of productions of *The Merry Widow* in many different languages, or details of English-language productions, appeared regularly in US and Canadian immigrant-oriented newspapers before World War II. For example, in 1909 the Icelandic population of Winnipeg, Manitoba, Canada—which had the largest number of Icelanders outside of Iceland—read about the upcoming appearances in Winnipeg's Walker Theatre of Savage's *Merry Widow* touring company in both the *Winnipeg Tribune* (1 May, 10) and in their own local Winnipeg Icelandic-language newspaper, *Lögberg* (6 May, 5).[66] In 1911 Chicago's Danish-language Scandinavian Theatre Company presented Lehár's operetta as *Den glade Enke* (*Revyen*, 8 April, 4), and performances in Swedish were given in Swedish communities in the Upper Midwest. *Denní Hlasatel* (16 February 1922), Chicago's major Czech-language newspaper, noted that because of the tremendous success of *Veselá Vdoya*, the National Bohemian-American Theatre decided to reprise Lehár's operetta, starring their own local Chicago Czech soprano, Mařenka Havelka, as Hanna and their stage manager, Mr. V. Havelka (her husband), as Danilo.

Besides German American companies, the immigrant theatrical groups that seemed to have performed *The Merry Widow* most often were touring and resident Mexican and Italian troupes. In the 1910s the fifty-member Compañia Mexicana de Operetas (Mexican Operetta Company), led by Ricardo de la Vega, performed frequently in venues throughout the American southwest and northern Mexico, including the Texas border cities of El Paso and Laredo. They included *La viuda alegre* in their regular touring repertory of Viennese and other European operettas, along with Spanish and Mexican zarzuelas.[67] One of the most important Mexican American companies performing *La viuda alegre* for enthusiastic Spanish-speaking immigrant working-class audiences was the troupe led by Romualdo Tirado, who was a leading light of Los Angeles's very active Mexican musical theatre scene in the 1920s and 1930s.[68] Tirado frequently appeared as a dashing Conde Danilo (Count Danilo) in *La viuda alegre* throughout California. On 27 December 1920 the *Calexico Chronicle* (Calexico, California, 2) announced that Tirado and his operetta-zarzuela company would perform *La viuda alegre* in 'the splendid new theatre' in Calexico's cross-border Mexican sister city Mexicali (in the northern Mexican state of Baja California).

Numerous Italian companies performed *La vedova allegra* before World War II in Italian American communities throughout the United States, and they celebrated their Italian American heritage in doing so. For example, in 1917 the Eduardo Migliaccio ('Farfariello') Company performed *La vedova allegra* at the Teatro Liberty in San Francisco's famed North Beach Italian American neighborhood (*L'Italia*, 25 September, 5). In 1918 his company performed *La vedova allegra* and other German-language operettas in Italian for Italian American fishermen, tuna cannery employees, and their families living in Fish Harbor at the southern California port of San Pedro (part of the city of Los Angeles).[69] In San Jose, California in 1920 the Italian Compagnia La Moderna Opera presented Lehár's work at the Victory Theatre (*San Jose Evening News*, 24 January, 2). And in 1929 *La Sentinella* of Bridgeport, Connecticut reported that the 'Compagnia Magni will delight our colony with their performance of *La vedova allegra* in Columbus Auditorium in Stamford, Connecticut' (23 November, 5).

## PARODIES AND REFUNCTIONINGS

In addition to the fervor and enthusiasm with which *The Merry Widow* has been received in live performance in hundreds of cities around the world over more than a century, the operetta has also caught the attention of a global public through a wide range of productions and products, perhaps more than almost any other musical. These refunctionings include stage and silent film parodies and adaptations, sheet music tie-ins, commercial recordings, pianola rolls, music box tunes, several musical sound film and television versions, YouTube clips, and other reuses.

Among the first commercial tie-ins to *The Merry Widow* were the stage parodies—listed in Table 4.4—that began to appear in 1906, the year after the operetta's world première, and that seem to have ended about 1914, when the fashion for stage parodies of *The Merry Widow*

**Table 4.4  *Merry Widow*–Related Stage Parodies, 1906–1914[a]**

| Première | City/country | Title/translation | Composer/librettist(s) | Additional information |
|---|---|---|---|---|
| 1906 | Germany | *Die lustige Witwe in ihrer zweiten Ehe* (*The Merry Widow's Second Marriage*) | A. Robert and K. Leopold | Play? |
| 1/1907 | Vienna, Austria | *Mitislaw der Moderne* (*Fashionable Mitislaw*) | Franz Lehár/Fritz Grünbaum and Robert Bodanzky | Play? |
| ca. 1907 | Germany | *Der lustige Witwer* (*The Merry Widower*) | J. Jarno and H. Fischer | Play? |
| 2 January 1908 | New York, USA | *Merry Widow Burlesque* | Franz Lehár/George V. Hobart | Opened at Weber's Theatre; produced by Joseph Weber |
| August 1908 | Germany | *Die lästige Witwe* (*The Annoying Widow*) | | Play? |
| 1908 | USA | *Merry Kiddow and the Widow* | | Play? |
| 11/1908; 1/1909 | New York, USA | *The Merry Widow and the Devil* | Franz Lehár et al./George V. Hobart | Played first at the West End Theatre, later at Weber's Music Hall; produced by Joseph Weber |
| 21 July 1909 | Madrid | *Dora, la viuda alegre* (*Dora, the Merry Widow*) | Franz Lehár/Felipe Pérez Capo | Opened at the Gran Teatro; also played Mexico City in Fall 1909 |
| November 1909 | Mexico City, Mexico | *El viudo triste* (*The Sad Widower*) | | Opened at the Teatro Lírico |
| 17 July 1909 | Madrid, Spain | *La viuda mucho más alegre* (*The Much Merrier Widow*) | Álvarez del Castillo/Luis Pascual Frutos | Opened at the Teatro Cómico |
| 1909 | USA | *The Merry Widow Remarried* (*Die Lustige Witwe in zweiter Ehe*) | Carl von Wegern/Max Hanisch | Operetta; English and German versions |
| 1911 | Spain | *Flora, la viuda verde* (*Flora, the Naughty Widow*) | Francisco A. de San Felipe and Cayo Vela/Federico Riera | Musical parody of *Dora, la viuda alegre* |
| 1912 | France | *Ni veuve, ni joyeuse* (*Neither a Widow Nor Merry*) | Paul Fauchey/Altéry and Paul Gordeaux | Operetta |
| 1914 | USA | *The Swede and the Merry Widow* | Alfred Thomas | Toured in Upper Midwest, United States |

[a] Sources used include online catalogues of Biblioteca Nacional de España and Biblioteca Nacional de México; *Deutscher Bühnen-Spielplan* (1907–1911); Internet Broadway Database; and Richard C. Norton, *A Chronology of American Musical Theater*, 3 vols. (New York: Oxford University Press, 2002).

seems to have waned. Some of these parodies reused and reworked the music and plot of the original operetta, while others only made reference to the work in their titles and some plot aspects. Franz Lehár even wrote his own parody of *Die lustige Witwe*, titled *Mitislaw der Moderne* (Fashionable Mitislaw), which premiered in 1907. One of the most successful of the authorized stage parodies was Joe Weber's very popular *Merry Widow Burlesque*, which opened in New York's Weber's Theatre on 2 January 1908 and used Lehár's original music. Baron Zeta (Baron Popoff) became Baron Copoff, the Farsovian ambassador in Paris; Count Danilo became Prince Dandilo, a waiter at Maxim's; and Sonia/Hanna became Fonia, the richest woman in Farsovia. It was a riot and ran for 156 performances in New York; it also played successfully in Chicago at the Colonial Theatre after opening there on 18 May 1909.[70]

Less than a year after *Die lustige Witwe* opened in Vienna in December 1905, the first of the motion-picture adaptations of the work appeared as *Den glade Enke* in a short film released in Denmark in November 1906 by the film company Nordisk. Many film and television versions would follow. Most of the silent film adaptations, excerpts, or parodies were released without permission of Lehár or his librettists, their publisher, or the different rights holders that controlled the work in various parts of the world. Laws governing copyright and performance rights and royalties varied widely from country to country, so the very successful and commercially valuable music and libretto of *The Merry Widow* were highly susceptible to piracy and unauthorized uses, despite the best efforts of the various rights holders. Table 4.5 lists these film and television releases and includes adaptations and film parodies. (It does not include filmed live opera house performances, however.) As with the stage parodies, the film parodies or adaptations capitalized on the great popularity of *The Merry Widow* by making reference to the operetta's title and/or plot in their own titles or stories.

Two notable examples demonstrate the quick spread of *The Merry Widow* throughout the world via the medium of film. In December 1907 the Kalem Company released a 1,000-foot version filmed by the cast of a local New York City German operetta company and starring the soprano Nellie Morena. This version was distributed nationally and was billed falsely as featuring the original Viennese cast.[71] Savage fought back and succeeded in having the film suppressed for a time.

An early Brazilian film adaptation of *A viúva alegre* was directed by Júlio Ferrez and released by William & Cia. in 1909. A notice published in the newspaper *O Norte* in Parahyba do Norte (Paraíba state) on 24 September 1911 advertised that *A viúva alegre* would be shown at the Cinema Pathé as a form of *cinema fallante* (talking picture), with live musical accompaniment 'sung and spoken' by numerous artists. *O Norte* also reported that this *Merry Widow* silent film version with live musical accompaniment had been 'shown 856 times in Rio de Janeiro'.

Lehár's very popular work probably has had more film and television adaptations and parodies than any other musical. The most important, most artistic, and best loved of the musical film adaptations is director Ernst Lubitsch's 1934 MGM film version, starring Jeanette MacDonald and Maurice Chevalier (also released in a French-language version directed by Lubitsch with these same Hollywood stars). However, Lubitsch's version, like the director Erich von Stroheim's highly eroticized 1925 MGM silent film adaptation, takes liberties with the original libretto and story. (Von Stroheim's version includes

**Table 4.5** *Merry Widow*–Related Films and TV Broadcasts[a]

| Released/broadcast | Country | Title (translation) | Medium | Director | Producer/series | Additional information |
|---|---|---|---|---|---|---|
| November 1906 | Denmark | *Den glade Enke* | Film | Viggo Larsen | Nordisk | Excerpts |
| August 1907 | Sweden | *Den glade änkan* | Film | | Apollo Film Company | Excerpts |
| November 1907 | Germany | *Ballsirenenwalzer aus Die lustige Witwe* (*The Merry Widow Waltz*) | Film | | Deutsche Bioscope-Film | Excerpts |
| 28 December 1907 | USA | *The Merry Widow* | Film | | Kalem | Excerpts |
| September 1907 | Denmark | *Den glade Enke* | Film | Viggo Larsen | Nordisk | Excerpts |
| 1907 | Brazil | *A viúva alegre* | Film | | | Excerpts |
| April 1908 | USA | *The Merry Widow Waltz Craze* | Film | | Edison | Parody |
| April 1908 | USA | *The Merry Widow at a Supper Party* | Film | | American Mutuoscope; Biograph Co. | Parody |
| May 1908 | USA | *The 'Merry Widow' Hats* | Film | | Lubin Films | Parody |
| August 1908 | USA | *The Merry Widower, or, The Rejuvenation of a Fossil* | Film | | Vitagraph | Parody |
| October 1908 | USA | *The Merry Widow Hat* | Film | | Vitagraph | Parody |
| 1908 | France | *La valse de La Veuve joyeuse* (*The Merry Widow Waltz*) | Film | Ferdinand Zecca | Pathé Frères | Excerpts |
| May 1909 | UK | *Won't You Waltz the Merry Widow Waltz with Me?* | Film | | Warwick Trading Company | Parody |
| 1909 | Brazil | *A viúva alegre* | Film | Júlio Ferrez | William & Cia. | Excerpts |

(*continued*)

**Table 4.5 Continued**

| Released/broadcast | Country | Title (translation) | Medium | Director | Producer/series | Additional information |
|---|---|---|---|---|---|---|
| 1909 | Brazil | *Valsa da Viúva alegre* (*The Merry Widow Waltz*) | Film | Júlio Ferrez | William & Cia. | Excerpts |
| March 1910 | USA | *The Courting of the Merry Widow* | Film | | Vitagraph | Parody |
| April 1910 | USA | *The Merry Widower Takes Another Partner* | Film | | Vitagraph | Parody |
| 1910 | Brazil | *O viúvo alegre* (*The Merry Widower*) | Film | | | Parody |
| 1912 | Hungary | *Víg Özvegy* | Film | Sándor Góth | | Excerpts |
| January 1913 | France | *La Veuve joyeuse* | Film | Émile Chautard | Société Française des Films Éclair | Excerpts |
| 1920 | Germany | *Der lustige Witwer* (*The Merry Widower*) | Film | Heinrich Bolten-Baecker | BB-Film-Fabrikation | Parody |
| 1920 | Hungary | *A Víg Özvegy* | Film | Michael Curtiz | Semper Filmvállalat | Excerpts |
| 1925 | USA | *The Merry Widow* | Film | Erich von Stroheim | MGM | Silent film adaptation |
| November 1934 | USA | *The Merry Widow* | Film | Ernst Lubitsch | MGM | Musical film adaptation |
| December 1934 | USA | *La Veuve joyeuse* | Film | Ernst Lubitsch | MGM | Musical film adaptation; in French |
| 1941 | Philippines | *Ang viuda alegre* | Film | Enrique H. Davila | X-Otic Films | Musical film adaptation; in Tagalog |
| October 1950 | USA | *The Merry Widow* | TV | | *Musical Comedy Time Show* series | Musical Adaptation |
| September 1952 | USA | *The Merry Widow* | Film | Curtis Bernhardt | MGM | Musical film adaptation |

| 1952 | Brazil | *A viúva alegre* | TV | | | Musical adaptation; in Portuguese |
|------|--------|------------------|-----|---|---|------------------------------------|
| 1952 | USA | *The Merry Widow* | TV | | | Musical Adaptation |
| December 1955 | USA | *The Merry Widow* | TV | | *Omnibus Series* | Musical adaptation |
| 1955 | USA | *The Merry Widow* | TV | | Max Liebman | |
| | | | | | | Musical adaptation; dialogue by Neil Simon and others |
| 1958 | Germany | *Die lustige Witwe* | TV | | | Musical adaptation |
| April 1959 | UK | *The Merry Widow* | TV | Charles Hickman | BBC | Musical adaptation |
| 1959 | UK | *The Merry Widow* | TV | Mark Lawton | | Musical adaptation |
| 1961 | Egypt | *Al-Armalah al-taroub* | TV | | Cairo Opera House | Musical adaptation; in Arabic |
| December 1962 | Austria | *Die lustige Witwe* | Film | Werner Jacobs | Wien-Film | Musical film adaptation |
| 1963 | Italy | *La vedova allegra* | TV | | RAI | Musical adaptation; in Italian |
| 1968 | UK | *The Merry Widow* | TV | John Gorrie | BBC | Musical adaptation |
| 1968 | Italy | *La vedova allegra* | TV | Antonello Falqui | RAI | Musical adaptation; in Italian |

[a] Film and TV adaptations listed here were in English, unless silent versions or otherwise indicated. Sources used include AFI Catalog, American Film Institute, https://aficatalog.afi.com; Internet Broadway Database, www.imdb.com; and YouTube.

FIG. 4.5 Italian postcard of the 1925 MGM screen adaptation of *The Merry Widow* (*La vedova allegra*), directed by Erich von Stroheim, with John Gilbert as Count Danilo and Grisettes. Postcard provided by the author.

only about one-third of the original plot.) The Broadway songwriting team of Richard Rodgers and Lorenz Hart contributed new material to MGM's 1934 film version. MGM's 1952 film version starred Lana Turner as the American-born widow Crystal Radek and Fernando Lamas as Count Danilo; it retained only the basic plot elements of the original stage version. When *The Merry Widow* was adapted for television beginning in the 1950s, additional liberties were taken to fit the new medium, although Lehár's music continued to shine through, even if the original libretto was changed and often truncated. The famous American playwright Neil Simon got his start in television by adapting the libretti for classic operettas in reduced versions for the producer Max Liebman, including a 1955 television broadcast of *The Merry Widow* (available today on DVD).[72]

*The Merry Widow* has been parodied in other ways as well. Several leading composers have included ironic or parodistic references to the music of Lehár's famous operetta in their works. Dimitri Tiomkin included its famous waltz as a recurring, ominous motive in his score to Alfred Hitchcock's classic 1943 film *Shadow of a Doubt*. In 1942 the Hungarian composer Béla Bartók heard a radio broadcast of Dimitri Shostakovich's Symphony No. 7, the 'Leningrad', conducted by Arturo Toscanini. As Richard Taruskin explains, Bartók was so enraged by Shostakovich's work that he parodied its 'invasion' theme (which resembles a section from *Die lustige Witwe*), heard multiple times in Shostakovich's first movement, in the fourth movement of his own Concerto for Orchestra (1943). Bartók claimed he was quoting Danilo's song 'Da geh' ich zu Maxim' ('I'm Off to Chez Maxime') from *Die lustige Witwe*, the melody that according to Taruskin 'may in fact have served as Shostakovich's model for caricaturing the Nazis.'[73]

## WALTZING ALONG

Over the decades, the role of Hanna Glawari has attracted the attention of many operatic sopranos, who have performed the role of the Widow in both opera houses and commercial theatres, on tour around the globe, and in the television and recording studio. Some of the most prominent operatic Hannas/Sonias include Marta Eggerth, Ratiba El-Hefny, Maria Jeritza, Dorothy Kirsten, Anna Moffo, Patrice Munsel, Roberta Peters, Elisabeth Schwarzkopf, Beverly Sills, Risë Stevens, and Joan Sutherland.[74]

FIG. 4.6 Joan Sutherland taking a curtain bow after performing in the 1989 Dallas production of *The Merry Widow*. Photo: Photo: Ira Nowinski/Corbis/VCT © Getty Images.

**Table 4.6 *The Merry Widow* in the Opera House**

| Company | City | Country | Company | City | Country |
| --- | --- | --- | --- | --- | --- |
| Cairo Opera House | Cairo | Egypt | Opera Australia | Sydney | Australia |
| Dubai Opera House | Dubai | United Arab Emirates | Opéra National de Lyon | Lyon | France |
| Edmonton Opera | Edmonton | Canada | Opera North | Leeds | UK |
| English National Opera | London | UK | Opera Saratoga | Saratoga | USA |
| Gran Teatre del Liceu | Barcelona | Spain | San Francisco Opera | San Francisco | USA |
| Grand Théâtre de Genève | Geneva | Switzerland | Santa Fe Opera | Santa Fe | USA |
| Hungarian State Opera | Budapest | Hungary | Seefestspiele Mörbisch | Mörbisch | Austria |
| Lithuanian National Opera | Vilnius | Lithuania | Semperoper | Dresden | Germany |
| Los Angeles Opera | Los Angeles | USA | State Opera of South Australia | Adelaide | Australia |
| Lyric Opera of Chicago | Chicago | USA | Tacoma Opera | Tacoma | USA |
| Metropolitan Opera | New York | USA | Teatro del Bicentenario | Guanajuato | Mexico |
| New York City Opera | New York | USA | Theatro Municipal | Rio de Janeiro | Brazil |
| Northwest Opera Spokane | Spokane | USA | Vancouver Opera | Vancouver | Canada |
| Ohio Light Opera | Wooster | USA | Wichita Grand Opera | Witchita | USA |
| Opéra Bastille, Opéra National de Paris | Paris | France | Zurich Opera House | Zurich | Switzerland |

The Metropolitan Opera in New York, whose main operetta production has always been Johann Strauss's frothy comic *Die Fledermaus* of 1874 (226 performances at the Met since 1905), has in recent decades also presented *The Merry Widow* (forty times since 2000), with the soprano Renée Fleming and the mezzo-sopranos Susan Graham and Frederika von Stade taking turns as the Widow.[75] Table 4.6 lists some of the opera houses throughout the world that have performed *The Merry Widow* in recent decades. It shows the global reach and appeal of this operetta and that the opera house is today one of the main venues for performances of the work, in addition to the many community, regional, and college and university opera theatre productions each year. These opera houses (and other companies) perform *The Merry Widow* in different languages, venues, performing styles, and stagings, but they retain most or all of Franz Lehár's original music.

More than 115 years after its première, and despite—or because of—the many adaptations, reworkings, refunctionings, tie-ins, and other forms of extensive exploitation of Franz Lehár's *Die lustige Witwe*, the work is still a very successful musical, theatrical, and commercial property, performed today throughout the world. *The Merry Widow* continues to enchant audiences and to represent the practice of the globalisation of musical theatre that the work began more than a century ago and that continues unabated today.

# DIGITAL NEWSPAPER SOURCES

- California Digital Newspaper Collection, University of California, Riverside, https://cdnc.ucr.edu
- Chicago Foreign Press Survey, Newberry Library, translated transcripts from non-English-language Chicago newspapers, https://flps.newberry.org
- Chronicling America: Historic American Newspapers, Library of Congress, https://chroniclingamerica.loc.gov
- Cuban Newspapers and Periodicals, University of Florida, Digital Library of the Caribbean, *El Diario de la Marina* (Havana), https://dloc.com/UF00001565/02436
- Delpher, Dutch and Dutch colonial newspapers, https://www.delpher.nl/nl/kranten/
- Digital Brasileira, Biblioteca Nacional Brazil, Brazilian newspapers, http://bndigital.bn.gov.br
- Gallica, Bibliothèque nationale de France, French and French colonial newspapers, https://gallica.bnf.fr
- Genealogybank.com, US newspapers, https://genealogybank.com
- Hemeroteca Nacional Digital de México, Biblioteca Nacional de México, Mexican newspapers, http://www.hndm.unam.mx/index.php/es/

- National Library of Australia, Australian newspapers, https://trove.nla.gov.au/newspaper/
- Newspapers.com, US newspapers, http://newspapers.com
- NewspapersSG, Singapore newspapers, http://eresources.nlb.gov.sg/newspapers/
- Papers Past, New Zealand newspapers, https://paperspast.natlib.govt.nz/newspapers
- Texas Digital Newspaper Program, The Portal to Texas History, University of North Texas, Texas newspapers, https://texashistory.unt.edu/explore/collections/TDNP/
- ProQuest Historical Newspapers: Chinese Newspaper Collection (including Hong Kong)
- ProQuest Historical Newspapers: South Asian Newspaper Collection
- Timarit.is, newspapers from Iceland, Greenland, Faroe Islands, and Canada (Canadian Icelandic papers only), http://timarit.is
- University of Manitoba, UM Digital Collections, *Winnipeg Tribune*, https://digitalcollections.lib.umanitoba.ca/islandora/object/uofm:1243378

## NOTES

1. For some early Viennese press coverage of the première of *Die lustige Witwe*, see 'Theater und Musik', *Wiener Zeitung*, 2 January 1906, 10; H. H., 'Theater, Kunst und Literatur', *Sport & Salon*, 6 January 1906, 7; and *Le Figaro*, 6 January 1907, 7. According to one Viennese newspaper, *Die lustige Witwe*'s 'great success was due to its extraordinarily graceful music and colorful instrumentation'. *Wiener Sonn- und Montags Zeitung*, 1 January 1906, 7.

2. Henry T. Finck, *Success in Music and How It Is Won* (New York: Charles Scribner's Sons, 1913), 15; and '*The Merry Widow* Making a Million', *New York Times*, 22 December 1910, C8.

3. Stefan Frey, *Was sagt ihr zu diesem Erfolg: Franz Lehar und die Unterhaltungsmusik des 20. Jahrhunderts* (Frankfurt: Insel, 1999), 91. It is difficult to establish a close estimate of the number of performances of *The Merry Widow* given since its 1905 première, although the Lehár biographer Bernard Grun guessed that it was performed about half a million times in its first sixty years. Bernard Grun, *Gold and Silver: The Life and Times of Franz Lehár* (London: W. H. Allen, 1970), 129. However, there are accurate performance statistics for German-speaking Europe, not including Berlin. For example, 441 performances were given from December 1905 through to August 1906. In the season from September 1906 through to August 1907 alone, the operetta was scheduled 2,738 times. Later performances numbered 1,778 (1907–1908), 671 (1908–1909), and 309 (1909–1910), according to the *Deutscher Bühnen-Spielplan* (Leipzig: Breitkopf & Härtel, 1906–1908), 1910–1911.

4. Marlis Schweitzer, '"Darn That Merry Widow Hat": The On- and Offstage Life of a Theatrical Commodity', *Theatre Survey* 50, no. 2 (2009): 189–221.

5. The J. C. Williamson Royal Comic Opera Company gave the Australian première of *The Merry Widow* at Her Majesty's Theatre, Melbourne, on 16 May 1908. 'Her Majesty's

Theatre', *Argus* (Melbourne), 18 May 1908, 9. See also Veronica Kelly, 'Australasia: Mapping a Theatrical "Region" in Peace and War', *Journal of Global Theatre History* 1, no. 1 (2016): 62–77.

6. J. C. Williamson presented the New Zealand première at the Wellington Opera House on 10 April 1909; see the announcements in the *New Zealand Times*, 2 April 1909, 7–8.

7. *La Veuve joyeuse* was performed in French colonial Vietnam in the opera houses in Hanoi and Saigon. A pair of contrasting newspaper reviews appeared in the same periodical, dated two days apart: 'The striking production of *La Veuve joyeuse* will be repeated, with the Saigon debut of Mlle Paule France, our golden voice singer, as the widow' ('Chronique théâtrale', *L'Echo annamite* (Saigon), 10 December 1928, 6); and 'Mlle. France is a good comedienne, but it is too bad that her voice was not up to the task in *La Veuve joyeuse*' ('Chronique théâtrale', *L'Echo annamite*, 12 December 1928, 5). See also *La Plume indochinoise* (Hanoi), 1 April 1913, 272, as well as Michael E. McClellan, 'Performing Empire: Opera in Colonial Hanoi', *Journal of Musicological Research* 22 (2003): 135–166.

8. From at least 1908 through the 1920s, the Maurice Bandmann Company performed *The Merry Widow* in English innumerable times on tour to Hong Kong, Singapore, Burma (Myanmar), Japan, China, India, and the Dutch East Indies (Indonesia), as well as other locations.

9. Although it was not the Cairo première of Lehár's operetta, an Arabic-language *Merry Widow* was produced at the old Cairo Opera House that was also broadcast on Egyptian television in 1961. The prominent Egyptian operatic soprano Ratiba El-Hefny (1931–2013) starred as Hanna, and the Iraqi actor-singer Kanaan Wasfi (1932–1992) was her Danilo. Since then, *The Merry Widow* has returned to Cairo.

10. *The Merry Widow* appeared in South Africa and in other locations in Africa. For example, it was performed in Victoria Falls in 1908 and 1910 by European touring companies. *New Zealand Herald* (Auckland), 8 August 1908, 16; 'Die lustige Witwe am Zambesi', *Berliner Tageblatt*, 22 February 1910, 3; and John Creewel, *90 Glorious Years: A History of the Victoria Falls Hotel* (Harare: Harper Collins Zimbabwe, 1994), 29. Victoria Falls, on the Zambezi River, then in the British colony of Northern Rhodesia and now in Zimbabwe along its border with Zambia, was long a tourist site with a famous tourist hotel that opened in 1904, and it was connected to the never-completed British Cape-to-Cairo Railway. It 'became a symbol of British Southern Africa's aspirations'; Andrea L. Arrington-Sirois, *Victoria Falls and Colonial Imagination in British Southern Africa* (New York: Palgrave Macmillan, 2017), 11.

11. The *Canton Repository* (Canton, Ohio) noted on 2 February 1908 (on p. 9) that *The Merry Widow* was being performed in eleven different languages 'in over 300 cities throughout the world'.

12. Tobias Becker, 'Globalizing Operetta before the First World War', *Opera Quarterly* 33, no. 1 (2017): 7–27; here: 23.

13. Mitzi Günther and Louis Treumann, the original Hanna and Danilo in the 1905 Viennese cast, recorded eight songs from *Die lustige Witwe* on 10-inch discs for Deutsche Grammophon in 1906. That this record album traveled far and wide was noted in the 11 March 1909 advertisement for the set published in *De Preanger-bode*, in Bandoeng, Dutch East Indies (Indonesia). Original 1906 and 1907 creator recordings from *Die lustige Witwe* were re-released by Christian Zwarg on his Truesound Transfers compact disc set TT 4014.

148   JOHN KOEGEL

14. Victor Léon (né Victor Hirschfeld, 1858–1940) and Leo Stein (né Leo Rosenstein, 1861–1921), separately or together, wrote operetta libretti for Lehár, Johann Strauss II, Emmerich Kálmán, and Leo Fall, among others. See Paul D. Seeley, 'Franz Lehár: Aspects of His Life with a Critical Survey of His Operettas and the Work of His Jewish Librettists' (PhD diss., University of Liverpool, 2004). Léon and Stein's knowledge of the history of the real Montenegro and its customs, folklore, and poetry is reflected in their famous operetta.

15. Henri Meilhac, *L'Attaché d'ambassade* (Paris: Michel Lévy Fréres, 1861).

16. For a profile of the Montenegrin Crown Prince Danilo Petrović-Njegoš (1871–1939) and the Balkan connections to *Die lustige Witwe*, see Jelena Milojković-Djurić, 'Franz Lehár's *The Merry Widow*: Revisiting Pontevedro', *Serbian Studies* 25, no. 2 (2011): 259–272. The first Hanna and Danilo, Mitzi Günther and Louis Treumann, dressed in traditional Montenegrin costume on stage. Treumann looked very much like the real Prince Danilo, who often visited Paris and appeared in Montenegrin apparel.

17. For more information about the composer, see Ernst Decsey, *Franz Lehár* (Berlin: Drei Masken Vertlag, 1930); Maria von Peteani, *Franz Lehár: Seine Musik, sein Leben* (Vienna: Gloken Verlag, 1950); W. MacQueen-Pope and D. L. Murray, *Fortune's Favourite: The Life and Times of Franz Lehár* (London: Hutchinson, 1952); Stefan (Stan) Czech, *Schön ist die Welt: Franz Lehárs Leben und Werk* (Berlin: Argon Verlag, 1957); Grun, *Gold and Silver*; Otto Schneidereit, *Franz Lehár: Eine Biographie in Zitaten* (Berlin: Lied der Zeit, 1984); Edward Michael Gold, 'On the Significance of Franz Lehár's Operettas: A Musical-Analytical Study' (PhD diss., New York University, 1993); Stefan Frey, *Franz Lehár, oder das schlechte Gewissen der leichten Musik* (Berlin: De Gruyter, 1995); and Franz Endler, *Immer nur lächeln . . . : Franz Lehár, Sein Leben—Sein Werk* (Munich: Wilhelm Heyne Verlag, 1998).

18. 'Dvořák sagte mir damals, ich solle die Geige an den Nagel hängen und mich nur der Komposition widmen'. Franz Lehár, 'Vom Schreibtisch und aus dem Atelier: Bis zur Lustigen Witwe', *Velhagen & Klasings Monathefte* 26, no. 6 (1912): 212–216; here: 212.

19. Friedrich Anzenberger, '"Vom Passionswege des Komponisten": Ein bisher unbekannter Text Franz Lehárs zur Rezeption seines Schaffens', *Die Musikforschung* 48, no. 2 (1995): 167–168.

20. 'Mit der *Lustigen Witwe* hatte ich meinen Stil gefunden, den ich in meinen seitherigen Werken zu vervollkommnen trachte'. Lehár, 'Vom Schreibtisch und aus dem Atelier', 216.

21. According to Grun, a certain type of 'orchestral colouring, as used till now only by Richard Strauss, Mahler, or Debussy, suddenly became part of the operetta palette' (*Gold and Silver*, 120). See also Gold, 'On the Significance of Franz Lehár's Operettas', 87–88.

22. Micaela Baranello, '*Die lustige Witwe* and the Creation of the Silver Age of Viennese Operetta', *Cambridge Opera Journal* 26, no. 2 (2014): 175–202; here: 192.

23. Ibid., 189–190.

24. Czech, *Schön ist die Welt*, 121 and 126, quoted in translation in Henry-Louis de La Grange, *Gustav Mahler*, vol. 3, *Vienna: Triumph and Disillusion (1904–1907)* (New York: Oxford University Press, 1999), 476.

25. Grun, *Gold and Silver*, 119.

26. La Grange, *Gustav Mahler*, 473–476.

27. Siegfried Kracauer, *Offenbach and the Paris of His Time* (London: Constable, 1937), and Richard Traubner, *Operetta: A Theatrical History* (Garden City, NY: Doubleday, 1983;

later eds., New York and London: Oxford University Press, 1989; New York: Routledge, 2003, 2016).

28. The Hungarian historian Péter Hanák (1921–1997), for example, found operetta of interest while at the same time ironically—and unfairly—damning it artistically: 'Operetta is one of the most rewarding topics of cultural history. Imagine a performance in an average musical theater. Its libretto is primitive and silly (if not idiotic), unbelievable, and ridiculous. Its music is a mélange of cheap opera arias and fashionable dance music full of sentimental commonplaces and a few melodious hits for everyone to whistle at home'. Péter Hanák, *The Garden and the Workshop: Essays on the Cultural History of Vienna and Budapest* (Princeton, NJ: Princeton University Press, 1998), 135.

29. Michael Heinemann points out that '[t]he caution with respect to operetta in academic musicology is not only due to prejudices against the genre itself, but also because descriptions and analyses of the score and libretto are insufficient for an adequate construction of a work's reception history'. Michael Heinemann, 'Das Erlebnis Operette: Zur Historizität von Performanz', *Archiv für Musikwissenschaft* 73, no. 4 (2016): 250–263; here: abstract. This prejudice against operetta has lessened, as evidenced especially by the recent publication of Derek B. Scott's seminal book *German Operetta on Broadway and in the West End, 1900–1940* (Cambridge: Cambridge University Press, 2019), and by Anastasia Belina and Derek B. Scott, eds., *The Cambridge Companion to Operetta* (Cambridge: Cambridge University Press, 2019).

30. Although Baranello describes the scholarly literature on operetta as 'scant', it is indeed growing; Baranello, '*Die lustige Witwe* and the Creation of the Silver Age of Viennese Operetta', 176. A short list of recent books on operetta includes Moritz Csáky, *Ideologie der Operette und Wiener Moderne: Ein kulturhistorischer Essay zur österreichischen Identität* (Vienna: Böhlau, 1996); Marion Linhardt, '*Warum es der Operette so schlecht geht'*: *Ideologische Debatten um das musikalische Unterhaltungstheater (1880–1916)* (Vienna: Böhlau, 2001); Kevin Clarke, ed., *Glitter and Be Gay: Die authentische Operette und ihre schwulen Verehrer* (Hamburg: Männerschwarm Verlag, 2007); William A. Everett, *Sigmund Romberg* (New Haven, CT: Yale University Press, 2007); William A. Everett, *Rudolf Friml* (Urbana: University of Illinois Press, 2008); Len Platt, Tobias Becker and David Linton, eds., *Popular Musical Theatre in London and Berlin 1890 to 1939* (Cambridge: Cambridge University Press, 2014); Albert Gier, *Poetik und Dramaturgie der komischen Operette* (Bamberg: University of Bamberg Press, 2014); and Bettina Brandl-Risi, Clemens Risi and Rainer Simon, *Kunst der Oberfläche: Operette zwischen Bravour und Banalität* (Leipzig: Henschel Verlag, 2015).

31. See Alain Duault, ed., 'Franz Lehár: *La Veuve joyeuse*', *L'avant-scène: Opéra, opérette, musique* 45 (1982): 1–139; Carl Dahlhaus, 'Zur musikalischen Dramaturgie der *Lustigen Witwe*', *Österreichische Musikzeitschrift* 12, no. 40 (1985): 657–664; Franz Anton Meyer, *Lehár—Die lustige Witwe: Der Ernst der leichten Muse* (Vienna: Edition Steinbauer, 2005); and *Weiber, Weiber, Weiber, Weib! Ach! 100 Jahre Die lustige Witwe* (Vienna: Wiener Stadt- und Landesbibliothek, 2005).

32. Baranello, '*Die lustige Witwe* and the Creation of the Silver Age of Viennese Operetta'.

33. Kiril Tomoff, 'Of Gypsy Barons and the Power of Love: Operetta Programming and Popularity in the Postwar Soviet Union', *Cambridge Opera Journal* 30, no. 1 (2018): 29–59. The classic text on real and imaginary themes on the Balkans in literature and theatre is Vesny Goldsworthy, *Inventing Ruritania: The Imperialism of the Imagination*, rev. ed. (London: Hurst, 2013).

34. Becker, 'Globalizing Operetta before the First World War'. On globalisation in theatre, see Rustom Bharucha, *The Politics of Cultural Practice: Thinking through Theatre in an Age of Globalization* (Hanover, NH: Wesleyan University Press, 2000); and Dan Rebellato, *Theatre and Globalization* (New York: Palgrave Macmillan, 2009).

35. Stefan Schmidl, '"Dort ist die ganze Welt noch rotweißgrün!" Diskurse über Kollektive, Alteritäten und Nation in der Operette Österreich-Ungarns', *Studia Musicologica* 52, no. 1–4 (2011): 109–121; here: abstract.

36. Platt, Becker and Linton, *Popular Musical Theatre in London and Berlin 1890 to 1939*.

37. Lawrence Senelick, 'Musical Theatre as a Paradigm of Translocation', *Journal of Global Theatre History* 2, no. 1 (2017): 22–36.

38. Some writers on musical theatre believe that Budapest saw the first non-German-language performance of *Die lustige Witwe*. However, Copenhagen was the more likely city; the work was given at the Casino Theatre on 18 August 1906. See *Den glade Enke*, http://wayback-01.kb.dk/wayback/20100902125838/http://www2.kb.dk/kb/dept/nbo/ma/fokus/enke.htm,, accessed 5 January 2020.

39. Kurt Gänzl, 'Die lustige Witwe', in *The Encyclopedia of the Musical Theatre*, 2nd ed., 3 vols. (New York: Schirmer Books, 2001), 2: 1270–1275; here: 2:1272. For performance information about *The Merry Widow*, see Frey, *Was sagt ihr zu diesem Erfolg*, 87–103, 395–398.

40. William Boosey, *Fifty Years of Music* (London: Ernest Benn, 1931), 166–169.

41. Brown v. Select Theatres Corporation, Title (Related Documents), File SJJA-2, Show Series, *The Merry Widow*, Box 105, Shubert Archive, New York.

42. Purchase of rights: District Court of the United States, District of Massachusetts, Daniel E. Brown v. Select Theatres Corporation, Findings of Fact and Conclusions of Law, 30 June 1944, p. 2; legal document in Trials and Settlement Papers folder, Show Series, *The Merry Widow*, Box 105, Shubert Archive, New York. London première: Thomas Postlewait, 'George Edwardes and Musical Comedy: The Transformation of London Theatre and Society, 1878–1914', in *The Performing Century: Nineteenth-Century Theatre's History*, ed. Tracy C. Davis and Peter Holland, 80–102 (Basingstoke and New York: Palgrave Macmillan, 2007).

43. Brown v. Select Theatres Corporation, Title (Related Documents), SJJA-2, Show Series, *The Merry Widow*, Box 105, Shubert Archive, New York.

44. 'Syracuse Enthuses over First Production', *Democrat and Chronicle* (Rochester), 24 September 1907, 14.

45. H. E. K. [Henry E. Krehbiel], 'The Merry Widow', *New-York Tribune*, 22 October 1907, 7.

46. Although Lina Abarbanell was a major operetta and musical comedy star, and later an important theatrical agent, she did appear in opera—fifteen times at the Metropolitan Opera as Hänsel in *Hänsel und Gretel* in the 1905–1906 season, in the Met's first production of Engelbert Humperdinck's popular opera. Met Opera Database, Metropolitan Opera Archives, http://archives.metoperafamily.org/archives/frame.htm, accessed 5 January 2020.

47. Advertisement, *The Inter-Ocean* (Chicago), 1 December 1907, 50; and Burns Mantle, '*The Merry Widow* Wins', *The Inter-Ocean*, 4 December 1907, 6. See also Jim McPherson, 'The Savage Innocents, Part 2: On the Road with *Parsifal*, *Butterfly*, the *Widow*, and the *Girl*', *Opera Quarterly* 19, no. 1 (2003): 28–63.

48. '*Merry Widow* Record Maker: 5,000th Performance Sunday', *San Francisco Examiner*, 26 March 1913, 13.

49. Christopher B. Balme, 'The Bandmann Circuit: Theatrical Networks in the First Age of Globalization', *Theatre Research International* 40, no. 1 (2015): 19–36; Christopher B. Balme, 'Managing Theatre and Cinema in Colonial India: Maurice E. Bandmann, J. F. Madan, and the War Films' Controversy', *Popular Entertainment Studies* 6, no. 2 (2015): 6–21; Christopher B. Balme, 'Maurice E. Bandmann and the Beginnings of a Global Theatre Trade', *Journal of Global Theatre History* 1, no. 1 (2016): 34–45; and Christopher B. Balme, *The Globalization of Theatre, 1870-1930: The Theatrical Networks of Maurice E. Bandmann* (Cambridge: Cambridge University Press, 2019).

50. John Koegel, *Music in German Immigrant Theater: New York City, 1840-1940* (Rochester, NY: University of Rochester Press, 2009), Chap. 4.

51. Tobias Becker, 'Entertaining the Empire: Theatrical Touring Companies and Amateur Dramatics in Colonial India', *Historical Journal* 57, no. 3 (2014): 699–725; here: abstract.

52. On foreign artistic influences on treaty port–era Shanghai (1842–1946), see J. H. Haan, 'Thalia and Terpsichore on the Yangtze: A Survey of Foreign Theatre and Music in Shanghai, 1850–1865', *Journal of the Hong Kong Branch of the Royal Asiatic Society* 29 (1989): 158–251; Xuelei Huang, 'Through the Looking Glass of Spatiality: Spatial Practice, Contact Relation and the Isis Theater in Shanghai, 1917–1937', *Modern Chinese Literature and Culture* 23, no. 2 (2011): 1–33; and Hon-Lun Yang, 'From Colonial Modernity to Global Identity: The Shanghai Municipal Orchestra', in *China and the West: Music, Representation, and Reception*, ed. Hon-Lun Yang and Michael Saffle (Ann Arbor: University of Michigan Press, 2017), 49–64.

53. Tom Hoogervorst and Henk Schulte Nordholt, 'Urban Middle Classes in Colonial Java (1900–1942): Images and Language', *Bijdragen tot de Taal-, Land- en Volkenkunde* 173, no. 4 (2017): 442–474.

54. Historical sources used include digitised editions of the following newspapers: *El Correo Español* (Mexico City), *Correio Paulistano* (São Paulo), *Diario Oficial* (Mexico City), *El Diario de la Marina* (Havana), *Jornal do Comercio* (Rio de Janeiro), *The Mexican Herald* (Mexico City), *O Norte* (Parahyba do Norte, Brazil), and *O Paiz* (Rio de Janeiro). See also John Rosselli, 'The Opera Business and the Italian Immigrant Community in Latin America 1820–1930: The Example of Buenos Aires', *Past & Present* 127 (May 1990): 155–182; Kristen McCleary, 'Popular, Elite and Mass Culture? The Spanish Zarzuela in Buenos Aires, 1890–1900', *Studies in Latin American Popular Culture* 21 (2002): 1–27; Claudio E. Benzecry, 'An Opera House for the "Paris of South America": Pathways to the Institutionalization of High Culture', *Theory and Society* 43, no. 2 (2014): 169–196; and Luísa Cymbron, 'Camões in Brazil: Operetta and Portuguese Culture in Rio de Janeiro, circa 1880', *Opera Quarterly* 30, no. 4 (2014): 330–361.

55. Susana Salgado, *The Teatro Solís: 150 Years of Opera, Concert, and Ballet in Montevideo* (Middletown, CT: Wesleyan University Press, 2003), 303.

56. *El Diario de la Marina* (Havana), 17 September 1908.

57. *Diario Oficial* (Mexico City), 2 June 1909, 533, a notice of Mexican copyright granted to José Castellanos Haaf and Alberto Michel for their adaptation into Spanish of the English-language libretto of *The Merry Widow*.

58. Historical sources used include digitised editions of the following newspapers: *Calexico Chronicle* (Calexico, California), *El democrata fronterizo* (Laredo, Texas; Spanish-language), *Denní Hlasatel* (Chicago, Illinois; Czech-language), *El heraldo de México*

(Los Angeles, California; Spanish-language), *L'Italia* (San Francisco, California; Italian-language), *Lögberg* (Winnipeg, Manitoba; Icelandic-language), *New-York Tribune*, *New Yorker Volkszeitung* (German-language), *El Paso Times* (El Paso, Texas; English- and Spanish-language), *Revyen* (Chicago; Danish-language), *San Jose Evening News* (San Jose, California), *La sentinella* (Bridgeport, Connecticut; Italian-language), and *Winnipeg Tribune*.

59. See Koegel, *Music in German Immigrant Theater*; and John Koegel, 'Non-English-Language Musical Theater in the United States', in *The Cambridge Companion to the Musical*, ed. Paul Laird and William Everett, 3$^{rd}$ ed., 51–78 (Cambridge: Cambridge University Press, 2017).

60. 'Not Copyrighted Here', *New York Times*, 31 October 1907, 9.

61. '*Die Lustige Witwe* Banished', *New-York Tribune*, 14 January 1908, 3; 'Says *Merry Widow* Copyright Is Faulty', *Los Angeles Herald*, 19 January 1908, III 8; and 'Forced to Stop the *Merry Widow*', *Dixon Evening Telegraph* (Dixon, Illinois), 4 March 1908, 1.

62. Marion Winthrop, 'The Transplanted Teuton and His Amusements', *The Craftsman* 14, no. 4 (1908): 395–396.

63. '*Merry Widow* Seen through German Glasses', *New York Times*, 16 February 1908, V9; 'East Side *Widow* the Jolliest Yet', *Evening World* (New York), 18 March 1908; and '*Merry Widow* with Beer', *Sun* (New York), 12 April 1908, 7.

64. 'Another *Merry Widow*', *Sun* (New York), 5 June 1908, 7.

65. Originally founded as the White Rats of America, a fraternal organisation of male vaudeville performers, the White Rats Actors Union also had a German American branch.

66. Winnipeg's *Lögberg* newspaper is published today as *Lögberg-Heimskringla*.

67. *El democrata fronterizo* (Laredo), 31 August 1912, 3; 'Gran Teatro Texas', *El Paso Times*, 25 January 1925, 1; and 'El Teatro Lincoln', *El democrata fronterizo* (Laredo), 16 November 1918, 4.

68. John Koegel, 'Mexican Musical Theater and Movie Palaces in Downtown Los Angeles before 1950', in *The Tide Was Always High: The Music of Latin America in Los Angeles*, ed. Josh Kun (Oakland: University of California Press, 2017), 49–64; and John Koegel, 'Mexican Music, Theater, and Circus at the Los Angeles Plaza, 1850–1900', in *De Nueva España a México: El universo musical mexicano entre centenarios (1517–1917)*, ed. Javier Marín López (Seville: Universidad Internacional de Andalucía, 2020), 29–113.

69. 'Farfariello', *El heraldo de México* (Los Angeles), 9 May 1918, 1.

70. 'News of the Theatres', *Chicago Daily Tribune*, 19 May 1908, 10.

71. Theatre advertisements: Scenic Theatre, Sioux City, Iowa, *Sioux City Journal*, 2 February 1908, 12; and Wonderland Theatre, Lincoln, Nebraska, *Lincoln Journal Star*, 13 February 1908, 4.

72. On *The Merry Widow* on film, see Nancy Schwartz, 'Lubitsch's *Widow*: The Meaning of a Waltz', *Film Comment* 11, no. 2 (1975): 13–17; Bo Berglund, 'À la recherche des films perdus: A Substantial Find of Early Danish Cinema', in *Nordic Explorations: Film before 1930*, ed. John Fullerton and Jan Olsson, 63–74 (Sydney: John Libbey, 1999); Maud Nelissen, '"Hab mich lieb": The Development of a Music Score for Erich von Stroheim's *The Merry Widow*', *Journal of Film Preservation* 94 (April 2016): 77–83; and Steve Neale, *Screening the Stage: Case Studies of Film Adaptations of Stage Plays and Musicals in the Classical Hollywood Era, 1914–1956* (Bloomington: Indiana University Press, 2017).

73. Richard Taruskin, 'Review of Facsimile Edition of Dimitri Shostakovich, Symphony No. 7, *Leningrad*', *Notes: Quarterly Journal of the Music Library Association* 50, no. 2 (1993): 756–761; here: 757; and Benjamin Suchoff, 'Background and Sources of Bartók's Concerto for Orchestra', *International Journal of Musicology* 9 (2000): 339–361, esp. 355.

74. The American opera star Beverly Sills (1929–2007) was particularly associated with *The Merry Widow*, having sung the role of Hanna (Sonia) many times on tour throughout the United States, for the first time at age eighteen in 1947 and the last time in 1979, one year before her last performances. See *Beverly Sills Performance Annals Database*, http://www.beverlysillsonline.com/index.htm, accessed 5 January 2020.

75. Met Opera Database, Metropolitan Opera Archives, http://archives.metoperafamily.org/archives/frame.htm, accessed 5 January 2020.


## BIBLIOGRAPHY

Advertisement. *The Inter-Ocean* (Chicago), 1 December 1907, 50.

'Another *Merry Widow*'. *Sun* (New York), 5 June 1908, 7.

Arrington-Sirois, Andrea L. *Victoria Falls and Colonial Imagination in British Southern Africa*. New York: Palgrave Macmillan, 2017.

Balme, Christopher B. 'The Bandmann Circuit: Theatrical Networks in the First Age of Globalization'. *Theatre Research International* 40, no. 1 (2015): 19–36.

Balme, Christopher B. *The Globalization of Theatre, 1870-1930: The Theatrical Networks of Maurice E. Bandmann*. Cambridge: Cambridge University Press, 2019.

Balme, Christopher B. 'Managing Theatre and Cinema in Colonial India: Maurice E. Bandmann, J. F. Madan, and the War Films' Controversy'. *Popular Entertainment Studies* 6, no. 2 (2015): 6–21.

Balme, Christopher B. 'Maurice E. Bandmann and the Beginnings of a Global Theatre Trade'. *Journal of Global Theatre History* 1, no. 1 (2016): 34–45.

Baranello, Micaela. '*Die lustige Witwe* and the Creation of the Silver Age of Viennese Operetta'. *Cambridge Opera Journal* 26, no. 2 (2014): 175–202.

Becker, Tobias. 'Entertaining the Empire: Theatrical Touring Companies and Amateur Dramatics in Colonial India'. *Historical Journal* 57, no. 3 (2014): 699–725.

Becker, Tobias. 'Globalizing Operetta before the First World War'. *Opera Quarterly* 33, no. 1 (2017): 7–27.

Belina, Anastasia and Derek B. Scott, eds. *The Cambridge Companion to Operetta*. Cambridge: Cambridge University Press, 2019.

Benzecry, Claudio E. 'An Opera House for the "Paris of South America": Pathways to the Institutionalization of High Culture'. *Theory and Society* 43, no. 2 (2014): 169–196.

Berglund, Bo. 'À la recherche des films perdus: A Substantial Find of Early Danish Cinema'. In *Nordic Explorations: Film before 1930*, ed. John Fullerton and Jan Olsson, 63–74. Sydney: John Libbey, 1999.

Bharucha, Rustom. *The Politics of Cultural Practice: Thinking through Theatre in an Age of Globalization*. Hanover, NH: Wesleyan University Press, 2000.

Boosey, William. *Fifty Years of Music*. London: Ernest Benn, 1931.

Brandl-Risi, Bettina, Clemens Risi, and Rainer Simon. *Kunst der Oberfläche: Operette zwischen Bravour und Banalität*. Leipzig: Henschel Verlag, 2015.

'Chronique théâtrale'. *L'Echo annamite* (Saigon), 10 December 1928, 6.

'Chronique théâtrale'. *L'Echo annamite* (Saigon), 12 December 1928, 5.

Clarke, Kevin, ed. *Glitter and Be Gay: Die authentische Operette und ihre schwulen Verehrer*. Hamburg: Männerschwarm Verlag, 2007.

Creewel, John. *90 Glorious Years: A History of the Victoria Falls Hotel*. Harare: Harper Collins Zimbabwe, 1994.

Csáky, Moritz. *Ideologie der Operette und Wiener Moderne, ein kulturhistorischer Essay zur österreichischen Identität*. Vienna: Böhlau, 1996.

Cymbron, Luísa. 'Camões in Brazil: Operetta and Portuguese Culture in Rio de Janeiro, circa 1880'. *Opera Quarterly* 30, no. 4 (2014): 330–361.

Czech, Stefan (Stan). *Schön ist die Welt: Franz Lehárs Leben und Werk*. Berlin: Argon Verlag, 1957.

Dahlhaus, Carl. 'Zur musikalischen Dramaturgie der *Lustigen Witwe*'. *Österreichische Musikzeitschrift* 12, no. 40 (1985): 657–664.

Decsey, Ernst. *Franz Lehár*. Berlin: Drei Masken Verlag, 1930.

*Den glade Enke*. http://wayback-01.kb.dk/wayback/20100902125838/http://www2.kb.dk/kb/dept/nbo/ma/fokus/enke.htm, accessed 5 January 2020.

*Deutscher Bühnen-Spielplan*. Leipzig: Breitkopf & Härtel, 1906–1908, 1910–1911.

'*Die lustige Witwe* am Zambesi'. *Berliner Tageblatt*, 22 February 1910, 3.

'*Die Lustige Witwe* Banished'. *New-York Tribune*, 14 January 1908, 3.

Duault, Alain, ed. 'Franz Lehár: *La veuve joyeuse*'. *L'avant-scène': Opéra, opérette, musique* 45 (1982): 1–139.

'East Side *Widow* the Jolliest Yet'. *Evening World* (New York), 18 March 1908.

'El Teatro Lincoln'. *El democrata fronterizo* (Laredo), 16 November 1918, 4.

Endler, Franz. *Immer nur lächeln . . . : Franz Lehár, Sein Leben—Sein Werk*. Munich: Wilhelm Heyne Verlag, 1998.

Everett, William A. *Rudolf Friml*. Urbana: University of Illinois Press, 2008.

Everett, William A. *Sigmund Romberg*. New Haven, CT: Yale University Press, 2007.

'Farfariello'. *El heraldo de México* (Los Angeles), 9 May 1918, 1.

Finck, Henry T. *Success in Music and How It Is Won*. New York: Charles Scribner's Sons, 1913.

'Forced to Stop the *Merry Widow*'. *Dixon (Illinois) Evening Telegraph*, 4 March 1908, 1.

Frey, Stefan Frey. *Was sagt ihr zu diesem Erfolg: Franz Lehár und die Unterhaltungsmusik des 20. Jahrhunderts*. Frankfurt: Insel, 1999.

Frey, Stefan. *Franz Lehár, oder das schlechte Gewissen der leichten Musik*. Berlin: De Gruyter, 1995.

Gänzl, Kurt. 'Die lustige Witwe'. In *The Encyclopedia of the Musical Theatre*, vol. 2, 1270–1275. 3 vols., 2nd ed. New York: Schirmer Books, 2001.

Gier, Albert. *Poetik und Dramaturgie der komischen Operette*. Bamberg: University of Bamberg Press, 2014.

Gold, Edward Michael. 'On the Significance of Franz Lehár Operettas: A Musical-Analytical Study'. PhD diss., New York University, 1993.

Goldsworthy, Vesny. *Inventing Ruritania: The Imperialism of the Imagination*. Revised ed. London: Hurst, 2013.

'Gran Teatro Texas'. *El Paso Times* (El Paso), 25 January 1925, 1.

Grun, Bernard. *Gold and Silver: The Life and Times of Franz Lehár*. London: W. H. Allen, 1970.

Haan, J. H. 'Thalia and Terpsichore on the Yangtze: A Survey of Foreign Theatre and Music in Shanghai, 1850–1865'. *Journal of the Hong Kong Branch of the Royal Asiatic Society* 29 (1989): 158–251.

Hanák, Péter. *The Garden and the Workshop: Essays on the Cultural History of Vienna and Budapest*. Princeton: Princeton University Press, 1998.

Heinemann, Michael. 'Das Erlebnis Operette: Zur Historizität von Performanz'. *Archiv für Musikwissenschaft* 73, no. 4 (2016): 250–263.

H. E. K. [Henry E. Krehbiel]. 'The Merry Widow'. *New-York Tribune*, 22 October 1907, 7.

'Her Majesty's Theatre'. *Argus* (Melbourne), 18 May 1908, 9.

H. H. 'Theater, Kunst und Literatur'. *Sport & Salon*, 6 January 1906, 7.

Hoogervorst, Tom and Henk Schulte Nordholt. 'Urban Middle Classes in Colonial Java (1900–1942): Images and Language'. *Bijdragen tot de Taal-, Land- en Volkenkunde* 173, no. 4 (2017): 442–474.

Huang, Xuelei. 'Through the Looking Glass of Spatiality: Spatial Practice, Contact Relation, and the Isis Theater in Shanghai, 1917–1937'. *Modern Chinese Literature and Culture* 23, no. 2 (2011): 1–33.

Kelly, Veronica. 'Australasia: Mapping a Theatrical "Region" in Peace and War'. *Journal of Global Theatre History* 1, no. 1 (2016): 62–77.

Koegel, John. 'Mexican Musical Theater and Movie Palaces in Downtown Los Angeles before 1950'. In *The Tide Was Always High: The Music of Latin America in Los Angeles*, ed. Josh Kun, 49–64. Oakland: University of California Press, 2017.

Koegel, John. 'Mexican Music, Theater, and Circus at the Los Angeles Plaza, 1850–1900'. In *De Nueva España a México: El universo musical mexicano entre centenarios (1517–1917)*, ed. Javier Marín López, 29–113. Seville: Universidad Internacional de Andalucía, 2020.

Koegel, John. *Music in German Immigrant Theater: New York City, 1840–1940*. Rochester, NY: University of Rochester Press, 2009.

Koegel, John. 'Non-English Language Musical Theater in the United States'. In *The Cambridge Companion to the Musical*, ed. Paul Laird and William Everett, 51–78. 3rd ed. Cambridge: Cambridge University Press, 2017.

Kracauer, Siegfried. *Offenbach and the Paris of His Time*. London: Constable, 1937.

La Grange, Henry-Louis de. *Gustav Mahler*. Vol. 3, *Vienna: Triumph and Disillusion (1904–1907)*. New York: Oxford University Press, 1999.

Lehár, Franz. 'Vom Schreibtisch und aus dem Atelier: Bis zur *Lustigen Witwe*'. *Velhagen & Klasings Monathefte* 26, no. 6 (1912): 212–216.

Linhardt, Marion. '*Warum es der Operette so schlecht geht*': *Ideologische Debatten um das musikalische Unterhaltungstheater (1880–1916)*. Vienna: Böhlau, 2001.

MacQueen-Pope, W., and D. L. Murray. *Fortune's Favorite: The Life and Times of Franz Lehár*. London: Hutchinson, 1952.

Mantle, Burns. '*The Merry Widow* Wins'. *Inter-Ocean*, 4 December 1907, 6.

McCleary, Kristen. 'Popular, Elite and Mass Culture? The Spanish Zarzuela in Buenos Aires, 1890–1900'. *Studies in Latin American Popular Culture* 21 (2002): 1–27.

McClellan, Michael E. 'Performing Empire: Opera in Colonial Hanoi'. *Journal of Musicological Research* 22 (2003): 135–166.

McPherson, Jim. 'The Savage Innocents, Part 2: On the Road with *Parsifal*, *Butterfly*, the *Widow*, and the *Girl*'. *Opera Quarterly* 19, no. 1 (2003): 28–63.

Meilhac, Henri. *L'Attaché d'ambassade*. Paris: Michel Lévy Fréres, 1861.

'*Merry Widow* Record Maker: 5,000th Performance Sunday'. *San Francisco Examiner*, 26 March 1913, 13.

'*Merry Widow* Seen through German Glasses'. *New York Times*, 16 February 1908, V9.

'*Merry Widow* with Beer'. *Sun* (New York), 12 April 1908, 7.

Meyer, Franz Anton. *Lehár—Die lustige Witwe: Der Ernst der leichten Muse*. Vienna: Edition Steinbauer, 2005.

Milojković-Djurić, Jelena. 'Franz Lehár's *The Merry Widow*: Revisiting Pontevedro'. *Serbian Studies* 25, no. 2 (2011): 259–272.

Neale, Steve. *Screening the Stage: Case Studies of Film Adaptations of Stage Plays and Musicals in the Classical Hollywood Era, 1914–1956*. Bloomington: Indiana University Press, 2017.

Nelissen, Maud. '"Hab mich lieb": The Development of a Music Score for Erich von Stroheim's *The Merry Widow*'. *Journal of Film Preservation* 94 (April 2016): 77–83.

'News of the Theatres'. *Chicago Daily Tribune*, 19 May 1908, 10.

Norton, Richard. *A Chronology of American Musical Theater*. 3 vols. New York: Oxford University Press, 2002.

'Not Copyrighted Here'. *New York Times*, 31 October 1907, 9.

Platt, Len, Tobias Becker and David Linton, eds. *Popular Musical Theatre in London and Berlin 1890 to 1939*. Cambridge: Cambridge University Press, 2014.

Postlewait, Thomas. 'George Edwardes and Musical Comedy: The Transformation of London Theatre and Society, 1878–1914'. In *The Performing Century: Nineteenth-Century Theatre's History*, ed. Tracy C. Davis and Peter Holland, 80–102. Basingstoke and New York: Palgrave Macmillan, 2007.

Rebellato, Dan. *Theatre and Globalization*. New York: Palgrave Macmillan, 2009.

Rosselli, John. 'The Opera Business and the Italian Immigrant Community in Latin America 1820–1930: The Example of Buenos Aires'. *Past & Present* 127 (May 1990): 155–182.

Salgado, Susana. *The Teatro Solís: 150 Years of Opera, Concert, and Ballet in Montevideo*. Middletown, CT: Wesleyan University Press, 2003.

'Says *Merry Widow* Copyright Is Faulty'. *Los Angeles Herald*, 19 January 1908, III 8.

Schmidl, Stefan. '"Dort ist die ganze Welt noch rotweißgrün!" Diskurse über Kollektive, Alteritäten und Nation in der Operette Österreich-Ungarns'. *Studia Musicologica* 52, no. 1–4 (December 2011): 109–121.

Schneidereit, Otto. *Franz Lehár: Eine Biographie in Zitaten*. Berlin: Lied der Zeit, 1984.

Schwartz, Nancy. 'Lubitsch's Widow: The Meaning of a Waltz'. *Film Comment* 11, no. 2 (1975): 13–17.

Schweitzer, Marlis. '"Darn That Merry Widow Hat": The On- and Offstage Life of a Theatrical Commodity, circa 1907–1908'. *Theatre Survey* 50, no. 2 (2009): 189–221.

Scott, Derek B. *German Operetta on Broadway and in the West End, 1900–1940*. Cambridge: Cambridge University Press, 2019.

Seeley, Paul D. 'Franz Lehár: Aspects of His Life with a Critical Survey of His Operettas and the Work of His Jewish Librettists'. PhD diss., University of Liverpool, 2004.

Senelick, Laurence. 'Musical Theatre as a Paradigm of Translocation'. *Journal of Global Theatre History* 2, no. 1 (2017): 22–36.

Suchoff, Benjamin. 'Background and Sources of Bartók's Concerto for Orchestra'. *International Journal of Musicology* 9 (2000): 339–361.

'Syracuse Enthuses over First Production'. *Democrat and Chronicle* (Rochester), 24 September 1907, 14.

'Theater und Musik'. *Wiener Zeitung* (Vienna), 2 January 1906, 10.

'*The Merry Widow* Making a Million'. *New York Times*, 22 December 1910, C8.

Tomoff, Kiril. 'Of Gypsy Barons and the Power of Love: Operetta Programming and Popularity in the Postwar Soviet Union'. *Cambridge Opera Journal* 30, no. 1 (2018): 29–59.

Traubner, Richard. *Operetta: A Theatrical History*. Garden City, NY: Doubleday, 1983; later eds., New York: Oxford University Press, 1989; New York: Routledge, 2003.

Von Peteani, Marie. *Franz Lehár: Seine Musik, sein Leben*. Vienna: Gloken Verlag, 1950.

*Weiber, Weiber, Weiber, Weib! Ach! 100 Jahre Die lustige Witwe*. Vienna: Wiener Stadt- und Landesbibliothek, 2005.

*Wiener Sonn- und Montags Zeitung* (Vienna), 1 January 1906, 7.

Winthrop, Marion. 'The Transplanted Teuton and His Amusements'. *Craftsman* 14, no. 4 (1908): 395–396.

Yang, Hon-Lun, 'From Colonial Modernity to Global Identity: The Shanghai Municipal Orchestra'. In *China and the West: Music, Representation, and Reception*, ed. Hon-Lun Yang and Michael Saffle, 49–64. Ann Arbor: University of Michigan Press, 2017.

CHAPTER 5

# MUSICAL TRAVAILS IN THE BRITISH EMPIRE

*South Africa and Australia*

DAVID PEIMER

## INTRODUCTION

AFTER World War I, British influence remained widespread across the globe. Its colonies included countries as diverse and far-flung as Canada, New Zealand, Australia, India, Egypt, South Africa, Rhodesia (now Zimbabwe), Ghana, Nigeria, Kenya, Singapore, Burma (now Myanmar), Hong Kong, and Jamaica. The primary purpose of musicals exported from Britain to these countries was to entertain expatriates—including diplomats, civil servants, military top brass, and British settler families—as well as, in an implicit aim, to 'educate' indigenous subjects and earn financial profits for commercial theatre companies. The covert function was to help inculcate notions of the cultural superiority of white settlers in order to justify the colonial hierarchy of values and peoples or races.

While in some regions the performances of Gilbert and Sullivan, Edwardian musical comedy, and operetta remained mainly in the hands of amateur societies, other colonies and Commonwealth countries had a highly developed professional production system. Among the latter are Australia and South Africa. In the former, J. C. Williamson Management consolidated its control of Australian theatre in 1920 when it merged with its most significant rival, J. & N. Tait, to create a de facto monopoly. A comparable development was observed in South Africa, where African Consolidated Theatres (ACT), founded by J. W. Schlesinger and A. H. (Harry) Stodel in 1913, reorganised the theatre industry in the new Union of South Africa after the Boer Wars. ACT became a powerful producing entity between 1920 and 1960 and gained control of most commercial South African theatres and productions.

The development of the empire's ready-made touring circuit for British theatre exported from the West End preceded a postcolonial era of growth and development of indigenous theatre in Australia and South Africa, some of which was initially exported to London and later to New York. Far more new shows were created in South Africa than in Australia. To do justice to the number of productions meriting discussion, this investigation is not directly comparative but seeks to explore each country in relation to its own history and culture. Importantly, the overall context of colonial and especially postcolonial cultural frameworks informs both narratives.

The making and exporting of new indigenous musicals by previously colonised peoples reflects new paradigms of identity forged in contestation with those constructed during colonialism and, later in South Africa, apartheid. In many musicals, the apartheid system of institutionalised racism is directly contested. A few of the musicals examined do not do this, and the chapter investigates why. In Australia, changing expressions of gender and in particular masculinity as well as (at times) class are crucial to the meaning of the works.

Stuart Hall's work on identity provides a framework for the musicals discussed. Emerging interest in indigenous musical theatre in Australia, and even more so in South Africa during and after apartheid, is reflected in the exploration of ways in which representations of identity determine the form and meaning of individual shows. Most helpful in addressing this issue is Hall's view that 'cultural identity is not an essence but a positioning'. He thereby contends that 'identities are the names we give to the different ways we are positioned by, and position ourselves within, the narratives of the past.' For Hall, identity is not fixed but 'undergoes constant transformation [and is] subject to the continuous "play" of history, culture, and power'.[1]

Thus, identity is nuanced and variable—a site of shifting attitudes, a multiplicity of reference points, and never a stable entity. Further, I would suggest that it is precisely when identity is essentialised that the ideology of the binary replaces one of fluidity: when that happens, the result is prejudice and stereotyping. Critiquing the musicals of these countries from Hall's perspective on identity leads to the question of how the works contest the cultural inheritance of the colonial paradigm—or, in some South African musicals, romanticise the colonial subjects as the 'primitive [and] exotic', devoid of an historical context.

# British (and Broadway) Exports to South Africa

The colonial South African theatre story really begins with ACT, which effectively controlled the theatre and film industry between 1913 and 1961. The company also imported numerous drama, musical, and pantomime companies to tour the country. It was a de facto monopoly, and whilst it certainly gave work to local professional performers and introduced shows from London and New York, the company dominated the industry.

Representing colonial perceptions of identity and socio-political hierarchies while mostly ignoring indigenous black voices, ACT during this period was responsible for presenting many shows or staging productions from London with South African performers,[2] including *The Sleeping Beauty* (1890), *Alice in Wonderland* (1941), *Oklahoma!* (1948), and *The Desert Song* (1970). ACT imported Irving Berlin's *Annie Get Your Gun* in 1949 with Bonita Primrose and Bob Lyon, both of *Oklahoma!* fame. *Brigadoon* (1950) was brought out with Louise Boyd and Michael O'Dowd in the leading roles. The pantomimes *Cinderella* (1950) and *Dick Whittington* (1952), starring the British actor Terry-Thomas, all achieved notable success. In the mid-1950s ACT presented Bernard Delfont's London version of *Folies Bergère* (1957). The Broadway musical *The Pajama Game* was first staged in South Africa in 1958 and starred the young English actor Michael McGovern, who stayed on to become one of South Africa's leading actors. Importantly, Bertha Egnos (later to achieve international success with *Ipi Tombi*) staged *Bo Jungle* in association with ACT in 1959. One of the company's final productions was *My Fair Lady*, starring Diane Todd and David Oxley, in 1962. It played to 234 packed houses in Johannesburg before repeating its success in Cape Town and Durban. Other very successful productions under the aegis of ACT include the operetta *Lilac Time* and performances by a company from the Moulin Rouge in Paris in 1964.

In 1966 the South Africans Joan Brickhill and Louis Burke co-directed and co-devised *The Minstrel Scandals* for ACT; typically, this box-office hit, which toured nationally for over a year, featured 'blacked-up' male performers. Three years later the director Taubie Kushlick directed *Cabaret* (1969) and staged *Fiddler on the Roof* (1969) for an ACT tour. The team of Brickhill and Burke became highly successful producers of musicals in South Africa, presenting a series of Las Vegas–style revues as well as *South Pacific* (1969), *Gypsy* (1975), *The Sound of Music* (1976), *I Love My Wife* (1978), *Hello, Dolly!* (1980), and *Mame* (1982) in Johannesburg and elsewhere. Although Brickhill-Burke produced a slickly commercial indigenous musical titled *Meropa* (later *Kwa-Zulu*), which was also enthusiastically received in London in 1975, the vast majority of these productions enhanced colonial notions of the cultural superiority of the capital (i.e., London or New York). This was because the musicals often marginalised the culture of the colonial subject, who was deemed unworthy of serious attention. Stories were told from the white, colonial point of view, which framed the black subject as the primitive or noble savage, physically strong and beautiful but intellectually naive. In short, black history and culture were ignored or traduced.

# British Exports to Australia

As in South Africa, Australia's theatre industry was dominated by one company, J. C. Williamson, which offered colonial depictions of other identities and cultures.

The voices of the Aboriginal and even of the local white culture were ignored. J. C. Williamson brought international stars and productions of all genres to Australia, from dance to theatre to opera and musical theatre.[3] The company was set up in 1881, when it leased the Theatre Royal and the Princess Theatre in Sydney; it soon began to play a highly influential role in the establishment of professional Australian theatre and performance. The 1880s was a very successful decade, with seasons of Gilbert and Sullivan's *Patience* (1882). In 1911 Williamson merged with the theatre entrepreneurs Rupert Clarke and Clyde Meynell and was renamed J. C. Williamson. After the death of Williamson in 1913, the business was led by the Tait brothers for the next fifty years. The company staged many musicals that provided employment for Australian performers throughout the 1940s, 1950s, and 1960s—decades during which they imported many Broadway musicals, including *Annie Get Your Gun* (1947), *Oklahoma!* (1949), *Brigadoon* (1951), *Kiss Me, Kate* (1952), *South Pacific* (1952), *The Pajama Game* (1958), and *My Fair Lady* (1959).

In the 1950s competition from developing entertainment media, specifically television and cinema, and the deaths of the Tait brothers resulted in the company's losing its role as the most powerful Australian theatre production company. In 1976 the company's theatres were sold, and in 1984 J. C. Williamson Ltd. was acquired by the Danbury Group. As with productions exported from Britain to South Africa, the commercial repertoire in Australia included almost no indigenously created musicals, no portrayals of Aboriginal experience, no storytelling from the perspective of the colonised subject, and no reference to local culture or history.

# INDIGENOUS SOUTH AFRICAN MUSICALS

In South Africa the apartheid experience frames the post–World War II period. Apartheid, which was the law of the land from 1948 to 1994, created a social, legal, and economic hierarchy of racially categorised subjects: black, white, Cape Coloured (mixed race), and Indian. Black, mixed-race, and Indian individuals were denied the vote, access to almost all higher education institutions, and most skilled jobs, and were forced to live in racially defined areas. Racial intermarriage and cohabitation were banned, as was access to public spaces such as schools, hospitals, beaches, parks, and buildings. A highly repressive system, apartheid legalised systematic arrests, torture, and killings that enabled police and military to ensure the system was strictly enforced.

This essay argues that the colonial/apartheid and post-apartheid eras have given rise to new representations of identity which contest and/or embrace the colonial legacy. Indigenous South African musicals have responded to the regimes of British colonialism and apartheid to showcase the vast range and variety of indigenous dance and music. Whilst some productions are testament to the exploitation of ethnic 'black' culture for white British consumption, overall one can observe the dynamic contribution that musicals have made to evolving identities forged in contestation with the colonial legacy. The rich and dynamic story of South African indigenous musical theatre begins in 1959 with *King Kong*.

## FOREGROUNDING BLACK PROTAGONISTS' VOICES: THE SOUTH AFRICAN *KING KONG*

*King Kong* is widely regarded as the first indigenous South African musical. Created in 1959, it toured the United Kingdom in 1961 and has since taken on iconic status in South Africa. In London it ran for 201 performances. Cast members who remained in the United Kingdom or United States, such as the singer Miriam Makeba, the composer and jazz musician Hugh Masekela, and the composer and writer Todd Matshikiza became international stars. They remained in exile because they knew that if they went back home the regime could ban them from future travel.

This jazz musical, based on the true story of the South African boxer Ezekiel 'King Kong' Dlamini, begins with the song 'Sad Times, Bad Times', which tells of the fate of 'men accused of committing a crime which no one knows is a crime'[4]—a reference to the Treason Trial of 1956 in which Nelson Mandela and his co-accused were sentenced to imprisonment on Robben Island. The production depicts Dlamini's birth in poverty in 1921, his meteoric rise to national renown as the 'non-white' champion who wished to test himself against white boxers but knew this could never happen in apartheid South Africa. Disillusionment led him to neglect his training, which ultimately cost him his title. He 'lapsed into reckless drinking' and took up with a girl who 'was the partner of a gang leader'[5]. Gang violence dominated the rest of his life; eventually, he killed his lover. In court, he requested the death sentence but was instead sentenced to fourteen years' hard labour in Leeuwkop Prison, near Johannesburg. In 1957, two weeks after being sentenced, he was found drowned in a dam near where prisoners worked—a presumed suicide. He was thirty-four.

Given the enforced segregation of the apartheid period, it is significant that the creative team was mostly white, interracial theatrical activity being extremely problematic under the regime. The libretto was written by the white Harry Bloom and the black Todd Matshikiza, who composed much of the music and developed the concept with Pat Williams. Matshikiza employed some Xhosa and Zulu in the lyrics. Kippie Moketsi, often regarded as South Africa's Charlie Parker, played in the fourteen-piece orchestra, while Miriam Makeba played the role of Joyce, who runs the legendary Back of the Moon *shebeen* (township tavern). The production opened in February 1959 at the University of the Witwatersrand Great Hall in Johannesburg and was an immediate critical and financial success. 'It ran for two years and over 200,000 persons saw it', with blacks making up about one-third of the audience.[6] The music was played in many shebeens and on most black radio stations around the country.

The show foregrounds the black protagonist's 'voice'; in this work, the 'political is embodied in the personal', rather than its being overtly polemical (had it been politically outspoken, it might well have been banned). One significant scene helps inform this interpretation: when King Kong was sentenced to hard labour for killing his girlfriend, he asked the court to hang him instead—a plea staged in the musical. A few weeks later he took his own life in prison. For black South Africans, this was an act of agency: he had always refused to be dictated to by apartheid laws, and this was his final act of defiance. They saw him as a 'popular hero—an inspiration for black persons struggling for emancipation'.[7] The court scene represents the hero as a contradictory, multifaceted, and complex character. To adapt Hall's terms, the cultural identity of Dlamini is represented as non-binary—a positioning in relation to history and power, a multiplicity of identities, not an essence. We observe King Kong 'presenting his narrative from the subaltern point of view',[8] and it is his subjectivity that contests the inherited legacy of the colonial, racialised binary.

A collaboration of black and white authors, this was the first South African musical to be performed by an all-black cast, and it influenced much township work to come. Further, the black male is partly portrayed as physically strong (although this is not a racial stereotype, since he is a boxer) and perhaps, while he may seem exotic to some, we see that he is flawed, vulnerable, tormented. He is an astute and impulsive character, a man who strives to overcome his harsh upbringing under apartheid. Overall, *King Kong* rejects the legacy of colonialism by foregrounding the black protagonist's voice, a vital first step to forging a new representation of black identity in South African musicals.

## SATIRISING APARTHEID: *WAIT A MINIM!*

Another fascinating addition to the variety of indigenous musicals was *Wait a Minim!* (1962), which employed satire to indict the harsh absurdity of apartheid. Appearing five years after *King Kong*, the revue extended the range of South African approaches to the genre of musical theatre. This revue was created by an all-white group; conceived by the well-known actor and director Leon Gluckman, it featured original songs by the English-born folk musician Jeremy Taylor. The production consisted of a collection of international folk music arranged by Andrew Tracey, an expert in indigenous southern African musical instruments. Most of the instruments heard in *Wait a Minim!* were authentic to various cultures and incorporated to enhance the show's subject matter, which satirised the social mores of numerous countries. Dialogue only occurred when the cast was introduced, and in the South African scene where apartheid was ridiculed for its cruel absurdity.

There was clearly an international market for satire and for the musically exotic: in London this commercial production ran for two years (1962–1964), and on Broadway (1966–1967) it had 456 performances. It was also performed in Japan, New Zealand, and Australia. However, in South Africa itself, the rest of the 1960s was dominated by the presentation of more slickly professionalised whites-only musicals from Broadway and the West End (*Oliver!*, *Fiddler on the Roof*, *Robert and Elizabeth*, and *Cabaret*), locally produced by Brian Brooke, Brickhill-Burke, and Taubie Kushlick managements.

# SHAKESPEARE AS ZULU MUSICAL: *uMABATHA*

One of the most critically debated shows to emerge from South Africa was *uMabatha* (1971). Here, a new approach to making musicals evolved as Shakespeare was blended with Zulu myth, history, rituals, dance, music, song, and costumes in a production which embraced colonial representations of identity involving the primitive black individual in a financial exploitation of pre-apartheid Zulu culture.

Elizabeth Sneddon, head of speech and drama at the University of Natal, Durban, suggested to her then-student Welcome Msomi that instead of the new play he had initially written for performance, he should 'prepare a play that presented his people in a more worthy light and drew his [attention] to the many parallels existing between *Macbeth* and the tribal history of the Zulu'.[9] Sneddon's language suggests from the inception of this project a 'superior', paternalistic, colonialist view, for her assumption was that projecting the high cultural status of Shakespeare onto certain elements of Zulu history would help Msomi dignify the subject. Directed by a white lecturer in the department, Pieter Scholtz, *uMabatha* was composed and written by Msomi in 1971.

In 1972 *uMabatha* ran at the Aldwych Theatre (then the London home of the Royal Shakespeare Company) as part of its World Theatre Season. 'Every performance received a standing ovation and box office returns broke the record set by Brook's 1970 production of *A Midsummer Night's Dream*.'[10] Revealing his colonial perception of Zulu culture, Peter Daubeny, the British founder of the Season, described the production as 'the greatest hit of all his years of bringing exotic theatre to London'.[11] The production also played in London the following year and was later invited to tour the United States, France, Belgium, Holland, Germany, Italy, Denmark, Japan, Australia, and Scotland, finally arriving off-Broadway in 1978.

Msomi's text remained close to Shakespeare, and his production is categorised by most critics as an 'adaptation'.[12] It is interesting to note that there are only superficial similarities between *Macbeth* and the Zulu history of the murder of Shaka by his half-brother, Dingane, in 1828, the premise of the piece. As a backdrop, this constitutes only in a very general sense a parallel to the Scottish kingdom evoked in *Macbeth*. Laurence Wright sums up the British perception of the show: '*uMabatha* directs the informed European gaze—those sophisticated consumers of post-colonial Shakespeare—to colonial and pre-colonial Africa. This stimulates touristic voyeurism; it suggests a primal Africa destroyed by colonial incursion, a reductive notion of the primitive, a heart of darkness'.[13] The musical showed Zulu factory workers engaged in military, marital, and

FIG. 5.1 The final scene from the 1978 off-Broadway production of *uMabatha: the Zulu Macbeth*: Mafudu (MacDuff) slays Mabatha (Macbeth). Photo: Jack Vartoogian © Getty Images.

other primal rituals, costumes, dancing, bare-breasted women, drums—all with an emphasis on the muscular prowess of the objectified black body. In short, historical context is denied. Wright suggests that 'global theatre tends to smooth out, homogenise, or simply eviscerate ideological and theatrical elements.'[14] When making indigenous 'African' theatre for international consumption, aesthetic choices involve a rejection of the fluid positionality of cultural identity in favour of an essentialist binary between tribal and Western/modern.[15] Robert Malcolm McLaren highlights why this might be considered problematic:

> Your saying of lines tends to be superficial and careless, you take advantage of audience ignorance by relying on sound instead of meaningful expression. This happened in *uMabatha* where the interpretative work of the actor was hardly touched on. What one had instead was a grand and sonorous recitation of rich Zulu melody.[16]

Thus, the spoken language constructed a primitivist, exotic mode of verbal expression invoking a cultural identity reduced to an essentialist paradigm, very different to the intercultural approach adopted in *King Kong*, where the experience of urban black authors and performers enabled a believable articulation of the inner world of the protagonists. This essentialist notion of identity enables the production to propose a universalist interpretation of *Macbeth*, denying the complexity of historical processes by providing an exotic stereotype for the global consumer. The critic Michael Feingold's comment on a performance at the Lincoln Centre Festival in 1997 typifies the naive

## 166   DAVID PEIMER

colonialist assumptions of Western audiences: 'How thrilling it must be for citizens of Zulu ancestry to see the music and dance, ritual and history, of their culture onstage.'[17]

# THE BLAXPLOITATION MUSICAL: *IPI TOMBI*

If *uMabatha* articulates identities brought together by the indiscriminately syncretic mix of Shakespeare, Zulu history, rituals, dance, music, song, and costume for financial exploitation, *Ipi Tombi* takes a step further into this realm by reducing colonial/apartheid representations of black culture to voyeurism for profit. As the musical theatre equivalent of blaxploitation,[18] the show is a low point in the representation of precolonial South African cultures.

*Ipi Tombi* (*Where Is the Girl?*) was created by two white South African composer-writers, Bertha Egnos and Gail Lakier, in 1974. The production clearly represents black South Africans as the colonised 'other'—exotic and primitive. The story is minimal, and the characters/performers are primarily vehicles for touristic mixtures of 'tribal' dances (Xhosa and Zulu), singing, costumes, and rituals. Its commercial success is attested by the fact that it was performed in Nigeria, South Africa, Europe, Canada, Australia, and the West End, and on Broadway.

The musical tells the story of a rural young black man who leaves his wife and goes to Johannesburg to work in the gold mines. He hopes for a better life but experiences hardships and disappointments, with few moments of reprieve. Disillusioned, he returns to his village and, in the powerful finale, discovers people there are preparing for a battle. Critical responses to the West End production revel in the colonialist romanticisation of the 'African indigenous', admiring a musical which 'is presented with verve, a richness of singing and excitement in the dancing. A riot of colour.'[19] Others praised 'the beat of a drum, the sheer primitive beauty!'[20] When *Ipi Tombi* was later produced at the Lincoln Centre Festival in 1976, there were protests against its representation of the indigenous African as exotic, naive, and primitive—against 'the show's exploitation of South Africa's black culture and of the political conditions there.'[21]

Another example of this subgenre was *Meropa* (1974), which was renamed *Kwa Zulu* for its UK transfer and displayed a similarly uncritical attitude to the representation of an historically inaccurate idealisation of the tribal African. Its minimal storyline was an excuse to produce a voyeuristic spectacle of black bodies combined with indigenous music. One British critic naively celebrated the 'magnificently harmonised chanting of [the] troupe [and the] drumming and dancing in a blaze of African splendor.'[22] While the music was drawn from traditional folklore, with original songs and music by the South African jazz composer Victor Ntoni, its producers and directors were Joan Brickhill and Louis Burke, the leading producers of commercial musicals in the apartheid area, so its slickly packaged aesthetic was in fact an adaptation of their Las Vegas–style revues, referenced earlier.

All three shows, *uMabatha*, *Ipi Tombi*, and *Meropa*, are examples of blaxploitation in their romanticisation of black South Africans in the terms of Rousseau's noble savage, a trope which reflects the dominant ideological structure of identity during the colonial and apartheid eras.

# CREATING MUSICAL THEATRE DURING THE STATE OF EMERGENCY: *SOPHIATOWN*

Profoundly different to these three productions is the musical *Sophiatown* (1986). which directly confronts the apartheid reality of forced removals of black, Indian, and mixed-race South Africans to racially designated areas. The primary aim of this show was to take a political stand, not turn a profit, although *Sophiatown* later toured internationally. As an a cappella musical sung in a jazz idiom, the piece represents another major development in the story of indigenous theatre. Long after the stage is empty, we recall the echo of voices, of a life long gone.

*Sophiatown* was created by the Junction Avenue Theatre Company in Johannesburg during the height of the South African State of Emergency, which held from 1985 to 1989. This four-year period saw the suspension of what minimal legal rights ordinary citizens had under apartheid—a development that primarily affected black South Africans. Thousands were killed, arrested, and imprisoned. This is the historical context in which *Sophiatown* was created, and it is important because during that time many artists and activists articulated the hope for racial reconciliation which was part of Junction Avenue's rationale in devising the work.

The company was founded in 1976 by white students of the University of the Witwatersrand, led by Malcolm Purkey (who, after the demise of apartheid, became the artistic director of the Market Theatre in Johannesburg). Their goal was to devise musicals and text-based theatre which directly challenged the apartheid state. They were joined by black performers and theatre makers, including Arthur Molepo, Doreen Mazibuko, Ramalao Makhene, and others. In those times, having a theatre company of white and black performers was discouraged by the state, so they were constantly harassed by the police.

During the early years of apartheid, from 1948 to the mid-1950s, Sophiatown had been a legendary multicultural suburb in Johannesburg. In spite of apartheid legislation, it was the nation's centre for writers, musicians, activists, and intellectuals of all ethnic groups—a hub of interculturalism and interracial mixing, where Mandela's African National Congress (ANC) party had its most important office. In 1955 the apartheid government sent in two thousand armed police and bulldozed Sophiatown to the ground as part of their systematic enforcement of racial segregation throughout the country. Blacks were moved to the new township of Soweto, mixed-race persons to El Dorado Park, and Indians to Lenasia; what had been Sophiatown was rezoned the whites-only

Johannesburg suburb of Triompf—Afrikaans for 'triumph'. As we learn in the play, people were evicted three days before the announced date on the notice and were given time only to collect a few items to take to Soweto, twenty miles outside Johannesburg.

The production was inspired by a real-life event: two black South African writers, Nat Nakasa and Lewis Nkosi, had set up house together in Sophiatown and advertised for a Jewish girl to come and live with them. It has often been speculated that they did this to test the degree of tolerance in the application of apartheid laws.

In the musical, Jakes, the black journalist who lives in Sophiatown, has written the advertisement: he wants to see if racial reconciliation is possible or the notion is naive. When asked, the white character, Ruth, says she came out of 'curiosity.'[23] *Sophiatown's* characters live in a 'cramped but comfortable house, suggesting care and warmth.'[24] Mamariti, the owner, runs a shebeen where she brews and sells alcohol. Ruth is regarded as 'a Sophiatown phenomenon',[25] and Jakes writes an article about her living with them: 'This crazy white girl! It was a scramble when word went round Sophiatown that a Jewish girl was living at Mamariti's Diamond *shebeen*. . . . A Jewish girl living in Softown! Is she crazy as a bedbug? . . . an eager intellectual? A wide-eyed jazz maniac? A daring do-gooder? . . .just a gal with a golden heart?'[26] They 'want life to be easy for the lady',[27] so they search all over for a bath for her—an important moment in the production. Ruth is embarrassed by the special treatment and insists on wanting 'to be like everybody else.'[28] Nevertheless, as the scholar Gugu Hlongwane observes, she 'remains of another world.'[29] Jakes slowly realises that the inherited and legislated cultural divide is too great and cannot be overcome. For him, the mixing of cultures and ethnicities remains a dream.

Recognising his sexual attraction to Ruth, Jakes states, 'White skin, it's a fatal attraction', highlighting that interracial love affairs—even just holding hands—are illegal.[30] The potential relationship never materialises, and eventually the black characters are forced to move out of Sophiatown. Despite Loren Kruger's suggestion that this brief period in South African history might be termed a 'fragile moment of racial tolerance',[31] Hlongwane believes the musical's promise of reconciliation is not realistic. The question of representation in *Sophiatown* is complex. Hlongwane posits that 'the black characters are stereotyped, while Ruth is a more well-rounded character, she is the narrative's catalyst [and] sets the parameters of the plot.'[32] From Hall's perspective, Ruth's and Jakes's identities are positioned complementarily and in constant transformation: Ruth is positioned as Jewish, and privileged because she is white; Jakes is a journalist and an activist, yet without power because he is black. Through them the audience gains a sense of the historical situation of apartheid ideology and the suffering, courage, and fear concomitant on the characters' positions in relation to its hegemony. Even though there is minimal concern with the inner lives of the other characters, the historical causes of the horror engulfing them all in the geographically determined fracturing of their social lives is clearly articulated.

As one discovers the impressive range of South African indigenous musicals, one can see how the productions explored so far contribute to showing the richness of postcolonial and apartheid-era work. Developing the trajectory of South African musicals, we see that *Sophiatown* presents a directly political reaction to forced removals based on a highly significant historical event. *Sarafina!* (1987) is similarly focused in its politics, depicting another major historical event, the Soweto uprising of 1976, which saw the real beginning of the demise of apartheid.

Before exploring *Sarafina!* in more detail, it is appropriate to briefly investigate another important musical that dealt with forced removals: *District Six: The Musical* (1986). Created by the composer Taliep Peterson, with book and lyrics by David Kramer, the work was staged in Cape Town in 1986, at the height of the State of Emergency. It was later performed at the 1988 Edinburgh Festival. The show concerned the forced removal of Cape Coloured people from District Six in Cape Town as part of the social engineering of apartheid during the mid-1950s, when all buildings except churches, mosques, and some schools were bulldozed. The show is set at the moment when every single home was being destroyed and the sense of community fractured as people were sent to forlorn areas outside the city. As in *Sophiatown*, the musical told the story of the removals, community life, and effect of apartheid on Cape Coloured family lives. It captured both the vivid language and the histrionic versatility of the people who lived there: the distinctive rhythms of their Kaapse Klopse (Cape New Year carnival) was juxtaposed with lyrics that illustrated the pathos of the process of destruction.[33] In contradistinction to *Sophiatown*, identity was not located in individual characters, but in a social group. Attesting to its impact was the fact that in South Africa the production ran for 550 performances between 1987 and 1990.

## STAGING THE SOWETO UPRISING: *SARAFINA!*

Written and composed by Mbongeni Ngema, who had devised the celebrated anti-apartheid play *Woza Albert!* (1981) together with Percy Mtwa and Barney Simon, *Sarafina!* dramatises the 1976 Soweto uprising. The catalyst for the revolt was the regime's new law forcing all black South African schoolchildren to study in the hated Afrikaans language. When the police and army sought to break up the protest, many children were injured or killed. The Soweto 'riots', as they were first called, had begun. What started as a protest at a local high school in 1976 spread throughout the country as over 200,000 black students took to the streets in protest. Most of the thousands subsequently killed by the army were children.

First staged in Johannesburg in 1987, this musical, like *Sophiatown*, dramatises a crucial historical turning point. With powerful music and dancing, it tells the story of Sarafina, a young schoolgirl who inspires her peers to rise up in protest and challenge the apartheid state after her teacher, Mary Masombuka (played by Whoopi Goldberg in the 1992 film), is imprisoned and murdered for her activism. *Sarafina!* follows the activities of a fictional class at the school against the backdrop of the nationwide revolt. The musical shows the political awakening of Sarafina (performed by Leleti Khumalo in the film), her involvement in leading the revolt, and her eventual capture and torture by the South African police.

At the funeral of pupils shot dead by a policeman as 'Communists', their friends share the real story of Victoria Mxenge, a black female lawyer and activist who was axed to death by white policemen in front of her children. In 1987 some black South African critics challenged Ngema for weaving Mxenge's murder 'very artificially into the texture of the production',[34] one of numerous sequences that seem 'artificially' shoehorned into the libretto, undermining the narrative's coherence in favour of political didacticism.

In the piece, the entanglements of colonial and apartheid eras are reflected in the time-table of an average school day: a musical rendition of 'The Lord's Prayer', an English class discussing Wordsworth's poem 'Upon Westminster Bridge', algebra lessons in a mixture of languages, and the history of Britain, taught in English. Whilst highly polemical in its portrayal of the tragic events, the show's innovative adaptation of contemporary and traditional South African ethnic dance and song was often accused of exploiting black culture for financial gain, and thus of conflating contestation against the colonial legacy with embrace of its economic structures in the attempt to represent new identities.

Before *Sarafina!*, Ngema had been seen as an artist of the 'struggle' who, with his in-volvement in the plays *Woza Albert!* and *Asinamali!* (1985), had contributed to the crea-tion of some of the most significant anti-apartheid theatre. Yet his musical became part of a local debate which focused on the ethics of producing 'protest theatre.' The South African theatre director Jerry Mofokeng contended that 'theatrical expressions cen-tering on blacks have [ ... ] provided South Africa with a viable commodity for export, paradoxically bolstering and validating the state in the process.'[35] In retrospect, Gibson Cima concluded that 'the crassly commercial 1987 Market Theatre production was clearly on its way to Broadway',[36] where it arrived in early 1988. Most perceptively, Safu Mofokeng summed up the show as 'the commercialisation of the black people's struggle in South African musicals.[37]

In this context, the scholar, playwright, and novelist Zakes Mda has noted that the international tours of *Sarafina!* 'created the illusion of a democratic environment.'[38] Interestingly, when *Sarafina!* opened at Lincoln Center in New York in 1987, the critic Frank Rich observed: 'Dissident productions from Johannesburg's Market Theatre, ur-gently telling and retelling the atrocities of apartheid, now reach New York faster than new plays from Louisville or London.'[39]

From *King Kong* to *Sarafina!*, 1959 to 1987, the trajectory of indigenous South African musicals shows an immediate awareness of significant political events, whether they are challenging the colonial/apartheid era or not. Undeniably inspirational is the foregrounding of the suppressed, indigenous black voices in most of the works, espe-cially those created by authors who were politically aware of the historical context. In Hall's terms, the central question is whether South African musicals show the complex dialectical relation of identity to culture, power, and history or are based on notions of essentialised black identity, which—however romanticised—ignore those historical contexts.

FIG. 5.2 The young cast of *Sarafina!* at the Cort Theatre in 1988. Photo by Martha Swope © The New York Public Library for the Performing Arts.

## Post-Apartheid Musicals: The 'Rainbow Nation' Era (1994–Present)

The brief period after apartheid ended (1990) and before the first democratic elections (1994), which ushered in a Mandela (ANC) government, can be categorised as one of historical contradictions, reflecting Gramsci's notion of interregnum: it was characterised by hope, fragile euphoria, a lack of justice for apartheid's victims, attempts at racial reconciliation, and efforts to prevent a racial civil war. Ironically, and in contrast to the apartheid period, these years often led to a dehistoricised paradigm for original musicals. In Hall's terms, concepts of identity reverted to an essentialist construction, but instead of stereotypes of apartheid's black 'victims,' a new kind of stereotype emerged in the exuberant celebration of racial difference—'the rainbow nation'. Furthering the irony of the times was the sense that theatrical representations of the post-apartheid experience often fetishised the 'exotic' black body for the pleasure of the white consumer. Such an identity was partly constructed in the 'new South Africa' as the poster image for multicultural 'reconciliation' in a progressive attempt to redress the apartheid notion of the 'primitive' black person.

Numerous shows reflected this interpretation; one was *Kat and the Kings* (1998). Created by Taliep Peterson and David Kramer, the musical is set in 1950s District Six in Cape Town, when over sixty thousand mixed-race people were forcibly moved to a Cape Coloureds–only shanty township, the Cape Flats. The story is narrated by an older Kat, in his late fifties, who is shining shoes on the streets of Cape Town. The show presents the memories of his youth, when he was known as a singer, and is mostly told through as 'a crowd-pleasing, foot-stomping, singing and dancing joyfest: a musical that entertains and uplifts with high spirits and high energy. It is deceptively simple: six dazzlingly talented performers, an onstage band, some snappy costumes, two dozen tuneful numbers.'[40] However, the show is more complex than that. Although it does show the indignity and suffering of mixed-race characters under apartheid, their mimicry of American singers suggests a satirising of the colonial perspective in which they existed. The musical is thus not merely an ahistorical portrayal of stereotyped identities.

The work was small in scale and staged in a small West End theatre in a revue-like format. It opened in 1997 at London's Tricycle Theatre and in 1998 moved to the Vaudeville Theatre, where it ran for more than four months. It won the Laurence Olivier Award for Best New Musical and was nominated for a number of other awards in London and later on Broadway.

Perhaps inevitably, the musicals produced in this period reflected a mythical, idealistic future and a glossing over of the immediate legacy of apartheid; the euphoria of the Mandela years was framed by a sense of negotiated togetherness, a desire for reconciliation after so many exhausting decades of division, racial hatred, and violent conflict. Ironically, this ultimately led to some shows' being created and received without consideration of the ahistorical context, such as *Umoja*.

## COMING TOGETHER AS A RAINBOW NATION: *UMOJA: THE SPIRIT OF TOGETHERNESS* (2001)

The title of *Umoja: The Spirit of Togetherness* (2001) captures the essence of certain works devised post-apartheid and at the beginning of the new millennium. The concept of South Africa as a 'rainbow nation' had become mandatory, with reconciliation being 'staged' most days on television, with the Truth and Reconciliation Commission, and in general political discourse. A desire to 'come together' swept through the country as it tried to come to terms with the injustice and suffering of apartheid and to forge new identities representing the post-revolution ideal. The Zulu word *umoja* means 'togetherness', and like other South African musicals, *Umoja* presents a 'singing and dancing joyfest'. The production, created by Todd Twala and Thembi Nyandeni in collaboration with the writer and director Ian von Memerty, had a cast of thirty singers and dancers; it toured over thirty countries and was seen by over four million people.[41] *Umoja* was first performed in the West End in 2001 and returned for a second season in 2012. The show is more a revue than a conventional musical; a narrator explains in a celebratory style how South African music and sounds emerged from tribal roots to develop into traditional, gospel, and contemporary township music and dance. This is then linked to the overall theme of the spirit of 'togetherness' or political reconciliation.

When *Umoja* was exported, many reviewers wanted to show their appreciation and offered 'kind words' for the performers: 'Apparently many of the cast members come from disadvantaged communities and townships so it is a joy to see what has been achieved, and although some of their routines are not perfectly executed, they more than make for this with their enthusiasm.'[42] This verdict reflects Western critics' patronising attitude and reveals an unconscious racism: it pays lip service to the injustice, poverty, and devastating legacy of colonisation and apartheid. By comparison, Sophie Constanti opined in London's *Evening Standard* that *Umoja* was 'the kind of show which shuns theatrical complexity in favour of airbrushed stereotype endorsement.'[43] Essentially, the show puts black bodies on display as an exotic, idyllic celebration of an Edenic primitive produced for global consumption, marketing the post-apartheid aspiration of a binary version of reconciliation internationally. In fact, *Umoja* was a continuation of the commercial blaxploitation musicals by white producers at the height of the apartheid era before the explosion of political protest theatre in the late 1970s discussed above.

*African Footprint* (2000) also articulates the post-apartheid hope of reconciliation, a 'coming together of peoples' under the rainbow-nation label. The show set the poems of the South African writer Don Mattera to music by Richard Loring, an expatriate Brit who began his career in England in the 1960s and who also directed the musical. The narrative starts in ancient Africa: the audience views song and dance sequences that illustrate idealised harmony in nature and in ethnic diversity from that time to the present. It is a fantasy devoid of history, power struggles, or cultural differences and creates a fiction without anthropological foundation. The production travelled to Monte Carlo, India, Mexico, France, Lebanon, Germany, and Canada, racking up over 3,800 performances worldwide; in Great Britain it was featured on the Royal Variety Show in 2000, reaching a television viewership of millions.

# A SOUTH AFRICAN TAKE ON MOZART: *IMPEMPE YOMLINGO* (*THE MAGIC FLUTE*)

Most post-apartheid musicals also exhibit a desire to incorporate global influences from European and other cultures in order to find new ways to adapt these works to the South African context. However, this attempt often embraces colonial legacies in how identities were represented in the forgiving spirit of *Umoja*, where the hardships of township life and the devastating legacy of apartheid were portrayed by seemingly carefree, ahistorical characters. A typical example is *Impempe Yomlingo* (*The Magic Flute*, 2007).

This musical theatre piece was adapted from Mozart's 1791 singspiel by the British expat Mark Dornford-May, who also directed. Words and music were by Mandisi

Dyantyis, Mbali Kgosidintsi, and Nolufefe Mtshabe. Mozart's music was transposed for marimbas, steel and oil drums, water-filled glass bottles, and a jazz trumpet, interspersed with township and traditional singing and dancing. *Impempe Yomlingo* reimagined the opera from a poverty-stricken township perspective: Sarastro is an African tribal leader, while Tamino and Pamina are Xhosa-speaking teenagers who undergo traditional initiation rituals. The performers were from the Khayelitsha township, outside Cape Town. After a critically successful West End run in 2008, the show played in Dublin, Chichester, Canterbury, and Singapore. Although more sophisticated in its intercultural hybridity, its easy invocation of the hardships of township life for the entertainment of sophisticated global consumers calls to mind the neocolonialist attitudes of *uMabatha*, now asserting the superiority of Mozart rather than Shakespeare as the European cultural master. The one feature of the show that seems authentically to express contemporary South African culture is the highly effective use of the marimbas. The *Irish Times'* response to the production's 'glorious outpouring of joy' is surely a sign, however, that the realities of post-apartheid poverty were mostly ignored.[44] If some musicals from this period represented township life within the ahistorical context of 'joy', it is interesting to note that Nelson Mandela himself was portrayed as, I would argue, a noble sufferer. We can see this in musical theatre work dramatising his life.

## REPRESENTING A POLITICAL ICON: *THE MANDELA TRILOGY*

A fusion of musical and opera, *The Mandela Trilogy* (2010) featured a combined group of sixty performers and musicians from the Cape Town Opera and Philharmonic Orchestra, respectively, to represent Nelson Mandela's activism and personal experiences in three acts. Using multimedia projections, newsreels, and video material, the production featured three singers playing Mandela at various stages of his life. The work depicts his youth in rural Qunu, in the Transkei; his marriages; the period in Sophiatown; his leadership of the ANC; his incarceration on Robben Island; and his election as president in 1994. The music combined arias with village chants, ritual dances, jazz, traditional choral Xhosa music, and contemporary opera. The libretto was in Xhosa and English. The show has been performed only a few times internationally; the aim was not commercial profit, but the artistic and political representation of an extraordinary icon's life. The question of authenticity raised by this well-meaning but still somewhat touristic show might be better directed at the representation of Mandela the man, whose life is reduced to a nascently colonialist myth as the 'noble' sufferer—a new post-apartheid stereotype.

Looking back at the colonial/apartheid and immediate post-apartheid periods, one can contend that the dominant theme running through the South African musical is how greatly constructions of black identity in times of oppression vary over time.

Whether foregrounding black voices, being caught in the tension between embracing and contesting the dominant regime, or doing theatre for export, the ultimate result is a unique contribution to the genre of performance and the position of the black subaltern in South Africa. This is accompanied by dynamic variations of indigenous dance, song, performance styles, and characters. Yet, given the adverse conditions of the colonial/apartheid era, it is astonishing that these artistic expressions somehow found a way of being created and staged.

# FORMER COLONIES: SOUTH AFRICA AND AUSTRALIA

Although the histories of South African and Australian musical theatre after World War II are markedly different, what they have in common is the cultural process of emerging from a colonial era. In the former, the production of popular cultural was determined by a harsh, institutionalised racism, which the postwar apartheid system inherited from centuries of British colonial rule, while the latter to a large extent effaced the culture of its indigenous people and thus the whole Aboriginal experience. Instead, the genre explored representations of gender and in particular white masculinity, starting with *Reedy River* (1953), an early postwar example. In both societies the post-colonial period reveals how in musical theatre the 'inferior' colonised person either contests or embraces the narrative of the coloniser. While it can be proposed that this process underlies musical theatre production in both countries, they are culturally very different, so each requires investigation on its own terms rather than direct comparison. It might be helpful in the future to ask why institutionalised racism in South Africa produced a prolific and varied range of musicals, while centuries of covert racism in Australia have seldom produced musicals which interrogate that very phenomenon.

# MASCULINITIES IN THE AUSTRALIAN MUSICAL: *REEDY RIVER*, *THE SENTIMENTAL BLOKE*, AND *SHANE WARNE: THE MUSICAL*

In 1953 the English-born journalist Dick Diamond dramatised essentialist Australian notions of male identity as hypermasculine, which were reinforced by male bonding in the context of major political and cultural changes. His *Reedy River* is a folk musical about the 1891 sheep-shearer's strike, one of the earliest and most important in Australian history. The narrative focuses on a farmhand who urges colleagues to strike because of poor wages, bad working conditions, and maltreatment. Many of the show's numbers were accompanied by a single guitar; the piece was performed in period costume with a simple farm wagon as the set.

Like numerous other works of this and subsequent periods, the show offers insights into the development of theatrical representations of masculinity. As noted by Jonathan Bollen, Adrian Kiernander, and Bruce Parr:

> *Reedy River* links the values of unionism with those of traditional Australian male bonding as two compatible versions of mateship; an idealised masculinity with hard-working comrades who are loyal to fellow workers and suspicious of strangers. The man alone; yet bonded in the trade union movement. It was written after the election of a conservative government, in 1949, and its repeated attempts to outlaw the Communist Party.[45]

Australian masculinity here is represented as having been derived from the immigrant/ frontier farm worker, soon transformed into a notion of moral integrity and rugged strength combined with a strong sense of justice, which was developed during the fight to assert individual rights. Although masculinity is romanticised, it is portrayed in relation to the protagonist's struggles with his fellow workers and to hegemonic power. The male characters of *Reedy River* gain complexity by being dramaturgically located in a moment of historical injustice and class conflict; the show expresses the lived experience of a specific kind of masculinity which has remained notable to this day.

The musical was hugely popular,[46] probably because of its local themes and its novel use of traditional folk songs reflecting Australian bush culture. With orchestrations that included the bush bass (or tea-chest bass) and the lagerphone (or Murrumbidgee river rattler) as well as the button or bush accordion, the mouth organ, and the tin whistle, the show also helped foster the Australian folk music revival of the 1950s, not least because the bush band the Bushwackers were hired to provide the musical accompaniment for the 1953 Sydney production.[47]

Written and composed by Albert Arlen and Nancy Brown, *The Sentimental Bloke* became one of the most successful Australian musicals of the twentieth century. Based on songs and poems published by C. J. Dennis in 1915, it was first performed in 1961; J. C. Williamson and then toured the country with it in 1962. A film adaptation was released in 1963,[48] and another production toured between 1986 and 1988.

*The Sentimental Bloke* tells the story of Bill, beginning with his decision to abandon his life of gambling and drinking after being in prison. The show then focuses on Bill's relationship with Doreen, who works in a pickle factory, and his rivalry with another suitor, portrayed as a sophisticated, urbane male. In scenes of humour and sentiment, the narrative then depicts the couple's marriage and the protagonist's transformation as he adapts to domestic life on the farm. In Arlen and Brown's show, notions of masculinity are represented by the Bill's 'larrikin' persona. This type of Australian male character can be described as a 'person of comical or outlandish behavior, a brash and impertinent hooligan, a high-spirited person who playfully rebels against authority and convention'.[49] The larrikin is central to the portrayal of the playful, rugged, unsophisticated, rowdy male hero in Australian folklore; a highly popular type, he is a well-intentioned

FIG. 5.3 The Bushwackers on the set of the 1953 Sydney production of *Reedy River*. Photo: J. C. Parker © Alamy Stock Photo.

rogue who needs to buck authority and follow his own individualistic path rather than belong to a group. The larrikin has a moral code which is not dictated by social mores, giving his masculine character charm and provoking empathy.

Written and composed by Eddie Perfect in 2008, *Shane Warne: The Musical* is in a similar vein. It tells the story of one of the greatest Australian cricketers, who caused controversy with his drug use, infidelity, and illicit deal with a bookmaker from India in1994–1995. One newspaper notes that '[t]he musical is billed as a warts-and-all account of the spin bowler's controversy-laden career and roller-coaster personal life set to soul, rock, opera, gospel music—and even a bit of Bollywood.'[50] It finishes with the chorus singing the refrain 'Everyone's a Little Bit like Shane,' implicating all Australian men in the protagonist's larrikin persona. The show's creator adds: 'There's a *Truman Show* quality to [Shane's] life, as if he's been thrown on to the set of his own story and doesn't really know his lines.'[51] Among the highlights of Warne's career is the 1993 Ashes series, when he bowled the 'Ball of the Century'—also known as 'That Ball'—to dismiss an astonished Mike Gatting, then captain of the English team; but the musical also shows him being stripped of the Australian vice-captaincy in 2000 after bombarding an English nurse, Donna Wright, with text messages.[52] Eddie Perfect asserts: 'Here is this incredibly gifted guy who bowls with such grace and beauty [ … ] but off the field his life is a shambolic disaster.'[53] Warne's comment after seeing the show was: 'They have captured my fun, "larrikin" side.' Once again, satire is the vehicle for the deconstruction

FIG. 5.4 Stymied by the googlies bowled by life: Shane Warne (1969–2022) ponders his options. Eddie Perfect, creator and star of *Shane Warne: The Musical*, as the beloved cricketer in the 2009 Sydney production. Photo: Robert Wallace © Alamy Stock Photo.

of a certain kind of masculinity, and with its mix of cricket, celebrity, and musical theatre the show brought 'sports fans into venues they hadn't visited before'.[54]

## THE HOMOSEXUAL AS A DIFFERENT KIND OF MALE: *THE BOY FROM OZ* AND *PRISCILLA, QUEEN OF THE DESERT*

With an original book by Nick Enright, later rewritten by Martin Sherman, *The Boy from Oz* is a jukebox musical based on the life of the Australian singer-songwriter Peter

Allen and features his songs. The show opened in Australia in 1998 before being staged in a revised version on Broadway in 2003, with a highly acclaimed Hugh Jackman in the title role. As well as being hugely popular in New York and Australia, the show broke new ground in relation to Australian musical theatre with its celebration of homosexuality, its articulation of masculine pride, and its focus on the subjects of AIDS and the nature of celebrity. Allen's life is portrayed in a series of flashbacks: he is depicted as a child; battling homophobia in his bush town; and working in a local pub, where he sings, dances, and plays the piano while dreaming of escaping small-town life and his abusive, alcoholic father. When Allen performs in the Hilton Hotel in Hong Kong, he meets Judy Garland, who enables him to realise his dream of performing in New York. After a brief marriage to Garland's daughter Liza Minnelli, he finds success on his own and personal happiness as a gay man.

Masculine identity is explored by the fluidity of Allen's gender positioning and the rejection of social discrimination against homosexuality. *The Boy from Oz* reflects how Australian conceptions of masculinity have changed over the last few decades, since Allen's story ends with the recognition of a non-stereotypical homosexual character, with his vulnerabilities, charm, ambition, and determination. In addition, the multiplicity of identity reference points is furthered in the contestation of celebrity myth and the assertion of a contemporary masculine agency.

Based on the film released in 1994, *Priscilla, Queen of the Desert* was first staged in 2006.[55] The show, written by Stephan Elliott and Allan Scott, toured Australia in 2006; it was performed in the West End in 2010 for two years and on Broadway in 2011. It also toured the United Kingdom and between 2009 and 2019 played in Milan, São Paulo, Madrid, Norway, New Zealand, Tokyo, Paris, Cape Town, and Munich. In Australia, the show's overt presentation of drag performers broke new ground in the portrayal of masculine identity. The campy self-awareness of the othered subjects allowed them to satirise themselves and others, enabling the audience to grasp the complexities of gender identity and sexual orientation by means of carnivalesque spectacle. Most important, the musical presents a knowing satire on essentialist gender stereotypes and homophobic prejudice, attaining its humanising effect through the ironic deconstruction of the hegemonic type of rugged masculinity seen as typical of 'real' men in the outback.

In a rather different way *Strictly Ballroom, the Musical* (2014) also addresses identity formation. The narrative, constructed around the theme of a corrupt ballroom competition, was adapted from Baz Luhrmann's 1992 film, and he himself created and directed the stage musical twenty-two years later. The jukebox show had a book by Luhrmann and Craig Pearce and was staged first in Melbourne and then the following year in Brisbane. A West End production opened in 2018, with Will Young as Wally, the master of ceremonies. Michael Billington, writing in the *Guardian*, wasn't overly impressed, calling the musical 'laborious, a Cinderella story, like a holiday camp.'[56]

Although there are no LGBTQ characters in *Strictly Ballroom*, it has a queer sensibility that echoes the postmodern approach of Luhrmann's films. Masculinity is portrayed as an attempted imitation of current Western stereotypes of dancer/contestant, inverting the traditional image of the male dancer as homosexual by presenting the young protagonist in an intensely romantic relationship with his female dance partner.

# COMING OF AGE: *BRAN NUE DAE*

The one significant Australian musical to focus on the Aboriginal experience was *Bran Nue Dae* (Brand New Day). The show premiered in 1990 at the Octagon Theatre in Broome, Western Australia, as part of the Festival of Perth, and combines the road-trip genre with a coming-of-age narrative incorporating blues, rock, and R&B. It was written by Jimmy Chi with his band, Knuckles. The musical was originally directed by Andrew Ross, a prominent theatre director of the region. The show won the prestigious Sidney Myer Performing Arts Awards in 1990 and later toured nationally. The following year the published script and score won the Special Award in the Western Australian Premier's Book Awards. A screen adaptation, directed by Rachel Perkins, was presented at a number of international film festivals (Melbourne and Toronto, 2009; Sundance, 2010), In the wake of the film's success—it became one of the top fifty local releases at the Australian box office—the stage musical was revived for an Australian tour in 2010.

Set in Broome in 1960, the story follows an Aboriginal teenager, Willie, who has problems with his girlfriend, Rosie. His mother, Theresa, sends him to boarding school in Perth. He is caught stealing food and runs away, spends a night on the streets of Perth, and meets 'Uncle' Tadpole, who wants to help Willie get home. At the same time, the head of the boarding school, Father Benedictus (played in the movie by Geoffrey Rush), who has noticed Willie's potential, starts searching for him. The road trip begins when two hippies agree to drive Willie and Tadpole to Broome in their camper van. On the way they have various adventures, including being arrested by the police. Willie meets Rosie at the beach in Broome and confesses his love for her. The story ends with Theresa's revelation that she had another son with Father Benedictus and that Tadpole is Willie's father.

The narrative has numerous comic scenes replete with uncovered identities and unlikely or surprising coincidences, built around a series of love stories. Two aspects of the writing undermine the artistic integrity of the show. One is that the Aboriginal experience is minimised so as to foreground the romantic events. In the context suggested by Hall's theory, the musical lacks a coherent representation of how Aboriginal identities are positioned in relation to the history of cultural and social hegemony. Whilst *Bran Nue Dae* deserves recognition as the first musical with an Aboriginal protagonist, it could be argued that the identities of the indigenous characters are framed as limited stereotypes. The young Aboriginal man at the centre of the musical is given a binary identity reminiscent (albeit in a sentimental and romanticised way) of the colonised 'noble savage', a representation that echoes certain South African musicals such as *uMabatha*, *Kwa Zulu*, and *The Mandela Trilogy*. Furthermore, one could argue that even after his coming of age Willie remains boyish—yet another naive and binary conception of 'tribal' masculine identity. Since the representation of the father amounts to a cliché of the street hobo as 'noble sufferer', Aboriginal adulthood and agency seem barely reflected. Here, manhood is infantilised and very different from the range of masculinities one can observe in 'white' musicals.

Homing in on these limitations, Stephen Holden, who reviewed the film version for the *New York Times*, noted that it is a 'deceptively slap-happy Australian pop fable', opining that its 'singsongy score is a mostly forgettable potpourri of folk, reggae, country and gospel poorly lip-synced. The bits of Aboriginal lore imparted along the way add flavoring to a sugar-coated romp that has the craft of a high school revue.'[57] However, a counter argument is advanced by Steve Dow, who saw the show's revival at the 2010 Sydney Festival:

> [The] work is a blend of lacerating truths [of] historical indigenous genocide and continuing dispossession. The production instills hope that there is a way to reconciliation. The ensemble sings 'Is this the end of our people?' moments after the men reenact a projected historical photograph of Aboriginal men chained together by their necks.[58]

In this view, the masculine coming-of-age trope makes it possible to attain adult agency because the context of Aboriginal history frames the dramaturgy; this is achieved by the use of historical photographs, references to land appropriation, and the males being chained, an image that suggests convicts or animals and thus portrays the Aboriginals as being 'inferior, primitive'. The history of the genocide of Aboriginal persons is almost an undertone in the production, one that acts as a point of reference for the narrative. History is a partial frame for the production; it is not entangled in the colonial master narrative.

Like *Sarafina!* and other South African musicals, *Bran Nue Dae* can be read in contrasting ways. I contend that the work is more than merely a commercially driven representation of stereotyped Aboriginal identities, devoid of any historical perspective. The stage production may at times consist of an unwieldy yoking together of subject matter and musical dramaturgy, but it does attempt a degree of contestation of colonial history and its legacies of identity construction. As Willie begins to mature and act independently, the show hints at his developing adult masculinity in conjunction with his acceptance of his Aboriginal origins. The coming-of-age narrative, the road trip to Broome, and the guidance of Uncle Tadpole combine with the projections and dialogues about land ownership and historical identity to indicate Willie's inner journey towards the realisation of an historically and culturally unique masculinity.

# The Black Beast Unleashed: the Australian *King Kong* (2013)

The final musical to be discussed in this overview couldn't be more different from *Bran Nue Dae*. The Australian *King Kong* has nothing to do with the South African work of the same title; rather, it is based on the classic 1933 film about a giant ape and a blonde damsel in distress, culminating in the famous scene of King Kong climbing the Empire State Building and being shot down by airplanes—to the dismay of Ann, the heroine.

The musical featured a score by Marius de Vries, with lyrics by Michael Mitnick and Craig Lucas and book by Lucas. It opened in Australia in 2013. The primary technological innovation was a one-ton, six-metre animatronic silverback gorilla as the title character, created by the Creature Technology Company. This was the largest puppet ever made for the stage. The 2013 press release specified that Kong was a highly sophisticated animatronic-marionette hybrid, controlled by the integration of hydraulics, automation, and manual manipulation from a team of puppeteer aerialists: 'A group of 35 on-stage and off-stage puppeteers manipulate the large-scale puppet. Several puppeteers are positioned on swinging trapezes and others launch themselves as counterweights off the puppet's shoulders to raise Kong's massive arms as he runs and swipes at planes during the performance.'[59] Following its 2013 première, the screen-to-stage transfer received mixed reviews. The reviewer for the *Aussie Theatre* wrote, 'It's spectacular. Visually and technically, this is theatre that we haven't seen before.' However, she went on:

> The story isn't there. There's a plot based on assuming the audience know King Kong's film story, but it's filled with illogical leaps, clunky dialogue and the melodrama of unearned emotion. It feels like it was written around the spectacle [ ... ] The music is forgettable. It's not boring, but it doesn't move the story, show character or add much more than a beat for the spectacle that it's supporting. [ ... ] The most successful number is Ann's lullaby to Kong on Skull Island.[60]

*Australian Stage* was similarly skeptical: 'The storyline does suffer from a lack of character development and an over-use of musical numbers that are sometimes more razzle-dazzle than relevant to the actual story.'[61] The *Sydney Morning Herald* believed that the show '[succeeds] on many levels [ ... ] if it falls short, it's because our expectations are so sky high. As such, it is a showcase for a technology's potential and also its limitations. It is a novel, intermittently powerful but synthetic spectacle that seeks to be more.'[62] In spite of its less-than-stellar reception, the show moved to Broadway. The playwright Marsha Norman was commissioned to rewrite certain sections of the script. In its revised version, the musical opened on Broadway on 8 November 2018 and closed on 18 August 2019 after 324 performances.

The musical clearly embraces the colonial legacies of the stereotyped identities already ingrained in its source material: the female is the demure, submissive, compliant, feminine *white* type and Kong an emblem of the primitive, wild, yet morally noble 'savage' who ultimately saves the white woman from harm at the cost of his own life. The stereotyped tropes of colonial/colonised relationships are obvious: a fantasy of black masculinity as sexually potent is grafted on to the colonially defined categories of the 'buck Negro'/animal of antebellum American slavery, the male being conceived as naïve, childlike, and primitive, yet having a moral core which redeems him from being merely savage. In a word, masculinity is infantilised in a trope often seen in the representation of the colonised male subject. This provokes the question of why—eighty years after the film was first released in cinemas—an Australian stage musical felt the necessity to revive those stereotypes without giving them a contemporary makeover.

# Conclusion

The contrasting trajectories of musical theatre as it developed in the very different cultures of South Africa and Australia distinctly reveal the dialectical process through which notions of colonial and postcolonial identity have developed and changed. The indigenous Australian musical can be seen to involve a continuing preoccupation with expressing a peculiarly Australian paradigm of masculinity; the works are not especially notable for innovations in musical and theatrical dramaturgy but are by and large limited to the formal imitation of first-world American and British models. Perhaps *Bran Nue Dae* signals a new approach to the representation of indigenous Australian identity, but otherwise there is a surprising lack of Aboriginal perspectives. In contrast, the subject matter of South African musical theatre has almost obsessively reflected or openly contested the oppressive regimes of British colonialism and apartheid in its foregrounding of black colonised or subaltern identities. Aesthetically, most South African musicals showcase a surprising variety of indigenous African music and dance, which, though often masking the exploitative conditions of their creation and reception, have been both distinctive and internationally popular since 1959. As globalisation causes the postcolonial story of musical theatre in both countries to become more syncretic over time, it is to be hoped that there will be room for genuinely original postcolonial versions of indigenous narratives and identities.

## Notes

1. Stuart Hall, 'Cultural Identity and Diaspora', in *Colonial Discourse and Post-Colonial Theory*, ed. Patrick Williams and Laura Chrisman (New York: Columbia University Press, 1994), 231.

2. A rival commercial management that emerged in Johannesburg in the 1950s was Brian Brooke, which occasionally produced musicals.
3. 'J. C. Williamson's LTD', *Australian Variety Theatre Archive*, 27 August 2015, http://ozvta.com/organisations-a-l/, accessed 17 November 2019.
4. Mxolisi Norman, 'South African Musical Theatre' (PhD diss., Edge Hill University, 2019), 13.
5. Ibid.
6. Ibid., 16.
7. Ibid., 17.
8. Ibid., 17.
9. Mervyn McMurtry, 'Doing Their Own Thane: The Critical Reception of *uMabatha*, Welcome Msomi's Zulu *Macbeth*' (PhD diss., University of Natal, South Africa, 1999), 311.
10. Ibid., 309.
11. Quoted in Percy Baneshik, 'Impact in London Must Have Been Overwhelming', *Johannesburg Star*, 22 July 1972, 22.
12. Welcome Msomi, *uMabatha*, in *Adaptations of Shakespeare: An Anthology of Plays from the 17th Century to the Present*, ed. Daniel Fischlin and Mark Fortier (London: Routledge, 2014), 164–188; here: 164.
13. Laurence Wright, '*uMabatha*: Global and Local', *English Studies in Africa* 47, no. 2 (2004), 61, https://core.ac.uk/download/pdf/145045912.pdf, accessed 20 November 2019.
14. Ibid.
15. Ibid.
16. 'Mshengu' [pseud., Robert Malcolm McLaren], '*uMabatha*: To Be or Not To Be; Review of *uMabatha* by Welcome Msomi', *S'ketsh* (Summer 1974–1975): 15.
17. Quoted in Graham Bradshaw, Tom Bishop, and Laurence Wright, eds., *The Shakespeare International Yearbook 9: Special Section, South African Shakespeare in the Twentieth Century* (Farnham: Ashgate, 2009), 127, n. 9.
18. *The Oxford History of World Cinema* defines blaxploitation films as those which 'romanticized the iconography of the black ghetto—its subcultural styles in dress, speech, behaviour and attitudes and glorified the ghetto as a kind of noble jungle' (Geoffrey Nowell-Smith, ed., *The Oxford History of World Cinema* [Oxford: Oxford University Press, 1996], 505).
19. Quoted in Mel Atkey, *A Million Miles from Broadway: Musical Theatre beyond New York and London* (Canada: Friendlysong, 2012), 188.
20. Quoted in Eddy De Clercq, 'Eureka! Tribute to Bertha Egnos', *Soul Safari: South African Musicals & Movies*, 6 October 2013, https://soulsafari.wordpress.com/2013/06/10/eureka-tribute-to-bertha-egnos/, accessed 15 November 2019.
21. Charles Gerald Fraser, 'Black Committee Urges Boycott of *Ipi Tombi*', *New York Times*, 28 December 1976, https://www.nytimes.com/1976/12/28/archives/black-committee-urges-boycott-of-ipi-tombi-from-south-africa.html, accessed 16 November 2019.
22. Quoted in Richard Anthony Baker, 'Joan Brickhill', *Stage*, 29 January 2014, https://www.thestage.co.uk/features/obituaries/2014/joan-brickhill/, accessed 16 November 2019.
23. Gugu Hlongwane, 'The Junction Avenue Theatre Company's *Sophiatown* and the Limits of National Oneness', *Postcolonial Text* 2, no. 2 (2006) https://www.postcolonial.org/index.php/pct/article/view/425/829, accessed 18 November 2019.
24. Ibid.
25. Ibid.
26. Ibid.

27. Ibid.

28. Ibid.

29. Ibid.

30. Ibid.

31. Loren Kruger, 'The Uses of Nostalgia: Drama, History, and Liminal Moment in South Africa', *Modern Drama* 38, no. 1 (1995): 60–70; here: 60.

32. Hlongwane, 'The Junction Avenue Theatre Company's *Sophiatown*', 18.

33. Eddy De Clercq, 'Remember District 6', *Soul Safari South African Musicals & Movies*, 18 May 2015, n.p., https://soulsafari.wordpress.com/2015/05/18/remember-district-6/, accessed 20 November 2019.

34. 'Freedom Coming Through Tomorrow! Dynamic, Passionate *Sarafina!* Portrays a People Confident of Winning Through', *New Nation*, 18–24 June 1987, 12.

35. Jerry Mofokeng, 'Theatre for Export: The Commercialization of the Black People's Struggle in South African Export Musicals,' in *Theatre and Change in South Africa*, ed. Geoffrey V Davis and Anne Fuchs (Amsterdam: Harwood Academic, 1996), 85–87; here: 86.

36. Cima, 'Sarafina! In Black and White: Revival, Colour-conscious casting and new social cohesion paradigms'.

37. Quoted in ibid, 51. Confirming the musical's international reach, Leleti Khumalo, who played Sarafina, received a Tony Award nomination for Best Featured Actress in a Musical as well as an NAACP Image Award. The production itself was nominated in 1988 for four Tony Awards: Best Musical, Best Original Score, Best Choreography, and Best Direction of a Musical.

38. Zakes Mda, 'Politics and the Theatre: Current Trends in South Africa,' in *Theatre and Change in South Africa*, ed. Geoffrey V. Davis and Anne Fuchs (Amsterdam: Harwood Academic, 1996), 193–218; here: 205.

39. Frank Rich, 'Stage: South African *Sarafina!*', *New York Times*, 26 October1987, https://www.nytimes.com/1987/10/26/theater/stage-south-african-sarafina.html, accessed 17 November 2019.

40. Martin Denton, '*Kat and the Kings*', www.theatermania, 27 October 1999, https://www.theatermania.com/new-york-city-theater/reviews/kat-and-the-kings_65.html, accessed 16 November 2019.

41. '*Umoja* by Todd Twala and Thembi Nyandeni', *Afridiziak Theatre*, January 2012, 17, http://www.afridiziak.com/theatrenews/whatson/january2012/umoja.html, accessed 15 November 2019.

42. Darren Dalglish, '*Umoja: The Spirit of Togetherness*', *London Theatre*, 22 November 2001, https://www.londontheatre.co.uk/reviews/umoja-the-spirit-of-togetherness, accessed 18 November 2019.

43. Sophie Constanti, 'Shout of Africa', *Evening Standard*, 16 November 2001, https://www.questia.com/newspaper/1G1-80126524/shout-of-africa, accessed 18 November 2019..

44. Arminta Wallace, '*Magic Flute* Finds Its African Edge', *Irish Times*, 20 September 2008, https://www.irishtimes.com/news/magic-flute-finds-its-african-edge-1.939970, accessed 20 November 2019.

45. Jonathan Bollen, Adrian Kiernander, and Bruce Parr, *Men at Play: Masculinities in Australian Theatre since the 1950s* (Amsterdam and New York: ProQuest Ebook Central, 2008), 21.

46. Melissa Bellanta, 'A Masculine Romance: *The Sentimental Bloke* and Australian Culture in the War and Early Interwar Years', *Journal of Popular Romance Studies* 4, no. 2 (2014): 1–20; here: 1.

47. 'Bushwackers, The, Musical Group (–1957)', *Trove, National Library of Australia*, 2019, https://trove.nla.gov.au/people/1307511?c=people, accessed 20 November 2019.

48. A copy of the film, starring Maxwell Collins, Carolyn Harrison and Jack Manue,l is held by the Australian National Film and Sound Archive, http://colsearch.nfsa.gov.au/nfsa/search/display/display.w3p;adv=;group=;groupequals=;holdingType=;page=1;parentid=;query=sentimental%20bloke%20Media%3A%22TELEVISION%22;querytype=;rec=2;resCount=10, accessed 20 November 2019..

49. *Webster's New World College Dictionary*, 5th ed. (United States: Houghton Mifflin Harcourt, 2014), s.v. 'larrikin'.

50. Bonnie Malkin, 'Shane Warne Backs Musical Based on His Life', *Telegraph*, 10 December 2008, https://www.telegraph.co.uk/sport/cricket/3699759/Shane-Warne-backs-Musical-based-on-his-life.html, accessed 20 November 2019.

51. Quoted in Kathy Marks, '*Shane Warne: The Musical*', *Independent*, 3 December 2008, https://www.independent.co.uk/arts-entertainment/theatre-dance/features/shane-warne-the-musical-1048567.html, accessed 20 November 2019.

52. Ibid.

53. Quoted in ibid.

54. Craig Mathieson, 'Warne Out? Not Even a Half-Chance', *Sunday Morning Herald*, 14 June 2013, https://www.smh.com.au/entertainment/musicals/warne-out-not-even-a-halfchance-20130613-2o6go.html, accessed 20 November 2019..

55. The plot of the show can be summed up as follows: Anthony Belrose is appearing in Sydney under his drag pseudonym Mitzi Del Bra when his ex-wife, Marion, asks him to perform for a few weeks at her business resort in distant, rural Alice Springs. She also wants him to meet their son, Benji, now eight years old. Mitzi invites his transgender friend Bernadette and another drag queen, Felicia, to join him. The travelers purchase a camper van they nickname 'Priscilla, Queen of the Desert', which initiates a picaresque journey through the outback culminating in Benji's acceptance of his father's sexuality and lifestyle. At the end of their performances in Alice Springs, the group makes plans to travel Australia performing their drag show.

56. Michael Billington, '*Strictly Ballroom the Musical* Review: Baz Luhrmann's Dancefloor Disaster', *Guardian*, 14 February 2018, https://www.theguardian.com/stage/2018/apr/24/strictly-ballroom-the-musical-review-baz-luhrmann-dancefloor-disaster, accessed 20 November 2019.

57. Stephen Holden, 'Aboriginal Teenager's Australian Road Trip', *New York Times*, 9 September 2010, https://www.nytimes.com/2010/09/10/movies/10bran.html, accessed 21 November 2019.

58. Stephen Dow, '*Bran Nue Dae* Review: Great Australian Musical with Vibrant Cast Resonates at Sydney Festival,' *Guardian*, 18 January 2020, https://www.theguardian.com/culture/2020/jan/18/bran-nue-dae-review-great-australian-musical-resonates-with-vibrant-cast-at-sydney-festival, accessed 20 January 2020.

59. Adam Hetrick, 'King Kong Musical May Conquer Broadway Next', www.playbill, 26 June 2013, https://www.playbill.com/article/king-kong-musical-may-conquer-broadway-next-com-206968, accessed 20 November 2010.

MUSICAL TRAVAILS IN THE BRITISH EMPIRE    187

60. Anne-Marie Peard, 'Oh King Kong! You Gorgeous, Sexy, Magnificent Beast', *Aussie Theatre*, 16 June 2013, https://aussietheatre.com.au/reviews/oh-king-kong-you-gorgeous-sexy-magnificent-beast, accessed 20 November 2019.
61. Vito Mattarelli, '*King Kong*—Global Creatures', *Australian Stage*, 16 June 2013, https://www.australianstage.com.au/201306166377/reviews/melbourne/king-kong-|-global-creatures.html, accessed 20 November 2019.
62. Jason Blake, '*King Kong* Clings On to Audience's Sky-High Expectations', *Sydney Morning Herald*, 16 June 2013, https://www.smh.com.au/entertainment/musicals/king-kong-clings-on-to-audiences-skyhigh-expectations-20130616-20brb.html, accessed 20 November 2019.

## Bibliography

Atkey, Mel. *A Million Miles from Broadway: Musical Theatre beyond New York and London*. Canada: Friendlysong, 2012.

Baker, Richard Anthony. 'Joan Brickhill'. *Stage*, 29 January 2014, n.p., https://www.thestage.co.uk/features/obituaries/2014/joan-brickhill/, accessed 16 November 2019.

Baneshik, Percy. 'Impact in London Must Have Been Overwhelming'. *Johannesburg Star*, 22 July 1972, 22.

Bellanta, Melissa. 'A Masculine Romance: *The Sentimental Bloke* and Australian Culture in the War and Early Interwar Years'. *Journal of Popular Romance Studies* 4, no. 2 (2014): 1–20.

Billington, Michael. '*Strictly Ballroom the Musical* Review: Baz Luhrmann's Dancefloor Disaster'. *Guardian*, 14 February 2018, n.p., https://www.theguardian.com/stage/2018/apr/24/strictly-ballroom-the-musical-review-baz-luhrmann-dancefloor-disaster, accessed 20 November 2019.

Blake, Jason. '*King Kong* Clings On to Audience's Sky-High Expectations'. *Sydney Morning Herald*, 16 June 2013, n.p., https://www.smh.com.au/entertainment/musicals/king-kong-clings-on-to-audiences-skyhigh-expectations-20130616-20brb.html, accessed 20 November 2019.

Bollen, Jonathan, Adrian Kiernander, and Bruce Parr. *Men at Play: Masculinities in Australian Theatre since the 1950s*. Amsterdam and New York: ProQuest Ebook Central, 2008.

Bradshaw, Graham, Tom Bishop, and Laurence Wright, eds. *The Shakespeare International Yearbook 9: Special Section, South African Shakespeare in the Twentieth Century*. Farnham: Ashgate, 2009.

'Bushwackers, The, Musical Group (–1957)'. *Trove, National Library of Australia*, 2019, n.p., https://trove.nla.gov.au/people/1307511?c=people, accessed 20 November 2019.

Cima, Gibson Alessandro. 'Sarafina! in Black and White: Revival, Colour-conscious casting and new social cohesion paradigms'. *South African Theatre Journal*, 27, 2014, 207–221. Available from: https://journals.co.za/doi/abs/10.1080/10137548.2014.974310

Constanti, Sophie. 'Shout of Africa'. *Evening Standard*, 16 November 2001, n.p., https://www.questia.com/newspaper/1G1-80126524/shout-of-africa, accessed 18 November 2019.

Dalglish, Darren. '*Umoja: The Spirit of Togetherness*'. *London Theatre*, 22 November 2001. https://www.londontheatre.co.uk/reviews/umoja-the-spirit-of-togetherness, accessed 18 November 2019.

De Clercq, Eddie. 'Eureka! Tribute to Bertha Egnos'. *Soul Safari: South African Musicals & Movies*, 6 October 2013. https://soulsafari.wordpress.com/2013/06/10/eureka-tribute-to-bertha-egnos/, accessed 15 November 2019.

De Clercq, Eddy. 'Remember District 6'. *Soul Safari: South African Musicals & Movies*, 18 May 2015. https://soulsafari.wordpress.com/2015/05/18/remember-district-6/, accessed 20 November 2019.

Denton, Martin. '*Kat and the Kings*'. www.theatermania, 27 October 1999. https://www.theatermania.com/new-york-city-theater/reviews/kat-and-the-kings_65.html, accessed 16 November 2019.

Dow, Stephen. '*Bran Nue Dae* Review: Great Australian Musical with Vibrant Cast Resonates at Sydney Festival'. *Guardian*, 17 January 2020. https://www.theguardian.com/culture/2020/jan/18/bran-nue-dae-review-great-australian-musical-resonates-with-vibrant-cast-at-sydney-festival, accessed 20 January 2020.

Fraser, Charles Gerald. 'Black Committee Urges Boycott of *Ipi Tombi*'. *New York Times*, 28 December 1976. https://www.nytimes.com/1976/12/28/archives/black-committee-urges-boycott-of-ipi-tombi-from-south-africa.html, accessed 16 November 2019.

'Freedom Coming Through Tomorrow! Dynamic, Passionate *Sarafina!* Portrays a People Confident of Winning Through'. *New Nation*, 18–24 June 1987, 12.

Hall, Stuart. 'Cultural Identity and Diaspora'. In *Colonial Discourse and Post-Colonial Theory*, edited by Patrick Williams and Laura Chrisman, 207. New York: Columbia University Press, 1994.

Hetrick, Adam. 'King Kong Musical May Conquer Broadway Next'. www.playbill, 26 June 2013. https://www.playbill.com/article/king-kong-musical-may-conquer-broadway-next-com-206968, accessed 20 November 2010.

Hlongwane, Gugu. 'The Junction Avenue Theatre Company's *Sophiatown* and the Limits of National Oneness'. *Postcolonial Text* 2, no. 2 (2006): 127–136. https://www.postcolonial.org/index.php/pct/article/view/425/829, accessed 18 November 2019.

Holden, Stephen. 'Aboriginal Teenager's Australian Road Trip'. *New York Times*, 9 September 2010. https://www.nytimes.com/2010/09/10/movies/10bran.html, accessed 21 November 2019.

'J. C. Williamson's LTD'. Australian Variety Theatre Archive, 27 August 2015. http://ozvta.com/organisations-a-l/, accessed 17 November 2019.

Kruger, Loren. 'The Uses of Nostalgia: Drama, History, and Liminal Moment in South Africa'. *Modern Drama* 38, no. 1 (1995): 60–70.

Malkin, Bonnie. 'Shane Warne Backs Musical Based on His Life'. *Telegraph*, 10 December 2008, n.p., https://www.telegraph.co.uk/sport/cricket/3699759/Shane-Warne-backs-Musical-based-on-his-life.html, accessed 20 November 2019.

Marks, Kathy. '*Shane Warne: The Musical*'. *The Independent*, 3 December 2008. https://www.independent.co.uk/arts-entertainment/theatre-dance/features/shane-warne-the-musical-1048567.html, accessed 20 November 2019.

Mathieson, Craig. 'Warne Out? Not Even a Half-Chance'. *Sunday Morning Herald*, 14 June 2013, n.p., https://www.smh.com.au/entertainment/musicals/warne-out-not-even-a-halfchance-20130613-206g0.html, accessed 20 November 2019.

Mattarelli, Vito. '*King Kong*—Global Creatures'. *Australian Stage*, 16 June 2013, n.p., https://www.australianstage.com.au/201306166377/reviews/melbourne/king-kong-|-global-creatures.html, accessed 20 November 2019.

McMurtry, Mervyn. 'Doing Their Own Thane: The Critical Reception of *uMabatha*, Welcome Msomi's Zulu *Macbeth*'. PhD diss., University of Natal, South Africa, 1999.

Mda, Zakes. 'Politics and the Theatre: Current Trends in South Africa.' In *Theatre and Change in South Africa*, edited by Geoffrey V. Davis and Anne Fuchs, 193–218. Amsterdam: Harwood Academic, 1996.

Mofokeng, Jerry. 'Theatre for Export: The Commercialization of the Black People's Struggle in South African Export Musicals.' In *Theatre and Change in South Africa*, edited by Geoffrey V Davis and Anne Fuchs, 85–87. Amsterdam: Harwood Academic, 1996.

Mshengu [pseud., Robert Malcolm McLaren]. '*uMabatha*: To Be or Not To Be; Review of *uMabatha* by Welcome Msomi'. *S'ketsh*, 1(2) (Summer1974–1975): 15.

Msomi, Welcome. *uMabatha*. In *Adaptations of Shakespeare: An Anthology of Plays from the 17th Century to the Present*, edited by Daniel Fischlin and Mark Fortier, 164–188. London: Routledge, 2014.

Norman, Mxolisi. 'South African Musical Theatre'. PhD diss., Edge Hill University, 2019.

Nowell-Smith, Geoffrey. *The Oxford History of World Cinema*. Oxford: Oxford University Press, 1996.

Peard, Anne-Marie. 'Oh King Kong! You Gorgeous, Sexy, Magnificent Beast.' *Aussie Theatre*, 16 June 2013, n.p., https://aussietheatre.com.au/reviews/oh-king-kong-you-gorgeous-sexy-magnificent-beast, accessed 20 November 2019.

Rich, Frank. 'Stage: South African *Sarafina!*' *New York Times*, 26 October1987. https://www.nytimes.com/1987/10/26/theater/stage-south-african-sarafina.html, accessed 17 November 2019.

'*Umoja* by Todd Twala And Thembi Nyandeni'. *Afridiziak Theatre*, January 2012, n.p., http://www.afridiziak.com/theatrenews/whatson/january2012/umoja.html, accessed 15 November 2019.

Wallace, Arminta. '*Magic Flute* Finds Its African Edge'. *Irish Times*, 20 September 2008. https://www.irishtimes.com/news/magic-flute-finds-its-african-edge-1.939970, accessed 20 November 2019.

*Webster's New World College Dictionary*. 5th ed. United States: Houghton Mifflin Harcourt, 2014.

Wright, Laurence. '*uMabatha*: Global and Local'. *English Studies in Africa* 47, no. 2 (2004): 67–74, https://core.ac.uk/download/pdf/145045912.pdf, accessed 20 November 2019.

CHAPTER 6

# MY UN-FAIR LADY?

*Celebrity Producer Lars Schmidt and the Postwar
International Success of Broadway Shows*

DIRK GINDT

> *You don't go into theatre to make money. It's not the place for it. And you
> have to be a little naïve. It is only afterwards that you understand what kind
> of dangers you have avoided.*
>
> Lars Schmidt[1]

IT seems preposterous, at least at first, that one of the postwar period's most successful individual theatre producers who ruled a financial empire that stretched from Scandinavia to France and who became a millionaire by his mid-forties, would complain about financial hazards. In a career that stretched from 1941, when he founded a publishing house in Gothenburg, to 1996, when he produced his last theatre project in Paris, the Swedish impresario Lars Schmidt (1917–2010) was the first to introduce Nordic and continental European audiences to such seminal works as *The Glass Menagerie*, *The Diary of Anne Frank*, and *Cat on a Hot Tin Roof*. Schmidt also played a pivotal role in successfully helping to introduce and establish the postwar Broadway musical, including the blockbuster hits *Oklahoma!*, *My Fair Lady*, and *Jesus Christ Superstar*, first on Nordic and then on continental stages.

In this chapter I identify and explain some of Schmidt's key artistic choices and financial strategies, which paved the way for the transatlantic breakthrough of the American musical. By presenting heretofore unmined archival and original sources (including reviews, interviews, letters, and contracts), many of which have until now been unavailable to English-speaking scholars, the chapter proposes to offer a significantly more nuanced understanding of the Swedish agent-*cum*-producer than has been available thus far. I aim to shift the prevailing perception of Schmidt as a financial profiteer and ruthless businessman who sold 'prefabricated' productions to European theatres with little interest in artistic quality or creative processes. Instead, I emphasise his drive and passion for the performing arts as well as his profound understanding of the financial realities of producing live theatre. Although Schmidt caused no little controversy, and although his increasing influence as a producer triggered numerous anxieties among theatre critics and managing directors in many European countries, he ultimately played a central role both in bringing postwar Broadway musicals and plays to the other side of the Atlantic and in making it culturally intelligible to European audiences as well as financially viable for European theatres.

The essay begins by briefly charting the efforts of Swedish theatres to culturally translate the new American musical genre for their audiences before summarising some of the defining moments of Schmidt's career, including his adventurous trip to the United States in the middle of World War II and his move to Paris in 1956. As a primary case study, the 1959 production of *My Fair Lady* in Stockholm is representative of how European audiences came to embrace the Broadway musical. Not only did it mark one of the most expensive theatrical events produced in Sweden up to that point, but it also engendered significant anxieties around 'prefabricated' theatre that seemingly valued profit over art. I will put this criticism to the test by presenting various sides of the debate and teasing out the complexity of the (arguably very shrewd) business strategies used by Schmidt to launch *My Fair Lady* as one of the defining cultural events of the postwar period in Northern and Western Europe, one that became a turning point for the financial and conceptual organisation of live theatre. Also at play in this moment are the intertwined fears around commercialisation and Americanisation that served to heighten the tensions between theatre as art and theatre as mass entertainment.

# THE CULTURAL TRANSLATION OF A NEW GENRE

For a variety of cultural, political, and financial reasons, Sweden provided a gateway for postwar American theatre and Broadway culture in the immediate postwar era. The country was never occupied by Nazi Germany and thus retained a relatively intact infrastructure after the war. The social democratic government not only built the country's famous welfare state but also initiated a rapidly unfolding process of cultural democratisation that led to the opening of numerous regional and city theatres whose managing and artistic directors were eager to present contemporary and international works to their audiences. Moreover, the first Swedish translations of the Russian director Konstantin Stanislavsky appeared in 1944, which led to a new generation of actors trained (or self-educated) in a realistic style, which in turn facilitated the successful staging of new American plays. Dramas like *Cat on a Hot Tin Roof* (1955) and *Long Day's Journey into Night* (1956) had their first European performance in Sweden, while many musicals celebrated their non-English premieres in Sweden, including *Oklahoma!* (1948), *Annie Get Your Gun* (1949), and *My Fair Lady* (1959).[2]

The theatre scholar Sven Åke Heed identifies 1942 as the starting point for a new wave of musical theatre, when the private Oscar Theatre (Oscarsteatern) in Stockholm produced Jerome Kern and Oscar Hammerstein II's *Show Boat*. By then, audiences were already familiar with some of the tunes, not least because of the two movie versions (from 1929 and 1936), which were also screened in Swedish movie theatres. Although theatre reviewers realised that they were confronted with a new genre that was significantly different from the well-established and very popular operetta, they were unsure how to label it, and the term musical (*musikal*) had yet to establish itself in Swedish. They agreed, however, that neither 'show' nor 'operetta', let alone 'melodrama', was an appropriate designation.[3]

Managing directors recognised this confusion, so the playbills for the Swedish productions of *Oklahoma!* and *Annie Get Your Gun* contained didactic essays that marked an attempt to culturally translate the genre to Swedish audiences. The designations of American singspiel, operetta, or musical play were purposely employed to distinguish a particularly American form of musical theatre that was different from European operetta, with its connotations of nineteenth-century and pre-war Viennese and Parisian culture. Heed suggests that the outmoded romances and intrigues of European aristocracy no longer appealed to postwar audiences; instead they were drawn to musicals that presented a larger variety of social classes, which in turn demanded a more natural acting style. Musicals symbolised the dawn of a new age and epitomised American modernity, optimism, and sense of progress. Moreover, they imbued Swedish theatre with a much-needed revitalisation of entertainment culture and a renewed appreciation of popular music.[4]

## FROM GOTHENBURG TO NEW YORK AND PARIS

Born in Gothenburg, Schmidt initially envisaged a career in shipping before he attended the inaugural production of Gothenburg City Theatre in 1934, Shakespeare's *The Tempest*, which led to his decision to pursue a life serving the muse Thalia. Together with Per Thorsten Hammarén, who was the son of Gothenburg City Theatre's managing director Torsten Hammarén, he co-founded the publishing house Lars Schmidt & Co. in 1941. Because of the ongoing war, there was a shortage of newly written stage works, so the twenty-four-year-old Schmidt booked a ticket on the M.S. *Carolina Thordén*, bound for Philadelphia, to purchase the rights to new American plays for Gothenburg City Theatre. The journey started in Liinakhamari, an ice-free harbour in the north of Finland (today part of Russia), which was the only route for Swedish and Finnish boats to travel westbound during the early years of the war. The trip, which was initially supposed to take only a couple of weeks, took over two months. On 26 March, soon after passing the Faroe Islands in the North Atlantic, the ship was attacked by German fighter planes. Schmidt's cabin was completely destroyed by a bomb, and of the seventy people on board, one Finnish courier died when the ship caught fire and eventually sank. Schmidt was among the survivors who were led to safety by British troops. He found himself stranded on the Faroe Islands for a few weeks, where he debated whether he should instead become a farmer and wait there for the end of the war. Swedish newspapers were informed about the attacks by the consulate in Tórshavn and eagerly reported on the aspiring publisher's adventures. Eventually an opportunity presented itself to continue his journey via Havana to Miami.

By the time he arrived in New York he had lost his travelling funds, his passport, and his letters of introduction. Thanks to the contacts of his father, a high-ranking army officer, his permit to visit the United States was extended. Schmidt had an exciting story to tell his new American friends and acquaintances, at a moment when the country had not yet entered the war, and the fact that he was fluent in English served him well. Soon he became a welcome guest at cocktail parties, where he was introduced to the leading playwrights, lyricists, and composers of the period, including Tennessee Williams, Lillian Hellman, Clifford Odets, Maxwell Anderson, Robert Sherwood, Irving Berlin, Cole Porter, Oscar Hammerstein II, and Richard Rodgers.[5] Schmidt made sure to cherish and actively cultivate these personal contacts, which allowed him to bypass agents and gatekeepers ('the raging wolves',[6] as he called them), gain access to writing workshops, and attend try-out openings in Boston and New Haven.

On 3 July 1941 the *New York Herald Tribune* reported that the rights for Joseph Kesselring's farce *Arsenic and Old Lace* had been purchased by a Swedish producer who aimed to have the play staged at Gothenburg City Theatre and the Royal Dramatic Theatre in Stockholm.[7] When Schmidt returned to Sweden in August, he eagerly recounted his adventures to the press and raved about New York theatre: 'On Broadway, the entertainment life is flourishing [ ... ] and the question is whether there have ever been such great financial successes as now.'[8] In his 1995 biography Schmidt reminisced: 'Getting to experience Broadway in 1941 was incredible. Everything I dreamed of was there. Plays that had run for three to four years, the musical that was emerging. I established contact with many of the big authors.'[9]

The Swedish production of *Arsenic and Old Lace* turned out to be a success, and Schmidt was able to solidify his position with a second trip to New York in late 1945. Upon his return in December, he had secured the rights to over a hundred American plays, amongst them Tennessee Williams's *The Glass Menagerie*, which would have its European debut at the Royal Dramatic Theatre in Stockholm in February 1946. Soon Schmidt's publishing house held a unique position in the entire Nordic region: he was the first person to bring new American works to Europe. Schmidt understood early on that, as a consequence of the war, the United States was bound to become a dominant player in international theatre: 'There is no doubt', he explained, 'that America will become the strongest theatre country in the near future. This is where the best plays are being written right now, and the Americans have received a great addition through all the skilled refugee writers in recent years.'[10]

It is during these two initial trips that we find the seeds not only of Schmidt's fascination with Broadway culture, American drama, and musicals, but also of his increasing admiration of American production methods. The young entrepreneur was in awe of the large sums of money that were being invested in American productions—'$80,000 for a spoken drama and $150,000 for an operetta are not unusual', he told the Swedish press. To afford such endeavours, American theatres were dependent on outside investors, 'so called backers who speculate in theatrical successes. Some of them always get lucky and get themselves a mighty income—they are called "angels"'.[11] Schmidt also emphasised how much he appreciated the try-out system, which allowed the author, the director, and the cast a chance to finesse and perfect a production before transferring it to New York.

As a publisher, Schmidt purchased the licences for foreign productions of mostly American and some British plays and forwarded the scripts to managing directors in the Nordic region. Once a playhouse showed interest in producing a certain work, a translation was commissioned. Over time this would create intense competition among theatres to be the first to host the Scandinavian or even European opening of established American playwrights. In a race to be the first in Scandinavia to host *A Streetcar Named Desire*, for example, Gothenburg City Theatre opened a mere fifteen minutes ahead of Malmö City Theatre's production on 1 March 1949.

Williams came to play a crucial part in Schmidt's professional life. Impressed by his Nordic representative's efforts, Williams convinced him to produce the French opening of *Cat on a Hot Tin Roof* in Paris in 1956. Directed by Peter Brook, the production caused significant sexual anxieties among audiences and critics owing to the play's provocative subject matter and a sexually charged performance by Jeanne Moreau as Maggie.[12]

Encouraged by the success of the production, Schmidt decided to settle in Paris, founded his own production company, Lars Schmidt Productions Société Anonyme, and within a few years had become the co–managing director of four private theatres, each of which received little public subsidy.[13] In addition, he continued to hold a stake in his publishing house in Gothenburg (which he sold in 1975). As producer, he either financed an entire production (alone or, more often, with the help of outside investors) or leased out one of the theatres that he managed for an outside production. Within two years he had established himself as a cultural force to be reckoned with in the City of Light, and French theatre magazines started portraying him as *l'homme du jour* ('the man of the day'), who had quickly consolidated his first success with Williams's play with a production of *The Diary of Anne Frank* that ran for three years. Soon critics had altered their title for him to *le premier producteur de Paris* ('Paris's foremost producer').[14] He participated in lively theatre debates and, unafraid of the wrath he sometimes caused among his peers, was not shy to make his own recommendations on how best to handle the theatre crisis of the 1950s, which was partly caused by new modes of consumption and the burgeoning medium of television. On one occasion, Eugène Ionesco famously dismissed him as a *commerçant du théâtre* ('theatre's wholesale dealer').[15]

In early 1966 Schmidt bought the Théâtre Montparnasse, where he had previously produced Henrik Ibsen's *Hedda Gabler*, with Ingrid Bergman in the title role. The two

FIG. 6.1 Lars Schmidt in front of the poster for his groundbreaking 1956 French production of *Cat on a Hot Tin Roof*. Photo: Photo: IMS/Borglund © Camera Press London.

of them had met during the run of *Cat on a Hot Tin Roof* while Bergman was playing the female lead in Robert Anderson's *Tea and Sympathy*. Once rumours of their romance broke in the press, Schmidt all of a sudden found himself propelled to fame even beyond theatre circles, as international tabloids and lifestyle magazines started writing about the new man in Bergman's life. The couple were married in 1958 and remained friends even after their divorce in 1978.

## A Spanish Fox in Stockholm

As early as 1947 Schmidt organised a tour throughout Scandinavia for Oscar Hammerstein II to familiarise him with the major theatres and introduce him to key artists in order to convince him of the prospects for launching Broadway musicals in Europe. The move was successful, and during another trip to New York Schmidt negotiated the exclusive rights to Rodgers and Hammerstein's collected works for the entire Nordic region.[16] In collaboration with the Oscars Teatern in downtown Stockholm (which opened its doors in 1906), Schmidt helped launch *Oklahoma!*, *Annie Get Your Gun*, *Kiss Me, Kate*, *South Pacific*, *Guys and Dolls*, and, later, *West Side Story*. As Stockholm's largest private theatre, Oscars Teatern was mostly known for its first-class operettas, performed by some of the leading stars in the pre- and inter-war periods. Named after King Oscar II, the playhouse had already hosted the Swedish opening of *Show Boat* in 1942.[17] Key collaborators at Oscars Teatern who helped introduce the American musical to Swedish audiences included the composer and managing director Nils Perne; Anders Sandrew, who ran a large theatre and movie company; and the managing director Gustav Wally, who was known as the 'revue king' of the city. All three men were equally enthusiastic about American musicals, regularly travelled to New York to see new works, and quickly learned that a successful launch entailed more than an excellent production—it also necessitated a carefully orchestrated publicity campaign and more than a touch of Hollywood-style glamour on opening night.[18]

The Swedish opening of Alan Jay Lerner and Frederick Loewe's *My Fair Lady* took place on 14 February 1959 at the Oscars Teatern. By this point the musical had been running for three years in New York and one year in London, showing no sign of closing. Oscars Teatern thus hosted what was only the third production worldwide and, crucially, the first non-English production. Securing the rights for this project was a drawn-out process that involved numerous lawyers, rights holders, and artists. Once again Schmidt pointed to the importance of personal contacts and graciously credited Lerner for his support.[19]

Gösta Rybrant, the author and lyricist who was regularly commissioned by Schmidt, became the first international translator of the musical and received almost universal praise by the Swedish press for his imaginative interpretation of Lerner's libretto, including the difficult task of making Eliza's cockney dialect and Higgins's speech lessons culturally intelligible to Swedish audiences.[20] Rybrant focused on pronunciation and played around with the phonetic differences between the long vowel sounds ä [æ:] and e [e:], which are often mixed up in certain Stockholm dialects. Thus, the Swedish Eliza had to learn to properly enunciate the tongue-twister 'En spansk räv klev bland säv och rev en annan räv' ('A Spanish fox stepped among the reeds and tore another fox'), which became the equivalent of the famous 'The rain in Spain stays mainly in the plain'. Not only was this a very innovative solution, but Rybrant also managed to respect the paso doble rhythm of the song. Furthermore, he made Eliza struggle with the arguably quite difficult pronunciation of the Swedish sj- sound [ɧ], which is a voiceless fricative phoneme that has produced a wide variety of pronunciations in different dialects. Finally, he came up with some inspired plays on words and introduced a number of slang expressions that at the time were unheard of on Swedish stages and potentially shocking for some audiences. Rybrant worked with Schmidt for two decades and translated other musicals such as *Show Boat*, *Kiss Me, Kate*, *Guys and Dolls*, and *West Side Story*. He had a background in revue culture and was well equipped to translate the humour, smart rhymes, and jazzy idiomatic phrases of the Broadway musical, no matter how difficult a task this seemed at first.[21]

Throughout his career, Schmidt continuously emphasised the importance of finding the right translator, one who would do justice to the original work and its style. 'It is one's duty to the author to ensure that the first Swedish version is as ideal as possible' to secure the play's long-term success, he once explained to a journalist.[22] One of the longest and most detailed clauses in a standard contract between Schmidt's publishing house and the respective playhouse addressed the issue of translation and the obligation of the theatre to respect the translation provided and to communicate any changes made during the rehearsal process for the publisher's approval. Moreover, should the publisher approve these new translations and deem them superior, Schmidt had the right to incorporate these for future productions without having to meet any compensatory demands.[23] More than just a business move, this respect for the process of translation needs to be understood as a key ingredient of Schmidt's success and contributed to the popularity of postwar Broadway shows in Europe, at least for those productions that he was directly involved in.

To successfully stage *My Fair Lady*, Schmidt commissioned the Danish director and choreographer Sven Aage Larsen. Larsen had already directed numerous versions of *Oklahoma!* (1948, Malmö City Theatre), *Annie Get Your Gun* (1949, Oscars Teatern, Det Norske Teatret in Oslo, and Stora Teatern in Gothenburg), and *Kiss Me, Kate* (1951, Oscars Teatern, Nørrebro Teater in Copenhagen, and Oslo Nye Teater) and had by that point established himself as the primary interpreter of American musicals in Scandinavia. He was trained as both a director and choreographer who worked in the performing arts as well as the film industry. As a choreographer he could stage the musical numbers, and as a director he could guide the performers, who needed to be trained singers and actors. Larsen was one of the first Scandinavian directors who understood that the American musical signified a fully integrated combination of song, dance and spoken dialogue: 'The modernity [of the musical] is the intimate collaboration between director and choreographer. Preferably they should be one and the same person.'[24] The dance historian Sigrid Øvreås Svendal identifies Larsen as a key transnational link between American musical culture and Scandinavian productions of these. It was through Larsen that Scandinavian stages were introduced to the key innovations of this new genre. In the long run, Svendal suggests, this also led to an Americanisation of European popular culture. Larsen made regular trips to the United States to remain *au courant* with recent developments in musical theatre. By the time he directed *Oklahoma!*, Larsen made no secret of the fact that he was following the original Broadway version and did not see the point of trying to improve upon it. In other words, Larsen allowed himself to be inspired by the original productions and borrow heavily from them, to the point of copying their blocking and choreography.[25] Schmidt encouraged this method of working and made sure to send Larsen to see the West End production of *My Fair Lady* (which itself was a more or less exact replica of the Broadway production, directed by Moss Hart, and saw the lead actors reprise their roles) in preparation for his engagement at Oscars Teatern.

A key ingredient of Schmidt's success, for which he is rarely credited to this day, was to assemble the right people for each production, including the casting of the ideal performers. In Stockholm, the leading roles were performed by Jarl Kulle (Professor Higgins) and Ulla Sallert (Eliza Doolittle).[26] Kulle was a popular actor who was mostly known for his work at the Royal Dramatic Theatre, where he had performed leading roles in plays by Shakespeare, Aeschylus, Strindberg, and Molière. Not a trained singer, he recited his songs in a more casual and rhythmic manner, which fit the restrained disposition of the character of Higgins (not unlike Rex Harrison's style in the Broadway production). Sallert was a trained singer who had already made a name for herself by appearing in *Annie Get Your Gun, Kiss Me, Kate,* and *Guys and Dolls.* Casting her as Eliza was an important move: she had clearly mastered the new genre of the musical, unlike an earlier generation of operetta stars, who struggled with the demands of combining acting, singing, and dancing. Fully aware that *My Fair Lady* marked a watershed in Swedish and European theatre, she became a proponent of and cultural ambassador for the American musical:

> A musical is simply a play with music illustrations. The music aims to enhance the play, make it more accessible to a wide audience. In operetta, on the other hand, music remains the main point. Hence the characters in a musical are much more rewarding for an actor to perform. The parts are made of flesh and blood, the characters are real.[27]

Given Sallert's popularity and outreach at the time, her efforts to spread knowledge about the cultural translation of American musicals must not be underestimated.[28]

## 'FAMOUS PEOPLE SMOKE KENT'

Oscars Teatern's production of *My Fair Lady* was a meticulously planned event, designed to make the biggest possible cultural impact. A month ahead of opening night, Oscars Teatern and Schmidt hired the advertising agency Tessab to conduct a large-scale opinion poll and test the average Stockholmer's and potential theatre-goer's knowledge about *My Fair Lady.* In total, three hundred people were interviewed across a wide demographic range of gender, age, and income. An impressive 69 percent had heard of *My Fair Lady* and knew that it was an 'operetta' that was soon going to open at Oscars Teatern. Perhaps not surprisingly, 74 percent of representatives of the upper classes knew that the work was based on George Bernard Shaw's play *Pygmalion.* More interesting, however, was how 53 percent of young people (under the age of thirty) displayed a solid knowledge of the plot. Additionally, younger interviewees showed an accurate awareness of who were performing the leading roles.[29] This active interest in popular culture on the part of young people represented an enthusiastic embrace of American culture. Moreover, the high level of attentiveness displayed by upper- and middle-class audiences proved to be relevant for the large-scale advertising campaign, which became one of the most striking by-products of *My Fair Lady*.

To coincide with the opening, clothing stores started advertising casual 'Professor Higgins cardigans' in different colours, as well 'Eliza scarves'; a local jeweller designed a special watch bracelet called 'My Fair Lady'; and the country's most luxurious department store, Nordiska Kompaniet, proudly announced that its tailors had designed Kulle's costumes. Advertisements for throat pills and tea were accompanied by photographs of Higgins and Eliza's speech lessons, and in a clever reference to Eliza's father, a manufacturer of garbage trucks pompously proclaimed that their system of collecting garbage was significantly more effective than old Doolittle's. Moreover, the LP of the American recording was a success on the charts, and Rybrant's translation was published in various editions in time for the Swedish opening. Finally, innumerable press reports began to circulate long before the leading roles were cast, helping to generate free publicity that only increased in intensity in the weeks leading up to opening night.

The most striking advertisement from the period is a picture of Schmidt endorsing Kent cigarettes, feeding into the then-popular advertising slogan 'Känt folk röker Kent' ('Famous people smoke Kent'), an expression that remains recognisable to most Swedes even today. The picture in question was originally taken by an unidentified press photographer at Bromma Airport in Stockholm when Schmidt, accompanied by Bergman, stepped out of a plane to oversee the final weeks of rehearsal. As he descended the stairs, Schmidt conspicuously carried a manuscript and a carton of the American cigarette brand under his right arm. He then proceeded to happily distribute cigarettes amongst the assembled journalists while explaining that he was currently the producer of four simultaneously running productions in Paris. The photograph was initially printed to illustrate an article published in *Svenska Dagbladet* on 27 January 1959, reporting on the arrival of Schmidt and Bergman. What at first seemed like a casual gesture revealed itself to be a skilfully planned marketing strategy. Two days later the same photograph was blown up into a full-page advertisement and once again published in the same newspaper, this time as an advertisement for both *My Fair Lady* and the new micro-filter of the cigarette brand.

Advertisements for Kent had already featured prominently in the playbill of the musical's original production at the Mark Hellinger Theatre in New York, so it is not surprising that this early example of a sponsorship agreement was continued in Stockholm. The true cultural significance of the marketing ploy, however, lies in how it cast the producer as a celebrity. While his marriage to Bergman had undeniably contributed to Schmidt's fame, it speaks to his acumen that a theatre producer in 1959 would be recognisable to the extent of being an attractive advertising face for an international brand.

Due to the high demand for tickets for *My Fair Lady*, there were two pre-openings and a highly publicised gala premiere that provided fodder for gossip columns and lifestyle magazines for weeks to come. Hundreds of people had come to catch a glimpse of the arriving celebrities, who included ambassadors, bankers, doctors, and politicians, and the premiere caused significant traffic interruptions. The red-carpet event climaxed

FIG. 6.2 The combined advertisement for *My Fair Lady* and Kent cigarettes, using the photograph of Lars Schmidt arriving at Stockholm Airport. Used with permission by *Svenska Dagbladet*.

with the arrival of the king and queen of Sweden. The foyer at Oscars Teatern was decorated with 'Doolittle carnations', during the interval audiences were treated to specially mixed 'Eliza cocktails', and ushers carried trays to offer nothing other than Kent cigarettes.

The only ones who refused to be entirely blinded by the bright lights and surrender to the spectacle, both on- and offstage, were the critics. Most were fully aware of the efforts to turn *My Fair Lady* into the theatrical event of the century, and all of the major newspapers devoted long sections to debates and evaluations of the merits of the production. In short, reviewers generally applauded Lerner's lyrics, even though several of them noted how the perceived happy ending appeared forced and regretted that the love story between Eliza and Higgins was privileged over the social satire of Shaw's play. The second act was said to be too long. Lerner's music received mixed reviews; while the melodies were considered catchy and contemporary, they also seemed too sentimental and simple. The costumes were praised, with many reviewers singling out the climax of the first act as a particular highlight. The scenography, on the other hand, was less well received and compared unfavourably to the finesse of Swedish set designers. Rybrant's translation was applauded, even deemed to be superior to the original. With few exceptions, the leading actors received excellent reviews for their performances. However, some critics were sceptical that Kulle, one of the most promising actors of his generation, had taken a sabbatical from his engagement at the Royal Dramatic Theatre to perform in a musical, which was not only an American import but also regarded as light entertainment.[30]

## HOW TO SUCCEED IN BUSINESS

With seating for approximately a thousand spectators, Oscars Teatern was sold out for months. The musical eventually ran for 776 performances, making it the longest-running production in Sweden at the time, with an estimated audience of 750,000 people. With 178 actors, dancers, chorus members, musicians, and technicians involved, *My Fair Lady*, as Schmidt repeatedly emphasised, marked the most expensive endeavour in Swedish theatre until that point. The high costs associated with the production also included the advance of the percentage fee for the creators, the rights for the set design and costumes, and trips for the director and cast to see the London production.[31]

Within a year Schmidt produced three additional productions in the Nordic capitals: first at the Swedish-speaking Svenska Teatern in Helsinki and thereafter a particularly ill-fated production at the Falkoner Centret in Copenhagen. Two days before the scheduled opening, the main actor attempted suicide; the understudy made a heroic effort to learn the part of Eliza on such short notice but failed owing to exhaustion. Three hours before the scheduled opening, Schmidt informed the audience that the event would have to be postponed for a week.[32] However, it was the Norwegian production at the Folketeateret in Oslo that created a public outrage, which soon spread to the neighbouring countries. Led by *Dagbladet*, the Norwegian press started a campaign to question the monopoly position that Schmidt's publishing house held in the region and protested against his unusually high profit share of 40 percent. *Göteborgs-Tidningen* was among the Swedish papers that reported on the case and deemed it 'not only distasteful but also impertinent' that the publisher was raking in 40 percent of the profits.[33] A more nuanced account was provided by the Swedish *Dagens Nyheter* whose reporter pointed out that while it was true that Schmidt's publishing house was receiving the unusually high royalty of 12 percent (as opposed to the more regular 9 to 10 percent) as a mediation fee for *My Fair Lady*, which had to cover royalties paid to Loewe and Lerner, the estate of

Shaw, and the American publisher, this was not to be confused with Schmidt's position as producer, a role he himself described as 'scout, pathfinder and initiator'. His French-based production company had invested almost half of the necessary sum to mount *My Fair Lady*, which cost 500,000 Swedish kronor. Within less than a year and three hundred performances, the production had generated enough profit for Schmidt and his co-investors not only to recoup their investment, but also to enjoy a healthy profit of nearly half a million kronor each.[34]

Most critics, however, erroneously assumed that Schmidt's publishing house was enjoying hefty profits, when in fact it was his production company that generated the higher income (while also carrying the biggest financial risk through his investment). The media scandal that accompanied the Norwegian opening of *My Fair Lady* revealed the confusion that the relatively unknown role of the producer, which was a postwar phenomenon, entailed. Previously, Nordic theatres were run by managing directors, who were financially accountable to their board and, in the case of public theatres, to their respective city council and the Ministry of Culture. As a producer, Schmidt was investing his own money (and that of his co-investors), which, according to the logic of capitalism, made it legitimate that he would receive the contractually agreed percentage of the profits. A so-called fifty-fifty clause was unknown to many reviewers, who failed to properly grasp the implications and therefore painted Schmidt as a financial shark who imported not only American popular culture, but also American business models.

Heed notes that, while American business strategies had been established in large sectors of entertainment culture by that point, *My Fair Lady* marked their first foray into the performing arts industry, which is why the production marked a moment in Swedish theatre history when the opening of a new stage work was intimately tied to the launch of a particular business model. *My Fair Lady* became an intriguing mixture of Broadway culture, new forms of marketing, sponsorship and advertisement, and the launch of 'pre-packaged' theatre where each new production and national opening was apparently nothing more than a copy of the original Broadway version.[35] The many intricacies of this process, however, need to be teased out, so Schmidt's position in Swedish theatre specifically and European theatre more broadly cannot be easily dismissed as that of a profiteer. First, Schmidt's perceived role as the embodiment of American capitalism has to be considered in all its nuances. As I have argued elsewhere, Schmidt invested a significant part of the profit he made from large-scale musical productions to finance some highly risky and less profitable productions of avant-garde plays and works by young and upcoming playwrights in Paris.[36] Secondly, a production of the scale and magnitude of *My Fair Lady* would never have been feasible on Nordic and continental European stages without the efforts and concrete financial investments made by Schmidt and his associates. Thirdly, it is important to analyse how he skilfully negotiated national anxieties and tensions between theatre as art and theatre as commerce engendered by a blockbuster like *My Fair Lady*.

An article by Nils Beyer, one of the country's most respected theatre critics, marked a crucial turning point in the public perception of the producer. Under the headline 'Showbusiness', Beyer claimed that, because the director had received specific directions from the American rights holders and because the set and costumes were a copy of the American originals, the production was no more than a simple import. In addition, he alluded that Kulle, one of his generation's most promising actors, was dangerously close to selling out by performing in this 'vacuous musical'. Beyer regretted this development and contrasted it with what he perceived to be the core values of Swedish theatre artists, including their 'spiritual life' and a determination to put art above profit. Moreover, he pointed to postwar developments in the art of direction that had made large contributions to the 'Swedish art of theatre that we can feel proud of' and that had 'started to develop its own national characteristics'. Beyer condemned the fact that Schmidt, 'a man who knows the art of producing American showbusiness on a large scale,' received up to 50 percent of the profits, while clairvoyantly predicting that the musical marked a turning point in theatre history: 'Maybe it will even usher in a new era which future scholars in that case could designate as the triumph of Americanism.'[37]

*Svenska Dagbladet* went so far as to suggest placing successful productions like *My Fair Lady* 'under state control', only allowing 'soulless musical actors' to perform in them and restricting their run 'to a maximum of three months'.[38] Even regional newspapers participated in the debate and brought the implied national chauvinism further to the surface. It was deemed unacceptable that Kulle, whose task it was to 'enrich our national stage', was taking a leave from the Royal Dramatic Theatre to 'make money for Americanised musical theatre that entirely ignores our domestic theatre tradition'. Musical culture, moreover, was said to be diametrically opposed to Swedish theatre, with its 'constructive, social mandate'; hence, the long-term success of such imported works posed a serious threat to 'Sweden's internationally recognised exclusive theatre standard'.[39]

Sveriges Radio scheduled a special broadcast to discuss the commercialisation of culture. The programme focused its attention almost exclusively on *My Fair Lady*. At stake was the curious and previously unknown combination of a theatre publisher asking for an exceptionally high agent's fee while at the same time acting as a producer of the production and thus securing an even larger profit. Among the invited representatives of Swedish and Nordic theatre was Kåre Fasting, the critic who had started the debate in the Norwegian *Dagbladet* by accusing Schmidt of having too much influence over Nordic theatre in general. Another guest was Kulle, who had to defend himself against the accusations of being a mere puppet whose strings were being pulled by the American rights holders and who had no artistic freedom.[40] Schmidt was conspicuously absent from the broadcast. Never one to shy away from a public debate, however, he defended himself in an interview with *Dagens Nyheter* and pointed out some of the concrete achievements of the Nordic productions of *My Fair Lady*:

> *My Fair Lady* brings joy to about 5,500 people in the Nordic countries every night. It provides livelihoods to infinitely more people. It has put a halt to all talk of a theatre crisis. It pulls up with it other theatres—a big audience success also breathes life into other performances.[41]

Schmidt further emphasised that it was time to stop sneering at musicals, which were a legitimate theatrical genre that, if staged properly, had the truly democratic potential to attract a variety of spectators.

*My Fair Lady* thus provoked a number of intersecting cultural and national anxieties around art, commerce, artistic freedom, mass entertainment, and notions of Swedishness. Postwar American spoken drama brought a lot of national apprehensions, sexual anxieties, and racial fantasies to the surface when performed on the other side of the Atlantic.[42] Musicals added another dimension to these fears, namely the seemingly intertwined commercialisation and Americanisation of the performing arts. Schmidt was seen as the embodiment of American production values and business methods, which were perceived as a threat to the Swedish organisation of theatrical life. Critics were horrified by the fact that an American musical could become the country's biggest commercial success—without, ironically, any state subsidies, and thus without the investment of taxpayers' money.

Some of these anxieties were already manifest during the initial reviews of the Stockholm production, best illustrated by the author and filmmaker Vilgot Sjöman's scathing critique of the capitalist forces propelling *My Fair Lady*. Sjöman correctly recognised that the musical's commercial triumph was more than the result of a well-oiled advertising machine—it needed to be understood in relation to the social context. He pointed to new patterns of consumption in the postwar era and also noted his country's fascination with all things American.[43] It was an era characterised by more people buying cars, supermarkets competing successfully with local grocery stores, large-scale suburban development projects, and, of course, the breakthrough of television, and theatre did not remain immune to these new, centralizing economic principles.[44] In other words, the success of *My Fair Lady* would never have been possible had Swedish (and Western European) society not invited it.

Svendal argues that cultural diplomacy played a crucial part and emphasises that the success of Broadway culture needs to be seen in relation to the political efforts of the American government to establish the United States as superior to the Soviet Union and other communist countries not just on a military and technological, but also on a cultural level. The previously outlined modernity of the musical, as opposed to the perception of European operetta as outmoded, appealed to large segments of the population and thus resulted in a new form of genuinely *popular* entertainment. At the same time, the tremendous success of these works provoked anti-American sentiment among some critics.[45] Building upon Svendal's argument, I would add that Swedish critics saw themselves not only as gatekeepers for art and culture, but also as supporters of the social democratic model of organising theatrical life that was becoming hegemonic. The American musical posed a challenge to cultural politics in the Nordic region, not because of its form and content, but because it required and facilitated a new way of approaching and producing live theatre on a large scale.

However, it would be incorrect to presume that Schmidt suddenly found himself isolated as *persona non grata*. Amongst those who came to the producer's defence was the respected cultural journalist and editor Gustaf von Platen, who throughout his life remained a vital supporter of Schmidt. Von Platen wrote a long, slightly romanticised feature in the weekly magazine *Vecko-Journalen* with the headline 'Is His Lady Really Fair?'[46] Starting with a number of provocative questions, he wondered if Schmidt had been chosen as 'Lady Luck's golden boy'. To counter the accusations against Schmidt, von Platen pointed out that the management of Oscars Teatern had approached the producer with a specific request to share the financial burden, and that a close comparison of the four Nordic productions revealed both subtle and significant differences between them. According to von Platen, the management was well aware of the commercial success of *My Fair Lady* on Broadway but initially hesitated to produce it. Only a few years prior the playhouse had experienced a painful flop with their production of *Guys and Dolls*, which generated good reviews but failed to attract audiences and therefore cost the theatre 250,000 kronor. To compensate, Oscars Teatern scheduled a revival of *Annie Get Your Gun*, which also failed to become a box-office success. It was therefore hardly surprising that the theatre was reluctant to schedule yet another Broadway musical, no matter how successful it might have been in New York. Thus, according to von Platen, it was Oscars Teatern that approached Schmidt with a suggestion to share the financial risk—hence the infamous fifty-fifty agreement—and not the producer who insisted on such an arrangement.

The second criticism that von Platen addressed, albeit less convincingly, was the critics' outrage that all four Nordic productions of *My Fair Lady* were almost identical copies of the Broadway and London productions. His explanation was that the board of directors had become so enamoured with the London production that they approached Schmidt to acquire the rights for the original décor and costumes. Once Larsen was hired as the director, he too attended a London performance, which he carefully studied in order to use it as a source of inspiration. In other words, the similarities were mostly due to the uniform set and costumes, which, in turn, affected the actors' blocking. However, each production had its own distinct choreography, and each actor brought their own interpretation of the character, which resulted in four very different takes on Eliza and Higgins.

A valid point that von Platen made was that the New York producers had never made the demand for Nordic and European productions to follow and copy the original Broadway production. This had always been Schmidt's idea and was realised to a large extent by hiring Larsen as the director. A look at the various preserved contract drafts and correspondence between Schmidt and the creative team of the Broadway production sheds some important light on this process. Clause 12 in the agreement with the musical's originators clearly states that, while Lerner and Loewe had the right to approve the director and the main cast of each production prior to the start of rehearsals, the choice of set and costume design was the prerogative of the licensee, that is, Schmidt.[47] Since Schmidt decided that he wanted to use the original set and costumes, he had to negotiate the rights independently with the designers Oliver Smith and Cecil Beaton. Schmidt later explained his reasoning for this controversial move in very pragmatic terms: 'I realised that we, in order to succeed, had to learn to take the best from the original productions in New York and London.'[48]

In a letter written in September 1958, Smith offered to grant Schmidt the rights to use his original set design for a fee of $500, in addition to an additional $25 for each week that the production was running. He explained that the reason that he did not ask for a significantly higher compensation (as he had done for the London production) was that he was very fond of Schmidt.[49] Once again, Schmidt's social skills, charm, and winning personality must not be underestimated. Ever the shrewd negotiator, Schmidt suggested in his response that the agreement would cover the four Nordic capitals in which he was planning to produce the musical and proposed a slight amendment to the additional fee, namely to pay another $500 if the play ran for more than half a year.[50] This was, in fact, the same agreement Schmidt had struck with Beaton for the rights to use the original costume designs. These conditions are spelled out in a preserved contract that further states that Beaton's name was to appear along with and in the same font size as the name of the director.[51]

While critics lamented the perceived danger that Schmidt represented to the performing arts and cultural politics, the general audience remained seemingly unconcerned, and tickets continued to sell. Weekly journals and regional newspapers organised various competitions that offered rural audiences a chance to win a trip to Stockholm that included dinner at a fancy restaurant and tickets to the country's most discussed theatrical event. During a state visit in May 1960, even the shah of Iran requested to see a performance of *My Fair Lady*, which generated further publicity. By 12 September 1960, *My Fair Lady* was celebrating its five hundredth performance, an achievement that was celebrated by means of a special soirée with dinner and dancing.

Once the four Nordic premières were successfully launched, Schmidt spent a large part of the next four years conquering other western European countries with productions of *My Fair Lady* in Amsterdam, Antwerp, Brussels, Hamburg, Milan, Munich, Rome, Rotterdam, The Hague, Vienna, and West Berlin. It is of course ironic that the one city in which he failed to produce the musical was his adopted home of Paris, a city that only reluctantly embraced American plays and seemed to draw the line at musicals. That was but a minor setback, however, in light of how 'Fair Ladies swept Europe like nothing since the Black Plague,' as *Life* magazine mused in 1964 in a lengthy feature that highlighted Schmidt's efforts to introduce postwar American theatre to European audiences and commended him for being 'the first man to bring the ineffable qualities of Broadway to Europe and make them both understandable and profitable.'[52]

As *My Fair Lady* was opening in continental theatre capitals, the presence of the international celebrity couple Schmidt and Bergman never failed to add some extra glamour to the press reports. Several of these productions were directed by Larsen and followed his well-established working method of copying the original production, including the blocking and choreography. Schmidt (who, in addition to speaking Swedish and English, was fluent in French, German, and Danish and managed to get along in Italian) explained their working process during those years: he and Larsen picked the most appropriate translators, conductors, and designers and organised auditions to assemble the right cast. Larsen then oversaw the rehearsal process, and Schmidt returned a couple of weeks before opening night to see if any final changes, additions, or corrections were necessary. 'We worked in many languages, but Sven Aage's treatment of the various

FIG. 6.3 Schmidt and his first wife, Ingrid Bergman. His marriage to the three-time Oscar-winner lasted seventeen years, from 1958 to 1975. Photo: UPI.

languages was probably not particularly nuanced', he later reflected.[53] The combination of Schmidt's production methods and Larsen's directing style resulted in *My Fair Lady* becoming the defining American musical on European stages while simultaneously turning it into a distinctly American *brand* with a transnational appeal that was slightly adapted to please local tastes but never changed its outward appearance. It is noteworthy that the title was never translated, which helped to establish the distinct Americanness of the work. Even the cover of the playbill for most European productions was an exact replication of that of the Broadway production, with the famous drawing of Shaw lying on a cloud and playing both Higgins and Eliza like marionettes on strings.

Many decades later, when Schmidt was promoting the release of his memoirs in 1995, he reminisced about how cultural snobs back in the day accused him of producing 'prefabricated theatre' (*paketteater*) and called him 'culture's gravedigger'.[54] However, he also finally admitted in his book that there was not an ounce of truth to the claims he once made about the American rights holders stipulating that no major changes were allowed to be made to *My Fair Lady* in international productions and added: 'The consequences would have been serious. The original creator would certainly have demanded additional compensation for plagiarism. [ . . . ] To a large extent we "stole" the best directing ideas without paying for them.'[55] Schmidt remained unruffled by the many accusations that had been levelled against him and reminded readers that he helped many theatres to make a lot of money while seemingly being the exclusive scapegoat for critical attacks.

# Conclusion

With a career that covered almost six decades, Schmidt witnessed countless changes in both the American and the European theatre landscape, not least the escalation in production costs for live performances. In 1978 he explained that the only genre that made a real profit was big musicals, and in 1989 he lamented the fact that live theatre had become such a risky endeavour that young and upcoming writers were often tempted to go into the television and movie industries, which seemed to offer more financial stability.[56] Throughout his professional life, Schmidt never downplayed the harsh realities of being a producer, a profession which involved constant risks and financial gambles. On more than one occasion he experienced the fickleness of Thalia, such as when *Oliver!* flopped in Sweden in 1961 or when a play that Jean Anouilh had specifically written for the reopening of the Théâtre Montparnasse in 1965 had to be cancelled after just six nights. Even *My Fair Lady* did not strike gold everywhere, as manifested by French audiences' resistance to it. Schmidt never made a secret of these failures or other difficulties and challenges he had met along the way and spoke honestly about them in interviews and in his memoirs.[57]

When a reporter once asked him why he ended up behind the scenes as opposed to becoming an actor or director, Schmidt responded: 'It wasn't unrequited love for the stage [ ... ]. It was the interest in books and the desire to sit in the auditorium as often as possible. I was lucky in love, thus.'[58] He always approached theatre from the position of the passionate and intelligent spectator who placed high demands on live performance but refused to engage in value judgments or foolish comparisons between an avant-garde play and a blockbuster musical. Thanks to a combination of almost impeccable financial instinct, an undeniable passion for the performing arts, a consistent refusal to make a qualitative distinction or judgment between high art and popular culture, and the necessary social and linguistic skills to befriend international actors, playwrights, lyricists, and composers, Schmidt managed to become one of the most influential personalities in postwar European theatre. His most distinctive talent, I suggest, was his genuinely transnational outlook on and understanding of cultural production. Instead of dismissing American postwar culture, as so many of his contemporaries did, Schmidt genuinely attempted to study and understand it in addition to successfully translating it onto European stages. In the process he also introduced business methods that were perceived (and denigrated) as distinctively American. Schmidt was both a genuine global citizen—a privileged position made possible only by his financial security—and a cultural ambassador for postwar Broadway culture in Europe.

# Acknowledgements

My sincere gratitude goes to John Potvin for reading and commenting on various drafts of this chapter.

MY UN-FAIR LADY?    209

## NOTES

1. Lars Schmidt, quoted in Gaby Wigardt, 'Det enda som går är de stora musikalerna', *Svenska Dagbladet*, 3 November 1978. Unless otherwise stated, all translations in this essay from Swedish and French are my own. Page numbers for original reviews and articles are not available: newspaper items about Schmidt and various productions of *My Fair Lady* were cut out of the papers before they were archived, and page numbers were not included in the source information recorded. Archives consulted for this article include the Swedish Performing Arts Agency and the Music and Theatre Library of Sweden in Stockholm, the National Library of Sweden in Stockholm, Gothenburg University Library, the Département des Arts du Spectacle at the Bibliothèque nationale de France in Paris, and the Bibliothèque historique de la Ville de Paris.

2. Dirk Gindt, *Tennessee Williams in Sweden and France, 1945–1965: Cultural Translations, Sexual Anxieties and Racial Fantasies* (London: Bloomsbury Methuen Drama, 2019); Sven Åke Heed, 'Stadsteatertanken i svensk teater', in *Ny svensk teaterhistoria*, vol. 3, ed. Tomas Forser and Sven Åke Heed (Hedemora: Gidlunds, 2007), 195–235; Karin Helander, *Teaterns korsväg: Bengt Ekerot och 1950-talet* (Stockholm: Carlssons, 2004).

3. Sven Åke Heed, 'Operett och musikal', in *Ny svensk teaterhistoria*, vol. 3, ed. Tomas Forser and Sven Åke Heed (Hedemora: Gidlunds, 2007), 260–262.

4. Ibid., 262–269.

5. Schmidt's scrapbook meticulously collected newspaper articles about the bombing in Nordic newspapers, Cuban reports about the stranded Swedes and Finns arriving in Havana, and US papers reporting that the group had finally arrived on American soil. The scrapbook also contains invitations to various dinner parties, postcards from different locations, and articles about plays he had seen. Lars Schmidt, *Scrapbook, 1941–1946*, Library of Congress, https://www.loc.gov/item/muslarsschmidt.200221551/, accessed 7 June 2019.

6. Schmidt, quoted in Thorleuf Hellbom, 'Strapatser ledde till stjärnorna', *Dagens Nyheter*, 20 April 1995.

7. Alan Brixey, 'News of the Theater', *New York Herald Tribune*, 3 July 1941.

8. 'Dramatik-spanare nära bombdöd', *Aftonbladet*, 28 August 1941.

9. Lars Schmidt, *Mitt livs teater* (Höganäs: Bra böcker, 1995), 23.

10. Schmidt quoted in Roddy, 'Den amerikanska dramatiken tongivande de närmaste åren', *Göteborgs-Tidningen*, 4 September 1945.

11. Schmidt quoted in Hax, 'Författarekomet i USA introduceras i Göteborg', *Göteborgs Handels- och Sjöfartstidning*, 11 December 1945.

12. For a detailed analysis of that production and Schmidt's involvement, see Gindt, *Tennessee Williams*, 111–136.

13. Schmidt had already gained valuable experience as managing director of a theatre when he leased a boat in Gothenburg harbour. Named *Teaterbåten* (The Theatre Boat) as an homage to *Show Boat*, it presented revues with some of the period's most popular performers between 1948 and 1953. In 1947 he produced the London production of Ingmar Bergman's *Frenzy* (*Hets*), directed by Peter Ustinov, at the St Martin's Theatre.

14. "Lars Schmidt: 'L'homme du jour', *Paris-Théâtre* 137 (1958): 6–9; A. Parinaud, 'Le premier producteur de théâtre de Paris: Lars Schmidt présente sa "charte"', *Arts* 693 (1958): 6.

15. Eugène Ionesco, 'Gardez vos conseils M. Lars Schmidt', *Arts* 694 (1958): 1 and 6. For a detailed study of the debate between the French theatre establishment and Schmidt, see Dirk Gindt, 'Transatlantic Translations and Transactions: Lars Schmidt and the

210 DIRK GINDT

Implementation of Post-War American Theatre in Europe', *Theatre Journal* 65, no. 1 (2013): 19–37.

16. Schmidt, *Mitt livs teater*, 94–97.
17. Sveriges Teatermuseum and Stockholms Stadsmuseum, *Oscars Teatern: Oscars genom åren* (Stockholm: Drottningholms Teatermuseum, 1974).
18. Schmidt, *Mitt livs teater*, 103–108.
19. Ibid., 119–120.
20. For a detailed study of the Swedish, Danish, and Norwegian translations, see Johan Franzon, 'My Fair Lady på skandinaviska: En studie i funktionell sångöversättning' (PhD diss., University of Helsinki, Department of Translation Studies, 2009).
21. 'Gösta Rybrant, *Svenskt översättarlexikon*, https://litteraturbanken.se/%C3%B6v ers%C3%A4ttarlexikon/artiklar/G%C3%B6sta_Rybrant, accessed 7 June 2019.
22. Schmidt, quoted in Perpetus, 'Trehundra pjäser om året teaterförläggarens pensum', *Dagens Nyheter*, undated clipping, ca. mid-1950s, Musikverket Stockholm.
23. 'Överenskommelse', Teaterförlag Lars Schmidt & Co., archived at Musikverket Stockholm. In the case of *My Fair Lady*, these rights would ultimately return to Lerner and Loewe. Agreement between A. B. Lars Schmidt and Lowal Corporation. Annotated Draft, 20 October 1958, Library of Congress, Music Division, https://www.loc.gov/resource/mus larsschmidt.200221709.0/, accessed 5 June 2019.
24. Larsen, quoted in Sigrid Øvreås Svendal, 'Alles øyne på Broadway: Amerikansk innflytelse på musikalscenen i Norge', *Temp: Tidsskrift for Historie* 3, no. 6 (2013): 65.
25. Svendal, 'Alles øyne på Broadway', 55–58.
26. Unlike the Royal Dramatic Theatre or the many regional and city theatres, the privately run Oscars Teatern did not have a stable ensemble but hired different actors for every production.
27. Sallert, quoted in Stig Gränd, 'Champagnekorkarna har tystnat', *Röster i Radio* 28 (1959).
28. It is slightly anachronistic that the lavishly illustrated souvenir book of *My Fair Lady* still announced the work as an operetta co-produced by Oscars Teatern and Lars Schmidt. Teddy Nyblom, 'Nobelpristagaren på operettscenen', souvenir book, *My Fair Lady* (Stockholm: Oscar Theatre, 1959).
29. Hans Olof Stjernström, 'En undersökning av allmänhetens kunskaper om *My Fair Lady*', Tessab, Stockholm, 23 January 1959, archived at Musikverket Stockholm.
30. Reviews consulted for this section include those in *Aftonbladet*, *Dagens Nyheter*, *Göteborgs-Posten*, *Kvällsposten*, *Ny Tid* and *Sydsvenska Dagbladet* (all published on 15 February 1959), and *Scen och salong* (no. 3, 1959).
31. Lars Schmidt, letter to Irving Cohen, 3 December 1958, Library of Congress, Music Division, https://www.loc.gov/resource/muslarsschmidt.200221708.0?r=-0.751,-0.002,2.503,1.409,0/, accessed 5 June 2019. The advance paid was $10,000, the royalty rate to the authors was 9 percent and the royalty to the Shaw estate was 3 percent. See the agreement between A. B. Lars Schmidt and Lowal Corporation.
32. Schmidt, *Mitt livs teater*, 128–132.
33. Lars Åhrén, 'Lasse Schmidt i blåsväder för höga priser', *Göteborgs-Tidningen*, 9 January 1960.
34. Tell, 'Halv miljon till Schmidt från *Ladyn* i Stockholm', *Dagens Nyheter*, 9 January 1960.
35. Heed, 'Operett och musikal', 269–275.
36. Gindt, 'Transatlantic Translations and Transactions', 34–36.
37. Nils Beyer, 'Showbusiness', *Stockholms-Tidningen*, 14 January 1060.

MY UN-FAIR LADY? 211

38. Kar de Mumma, 'Dagens Kar de Mumma', *Svenska Dagbladet*, 15 January 1960.

39. Lars Törnqvist, 'En gång Ladyn men aldrig mer', *Sundsvalls Tidning*, 15 January 1960.

40. Sveriges Radio, 'Tidsspegeln', radio broadcast, 19 January 1960.

41. 'Lars Schmidt: Ingen påtvingas "teater i paket"; *Ladyn* avbröt norsk teaterkris', *Dagens Nyheter*, 31 January 1960.

42. Gindt, *Tennessee Williams*.

43. Vilgot Sjöman, 'Varför köper vi den damen?', *Vi* 8 (1959).

44. Heed, 'Operett och musikal', 274.

45. Svendal, 'Alles øyne på Broadway', 61–67.

46. Gustaf von Platen, 'Är hans lady riktigt fair?', *Vecko-Journalen*, 10 January 1960.

47. Agreement between A. B. Lars Schmidt and Lowal Corporation.

48. Schmidt, *Mitt livs teater*, 110.

49. Oliver Smith, letter to Lars Schmidt, September 1958, Library of Congress, Music Division, https://www.loc.gov/item/muslarsschmidt.200221704/, accessed 27 June 2023.

50. Lars Schmidt, letter to Oliver Smith, 3 October 1958, Library of Congress, Music Division, https://www.loc.gov/item/muslarsschmidt.200221705/, accessed 5 June 2019.

51. Lars Schmidt, letter to Cecil Beaton, 21 October 1958, Library of Congress, Music Division, https://www.loc.gov/resource/muslarsschmidt.200221706.0/, accessed 5 June 2019.

52. Dora Jane Hamblin, 'Hardly Anybody Knows Him—That's the Way He Wants It', *Life*, 16 October 1964, 133–144; here: 135.

53. Schmidt, *Mitt livs teater*, 109.

54. Schmidt quoted in Kerstin Hallert, 'Ett teaterliv av katastrofer och äventyr', *Svenska Dagbladet*, 28 March 1995.

55. Schmidt, *Mitt livs teater*, 110. For a discussion of how these attempts at 'prefabricated' theatre affected the productions of *Kiss Me, Kate* and *West Side Story* in Norway, see Svendal, 'Alles øyne på Broadway', 55–59.

56. Wigardt, 'Det enda'; Richard Hummler, 'In Paris and New York, *Metamorphosis* Posts Similar Cost, Nut and Scale', *Variety*, 1 February 1989.

57. Sveriges Radio P1, 'Lars Schmidt 2002', radio broadcast, 5 July 2002.

58. Schmidt, quoted in Perpetus, 'Trehundra pjäser'.

## APPENDIX 6.1

### Selected List of Musicals Produced with the Involvement of Lars Schmidt

| Musical | Year | Country | City |
| --- | --- | --- | --- |
| *Oklahoma!* (1943) | 1948 | Sweden | Malmö |
| | | Finland | Helsinki |
| | 1949 | Denmark | Copenhagen |
| | 1950 | Sweden | Gothenburg |
| *Annie Get Your Gun* (1946) | 1949 | Sweden | Gothenburg/Malmö/Stockholm |
| | 1957 | Austria | Vienna |
| | 1963 | West Germany | Berlin |

*(continued)*

| Musical | Year | Country | City |
|---|---|---|---|
| Kiss Me, Kate (1948) | 1951 | Sweden | Stockholm/Malmö |
| | | Norway | Oslo |
| | | Denmark | Copenhagen [+ tour through Denmark] |
| | 1953 | Sweden | Gothenburg |
| | 1957 | Finland | Tampere [+ tour through Finland] |
| | 1958 | Iceland | Reykjavik |
| South Pacific (1949) | 1952 | Sweden | Stockholm |
| Guys and Dolls (1950) | 1953 | Sweden | Stockholm |
| My Fair Lady (1956) | 1959 | Sweden | Stockholm |
| | | Finland | Helsinki |
| | 1960 | Denmark | Copenhagen |
| | | Norway | Oslo |
| | | The Netherlands | Rotterdam [+ tour to Amsterdam and The Hague][I] |
| | 1961 | West Germany | Berlin [+ transfer to Hamburg in 1962]/ Munich [+ transfer to Frankfurt in 1963] |
| | 1963 | Belgium | Antwerp |
| | | Austria | Vienna |
| | | Italy | Milan [+ transfer to Rome][II] |
| West Side Story (1957) | 1962 | Sweden | Stockholm |
| | | Denmark | Copenhagen |
| Oliver! (1960) | 1961 | Sweden | Stockholm |
| | 1963 | The Netherlands | Rotterdam |
| How to Succeed in Business Without Really Trying (1961) | 1963 | Sweden | Stockholm |
| | | Denmark | Copenhagen |
| | 1965 | France | Paris |
| Hello, Dolly! (1964) | 1966 | Sweden | Stockholm |
| Jesus Christ Superstar (1971) | 1971 | Denmark | Copenhagen |
| | 1972 | Sweden | Gothenburg |
| | | West Germany | Münster [+ tour to Berlin and Frankfurt] |
| Abbacadabra (1983) | 1983 | UK | London |

Source: Schmidt, *Mitt livs teater*, 232–235; Library of Congress, List of Lars Schmidt Papers, 1910–2010, http://findingaids.loc.gov/db/search/xq/searchMfer02.xq?_id=loc.music.eadmus.mu015009&_faSection=overview&_faSubsection=bioghist&_dmdid=d13204e20, accessed 27 August 2019.

[I] Between 1960 and 1962 there were also various productions by regional theatres throughout the Nordic region.

[II] In the 1960s and 1970s the show was also revived in various European countries.

## Bibliography

Agreement between A. B. Lars Schmidt and Lowal Corporation. Annotated draft, 20 October 1958. Library of Congress, Music Division. https://www.loc.gov/resource/muslarsschmidt.200221709.0/, accessed 5 June 2019.

Åhrén, Lars. 'Lasse Schmidt i blåsväder för höga priser'. *Göteborgs-Tidningen*, 9 January 1960.

Beyer, Nils. 'Showbusiness'. *Stockholms-Tidningen*, 14 January 1960.

Brixey, Alan. 'News of the Theater', *New York Herald Tribune*, 3 July 1941.

de Mumma, Kar. 'Dagens Kar de Mumma', *Svenska Dagbladet*, 15 January 1960.

'Dramatik-spanare nära bombdöd'. *Aftonbladet*, 28 August 1941.

Franzon, Johan. 'My Fair Lady på skandinaviska: En studie i funktionell sångöversättning'. PhD diss, University of Helsinki, Department of Translation Studies, 2009.

Gindt, Dirk. *Tennessee Williams in Sweden and France, 1945–1965: Cultural Translations, Sexual Anxieties and Racial Fantasies*. London: Bloomsbury Methuen Drama, 2019.

Gindt, Dirk. 'Transatlantic Translations and Transactions: Lars Schmidt and the Implementation of Post-War American Theatre in Europe'. *Theatre Journal* 65, no. 1 (2013): 19–37.

'Gösta Rybrant'. *Svenskt översättarlexikon*. https://litteraturbanken.se/%C3%B6v ers%C3%A4ttarlexikon/artiklar/G%C3%B6sta_Rybrant, accessed 7 June 2019.

Gränd, Stig. 'Champagnekorkarna har tystnat'. *Röster i Radio* 28 (1959).

Hallert, Kerstin. 'Ett teaterliv av katastrofer och äventyr'. *Svenska Dagbladet*, 28 March 1995.

Hamblin, Dora Jane. 'Hardly Anybody Knows Him—That's the Way He Wants It'. *Life*, 16 October 1964, 133–144.

Hax. 'Författarekomet i USA introduceras i Göteborg', *Göteborgs Handels- och Sjöfartstidning*, 11 December 1945.

Heed, Sven Åke. 'Operett och musikal.' In *Ny svensk teaterhistoria*, vol. 3, Edited by Tomas Forser and Sven Åke Heed, 258–284. Hedemora: Gidlunds, 2007.

Heed, Sven Åke. 'Stadsteatertanken i svensk teater.' In *Ny svensk teaterhistoria*, vol. 3, Edited by Tomas Forser and Sven Åke Heed, 195–235. Hedemora: Gidlunds, 2007.

Helander, Karin. *Teaterns korsväg: Bengt Ekerot och 1950-talet*. Stockholm: Carlssons, 2004.

Hummler, Richard. 'In Paris and New York, *Metamorphosis* Posts Similar Cost, Nut and Scale'. *Variety*, 1 February 1989.

Ionesco, Eugène. 'Gardez vos conseils M. Lars Schmidt'. *Arts* 694 (1958): 1, 6.

'Lars Schmidt: L'Homme du jour'. *Paris-Théâtre* 137 (1958): 6–9.

Nyblom, Teddy. 'Nobelpristagaren på operettscenen'. Souvenir book, *My Fair Lady*. Stockholm: Oscar Theatre, 1959.

'Överenskommelse'. Teaterförlag Lars Schmidt & Co. Musikverket Stockholm.

Parinaud, A. 'Le premier producteur de théâtre de Paris: Lars Schmidt présente sa "charte"'. *Arts* 693 (1958): 6.

Perpetus. 'Trehundra pjäser om året teaterförläggarens pensum'. *Dagens Nyheter*, undated clipping, ca. mid-1950s. Musikverket Stockholm.

Roddy. 'Den amerikanska dramatiken tongivande de närmaste åren'. *Göteborgs-Tidningen*, 4 September 1945.

Schmidt, Lars. 'Ingen påtvingas "teater i paket", *Ladyn* avbröt norsk teaterkris'. *Dagens Nyheter*, 31 January 1960.

Schmidt, Lars. Letter to Cecil Beaton, 21 October 1958. Library of Congress, Music Division. https://www.loc.gov/resource/muslarsschmidt.200221706.0/, accessed 5 June 2019.

Schmidt, Lars. Letter to Irving Cohen, 3 December 1958. Library of Congress, Music Division. https://www.loc.gov/resource/muslarsschmidt.200221708.0?r=-0.751,-0.002,2.503,1.409,0/, accessed 5 June 2019.

Schmidt, Lars. Letter to Oliver Smith, 3 October 1958. Library of Congress, Music Division. https://www.loc.gov/item/muslarsschmidt.200221705/, accessed 5 June 2019.

Schmidt, Lars. *Mitt livs teater*. Höganäs: Bra böcker, 1995.

Schmidt, Lars. Scrapbook, 1941–1946. Library of Congress. https://www.loc.gov/item/muslars
schmidt.200221551/, accessed 7 June 2019.

Sjöman, Vilgot. 'Varför köper vi den damen?' *Vi* 8 (1959).

Smith, Oliver. Letter to Lars Schmidt, September 1958. Library of Congress, Music Division.
https://www.loc.gov/resource/muslarsschmidt.200221704/, accessed 5 June 2019.

Stjernström, Hans Olof. 'En undersökning av allmänhetens kunskaper om *My Fair Lady*'.
*Tessab*, Stockholm, 23 January 1959. Musikverket Stockholm.

Svendal, Sigrid Øvreås. 'Alles øyne på Broadway: Amerikansk innflytelse på musikalscenen i
Norge'. *Temp: Tidsskrift for Historie* 3, no. 6 (2013): 54–67.

Sveriges Radio P1. 'Lars Schmidt 2002'. Radio broadcast, 5 July 2002.

Sveriges Radio. 'Tidsspegeln'. Radio broadcast, 19 January 1960.

Sveriges Teatermuseum and Stockholms Stadsmuseum. *Oscars Teatern: Oscars genom åren*.
Stockholm: Drottningholms Teatermuseum, 1974.

Tell. 'Halv miljon till Schmidt från *Ladyn* i Stockholm'. *Dagens Nyheter*, 9 January 1960.

Thorleuf Hellbom, Thorleuf. 'Strapatser ledde till stjärnorna'. *Dagens Nyheter*, 20 April 1995.

Törnqvist, Lars. 'En gång Ladyn men aldrig mer'. *Sundsvalls Tidning*, 15 January 1960.

von Platen, Gustav. 'Är hans lady riktigt fair?' *Vecko-Journalen*, 10 January 1960.

Wigardt, Gaby. 'Det enda som går är de stora musikalerna'. *Svenska Dagbladet*, 3 November 1978.

# PART III

## GLOBAL PRODUCTION ENTITIES

CHAPTER 7

# PAVING THE WAY: CAMERON MACKINTOSH AND THE DEVELOPMENT AND IMPACT OF THE GLOBAL MUSICAL

RICHARD M. SHANNON

## INTRODUCTION

CATS (1981), *Les Misérables* (1985), *The Phantom of the Opera* (1986), and *Miss Saigon* (1989)—the works for musical theatre produced by Cameron Mackintosh have had a profound impact on both producing business models and artistic practice globally. Although musicals have often toured the world, most notably *Jesus Christ Superstar* (1971), originally produced by Robert Stigwood, it was the series of shows produced by Mackintosh in the 1980s that created a global market and transformed the way musical theatre is produced internationally.

Thomas Schumacher, the president of Disney Theatrical, once commented:

> Cameron changed the face of the theatrical industry in terms of musicals. Our success at Disney theatrical, we owe to the model that Cameron created with his mega-hits and his commitment to the role of the producer being all over the show and at the centre of it with the creative team.[1]

His statement, underlining Disney's debt to Mackintosh, points to a key factor in this remarkable achievement: the role of the producer, which lies at the heart of every process. This chapter will focus initially on this role and then discuss production methods and business models in more detail, beginning with the game-changing musical *Cats* and examining how it set the template for innovations that would be applied to the works that followed, including the use of global branding, reproduction and quality control, translation for foreign markets, tourism, and ticket sales.

# Cameron Mackintosh: The Producer Is the Key

Thomas Schumacher's statement attests to Mackintosh's personal contribution: an intense focus on every aspect of the process that has made the real difference to both the quality and the dissemination of his work. By his own admission, Mackintosh meddles 'constantly in every aspect' of his productions, and he is clear that this is 'what makes a producer'.[2] The success of a number of important shows would seem to confirm his abilities and instincts. But what are the building blocks of his talent as a producer?

He has a consummate eye for the details that improve not just a show but also the overall audience experience, even taking a keen interest in the toilet facilities and the placement of artwork in his theatres. Mackintosh's work reflects Florenz Ziegfeld's views: 'Details are what make a show's personality. I hunt for chances for putting in a laugh or taking out a slow bit'.[3]

From the outset, Mackintosh was willing to learn from established producers, and two of his key models were David Merrick and Harold Fielding, [4] both of whom realised that the only stars needed were the producer and the show itself. Once a show depends on a star name, it becomes vulnerable when that star leaves the show. In contrast to Andrew Lloyd Webber's Really Useful Group, where some shows have been tied to star names,[5] Mackintosh has focused on promoting the show and himself as producer.

Most critically, Cameron Mackintosh has a real sense of what will work for a mass audience, founded on a strong sense of what works as a story. *Les Misérables* exemplifies this, written, as Megan Behrent puts it, 'for the masses'.[6] Mackintosh recognises that 'no matter how many great songs there are in a score, it is no good unless you get the book right'.[7] This is not to say that Mackintosh's judgement is always perfect. In the case of *Martin Guerre*, Mackintosh has admitted that the book was the problem: 'It's very hard when you're doing a show about lies to be direct, and in musical theatre most songs are direct'.[8]

Despite this realisation, Mackintosh is still trying to find solutions, and he has discussed further development of *Martin Guerre*'s book with Richard Eyre. Eyre has resisted these approaches, convinced that the story is 'inherently faulty'.[9] He goes on to speculate that Mackintosh is perhaps a 'victim of his own success, believing that he can take imperfect musicals, such as *Barnum* and *Half a Sixpence* and be an alchemist',[10] turning a story's base metal into musical gold.

In addition to an overall eye for story, Mackintosh understands structure; for instance, he was quick to realise that the Phantom needed his own aria in act 1 in order to establish his identity and build empathy with the audience. Luckily, Andrew Lloyd

Webber had a song that was written for *Song and Dance* (1982) called 'Married Man'. Richard Stilgoe suggested it be renamed 'Music of the Night', 'and that song went into the middle of the first act to fantastic effect.'[11] Mackintosh draws heavily on 'the craft of Rodgers and Hammerstein', noting, 'There's not a wasted word in the book or a lyric that doesn't inform the plot or character, and . . . all the music has a dramatic reason for being precisely where it is in the score.'[12]

In addition to his dramaturgical understanding, Mackintosh possesses that essential skill of being able to match any given show to the right space. He learnt this lesson early with the failure of his production of Cole Porter's *Anything Goes* when it transferred to the 1,500-seat Saville Theatre in 1969 (now the Odeon, Covent Garden). The show simply wasn't big enough to fill the space. By contrast, the choice of the New London Theatre for *Cats* was perfect.[13] Not only was Napier's set able to dominate the space and give the audience an immersive experience, but the number of seats was small enough to sustain a long run. As Mackintosh himself said in an interview in the *Times* in 1999: 'If *Cats* had been in a 2,000 seat theatre, it would have come off years ago.'[14]

One of the most crucial talents for any producer is the 'ability to bring the right people together at the right time on the right project',[15] and Mackintosh has made bold choices; perhaps no more so than in the selection of Nicholas Hytner to direct *Miss Saigon*. Although Hytner had directed opera,[16] this was his first large-scale musical. However, when Cameron trusts the team he has appointed—and normally they have long track records—he will respect their approach whilst remaining fully in touch with the process throughout. With the first production of *Miss Saigon*, after he met the cast, he wished them and Hytner good luck and told them he would see them in 'eight weeks'.[17]

A more recent example of Cameron's ability to assemble first-class teams is *Mary Poppins*. As the director Richard Eyre points out, it was 'quite a coup' to secure both himself and the designer Bob Crowley,[18] and to add Matthew Bourne alongside Stephen Mear as co-choreographers was a masterstroke. These choreographers complemented one another, Bourne being a '[modern-]dance savant' and Mears, a 'wonderful, old school' choreographer.[19] Eyre adds that Cameron's skill in assembling teams extends to casting and that he has 'really good instincts'.[20] The casting of Zizi Strallen as Mary Poppins and Charlie Stemp as Bert in the West End revival were Cameron's choices, and Eyre was 'thrilled' with both.[21]

With less experienced directors he can be much more interventionist. At a rehearsal of his show *Barnum*, he made it clear to the co-director, Timothy Sheader,[22] that the beginning of the production did not work: 'The opening is wrong. I absolutely feel it in-credibly strongly. I just know you have to be so careful in the first five minutes of a show . . . how you give the audience a language, and simplicity is always better. There's just too many things coming in too fast'.[23] The fact that this dressing-down was given on camera as part of a Channel 4 documentary added to Sheader's discomfort; tellingly, there have been no subsequent collaborations.

The speed with which any show can establish its theatrical language and conventions is critical to engaging the audience in the narrative; Mackintosh is keenly aware of this. He is always the first audience for his shows and seems physiologically affected by what he sees. In the words of the lighting designer Paule Constable, 'He lives and breathes every moment of a show as he is watching it'.[24]

Mackintosh is driven by a desire to give the audience the most exciting and immersive experience possible. The musical must pull the 'audience into another world' and take them 'on a journey'.[25] He demands this of all his shows. The set plays a critical role in this process. His early experience, as an acting assistant stage manager working in 1965 on Sean Kenny's sets for *Oliver!* by Lionel Bart, taught him the importance of visual language in a musical and that 'the sets have to dance with the action'.[26]

Each of the major productions required varying degrees of risk in their commissioning and production, and this is another vital ingredient in Mackintosh's work. Whether this practice has inspired others to take similar risks is a moot point. Certainly Mackintosh encouraged Judy Craymer in the development of *Mamma Mia!*, offering her the Prince Edward Theatre in 1999 for the opening of the show.[27] She makes it clear that he was a major influence: 'Cameron Mackintosh was a mentor to me and I like to think I learned a lot from him, right down to giving good parties, which has always been very important'.[28]

On the other hand, Disney's musical adaptation choices are far more conservative and rely heavily on established film brands. The company is highly unlikely to have commissioned a major musical from a series of poems by T. S. Eliot. Its theatrical endeavours are primarily motivated by the potential profit to be made, and this is more likely to be achieved with existing titles drawn from their film catalogue. However, it is notable that it was Mackintosh who secured the permission of P. L. Travers to adapt *Mary Poppins* for the stage as a musical. She had steadfastly refused any approach from Disney. Cameron also got her to agree to include some of the famous songs from the film, and then he brokered the deal with Thomas Schumacher, the head of the Disney Theatrical Group.

*Cats*, the first notable global success of the 1980s, was regarded as extremely daring—the first attempt at a British dance musical and one furthermore built on the thinnest of story lines. Nick Allott makes it clear that it was the riskiest thing they had ever done: 'We got into preview without having the last little bit (of finance) in place'.[29] Normally, even to engage performers without being fully capitalised would be regarded as extremely foolhardy. The process of raising money for the show had been incredibly difficult, with Mackintosh having to secure 220 backers, each investing 'an average of £750 into a show capitalised at £450,000'.[30] Even at the interval of the first performance Mackintosh was convinced the show 'was a total disaster'.[31]

The financial success of this unlikely show reinforced Cameron's ability to continue to take risks. The next key decision would be to transfer *Les Misérables* from the Barbican to the West End at a cost of £300,000, despite a series of terrible reviews.

Mackintosh was told by the box office that 'since 10 am this morning there has been a queue snaking around the Barbican. All of them want tickets to *Les Miz*'.[32] This information tipped the balance in favour of taking the risk. Years later, Judy Craymer demonstrated a similar ability to take risks in her determination to create *Mamma Mia!*—in her case, she sold her flat and gave up her job to focus on producing the show.

In addition to providing the Prince Edward theatre, Mackintosh encouraged her to develop the idea of a jukebox musical. Cameron Mackintosh had in fact already supported a musical using ABBA songs, written by David Wood, Mike Batt, and Don Black. This production was *Abbacadabra* (original French book by Alain and Daniel Boublil),[33] which opened at the Lyric Hammersmith in 1983. Although the show only ran for eight weeks, it proved the effectiveness of using the back catalogue of the Swedish pop group in a musical, and this may have fed into Mackintosh's decision to take a risk in supporting Craymer.

# *Cats*: The Key to the Global Market

It is important to emphasise that the market for global musicals was built incrementally, and that it was only the massive financial success of *Cats* that enabled Mackintosh to develop the other works. The fact that the first of his international successes told its story through dance and music made it 'the ideal exportable international entertainment',[34] with a minimal language barrier. The story itself is instructive in terms of what Mackintosh looks for in a narrative and what ultimately can succeed with a global audience: universality and emotional engagement.

For *Cats*, Trevor Nunn, who acted both as director and dramaturge, developed a simple but powerful narrative thread: an outsider who achieves acceptance by the tribe and a form of redemption—in this case, Grizabella, the Glamour Cat, emblematic of a 'fallen woman'. She was also given the song 'Memory', which turned out to be an enormous hit and thus an important factor in the show's global success.

The importance of the choreography also cannot be overstated. Gillian Lynne, who created the dances, makes the point that 'a lot of the storytelling is inherent in the choreography', but also that she deliberately built 'sensuality and sexuality' into the show. She goes on to describe how 'a lot of the movements' were 'for performers' bottoms', and this was deliberately designed to 'turn [the audience] on'.[35]

This insight into the choreographic strategy reveals how *Cats* was designed to engage its family audience on very different levels. *Cats* was always planned as a family show and to appeal to this larger audience, rather than just children. David Wood recounts a conversation he had with Cameron Mackintosh in 1979, where the producer made it clear that 'the future is going to be family shows'.[36]

Mackintosh has stated that he is 'most proud' of having 'raised the standard of the musical by putting on shows to a Broadway and London standard, in parts of the world which have never seen that', but that was never his 'intention'.[37] This points clearly to the fact that originally there was no grand corporate strategy, but merely a series of responses to invitations to transfer successful productions. While there was always the hope that a successful UK show might transfer to Broadway, the way *Cats* was to make that leap was to have a profound impact on how the global market would develop. Up to this point, the standard practice was for UK producers to sell 'foreign rights, allowing

FIG. 7.1 Betty Buckley as Grizabella in the 1982 Broadway production of *Cats*. Photo by Martha Swope © The New York Public Library for the Performing Arts.

overseas buyers total control over the show thereafter'.[38] Gerry Schoenfeld of the Shubert Organization in New York wanted the show but gave Mackintosh 'carte blanche to reproduce' the staging.[39]

The same request came from the Theater an der Wien in Vienna and the Operettenhaus in Hamburg. In each case the overseas producer carried the financial risk. This model of taking the original production out first, following a request, has become standard practice. However, at the time it was exceptional. Frank Rich, the theatre critic of the *New York Times*, made it clear that British imports were always 'tweaked by American producers and so to bring something over lock, stock and barrel was unusual'. He went on to point out that for a British musical to be such a hit 'was unheard of':[40] before its Broadway opening *Cats* had already taken an advance of $6 million.[41]

## Protecting the Brand

The export of an original production was in response to the demand for the actual experience and the desire to see something of a high standard. Mackintosh had learnt from Robert Stigwood, who had to protect his productions of *Jesus Christ Superstar* from unlicensed stagings. These were often second-rate, and Stigwood pursued 'any unauthorised companies with legal action'.[42]

In the same way, Richard O'Brien's cult musical *The Rocky Horror Show* had received poor productions in theatres such as the Theatre Royal, Hanley, Stoke-on-Trent. This theatre, in co-production with the Kenneth More Theatre, had toured *Rocky Horror* from 1984 to 1988, but when the show attempted to enter the West End, O'Brien refused permission, describing the production as 'too vulgar',[43] as well as 'amateur', lacking 'excitement' and 'danger'.[44] The show, however, continued to tour, and the producer, Charles Deacon, attempted to introduce new elements, such as an egg out of which Rocky was to be born, a gag about an offstage cat and a statue of the Venus de Milo, employed for various sex gags.[45]

The tour was brought to a halt once O'Brien's own production opened in the West End in 1988. Only when O'Brien was able to partner with the Ambassadors' Theatre Group (ATG) and retitle the work *Richard O'Brien's Rocky Horror Show* was he able to preserve the integrity of the original work.[46] It is interesting to note that Mackintosh produced the UK and German tours of *Rocky Horror* (1979–80), a production that maintained the quality of O'Brien's vision.[47]

For the impresario the challenge is not simply how to ensure a quality product, but, crucially, how that product will be 'inextricably linked to the establishment of his brand in the minds of the consumers'.[48] The brand would guarantee quality, in terms of music, book, and performance.

## Global Branding: Logos, Marketing, and 'Event' Productions

Essential to this process was the creation of a memorable logo. Mackintosh points out that he was inspired by two major films, *Raiders of the Lost Ark* (1981) and *Star Wars* (1977): 'They had very strong logos and I said we need something like that'.[49] It was Mackintosh's instinct for effective marketing rather than a pre-planned global release for *Cats* that led the development of the show's striking logo. As Richard Eyre notes, this was exceptional: 'Cameron Mackintosh showed a conviction, more or less unique in British theatre when he started, that marketing was an essential tool, rather than an optional extra'.[50] The logo had instant impact; as Frank Rich points out, the cat's eyes were 'a stroke of marketing genius, that no-one had thought of before. It changed the whole industry.'[51]

The logo was designed by Russ Eglin of the Dewynters Agency and was inspired by a suggestion from the show's designer, John Napier. He told Russ Eglin that, at the beginning of the show, cats appeared out of tunnels wearing LED glasses, to give the illusion of cats' eyes. He went on to say that 'I think [the show's image] should be something you know is a cat, but you can't see it. You're not giving any literal dimension to it.'[52] The fact that the concept for the logo was generated by the designer in response to his own design would seem to suggest that the choice was primarily aesthetic and not driven by the need for an image that could be read by an international audience.

The logo was designed to be mysterious, and this mystery extended to every aspect of the marketing campaign. No production stills were ever released in advance of the opening of the show. If people wanted to know what *Cats* was, they had to see it live. Of course, once the show premiered, the campaign utilised striking images from the production which were then used to stimulate audience interest.

Perhaps the most intriguing element of the logo is that it has to be decoded by the audience; it demands closer scrutiny. Only at a second glance does it become apparent that the cat's pupils are dancers. The same appeal to interactivity is adopted in the logo for *Miss Saigon*, where the central graphic appears to be a Chinese character, a helicopter, and to contain a melancholy female face. That the logos for the successful musicals convey a sense of energy and/or evoke an emotional response points to why they work. By contrast, the logo for the Mackintosh production of *Martin Guerre*, by Claude-Michel Schönberg and Alain Boublil, is simply an abstract face, which fails to communicate any of these qualities.

Although such logos create a unified image for productions all over the world, regional variants are allowed. The key image for *Les Misérables*, the etching of Cosette by Émile Boyard, has taken many different forms depending on where the show is playing. The first production in South Africa had an image of Cosette on the back of a springbok with the strap line, 'Let the people spring!'[53] The playful image works only because the brand and the story are so strongly established in the public mind that it did not serve to undermine the power of the narrative.

Adaptation is actually a key element in the successful marketing of Mackintosh shows. The logo for *The Phantom of the Opera* was changed to include a single red rose after the attacks on 11 September 2001 to emphasise the show's romantic nature and to tone down its more gothic and supernatural overtones.[54] The rose was included on the sleeve of the original cast recording, published in 1987, but not in the advertising for the first New York opening.[55]

Cameron Mackintosh's use of production logos has been successfully imitated. In each case the logo has to give the audience an instant sense of what the show might be like. Disney's logo for *The Lion King* was in fact designed by Dewynters; the African location and production style are hinted at by both the colour and the non-naturalistic lion's head. Unlike the poster for the original animated cartoon, it makes no attempt to illustrate the story.

FIG. 7.2 The logos for the Cameron Mackintosh productions of *Cats* (1981), *Les Misérables* (1985), *The Phantom of the Opera* (1986), *Miss Saigon* (1989), and *Martin Guerre* (1996). Reprinted by kind permission of Cameron Mackintosh Ltd.

By contrast, the logo for Little Star's *Mamma Mia!* is designed to clearly convey the fact this musical is about nuptial joy, evoked effectively by the image of a laughing bride set against a bright white background. As Phyllida Lloyd, the show's director, states: 'The logo for *Mamma Mia!* is more human, less graphic and more jolly'.[56] Interestingly, the image is strikingly similar to the poster for the 1994 Australian film *Muriel's Wedding*, in the plot of which ABBA songs also play an important role. As Peter Bradshaw noted in *The Guardian* in 2008: 'That ecstatic-bride logo for the *Mamma Mia!* stage show, on display outside theatres from Antwerp to Las Vegas, owes a great deal to the *Muriel's Wedding* poster',[57] reflecting the continuing influence of film publicity design on theatre.

The logos for these productions offer the headline image for the standardisation of any global marketing campaign, and this in turn reduces costs. An equally important consequence of unified global marketing is that you manufacture a sense of a high-quality, communal experience. This sense of community is perhaps reinforced by the statistics trumpeted in the musical's programme. In the London production of *Les Misérables*, for example, two pages are taken up with mind-boggling statistics, with the audience at '130 million (and counting!) in 425 cities in 52 countries in 22 languages'.[58]

Theodor Adorno points to the seductive role of such figures: 'Whatever is to pass muster must already have been handled, manipulated and approved by hundreds of thousands of people before anyone can enjoy it'.[59] The statistics certainly seem to play on our fear of missing out on a major experience. Mackintosh has further developed the sense that his musicals are important events by running massive merchandising programmes, where every mug and T-shirt carries the production logo and becomes a mobile advertisement for the show, a trail blazed by the hugely successful merchandising of *Star Wars*.

Despite the fact that Western cultural hegemony is being reinforced, there is little doubt that many non-English-speaking nations are keen to be part of a perceived mainstream. Japan in particular has been importing Western musicals since the late 1960s. Toho, one of the two major Japanese theatre producers, had already worked with Harold Fielding on the staging of *Half a Sixpence* in 1968 and was the first production company to stage *Les Misérables* in Asia.[60]

The scale of any marketing campaign is generally related to the length of run needed for a production to recoup its initial production budget. Mackintosh, however, will continue heavy marketing even when a show is sold out: 'That is the best time to beat the drum—when people can't buy tickets you have to let them know what they are missing. That is the difference between a hit and a mega-hit'.[61]

The global success of his major musicals meant that Mackintosh was able to sustain the marketing campaigns and nurture the work; other producers felt that they couldn't compete. Rob Bettison, producer of the musical *Buddy: The Buddy Holly Story*, commented in 2002: 'Now marketing has become an industry in itself. It affects you because if you haven't got the money to market at that level, it is almost as if you are not-existent'.[62]

Disney has acknowledged its debt to Cameron Mackintosh's marketing innovations but has been able to take promotion to a whole new level 'through cross fertilisation and corporate synergy [which] provides such corporations with an unmatchable advantage'.[63] The repeated images and stories carried by Disney films and theme parks act as permanent marketing tools for the musicals.

# GLOBAL REPRODUCTION AND QUALITY CONTROL

At the heart of the unease around global replication is the sense that new creative interpretation is stifled, that theatre is by its very nature ephemeral, and that attempts to repeat a specific production will simply be a dilution of the original. Groundbreaking productions such as Peter Brook's *A Midsummer Night's Dream* (1970) arose out of a particular period and rehearsal process. The production was toured internationally for over a year after its première, but Brook took pains to keep the performances fresh. To replicate this staging now, detached from its originator and period, would simply be to create a curiosity.

Cameron Mackintosh's global productions do not feel like pale imitations of their originals, in part because, unlike that of Brook's *Midsummer Night's Dream*, their staging does not feel tied to a particular period, but also because he engages in similar efforts to keep his productions sharp over the long term. To this end he has created an entire system wherein associate directors, choreographers, musical directors, and other key personnel supervise the remount—the *reproduction*. This is perhaps the most significant production innovation that Disney, Little Star, and other major players such as Universal have adopted.[64] Mackintosh has always insisted that the reason he requires touring shows to be essentially clones of the original production is that he wants to provide audiences all around the globe with the best possible experience. As Richard Eyre notes, this is a 'guarantee of quality'.[65] As I will discuss, the notion that the productions are simply clones of the original is not strictly correct: there is a wide spectrum of reproduction. The key common factor is Mackintosh's quality control.

To ensure that the quality of the original production is preserved, Mackintosh takes a close interest in every new opening of his shows and intervenes immediately if he feels a high standard is not being met. In 2002, prior to the opening of *Miss Saigon* at the Manchester Palace Theatre in the United Kingdom, Cameron Mackintosh noticed that the statue of Ho Chi Minh was too small, meaning that its impact would be lost. He ordered a new statue to be built at the last minute.[66] In the same vein, in 1996 he sacked twelve members of the cast of the Broadway production of *Les Misérables* because he felt they were not delivering performances of the required standard. John Caird, the co-director, described the cast at the time as 'Madame Tussaud's waxworks' and 'far too old to play students'.[67] Given that American Equity's Broadway contract at this time allowed the cast to remain in a show until it closed,[68] this was a very bold move and demonstrated Mackintosh's determination to defend the brand and the invaluable word of mouth that continues to underpin the success of all the shows.

Chris Grady, Mackintosh's former director of international licensing, made it clear that the reproduced shows would be 'as close to identical' to the original 'as was possible to do in a particular territory'. The production would be 'done with a local cast singing in the local language'.[69] A Cameron Mackintosh team would create the show and then leave 'resident directors' to maintain the standard.

This model has worked well. In some cases the local directors have even been able to develop the shows further, to the extent that some of their changes have been adopted by the main UK production. The producer of the Japanese production of *Les Misérables* has stated that the way Gavroche's body is displayed in the new UK touring production originated in Japan.[70]

Judy Craymer also embraces discoveries by her associate directors in the replica productions around the world; changes to the lighting design and set are key examples.[71] Innovations are welcomed so long as 'such changes in no way undermine the brand image'.[72]

The freedom given to both local and associate directors sent out to restage shows must be set within this clear boundary. They are however encouraged to solve persistent production problems and to explore potential improvements. This model also applies to the original creative teams. Eyre has pointed out that since the opening of *Mary Poppins* in the West End in 2004 at the Prince Edward Theatre, the production has been 'refined' on tour: a rather cumbersome set was eliminated, and the production that opened in 2019 was much 'more light-footed'.[73] Eyre develops this point, stating that in redirecting the show, he has made 'one or two substantial changes'. Such changes are 'debated in immense detail and often argued with some passion by Cameron', who has the final say but is not 'resistant to change' in principle.[74]

This model 'of learning from, refining and distilling productions' has been adopted by Disney,[75] making possible useful changes within a tightly controlled framework. Christian Durham, the associate director of Disney's *The Little Mermaid*, produced in Japan by the Shiki theatre company (set up in 1953), has introduced a number of innovations. Shiki, for example, wanted to make the show even more spectacular and requested additional puppets. Durham commissioned the making of a massive shark, and this now adds a frisson of fear at certain key moments in the Japanese production.[76]

Chris Grady illuminates another important element in the Mackintosh business model: after the first major replica production, Mackintosh would be 'open to "local" production licenses'.[77] For such a production, Cameron's subsidiary, Music Theatre International, would supply the book, music, and lyrics. This version would have to be substantially different from the original show.

The local producers would engage a new artistic team to create their own design and concept (subject to approval by Cameron), obviating the need to 'pay for any original creative input because they are not using it. This has allowed amazing new interpretations of his shows in many local productions around the world.' Grady described a Swedish production of *Miss Saigon* for which twelve helicopters were flown in, and a Czech production which had the helicopter 'lowered from the centre of the auditorium and soldiers and embassy staff run in and up a ladder into the helicopter.'[78]

## PAVING THE WAY: CAMERON MACKINTOSH

FIG. 7.3 Cameron Mackintosh in front of London's Prince Edward Theatre, home of his productions of *Martin Guerre* (1996), *Mary Poppins* (2004; 2019 revival) and *Miss Saigon* (2014 revival). Photo: Eric Roberts © Telegraph Media Group Limited 1995.

In smaller countries, Cameron sometimes waives the requirement of a 'reproduction first' production and grants a 'first in time, first in territory' local production. The first production of *Miss Saigon* in Estonia was staged by a local team. However, even in these unusual cases, Mackintosh approves all design concepts and casting to ensure that the audience has the best experience possible.

## Restaging, Remounting or Reconceiving?

The 'local' model seems to underpin the decision in 2019 to replace the original production of *Les Misérables* with the touring production. Aside from the financial advantage obtained by no longer having to pay royalties to the original creative team of the directors Trevor Nunn and John Caird and the designer John Napier, the change allows the show to be remarketed as having 'glorious new staging and dazzlingly re-imagined scenery inspired by the paintings of Victor Hugo'.[79] This 'acclaimed new production' opened in December 2019 in the newly renamed Sondheim Theatre:[80] '*Les Miserables* for the 21st century'.[81] Even this rebranding of what was formerly the Queen's Theatre lends the production a new gloss. The opening was prepared by the run of a concert version of *Les Misérables* at the Gielgud Theatre with an all-star cast, including Alfie Boe and Michael Ball. This version also ensured that the title was kept in the public eye and acted as a living advertisement for the new production.

In fact, the 'new version' of *Les Misérables*, directed by Laurence Conner and James Powell and designed by Matt Kinley and Paule Constable, has been running on tour since 2010. The business model described by Grady was already in operation: Napier did not receive any royalties, although he was offered a buyout of his intellectual property for $50,000, which he refused. The new production abandons the famous revolve and replaces it with projections. The most important part of Napier's original design is the revolve, and it arose out of Nunn's feeling that the production needed a 'dynamic that is sculptural and not painterly'.[82] This dimension has now been lost.

Napier criticises Mackintosh for not reconceiving the production: "I would have celebrated another production of *Les Misérables*—a new take on it. But it seems to me this is a fudged take on the old production'.[83] Nunn was similarly critical: 'It is not a new production. It is a variant production that owes everything that's good about it to the original production. And everything that's not so good about it, and is uncomfortable about it, is the work of a group of assistants'.[84]

This view seems in some measure to be borne out by Mark Shenton's comments in *The Stage*: 'Many of its iconic gestures are replicated identically—the flag-waving and the marching on the spot for the act 1 curtain song 'One Day More'—and visual continuity is provided by retaining Andreane Neofitou's shabby-chic costumes and the physical representation of the barricade. In many ways, fans of the original will see a replica'.[85] Writing in the same publication, Lyn Gardner makes the point that a 'theatre too much in thrall to the past is a dead theatre'.[86] It could be argued that Mackintosh did not go far enough in reconceiving *Les Mis*.

What is certain is that a remounted and more streamlined production both reduces the financial outlay in terms of royalties to the original team and ensures that the show can be marketed as a new experience to a whole new audience. The fact that the profits of the Cameron Mackintosh Organisation were down 57 percent over the year 2017–18, due in part to the refurbishment of the Victoria Palace Theatre, meant that Mackintosh had to find savings.[87]

The new production does attempt to realise some of the images originally conceived by Claude-Michel Schönberg. Now, instead of a chain gang opening the show, the image is of galley slaves, and this does have a tremendous impact. Alfonso Casado Trigo, the musical supervisor of the original West End and the restaged productions worldwide, also made the point that 'the new version of *Les Miz* aimed for a more cinematic and faster dynamic'.[88] This insight would seem to bear out Lyn Gardner's comment that 'the new staging might have greater appeal to younger audiences who were not even born when *Les Misérables* began its West End run'.[89] Such audiences might also be familiar with the Oscar-winning film version (2012) starring Hugh Jackman, which opens in a vast shipyard and a vision of the hellish world of the galley slave.

Perhaps the key point is that the original artistic team do not think their foundational work has been properly acknowledged either financially or artistically. The closure of the original production will also lead to 50 percent of the musicians being laid off and cuts in backstage staff. The band will, however, remain at fourteen, with new musicians being engaged, so the redundancies seem designed primarily to refresh the band with new talent.[90]

For Cameron Mackintosh, perhaps the main issue is to refresh the production whilst relaunching it and in the process freeing the budget from onerous royalties, not least from the percentage owing to the Royal Shakespeare Company (RSC) 'in perpetuity'.[91] Since the show first opened, the RSC has made £25 million in royalties.[92] The touring production has been hugely successful, grossing over $250 million in the United States and Canada alone. It continues to play to 95 percent attendance and is booking at least until 2021.[93] The touring productions generate 'road money', and according to Nick Allott, the CEO of the Cameron Mackintosh Organisation, this is a key source of revenue globally. He also pointed out that the livestreaming of the concert version of *Les Misérables* (2010) and the release of the film led to major spikes in the live audiences for the touring production in the United States in 2012.[94]

Exactly the same remount process was carried out in early 2004 with *Miss Saigon*. Nick Allott has described the difficulty of touring the original production in the United Kingdom: 'Each move took more than two weeks and cost three-quarters of a million pounds. So we decided to create a lighter production'.[95] It was this production that ran most recently (2014) at the Prince Edward Theatre. In 2019 the production toured the United States, where it came to more than thirty cities, from Los Angeles, California, to Milwaukee, Wisconsin.[96]

The opening in New York was not without controversy. The Pulitzer Prize–winning novelist Viet Thang Ngyuen wrote a front-page article for the *New York Times* condemning the production as perpetuating damaging racist stereotypes: 'Why is a musical that perpetuates a Western fantasy of Asians as small, weak and effeminate people, still so popular?'[97]

*The Phantom of the Opera* was also reconceived for its twenty-fifth anniversary British tour with 'a new design and a very different staging, but retaining Maria Björnson's wonderful costumes'.[98] The retention of original costume designs seems to be a key signifier of quality.[99]

# Cultural Sensitivity and Taste

Meryl Faiers, executive producer of *The Rocky Horror Show* for the Trafalgar Entertainment Group, has stated that 'taste and culture underlie everything you do internationally; what works at home ... may not work anywhere else'.[100] The 2019 production of *Rocky Horror* in South Africa had a black Janet, who was cast on merit, but in itself has generated a lot of positive publicity. In a similar vein, Judy Craymer underlines that she aims to make *Mamma Mia!* familiar to the country where it is playing, and so on Broadway the female holiday makers are American.[101]

By contrast, Nick Allott made it clear that, despite approaches from Saudi Arabian producers, he would not be comfortable taking *Les Misérables* or *Miss Saigon* there, as there is a risk of causing real offence, particularly with the scenes involving actors playing prostitutes. Meryl Faiers makes the same point in relation to *The Rocky Horror Show*, which, despite its intrinsic innocence, does portray sexual fluidity in ways which might even be illegal in some Muslim countries.[102] Chris Grady describes a request from the local producer of a South Korean *Miss Saigon* to add a 'mega-mix of the all the songs' at the end of the show during which Kim comes back to life and sings a romantic duet with Chris.[103] Unsurprisingly, this request was turned down; clearly, adapting to local tastes has its limits.

In Japan, Kazuhiko Matsuda, the producer of *Les Misérables* for Toho, points out that although the production is very popular and the collaboration with Mackintosh a long-standing one, he still encountered difficulties with trying to get Mackintosh to sign off on promotional materials, merchandise, and cast photographs which appeal to a Japanese audience. A more difficult producing issue is that the Japanese system does not permit previews, which means that the first public performance is opening night, placing cast and crew under considerable pressure.[104] However, above and beyond such details, the macroeconomic state of any country will determine how successful Western productions will be. In Japan, for example, the economy has remained relatively stagnant, and although ticket prices were amongst the highest in the world twenty years ago, they have not increased significantly, so profits for musicals remain static.[105]

In all countries and regions, judging the length of a run can be critical to the success of a show. In Japan the runs are relatively short, with shows allowed to lie fallow and only brought back at intervals when demand is judged to have built. Meryl Faiers, commenting on a tour to Australia of *West Side Story*, has pointed out that shorter runs almost always meet capacity, and in Australia, where distances between cities are so vast, you need to have two sets—each one ready and waiting for the cast.[106] This means that as soon as the cast arrive, the show can open and generate revenue.

Politics also play a role in navigating a new culture. Nick Allott described how, although the audience in Shanghai for the première of *Les Misérables* (2002) went wild after 'Do You Hear the People Sing',[107] the Communist Party officials, who were seated in the front two rows, were silent.[108] The song has now been banned from QQ Music, China's most popular music-streaming service.[109] It was also not immediately apparent why, despite full houses, the box office was always lower than expected. Eventually the local producer revealed that large sections of the audience were made up of party officials and the police, and these seats were all complimentary.

## TRANSLATION FOR FOREIGN MARKETS

Aside from taste and culture, translation is a critical issue. Many productions playing in the non-English-speaking world are now sung and spoken in the language of the producing country. The process followed by Mackintosh and other major producers is to commission a translation and then have it back-translated into English to see how accurate it is. Idioms present a particular problem. In the Disney production of *The Little Mermaid*, a joke bound up with the expression 'a school of fish' made no sense in Japanese, so a new joke had to be found.[110] Problems also arise out of the structure of Japanese words, which do not easily match the rhythm of English. Matsuda pointed out that *Les Misérables* is regularly taken out of the repertoire to allow time for the translation to be continually improved.[111]

Particular challenges are offered by tonal languages such as Mandarin. In the Chinese production of *Cats*, the name of one of the felines, when translated, became 'genitalia'.[112] Chris Grady points out that the music often determines the length of a word, which can present significant challenges in other languages. In Mandarin, for example, if the length of a word is changed, so can its meaning be. There is a Mandarin word that can mean 'mother, horse or whore and so if you sing it the wrong way, you are suddenly translating your mother into a horse or a whore',[113] which clearly would present problems. In advance of the Chinese version of *Les Misérables*, Annie Guo, the assistant producer, was employed to record the songs in Mandarin in London to test how the translated lyrics worked with the music.[114]

# THEATRE INFRASTRUCTURE

Another element affecting a Western musical's ability to work in a new territory, such as China, is the theatre infrastructure. China now has a vast range of large theatres, some of which are not appropriate for musical theatre. *Les Misérables* was initially offered the Great Hall of the People in Beijing, where the first row of the audience is so far from the stage that any sense of intimacy would be impossible.[115] By contrast, in Taiwan the development of imported Western musicals of scale has been limited by a lack of theatres large enough to stage the work. Another limitation on the longevity of a show is the available talent pool. The Cameron Mackintosh Organisation considered setting up a musical theatre academy in China in order to develop local talent to feed the imported productions, but to date this has not happened.

The key European markets are Germany/Austria, the Netherlands, and Spain. A major partner for Mackintosh and other global producers is Stage Entertainment, founded by Joop van den Ende, who 'is often credited with creating an audience from scratch in the Netherlands... he started with *Les Misérables*... and now an audience of up to two million people (out of a population of 17 million) visit a musical each year'.[116] Other major European productions include *Mary Poppins*, a co-production between Mackintosh and Disney that was presented in Sweden at the Gothenburg Opera House in 2008;[117] and *The Lion King*, which has been playing in Hamburg for sixteen years.

The only major European country that has yet to embrace the so-called mega-musicals is France. Mackintosh himself observed, 'The French have hardly taken to modern musicals, and Paris has proved an early graveyard for most of the worldwide musical successes of the last fifty years'.[118] There is little hard evidence of this, but perhaps it is a symptom of French nationalism and resistance to foreign cultural imports, much in the way the French government protects its indigenous film industry from domination by Hollywood.[119] More significantly, France has developed a distinctive form of music theatre, the *spectacle musical*. This form has its origins in rock opera, and as Rebecca-Anne C. Do Rozario points out, 'For these musicals, the songs are the musical and what occurs on stage is configured according to the songs, rather than the narrative as in traditional Broadway or blockbuster musicals'.[120]

## Tourism and Ticket Sales

An important factor in Mackintosh's success has been his awareness of the link between his brand, the audience's perception of the show and ticket sales. The key is manipulating ticket distribution to stimulate demand. He 'is unwilling to discount tickets in such a way that consumers would gain the impression that a show was struggling' but does not hesitate to give unsold seats to charity to make it look as though it is sold out,[121] thereby increasing demand. Mackintosh has always been aware of the close relationship between travel and ticket sales. He came up with the idea of 'Hair Rail'—a combined train and theatre ticket to the musical *Hair* in 1968.[122] This model has been developed in relation to air travel, and Mackintosh acknowledges the growth in international air travel as a key influence on his global success.[123] It has yet to be seen how coronavirus, climate change, and consequent opposition to long-haul flights will impact West End musicals in the long term.

Mackintosh has cultivated strong relationships with ticket distribution networks and travel agents all over the world. Musicals are now treated by travel companies as tourist attractions that may be visited like any other traditional landmarks. Indeed, the phrase 'landmark' production is constantly used in relation to Mackintosh musicals, and repeat visits become part of the tourist agenda. The phrase currently used in the marketing for *Phantom* indicates this strategy: 'Remember your first time'.

## Conclusion: Setting the Standard

It is clear that Cameron Mackintosh has paved the way for the globalisation of musical theatre. His contributions have been acknowledged not only by Thomas Schumacher, the president of Disney Theatrical, but also by other key players, including Michael McCabe, marketing manager for *Mamma Mia!*:

> He has created new markets for musical theatre ... so when it comes to Europe, Russia, Japan and China ... we are very lucky that there was this pioneer. So there

is now an audience who is ready to engage in musical theatre in some extremely obscure places and so *Mamma Mia!* is able to roll itself around the world.[124]

The charge that Mackintosh's musicals are mere reproductions, like McDonald's
hamburgers, and are sold merely for profit is not sustainable. His careful restaging of
high-quality shows ensures that global audiences get the best possible versions; but, as
this chapter has demonstrated, the replica and local productions reflect regional variation and leave space for developments that can be applied to the home productions. In
the words of Schumacher, 'There is no doubt that works like *Cats* and *Phantom* set the
standard for the musical as event';[125] but I would argue that the spectacular elements of
the Mackintosh musicals, from the crashing chandelier in *Phantom* to the helicopter in
*Miss Saigon*, are dramaturgically essential, not merely gratuitous crowd pleasers.

The critic Anne Marie Walsh is scathing about these elements, claiming that 'cast-
proof, critic-proof and saturation marketed, these shows rely as much on visual spectacle as music for their effect.... They've divided the Broadway audience into two
camps—theme park visitors and serious theatre goers'.[126] Such criticism misses the point
that spectacle is often a key element in the storytelling. In the case of *Miss Saigon*, the
helicopter not only powerfully evokes the actual moment when a tiny number of select Vietnamese and American staff are evacuated from the roof of the US embassy, but
underscores how American power has been diminished. Like a number of other (in)
famous moments in Mackintosh productions—most obviously, perhaps, the barricade
scenes in *Les Miz*—it is not literal, but a theatrical illusion evoked with minimal means.

Richard Eyre points to a more problematic legacy: 'Cameron Mackintosh's
commodified approach to musical theatre paved the way' for productions such as
Disney's *Beauty and the Beast*, which 'has all the liveliness of a wax museum and
the charm of a yawning grave'.[127] Whilst I have taken issue with the notion that the
Mackintosh musicals are in some sense second-rate because they are essentially carbon-
copied across the globe, Eyre's criticism of this particular Disney musical is instructive.
I would suggest that his pejorative use of 'commodification' arises from the fact that the
1994 screen-to-stage musical represented a way for Disney to exploit their back catalogue for profit, where 'marketability takes precedence over quality, artistry, integrity,
and intellectual challenge. The origin of the live version of *Beauty and the Beast* determined its form. It was the first musical adaptation of a Disney animated film, and its
close adherence to the film betrays a lack of confidence in tackling a new form. This is
borne out by the exact reproduction of the design of the film on stage, from the costumes
to the set. The playwright David Wood attests to this lack of theatricality, describing the
experience as watching a show 'behind a glass screen . . . just like in a cinema'.[128] The cinematic experience was reinforced by the sale of popcorn. Wood goes on to point out that
the performance was so locked down that no spontaneous reaction from the audience
could alter the rhythm of the performance, rendering it 'inert'.[129]

The earliest versions of *Beauty and the Beast* were conceived as theme park or arena
productions. They relied heavily on spectacular set pieces, which are not impelled by
critical dramatic need and in which the characters are often merely sketched. Problems

FIG. 7.4 The notorious helicopter scene from *Miss Saigon*. Photo: Michael Le Poer Trench © Cameron Mackintosh Ltd.

arise in part because the truncated time frame of this type of show does not allow significant plot or character development. Another factor which may play a role here is that 'happiness' is a key element of the Disney brand, and this can lead to work that is uniformly sentimental or cheerful in tone and execution.

However, with their later stage adaptations, including their co-production of *Mary Poppins*, Disney became more creative. Richard Eyre emphasises that Thomas Schumacher was feeling his way with *Beauty and the Beast* but 'found his feet' with *The Lion King*.[130] The latter, directed by Julie Taymor, is a highly theatrical evocation of the original film, using masks and puppets to create an exciting theatrical language expressing a mythic story. *The Lion King* was the second adaptation of a Disney film, and it is clear that the company understood by then that any adaptation had to be reconceived in a wholly theatrical style.

In a similar vein, *Mary Poppins*, directed by Richard Eyre, is not a simply a retread of the film, and whilst it includes all the iconic songs, there are also new scenes and songs to surprise the audience. These include a memorable upside-down walk over the proscenium arch and a wonderful ensemble dance sequence with a new version of the famous song 'Supercalifragilisticexpialidocious'. The fact that this is a joint production with Cameron Mackintosh ensured that a detailed and very theatrical approach was taken from the outset; thus, a new benchmark was established for the adaptation of musicals from film to the stage.

## Notes

1. *The Story of Musicals*, broadcast on BBC4, 19 January 2012, 60 mins; https://learningonscr een.ac.uk/ondemand/index.php/prog/023B4DDF?bcast=77601919, accessed 26 July 2019.
2. Sheridan Morley and Ruth Leon, *Hey Mr Producer! The Musical World of Cameron Mackintosh* (London: Weidenfeld & Nicholson, 1998), 17.
3. Charles Lee, 'Cameron Mackintosh and the McDonaldisation of Musical Theatre Marketing' (PhD thesis, Goldsmiths College, University of London, 2000), 77.
4. David Merrick, born David Margulois (b. 27 November 1911, St. Louis, Missouri, US–d. 25 April 2000, London, England), was a prolific American theatrical producer who staged many of the most successful plays in American theatre during the 1960s; https://www. britannica.com/biography/David-Merrick, accessed 29 July 2019. The credits of Harold Fielding, one of Britain's foremost theatrical producers, include the London-originated hits *Half a Sixpence* and *Charlie Girl*, as well as Broadway imports such as *Mame* and *Sweet Charity*; https://www.latimes.com/archives/la-xpm-2003-oct-04-me-fielding4-story. html, accessed 29 July 2019.
5. The role of Norma Desmond is a star vehicle and has been played by (among others) Patti LuPone, Diahann Carroll, Glenn Close, Petula Clark, and Elaine Page. There are a limited number of performers of such stature, so the part is difficult to cast.
6. https://isreview.org/issue/89/enduring-relevance-victor-hugo, accessed 26 March 2020.
7. *Imagine . . . Cameron Mackintosh: The Musical Man*, broadcast on BBC1, 11 September 2017, 90 mins; https://learningonscreen.ac.uk/ondemand/index.php/prog/0FB1E42D?bcast= 125145592, accessed 29 July 2019.
8. Ibid.
9. Interview with Richard Eyre, director, 28 January 2020.
10. Ibid.
11. 'The Story of *The Phantom of the Opera*', *The Phantom of the Opera*, dir. Joel Schumacher, 2004 (DVD, Entertainment in Video, 2005, ASIN B0052YT370).
12. *Imagine . . . Cameron Mackintosh*.
13. In June 2018 the New London Theatre was renamed the Gillian Lynne Theatre; https:// officiallondontheatre.com/news/new-london-theatre-renamed-gillian-lynne-theatre-111410734/, accessed 29 July 2019.
14. Miranda Lundskaer-Nielsen, 'Cameron Mackintosh: Control, Collaboration and the Creative Producer', in *The Oxford Handbook of the British Musical*, ed. Robert Gordon and Olaf Jubin (Oxford and New York: Oxford University Press, 2016), 537–59.
15. Morley and Leon, *Hey Mr Producer!*, 37.
16. Hytner's first opera was Benjamin Britten's *The Turn of the Screw*, which he staged for Kent Opera; https://www.independent.co.uk/news/obituaries/norman-platt-37758.html, accessed 29 July 2019.

17. *The Heat Is On: The Making of* Miss Saigon (DVD, Freemantle Home Entertainment, 2008, ASIN B009LPYFBU).
18. Interview with Richard Eyre.
19. Ibid.
20. Ibid.
21. Ibid.
22. *Barnum* was co-directed by Liam Steel, who also acted as choreographer; https://www.cameronmackintosh.com/news/view/barnum-cast-announced, accessed 29 July 2019.
23. *The Story of Musicals.*
24. *Imagine . . . Cameron Mackintosh.*
25. Morley and Leon, *Hey Mr Producer!*, 46.
26. Cameron Mackintosh, quoted in ibid.
27. https://www.delfontmackintosh.co.uk/theatres/prince-edward-theatre/, accessed 1 April 2020
28. Jo Caird, 'Producer Judy Craymer: *Mamma Mia!* Was the Dark Horse That Surprised Everyone', *The Stage*, 20 March 2019; https://www.thestage.co.uk/features/interviews/2019/producer-judy-craymer-mamma-mia-dark-horse-surprised-everyone/, accessed 29 July 2019.
29. *Imagine . . . Cameron Mackintosh.*
30. Cameron Mackintosh, quoted in Morley and Leon, *Hey Mr Producer!*, 63.
31. Ibid., 65.
32. Ibid., 98.
33. The original book for *Abbacadabra* was written by Alain and Daniel Boublil. David Wood, Don Black, and Mike Batt wrote new material for the English production. Despite an offer from a Japanese company to restage the show, Mackintosh decided not produce it again, telling Wood at the time that he felt the musical was too 'christmassy', because the characters, such as Cinderella and Pinocchio, were all drawn from fairy tales. Interview with David Wood, playwright, 7 August 2019.
34. Lee, 'Cameron Mackintosh', 111.
35. 'Interview with Gillian Lynne', *Cats: Ultimate Edition* (DVD, Universal Pictures, 1998, ASIN B000064215).
36. Interview with David Wood.
37. David Thomas, 'I Always Think I'm Tigger', *Sunday Telegraph*, 8 July 2011, 5.
38. Morley and Leon, *Hey Mr Producer!*, 71
39. Ibid.
40. *Imagine . . . Cameron Mackintosh.*
41. Morley and Leon, *Hey Mr Producer!*, 71.
42. Lee, 'Cameron Mackintosh', 106.
43. The costumes for this touring production were not designed by Sue Blane, the original designer. From photographic records of the production, the designs by Margaret Brice and Nigel Ellacott were clearly much more overtly based on bondage gear; http://www.overthefootlights.co.uk/The%20Rocky%20Road.pub.pdf, accessed 29 July 2019.
44. Ibid.
45. Ibid.
46. Interview with Meryl Faires, executive producer, Trafalgar Entertainment Group, 24 July 2019.
47. Morley and Leon, *Hey Mr Producer!*, 42.

48. Lee, 'Cameron Mackintosh', 106.
49. *Imagine ... Cameron Mackintosh*.
50. Richard Eyre and Nicholas Wright, *Changing Stages: A View of British Theatre in the Twentieth Century* (London: Bloomsbury, 2000), 343–44.
51. *Imagine ... Cameron Mackintosh*.
52. Matthew Hemley, '*Les Mis* Designer John Napier Hits Out at Plans to Replace West End Production with "Fudged" Update', *The Stage*, 6 February 2019; https://www.thestage.co.uk/news/2019/les-mis-designer-john-napier-hits-out-at-plans-to-replace-west-end-production-with-fudged-update/, accessed 16 May 2019.
53. Morley and Leon, *Hey Mr Producer!*, 100.
54. Lee, 'Cameron Mackintosh', 118.
55. https://www.amazon.co.uk/Phantom-Opera-VINYL-Various/dp/B000091F0F.
56. Lee, 'Cameron Mackintosh', 167.
57. Peter Bradshaw, 'Film Review: *Mamma Mia!*', *The Guardian*, 10 July 2008; https://www.theguardian.com/culture/2008/jul/10/film.reviews, accessed 29 July 2019.
58. *Les Misérables*, programme, Queens Theatre, London, June 2019.
59. Theodor Adorno and Max Horkheimer, *Gesammelte Schriften III: Dialektik der Aufklärung* (Frankfurt am Main: Suhrkamp,1981), 58.
60. Interview with Kazuhiko Matsuda, producer, Toho Theatre Company, Japan, 4 June 2019.
61. Morley and Leon, *Hey Mr Producer!*, 131.
62. Lee, 'Cameron Mackintosh', 220.
63. Ibid., 178.
64. Musicals produced by Universal include *Wicked* (2003), *Billy Elliot: The Musical* (2005), and the Broadway revival of *Carousel* (2018); https://www.ibdb.com/broadway-organizat ion/universal-pictures-stage-productions-490376, accessed 28 July 2019.
65. Interview with Richard Eyre.
66. Lee, 'Cameron Mackintosh', 134.
67. Laurette Ziemer, '*Les Mis* Purge Causes Fury on Broadway', *Evening Standard*, 30 October 1996, V&A Theatre and Performance Collection.
68. Robert Viagas and David Lefkowitz, 'Equity Calls Meeting on *Les Miz* Firings Nov. 5', www.playbill.com, 5 November 1996; http://www.playbill.com/article/equity-calls-meet ing-on-les-miz-firings-nov-5-com-329048, accessed 29 July 2019.
69. Interview with Chris Grady, former licensing director for Cameron Mackintosh, 26 February 2019.
70. Interview with Kazuhiko Matsuda.
71. Kramer cites as an example improvements to the lighting design: 'We continue to improve the show every time it is re-lit, for example, and Howard Harrison has the chance to go in there and re-light it. I mean, in Las Vegas he will probably give us even more bloody lamps and then he will come back and he will say, 'Right, I want to go into London again or Toronto and do the same.' Quoted in Lee, 'Cameron Mackintosh', 164.
72. Ibid., 163.
73. Interview with Richard Eyre.
74. Ibid.
75. Ibid.
76. Interview with Christian Durham, associate director of Disney's *The Little Mermaid*, 8 June 2019.
77. Interview with Chris Grady.

78. Ibid.
79. Trailer for *Les Misérables*; https://www.youtube.com/watch?v=5s5ImbMCxtE, accessed 29 July 2019.
80. See the official website of *Les Misérables*: https://www.lesmis.com/london?landing, accessed 29 July 2019.
81. Ibid.
82. '*Les Mis* Designer ...'
83. Ibid.
84. Jasper Rees, 'Trevor Nunn: I Feel Betrayed by New *Les Mis*', *Daily Telegraph*, 29 June 2010, https://www.telegraph.co.uk/culture/theatre/theatre-features/7861715/Trevor-Nunn-I-feel-betrayed-by-the-new-Les-Mis.html, accessed 30 July 2019.
85. Mark Shenton, 'Theatre Shouldn't Be Preserved in Aspic, even *Les Misérables*', *The Stage*, 17 January 2019; https://edition.thestage.co.uk/2019/01/16/mark-shenton-theatre-shouldnt-be-preserved-in-aspic-even-les-miserables/pugpig_index.html, accessed 29 July 2019.
86. Lyn Gardner, 'We Can Cherish Beloved Shows Such as *Les Misérables* but Let's Not Resist Change', *The Stage*, 14 January 2019; https://edition.thestage.co.uk/2019/01/14/lyn-gard ner-we-can-cherish-beloved-shows-such-as-les-miserables-but-lets-not-resist-change/pugpig_index.html, accessed 29 July 2019.
87. Matthew Hemley, 'The RSC Begins Crunch Talks with Cameron Mackintosh over *Les Misérables* Royalties', *The Stage*, 16 January 2019; https://www.thestage.co.uk/news/2019/rsc-begins-crunch-talks-cameron-mackintosh-les-miserables-royalties/.
88. Asako Kajiwara, 'A Comparison of the Original West End *Les Misérables*, and Its Newly Staged Japanese Production' (MA essay, Goldsmiths College, University of London, 2019), 36.
89. Gardner, 'We Can Cherish'.
90. Matthew Hemley, '*Les Misérables*' Backstage Staff Facing Redundancy as 50% of Musicians Are Axed', *The Stage*, 1 May 2019; https://www.thestage.co.uk/news/2019/les-miserables-backstage-staff-facing-redundancy-threat-50-musicians-axed/, accessed 30th July 2019.
91. Morley and Leon, *Hey Mr Producer!*, 92.
92. Hemley, 'RSC Begins Crunch Talks.'
93. Kajiwara, 'A Comparison', 26.
94. Interview with Nick Allott, CEO of the Cameron Mackintosh Organisation, 9 July 2019.
95. *The Story of Musicals*.
96. https://www.miss-saigon.com/us-tour/tour-dates, accessed 30 July 2019.
97. Viet Thanh Nguyen, 'Close the Curtain on *Miss Saigon*: Why Is a Musical that Perpetuates a Western Fantasy of Asians as Small, Weak and Effeminate People Still So Popular?', *New York Times*, 3 August 2019; https://www.nytimes.com/2019/08/03/opinion/miss-saigon-play.html, accessed 20 January 2020.
98. Cameron Mackintosh, 'The Phantom's Trial', *The Phantom of the Opera*, programme, Her Majesty's Theatre, London, 2019.
99. A key element in the rebranding of *The Rocky Horror Show* is Sue Blane's 'iconic' costumes.
100. Interview with Meryl Faires.
101. Lee, 'Cameron Mackintosh', 166.
102. Interview with Meryl Faires.
103. Interview with Chris Grady.

104. Interview with Kazuhiko Matsuda.

105. The average rate of inflation in Japan from 1958 to 2019 is 2.95 percent; https://tradingec onomics.com/japan/inflation-cpi, accessed 1 August 2019.

106. This allows the show to go into performance and begin earning money much faster. The second set will be sent onto the next city or region, ready for the next leg of the tour. Interview with Meryl Faires.

107. '*Les Mis*' Shanghai Opening to Make History, *South China Morning Post*, 22 June 2002; https://www.scmp.com/article/382910/les-mis-shanghai-opening-make-history, accessed 30 July 2019.

108. Interview with Nick Allott.

109. Simon Rabinovitch, 'Do You Hear the People Sing? Not in China', *The Economist*, 14 June 2019; https://www.economist.com/prospero/2019/06/14/do-you-hear-the-people-sing-not-in-china, accessed 29 July 2019.

110. Interview with Christian Durham.

111. Interview with Kazuhiko Matsuda.

112. Interview with Tim MacFarlane, executive chairman of Trafalgar Entertainment Asia-Pacific, 20 July 2019.

113. Interview with Chris Grady.

114. Interview with Annie Guo, assistant producer of the Chinese production of *Les Misérables*, 20 May 2019.

115. Ibid.

116. Lisa Martland, '*Mamma Mia!* Why Musical Theatre Has Taken Off across Europe', *The Stage*, 6 July 2017; https://www.thestage.co.uk/features/2017/mamma-mia-musical-thea tre-across-europe/, accessed 28 July 2019.

117. For more information, see the official website: https://en.opera.se/forestallningar/mary-poppins-2008-2009/, accessed 1 August 2019.

118. *Imagine . . . Cameron Mackintosh*.

119. The following statement appeared in 25 May 2016, published in a Ministry of Culture and Communication communiqué: 'In 2013 France secured the exclusion of cinema and the audiovisual sector from the negotiation mandate for the draft free trade agree-ment with the United States. True to its values, France refused to reduce culture to a mere commodity, whatever its economic weight.' 'Policy to Support French Cinema Bringing Results—Minister', https://uk.ambafrance.org/Policy-to-support-French-cinema-bear ing-fruit-says-Minister, accessed 2 August 2019.

120. Rebecca-Anne C. Do Rozario, 'The French Musicals: The Dramatic Impulse of *Spectacle*', *Journal of Dramatic Theory and Criticism* 19, no. 1 (2004): 125–42; https://journals. ku.edu/jdtc/article/download/3504/3380/, accessed 2 August 2019.

121. Lee, 'Cameron Mackintosh', 118.

122. Morley and Leon, *Hey Mr Producer!*, 31.

123. Lee, 'Cameron Mackintosh', 106.

124. D. F. Walsh, *American Popular Culture and the Genesis of the Musical*, Goldsmiths Sociology Papers 1 (London: Goldsmiths College, University of London, 1996). Quoted in Lee, 'Cameron Mackintosh', 190.

125. *The Story of Musicals*.

126. Quoted in Lee, 'Cameron Mackintosh', 97.

127. Eyre and Wright, *Changing Stages*, 346

128. Interview with David Wood.

## 129. Interview with Richard Eyre.
130. Ibid.
131. Ibid.

## BIBLIOGRAPHY

### Interviews

Interview with Nick Allott, CEO of the Cameron Mackintosh Organisation, 9 July 2019.

Interview with Christian Durham, associate director of Disney's *The Little Mermaid*, 8 June 2019.

Interview with Richard Eyre, director, 28 January 2020.

Interview with Meryl Faires, executive producer, Trafalgar Entertainment Group, 24 July 2019.

Interview with Chris Grady, former licensing director for Cameron Mackintosh, 26 February 2019.

Interview with Annie Guo, assistant producer of the Chinese production of *Les Misérables*, 20 May 2019.

Interview with Tim MacFarlane, executive chairman of Trafalgar Entertainment Asia-Pacific, 20 July 2019.

Interview with Kazuhiko Matsuda, producer, Toho Theatre Company, Japan, 4 June 2019.

Interview with David Wood, playwright, 7 August 2019.

### Secondary Sources

Adorno, Theodor, and Max Horkheimer. *Gesammelte Schriften III: Dialektik der Aufklärung.* Frankfurt am Main: Suhrkamp, 1981.

Caird, Jo. 'Producer Judy Craymer: *Mamma Mia!* Was the Dark Horse That Surprised Everyone'. *The Stage*, 20 March 2019. https://www.thestage.co.uk/features/interviews/2019/producer-judy-craymer-mamma-mia-dark-horse-surprised-everyone/, accessed 29 July 2019.

Bradshaw, Peter. 'Film Review: *Mamma Mia!*' *The Guardian*, 10 July 2008. https://www.theguardian.com/culture/2008/jul/10/film.reviews, accessed 29 July 2019.

Do Rozario, Rebecca-Anne C. 'The French Musicals: The Dramatic Impulse of *Spectacle*'. *Journal of Dramatic Theory and Criticism* 19, no. 1 (2004): 125–42. https://journals.ku.edu/jdtc/article/download/3504/3380/, accessed 2 August 2019.

Eyre, Richard, and Nicholas Wright. *Changing Stages: A View of British Theatre in the Twentieth Century*. London: Bloomsbury, 2000.

Garner, Lyn. 'We Can Cherish Beloved Shows Such as *Les Misérables* but Let's Not Resist Change'. *The Stage*, 14 January 2019. https://edition.thestage.co.uk/2019/01/14/lyn-gardner-we-can-cherish-beloved-shows-such-as-les-miserables-but-lets-not-resist-change/pugpig_index.html, accessed 29 July 2019.

*The Heat Is On: The Making of 'Miss Saigon'*. DVD. Freemantle Home Entertainment, 2008, ASIN B009LPYFBU.

Hemley, Matthew. '*Les Mis* Designer John Napier Hits Out at Plans to Replace West End Production with "Fudged" Update'. *The Stage*, 6 February 2019.

Hemley, Matthew. '*Les Misérables*' Backstage Staff Facing Redundancy as 50% of Musicians Are Axed'. *The Stage*, 1 May 2019.

Hemley, Matthew. 'The RSC Begins Crunch Talks with Cameron Mackintosh over *Les Misérables* Royalties'. *The Stage*, 16 January 2019. https://www.thestage.co.uk/news/2019/rsc-begins-crunch-talks-cameron-mackintosh-les-miserables-royalties/, accessed 30 July 2019.

http://www.overthefootlights.co.uk/The%20Rocky%20Road.pub.pdf, accessed 29 July 2019.

https://en.opera.se/forestallningar/mary-poppins-2008-2009/, accessed 1 August 2019.

https://officiallondontheatre.com/news/new-london-theatre-renamed-gillian-lynne-theatre-111410734/, accessed 29 July 2019.

https://tradingeconomics.com/japan/inflation-cpi, accessed 1 August 2019.

https://www.amazon.co.uk/Phantom-Opera-VINYL-Various/dp/B000091F0F.

https://www.cameronmackintosh.com/news/view/barnum-cast-announced, accessed 29 July 2019.

https://www.ibdb.com/broadway-organization/universal-pictures-stage-productions-490376, accessed 29 July 2019.

https://www.independent.co.uk/news/obituaries/norman-platt-37758.html, accessed 29 July 2019.

https://www.lesmis.com/london?landing, accessed 29 July 2019.

https://www.miss-saigon.com/us-tour/tour-dates, accessed 30 July 2019.

https://www.thestage.co.uk/news/2019/les-mis-designer-john-napier-hits-out-at-plans-to-replace-west-end-production-with-fudged-update/, accessed 16 May 2019.

https://www.thestage.co.uk/news/2019/les-miserables-backstage-staff-facing-redundancy-threat-50-musicians-axed/, accessed 30 July 2019.

*Imagine . . . Cameron Mackintosh: The Musical Man*. Broadcast on BBC1, 11 September 2017. 90 mins. https://learningonscreen.ac.uk/ondemand/index.php/prog/0FB1E42D?bcast=125145592, accessed 29 July 2019.

'Interview with Gillian Lynne'. *Cats. Ultimate Edition*. DVD, Universal Pictures, 1998, ASIN B000064215.

Kajiwara, Asako. 'A Comparison of the Original West End *Les Misérables*, and Its Newly Staged Japanese Production'. MA essay, Goldsmiths College, University of London, 2019.

Lee, Charles. 'Cameron Mackintosh and the McDonaldisation of Musical Theatre Marketing'. PhD diss., Goldsmiths, University of London, 2000.

'*Les Mis* Shanghai Opening to Make History'. *South China Morning Post*, 22 June 2002, https://www.scmp.com/article/382910/les-mis-shanghai-opening-make-history, accessed 30 July 2019.

*Les Misérables*. Programme, London, Queens Theatre, June 2019.

Lundskaer-Nielsen, Miranda. 'Cameron Mackintosh: Control, Collaboration and the Creative Producer'. In *The Oxford Handbook of the British Musical*, edited by Robert Gordon and Olaf Jubin, 537–59. Oxford and New York: Oxford University Press, 2016.

Mackintosh, Cameron. 'The Phantom's Trial'. In *The Phantom of the Opera*, programme, Her Majesty's Theatre, London, 2019.

Martland, Lisa. '*Mamma Mia!* Why Musical Theatre Has Taken Off across Europe'. *The Stage*, 6 July 2017. https://www.thestage.co.uk/features/2017/mamma-mia-musical-theatre-across-europe/, accessed 28 July 2019.

Morley, Sheridan Morley, and Ruth Leon. *Hey Mr Producer! The Musical World of Cameron Mackintosh*. London: Weidenfeld & Nicholson, 1998.

'Policy to Support French Cinema Bringing Results—Minister'. https://uk.ambafrance.org/Policy-to-support-French-cinema-bearing-fruit-says-Minister, accessed 2 August 2019.

Rabinovitch, Simon. 'Do You Hear the People Sing? Not in China'. *The Economist*, 14 June 2019. https://www.economist.com/prospero/2019/06/14/do-you-hear-the-people-sing-not-in-china, accessed 29 July 2019.

Rees, Jasper. 'Trevor Nunn: I Feel Betrayed by New *Les Mis*'. *The Daily Telegraph*, 29 June 2010. https://www.telegraph.co.uk/culture/theatre/theatre-features/7861715/Trevor-Nunn-I-feel-betrayed-by-the-new-Les-Mis.html, accessed 30 July 2019.

Shenton, Mark. 'Theatre Shouldn't Be Preserved in Aspic, Even *Les Misérables*'. *The Stage*, 17 January 2019. https://edition.thestage.co.uk/2019/01/16/mark-shenton-theatre-shouldnt-be-preserved-in-aspic-even-les-miserables/pugpig_index.html, accessed 29 July 2019.

*The Story of Musicals*. Broadcast on BBC4, 19 January 2012. 60 mins. https://learningonscreen.ac.uk/ondemand/index.php/prog/023B4DDF?bcast=77601919, accessed 26 July 2019.

'Story of *The Phantom of the Opera*'. *The Phantom of the Opera*. Directed by Joel Schumacher, 2004. DVD, Entertainment in Video, 2005, ASIN B0052YT370.

Thanh Nguyen, Viet. 'Close the Curtain on *Miss Saigon*: Why Is a Musical That Perpetuates a Western Fantasy of Asians as Small, Weak and Effeminate People So Popular?' *New York Times*, 3 August 2019. https://www.nytimes.com/2019/08/03/opinion/miss-saigon-play.html, accessed 20 January 2020.

Thomas, David. 'I Always Think I'm Tigger'. *Sunday Telegraph*, 8 July 2011, 5.

Viagas, Robert, and David Lefkowitz. 'Equity Calls Meeting on *Les Miz* Firings Nov. 5', 5 November 1996. http://www.playbill.com/article/equity-calls-meeting-on-les-miz-firings-nov-5-com-329048, accessed 29 July 2019.

Ziemer, Laurette. '*Les Mis* Purge Causes Fury on Broadway'. *Evening Standard*, 30 October 1996. V&A Theatre and Performance Collection.

CHAPTER 8

# EXTENDING THE BRAND TO THE STAGE

*The Walt Disney Company*

SANNE THIERENS AND JEROEN VAN WIJHE

'IT wasn't easy for me, disagreeing with Phil Collins.'[1] But disagree she did, and often: Martine Bijl, translator of several Disney musicals for the Dutch stage, had a somewhat different perspective on translation from the famous singer-songwriter. When *Tarzan* transferred from Broadway to the Netherlands in 2007, the songwriter expected literal translations of his hit songs, regardless of rhyme schemes.[2] Bijl preferred to practise *hertalen* (transposing) rather than *vertalen* (translating): instead of translating the English original as literally as possible, her vision dictated that the new lyrics should adapt to Dutch language and culture. 'Of course', Bijl stated, musical lyrics have a 'robust corset of rhythm, emphasis, rhyme and internal rhyme that you should not untangle. But sometimes you have to change a sentence or a joke—the mentality, the sentimentality and the sense of humour of the Dutch are different from those of the Americans.'[3] To Collins's dismay, the opening number's 'one world, one family' became 'een huis, een hemelboog' (one house, one heaven's arch) in Bijl's translation. A far cry from the original, but the end result was successful; Bijl's *hertaling* eventually won Collins's approval and was well received by critics.[4] It was her command of the Dutch language, the producer Joop van den Ende recalled, that lifted the Disney musicals that she 'transposed' to a higher level.[5]

This tension between literal translation and adaptation to a local context is common for the so-called megamusical, the category which best describes *Tarzan* and most other Disney musicals. Borrowing the term 'McTheatre' from others, such as Jonathan Burston, Dan Rebellato argues that megamusicals favour reproducibility over the uniqueness of live performance.[6] Producers of megamusicals strive for nearly identical reproductions of the original show, allowing audiences across the globe to see a production as it was first envisaged on Broadway or in the West End.[7] According to Rebellato and Burston, this standardisation of theatre diminishes its distinctive qualities: it suppresses theatre's potential to respond to a specific time and place and instead creates productions that are intended to look and sound the same, regardless of the country where they are performed.[8]

David Savran disagrees with the presumption that international reproductions of megamusicals are identical. He argues that the McTheatre thesis does not account for the glocalisation that inevitably occurs when megamusicals travel to another country. These productions cannot be exactly replicated but instead are mediated by translations, local performers and creatives, performance venues, different theatrical traditions, and audiences with different cultural backgrounds. Furthermore, the relationship between the original producer and the foreign creative teams tends to be more collaborative than one might expect. The 2000s saw several Broadway producers seeking to exploit and expand flourishing foreign markets. As an alternative to the costly development of new musicals on Broadway, American producers engaged in partnerships with South Korean and German producers to develop musicals such as *Dreamgirls* (2009; a reworking of the 1982 original) and *Rocky* (2012). Rather than characterising the relation between Broadway and cities such as Seoul and Hamburg as culturally imperialist, Savran opts for the term 'transnational.' This suggests a relationship in which both parties have creative influence on the development of a new musical.[9]

In Savran's discussion of transnational musicals, the Netherlands remains notably absent. Savran mentions the fact that Stage Entertainment, founded by van den Ende, is the largest producer of musicals in the world but refers mainly to its creative involvement in the German musical theatre market. A closer analysis of transnational dynamics in Dutch musical theatre has not yet been undertaken. Ironically, one of the most striking examples of a Dutch transnational musical was not produced by Stage Entertainment. *Soldaat van Oranje (Soldier of Orange)*, a record-breaking musical about an iconic resistance fighter during World War II, was produced by NEW Productions and created in close collaboration with American creatives before premiering in 2010.

Nevertheless, it was van den Ende, with his revised production of *Tarzan*, who set the stage for fruitful creative partnerships between Dutch and American producers. Whereas *Dreamgirls'* 2009 revival had its first try-outs in Seoul and *Prince of Broadway* premiered in Japan in 2015 before embarking on Broadway, in 2007 van den Ende's Circustheater in Scheveningen (near The Hague) became the place where Disney Theatrical Productions could experiment with a new *Tarzan* without facing the financial risks that another try-out period on Broadway would entail. After a successful run in the Netherlands, the reworked production of *Tarzan* was green-lit to swing onto a larger European stage. It became a huge success in Germany, with runs in Hamburg, where it earned over $224 million (compared to a $12 million loss on Broadway)[10], Stuttgart, and Oberhausen. In 2012 the process was repeated when Stage Entertainment revised *The Little Mermaid*.

## The Case of *Tarzan*

Founded in 1993, Disney Theatrical Productions produced its first stage musical in 1994, an adaptation of the 1991 animated film *Beauty and the Beast*. Since then the company has produced over a dozen musicals, which include not only adaptations of animated films such as *The Lion King* (1997) and *Frozen* (2018), but also live-action adaptations such as *Mary Poppins* (2004) and *Newsies* (2011). Some of these have been produced by Disney Theatrical Productions as a sole producer, some in collaboration with other producers, such as Cameron Mackintosh (*Mary Poppins*).[11]

Starting with *Beauty and the Beast*, which, having opened on Broadway in 1994, received its Australian première in 1995 before opening in London in 1997, Disney musicals have quickly spread over the world, from Europe to Asia, where productions have been adjusted—sometimes slightly, sometimes radically—to cater to a specific country's demographic. Disney Theatrical Productions has both collaborated with European producers on mounting replicas of Broadway productions and licensed independent productions of Disney musicals. One of its least successful shows on Broadway surprisingly became one of its biggest successes in Europe: *Tarzan* (2006).

Disney's fifth Broadway musical was created by the composer-lyricist Phil Collins and the book writer David Henry Hwang. Like *Beauty and the Beast* and *The Lion King*, the Broadway stage production of *Tarzan* was an adaptation of the 1999 animated film. Adapting *Tarzan* for the stage, however, posed new challenges that earlier Broadway adaptations of Disney films had not. To begin with, the music by Collins was not written in the traditional Broadway style, with book songs sung by the characters, but rather consisted of non-diegetic songs that were used as commentary or underscoring. This had to change in order to make the show work as a Broadway musical, requiring the writing of a variety of new book songs but nevertheless leaving several comment songs sung by an all-knowing voice, such as the opening song, 'Two Worlds', which proved difficult to assign to specific characters. The decision was made, moreover, to keep Collins's synthesised sound, which had characterised the animated film, for the Broadway score, which, according to Amy Osatinski, 'felt more like a pop album on stage than a pop-inspired Broadway score'.[12]

Another major challenge was posed by the setting of the story and the characters, centring on the issue of how to bring the gorillas to the stage and how to evoke the jungle, with Tarzan flying through it.[13] Initially, the set designer, Bob Crowley, came up with a circus-inspired concept that would transpose the audience to a different world once they entered the building; it would be especially designed for the show and situate the audience in the round. Owing to the cost, Crowley finally settled for a more conventional proscenium-style Broadway auditorium, thus shifting the scale from epic and immersive to intimate, a factor later cited as one of the reasons for *Tarzan*'s lack of success.[14] As for the staging and choreography, the producer, Thomas Schumacher, hired the Australian contemporary ballet dancer Meryl Tankard, who had experience in aerial ballet, for the choreography, while the movement team opted for a hybrid system of rock-climbing equipment and theatrical flying technology.[15] Though this made for an impressive opening, Osatinski states that 'the show never managed to return to its initial visual magic'.[16] Indeed, when *Tarzan* premiered on Broadway on 10 May 2006, it received mixed reviews. The criticism was directed mainly at the fact that the high level of spectacle could not hide the lack of depth in the story and characters.[17]

The latter were enacted by performers who were, one could argue, faced by a deceptively difficult task. In the DVD commentary of Disney's animated film of *Tarzan*, the animator Glen Keane makes a convincing case for portraying Tarzan as an animated character: 'This Tarzan moves and thinks and acts like an animal. He is like a genius of adaptation. He takes the movement of a leopard, he takes the movement of a gibbon, he can imitate the movement of a serpent'.[18] The director, Chris Buck, adds: 'No actor can move like that. It is not physically possible'.[19] The irony of adapting *Tarzan* for the stage, with live actors emulating their animated counterparts, was not entirely lost on the critic of the *New York Times*. After referencing the DVD commentary, Ben Brantley noted in his review that 'we now have conclusive evidence that the Disneyfied Tarzan does indeed flatten perversely when translated from two dimensions into three'.[20] The protean physicality that worked so well in animation was much more difficult to put onto the stage.

Brantley's remark illustrates the challenges of casting this particular role. The ideal Tarzan should be a quintuple-threat performer: he needs to act, sing, and dance well, handle aerial stunts, and be the physical 'genius of adaptation' that Keane once created on a drawing board. Moreover, he should be established enough to draw in large audiences, preferably children and teenagers familiar with the performer and the source material. Enter Josh Strickland, a twenty-two-year old ex–*American Idol* contestant who swung onto the Broadway scene in December 2005, when the cast was officially announced. From a marketing perspective, the decision to cast Strickland as *Tarzan*'s leading man seems sensible. When he participated in the 2003 edition of *American Idol*, the show was in its second season and did not yet suffer from the declining ratings that plagued later editions. Averaging around 21.93 million viewers, its Wednesday episodes made it the third-most-watched show of the year.[21] The season finale still ranks as the most-watched episode in the history of *American Idol*, with 38.1 million viewers tuning in to see Ruben Studdard narrowly winning over Clay Aiken.[22] A singer coming off a national platform like that, especially one that was popular with family audiences, was an appealing choice for a Disney musical.

However, the amount of screen time that Strickland had on *American Idol* was limited. After regional auditions, he was selected for the 'Hollywood week', where he was eliminated before the semi-finals and the live shows.[23] Moreover, when *Tarzan* premiered in May 2006, *American Idol* was well into its fifth and most popular season. At the peak of its popularity, the show had produced a catalogue of more recognisable singers to idolise. While Strickland's connection to the show could still be capitalised on by Disney's marketing team, it did not make him a household name that would bring children and teenagers to the theatre.

What appeared to be a logical choice in the heyday of televised talent shows was thus in fact a risky decision. Besides his slight celebrity value, Strickland was an upcoming singer in his early twenties, with no prior experience of Broadway theatre. His co-star, Jennifer Gambatese, was a more seasoned Broadway performer. A graduate of New York University's Tisch School of the Arts, Gambatese had played Penny Pingleton in *Hairspray* and Natalie Haller in *All Shook Up* before creating the role of Jane Porter in *Tarzan*.[24] While not inexperienced on the Broadway scene, Gambatese was not a familiar face for a larger audience. With both leads being relative unknowns, the most obvious selling points of *Tarzan* were Phil Collins and the Disney animated film. While the lack of celebrity of its leads does not fully explain *Tarzan*'s disappointing box-office results (the hit musical *The Lion King* also depended more on its source material and well-known creatives than the familiarity of its performers), it did little to boost its success.

The Dutch producer Joop van den Ende became involved in the Broadway production of *Tarzan* early in the process, attending initial readings and workshops of the show.[25] Having previously produced licensed replica productions of *The Lion King* (2001, Germany), *Aida* (2003, Germany) and *Beauty and the Beast* (2005, the Netherlands and Germany) with his company Stage Entertainment, van den Ende was a partner well known to Disney Theatrical Productions. Often credited with introducing megamusicals to the Netherlands in the late 1980s and founder of the biggest Dutch musical theatre production company to date, van den Ende conquered the German musical theatre market in the early 2000s and became an active player in the United Kingdom (with, for example, *Sister Act* in 2009) and on Broadway, with productions such as *Big Fish* in 2013 and *Anastasia* in 2017.

Although the German company Stella AG had initially gained the exclusive rights to stage Disney musicals in Germany, producing, amongst others, *Der Glöckner von Notre Dame* in 1999,[26] Stage Entertainment soon sidelined Stella AG and took over its role.[27] The fact that van den Ende owned theatres all over Europe made him an attractive partner for Disney Theatrical Productions: he could produce a Disney musical in several countries at the same time. After mainly producing in the Netherlands and Germany, Stage Entertainment brought Disney musicals such as *Beauty and the Beast*, *Mary Poppins*, and *High School Musical* to France, Spain, Belgium, Italy, and Russia.

Van den Ende, clearly aware of his production monopoly, was not merely interested in staging Disney musicals, but also wanted to have an artistic influence over them as a creative producer. Whereas the first few European productions of Disney musicals, such as the Dutch and German *Aida* and *The Lion King*, closely followed the original Broadway productions in terms of looks and execution, Disney became increasingly open to van den Ende's suggestions for adjustments.[28] Thus he became involved with *Tarzan* around the time of its conception and secured the rights for a Dutch production even before the show had opened on Broadway and it became clear that *Tarzan* would fail to achieve success in New York.[29]

For van den Ende it was clear what the Broadway production lacked, and he shared his views with Disney Theatrical Producer, Thomas Schumacher:

> It was all wrong. The choreography wasn't show business, but hopping and skipping. Jane was a goody-two-shoes, whereas it should be a comical woman's role. The love duet was situated at the wrong moment. The set consisted mainly of things coming from the ground, and the actors barely flew on lianas, but were constantly crawling on the floor.[30]

Still, the show appealed to van den Ende, and he offered to produce *Tarzan* in the Netherlands provided that the necessary changes would be made.[31] In collaboration with Disney, he started working on a new version for the Circustheater in Scheveningen, near The Hague.

The following section will look at the changes made to *Tarzan* in order to adapt it to the Dutch market, most importantly exploring the artistic choices that were made concerning staging, mise-en-scène, and direction of the musical. In addition, the marketing approach that Stage Entertainment adopted for *Tarzan* will be considered to identify how it differed from that of Disney. Whereas the original marketing campaign had focused on attracting a family audience, Stage Entertainment decided to shift this focus to dating couples, marketing *Tarzan* as a date-night show.

Intertwined with the marketing strategy is the somewhat unusual casting process, which will be explored last. *Tarzan* became the first musical in the Netherlands to feature a televised audition show for the titular role. A Former *Idols* (the Dutch equivalent of *American Idol*) contestant, Ron Link, was chosen by popular vote and a professional jury to play Tarzan. The leading lady was already cast: Chantal Janzen, one of the best-known musical actresses in the country, would be Jane. The reality show *Wie Wordt Tarzan?* (*Who Will Be Tarzan?*), featuring both Link and Janzen, became the first in a series of Dutch talent shows in which potential theatre visitors could feel invested in the casting process of productions of musicals like *Fame*, *Evita*, *Zorro*, *Mary Poppins*, and *Saturday Night Fever*.

# CASE STUDY: STAGE ENTERTAINMENT'S DUTCH PRODUCTION OF *TARZAN*

One of the most important elements redeveloped for the Dutch production of *Tarzan*, which premiered barely one year after the Broadway original, was its visual aesthetic. According to van den Ende, the original *Tarzan* staging lacked 'the epic nature and feel that this jungle adventure deserved', suggesting the need for a change in the mise-en-scène.[32] Interestingly, Jeff Lee, Disney Theatrical Productions' staff associate director, believed that Broadway audiences were unprepared for the show's aesthetic, suggesting the spectacle was too big.[33] On the other hand, European audiences, according to Ron Kollen, the senior vice president of Disney's International Theatrical Productions, 'tend to love spectacle as well and we did add more spectacle to *Tarzan* [in the Netherlands]'.[34] This was done by adapting the musical, which originally had a proscenium set, for the Dutch Circustheater, with its semi-round auditorium free from obstructive balconies, which was closer to Crowley's original circus-inspired idea. The Circustheater, with approximately 1,850 seats, is significantly larger than the 1,300-seat Richard Rodgers theatre and has a lot of room in the house, which allowed the set to project beyond the proscenium 'so that it enveloped the audience and you got the feeling you were actually in the jungle with the characters'.[35]

The focus included everything from movement on the ground to aerial movement; in the words of Disney Theatrical Productions' dramaturge Ken Cerniglia, there was '60% more flying and 30% more "jungle"', while new moments were created for the actors to fly on lianas over the audience and into the centre of the Circustheater.[36]

Meanwhile, Tankard's contemporary ballet-inspired dance was replaced by a 'more entertaining and explosive choreography' by Sergio Trujillo,[37] with acrobatic jumps, flips, somersaults, and bounces from lianas dangling from the air. These changes made the Dutch production more spectacular in 'sheer scope and size' than the Broadway production.[38] As Schumacher wrote in the souvenir booklet of the Dutch production:

> The *Tarzan* that you are going to see tonight has been developed especially for the Netherlands, with this particular theatre in mind. It is an improved version of the Broadway production with more 'special effects', more flying and more magical moments that can only be realised in this special theatre.[39]

For Bob Crowley and Phil Collins, the Dutch production was a second chance, one that allowed them to improve the dialogue and music—or. as Collins stated, to 'do what we kind of wanted to do but couldn't do' on Broadway because of the tight time schedule.[40] In practice, this resulted in new music and arrangements, new scenes, and a bigger cast.[41] Though Collins initially wanted all songs to be translated literally into Dutch, ignoring rhyme, he eventually collaborated closely with the Dutch translator Martine Bijl, who had previously worked on *Aida*, *The Lion King*, and *Beauty and the Beast*. Bijl included local references that resonated with the Dutch audience.[42] Her translation of *The Lion King*, for example, features references to wooden clogs, local carnival songs, and shower curtains from HEMA, a well-known Dutch store.[43] In *Tarzan*, her translation of 'Who Better than Me' gave a nod to the local political situation. At the time, integration policy was a hot topic in the public debate, partly because of scandals surrounding the minister for integration and immigration, Rita Verdonk. It was Verdonk's attempted expulsion of the Somali-born politician Ayaan Hirsi-Ali that led to the fall of the Dutch cabinet in December 2006.[44] Bijl's translation of the lyric 'though you're weird, you can make it', which became 'maar je moet best nog integreren' ('but you still have to integrate'), thus aptly reflected the political climate of 2007.[45]

FIG. 8.1 A scene from the 2008 Dutch production of *Tarzan*: Terk (Clayton Peroti) flies above the audience of the Circustheater in Scheveningen. Photo: Deen van Meer. Used by permission of Disney & Burroughs Tarzan® ERB, Inc.

According to Kollen, implementing such local references is actually standard practice when it comes to exporting Disney musicals abroad. Usually, the director and the book writer review the script and ask how they can adapt it for a local audience.[46] Local jokes or dialects are inserted to enhance audience recognition. Kollen explains: 'It is mainly with the humor. We work with our local partners and the script adaptor to find local nuances and references that connect to the audience. Often times our adaptors are writers themselves, never just translators'.[47]

In terms of marketing, the original stage production of *Tarzan* struggled more than earlier Disney musicals. The timing of the musical adaptation was arguably less fortunate than that of its predecessors, *Beauty and the Beast* and *The Lion King*. Both of these musicals premiered within three years after the release of the motion pictures on which they were based. The interval between the film and stage adaptation of *Tarzan* was significantly longer: the musical premiered seven years after the 1999 film. Although the film did well with critics and audiences alike, it did not have the lasting cultural impact that *The Little Mermaid, Beauty and the Beast, Aladdin*, or *The Lion King* had. In retrospect, *Tarzan* was the closing chapter of a decade of renewed artistic and commercial success now commonly known as the Disney Renaissance.[48]

*Beauty and the Beast* and *The Lion King* also profited from marketing campaigns that emphasised the universal appeal of their themes to a broad Western audience. In *Beauty and the Beast,* the 'tale as old as time' is a classic heterosexual romance between two young and (eventually) attractive people. Like the 1991 Disney film, the musical was effectively marketed towards young couples looking for a night out. While *The Lion King* has its own romantic arc, its main focus is on the circle of life. It celebrates the constant renewal of the nuclear family and chronicles how a new generation comes of age. That musical directed its marketing less towards couples and more towards families, whose various generations can relate to the parental struggles of Mufasa or the growing pains of Simba and Nala.

Like *The Lion King*, the initial Broadway run of *Tarzan* was marketed towards a family audience. That seemed a logical choice, since the most memorable songs in the film reflect on parenthood and belonging. The Oscar-winning 'You'll Be in My Heart' underscores Tarzan's transition from boy to man under the watchful eye of his adoptive mother, Kala. The opening number, 'Two Worlds', reinforces the central theme of the film: that true family is bound not by bloodlines, but by love.

Nevertheless, in that particular type of love also lies the complexity of *Tarzan*'s family trope and its subsequent marketing. Where *The Lion King* reinforces a heteronormative notion of family—one where bloodline determines both belonging and one's place in the circle of life—*Tarzan* is susceptible to a queer reading. It reflects on adoption and the idea of belonging to multiple communities: a biological family, with parents who gave birth to you, and an adopted family, which takes you in and loves you. This experience undoubtedly resonated with families watching the show, as most spectators will relate to the struggles of growing up, the trauma of losing parents, or the blossoming of first love. However, the same may not be true for the negotiation between two cultural identities, which is arguably the musical's main source of conflict. As a consequence, the appeal of *Tarzan* as a musical for families may not have been as self-evident as Disney Theatrical Productions hoped.

For the Dutch iteration, van den Ende's marketing team had to come up with another way to attract audiences, which they did by inventing a new advertising campaign.

Rather than following the model of *The Lion King*, the Dutch *Tarzan* was promoted in the vein of *Beauty and the Beast*: as an ideal date night for young couples.[49] Putting the focus on the love story between Tarzan and Jane gave the marketing department an arguably more recognisable story to sell. Kollen states that Stage Entertainment's marketing team 'rightly told us that this musical would be more attractive for young adults, couples on dates, and teenagers. We targeted that demographic with advertising creative copy that was more "sexy" than in New York and it worked!'[50] Marketing outlets included Valentine-themed promotions and a Tarzan Dating Event in collaboration with dating website Relatieplanet, where five hundred singles gathered, hoping to find their own Tarzan or Jane through speed dating; eight successful matches were given tickets for the show.[51]

Describing the new marketing campaign as 'more sexy' is revealing. Throughout its history, *Tarzan* has been read and watched through a lens of sexuality rather than family dynamics. When Edgar Rice Burroughs started publishing his *Tarzan* novels in 1912, it provided women with a new outlet for sexual imagination. Unlike the wholesome heroes in the novels of Jane Austen or the emotionally troubled ones in those of the Brontë sisters, Burroughs did not shy away from describing Tarzan's alluring physique.[52] In pre–Hays Code Hollywood, the muscled and semi-naked Tarzan became a popular, transgressive figure. MGM wasted no opportunity to advertise the jungle king as a sex object: 'Girls! Would you like to live like Eve if you found the right Adam? Modern marriages could learn plenty from this drama of primitive jungle mating! If all marriages were based on the primitive mating instinct, it would be a better world'.[53] In the early twenty-first century, the figure of Tarzan is still perceived as both a sexual and a romantic fantasy: he will treat you well and look good doing it.

*Tarzan* had a built-in aura of fantasy for straight women who could imagine a romance with a physically desirable man whilst identifying with a strong female character. Disney's rendition of Jane stands in a tradition of stronger Disney heroines like *The Hunchback of the Notre Dame*'s Esmeralda or *Hercules*' Megara. Although Jane is still rescued by a strong man, her character is more independent and three-dimensional than classic Disney princesses. Furthermore, Jane is an independent wildlife explorer, a profession that was typically occupied by men.[54]

The Dutch production of *Tarzan* re-envisaged Jane as less wholesome and more comic, making her an even more pronounced character than previous iterations on screen and stage. This was largely accomplished by casting the established musical theatre star Chantal Janzen as Jane. By the time Janzen's casting was announced, she was one of the most famous musical theatre actresses in the Netherlands. After appearing in the ensemble of *42nd Street* (2000), her notable talent led van den Ende to cast her as the female lead in *Saturday Night Fever* (2001). Prominent roles in *Kunt u mij de weg naar Hamelen vertellen, Mijnheer?* (*Could You Tell Me the Way to Hamelen, Sir?*, 2003), *Crazy for You* (2004), and *Beauty and the Beast* (2005) followed, with Janzen winning Dutch Musical Awards for her roles in *Saturday Night Fever* and *Crazy for You*. Janzen's public profile was boosted by her decision to branch into television: starting as the co-host of the third edition of *Idols*, she gained a reputation as an accessible presenter and a prankster who subverted her own wholesome image. As Jane, she could evoke sympathy in her opening number 'Van zo ver' ('Waiting for This Moment'), and then change the first meeting with Tarzan into a comic sequence.

Janzen's public profile further raised the profile of the role: rather than being Tarzan's love interest in the second act, Janzen's Jane became one of the show's chief selling points. She was an important part of the appeal of the prime-time live television show *Wie Wordt Tarzan?*. This one-episode program, broadcast on 24 November 2006, aimed to cast the titular role for the Dutch production of *Tarzan* live on television in order to maximise media exposure. *Wie Wordt Tarzan?* marked the first time that a television audience would influence the casting process of a musical, giving them a sense of participation. *Wie Wordt Tarzan?*, televised in the same year as the BBC's *How Do You Solve a Problem like Maria?*, would prove a successful format and lead to a host of similar audition shows like *De weg naar Fame* (*The Road to Fame*), *Op zoek naar Evita* (*Searching for Evita*), *Op zoek naar Joseph* (*Searching for Joseph*), *Op zoek naar Zorro* (*Searching for Zorro*), and *Op zoek naar Mary* (*Searching for Mary*).

Besides casting the lead role, *Wie Wordt Tarzan?* gave potential theatre-goers a peek behind the scenes, allowing them to watch short performances of Janzen as Jane, who appeared on the show as a singing and acting partner for the potential Tarzans. Creatives of Stage Entertainment and Disney, including Jeff Lee, van den Ende, and Collins, also appeared on the programme and selected their favourite Tarzan out of five remaining candidates who had made it through the off-screen audition rounds. In the final round, the public could also cast their vote, finally choosing Ron Link as the winner.

Twenty-six-year old Link, like Strickland, had been a contestant in a local version of *American Idol*. Participating in the second season of *Idols*, Link finished in eighth place. Even though he did not win the competition, his participation in the talent show had contributed to his fame. *Idols* was a bit of a phenomenon in the Netherlands: the season 2 finale ranks as one of the 25 most-watched television programs in 2004.[55]

Although Link was, like Strickland, a newcomer to the Dutch musical theatre, his profile was arguably stronger than Strickland's by the time he started rehearsing for *Tarzan*. Thanks to the relatively small population of the Netherlands and the great success of the first *Idols* seasons, Link's face was recognisable to a young audience. Although, with a viewership of 958,000, *Wie Wordt Tarzan?* was not nearly the success that *Idols 2* was, it was more specifically aimed at musical theatre fans, who were naturally more likely to buy tickets for the show.

If there remained any risk of casting newcomer Link as the lead in Stage Entertainment's biggest musical of the season, it was mitigated by the prospect of Janzen as the female lead. She was experienced enough to carry a large-scale musical and had the public profile to guarantee potential audiences of *Tarzan's* quality. By building up the public reputation of a new male lead and casting an experienced, well-known performer as Jane, Stage Entertainment invested in not one but two familiar faces to help attract their audience.

*Wie Wordt Tarzan?* thus proved an invaluable marketing tool for enhancing *Tarzan's* brand awareness with Dutch audiences, boosting ticket sales months before the show opened in Scheveningen.[56] The format allowed Stage Entertainment to start building a relationship with its target audience, attracting potential ticket buyers early in the production process. In this sense, Stage Entertainment had a smart strategy for boosting its pre-première popularity.

With all its adjustments, the Dutch production of *Tarzan* is a prime example of a transnational musical that became a triumph, playing for two years to 1.6 million people in a country of (at the time) 16 million people.[57] The case shows how the Dutch production process functioned as a sort of belated workshop phase for a musical that had failed to achieve success on Broadway. By contributing to the success of *Tarzan*, van den Ende proved himself a fully fledged creative partner for Disney Theatrical Productions.

Although *Tarzan* did well with Dutch audiences, its critical reception was lukewarm. Despite its many revisions, reviews in Dutch newspapers were not unlike those of the original production. In both cases, critics saw a visually impressive but emotionally unsatisfying production that failed to sustain momentum. Bianca Bartels from *Trouw* called *Tarzan* a 'lightweight musical with big effects', strong in entertainment value but lacking in vocal or choreographic innovation. The prologue, she argued, was the standout moment and was never surpassed in the rest of the show:

> When a bright green jungle appears, full of gorillas on vines swinging over the audience, the 'oohs' and 'aahs' are abundant. In the first five minutes, it leads to three ovations for set designer/director Bob Crowley, and deservedly so. But he makes it difficult for himself, since he never manages to surpass this effect.[58]

Bartels's observation was shared by Patrick van den Hanenberg, critic of *De Volkskrant*, and similar to Ben Brantley's critique of the original production in the *New York Times*. Once the prologue is over, Brantley argued, 'the thrill is gone'. He described the rest of *Tarzan* as a musical where 'no moment seems to carry more dramatic weight than any other'.[59] Van den Hanenberg saw a stronger emphasis on family loyalty in the Dutch reworking but criticised its technical display for 'suppressing any emotionality'.[60] Henk van Gelder, critic for *NRC Handelsblad*, saw a 'show to marvel at, greater in scope than its American predecessor', but one with a substantially simplified story.[61] Then again, Chantal Janzen's humorous interpretation of Jane, supported by Bijl's translation, was well-liked. Van den Hanenberg remarked on how Janzen's cool intonation provided the musical with much-needed humour, whilst Bartels credited Bijl's translation for creating a 'delightfully ironic Jane'.[62]

The mixed reviews notwithstanding, van den Ende and his business partner at the time, Erwin van Lambaart, concluded their preface of *Tarzan*'s souvenir booklet with hope for the future: 'The intention is that *Tarzan*, with these adjustments that have been made in the Netherlands, is now ready for musical theatres in the rest of the world'.[63] In 2008 the production was indeed exported to Germany, where even more changes were made; this production ran until 2018.[64] The partnership of Disney Theatrical Productions and van den Ende has since resulted in Russian, Spanish, Italian, French, Dutch, and German productions of such musicals as *The Little Mermaid* (which was, again, rather radically reworked and even exported to Russia in 2012), *Mary Poppins*, *Aladdin*, and the European première of the new version of *The Hunchback of Notre Dame*. It shows how important it is for international producers to work together with locals and adapt a musical for the national market.

Interestingly, Stage Entertainment, which van den Ende sold in August 2018,[65] became somewhat of a competitor for Disney Theatrical Productions when in 2017 it produced a stage version of the Twentieth Century Fox animated film *Anastasia* on Broadway, with a score by Stephen Flaherty and Lynn Ahrens, and a libretto by Terrence McNally. Stage Entertainment has since brought that production to Spain, Germany, and the Netherlands, arguably tapping into the same European market as their partners at Disney. Stage Entertainment nevertheless remains in partnership with Disney Theatrical Productions to this day, with several European productions of *The Lion King* simultaneously running in their theatres as of the spring of 2019. This demonstrates the fascinating interaction between collaborating on and creating autonomous work at a transnational level.

# Non-replica Disney Musicals in Europe

Whereas Stage Entertainment created the Dutch production of *Tarzan* in close collaboration with Disney, a divergent path is possible. On 16 February 2008, one year after the Dutch production, a completely different staging of *Tarzan* opened in Kristianstad, Sweden. Rather than being a copy of the original, this was an independent production, though still licensed by Disney. Kollen states that Disney Theatrical Productions 'license[s] the script and the score to smaller theater producers whom we trust, in countries where the original large-scale productions are not feasible.'[66] Indeed, the Swedish production was on a smaller scale and performed by a mixture of amateurs and professionals; the producer, Emil Sigfridsson, who had previously produced *Aida* with his one-man theatre company, employed professional singers in the leading roles, with amateurs playing the supporting roles. Sigfridsson used the score of the Dutch production but had new arrangements made for his smaller orchestra as well as new aerial movements designed by a Swedish company. Furthermore, the allocation of the songs was altered—for example, the opening song, 'Two Worlds', was assigned to Terk instead of Tarzan.[67]

Making any changes to the plot and songs of a Disney musical is highly unusual, however, even for a non-replica licensed production. The changes that production companies are permitted to make mainly concern the design and production set-up of the show. These, in fact, are *required* to be different from the original Broadway production. Kollen explains: 'The nature of the non-replica license is that we do not control the design, direction, choreography so that it cannot be confused with the original Disney production. Ideally the consumers understand the difference between a locally produced show and one that originates in London or New York.'[68] This philosophy seems to go against the general image of Disney, which is often associated with commodification and the McTheatre paradigm. But Ken Cerniglia emphasises the importance of creativity, stressing that Disney wants to encourage 'a number of interpretations': 'We are theatre people, we love to see someone's interpretation'.[69]

Some of the most striking interpretations have come from the Belgian company Marmalade, which was founded by Yoshi Aesaert, a young producer who was in his late twenties when he produced his first Disney musical, *Beauty and the Beast*, in 2016. 'Belgium has not historically been a big enough market to support a full-scale Broadway musical', says Kollen, so Disney Theatrical Productions 'engaged Marmalade to do its own productions of our script and score, at much lower cost than a large Disney replica production'.[70] By this time, however, Stage Entertainment's 2005 Dutch replica production of *Beauty and the Beast* had already toured through Belgium, replacing the leading roles with Flemish actors for the Belgian performances. This suggests that there *was* a market for replica productions. Furthermore, Marmalade's 2016 non-replica licensed production of *Beauty and the Beast* was much bigger than Stage Entertainment's replica production. The large-scale staging was called for by the theatre, as Marmalade had chosen a non-traditional venue: the Flanders Expo in Ghent, a multi-purpose arena and convention centre with a large auditorium accommodating 3200 people.

This huge stage and large, flat auditorium called for new scenography, direction, and choreography. The director, Christophe Ameye, regarded the scene changes as choreography in itself, incorporating them in his direction of the show. Ish Ait Hamou furthermore created new musical staging based on a combination of contemporary and traditional musical theatre dance styles.[71] Meanwhile, the set designer, Stefaan Haudenhuyse, opted for a rose-shaped stage and used projections, an LED wall behind the stage, and moving and flying props. The production used many special effects that made the show more immersive, such as flying books controlled by drones and trees dropping amongst the audience.[72]

Similarly, for their 2017 non-replica production of *The Little Mermaid*, Marmalade delivered a spectacular set design with 'a five-ton pirate boat that breaks into pieces, tele-guided and moving rocks, an electrically driven swan boat, automated chairs', and six hundred square metres of LED screens.[73] Significantly, Aesaert, the producer, presented the changes as being made especially for a Belgian audience:

> This unique performance has been created especially for the Belgian fans and is a once-in-a-lifetime experience that you cannot even watch in London or New York. Except for the story and the songs, everything has been restyled. Literally and figuratively.[74]

Though the musical was largely overlooked by the main Belgian newspapers, the regional newspaper *Krant van West-Vlaanderen* praised 'the visual effects and extremely clever lighting': 'at times the spectacle is simply astounding'.[75] In the daily newspaper *Het Nieuwsblad*, Magali Degrande described the exciting, colourful costumes and the 'special use of space (soap bubbles above the tribune, check!) and that unexpected

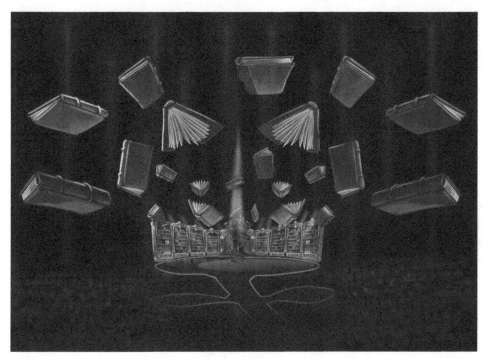

FIG. 8.2 A scene from 'Be Our Guest' showcasing the immersive design for Marmalade's 2016 non-replica production of *Beauty and the Beast*. Photo: Luk Monsaert, courtesy of Production: Marmalade Ghent 2016.

combination of calm and excitement that put the finishing touch on the aesthetics', concluding: 'our underwater desires have been fulfilled'.[76]

Marmalade's marketing manager, Lieve Hendriks, confirms that creativity is not merely encouraged; rather, 'you *have* to be original' where non-replica productions are concerned.[77] Frank van Laecke, who directed Marmalade's 2017 non-replica production of *The Little Mermaid*, adds that the overall look of the show and its characters needed to be distinguishable from the original franchise production, as well as from the original motion picture, because otherwise the production would run a risk of copyright infringement.[78] Furthermore, non-replica productions cannot resemble each other, says Hendriks: 'You cannot reproduce a non-replica concept that has been done before'.[79]

Nevertheless, reinterpretations should not be too experimental either. 'It was not encouraged', states Hendriks, referring specifically to *The Little Mermaid*. 'Frank van Laecke is a famous director in Belgium but also a wilful one. We were told repeatedly that we had to make certain the director would not go freewheeling too much. He had to be restrained a little. In that sense Disney Theatrical Productions are very careful'.[80] At least one critic noticed this, as Degrande stated in her review in *Het Nieuwsblad*: '*The Little Mermaid* is bound to strict Disney rules. So there is not much space for creativity at the Marmalade production company. Yet, director Frank van Laecke knows how to leave his mark on the story'.[81]

Indeed, Disney maintains control of the end result and has the final approval rights for everything. Changing the story, the music, and even the translation is off-limits. Their power extends beyond the show; Hendriks states that all communication had to be approved by Disney, including press releases, television commercials, invitations for the premiere, and visuals.[82] She illustrates:

> The logo could not be the same as the logo of the motion picture, but it had to be the same style. However, we were not allowed to include characters from the motion picture. We tried to make themed advertisements around Christmas with a snow-covered logo, which was rejected because it 'did not match Disney and the character of the show'.[83]

In that sense non-replica productions are ambiguous, Hendriks says: 'On the one hand they give you creative freedom, but on the other they try to restrict you. It would be easier if they just set clear rules'.[84]

# CONCLUSION

Disney Theatrical Productions have found their way to other countries, whether as nearly exact copies, as reworked in close collaboration with Disney, or reinvented as non-licensed productions. Whereas Stage Entertainment's Dutch production of *Tarzan* shows how creative and commercial ideas of a local theatre producer helped Disney turn a financial disappointment into a huge commercial success, the case of Marmalade illustrates the thin line between creative freedom and Disney's control. In any case, Marmalade's massive productions of Disney musicals demonstrate that non-replica licensed productions are not limited to small-scale productions.

It is worth noting, however, that Marmalade's non-replica production of *Beauty and the Beast* was significantly less successful than Stage Entertainment's tour of the replica production. Whereas the latter drew 138,000 visitors, only 65,000 spectators watched one of the thirty Marmalade performances.[85] Even though Disney engaged Marmalade to do their own production at a much lower cost than an original Disney replica, Marmalade's production of *Beauty and the Beast* left the company with a €700,000 loss, which can be explained in part by the scale of the production.[86]

All the productions discussed in this chapter were based on collaborations between Disney Theatrical Productions and European producers. Although the extent of creative control differs, Stage Entertainment, Sigfridsson, and Marmalade all exercised significant influence over their adaptations of Disney musicals. This contradicts the McTheatre thesis, which presupposes exact reproductions of the original staging and a hierarchical relationship between Anglo-American and local producers. Instead, the exportation of Disney's musicals to the Netherlands, Sweden, and Belgium is strongly transnational by nature. In collaboration with Disney Theatrical Productions, several of Disney's musicals were re-envisaged by European creatives with a deeper understanding of local culture and sensibilities. 'One does not translate from language to language, but from another country to your own country', Bijl remarked when asked about her work.[87] Her statement holds true for the libretto but can also be applied on a larger scale. The staging, directing, casting, and promotion of musicals such as *Tarzan, Beauty and the Beast,* and *The Little Mermaid* have significantly changed when exported from Broadway to European theatres, which, one could argue, makes them all the more interesting to study and watch in their variety.

## NOTES

1. Martine Bijl, 'Phil en ik', *Zin* (April 2007), 119.
2. Ibid.
3. Martine Bijl, 'Musical', in *Hindergroen* (Amsterdam: Atlas Contact, 2016), 86.
4. Monic Slijngerland, 'Soepele perfectionist', *Trouw*, 20 April 2007; Bianca Bartels, 'Tarzan, een spektakel met veel kunst- en vliegwerk', *Trouw*, 17 April 2007; Henk van Gelder, 'Tarzan', *NRC Handelsblad*, 16 April 2007.
5. Max van Daag, 'Martine Bijl: Eerbetoon aan een groot en geestig talent', 7 June 2019, Hilversum, https://pers.omroepmax.nl/martine-bijl-eerbetoon-aan-een-groot-en-gees tig-talent/, accessed. Accessed 8 June 2019.
6. Jonathan Burston, 'Enter, Stage Right: Neoconservatism, English Canada and the Megamusical', *Soundings* 5 (Spring 1997): 179–190; here: 188; Dan Rebellato, *Theatre and Globalization* (Basingstoke: Palgrave Macmillan, 2009), 39–46.
7. Jessica Sternfeld, *The Megamusical* (Bloomington: Indiana University Press, 2006), 4.
8. Ibid.
9. David Savran, 'Trafficking in Transnational Brands: The New "Broadway Style" Musical', *Theatre Survey* 55, no. 3 (September 2014): 318–342, doi: https://doi.org/10.1017/S00405 57414000337.
10. Marc Hershberg, 'Springtime for *Hamilton* as Hit Show Heads to Hamburg', *Forbes*, 28 February 2019, https://www.forbes.com/sites/marchershberg/2019/02/28/springtime-for-hamilton-as-hit-show-heads-to-hamburg/, accessed 17 August 2919.
11. Amy S. Osatinski, 'Disney Theatrical Productions: Anything Can Happen If You Let It', in *The Palgrave Handbook of Musical Theatre Producers*, ed. Laura MacDonald and William A. Everett (New York and London: Palgrave Macmillan, 2017), 413.
12. Ibid., 415.
13. Ibid., 419.
14. Ken Cerniglia, '*Tarzan* Swings onto Disney's Broadway Stage', in *Global Perspectives on Tarzan: From the King of the Jungle to International Icon* (New York: Routledge, 2012), 47–48.
15. Amy S. Osatinksi, *Disney Theatrical Productions: Producing Broadway Musicals the Disney Way* (New York and London: Routledge, 2019), 104.
16. Osatinski, 'Disney Theatrical Productions: Anything Can Happen', 420.
17. Ben Brantley, '*Tarzan* Arrives on Broadway, Airborne', *New York Times*, 11 May 2006, https://www.nytimes.com/2006/05/11/theater/reviews/11tarz.html, accessed 15 August 2019; Peter Marks, 'Fumble in the Jungle: Disney's Tame *Tarzan*', *Washington Post*, 11 May 2006, https://www.washingtonpost.com/archive/lifestyle/2006/05/11/fum

ble-in-the-jungle-disneys-tame-tarzan/9cdd3fd8-5481-4d56-87d2-d6b0b1439846/, accessed 15 August 2019.

18. *The Making of Tarzan* (n.d.), https://www.youtube.com/watch?v=drOxNNGwop4, accessed 15 August 2019.

19. Ibid.

20. Ibid.

21. 'Top 20 Most-Watched TV Programs in 2002–2003', *Television Blog*, 12 January 2010, https://archive.is/20120629135522/http://blog.newsok.com/television/2010/01/12/top-20-most-watched-tv-programs-in-2002-03/, accessed 15 August 2019.

22. Joe Lynch, '*American Idol* Finale Ratings: See the Up-Down Journey over 13 Seasons', *Billboard*, 5 December 2015, https://www.billboard.com/articles/news/6561370/american-idol-ratings-season-finale-ratings-graphic

23. Brandon Voss, 'Josh Strickland, Stripped', *Advocate*, 10 June 2010, https://www.advocate.com/arts-entertainment/television/2010/06/10/josh-strickland-stripped, accessed 15 August 2019.

24. 'Jenn Gambatese', *Internet Broadway Database*, https://www.ibdb.com/broadway-cast-staff/jenn-gambatese-395046, accessed 15 August 2019.

25. Ron Kollen, email to the authors, 2019.

26. Hubert Schäfer, *Musicalproduktionen: Marketingstrategien und Erfolgsfaktoren* (Wiesbaden: Deutsche Universitäts-Verlag, 1998).

27. Sanne Thierens, 'From Amsterdam with Love: Stage Entertainment's Global Success', in *The Palgrave Handbook of Musical Theatre Producers*, ed. Laura MacDonald and William A. Everett (New York and London: Palgrave Macmillan, 2017), 353.

28. Henk van Gelder, *Joop van den Ende: De biografie* (Amsterdam: Nijgh & Van Ditmar, 2012), 337.

29. van den Ende, quoted in ibid., 337.

30. Ibid. All translations from Dutch into English by the authors.

31. Ibid.

32. Patrick Healy, 'Flops on Broadway? Fix Them Overseas', *New York Times*, 29 July 2011, https://www.nytimes.com/2011/07/31/theater/flop-broadway-musicals-find-life-overseas.html, accessed 15 August 2019..

33. Amy Osatinski, 'Disney Theatrical Productions: Anything Can Happen', 420.

34. Ron Kollen, email to the authors, 2019.

35. Ibid.

36. Cerniglia, 'Tarzan Swings onto Disney's Broadway Stage', 55; Joop van den Ende and Erwin van Lambaart, 'Preface', in *Tarzan* (2006).

37. Cerniglia, '*Tarzan* Swings onto Disney's Broadway Stage', 55.

38. Ron Kollen, email to the authors, 2019.

39. 'De *Tarzan* die u vanavond gaat zien is speciaal voor Nederland geproduceerd, met dit theater in het achterhoofd. Het is een verbeterde versie van de Broadwayproductie met meer "special effects", waarin meer gevlogen wordt en met meer magische momenten die alleen in dit bijzondere theater kunnen worden gerealiseerd.' Thomas Schumacher, quoted in van den Ende and van Lambaart, 'Preface', in *Tarzan* (2006).

40. Maxim Bezembinder, *De Making Of: Tarzan de Musical* (2006), https://www.youtube.com/watch?v=WhkLdMbYCcs, accessed 15 August 2019.

41. van den Ende and van Lambaart, 'Preface', in *Tarzan* (2006); van Gelder, *Joop van den Ende*, 337.

EXTENDING THE BRAND TO THE STAGE    263

42. Bijl, 'Phil en ik', 119.
43. Ben Hertogs, 'Recensie *The Lion King*', *Concertnews.be*, 9 April 2017, http://www.concertn ews.be/recensietonen.php?id=3424&kop=The%20Lion%20King&waar=AFAS%20Ci rcustheater%20Den%20Haag, accessed 15 August 2019.
44. 'Hirsi Ali Brings Down Government', *Der Spiegel*, 30 June 2006.
45. Phil Collins, ' "Who Better than Me?"', recorded by Chester Gregory II and Daniel Manche', in *Tarzan: The Broadway Musical*, original Broadway cast (Walt Disney Records, 2006; ASIN B01KAVJVEO); Phil Collins and Martine Bijl (trans.), 'Bij mij moet je zijn', recorded by Clay Peroti and Tjeerd Melchers', in *Tarzan: Het Nederlandse Castalbum* (Universal Music, 2007; ASIN B004D3R1FC).
46. Ron Kollen, quoted in Robert Diamond, 'Industry Interview: Expanding the Kingdom— How Disney Theatrical Continues to Bring Pride Rock around the World', *BroadwayWorld. com*, 6 September 2017, https://www.broadwayworld.com/article/Industry-Interview-Expanding-the-Kingdom--How-Disney-Theatrical-Continues-to-Bring-Pride-Rock-Around-the-World-20170906, accessed 15 August 2019.
47. Ron Kollen, email to the authors, 2019.
48. Chris Pallant, *Demystifying Disney: A History of Disney Feature Animation* (New York: Continuum, 2011).
49. Healy, 'Flops on Broadway?'
50. Ron Kollen, email to the authors, 2019.
51. 'Tarzan en Jane Helpen Singles', in unknown (n.d.).
52. Maria Teresa Hart, 'An Earl in the Streets and a Wild Man in the Sheets: Tarzan and Women's Sexuality', *Media.com*, 22 June 2016, https://www.bitchmedia.org/article/earl-streets-and-wild-man-sheets-tarzan-and-women%E2%80%99s-sexuality, accessed 15 August 2019.
53. Thomas Doherty, *Pre-Code Hollywood: Sex, Immorality and Insurrection in American Cinema 1930–1934* (New York: Columbia University Press, 1999).
54. Hart, 'An Earl in the Streets'.
55. Stichting Kijkonderzoek, 'Persbericht kijkcijfers 2005', *Kijkcijferonderzoek*, 1 Januari 2005, <u>Microsoft Word - 050101 Stijging televisie kijken zet door in 2004.doc (kijkonderzoek.nl)</u>, accessed 5 July 2023.
56. *Wie Wordt Tarzan?* was broadcast on 24 November 2006. With opening night planned on 15 April 2007, 100,000 tickets had been sold by 12 January 2007 ('100.000 kaarten voor Tarzan', *Omroep West*, 12 January 2007, https://www.omroepwest.nl/nieuws/9993753/100-000-kaarten-voor-Tarzan, accessed 15 August 2019).
57. Healy, 'Flops on Broadway?'.
58. Bianca Bartels, 'Tarzan, een spektakel met veel kunst- en vliegwerk', *Trouw*, 17 April 2007, https://www.trouw.nl/cultuur-media/tarzan-een-spektakel-met-veel-kunst-en-vliegw erk~b6152014/, accessed 15 August 2019.
59. Brantley, '*Tarzan* Arrives on Broadway, Airborne'.
60. Patrick van den Hanenberg, 'Ook in vertaling lukt het Tarzan niet te ontroeren', *De Volkskrant*, 17 April 2007, https://www.volkskrant.nl/cultuur-media/ook-in-vertaling-lukt-het-tarzan-niet-te-ontroeren~b17c0ae9/, accessed 15 August 2019.
61. Henk van Gelder, '*Tarzan*', *NRC Handelsblad*, 21 April 2007, https://www.nrc.nl/nieuws/2007/04/21/tarzan-11311425-a1205266, accessed 15 August 2019.
62. Patrick van den Hanenberg, 'Ook in vertaling lukt het *Tarzan* niet te ontroeren', *De Volkskrant*, 17 April 2007, https://www.volkskrant.nl/cultuur-media/ook-in-vertal

ing-lukt-het-tarzan-niet-te-ontroeren~b17c0ae9/, accessed 15 August 2019. Bianca Bartels, 'Tarzan, een spektakel met veel kunst- en vliegwerk', *Trouw*, 17 April 2007, https://www.trouw.nl/cultuur-media/tarzan-een-spektakel-met-veel-kunst-en-vliegwerk~b6152014/, accessed 15 August 2019.

63. 'Het is de bedoeling dat *Tarzan* met deze aanpassingen die nu in Nederland zijn doorgevoerd, gereed is voor musicaltheaters in de rest van de wereld'; van den Ende and van Lambaart, 'Preface', in *Tarzan* (2006).

64. van den Ende, quoted in van Gelder, *Joop van den Ende*, 337.

65. 'Theaterbedrijf Stage Entertainment van Joop van den Ende verkocht', *AD*, 23 August 2018.

66. Ron Kollen, email to the authors, 2019.

67. *Tarzan The Musical in Europe: Sweden* (n.d.), http://www.erbzine.com/sweden/, accessed 15 August 2019.

68. Ron Kollen, email to the authors, 2019.

69. Quoted in Osatinksi, *Disney Theatrical Productions*, 176.

70. Ron Kollen, email to the authors, 2019.

71. Glen Vandenberghe, '*Beauty and the Beast* heruitgevonden door Marmalade', *Vlaams Musical Magazine*, 2 December 2016, http://vlaamsmusicalmagazine.weebly.com/reportages/beauty-and-the-beast, accessed 15 August 2019.

72. Lieve Hendriks, video call with Sanne Thierens, 2019.

73. Didier Verbaere, 'Ongezien totaalspektakel', *Deze Week/Gent*, 13 December 2017, 12.

74. '*The Little Mermaid*: Disneyklassieker', *Imago*, 1 December 2017, 94–95.

75. '*The Little Mermaid* zorgt voor magie', *KW Weekend*, 29 December 2017, 38.

76. Magali Degrande, 'Onderwaterverlangens', *Het Nieuwsblad*, 19 December 2017, 20–21.

77. Lieve Hendriks, video call with Sanne Thierens, 2019.

78. Frank van Laecke, telephone call with Jeroen van Wijhe, 2019.

79. Lieve Hendriks, video call with Sanne Thierens, 2019.

80. Ibid.

81. Degrande, 'Onderwaterverlangens'.

82. Lieve Hendriks, video call with Sanne Thierens, 2019.

83. Ibid.

84. Ibid.

85. Ben Serrure and Thomas Peeters, 'Productiehuis Marmalade redt zich met nieuwe investeerder', *De Tijd*, 14 September 2017.

86. Ibid.

87. Van Geelen, 'Elke schrijver heeft zijn eigen grondslag', *Trouw*, 24 July 2009.

## BIBLIOGRAPHY

Bijl, Martine. *Hindergroen*. Amsterdam: Atlas Contact, 2016.

Burston, Jonathan. 'Enter, Stage Right: Neoconservatism, English Canada and the Megamusical.' *Soundings* 5 (1997): 179–190.

Cerniglia, Ken. 'Tarzan Swings onto Disney's Broadway.' In *Global Perspectives on Tarzan: From the King of the Jungle to International Icon*, edited by Annette Wannamaker and Michelle Ann Abate, 41–56. New York: Routledge, 2012.

Gelder, Henk van. *Joop van den Ende: De biografie*. Amsterdam: Nijgh & Van Ditmar, 2012.

Osatinski, Amy S. 'Disney Theatrical Productions: Anything Can Happen If You Let It.' In *The Palgrave Handbook of Musical Theatre Producers*, edited by Laura MacDonald and William A. Everett, 413–426. New York and London: Palgrave Macmillan, 2017, doi: 10.1057/978-1-137-43308-4_42.

Osatinksi, Amy S. *Disney Theatrical Productions: Producing Broadway Musicals the Disney Way*. New York and London: Routledge, 2019.

Rebellato, Dan. *Theatre and Globalization*. London: Macmillan Education UK, 2009.

Savran, David. 'Trafficking in Transnational Brands: The New "Broadway Style" Musical'. *Theatre Survey* 55, no. 3 (September 2014): 318–342, doi:10.1017/S0040557414000337.

Thierens, Sanne. "From Amsterdam with Love: Stage Entertainment's Global Success.' In *The Palgrave Handbook of Musical Theatre Producers*, edited by Laura MacDonald and William A. Everett, 351–357. New York and London: Palgrave Macmillan, 2017, doi: 10.1057/978-1-137-43308-4_35.

# CHAPTER 9

# GOING DUTCH

## *Stage Entertainment*

JONAS MENZE

## INTRODUCTION

EVER since the so-called megamusical arrived in continental Europe in the 1980s, musical theatre has (re-)evolved into big business across the continent.[1] One of the key players is the Dutch producer Stage Entertainment, 'a multinational corporation of more than thirty-five companies' employing about three thousand people worldwide.[2] In the last twenty years it has developed into the market leader of popular musical theatre production in continental Europe and has become one of the largest producers in the world.[3] For the 2016–2017 season, the company has reported 6.7 million visitors, 6,639 performances, and 33 productions.[4] Today it operates eighteen theatres in eleven cities across five countries: Germany, the Netherlands, Spain, France, and Italy.[5] Its founder, Joop van den Ende, earned the reputation of having created 'an audience from scratch in the Netherlands', turning the company into 'a major player.'[6] The company is credited with having 'almost singlehandedly turned Hamburg into "the Broadway of Europe" '.[7] This may be a slight exaggeration; however, Hamburg promotes itself as a 'musical metropolis' and the 'world's third-biggest musical city just after New York and London,'[8] relying heavily on the four large theatres which Stage Entertainment runs in the city. On the artistic side, the Dutch company established itself as an important originator of local musicals and supporter of local musical theatre talent. The portfolio of musicals developed and staged by Stage Entertainment includes the Dutch *3 Musketiers* (*Three Musketeers*, 2003) and *Ciske de Rat* (*Ciske, the Rat*, 2007), as well as the German *Ich war noch niemals in New York* (*I Have Never Been to New York*, 2007) and *Hinterm Horizont* (*Beyond the Horizon*, 2011).

# History

The company's history is inseparable from that of its founder, Joop van den Ende, whose career may be described as leading him from carpenter to billionaire.[9] Van den Ende was born into a Dutch working-class family in 1942. After becoming a trained carpenter, he started working at the Dutch National Opera at the age of sixteen. He soon set up a cabaret group called De Pijpers (The Pipers), in which he himself performed and which led him to book and organise shows.[10] When he realised that his talent as performer would not meet his own high standards, he concentrated on the organisational side of entertainment. In his mid-twenties he founded his first booking agency under the name Spotlight, followed by the Joop van den Ende Theaterproducties a few years later.[11] Although his first activities as a theatre producer date from 1970, his first musical production, *Barnum*, premiered in 1988 in Scheveningen.[12] It was followed by touring productions of *Sweet Charity* and *Cabaret* (both 1989).[13] As a first large-scale production, van den Ende brought *Les Misérables* to Amsterdam in 1991. His first original musical production was *Cyrano de Musical*, which opened in 1992 in Amsterdam and was subsequently exported to Broadway (1993) and Germany (1999 and 2015), as well as licensed for production in Tokyo in 2000.[14]

During the 1970s van den Ende had primarily made a name for himself as a television producer. Besides his theatrical activities, in these years mostly involving touring productions of plays, he produced drama- and entertainment-show formats for Dutch television, which were also sold to other countries. These activities led to financial wealth, giving him the freedom to follow his interests and to invest in creative development of new formats and theatre works, as well as laying the foundation for his theatre portfolio: in the early 1990s van den Ende bought the Circustheater in Scheveningen, which he renovated, transforming it into the first Dutch theatre to house a specific long-run musical production. It re-opened with *The Phantom of the Opera* in 1993.[15]

In 1994 van den Ende partnered with his competitor John de Mol to found Endemol, a media and entertainment company that became prominent for creating and franchising television formats such as *Big Brother*.[16] In 1999 he completely took over Endemol's live entertainment division, which had been split off from the company's TV production arm, bundling it with his several of his companies under the name of Stage Holding.[17] The company was subsequently renamed Stage Entertainment in 2005. When Endemol was sold to the Spanish communications company Telefónica in 2000, van den Ende became a billionaire.[18]

*Chicago*, which opened in the newly acquired Beatrix Theater in Utrecht in 1999, was the first production under the aegis of the newly established company. The engagement of the popular leading actors Pia Douwes and Simone Kleinsma as well as rave reviews helped make the production a success that paved the way for further expansion.[19] In only about ten years, the musical as a genre had established itself in the Netherlands,

FIG. 9.1 Joop van den Ende, founder of Stage Entertainment, on 30 January 2014 at a press call for screen-to-stage musical *Das Wunder von Bern* (*The Miracle of Bern*). Photo: Panther Media, © Alamy Stock Foto.

with ten to thirteen new productions each season attracting 1.2 million visitors annually,[20] a remarkable proportion of a population of only 16 million citizens in 2000.[21]

## INTERNATIONAL EXPANSION IN CONTINENTAL EUROPE

With the founding of Stage Holding, van den Ende had managed to become the biggest musical producer in the Netherlands.[22] But obviously, the Dutch market for big-budget musicals was limited. Germany, with its eighty-two million citizens and a struggling market leader in musical theatre production, was an easy target for the company's expansionist strategy. For van den Ende, expansion was essential to enhancing his reputation as the most important player on the European market, which made it easier to negotiate licences. Even more important, access to the larger German market gave him status in the eyes of the American producers and publishers behind the most attractive and successful shows.[23]

Van den Ende seized an opportune moment. At the end of the century, the German musical market was dominated by Stella AG, a company founded by Friedrich Kurz, who had witnessed the enormous success of *Cats* in Vienna and brought the show to Hamburg in 1986. Despite doubts about its attraction for German audiences, the show ran there for about fifteen years, and its huge success heralded the beginning of a musical theatre boom in Germany that continued throughout the 1990s. Stella grew fast by bringing *Starlight Express* to Bochum and *The Phantom of the Opera* to Hamburg, all the while building new venues and producing new shows. In 1999 it operated eight theatres. But other producers had seen their chances too, so more and more productions opened all over the country. The market soon became saturated, and Stella—also heavily involved in real estate projects—got into financial difficulties. This is when van den Ende grabbed his opportunity. In 2000 Stage Holding bought the Colosseum Theater in Essen from the struggling Stella, establishing its entry into the German market in 2001, after extensive renovations with the German debut of *Elisabeth*. This was followed shortly afterwards by the acquisition of a theatre tent in Hamburg's harbour, which had been showing *Buddy—The Buddy Holly Story* and which was then turned into a permanent venue that became the home of *The Lion King*.[24]

Now van den Ende prepared for his final attack. He was in a lucky position: he had the financial security to pay literally any sum of money to acquire the rights for blockbuster shows or for taking an option on them, thereby preventing others from producing them on German stages—a strategy described as a 'war on musicals' by Peter Schwenkow, who at this time owned half of the shares in Stella.[25] When Stella finally went bankrupt in 2002, van den Ende could conveniently choose from its portfolio, taking over its two theatres in Hamburg, two further venues in Stuttgart's SI-Centrum entertainment complex, and the Theater am Potsdamer Platz in Berlin.[26] The Starlight-Halle in Bochum, which had been running Andrew Lloyd Webber's *Starlight Express* since 1988, was not purchased, as the show was assumed to have already passed its prime. Although the latter proved a mistake, since the production achieved cult status and is still running (currently in its thirty-first year), Stage Entertainment kept growing. The next acquisitions included Berlin's Theater des Westens and the TheatrO CentrO, which is located in one of Germany's biggest shopping malls in Oberhausen. Thus, in only a few years Stage Holding became the market leader in Germany. From this position it expanded to embrace more European markets.

In 2003 Stage Holding and the Mexican Grupo CIE joined forces in the Spanish market, founding CIE Stage Holding,[27] which was completely taken over by Stage Holding and renamed Stage Entertainment Spain in 2005. At this time, the company ran three theatres in Madrid—Teatro Lope de Vega, Teatro Alcalá, and Teatro Coliseum—and further productions staged in Barcelona followed.[28] Spain was a growing market for musical theatre in these years, where Stage Entertainment soon managed to become an important player with Spanish-language productions of *Cabaret* (2003), *Cats* (2003), and *Mamma Mia!* (2004).[29] The importing of licensed productions was considered to be filling 'a socio-cultural and artistic gap' in Spanish popular musical theatre.[30] Stage Entertainment and Rockspring joined forces to acquire the Teatro Coliseum and Teatro Lope de Vega in Madrid in 2017, while the Dutch corporation's production activities in the other Spanish theatres were discontinued. The deal underpinned the company's ambitions to play a major role on Madrid's Gran Via. Plans to acquire another theatre in Madrid were announced in 2019.[31]

Expansion into Eastern Europe started in 2004 with the launch of Stage Holding Russia. Its first production was *Cats*, which opened in 2005 in Moscow's MDM Theatre, followed by *Mamma Mia!* (2006) and *Beauty and the Beast* (2008), which established the MDM as a home for open-ended runs of musical theatre productions. In 2012 Stage Entertainment took over a five-year lease of Moscow's Rossia Theatre, a former movie house, where it first produced Disney's *The Little Mermaid*. But the MDM Theatre disappeared from the company's portfolio without further notice in 2019, leaving it unclear whether and how the company's activities in Russia will be continued.

In France, Stage Entertainment acquired Paris's Théâtre Mogador in 2005. This is a variety theatre built in 1919 where Sergei Diaghilev's Ballets Russes once performed and where operettas, light operas, and other shows had been produced.[32] Owing to its critical reception of the megamusical blockbusters and French *spectacles* showing a somewhat different approach to musical entertainment[33], Paris was considered a difficult market. Stage Entertainment initially tested its potential by renting the Folies Bergère and launching a production of *Cabaret* in 2006.[34] Its success proved the company right, and in 2009 the Folies Bergère saw another production, *Zorro*. After extensive renovations, the Mogador finally re-opened with *The Lion King* in 2007, which ran nearly three years and sold 1.3 million tickets, making it a decent success. It was followed by *Mamma Mia!* (2010), *Sister Act* (2012), and *Beauty and the Beast* (2013), which faced a steady decline in ticket sales.[35] With the exception of *Dance of the Vampires* (2014), which closed after five months, runs of about nine months became standard at the Mogador, an indication that profits were not huge. A production of *The Phantom of the Opera* had to be cancelled in 2016 just a few days before its opening after a fire broke out in the basement, necessitating extensive repairs and preventing performances for nearly a year.[36]

The Italian branch of Stage Entertainment was founded in 2007 and now operates the Teatro Nazionale CheBanca! in Milan, which opened in 2009 with a production of Disney's *Beauty and the Beast*. But in contrast to its success in other European markets, the company was not able to establish a local musical theatre audience. Rather than offering long-running productions, Stage Entertainment has since the 2013–2014 season presented a variety of shows,[37] using a stagione system.[38]

# Expansion into the English-Language Musical Theatre Market

As it had been for many producers, Broadway had been van den Ende's dream and goal right from the start. He launched his first attempt as early as 1993 with the New York production of *Cyrano - The Musical*. But the Dutch producer faced strong opposition. He felt that as a foreign impresario, insiders of the Great White Way considered him an amateur, which became evident in the difficulties he experienced when trying to cast the leading roles and putting together a creative team for *Cyrano*. He reacted by entrusting the title role to the Dutch actor Bill van Dijk and the staging to the Dutch director Eddy Habbema, which certainly did not help in overcoming the prejudice against the creation of a show that was deemed 'too Dutch',[39] even after the production received two Tony Award nominations for its book and score.[40] To counteract this impression, he entered into a partnership with Dodger Theatricals; together they developed *Titanic* (1997), which would win five Tony Awards.[41] This finally provided him with access to the key players in the business: 'The Dutch company had found an experienced and respected Broadway producer to help crack the American marketplace and generate exports for European theaters.'[42]

In spite of its critically acclaimed productions of *Urinetown* (2001), *42nd Street* (2001), and *Into The Woods* (2002), the partnership was not blessed with financial success. The joint venture was dissolved in 2004 after controversies about inadequate programming for the recently opened Dodger Stages, a former cinema complex with five separate theatres in Manhattan's Fiftieth Street.[43] Additionally, van den Ende had to face the failure of two big productions: *Dracula, the Musical* (2004) shuttered after 157 performances at a US$7.5 million loss,[44] while *Good Vibrations* (2005), a musical built around the hits of The Beach Boys, limped through only ninety-four performances after being torn apart by the critics.[45] These setbacks on Broadway led Stage Entertainment to redirect its focus on to the European market, which included the development of original productions that were not intended to run on Broadway.[46] It was years before a new attempt to break onto Broadway was made with *Sister Act* in 2011.

Some years earlier the company had already taken steps into London's West End, launching its UK office in 2002.[47] To expand its initial production activities, Stage Entertainment's UK division appointed Really Useful Group's chief executive, Bill Taylor, in 2006 and acquired the producer Adam Spiegel Productions the same year to serve as its production unit.[48] The company made another important move in 2007 when it announced a temporary lease of the struggling Shaftesbury Theatre, which led to a successful two-and-a-half-year run of *Hairspray* (2007).[49]

The most successful UK opening was the stage adaption of the musical film comedy *Sister Act* (1992), in which Whoopi Goldberg had played the nightclub singer Deloris. The struggling performer accidentally witnesses a murder committed by her gangster boyfriend. After entering a witness protection scheme, Deloris hides out in a Catholic convent, where her unconventional attitude is causing chaos. At the end, she revives the convent's choir by introducing a gospel programme which receives the highest praise, even from Pope John Paul II.

Van den Ende had been invited by the former Disney manager Peter Schneider to see a workshop production of *Sister Act* in Los Angeles in 2004 and invested in the show on condition that changes were made to the stage design and the book, which in his opinion lacked a love story. The movie had featured a couple of Motown hits, but for the stage production an original score was composed by eight-time Oscar-winner Alan Menken, who wrote numbers in the styles of Motown and disco.[50] The lyrics were written by Glenn Slater and the book by Cheri and Bill Steinkellner, and direction was provided by Schneider himself.[51] Whoopi Goldberg was involved in the creative development. Although she had no creative control, she was given credit as co-producer, which assured the show public attention.[52] When the musical later hit the boards in London, Goldberg herself joined the cast in the role of Mother Superior during select performances, boosting weak ticket sales.[53] *Sister Act* saw further tryouts in Los Angeles and Atlanta in 2006 and 2007 respectively, during which time much of the show was revised. The book was supplemented by additional material provided by Douglas Carter Beane.[54] But van den Ende was still not satisfied: in his attempts to solve the show's problems, he did not shy away from firing Schneider as director only a short time before opening and replacing him with the Dutch casting director Carline Brouwer.[55]

*Sister Act* finally opened in June 2009 in London's Palladium Theatre—with approximately 2,300 seats, one of the biggest venues in the West End,[56] and thus actually a theatre unsuited for what was basically a traditional musical comedy—where it ran until October 2010. It received mixed reviews by the critics for being highly entertaining while at the same time 'hyping up' and coarsening a 'rather sweet, sentimental film' to an 'ear-blasting, eye-scalding' production and thus losing the specific strengths of the screenplay when it was adapted to the stage.[57] Leading actress Patina Miller received much praise for her outstanding performance.[58]

While the original London production's run may be considered merely a modest success, it engendered a series of international productions. In the following years, *Sister Act* was brought to Stage Entertainment theatres in Germany, Italy, France, the Netherlands, and Spain as well as being licensed to Austria and Brazil.[59] The Broadway production opened in 2011 and ran for 561 performances, followed by a US tour.[60] Its reviews matched those of the London production:[61] '[W]hen the jubilant choral numbers subside, as inevitably they must, *Sister Act* slumps back into bland musical-theater grooves and mostly lacks the light of invigorating inspiration [ ... ] the show remains tame, innocuous and frankly a little dull.'[62] The show received major attention when it was visited by US President Barack Obama on special invitation by Whoopi Goldberg.[63] It also was nominated for a variety of awards, including five Tony Awards, finally winning a Theatre World Award for the lead actress, Patina Miller.[64]

Regarding Stage Entertainment's UK activities, even the success of *Hairspray* and *Sister Act* could not hide the fact that other original musical productions in London

FIG. 9.2 Patina Miller (*right*) as Deloris Van Cartier leading the nun's choir in the 2009 London production of *Sister Act*. Photo: John Phillips © Getty Images.

did not perform well: *Made in Dagenham* (2014), a musical based on the historical strike at Ford's Dagenham River Plant in 1968, did not last longer than five months at the Adelphi (approximately fourteen hundred seats), failing to reach its target audience of working- and middle-class women because of poor marketing. A UK tour was discussed by the producers but never materialised.[65] Another misfire that opened in the same year at the Palladium was *I Can't Sing! The X-Factor Musical*. Lasting a mere six weeks, it is regarded as 'one of the biggest failures in West End history'.[66] In 2016 Stage Entertainment announced it would cut down on its UK production activities after this string of unsuccessful productions, including a touring production of *Anything Goes* (2015), which closed early. The company maintained an office in London under the name Stage Entertainment UK but was instructed to refocus its efforts towards 'developing, sourcing and supporting [ ... ] European operations'.[67] An explanation for its failure may be that the company chose the wrong theatres, producing comedies that may have had more successful runs if they had been shown in smaller—and thus easier to sell out—venues, thereby enhancing the audience experience. While Stage Entertainment explored evolving markets in continental Europe, it faced a completely different situation in London, with well-established traditions and networks in musical theatre production and the most attractive theatres being operated by other big producers, such as the Really Useful Group, and occupied by their own productions. Regardless, Stage Entertainment's latest effort on the UK market is *Tina: The Tina Turner Musical*, based on the famous pop singer's biography, which opened in April 2018 at London's Aldwych Theatre (approximately twelve hundred seats) and is now in its second year after mostly receiving good reviews for telling an unadventurous and predictable story but excelling with 'a thumping catalogue to belt out, and a central performer as magnificent and magnetic as Adrienne Warden'.[68] The show was developed by a carefully assembled creative team around the director Phyllida Lloyd and her designer, Mark Thompson; it lists Tina Turner as executive producer, which provided a huge amount of publicity for the première. A second production is currently being presented at Hamburg's Operettenhaus, and a Broadway production opened in early November 2019.

# THE COMPANY'S CURRENT BUSINESS STRATEGY

At present, Stage Entertainment's strategy rests upon three pillars:

1. bringing internationally renowned and successful musical productions to continental Europe,
2. operating a network of its own theatres which host these productions and provide the infrastructure for a wide variety of events, such as the production of TV shows or—in the case of the Theater am Potsdamer Platz—which are the home of the annual Berlin International Film Festival, and
3. the creative development of original productions, such as 3 *Musketiers* (2003) or *Rocky* (2012).

Until recently, ticketing has been a fourth pillar of the company's strategy. In 1990 van den Ende founded the TopTicketLine,[69] which enabled him to build a customer database and keep in close contact with potential theatre-goers.[70] To this were added in 2005 the German company Ticket Online and in 2008 the British See Tickets, which was bought from Lloyd Webber's Really Useful Group.[71] Consequently, the ticketing subdivision grew into one of Europe's 'biggest [ ... ] ticket agencies'.[72] Yet in the same year, a majority share in the UK division of See Tickets was sold to the private equity group Parcom Capital. In 2011 the entire share was acquired by the French media group Vivendi.[73] The remaining international dependencies of See Tickets were sold to the German ticketing market leader CTS Eventim between 2010 and 2014.[74] In a press release, the sale was briefly justified by the announcement of Stage Entertainment's plans to concentrate on its growth ambitions in the field of musical production,[75] leaving the impression of a rather erratic business strategy related to the market for event ticketing.

# LICENSED PRODUCTIONS

Stage Entertainment differs from the majority of other musical producers in that the company combines production activities and theatre management. As a 'vertically integrated' corporation, they programme their own productions in their own venues.[76] The company's website lists more than four hundred productions that since 1971 have been realised by either Joop van den Ende, Endemol, Stage Holding, or Stage Entertainment.[77] A major part of the company's production portfolio is the result of joint ventures with other big players in the musical theatre industry: 'Most of Stage Entertainment's musicals have been launched in partnership with producers such as Disney Theatrical Productions, the Really Useful Group, Blue Man Productions, Cameron Mackintosh, and Vereinigte Bühnen Wien.'[78] Littlestar Services—the producer behind hit musical *Mamma Mia!*—also needs to be added to that list. However, the most important business relation is the long-term licensing partnership with Disney, which was established in 2000. Stage Entertainment regularly brings Disney shows to continental Europe. So far, the most successful cooperation has been *The Lion King* (1997), which has been running in Hamburg since 2001 and in Madrid since 2011.

Again, the company's profile is heavily influenced by its founder's talents and ambitions. Van den Ende worked hard to achieve his status as a producer who is respected even on Broadway. He not only proved his ability to successfully produce and promote local productions of hit shows, but also demonstrated his know-how in creative development and revision by positioning existing works in ways that target the local market,[79] or even making major changes, as in the case of the Broadway flop *Tarzan* (2006), which he turned into a major European success by adding new songs and arrangements and reworking the staging and choreography.[80] When Stage Holding acquired the continental European license for *Mamma Mia!* and produced its German debut at the Operettenhaus in Hamburg in 2002, it was the first production with lyrics translated into the audience's native tongue, preserving the playwright Catherine Johnson's congenial way of integrating the lyrics with the book. Its artistic and financial success finally set the track for adopting the practice of translating the lyrics for all subsequent productions in non-English-speaking countries.[81]

Furthermore, Stage Entertainment's portfolio has always been amplified by touring productions which are not specifically musicals, such as *Holiday on Ice*. It had been part of the portfolio for about twenty years before its full share was sold to CTS Eventim's subsidiary company Medusa in 2016.[82] With productions such as the play *War Horse*, which was brought to Berlin in 2013 and to Amsterdam in 2014, or the Cirque du Soleil show *Paramour*, which has been running in Hamburg since 2019, the company still seeks to broaden its repertoire. Most successful have been the performances of the Blue Man Group, which has been presented in Berlin since 2004. In 2006 the show moved from the Theater am Potsdamer Platz into the much smaller BlueMax Theater located across from the larger theatre. With its six hundred seats, the new venue provided the optimal size for continued economic success.

More recently, Stage Entertainment generated excitement when the producer revealed plans to bring the Broadway hit *Hamilton* to Germany. Its première was scheduled for the autumn of 2020 in one of the company's four large theatres in Hamburg.[83,84]

# THEATRES

At present, Stage Entertainment controls eighteen theatres: twelve in Germany, two each in the Netherlands and Spain, and one each in Italy and France. Not all venues are actually owned by the company; some are subject to long-term rental agreements. This applied, for instance, to the Operettenhaus, which was finally bought from the city of Hamburg in 2011.[85] Other venues in London, New York, and Moscow were sold or closed over the past years. The size of most of the company's theatres is between thirteen hundred and two thousand seats, making them suitable for hosting large-scale productions in open-ended runs. A selection of smaller venues, such as the Kehrwieder Theater in Hamburg or the New World Stages (the former Dodger Stages), which were run by the company between 2004 and 2014 before being sold to the Shubert Organization, allowed room for small-budget experiments and workshop development of new musicals. One of the latest acquisitions is the Werk 7 theatre in Munich, situated in an industrial complex and providing space for 650 attendees in a rough but intimate setting. This is where *Fack ju Göhte—Se mjusicäl* (*Suck Me Shakespeer*, 2018) and *Amélie* (*Die fabelhafte Welt der Amélie*, 2019) premiered. But it once again became apparent that producing on a small scale was not the company's core competency, and the Werk 7 theatre, too, ceased operations before the end of 2019.

A key factor in van den Ende's strategy was that his company not only offered first-class productions, but also facilitated the highest standards in hospitality and comfort for audiences. Aiming to sell a premium product at a premium price necessitates offering audiences an outstanding experience. Thus, in contrast to most venues on Broadway or even in the West End, the company's theatres are equipped with a generous-sized lobby as well as catering facilities and are decorated with pieces of art—selected by van den Ende's wife, Janine—in order to offer customers a '360° experience' from the moment they arrive at the theatre.[86]

# CREATIVE DEVELOPMENT

An increasingly important part of the company's business is the development of new stage works. Since its vertical integration required Stage Entertainment to have sufficient product to fill its theatres, creative development of new shows became an important element in its corporate strategy.[87] Starting with *Cyrano de Musical* and leading up to *Sister Act* and *Tina*, the company promotes itself as having developed and presented more than thirty original productions.[88]

Perhaps the company's most ambitious and widely recognised production was the musical adaption of Sylvester Stallone's 1976 low-budget movie *Rocky*, with a book by Thomas Meehan and an original score by Lynn Ahrens (lyrics) and Stephen Flaherty (music). It was developed by the German branch of Stage Entertainment and premièred at the Operettenhaus in Hamburg in 2012 before a second production opened at Broadway's Winter Garden Theatre in 2014. The show depicts the story of the underdog Rocky Balboa, a boxer from Philadelphia, who by chance gets the opportunity to fight against the world heavyweight champion, Apollo Creed. Aware that he has not the slightest hope of beating Creed and winning the championship, he decides to go the distance and prove to himself he is not another aging loser. His love of the shy sales assistant Adrian helps him to 'Keep On Standing', epitomising the other major ingredient of the plot: 'a love story between two lonely people who struggle to express themselves and ultimately persevere because of each other'.[89]

Whereas earlier original productions of the company's German division, such as *Ich war noch niemals in New York* (2007) or *Der Schuh des Manitu* (*The Shoe of Manitu*, 2008), were aimed first and foremost at the German-speaking theatre market (including Austria and Switzerland), *Rocky*, with its US$15 million budget and a creative team of Broadway specialists, including the director Alex Timbers, was from the very beginning of its development intended for Broadway.[90] The show was written in English and translated into German by Wolfgang Adenberg (lyrics) and Ruth Deny (dialogue) for its world première. While the creative team remained more or less the same for the New York production, the show was dramaturgically tightened and its video design reworked after the Hamburg première. Two songs were cut.[91] The score is influenced by the Philadelphia pop sound of the 1970s but also includes 'Eye of the Tiger', taken from the soundtrack of *Rocky III*, the second instalment in the franchise. Yet it was the production's strikingly bold scenic design which grabbed most of the attention: for the show's finale, the theatre was transformed into a boxing arena by bringing the audience in the first few rows up onto the stage while moving the boxing ring into the auditorium, thus setting the scene for a fifteen-minute choreographed full-contact boxing prizefight.

The show received faint praise from reviewers. The German production was criticised for its translation of the lyrics; they may have tried carefully to render the idiom of the warm-hearted but not necessarily eloquent characters, yet the lyrics came across as simply clumsy. German and Broadway critics alike appeared to be more impressed by its technical spectacle than by the musical quality of its score.[92] In the *New York Times*, Ben Brantley praised the show's finale as 'a hell of a fight, a brutally balletic coup de théâtre that shakes up the joint in more ways than one [ ... ] an all-out, multimedia assault on the senses that forces much of the audience to its feet',[93] while at the same time denigrating the first two hours of the show as flat and uninspired as well as too strongly relying on the movies' iconic images and attractions. Finally, Brantley could not resist

FIG. 9.3 Drew Sarich (*centre*, as Rocky Balboa) and Terence Archie (*left*, as Apollo Creed) in *Rocky*'s spectacular final fight scene; the musical premiered in 2012 at the Operettenhaus, Hamburg. Photo: Franziska Krug © Getty Images.

taking a swipe at the show's origin as a big-budget production made in Germany ('I said, no snickers'[94]).

The Hamburg production was awarded the German Live Entertainment Award (LEA). The Broadway production was also nominated for numerous awards, with the scenic design by Christopher Barreca winning a Tony Award as well as a Drama Desk Award and an Outer Critics Circle Award, while the lighting design by Christopher Akerlind received a Drama Desk Award. Nevertheless, the Hamburg production had to close in 2015 after a two-and-a-half-year run. It was then transferred to Stuttgart, where it ran for another fourteen months. The Broadway production, however, shuttered after only 180 performances.[95]

## Reorganisation and Improvement

In the first decade of the millennium, Stage Entertainment had high hopes that its new works and licensed productions would play for several years in the place where they premièred, but since then shorter runs have become the norm. This comes along with a decline in audience interest. In its core market, Germany, ticket sales fell dramatically from 5.3 million in 2007 to 3.3 million in 2017, according to the company's annual consolidated financial statements.[96] As a consequence, it is not unusual for a new show to end its first run after only a year and thereafter to tour the company's theatres, bringing the show to the people instead of having the people travel across the country to see a selected show.[97] Development of small-scale productions, not necessarily intended to run in the company's own houses but rather to enrich the license portfolio, as well as partnerships with state-funded theatres in the development of new works have recently marked Stage Entertainment's strategic efforts to adapt to the changing markets.[98] Around 2010 the company applied a yield management system that optimises revenue by dynamic pricing (as it is known from airlines and tourism in general),[99] leading to criticism for a steady rise in ticket prices.

In addition, the past years have seen crucial changes in the company's ownership and organisational structure. This development began when Johannes Mock-O'Hara, the CEO of Stage Entertainment Germany, the biggest national branch of the company, suddenly left Stage Entertainment in 2013. His departure was explained as the result of 'fundamentally different views on strategy, necessary actions and timelines' between him and the board of directors.[100] Two years later, at the age of seventy-three, founder van den Ende sold a 60 percent share in Stage Entertainment to the private equity and investment firm CVC Capital Partners. According to press releases, the deal was meant to secure the company's continuity and success in international markets. Van den Ende's own role as co-chairman of the supervisory board was described as concentrating on the development of new original musicals.[101] Under the new owner, yield targets rose, and parts of the company were restructured. In early 2016 Stage Entertainment announced a performance improvement programme which included a reduction of between 300 and 350 employees worldwide.[102] In the following months, it closed down its production unit in London, shut its academy in Hamburg (where young German-speaking performers had been trained for the German market since 2003),[103] and stopped presenting productions in Berlin's Theater am Potsdamer Platz. Owing to a long-term lease agreement, the theatre remained part of the portfolio until 2019, when it was taken over by Live Nation.[104] These cuts mark a turning point in the company's activities, which until then had clearly been shaped by van den Ende's passion for theatre, his interest in promoting young talent, and his ideal of giving back something to the people. The aim now was simply to generate the largest profit possible.[105]

As is customary for a private equity company, CVC held its share in Stage Entertainment for just three years. In 2018 CVC and van den Ende sold 100 percent of the share to Advance Publications, a global American media, communication, and technology company. But even since selling his share, van den Ende has maintained close links to Stage Entertainment as a 'special advisor'. Advance announced the acquisition in a press release, thanking van den Ende 'for his creative vision and [ ... ] CVC for their operational excellence, both of which have positioned Stage Entertainment well for long-term growth'.[106] In its own public statement, Stage Entertainment announced a further expansion of its activities, with productions planned for Mexico, Japan, Brazil, and Australia.[107] Recently Stage Entertainment Germany revealed plans to stop productions at the Metronom Theater (the former TheatrO CentrO) in Oberhausen due to persistently weak ticket sales and to sell its Colosseum Theater in Essen, thus completely withdrawing from the densely populated Ruhr area.[108] This demonstrates how the company increasingly experiences pressure in its core market, Germany.

# OUTLOOK

Since its founding as Stage Holding in 1999, Stage Entertainment has evolved from an owner-operated enterprise into a transnational corporation with a strong brand. With its production activities in continental Europe, its international licensing, and its dominant market position, especially in Hamburg's commercial musical theatre landscape, the company today is a leading global player in commercial theatre production. As a Dutch company that produces Broadway shows and original musical productions on a large scale across continental Europe and beyond, it may be seen as a paradigm of the globalisation of the Broadway-style stage musical: 'The increasing economic clout of transnational entertainment conglomerates and the development of Broadway musical–like products in many parts of the world have meant that the most U.S. American form of theatre is becoming increasingly stateless.'[109] Although van den Ende proved savvy in changing Broadway flops into European hits through his broad knowledge of the Dutch and German/Austrian market, he did not succeed in conquering the Anglophone markets, where Stage Entertainment's international partners welcomed his investment but tended to rely on their own expertise. Today Stage Entertainment builds strongly upon its success in Germany. Nevertheless, since the general conditions for musical theatre production have changed owing to a decline in audience interest, the company had to adapt to these challenges by calculating for shorter runs and increasing the frequency of rotating productions between its theatres.

As an enterprise initially driven by the enthusiasm, expertise, and financial success of its founder, Stage Entertainment had developed a unique corporate culture, where van den Ende's artistic visions as well as his ability and willingness to provide the necessary funds to realise them for years characterised creative development and production activities.[110] With van den Ende preparing for his retirement, the company had to reshape its decision-making processes to set the stage for future competitiveness and growth. Thus, on the one hand, incisive strategic decisions taken in the CVC era may well be considered an important means of strengthening the company's operating business and focus on efficiency. On the other hand, the company runs the risk of focusing too much on short-term revenue without maintaining its ambitious aim 'to exceed the expectations' of its audiences,[111] as well as releasing the essential creative energy which prepares the ground not only to please dwindling crowds but also to develop relevant and innovative musical theatre that attracts new audiences.

As a key player in the musical landscape, Stage Entertainment has been pivotal in advancing the musical in continental Europe after the first wave of megamusicals had subsided. With his passion as well as with his financial investments, van den Ende has brought numerous important shows to Europe, revamped theatres or even built new ones, promoted the genre, and, last but not least, fostered expertise in popular musical theatre production. At the same time, the company represents like no other big business in continental European musical theatre. Although in the past the company concentrated on the development of shows tailored to local markets, its big-budget original productions increasingly follow the trend to exploit existing brands, such as well-known movies, for global audiences.[112] This leaves only limited room for the creative testing of artistic boundaries. But the entire continental European musical scene has developed in the slipstream of Stage Entertainment's productions.[113] When trying to assess the significance of the company in the development of the European musical, an ambiguous impression emerges. On the one hand, there have been repeated complaints that continually trying to bring about the next big hit by blowing up well-known material into spectacular stage events limits both the company's and the public's perception and understanding of the musical as a genre. On the other hand, although the financial scale of its productions may be criticised, the independent musical scene has also benefited from Stage Entertainment's success. Actor training has been professionalised, experts in show production have been imported, and networks dedicated to the further development of the genre have emerged.

With Mexico, Japan, Brazil, and Australia, the company aims to explore new markets in the future. Time will tell if the plans for increased efficiency will succeed and pave the way for further international expansion and more global productions. With the imminent departure of its founder and creative mind, with shaking up its organisational structure, with rising yield targets, and by becoming part of an even bigger media conglomerate unexperienced in stage production, the key question will be whether Stage Entertainment will be able to keep its creative development processes vigorous and innovative and to stay connected to its local audiences in the long run. Referring to the German market for musicals in general, Frédéric Döhl observes: 'What is perhaps most needed now is a kind of German *Hamilton*: a socially relevant piece that will reach the popular culture mainstream and find enormous economic success while also being aesthetically ambitious, unique, and local in both musical approach and storyline.'[114] If Stage Entertainment wants to build on its past success, to stay a relevant producing powerhouse and not be merely another cash cow for its current owner, it should make sure to be the producer behind it.

## Notes

1. Before World War II, popular musical theatre was among the commercially most influential forms of entertainment on Continental Europe with important centres in Paris, Vienna, Budapest, and Berlin. See Len Platt, Tobias Becker, and David Linton, 'Introduction', in *Popular Musical Theatre in London and Berlin: 1890–1939*, ed. Len Platt, Tobias Becker, and David Linton (Cambridge: Cambridge University Press, 2014), 1–22. Especially in the German-speaking countries, 'popular musical theater never fully recovered from the massive losses in expertise and artistic excellence due to murder or

migration while the region was under the Third Reich (1933–1945)'; see Frédéric Döhl, 'The Third Biggest Market: Musical Theater in Germany since 1990', in *The Routledge Companion to the Contemporary Musical*, ed. Jessica Sternfeld and Elizabeth L. Wollman (New York and Abingdon: Routledge, 2020), 427–436; here: 427.

2. David Savran, 'Trafficking in Transnational Brands: The New 'Broadway-Style' Musical', *Theatre Survey* 55, no. 3 (2014): 328.

3. Ibid.

4. 'Stage Entertainment Company Update FY 2016 | 2017', https://www.stage-entertainment.com/news/company-update1, accessed 27 January 2019.

5. 'Theatres', https://www.stage-entertainment.com/theatres, accessed 12 May 2019.

6. Lisa Martland, 'Mamma Mia! Why Musical Theatre Has Taken Off across Europe', https://www.thestage.co.uk/features/2017/mamma-mia-musical-theatre-across-europe, accessed 14 March 2019.

7. Savran, 'Trafficking in Transnational Brands', 328.

8. 'Hamburg—Musical Metropolis', https://marketing.hamburg.de/musicals.html, accessed 15 June 2019.

9. Sanne Thierens, 'From Amsterdam with Love: Stage Entertainment's Global Success', in *The Palgrave Handbook of Musical Theatre Producers*, ed. Laura MacDonald and William A. Everett (New York and London: Palgrave Macmillan, 2017), 351–357; here: 351.

10. Ibid., 351–352.

11. Elisa Mutsaers, 'Een professionele start', http://www.eenlevenlangtheater.nl/Joop%20van%20den%20Ende/Biografie/Een%20professionele%20start, accessed 5 April 2019.

12. 'History', https://www.stage-entertainment.com/about-us/history/the-netherlands, accessed 12 May 2019.

13. Information on production dates and theatres in this chapter are taken from Stage Entertainment, 'Productions', https://www.stage-entertainment.com/productions, accessed 20 June 2019.

14. Koen van Dijk, 'Cyrano das Musical: 1999 / 2015', http://koenvandijk.com/portfolio/cyrano-das-musical, accessed 2 June 2019. See also Koen van Dijk, 'Cyrano on Broadway: 1993 / 2000', http://koenvandijk.com/portfolio/cyrano-on-broadway, accessed 2 June 2019.

15. Wolfgang Jansen, *Cats & Co.: Geschichte des Musicals im deutschsprachigen Theater* (Leipzig: Henschel, 2008), 244.

16. Thierens, 'From Amsterdam with Love', 353.

17. Savran, 'Trafficking in Transnational Brands', 328–329.

18. Henk van Gelder, *Joop van den Ende: De biografie* (Amsterdam: Nijgh & Van Ditmar, 2012), 307.

19. Ibid., 295.

20. Ibid., 297.

21. 'Netherlands Population (Live)', https://www.worldometers.info/world-population/netherlands-population, accessed 15 June 2019.

22. Thierens, 'From Amsterdam with Love', 353.

23. van Gelder, *Joop van den Ende*, 304.

24. Jansen, *Cats & Co.*, 241–244.

25. Thierens, 'From Amsterdam with Love', 353.

26. Jansen, *Cats & Co.*, 249.

27. Fernando de Luis-Orueta, 'Dos grandes productoras se unen para crear el primer gigante des teatro en España', https://elpais.com/cultura/2003/07/04/actualidad/1057269601_850215.html, accessed 11 May 2019.

28. 'History', https://www.stage-entertainment.com/about-us/history/spain, accessed 12 May 2019.
29. Marta Mateo, 'Anglo-American Musicals in Spanish Theatres', *Translator* 14, no. 2 (2008), 319–342.
30. Ibid., 339.
31. 'Stage Entertainment Plans to Acquire a Third Theatre in Madrid', https://www.stage-entertainment.com/news/stage-entertainment-plans-to-acquire-a-third-theatre-in-madrid, accessed 11 May 2019.
32. van Gelder, *Joop van den Ende*, 327.
33. Judith Sebesta and Laura MacDonald, "'Tonight I Will Bewitch the World": The European Musical', in *The Cambridge Companion to the Musical*, ed. William A. Everett and Paul R. Laird (Cambridge: Cambridge University Press, 2017),339–355; here: 349–352.
34. van Gelder, *Joop van den Ende*, 327.
35. Jamal Henni, 'Cet Hollandais qui impose en France les succès de Broadway', https://bfmbusiness.bfmtv.com/entreprise/cet-hollandais-qui-impose-en-france-les-succes-de-broadway-894290.html, accessed 27 September 2019.
36. Adam Hetrick, 'Mogador Theatre Will Re-Open in September; Paris Phantom Shelved Indefinitely', http://www.playbill.com/article/mogador-theatre-will-re-open-in-september-paris-phantom-shelved-indefinitely, accessed 11 May 2019.
37. 'Chi siamo', http://www.stage-entertainment.it/teatro-nazionale/chi-siamo, accessed 11 May 2019.
38. Stagione refers to a way of presenting a variety of shows for a limited series of performances. In contrast to a repertory system, every production is cast separately.
39. Thierens, 'From Amsterdam with Love', 353–354. See also Marlise Simons, 'A Musical *Cyrano*: Can a Dutch Hit Sell on Broadway?', https://www.nytimes.com/1993/11/21/theater/theater-a-musical-cyrano-can-a-dutch-hit-sell-on-broadway.html, accessed 27 October 2019.
40. van Dijk, 'Cyrano on Broadway: 1993 / 2000'.
41. 'Titanic', http://www.playbill.com/production/titanic-lunt-fontanne-theatre-vault-0000005013, accessed 1 June 2019.
42. Jesse McKinley, 'Starved for Hits, Producer Finds Hard Times on Street of Dreams', https://www.nytimes.com/2005/03/17/theater/starved-for-hits-producer-finds-hard-times-on-street-of-dreams.html, accessed 1 June 2019.
43. van Gelder, *Joop van den Ende*, 328.
44. 'Dracula, the Musical', http://www.playbill.com/production/dracula-the-musical-belasco-theatre-vault-0000010754, accessed 1 June 2019.
45. van Gelder, *Joop van den Ende*, 328. See also McKinley, 'Starved for Hits'. In the *New York Times*, Ben Brantley criticised the show for being aimless, goofy, and clichéd, describing it as "a lumbering, brainless Frankenstein's monster, stitched together from stolen body parts and stuffed into a wild bikini'; see Ben Brantley, 'To Everything There Is a Purpose', https://www.nytimes.com/2005/02/03/theater/reviews/to-everything-there-is-a-purpose.html, accessed 27 October 2019.
46. van Gelder, *Joop van den Ende*, 336.
47. Matthew Hemley, 'Stage Entertainment Axes UK Production Department', https://www.thestage.co.uk/news/2016/stage-entertainment-axes-uk-production-department, accessed 25 February 2019.

48. Nuala Calvi, 'Stage Entertainment Snaps Up *Fame* Producer Adam Spiegel', https://www.thestage.co.uk/news/2006/stage-entertainment-snaps-up-fame-producer-adam-spiegel, accessed 14 March 2019.
49. Alistair Smith, 'Independent Thinking', https://www.thestage.co.uk/features/interviews/2013/shaftesbury-theatre-revamp, accessed 14 March 2019.
50. van Gelder, *Joop van den Ende*, 346.
51. 'Sister Act', http://www.playbill.com/production/sister-act-broadway-theatre-vault-000 0013729, accessed 15 June 2019.
52. van Gelder, *Joop van den Ende*, 346.
53. Natalie Woolman, 'Whoopi Goldberg Returning to *Sister Act*', https://www.thestage.co.uk/news/2010/whoopi-goldberg-returning-to-sister-act, accessed 16 June 2019.
54. David Ng, '*Sister Act* on Broadway: What Did the Critics Think?', https://latimesblogs.latimes.com/culturemonster/2011/04/sister-act-on-broadway-what-did-the-critics-think.html, accessed 16 June 2019.
55. van Gelder, *Joop van den Ende*, 347.
56. Sophie Thomas, 'The A–Z List of Theatres in the West End', https://www.encoretickets.co.uk/articles/every-theatre-in-the-west-end, accessed 12 October 2019.
57. 'Hyping up . . . sentimental film': Benedict Nightingale, quoted in Carson Vaughan, 'What Is the Fate of *Sister Act*? Critics Chime In on the Tuner', https://variety.com/2009/film/news/what-is-the-fate-of-sister-act-1118004819, accessed 16 June 2019. 'Ear-blasting, eye-scalding': Ben Brantley, 'London's Musicals: Intimate or Outsize', https://www.nytimes.com/2009/07/08/theater/08brantley.html, accessed 12 October 2019.
58. Vaughan, 'What Is the Fate of *Sister Act*?'
59. van Gelder, *Joop van den Ende*, 359.
60. 'Sister Act', http://www.playbill.com/production/sister-act-broadway-theatre-vault-000 0013729, accessed 15 June 2019.
61. 'SISTER ACT Broadway Reviews', https://www.broadwayworld.com/reviews/Sister-Act, accessed 27 October 2019.
62. Charles Isherwood, 'Different Church, More Sequins: *Sister Act* Comes to Broadway', https://www.nytimes.com/2011/04/21/theater/reviews/sister-act-comes-to-broadway-review.html, accessed 27 October 2019.
63. van Gelder, *Joop van den Ende*, 359.
64. 'Sister Act', http://www.playbill.com/production/sister-act-broadway-theatre-vault-000 0013729, accessed 15 June 2019.
65. Matthew Hemley, '*Made in Dagenham* to Close after Five Months in West End', https://www.thestage.co.uk/news/2015/made-dagenham-close-five-months-west-end, accessed 14 March 2019.
66. Richard Jordan, 'Lessons to Learn from X-Factor Musical's Flop', https://www.thestage.co.uk/opinion/2014/lessons-learn-x-factor-musicals-flop, accessed 14 March 2019.
67. Stage Entertainment, quoted in Matthew Hemley, 'Stage Entertainment Axes UK Production Department'.
68. Fergus Morgan, '*Tina*: The Tina Turner Musical at Aldwych Theatre, London—Review Round-Up', https://www.thestage.co.uk/opinion/2018/tina-the-tina-turner-musical-at-aldwych-theatre-london-review-round-up, accessed 27 October 2019.
69. 'History', https://www.stage-entertainment.com/about-us/history/headquarters.
70. Thierens, 'From Amsterdam with Love', 356.

## GOING DUTCH: STAGE ENTERTAINMENT    285

71. Alistair Smith, 'Stage Entertainment Buys Really Useful's See Tickets', https://www.thest age.co.uk/news/2008/stage-entertainment-buys-really-usefuls-see-tickets, accessed 14 March 2019.

72. Thierens, 'From Amsterdam with Love', 355.

73. Michael Quinn, 'See Tickets Bought by Vivendi for £86m', https://www.thestage.co.uk/news/2011/see-tickets-bought-by-vivendi-for-86m, accessed 14 March 2019.

74. Wolfgang Spahr, 'CTS Eventim Acquires See Tickets Germany', https://www.billbo ard.com/biz/articles/news/global/1204153/cts-eventim-acquires-see-tickets-germany, accessed 2 June 2019. See also 'BRIEF-CTS Eventim Acquires Ticketing Companies in Spain, Netherlands and France', https://www.reuters.com/article/ctseventim-brief/brief-cts-eventim-acquires-ticketing-companies-in-spain-netherlands-and-france-idUSW EB00JUQ20140306, accessed 2 June 2019.

75. 'Stage Entertainment and CTS Eventim Enter into Pan-European Partnership', https://www.stage-entertainment.com/news/stage-entertainment-and-cts-eventim-enter-into-pan-european-partnership, accessed 30 January 2019.

76. Alistair Smith, 'The Rise and Fall of Stage Entertainment', https://www.thestage.co.uk/opinion/2016/alistair-smith-the-rise-and-fall-of-stage-entertainment, accessed 25 February 2019.

77. This list does not include touring productions which have followed a long running pro-duction in the same country.

78. Savran, 'Trafficking in Transnational Brands', 329.

79. Ibid., 335.

80. van Gelder, *Joop van den Ende*, 337.

81. Ibid., 324.

82. 'Konzern-Zwischenbericht zum 30. Juni 2016', http://www.equitystory.com/Download/Companies/cts-eventim/Quarterly%20Reports/DE0005470306-Q2-2016-EQ-D-00.pdf, accessed 15 June 2019, 46.

83. Because of the pandemic, Hamilton finally opened in Hamburg on 6 October 2022.

84. 'Stage Entertainment: Broadway-Musical 'Hamilton' in Hamburg', *Welt*, https://www.welt.de/regionales/hamburg/article189107435/Stage-Entertainment-Broadway-Musical-Hamilton-in-Hamburg.html, accessed 19 May 2019.

85. 'Stage Entertainment kauft Operettenhaus am Spielbudenplatz', *Hamburg*, https://www.hamburg.de/pressearchiv/3112972/2011-10-13-fb-verkauf-operettenhaus, accessed 15 June 2019.

86. '360° experience': Arthur de Bok, quoted in Lisa Martland, 'Stage Entertainment: The Europe-Wide Powerhouse Producer with a Local Touch', https://www.thestage.co.uk/features/2017/stage-entertainment-the-europe-wide-powerhouse-producer, accessed 7 February 2019. This comprehensive approach to hospitality and understanding of quality is still an important part of the company's strategy and PR: 'Everyone who visits a Stage Entertainment venue feels warmly welcomed the moment they walk through the door. We aim to deliver a total night-out experience second to none and to exceed our visitors' expectations before the show begins with our friendly and professional staff, comfortable bars and restaurants, spacious and elegant foyers, high-quality merchandise booths and beautiful art exhibitions.' See: Stage Entertainment, 'Theatres', https://www.stage-entert ainment.com/theatres, accessed 12 May 2019.

87. The company also understands its development activities as an opportunity to mine the professional experience of its creative staff and artists as well as an impulse for the

enrichment of local musical theatre. See 'A Rich Palette of Quality Musical Theatre', https://www.stage-entertainment.com/news/a-rich-palette-of-quality-musical-theatre, accessed 27 January 2019.

88. 'Creative Development', https://www.stage-entertainment.com/creative-development/licensing-productions, accessed 18 May 2019. This obviously does not include recurring show formats such as *Holiday on Ice, Holland zingt Hazes,* or *Strictly Come Dancing.*

89. Patrick Healy, 'Yo, Adrian! I'm Singin'!', https://www.nytimes.com/2012/12/09/theater/a-hit-in-germany-a-rocky-musical-aims-at-broadway.html?action=click&contentCollection=Theater&module=RelatedCoverage&region=Marginalia&pgtype=article, accessed 1 June 2019.

90. Savran, 'Trafficking in Transnational Brands', 329.

91. These two songs were 'Philly Pie' and 'Holiday'. Another song, 'I Got Ideas', had already been cut during the German previews.

92. 'ROCKY Broadway Reviews', https://www.broadwayworld.com/reviews/Rocky, accessed 27 October 2019. See also Gerhard Knopf, 'Rocky. Grandiose Produktion—Grandiose Protagonisten', *Musicals: Das Musicalmagazin* 158 (2012): 4–7, and Armgard Seegers, 'Große Gefühle, Großes Theater: Die 'Rocky'-Weltpremiere', http://www.abendblatt.de/kultur-live/article111262505/Grosse-Gefuehle-grosses-Theater-Die-Rocky-Weltpremiere.html, accessed 27 October 2019.

93. Ben Brantley, 'Swinging at Fighters and Serenading Turtles', https://www.nytimes.com/2014/03/14/theater/rocky-the-musical-brings-songs-to-a-film-story.html, accessed 19 May 2019.

94. Ibid.

95. 'Rocky', http://www.playbill.com/production/rocky-winter-garden-theatre-vault-000 0014010, accessed 18 May 2019.

96. Consolidated financial statements can be retrieved from Bundesministerium der Justiz und für Verbraucherschutz, 'Bundesanzeiger', https://www.bundesanzeiger.de, accessed 19 September 2019.

97. Jonas Menze, 'Der Schuh des Manitu: Zum Einfluss des Broadway-Megamusicals auf die deutsche Musical-Landschaft', in *Die Rezeption des Broadwaymusicals in Deutschland,* ed. Nils Grosch and Elmar Juchem (Münster: Waxmann, 2012), 203–216; here: 209.

98. Jonas Menze, *Musical Backstages: Die Rahmenbedingungen und Produktionsprozesse des deutschsprachigen Musicals* (Münster: Waxmann, 2018), 233. See also Frederik Hanssen, 'Die Musical-Konkurrenz in Berlin ist enorm', https://www.tagesspiegel.de/kultur/geschaeftsfuehrerin-von-stage-entertainment-die-musical-konkurrenz-in-berlin-ist-enorm/20191986-all.html, accessed 16 June 2019.

99. Leonie Miserre, *Dynamic Pricing im Kulturbetrieb: Eine Machbarkeitsstudie am Beispiel der Staatsoper Berlin und der Stage Entertainment GmbH* (Berlin: Siebenhaar, 2016). See also Stef Driessen, 'Podiumkunsten stimuleren kaartverkoop met inzet doelgroepmarketing en prijsstratgieën', https://insights.abnamro.nl/2014/09/podium kunsten-stimuleren-kaartverkoop-met-inzet-doelgroepmarketing-en-prijsstratgieen, accessed 21 September 2019.

100. 'Change of Senior Management at Stage Entertainment Germany', https://www.stage-entertainment.com/news/change-of-senior-management-at-stage-entertainment-germany, accessed 30 January 2019.

101. 'New Investor for Stage Entertainment', https://www.stage-entertainment.com/news/new-investor-for-stage-entertainment, accessed 27 January 2019.

102. 'Stage Entertainment Announces Improvement Plan', https://www.stage-entertainm ent.com/news/stage-entertainment-announces-improvement-plan, accessed 27 January 2019.

103. When the big-budget en-suite musical productions came to continental Europe in the 1980s, local producers struggled to find performers who were able to sing, act, and dance well enough to meet the genre's requirements, since theatre in continental Europe had different traditions and educational programs for actors and performers. Thus, the producer's engagement in actor training originally was a reaction to the rising demand of the market. However, it later evolved into a prestige project to support young musical theatre talent, when admission to the school came with a full scholarship from 2011 onwards. Shutting down the school clearly demonstrates the investor's focus on short-term revenue growth and its lack of interest in long-term artistic development or commitment, not least since there remains a 'lack of first-class, versatile, "triple threat" performers'; see Döhl, 'The Third Biggest Market', 433.

104. Andreas Conrad, 'Cirque du Soleil zieht an den Potsdamer Platz', https://www.tagesspie gel.de/berlin/ein-neuer-glanzpunkt-unserer-metropole-cirque-du-soleil-zieht-an-den-potsdamer-platz/25114590.html, accessed 31 October 2019.

105. Frederik Hanssen, 'Wie ein Finanzinvestor Joop van den Endes Lebenswerk zerstört', https://www.tagesspiegel.de/kultur/stage-entertainment-wie-ein-finanzinvestor-joop-van-den-endes-lebenswerk-zerstoert/12868850.html, accessed 12 October 2019.

106. 'Advance to Acquire Stage Entertainment from CVC Fund VI and Joop van den Ende', https://www.stage-entertainment.com/news/advance-to-acquire-stage-entertainment-from-cvc-fund-vi-and-joop-van-den-ende, accessed 20 January 2019.

107. Ibid.

108. 'Stage Entertainment plant Beendigung des Spielbetriebs in Oberhausen und Verkauf des Colosseum Theaters Essen zur Fokussierung auf die starken Kernmärkte in Deutschland', https://www.stage-entertainment.de/unternehmen/presse/presse-detail seite_19840.html, accessed 31 October 2019.

109. Savran, 'Trafficking in Transnational Brands', 319.

110. Menze, 'Musical Backstages', 266.

111. 'Making Moments Magical', https://www.stage-entertainment.com, accessed 22 September 2019.

112. Sebesta and MacDonald, ' "Tonight I Will Bewitch the World" ', 343–344.

113. Döhl, 'The Third Biggest Market'.

114. Ibid., 434.

## BIBLIOGRAPHY

Jansen, Wolfgang. *Cats & Co.: Die Geschichte des Musicals im deutschsprachigen Theater* (Leipzig: Henschel, 2008).

Martland, Lisa. 'Stage Entertainment: The Europe-Wide Powerhouse Producer with a Kocal Touch', 29 November 2017, https://www.thestage.co.uk/features/stage-entertainment-the-europe-wide-powerhouse-producer-with-a-local-touch, accessed 7 February 2019.

Mateo, Marta. 'Anglo-American Musicals in Spanish Theatres'. *Translator* 14, no. 2 (2008): 319–342.

Menze, Jonas. 'Der Schuh des Manitu: Zum Einfluss des Broadway-Megamusicals auf die deutsche Musical-Landschaft.' In *Die Rezeption des Broadwaymusicals in Deutschland*, edited by Grosch and Elmar Juchem, 203–216. Münster: Waxmann, 2012.

Menze, Jonas. *Musical Backstages: Die Rahmenbedingungen und Produktionsprozesse des deutschsprachigen Musicals*. Münster: Waxmann, 2018.

Savran, David. 'Trafficking in Transnational Brands: The New "Broadway-Style" Musical.' *Theatre Survey* 55, no. 3 (2014): 318–342.

Thierens, Sanne. 'From Amsterdam with Love: Stage Entertainment's Global Success' In *The Palgrave Handbook of Musical Theatre Producers*, edited by Laura MacDonald and William A. Everett, 351–357. New York and London: Palgrave Macmillan, 2017.

Sebesta, Judith, and Laura MacDonald. "Tonight I Will Bewitch the World': The European Musical'. In *The Cambridge Companion to the Musical*, edited by William A. Everett and Paul R. Laird, 339–355. Cambridge: Cambridge University Press, 2017.

van Gelder, Henk. *Joop van den Ende: De biografie*. Amsterdam: Nijgh & Van Ditmar, 2012.

# PART IV

## GOOD NEIGHBOURS?

# CHAPTER 10

## CANADIAN MUSICALS AND THE COMMERCIAL THEATRE OF BROADWAY AND THE WEST END

### MEL ATKEY

FOR most of the past century Broadway (and to a lesser extent London) has, rightly or wrongly, been a mecca for Anglophone musical theatre. Canadians have been fed a steady diet of Horatio Alger stories from their southern neighbours stressing the need to 'make it' in the 'big time'. As the Canadian humorist Eric Nicol says, 'It is the ambition of every Canadian playwright to have his play run on Broadway for more than one night.'[1] Nicol knew whereof he spoke: his 1965 Vancouver hit *Like Father, Like Fun* actually managed three performances at the Brooks Atkinson Theatre in 1967 under a new title imposed by the producers—*A Minor Adjustment*. Still, some would argue that Canadians ought to concentrate on developing their own domestic audience first and then worry about exports.

In fact, Canadians have been making musicals for well over a century, beginning in 1880 with the pastiche *H.M.S. Parliament* by William Henry Fuller (which borrowed its music from *H.M.S. Pinafore*), and *Ptarmigan* (1895), with music by J. E. P. Aldous and a libretto by J. N. McIlwraith. Neither of these shows attempted to go to Broadway, but twenty-one years later the first hit Canadian show tune emerged when a young actor named Eugene Lockhart wrote the book and lyrics for a travelling show called *Pierrot Players* which toured Ontario's vaudeville and Chautauqua circuits. The music was by a classical pianist from Toronto named Ernest Seitz. Among the half dozen songs was one called 'The World Is Waiting for the Sunrise', which would later be recorded by everybody from Les Paul and Mary Ford to Laurel and Hardy and remains a standard to this day.

Many Canadian actors—Robert Goulet, Len Cariou, Victor Garber, and others— have made it on Broadway, as have the choreographer Onna White and the director Des

MacAnuff, as well as a couple of composers, such as Galt MacDermot, who wrote the music for *Hair*, and the team of Ray Jessel and Marian Grudeff (*Baker Street*)—but not with shows that originated in Canada.

They say that on Broadway, only one show in five pays off.[2] To date, five Canadian book musicals have been produced on Broadway. Three were reckoned flops. *Rockabye Hamlet* (1976) was slated by the critics and lasted only three performances, although it was later revived in Los Angeles for a healthy run. *Billy Bishop Goes to War* (1980) received mixed notices and transferred for a three-month run off-Broadway; it has subsequently been successful in US regional theatres. *The Story of My Life* (2009) was panned by most critics and enjoyed only a brief Broadway run, although it too has had a further life in regional theatres. Two were accounted hits: *The Drowsy Chaperone* (2006) and *Come from Away* (2017). Thus, two Canadian shows out of five have succeeded on Broadway—twice the average.

It must be noted, however, that these are not the only Canadian musicals that have tried to make the big move; there have been many other attempts. These include *Duddy* (1984), based on Mordecai Richler's novel *The Apprenticeship of Duddy Kravitz*. Although it had a score by the American pop songwriters Jerry Leiber and Mike Stoller, it was Canadian in the sense that it was set in Montreal and based on a Canadian novel; it also had a Canadian director (Brian Macdonald) and producer (Sam Gesser). It closed on tour and never even reached Toronto, much less Broadway. *Durante*, a 1989 biomusical of Jimmy Durante with a book by the Canadian comedy legends Frank Peppiatt and John Aylsworth, also closed out of town without reaching New York, while others, such as *2 Pianos, 4 Hands* (1997) and *Evil Dead: The Musical* (2006), have played successfully off-Broadway.

# THE DUMBELLS

In fact, the first Canadian show to make it to the Great White Way premiered more than a century ago: Captain Merton Plunkett (1888–1966), a YMCA social director turned World War I morale officer, put together an entertainment troupe known as *The Dumbells*. Their act combined sketches, popular songs like 'These Wild, Wild Women Are Making a Wild Man out of Me', and some original tunes composed by Plunkett and the pianist Jack Ayre. In the autumn of 1918, as the war was winding down, Plunkett tested the peacetime waters by booking the troupe into London's Victoria Palace Theatre. They were such a hit that the London Coliseum booked them for a four-week engagement.

Within two years they were on Broadway at the Ambassador Theatre for a twelve=week run of *Biff! Bing! Bang!* The *New York Telegraph* wrote, 'No American soldier show seen in New York has *Biff! Bing! Bang!*'s shape and vigor, nor its talent.'[3] Their material was intensely patriotic, including such numbers as 'Canada for Canadians' and 'Goodbye Broadway, Hello Montréal.' Although the patriotism was for another country, their

## CANADIAN MUSICALS, BROADWAY, AND THE WEST END    293

talent carried the day, or perhaps the production assuaged the guilt of some Americans who felt they should have been more involved in this European war than they actually were. As the *Telegraph*'s critic put it, 'If this be treason, make the most of it.'[4]

The next serious Canadian attempt to conquer Broadway wouldn't come for more than fifty years, but the country was busy laying the groundwork for a specifically Canadian musical theatre. The notion of a musical show targeted expressly at a local audience began to develop shortly before World War II, when Gratien Gélinas created the Montréal revue *Les Fridolinades*. Michel Vaïs wrote:

> For the first time, audiences were seeing one of their own on stage. The costumes, the frankness of the language and the situations reflected the reality of French Canada, which unconscious modesty—ascribed by some to an inferiority complex, by others simply to good taste—had never before permitted in the theatre.[5]

'Gélinas deserves the credit for insisting that Canadian theatre had to start putting its audience on stage',[6] said Mavor Moore, the man whom the York University professor Ross Stuart called the 'father of the modern Canadian musical theatre'.[7] As a university student, young Mavor had lived in a rooming house kept by Pat Rafferty, a veteran of the Dumbells troupe. Thus he was inspired to found what would become the world's longest-running annual satirical revue. *Spring Thaw*'s name was suggested by the Canadian Broadcasting Corporation director Andrew Allan 'for the time in Canada when the snow melts and exposes the old galoshes and Christmas trees and iron bedsteads of winter'.[8] As he had with *Les Fridolinades*, Mavor Moore wanted 'to make [his revue] so Canadian in subject matter and personality that it would inevitably give the audience something they could not get from an American show or a British show.'[9] The aim was to hold a mirror up to the audience. It is difficult to describe to a non-Canadian exactly what this quality is. Few people in Canada can describe what makes something 'Canadian', but they know that they will recognise it when they see it. Perhaps it is an ironic detachment, or a sense of looking at the world from the perspective of a powerless outsider, although nobody who can make the world laugh is truly powerless.

In this context, William Littler highlights: 'The congeniality of the revue's format to the Canadian scene is readily understandable, given the habit of self-deprecation that Canadians evidently develop during the early stages of their toilet training.'[10] Appraising *Spring Thaw*, the playwright John MacLachlan Gray adds, 'If you can't see something unique to your own area where you live in a theatre, what's the point of going?'[11]

There were some major obstacles to be overcome. The 'national inferiority complex' was no laughing matter. In 1947 the Canadian author Margaret Laurence wrote:

> It seems to be very difficult to capture the much more rugged atmosphere of Canada in a musical comedy. [ . . . ] They must deal in subtle wit, and the wit of this country is not generally found in the super-civilized repartee. They must be gay, and while this country has great potentialities for humorous writing, it is not basically gay[ . . . . ] I feel that the Canadian scene simply does not lend itself to good musical comedy. Just

as great tragic drama flourished in Elizabethan England, the time and the tone of a country almost always sets the pattern of its artistic creation. Until musical comedy actually fits in with the life of our people, and until it can be written with more spontaneity than at present, I think we would be better to forget about it for a while.[12]

It is, perhaps, no coincidence that Laurence wrote these words in the same year that *Spring Thaw* began its run, and yet the latter caught on. 'Everybody loved to see *Spring Thaw*', says the choreographer Blanche Lund, 'because it was political and it was well written. [... The Americans] couldn't spoof their government the way we could.'[13] Somehow, being less than a superpower liberated people's sense of irony. Those who have nothing to defend have nothing to lose. Over the next quarter of a century *Thaw*'s contributors would include the author Pierre Berton; the comedian Dave Broadfoot, who would co-found Royal Canadian Air Farce, *Spring Thaw*'s direct offspring; Stan Daniels, creator of the 1970s television show *Taxi*; the Oscar-nominated film director Norman Jewison (*In the Heat of the Night*, 1967; *Fiddler on the Roof*, 1971; *Jesus Christ Superstar*, 1973; *Moonstruck*, 1988); and the songwriters Jessel and Grudeff, whose musical *Baker Street* would later be staged on Broadway by Harold Prince. Although they never appeared in the show, the comedy legends Wayne and Shuster contributed sketches.

Historically, Canadian musicals attempting the move to Broadway had been up against some pressures that American shows didn't necessarily face, such as the presumption that only Americans could write musicals. When Julius Novick of the *New York Times* reviewed a Washington, DC production of George Ryga and Ann Mortifee's play with music *The Ecstasy of Rita Joe* in 1973, he said: ' "Canadian Playwright". The words seem a little incongruous together, like "Panamanian Hockey Player", almost, or "Lebanese Fur Trapper" . [ ... ] Isn't there a natural tendency in newly self-conscious small countries to overpraise local talent if only it is earnest enough, to take the wish for the deed?'[14] It should be explained here that the Americans have long had their own deep-seated fear of being 'Rome to Britain's Greece'.[15] At the time, the US media tended to ignore Canada. It was, for them, an embarrassment to live next to a country that had said 'no' to their revolution, yet was prosperous and democratic. As a result, the then-prevalent belief that musicals inevitably required New York's seal of approval made it very difficult for a writer to defend his or her work against what uninformed producers may wish to do to it.

## ANNE OF GREEN GABLES

There is one notable Canadian musical that has never been attempted on Broadway yet can be considered the granddaddy of all that followed. Although it has been playing for more than fifty summers at the Charlottetown Festival in Prince Edward Island and was the first Canadian book musical to reach an international audience, the creators of *Anne of Green Gables* have consciously avoided the Great White Way.[16] 'We learned long ago it's not that kind of show', says the actor and book writer Don Harron. '*Anne of Green Gables* is not *Annie*'.[17]

The show was conceived in the late 1950s, when Norman Campbell approached Harron saying, 'I've got ninety minutes to fill on CBC Television. What'll I do with it?' Harron replied, 'I've been reading a book to my kids that sounds like it would make a good musical. It's *Anne of Green Gables*'.[18] Based on the novel by Lucy Maud Montgomery, *Anne* was first seen as a live TV production in 1956 starring John Drainie as Matthew, Margot Christie as Marilla, and Toby Tarnow as Anne. The music was arranged and conducted by Phil Nimmons. Its composer, Norman Campbell, was an Emmy Award–winning producer of opera and ballet for television. 'I think it was just instinct that, as a TV producer, I understood dramatic construction',[19] he says. Musically, the show reflected Campbell's love of Offenbach, Gilbert and Sullivan, Victor Herbert, Lerner and Loewe, and, most of all, Rodgers and Hammerstein.

Having been written in 1956, *Anne of Green Gables* is stylistically rooted in that period. Mavor Moore maintained that *Anne* 'simply does not have the hard edge that Broadway absolutely requires. It's gentle, it's flowing. There is, for instance, in all of *Anne of Green Gables*, scarcely anything in a minor key'.[20] Nevertheless, the composer-lyricist Leslie Arden, whose mother, Cleone Duncan, was a member of the *Anne* cast for many years, says, 'The reason *Anne of Green Gables* has lasted so long is that there are actual stakes. She is an orphan and she almost doesn't get adopted, and then in the end, Matthew does die. It's not "he almost dies but he's okay and it's a happy ending." No, he dies. And she doesn't go to university; she stays home to look after Marilla. There are stakes, and they don't shy away from them. At the same time, the lines are truly funny. So, yes, it's old-fashioned, but the reason it's lasted and is so successful is that it's a well-constructed show and you believe that they have something at stake'.[21]

It then lay on the shelf for the next few years until 1964, when Moore was appointed director-general of the new Confederation Centre of the Arts in Charlottetown, Prince Edward Island. At the opening ceremony, Queen Elizabeth II remarked on one of the songs that had been sung by Diane Stapley. Moore explained that it was from *Anne of Green Gables*. 'I'd like to hear the rest of it', replied Her Majesty.

Moore wanted to develop a festival of all-Canadian work to honour the Fathers of Confederation, who had first met in Charlottetown a century earlier 'in a great fog of bonhomie—drank themselves into merriment, much to the scandal of the local newspapers. They had a great party. I felt the idea of having a good time at the birth of a nation was a marvellous excuse for a festival'.[22] Thus, he called it a 'Festival of Music and Laughter'.

Part of this all-Canadian season was the world stage premiere of *Anne of Green Gables*, put together by the choreographer Alan Lund—a *Spring Thaw* veteran—making his solo directorial debut with only three weeks' rehearsal on a budget of $60,000. In that initial 1965 season, much of the company, both backstage and onstage, came from *Spring Thaw*, including Peter Mews as Matthew, Barbara Hamilton as Marilla, and Dean Regan as Gilbert, in addition to Lund and the musical director, John Fenwick. *Anne of Green*

*Gables* is in fact thoroughly grounded in *Spring Thaw*: the Festival was run by *Thaw*'s founder, and the core of the company, including its librettist, were all *Thaw* veterans. As Moore remarks: 'Only an acting company drilling together for years could have prepared two new musicals in one month while performing a third and added a fourth while performing the first three.'[23]

Nathan Cohen's initial review in the *Toronto Star* seemed to damn *Anne of Green Gables* with faint praise: 'There's no doubt that it will be much improved when it returns to the Charlottetown Festival next summer. It won't be then, and it isn't now, a musical of world-shaking consequence, but even now it has a commendable steadiness.'[24] The *New York Times* reported: 'Prince Edward Island has a reputation for friendliness, but nowhere has sociability gone as far as it has the nights that *Anne* is on.'[25] Seemingly, at this time, the notion of anything of artistic merit coming out of Canada was novel to American ears, for the reviewer added: 'Whether critics in New York or producers in Hollywood would agree remains to be seen'.

In 1967 the piece toured across the country as part of the centennial of confederation. After that, Lund succeeded Moore as artistic director of the Festival. Two years later the expatriate Canadian Bill Freedman, who had seen the show during its 1967 tour, brought *Anne* to London. 'Everybody told me not to do it', he said at the time. 'They said no-one wants to see a sentimental kid's classic on stage.'[26] Freedman, who had another play called *Hadrian the Seventh* running at the same time, said more recently, 'I could have bought a couple of Picassos instead of putting it on.'[27] Instead, he has a painting of the *Anne* set hanging in his Covent Garden office. 'The man who was putting up all the money fled about two weeks before it went into rehearsal and [looking at the painting] I ended up spending a lot of money on that particular masterpiece.'

*Anne* opened on 16 April 1969 at what is now the Noël Coward Theatre to largely enthusiastic notices. Because the show had been launched in a so-far disappointing season with little advance publicity, not much was expected of it. 'All my colleagues and I came into the New Theatre expecting to see a complete failure', wrote Harold Hobson in the *Christian Science Monitor*, but he conceded: 'It can, and does, give the highest pleasure.'[28] A young Cameron Mackintosh saw it at least once (describing it to me when I met him in 1990 as 'folksy'), as did the actor Simon Callow, who remembered it to me in 2003 as a 'charming show'.

The family show concluded its London run on 17 January 1970 after 319 performances. Although *Plays and Players* magazine voted it the year's best musical, '[i]t never caught on with adult audiences', Freedman says. 'We used to sell out in the summer, half-term and Saturday matinees. They considered it to be a children's show. I was very unsophisticated in 1969. I should have toured it.'[29] Duncan Weldon and Paul Elliot enquired about mounting a provincial tour, but nothing came of it. Barbara Kelly and Bernard Braden, a married couple from Vancouver who had become stars in Britain, were offered it at the time, but turned it down. Says Freedman, 'I would not have done it today without two stars.'[30]

But what about Broadway? At Christmastime of 1971 *Anne* made a two-week stop at New York's City Centre as a part of a regional tour. Walter Kerr wrote in the *New*

FIG. 10.1 The ensemble number 'Open the Window' from *Anne of Green Gables*, as performed at the Charlottetown Festival in 1981. Photo: George Zimbel, provided by the editors.

York Times: 'As staged, the show's deliberate simplicity seemed to me synthetic and a bit pushy, its pig-tailed heroine seemed constantly on the verge of turning herself into Donald Duck in her eagerness to be recognised as a pint-sized force of nature, and its jokes—what [sic] might have been good enough if anyone had shushed them a little—kept spelling themselves out in the capital letters that belong on children's play-blocks, and should be swept right back under the Christmas tree.'[31] Other reviews were more positive. Richard Watts in the *New York Post* found it 'surprisingly disarming and likeable.'[32] To United Press International, it was 'warmly charming.'[33]

Still, Harron sensed that *Anne* was not a show for Broadway. He says, 'I have been at many Broadway opening nights and seen the brittle sophistication of the first niters [*sic*] who were much more interested in being seen than seeing anything on that stage. [ ... ] Londoners were different, in their ratty fur stoles they wanted to see a show and enjoy it.'[34]

In the early 1990s the English lighting designer Benny Ball remarked to the author that if somebody were really clever, they would mount a UK provincial tour of *Anne of Green Gables*, as Duncan Weldon and Paul Elliot had failed to do twenty years earlier, to give the musical another chance at international exposure and turn it into a work with title recognition, both of which so far have eluded the show outside of its native country. Still, as Canada's first 'international' musical, *Anne of Green Gables* helped to give other creators the confidence they needed for the shows that would follow.

# ROCKABYE HAMLET

In 1976 *Rockabye Hamlet* opened at the Minskoff Theatre, where it lasted for twenty-one previews and seven performances. Cliff Jones, the musical's composer, lyricist, and book writer, was a capable composer, but his work was saddled with a concept that couldn't quite decide whether to be serious or a send-up.

It had begun its life three years earlier as *Hamlet: The Musical* on the Canadian Broadcasting Corporation's radio program *The Entertainers*. Reportedly written in only three weeks, it aired on 1 December 1973 with Cal Dodd as Hamlet and Nancy White as Ophelia. Jones was a TV variety script writer specialising in children's shows. At the age of twenty-four, for a year before *Hamlet*, he had been writing satirical songs for a radio series called *Inside from the Outside*.

*Hamlet* opened under its new title, *Kronborg 1582* (changed after Jones and his wife visited Kronborg Castle in Elsinore) at the Charlottetown Festival in the summer of 1974, directed by Alan Lund and starring Cal Dodd as Hamlet and Roma Hearn as Gertrude. *Variety* wrote that 'this *Hamlet* is something special. Lacking dialogue, it rolls with ease from ballads to boogie woogie, blues, country and western and campy musical style and yet maintains the basic tragic plotline right to the bloody finale.'[35] Champlain Productions, owned by the Bronfman family (of Seagram fame), bought an option on the show with a view to taking it to Broadway.

Its actual path to Broadway was pure serendipity. The actress Colleen Dewhurst, who had a summer home on Prince Edward Island, was a fan of the show, and she introduced Cliff to her agent Clifford Stevens. He in turn brought in the producer Lester Osterman, with whom Dewhurst had worked on a Broadway revival of *A Moon for the Misbegotten*; Osterman then took over the option from the Bronfmans.

The following year *Kronborg* returned to the Charlottetown stage. Osterman sent Gower Champion to check it out. Champion, it turns out, was a recent convert to the idea of rock musicals. 'It's so damned ironic', he declared. 'There's been this incredible proliferation of music, but not one note of it has made it to the Broadway stage.'[36] After the disappointing fate of his last show, *Mack and Mabel*, Champion was desperate for a hit.

The show then mounted a regional tour to Toronto, Montréal, Ottawa, and Hamilton. Here things began to unravel. Hampered in his ability to rewrite the show by the fact that the rhythm section of the music was pre-recorded, and with no budget to make changes, Jones felt helpless. It did not play as well on the major urban stages, and critics were not kind. The *Toronto Star*'s Urjo Kareda said, '*Kronborg 1582* trivialises *Hamlet*, turning a famous play into a series of jukebox solos.'[37] *Starweek*'s music critic William Littler stated: 'We'll pause a moment now to give time for the ghost of Will Shakespeare to roll over.'[38]

Lund was out, Champion was in. According to Blanche Lund, Champion offered her husband the position of associate director, which he turned down. A proposed pre-Broadway tour to Washington and Boston fell through, and Osterman decided to once again change the show's title: it opened as *Rockabye Hamlet* on 17 February 1976 at the Minskoff Theatre. A strange blend of gothic melodrama and very high camp, it began with the lyric 'Why did he have to die?/Didn't you hear him laugh?/Didn't you hear him cry?' As it wasn't quite clear whether the show was a tongue-in-cheek send-up or serious in its approach to the source material, the critics were out for blood. Clive Barnes in the *New York Times* proclaimed Jones 'a second-rate musician with a third-rate mind.'[39] Doug Watt of the *New York Daily News* opined: 'To watch *Rockaby* [*sic*] *Hamlet*, a gaudy and anachronistic exercise in musical kitsch that flopped about the stage of the Minskoff last night like a dying swordfish, is to marvel at the heights of folly attainable along Broadway.'[40] With song titles like 'He Got It in the Ear', Jones seemed to be playing it for laughs, but the people attending the production were never quite sure. Barnes conceded: 'The audience seemed to like the show. But perhaps they wouldn't have liked *Hamlet*.'

The musical closed after less than a week. That 'thoroughly devastated me',[41] Jones told the news agency Canadian Press in 1980. The national fascination at that time with the prospect of international failure caused CBC Radio to produce a mammoth eight-hour post-mortem documentary, *A Bite of the Big Apple*. The *Toronto Globe and Mail* critic Blaik Kirby stated: '[The program] required such a huge investment of time and skill that a solid block of results had to come out of it.'[42] Its producer, Malka Cohen (now Malka Marom), told the *Globe and Mail* that the show which had flopped on Broadway was inferior to the Canadian production: 'The transformation of the show for Broadway removed all its heart and warmth.'[43] This comes down to one of the presumed differences between Canadian and American culture: the assumption that American shows are all glitz and glamour, and that Canadian works are either deadly earnest or ironically detached. This may not necessarily be true, but the stereotype has taken roots in the minds of many Canadians. It is a common fear among foreign (not just Canadian) shows going to Broadway that their delicate little show will be polished to death by New York. It happened when the US producers of *The Boy Friend* (coming over from its London success in 1954) barred its author, Sandy Wilson, from rehearsals and then transformed it from a little fringe show with just one piano and drums into a full-blown Broadway opus. Although it ran for 485 performances on Broadway,[44] in its creator's eyes it was a weakened show.[45]

Gower Champion's biographer, John Anthony Gilvey, has another explanation for why *Rockabye Hamlet* failed to win over either the critics or the public:

> The Canadian production had appeared during the Vietnam War at a time when the social order in the United States was under fire by numerous dissenters critical of its injustices and failures. For many, especially American youth, social protest was a way to express dissatisfaction with a nation seen as rotten with war, injustice and political intrigue as Denmark itself. [ ... ] But since the climax of Watergate, with President Nixon's resignation, and the fall of Saigon, which ended the war, the era of social protest was rapidly drawing to a close as the nation put behind itself over a decade of unrest in preparation for its bicentennial.[46]

Unbowed, Jones rewrote the show again, and this time it was a hit at the Odyssey Theatre in Santa Monica in November 1981 under the title *Something's Rockin' in Denmark*. 'It was supposed to run only a month, there,' Jones explained, 'but played for a year and won twelve Dramalogue awards.'[47] The *Los Angeles Times* concluded: 'It's got energy. It's got talent. It's got a sense of humor—sometimes. [ ... ] For all its good points, this pop opera takeoff on *Hamlet* [ ... ] falls more frequently slightly to the left or right of the mark than on it', but the reviewer nonetheless conceded that 'you don't walk away bored.'[48] On the more modest scale of its Los Angeles production, *Rockabye Hamlet* was able to find a cult audience to sustain it. There were hints of that kind of audience in New York, but the producers couldn't keep the piece going in that high-stakes environment, since it is more risky to allow a show to run and find its audience when it is big and expensive.

Meanwhile, in Canada, the critical drubbing the work received merely reinforced the country's national inferiority complex. It seems people happily read the news of its demise in the way some are drawn to watching car accidents and fires.

## *BILLY BISHOP GOES TO WAR*

In Canada, regional theatres are the 'establishment' and commercial theatre is the maverick intruder. The country has had a system of regional theatres since the early 1960s and fringe or 'alternate' theatres since the end of that decade. These organisational forms became the traditional two halves of Canadian theatre. Then, in 1985, when the producer Marlene Smith presented *Cats* with an all-Canadian cast, that changed everything, at least in Toronto. Today the commercial enterprise Mirvish Productions, run by David Mirvish following in Smith's footsteps, runs four theatres. Toronto has seen sit-down productions of *Les Misérables*, *Miss Saigon*, *Crazy for You*, and a host of other shows, but to date the only Canadian-written show to be staged on a big scale has been Marlene Smith's production of *Napoleon* in 1994, which later 'enjoyed' a tortuous six-month run in London in 2000. Because of its apparent lack of interest in presenting new work, the commercial theatre has been regarded with a certain distrust by some members of the theatrical establishment.

On the other hand, the so-called alternate theatres do little besides original work, even though little of it falls into the category of the musical. One of the most notable exceptions has been *Billy Bishop Goes to War*. At home, it is known as a show that triumphed across the country,[49] but in New York, where a musical doesn't officially exist until it has opened on or off-Broadway, *Billy Bishop*, although highly regarded in some circles, is known only for its all-too-brief run at the Morosco Theatre.

The show's author, John MacLachlan Gray, has carved out his own distinctive artistic path. 'Each show John does is a little different', explains Mavor Moore: 'He's got a voice all his own, out of his own period, his rock and roll experience.'[50] Gray says, 'I don't know very many writers of musicals that came out of the background I did.'[51] As a teenager he played keyboards in a rock and roll band; he claims that he never saw a Broadway show until after he had written his first musical. He was influenced more by nightclub acts and by Brecht and Weill than by the American musical. He graduated from the University of British Columbia—'The only place you could study directing'[52]—with an MA in 1972 and later became a founding member of Vancouver's Tahmanhous Theatre Workshop. His first full-length musical was *Eighteen Wheels*, a show about truckers that Paul Thompson directed at Theatre Passe Muraille in Toronto. It broke attendance records when Richard Ouzounian presented it at Festival Lennoxville.

Gray has very strong feelings about tailoring theatrical forms to suit the subject: 'I think that if you're going to write something unique in Canada, you have to write something in a form that comes out of the country.'[53] *Billy Bishop* is a case in point. Gray's shows tend to be small, but *Billy Bishop* was small even by his standards. His music may not be sophisticated, but it is simple and effective. To what extent his style actually 'comes out of the country' is debatable: it is largely a blend of English music hall and German cabaret. However, Gray points out that 'Canadians don't much like listening in on other people's conversations. They think it's impolite. This plays havoc with the basic convention of theatre itself, so what do you do? Well, you drop the fourth wall and simply talk to the audience. They tend to relax a bit because they are in an arena whose aesthetics they understand: the arena of the storyteller.'[54] The actor Eric Peterson had told Gray about a book he had been reading, *Winged Warfare*, by Captain William Avery Bishop, at the time considered to be the top fighter pilot of the Royal Flying Corps in World War I. This set the wheels in motion. The show takes place in an officer's mess, with Bishop addressing new recruits for World War II. Gray and Peterson were both in Royal Canadian Air Force uniforms, with the composer seated at a grand piano. Using only his microphone and a toy plane, Peterson re-enacted the battles, playing Bishop in addition to sixteen other characters, including his aunt Lady St. Helier and a French chanteuse.

When *Billy Bishop* opened at the Vancouver East Cultural Centre in November 1978, audiences were small owing to a newspaper strike, but word of mouth slowly set in. The late New York producer Lewis Allen was brought to see it. 'It's a very Canadian show, set in its own very specific milieu, that can speak to people everywhere in a terribly entertaining way,'[55] he enthused. Allen and his partner Mike Nichols both had Vancouver connections: Nichols had directed one of his first plays for the Vancouver Festival a couple of decades earlier, and Allen had some mining investments there. Perhaps he thought that the show's small scale and Canadian references, something New York audiences had not seen before, would be intriguing. He took Nichols, with whom he'd produced a perennial cash cow named *Annie* four years earlier, to see it as well. In Toronto, *Billy Bishop* enjoyed its greatest success at Theatre Passe Muraille, and this is where Nichols and Allen saw it for the second time, with the latter stating: 'We thought it was original and funny and moving.'[56]

Then came the Broadway première at the Morosco Theatre where, following seven previews, it opened on 29 May 1980. The first night was a media sensation; Candice Bergen, Phyllis Diller, Dick Cavett, and Paul Simon all came to the after-party at Sardi's. Andy Warhol exclaimed: 'I love it! It's so Canadian!'[57] (Gray confided in a letter home, 'I wonder what he meant by that.'[58]) Even the Broadway guru Lehman Engel loved it, but something was wrong. Gray and Peterson detected a 'yawning gulf of uncomprehending silence' from the audience.[59] 'We had been hoping for a little more appreciation of irony, but Americans, it seems, aren't into irony.'[60] It could also be argued that some American audiences will only accept a foreign show if it relates to their own history or fits into their world-view. This explanation would account for the failure of *Billy Bishop Goes to War* as well as the later success of *Come from Away*.

The reviews were generally upbeat. In the *New York Post*, Clive Barnes announced: '*Billy Bishop* flies high!'[61] But Walter Kerr, writing for the *New York Times*, begged to differ:

> When Billy Bishop realises that so long as he is in the ground forces, he is 'a casualty in training, and the only way out is up', you understand him and you're with him. It would be a saving grace to understand the Billy Bishop who came down as well.[62]

The musical closed on 6 June after twelve performances (plus seven previews), but Gray, Peterson, Nichols, and Allen did not give up. They moved it to the three-hundred-seat Theatre de Lys (now the Louise Lortel Theatre) in Greenwich Village, where Gray concedes it probably should have gone in the first place. A further cash infusion of $50,000 kept the show running until the end of August, when the actors left for the Edinburgh Festival, where they were again greeted by standing ovations.

In London, Ken Renton brought the show to the Comedy (now Harold Pinter) Theatre. At last they were in another country that actually fought in that war all the way through, and the reviews were largely positive. Michael Coveney wrote in the *Financial Times* that 'the presentational conjunction of lights, music and sound effects is truly breathtaking.'[63] But other critics had nagging reservations. The *Observer* complained: 'Its opening lyrics [ ... ] "Somehow it never seemed like war at all" are simply and

FIG. 10.2 Eric Peterson and John Gray (at the piano) in the 1980 Broadway staging of *Billy Bishop Goes to War*. Photo: Harry Naltchayan, provided by the editors.

hauntingly set and suggest irony. But it never materialises. Ambiguities are bypassed, the evolution of a killer-hero unexamined.'[64] So, according to the critics, the show was too ironic for New York but not ironic enough for London, where *Billy Bishop* closed on 11 July 1981.

The difference between its Canadian reception and the response on Broadway and later in the West End may not be so much a difference between the cultures of the three countries as one between the subsidised and commercial sectors, for *Billy Bishop* has been successfully staged in many regional theatres in the United States since then. Some will also say that the show was too intimate for the large theatres of Broadway or the West End. New York audiences generally pay a lot of money for their tickets and are financially well-off, so they may demand high production values in exchange, whereas an off-Broadway or a regional theatre audience may have different expectations of an evening in the theatre.[65]

# THE DROWSY CHAPERONE

The next attempt to transfer a Canadian musical to Broadway proved to be luckier. In 2006 *The Drowsy Chaperone*, with a book by Bob Martin and Don McKellar and music and lyrics by Greg Morrison and Lisa Lambert, opened at the Marquis Theatre on Broadway, where it broke box-office records after winning five Tony Awards (including Best Book and Best Score). The musical, in which a lonely divorcé sits in his apartment listening to the cast recording of his favourite 1920s musical, had begun on the fringe in Toronto in 1998 and progressed through many incarnations before making its move south.

Bob Martin had attended Lawrence Park Collegiate Institute with two of his future collaborators, Lisa Lambert and Don McKellar. Even then they dreamed up mock musicals. The late Marian Grudeff, a veteran of *Spring Thaw*, remembered Don as an English student at Victoria College. 'He looked like a rabbinical student', she said in 2004. 'He played Hysterium in *A Funny Thing Happened on the Way to the Forum*. He had a lot of charisma on stage. He's a very musical man. He'd come over and sit beside me on the piano and we'd go over a whole book of different songs.' McKellar added, 'We never would have written a musical if we hadn't met Marian. It's inconceivable. She simultaneously glamorised and demystified Broadway. Her affectionate and irreverent anecdotes made it irresistible and somehow within reach. Heaven for 'Man in Chair' would have been an evening with Marian Grudeff: trading tidbits of musical comedy arcana, laughing himself silly and singing into the night.'[66]

When Bob asked Lisa to be the 'best man' at his wedding to Janet Van de Graaff, the idea for *The Drowsy Chaperone* was born. Lisa and Don, together with Greg Morrison, a composer to whom Bob had introduced them, began to write a forty-minute pastiche 1920s musical about the marriage of two people (who happened to be named Robert Martin and Janet Van de Graaff) as a stag-night entertainment. This very first incarnation was performed on 9 August 1998 at the Rivoli on Toronto's Queen Street. It was open to the public and was advertised in the newspaper. The show at that point contained a half dozen songs, of which two, 'Aldolpho' and 'An Accident Waiting to Happen', survived into the Broadway production. That first book, which contained the basic plot of the musical within the show, was written by McKellar in collaboration with Matt Watts and the actors.

They decided it shouldn't end there. Bob Martin joined the team as a co-writer, and the character of the Man in Chair was born—a would-be raconteur, an obsessive show nerd who can—and does—recount every detail about his favourite 1928 musical, *The Drowsy Chaperone*. Lisa Lambert explained: 'It's all about the private place—the bedrooms where musical-theatre-fan teenagers record their YouTube renditions, etc.'[67] Lambert herself played the title role, and McKellar played the Latin lover, Aldolpho, while Janet Van de Graaff played her own namesake. Also in the cast was Jonathan Crombie, who would later replace Martin as the Man in Chair on Broadway and on tour. This version, now an hour long, opened on 2 July 1999 at the 181-seat George Ignatief Theatre as a part of the Fringe of Toronto Festival, directed and choreographed by Steven Morel. John Karastamatis, director of communications for Mirvish Productions, waited in line for one of the half dozen sold-out performances.

Over the next couple of years the show went through two more incarnations in Toronto—first at Theatre Passe Muraille in 1999 and finally at the Winter Garden Theatre in 2001. Each time it grew in length, adding songs, receiving rave reviews, and winning awards. The American producer Roy Miller saw the show at the Winter Garden and with Paul Mack presented a showcase of it at the National Alliance for Musical Theatre's Festival of New Musicals in New York in 2004. Kevin McCollum and Bob Boyett came on board as co-producers at this point.

A new director was brought in: Casey Nicholaw, who had been nominated for a Tony Award for best choreography for *Spamalot*, would make his Broadway debut as director-choreographer. 'We knew that in order for the show to be truly effective, the musical within the show had to be fully realised, with great voices, great dancers, great costumes,'[68] Martin told the Working in the Theatre symposium. 'We were excited when we thought about the idea of a director-choreographer, because the show is not just about dancing, it's about movement, and the set itself is almost like another character in the show. It's constantly transforming, and it's absolutely crucial that we had somebody at the helm who knew how to move the action around with the characters in and out of these two worlds that we're presenting.'

Many shows from other countries have gone to New York and lost their souls to producers who had no understanding of their original concepts. 'It was certainly something we were really scared of,' McKellar told Phil Hahn of CTV News,

> but it never entered into that territory where we sold out or betrayed our initial impulse. [ . . . ] At first, when we had our American partners involved we were sure that was going to be an issue, and it would lose its irony [ . . . ] but fortunately we had, in our producers and our director and our creative team, collaborators who were able to understand the importance of the tone, and the irony that we came with—and encouraged us to stick with that.[69]

Of course, this is a show that benefited from Broadway gloss, as opposed to one smothered by it (as others have been, including British imports such as *The Boy Friend*). There is a perception, especially among the British, that American audiences don't 'get' irony, but the success of the television series *Frasier* would appear to give the lie to that idea. Having seen it play so successfully in its original pared-down incarnation, the American producers knew that they mustn't throw the baby out with the bath-water. *The Drowsy Chaperone* was closely associated with Toronto's Second City comedy tradition[70]—Bob Martin was a former Second City artistic director—and with Canada's firm reputation in the United States for great comedy, the producers may have been more inclined to trust its authors than on previous shows.

*The Drowsy Chaperone* opened at the Marquis Theatre on 1 May 2006. The Associated Press's Michael Kuchwara called it a 'disarming, delightful soufflé'.[71] Howard Kissel of the *New York Daily News* found 'cause for rejoicing. It's full of wit and high spirits'.[72] The all-important *New York Times* critic Ben Brantley acknowledged: 'The gods of timing, who are just as crucial to success in show business as mere talent is, have smiled brightly upon *The Drowsy Chaperone*, the small and ingratiating musical that opened last night at the big and intimidating Marquis Theater.' But, he added, '[t]hough this revved-up spoof of a 1920's song-and-dance frolic, as imagined by an obsessive 21st-century show queen, seems poised to become the sleeper of the Broadway season, it is not any kind of a masterpiece.'[73]

The show won seven Drama Desk Awards, including Best Musical, Best Book, and Best Score. It also won the Best Musical award from the Drama Critics Circle and was nominated for thirteen Tony Awards, including every category for which it was eligible. The first Canadian show since *The Dumbells* to be an unqualified Broadway hit, it repaid its $8 million cost within thirty weeks before finally closing at the end of December 2007 after 674 performances.

Its London production was not quite so lucky. Its producers cast a star—Elaine Paige, who had an entire floor set aside as her dressing room—in the title role, a character who was barely on stage for ten minutes, whereas in New York it had been sold as an ensemble piece. If there was any starring role in the show it would have been the Man in Chair, who is the heart and soul of the piece. (In Toronto, Richard Ouzounian said, 'What makes it special? I call tell you that in two words. Bob Martin. He's always been *The Drowsy Chaperone* 's secret ingredient.'[74]) It was later successfully revived off–West End.

How Canadian is *The Drowsy Chaperone*? It has often been described as a love letter to the American musical—but that letter was definitely postmarked Toronto. 'We've always felt that there is a Canadian angle,' expounds Don McKellar, 'which is sort of the Man in Chair, that he has this perspective outside of Broadway. In a way, he's watching as we watched from across the border and imagining what it's like and being titillated by it, and also critical.'[75] 'I love this Canadian focus,' confirms Amon Miyamoto, who directed the Japanese production. 'This is how they loved musicals long distance. That's good for me. It's all in his imagination, his own creation. This is a Canadian viewpoint. That's what made me very excited when I saw it on Broadway. It touched my heart. [ ... ] Japanese people looking at Broadway and Canadian people looking at Broadway, the distance is similar.'[76]

Through the character of the Man in Chair, who constantly interjects his often sardonic commentary into the action of the show-within-a-show, *Chaperone* possesses that detached irony that has long been presumed to be a trademark of Canadian humour. Lisa Lambert explicates: 'For me, the apartment is my bedroom in the North Toronto house I lived in growing up in Toronto—my crappy record player and Broadway cast recordings I stole from my mother's collection.'[77] *The Drowsy Chaperone* built on a tradition that began with *The Dumbells* and *Spring Thaw* and developed through the Toronto branch of Second City. Comedy is something at which Canadians have long succeeded,

FIG. 10.3 A scene from the London production of *The Drowsy Chaperone*: (*left to right*) Summer Strallen, Paul Iveson, and Elaine Paige. Photo: Nigel Norrington © ArenaPal.

so it's hardly surprising that they would eventually conquer Broadway with a musical comedy.

## *The Story of My Life*

In 2006 Canadian Stage presented a new homegrown musical called *The Story of My Life*, with songs by Neil Bartram and a book by Brian Hill, and starring Brent Carver and Jeffrey Kuhn. Bartram, from Burlington, Ontario, and Hill, from Kitchener, met in Toronto while performing in the revue *Forever Plaid* in the early 1990s. Their previous musical, *Somewhere in the World*, had run for five seasons in Charlottetown. *The Story of My Life* tells of a lifelong relationship between a writer named Thomas and his childhood friend and muse Alvin, told in flashbacks after the latter's death. Alas, the *National*

*Post*'s Robert Cushman found its overt emotionalism 'close to unbearable'.[78] However, that was not the end of the line for *The Story of My Life*. On 19 February 2009, it opened at the Booth Theatre on Broadway in a production directed by Richard Maltby, Jr., and starring Will Chase and Malcolm Gets. Unfortunately, most of the critics didn't clue in to its low-key approach. Ben Brantley berated the piece in the *New York Times*: 'In addition to jettisoning the usual excesses of tourist-trapping extravaganzas, they have tossed away such niceties as originality, credibility, tension and excitement.'[79] The verdict of *Variety*'s David Rooney was that '[t]his flavorless new musical is not exactly terrible, but it's not terribly interesting, either.[80]

Michael Kuchwara of the Associated Press disagreed. He called it 'a heartfelt little musical that has the courage of its sweet-tempered, low-key convictions.[81] Peter Filichia, in his Theatremania blog, concluded that 'it deserved far more respect than it got.'[82] Perhaps 'sweet-tempered' and 'low-key' is just too Canadian for New York. New York critics may expect Broadway shows to be bigger than life, and any that attempt to defy this notion will be shot down. As a two-hander, *The Story of My Life* may very well have fared better if it had contented itself with an off-Broadway engagement. It closed after only five performances, although it received four Drama Desk Award nominations for book, music, lyrics, and outstanding production of a musical. It has since been successfully mounted in Korea and appears to have a future in regional theatre productions. Brian Hill has stated: 'The Broadway production of *Story* was quite beautiful and benefitted greatly from having the CanStage tryout. As for the critics, we don't read or care about reviews so we can't really comment.'[83]

*The Story of My Life* is another example of a show that should probably have remained off-Broadway. However, given that it received an equally hostile critical reception in its home country, it's very hard to draw any conclusions regarding national cultural differences. It seems more likely that it comes down to a difference in what people believe a musical can and should be. To some critics, musicals are expected to be broad and brash and camp; others want them to be subtle and tender. *The Story of My Life* is not for those who espouse the former.

All of these shows have contributed in some way to the establishment of what may prove to be the turning point in Canadian musical theatre history: the Canadian Music Theatre Project at Toronto's Sheridan College.[84] Michael Rubinoff, who heads the Project, explains, 'I've always believed you need two things for a musical: you need a compelling story and a compelling reason to musicalise it.'[85]

# COME FROM AWAY

This brings us to the second Canadian musical to become a hit on Broadway: *Come from Away*, about the people of Gander, Newfoundland, who took in the airline passengers stranded after the World Trade Center attacks on 11 September 2001. The show tells the true stories of how the Gander residents interacted with their foreign visitors and the generosity they showed them. Rubinoff explains:

> There was something really special that happened in Gander, Newfoundland. Learning about that story, immediately and then the aftermath, I was quite moved. I was proud to be a Canadian. [...] The other benefit was [ ... ] that the way Newfoundlanders tell their stories and record their stories is through music. Storytelling, kitchen parties; that is so much a part of their culture.[86]

However, Rubinoff is neither a composer nor a writer. As a creative producer, he set out to find authors to musicalise the event, approaching several teams—who all turned him down. Then he saw a show called *My Mother's Lesbian Jewish Wiccan Wedding*, with book, music, and lyrics by the husband-and-wife team David Hein and Irene Sankoff. Hein had a degree in set and lighting design, but it was his wife who introduced him to musicals: Sankoff grew up on black-and-white movies and *Les Miz* at the Royal Alexandra Theatre, which she saw countless times, whereas her husband was mainly influenced by Newfoundland music, folk music, and rock music.[87] The couple approached the project as follows:

> We [ ... ] dove into researching it like crazy and found out there was a commemoration ceremony that was going to be happening in Newfoundland on [the tenth anniversary of] 9/11, and all of these passengers who were stranded there were returning to commemorate the kindness they had seen, and to reunite with the friends they had made there ten years earlier. So we applied for a grant from the Canada Council for the Arts and were able to travel out there for almost a month.[88]

*Come from Away* has not been fictionalised; instead, its authors tried to stay as true to what had happened as possible, so that the people whose stories they dramatised would be able to recognise themselves on-stage.[89] The project was first presented as a showcase at Toronto's Panasonic Theatre on 10 April 2012. According to Hein, the show wasn't always meant to have a one-act structure: '[O]riginally we had an interval after [the song] "Screech In" and before "Me in the Sky". Our producers suggested that it be one act, because the people who were stranded in 2001 didn't get a break.'[90]

*Come from Away* opened on Broadway at the Gerald Schoenfeld Theatre on 12 March 2017. Ben Brantley advised:

> Try, if you must, to resist the gale of good will that blows out of *Come from Away*, the big bearhug of a musical that opened on Sunday night at the Gerald Schoenfeld Theater. But even the most stalwart cynics may have trouble staying dry-eyed during this portrait of heroic hospitality under extraordinary pressure.[91]

The show's warm reception in New York paved the way for a West End transfer, where, following its opening in London in 2018, the *Evening Standard* was equally impressed:

There are moments when *Come from Away* feels like an advertisement for Canadian decency and its capacity to improve the lives of malcontent Americans. [ ... ] But in the end its defining features are charm, energy and a real generosity of spirit, and audiences are left with a nagging question: in a situation like the one the people of Gander faced, would we do the same?[92]

A new open-ended production began its run at the Royal Alexandra Theatre in Toronto on 13 February 2018, following a sold-out run at the Royal Manitoba Theatre Centre in Winnipeg. There is even talk of a movie,[93] which will of course be filmed in Gander.

# THE END OF THE NATIONAL INFERIORITY COMPLEX?

The productions suggest there has been a steady progression in the profile of Canadian musical theatre on Broadway. *Anne of Green Gables* proved that Canadians can write musicals. *Billy Bishop Goes to War* suggested a new and distinctly Canadian way of doing them by drawing on the alternate theatre movement. *The Drowsy Chaperone*, while superficially a love letter to the American musical, was actually a product of Toronto's well-established improv comedy movement. (Although the Broadway version of *The Drowsy Chaperone* was performed by 'triple threats', the original Toronto incarnation was acted by improv comedians.) *Come from Away*, at the time of writing the most commercially successful of all of them, has found a happy coincidence between what interests an American audience and what is paradoxically a unique reflection of Canadian culture.

Would the show have worked on Broadway if the stranded passengers had been Polish or Chinese, rather than American, or if the terrorist attack had been in Rome rather than New York? Possibly not. Yet *Come from Away* proves two things: first, each Canadian show discussed here has succeeded or failed for reasons that are different but are closely linked to the individual work. Secondly, when it comes to musical theatre, Canada continues to forge its own path, gradually overcoming its former inferiority complex.

## NOTES

1. Eric Nicol and Dave More, *Canada Cancelled Because of Lack of Interest* (Edmonton: Hurtig, 1978), 128.
2. N.B.: Wherever possible I have given the full citation of author, title and page number. However some of the newspaper articles quoted were provided by theatrical producers some years ago in the form of clippings and photocopies, and in a few cases, the page number and author's name are missing.
   'No Business like Show Business', *Economist*, 16 June 2016, https://www.economist.com/business/2016/06/16/no-business-like-show-business, accessed 22 November 2019.

3. *Globe and Mail*, June 27, 1977 (as cited in Library and Archives Canada, https://www.bac-lac.gc.ca/eng/discover/films-videos-sound-recordings/virtual-gramophone/Pages/the-dumbells-bio.aspx, accessed 19 November 2019

4. Ibid.

5. Michel Vaïs, in Contemporary Canadian Theatre: New World Visions (Toronto: Simon & Pierre, 1985); here: 118.

6. Mel Atkey, *Broadway North: The Dream of a Canadian Musical Theatre* (Toronto: Dundurn Press, 2006), 54.

7. Ross Stuart, *Encyclopaedia of Music in Canada* (Toronto: University of Toronto Press, 1981), 657.

8. Andrew Allan, *A Self-Portrait* (Toronto: Macmillan of Canada, 1974), p. 119.

9. Atkey, *Broadway North*, 54.

10. William Littler, 'Developing Opera and Musical Theatre', in *Contemporary Canadian Theatre* (Toronto: Simon & Pierre, 1985), 280.

11. Atkey, *Broadway North*, 54.

12. Margaret Laurence., 'In the Air', *Winnipeg Citizen*, 14 July 1948. Quoted in Christian Riegel, *Challenging Territory: The Writing of Margaret Laurence* (Edmonton: University of Alberta Press, 1997), 204–205.

13. Atkey, *Broadway North*, 56.

14. Julius Novick, ' "Ecstasy": The Indian's Agony', *New York Times*, 13 May, 1973, quoted in *Edmonton Journal*, 25 May 1973, 83.

15. See Anthony Sampson, *MacMillan: A Study in Ambiguity* (Penguin, 1968), 61.

16. The Charlottetown Festival, part of the Confederation Centre of the Arts, was established in 1965 and was the first professional company to be dedicated almost exclusively to the development of original Canadian musicals.

17. Don Harron, *Anne of Green Gables the Musical: 101 Things You Didn't Know* (Toronto: White Knight Books, 2008), p. 133.

18. Atkey, *Broadway North*, 105–106.

19. Ibid., 114.

20. Ibid., 231.

21. Ibid., 115.

22. Ibid., 107.

23. Mavor Moore, *Reinventing Myself* (Toronto: Stoddart, 1994), 316. Since he doesn't specify the year here, it is not clear which other musicals he is referring to, only that the Charlottetown Festival functioned as a repertory company. In its first year, *Anne of Green Gables* was performed in repertory with *Laugh with Leacock*, *Wayne and Shuster* and *Spring Thaw*. In its second year, it was with *The Ottawa Man* (an adaptation of Gogol's *The Inspector-General*) and *Private Turvey's War*. In its third season, it was with *Paradise Hill*, *Yesterday the Children were Dancing* and *Rose Latulippe*. In its fourth season, which may be the one he is referring to, it was with *Johnny Belinda*, *Sunshine Town*, and *Beyond the Fringe*.

24. Nathan Cohen, 'All about *Anne*', *Toronto Star*, 19 August 1965, 32.

25. '*Anne of Green Gables* Catches Charlottetown's Fancy', *New York Times*, 22 August 1965, 82.

26. *Times* (London), 18 April 1969.

27. Atkey, *Broadway North*, 110.

28. Harold Hobson, '*Anne* Revisited . . ', *Christian Science Monitor*, 22 October 1969, 4.

29. Atkey, *Broadway North*, 112.

30. Ibid.
31. Walter Kerr, 'Is Pollyanna Just Around the Corner?', *New York Times*, 2 January 1972, 1.
32. Richard Watts, 'Ceremony of Innocence', *New York Post*, 27 December 1971, 38.
33. Jack Gaver, '*Anne of Green Gables*: A Warm Change of Pace', *United Press International*, n.d.
34. Atkey, *Broadway North*, 72.
35. Quoted in www.olympusarts.com/hamlet.html, accessed 30 October 2005.
36. Marilyn Stasio, '. . . And Still Champion', *Cue*, 30 September 1974, 10.
37. Urjo Kareda, '*Hamlet* Rip-off Plays It Too Safe', *Toronto Daily Star*, 7 May 1975, E20.
38. William Littler, '*Kronberg: 1582*; A Pop/Rock *Hamlet* Complete with the Rosencrantz and Guildenstern Boogie', *Starweek*, 3–10 May 1975, n.p.
39. Clive Barnes, 'Play: *Rockabye Hamlet*', *New York Times*, 18 February 1976, quoted in *Maclean's*, 8 March 1976, 62.
40. Douglass Watt, 'Rock *Hamlet* Gaudy, Lifeless', *New York Daily News*, 18 February 1976, quoted in *Kansas City Times*, 19 February 1976, 70.
41. 'Cliff Pins His Hopes on Musical *Marilyn*', *Globe and Mail*, 15 January 1980.
42. Blaik Kirby, "*Hamlet*'s Birth and Death Pains on Broadway", *Toronto Globe and Mail*, 6 January 1977, 15.
43. Ibid.
44. Compared to 2085 in London's West End.
45. Vida Hope, '*The Boy Friend* on Broadway', *Plays and Players*, 25 December 1954, 12.
46. John Anthony Gilvey, *Before the Parade Passes By* (New York: St. Martin's Press, 2005), 259.
47. Atkey, *Broadway North*, 180.
48. Sylvie Drake, '*Hamlet* Takeoff at the Odyssey', *Los Angeles Times*, 25 November 1981, 4.
49. It may be instructive to note that at the time of its original Canadian production, it was often described as a play. Only after its international exposure have certain of Canada's cultural vanguards admitted, however condescendingly, that it is in fact a musical.
50. Atkey, *Broadway North*, 167.
51. Ibid.
52. Gregory Strong, 'UBC Grads Steal the Scene in Canadian Theatre', *UBC Chronicle*, Summer 1985, 14.
53. Atkey, *Broadway North*, 168.
54. John Gray, with Eric Peterson, *Billy Bishop Goes to War: A Play* (Vancouver: Talonbooks, 1981), preface.
55. Max Wyman, 'From the Wild Blue Yonder to the Great White Way', *Vancouver*, July 1979, n.p.
56. Ibid.
57. John Gray, 'Letters from the Front', *Vancouver*, October 1984, 42.
58. Ibid.
59. Ibid., 46.
60. Gray, *Billy Bishop Goes to War*, 379–404. It may be the Broadway audiences that he is talking about. Off-Broadway and regional theatre audiences might react differently.
61. Clive Barnes, *Daily News*, 9 June 1980, 580
62. Walter Kerr, '*Billy Bishop* Flies In', *New York Times*, 30 May 1980, C3.
63. Michael Coveney, '*Billy Bishop Goes to War*', *Financial Times*, 4 June 1981, n.p.
64. *Observer*, 7 June 1981, n.p.
65. Very recently, *Billy Bishop* was revived in an off–West End theatre with a rather clever variation: rather than having one actor play Bishop and the other accompanying him on the

piano, in this version the pianist also played the older Billy Bishop, while a much younger colleague played him in flashbacks.

66. Sandy Thorburn, 'Who Is the *Drowsy Chaperone*'s Muse?', Thousand Islands Theatre programme, 2009 (courtesy of Lisa Lambert and Sandy Thorburn).

67. Email to the author, 2 August 2009.

68. *The Drowsy Chaperone: Working in the Theatre*, American Theater Wing/City University Television, April 2006.

69. Phil Hahn, 'From the Fringes to Broadway: *The Drowsy Chaperone*', CTV, 7 June 2006, http://edmonton.ctv.ca/servlet/an/local/CTVNews/20060607/drowsy_chaperone_060 607, accessed 30 July 2009.

70. Second City is an improv comedy troupe originally founded in Chicago by Bernard Sahlins and Paul Sills in 1959. In 1973 a branch in Toronto was founded by Andrew Alexander. It was the Toronto offshoot that launched the television series *SCTV*, and Alexander eventually took over the Chicago operation as well. Among the graduates of the Toronto operation are Dan Ayckroyd, John Candy, and Catherine O'Hara.

71. Michael Kuchwara, Associated Press, 1 May 2006.

72. 'Howard Kissel, 'Drowsy Chaperone a Sleeping Beauty', *New York Daily News*, 2 May 2006, 40.

73. Ben Brantley, 'Nostalgic *Drowsy Chaperone* Opens on Broadway', *New York Times*, 1 May 2006, https://www.nytimes.com/2006/05/02/theater/reviews/nostalgic-drowsy-chaper one-opens-on-broadway.html, accessed 30 November 2019.

74. Richard Ouzounian, *Toronto Star*, 24 September 2007, L4.

75. *The Drowsy Chaperone: Working in the Theatre*.

76. Mel Atkey, *A Million Miles from Broadway: Musical Theatre Beyond New York and London* (Vancouver: Friendlysong Books), 143.

77. Ibid.

78. Robert Cushman, 'Quaint Musical Demands We Care', *National Post*, 11 November 2006, p. TO20.

79. Ben Brantley, 'Male Bonding—It's a Wonderful Friendship', *New York Times*, 20 February 2009, https://www.nytimes.com/2009/02/20/theater/reviews/20stor.html

80. David Rooney, *Variety*, 20 February 2009. https://variety.com/2009/legit/markets-festiv als/the-story-of-my-life-1200473571/

81. Michael Kuchwara, 'Friendship Flowers in *The Story of My Life*', *Associated Press*, 20 February 2009, http://archive.boston.com/ae/theater_arts/articles/2009/02/19/review_ friendship_flowers_in_story_of_my_life_1235078167/.

82. Peter Filichia, 'The Story on *The Story of My Life*', 23 February 2009, www.theatermania. com, accessed .

83. Email to the author, 6 August 2009.

84. The Canadian Music Theatre Project is a program at Sheridan College initiated by Michael Rubinoff to develop new Canadian musicals. Their first project was *Come from Away*.

85. Interview by the author with Michael Rubinoff, 4 May 2018.

86. Ibid.

87. Facebook message from David Hein to the author, 31 May 2019.

88. Ibid.

89. 'It is all true [ ... ] We sometimes joke about how there were 7,000 people on the planes and 9,000 people in the town, so we're trying to tell 16,000 stories in a hundred-minute

musical. [ ... ] Our goal was for the people we interviewed to come to the show and say, "You got it right, that's exactly how it happened" ' (ibid.).

90. Ibid.

91. Ben Brantley, 'Review: *Come from Away*, a Canadian Embrace on a Grim Day', *New York Times*, 12 March 2017, https://www.nytimes.com/2017/03/12/theater/come-from-away-review.html, accessed 25 November 2019.

92. Henry Hitchings, 'Touching Tale of Kindness in Face of Terror Sees Human Spirit Soar', *Evening Standard*, 19 February 2019, https://www.standard.co.uk/go/london/theatre/come-from-away-review-phoenix-theatre-a4070281.html, accessed 25 November 2019.

93. *The Drowsy Chaperone*, https://www.imdb.com/title/tt2298262/, accessed 22 November 2019.

## BIBLIOGRAPHY

Atkey, Mel. *Broadway North: The Dream of a Canadian Musical Theatre*. Toronto: Dundurn Press, 2006.

Atkey, Mel. *A Million Miles from Broadway—Musical Theatre Beyond New York and London*. Vancouver: Friendlysong Books, 2012.

Gilvey, John Anthony. *Before the Parade Passes By*, New York: St. Martin's Press, 2005.

Harron, Don. *Anne of Green Gables the Musical: 101 Things You Didn't Know*. Toronto: White Knight Books, 2008.

Moore, Mavor. *Reinventing Myself*. Toronto: Stoddart, 1994.

Michel Vaïs. *Contemporary Canadian Theatre: New World Visions*. Toronto: Simon & Pierre, 1985.

Wagner, Anton, ed. *Contemporary Canadian Theatre: New World Visions*. Toronto: Simon & Pierre, 1985.

## DISCOGRAPHY

NB: Many of these recordings are independently released and lack labels and/or catalogue numbers.

*Anne of Green Gables*. CD. Charlottetown Festival Cast. Music by Norman Campbell. Book by Don Harron. Lyrics by Don Harron, Norman Campbell, Elaine Campbell, and Mavor Moore. 1984, Attic ACDM1225.

*Billy Bishop Goes to War*. CD. Twentieth Anniversary Recording. Colonial Theatre Repertory Theatre Company. Book, music, and lyrics by John Gray. 1999, CD rl14183.

*Come from Away*. CD. Original Broadway Cast. Music and lyrics by David Hein and Irene Sankoff. The Musical Company. 2017, B06WRPXNZ5.

*The Drowsy Chaperone*. CD. Original Broadway Cast Recording. Music by Greg Morrison. Lyrics by Lisa Lambert. Book by Bob Martin and Don McKellar. 2006, Ghostlight 7915584411-2.

*Evil Dead: The Musical*. CD. Off-Broadway Cast. Music by Frank Cipola, Christopher Bond, Melissa Morris, and George Reinblatt. Book and lyrics by George Reinblatt. 2006, Time Life M19407.

*Field of Stars: Songs of the Canadian Musical Theatre*. CD. 2005. Compiled by Jim Betts. Northern River Music.

*Strike!* Demo CD. 2006. Music and lyrics by Danny Schur. Book by Danny Schur and Rick Chafe.

*Tristan.* CD. 2007. Shaw Festival Cast. Book, music, and lyrics by Jay Turvey and Paul Sportelli. JPCD04.

## Videography

*Billy Bishop Goes to War.* DVD. 2020. Directed by Barbara Willis Sweete. Brightspark Productions. BSPK779.

# CHAPTER 11

······································································

# MUSICALS IN MEXICO
## *Borders and Bridges*

······································································

### EMILIO MÉNDEZ

MEXICO City theatres have been importing Broadway and West End musicals since the mid-1950s. There have been explicitly Mexican adaptations or reterritorialisations of musicals such as *Grease* (1973),[1] *Cats* (1991), *The Best Little Whorehouse in Texas* (1996), *Starlight Express* (1997), and *Blood Brothers* (1998). In the parallel reality of these shows with their localized translations, Mexican high school girls have Marine boyfriends posted in Korea; Bustopher Jones, uprooted from his St. James Street origins, is transmogrified into a mariachi cat; and the best little pleasure house gets Tex-Mexified and migrates south of the border. The mixed results of these modifications prove that while audiences demand certain concessions, they also need to be targeted with caution. Julissa's production of *Grease* raised a level of enthusiasm that her adaptations of *Little Whorehouse* and *Blood Brothers* could not match.[2] Although the company's drive kept *Cats* running for over a year, many of its performers and creatives met with indifference when they teamed up again to present *Starlight* for just over a hundred performances.

Reviewing the history of the Mexican importation of musicals, in terms not just of the aspirations of their producers but also of their tangible successes and failures, casts further light on the reticence of national audiences. Enthusiastic musical-minded impresarios built theatres such as Teatro San Rafael (1977), the two Televiteatros (1983), and Teatro Telcel (2013). Ambitious refurbishments turned the Nuevo Ideal into the Teatro Manolo Fábregas (1965), made the Teatro-Cine Estadio over into Teatro Silvia Pinal (1988), and repurposed the Orfeón and Polanco cinemas (1997). By the turn of the millennium, Teatro Silvia Pinal had been bought out and converted into a megachurch; the Orfeón, having squandered its $10 million renovation, has been dark ever since *Beauty and the Beast* (1997) closed after only one year. As successful runs go, *Fiddler on the Roof* (1970) broke a local record for a musical with four hundred performances; *Sugar* (1975) overtook this with five hundred; *Joseph and the Amazing Technicolor Dreamcoat* (1983) reached almost nine hundred;[3] and the first production of *Les Misérables* (2002) achieved a little over seven hundred. Conversely, *A Funny Thing Happened on the Way to the Forum* (1962) ran for a mere nineteen performances, and *Billy* (1975), one of the few direct transfers from the West End, lasted barely a month.

Against this backdrop, the Mexican theatre industry has built its own catalogue of original musicals haunted by the aims and structures of imported shows. *Evita* (1981) was followed by musicals based on a number of influential Mexican women: Hernán Cortés's interpreter (*Malinche*, 1987); the country's most iconic artist (*Frida*, 2007); and an insurgent from the War of Independence (*Josefa*, 2017). These were constrained by the same 'naïve and simplistic historical view' that Frank Rich identified in *Evita*,[4] and they also lacked the traditional political punch of the Mexican *revista*.[5] In certain respects, *Frida*—a resounding flop—is symptomatic of the state of the homegrown musical, suffering both from production problems and a harsh critical reception: backers withdrew over the opening weekend, and reviewers denounced the biographical work as gender-regressive. The critic Estela Leñero noted that the onstage Kahlo claimed that all she wanted in her life was to give her husband, Diego Rivera, a child. Calling the musical's dramaturgical research 'poor and schematic', Leñero regretted the way the artist's portrayal sidestepped her political views and personal panache in favour of emphasising Kahlo's pain and suffering.[6]

Rock musicals have taken on Goethe (*Fausto-rock*, 1984), Shakespeare (*Hamlet*, 1984) and Bram Stoker (*Drácula*, 1998). All of these echo *Jesus Christ Superstar* (1975). Even before the local productions of *Cats* and *Starlight Express*, an ecological musical tapped a similar anthropomorphic vein, but with plants: *¡Qué plantón! (Supplanters!* 1989). *Houdini, la magia del amor* (*Houdini, the Magic of Love*, 1997), ghosted by *The Phantom*

FIG. 11.1 Itati Cantoral as Frida Kahlo in the bio-musical *Frida, un canto a la vida* (*Frida, a Tribute to Life*, 2007), composed by Marcos Lifshitz. Photograph: Marcos Delgado/EPA © Shutterstock.

*of the Opera's* (1999) flashback opening and penchant for smoke and mirrors, was a sung-through love story about the world's most famous escapologist. Finally, *Mentiras* (*Lies*, 2009), the longest-running Mexican musical, recalls *Mamma Mia!*'s (2009) 'who's-the-father' plot line in a Mexican whodunit jukebox musical of schmaltzy 1980s Mexican pop hits commenting on the story of four women romantically and sexually involved with the same man. Although these national musicals either draw on themes directly concerning Mexico or address universal issues occasionally incorporating Mexican motifs, their dominant style is the result of choices made within the set of constraints of the Broadway and West End models.[7]

Mexican theatre artists were slow to push against these constraints, despite decades of political and aesthetic reservations which characterized the ambivalent reception of the foreign musical in Mexico. The critic, journalist, and political activist Carlos Monsiváis noted that between 1945 and 1960, 'regardless of the cinema's absolute drawing power, the theatre attracts bourgeois and middle-class audiences; enthralled by the performances, they discuss the plots over dinner'.[8] Spectators, Monsiváis argued, began deserting Hispanic comedies, drawn instead to translated American theatre and musicals in particular. He found Mexican society to fall 'halfway between Americanisation and nationalism': no longer satisfied by Spanish comedies and melodramas but also avoiding unconditional surrender to Broadway.[9] Such reluctance was framed in what the Mexican author Carlos Fuentes considered the 'psychological, historical problem' of the US-Mexican border. For him, that unique frontier represents a scar 'because it's the place where we lost half our territory to [the US] in the War of 1847–48. We don't forget that'.[10] Mexican cultural memory has caused spectators and critics alike to pick uncomfortably at this symbolic scar throughout the second half of the twentieth century in their reception of the very foreign institution of the musical.

A yearning to participate in the global conversation led the Mexican middle classes to shift gradually from a stance of resistance to one of acceptance. Monsiváis described a 'submissive and meticulous importing of Broadway musical hits' from the mid-1950s onwards, leading to 'the assimilation of musicals which, in the space of a few years, go from "gringada" to the irreversible predilection of the middle class'.[11] There are four major stages in this process of assimilation. The first, from 1956 to 1967, saw the earliest Anglophone imports, even though at the same time theatres in Mexico City were prohibited from charging more than twelve pesos per ticket, and the Bank of Mexico had set a fixed currency exchange of twelve and a half pesos per US dollar.[12] Musicals flourished during a second stage, from the liberation of ticket prices in 1968 up until Mexico City's devastating earthquake of 1985. A patchy third stage followed, ending only in 1997–2000 with the involvement of OCESA Entretenimiento, a leading promoter of live entertainment in the region, and with the 1999 announcement of Televisa, the most powerful media corporation in Latin America, of its intention to leave the theatre business,[13] as well as the sale of its subsidiary company Televiteatro in 2000.[14] Finally, an ongoing fourth phase has seen the consolidation of OCESA, the emergence of new producers, and the condescending lack of interest on the part of many professional critics in reviewing musicals.[15]

The *gringada* discourse, a distinctive approach to criticism developed by Mexican reviewers, insisted on the alien and commodified nature of the musical. Its precedents go back to the 'first phase' period of globalisation. In 1884 Mexico began to discover Gilbert and Sullivan's repertoire. The touring Charles D. Hess's Acme Opera Company presented original-language versions of *H.M.S. Pinafore, Iolanthe*, and *The Pirates of Penzance* in Mexico City, along with Michael Balfe and Alfred Bunn's *The Bohemian Girl* and Vincent Wallace and Edward Fitzball's *Maritana*. José Joaquín Moreno, impresario of Mexico's Gran Teatro Nacional, hired 'The Largest, Strongest and Most Complete Organization performing English Opera in America'.[16] Newspapers proclaimed that Hess had 'the honour of introducing to Mexico the first English Opera Company'.[17] Critics did not receive the company enthusiastically, however.

The most vehement objections to the English-language catalogue came from Manuel Gutiérrez Nájera, one of Mexico's leading literary, theatre, and music critics. In his review he conflated British and North American perspectives regarding the relationship between aesthetic and commercial decisions. His arguments would be echoed in the Mexican reception of musicals for generations to come. They also betray the compulsion to reopen old cultural wounds:

> I do not mean to judge English music lightly. [ ... ] I am referring only to *Maritana, Bohemian Girl, Pinafore*, the only English operas [ ... ] I shall hear, since I lack the required courage to attend the performance of any other. [ ... ] These are neither operas, nor bouffes, but nuisances in three or four yawns, with three or four notes distributed among thirty or forty characters. These operas without plot and without music are not as typical of England as they are of the US. [ ... ] Believing as I do that the French bouffes degrade art, I still prefer them to the gullible and clownish Yankees. [ ... ] I am the first to admire the North American people; the marvels they achieve through labour astonish me. I wish we had learned their industriousness and determination, but I abhor, loathe and detest that art of theirs that is not art, but a pretext to earn money. [ ... ] Let us stand, then, against the first charge of the Yankee art, without handing our theatres over to the clowns. Above all, let us avoid the contagion.[18]

Gutiérrez Nájera's stance has reverberated throughout the history of the assimilation of musicals. His rationale introduces capitalism into the discussion, and with it the economic considerations for assessing the response to these forms of theatre. When judging musicals such as those by Gilbert and Sullivan as expressions of a mercenary non-art, he anticipates a critical view common to theatre critics well into the twenty-first century. *La cultura en México* dismissed *No, No Nanette* as 'theatre with a capitalist mentality, but a socialist professionalism; to make money you have to spend money', and its only result was transposing 'a faithful enough facsimile of Broadway's least transcendental trifle' to Mexico.[19] Félix Cortés Camarillo denounced the commodification of protests and nostalgia in *Jesus Christ Superstar* and *Grease*, respectively.[20] In 1977 Juan Jaime Larios accused Mexican producers of being carried away by their commercial instincts in always considering a foreign show to be potentially more lucrative than a Mexican one.[21] Rafael Solana, recognising that New York also had 'good' theatre to offer, dismissed the 1981 revival of *The Fantasticks* as 'for gringos only', objecting to its simple-mindedness.[22] Estela Leñero regretted OCESA's investment in the Mexican 'manufacturing' of *The Producers* (2007), a show she found alien to the country's 'artistic universe'. While acknowledging that it might make its producers a profit, she feared it would keep them from contributing to the development of national culture.[23] Mexican critics of this phenomenon of theatrical globalisation and the theatrical standardisation they believe it promulgates attest to the history of journalistic resistance to its consequences.

Mexican spectators have longed to be included in the global conversation on theatre, and they have struggled for over a century to come to terms with the alien form and content of the musical.[24] Around the end of the twentieth century, however, Monsiváis found that the local response to *Beauty and the Beast*, *The Phantom of the Opera*, and *Les Misérables* validated the musical's assimilation.[25] Overlapping cultural-aesthetic and economic considerations, together with the 'gringada' discourse, have hindered the assimilation of the foreign form and spurred the development of Mexico's own contemporary musical theatre.

## THE *NI FU NI FA* OVERTURE: NEITHER A MEXICAN *REVISTA* NOR AN INTEGRATED MUSICAL

In 1955, one year before Mexico began importing shows, a young, eager, and inexperienced team attempted to produce the first Mexican musical of the twentieth century: *Ni fu ni fa*.[26] Edmundo Mendoza, who was to become one of the busiest musical choreographers in Mexico, created what he called a 'musical comedy' in collaboration with his fellow dancer and journalist Beatriz Querol,[27] backed by the prominent lawyer and presidential advisor Antonio Luna Arroyo.[28] The experiment promised to foster multidisciplinary and international connections. The direction was by Salvador Novo, one of the country's pre-eminent directors, playwrights, and producers, a poet in his own right and chronicler of Mexico City. Arnold Belkin, a painter of Canadian origin who had assisted the muralist David Alfaro Siqueiros, was responsible for the stage design. John Sakmari, a Pennsylvanian dancer and alumnus of New York's New Dance Group, was in charge of the choreography. Rosenda Monteros, the young actress who had first billing in the programme, was part of the dance company of Katherine Dunham and would go on to be one of Mexico's foremost theatre artists, while Sergio Magaña, a young but already esteemed playwright, wrote the song 'The Inferiority Complex' especially for the show.

*Ni fu ni fa* translates, perhaps inauspiciously, as 'neither here nor there' or 'neither one thing nor the other', and the show was a resounding flop. Its artistic and economic failure notwithstanding, *Ni fu ni fa* demonstrates Mexico's complex negotiation with its particular heritage of musical performance, the local conditions for theatrical production, and the desire to partake in the cross-cultural interactions of musical theatre. While asserting in the programme note that through willpower and talent, Edmundo Mendoza had 'resolved to conquer a dream, to stage a musical comedy',[29] the actor Castillón Bracho suggested that this show would bridge traditions and, by aspiring to 'musical comedy', border the integrated musical. *Ni fu ni fa*, he claimed, was 'an ensemble composed of [ ... ] songs, dances, and jokes united in a plot that says something while justifying what is seen on stage', instead of the 'series of songs, dances, and jokes in isolation' characteristic of revues and variety acts that Mexican audiences could see at venues such as the Tívoli, Lírico or Follies.[30] Such a claim conveys a local need for a more coherent and cohesive musical dramaturgy. This urge was developing, perhaps as a reaction to the dramaturgical decline of the Mexican revue, and was already spreading among theatre-goers and critics alike.

The Mexican revue or *teatro de revista* had a musical dramaturgy all of its own, which began to decline in the 1930s. The plots of these one-hour shows revolved around an often satirical central theme, as Pablo Dueñas and Jesús Flores y Escalante describe, of either a patriotic, nostalgic, erotic, or political nature. These authors note that 60 percent of the musical numbers in a Mexican revue have at least something to do with the plot. Lyrics, they say, 'kept a continuity with the plot, since the writers of the book wrote them along with the musicians'. Popular songs of the moment made up another 20 percent of the numbers by accommodating their lyrics to the plot. The remaining 20 percent were numbers entirely unrelated to the plot that, as Dueñas and Flores put it, would lend a certain beauty to the show.[31]

A number of factors contributed to the *revista*'s decline. Dueñas and Flores y Escalante note that by the 1930s it had become common practice to cobble together a weak plot around a single song based solely on its popularity, a move which began to dictate set design and even the casting, with multiple orchestras and up to five singers required to capitalize on the tune's appeal, such that the *revista* increasingly began to resemble a variety act. The Principal, the *revista* genre's main theatre, burned down and gave way to venues dedicated to variety acts and rapid-fire political sketches, a trend that lasted until the 1960s.[32] By 1955 Maria y Campos considered that decades of politically motivated, even revolutionary Mexican music theatre 'had been reduced to the work of a single comedian: Palillo'.[33] According to Dueñas and Flores y Escalante, Palillo emerged from the marked shift in which the Mexican musical *revista* eliminated its book almost completely, giving way to the improvisation and personal showcasing of individual performers.[34] On the other hand, the growing film and radio industry began recruiting theatre writers, composers, and performers. Radio in particular took the place of *revistas* in popularising new songs and reporting on current events.[35]

While Castillón had promised that *Ni fu ni fa* would counteract the excesses of the *revista* structure, his praise of willpower and talent foreshadows the misleading discourse that prized imagination, drive, and even youth over proper training and craft. Such praise is especially relevant in a country which even today lacks formal musical theatre training programmes at universities and conservatoires, furthering the general perception that there is no real need to foster musical performers and creators. Although in his self-penned résumé there is no mention of his having taken playwriting or dramatic courses, Edmundo Mendoza had previously trained as a dancer.[36] In 1951 he entered the Academia de la Danza Mexicana (Mexican Academy of Dance) and later became a member of the company of the dancer José Limon.[37] *Cine mundial* underlined the fact that he wrote *Ni fu ni fa*'s libretto with great enthusiasm.[38] In contrast, Sergio Magaña, the author of the show's one original song, studied in the School of Philosophy and Literature at the National Autonomous University of Mexico. He attended the class on dramatic theory and composition taught by Mexico's leading playwright of the time, Rodolfo Usigli.[39] Magaña declared that Usigli threw him out of his class: typically, he considered himself an autodidact.[40]

Mendoza made a number of amateurish mistakes. Salvador Novo, in his weekly column, charted the one technical and dress rehearsal the company ever had in its chaotic hours before opening night. He praised the group's guts and zeal but noted that in embarking upon this enterprise, the inexperienced twenty-four-year-old Mendoza had gone all out by renting an essentially unequipped theatre and had to hire lighting equipment independently at last-minute prices. Novo claimed that his personal participation was limited to advising the troupe on the nuances and gestures of the brief dialogues linking their musical numbers.[41]

Some reviewers, however, could not find Novo's direction of *Ni fu ni fa* anywhere in the show. Rafael Solana contended that the young ensemble exposed the 'almost entirely negative portrait of their director, who evidently had not marked them with any of his distinctive features'.[42] *Cine mundial* had the same impression; for them it was doubtful that Novo had actually directed the show at all: 'if he had, it would not lack such agility and rhythm'.[43]

Although branded as *comedia musical* (musical comedy), *Ni fu ni fa* was dramaturgically closer to a *revista*. There is no copy of the libretto at the Biblioteca de las Artes in Mexico City,[44] but certain elements can be reconstructed from reviews. Its three acts revisited scenes from the lives of the mother and grandmother of a contemporary Mexican woman.[45] Aside from Magaña's song, the show lacked original music, resorting to a 'musical retrospective' and rehashing numbers from different eras from the 1920s to the 1950s.[46] González Márquez at *Cine mundial* accused Mendoza of plagiarising musical numbers from previous *revistas*, such as 'El Deshollinador' ('The Chimney-Sweep') from *Señoritas garantizadas* (*Ladies Guaranteed*).[47] Indeed, Mendoza had worked on that show the previous year,[48] and now he reprised his Chimney-Sweep role.[49] The actresses and dancers Beatriz Querol and Rosenda Monteros portrayed, respectively, a flapper from the silent-film era and a 1950s femme fatale.[50] The latter performed a number in which, during a session of psychoanalysis, her character remembered past boyfriends, to the strains of French music, mambo, and jazz.[51]

However, 'The Inferiority Complex', the original number with music and lyrics by Sergio Magaña, promised to be a potential hit. Magaña's playwriting career had taken off four years before,[52] and his name alone was deemed a guarantee of success. *Cine* mundial called 'The Inferiority Complex' 'a superb song'. Moreover, the newspaper speculated that its title alone dramaturgically motivated Mendoza in the development of his dialogue. It described people coming out of the theatre merrily humming 'The Inferiority Complex', even though the cast, lacking singing capabilities, spoke it rather than properly singing it.[53]

The *gringada* discourse surfaced in *Ni fu ni fa*'s critical reception. *Cine mundial* resented the fact that 'North American dances of the silver screen' had overly influenced John Sakmari's choreography.[54] The objection was more over creative than cultural issues. If it had not been for that influence, *Cine mundial* argued, the choreography would have to have been created from scratch.

The failure of *Ni fu ni fa* posed challenges and questions for Mexican musical theatre artists and their future endeavours. It ran from 3 to 18 November, performing twice daily, with all tickets priced at twelve pesos. In hindsight, Novo would call *Ni fu ni fa* a 'premature musical venture',[55] but in an already premature enterprise, its structure appears naively avant-garde. Although its programme committed the show to pushing the storytelling boundaries of the *revista* in the direction of the integrated musical in this respect it emphatically failed to deliver. While some cast members were capable dancers, the show's profligate use of stage conventions came off as sophomoric. The integrated musical calls for an integrated collaboration, dramaturgical guidance, and attention to detail in order to articulate the drive of enthusiastic newcomers, and what lessons *Ni fu ni fa* offered would go unheeded.

# 'WE'D SAVE FOR [IT]/AND SLAVE FOR [IT]/ WE'D EVEN MISBEHAVE FOR [IT]/THAT CERTAIN THING CALLED . . .' THE MUSICAL

The twelve-peso stage in the assimilation of the musical reflected global economic norms as well as Mexico City's socio-political conditions. The Bank of Mexico maintained a fixed currency exchange rate of twelve and a half pesos per US dollar between April 1954 and August 1976, coinciding with the twelve-peso regulation (1954–1968). The Federal District Bureau of Spectacles fixed this maximum price regardless of the size, capacity, or location of the theatre. The first Broadway musical presented in Mexico was *Bells Are Ringing* (1957). A month before its Mexican premiere, the most expensive evening ticket at New York's Shubert Theatre had cost $8.05; the cheapest one, for matinées, went for $1.75.[56] The audience capacity of 1,460 seats at the Shubert Theatre should be compared with that of the 1,200-seat Teatro del Bosque, where *Bells Are Ringing* opened in October 1957, with all seats at twelve pesos, or less than one dollar.

There was also a socio-political condition that overlapped with the economic restrictions for producing any theatrical entertainment in Mexico City in the mid-1950s—the fourteen-year administration of Ernesto Uruchurtu, known as the 'Iron

Mayor'. Producers presented all sorts of arguments to the Bureau of Spectacles in favour of removing restrictions on ticket prices, but to no avail. Although he contributed to Mexico City's modernisation, the mayor also spearheaded a moral crusade against what he considered pornographic theatre, closing *revista* venues and cabarets and enforcing tight censorship. Producers willing to risk the hazards of importing foreign shows to Mexico City had to face the music and dance to Uruchurtu's tune.

Framed by such conditions, it becomes clearer why the very first musical ever to be performed in Mexico City was the small-scale British show *The Boy Friend*, which premiered in 1956, somewhat surprisingly capturing the attention of audiences and critics alike. The principal agents in charge of this production were the Bostonian Reynold 'Rene' Anselmo and Spanish Civil War refugee Luis de Llano Palmer. Both had worked as producers in the emerging television industry,[57] and both would play decisive roles in its development.[58]

They met in 1955 and agreed that Mexico 'was ripe for musical comedy in the Cole Porter tradition, and they started casting about for a likely musical'.[59] Indeed, after considering *Can-Can* and *Silk Stockings*,[60] de Llano decided on Sandy Wilson's musical because he found it dealt with a period familiar to Mexican audiences, was easily translatable,[61] and required only a small cast, thereby proving to be the most viable option for Mexico City in the mid-1950s.

The press, including the *New York Times* and *Time* magazine, was unanimous in hailing the Mexican production of *The Boy Friend* a hit. Bill Llano wrote that the performers received warm ovations every night,[62] while Alberto Catani concluded that this was clean entertainment which would amuse both young and old and was well worth its ticket price.[63] An American reviewer known only as 'Pete' recorded that the show had the 'audience Charlestoning in the aisles'.[64]

Although the quandary of how to classify this new form remained, *The Boy Friend* did function as a connection between Mexican traditions of music theatre and the integrated Anglophone musical. The program and playbills announced it as *comedia musical* (musical comedy). Journalists such as Luis Granados, Bill Llano, and Maria y Campos held fast in ascribing it to the local tradition of *revista*.[65] Maria y Campos asserted that *The Boy Friend* would trigger the renaissance of a genre that, in his opinion, had been in a state of shameful decline for over fifteen years. By contrast, Octavio Alba chose to employ the production's own denomination: he called it a

> theatrical innovation [and an] authentic musical comedy, not the Palillo sketches with political satire; not a string of disjointed musical numbers; not a parade of variety acts. A clean musical comedy, with original music, simple dialogues, above all else, very dynamic.[66]

In contrasting *The Boy Friend* with Palillo's brand of political satire, Alba distinguishes what he considered an authentic musical comedy from shows pushing a political agenda. For Alcaraz, the original *revista* managed to be 'comical, political, amusing, musical, engaging [ ... ] when society was settling after the Mexican Revolution'.[67] He believed the *revista* was 'for everybody', as opposed to music theatre forms 'born in the Japanese Empire or the Operetta (of Paris and Vienna) aimed at a specific sector of their respective societies.' He even drew a parallel to the musicals of Gilbert and Sullivan, finding that 'thanks to their parody of everyday Victorian life they could travel to other times and places [ ... ] even on Broadway or film'.[68] The dumbing down of satire, however, was one of the factors in the *revista*'s decline. As Luis de Tavira noted, it 'succumbed to the ease of its success [ ... ] corrupted by the political interest to which it was once committed'.[69] Consequently, Mexican musicals would have to break with their forerunners' political aims.

The critical praise of *The Boy Friend* contrasted dramatically with its poor box-office take. Luis Vicent postulated an income of 720,000 pesos over the three-month run of the show, with expenses amounting to 707,000—a net profit of just 13,000 pesos ($1,040). He predicted that few others would now dare produce musicals in Mexico City,[70] but despite the daunting prospect of charging less than a dollar for the most expensive seats in the house, some pioneers did take the risk. The actors Sergio Corona and Alfonso Arau teamed up to import and perform in the British musical *Cranks* (1957).[71] De Llano and Anselmo managed throughout the twelve-peso period to produce *Bells Are Ringing*, *Redhead* (1960), *The Fantasticks*, and *Where's Charley?* (both 1961). Robert W. Lerner's Mexican productions of his brother Alan's musicals *My Fair Lady* (1959) and *Brigadoon* (1960) soon followed, as did Stephen Sondheim's *Forum*. What the industry lost in revenue, it gained in experience, which would become especially evident during the period between the unfreezing of ticket prices in 1968 and the 1985 earthquake.

# 'ALMOST LIKE BEING IN LOVE': MEXICAN EXPERIMENTS WITH THE INTEGRATED MUSICAL

The struggle to create integrated Mexican musicals emerged from the importation of shows during the twelve-peso period that provided a gradual familiarisation with the form's diversity. Tensions between the *revista* tradition and the relative novelty of the musical form remained at the forefront of the theatrical scene. The first two Mexican musicals of the decade—indeed, of the modern era—were *Rentas congeladas* (*Rent Freeze*, 1960) and *Las fascinadoras* (*Fascinating Girls*, 1961).

*Rent Freeze* raised high expectations, with its book, lyrics, and music by Sergio Magaña, by this point one of Mexico's leading playwrights. He first previewed the work as a one-man show, which further heightened the anticipation of a full production. Magaña proved to be a capable composer of catchy and ironic tunes, pastiching musical styles such as the *ranchera* and the *corrido* with rock 'n' roll, ballads, and even opera.[72] These musical numbers were an improvement over the one song he had composed for

FIG. 11.2 Mexican spectators at Esperanza Iris Theatre watch a crowded musical number from *Rentas congeladas* (*Rent Freeze*), directed by Virgilio Mariel and choreographed by Raul Flores and Xavier Fuentes. Photograph: INBAL/CITRU, Archivo Sergio Magaña, provided by the author.

*Ni fu ni fa*, even if one critic considered them to be, for the most part, a rehash of already-known melodies.[73]

The libretto, however, seemed overburdened with songs and failed to develop the plot, which revolved around how Mexico City ended its rent freeze around the end of the 1950s, including the resulting class conflict between tenants and landlords. Magaña articulated this theme with a doppelganger trope and added a dash of Shakespeare's *Measure for Measure* and Mark Twain's *The Prince and the Pauper*: the Mayor of the city just happens to be identical to Juan, one of the anguished tenants. Most critics, however, expressed their disappointment at an unbalanced, non-partisan show that defined itself as '¡Authentic Mexican *Revista*!'[74] and 'musical comedy (operetta)' in the same billing.[75]

The *gringada* discourse resurfaced in the press, this time regarding an original Mexican musical. Solana, its most lenient reviewer, considered *Rent Freeze* more akin to Mexican *revistas* and attempted to establish the show's artistic and idiosyncratic heritage: 'It shares with those *revistas* the popular and the typically Mexican traits which have maintained them for years'.[76] Marcela del Río disagreed. For her, it required

MUSICALS IN MEXICO: BORDERS AND BRIDGES      327

more than a Mexican author for a musical to be authentically Mexican: she held that the melodies and structure were 'of a distinctly North American nature'.[77] Broadway's haunting of this Mexican musical, she believed, was a drawback to Magaña's original intention. She asked some critical questions of the production: 'Why not rely on the characteristics of our music? Why not examine our own ways? Why this eagerness to imitate? In the United States they have a lot of experience in this arena. Why not try to follow a more genuine trajectory, then, a less artificial one?'[78] For the critic Fernando Mota,[79] this was *Rent Freeze*'s central issue—its determined resolve to imitate a foreign model:

> A stage entertainment of this nature that imitates [ ... ] this type of theatrical entertainment in the American style turns out to be, for a local audience still uncontaminated by these sorts of tastes, a stage-show more disconcerting than amusing.[80]

*Rent Freeze* ran from 31 August to 11 September 1960. It was only revived in 2019, with dramaturgical revisions but this time without Magaña's score, which appears to have been lost. The stylistic ambivalence between *revista* and musical persisted, bringing the show closer to what Julian Woolford describes as a 'play with songs', its drama advanced primarily through the spoken text.[81]

*Fascinating Girls* was the first truly successful Mexican musical, especially compared to its predecessors. Many critics reacted positively, the press celebrated its excellent box-office take, and the audience kept it running for over a hundred performances at the 1,100-seat Teatro de los Insurgentes.[82] This 1961 show by the agronomist and actor Felipe Santander, based on an idea by Jaime Rojas, with music by Raúl Sáyago, came closer than its forerunners to the experience of a fully integrated musical. It not only ran longer than previous Mexican musicals, but also for longer than *Brigadoon* and *Bells Are Ringing*. Lya Engel called the *Ni fu ni fa* veteran Edmundo Mendoza 'an ace at musical comedy and one of its initiators in Mexico'.[83] He brought to the staging of *Fascinating Girls* his experience choreographing *Bells Are Ringing* and *The Boy Friend*, and it is conceivable that his latest dance numbers networked inter-theatrically with these imported shows.[84] With this musical, Engel divined 'an overpowering movement' in Mexican theatre.[85] Although critics continued to romanticize the enthusiasm and willpower of the company, they also praised the size and scope of their effort. Rafael Solana pegged *Fascinating Girls* as a hit, 'one of the happiest musical comedies yet seen in Mexico'. For him, only *My Fair Lady* was superior, but he believed that Santander and Sáyago's show actually equaled *Redhead* and *Bells*, and in his judgement *Fascinating Girls* was far more noteworthy than *The Fantasticks* and *Brigadoon*.[86] Maria y Campos claimed it 'blazed a trail for the genre's renaissance' in Mexico.[87]

The meta-theatrical plot of *Fascinating Girls* gave the show some appeal, but it can also be read as a commentary on the history of Mexican musicals up to that moment. The show was about a group of university students with showbiz aspirations confronting the obstacles of putting on a musical. The company's youthfulness provided it with 'a pleasant freshness and an authentically young atmosphere', according to Maria y

Campos.[88] Whether or not *Ni fu ni fa* or *Rent Freeze* was a direct reference for Santander and Sáyago, both were evoked in the plot of *Fascinating Girls*, which is indicative of how appealing audiences in Mexico find the ups and downs of show business.

However simplistic, the musical's structure connoted an evolution from *Ni fu ni fa* and *Rent Freeze*. Although most reviews chastised the overly melodramatic tone of the show, it received generally sympathetic, if slightly condescending, appraisals. Solana and Engel agreed in finding the plot appropriately entertaining for the genre. More demanding assessments identified the book as the central problem. 'That a piece of theatre contains song and dance does not excuse the neglect of the dramatic dynamic of the entire comedy', judged Mara Reyes, who accused Santander and Sáyago of exaggerating the importance of the musical aspects.[89] The show was unbalanced, according to François Baguer, since the first act ran to an hour and a half and the second lasted only around half an hour. Having such a lengthy first act was, for Baguer, a 'capital offense for a *revista* or "musical comedy", in which lightness should prevail', and he called for them to recalibrate the show.[90]

Unusually for Mexican musicals, the creators of *Fascinating Girls* paid dramaturgical attention to reviews. Antonio Magaña Esquivel revisited the show a month after its opening and discovered significant adjustments to the production based on Baguer's critique which had made the book lighter and given the show a better balance. Magaña Esquivel reported that the cuts 'alleviated' the musical's more exorbitant melodramatic touches.[91] There remained scenes in need of editing, but the production's immediate response to dramaturgical criticism was sincere and should have remained standard procedure in the development of Mexican musicals.

Raúl Sáyago's music proved to be one of *Fascinating Girls*' main assets.[92] Maria y Campos described the score as 'easy and playful as behooves the genre' while characteristic of a skillful and original composer,[93] and Engel found it 'catchy', claiming that 'all Mexico would be singing it soon'.[94] As with *Rent Freeze*, the cultural identity of the music was subject to question. Jazz and calypso stood out as the most striking rhythms of *Fascinating Girls*, and Magaña Esquivel regretted that the show did not remember, 'even for a moment', Mexico, 'so rich in rhythms, dancing styles, colour, and folklore'.[95]

During this initial phase a daring and innovative musical emerged from what was at the time an unexpected combination of sources. The book and exceptional lyrics were by the poet Alfonso Reyes and the direction by the reckless young Juan José Gurrola, who earned the title '*l'enfant terrible* of Mexican theatre'; their work narrated the story of Henry Désiré Landru, the notorious French serial killer. Even though Reyes had written it between 1929 and 1953 and had himself called it an operetta, the *Landrú* that premiered in 1964 can be considered an integrated Mexican musical in its own right, both in its libretto and in its staging.[96] Rafael Elizondo composed the score for this production, which incorporated styles such as tango, march, and Charleston, with a touch of Charlie Chaplin and Kurt Weill,[97] and received general acclaim for its catchiness and for accommodating Reyes's irony-laden verse. Elizondo orchestrated his music with drums, bass guitar, and a piano that he himself played in every performance. The writer and music critic Juan Vicente Melo believed that with the inspired Elizondo, 'Mexican musical comedy had found the musician it needed and deserved'.[98] The intimate space and experimental spirit of Casa del Lago, where *Landrú* was developed and performed, fostered the theatricality and innovative character of the production. The playwright and critic Jorge Ibargüengoitia, despite being *Landrú's* principal detractor, nonetheless considered it a hit, finding in it two saving graces: 'First, there is no single romantic moment, which is the plague and death of lyric theatre; second, the reduced cast and the unfinished text achieve very interesting surrealist effects, such as having the actor that plays Landrú (and who looks a lot like Alfonso Reyes) entering as the Police Chief, so that it is never quite clear who is talking'.[99] *Landrú* had only one weekly performance, on Sundays, but the enthusiastic audience response encouraged the producers to introduce a second performance, which also played to a packed house. Critics hailed Gurrola's staging, and Melo went as far as to envisage a revitalisation that Gurrola and Elizondo might bring to musical theatre, possibly even creating an entirely new genre. However, the theatrical trail they blazed with *Landrú* took them further afield.

# 'OPEN A NEW WINDOW/OPEN A NEW DOOR': THE NEW RHYTHM OF SUCCESSFUL MUSICALS IN MEXICO CITY

From 1968 to 1985 productions of certain musicals, both imported and indigenous, became profitable enterprises in Mexico City. The four-month run of *Hello, Dolly* (1968) was not a commercial success, but it was the first musical production allowed to charge a range of seat prices, at twelve, twenty-five, or forty pesos. Novo recorded how this shift in the box office was reflected in the house:

> Curiously, all 40-peso seats were occupied, as were all the 12-peso seats, where we had the chauffeurs sit. The 25-peso section, however, was almost empty, as if in demonstration of the middle-class's non-existence. There's only rich and poor, or maybe the rich like to show off, and the less-so like to act as if they were rich and that the 40 pesos doesn't scare them.[100]

The box office began to stabilize the following year, earning the partnership of Lew Riley and Manolo Fábregas a record five and a half million pesos for their production of *Man of La Mancha*.[101]

Fábregas, who directed and starred in *My Fair Lady* in 1959, became a prominent producer of hits such as *Fiddler on the Roof*, and, in association with Robert W. Lerner, *No, No, Nanette* (1972). Silvia Pinal, the leading lady in *Bells*, went on to play *Mame* in the successful Lerner production (1973). Lerner established the practice of bringing in a choreographer and technical advisors from the United States while entrusting the direction to local talent. This method, also adopted by Fábregas, ensured that the original technical demands of choreography and technical stagecraft were met, while a native-Spanish-speaking director attuned the shows to local perspectives. José Luis Ibáñez, Lerner's top-shelf director for the period, became an expert in the genre. His work directing early modern Spanish theatre and his interest in its verbal demands and poetry also made him the foremost translator of musicals. The Lerner-Ibáñez duo produced a technically accomplished *Pippin* (1974), which nonetheless failed to move the audience. In 1979, however, they scored a hit with *Annie*, which played twice daily from Tuesdays to Sundays and lasted a year. This conjunction of well-honed productions and genuine expertise contributed decisively to the assimilation of musical theatre and its conventions.

While Anselmo and de Llano persevered in television, the latter's daughter, Julissa, went on to become a producer, translator, and star in her own right. Her localized translation of *Grease* has made it the most frequently revived musical in Mexico.[102] Instead of faithfully replicating the Broadway production, her *Joseph and the Amazing Technicolor Dreamcoat* was designed by a Mexican team led by David Antón and proved an enormous hit. In this promising climate, Mexican producers felt more confident in undertaking their own original musicals. Their source materials included a romantic comedy by the nineteenth-century Mexican playwright Manuel Eduardo de Gorostiza (*Contigo pan y cebolla* [*For Poorer, for Stone-Broke*, 1972]), a novel by Émile Zola (*Nana*, 1974), and a sci-fi/Tarzan crossbreed in rock opera style (*Kumán*, 1984).

*Papacito piernas largas* (*Daddy Longlegs*, 1977), the most successful Mexican musical up to that moment, opened during this burgeoning phase. The show was a local theatrical adaptation by the producer Angélica Ortiz, who engineered the show for her daughter, the actress and pop idol Angélica María, nicknamed 'Mexico's Girlfriend'. Ortiz set Jean Webster's story in Mexico City in the early 1900s. José Luis Ibáñez's staging brought even the most recalcitrant critics together in their praise. In producing a Mexican musical of this scope, *Daddy Longlegs* was an unprecedented case: a joint venture between a private producer and a public institution, Teatro de la Nación. The critic Marco Antonio Acosta objected to the organisation's forsaking its artistic policy by allowing an impresario to benefit from subsidies in order to stage a patronising story about 'the good life of the high bourgeoisie'.[103] The playwright Óscar Liera regretted the show's individualism, finding it to revolve entirely around its long-suffering heroine, whom he compared to Mexican soap opera protagonists.[104] Nevertheless, *Daddy Longlegs* broke records, running for fifteen months and a thousand performances attended by over 520,705 spectators.[105]

In 1976 producers inaugurated the tradition of reviving musicals. Rather bizarrely, they first chose to bring back from the dead that most inauspicious production from the previous period. Sondheim's *Forum*, cautiously billed as a four-week limited engagement, was slightly more favourably received than its 1962 predecessor.

In contrast, the revival of *Mame* (1985) enjoyed outstanding success, even surpassing its first Mexican iteration, according to the critics.[106] Silvia Pinal not only reprised her role but actually produced the show in association with Televisa. The 1985 earthquake destroyed both Televiteatros, bringing the run to a premature end. In August 1976 the price of the US dollar rose to 20.50 pesos; around the time of the earthquake, one dollar sold for over 300 pesos. These incessant devaluations, alongside the post-quake changes in city life, brought a period of thriving musical theatre in Mexico to an end, a period also marked by the death of the pioneer Robert W. Lerner just after the opening of his production of *Evita*, the last musical in Mexico City to play twelve times a week.[107]

# 'Easy Terms'

The number of weekly musical performances in Mexico City could be considered an expression of the adversity theatre had begun to face in the 1985–2000 period. Around the time of the earthquake, most musicals played nine times a week from Tuesdays to Sundays. When *Beauty and the Beast* opened, performances had been reduced to seven, and many productions only played from Thursdays to Sundays. Televisa would continue to produce musicals independently throughout this period. These included the second revival of *A Chorus Line* (1989), *Cats*, and the Mexican revival of *Woman of the Year* (1995). Televisa also partnered with impresarios for *Kiss of the Spider Woman* (1996), *Fame* (1997), *Blood Brothers*, and even a third revival of *Forum* (1998). Nevertheless, with the collapse of both Televiteatros, two theatres of considerable size and technical resources, Televisa lost one of its main assets in the production of musicals. Furthermore, this loss implied a slowing down of the importation of blockbuster musicals that Televisa might well have produced in Mexico at an earlier date. By the turn of the century, Televisa, despite its abundant economic resources, found fewer and fewer reasons to invest in theatre and sold Televiteatro, its subsidiary company dedicated to theatrical production, which was named after the venues it lost in 1985. This period saw other producers exhausting their capacities or disappearing altogether. *Phantom* and *Les Misérables* ended up being presented by OCESA, a commercial behemoth that had risen to prominence by the end of this period, and that, with *Beauty and the Beast* in association with Walt Disney Productions, had started producing musicals in Mexico. Notwithstanding the tepid response *Rent* (1999) received—it ran for a mere two hundred performances—OCESA premiered *The Phantom of the Opera*. Even though the Mexican production was more opera than musical, principally because opera-trained singers and ballet-trained dancers dominated the Mexican cast,[108] it achieved a thirteen-month run and celebrated four hundred performances. Acknowledging OCESA's established infrastructure, the critic Gonzalo Valdés Medellín signalled its failure to achieve 'artistic soundness' overall: 'All that remains is empty *maquila* [the mere importation of raw materials for local assembly], well presented on the outside, but disastrously fatuous on the inside'.[109] Comparing OCESA's endeavours with those of its forerunners, he found that it failed to match the 'historical gravitas' of Fábregas, Pinal, and Julissa, who he believed prioritized a 'passion for art over passion for money'.[110]

*¡Qué plantón! (Supplanters!*, 1989) stands out among Mexican musicals of the period for its enthusiastic audience and critical response. Marina del Campo and Guillermo Méndez, the star of 1983's *Joseph and the Amazing Technicolor Dreamcoat*, devised

a musical around ecological concerns with characters drawn from the plant world. *Supplanters!* is haunted not only by the colourful tights and anthropomorphic model of *Cats* and *Starlight Express* but also by the journey narrative found in the Farid ud-Din Attar poem *The Conference of the Birds*, adapted for the stage by Peter Brook and Jean-Claude Carrière. The plot has divine forces granting plants the powers of communication and movement, in order that they might supersede man's dominion over the planet—and to give legs to what could have been a fairly static musical. The songs not only serve the purpose of exposition and personification, but also permit the characters to reveal their unstated urges and reinforce the ecological theme. While Grizabella the Glamour Cat's transgressions are not portrayed on stage, here Poison Ivy manipulates the other plants throughout the course of their quest, only redeeming herself in the show-stopping 'Quiero pedir perdón' ('I Want to Ask Forgiveness'). Although the structure and aesthetics of *Supplanters!* remained beholden to the stage conventions of the foreign shows that inspired it, this musical, rooted in a relatively immature tradition, nonetheless transcended the boundaries of its models by addressing a global concern: the environmental dangers to the planet.

# 'Tell Me Sweet Little Lies ... Oh, No, No, You Can't Disguise': *Mentiras* and the *Revista* Cycle

In hindsight, the quest for a genuinely Mexican musical appears to have been somewhat cyclical. *Lies*, the longest-running musical in the country's history, is constructed around Mexican hits from the 1980s, but this twenty-first century show also has deep roots in the *revista* tradition. In examining the decadence of that tradition in 1955, Maria y Campos noted the name of the genre had become quite apt, since by then the audience already knew musical numbers by heart, thus they were *re*-viewing them.[111] For Bud Coleman, 'similar to the revue, the jukebox musical is an assemblage of pre-existing songs where the emphasis is clearly on the songs, not on plot and/or character'.[112] *Ni fu ni fa*'s rehashing of numbers from different eras, and indeed from previous *revistas*, fits Coleman's description, and *Lies* is cut from similar cloth.[113]

The fact that a significant part of the audience already knows the songs has been decisive for its success. Lyrics, from both translated musicals and original local shows, have tended to alienate spectators, and critics have often stressed their unintelligibility.[114] Belaboured word inversions,[115] forced rhymes, and erroneous stresses are just some of the charges that have been leveled.[116] The author of *Lies*' book, José Manuel López Velarde, had previously studied communication science, and 'with the intention of becoming a better director he started studying acting'.[117] He declared: 'Part of my formation as spectator was watching music videos. [ ... ] I consider myself more a director than a playwright; if I write it is because I can't find material that interests me'.[118] Regarding

FIG. 11.3 The finale of the long-running local hit *Mentiras* (*Lies*), with Crisanta Gómez, Leticia López, Ana Cecilia Anzaldúa, Lolita Cortés, and Mauricio Martínez, at the Manolo Fábregas Theater Center in Mexico City. Photo: Leonel Martínez © Getty Images.

*Lies*, he has stated: 'The characters are archetypes: the sweet pregnant woman, the sexy and liberated woman, the broody housewife, the independent and successful woman. They're iconic characters'.[119]

This misreading of stereotype for archetype is exacerbated by production choices— the homemaker, pretty in pink; the 'sexy and liberated woman' in orange leather and leopard print; and the college-educated lawyer, the only one accomplished enough to wear trousers—and explains the production's reliance on musical numbers. With its loose grasp of plot and character, its performers occasional resorting to improv, and the show's humour depending so significantly on sexual puns, *Lies* backslides unconsciously into the realm of the *revista*. Audiences have found this combination entertaining and have kept the show running for a decade. In its tenth year, the show is advertised as '[t]he musical that enriches the history of theatre in Mexico'.[120] López Velarde teamed up with the composer Iker Madrid to devise a more daring show: *El último teatro del mundo* (*Last Theatre in the World*, 2015), a small-scale children's musical flirting with actor-musicianship. By embracing theatricality in its entirety, this musical represents a promising result of the processes of imitation, assimilation, and recreation.[121]

Mexico is a cultural powerhouse, with many paths to choose from in the development of its own tradition of musical theater. Following the Anglophone model has helped it to explore one possible way of coordinating form and content. If Mexico still has anything to learn from the Anglophone musical theater tradition, it is the laborious process of workshopping to develop new works. Unfortunately, when foreign shows are imported to Mexico, they arrive with many of their dramaturgical and production questions already resolved, depriving the local industry of valuable learning opportunities. In creating musicals, Mexican producers, authors, composers, and directors have yet to actively promote workshops or to seek feedback for works in progress. If cases such as *Rent Freeze*, *Fascinating Girls*, and *Supplanters!* provide any lesson at all, it is that while inspired and imaginative composers abound in Mexico, it still needs a more comprehensive understanding of musical storytelling. Playwrights and book authors would certainly benefit from meaningful collaboration with dramaturges. As globalisation increasingly renders theatrical borders porous, greater dramaturgical interaction is encouraged, fostering more efficient song spotting, a greater dynamism in book writing, the diversification of storytelling approaches, and the development of succinct yet expressive lyrics, of which Mexican musicals are sorely in need.

While there are skilled and ambitious musical theatre performers in the country, what professionalisation there has been in the industry has depended to a disconcerting extent on the survival skills of individuals. Traditionally, they have had to seek singing, dancing, and acting training on their own initiative, often with private tutors and at their own cost. In recent years those young Mexican performers who were able to do so have gone abroad to obtain their formal education in musical theatre. Fundamentally, in Mexico there exists a profession for which there are no educational foundations.[122] Both endeavours to create an authentic national musical and the industry as a whole would benefit, commercially and artistically, from the funding and deployment of formal university training programmes in the performance and creation of musical theatre.

Musicals have captured the Mexican imagination and prompted an erratic series of reappraisals of the country's own heritage of musical performance forms, including the *revista*, with all its political bite. Mexico has confronted the Broadway and West End challenge and assimilated the musical theatre form. Broadening critical perspectives on Mexico's musical theatre history is paramount if theatre makers are to challenge and evolve the form and force their traditionally complacent industry from its comfort zone in order that it might cultivate a national audience and compete for a global one.[123]

## NOTES

1. I will refer throughout to the year of the first Mexican production, unless otherwise stated.
2. Julissa is the professional name of the Mexican actress, producer, and translator Julia Isabel de Llano Macedo. She has also produced Mexican versions of *Jesus Christ Superstar* (1975), *The Rocky Horror Show* (1976), *John, Paul, George, Ringo . . . and Bert* (1977), *I'm Getting My Act Together and Taking It on the Road* (1982), and *Menopause: The Musical* (2004).
3. The Mexican *Joseph and the Amazing Technicolor Dreamcoat* premiered in 1983 and was the inaugural production of the Televiteatro 1. By early 1985 it had relocated to Teatro San Rafael, and by the summer of that year it was back at Televiteatro 1, playing only four matinées on the weekend. The season was supposed to close with its nine hundredth performance on Sunday, 22 September 1985. The earthquake on the morning of 19 September

1985, however, brought down the two Televiteatros, and so *Joseph*'s two-year run came to an end.

4. "The Andrew Lloyd Webber Story," in *The South Bank Show*, season 10, episode 7, ITV, 15 November 1986.

5. The *revista* was the ultimate popular form of Mexican music theatre during the first half of the twentieth century. Audiences engaged with political issues through musical numbers brimming with topical references, in a diversity of national and foreign styles. Spectators actively participated, often rebuking both the performers and characters they played. As the Mexican anthropologist and ethnologist Guillermo Bonfil observed, it was a theatre that belonged to the people, devised by 'librettists (mainly journalists, down in the street, in the café, in the cantina) using common slang and puns, with an irreverent stance and iconoclastic jokes' and composers 'capable of writing the score to an entire show in a week'. Guillermo Bonfil Batalla, 'Cuando el teatro fue del pueblo', in *El país de las tandas: Teatro de revista 1900–1940*, ed. Alfonso Morales, 2$^{nd}$ ed. (Mexico: Museo Nacional de Culturas Populares, SEP,1986), 9–10. Carlos Monsiváis believed that *revistas* 'cast elementary political judgments in a depoliticised society', and that this form of theatre allowed for a level of political criticism otherwise unadvisable in a minimally democratic system, at least for a time. Carlos Monsiváis, 'Notas sobre la cultura mexicana en el siglo XX', in *Historia general de México*, 2$^{nd}$ ed., vol. 4 (Mexico: El Colegio de México, 1977), 466.

6. All translations in the chapter are my own. Estela Leñero, 'El fracaso del Frida musical', *Una mirada al teatro en México (2000–2010)* (Mexico: Secretaría de Cultura, 2017), 332.

7. For a further exploration of the concept of style resulting 'from a series of choices made within some set of constraints', see Leonard B. Meyer, 'Toward a Theory of Style', in *The Concept of Style*, ed. Berel Lang (Ithaca, NY: Cornell University Press, 1987), 21–71. Furthermore, two factors explain the adjectivisation of the term 'Broadway'. The most significant is an aesthetic homogenisation, the pervasive impulse among Mexican spectators and even certain critics to associate any Anglophone integrated musical with the Great White Way's dramaturgical and theatrical hallmarks. The other is that the British musicals which have been produced in Mexico since the late 1800s have always had a previous stopover in Manhattan.

8. Carlos Monsiváis, *Salvador Novo: Lo marginal al centro*, 2$^{nd}$ ed. (Mexico: Ediciones Era, 2004), 187.

9. Ibid., 187–188.

10. Bill Moyers, 'Carlos Fuentes: Mexican Novelist', in *A World of Ideas: Conversations with Thoughtful Men and Women about American Life Today and the Ideas Shaping the Future* (New York: Doubleday, 1989), 506–507.

11. Carlos Monsiváis, 'El teatro: Que el telón se desplome sobre la conciencia', in *Historia mínima de la cultura mexicana en el siglo XX*, ed. Eugenia Huerta (Mexico: El Colegio de México, 2010), 474.

12. 'Serie histórica diaria del tipo de cambio peso-dólar—(CF373)', *Banco de México*, https://www.banxico.org.mx/SieInternet/consultarDirectorioInternetAction.do?accion=consultarCuadro&idCuadro=CF373&sector=6&locale=es#, accessed 30 January 2020.

13. Alberto Aguilar, 'Nombres, nombres y . . . nombres', *Reforma*, 21 April 1999, Negocios 3A.

14. Fernando Pedrero, 'Reporte de empresas: Cae utilidad neta de Televisa 18.2%', *Reforma*, 27 April 2000, Negocios 5A.

15. Although Mexican newspapers did not wait for professional theatre reviews, critics such as Armando de Maria y Campos and Antonio Magaña Esquivel published their reviews

two or three days after opening; they committed to critiquing all theatrical expressions in Mexico City. Marcela del Río Reyes ('Mara Reyes'), Rafael Solana, and Félix Cortés Camarillo, in their weekly columns, presented more thoughtful insights. Daily theatre reviews began to disappear during the 1980s as productions decreased their weekly performances, while weekly reviewing prioritised other genres over musicals. Two of the few professional reviews of *Lies*, the longest-running Mexican musical, only appeared in April and July 2011, over two years after the show's opening.

16. '[Pittsburgh] Opera House: Program of Entertainment', *Opera News* 26 (26 Februrary 1883), 2

17. 'Diversiones públicas: Gran Teatro Nacional / Gran Compañía de Ópera Inglesa del Sr. C. D. Hess', *El monitor republicano*, 13 February 1884, 4.

18. El Duque Job [Manuel Gutiérrez Nájera], 'Crónicas deshilvanadas', *La libertad*, 2 March 1884, 1–2.

19. 'Cartelera Teatro', *La cultura en México* 527 (15 March 1972): XIV .

20. *Jesus Christ Superstar*: Félix Cortés Camarillo, 'Si allá existe un off-Broadway ¿aquí se da un off-Fábregas', *La cultura en México* 581 (28 March 1973): XVI; *Grease*: Félix Cortés Camarillo, 'Remember When: Yo no soy un rebelde sin causa, ni tampoco un desenfrenado', *La cultura en México* 603 (29 August 1973): XVI .

21. Juan Jaime Larios, 'Microcomentarios', *El universal*, 18 April 1977, Espectáculos-1.

22. [Rafael Solana], 'Espectáculos: Rogelio', *Siempre!* 1458 (3 June 1981): 51.

23. Estela Leñero, '*Los productores* de Broadway', *Una mirada al teatro en México (2000–2010)* (Mexico: Secretaría de Cultura, 2017), 329–330.

24. The assimilation process included Mexican productions of Italian musicals such as *Alleluja brava gente* (*Alleluya, brava gente*, 1973); *Buonanotte Bettina* (*¡Buenas noches . . . Betina!*, 1974); *Ciao, Rudy* (*Chao Valentino*, 1975); *Forza venite gente* (*Venga toda la gente*, 1983); and the successful *Aggiungi un posto a tavola* (*El diluvio que viene*, 1978), which had a record-breaking first run of three years and revivals in 1993 and 2007. There has been also a local production of a Spanish jukebox musical, *Hoy no me puedo levantar* (*I Can't Get Up Today*, 2006 and 2014).

25. Monsiváis, 'El teatro', 474.

26. *Ni fu ni fa* premiered on 3 November 1955 at Teatro Sullivan. This 348-seat venue had been inaugurated earlier that year, on 28 April 1955. Antonio Magaña-Esquivel, *Imagen y realidad del teatro en México (1533–1960)* (Mexico: CONACULTA, INBA, Escenología AC, 2000), 587. It was originally named, like the street it was on, after James Sullivan, a US special agent of the Mexican National Railroad Company from the 1880s. The theatre was briefly renamed Pardavé after the film star Joaquín Pardavé, a comedian who had recently passed away. *Ni fu ni fa*'s programme reads: 'Teatro Pardavé (formerly Sullivan)'. However, Salvador Novo kept calling it Sullivan in his chronicle about the show's opening night, since he noted that 'the name Pardavé seems out of place'. Salvador Novo, *La vida en México en el periodo presidencial de Adolfo Ruiz Cortines*, vol. 2 (Mexico: CONACULTA, 1996), 201.

27. *Ni fu ni fa*, Mexico City, 1955, programme, November [1955] (Mexico City: Teatro Pardavé-Edmundo Mendoza, [1955]), n.p., Biblioteca de las Artes.

28. Emma Grissé, 'Corrillos de teatro', *Atisbos*, 22 November 1955, 14.

29. [Mario] Castillón Bracho, programme note, *Ni fu ni fa* programme, n.p.

30. Ibid.

31. Pablo Dueñas and Jesús Flores y Escalante, 'Estudio introductorio', in *Teatro de revista (1904–1936)*, ed. Pablo Dueñas and Jesús Flores y Escalante (México: CONACULTA, 1995), 11–35; here: 11.
32. Ibid., 31.
33. Armando de Maria y Campos, *El teatro de género chico en la Revolución Mexicana* (Mexico: CONACULTA, 1996), 460.
34. Dueñas and Flores y Escalante, 'Estudio', 34.
35. Ibid., 32.
36. Edmundo Mendoza, 'Edmundo Mendoza', résumé, manuscript 1987, Biblioteca de las Artes, Archivo vertical de personalidades, I.
37. Ibid., I–V.
38. 'Siguen los ensayos de la revista musical que dirigirá maese Novo', *Cine mundial*, 2 November 1955, 12.
39. Rodolfo Usigli, in turn, had studied at Yale University under Barret H. Clark.
40. Sergio Magaña, interview with Leslie Zelaya and Julio César López, in Leslie Zelaya, Imelda Lobato, and Julio César López, *Una mirada a la vida y obra de Sergio Magaña* (Mexico: Secretaría de Cultura de Michoacán, CITRU, CONACULTA, 2006), 28.
41. Novo, *La vida en México en el periodo presidencial de Adolfo Ruiz Cortines*, 2:201.
42. [Rafael Solana], 'Espectáculos: Ni Fu Ni Fa', *Siempre!*, 30 November 1955, 50–51.
43. 'Farandulerías: Rostros nuevos y cuerpos bellos en la obra musical "Ni fu ni fa"', *Cine mundial*, 7 November 1955, 4.
44. It is neither in the libretti collection nor in the file on Edmundo Mendoza in the archive.
45. 'Por nuestros teatros: Pardavé "Ni fu, ni fa"', *El redondel*, 6 November 1955, section 2, 18.
46. Ibid.
47. González Marquez, 'Tanda', *Cine mundial*, 13 November 1955, 12.
48. Mendoza, 'Edmundo Mendoza', III.
49. 'La comedia musical', *El universal gráfico*, 11 November 1955, 11.
50. 'Farandulerías', 4.
51. Fausto Castillo, 'Cabeza de playa', *Esto*, 5 November 1955, 4-B.
52. In 1951 he premiered *Los signos del zodíaco* (*The Signs of the Zodiac*) with a lavish production fostered by Novo, who directed it for Mexico's most prestigious theatre: the Palacio de Bellas Artes. Magaña was only twenty-six years old.
53. 'Farandulerías', 4.
54. Ibid.
55. Salvador Novo, *La vida en México en el periodo presidencial de Adolfo Ruiz Cortines*, vol. 3 (México: CONACULTA, 1997), 181.
56. 'Calendar', *Theatre Arts* 41, no. 4 (April 1957): 6.
57. Media technologies, which played a part in the *revista*'s fall from favour, also assisted in the acclimatisation of the Anglophone musical in Mexico. In the context of *The Boy Friend*'s opening, *Time* magazine observed: 'Paradoxically, the Mexican theater apparently owes its robust health to the growth of Mexican television. By bearing down heavily on dramatic shows, TV producers fanned an interest in the drama which television alone has not been able to satisfy. The number of legitimate theaters in Mexico City has increased from 4 to 30 in only four years. And with the boom has come a sudden flowering of Mexican acting, producing and directing talent'. 'Hit Season', *Time: The Weekly Magazine Mexico*, [1956], unidentified clipping, Edmundo Mendoza Archive, Biblioteca de las Artes, Archivo

vertical de personalidades. Salvador Novo concurred: 'All the years that radio has domesticated the audience, and the way small theatres and television have imparted to them a taste for theatre, have come together in the opportunity to begin producing musical comedies with considerable success'. Novo, *La vida en México en el periodo presidencial de Adolfo Ruiz Cortines*, 2:435.

58. Anselmo would establish the Spanish-speaking American network Univision. De Llano worked in the International Division of the National Broadcasting Company, based in New York; when he returned to Mexico, he played a crucial role in developing the Mexican soap opera or *telenovela*.

59. 'Hit Season', *Time: The Weekly Magazine Mexico*, [1956], unidentified clipping.

60. Paul F. Kennedy, 'Musical Crisis in Mexico', *New York Times*, 23 December 1956, 39.

61. 'Hit Season'.

62. Bill Llano, 'Los espectáculos: Un gran éxito; "Los novios", en el Teatro de los Musicos', *Impacto*, 17 October 1956, 44.

63. Alberto Catani, 'Pasarela', *Jueves de excélsior*, 18 October 1956, 8.

64. Pete, 'Los novios (The Boy Friend)', unidentified clipping, Edmundo Mendoza Archive, Biblioteca de las Artes, Archivo vertical de personalidades.

65. Luis Granados, 'En "Los novios" participan, en forma inesperada, los artistas y el público', 4 December 1956, unidentified clipping, Edmundo Mendoza Archive. Biblioteca de las Artes, Archivo vertical de personalidades. Llano, 'Los espectáculos', 45. Armando de Maria y Campos, 'Estreno del Teatro del Músico con el estreno de la revista *Los novios*', *Veintiún años de crónica teatral en México*, vol. 1, pt. 1, *1956–1959*, ed. Marta J. Toriz (México: INBA-CITRU-IPN, 1999), 137.

66. O[ctavio] A[lba], 'Farandulerías: Una ráfaga artística "distinta" en la escena Mexicana', *Cine mundial*, 6 October 1956, 8–9.

67. José Antonio Alcaraz, 'Teatro y sociedad: Espejos que se acechan', *Al sonoro rugir del telón (Anuario teatral del DF, 1987)* (Mexico: Editorial Posada, 1988), 238–239.

68. Ibid.

69. Luis de Tavira, 'El otro teatro', prologue to Maria y Campos, *El teatro*, XVII.

70. Luis D. Vicent, 'Teatro: El negocio del teatro musical en México', *La familia para la familia* (2 February 1957), 60.

71. He later gained international attention for directing the films *Like Water for Chocolate* (1992) and *A Walk in the Clouds* (1995).

72. The *canción ranchera* is an energetic, popular type of love song which originated in a rural environment, as its very name suggests: from the ranches. It has been ubiquitous on the screen, from classic Mexican films to Disney's *Coco*. For Monisváis, its thunderous delivery and pleading melody sketch out an attitude far from or even adversarial to the 'urban' or 'contemporary'. Carlos Monisváis, *Amor perdido* (Mexico: Secretaría de Educación Pública, Ediciones Era, 1986), 90. The *corrido* is a popular Mexican form of song and dance usually set to guitars, or accordion or accompanied by a mariachi band. Vicente T. Mendoza, a specialist in *corrido*, defines it as an 'epic-lyrical-narrative genre [ . . . ] it tells of occurrences that deeply move the masses' "sensibilities" '. For illiterate crowds at the end of the nineteenth century, corridos 'constituted the sole source of information on the current events'. Vicente T. Mendoza, *Corridos mexicanos* (Mexico: Fondo de Cultura Económica, 1985), 7–8.

73. Antonio Magaña Esquivel, 'Teatro: "Rentas congeladas", de Sergio Magaña en el Iris', *El nacional*, 3 September 1960, 5.

## MUSICALS IN MEXICO: BORDERS AND BRIDGES    339

74. Among them: Luis G. Basurto, 'Teatro: "Rentas congeladas", *Excélsior*, 2 September 1960, 4B; Fernando Mota, 'Se levanta el telón: "Rentas congeladas", en el Iris', *Últimas noticias de Excélsior*, 2nd ed. (5 September 1960), 6; and the anonymous 'Las rentas', *Cuadernos de Bellas Artes* 1, no. 3 (October 1960): 24–25.

75. Teatro Iris, *Rentas congeladas*, billing, *Últimas noticias de Excélsior*, 2nd ed., (7 September 1960), 6.

76. Rafael Solana, 'Rentas congeladas', in *Noches de estreno* (Mexico: Ediciones Oasis, 1963), 207.

77. Marcela del Río, 'Diorama teatral: Rentas congeladas', *Diorama de la cultura*, 11 September 1960, 2.

78. Del Río, 'Rentas congeladas', 2.

79. In juxtaposing stances like Mota's and Del Río's with the artistic intentions of Mexican theatre over the previous three decades, an aesthetic and critical paradox emerges. Back in 1928, the group Theatre of Ulysses, to which Salvador Novo belonged, believed that what was felt to be 'Mexican' actually formed part of a universal culture. They claimed that a break with tradition was in order and turned towards Europe in search of models. Luis Mario Schneider, *Fragua y gesta del teatro experimental en México* (Mexico: UNAM, El Equilibrista, 1995), 16. In outlining their objectives, the group's patron, Antonieta Rivas Mercado, claimed: 'We are opening contemporary Mexican sensibilities to the mature creations of foreign theatre.' Quoted in ibid., 19.

    From the 1930s to the 1950s many other reformist groups, such as Teatro de Orientación, Panamerican Theatre, and Poesía en Voz Alta, followed in Ulysses' steps, producing both Mexican and foreign plays. Musical theatre, however, remained marginalised from this conversation, perhaps because, as Margarita Mendoza López noted, for the renovators of the Mexican stage theatre meant comedy, drama, and tragedy; the musical or lyric genre was scorned as 'show', not embraced as theatre. Margarita Mendoza López, *Primeros renovadores del teatro en México 1928–1941* (Mexico: IMSS, 1985), 27. This aesthetic and critical marginalisation has curbed the pace of musical theatre development in Mexico.

80. Mota, 'Se levanta el telón', 6.

81. Julian Woolford, *How Musicals Work and How to Write Your Own* (London: Nick Hern Books, 2012), 21.

82. Vicente Leñero, *El Teatro de los Insurgentes: 1953–1993* (Mexico: El Milagro, 1993), 116.

83. Lya Engel, 'Teatro: Teatro de los Insurgentes "Las fascinadoras", *Impacto*, 18 October 1961, 45.

84. Jacky Bratton's concept of inter-theatricality serves in the understanding of Edmundo Mendoza's experience and memory as a bridge between musical theatre practices and traditions. Bratton considers an intertheatrical reading as transcending the written and seeking 'to articulate the mesh of connections between all kinds of theatre texts, and between texts and their users'. She posits that all entertainments 'performed within a single theatrical tradition are more or less interdependent', and that 'they are uttered in a language, shared by successive generations', including 'speech, [ ... ] the systems of the stage—scenery, costume, lighting, and so forth', as well as 'genres, conventions and, very importantly, memory'.

    Mendoza's visceral memory of his previous experiences as dancer and choreographer of musicals sits at the core of *Fascinating Girls*' inter-theatrical transactions with local and foreign musicals. 'The fabric of that memory, shared by audience and players,' Bratton asserts, 'is made up of the dances, spectacles, plays and songs, experienced as particular performances—a different selection, of course, for each individual—woven upon knowledge of the performers' other current and previous roles, and their personae on and off the stage'. Jacky Bratton, *New Readings in Theatre History* (Cambridge: Cambridge University Press, 2003), 37–38.

However unconsciously, in acknowledging Mendoza as an 'ace at musical comedy and one of its initiators in Mexico', Engel is reading inter-theatrically the dancer and choreographer's role in the history of Mexican musicals. So did Maria y Campos, who claimed, 'Edmundo Mendoza naturally assumes the spotlight because he is a master choreographer', a mastery perhaps developed through his theatrical interactions.

85. Engel, 'Teatro de los Insurgentes', 45.

86. Rafael Solana, 'Las fascinadoras', *Noches de estreno* (Mexico: Ediciones Oasis, 1963), 265.

87. Armando de Maria y Campos, 'Las fascinadoras, en el Teatro de los Insurgentes', *Veintiún años de crónica teatral en México*, vol. 2, pt. 2 (1960–1965), ed. Marta J. Toriz (Mexico: INBA-CITRU-IPN, 1999), 824.

88. Ibid., 825.

89. Mara Reyes [Marcela del Río], 'Diorama teatral: "Las fascinadoras"', *Diorama de la cultura*, 15 October 1961, 3.

90. François Baguer, '"Las fascinadoras", comedia musical, en el "Insurgentes"', *Excélsior*, 7 October 1961, 4B.

91. Antonio Magaña Esquivel, 'Teatro: "Las fascinadoras" en el Insurgentes', *El nacional*, 11 November 1961, 5.

92. Unfortunately, no cast recording was produced. Felipe Santander revisited the show, but in title only, and five years later he produced, composed, designed, directed, and starred in *Las fascinadoras 66*. This new musical revolved around an international conference of beauty queens, creating, as Santander himself put it, a 'feminist coalition that benefits from their popular drive, channeling their market value towards social good'. Felipe Santander, 'Las fascinadoras 66', *Teatro mexicano del siglo XX, 1900–1986: Catálogo de obras teatrales*, ed. Margarita Mendoza López, Daniel Salazar, and Tomás Espinosa, vol. 2 (Mexico: IMSS, 1987), 238. Although harshly reviewed, the show issued a cast recording with Santander's musical numbers under the Polydor label.

93. Maria y Campos, 'Las fascinadoras', 825.

94. Engel, 'Teatro de los Insurgentes', 45.

95. Magaña Esquivel, '"Las fascinadoras"', 5.

96. Marcela del Río Reyes, *El teatro de Alfonso Reyes: Presencia y actualidad* (Monterrey: Universidad Autónoma de Nuevo León, 2013), 177.

97. Chaplin himself starred as the murderer in *Monsieur Verdoux* (1947), a film version of the story he directed and wrote himself.

98. Juan Vicente Melo, 'Alfonso Reyes: *Landrú*—opereta y la mano del comandante Aranda', *La cultura en México* 107 (4 March 1964): XV.

99. Jorge Ibargüengoitia, 'Teatro: El Landrú degeneradón de Alfonso Reyes', *Revista de la Universidad de México* 18, no. 10 (1964): 27.

100. Novo, *La vida en México en el periodo presidencial de Gustavo Díaz Ordaz*, 2:382.

101. Rafael Solana, 'Violinista en el tejado', *Cine mundial*, 9 March 1970, 8.

102. Julissa set *Grease* in the Mexican 1950s. Rydell High became 'la Prepa Nacional', the national public high school. Many characters were rebaptized with Spanish names, so Kenickie became Quico and Marty became Licha, although she retained her Marine boyfriend, now based in Tokyo rather than Korea. Original allusions to Troy Donahue were

now made to local rock 'n' roller Enrique Guzman, and Julissa's media rival in the 1950s, Angélica María, even stepped in for Doris Day in 'Look at Me I'm Sandra Dee'. The ferocious critic Félix Cortés Camarillo, objecting to the adaptation or 'Mexicanisation' of the plot, noted: 'Marine boyfriends, even those based in Tokyo, remain a North American privilege'. Cortés Camarillo, 'Remember When', 16.

103. Marco Antonio Acosta, 'La escena: "Papacito Piernas Largas"', *El nacional*, 16 November 1977, 16.

104. Óscar Liera, 'Sobre las piernas largas de papacito', *Diorama de la cultura*, 30 October 1977, 11.

105. Instituto Mexicano del Seguro Social, *Teatro de la Nación: Memoria 1977–1981* (Mexico: IMSS, 1982), 174.

106. Marilyn Ichaso claimed that 'Silvia [Pinal] is now even more Mame than when she first played her [ ... ] years ago, a more beautiful, elegant and star-like Mame than ever. [ ... ] In the face of this spectacular revival, let us concur that no revival could have been better than this new *Mame* that Pinal is currently offering us'. Marilyn Ichaso, 'En la cuarta pared: Mame', *Excélsior* [1985], unidentified clipping.

Mirabal agreed. In a public letter addressed to his 'Admired Silvia Pinal' in his daily column, he asserted: 'We were thrilled to offer you such unanimous, long, ever so long, applause, not once or twice but many times. In reviving the precious musical comedy *Mame* you pulverised the belief that "sequels always suck"'. Mirabal, 'Crisol', *Novedades*, 11 June 1985, 6D.

Although Malkah Rabell judged *Mame* to be a 'classist [ ... ] stupid comedy', even she, when reviewing the one hundredth performance of the revival, packed as it was with press and theatre people, acknowledged: 'I can't remember a time when I had seen such a triumph: a standing audience, tirelessly applauding, not just at the end of the show, but at every scene, regardless of its insignificance'. Malkah Rabell, 'Se alza el telón: Las cien representaciones de Mame', *El día*, 26 August 1985, 23.

107. Given that the show performed twice daily from Tuesday to Sunday, two actresses were cast as Evita: the Argentine Valeria Lynch and the Mexican Rocío Banquells. Similarly, Jaime Garza alternated the role of Che with Javier Díaz Dueñas, although the former received top billing. The role of Peron's mistress was played by Carmen Delgado and, in certain performances, by Ga-Bi. *Evita*, Latin American première, Mexico City, 1981, programme (Mexico: Teatro Ferrocarilero, 1981), unpaginated. The intense performance schedule allowed the production to run for over three hundred performances at Teatro Ferrocarrilero by December 1981.

108. According to the programme, out of a cast of thirty-nine performers, including swings, only nine mentioned previous work in musicals. Only two, Bianca Marroquín and Ricardo Villareal, gave information related to their training in their bios. Marroquín had studied dance styles such as tap, jazz, and ballet in Brownsville, Texas; Villareal, also a communications engineer, had trained at the acting school of Televisa. The latter starred as Rusty (Ferro) in the failed Mexican production of *Starlight Express*; the former would go on to star in the Mexican production of *Chicago* as Roxie Hart and would reprise the role on Broadway. The cast also featured Laura Morelos, the prima ballerina of Mexico's National Dance Company, as Meg Giry. *El fantasma de la ópera*, Mexico City, 1999, programme (Mexico: Teatros Alameda, Teatro Alameda 1, 1999), 5–9.

Luz Emilia Aguilar held that the voices were 'uneven [ ... ] some were trained like that of Tatiana Marouchtchak [playing Carlotta] and some were out of tune and opaque like

Jose Joel's, [playing] Raoul'. Luz Emilia Aguilar Zinser, 'Prófugos de la realidad', *Reforma*, 16 December 1999, 11E. Pablo Espinosa found in the Mexican *Phantom* 'the standardized tone adopted in the voice modulation and impostation proper of documentary dubbing'. Pablo Espinosa, 'El fantasma de la ópera, spectacular montaje de 8.5 mdd en versión meshica', *La jornada*, 18 December 1999, https://www.jornada.com.mx/1999/12/18/cul1.jpg.html, accessed 9 April 2019.

109. Gonzalo Valdés Medellín, 'El show business en el teatro mexicano', in *Un siglo de teatro en México*, ed. David Olguín (Mexico: Fondo de Cultura Económica, CONACULTA, 2011), 202.

110. Ibid. Despite being a foreigner, Robert W. Lerner deserves to be added to this list: he consistently put his faith in national artists and even helped launch the musical theatre careers of the three artists mentioned by Valdés Medellín.

111. Maria y Campos, *El teatro*, 459.

112. Bud Coleman, 'New Horizons: The Musical at the Dawn of the Twenty-first Century', in *The Cambridge Companion to the Musical*, 3rd ed., ed. William A. Everett and Paul R. Laird (Cambridge: Cambridge University Press, 2017), 360.

113. *Lies* appears to be haunted by a particular *revista* subgenre, the *revista de evocación* (evocative review). According to Maria y Campos, veteran authors exploited this approach during the 1930s, granting them steady hits for over ten years (Maria y Campos, *El teatro*, 365). It was an amalgam of old songs, folk dances, historical episodes, and any other element useful in building up a nostalgic libretto (Dueñas and Flores y Escalante, 'Estudio', 30).

The public discourse of *Lies* has insisted on the alleged persistence of 1980s culture well into the twenty-first century. 'That decade stayed in Mexico', declared the author of the book and director of the show; 'I go out to the street, and I see people dressed as they were back then' (Arturo Cruz Bárcenas, 'Mentiras recrea la vida en los años 80, época que se quedó: el director', *La jornada*, 30 January 2009), 11a. . The evocative review, however, in deploying permanent comparisons between the 'now' and the 'then', with the latter always prevailing, relied on political commentaries for its success.

114. The critic Rosa Margot Ochoa, for instance, found the lyrics for *Cats* in Spanish to be 'unintelligible'. Trying to reconcile her experience with book musicals and the sung-through structure of Lloyd Webber's show, she went on to suggest the production hand out 'a synopsis of the plot' along with the programmes, 'as they do in opera.' (Rosa Margot Ochoa, '*Cats* México,' *Entretelones* (Mexico: CEID, 1997), 43–44.) Responses to local cast recordings reveal another level of audience alienation: until fairly recently, Mexican theatre-goers simply did not buy them. In the early 1990s Monsiváis assessed audience responses to the acclimatisation of the musical: 'In contrast to their Broadway counterpart, [Mexican audiences] won't memorize song lyrics by heart, nor will they collect programmes.' (Carlos Monsiváis, 'Introducción: Apúrate, vieja, que vamos a llegar tarde', in Vicente Leñero, *El Teatro de los Insurgentes 1953–1993* (Mexico: El Milagro, 1993), 14).

115. Spanish sentences, like English, tend to be constructed in the order subject-verb-object. Sometimes lyric translations resort to word inversion to fit scansion, producing an artificial structure that can alienate audiences and sacrifice clarity. For example, Christine's reply to the Phantom in the original 'The Phantom of the Opera' follows the natural structure: 'Those who/have seen your face/draw back/ in fear'. 'The Libretto', in George Perry, *The Complete Phantom of the Opera* (New York: Henry Holt and Company, 1988), 145. In order to fit the scansion, the Mexican Spanish version became the slightly

off-sounding structure subject-object-verb (S-V-O): S ['Quien ya tu rostro vio']; O: ['terror'] V: ['sintió'], which back-translates as: 'Who already your face saw, terror felt'. From 'El fantasma de la ópera', *El fantasma de la ópera*, Grabación de la premiere mundial en español, CD Booklet, Columbia-Really Useful Records CDIM 501397, 2000.

116. Criticisms of translations have included José Antonio Alcaraz's reviews of the Mexican production of *Anything Goes* (1984), *Starlight Express*, and *Evita*'s 1998 revival. See José Antonio Alcaraz, 'Aburrición eterna a quien vea esta obra', in *Suave Teatro: 1984* (México: Universidad Autónoma Metropolitana, 1985), 128–132; José Antonio Alcaráz, 'Harina de Otro Costal: Dos de Lloyd Webber', *Reforma*, 20 February 1998, 3C. See also Bruno Bert's review of *Cats*: Bruno Bert, 'Ahora, gatos de importación' *Tiempo libre*, 9–15 May 1991, 29; and Silvia Peláez's and Emmanuel Haro Villa's reviews of *Rent*: Silvia Peláez, '¡Ábrete sésamo!: Rent', *Reforma*, 2 July 1999, primera fila 18; and Emmanuel Haro Villa, 'Rent, talento desperdiciado en pobre obra', *Novedades*, 26 June 1999, 1-E.

117. Mariana Mijares, 'Apuesta por su vocación teatral', *Reforma*, 18 September 2011, 6-Gente.

118. Ibid.

119. Arturo Cruz Bárcenas, 'Los temas del musical *Mentiras* cuentan el drama de la rebelión de la mujer', *La jornada*, 23 April 2011, 8a.

120. *Mentiras*, Mexico City, 2009, programme, 36th ed (Mexico: Centro Teatral Manolo Fábregas, Teatro México, 2019), cover. Differences between the author and director of *Lies*, Jose Manuel López Velarde, and the show's producers, OCESA's theatre division rebranded as Mejor Teatro, arose before this chapter came to press and performances ceased. 'Termina, por disputa, la era de *Mentiras*', *Reforma*, 26 March 2021, 1-Gente. A new agreement between the author and producer Alejandro Gou allowed for the show's relaunching in 2022.

121. Between 2015 and 2020 the show had back-to-back revivals, shifting between private and state-funded venues.

122. Programmes do exist in the general field of theatre called *licenciaturas* (licentiate degrees, equivalent to a bachelor of arts) at the National Autonomous University of Mexico (UNAM) (BA in Dramatic Literature and Theatre, School of Philosophy and Literature; BA in Theatre and Acting, University Centre of Theatre); at the National Institute of Fine Arts (INBA) (BA in Acting); and at regional universities. A private institution belonging to the Catholic religious congregation of the Legionaries of Christ, Universidad Anáhuac, launched its BA in Theatre and Acting in 2012, which includes a seminar in musical theatre.

Sporadically, alumni from these public programmes who have pursued supplementary musical theatre training have been cast in professional productions. From UNAM: Javier Díaz Dueñas (*Evita*, *The Three Musketeers* [1983], *Fausto-rock*, *Cats*, *La Cage aux Folles* [1992], *The Most Happy Fella* [1994], and *Ciudad Blanca* [2006]); Lilia Sixtos (*Mame* [1988], *Cats*, and *Starlight Express*); Lenny Zundel (*Cats*, *La Cage aux Folles*, *Singin' in the Rain* [1996], and *Beauty and the Beast*); Enrique Chi (*Houdini*, *Rent*, and *Man of La Mancha* [2001 and 2016]); and, most recently, Javier Oliván (*Man of La Mancha* [2016] and *Rent Freeze* [2019]) and Jorge Viñas (*Avenue Q* [2019]). From INBA: Héctor Bonilla (*Sugar*, *Barnum* [1986], and *The Drowsy Chaperone* [2014]); Samantha Salgado (*Rent*, *Cabaret* [2006], and *The Addams Family* [2014]).

123. In April 1939, *Mexicana*, a show presented by the Republic of Mexico, premiered on Broadway at the Forty-sixth Street Theatre, now known as the Richard Rodgers. According to Sam Stephenson, '*Mexicana* was the first Broadway show presented by a

foreign government'. Sam Stephenson, *Gene Smith's Sink: A Wide-Angle Review* (New York: Farrar, Straus & Giroux, 2017), 11. The production began in Mexico as *Upa y apa* earlier that year. The Austrian impresario Sam Spiegel received a 'refundable credit' from the Mexican government to produce this folkloric musical, branded as '[a] spectacle made in Mexico to triumph in New York'. Jovita Millán Carranza, *70 años de teatro en el Palacio de Bellas Artes 1934–2004* (Mexico: INBA, 2004) 49–50. The score brought together such celebrated composers as Silvestre Revueltas, Blas Galindo, José Rolón, and Candelario Huízar with popular musicians like Tata Nacho, Gabriel Ruiz, and Alfonso Esparza Oteo. The libretto included contributions from such prominent Mexican authors as Xavier Villaurrutia, Octavio G. Barreda, José Gorostiza, and Jorge Cuesta. *Upa y apa*, Mexico City, 1939, programme (Mexico: Palacio de Bellas Artes, 1939). After only a single performance, the show was branded as 'the theatre scandal of the year' by the critic Roberto Núñez y Domínguez, largely due to its excessive costs. Roberto Núñez y Domínguez, *Descorriendo el telón: Cuarenta años de teatro en México* (Madrid: Editorial Rollán, 1956), 561. Nevertheless, the show did make it to the World's Fair in New York, rebaptized as *Mexicana*. Brooks Atkinson found that it 'lack[ed] showmanship' and that the 'big production numbers' were 'so monotonously balanced in design that most of them lack spontaneity'. The *New York Times* critic observed that other expressions of Mexican art were familiar in American culture, but not Mexico's 'theatre arts as a whole'. 'It would be worthwhile looking into them', he claimed, 'for some of the scenery and many of the costumes in "Mexicana" suggest an unspoiled vitality that would enrich the theatre. [ . . . ] The gay things [*Mexicana*] has generously brought to Broadway deserve versatile theatre support'. Brooks Atkinson, 'The Play: Republic of Mexico Produces Musical Revue of Native Arts With Mexican Dancers and Performers', *New York Times*, 22 April 1939, 14L+. George Jean Nathan, on the contrary, considered that the alleged absence of showmanship was what 'made and makes the show the immensely delightful thing it is.' He thought that anyone who couldn't 'discern [*Mexicana*'s] natural and unmechanical element of speed in its dance movement, its variety in music and smashing color, and its alternation of moods in its terpsichorean interpretation of tragedy, glee, pity, and passion should go out and bury his head in the Broadway sands.' George Jean Nathan, 'Through Rose-Colored Spectacles', *Newsweek*, 22 May 1939, 34.

In 1976, Mexican musical producers were still yearning for exportation to Broadway, but to no avail. That year the press reported that the New York producers Samuel Taylor and Irving Lewis would take the original Mexican production of *El fantasma de la ópera* (*The Phantom of the Opera*, 1976), by Raúl Astor and Marcial Dávila, to Broadway. Bob Fosse and Jerome Robbins were even mentioned as potential directors. Félix Zúñiga, 'Vaya, vaya: Exportaremos obra musical', *Novedades*, 18 September 1976, Espectáculos 1–3.

Through the early 1990s there were also reports about Ed Robinson and Candi Carrel producing *Supplanters!* in New York. *El economista* even reported that the contract would be signed in February 1995. 'La Plaza Chica: ¿Qué Plantón, a Broadway?', *El economista*, 31 January 1995, 54. Playbill.com reported in 1998 that Antonio Calvo, the composer and co-producer of *Houdini*, had been in negotiation with producers to export his show. He declared: 'Madrid, Buenos Aires, Tokyo, New York and London are the cities that might feel Houdini's *Magic of Love* in the following years'. Claudio Carrera, 'Mexico City Houdini Celebrates 200th Performance', *Playbill*, 7 August 1998, http://www.playbill.com/article/mexico-city-houdini-celebrates-200th-performance-com-76844, accessed 24 September 2019.

# CHAPTER 12

# STUDIES IN CONTRAST

## *Chile and Brazil*

### TIAGO MUNDIM

FROM 1933 onwards, the American government under President Franklin D. Roosevelt pursued a good-neighbour policy of non-intervention with the countries south of its borders. Not only was that foreign policy totally abandoned by later US presidents, but even in the 1930s and 1940s Latin American countries remained highly sceptical of Roosevelt's promise not to interfere with their national development, so the hoped-for reciprocal trade agreements never materialised. What the United States has managed to export successfully to South America since then, however, is musicals. This chapter will chart how Anglophone musical theatre has been produced and received in two important foreign markets of very different sizes—small Chile, with its population of just 19 million, and huge Brazil, with its 213 million people and fast-growing economy. Both countries have a special characteristic that makes them stand out from the other manifestations of global musical theatre: not only do they successfully import Anglophone shows, but they have also developed a flourishing approach to the creation of their own musicals, which are based on Latin America culture.

In this essay I will contrast data collected on the production of musical theatre in Chile with what has been produced in Brazil regarding both Anglophone musical theatre imports and homegrown musicals. I will outline the specific characteristics of each country's productions, including how they transformed their own culture into narrative-driven spectacles and expressed through them a political stance against the repressions suffered throughout the history of both countries. As a Brazilian musical theatre producer and scholar connected with its industry, I will also present detailed information on how productions in my country make use of federal tax incentives for sponsoring the performing arts, thereby encouraging private investment in Brazilian theatre.

# CHILE

The Chilean theatre experiments consistently with its own artistic forms; local companies consolidate an indigenous dramaturgy. According to Javiera Larraín and Jimmy Gavilán,[1] the first milestone of musical theatre in Chile was produced in 1958 when the playwright Luis Alberto Heiremans wrote *Esta Señorita Trini* (*This Miss Trini*), with music by the singer and actress Carmen Barros. The work was created in the form of American musical comedy but maintained its roots in Chilean culture, resulting in an unprecedentedly effective production. *Esta Señorita Trini* paved the way for the rapid development of Chilean musical theatre, peaking in 1960 with the première of *La pérgola de las flores* (*The Pergola of Flowers*), which contributed massively to the popularisation of the genre in the whole country.

A musical movement called Nueva Canción Chilena (NCCh; New Chilean Song) had great repercussions in the country between the years 1960 and 1973, combining political and social content (i.e. critical engagement) with a creative and original form that mixed 'modern' sounds and resources deriving from its roots in folk music and popular song.[2] The movement acquired its name in 1969 when Ricardo García, a journalist and radio announcer, together with the vice chancellor of communications at Catholic University, organised a seminar on the state of Chilean music. The seminar ended in a festival that became known as the Primer Festival de la Nueva Canción Chilena (First Festival of the New Chilean Song). Its objective was to disseminate the musical and theatrical expressions that had emerged in the previous years, which, by distinguishing themselves from 'typical' song, made use of new modes of musical and poetic structure as well as modern styles of acting and scenic presentation, engaging with changes occurring on the world stage and, more specifically, in Latin America.[3]

However, between 1973 and 1990 Chile experienced a period of military dictatorship led by the authoritarian government of Augusto Pinochet, which exploited all available means to prevent those who attacked the government—especially the NCCh movement, with its protest songs—from publicly voicing their criticism. The political persecution of the movement peaked with the murder of Vitor Jará, who was one of its chief exponents. Alongside Violeta Parra, Payo Grondona, Angel Parra, Isabel Parra, Rolando Alarcón, and the groups Quilapayún and Inti Illimani, Jará was one of the main exponents of the radical group, whose members were all regarded as militant communists. Yet, since the 1960s this widespread artistic movement had been renewing Chilean cultural production by returning to traditional musical folklore. After the imposition of the dictatorship, their music became an instrument of protest and denunciation against any and all forms of repression.[4]

The Chilean cultural scene was rebuilt when the authoritarian regime ended in 1990 after sixteen years. The first artistic manifestation of Chile's cultural recovery was the Festival de Teatro de las Naciones (Theatre of Nations Festival), which was organised by the Instituto Internacional del Teatro (ITI; International Theatre Institute) in collaboration with UNESCO. Held in April 1993, the festival not only brought together playwrights, actors, theorists, and internationally known theatre personalities, but also provided the Chilean public with the opportunity to see shows from around the world. It fulfilled an important political role for Chile by making national democracy internationally visible and providing a symbol for the return to a cultural life without restrictions.[5]

Nowadays, one of the most important musical theatre producers in Chile is Luis Fierro Producciones, which has managed to produce musicals of international acclaim in Chile since 2017, in association with international agencies such as MTI (Music Theatre International), the Rodgers and Hammerstein Organization, and Theatrical Rights Worldwide. Luis Fierro Producciones has produced the first Chilean productions of such huge international successes as *Annie* (2017), *Mamma Mia!* (2018), *The Sound of Music* (2018), and *Billy Elliot* (2019).

It was the producer Luis Fierro who contacted MTI to acquire the rights to *Billy Elliot*, which had its West End debut in 2005. Fierro said that he had been trying to bring this work to the Chilean stage for a long time but had to prove himself before getting its rights, because local producers must demonstrate sufficient ability and resources to produce a musical of such magnitude.[6] So, in order to obtain the licence for *Billy Elliot*, his company had to 'audition' by first producing *Annie* and *Mamma Mia!* to demonstrate that they had the requisite experience.

In addition to the blockbuster hits imported from Anglophone culture (especially from the Broadway and West End stages), Chile has also been a sponsor of original musical theatre works, reaffirming its concern with the conservation and development of a specifically Chilean dramaturgy in the field of musicals as in other types of theatre. Examples include two works that opened in 2019: a children's show inspired by *El viejo del saco* (*The Sack Man*) and a new musical created by the Contadores Auditores company, the musical soap opera *Morir de amor* (*Dying of Love*, 2018). The latter premiered at the Teatro Nescafé de las Artes in Santiago, with both plot and songs based entirely on Chilean culture.

*El viejo del saco* is a cautionary tale in the Chilean popular imaginary: in order to frighten their children into finishing their meals, parents used to tell children about the 'Sack Man', who would steal them away if they did not eat all their food. It was the first time that this legend reached the theatre in a musical version, which was created by the musician Alejandro Miranda, the director Omar Morán, and the playwright Isidora Stevenson. It tells the story of a child who is overprotected by his mother and one day believes he sees and is chased by the evil character.[7]

Totally different in style and content, *Morir de amor* was as great a success as the mega-productions that have travelled globally. The story is a full-blown Latin American melodrama focusing on Ana Luisa del Rio, the eldest daughter of a millionaire family of women. At first, everything goes smoothly in the mansion where Ana Luisa lives with her unbearable husband, until a lover from her stormy past reappears, confusing her feelings and unleashing passion, rivalries, envy, and heartbreak. This melodrama is

FIG. 12.1 A scene from the Chilean musical *Morir de amor* (2018), a full-blown Latin American melodrama. Photo: Teatro Nescafé de las Artes, Chile, provided by the author.

accompanied by a soundtrack featuring Latin American AM radio classics, which are played live by the actors and the band.[8]

Attendance at Chilean musical theatre productions is also promising. A survey of the Chilean artistic landscape in 2018 reveals at least eight huge and significantly different musicals that debuted in Santiago alone. There were modern classics like *Mamma Mia!*, with more than twenty thousand spectators, and *The Sound of Music* (fifteen thousand tickets sold), both at the Municipal de Las Condes and staged by Luis Fierro.[9] Also very popular was a tribute concert to John Lennon (*John: El último día de Lennon*, 2018) by Capital Culture (ten thousand spectators) and a local version of the Spanish text *La llamada* (*The Call*, 2013), produced by the Cow Company (six thousand spectators), in addition to the American *Murder for Two* (*Asesinato para dos*, 2011), at the Corporación Cultural de Las Condes (three thousand spectators). Finally, the Chilean originals *Condicional* (*Conditional*, 2018), *Morir de amor* (with more than 22,000 spectators), and *1995: El año que nos volvimos todos un poco locos* (*1995: The Year That We All Went a Little Crazy*, 2018), with book, lyrics, and music by Marco Antonio de la Parra and directed by Maitén Montenegro at the Teatro Nescafé de las Artes, which in the late 2010s founded the first musical theatre company in Chile.[10]

It was estimated that more than 75,000 people have seen musicals which premiered during the 2018 season; this number does not include the revivals of *La pérgola de las flores* and *La negra Ester* (*The Black Ester*, 1988) or the tour of *Mercury, la leyenda* (*Mercury, the Legend*, 2016), which has in recent years been the most popular show in

Chile, with more than a hundred thousand spectators. *Mercury, la leyenda* is about the life and career of Freddie Mercury and depicts the tense days before the monumental concert that Queen gave at London's Wembley Stadium in 1986, showing the intensive media scrutiny of his private life as well as his extravagance and genius on stage and in his compositions.

This growth of the Chilean musical theatre industry has also generated a demand for professionalisation of the artists involved in these productions. A career as a performer in musical theatre is a well-established profession around the world: in the United States, for example, there are around 140 universities that offer this kind of specialist training. As a consequence, the Chilean theatre industry has established musical theatre schools and courses in universities in order to develop the skills of acting, singing, and dancing and thereby improve the standard of multi-disciplinary performances required for stage musicals.

One of the most important musical theatre training institutions in Chile is the Projazz Instituto Profesional (Projazz Professional Institute), an independent Chilean music school recognised by the Ministry of Education of Chile.[11] George Abufhele Bus and Ana María Meza originally founded it as Projazz Music Academy in 1982. The initial initiative for it stemmed from the need for places where musicians could improve their skills in jazz and popular music. There was not sufficient training in these areas, since the only academic alternatives were in conservatories and universities dedicated to classical music and contemporary avant-garde music. In 2005 Bus and Meza decided to join the Chilean system of higher education with the assurance that this step would give recognition to their educational project, which by then had been in existence for over two decades. Thus in 2007 it became the Projazz Professional Institute, the first teaching institution to devise a professional-level jazz programme, approved by the Ministry of Education, teaching jazz, popular music, and music composition.

In 2012 two academic teams from Texas State University visited Projazz to conduct master classes. Thus an academic exchange between the two institutions was established with the graduate program in jazz and the musical theatre program. With the support of the US embassy, Projazz invited Kaitlin Hopkins, director of Texas State University's musical theatre program, and Jim Price, an acting professor—both with ample Broadway experience—to lead an open master class for the entire national community and also to hold work sessions based on the academic curriculum they intended to teach at Projazz in 2013, directed by the renowned actor and theatre director Felipe Ríos. The same year, Projazz became the first institution of higher education in the country to offer training for professional careers in musical theatre, leading to the improvement of the integrated performing arts curriculum in Chile overall; in 2015 it was given the status of 'institutional autonomy' by the Ministry of Education. Its design of musical theatre courses was modelled on plans and programmes from the most prestigious schools in North America and Europe.[12]

Besides this tertiary-level Projazz programme, there are today many other schools and training centres for musical theatre around the country, among which we can highlight the TMD (Teatro-Música-Danza [Theatre-Music-Dance]), a musical theatre company that in 1993 pioneered actor training for musical theatre in Chile. In 1998 they created the country's first musical theatre school: the Escuela de Teatro Musical Hernán Fuentes, with twenty hours of instruction per week, designed to train everyone from beginners to advanced and professional-level students.[13]

Although Chile is much smaller than Brazil, it is exceptional in its provision of higher-education training for musical theatre, offering a bachelor's degree for performers in this particular field. In Brazil, on the other hand, it is possible to identify several specialised schools and technical courses, but there are still no universities offering an undergraduate degree programme in musical theatre, even though the country is the fifth-largest musical theatre producer in the world[14].

# Brazil

The country's first school providing musical theatre training opened in 1986: the Oficina dos Menestréis in Rio de Janeiro, which initiated specialised musical theatre training in Brazil. Later on other important schools followed, such as OperÁria in 1993 and TeenBroadway in 1996, both in São Paulo, which are still in operation as of 2023.

With the subsequent growth of the musical theatre industry in Brazil and the demand for actors to perform in the Brazilian versions of the Anglophone musicals being staged around the country came the growing need for skilled casts. Large schools emerged as a consequence, such as the Escola de Atores Wolf Maya in São Paulo, which in 2001 opened a programme focused on musical theatre, with acting, singing, and dance classes modeled on the Broadway and West End musical style.[15]

In the years that followed, other important schools and training centres were established in Brazil, such as 4Act in 2009 and Curso Técnico de Teatro Musical—SESI-SP in 2018, both in São Paulo, as well as Centro de Estudos e Formação em Teatro Musical (CEFTEM) in 2013 and Instituto Brasileiro de Teatro Musical (IBTM) in 2014 in Rio de Janeiro. In addition, the success of musicals in the country was so great that in 2007 the musical schools moved beyond the boundaries of São Paulo and Rio de Janeiro to incorporate the capital of the country, with the opening of the Escola de Teatro Musical de Brasília (ETMB), which prepared actor-singer-dancers to perform not only locally and nationally, but also to work in musical productions in the United States, the United Kingdom, and Germany.[16]

Since Brazil's colonial period, theatre there has maintained a strong relationship with song and dance. The Jesuits in the mid-sixteenth century used a lot of music and dance to catechise the indigenous people, who were sensitive to these elements because they employed them in their own rituals. The church's mission to convert the 'unbelievers' employed the theatrical and musical elements present in those rituals and thus generated an appealing mood to effectively influence the natives; this purpose was not necessarily artistic, but rather was part of a religious mission to convert the Indians through art.[17] However, one early version of Brazilian musical theatre debuted in 1859, when the play

As surpresas do Senhor José da Piedade (*The Surprises of Mister José da Piedade*) marked the first musical theatre production in the country. The piece did not have a linear narrative but described social events that had taken place the previous year, with short scenes full of diverse satirical elements—typical ingredients of French revue, which served as the reference point for the creation of the show.[18]

Nevertheless, this first attempt to create an authentically national form of musical theatre was a failure, as was the second attempt in 1875: *A revista de 1874* (*Revue of 1874*). This show was pure political satire and was not well received by either the audience or the critics at the time, a politically unstable period which saw the end of the Paraguayan war and a growing number of republicans. In spite of some flops, by appealing to an audience increasingly enchanted by parodies, vaudevilles, operettas, and magicians, musical theatre eventually succeeded in the country with revues.

The national revue changed as a consequence of World War I, which hindered cultural influences from abroad. Thus, the genre was greatly influenced by the rhythms, grace, sensuality, and uniqueness of Brazilian popular music, in the process turning this style into a form that swept the nation. In the years between 1914 and 1918, the musical formula of Brazilian revues became standard all over the country. These shows had a different structure, far removed from the Portuguese or French models, so they may be deemed 'typically Brazilian'. Partly because they gave music more weight, they became the main means of promoting Brazilian popular music.[19]

The Brazilian revue established itself as one of the country's major and constantly surprising forms of theatre; no other genre was as widely produced between the 1920s and 1940s. Rio de Janeiro was transformed into a veritable theatrical hub where tourists and audiences went looking for fun, music, and beauty.[20] Even so, in the 1960s, after more than half a century of growth, musical theatre eventually lost currency as a result of political censorship under the Brazilian military government and in competition with other types of entertainment, such as dramatic theatre, cinema, and the chief mass medium of the time, television.

Conversely, as a reaction to the dictatorship of the 1960s and 1970s, political theatre took the form of musicals that responded critically to the military regime. Because of this appropriation, much political drama in Brazil in this period was presented through the medium of musical theatre. As popular entertainment, created by artists with strong political convictions, these musicals were designed to capture the audience by amusing them while at the same time expressing political views.[21]

One of the first musicals to use this approach was Augusto Boal's *Revolução na América do Sul* (*Revolution in South America*), directed by José Renato in 1960. It tells the story of the worker José da Silva—a symbol of the Brazilian people—whom corrupt politicians trap in a very precarious situation, so that he suffers from hunger and misery. These politicians used bribery to be elected to power in order to plunder the national industries and exploit the workers while ignoring the basic living conditions they were forced to endure. Structured in the form of frames, the piece was intended to present the actual social conditions of the time, in all their contradictions.

In addition to this kind of political theatre, Brazilian versions of certain famous Anglophone musicals also began to be staged in the country during the 1960s, but these were produced independently on a small scale by various local artists, because censorship also applied to shows from other nations.[22] While political musicals managed to outmanoeuvre censorship through poetic and metaphoric lyrics, adding another meaning to what was being staged, imported musicals had no such freedom of creation and adaptation. As a result, the only musicals produced were those which were not a threat to the order imposed by the military dictatorship and which had passed through the sieve of censorship.

In 1999 the Brazilian musical industry achieved a new milestone, when the CIE company (currently known as T4F—Time for Fun) organised an audition for *Rent*, adapted into Portuguese that year. Despite the show's success on international stages, the Brazilian version was not widely accepted by the audience, probably because they were not used to its musical and theatrical language, which openly addressed such sensitive issues as illicit drug use, AIDS, and various LGBTQ+ identities.[23]

Notwithstanding this failure, CIE survived to form a partnership with the Abril Group to renovate the Paramount Cine-theatre in São Paulo, which was inaugurated in 2001 with the musical *Les Misérables*, a production that attracted around 350,000 spectators in just over a year. This musical was the landmark that consolidated CIE's position and strengthened the musical theatre industry in Brazil as a whole.[24]

From this moment onwards the way the Brazilian industry produced theatre in the metropolis changed: the 'musical revolution' had begun, leading to a proliferation of productions inspired by successful Anglophone musicals. The 2001 production of *Les Misérables* can be considered ground zero of a process that developed more extensively and incrementally in the following decade, with the import of international shows and the creation of homegrown works that employed Anglophone musicals as a reference. By the end of the millennium, basic conditions were in place to promote all those musicals based on successful Anglophone productions. Generous budgets, aided by federal tax incentives for sponsorship, permitted the staging of huge shows and accelerated the professionalisation of the sector.[25]

Musical theatre as a cultural phenomenon was increasingly perceived as a marketing opportunity—that is, as a mechanism for producing a brand or a label. Thus, artistic products turned into coded interactions between companies and their target public. In 2000 Luiz Calainho, an entrepreneur who had long worked as chief executive at Sony Records, left the multinational company and assumed the role of negotiator between producers and the marketing executives of big companies. Calainho created a new model of collaboration between these two potential partners, demonstrating that a musical can be an effective signifier capable of communicating all kinds of messages to an audience.[26] For instance, the Bradesco Seguros insurance company is not interested in sponsoring a play performed in a small theatre without a safety exit and to have its name associated with an unsafe building or with a drama that is not wholesome family fare. On the contrary, companies are looking for shows in large theatres, which deal with familiar and light-hearted subject matter. Thus, Bradesco Seguros invests in works such as

FIG. 12.2 Scene from the first Brazilian production of *Les Misérables*, staged in 2001 in São Paulo. Photo: T4F, Brazil, provided by the author.

*The Lion King* (2013) precisely because it is a family show, presented in a huge, beautiful, and safe theatre.[27]

Other important entrepreneurs of musical theatre in Brazil are the team of Charles Möeller and Claudio Botelho (Möeller and Botelho). They have produced Brazilian versions of famous Anglophone musicals such as *Company* (2000), *The Sound of Music* (2008 and 2018), *Spring Awakening* (2009), *The Wizard of Oz* (2012), and *Pippin* (2019). But they do not finance only imported musicals. The pair are also known for original Brazilian musicals, such as:

- *As malvadas* (*The Cold-Eyed*, 1997), a tribute to musical comedy in the spirit of B movies, which was their first original musical;
- *Ópera do malandro* (*The Wheeler-Dealer Opera*, 2003), based on *Der Dreigroschenoper* (*The Threepenny Opera*) by Bertolt Brecht and Kurt Weill, with new text and music by Chico Buarque;
- *7: O musical* (*7: The Musical*, 2007), which incorporates elements from well-known Grimm tales, specifically *Snow White*, but has a contemporary noir mood and adult themes;

- *Cole Porter: Ele nunca disse que me amava* (*Cole Porter: He Never Said He Loved Me*, 2000 and 2019); this show tells the life story of the American composer Cole Porter from the perspective of six different women.[28]

The pair also created several other musicals; they were always concerned to add Brazilian characteristics to their shows, in their books as well as in their musical elements. Many of their musicals revolved around the biographies of Brazilian celebrities and exploited the music of different national composers, such as Chico Buarque (*Todos os musicais de Chico Buarque em 90 minutos* [*All Chico Buarque's Musicals in 90 Minutes*, 2014]) and Milton Nascimento (*Milton Nascimento: Nada será como antes; O musical* [*Milton Nascimento: Nothing Will Be Like Before; The Musical*, 2016])—two important Brazilian artists from the period of military dictatorship.[29]

In addition to Möeller and Botelho, another production company that has invested in original musicals reflecting Brazilian culture is Chaim Produções, which in 2011 premiered *Tim Maia: Vale tudo; O musical* (*Tim Maia: Everything Is Allowed; The Musical*), a show which dramatises the life of the Brazilian singer Tim Maia. Starting with his childhood in Tijuca, when he used to deliver packed lunches for a living, it covers the period when he worked in New York and finally his premature death in 1998, aged fifty-five, as a result of his addiction to drugs and alcohol. The show presents Maia's various bands, incorporating their pop hits from the 1970s, 1980s, and 1990s.

In 2013 Chaim Produções chose another Brazilian rock singer as the subject of a musical: *Cazuza: Pro dia nascer feliz* (*Cazuza: For the Day Is Born Happy*). The show depicts both the career and personal lifestyle of the eponymous singer and composer, from Cazuza's humble beginnings at the Circo Voador in 1981 until his early death from AIDS in 1990 at the age of thirty-two. It highlights his success with the band Barão Vermelho, his solo career, and his relationships with parents, friends, and lovers, as well as showcasing his passionate songs, which spoke of the yearnings of a whole generation.[30] Cazuza represented those Brazilians raised during the military dictatorship, when everything was forbidden and nothing could be said. Transgressive in his behavior, he used his music as the mouthpiece of dispossessed groups. He led a bohemian life, using drugs and promoting free love as a means to oppose the system, thus representing many dissatisfied youth. He declared himself bisexual in a period characterised by the oppression of individual freedoms and the growing fear of AIDS, increasingly stigmatised even in the LGBTQ+ community.[31]

Analysing the successful production of musicals in São Paulo and Rio de Janeiro in 2018 and 2019, it is possible to discern a huge increase in both productions of international shows and original Brazilian musicals. Among the forty musicals that premiered in São Paulo and Rio de Janeiro in 2018, twenty-two were original musicals, such as the hits *Ayrton Senna: O musical* (*Ayrton Senna: The Musical*, a biographical show about the famous Formula 1 race car driver who died in 1994), *Bibi: Uma vida em musical* (*Bibi: Life as a Musical*), concerning the career of one of the greatest Brazilian musical theatre actresses, Bibi Ferreira, and *MPB: Musical popular brasileiro* (*MPB: Brazilian Popular*

*Musical*), the fictional story of a Brazilian subsidiary of a multinational company, which prepares a show to impress visiting foreign investors, with the famous songs of MPB (popular Brazilian songs) under the supervision of a former musical theatre director. In addition, eighteen Brazilian versions of international musicals were produced in 2018, ranging in size and style from Broadway and West End successes such as *Wicked*, *Beauty and the Beast*, *The Sound of Music*, *The Little Mermaid*, *Peter Pan*, *Shrek*, and *The Phantom of the Opera* to off-Broadway musicals like *Bare: A Pop Opera*, *Tick, Tick . . . Boom!*, and *The Last Five Years*.

The first half of 2019 alone saw the premières of thirty-seven musicals, twenty original Brazilian shows, and seventeen Brazilian versions of international musicals. Among the original ones that debuted on the Rio de Janeiro–São Paulo circuit, there were musicals addressing all aspects of Brazilian culture. There were musicals about Brazilian religiosity, like *Aparecida: Um musical* (*Our Lady Aparecida: A Musical*), which follows a non-religious young couple on their journey of spiritual discovery in the hope of healing the protagonist's brain cancer, a journey that leads them to the greatest symbol of faith for Brazilians, Our Lady Aparecida, the patron saint of Brazil. There were other musicals about Brazilian regional phenomena, like *Bem sertanejo: O musical* (*Pretty Country: The Musical*), which depicts the creation and trajectory of Brazilian country music and its culture, allowing direct contact with the country's cultural roots and individual psychology. *Macunaíma: Uma rapsódia musical* (*Macunaíma: A Musical Rhapsody*) presents the saga of the indigenous Macunaíma from his birth in a village in the Amazon region of northern Brazil and his relationship with his family to his trip to southeastern Brazil, where he is confronted with a completely different culture, before he finally returns to his native tribe.

Moreover, in the same year, there were also traditional musicals about famous Brazilian personalities, such as *Carmen, a grande pequena notável* (*The Great Little Remarkable Carmen*), which portrays the life of Carmen Miranda. This Brazilian samba singer, dancer, Broadway actress, and film star was popular from the 1930s to the 1950s and was nicknamed 'the Brazilian Bombshell'; she was notorious for the signature headdress of a huge arrangement of fruit that she wore in her American films and became an international symbol of Brazil. In contrast, *Nelson Gonçalves: O amor e o tempo* (*Nelson Gonçalves: Love and Time*) is built around remarkable moments in the life of one of the greatest idols of Brazilian music, who sold over eighty million records throughout his career and was considered Brazil's 'King of Radio' in the early twentieth century.

Regarding imported Anglophone musicals that premiered at Brazilian playhouses in 2019, the great successes were *The Color Purple*, *The Phantom of the Opera*, *Peter Pan*, *Annie*, *Billy Elliot*, and *School of Rock*. The last three works showcased the talent of the Brazilian juvenile performers who led these musicals and who had trained at the numerous musical theatre schools mentioned previously. The productions evidence not only the thorough acting, singing, and dance training of these children, but that of the whole cast and technical teams currently presenting musicals to public and critical acclaim in the country.

# Federal Tax Incentives for Sponsorship

One significant reason for the major expansion of Brazil's musical theatre industry in recent years has been legislative schemes: the laws governing federal tax incentives for sponsorship such as the Lei Sarney (1986) and the Lei Rouanet (Rouanet Law, 1991), are both based on the model of patronage and regulate fiscal compensation as a way to encourage cultural production.[32]

On 23 December 1991 the Brazilian President Fernando Color established Federal Law No. 8.313 (Lei Rouanet, or Rouanet Law), which reinstates principles of Law No. 7.505 (Lei Sarney, or Sarney Law) of 2 July 1986. The latter was promulgated by Color's predecessor José Sarney one year after the creation of the Ministry of Culture; Sarney thus implemented the country's first tax incentive for cultural productions. However, after several reports of losses and fraud, owing to the state's refusal to intervene in negotiations between companies and producers, the Lei Sarney, was repealed.[33]

With the publication of the Lei Rouanet, a name chosen in honor of its originator, Sergio Paulo Rouanet, who was secretary of culture in the Color government, the Programa Nacional de Apoio à Cultura (National Cultural Incentive Program, PRONAC) was introduced; its intent was to secure and channel resources in order to promote, stimulate, and support access to cultural goods. PRONAC has since established the Fundo Nacional de Cultura (National Fund for Culture, FNC) to obtain resources primarily from public funds, such as the national treasury, lottery funds, investment funds, and others,[34] in order to distribute funding within the cultural sector. It primarily increases the diversity of funding sources for cultural production in such a way that their distribution becomes as broad as possible. The FNC aims at producing a culture geared much more towards the popular and to small producers, in opposition to the neoliberal character of the Lei Rouanet, so that the FNC plays a much smaller role in relation to patronage.[35]

The Lei Rouanet promotes investment in cultural production by companies and individuals through deductions from the sponsor's income tax, that is, 6 percent in the case of an individual and 4 percent for a registered company. As a consequence, the Lei Rouanet ties most cultural production in Brazil to sponsoring companies—a double-edged sword, because it leaves it up to sponsors to decide which types of projects they want to support. Yet it also has been one of the main vehicles for financing Brazilian musicals, thus allowing the country to develop this particular market. As the managing body, the Ministry of Culture does not try to monitor the projects receiving incentives in terms of their community impact; on the contrary, their performance is measured by accountants entirely in financial terms, and that criterion applies to both patronage and financing via the FNC.[36]

Over the years the legislation has undergone changes in order to diversify its funding mechanisms. Among these changes is that now 100 percent of the amount invested by the sponsors is deducted from their tax; therefore, the capital invested by the sponsoring company is actually reimbursed by public funds, since the money is treated as taxes owed to the government. In other words, the company converts its tax budget into marketing by means of cultural projects.[37]

Within this neoliberal culture, private initiative assumes responsibility for cultural mediation and often acts according to its own logic, resulting in a capitalist market where capital is the main objective, while culture—the creative work of cultural agents—is marginalised.[38] Brazil's cultural policy merely transfers to the private sector the choice of which projects will be supported by means of patronage[39].

This possibility of diverting government taxes into sponsorship opportunities was and remains highly attractive to private companies, since their financial investment is more than just a means to advertise their companies. In fact, the manifold positive effects generated by the overwhelming success of many musicals has fanned the desire of a wide range of important and powerful Brazilian companies to sponsor large-scale musicals. Musicals have become excellent business prospects for both sponsors and regular producers, ensuring an exponential growth of the Brazilian musical theatre industry.

# THE BRAZILIAN MUSICAL INDUSTRY AND THE LEI ROUANET

Musical theatre producers have raised millions of dollars through Lei Rouanet to promote theatrical culture and to bring some of the most famous international musicals to Brazilian stages. In view of the enormous costs of producing these musicals, it was only because of the laws incentivising cultural production that it was possible to reproduce them in Brazil along the same spectacular lines seen on Broadway or in the West End, carefully maintaining the production values of each show while adapting the dialogue and lyrics to ensure they were appealing and understandable in a Brazilian idiom.[40]

For example, *Les Misérables* was produced by T4F in 2001 for R$9,587,900 (US$3.5 million at that time), attracting an audience of 350,000 during its eleven-month run. The production featured more than 130 professionals, a revolving stage, original costumes, and imported props. A year later *Beauty and the Beast* debuted with a budget of more than double that of *Les Miz*: R$21,738,400 (around US$9 million at that time). The results were even more impressive: 600,000 spectators over nineteen months.

Since *Beauty and the Beast*, T4F has been producing one musical after another. In 2014 the company simultaneously staged blockbusters like *The Lion King* at the Teatro Renault and *Jesus Christ Superstar* at the Teatro Tomie Otake, both funded with resources capitalised by means of the Lei Rouanet. T4F followed the successful three-month season of *The Lion King*, with *Mudança de hábito*, the Brazilian staging of *Sister Act*, and *Antes tarde do que nunca*, a local version of *Nice Work If You Can Get It*.

Since *Les Misérables* in 2001, the number of shows opening in Brazil has increased. In addition to new shows, there were also new producers specialising in the production of original work, such as Aventura Entretenimento, created in 2008 by the union between Luiz Calainho, Aniela Jordan, and the partners Charles Möeller and Claudio Botelho. That same year the company had already produced several musicals on the Rio de Janeiro–São Paulo circuit, and 2012 alone saw their shows grossing R$19,881,046 (approximately US$8 million).[41]

In this crowded marketplace, the Australian musical *Priscilla, Queen of the Desert* premiered at the majestic and modern Teatro Bradesco in São Paulo, produced by Geo Eventos, a company linked to the Brazilian television company Organizações Globo, which was set up in 2010 but ended its activities in 2013. The show was immense: the stage of the theatre had to be reinforced in order to support the size and the weight (twenty-three tons) of the show's scenery, including the famous eight-ton bus, Priscilla. There were twenty-eight actors onstage, and the production directly or indirectly involved more than a hundred people and featured five hundred costumes and two hundred wigs. The bus alone was estimated to cost more than R$5,000,000 (US$1,500,000). Maintaining a production of this size for a lengthy period of time demands a lot of money, which was acquired through the funding system outlined above.[42]

Unlike Geo Eventos, the partnership of Claudia Raia and Sandro Chaim has had great success. After the tour of *Cabaret* in 2011, Raia showed even more ambition by bringing the classic Gershwin tap-dance musical *Crazy for You* to São Paulo. Although they had high production values, both of these shows toured Brazil's main theatres without making concessions to their elaborate scenography. Touring a show with a budget of more than R$5,000,000 (US$1,000,000) was only possible with a guarantee that all costs would be paid, including the transportation of sets and costumes, technical staff (some cities do not have technicians skilled in musical theatre), and all the artists involved. Just like every other production, *Crazy for You* depended on the tax incentive to cover its entire production costs.[43]

The box-office take alone cannot always cover the full expense of a musical, even if all its performances are sold out, because the Lei Rouanet stipulates that the vast majority of tickets must be offered at affordable prices. This was the case with the musicals toured by Claudia Raia and Sandro Chaim, which always performed to huge crowds around the country but could not rely on ticket sales alone to cover the expenses of the tour, making the tax incentives vital for the production to recoup its costs.

For a musical to sustain itself without tax incentives, tickets would have to be sold at a much higher price than is currently the case, which would pose a great risk to producers, who normally do not have enough money to run that risk, especially when it comes to large productions. At the moment, relying on box-office returns is only possible for those productions with a small cast and crew; and even in those cases, there is no guarantee of recovering all the costs, which makes the production of musicals in Brazil without tax incentives a high-risk business.

# Local Tax Incentives

Beyond the aforementioned national programmes such as the Lei Rouanet, PRONAC, and FNC, there are also local alternatives for raising funds as well as tax incentives for cultural productions outside the large urban centres, which aim to decentralise tax incentives in order to encourage cultural production in smaller cities. Customarily, the Lei Rouanet mainly covers shows and events that are part of the São Paulo–Rio de Janeiro circuit; the high population density of these cities (the two most populous cities in the country, with twelve million and six million inhabitants respectively) makes it even more attractive for sponsors to reach out to those people via a musical's advertising.

Other states and municipalities are allowed to create their own systems to encourage local cultural production. For instance, Brasília, the federal capital, operates a fund for supporting culture called the Fundo de Apoio à Cultura (FAC, Culture Support Fund), which awards public money to selected projects, subdivided into specific artistic fields, from audiovisual, theatre, dance, and musicals to art exhibitions and book launches, supporting about four hundred small projects every year. FAC has a far less neoliberal approach than the Lei Rouanet, since the projects are chosen on artistic merit and not to further the specific interests of the sponsoring companies.

Although Brasilia is the third most populous city in the country, with three million inhabitants and much of its population being made up of members of the higher social classes, it is still a very young city—it was founded in 1960—and throughout its existence has undertaken few initiatives in the area of culture. For example, the city has few theatres, and most of these are small venues with between one hundred and three hundred seats. The only public theatre in the city, the Teatro Nacional (National Theatre), which has two large stages (the Villa-Lobos room, which seats fourteen hundred and is the only stage in the city designed to host opera, musicals, and ballet, and the Martins Penna room, which holds four hundred) has been closed since 2014 for a refurbishment that has so far not happened, owing to a lack of public funding. The city also possesses three large private theatres that can accommodate around five hundred people each, but they charge a great deal of money for rent and equipment. Consequently, there are not enough theatres in Brasilia for all of the city's productions—especially venues with stages large enough to host a musical, with its complex scenery, large cast, technical staff, and musicians. Besides, the budget for most productions is so small that it only allows them to run for a few weeks.

Owing to the constant lack of investment in Brasília's theatrical venues, the Lei Rouanet does not attract much investment from big sponsors to the city, since the shows in the federal capital cannot attract large audiences, playing for a much shorter period of time (normally two weeks) than the musicals in São Paulo and Rio de Janeiro, where some may run for a year. This problem also extends to the rest of the country, which necessitates the creation of local incentives to foster theatrical production in Brasilia and other small cities around Brazil.

Therefore, supported by FAC resources, ETMB in Brasília has been producing original musicals since 2010. Although the shows are put together on smaller budgets—the FAC has a limit of R$120,000 (around US$35,000) for each project—ETMB has devised new works with books, songs, and musical arrangements that express Brazilian culture. Their first original musical was the show *Um homem para chamar de Sir* (*A Man to Call Sir*), which premiered in 2010, with an original libretto by Rafael Oliveira and musical direction by Michelle Fiúza, meta-theatrically presenting the story of a theatre group trying to relaunch a musical that had premiered more than twenty years prior. A jukebox musical, it used songs by Elton John to reveal the love affairs (actually, mismatches) of the various members of the two ensembles performing the show.

In 2011 ETMB produced another original show with the title *Correndo atrás* (*Chasing*), about three strong women chasing their dreams. It was again a jukebox musical, with songs from several Anglophone musicals (including some of the ETMB librettist's favourite numbers) that helped to tell the story of women who are involved in a typically Brazilian wedding ceremony and who throughout the event seek to achieve their dreams of love, family, sexual fulfilment, and professional satisfaction.[44]

As early as 2014, ETMB produced their first musical featuring both an original libretto and an original score. With a book and lyrics by Walter Amantéa, musical direction and arrangements by Michelle Fiúza, direction by Camila Meskell, and choreography by Aleska Ferro, the show *Entre sonhos e sonhos* (*Between Dreams and Dreams*) was seen at the Teatro La Salle in Brasília by nearly two thousand spectators over six performances in one week. The show told the story of a boy who is attending an undergraduate college course in social communication but dreams of becoming a great national rock star. Since pursuing a music career in Brazil is a major challenge and not culturally acceptable, his parents do not support him in his endeavour, forcing the boy to choose between pursuing his dreams and continuing to try to live according to the social standards that have been set for him; in the end, despite all of the hardships, he still attempts to realise his dreams.

Two years later ETMB premiered the musical *Domingo no parque* (*Sunday in the Park*), with an original book authored by Diógenes Rezende, Rafael Oliveira, and Wilson Granja; it incorporates the music of Gilberto Gil but presents songs that over the years have achieved immense success in Brazilian musicals in new arrangements by the musical director, Michelle Fiúza.[45] This musical was produced with FAC resources in the cities of Brasília, Ceilândia, Gama, and Taguatinga, reaching an audience of around three thousand people. It follows the love triangle between Juliana, João, and José (characters in the homonymous music by Gilberto Gil that inspired the musical's libretto) who live in the interior of Brazil; it features many Brazilian songs and scenography that portray the typical culture of the country's interior.

The following year, also with the support of FAC, ETMB produced the musical *Quem um dia irá dizer* (*Who Will Say It One Day*), based on the story of Eduardo and Mônica, two characters from a famous Brazilian song by the rock band Legião Urbana. With a new plot and arrangements, the show was presented in 2017 to an audience of approximately two thousand people in the cities of Brasília and Taguatinga. The original libretto

FIG. 12.3 A scene from Brazilian musical *Domingo no parque* (2016), performed in Brasilia. Photo: Tiago Mundim.

was written by Fernanda Resende, and it had musical direction by Michelle Fiúza, direction by Tiago Mundim, and choreography by Aleska Ferro. The musical uses songs by artists that came to prominence in the city of Brasilia and who were nationally or internationally successful, focusing on the show's fictional couple. Eduardo and Mônica represent the local culture of the country's capital, and there are passing references to the Brazilian rock revolution and to the city's growth in the 1960s, even allusions to Brasília's modernist architecture in the show's design.

In the same year, ETMB also produced *Agreste*, using a local Brazilian word which signifies both 'rural' and 'arid'. Written by Thais Uessugui, the piece tells the story of a northeastern family who moves to Brasilia to seek a new life during the period of its construction in the 1960s. Under the same funding system, *Agreste* toured Brasília, Taguatinga, and Ceilândia, attracting an audience of approximately two thousand people, illustrating the family's experiences with the help of popular Brazilian songs from the 1960s. Filled with dance numbers evoking a playful ambience, it addresses important social issues such as the hunger of the people of Brazil's northeast and the prejudice against those immigrants who left their homeland to build the Brazilian capital in the middle of the country. Because of the positive audience reaction and because they received small amounts from the FAC, there were talks of relaunching both *Agreste* and *Entre sonhos e sonhos* in 2020, but since FAC resources have been cut to almost one-fifth of what they had been in 2019, these new tours never materialized. With the revival of these two projects, a musical theatre market is being established in Brazil's federal capital. While this development may be slow compared to São Paulo and Rio de Janeiro,

FIG. 12.4 A scene from the Brazilian musical *Agreste* (2017), staged in Brasília. Photo: Tiago Mundim.

the city at the same time is also intensifying specialised training for Brazilian actor-singer-dancers, preparing the performers for both the national and the international industry.[46]

## FINAL CONSIDERATIONS

Despite the many differences between their cultures and industries, it is possible to see that musical theatre in both Brazil and Chile has been growing year by year as a consequence of the successful creation of a new market in each nation. So while it is possible in both countries to see blockbuster hits from Broadway and the West End such as *The Sound of Music* in 2018 and *Billy Elliot* in 2019, one can also observe an increase in the number of musicals that mix aspects of the Anglophone forms of the genre with local cultural features, as in the Chilean *Morir de amor* or the Brazilian *Quem um dia irá dizer*, emphasising the unique culture of each respective Latin American country.

One of the current obstacles to the production of musical theatre in Brazil is connected to the rise of extreme right-wing political representatives. As soon as Jair Bolsonaro took over as the nation's new president in 2019, he dismantled the Ministry of Culture and cancelled many of the cultural funding programmes. These changes also directly affected the Lei Rouanet by establishing a new investment limit of only R$1 million for each project (US$270,000). The repercussions for the mounting of large musicals on the Rio de Janeiro–São Paulo circuit are palpable, since those productions usually cost more than R$10,000,000 per show. The FAC is a regional program affected by this government policy of dismantling culture: it had funds earmarked for projects already approved in 2018 and, as mentioned above, had its resources drastically slashed to one-fifth of their original value.

In spite of countless industry challenges, the success of musical theatre productions in Brazil has been so great that new producers are emerging and establishing innovative forms of partnership to generate financing for small musicals, such as *Cargas d'água* (*Out of Water: A Brazilian Pocket Musical*), which was performed with only three actors and toured in several Brazilian states in 2018–2019. This was an independent, low-budget production that raised money through crowdfunding before eventually establishing international partnerships,[47] which allowed the show to debut its English version in 2019 in both New York and London.

The musical *Cargas d'água* is a coming-of-age story about a young boy's determination to save his best friend by returning him to the sea. The protagonist Kid has forgotten his name, identity, and former life. When he makes a new friend, Mr Out of Water, they venture out to find the sea. Along the way the pair meet traditional Brazilian characters who help them on their journey. With a book and lyrics by Vitor Rocha and music by Rocha and Ana Paula Villar, the musical won the Brazilian Bibi Ferreira Award for Best New Playwright in 2018. The musical also received Aplauso Brazil nominations for Best Musical and Best Original Score and Lyrics in addition to a Bibi Ferreira nomination for its original score.[48]

Since then other low-budget musicals have been produced seeking to maintain high artistic quality in spite of more limited financial resources, leading Brazilian musical theatre producers to invest in shows with minimal casts and scenography, thereby decreasing the production costs to allow a small financial return that in the long run may enable the Brazilian musical theatre industry to prosper.

## Notes

1. Javiera Larraín and Jimmy Gavilán, Reseña de Martín Farías Zúñiga, *Encantadores de serpientes: Músicos de teatro en Chile 1988–2011 y Reconstruyendo el sonido de la escena: Músicos de teatro en Chile 1947–1987*', Apuntes de teatro 139 (2014): 146–150, http://www.rev istaapuntes.uc.cl/images/indice_139.pdf, accessed 3 February 2021
2. Sílvia Sônia Simões, 'La nueva canción chilena: O canto como arma revolucionária', *História social* 1, no. 18 (2010): 151.
3. Ibid., 138.
4. Cassio Michel dos Santos Camargo and Rafael Souza Alves, 'Ditadura, repressão e música no Chile', *Oficina do historiador* 3, no. 2 (2011): 118.
5. Juan Villegas, 'El teatro chileno de la postdictadura', *Revista de literatura hispánica* 69, no. 13 (2009), 190.
6. 'Creamos sueños y los hacemos realidad', Luis Fierro Producciones, https://www.luisfierrop roducciones.com/, accessed 1 June 2019.
7. 'Un género pop: El teatro musical se afina para el 2019', *Culto: La tercera: Una guía de cultura pop*, 11 November 2018, http://culto.latercera.com/2018/11/11/genero-pop-teatro-musical-se-afina-2019/, accessed 30 September 2019.

8. 'Morir de amor con este musical cebollero y kitsch', *Finde Latercera*, 27 July 2018, http://finde. latercera.com/cultura-pop/morir-de-amor-teatro-nescafe/, accessed 30 September 2019.

9. The Teatro Municipal de Las Condes opened on 25 August 2010 and has 809 seats. It has presented more than five hundred works, which were attended by over a million spectators in the first nine years of its existence; https://www.tmlascondes.cl/teatro/, accessed 30 September 2019.

10. 'Creamos sueños y los hacemos realidad'.

11. 'El Instituto Profesional Projazz cumple 9 años en 2016', *Projazz—Instituto Professional*, http://www.projazz.cl/, accessed 1 June 2019.

12. Ibid.

13. 'La Escuela de Teatro Musical *Hernán Fuentes*', TMD Escuela y Compañía de Teatro Musical, http://www.hernanfuentescruz.com/, accessed 1 June 2019.

14. Ery Filho, Lima Requena, and Patrícia Bieging, 'Lei Rouanet e a Broadway paulista: O teatro musical na cidade de São Paulo', *Revista estética* 1 (2015): 1–17.

15. Tiago Elias Mundim, 'Contextualização do teatro musical na contemporaneidade: Conceitos, treinamento do ator e inteligências múltiplas' (master's thesis, Universidade de Brasília, 2014), 73.

16. Tiago Elias Mundim, 'A utilização de tecnologias em processos de aprendizagem, treinamento e performance do ator-cantor-bailarino de Teatro Musical' (PhD diss., Universidade de Brasília, 2018).

17. Sábato Magaldi, *Panorama do teatro brasileiro* (São Paulo: Global Editora, 1997), 16–17.

18. Mundim, 'Contextualização do teatro musical na contemporaneidade', 66.

19. Neyde Veneziano, *De pernas para o ar: Teatro de revista em São Paulo* (São Paulo: Imprensa Oficial, 2006), 126.

20. Neyde Veneziano, 'É brasileiro, já passou de americano', *Revista poiésis* 11, no. 16 (2010): 52–61, https://periodicos.uff.br/poiesis/article/view/26977, https://doi.org/10.22409/poie sis.1116.52-61, accessed 15 February 2021.

21. Mundim, 'Contextualização do teatro musical na contemporaneidade', 66–67.

22. Ibid., 68.

23. Ibid., 72.

24. Ibid., 72–73.

25. Bernardo Fonseca Machado, 'Empreendedorismo na "Broadway Brasileira": Análise do discurso de produtores nacionais de Teatro Musical', paper presented at the 29th Reunião Brasileira de Antropologia, Natal, Rio Grande del Norte, 3–6 August 2014, 2.

26. Ibid., 8–9.

27. Ibid., 10.

28. Tânia Carvalho, *Charles Möeller e Claudio Botelho: Os reis dos musicais* (São Paulo: Imprensa Oficial do Estado de São Paulo, 2009), 157.

29. Mundim, 'Contextualização do teatro musical na contemporaneidade', 76.

30. Ibid., 78–79.

31. Cazuza, 'Cazuza: O poeta está vivo', 2019, http://cazuza.com.br, accessed 30 September 2019.

32. Cristiane García Olivieri, *Cultura neoliberal: Leis de incentivo como política pública de cultura* (São Paulo: Escrituras, 2004).

33. Lusia Angelete Ferreira and Manoel Marcondes Machado Neto, *Economia da cultura: Contribuição para a construção do campo e histórico da gestão de organizações culturais no Brasil* (Rio de Janeiro: Editora Ciência Moderna, 2011).

34. Ibid.
35. Olivieri, *Cultura neoliberal*.
36. Ibid.
37. Filho, Requena, and Bieging, *Lei Rouanet e a Broadway paulista*, 4–5.
38. Marilena Chaui, *Cidadania cultural: O direito à cultura* (São Paulo: Editora Fundação Perseu Abramo, 2006), 75.
39. Filho, Requena, and Bieging, *Lei Rouanet e a Broadway paulista*, 4.
40. Ibid., 1.
41. Machado, 'Empreendedorismo na "Broadway Brasileira"', 2–3.
42. Filho, Requena, and Bieging, *Lei Rouanet e a Broadway paulista*, 11–12.
43. Ibid., 13.
44. Mundim, 'Contextualização do teatro musical na contemporaneidade', 80.
45. Mundim, 'A utilização de tecnologias', 129.
46. Ibid., 130.
47. 'Notícias sobre o teatro musical brasileiro', *Entre Atos*, 26 October 2018, https://www.entreatosloja.com.br, accessed 30 September 2019.
48. *Cargas d'água* (*Out of Water: A Brazilian Pocket Musical*), https://www.outofwatermusical.com/, accessed 30 September.

## BIBLIOGRAPHY

Aragão, Helena. '*My Fair Lady* em versão nacional: O musical com Bibi Ferreira foi sucesso de público', 15 July 2014, http://www.funarte.gov.br/brasilmemoriadasartes/acervo/foto-carlos/my-fair-lady-emversao-nacional/, accessed 30 September 2019.

'Archivo de la música en el teatro chileno'. Musica Teatral, http://www.musicateatral.cl/, accessed 30 June 2019.

Aristotle. *Poetics*. Translated with an introduction and notes by Malcolm Heath. London: Penguin Books, 1996.

Atkey, Mel. *A Million Miles from Broadway: Musical Theatre beyond New York and London*. Vancouver and London: Friendlysong, 2012.

Academia Verónica Villarroel. 'Taller integral que busca la práctica de las disciplinas de canto, actuación y baile con repertorio del teatro musical.' Academia Verónica Villarroel, 1 June 2019, https://www.avv.cl/index.html#cursos-p, accessed 30 September 2019.

Balk, H. Wesley. *The Complete Singer-Actor Training for Music Theatre*. Minneapolis: University of Minnesota Press, 1977.

Bartow, Arthur. *Training of the American Actor*. New York: Theatre Communications Group, 2006.

Berk, Ronald. 'No Teacher Left Behind: Teaching Strategies for the Net Generation'. *Transformative Dialogues: Teaching and Learning Journal* 3, no. 2 (2009): 77–90, https://journals.kpu.ca/index.php/td/article/view/983, accessed 22 January 2021.

Bogart, Anne. *And Then, You Act: Making Art in an Unpredictable World*. London and New York: Routledge, 2007.

Brasil. *Lei Rouanet*. Law no. 8.313, 23 December 1991, http://www.planalto.gov.br/ccivil_03/leis/l8313cons.htm, accessed 30 September 2019.

Brook, Peter. *A porta aberta*. Rio de Janeiro: Civilização Brasileira, 2005.

Budasz, Rogério. 'Perspectivas para o estudo da ópera e teatro musical no Brasil do período colonial ao primeiro reinado'. In *Anais do VI Encontro de Musicologia Histórica, Juiz de Fora, 22 a 25 de julho de 2004*, 22–37. Juiz de Fora: Centro Cultural Pró-Música, 2006.

Calainho, Luiz. *Reinventando a si mesmo: Uma provocação autobiográfica*. Rio de Janeiro: Agir, 2013.

Camargo, Cassio Michel dos Santos, and Rafael Souza Alves. 'Ditadura, repressão e música no Chile'. *Oficina do Historiador* 3, no. 2 (2011): 112–125, 2 August 2011, https://revistas eletronicas.pucrs.br/ojs/index.php/oficinadohistoriador/article/view/8861, accessed 12 February 2021.

Cargas. *Cargas d'água (Out of Water: A Brazilian Pocket Musical)*, 2019, https://www.outofw atermusical.com/, accessed 30 September 2019.

Carvalho, Tânia. *Charles Möeller e Claudio Botelho: Os reis dos musicais*. São Paulo: Imprensa Oficial do Estado de São Paulo, 2009.

Cazuza. *Cazuza: O poeta está vivo*, 2019, http://cazuza.com.br, accessed 30 September 2019.

Chauí, Marilena. *Cidadania cultural: O direito à cultura*. São Paulo: Editora Fundação Perseu Abramo, 2006.

'Clases Integrales de Teatro Musical'. *Academia Dartis*, 1 June 2019, http://dartisacademia.cl/tea tro-musical/, accessed 30 September 2019.

Comparato, Doc. *Da criação ao roteiro: Teoria e prática*. São Paulo: Summus Editorial, 2009.

*Creamos sueños y los hacemos realidad*. Luis Fierro Producciones, 1 June 2019, https://www.lui sfierroproducciones.com/, accessed 30 September 2019.

Deer, Joe. *Directing in Musical Theatre: An Essential Guide*. London/New York: Routledge, 2014.

Duarte, Marcia de Freitas. *Práticas de Organizar na Indústria Criativa: a Produção de um Espetáculo de Teatro Musical em São Paulo—SP*. Tese de Doutorado, Escola de Administração de Empresas de São Paulo - Fundação Getúlio Vargas (EAESP/FGV), 2015.

'El Instituto Profesional Projazz cumple 9 años en 2016'. Projazz—Instituto Professional, http://www.projazz.cl/,, accessed 1 June 2019.

'Entrevista al director del musical *Mamma Mia!* Eduardo Yedro: "El público se va a ir con la experiencia de ver un musical de un alto nivel". *Fundación Culturizarte*, 11 April 2018, https://culturizarte.cl/entrevista-al-director-del-musical-mamma-mia-eduardo-yedro-el-publico-se-va-a-ir-con-la-experiencia-de-ver-un-musical-de-un-alto-nivel/, accessed 30 September 2019.

Evans, Mark. *The Actor Training*. London and New York: Routledge, 2015.

Ferreira, Lusia Angelete, and Manuel Marcondes Machado Neto. *Economia da cultura: Contribuição para a construção do campo e histórico da gestão de organizações culturais no Brasil*. Rio de Janeiro: Editora Ciência Moderna, 2011.

Filho, Ery, Lima Requena, and Patrícia Bieging. 'Lei Rouanet e a Broadway paulista: O teatro musical na cidade de São Paulo'. *Revista estética* 1 (2015): 1–17.

Harvard, Paul. *Acting through Song: Techniques and Exercises for Musical-Theatre Actors*. London: Nick Hern Books, 2013.

Hurtado, María de La Luz. 'Teatro chileno: Historicidad y autorreflexión'. *Revista Nuestra América* 7 (2009), http://hdl.handle.net/10284/2691, accessed 14 February 2021.

Koelsch, Stefan. 'Brain Correlates of Music-evoked Emotions'. *Nature Reviews | Neuroscience* 15 (March 2014): 170–180, https://www.nature.com/articles/nrn3666 – https://doi.org/10.1038/nrn3666, accessed 31 January 2021.

'La Escuela de Teatro Musical Hernán Fuentes'. TMD Escuela y Compañía de Teatro Musical, http://www.hernanfuentescruz.com/, accessed 1 June 2019.

Larraín, Javiera, and Jimmy Gavilán. 'Reseña de Martín Farías Zúñiga, *Encantadores de serpientes: Músicos de teatro en Chile 1988–2011 y Reconstruyendo el sonido de la escena: Músicos de teatro en Chile 1947–1987'. Apuntes de teatro* 139 (2014): 146–150, http://www.rev istaapuntes.uc.cl/images/indice_139.pdf, accessed 3 February 2021.

Lent, Roberto. *Cem bilhões de neurônios? Conceitos fundamentais de neurociência.* 2nd ed. Lisbon: Atheneu, 2010.

Machado, Bernardo Fonseca. 'Empreendedorismo na "Broadway Brasileira": Análise do discurso de produtores nacionais de Teatro Musical.' Paper presented at the 29th Reunião Brasileira de Antropologia, Natal, Rio Grande del Norte, 3–6 August 2014.

Magaldi, Sábato. *Panorama do teatro brasileiro.* São Paulo: Global Editora, 1997.

Molnar-Szakacs, Istvan, and Kate Overy. 'Being Together in Time: Musical Experience and the Mirror Neuron System.' *Music Perception: An Interdisciplinary Journal* 26, no. 5 (2009): 489–504, https://online.ucpress.edu/mp/article-abstract/26/5/489/62447/Being-Together-in-Time-Musical-Experience-and-the?redirectedFrom=fulltext—https://doi.org/10.1525/mp.2009.26.5.489, accessed 15 February 2021.

Molnar-Szakacs, Istvan, and Kate Overy. 'Music and Mirror Neurons: From Motion to "E"motion.' *Social Cognition and Affective Neuroscience* 1, no. 3 (2006): 235–241, https://academic.oup.com/scan/article/1/3/235/2362883—https://dx.doi.org/10.1093/scan/nsl029, accessed 15 February 2021.

'*Morir de amor* con este musical cebollero y kitsch.' *Finde Latercera,* 27 July 2018, http://finde. latercera.com/cultura-pop/morir-de-amor-teatro-nescafe/, accessed 30 September 2019.

Mundim, Tiago Elias. 'A utilização de tecnologias em processos de aprendizagem, treinamento e performance do ator-cantor-bailarino de teatro musical.' PhD diss., Universidade de Brasília, 2018, https://repositorio.unb.br/handle/10482/34744, accessed 3 January 2021.

Mundim, Tiago Elias. 'Contextualização do teatro musical na contemporaneidade: conceitos, treinamento do ator e inteligências múltiplas.' Master's thesis, Universidade de Brasília, 2014, https://repositorio.unb.br/handle/10482/16165, accessed 5 January, 2021.

'Musical "El Mago de Oz" vuelve con reestreno en Las Condes.' Radio Cooperativa, 4 May 2012, https://www.cooperativa.cl/noticias/entretencion/espectaculos/musical-el-mago-de-oz-vuelve-con-reestreno-en-las-condes/2012-05-04/201116.html, accessed 30 September 2019.

'Notícias sobre o teatro musical brasileiro.' *Entre Atos,* 26 October 2017, https://entre-atos.com/musical-regional-e-inedito-lanca-site-onde-o-publico-pode-colaborar-com-espetaculo/, accessed 30 September 2019.

Olivieri, Cristiane Garcia. *Cultura neoliberal: Leis de incentivo como política pública de cultura.* São Paulo: Escrituras, 2004.

Selioni, Vasiliki. 'Laban-Aristotle: ζώον (Zoon) in Theatre Πράξις (Praxis); Towards a Methodology for Movement Training for the Actor and in Acting.' PhD thesis, Royal Central School of Speech and Drama, University of London, 2013.

Simões, Sílvia Sônia. 'La nueva canción chilena: O canto como arma revolucionária.' *História social* 1, no. 18 (2010): 137–156, https://www.ifch.unicamp.br/ojs/index.php/rhs/article/view/355, accessed 14 February 2021.

Taylor, Millie. *Musical Theatre, Realism and Entertainment.* London and New York: Routledge, 2016.

'Um mundo cheio de conteúdo pra quem é fã de musicais.' *Mundo dos musicais,* https://mundo dosmusicais.com, accessed 30 June 2019.

'Un género pop: El teatro musical se afina para el 2019'. *Culto: La tercera; Una guía de cultura pop*, 11 November 2018, http://culto.latercera.com/2018/11/11/genero-pop-teatro-musical-se-afina-2019/, accessed 30 September 2019.

Veneziano, Neyde. *De pernas para o ar: Teatro de revista em São Paulo*. São Paulo: Imprensa Oficial, 2006.

Veneziano, Neyde. 'É brasileiro, já passou de americano'. *Revista poiésis* 11, no. 16 (2010): 52–61, https://periodicos.uff.br/poiesis/article/view/26977, https://doi.org/10.22409/poie sis.1116.52-61, accessed 15 February 2021.

Villegas, Juan. 'El teatro chileno de la postdictadura'. *Revista de literatura hispánica* 69, no. 13 (2009): 189–205, http://digitalcommons.providence.edu/inti/vol1/iss69/13, accessed 14 February 2021.

Wagner, Richard. *A obra de arte do futuro*. Lisbon: Antígona, 2003.

# PART V

## POPULAR IN BRITAIN

CHAPTER 13

# THAT SPECIAL RELATIONSHIP

*Dolores Gray, Mary Martin, and Elaine Stritch on the Postwar London Stage*

ROBERT GORDON

## INTRODUCTION: TRANSATLANTIC TRAFFIC

ALTHOUGH a two-way transatlantic exchange of performers between the United States and the West End began in the early nineteenth century,[1] American stars performing in London transfers of hit Broadway musicals had until the 1950s been the exception rather than the rule. The enormous success of Fred and Adele Astaire in George and Ira Gershwin's *Lady Be Good* (1924) was repeated in London in 1926. Paul Robeson, for whom the role of Joe in *Show Boat* (1927) had originally been written, did not in fact make his debut in the show until its West End première of 1928, when his performance in London immediately established his legend. Apart from the jazz singers Elisabeth Welch (who based herself in the British capital after her initial appearance there in 1933) and Adelaide Hall (who remained in the UK after her debut in London in 1938), it is notable that few American musical theatre stars made this kind of impact in London until after the war. Mary Martin and Dolores Gray were among the first wave of American stage performers whom the British took to their hearts in the immediate postwar years;[2] they were followed a few years later by Elaine Stritch.

Without the necessity of complicated cultural 'translation', these entertainers personified in cultural terms what Winston Churchill had since 1944 referred to as the 'special relationship'[3]—enhanced by the close co-operation between the two countries during the early years of the Cold War. The 'special relationship' between the United States and Britain may have reached its nadir in the era of Donald Trump and Boris Johnson; still, a chronological survey of the response of London audiences to Gray,

Martin, and Stritch—all three Broadway actors active between 1946 and 2002—enables one to trace the changes that have occurred in the British understanding of the relationship between the two cultures from the height of its Cold War urgency to its current status since the Russian invasion of the Ukraine.

The importation of American performers to the UK ceased during World War II. John Snelson has calculated that the number of 'alien permits' issued by British Actors' Equity 'declined from seventy-one in 1938 to two in 1940. From 1941 to 1946 no figures were given and, presumably, no permits were issued. [ ... ] In 1946, three permits were granted to alien performers, rising dramatically to 223 for the following year'.[4] Snelson has also argued persuasively that the idea of an 'American invasion' of the West End by Broadway musicals as a result of the postwar triumph of *Oklahoma!* and *Annie Get Your Gun* in 1947 was a myth readily perpetuated by journalists in the 1940s and 1950s to account for the overwhelming success of these two rambunctious and optimistic musicals and those such as *South Pacific* and *Guys and Dolls* that arrived in their wake in 1951 and 1953, respectively. Only a relatively small number of permits were in fact granted to American artists in *musicals*: between 1951 and 1957, the numbers varied annually between seven and twenty-six.[5]

Although the invasion might have been something of a journalistic myth, it was reinforced by the influential young reviewer Kenneth Tynan, who more accurately than most diagnosed the reasons for the overwhelming enthusiasm of London audiences after the war for the specifically 'American' qualities of the two Broadway shows, which opened almost simultaneously on West End stages in 1947:

> The powerful sunlight, the blithe pushfulness of shows like *Annie Get Your Gun* and *Oklahoma!* had an effect which [ ... ] no dogmatic pen can ever annihilate. The lesson they had to teach the English stage is easily stated: they taught abandon. The young people in them would catapult joyously onto the stage, kick off their shoes, shoot out the lights, and then dash out into the spacious air, shouting at the sky. An Englishman in *Oklahoma!* would have looked as stiff and static as a scarecrow.[6]

Tynan conveniently avoids mention of the comparable impact of Noel Gay's musical comedy *Me and My Girl* (1937), which he was too young to remember, but the gleeful sing-along effect of Lupino Lane's rumbustious belting and strutting of the 'The Lambeth Walk' had become legendary for just the sort of abandon to which he was referring, even generating a dance craze in the country shortly after the show's opening. Nevertheless, Tynan's response conveys a sense of the energy and classlessness that were hallmarks of American culture attractive to British audiences exhausted by the war and envious of the optimism of their American allies.

While British people may at times have had mixed feelings about the Americans they had encountered during the 'friendly invasion' between 1942 and 1945, when 500,000 GIs were stationed in Britain and almost three million passed through the country, the entry of the United States into the war had after all turned the tide against the Nazis by contributing both troops and military equipment, so by the end of the war the general population were on the whole warmly predisposed to Americans. Although superficially familiar with popular myths of American society perpetuated in Hollywood movies, the war was the first time most British people had actually met Americans—and then almost all were men.[7] Some may have regarded the GIs as 'oversexed, overpaid. and over here', but according to Neil Wynn, women in particular came to regard 'America as an ideal'.[8]

# RIVALS OF ETHEL MERMAN

While the appearance of a number of young female American stage and screen stars on the London stage immediately following the end of World War II was undoubtedly greeted by female and male theatre-goers alike as a welcome innovation, it is perhaps significant that the most important American musical theatre star did not perform in London for another twenty-nine years. Although known in the UK from some of the eleven films in which she had featured, Ethel Merman, the unrivalled star of Broadway musicals between 1930 and 1950, declined to repeat her triumphs on the English stage. By the time she did decide to appear in London in September 1974, she was sixty-six years old and her career in musical theatre was effectively at an end.[9]

In her place it was left to the American musical theatre stars Dolores Gray, Mary Martin, and—over a decade later—Elaine Stritch to win the affection of British audiences. For different reasons, each was or might easily be compared to the brassy Merman; however, their performances on the London stage presented the kind of images of American womanhood that would have been more comfortably embraced by a British audience than the tough New York persona of the somewhat overpowering Merman.

Between 1940 and 1969 the only American stage stars other than Merman who did *not* cross the pond were Carol Channing and Gwen Verdon. Verdon's absence from the West End, especially in *Sweet Charity*, is inexplicable, as her comic sweetness and definitive show dancing would undoubtedly have found favour with the British public. On the other hand, one can neither imagine Ethel Merman being taken to heart by British audiences in 1947 as Dolores Gray was in *Annie Get Your Gun* nor envisage Carol Channing in the early 1950s conquering the West End in the way Mary Martin had as Nellie Forbush.[10] In 1950 British audiences may have found both Merman and Channing to be lacking in feminine charm—too brash and devoid of sentiment.

Dolores Gray was to risk direct comparison with Merman as Annie. For a while she had understudied Merman as Annie on Broadway.[11] Unknown in London and hitherto undervalued on Broadway and in Hollywood,[12] Gray was propelled to stardom as a result of her West End debut in *Annie Get Your Gun* on 7 June 1947, a role to which she brought musical subtlety and variety as well as a dramatic range far surpassing that of Merman. By 1974, when Merman's Broadway career was at an end, Gray had replaced Angela Lansbury as Madame Rose in the London première production of *Gypsy*, another role designed for and originated by Merman in the legendary 1959 production. Although Gray performed standout numbers in four Hollywood films in the mid-1950s,[13] won a Tony in 1954 (for *Carnival in Flanders*), and performed successfully on television in the United States, she never achieved the type of iconic status that Merman, Martin, or Verdon did on Broadway. In Britain, however, she became a legend.

With *South Pacific* (1949) Mary Martin, who was already an established Broadway star with a successful but unspectacular Hollywood film career,[14] became Merman's only serious rival for the title of Broadway's leading lady over the next twenty years: Martin starred with notable success in roles associated with Merman (Annie in the national tour and Dolly Levi in an international tour of *Hello, Dolly!*, originally conceived as a vehicle for Merman). Her three appearances in the West End in Noël Coward's *Pacific 1860* (1946), *South Pacific* (1951), and *Hello, Dolly!* (1965) made Mary Martin an equally beloved star in the UK.

Almost the same age as Gray, Elaine Stritch spent more time in London (eleven years) than either of her compatriots. Her Broadway career in the 1940s and 1950s had been somewhat uneven;[15] she did not make her West End debut until 1962, as the star of Noël Coward's *Sail Away*, becoming a celebrated West End actress between 1971 and 1974 and a household name in the English television sitcoms *Two's Company* (1975–1979) and *Nobody's Perfect* (1980–1982). Stritch herself invited comparison with Merman in that she had been her Broadway standby in the role of Mrs Sally Adams in *Call Me Madam* (1951), which Stritch had performed during the national tour in 1952.[16]

# Views of Women during and after the War

Consideration of the popularity of Dolores Gray, Mary Martin, and Elaine Stritch in the UK reflects the changes and contradictions of gender identity consequent on the return of men to their pre-war occupations. The three Americans seemed to embody a range of complementary feminine types that men and women found attractive in the two decades after the war. Wartime experience changed British perceptions of women's capabilities and to a certain extent blurred the traditionally essentialist distinctions between masculine and feminine gender stereotypes by highlighting the success of women in doing jobs conventionally reserved for men.[17]

In spite of this fact, the predominant pre-war ideology valorising 'masculine' and 'feminine' as invariable attributes of the male and female sexes remained intact: women's wartime roles were thus represented as an exception that proved the rule.[18] Inevitably contradictions appeared between persistent ideological assumptions concerning gender and the subjective experience of groups of men and women at work and at home. These were recognised by way of the broad range of filmmakers' portrayals of wartime women: the title of one popular film, *The Gentle Sex* (1943),[19] plays on the traditional stereotype of women as the weaker sex, trying to have it both ways in its representation of women as both strong and at the same time sexually attractive (coded here as gentle). Although still for the most part denied equal pay with men, the war obviously increased women's sense of their own independence, responsibility, freedom of movement, and self-esteem.[20]

When the war was over it was necessary, in both the United States and the United Kingdom, to ensure that servicemen could return to the kind of jobs they had undertaken before the war, resulting inevitably in a severe reduction of career opportunities for women. After the excitement and newfound freedoms of wartime, women needed to be persuaded to accept as normative the virtue—and even pleasure—of being full-time housewives and mothers. In this context, popular entertainment forms might be expected to reinforce the values of the new status quo, yet successful engagement with the target film or stage audiences—a majority of whom were still female—would have necessitated a recognition of the desires of actual women, deprived in the immediate postwar period of the liberating sense of agency achieved doing war work.

Undoubtedly, too, men's images of women had been transformed from the stereotype of the unassertive wife and mother, who echoed her husband's opinions on important issues and assented to his dominance in family decision-making, to a bolder and more independent figure. Such a confident woman might well have indulged in a dalliance with a GI while her husband was away at the front, her personal experience challenging what had been perceived as eternal verities, thereby exposing traditionally gendered behavior as mere role-play.

In what ways, then, did the images of American femininity Martin and Gray presented on stage strike sympathetic chords with British audiences? On the London stage they projected down-to-earth charm, free of the social-class overtones typical of British performers. The country had in 1945 voted a Labour government into power in the expectation that it would abolish class-based inequalities by means of the introduction of free health care for all as part of a welfare state designed to enhance opportunities for working-class people, so the unfettered vitality and patent sincerity of both Martin and Gray were particularly appealing. Both pre-war resentment of the class system and fear of wartime destruction were replaced by an egalitarian belief in social justice that many British people had already come to recognise as characteristic of their American friends.

# THE (AMERICAN) GIRL NEXT DOOR

Kenneth Tynan's view of the impact of American performers immediately after the war is amplified by Ronald Bergen's *Guardian* obituary for Dolores Gray (3 July 2002):

> If one were to compile a list of entertainers who cheered up Britain in the austere years after the Second World War, the American singer and actor Dolores Gray [ ... ]

would be among the top names. On June 7 1947, the colourful Irving Berlin musical *Annie Get Your Gun* burst onto the stage of the London Coliseum, with the ebullient Gray in the title role. The show ran for three years, the longest run in the theatre's history, and Gray, in her first big success, became the toast of the town.[21]

Gray's powerful voice and her natural, jazz-inflected singing style, like that of Mary Martin, must have registered for a London audience as remarkably different from the cultivated operetta-style voices of Evelyn Laye and Peggy Wood, who had appeared in Coward's pre-war operettas, or Ivor Novello's female co-stars, Mary Ellis, Dorothy Dickson, Zena Dare, and Olive Gilbert, whose elegant style had graced the Drury Lane stage since the early 1930s with the idealised *politesse* of 'Ruritania'. To a great extent, West End stars enshrined the ethos of the reticent upper middle class, with its refined manners and rigid gender distinctions between masculine and feminine. Speech and singing styles for upper- or middle-class British actors and characters on the legitimate stage were formal and artificial, while the supposed 'naturalness' of working-class actors and characters was signified by means of eccentrically idiomatic dialects and the kind of belting or shouting voices deployed by music-hall singers before the advent of microphones.

Representation of the comparatively uninhibited behavior of the working classes was the province of the music hall and later variety, with its panoply of comic and sentimental types, from the grotesque eccentricity of Lily Morris's 'old maid' to the risqué cockney innuendoes of the universally adored Marie Lloyd. By the 1930s sound films had elevated the variety performers Gracie Fields and George Formby to the status of national icons, but these northern working-class stars did not attempt to express or provoke any degree of erotic response, all implications of romance being strictly confined to the comic register of 'naughtiness' or the pathos of unrequited attraction. The unabashed sexual attractiveness of both Gray and Martin helped to liberate desire as an affect of British stage entertainment.

The triumphant debut of *Oklahoma!* at Drury Lane less than a year after Coward's *Pacific 1860* had flopped there was followed within weeks by the equally popular *Annie Get Your Gun* at the Coliseum, London's largest theatre. The closely knit ensemble and innovatively integrated book, music, and lyrics of *Oklahoma!* emphasised characters rather than performers, so that even the promising young bass-baritone Harold (Howard) Keel, who played Curley, did not stand out as a personality in quite the same way as Dolores Gray. *Annie Get Your Gun*, on the other hand, had been constructed as a musical comedy vehicle for Ethel Merman, with an above-the-title role for its eponymous heroine, so the superb performance by Gray in the West End was bound to catapult the younger performer to stardom.

In retrospect it seems that the part might actually have been tailor-made for Dolores Gray, but the role of the markswoman Annie Oakley had initially been offered to the iconic Gracie Fields. While John Snelson has convincingly argued that Fields possessed the vocal range and the comic skills to encompass the role,[22] the great familiarity of audiences with her plucky film and stage persona made her image as a working-class Lancashire lass difficult to ignore; this, together with her habitual alternation between a powerful operatic head voice and a distinct chest register, would have contributed to the perception of her Annie as an elaborate impersonation rather than Gray's 'natural' incarnation of the character. Although the show proved to be the biggest hit of Ethel Merman's career, at thirty-eight she looked too old to play a teenager convincingly, so at forty-nine Fields would certainly not have been credible. Her Annie would have registered as not merely too old, but as a throwback to the class-based English musical comedy of the 1920s and 1930s, by contrast to the innocent and egalitarian aura projected by the American ingénue.

In the words of the *Daily Telegraph* reviewer, the young performer 'seems to have everything the part could need. She is exceedingly pretty, has a devastating sense of comedy, and her points are made with the clean smack of one of Annie's bullets hitting the centre

FIG. 13.1 Dolores Gray enrols at London's Royal Academy of Dramatic Arts (1947). Photographer unknown; image provided by the editors.

of the target'.[23] Gray possessed energy, warmth, and an extremely versatile contralto voice capable of everything from a strong belt to a smoky croon, while also boasting the fashionable hourglass figure admired in the two decades after the war. Her serious-mindedness as an artist was touchingly revealed when she enrolled at the Royal Academy of Dramatic Art (RADA) to take a diploma in acting during the first year of the run.

Having understudied Merman in New York for a brief period, Gray was familiar with the role and was able to offer a more nuanced interpretation of the role than its originator, who was a competent comedienne but by no means a dramatic actress. A cursory comparison of Gray's rendition of the love ballad 'They Say It's Wonderful' with Merman's serves to prove the point.[24] Gray's tender and heartfelt caressing of the lyrics exposes Merman's unvaryingly brassy belt as a grotesquely unconvincing expression of the character's feelings. In the event, London audiences embraced Dolores Gray in a way they had not any previous American theatre performer. Besides garnering rave reviews from the newspaper critics, the young star endeared herself to the British public in many ways: by her own account, fans waiting for her at the stage door gave her their food rationing coupons.[25] Having heard that the opening night was her twenty-third birthday, the audience brought her to tears by singing 'Happy Birthday' during a standing ovation at the curtain call. The *Recorder* headline announced that 'Men Stand in Their Seats and Shout "You're Wonderful." '[26]

Unusually, Gray and her co-star, Bill Johnson, played their roles throughout all of its unprecedented 1,304 performances in the largest theatre in the West End; audience attendance was estimated at 2,500,000 people[27]. After the production closed, its producer, Emile Littler, claimed that his two leads 'had done more for the promotion of goodwill between England and America in the previous three years [of the run] than any politician'.[28]

While both Martin and Gray were often complimented by reviewers on their physical attractiveness, the feminine images they conjured were a type of the Hollywood 'girl next door'. In 1947 Dolores Gray had not yet developed the exaggerated sultriness of the stereotypical vamp persona she later—almost parodically—assumed in *It's Always Fair Weather* (1955) and *The Opposite Sex* (1956), as well as Vincente Minnelli's *Kismet* (1955) and *Designing Woman* (1957). As Annie Oakley, she found in London audiences a warm response to her versatile and powerful singing voice, her pretty face, and her emotional directness, rather than any eroticised display of her hourglass figure,[29] which the costumes to a certain extent concealed.[30]

## From Career to Career

Gray's turn as Annie ('I've only seen it happen once or twice before in my lifetime'[31]) was not the only one Coward raved about. In her cabaret show a few years later, he found her 'quite enchanting and brilliantly professional',[32] while in *Two on the Aisle* on Broadway she was 'wonderful.'[33] Gray performed 'triumphant' seasons at the London Palladium in 1952 and 1958 and in cabaret at the Talk of the Town in 1963 before replacing Angela Lansbury as Madame Rose in the London production of *Gypsy* (1973).

Lansbury's definitive interpretation of Rose had received such overwhelming critical acclaim that she might have seemed an impossible act to follow;[34] although this may have been why the London producers chose a star as popular as Gray to succeed her, the star took some persuading to assay the role. Her performance radiated both warmth and vitality, making Gray's Rose less quirky than that of her predecessor, but just as driven.[35] In the final scene of act 1, Gray did not, as Lansbury had done, pinpoint the moment before "Everything's Comin' Up Roses" as the start of a gradual but inevitable descent towards the complete mental breakdown of 'Rose's Turn'. Her Rose emblematised the all-American pluck of those Depression-era breadwinners whose resourcefulness and sheer guts enabled them to survive unemployment and poverty. At forty-nine, Gray's sassy attractiveness made Rose a smiling yet persuasive bully, thoughtlessly cajoling Herbie and Louise into bewildered acquiescence. Her interpretation of 'Some People' was sunny and determined rather than willful and neurotic, the strength of her singing leaving audiences in no doubt that she would turn her daughters into stars.

Vocally she had even more power than Lansbury, her singing more mellifluous and jazz inflected, especially in numbers such as 'Small World' and 'Together, Wherever We Go'. Her rendition of the speech that introduces the legendary eleven o'clock number 'Rose's Turn' was not so much mentally disturbed as motivated by a lifetime of frustrated ambition.[36] The number became a showcase for Gray's talent as a singing actress, giving an opportunity never afforded her previously to display the full range of her dramatic ability.[37] By singing much more slowly and deliberately than Lansbury had done, Gray allowed every note its full sonic value. Whereas Lansbury's vocal texture had alternated between hoarse screaming and steely sung notes, the many variations in tempo echoing the hysterical dissonances of a fragmented conscious-ness, Gray hardly ever shouted, her evenly paced delivery of both speech and song supporting a somewhat different interpretation. In Gray's portrayal, the turning point for Rose occurred after Louise's successful transformation into Gypsy Rose Lee in 'Let Me Entertain You'. Her jealous incredulity that Louise could function independently of her spurred the enraged exhibition of her own talent, the mock striptease and vir-tuosity of her vocal delivery demonstrating the reason for her monstrous envy of her daughter's success.[38]

Gray's performance attested that Rose was indeed far more talented than either of her daughters. Her Rose was not so much mentally unhinged as blinded by rage at her own bad luck. Her version of 'Rose's Turn' functioned as a catharsis of the pain caused by the consistent repression of her own needs. Gray's mimicking of Louise's striptease substituted the aging Rose for the youthful Gypsy in a grotesque parody that revealed how she had molded her hopeless daughter into a crude approximation of the star she herself should have been, rather than merely as an uncontrolled revelation of mental collapse.

Although Dolores Gray never publicly expressed any bitterness or regret concerning missed chances, she was singularly unlucky in the vehicles she was offered after *Annie*.[39] Had her opportunity at MGM arrived as early as 1948, she might well have become a much bigger film star. She was certainly the equal of Mary Martin in her versatility, force, and subtlety as a singing actress. Indeed, as the most obvious successor to Merman and possessed of more consistent vocal power than Lansbury, she might well have expected to be the first choice for Rose in the London première.[40]

When Gray returned to play the show-business survivor Carlotta Campion in the West End première of Stephen Sondheim and James Goldman's *Follies* (1987), it was as if reality and theatrical fiction had become fused.[41] With the kind of alchemy evinced by great film and theatre stars, Carlotta uncannily appeared to morph into Gray as her song 'I'm Still Here' progressively unveiled its autobiographical recollection of American popular cultural history.[42] Mark Steyn's review in the *Independent* typically conflates Gray's star persona with her stage role:

> The tone of the evening is set by an all-star cast, in which even Dolores Gray, an above-the-title star for 40 years, only makes fifth billing. She does, though, bring all the personal resonances of her own career to 'I'm Still Here', Stephen Sondheim's hymn to showbiz survival.[43]

Many other reviewers praised her astonishing vocal power as a personal demonstration of Gray's undiminished ability over the forty years since her London debut: '[F]rom the moment the ageless Dolores Gray who plays Carlotta sings 'I'm Still Here' you know *Follies* will be around for a long time yet'.[44] Her warm and witty belting of the famous number prompted Clive Hirschhorn actually to begin his review in the *Sunday Express* with a kind of eulogy to Ms Gray:

> There is a spine-tingling moment in the Stephen Sondheim–James Goldman musical *Follies* when that veteran Broadway show-stopper Dolores Gray belts out Sondheim's diamond-sharp 'I'm Still Here' and is rewarded for the star-quality she brings to the number with a thrillingly spontaneous roar of audience approval. It's a song about survival and provides a steely backbone to much of the bitter-sweet mood of nostalgia that wafts across the footlights like theatrical mist. Miss Gray [ ... ] is simply wonderful. Although this is the only song she has, she brings just the right kind of pazazz to it.[45]

With self-deprecating irony, but without the calculated overlay of pathos that has marked some interpretations of Carlotta, Gray has perhaps come closest to performing the song and embodying the character in the way Sondheim and Goldman later intended—as the one character in *Follies* who is a genuine survivor.[46]

Recordings of her belting the song in the slow tempo in which it was originally conceived reveal her innate respect for the sophistication of the song itself. Never illustrating its dramatic subtext by imposing her own personal commentary upon the material through gesture and vocal emphasis, she wisely relied on her effortless accomplishment in the perfect enunciation of lyrics and her powerful vocal projection to allow both pathos and comedy to emerge from the interplay of music and lyrics. It appeared as

FIG. 13.2 Dolores Gray as Carlotta Campion in the 1987 London version of *Follies*. Photo: Clive Barda © ArenaPal.

if Carlotta, in refusing to countenance the type of traumatic orgy of regret experienced by the four central characters, had resigned herself philosophically to the devastation wrought by time. Dolores Gray was welcomed back to London by critics and the public as show business royalty. London had accorded her the diva status that, in spite of her Tony Award, had narrowly eluded her on Broadway.

## Postwar Heroine: From Fashion Plate to Tomboy

Mary Martin's debut in Noël Coward's *Pacific 1860* had an extremely high profile: the show reopened the Theatre Royal Drury Lane after the war,[47] making her the first

American stage performer to play for a British audience in a musical since 1939, albeit in a British show written by an English icon of the pre-war era.[48] Coward had first seen her in her cabaret season in New York in 1938, but it was her skillful performance as the star of *One Touch of Venus* (1943) that convinced him she was right for the role of the 'outrageous Elena Salvador [... an] opera singer who wears men's riding breeches and falls in love with Kerry [Stirling]' while visiting the fictional Pacific island of Samolo.[49] Coward had wanted Mary Martin because he believed she was not only capable of carrying most of the show's songs, yet while 'still a romantic heroine [ ... ] was capable of playing in a lighter and more cheerful convention'.[50]

Although *Pacific 1860* was a huge disappointment, Mary Martin received excellent notices, the reviewer of *Theatre World* regarding her performance as a 'sensation' and criticising Coward for failing 'so glamorous a star'.[51] According to Coward's secretary and friend, Cole Lesley, 'Mary was enchanting from every point of view (not her fault that she was somewhat miscast)'.[52] The *Times* praised Martin's 'charm'—a word that would be consistently employed to describe her quality as a performer.[53] In writing and producing *Pacific 1860*, Coward's great miscalculation was that Drury Lane audiences would wish to return to the nostalgic and class-ridden formula of 1930s operetta after the hiatus of the war. The enormous critical and popular success of *Oklahoma!* and *Annie Get Your Gun* which immediately followed the closure of *Pacific 1860* appealed to the new and very different postwar zeitgeist: in this altered cultural context Coward's show appeared hopelessly outmoded, while London audiences were more than ready for the raw energy and confident utopianism of the American musicals.

Appealing in a variety of ways to both men and women, Martin's Nellie Forbush in *South Pacific* reveals a change from the cute stereotype she had adopted in her legendary Broadway debut when she sang 'My Heart Belongs to Daddy' in *Leave It to Me!* (1938) as a comic striptease—more tease than strip, if her own recreation of her stage performance in the film *Night and Day* (1946) is an authentic replica. Even the idealised glamour of her portrayal of Venus in disguise as a mortal, in her first starring role on Broadway—*One Touch of Venus*, by Kurt Weill and Ogden Nash—was a gently comic, possibly even camp performance of sexiness rather than a straightforward representation of femininity as conceived in the 1940s. The latter show, with its gowns designed especially for her by the celebrated couturier Mainbocher, as well as *Pacific 1860*, with its beautiful nineteenth-century dresses, had demonstrated how poised and elegant she could be; yet the more transgressive role of 'an opera singer who wears men's riding breeches' highlights Martin's duality as both fashion plate and tomboy.

In her scrutiny of Martin's career as a star from a lesbian feminist perspective, Stacy Wolf has revealingly exposed the meanings of Martin's performance of gender onstage and off.[54] A viewing of the filmed performance of *South Pacific* at Drury Lane supports Wolf's interpretation of her tomboy persona, for which her portrayal of Annie Oakley in the national tour of *Annie Get Your Gun* must have prepared her by drawing on

FIG. 13.3 Mary Martin and Noël Coward at the dress rehearsal for *Pacific 1860* (1947). Photographer unknown; image provided by the editors.

deeper, more spontaneous impulses to communicate to her audiences the sheer joy of being alive. Annie was a role she was especially keen to play, having admired Merman's acclaimed performance on Broadway. The 1947 touring production was so successful that it not only assured her countrywide fame as a stage star but also earned her a Special Tony Award for 'spreading theatre to the rest of the country while the originals performed in New York'.[55] Playing the western girl Annie permitted Martin to invoke the charm of gender androgyny while at the same time allowing her to express emotional vulnerability.[56]

## CHALLENGING CONSERVATIVE GENDER STEREOTYPES IN POSTWAR MUSICALS

The Cold War ushered in a number of military conflicts between Western powers and Communist forces, which may also have touched on memories of World War II.[57] Clearly the anticommunist hysteria in the early period of the Cold War produced a defensive conservatism with respect to gender and sexuality in both the United States and the United Kingdom.[58] The normalisation of the nuclear family was supported by propaganda which often exploited various kinds of advertisements for consumer goods that illustrated the attractiveness for women of embracing a new, if paradoxically domestic, image of the pretty and subservient wife, who was nevertheless strong and supportive as a mother.

In various ways Mary Martin's transitions from sex symbol on stage in 1938 to her Peter Pan–like androgyny between 1947 and the late 1950s were responses to how cultural shifts altered perceptions of the feminine in American society after the pre-war epoch to fit the Cold War culture's heteronormative prescription of gender roles. Blurring on-stage the roles of loving and domesticated wife and transgressive tomboy as Nellie Forbush, the 'cock-eyed optimist' in Rodgers and Hammerstein's highly acclaimed *South Pacific* (1949), gained her another Tony Award while cementing her iconic status as a Broadway star. Writing in *Theatre Arts* a little more than three months before its London opening, Nathaniel Benchley commented on her performance, 'Miss Martin's personal charm is such that she could fall into a swamp and still be adorable, and on this occasion she broke all records for complete, sustained delight.'[59]

By the time she returned to Drury Lane in 1951 Martin had already been recognised as a star in the West End, while her status on Broadway was equal to that of Ethel Merman. The 'overpowering advance publicity' for the show may, however, have given rise to impossibly high expectations.[60] With the notable exception of Kenneth Tynan, the London critics were much less enthusiastic about the show's book than their eulogistic New York counterparts had been,[61] even if most praised the score. Yet all were enchanted by Mary Martin. Her adored co-star, the acclaimed operatic bass Ezio Pinza, was replaced in London by the wooden and uncharismatic Wilbur Evans, so most of the popular and journalistic attention now appears to have focused on Martin, who could appear physically attractive without projecting either the dangerous eroticism of a Hollywood vamp or the coy girlishness of an operetta soprano, as Tynan noted:

> When *South Pacific* opened in London, I heard people arguing during the intermission that realism and a pit orchestra didn't mix. [ ... ] I heard astringent voices [ ... ] loftily pointing out that the producers had overlooked the obvious theatrical possibilities inherent in erupting volcanoes and tribal dances. In these conversations I took no part, being transparently embarrassed by a huge sob of delight, of which I had suddenly found myself the custodian. Simple brilliance of execution had silenced my qualms. Mary Martin, skipping and roaming around that vast stage on

diminutive flat feet, had poured her voice directly into that funnel to the heart which is sealed off from all but the rarest performers. [ ... ] The sight of Miss Martin, with her defiantly projecting rump, standing astride with toes turned up and straw hat pulled down, singing uproariously at the sun, reminded me of something Aldous Huxley once wrote about the minor Caroline poets. 'They spoke in their natural voices,' he said, 'and it was poetry.'

# SEXUAL AMBIGUITY IN PERFORMANCE

Clearly Martin's appeal had something to do with the complex and androgynous image of femininity that she radiated.[62] Her boyish appearance in shorts and a blouse and the optimistic pluck with which she endowed Ensign Forbush might have proved attractive to heterosexual men and women as well as to gay men and women because the persona she constructed was never a threat to either sex.[63] The contrasts evoked by the conventionally girlish image in her scenes with Emile, her spunky interaction with her fellow nurses and her iconic appearance, dragged up in an oversized sailor suit to perform the show-stopping 'Honey Bun' two-thirds of the way through the musical, Martin's charm subtly subverted essentialist notions of gender identity. Like a Shakespearean boy actor playing a woman disguised as a young man, the sexuality on display in this number represents a type of gender fluidity which challenges normative categories of sexual desire.

Martin's ubiquitous charm may have stemmed from the sensitivity of a bisexual performer to the sexual fantasies of heterosexual and homosexual men and women. Her own gender fluidity clearly imbued her with the capability of appearing glamorous in her femininity, yet at other times roguish in her tomboy persona.[64] Seen today from a queer perspective, Nellie's comic wooing of the hyper-masculine Luther Billis's 'honey bun' provokes a kind of sexual fantasy, in which his crude female impersonation of her 'doll' parodies female burlesque dancing in a way that serves to highlight her own more attractive hint of bisexuality.[65]

In New York, *South Pacific* had appealed directly to the collective memory of its audience. As Brian Kellow has observed:

> It was a show that came along at the perfect moment in history. It could not have had the impact it had if it had opened while the combat was still raging. In 1949, audiences had the perfect vantage point of four years' distance on the war; seeing it years later, I noticed that the men and women in the audience who had actually lived through this tumultuous time were deeply moved—even nostalgic, although it must have been a complicated kind of nostalgia.[66]

As in New York, Martin's assertive can-do image needed somehow to be tempered in London by the postwar values of home and family. When Nellie finally overcomes the racial prejudice against Emile's previous interracial relationship to accept his marriage proposal, the reprise of 'Dîtes-moi' with his two children emphasises at the end her role as a homemaker rather than as an object of desire for an older man.[67] In this way the patriarchal order is naturalised at the musical's conclusion. Nevertheless, Martin's highly fluid and equivocal performance of gender and sexuality in *South Pacific* was subversive because of its unfettered appeal to the omnidirectional nature of sexual desire. Her universally acknowledged charm clearly conjured the kind of joy that is the artistic raison d'être of the genre.

# THE ART OF NOSTALGIA

After winning a Tony for her portrayal of Maria von Trapp in *The Sound of Music* (1959), a role created for her by Rodgers and Hammerstein, and having initially turned down the chance to originate the role of Dolly Levi,[68] Martin agreed to head an extensive national and international tour of *Hello, Dolly!* in 1965 that included Japan, in addition to performances for American troops in South Vietnam and South Korea. The *Variety* reviewer averred:

> Mary Martin gives title role [*sic*] her own interpretation and Miss Martin has never been known to take a backseat to anybody. As Mrs Dolly Levi, Mary Martin is a knockout. Her 'Dolly' is perhaps more whimsical, less boisterous than Carol Channing's but it's a rousing delineation of the role.[69]

The production, which toured for five months, was a personal triumph for its star, who immediately followed it with a further five-month run supported by a British ensemble at Drury Lane in London. According to Adrian Wright: 'When she [Martin] made her entrance for *Hello, Dolly!*'s title number [ . . . ] there was another whole something else going on at the Lane—much of the audience brought its own nostalgia with it.'[70] The *Times* opined that 'the show was single-mindedly bent on mobilising public enthusiasm for Mary Martin'.[71]

Whereas Channing had been arch and clever as Dolly, her deadpan delivery ironically emphasising the way the character cunningly outmanoeuvred everyone else in order to snare a wealthy husband, Mary Martin, true to form, was naughty and playful rather than calculating, imbuing Dolly's knowing attitude with an affectionate warmth and a mischievous joie de vivre, which won out against Horace van der Gelder's Puritan repressiveness. The critic of *Plays and Players* maintained:

> Until the second half, *Hello, Dolly!* is never dull, but never remarkable, and one wonders what Mary Martin is doing in it. After a beautifully choreographed piece of tomfoolery by the [ . . . ] waiters, Miss Martin appears, dressed to kill, at the top of a stairway, and proceeds to sing the title song. By the time the scene is over, the audience is limp with emotion, caught up in the schmaltz of it all, wracked by nostalgia,

FIG. 13.4 Mary Martin as Dolly Levi (with Loring Smith as Horace Vandergelder) in the international touring production of *Hello, Dolly!*, which arrived in London in December 1965. Photo: Friedman-Abeles © New York Public Library Digital Collections.

and bleary-eyed from sheer delight. It is the show-stopper of all time; and Miss Martin—whose business it is to be irresistible—has cemented her own legend for ever.[72]

As is often the case with musical theatre stars, Dolores Gray, Mary Martin, and, as will be apparent, Elaine Stritch ended their love affairs with the British theatre-going public in nostalgic tributes to the very notion of survival: each of their final appearances was imbued with the glow of a long-awaited comeback, tumultuous applause being accorded for being 'still here'.

## Rethinking the Special Relationship

In sharp contrast to the reasons for the popularity of Martin and Gray, London audiences' appreciation, starting in 1962, of Elaine Stritch's hard-bitten persona, reflects the changed nature of Anglo-American relations following the Suez conflict of 1957. No longer an equal partner in a cordial entente, Britain had become a junior partner in an unequal alliance with the dominant postwar imperial power. The historian Michael Dunne summed up the change that occurred as follows:

> [Anthony] Eden's successor, Harold Macmillan, held a summit with Eisenhower in Bermuda, which confirmed that any 'special relationship' was one of British dependence upon the United States, particularly in ultimate American control over the notionally independent British Thor nuclear missiles. In the vast area of the Middle East, defined ad hoc as ranging from Morocco east to Pakistan and Turkey, south to Sudan, the British were to follow guidelines set by Washington: there would be no more 'going it alone' by London.[73]

British resentment at having to concede global preeminence to the United States as their empire disintegrated was tempered by the greater familiarity of the British public with images of American lifestyles and individual American politicians, film stars, and ordinary citizens during the 1950s and 1960s. The increasing presence of television during this epoch brought American attitudes and values into British homes on a regular basis.[74] The design historian Andrew Jackson has commented:

> By the end of the 1950s, the American way of life had become key to the aspirations of the British public, in terms of both culture and material goods. After the deregulation of broadcasting in 1954, the way was cleared for the introduction of commercial television in 1955. This, coupled with the increased availability of colour magazines [ ... ] brought a proliferation of advertising for luxury commodities, much of it originating in America. In spite of the protestation of British intellectuals [ ... ] who viewed American culture as a symptom of cultural degeneration, Hollywood movies, commercial television, glossy magazines and consumer goods proved an instant hit with British consumers.[75]

In this context, Elaine Stritch represented a kind of American identity that was unlikely to have proven attractive to the British public before the 1960s. Acerbic, brash, and tough as nails, with a growling baritone belt, her image is in some respects comparable to that of Merman; yet unlike Merman, Stritch was not only supremely witty, she was also a superb dramatic actor, concealing a profound vulnerability under the sophisticated and self-deprecating cynicism of her fast-talking-dame persona.[76]

## UPPER-CLASS VERSUS CLASSY: ENGLISH SOPHISTICATION VERSUS AMERICAN CAMP

As he had done for Mary Martin in 1946, it was Noël Coward who in 1962 introduced Stritch to London audiences. He had admired her for some time before casting her in his

# THAT SPECIAL RELATIONSHIP    389

Broadway musical *Sail Away* (1961), having seen her in William Inge's drama *Bus Stop* (1955) and as the star of the musical *Goldilocks* (1958) by Walter and Jean Kerr:

> Noël Coward saw it [*Goldilocks*] and decided then and there he wanted me for *Sail Away*. [ ... ] And I [ ... ] started as the comic lead, but when the romantic lead wasn't cutting it, he combined the parts [ ... ] and gave it all to me. [ ... ] The thing about Noël Coward was that he got me. He didn't love everything about me, but [ ... ] he was one of the first really big players in this business that got me.[77]

Just as Coward's persona was perceived by Americans as that of a typically effete and witty upper-class English type, so, conversely, Stritch's arch stage persona registered with British audiences as that of an urbane New Yorker, the aggressive American individualism mitigated by an ironic attitude that betokened a degree of cosmopolitan poise beyond the reach of gauche countrymen from middle America.[78] Her attitude could be read as camp because the rowdy and frenetic aspects of her persona were on the surface at odds with her assumption of worldly ennui.

As Mimi Paragon in *Sail Away*, she played an American divorcée who is the cruise director aboard a British ship, the *Coronia*. While earning approval for her sparkling enunciation of Coward's supercilious 'English' sarcasm, Stritch's character exploited his type of British snobbery to mock the gallery of 'ugly Americans' on board:

> You're a long, long way from America,
> Be prepared to face the worst
> While guitars are strumming
> 'The Yanks Are Coming'
> You'll find the plumbing
> Rather frightening at first.[79]

Unlike the youthful innocents invariably associated with Mary Martin and Dolores Gray in their early London appearances, at thirty-seven Elaine Stritch played a middle-aged woman of the world who was having an affair with a younger passenger, Johnny Van Mier. Although in 1961 the 'bilious satire' of *Sail Away* may actually have offended some of the bourgeois Broadway patrons who were its satirical targets, much of its appeal to a London audience a year later was the chance to observe a funny and cynical Broadway performer voicing Coward's mockery of a 'cartoon gallery of variously pompous, ill-bred and boorish American tourists [including ...] camera-wielding Texans and rubes who imagine that the Parthenon is a ripoff of a Pennsylvania train station.'[80]

In 'Why Do the Wrong People Travel?', for instance, Stritch's inimitably deadpan delivery brilliantly highlighted Coward's hilariously funny lyrical observations:

> Why do the wrong people travel, travel, travel,
> When the right people stay back home?
> What explains this mass mania
> To leave Pennsylvania

>   And clack around like flocks of geese
>   Demanding dry martinis on the isles of Greece?[81]

By 1962 American tourists were a familiar sight to Londoners, so jokes about uncouth nouveau riche Americans would exploit the paradox that scorn for their naïveté and bad manners was yoked to envy of their material wealth. No longer simply admiring of the apparent classlessness of American democracy, the seventeen years spent in political cooperation with their closest postwar ally had familiarised the British with the nuances of difference consequent on being 'two nations separated by a common language'.[82] Culturally, Americans appeared as Romans to the British people's Greeks, the Cold War imperialism of the United States having inexorably superseded the global influence the British had wielded in the heyday of Empire.

FIG. 13.5 Elaine Stritch as Mimi Paragon with the author in Noël Coward's *Sail Away* (1961). Photo: Bettmann © Getty Images.

In comic terms, Stritch's characterisation, at the same time as it mocked American bad taste, was a wry comment on the persistent English sense of superiority, delighting London theatre-goers with her demonstration that New Yorkers were just as capable of the kind of 'English' wit and irony emblematised by Coward himself.[83] A slightly more sceptical reading might view Stritch's ability to get laughs from Coward's lines as an example of the colonial's mimicry of her former colonial masters, with Stritch as the dummy to Coward's imperialistic ventriloquist, the colonised still being manipulated by the sophisticated cultural and social superiority of the coloniser.

Given that she received rave reviews while the show itself was tepidly received, Coward's approval was perhaps a little condescending: 'Stritch can really speak my dialogue'.[84] Coward recorded in his diary that '*Sail Away* is a smash hit. [ ... ] The opening night was triumphant from beginning to end [ ... ] and, at the end[,] Stritchie got a tumultuous ovation.'[85] After interviewing Stritch in London, the New York critic Ward Moorhouse noted, 'She has suddenly become a fad and a craze in London's theatretown,' while she herself called Coward 'the best friend I've ever had in the theatre'.[86] Coward in turn telegraphed Elaine's mother: 'Your dear little blonde daughter has made a triumphant success and has all London at her feet. She is also behaving beautifully so don't be frantic'.[87]

# Honesty and Wit: A New Appraisal of the Relationship

As it happened, Elaine Stritch was later to spend eleven years working in the UK—far more time than either Dolores Gray or Mary Martin. Beginning with her first return to London as the brittle socialite Joanne in the 1971 *Company*, by Stephen Sondheim (music and lyrics) and George Furth (book)—her legendary delivery of 'The Ladies Who Lunch' regularly stopped the show in the West End, as it had on Broadway—Stritch became a regular fixture of the British theatre and television scene. While playing in the première production of Tennessee Williams's *Small Craft Warnings* on the fringe in London, she met and married the expatriate American actor John Bay; in 1974 she starred in the West End production of Neil Simon's *The Gingerbread Lady*, which was followed in 1975 by Bill Mcilwraith's television sitcom *Two's Company* for ITV, so popular that it ran through four series and spawned a successor, *Nobody's Perfect*, for which Stritch served in addition as co-writer. Starring opposite the well-known British farceur Donald Sinden, in *Two's Company* she became a household name as the American author Dorothy Macnab, a role especially tailored to showcase her individual persona and special comic talent.

In an interview with Dick Cavett in 1979, Stritch shared her perception of why she was so popular in the UK:

> The English people love Americans – if you level with them. You mustn't try to fool them. You must be very straightforward in your humour—and you must be very

FIG. 13.6 Elaine Stritch and Donald Sinden celebrate the start of the third season of their popular sitcom *Two's Company* at London's Savoy Hotel on 17 January 1978. Photo: Keystone Press © Alamy Stock Photo.

honest. They took to me because I guess my lack of inhibitions appealed to them, because the English people are a little more inhibited than we are.[88]

If it was the unguarded honesty of her delineation of a brittle Manhattan socialite in the process of an emotional breakdown in *Company* that both shocked and dazzled British audiences, it was the combination of uninhibited bluntness and arch self-mockery in her hilarious portrayal of a celebrated crime-fiction writer that channeled the viewers' affection for Stritch as a performer. Riffing on her established image as a forthright New York sophisticate, Dorothy lived in the salubrious London borough of Chelsea in a state of perpetual conflict with her stiff-upper-lip butler, Robert. While the wisecracking Dorothy is freewheeling, self-aware, and demanding, Sinden, as the sarcastic, cool, and calculating Robert, represents her nemesis, their games of mutual one-upmanship comprising the motor of the comedy.[89]

Each episode of the series was prefaced by the song 'Two's Company', especially written by Sammy Kahn and Dennis King to exhibit Stritch's signature style of droll irony, her world-weary belt reinforcing memories of her past stage musical performances. A number of episodes engineer opportunities for Dorothy to do an imitation tap dance, as if to remind television viewers of the performer's previous musical theatre career. The conflict of American values and British attitudes is both overt and affectionate, assuming the audience's long-established recognition of the limitations of both points of view.

The humour is founded on viewers' sly comprehension of the culture clash that underlies the unequal partners in the 'special relationship', portraying the narcissistic but egalitarian modernity of the New Yorker with as much affection as it exposes the traditionally supercilious snobbery of the Englishman. In their continuous warfare, Robert represents the view of the old class system:

> To the British establishment the American capitalist system that encouraged mass consumption and planned obsolescence was a threat to the old cultural order of stability and permanence. To the average Briton it offered a rich and desirable future.[90]

By the 1970s the huge affection in Britain for Elaine Stritch and the extremely popular reception of *Two's Company* was evidence of a more complex and nuanced understanding of the ironies of the special relationship. Here it is notable that Stritch, as a New Yorker and in particular a Broadway star, represents the exception that proves the rule—a sophisticate as scornful of the boorishness of her compatriots as the English are. In 2002, at the age of seventy-six, Stritch was to return to the Old Vic in London in the autobiographical revue of her life and times, *Elaine Stritch at Liberty*. Her enthusiastic critical reception showed how completely attuned London audiences had by this time become to the unique brand of East Coast self-mockery that characterised Stritch's live-wire theatrical personality.

# Conclusion

If the preeminence of Ethel Merman on Broadway made it necessary to begin this essay by comparing the three stars who *did* engage with London audiences in her absence, it would appear appropriate to end the attempt to sketch the paradoxical interaction of cross-cultural differences and connections between London and New York by considering why Noël Coward, the most ubiquitous Englishman abroad in the immediate postwar period, regarded each of these three American performers with such intense admiration. For mid-twentieth-century Americans, Coward was the figure who above all personified upper-middle-class English urbanity, while as a star personality he was perhaps even more highly praised in the United States than in Britain, garnering tremendous kudos from his cabaret seasons in Las Vegas and New York as well as playing opposite Mary Martin in the high-profile television special *Together with Music* in 1955.

His categorically English taste demanded that a great performer possess the kind of comic intelligence he implicitly perceived as the sine qua non of a sophisticated stage personality, as well as the skill to convey finely tuned emotions without crass sentimentality. His awareness of the kind of theatrical image that would translate most fully from the popular culture of Broadway to the West End was vindicated by the wonderful receptions that greeted Gray, Martin, and Stritch in their London performances.

Coward's supercilious attitude towards the culture that hailed him as a scion of upper-class Englishness in fact indicates the condescension and resentment of the imperialist towards the arriviste.[91] Between the end of World War II and 2002, British people traumatically experienced the entropic unravelling of global power from its position as the foremost Western nation to one of minor importance; this realignment has been accompanied by the corresponding rise of an American empire that has replaced the British Empire in the management of world affairs. Coward's oft-expressed contempt for the egalitarian values of the postwar British welfare state represents an attitude of aristocratic privilege concomitant on nostalgia for the lost empire.

Since the late 1960s, the displacement of British political preeminence has been accompanied by increasingly urgent demands to reshape the hierarchy of gender relations, with the ongoing conflict between masculinity and femininity producing an uneven series of challenges to patriarchical hegemony. As British people have acquired greater understanding of the cultural significance of America, so have they become increasingly aware of the historical aim of deconstructing and ultimately demolishing patriarchy. Both these forces can be observed at work in the comparative reception of the three female Broadway stars who are the subject of this chapter: a period of romance with two good-looking but independent-minded young women has been followed by a more cynical appraisal of the middle-aged Stritch's comic exposure of the gradual process of disillusionment inevitable in a long marriage. The intense affection for Gray and Martin immediately after the war exhibited the initial attraction to the freshness, classlessness, and glamour of all things American, while admiration for the ironic and more aggressive Stritch represents a more realistic embrace of the new dynamics of Cold War collaboration promoted between 1962 and 2002,[92] gesturing however towards the inevitability of the American empire's fall from grace.

## NOTES

1. Lewis Hallam brought the first British company of actors to Virginia, where their première performance was George Glanville's *The Jew of Venice* in Williamsburg in 1752, while American actors such as Ira Aldridge and Edwin Forrest have performed in Britain since the early nineteenth century.
2. This roster also famously included Danny Kaye and Judy Garland in their debuts at the London Palladium (in 1947 and 1950, respectively).
3. Although used earlier to describe an allegiance between Britain and the United States, the term 'special relationship' was popularised by Winston Churchill from 1944, becoming shorthand for their sharing of intelligence and military cooperation during the Cold War.
4. John Snelson, 'The West End Musical 1947–54: British Identity and the "American Invasion"' (PhD thesis, University of Birmingham, 2002), 70–71.

THAT SPECIAL RELATIONSHIP 395

5. Ibid.

6. Kenneth Tynan, 'Why London Likes American Musicals', *New York Times*, 13 April, 1952, movies2.nytimes.com/books/98/05/10/specials/tynan-musicals.htm, accessed 29 July 2019.

7. There are numerous accounts of how the catchphrase 'oversexed, overpaid, and over here' came into popular usage. See Kenneth Harris, 'Oversexed, Overfed, Over Here', *New York Times*, 12 February 1995, 26, for an explanation of how and why such phrases were applied to American GIs in Britain.

8. Quoted in Melissa Hogenboom, 'How the GI Influx Influenced Britain's View of America', BBC News (Magazine), 3 November 2012, www.bbc.co.uk>news>magazine-20160819, accessed 28 September 2019.

9. The role of Dolly Levi, which she had originally turned down in 1964, was finally played by Merman at the end of the run of *Hello, Dolly!*, beginning on 27 December 1970—the longest-running Broadway show at its closing. She was supported in her two-week engagement at the Palladium by a variety company. Her billing as 'Broadway's Ethel Merman' appeared to call attention to her qualities as a *foreign* performer.

10. British audiences were introduced to Carol Channing in the film musical comedy *Thoroughly Modern Millie* (1967), starring Julie Andrews. Essentially a clown, she became a star on Broadway for her definitive portrayal of Lorelei Lee in *Gentlemen Prefer Blondes* (1949), although her eccentric legend was truly established when she originated the role of Dolly Levi in Jerry Herman's *Hello, Dolly!* (1964), which she recreated in London in 1981 and continued to tour sporadically in the United States during the 1980s and 1990s.

11. See https://maxmcmanus.com/2019/07/23/dolores-gray-the-mgm-starlet-who-took-a-bullet-and-kept-on-belting/, accessed 29 January 2020.

12. Gray's career began in California, where she appeared in cabaret in Reno, Nevada, and San Francisco, in her own radio show, and then in two Broadway shows (1944 and 1945).

13. She appeared in the musicals *There's Always Fair Weather* (1955), *Kismet* (1955), and *Designing Women* (1957) and sang the title song in *The Opposite Sex* (1956).

14. Between 1939 and 1946 Mary Martin had featured in ten Paramount screen musicals, the most notable being *Rhythm on the River* (1940) and *The Birth of the Blues* (1941), both opposite Bing Crosby. None of these established her as a major movie star, so until *South Pacific* her face was most recognisable outside New York from the photograph on the cover of *Life* in 1938, celebrating her sensational Broadway debut performing Cole Porter's suggestive 'My Heart Belongs to Daddy'.

15. Stritch had appeared on Broadway in *Pal Joey* (1952) and *Bus Stop* (1956); in the national tour of *Call Me Madam* (1953); and in the Hollywood films *Three Violent People* (1956), *A Farewell to Arms* (1957), and *The Perfect Furlough* (1958). She also starred in the musical *Goldilocks* (1958).

16. In Stritch's words, 'I was 20. I looked 40. I got the part.' From *Elaine at Liberty*, quoted in Darryl H. Miller, 'Emotional Ride with a Larger-than-Life Elaine Stritch', 11 April 2003, https: //www.latimes. com/archives/la-xpm-2003-apr-11-et-daryl11-story.html, accessed 26 August 2019.

17. Aldgate and Richards note that by 1943, in addition to women who were conscripted into the armed forces, '90% of all single women between 18 and 40, and 80% of married women with children over 14 were working'. Anthony Aldgate and Tony Richards, *Britain Can Take It* (London: Tauris, 2007), 3.

18. '[The Second World War] was the first time that women's work had really been valued and celebrated, whether in the services, factories or running the home [nevertheless a . . .]

well-disguised [cinema] advert emphasises the importance of being able to make a good cup of tea (especially when a GI comes to call)'. [Josephine Botting, 'How British Film Celebrated the Role of Women in the Second World War', 24 April 2017, https://www.bfi. org.uk/features/british-cinema-women-second-world-war, accessed 28 August, 2019].

19. In fact this film was intended 'to encourage women to join the Auxiliary Territorial Service and was one of the most popular films of 1943.' Although 'rather patronizing [ . . . ] the film clearly had the right combination of glamour and realism to make war work seem attractive' (ibid.) A twenty-five-year-old bombardier believed it 'presents Britain and life as it is—we must have truth and integrity in our films.' Stephen Woolley, 'Behind the Lines: Women and WWII British film', 12 July 2017, https://www.watershed.co.uk/articles/beh ind-the-lines-women-and-wwii-british-film, accessed 29 August 2019.

20. *The Gentle Sex* was surprisingly successful at the box office. The film historian Antonia Caroline Lant observes that at the peak of female wartime employment in 1943, its appeal lay in the scope the film gave to female experience. Its director, Leslie Howard, asserted that the part played by women was 'so far-reaching and important that the least a mere maker of films' could do was 'express on the screen the significance of their work'. Antonia Caroline Lant, *Blackout: Reinventing Women for Wartime British Cinema* (Princeton, NJ: Princeton University Press, 1991), 93.

21. Ronald Bergan, 'Dolores Gray Obituary', *Guardian*, 2 July 2002, https://www.theguardian. com/news/2002/jul/03/guardianobituaries, accessed 5 August 2019

22. Snelson, 'The West End Musical 1947–54', 66.

23. 'Dolores Gray. Obituary', *Daily Telegraph*, 28 July 2002, https://www.telegraph.co.uk/ news/obituaries/1398599/Dolores-Gray.html, accessed 28 August 2019.

24. Although no original cast recording was made of the London production, Gray's vocal performance is preserved on a studio recording of medleys of selected songs made by members of the cast during the run: *Annie Get Your Gun*, CD reissue, original London cast, Lew Stone and His Orchestra, LaserLight Digital, Stanyan Records, 1994, 12 449. There is also a television recording of Gray performing 'You Can't Get a Man with a Gun' on a 1959 episode of *The Bell Telephone Hour*. 'Dolores Gray Can't Get a Man with a Gun', https://www.youtube.com/watch?v=ndYigf2aop8, accessed 5 August 2019.

25. This story was told by Ms Gray in an interview with Terry Wogan in 1987. Unfortunately the interview has not been preserved, but there is an extract from the show in which she sings 'I'm Still Here' on YouTube; see '"I'm Still Here" from *Follies* (London Revival 1987)', https://www.youtube.com/watch?v=NMupuOwK1AY, accessed 28 August 2019.

26. Quoted in Adrian Wright, *West End Broadway* (Woodbridge: Boydell Press, 2012), 44.

27. Ibid., 46.

28. Ibid.

29. The costumes were designed to flatter the somewhat plump Merman, so they would hardly have been shaped to emphasise an hourglass silhouette!

30. Neither of them at this time was directly comparable with such Hollywood screen sirens as Hedy Lamarr, Rita Hayworth, or Lana Turner, whom British audiences had admired during the war years, nor did they project the conspicuous sex appeal of the 'forces' favourite', Betty Grable.

31. Quoted in Michael Phillips's obituary, *Chicago Tribune*, 3 July 2002, https://www. chicagotribune.com/news/ct-xpm-2002-07-03-0207030029-story.html, accessed 2 September 2019.

32. Graham Payn and Sheridan Morley, eds., *The Noël Coward Diaries* (Basingstoke: Macmillan, 1982), 160.
33. Ibid., 189.
34. The choreographer Matthew Bourne declared: 'Angela Lansbury as Mama Rose in *Gypsy* [ ... ] changed my life. It captured the possibility of the theatre and what it could do. [ ... ] I've always revered Lansbury's performance—I can't imagine anyone doing it better. [ ... ] Lansbury tore the place down.' *Guardian*, 12 December 2010, https://www.theguard ian.com/stage/2010/dec/12/matthew-bourne-best-performance-ever, accessed. Also, see http://jameswilliamproductions.com/gypsy for a series of quotations from London reviews of Lansbury's performance.
35. I was fortunate enough to have seen Dolores Gray play Mama Rose while still a student; while disappointed to have missed Lansbury, I remember Gray's warmth and vocal versatility as distinctive features in her portrayal.
36. The recording made of her performance of 'Rose's Turn' in the London gala, *Stairway to the Stars* (1989, but released by First Night Records on CD in 1995), supports the view of some who saw her that her performance was vocally the most varied and powerful of anyone who has assayed the role.
37. In a 1989 interview with Skip E. Lowe, Gray herself said her only regret was not having taken the opportunity to play more dramatic roles, as she believed she had the range to do so. 'Dolores Gray, James Bacon—1989 TV Interview', https://www.youtube.com/watch?v= U-XcB_44gLM, accessed 28 September 2019.
38. Gray's distinctive interpretation of the little speech that leads into 'Rose's Turn' can be heard on *Stairway to the Stars*, recorded live at the London Palladium, Sunday, 12 November 1989, 1995, First Night Records.
39. Ellis Nassour, 'She's Still Here', http://www.totaltheater.com/?q=node/375, accessed 28 August 2019.
40. In fact, it is on record that Elaine Stritch had been led to believe she would be cast when it looked as though Lansbury might be unavailable; she regarded Lansbury as a very close rival. Alexandra Jacobs, *Still Here* (New York: Farar, Straus & Giroux, 2019), 199.
41. The role of Carlotta was reconceived by Goldman and Sondheim in 1987, in line with the more optimistic approach of the London version; in the rewrite, Carlotta is not a failure but a genuine survivor, making Gray perfect casting for the role.
42. For a full account of the changes made to the role of Carlotta in relation to the revised version of *Follies*, see Olaf Jubin, 'There's No Escaping Nostalgia: The 1987 London Version of *Follies*', *Studies in Musical Theatre* 6, no. 2 (2012), 199–212.
43. Mark Steyn, 'Review of *Follies*', *Independent*, 23 July 1987, reprinted in *London Theatre Record*, 16–29 July 1987, 894.
44. Rosalie Horner, 'Review of *Follies*', *Daily Express*, 22 July 1987, reprinted in ibid., 895.
45. Clive Hirschorn, 'Review of *Follies*', *Sunday Express*, 26 July 1987, reprinted in ibid., 893.
46. Other performers may have been funnier or more camp in the role, but a survey of twenty different performances on YouTube reveals that no other performer has possessed Gray's sheer vocal power.
47. Coward was even obliged to pay for some repairs to ensure that the theatre was ready to open in time for the scheduled first night.
48. Coward's diaries detail his progressive disillusionment with Martin and her manager-husband Richard Halliday, a typical pattern in Coward's working relationships. When he met the couple at Southampton on 27 September 1946, 'They were absolutely sweet and so

genuinely thrilled about everything [ … ] we showed them Drury Lane and then played them some of the music. They were madly enthusiastic. [ … ] Personally I think she has authentic magic. She is quite obviously an artist in the true sense. She is easy, generous and humble'. Payn and Morley, *The Noël Coward Diaries*, 64. After a rehearsal on 14 November, he noted, 'She is a dream girl, quick and knowledgeable; she has all the mercurial charm of Gertie [Gertrude Lawrence] at her best with a sweet voice and with more taste' (ibid., 69), and two days later he opined, 'Mary really is remarkable. [ … ] She is the only star I have ever worked with who has a real sense of the balance of the show. She is generous about everyone else in the company and never tries to snatch' (ibid.). Although Coward's biographer Philip Hoare attributes much of the blame to the designer Gladys Calthrop—a close friend of Coward—by 14 December there were unpleasant rows about her costumes and hat, with Coward blaming her husband for Martin's single display of temper, but on opening night he commented: 'A really triumphant first night. Mary wonderful' (ibid., 71). According to Coward, the writer Clemence Dane told him he had encased Mary Martin in a straitjacket … crushing her personality. Philip Hoare, *Noël Coward: A Biography* (London: Mandarin, 1996), 370.

49. Ibid., 368.

50. Sheridan Morley, *A Talent to Amuse* (Harmondsworth: Penguin, 1974), 311.

51. Quoted in Adrian Wright, *A Tanner's Worth of Tune* (Woodbridge: Boydell Press, 2010), 53.

52. Cole Lesley, *The Life of Noël Coward* (London: Jonathan Cape, 1976), 248.

53. Quoted in Wright, *A Tanner's Worth of Tune*, 53.

54. Stacy Wolf, *A Problem like Maria* (Ann Arbor: University of Michigan Press, 2002), 45–87.

55. See the entry on Mary Martin on The Official Masterworks Broadway website, https://www.masterworksbroadway.com/artist/mary-martin/, accessed 29 September 2019.

56. The role that Mary Martin became most closely associated with in the United States from the mid-1950s was Peter Pan. In her autobiography Martin claims to have identified since her childhood with 'the boy who never grew up'. She first appeared in the 1954 stage version of the musical by Jule Styne, Moose Charlap, Betty Comdon, and Adolph Green, directed by Jerome Robbins. One year later there was a television broadcast, which was followed in 1956 and 1960 by repeat television productions. The one from 1960 was rebroadcast in 1963, 1966, and 1973. However, this aspect of her performance persona was never known in the UK, which is why it is not discussed in the context of this chapter.

57. Beginning in 1948, the Malayan Emergency involved guerrilla warfare between British troops and the Communist Malayan National Liberation Army; in 1950 the United Nations sanctioned a retaliatory war against communist North Korea, led by the US military.

58. In both countries homosexuals were stigmatised as morally weak and mentally disturbed individuals whose 'abnormal' lifestyles made them suspect as potential communist traitors.

59. Nathaniel Benchley, 'Off Stage', *Theatre Arts*, September 1951, 47. Again, note the ascription of 'charm', which was practically ubiquitous in descriptions of Martin.

60. The *Stage* reviewer opined: '[T]here is too much story, and the story [ … ] is neither very good in itself nor of a character likely to appeal to British audiences as it has done to Americans. For it is not very easy for us to be interested in a complicated and not over-exciting yarn about the American-Japanese conflict in the South Pacific [ … ] or indeed in yet another colour-bar problem'. Quoted in Adrian Wright, *West End Broadway: The Golden Age of the American Musical in London* (Woodbridge: Boydell Press, 2012), 74.

61. *South Pacific* won the Pulitzer Prize for Drama.
62. The Hollywood costume designer Edith Head commented on Martin's 'audience appeal': 'First, she doesn't antagonize women. They regard her as wholesome, friendly, warm. Any housewife can vicariously live the role Mary enacts. Second, men like her because she is peppy and stimulating without making them feel inferior.' Quoted in Lloyd Shearer, 'Mary Martin: The Star Who Loves Everybody', *Parade*, undated, unpaginated, Billy Rose Theatre Collection, New York Public Library for the Performing Arts.
63. In fact there is considerable evidence that Martin, although twice married and with two children, was lesbian or bisexual. Her husband and manager Richard Halliday was regarded by most as a closeted gay man, so their marriage and close relationship, in addition to providing her with stability and professional support, conveniently disguised their sexual proclivities. Halliday's dictatorial and somewhat histrionic manner made him rather unpopular, but this enabled Martin, unlike many female stars in that era, to maintain in public the sweet-natured and sunny aspects of her personality while Halliday protected their business interests.
64. Unlike American audiences, the British public has in its traditions of music hall and pantomime almost compulsively surrendered to the appeal of transvestite performance. With gender and sexual stereotypes necesssarily subverted in many situations during the war, the wide-ranging attractiveness of drag performance needed no special pleading in London in 1951.
65. In the naturalistic logic of the dramatic fiction, Martin's uninhibited flirting with Luther's unconvincing woman could be construed as a means of normalising the inevitably homosexual friendships in wartime that often substituted for more usual heterosexual relationships, but in addition its double travesty of masculinity and femininity destabilises all stereotypes of gender and sexuality, depending on how you interpret the transvestite performance. The line 'I am caught and I don't wanna run' teasingly alludes to illicit homosexual and heterosexual activity alike. Although clearly a joke, the role-play permits the audience to identify with or feel attracted to Mary Martin's Nellie, no matter what their gender or sexual orientation.
66. Brian Kellow, 'There's Something about Mary', *Opera News* 78, no. 5 (November, 2013), https://www.operanews.com/Opera_News_Magazine/2013/11/Features/There_s_Something_About_Mary.html, accessed 20 July 2019.
67. This point was first developed by Stacy Wolf in *A Problem like Maria*.
68. The role of Dolly was initially offered to Ethel Merman, who turned it down.
69. Quoted in 'Mary Martin—Call on Dolly', www.callondolly.com/mary-martin/, accessed 12 September 2019.
70. Wright, *West End Broadway*, 222.
71. Quoted in ibid.
72. Quoted in ibid., 223.
73. Gianluca Spinato, 'The Suez Crisis and Britain's illusion of an Equal Relationship with Uncle Sam'. https://www.academia.edu/43508947/The_Suez_Crisis_and_Britains_illusion_of_an_equal_relationship_with_the_Uncle_Sam, accessed 26 August 2019. Sir Anthony Eden was the Conservative British prime minister, who, against the advice of the American government, formed a coalition with France and Israel to recapture the Suez Canal; as a result of the conflict over this action, he suffered a nervous breakdown and was forced to resign. He was succeeded by Harold Macmillan.
74. *I Love Lucy*, for instance, first appeared on ITV in 1955.

75. Andrew Jackson, 'Designing Britain 1945–75: Cultural Revolution 1950–1970,' https://vads.ac.uk/learning/designingbritain/html/crd_cultrev.html, accessed 26 September 2019. Speaking of the new age of consumerism, Harold Macmillan coined the slogan, 'Most of our people have never had it so good', first delivered to a group of Conservative Party members in 1958.
76. Belying her show-business persona, Stritch had in fact grown up in an affluent Catholic family in Michigan and was an alcoholic for much of her life.
77. John Bell, *Elaine Stritch: The End of Pretend* (New York: Page, 2019), 259–262.
78. Coward was actually a lower-middle-class arriviste from suburban Teddington.
79. Day, 324.
80. Charles Isherwood, 'Review: *Sail Away*', *Variety*, 14 November 1999, https://variety.com/1999/film/reviews/sail-away-1200459732/, accessed 29 September 2019.
81. Day, 327–328.
82. Since first being attributed to George Bernard Shaw in a *Reader's Digest* article in the 1940s, this apothegm has commonly been attributed to him.
83. Coward's friend the impresario Henry Sherek had for some reason expected Stritch to sing as broadly as a female minstrel performer, but he found her 'not only a splendid singer of songs where not a word is missed ... but a most sensitive actress with wonderful timing.' Jacobs, *Still Here*, 130.
84. Payn and Morley, The Noël Coward Diaries, 478.
85. Ibid., 507.
86. Jacobs, *Still Here*, 131.
87. Ibid.
88. 'Elaine Stritch—1979 TV Interview', https://www.youtube.com/watch?v=BTQXg_SpVkg, accessed 28 September 2019.
89. At the start of the series Sinden's *froideur* was apparently motivated as much by his distaste for Stritch's alcoholism as it was by fidelity to his character; their relationship improved when, with the aid of Alcoholics Anonymous, she became a complete teetotaler.
90. Jackson, 'Designing Britain.'
91. In spite of his admiration for Stritch's talent, he found her, 'like most Americans, dreadfully noisy'. Payn and Morley, *The Noël Coward Diaries*, 504.
92. The United States was in the dominant position after Suez; see Dunne, 'The Suez Crisis and the Politics of the Anglo-American Special Relationship'.

## Bibliography

Aldgate, Anthony, and Tony Richards. *Britain Can Take It*. London: Tauris, 2007.
*Annie Get Your Gun*. CD reissue. Original London Cast. Lew Stone and his Orchestra. LaserLight Digital, Stanyan Records, 1994, 12 449.
Bell, John. *Elaine Stritch: The End of Pretend*. New York: Page, 2019.
Benchley, Nathaniel. 'Off Stage'. *Theatre Arts*, September 1951, 47.
Bergan, Ronald. 'Dolores Gray Obituary'. *Guardian*, 2 July 2002, https://www.theguardian.com/news/2002/jul/03/guardianobituaries, accessed 5 August 2019.
Botting, Josephine. 'How British Film Celebrated the Role of Women in the Second World War', https://www.bfi.org.uk/news-opinion/news-bfi/features/british-cinema-women-second-world-war, accessed 28 August 2019.

Brown, Ivor. 'At the Theatre'. *Observer*, 22 December 1946, 2.

Day, Barry. *The Complete Lyrics of Noel Coward*. New York: Overlook Press, 1998.

'Dolores Gray Can't Get a Man with a Gun', https://www.youtube.com/watch?v=ndYigf2aop8, accessed 5 August 2019.

'Dolores Gray, James Bacon—1989 TV Interview', https://www.youtube.com/watch?v=U-XcB_44gLM, accessed 28 September 2019.

'Dolores Gray. Obituary'. *Daily Telegraph*, 28 July 2002, https://www.telegraph.co.uk/news/obituaries/1398599/Dolores-Gray.html, accessed 28 August 2019.

'Elaine Stritch—1979 TV Interview', https://www.youtube.com/watch?v=BTQXg_SpVkg, accessed 28 September 2019.

Harris, Kenneth. 'Oversexed, Overfed, Over Here'. *New York Times*, 12 February 1995, 26.

Hirschorn, Clive. 'Review of *Follies*'. *Sunday Express*, 26 July 1987, reprinted in *London Theatre Record*, 16–29 July 1987, 893.

Hoare, Philip. *Noël Coward: A Biography*, London: Mandarin, 1996.

Hogenboom, Melissa. 'How the GI Influx Influenced Britain's View of America'. BBC News (Magazine), 3 November 2012, www.bbc.co.uk>news>magazine-20160819, accessed 28 September 2019.

Horner, Rosalie. 'Review of *Follies*'. *Daily Express*, 22 July 1987, reprinted in *London Theatre Record*, 16–29 July 1987, 895.

Isherwood, Charles. 'Review: *Sail Away*'. *Variety*, 14 November 1999, https://variety.com/1999/film/reviews/sail-away-1200459732/, accessed 29 September 2019.

Jackson, Andrew. 'Designing Britain 1945–75: Cultural Revolution 1950–1970,' https://vads.ac.uk/learning/designingbritain/html/crd_cultrev.html, accessed 26 September 2019.

Jacobs, Alexandra. *Still Here*. New York: Farar, Straus & Giroux, 2019.

Jubin, Olaf. 'There's No Escaping Nostalgia: The 1987 London Version of *Follies*'. *Studies in Musical Theatre* 6, no. 2 (2012): 199–212.

Kellow, Brian. 'There's Something about Mary'. *Opera News* 78, no. 5 (November 2013) https://www.operanews.com/Opera_News_Magazine/2013/11/Features/There_s_Something_About_Mary.html, accessed 20 July 2019.

Lant, Antonia Caroline. *Blackout: Reinventing Women for Wartime British Cinema*. Princeton, NJ: Princeton University Press, 1991.

Lesley, Cole. *The Life of Noël Coward*. London: Jonathan Cape, 1976.

'Mary Martin: Call on Dolly', www.callondolly.com/mary-martin/, accessed 12 September 2019.

'Mary Martin'. https://www.masterworksbroadway.com/artist/mary-martin/, accessed 29 September 2019.

Maslon, Laurence, ed. *American Musicals 1927–1949*. New York: Penguin Random House, 2014.

Morley, Sheridan. *A Talent to Amuse*. Harmondsworth: Penguin, 1974.

Payn, Graham, and Sheridan Morley, eds. *The Noël Coward Diaries*. Basingstoke: Macmillan, 1982.

Shearer, Lloyd. 'Mary Martin: The Star Who Loves Everybody'. *Parade*, undated, unpaginated. Billy Rose Theatre Collection, New York Public Library for the Performing Arts.

Snelson, John. 'The West End Musical 1947–54: British Identity and the "American Invasion"'. PhD thesis, University of Birmingham, 2002.

Spinato, Giancluca, 'The Suez Cris and Britain's Illusion of an Equal Relationship with Uncle Sam', https://www.academia.edu/43508947/The_Suez_Crisis_and_Britains_illusion_of_an_equal_relationship_with_the_Uncle_Sam

*Stairway to the Stars*. 1989. CD. First Nights Records, 1995, .

Steyn, Mark. 'Review of *Follies*'. *Independent*, 23 July 1987, reprinted in *London Theatre Record*, 16–29 July 1987, 894.

Tynan, Kenneth. 'Why London Likes American Musicals'. *New York Times*, 13 April 1952, movies2.nytimes.com/books/98/05/10/specials/tynan-musicals.htm, accessed 29 July 2019.

Wolf, Stacy. *A Problem like Maria*. Ann Arbor: University of Michigan Press, 2002.

Woolley, Stephen. 'Behind the Lines: Women and WWII British film', July 2017, https://www.watershed.co.uk/articles/behind-the-lines-women-and-wwii-british-film, accessed 29 August 2019.

Wright, Adrian. *A Tanner's Worth of Tune*. Woodbridge: Boydell Press, 2010.

Wright, Adrian. *West End Broadway: The Golden Age of the American Musical in London*. Woodbridge: Boydell Press, 2012.

CHAPTER 14

························································································

# THE MOST BELOVED AMERICAN MUSICAL

## Guys and Dolls *in London*

························································································

JOHN SNELSON

IN the very top league of canonic American musicals sits *Guys and Dolls*: its premiere created 'the most unanimously ecstatic set of reviews in Broadway history'.[1] Damon Runyon's writings about New York and the Broadway–Times Square neighbourhood were precisely complemented by the songs of another New York resident, Frank Loesser. This chapter explores why a show synonymous with New York and portraying some of its most vivid and familiar archetypes has been presented in London so frequently, through productions over six decades: 1953, 1979, 1982–1997, 2005–2007, 2012, 2015, and 2018.[2]

When the show was new to the West End, Runyon's stories, characters and distinctive style were well-known to many in the London audience. Elements of London life and its archetypes, especially in relation to the Soho area, were well established in metropolitan literature and recognisable in London as analogues for Runyon's Broadway world. Indeed, such shared traits were to be amplified in British shows that followed fast in the West End wake of *Guys and Dolls*. From a British perspective. *Guys and Dolls* in London can be read not so much as a New York musical, but as a musical with a metropolitan topos shared by and understood locally in both cities. Such a connection beyond musical theatre repertoire alone has undoubtedly contributed to the show's West End prominence.

The performance reception of *Guys and Dolls* in 1953 was qualified by tensions around musical theatre exchanges between Broadway and the West End that had long been present, if not consistently so prominent as in the immediate wake of World War II.[3] With time, repertoire canonisation has been overtaken in prominence and been commercially matched (or even succeeded) by performative canonisation. Star casting and recurring imagery has established a certain Runyon-styled Broadway in the West End to the point of audience expectation, if not requirement. Considering the show's content alongside its performance context, *Guys and Dolls* can thus be understood not so much as an American in London, but as a balancing act of recognition between metropolitan and theatrical perspectives.

## THE LONDON PREMIÈRE OF *GUYS AND DOLLS*

*Guys and Dolls* had its Broadway premiere at the Forty-sixth Street Theatre on 24 November 1950 and ran for 1,200 performances, closing on 28 November 1953, four days after its third anniversary. The final six months of the Broadway production overlapped with the UK production, which opened at the London Coliseum on 28 May 1953 following a short regional tryout in Bristol. The London reception was informed by the profile of other American musicals that had opened there following the end of World War II, notably *Oklahoma!* in 1947.[4] In the aftermath of war, comparisons—of both writing and performance characteristics—between the nature of the imported US musicals and indigenous shows became symbolic of wider reflections on the successes and failures of the British national character. We see these preoccupations in 1953 in the responses to the opening of *Guys and Dolls*, when it replaced *Call Me Madam* at the Coliseum.[5]

The show was presented with Broadway authenticity. It followed George S. Kaufman's direction and Michael Kidd's musical staging, and it used Jo Mielziner's sets. Most of the leading parts were played by American actors: Jerry Wayne (Sky Masterson), Sam Levene (Nathan Detroit), Vivian Blaine (Miss Adelaide), Stubby Kaye (Nicely-Nicely Johnson), and Tom Pedi (Harry the Horse). In contrast, the only homegrown talent in a leading role came from the casting of Lizbeth Webb as Miss Sarah Brown. Such a national distinction marked a contested area: 'The success of the evening was our own Lizbeth Webb, always audible, in fine voice, and acting prettily. She has a leading part, and it is ridiculous and discourteous that her name on the programme should be in letters about half the size of those allotted to Vivian Blaine, Sam Levene, and Jerry Wayne'.[6] Some disturbance at the first night's curtain calls has been attributed to this nationalistic subtext, with 'a group of anti-American rowdies' objecting to Blaine.[7] Yet contemporary comments do not agree on either the cause of the negative response from some of those present or indeed its scale.

In the *Evening Standard* Kenneth Tynan enthused over 'a 100 per cent American musical caper'.[8] The opinion in the theatre journal *The Stage* was equivocal, finding that 'brassy and a little shrill, [the show] is tough, very modern in manner and utterly American in matter', if 'rarely other than vital and vigorous'. But the show gave 'a wan reflection of the author's distinctively satirical style', with the characters lacking 'essential likeability and innocence', being 'crude, childish and naive in their lack of the common virtues'.[9] The noted drama critic Harold Hobson (*Sunday Times*) was at an extreme, thinking 'in all parts of the house the reception seemed to me the coolest given to any American musical since the disastrous failure of *Finian's Rainbow*'. He could barely bring himself to write about 'this glorification of brutality, vice, illiteracy, and maudlin muddle-headedness', concluding that any good points were insufficient to prevent the work becoming 'an interminable, an overwhelming, and in the end intolerable bore'.[10] For Eric Keown (*Punch*), these negative qualities were signalled through a 'sinister' undertone to the booing, although he thought otherwise, finding instead 'childlike innocence' in the characters.[11] Beverly Baxter (*Sunday Express*) thought the booing was generated by a pro-Webb faction—unjustly so, as he considered Blaine the superior performer.[12]

Problematic too for a London audience were Runyon's distinctive speech patterns and vocabulary, compounded when taken off the page by marked American accents and rapid delivery. Walter Hayes wrote in *The Sketch* that inaudibility may have played a large part in the reception: 'Sitting, as I was, on the ultimate rim of the vast Coliseum ground floor, not all of the dialogue reached me. Maybe the gallery—which, at the première seemed to be bothered about something—had its own hearing troubles'.[13] The only hint of negativity in Tynan's review also came in a comment on the Coliseum's size as 'no rabbit hutch'.[14] Anthony Cookman summarised the interplay of factors:

> For *Guys and Dolls* is a genuine exotic, as strange to us as the Crazy Gang in Cockney extravaganza would be to New Yorkers; and in more intimate surroundings we should have a great deal better chance to get the hang of things. Among the things is the Damon Runyon argot. Easy enough in print, this lingo turns out to be teasingly difficult when given its proper American intonations, and the microphones are not so helpful as might be thought. Another thing is the wit of the songs. The wit is unmistakable when we hear it, but often it gets lost in the ingenious complications of the wording of the songs.[15]

When the show went on tour to Birmingham in 1955, J. C. Trewin delivered a 'final verdict' of 'just "nicely-nicely"': I doubt whether it will be any stronger. Damon Runyon is, first of all, for the printed page'.[16] The originality and stylistic integrity of *Guys and Dolls* were thus a source of both praise and criticism.

Questions of authenticity arise when a work is performed away from its home ground. As David R. Schwarz puts it, 'Runyon's Broadway [ ... ] was a state of mind as well as a specific location'.[17] The evocation is unusually complete, and thus the more convincing as Runyon's eye 'is the eye of a camera—the camera of tabloid newspapers for which he wrote', and his ear 'hears gossip, street lingo, and the cacophony of city sounds'.[18]

So, to what extent is a familiarity with its New York origins of sight, sound, and story fundamental to the success of *Guys and Dolls* in London? For all the exaggeration that goes with the territory of musical comedy and the show's remove from reality as 'a musical fable of Broadway', the language of New York in it is presented as real vocabulary, with authentic speech patterns.[19] Yet such authenticity is a conceit, a heightened variant of real speech developed idiosyncratically by Runyon for literary effect, the most prominent aspect of which is his unwavering restriction of tense. His son Damon Runyon, Jr.—also a writer and journalist—compared New York's reality with his father's depiction:

> It is true that some Broadwayites, especially in the Lindy's [restaurant] set, fall into the present tense in their gabble. [ ... ] However, even those to whom the present

FIG. 14.1 Journalist and short-story writer Damon Runyon (1880–1946) at his desk. Photographer unknown; image provided by the editors.

tense comes naturally usually mix in the past tense, too. In the Runyon stories this present tense was pure, carried out to every word, and it was laborious writing to make it read smoothly. If anyone talks like that along the Big Street they come after the fact, or rather fiction.[20]

But at a geographical and cultural remove in London, the potential for Runyon's literary use of the present tense to be taken as actual reported speech patterns was heightened to the extent that '[t]he controversy was taken seriously in England where the Runyon stories were as popular as they were [in the United States]. "Do guys and dolls really talk like that?" '[21] And the vocabulary itself was more performative than direct quotation, with the wide syndication of Runyon's writing readily spreading his linguistic inventions.[22] Within the context of vivid characterisations, the result is 'less imitation than simulacrum', whose holistic integration conveys the authenticity of a believable universe, albeit a parallel one.[23]

Identifiable distortions of fact about people and places are seldom far from the surface for those in the know, too: Mindy's, for example, was based on Lindy's restaurant, which was opened in 1921 by Leo and Clara Lindemann at 1626 Broadway, later relocating to Broadway and Fifty-first Street.[24] There was much discussion in Runyon's day over the extent to which Runyon embellished or copied, but his son confirms that the germ of inspiration was from life. Thus, 'The Brain' in *The Brain Goes Home* was drawn from the gambler, drug dealer, and Lindy's regular Arnold Rothstein, while the fictional journalist Waldo Winchester is an obvious allusion to Runyon's fellow New York journalist and friend Walter Winchell.[25] Closer to the *Guys and Dolls* cast list, Runyon's cop Brannigan was inspired by a local Broadway detective, Johnny Broderick.[26]

Some of those sitting in the audience at the Coliseum had gained a knowledge of the specifics of character, plot, and language through reading Runyon's work, which had been published from the mid-1930s on in collected volumes as well as in such British periodicals as the *London Evening Standard* and regional papers.[27] There was an assumption by journalists that Runyon's style was sufficiently familiar across the UK through print and film such that the term 'Runyonesque' could be used. In 1935 a film review in a Scottish periodical for Universal's film *Princess O'Hara* describes 'a racy comedy, which supplies a laugh a minute in the typical Runyonesque dialogue familiar to thousands of newspaper readers and movie-goers'.[28] In 1939 in the English home counties, a film review for *They're Off* was sufficiently informed to draw a distinction between elements of the Runyon style, questioning 'whether his style will be recognisable in either dialogue or story', although the characters are 'completely Runyonesque'.[29] An approach to gangsters provided a defining characteristic, with a 1938 film review of *A Slight Case of Murder* finding it 'unmistakably Runyonesque. This means, as anyone who has read the short stories knows, that it exploits the naivete of gangsters and makes them richly humorous characters.'[30] Even away from the writer's own work, a London review of the play *The Bowery Touch* at the Strand Theatre in 1937 could reference the same character type, such that 'the gangsters are so engaging in their naïve Damon Runyonesque way'.[31] More immediately, preceding *Guys and Dolls*' arrival in London in 1950, an omnibus edition of Runyon's stories was published in the UK.[32] Reviewers in 1953 made reference to a familiarity with Runyon's work, which 'had a tremendous vogue over here some years back',[33] enough to identify 'authentic Runyon raciness',[34] alongside his 'endearing New York underworld, which British managers have repeatedly toyed with and shunned for fear that the British public would find it too American'.[35] Unfamiliarity was not an issue for Tynan, who wrote his review of *Guys and Dolls* as a full-blown pastiche of Runyon's style: 'I found myself laughing ha-ha last night more often than a guy in the critical dodge has any right to. And I am ready to up and drop on my knees before Frank Loesser, who writes the music and lyrics.'[36] *Guys and Dolls* may not require foreknowledge of Runyon, but in 1953 it certainly helped.

## THE SHARED TERRITORIES OF BROADWAY AND SOHO

Many of the first London audiences were aware of Runyon's writing. But what of those who are increasingly not? Since Runyon's death, widespread familiarity with his stories has declined with a category shift from contemporary reportage to literary canon. Today, *Guys and Dolls* is more likely to bring Runyon's work to the attention of its audience than Runyon's work alone will prompt interest. For example, reprinting the principal source story for the musical, *The Idyll of Miss Sarah Brown*, in the accompanying programme book to productions in London has become a familiar method of filling in the literary origin and context. Qualities of the show transcend the New York geographical and Runyon literary specificity and allow the show to be viewed as 'wonderfully rootless: universal. [ ... ] About a technically illegal subculture operating with the main culture'.[37] The very things that seem to mark out its unique United States–New York–Broadway–Times Square identity can also be interpreted as localised incarnations of recognisable tropes of place, activity, accent, speech pattern, and vocabulary to be found in other large cities. In particular, they resonate with long-established portrayals of London.

In a novel from 1936, a description of London's main theatre and entertainment area, around Shaftesbury Avenue—an equivalent of the 'Great White Way'—on the lower edge of Soho, immediately suggests a version of Runyonland, where '[w]hores and clubmen, penniless outcasts and provincials, criminals and wage-slaves were walking along its pavements. Undoubtedly there was a detective or two among them: undoubtedly, he would have been delighted to have been able to capture the two prospective burglars who were sitting smugly like respectable citizens in the bus'.[38] The title of the novel, by James Curtis, compounds the connection: *The Gilt Kid*.[39] Its central character, just released from prison, returns to a life on the uneasy border between criminality and survival in central London, and is referred to mostly by his prison nickname, derived from his yellow hair.[40] Other characters are introduced into his story with the semi-concealed identities characteristic of the discrete social groupings of the underworld. Men have nicknames—Curly Simmonds, Scaley, Ginger—and women seem to have only forenames—Maisie, Isabella—which in the context of *Guys and Dolls* prompts the unanswered question, 'What is Miss Adelaide's surname before she finally becomes "Mrs Detroit"'? Runyon parallels continue: Curtis uses slang to emphasise social milieu and associated codes of behaviour. The Gilt Kid evokes Miss Adelaide's predicament when he justifies his avoidance of proposing marriage to his girlfriend because of his housebreaker values: '[B]ut who the hell had ever heard of a screwsman rolling up his mort's ken with a bunch of violets. [ ... ] A screwsman wanted to flash his dough around a bit. It showed that he was big-hearted, and what was a better way than by dolling up his jane?'[41]

Shady dealings, scams, and gambling in nightclubs and at dog tracks are the subject of Robert Westerby's *Wide Boys Never Work* (1937), whose central characters are morose British cousins of Nathan, Nicely-Nicely, and their circle.[42] Westerby foregrounds language as Runyon does to evoke locale, as with a dodgy Cockney mechanic fixing up a car for resale to a gullible customer: 'I s'pose abaowt noine outer twelve 'ave ter be faiked up some'ow. Ther's always loose bits ter pack up, an' things ter be woired up somewhere, y'know'.[43] *Guys and Dolls* could be cast from the seedy side of central London, to go by the narrator's summary of nightclub clientele as 'tarts, touts, ponces, louts, bookies, ex-pugs, petty gangsters, perhaps a stray newspaper reporter trying to feel tough and

THE MOST BELOVED AMERICAN MUSICAL    409

Metropolitan, and a few fools like me'.[44] At the dog track, appropriately transferrable skills from New York to London are much in evidence and referred to as 'American gangster stuff'.[45]

In 1937, Gerald Kersh published his most acclaimed novel *Night and the City*, to form with Curtis and Westerby a trilogy of novels with a 'gritty and then rare (and in some quarters unwelcome) portrayal of underworld and lowlife London'.[46] Kersh's uncompromising novel presents a cynical, dystopian version of *Guys and Dolls* before the event. Indeed, if there is an English equivalent of Runyon, it is Kersh.[47] Consider his self-description: 'Since I derive a certain enjoyment from it, I'm pretty good at covering most forms of [ ... ] 'lowlife': prizefights, dog fights, executions, jam sessions, orgies, booze-ups, whorehouses, etc., etc. I usually manage to get a certain zing into what I write'.[48] The protagonist of *Night and the City* is Harry Fabian, from London's East End but affecting to be an American songwriter with connections. The Hollywood-provoked lure of American gangster culture is evident in him, appropriately exaggerated, romanticised, and fake.[49] He painfully deceives no one more than himself and is increasingly recognisable as a failing, increasingly desperate alter ego of Nathan Detroit. A low dive for late-night drinkers that Fabian visits suggests a home-from-home for Runyon regulars, 'a meeting-place on the shifting frontier between the slough of small business and the quagmire of the underworld'.[50] A summary of the clientele is Runyonesque in conceit and literary execution when it concludes that '[m]any commercial gentlemen are called "business men" until they are found out; then they are described as "crooks". Many commercial gentlemen are called "crooks" until it is discovered that they are merely sharp business men'.[51] The importance of specific geography around Runyon's Times Square–Broadway parallels the precision of Kersh's Soho, in which Harry Fabian 'walked at top speed now, across Regent Street, thought Great Marlborough Street, up Wardour Street, back—inevitably back—towards Charing Cross Road', after which he 'walked up to New Compton Street, to one of the oldest and darkest of all the houses; passed through a stinking passage lit by one dim night-light bulb, and went downstairs to Bagrag's Cellar'.[52] The world of Soho in the 1930s that Kersh evokes is a de-romanticised Runyonland, stripped of its geniality. Sealing the West End–Broadway parallels, *Night and the City* was filmed twice, the first set in London (1950) and the second relocated to New York (1992).[53]

In 1970 the National Theatre in London announced *Guys and Dolls* for its very first production of a musical.[54] The critic Kenneth Tynan, who had been so effusive in his praise of *Guys and Dolls* when reviewing it in 1953, was a key architect in the development of the National Theatre project. He was its first dramaturge and the most significant influence on Sir Laurence Olivier, its director, for repertory planning, including encouragement for the scheduling of *Guys and Dolls*.[55] Tynan loved the novelty and energy he found in Broadway theatre, exemplified by American musicals and doubly so by *Guys and Dolls* in the combination of genre and setting.[56] He concludes his parody Runyon review of *Guys and Dolls* with a theatrical comparison that sets nightlife and underclass in London alongside those of New York: 'In fact, the chances are that *Guys and Dolls* is not only a young masterpiece but *The Beggar's Opera* of Broadway'.[57] By

1970 the perception of an emerging 'Golden Age' Broadway canon was beginning to take hold in response to significant shifts in the genre between the early 1940s and the 1960s in particular, not least with Hollywood film adaptations. Notably, *Guys and Dolls* benefited through its high-status film—featuring the iconic performers Frank Sinatra (Nathan Detroit) and Marlon Brando (Sky Masterson)—which allowed it (albeit in modified form) to be seen by vast numbers more than was possible in live theatre performance and also through repeat screenings during the long period when the show was not being staged.[58] Not only was it a superb stage show in its own right, but it was created in an era of musicals that swiftly attracted a stamp of nostalgic approval as the musical and dramatic landscape evolved towards the newer and strongly contrasting territory established by the 1970s. Its programming by the National Theatre could thus claim the dual authorities of high repertory status and public familiarity.

The National Theatre production was planned to open in mid-December 1970 at the Old Vic. Olivier defended his choice against the criticism of a British cultural institution taking on an American commercial show by stating, 'This is a classic and we are doing it as a classic', adding, 'Runyon in his way is the American Dickens'.[59] In the event, the production was cancelled, owing in part to Olivier's illness during the second part of 1970,[60] as well as through cost-cutting imposed by the Board of the National Theatre in the wake of a less financially successful year than anticipated.[61]

Olivier's reference to Charles Dickens immediately connects with Runyon through the authors' shared wealth of imagined colourful characters, complex plots, depiction of metropolitan society at all levels, and acute awareness of the struggles for survival within the city's disfigured sprawl. That New York developed its metropolitan hinterland most prominently in the first part of the twentieth century, represented in literature and on film, is predominantly the result of comparative chronology: London—one of many powerful capital cities—had long been established when America was put on the Western European map. New York became *the* defining city of the twentieth century as the New World embraced contemporary technology in skyscrapers and subways, elevators and electricity, and as its flood of immigrants alongside dynamic capitalism challenged the dominance of the Old World. Physically and systemically, it stood out against the eighteenth- and nineteenth-century imperialism of such great European capitals as Paris, Berlin, and St Petersburg and the grandeur of combined past eras in Rome. New York encapsulated the future in its technological environment and the diversity of its rapidly expanding population: not only do 'a million lights . . . flicker there', but 'a million hearts beat quicker there'.[62]

# THEMATIC AND STYLISTIC PARALLELS IN THE SOHO MUSICALS

Within the outward shell of novelty and innovation, the characteristics of Runyon's New York represent a recurring need to find ways through which to negotiate the concept of the metropolis, to shape its vastness into a manageable form and scale. One way this can happen is by the classification of types through their attitudes and their work. Such types rely on sheer numbers of people to make them identifiable, even as archetypes—enough to gamble, drink, jostle for position, and be grouped through shared aims and actions. This is where we can find gangsters, gamblers, nightclub owners, hostesses, and prostitutes. It is also where we find Londoners, summed up especially through the Cockney archetype.[63]

Garebian considers that *Guys and Dolls* has 'something undeniably American [ ... ] captured in its racy argot, breezy manner, high, raucous energy, and eager willingness to gamble on enterprises that could bring in the cops'.[64] But that description works too for significant elements of Noël Coward's musical *Ace of Clubs* (London, 1950), about the romantic and illegal goings on in a Soho nightclub. Coward's showgirls are sisters to those of the Hot Box in *Guys and Dolls* and the two clubs in *Pal Joey*. For example, their performance in the club of 'Time for Baby's Bottle' (act 2, scene 4) characterises them as a series of women's perfumes, identified through spoken rhyming couplets, just like the flowers in *Pal Joey*'s 'The Flower Garden of My Heart'. The choice of a night-time, night-club setting for *Ace of Clubs* retrospectively invites the acknowledgement of similarities with *Guys and Dolls* and *Pal Joey*.[65] But the resonance comes through the shared tropes around urban night life in the two major cities, not a specific lineage from show to show: Coward noted his conception for *Ace of Clubs* in his diary for 27 December 1949,[66] before he had seen either American show.[67] London audiences saw Coward's version of Soho high jinks first too, well in advance of the London openings of either *Guys and Dolls* (1953) or *Pal Joey* (1954).[68] Slang, energy, and frantic business around the avoidance of the local police further the comparison with *Guys and Dolls*.[69] Alan Dent's review of Coward's *Ace of Clubs* in the *News Chronicle* (July 1950) summarises the point: 'It is a show to make the visitor to London think that Soho is the heart of London, and it will make even the Londoner think that Soho has a heart'.[70] Substitute London and Londoners with New York and New Yorkers, and Soho with Broadway, and the show being described could easily be *Guys and Dolls*.

Later in the 1950s, *Expresso Bongo* (1958) and *The Crooked Mile* (1959), among others, are equally apt for Garebian's description. The origins of *The Crooked Mile* are in Peter Wildeblood's novel *West End People*, 'about Soho and London's low life'.[71] This was as much a Soho of invention as Runyon's Broadway '[p]eopled with small time crooks and prostitutes', a 'romanticised Soho. We all know that most of those who work in this district go home every night to Putney or Ilford. Mr Wildeblood would have us believe that the streets of Soho are full of gangsters and street women with marshmallow centres'.[72] The same reviewer cited *Guys and Dolls* as 'probably the nearest equivalent, for Jug Ears Jones and his henchmen are close relatives of the Nathan Detroit gang, the main difference being that the Soho types are more addicted to petty larceny than illegal gambling'.[73] A version of Miss Adelaide seeking her domestic settled life, but within the trope of the 'glorification of the common tart' in these later 1950s shows, is Cora.[74] She is one of the street women but longs to be a suburban gardener. In her sung aspirational musing about her ideal, respectable existence away from her Soho activities, the extreme sustaining of the first syllable of the word 'horticultural' provides the punch line.

A 'shpieler [illegal gambling club] in a back street in Soho' is the London location for a major London musical theatre hit that ran from 1959 to 1962: Lionel Bart's *Fings Ain't Wot They Used t'Be*. Each of those characteristics that Garebian views as distinctive to *Guys and Dolls* are equally applicable to *Fings*. The 'breezy manner [and] high, raucous energy' Garebian describes can be found in Bart's defining title song, which became a catchy popular hit, and runs through the whole show. 'Racy argot' is at the core of the verbal style in lyrics and dialogue, reinforcing the London location not least with Cockney rhyming slang.[75] Illegal activity is inevitable, given that the central character, Fred, has only just been released from prison, and the shpieler is a meeting-ground for various con artists, gang leaders, and prostitutes under the watchful eye of a policeman open to bribery. Chiming with Runyon's verbal presentation of Broadway, 'peculiarity of speech was the badge of the "cockney"' characters.[76] In a further parallel with *Guys and Dolls*, Lily has been hoping to marry Fred for twenty years and has carried a marriage licence around in readiness for ten years, and like Adelaide with Nathan, in the finale she does indeed get the vital wedding ring.[77] The origins of the work in the semi-improvisatory nature of director Joan Littlewood's Theatre Workshop Company, based at the Theatre Royal in the London district of Stratford East, ensured that character featured more than tightness of plot. This made it a British reflection of Runyon's focus on atmosphere and personality, not the slick, narrative structure of the musical realisation created for Broadway.

The geographical nature of these character types, with their associated areas of commercial activity of variable legality and their demotic speech patterns and vocabulary, contribute to the term frequently given to this series of musicals of the 1950s and early 1960s that reflect on British metropolitan life: the 'Soho' musicals.[78] They portray the Cockney-generated 'fantasy of a metropolitan community grounded in the good-humoured, if sometimes ironic, acceptance of social difference and subordination', and thus show how the community resonance of *Guys and Dolls* for a London audience need not be restricted to the specific evocation of New York.[79] Rather, the acknowledgement of generic metropolitan types and tropes common to both London and New York brings the concept of the city itself to the fore. Thus, through the reflexivity between stage and street, *Fings Ain't Wot They Used t'Be* could be described at the time of its revision and transfer to the West End in 1960—and by the same reviewer who noted the romanticism of the view of Soho in *The Crooked Mile*—as 'undoubtedly the most authentic slice of London life that has been produced in the theatre'.[80]

The evolution of a huge metropolis, embracing areas modified by immigrant cultures—Italian and Jewish in particular—alongside the desire of those drawn to city life to stand out from the packed throngs and succeed financially, not least with the resulting pull between morally or immorally gained fortunes, is as readily found in portrayals of London as it is in those of New York. But the gaze of one world capital directed towards another has tended to follow the timeline, looking from the nineteenth-century metropolis to one portrayed uniquely as embodying the contemporaneity of the twentieth. During the first half of the twentieth century, New York could become a vision of London updated, revitalised, and idealised by the romantic glow of transatlantic distance, reinforced through the importation of urban-centric American popular culture into the UK, especially on-screen and in music. In the atmosphere of postwar reassurance, *Guys and Dolls* sanitised its already partially defused source material in presenting violent gangsters of the Prohibition era as disarming, lovable comic types. British musicals tackling similar gangland-inspired material did so set in an identifiable 'now', with a matching sense of social awareness and hard-edged reality, albeit also tempered with humour. Runyon's gamblers and gangsters were to be observed vicariously through actors on a London stage, but the petty criminals and the prostitutes of Soho were on the streets right outside the theatre.

Whereas *Guys and Dolls* sidestepped any claim to historical authenticity, the Soho musicals embraced it. For example, the social commentary in *Fing's Ain't Wot They Used t'Be* arose in part in the repressive and judgemental atmosphere around the Sexual Offences Act (1956), and more particularly the introduction of the Street Offences Act (1959) that tried through law to tackle a rise in prostitution. And the meteoric rise of a popular skiffle singer named Bongo Herbert in *Expresso Bongo* was inspired by a similar story of the discovery of the real chart-topping pop singer, Tommy Steele. A broader backdrop was provided by the London theatre landscape, whose homegrown playwrights increasingly produced works of overt social criticism and debate that challenged mainstream, conservative postwar values.[81] The social context that made the Soho musicals vibrantly contemporary when new and their alignment with the tone of British theatre works of the time have inevitably faded in resonance, making them dated and distant. In contrast, the chronologically blurred nostalgia of *Guys and Dolls* within the regularly reinforced stereotypes of comedy gamblers and gangsters—a pair of whom brushed up their Shakespeare on Broadway and then in London two years before Big Jule moved in on both territories—has contributed to its popularity and longevity as a safe, fun alternative.

# *Guys and Dolls* as the Performance of Show Business

The London presentations of *Guys and Dolls* from 1953 to 2018 suggest that a widespread understanding of the show as an acted-out version of Runyon's literature in 1953 had been supplanted by 2018 with a view of it as a self-contained, sui generis musical theatre world. A *Guys and Dolls* 'authenticity' was established through the dominating performance presence of the National Theatre's landmark production from 1982 to 1997.[82] It was an extraordinary success, recalled as 'one of those shows that pleased everyone: critics, audiences and accountants',[83] and several revivals consolidated a reputation that has persisted for two decades. It is hard to overstate the impact of this production on the West End, the profile of director Richard Eyre, the acceptance and repertory choices of the National Theatre's subsequent staging of American musicals, and indeed the status

FIG. 14.2 A scene from the landmark 1982 National Theatre staging of *Guys and Dolls*, directed by Richard Eyre; *in the centre*: Jim Carter as Big Jule and Bob Hoskins as Nathan Detroit. Photo: John Haynes © Bridgeman Images.

of *Guys and Dolls* as even more of a London regular than a New York one.[84] It was a top-class show, imaginatively cast to the hilt, technically impressive, and a first in the National Theatre's repertory,[85] and the thrust stage and state-of-the art sound in a theatre with half the seating capacity of the Coliseum obviated the communication issues between stage and audience in evidence at the West End première three decades earlier.

The use of lighting was integral to John Gunter's stage design, in which large neon signs provided a backdrop that could fill the great height of the Olivier stage and animate the space. Twenty years after Julia McKenzie played Miss Adelaide in the first National Theatre cast, she recalled, 'Of all the images that stay in your head it is of those neon signs'.[86] The visual cue came from an archetypal image of Broadway, as exemplified by the establishing shot behind the title sequence of the film *The Big Street* (1942), produced by Runyon and based on his story *Little Pinks*. Cars drive up and down a long, straight street, illuminated by the lights of theatre marquees, club signs, and shops, brilliant through their contrast against the night-time dark. A following close-up on a signpost fixes the location at the intersection of Broadway and West Fiftieth Street, reinforced by an introductory text over the image: 'Loser's Lane—the sidewalk in front of Mindy's Restaurant on Broadway'. For Eyre's stage production, set in 1948, Gunter wanted 'that flavour of the post-War period'.[87] (The inherent anachronisms the work generates are discussed below.) Gunter referred to Andreas Feininger's photographs of New York in the 1940s for space and the daytime environment.[88] For night, his inspiration came from a related American image, of 'Las Vegas and its two personalities: the daytime Las Vegas and the night time Las Vegas', capturing the contrast 'when neon grew above it and transformed it into another society'.[89]

A stage image of brightly lit commercial promotion against a night-time background has become a convention in London productions of *Guys and Dolls* since.[90] From the National Theatre's production and revivals in the Olivier auditorium and transfer to the Prince of Wales Theatre, the production presented by the Donmar Theatre in the West End at the Piccadilly Theatre (2005–2007), and the transfer from the Chichester Festival Theatre to the Savoy then Phoenix theatres (2015–2016), the stage setting has remained recognisably consistent. Through it, the sense of the 'Big Street' dominates the visual aspect of the production and silently reinforces the essential city setting, with a London parallel in the 'little territory of the theatre world', as London novelist John Sommerfield described it in 1936, where '[t]he night quivered with multi-coloured explosions of advertising signs [ ... ] . The red-hot worms of neon bulbs squirmed and wriggled, forming themselves into luminous exhortations to drink beer, take bile beans, travel by air and go on pleasure cruises.'[91]

Visual conformity has also extended to costume: the sharply cut pinstripe suits of the male ensemble, Sister Sarah's formally drab Salvation Army uniform, and the more scanty and colourful costumes of Adelaide and her Hot Box ensemble. Julia McKenzie's

FIG. 14.3 The set of the 2015 London revival of *Guys and Dolls*, once again using commercial promotion—in this case, iconic billboards—as markers of the 'Big Street'. Photo © Donald Cooper/Photostage.

opinion that 'I don't think you can be revolutionary with this piece' has been widely shared.[92] The approaches of the subsequent Donmar and Chichester productions have encouraged this through their visual variations around the same themes. Each return of the show to the West End has thus strengthened an 'authentic' *Guys and Dolls* identity drawn not so much from Runyon per se or from historical precision as from reinforcement by performance practice.

However, there are elements of London productions that have shown interpretative flexibility, beginning twenty-five years after the London première, when the tiny Half Moon Theatre in Alie Street in London's East End staged a short revival (1–27 January 1979). The production pared the show down to just seven actors, with musical accompaniment from piano, bass, and drums and the audience packed around tables: this inverted the original conception of the musical such that the 'Big Street' externality of the show was transformed into a 'nightclub' internality. The city was characterised through the physical proximity of performers and audience, literally crowded in, rather than through a cityscape backdrop.[93] Maggie Steed (Miss Adelaide) recalls that the director, Rob Walker, 'had us all sitting as people in this bar, with macs on and with our heads in our hands like down-and-outs. [ ... ] The pianist, who was also sitting like a down-and-out, starts playing "I got the horse right here." And one body comes up and starts singing it, and then another person comes up [ ... ] and then everybody—only seven people. [ ... ] Everybody just threw off their macs, and did *Guys and Dolls*'.[94] It was a great success for such a small theatre, and in London in particular the profile of *Guys and Dolls* was raised among theatre people as a show that still had the drawing power of the popular.[95]

As the show can be reframed spatially, so it can be adapted musically. The arrangement alterations made for the National Theatre production reflect a changing relationship to the nature of the show, shifting from company novelty to repertory classic. Eyre's production put *Guys and Dolls* back at the top of the London musicals, with other large-scale presentations returning with a regularity that has probably only been exceeded by that of the seemingly ubiquitous *Sweeney Todd* (which shares the metropolitan topos). In 1982 the show did not have a pre-eminent position in the West End audience's mind, and the production was thus working more from 'first principles' than responding to a London audience's staging expectations, as have later revivals. As a result, the production blurred chronological boundaries, particularly in the approach to the music, as the show had in 1950 when new.

Runyon's stories and characters reflect the latter part of the Prohibition Era (1920–1933), notably shown through the bootleg suppliers of alcohol and their clients who regularly feature, with a direct social impact, as Runyon (and Winchell's) writing 'taught millions of formerly law-abiding citizens to break the law, and so broadened the base of organised crime in national life that Americans were still paying off the bar bill for the noble experiment half a century later'.[96] The characters and situations presented in *Guys and Dolls* function within the values of that age, not those of 1950.[97] Yet the show itself implied a generalised 'now' at the time of its 1950 opening, with the verse of the song 'Take Back Your Mink' referring to 'late forty eight'.[98] There is a negotiation in play between the era of the stories and the necessary contemporaneity of the musical for its audience at its première, which is the result of the inherent nostalgia of the show and its approach to Runyon and his characters. The precise time is elusive, and the action lacks such essential reality as violence appropriate to its Prohibition-gangster origins.[99] Responding to this, the musical style is also hard to pin down to a specific era, containing as it does a mixture of lively postwar swing showtune title song, popular romantic ballad ('I've Never Been in Love Before'), revivalist inflected chorus ('Sit Down You're Rockin' the Boat'), and ragtime-syncopated/barbershop-inflected character number ('Good Old Reliable'). The film score by Franz Waxman to the American release of *Night and the City* provides stylistic comparison to the early 1950s: the uneasy urban-noir sound-world contrasts with the tuneful immediacy of Loesser's popular-song world.[100] The characters, scenarios, and images of the film *The Sweet Smell of Success* (1957) provide a direct comparison in that the setting is the New York of Damon Runyon and Walter Winchell—the character of the newspaper columnist J. J. Hunsecker, played by Burt Lancaster, is based on Winchell—but clearly contemporary with the film's release. The film includes a rising jazz guitarist as a central character and shows him playing in a nightclub, and his is not the sound of the Hot Box band. From the later 1950s into the 1960s, the music of *Guys and Dolls* and its orchestral resources—five reed, five brass, strings, piano, and percussion—and style (orchestrated by George Bassman and Ted Royal)—reinforced a sense of the show's soundscape being 'older', but at that time not yet sufficiently distanced to be perceived as classic.[101]

The 1982 London production reduced the band size (for budgetary reasons) and shifted towards what the co-orchestrator, Tony Britten, described as 'a hard-swinging Big Band sound' with a distinctly jazz feel, as 'the Broadway version is quite tame; it's quite foursquare really. We were reinventing it in a style very much *New York, New York* [1977].[102] The reorchestration further blurred the chronological placing through the re-placement of acoustic piano by electric keyboards and the addition of bass guitar and guitar/banjo. It also pushed the sense of a cartoon world in heightening the orchestral colour palette with prominent percussion effects, points of animation with short instrumental fills and stabs, and tonal extremes, especially through high melodic doubling. For example, the opening (truncated) 'Runyonland' edges away from 1930s–1940s American city qualities (exemplified by Gershwin) towards Looney Tunes musical exaggeration.[103] The post-1950 jazz sense is furthered through such alterations as the sound and harmonisation of the introductory electric piano's accompanying chords for 'My Time of Day' and the interpolated obbligato on muted trumpet. 'If I Were a Bell' significantly shifts the musical era with a jazz electric walking bass and Julie Covington's pop/rock-inflected vocal delivery.[104]

For the 1996 revival, revised orchestrations toned down what seemed by then stylistically anachronistic: chronological distance had reversed the desire to reinterpret the sound of an old show into the preference for the nostalgic sound of a classic. By the time of the three semi-staged concert performances with celebrity cast in the vast Royal Albert Hall (2018), the sound was an enriched period magnificence, with the orchestra, which included a generous bank of strings and a grand piano, placed centre stage. The trajectory in London of arrangement and orchestration—from original to updated and back towards the original style—marks a shift in perception of the show from contemporary, to established older work, to self-contained period masterpiece reinforced by a 'classic' Broadway sound. The musical presentation's development, moving towards an accommodation with the contemporary and then retreating from it, is indicative of a more general shift of status for the show as it asserted itself anew in London.

Contemporary aspects of performance—notably the casting and stage-craft—suggest that a 1980s element of reinvention or even rediscovery was no longer required once the show's regained prominence in the active repertory had been consolidated. Later presentations have responded to this trajectory and reinforced it: as the status in London of *Guys and Dolls* has evolved from that of a new Broadway import in 1953 to one more than sixty years on of canonic veneration, audience expectations of what the show will look and sound like have narrowed. The most recent performances at the time of writing were the semi-staged concert performances at the Royal Albert Hall in London in 2018. This staging dispensed with any formal backdrop of New York. The space was that of the concert hall, the orchestra topped by the organ pipes in place of skyscrapers—a famous performance venue rather than the evocation of a city. Yet the staging did retain costumes: pinstriped suits with wide lapels paired with fedoras, the Salvation Army uniforms, and Miss Adelaide inevitably at some point in short skirt and stockings. But the advance attention these performances drew came from the casting. The matching of the score's ever-appealing variety to the text's speed and wit, alongside such dynamically drawn characters who can still convey much through stereotypic presentation, make the leading roles gifts for actors with more or—as the role of Nathan Detroit was conceived—less singing voice and a way of bridging a range of entertainment spheres. More often than not, celebrity status garnered beyond live theatre has been reflected in some part of the casting, which has shifted the promotional focus from 'see *Guys and Dolls*, with [ ... ]' to 'See [name of film and/or television star] in *Guys and Dolls*'. This continues in principle (if not necessarily in effect) the approach of the 1955 Paramount film version, for which the consequences of the star miscasting of Frank Sinatra as Nathan Detroit enraged Loesser.[105] The 1982 National Theatre cast Ian Charleson (Sky Masterson), fresh from his international fame playing Eric Liddell in the Academy Award–winning *Chariots of Fire* (1981). Bob Hoskins (Nathan Detroit) also brought a UK reputation beyond live theatre through his leading role in the acclaimed television series *Pennies from Heaven* (1979).[106] Neither was known for musical theatre roles. The established Hollywood film star Ewan McGregor played Sky Masterson in 2005, and the Australian film actor Rebel Wilson (*Bridesmaids*, *Pitch Perfect*) played Miss Adelaide in 2016. The director of that production did offer an interesting perspective on the casting of the boisterous and large comedian as a corrective to the show now seeming 'quaint. [ ... ] But I wanted to recapture the danger and the racy tone that it had in 1950, when the language and the sheer exposure of flesh made it pretty bold.'[107] The production had originated at the Chichester Festival and officially opened in the West End in January 2016. Rebel Wilson took the role for a limited time in July–August, to much praise. Although this approach to Miss Adelaide offered a refreshing perspective, it was tailored specifically

THE MOST BELOVED AMERICAN MUSICAL 419

to suit Rebel Wilson in a guest appearance and was not part of the characterisation for the production's original Miss Adelaide, Sophie Thompson.

The burlesque quality of Wilson's Miss Adelaide was echoed in the performance of Meow-Meow at the Royal Albert Hall performances two years later. Overall, the 2018 casting played to a broad audience demographic in taste and age by encompassing TV presentation, stand-up comedy, yesteryear pop star, and alternative cabaret celebrity alongside established names from West End musicals.[108] The venue, scale, and presentational style alongside such casting inevitably foregrounded *Guys and Dolls* not as a musical about a city, but as a performance event that revels in show business in its own right, Runyon's performance of the street having evolved into the self-reflexive performance of entertainment.[109]

*Guys and Dolls* is a summary of New York archetypes drawn from the 1920s and 1930s, the success of which has persisted and grown through the twentieth century into the twenty-first. The productions in London of 2005 and 2016 and the semi-staged concert performances of 2018 resonate with similarities: a *Guys and Dolls* style all its own sits alongside the familiar songs and lyrics as a summary package of all things Runyon, New York, Broadway, and musical theatre. The showbiz surface of a performance tradition, delightfully engaging and idiosyncratic, has grown to dominate in recent decades—a nostalgia for the musical and a golden age of musicals, as many portray it, more than for any reality of Prohibition New York. Nonetheless, the characters and their storylines arise from the deeper themes within the patterns and neuroses of aspects of city life that have proved especially recognisable and durable in London. This metropolitan condition—language, localised vocabulary, character types, activities, and values—can still resonate through the recognition that *Guys and Dolls* performs not only New York, but London, and even the idea of the city itself.

## NOTES

1. Steven Suskin, *Opening Night on Broadway: A Critical Quotebook of the Golden Era of the Musical Theatre, 'Oklahoma!' (1943) to 'Fiddler on the Roof' (1964)* (New York: Schirmer Books, 1990), 275.
2. For discussion of *Guys and Dolls* within the context of the Broadway canon see, for example, Keith Garebian, *The Making of Guys and Dolls* (Ontario: Mosaic Press, 2002); Thomas L. Riis, *Frank Loesser* (New Haven, CT: Yale University Press, 2008), 74–116; and Geoffrey Block, *Enchanted Evenings: The Broadway Musical from 'Show Boat' to Sondheim and Lloyd Webber* (Oxford and New York: Oxford University Press, 2009), 233–247.
3. For a detailed investigation of this area see John M. Snelson, 'The West End Musical 1947–54: British Identity and the "American Invasion"' (PhD thesis, University of Birmingham, 2003); and John M. Snelson, '"We Said We Wouldn't Look Back": British Musical Theatre, 1935–1969', in *The Cambridge Companion to the Musical*, 3rd ed., ed. William A. Everett and Paul R. Laird (Cambridge: Cambridge University Press, 2017), 159–184.
4. Subsequent Broadway imports, not all equally successful, were *Annie Get your Gun* and *Finian's Rainbow* (1947); *Lute Song* and *High Button Shoes* (1948); *Brigadoon* (1949); *Carousel* (1950); *Kiss Me, Kate* and *South Pacific* (1951); *Call Me Madam* and *Porgy and Bess* (1952).

5. *Call Me Madam* had finished its run two weeks previously; Rodgers and Hammerstein's *South Pacific*, just a few minutes' walk away at the Theatre Royal, Drury Lane, had five more months to go. Other London openings of Broadway shows in 1953 were *Paint Your Wagon* (11 February), *Wish You Were Here* (10 October), and *The King and I* (8 November).
6. [Ivor Brown], Review of *Guys and Dolls*, *Observer*, 31 May 1953, 14.
7. Garebian, *The Making of Guys and Dolls*, 125.
8. Kenneth Tynan, Review: *Guys and Dolls*, *Evening Standard*, 29 May 1953, 10; reprinted in Kenneth Tynan, *Theatre Writings*, selected and ed. Dominic Shellard, preface by Matthew Tynan, foreword by Tom Stoppard (London: Nick Hern Books, 2007), 29–31.
9. 'London Theatres: *Guys and Dolls*', *Stage*, 17 June 1953, 7. An interesting point of past–present comparison of values comes in the review's opening remarks, suggesting that '[s]hades from *The Belle of New York* seem to mingle with the gambling guys and dancing dolls of Damon Runyon's creation. As in the old musical play the activities of the Salvation Army in New York are an integral part of the story. But there the comparison ends'.
10. Harold Hobson, Review of *Guys and Dolls*, *Sunday Times*, 31 May 1953, 9.
11. Eric Keown, Review of *Guys and Dolls*, *Punch*, 10 June 1953, 698.
12. Beverley Baxter, 'Now There's the Doll for Me', *Sunday Express*, 31 May 1953, V&A Theatre Collection cuttings file.
13. [Walter Haynes], Review of *Guys and Dolls*, *Sketch*, 17 June 1953, 5.
14. Kenneth Tynan, Review of *Guys and Dolls*, *Evening Standard*, 29 May 1953, 10.
15. Anthony Cookman, 'At the Theatre: *Guys and Dolls*', *Tatler and Bystander*, 17 June 1953, 630. The Crazy Gang were a British comedy team (formed from three male double acts). They were popular on radio and film, and presented stage shows 1935–60. In 1953 Kenneth Tynan summarised their style: 'A stubboner quintet of rude uncles can never have existed than the Crazy Gang: they refuse to acknowledge that humour has developed in any way since Mr. Punch first murdered his wife with a mallet. [ ... ] Clapping and shoving each other, swapping puns and laying traps, they belong to the archaeology of farce.' Kenneth Tynan, *Profiles*, selected and ed. Kathleen Tynan and Ernie Eban, preface by Simon Callow (London: Nick Hern Books, 1989), 58.
16. J. C. Trewin, '*Guys and Dolls* at Theatre Royal', *Birmingham Daily Post*, 11 October 1955, 16.
17. Daniel R. Schwarz, *Broadway Boogie Woogie: Damon Runyon and the Making of New York Culture* (New York and Basingstoke: Palgrave Macmillan, 2003), 37.
18. Ibid., 64.
19. Through the American-British transfer postwar, the book and lyrics provide good examples of the oft-quoted notion of two countries divided by a common language. This general problem was widely recognised in both directions, enough that a later West End musical discussed below, *The Crooked Mile* (1959), could make reference in song lyrics through an observation from an American to a Londoner: 'I've seen lots of British movies/ And the only thing they prove is/If they had a few subtitles we might know what's going on.' 'Cousin Country', from *The Crooked Mile* (1959), lyrics by Peter Wildeblood, music by Peter Greenwell.
20. Damon Runyon, Jr., *Father's Footsteps: The Story of Damon Runyon by His Son* (London: Constable, 1955), 101.
21. Ibid., 100–101.
22.. William R. Taylor, 'Introduction', in *Inventing Times Square: Commerce and Culture at the Crossroads of the World*, ed. William R. Taylor (Baltimore, MD: John Hopkins University Press, 1991), xvii.

THE MOST BELOVED AMERICAN MUSICAL    421

23. William R. Taylor, 'Broadway: The Place That Words Built', in *Inventing Times Square: Commerce and Culture at the Crossroads of the World*, ed. William R. Taylor (Baltimore, MD: John Hopkins University Press, 1991), 222.

24. John Mosedale, *The Men Who Invented Broadway: Damon Runyon, Walter Winchell, and Their World* (New York: Richard Marek, 1981), 206.

25. Runyon, Jr., *Father's Footsteps*, 97–100.

26. Mosedale, *The Men Who Invented Broadway*, 206–207.

27. Damon Runyon, *More than Somewhat* (London: Constable, 1937) [selection and introduction by E. C. Bentley, pictures by Nicolas Bentley]; Damon Runyon, *Furthermore* (London: Constable, 1937); and Damon Runyon, *Take It Easy* (London: Constable, 1938).

28. 'Entertainments: Theatre Royal, Coatbridge', *Aidrie & Coalbridge Advertiser*, 28 December 1935, 3.

29. The Judge, 'The Week's Film Fare', *Surrey Advertiser*, 10 June 1939, 4.

30. Molly Hobman, 'This Film Angered General Franco', *Nottingham Journal*, 4 June 1938, 9.

31. M. R., 'Ghosts and Gangsters: Max Catto's *The Bowery Touch*', *The Era*, 25 November 1937, 15.

32. Damon Runyon, *On Broadway: Containing All the Stories from 'More than Somewhat', 'Furthermore', 'Take It Easy'* (London: Constable, 1950).

33. W. A. Darlington, Review of *Guys and Dolls*, *Daily Telegraph*, 29 May 1953, 10.

34. Review of *Guys and Dolls*, *Times*, 31May 1953, 6.

35. Cecil Wilson, Review of *Guys and Dolls*, *Daily Mail*, 29 May 1953, 8.

36. Tynan, review of *Guys and Dolls*.

37. Ethan Mordden, *Coming Up Roses: The Broadway Musical in the 1950s* (New York and Oxford: Oxford University Press, 1998), 31.

38. James Curtis, *The Gilt Kid*, introd. Paul Willetts (London: London Books, 2007), 122. First published in 1936 by Jonathan Cape.

39. Runyon's story 'The Lemon Drop Kid' was first published in *Collier's*, 3 February 1934; reprinted in Runyon, *On Broadway*, 289–301. First published 1950 by Pan Books.

40. Curtis, *The Gilt Kid*, 17. His name of William Kennedy is revealed a considerable way into the novel, and only clearly stated in the final chapter within the formality of a court appearance.

41. Ibid., 190.

42. 'They all sat round a table in the sitting room, trying to figure out what to do. They were all worried—except Benny. They were all Wide Boys, and only Mugs worked and saved money. All the Wide Boys were broke. Bill was inside for a spell, and they looked like being broke until he came out. Life could be a proper bastard sometimes.' Robert Westerby, *Wide Boys Never Work*, introd. Iain Sinclair (London: London Books, 2008), 113. First published 1937 by Arthur Baker.

43. Ibid., 83.

44. Ibid., 128.

45. Ibid., 122.

46. Ibid., dust jacket.

47. Kersh and Runyon were of similar generations, inhabited the same journalistic milieu in their respective capital cities, and became widely syndicated, and thus their writing was widely known. Kersh moved to the United States in 1954, where he was already established as a writer. Like Runyon, Kersh was a heavy smoker—as suited the journalistic haunts of London's Fleet Street where he made his name—and like Runyon, he died in New York of

## 422    JOHN SNELSON

throat cancer. As authors, they shared a love of detailed observation, which fed the creation of distinctive and exaggerated characters, and their prolific outputs generated for each recurring characters and character types. While Kersh's *Night and the City* is the tonal antithesis of Runyon's depiction of lovable roguery, Kersh's later novels, particularly his comic masterpiece *Fowlers End* (1957) and the Soho-centred *The Angel and the Cuckoo* (1967), make him Runyon's twin in wit, locale and storyline.

48. Gerald Kersh, *The Angel and the Cuckoo*, introd. Paul Duncan (London: London Books, 2011), 6. First published in 1967 by Heinemann.

49. 'Hell! *We* could of showed you some shooting back in 1927 in Chicago. Did you ever hear about Bugs Moran? ... Chicago? Sure I lived there most of my life. ... No I quit the racket while I had my health and strength [ ... ] I left the booze racket for the movie business. Acting? Hell no producing. I don't take the mug's end of any racket.' Gerald Kersh, *Night and the City*, introd. John King (London: London Books, 2007), 17. First published in 1938 by Jonathan Cape.

50. Ibid., 20.

51. Ibid.

52. Ibid., 48.

53. I am grateful to Gregory Dart of University College London for his suggestion of this film and Kersh early in my research for this chapter.

54. Garson Kanin was to direct a cast that includes Geraldine McEwan (Miss Adelaide), Laurence Olivier (Nathan Detroit), Louise Purnell (Miss Sarah), and Edward Woodward (Sky Masterson). Choreography was to be by Wally Strauss, with designs by Michael Annals. *Guys and Dolls* was programmed alongside the plays *A Woman Killed with Kindness*, *Cato Street*, and *Cyrano de Bergerac*. National Theatre, press release, 9 June 1970, National Theatre Archive RNT/PR/2/1/76.

55. Kathleen Tynan, *The Life of Kenneth Tynan* (London: Weidenfeld & Nicolson, 1987), 220, 302; and Richard Eyre, 'Directing the National Theatre *Guys and Dolls*', in *The Guys and Dolls Book* (London: Methuen, in association with the National Theatre, 1982), 34, reprinted in Richard Eyre, *Utopia and Other Places* (London: Bloomsbury, 1993), 151–156.

56. Tynan, *Theatre Writings*, xxiii, 29, 190, and 183.

57. Three years later Tynan invited the comparison again in considering George Bernard Shaw's observations on the lasting appeal of great art: 'After twenty hearings of *The Beggar's Opera* we weary and yearn for *Guys and Dolls*.' Kenneth Tynan, 'A Critic's Critic', *Observer*, 24 June 1956, reprinted in Tynan, *Theatre Writings*, 118. In 1982, the same year in which the National Theatre did eventually stage *Guys and Dolls*, the company also staged *The Beggar's Opera*. Both were directed by Richard Eyre.

58. In fact, *Guys and Dolls* was not staged in a large-scale production in London between 1955 and 1982.

59. 'The Inside Page: A Guy in the Peerage', *Daily Mirror*, 15 June 1970, 15.

60. Kathleen Tynan, *The Life of Kenneth Tynan*, 302.

61. Judith Cook [compiler], *The National Theatre* (London: Harrap, 1976), 33–34.

62. From lyrics by Arthur Freed for the song *The Broadway Melody* (1929), with music by Nacio Herb Brown.

63. Gareth Stedman Jones, 'The "Cockney" and the Nation, 1780–1988', in *Metropolis: London; Histories and Representations since 1800*, ed. David Feldman and Gareth Stedman Jones (London: Routledge, 1989), 315.

64. Garebian, *The Making of Guys and Dolls*, 1.

THE MOST BELOVED AMERICAN MUSICAL    423

65. The two musicals have often run in parallel in comment and production. Harold Hobson begins his review of the London opening of *Pal Joey* (1954) with such a comparison: '[T]here is nothing in *Pal Joey* to disquiet anyone robust enough to enjoy *Guys and Dolls*'; Harold Hobson, 'Black Musical', *Sunday Times*, 4 April 1954, 11. Frank Sinatra reinforced the association through his performances in both films as Nathan Detroit (1955) and Joey Evans (1957). The Half Moon Theatre in London followed its staging of *Guys and Dolls* (1979; discussed below) with a production of *Pal Joey* (1980), which transferred to the West End's Albery Theatre (now the Coward Theatre) for 327 performances (1980–1981). Richard Eyre considered creating a new production of *Pal Joey* for his final show as director of the Royal National Theatre in 1996 before deciding instead on a revival of his by-then classic staging *Guys and Dolls* (discussed below). Matt Wolf, *The Guys and Dolls Book* (London: Nick Hern Books, 1997), 91–92. Coward's scene-setting description of the Ace of Clubs' front man, Felix Felton, is more than a little reminiscent of Joey: '[T]he leading man, dance arranger and compère of the floor show, sings and dances adequately, has overwhelming vitality and an unqualified belief in his own charm and ability. He is quite amiable but inclined to be temperamental.' Noël Coward, *The Collected Plays of Noël Coward: Play Parade*, vol. 6 (London: Heinemann, 1962), 235.
66. Graham Payn and Sheridan Morley, eds., *The Noël Coward Diaries* (London: George Weidenfeld & Nicholson, 1982), 138.
67. Ibid., 161, 189. Coward saw both shows for the first time in New York: *Guys and Dolls* on 15 December 1950 ('Absolutely wonderful and brilliantly staged') and *Pal Joey* on 6 February 1952 ('thought it very common'). Ibid., 161, 189.
68. Coward claimed that *Ace of Clubs* 'anticipated the [late 1950s] rash of Soho-Gangster British musicals by some years, so I can always comfort myself with the reflection that it was "Before Its Time"'. Coward, Collected Plays, xiii. Graham Payn (Coward's life partner from the 1940s on, who performed the leading male role in *Ace of Clubs*) observed that in comparison to *Guys and Dolls*, 'It must have galled [Coward] to design and launch his own little ship, only to watch helplessly as this sleek ocean liner went steaming past.' Graham Payn and Barry Day, *My Life with Noël Coward* (New York and London: Applause, 1994), 61. Coward may also have noted that the self-explanatory subject of his satiric number on a contemporary sociological theme in *Ace of Clubs*, 'Three Juvenile Delinquents', significantly predated 'Gee, Officer Krupke' in *West Side Story*.
69. A significant difference in tone towards a tougher, up-front contemporary presentation of gangland confrontation is seen here, and which will run through the later British musicals on underworld-Soho themes discussed below. For example, the American show presents a comic brawl in a Cuban nightclub when the drunken mission doll turns 'slugger' after being provoked to alcohol-fuelled jealousy when a Cuban dancer moves in on Sky. At the end, Sky with amusement tells Sister Sarah, '[I]t's over and you're still the champ', and she then kisses him. Frank Loesser, Jo Swerling, and Abe Burrows, *Guys and Dolls: A Musical Fable of Broadway* (London: Frank Music, 1951), 38. The equivalent scene in Coward has the attempted physical domination of the nightclub singer Pinkie sparking a sailor in the audience (Harry) to come to her defence, in the process deflecting a gunshot fired by the aggressive gangster. After escaping the uproar in the nightclub, Pinkie tells Harry, '[Y]ou may be lucky and trained to fight the elements, but you're not trained to fight gangsters in night-clubs. They're liable to be a bit too quick for you. Snyder's a dangerous man, and unless you've killed him—which I doubt—you'll find yourself in a dark alley with your head bashed in.' Pinkie still kisses Harry, but only after two further pages of a dialogue and a

424    JOHN SNELSON

song. Noël Coward, "Ace of Clubs," in *The Collected Plays of Noël Coward: Play Parade*, vol. 6 (London: Heinemann, 1962), 246–252.

70. Quoted in Raymond Mander and Joe Mitchenson, *Theatrical Companion to Coward*, updated by Barry Day and Sheridan Morley (London: Oberon Books, 2000), 426. First published in 1957 by Rockcliff. For plot, numbers, performance, and reception of *Ace of Clubs*, see ibid., 419–430; and Kurt Gänzl, *The British Musical Theatre*, vol. 2, *1915–1984* (Basingstoke: Macmillan, 1986), 612–615.

71. Peter Greenwell, *The Crooked Mile*, CD, liner notes, 2002, MCSR [Must Close Saturday Records] 3002. The source for the musical was Peter Wildeblood, *West End People: A Novel* (London: Weidenfeld, 1958).

72. P. H., 'London Theatres: Great Stride Forward for British Musicals in *The Crooked Mile*', *Stage*, 17 September 1959, 17.

73. Ibid.

74. Ibid.

75. For example: FRED 'Gawd 'elp us, where did you get that peckham?' TOSHER (*fingering his tie*) 'Wot, the old peckham rye? I fort it was very tasteful.' ROSEY ''E nicked it orf a barrer, I saw 'im.' The name of the South London area of Peckham Rye is adopted in cockney rhyming slang for the word 'tie'. Frank Norman and Lionel Bart, *Fings Ain't Wot They Used t'Be* (London: Samuel French, 1960), 5. Norman wrote the book and Bart, the lyrics.

76. Stedman Jones, 'The "Cockney" and the Nation', 279.

77. Norman and Bart, *Fings Ain't Wot They Used t'Be*, 60–61.

78. For summary of this group of musicals, see Elizabeth A. Wells, 'After *Anger*: The British Musical of the Late 1950s', in *The Oxford Handbook of the British Musical*, ed. Robert Gordon and Olaf Jubin (New York: Oxford University Press, 2016), 273–289. Adrian Wright borrows somewhat loosely from opera the term 'verismo' for these works: Adrian Wright, *A Tanner's Worth of Tunes: Rediscovering the Post-War British Musical* (Woodbridge: Boydell Press, 2010), 139–168.

79. Stedman Jones, 'The "Cockney" and the Nation', 314.

80. P. H., 'Week in the Theatre: Revised *Fings Ain't Wot They Used t'Be* Finely Staged', *Stage*, 21 January 1960, 17.

81. For a contextual summary of London theatre, see Dominic Shellard, *British Theatre since the War* (New Haven, CT: Yale University Press, 1999), 1–97; and Dan Rebellato, *1956 and All That: The Making of Modern British Drama* (London: Routledge, 1999).

82. The production was staged at the National Theatre three times: 9 March 1982–15 October 1983, 2 April–15 September 1984, and 17 December 1996–29 March 1997. It was presented at the Prince of Wales Theatre in the West End 19 June 1985–26 April 1986. The production also toured to Bristol for thirteen performances, 5–16 October 1982.

83. Introductory remarks by Al Senter, Royal National Theatre, '25: *Guys and Dolls*', *Platform*, 16 May 2001, recording of public panel discussion, NT Archives RNT/PL/3/683.

84. At the time of writing, the professional Broadway presence of the show has covered the initial run in 1950–1953, brief revivals by New York City Light Opera Company in 1955 (16 performances) and 1965 (15 performances), an all-black production in 1976–1977 (239 performances), and productions in 1992–1995 (1,443 performances) and 2009 (121 performances). One small but telling indication of the continuing impact of the National Theatre's production comes in Eyre's published diaries for 1987–1997: his nineteen mentions of *Guys and Dolls*—beginning already five years into the sequence of première

and revivals—are equalled in number by Ibsen's *John Gabriel Borkman* and exceeded only by David O'Hare's *Racing Demon* (23) and by Shakespeare's *Richard III* (25), *Hamlet*, and *King Lear* (both 36). Richard Eyre, *National Service: Diary of a Decade* (London: Bloomsbury, 2003).

85. The final revival, in 1996, was also Eyre's final production as director of the National Theatre, thus concluding as he had begun. Concerned that his choice would be interpreted as self-indulgent or lacking confidence, he wrote in 1995 that '[w]e'll have to (a) clearly present the reasons for doing it and (b) do it better than before. But why should I apologise? It's the best musical *ever*.' As rehearsals concluded, on 21 October 1996 he wrote: 'It's probably as ill-advised as returning to an old love affair. I'm not sure it's right to be doing it again, without the excitement and danger of directing it for the first time, but everyone is full of good-will and generosity, the cast are immensely talented, and the piece *is* wonderful.' Eyre, *National Service*, 303 and 367. One sign of the almost mythic reputation the staging acquired is shown in the idealised recall by those involved. In a public discussion in 2001, Julia McKenzie (Miss Adelaide) and Jim Carter (Big Jule), both in the original cast, recalled that the orchestra had 'hardly any deps [i.e. deputies] in because they all enjoyed playing the show'—'We always had the same orchestra' (Royal National Theatre, *Platform*). In this context, a comparison with the stage manager's report for the thirty-third performance, on 14 April 1982, is instructive: 'Absentees: Dep. Woodwinds 1, 3 & 4, Trumpet 1, guitar & percussion. I'm afraid that, to me, it sounded like [an unrehearsed orchestra] although all the Deps had played before' (RNT/Guys and Dolls/Stage Manager Reports).

86. Royal National Theatre, *Platform*.

87. Matt Wolf, 'London 1996', in *The Guys and Dolls Book*, 103.

88. Eyre, 'Directing the National Theatre *Guys and Dolls*', 36.

89. Royal National Theatre, *Platform*, and Wolf, 'London 1996', 103.

90. And not only in London, as with Tony Walton's designs for Broadway in 1992.

91. John Sommerfield, *May Day*, introd. John King (London: London Books, 2010), 189. First published in 1936 by Lawrence & Wishart.

92. Royal National Theatre, *Platform*.

93. Loesje Sanders (administrator, Half Moon Theatre): 'It was the first time anyone had done *Guys and Dolls* for a very long time and the audience sat around tables in the theatre. Every time we did a show the whole space changed. The scenery could be built in any configuration, the audience seats could be in any configuration, so we set it in a kind of bar. [ . . . ] We just squeezed as many people as we could into that space, probably totally illegally. But there was always a queue and we were always turning people away.' 'Stages of Half Moon: Guys and Dolls (1979)', https://www.stagesofhalfmoon.org.uk/productions/guys-and-dolls/, accessed 22 August 2019.

94. Maggie Steed, interviewed by Kavana Joyett, ibid.

95. Richard Eyre knew of the production but did not see it. Its director told him 'that *Guys and Dolls* was so good that not even a director could mess it up.' Eyre, 'Directing the National Theatre *Guys and Dolls*', 34.

96. Mosedale, *The Men Who Invented Broadway*, 21. For discussion of the ambivalent moral attitudes expressed by Runyon and Winchell to criminality, see ibid., 22–23; Taylor, 'Broadway: The Place That Words Built', 229–230; and Schwarz, *Broadway Boogie Woogie*, 53–54.

97. Indeed, a similar dramatisation of Runyon stories in the film *Bullets over Broadway* (1994) is set in 1928 and seems indistinguishable from an archetypal *Guys and Dolls* production.

98. This causes a minor temporal wobble in Gunter's specified 1948 setting quoted above—a reference to 1948 would only make sense from 1949 or later.

99. It is worth noting again the resonance with the equivalent of the London Cockney, who 'always belongs to yesterday [ ... ] at best ill at ease in the present, and doomed in the future. Conversely, their past has become rich and concrete'. Stedman Jones, 'The "Cockney" and the Nation', 276 and 277.

100. The film score to the British release was by Benjamin Frankel. The BFI Blu-ray *Night and the City* BFIB1217 (2015) allows comparison of the edits and scores through both UK and US film releases, with accompanying notes by Lee Server, Paul Duncan, and James Hahn.

101. For details of the original orchestration and revisions, see Steven Suskin, *The Sound of Broadway Music: A Book of Orchestrators and Orchestrations* (Oxford and New York: Oxford University Press, 2009), 411–412.

102. Wolf, 'London 1996', 104. In an echo of Tynan's comparisons with *The Beggar's Opera* (above), Russell Davies considered the removal of strings, in particular, to have brought the sound 'sometimes a bit too close to the Brechtian wind-band tradition'. Russell Davies, 'The N. T. Production Reviewed', *Stage*, reprinted in *The Guys and Dolls Book* (London: Methuen, in association with the National Theatre, 1982), 104.

103. This is heard, for example, in the xylophone doubling the melody in bars 26–28 against the prominent electronic piano sound, and the woodwind smears in the 'Pug' section, bars 53–60. The bluesy countermelody introduced in 'Fugue for Tinhorns' at bar 19 marks a musical reinterpretation of mood towards jazz in tempo and modality.

104. Covington previously had sung the title role on the concept album of the Lloyd Webber–Rice show *Evita*. The original National Theatre cast recording was released on EMI CDMFP5978, with music arrangements by Tony Britten and Terry Davies. The results of Loesser's famously exacting requirements for the precise interpretation of his works, demonstrated by his obsessive approach to rehearsal, can be heard on the original Broadway cast recording. It shows how fundamentally different are the vocal interpretations for the 1982 production.

105. Susan Loesser, *A Most Remarkable Fella: Frank Loesser and the Guys and Dolls in His Life; A Portrait by his Daughter* (New York: Donald I. Fine, 1993), 117–19.

106. Julia McKenzie (Miss Adelaide) brought stage musical credentials, including performances in *Company* (1971) and the revue *Side by Side by Sondheim* (1976), which on its transfer to New York led to her Broadway debut (1977).

107. Ryan Gilbey, 'Rebel Wilson: From Pitch Perfect to a Pitch-Perfect West End Debut'. *Guardian*, https://www.theguardian.com/stage/2016/jul/15/rebel-wilson-west-end-guys-dolls, accessed 7 February 2021.

108. The cast featured the television comedian and presenter Jason Manford (Nathan Detroit) opposite the alternative cabaret performer and 'post-modern diva' Meow Meow (Miss Adelaide); Adrian Lester (Sky Masterson), known as a leading man in West End musicals and in prime-time TV drama, opposite West End musical performer Laura Pulver (Sister Sarah Brown); and the 1970s–1980s pop singer and actor Paul Nicholas in the cameo role of Arvide Abernathy with the comic television actor Stephen Mangan in an invented narrator role. Two long-established West End musical theatre performers reinforced the West End lineage of the show by returning to roles they had played for the National Theatre in 1996: Clive Rowe (Nicely-Nicely Johnson) and Sharon D. Clarke (General Cartwright).

THE MOST BELOVED AMERICAN MUSICAL    427

109. A short run of four performances in August 2012 at the small Cadogan Hall in London adopted a similar approach, but inevitably on a much smaller scale, with minimal staging and a reduced orchestra. Leading West End performers included Ruthie Henshall (Sister Sarah) and Graham Bickley (Nathan Detroit). The television drama and stage musical crossover actor Dennis Waterman took a narrator role in place of the full script and also played Arvide Abernathy and Lt Brannigan. Lance Ellington (Sky Masterson) was known for his big-band vocals on TV's *Strictly Come Dancing* rather than for acting roles.

## BIBLIOGRAPHY

Eyre, Richard. *Utopia and Other Places*. London: Bloomsbury, 1993.

Gänzl, Kurt. *The British Musical Theatre*. Vol. 2, *1915–1984*. Basingstoke: Macmillan, 1986.

Garebian, Keith. *The Making of Guys and Dolls*. Ontario: Mosaic Press, 2002.

Kersh, Gerald. *Night and the City*. With an introduction by John King. London: London Books, 2007.

Loesser, Susan. *A Most Remarkable Fella: Frank Loesser and the Guys and Dolls in His Life; A Portrait by His Daughter*. New York: Donald I. Fine, 1993.

Mander, Raymond, and Joe Mitchenson. *Theatrical Companion to Coward*. London: Oberon Books, 2000.

Mordden, Ethan. *Coming Up Roses: The Broadway Musical in the 1950s*. Oxford and New York: Oxford University Press, 1998.

Mosedale, John. *The Men Who Invented Broadway: Damon Runyon, Walter Winchell, and Their World*. New York: Richard Marek, 1981.

[National Theatre.] *The Guys and Dolls Book*. London: Methuen, in association with the National Theatre, 1982.

Norman, Frank, and Lionel Bart. *Fings Ain't Wot They Used t'Be*. London: Samuel French, 1960.

Payn, Graham, and Sheridan Morley, eds. *The Noel Coward Diaries*. London: George Weidenfeld & Nicholson, 1982.

Rebellato, Dan. *1956 and All That: The Making of Modern British Drama*. London: Routledge, 1999.

Riis, Thomas L. *Frank Loesser*. With a foreword by Geoffrey Block. New Haven, CT: Yale University Press, 2008.

Royal National Theatre. "25: Guys and Dolls." *Platform*. 16 May 2001. Recording of public panel discussion. NT Archives RNT/PL/3/683.

Runyon, Damon, Jr. *Father's Footsteps: The Story of Damon Runyon by His Son*. London: Constable, 1955.

Schwarz, Daniel R. *Broadway Boogie Woogie: Damon Runyon and the Making of New York Culture*. New York and Basingstoke: Palgrave Macmillan, 2003.

Shellard, Dominic. *British Theatre since the War*. New Haven, CT: Yale University Press, 1999.

Snelson, John "'We Said We Wouldn't Look Back": British Musical Theatre, 1935–1969'. In *The Cambridge Companion to the Musical*, edited by William A. Everett and Paul R. Laird, 159–184. Cambridge: Cambridge University Press, 2017.

Snelson, John M. 'The West End Musical 1947–54: British Identity and the "American Invasion"'. PhD thesis, University of Birmingham, 2002.

'Stages of Half Moon: Guys and Dolls (1979)', https://www.stagesofhalfmoon.org.uk/producti ons/guys-and-dolls/, accessed 22 August 2019.

Stedman Jones, Gareth. 'The "Cockney" and the Nation, 1780–1988'. In *Metropolis: London; Histories and Representations since 1800*, edited by David Feldman and Gareth Stedman Jones, 272–374. London: Routledge, 1989.

Suskin, Steven. *Opening Night on Broadway: A Critical Quotebook of the Golden Era of the Musical Theatre, 'Oklahoma!' (1943) to 'Fiddler on the Roof' (1964)*. New York: Schirmer Books, 1990.

Suskin, Steven. *The Sound of Broadway Music: A Book of Orchestrators and Orchestrations*. New York; Oxford: Oxford University Press, 2009.

Taylor, William R. 'Broadway: The Place That Words Built'. In *Inventing Times Square: Commerce and Culture at the Crossroads of the World*, edited by William R. Taylor, 212–231. Baltimore, MD: John Hopkins University Press, 1991.

Taylor, William R. 'Introduction'. In *Inventing Times Square: Commerce and Culture at the Crossroads of the World*, edited by William R. Taylor, xi–xxvi. Baltimore, MD: John Hopkins University Press, 1991.

Tynan, Kenneth. *Theatre Writings*. Selected and edited by Dominic Shellard. With a preface by Matthew Tynan and a foreword by Tom Stoppard. London: Nick Hern Books, 2007.

Wells, Elizabeth A. 'After *Anger*: The British Musical of the Late 1950s'. In *The Oxford Handbook of the British Musical*, edited by Robert Gordon and Olaf Jubin, 273–289. New York: Oxford University Press, 2016.

Westerby, Robert. *Wide Boys Never Work*. With an introduction by Iain Sinclair. London: London Books, 2008.

Wolf, Matt. *The Guys and Dolls Book*. London: Nick Hern Books, 1997.

CHAPTER 15

# BELOVED IN LONDON, IGNORED IN NEW YORK

## Starlight Express *and* We Will Rock You

### DAVID COTTIS

SINCE *Jesus Christ Superstar*'s 1971 opening on Broadway rather than the West End, or maybe since Andrew Lloyd Webber insisted that Harold Prince should direct the London opening of *Evita* in 1978, it has been assumed that British and American musicals are, to a large extent, playing to the same audience. The so-called megamusicals of Lloyd Webber, and later of Alain Boublil and Claude-Michel Schönberg, manifest a sensibility that's essentially mid-Atlantic, with little that needs footnoting to an American audience, and the days when key British talents like Vivian Ellis, Noel Gay, and Julian Slade were unknown outside the UK seem long gone. In 1986 Michael Billington suggested that the musical theatre had become internationalised to the point of blandness, with 'identical productions of *Les Misérables* opening all over the world, like Holiday Inns.'[1]

Of course, it isn't that simple. While the markets have come together to an extent that was unimaginable in the 1960s, there remain odd exceptions. *Dreamgirls*, one of the biggest hits of the 1981 Broadway season, didn't make it to the West End until 2016, following the success of the 2006 film version. Similarly, not all hits have transferred the other way: in 1990 *Aspects of Love* suffered the greatest financial losses in Broadway history.[2]

This chapter examines two shows, both major long-runners in the West End, which failed to translate their success to Broadway. *Starlight Express* (1984), Lloyd Webber's follow-up to *Cats*, ran from 1984 to 2002 at the Apollo Victoria in London but only managed two seasons on Broadway at the Gershwin theatre, losing much of its $8 million investment before tottering, in a cut-down version, to Las Vegas.[3] *We Will Rock You* (2002) wasn't quite as big a hit in London, running for twelve years at the Dominion Theatre, but still qualifies as 'the most successful British musical not to open on Broadway since the fabled, fusty *Salad Days* (1954);[4] instead playing in Las Vegas before going on a US tour.

As well as (comparative) failure in the United States the two shows have certain things in common. Both were visually spectacular, built round a central physical metaphor—roller skating in one case, an oversized statue in the other. Both are Cinderella stories, depicting the triumph of the underdog, albeit within a show that celebrates the power of the budget. Both ran, to a large extent, without stars—the biggest name in the original cast of *Starlight Express* was the singer P. P. Arnold, known to 1960s music buffs for her singles 'Angel of the Morning' and 'The First Cut Is the Deepest', while the most familiar cast members of *We Will Rock You* were the diva Sharon D. Clarke as the villainous Killer Queen and the comic actor Nigel Planer, best known as the hippie student Neil in the BBC TV series *The Young Ones* (1982–1984). Finally, both were choreographed, in energetic rock-video style, by Arlene Phillips. I will consider the reasons behind the shows' differing fates on the two sides of the Atlantic and look at the extent to which Great Britain and the United States remain, to paraphrase Oscar Wilde, two musical theatres separated by a common language.

## A Musical about the Value of Blind Self-Belief

Like Andrew Lloyd Webber's previous show *Cats* (1981), *Starlight Express* took its inspiration from a book (or, in this case, a series of books) that formed one of the touchstones of a British postwar middle-class childhood. Where *Cats* adapted the *Old Possum* poems of T. S. Eliot, the later show began as an attempt to stage the *Thomas the Tank Engine* stories, by the Reverend W. S. Awdry. Lloyd Webber had been intending to adapt these stories throughout the 1970s, even naming his production company, Really Useful, after a phrase from them.[5]

Even before the action begins, the script of *Starlight Express* emphasises the childlike nature of the story; the list of characters is headed 'The trainset', and the title page describes the show as taking place 'on the sort of train layout everyone would like to own, but only governments can afford'.[6] Lloyd Webber's score is self-consciously derivative, in a style that goes back to *Joseph and the Amazing Technicolor Dreamcoat*, with individual numbers that pastiche different, mostly American, musical styles—country ('U.N.C.O.U.P.L.E.D'), 1960s girl-group pop ('A Lotta Locomotion'), and blues, in a song ('Poppa's Blues') that, like a train set, provides its own instructions for assembly:

> Oh, the first line of a blues
> Is always sung a second time.
> Oh yes, the first line of a blues
> Is always sung a second time,

So that by the time you get to the third line
You've had time to think of a rhyme.[7]

At times, the show deliberately harks back to *Cats*; the leather-clad Greaseball is a direct descendent of the Rum Tum Tugger, while Belle, 'a sleeper [in the sense of sleeping car] with a heart of gold',[8] is clearly in the same long-established profession as Grizabella. The show's sexual politics are actually more retrograde than those of *Cats*; where that show was divided more or less equally between Toms and Tibs, in *Starlight Express*, until a 2017 rewrite, the engines were all male, the carriages female. The lyrics, by the TV satirist Richard Stilgoe, are faux-naïve, rarely aiming far beyond the next rhyme:

Freight is great
Freight is great
We carry weight
Cause we are freight
And freight is great.[9]

As in *Cats*, there are a large number of 'I am' songs, held together structurally by a competition. The earlier show had 'the Jellicle choice'; this has a competition to find the fastest train in the crew. This is won, inevitably, by the clapped-out steam train, Rusty, who, according to his opening stage direction, 'is small, and dreams a lot, because nothing outside his dreams is much fun'.[10]

Again, destiny is represented by a quasi-divine abstraction, in this case the Starlight Express for which the trains are competing.[11] Stilgoe and Lloyd Webber make clear the religious nature of this unknown force in lyrics that echo the title song of *Jesus Christ Superstar*, and particularly that show's pivotal line 'Do you think you're what they say you are?':

Starlight Express
You must confess
Are you real? Yes or no?
Starlight Express
Answer me yes
I don't want you to go.[12]

Where *Jesus Christ Superstar* was deliberately open-ended in its view of the divinity or otherwise of its title character, the Starlight Express (and, indeed, *Starlight Express*) makes an unambiguous statement about where the power resides:

Rusty—you're blind—look in your mind
I'm there—nothing's new.
The Starlight Express is no more or less
Than you, Rusty; I am you.[13]

FIG. 15.1 The original London cast of *Starlight Express*; (*left to right*): Stephanie Lawrence (Pearl), Chrissy Wikham (Ashley), Frances Ruffelle (Dinah), and Ray Shell (Rusty). Photo © Donald Cooper/Photostage.

In this respect, the show's philosophy was that of its decade, a motivational speaker's attitude towards the value of blind self-belief, employing some well-worn metaphors and showing a disdain for those who ask for help:

> Only you have the power within you,
> Just believe in yourself, the sea will part before you
> Stop the rain, and turn the tide.
> If only you use the power within you
> Needn't ask the world to turn around and help you
> If you draw on what you have within you
> Somewhere deep inside.[14]

The political/social subtext (if you can call it that) is very clear; both success and failure are doled out by destiny to those who deserve them. An earlier song, by three engines named Rocky I, Rocky II, and Rocky III, demonstrates the show's view of those who suggest that it may be otherwise: despite their names, these engines quote Marlon Brando in *On the Waterfront* (1954) rather than Sylvester Stallone's champion:

> If I'd had the chances
> If I'd had the brakes [*sic*]
> Could have been a winner

I had what it takes
But I wasn't in the right place
At the right time
[ ... ]
Could have been a contender
Could have been a star
Never reached the final
Didn't get that far.[15]

If the apparent moral of the show was the validation of the underdog, the production was all about the power of wealth. The show's Unique Selling Point came in the competition itself; the performance was punctuated by races, initially heats and then a final championship race, around the auditorium. For these, the designer, John Napier, and the lighting designer, David Hersey, redesigned the interior of the Apollo Victoria Theatre, installing retractable runways and bridges on which actors raced on roller skates.[16] These 'skating trains'—with Lycra-clad actors in make-up resembling 1950s rockers, television exercise queens, and, in one case, the briefly fashionable group Sigue Sigue Sputnik—became the show's symbol, achieving visual recognition among people who never visited a theatre in their lives and even being referenced in a television advertisement for British Rail. Nunn's programme note for the West End production sets the tone:

A great capital theatre like London boasts a comprehensively varied annual programme, but there has always been a place in it for circuses, spectacles, masques, pantomimes, operettas, vaudeville—every age has found its response to the public appetite for shows that are exuberant, light-hearted, eye-popping fun.[17]

Unlike previous Lloyd Webber shows, *Starlight Express* was not produced by Cameron Mackintosh, either in the West End or on Broadway; in one of the many unintentionally hilarious passages in his autobiography, Lloyd Webber argues that the show wasn't suitable for Mackintosh as the music was in 'rock and pop territory, far from Cameron's natural habitat.'[18]

Even in the West End, *Starlight Express* was a show that divided critics; Sheridan Morley in *Punch* described it, in a simile that's curiously evocative of the script's title page, as like 'being invited by a millionaire to watch him play with some expensive and ingenious but ultimately wasteful toys'.[19] Even the favourable reviews had a functional quality, praising the show as a business proposition rather than a piece of theatre: Milton Shulman, in the *Evening Standard*, predicted that '*Starlight Express* will make Mr. Webber even more filthy rich than he already is',[20] while Jack Tinker in the *Daily Mail* said the same thing in a pun: 'I can only say that this show could well set another track record for Mr Lloyd Webber.'[21]

In the end, *Starlight Express* was the defining example of an 'audience show'; the real star was the staging, and Lloyd Webber wisely treated it as an amusement park ride,

FIG. 15.2 A scene from the revised 1992 London *Starlight Express*. Photo: Alastair Muir, courtesy of the photographer.

providing rewrites in 1992 and 2017, as if updating a theme-park attraction. (The 2017 revision included new songs by the composer's son and addressed some of the accusations of sexism that had arisen in the intervening years.) The show also exists in foreign productions that incorporate local variations and topical references; the most successful of these, the German production, in a purpose-built theatre in Bochum, currently features a British train called Brexit, referred to as 'the train that goes nowhere'.[22]

## *Starlight Express* in New York and in Las Vegas

*Starlight Express* took its time to travel to Broadway, not opening until 1987. Lloyd Webber himself has said, perhaps with a degree of hindsight, that he never wanted the show to go to Broadway, preferring Robert Stigwood's idea of an arena tour, and suggested that the producer, Brian Brolly, was swayed by a large financial offer from the theatre owner Jimmy Nederlander.[23]

While it's possible to imagine a Broadway audience reacting favourably to a show that is, in essence, about the American dream, there are also cultural problems. Broadway veterans were certainly ill-disposed towards a show that, even more than *Cats*, was explicitly about the spectacle; Jule Styne reputedly came out of the London production with the words 'Who wants to come out of a show whistling the lightbulbs?'[24] The show's dressing-up box attitude to musical styles was also something that played better in the West End. Frank Rich, reviewing the show in the *New York Times*, summed up the difficulties that many American critics and audiences had with it, in particular the pastiches of American music:

> Instead of aspiring to his usual Puccini variations, Mr. Lloyd Webber has gone 'funky', English style, by writing pastiche versions of American pop music—with an emphasis on blues, gospel and rap. Short of a Lennon Sisters medley of the Supremes' greatest hits, soul music couldn't get much more soulless than this.[25]

However, Rich's major criticism struck at the heart of the Broadway production's problem. To put it simply, this production lost the main quality that had made the show worth seeing:

> In the London production of *Starlight*, there is at least the novelty of being surrounded by the skaters, who circle the entire auditorium. In New York, the tracks extend only a few rows in front of the proscenium; for most of the audience, the experience is about as involving as standing on the sidelines while other people take one of the lesser rides at Disneyland.[26]

Ethan Mordden makes the same two points while also criticising the attempted transcendence of the show's ending:

> Neither the story-line nor the score has led us to this point, however, it is simply presented to us. *Starlight Express* is thus a solution without the clues—and I hear that chorus of pop-opera haters crying, 'So aren't they all!' They aren't; this is the weakest of the group. For anyone who resists—who, to be candid, doesn't want the gaudy Andrew Lloyd Webber to succeed even at writing knockoffs of America's easiest music—*Starlight Express* is like a line written for the 1993 [*sic*] revision 'Forty tons of empty chrome.'
>
> Worse, the racecourses used in London, extending around the auditorium's side and rear and upstairs as well, could not be duplicated for Broadway. Not that the races were interesting in themselves: they involved too many characters we hardly knew and could be followed in toto only on a giant video screen. But at least it was all ... well, racy. Broadway's *Starlight* could not drop the races, but they were less elaborately run.[27]

This last point seems to strike at the core of why the show didn't run on Broadway; years before the phrase came into common parlance, *Starlight Express* was a 'site-specific' (or, at any rate, 'site-responsive') production. In this case, the location was not a variable but the central reason for the show's existence. (A UK tour, with videoed inserts capturing the races, proved similarly disappointing.)

The show found its natural US home years later, opening in 1993 in a shortened version at the Las Vegas Hilton where, as Jeremy Gerard put it in *Variety*, 'what was garish and soulless even by the standards of contemporary Broadway megamusicals, seems positively quaint in these surroundings.'[28] The show's philosophy also sits well in Las Vegas, a town that depends for its existence both on extreme conspicuous consumption and on an irrational faith in self-belief. The show was shortened to ninety minutes, losing several songs and the interval, and, crucially, the hotel was rebuilt to accommodate the show. Ironically, given its subject matter, *Starlight Express* has proved a show that doesn't travel easily.

# A JUKEBOX SHOW OF AGGRESSIVE INTERTEXTUALITY

Where *Starlight Express* found its natural US terminus in the Nevada desert, *We Will Rock You* started there: the show's US première was in 2004 at the Paris Las Vegas Hotel, followed by a US tour in 2013. By contrast with London, where the Freddie Mercury statue outside the Dominion Theatre became a West End landmark for more than a decade,[29] the show's American incarnation has existed much like a rock band: on the road.

*We Will Rock You* was the second of the big jukebox musicals, following the runaway success of *Mamma Mia!* (1999). Queen's immense following made them obvious candidates for this kind of treatment, as did the band's musical style; sometimes referred to as 'pomp rock', this was a built-up version of the glam rock that had dominated the British singles charts in the early 1970s, a consciously artifice-laden form that had arisen in response to the hippie era's emphasis on nature and authenticity.

Glam rock always had a vein of theatricality: David Bowie studied mime with the dancer and choreographer Lindsay Kemp and appeared on television in the title role of Bertolt Brecht's play *Baal* (1982); Sparks (an American duo resident in the UK, who had more success in their adopted than in their native country) showed off their influences from both Gilbert and Sullivan and German cabaret; and at the other end of the credibility spectrum, Gary Glitter's stage costume of built-up shoulders and shoes was inspired by the 1971 Royal Shakespeare Company production of Jean Genet's *The Balcony*.[30]

Queen, formed by the unlikely alliance of the Indian-born fashion and graphic design student Freddie Mercury with three thoroughly English scientists (the astronomer and guitarist Brian May, the engineer and bass player John Deacon, and—stretching the word 'scientist' a little—the dental student and drummer Roger Taylor),[31] epitomised this more than most; Mercury frequently mentioned his love of opera and musical theatre in interviews, saying of the group's breakthrough hit 'Killer Queen' that '[y]ou almost expect Noël Coward to sing it. [ ... ] It's one of those bowler hat, black suspender numbers—not that Noël would wear that.'[32] The singer who famously did wear a bowler

FIG. 15.3 The Dominion Theatre in London, for twelve years home to *We Will Rock You*; note the giant statue of Freddy Mercury above the marquee. Photo: Roberto Herrett © Alamy Stock Photo.

hat and suspenders, Liza Minnelli, appeared as the closing act at Mercury's memorial concert at Wembley Stadium in 1992, suggesting, as Mark Steyn pointed out, a counterfactual biography for the deceased singer:

> And you realized that poor Freddie had been in the wrong business all along. Like Liza, he dressed in basic black. Like Liza, he was a Broadway baby. He should have

graduated to being one of Jerry Herman's big ladies on the staircase in *Mame* or *Dolly*. Frankly, his legs were better than most of Jerry's girls.[33]

At times, Queen songs already sounded like part of an unwritten musical: 'I Want to Break Free' and 'I Want It Now' are (at the risk of stating the obvious) 'I want' songs, but so is 'Somebody to Love', and all three feature as such in *We Will Rock You*. 'Bohemian Rhapsody' and 'We Are the Champions' are eleven o'clock numbers, the former suggesting the multi-tune reprise structure of *Gypsy*'s 'Rose's Turn'. At the same time, the group's operatic and prog rock affectations were undercut with camp humour: the title of the album that includes 'Bohemian Rhapsody', *A Night at the Opera* (1975), is not just (as the 2018 movie *Bohemian Rhapsody* suggests) an invocation of the music's classical colourings, it's also a nod to the Marx Brothers.[34]

*We Will Rock You* signalled its serio-comic quality by employing the comedian and scriptwriter Ben Elton to write the book. Elton had come to national prominence as the co-writer of *The Young Ones*, then as the compère of the television show *Saturday Live*, combining the left-leaning subject matter of alternative comedy with a very traditional showbiz blokiness. After debuting as a playwright with *Gasping* (1990), he wrote the book and lyrics for Lloyd Webber's Irish-set musical *The Beautiful Game* (2000).[35]

Like *Mamma Mia!*, *We Will Rock You* is about the fans rather than the band. However, while *Mamma Mia!* takes place in a world where ABBA never existed, allowing their songs to emerge as the newly minted expression of middle-aged women and men, *We Will Rock You* is based on an idea that allows the band's repertoire to be performed both as well-loved standards and as spontaneous expressions of the characters singing them.

*We Will Rock You* takes place in a dystopian twenty-fourth century in which all music is controlled by the Globalsoft corporation and rock music has been forgotten. The protagonist, Galileo Figaro, described in a stage direction as 'the James Dean of his time',[36] finds himself troubled by odd music and lyrics that creep into his subconscious:

> I found it. [ ... ] In a dream. I have dreams, you see. And I hear noises, screeching, thudding b-hanging noises. And words, words, drop into my head, too many words. I'm a substitute for another guy, I look pretty tall but my heels are high.[37]

Later on, he describes the phenomenon in more detail, providing some of the script's very few references to any music made after 1990:

> Yes, I don't know where they come from, it drives me mad, all these phrases and sounds, useless phrases. I mean, what the hell is a Tambourine Man? What's the story, morning glory? Who was the real Slim Shady? It's torture, all I know, and I don't know why I know it, is that I really, really want to Zig-a-Zig Ah.[38]

Later on, Galileo meets the Bohemians, a countercultural group who, like him, have named themselves after half-remembered popular culture. This is mined for comic effect, as when one muscle-bound rebel introduces himself:

And I'm the biggest, baddest, meanest, nastiest, ugliest, most raging, rapping, rock and rolling, sick, punk, heavy metal, psycho bastard that ever got down funky. They call me Britney Spears.[39]

This memorial ability on the part of Galileo and some other characters, including his love interest Scaramouche, means that Queen songs slip from their mouth at the moments when the sentiments are most appropriate, enabling them both to quote the songs and to mean them. In this respect, the show places its central characters in the position identified by Umberto Eco as the definition of the postmodern condition:

> I think of the post-modern attitude as that of a man who loves a very cultivated woman and knows he cannot say to her 'I love you madly,' because he knows that she knows (and that she knows that he knows) that these words have already been written by Barbara Cartland. Still, there is a solution. He can say 'As Barbara Cartland would put it, I love you madly.' At this point, having avoided false innocence, having said clearly that it is no longer possible to speak innocently, he will nevertheless have said what he wanted to say to the woman, that he loves her, but he loves her in an age of lost innocence. If the woman goes along with this, she will have received a declaration of love all the same.[40]

FIG. 15.4 Sharon D. Clarke as the Killer Queen in the 2002 London production of *We Will Rock You*. Photo: Rowena Chowdrey © ArenaPal.

*We Will Rock You*'s central conceit allows its characters to say, 'As Freddie Mercury would put it, I want to break free.'

Eventually Galileo, Scaramouche, and the Bohemians overcome the Globalsoft Corporation with the aid of the Freddie statue, a replica of the one outside the theatre (which itself quotes the pose that adorned the poster for the 1992 memorial concert), and a guitar buried, Excalibur-style, in the location of that concert, Wembley Stadium.[41] The show also references the 1992 concert in its treatment of the Queen/David Bowie duet 'Under Pressure', which becomes, as at Wembley, a male/female duet (although this time it is Bowie's lines that are sung by a woman, whereas at Wembley Annie Lennox stood in for Mercury).

Ben Elton's public persona, both in his work and in interviews, is that of an anti-intellectual intellectual who will reference Dante's *Inferno* in his stand-up act or borrow the plot of *Twelfth Night* for a *Black Adder 2* episode but at the same time will argue that Morecambe and Wise were more interesting surrealists than Samuel Beckett,[42] or have one of his characters describe the RSC audience as 'eight rows of ponces on the mailing-list and fifteen hundred extremely pissed-off school kids'.[43] In keeping with this attitude, *We Will Rock You* is an almost aggressively intertextual work, throwing in both pop- and high-culture references with gleeful abandon. Galileo resembles not only King Arthur but also the chosen outsiders of many fantasy and young adult narratives, whether Harry Potter, Buffy Summers, or Neo in *The Matrix* (1999). Like Keanu Reeves's character in that film, Galileo becomes aware of a truth denied to others, linking him with both Joseph Campbell's *Hero with a Thousand Faces* and the visionaries of Plato's allegory of the cave in *The Republic*.

Similarly, the sterile, dystopian world echoes those of Aldous Huxley's *Brave New World* (1932), the Alan Moore and Ian Gibson comic *The Ballad of Halo Jones* (1984–1986), or the Fritz Lang film *Metropolis* (1927), from which the band had used extracts in the video for the song 'Radio Ga Ga'. The discovery of the Freddie statue inevitably recalls the reveal of the Statue of Liberty at the end of the original film of *Planet of the Apes* (1968), as well as the giant head in *Zardoz* (1974), another story based on a future misremembering of twentieth-century popular culture. Travelling further away from the audience's probable cultural backgrounds, Galileo himself, troubled by songs that he can't quite recall, resembles both Ormus Cama, the Parsi-born protagonist of Salman Rushdie's novel *The Ground Beneath Her Feet* (1999), who also inhabits a world in which iconic rock songs exist only in the central character's unconscious,[44] and Liza Elliot in Kurt Weill and Ira Gershwin's *Lady in the Dark* (1941), with 'Bohemian Rhapsody' fulfilling the function that 'My Ship' does in that show.

Indeed, *We Will Rock You*'s treatment of 'Bohemian Rhapsody' gives some indication of its tone. After spending the entire show troubled by the memory of the song, Galileo finally hears it for the first time through its original video. The character who plays him the song, the librarian Pop, played by Planer (and in a 2023 revival, by Elton himself) as a Dennis Hopper–ish hippie burnout, explains its significance:

> That's all there is. Those young men singing to us from over three centuries ago were members of a rock freedom fighter collective known as Queen and even then those

young soul visionaries knew that they existed in a world where real life was becoming just someone else's fantasy.[45]

To which Scaramouche replies, in a tone that many of the older members of the audience may have recognised, 'So that's what it meant? Blimey, it just sounded like a load of pretentious old bollocks to me.'[46]

The show mocks its own pretentions and those of the band themselves. We are told that the members of Queen were executed in the first decade of the twenty-first century:

> It is said that the hairiest of the gang, a man named Brian, was granted a final wish before execution, he asked to be allowed to play just one more guitar solo. [ ... ] And so he was able to delay his death by three and a half days.[47]

Like *Starlight Express*, which used a multi-million-pound budget to tell a story of the triumph of the underdog, or the film *School of Rock* (2003), which mocks MTV but was financed by its corporate owner,[48] *We Will Rock You* is a story that eats and retains its cake several times over, allowing a West End audience watching a show produced by millionaires both to position themselves as leather-jacketed rebels, and to laugh at themselves for doing so.

If *Starlight Express* received mixed reviews, *We Will Rock You* was a critical disaster, with Elton's book coming in for special criticism, particularly from the more right-wing papers. Toby Young wrote in the *Spectator* that '[i]f there are any lingering doubts about who was responsible for the best jokes in *Black Adder*, Ben Elton or Richard Curtis, *We Will Rock You* definitively lays them to rest'[49], while Charles Spencer in the *Daily Telegraph* borrowed a line from 'Killer Queen' to say that '[f]ar from being guaranteed to blow your mind, *We Will Rock You* is guaranteed to bore you rigid.'[50] The disjunction between the critical and popular response was so great that it prompted Janet Street-Porter to muse in the *Independent* about theatre critics' separation from their readership:

> Do these paragons of popular taste visit supermarkets like the rest of us? Do they know anyone who works shifts, gets paid by the hour, drives a Mondeo or proudly drinks Babycham? In other words, do they mingle with the people who read their opinions?[51]

Interestingly, Street-Porter didn't say that she herself enjoyed the show, adding that it 'wasn't my cup of tea, but I'm not that keen on panto either.'[52] She wasn't the only critic to make this connection; Michael Coveney opened his *Daily Mail* review with the words 'Pantomime has arrived a little early in the West End' before going on to add 'in the shape of this shallow, stupid and totally vacuous new musical.'[53] Indeed, at times the show's humour is that of a provincial pantomime:

> KHASHOGGI [a henchman]: You are an eager beaver.
> KILLER QUEEN: Leave my eager beaver out of this.[54]

# Queen and *We Will Rock You* in the United States, or, A Tale of Two Sensibilities

So what is the difference between a West End fixture and an American touring show? Part of the answer is quite a simple one: in Britain, Queen are an institution; in the United States, they were (at least until recently) a cult. Even 'Bohemian Rhapsody', which in Britain stayed at number one for six weeks over Christmas 1975, was only a minor hit in the United States; when Wayne and Garth headbang along to it in *Wayne's World* (1992), they are sharing a shibboleth rather than joining in the common culture.

However, the differing responses to the show in the United Kingdom and United States seems to me to point up a more fundamental difference between the two cultures in terms of the way in which they view rock music. When rock 'n' roll first came to Britain, it was absorbed initially into the variety tradition, with smiley crowd-pleasers like Tommy Steele, Cliff Richard, and Anthony Newley approaching it as an addition to music hall. Even the Beatles, whose success redefined the national relationship with the music, retained something of this ironic approach; both Lennon's idolisation of the Goons (and consequent willingness to work with their producer, George Martin), and Harrison's later bankrolling of the Monty Python troupe showed where the band's heart lay; the cover of *Sergeant Pepper's Lonely Hearts Club Band* included the comedians Max Miller, Tommy Handley, and Stan Laurel among its pantheon of influencers. When Street-Porter and Coveney mentioned pantomime, they were acknowledging a tradition that had been part of British rock history.

Some American critics are in sympathy with this: Myron Meisel described, in a generally unfavourable review, that he appreciated the way in which Queen's 'bombastic pomp is leavened by music hall humor and flamboyant campiness'.[55] Others find it harder to deal with. In a particularly dyspeptic article, the Britophobic music critic Dave Marsh analyses the place of rock music in 'a land without superhighways or elbow room, devoid of all-night TV or ice in your Coke, a place where blues and country, rockabilly and soul are fascinating affectations and purist obsessions rather than essential parts of the historical landscape':[56]

> England [*sic*] is a country with an openly articulated class structure, political parties that are meant to express the interests of each of those classes [ ... ], and a culture for centuries based on the fact of class privilege. There, popular music doesn't serve the function of communicating to a mass listenership its essential solidarity—its existence *as* a class. Certainly, the spirit of British rock is not critical in the way that American rock has been. Its mode is more often irony than commitment; its mood is more often detached than engrossed; its function is to entertain—whether entertaining with politicized sentimentality or just sentimentality often seems not to make much difference.[57]

One could take issue with some of Marsh's assumptions about the political element of British (and, indeed, American) rock, but there is an important point here; in Britain, irony and detachment have long been part of the rock package, a tradition seen throughout the twentieth century in the self-mocking vocals of John Lennon, Ray Davies, Jon Lydon, and Jarvis Cocker. In the United States, this kind of ironic approach has been more the stock-in-trade of singer-songwriters such as Randy Newman and some comedy acts within the fields of rap, such as the 2 Live Crew, and rock, such as Green Day, whose *American Idiot* (album 2004, stage musical 2009) forms a mirror image of *We Will Rock You*, a Broadway hit that existed in the UK as a touring and arena show. While many of these performers have a considerable following, they are all, to a large extent, cult acts, lacking the centrality to the culture that Queen possess in the UK.

In this respect, it is telling that the above-quoted Dave Marsh had a special antipathy to Queen, saying in a 1979 review of the album *Jazz* that they may have been 'the first truly fascist rock band.'[58] While 'fascist' is a strong word, there's no denying that the band did use authoritarian techniques and imagery, particularly in such crowd-marshalling songs as 'We Are the Champions' and, of course, 'We Will Rock You', as well as showing an instinctive identification, rare in popular music, with the rich and powerful; the band were notorious in the 1980s for their willingness to play in countries with oppressive or racist regimes, such as military junta–era Argentina in 1981 or apartheid South Africa the year before Live Aid.[59]

However, there is a curious paradox here. Although Queen's music does certainly flirt with the imagery of the far right, members of that movement never embraced the band. Even during the late 1970s, the period of the National Front's greatest engagement with popular culture, National Front skinheads were far more likely to attend concerts by the left-leaning Madness or the anarchistic Sham 69.[60] While it is, of course, possible that actual fascists would be put off by Mercury's sexuality or ethnicity, neither of these was well publicised in the 1970s.[61] The central issue here seems to be deeper than this; for Queen, the imagery of fascism was just another bowler hat or leotard, to be taken off after the show. Real fascists were never attracted to Queen's apparent fascism because they could tell, on some level, that the band weren't taking it seriously. As Susan Sontag has written, '[T]he camp sensibility is disengaged, depoliticized—or at least apolitical.'[62]

'Camp' is a word one has to be careful with here; while *We Will Rock You* adopts an ironic tone, it does so in a dad-rockish, heterosexual way that is very far from Mercury's own flamboyant on-stage (and offstage) persona. In this respect, it's less like Queen's output than that of 1970s rockers like Slade, Mud, and the Sweet, who combined a glam aesthetic with a thumping macho musical style, a combination memorably described by the punk singer Siouxsie Sioux as 'brickies in eyeliner'.[63] Of course, these groups were never successful in North America—while Canada and the United States supplied both camp glam rockers and stadium stompers, the two didn't coexist in the same bands.

In this respect, it's telling to compare *We Will Rock You* with an analogue that I didn't mention in my list above. In 1976, not long after Queen's *A Night at the Opera*, the Canadian hard rock band Rush brought out the concept album *2112*. As its title suggests, *2112* is set in the future, in this case, another dystopia where rock music is banned and

## 444 DAVID COTTIS

in which a single visionary locates a guitar, thus bringing back the music and liberating the world. However, unlike *We Will Rock You*, *2112* plays the allegory entirely straight; the protagonist is an unambiguous hero, modelled not just on the visionaries of Plato's cave but, according to the sleeve notes, on the Nietzschean supermen of the novelist, playwright, and (fascist-inclined) amateur philosopher Ayn Rand.[64] In the end, this is the difference between the two sensibilities: the divide between how British and North American bands view rock music is the difference between Ben Elton and Ayn Rand.

# CONCLUSION

It is perhaps dangerous to generalise too much about two large countries on the evidence of two shows; as I've argued, these shows failed on, or didn't get to, Broadway for very specific reasons, which don't necessarily apply to both of them. However, there is a slight similarity between the two shows: both were deliberately lightweight concoctions, drawing on popular theatrical forms such as the spectacle and pantomime and taking an omnivorous attitude towards musical styles. In Britain this is, for historical reasons, an aesthetic that has been far more part of the mainstream of postwar popular music; in the United States, it is one that sits more comfortably in Vegas than on Broadway.

## NOTES

1. Panel discussion at the National Student Drama Festival, Swansea, April 1986.
2. Ken Mandelbaum, *Not Since 'Carrie': Forty Years of Broadway Musical Flops* (New York: St. Martin's Press, 1991), 351.
3. Jeremy Gerard, 'Review: *Starlight Express*', *Variety*, 5 June 1995, https://variety.com/1995/ legit/reviews/starlight-express-1200442013/, accessed 15 July 2019.
4. Myron Meisel, 'Review: *We Will Rock You*', *Hollywood Reporter*, https://www.hollywoodr eporter.com/review/we-will-rock-you-theater-720064, accessed 21 July 2019.
5. Andrew Lloyd Webber, *Unmasked: A Memoir* (London: Harper Collins, 2018), 196–197.
6. Richard Stilgoe and Andrew Lloyd Webber, 'Starlight Express', typescript, British Library Manuscript Collection, MPS 2437, 1984, title page.
7. Ibid., act 1, 36.
8. Ibid., act 1, 38.
9. Ibid., act 1, 15.
10. Ibid., act 1, 4.
11. The classically trained Lloyd Webber was certainly aware of the incidental music and songs composed by Edward Elgar for a 1915 play entitled *The Starlight Express* by Algernon Blackwood and Violet Pearn.
12. Stilgoe and Lloyd Webber, 'Starlight Express', act 1, 47.
13. Ibid., act 2, 18.
14. Ibid.

15. Ibid., act 2, 16.
16. Lloyd Webber credits John Napier with the idea of roller-skating trains (Lloyd Webber, *Unmasked*, 400), although Nunn's programme note suggests that it was his idea. Trevor Nunn, 'Follies and Grandeur', programme note, *Starlight Express* programme (London: RUG, 1984), 4–5; here: 4. Lloyd Webber has more recently suggested producing a stripped-back production with 'absolutely no roller skates.' Lloyd Webber, *Unmasked*, 415.
17. Nunn, 'Follies and Grandeur', 4.
18. Lloyd Webber, *Unmasked*, 404.
19. Sheridan Morley, 'Review: *Starlight Express*', *Punch*, 4 April 1984, reprinted in *London Theatre Record* 4, no. 7 (1984): 239.
20. Milton Shulman, 'Review: *Starlight Express*', *Evening Standard*, 28 March 1984, reprinted in *London Theatre Record* 4, no. 7 (1984): 237.
21. Jack Tinker, 'Review: *Starlight Express*', *Daily Mail*, 28 March 1984, reprinted in *London Theatre Record* 4, no. 7 (1984): 234. It is worth noticing the way in which Lloyd Webber brings out a certain formality in London critics, as if the review had slipped across from the financial pages. It's hard to imagine Lloyd Webber's nearest contemporary rival being referred to in print as 'Mr. Sondheim'.
22. I am grateful to Olaf Jubin for this information.
23. Lloyd Webber, *Unmasked*, 472.
24. Mark Steyn, *Broadway Babies Say Goodnight: Musicals Then and Now* (London: Faber & Faber, 1997), 23.
25. Frank Rich, 'Review of *Starlight Express*', *New York Times*, 16 March 1987, https://www.nytimes.com/1987/03/16/theater/stage-andrew-lloyd-webber-s-starlight-express.html, accessed 15 July 2019.
26. Ibid.
27. Ethan Mordden, *The Happiest Corpse I've Ever Seen: The Last Twenty-Five Years of the Broadway Musical* (New York: Palgrave Macmillan, 2005), 76.
28. Gerard, 'Review: Starlight Express'.
29. The theatre's location, near the junction of Oxford Street and Tottenham Court Road, made the statue a useful reference point for people giving directions. It also functioned as a prompt to discussion; I once overheard two elderly South Asian men outside the theatre having a heated disagreement about the exact nature of the singer's Parsi origins.
30. Simon Reynolds, *Shock and Awe: Glam Rock and Its Legacy, from the Seventies to the Twenty-First Century* (London: Faber & Faber, 2016), 219. The singer himself mentioned the connection in Tom Hibbert, 'Who Does Gary Glitter Think He Is?', *Q Magazine*, January 1990. Glitter is also, together with David Essex (who played Che in the London production of *Evita*) and Steve Harley (who sang on the original single version of *The Phantom of the Opera*), one of the glam-era singers to have crossed professional paths with Andrew Lloyd Webber; under his real name of Paul Gadd, he featured as a priest on the original recording of *Jesus Christ Superstar*.
31. Reynolds, Shock and Awe, 463.
32. Quoted in Steve Irwin and Colin McLear, eds., *The Mojo Collection: the Ultimate Music Companion*, 3rd ed. (Edinburgh: Canongate, 2003), 304.
33. Steyn, Broadway Babies Say Goodnight, 200.
34. Indeed, the 2018 film's failure to portray this aspect of the band's output is, together with its sanitised view of Mercury's sexuality, one its most jarring features for those who were alive

at the time. The band made the connection clear by naming their next album *A Day at the Races*, after the Brothers' follow-up film.

35. A colleague who worked backstage on this show, and who will remain nameless for obvious reasons, once told me that the crew had a running sweepstake to find a line of dialogue in it that wasn't a cliché. The money remained unclaimed by the end of the run.

36. Ben Elton and Queen, 'We Will Rock You', typescript, 5 October 2002, British Library Manuscripts collection, MPS 9966, 2002, 5.

37. Ibid., 6.

38. Ibid., 38.

39. Ibid., 47.

40. Umberto Eco, *Reflections on 'The Name of the Rose'*, trans. William Weaver (London: Secker & Warburg, 1985), 67. Curiously, Ben Elton's former collaborator, Richard Curtis, made an oblique reference to this passage in his screenplay for *Four Weddings and a Funeral* (1993): '[I]n the words of David Cassidy, when he was still with the Partridge Family, "I think I love you." ' Richard Curtis, *Four Weddings and a Funeral* (London: Corgi, 1994), 72. Curtis's later screenplay for *Yesterday* (2019) is based on a premise that has a certain amount in common with both *We Will Rock You* and *The Ground Beneath Her Feet*, although this time with a protagonist who is aware of the source of the songs in his head.

41. Wembley Stadium was also, of course, the location of the band's triumphant set at Live Aid in 1985. Although YouTube has made this performance central to the myth of Queen, as evidenced by its placing as the third-act climax of the film *Bohemian Rhapsody*, it was less well remembered in 2002, whereas the memorial concert was widely available on video.

42. Ben Elton, 'Letter to My Younger Self', *Big Issue*, 2 July 2018, https://www.bigissue.com/int erviews/ben-elton-i-was-never-able-to-say-goodbye-to-rik-mayall/, accessed 21 July 2019.

43. Ben Elton, *Silly Cow* (London: Samuel French, 1991), 20.

44. Salman Rushdie, *The Ground Beneath Her Feet* (London: Jonathan Cape, 1999), 96. Cama's relationship with classic rock songs is slightly different from Galileo's in that he anticipates them (writing them a thousand and one days before their nominal authors) rather than remembering them.

45. Elton and Queen, 'We Will Rock You', 82.

46. Ibid., 83.

47. Ibid., 85.

48. Gary Mulholland, *Popcorn: Fifty Years of Rock 'n' Roll Movies* (London: Orion 2010), 378.

49. Toby Young, 'Review: *We Will Rock You*', *Spectator*, 25 May 2002. Reprinted in *Theatre Record* 22, no. 10 (2002): 618.

50. Charles Spencer, 'Review: *We Will Rock You*', *Daily Telegraph*, 15 May 2002, reprinted in *Theatre Record* 22, no. 10 (2002): 615.

51. Janet Street-Porter, 'Review: *We Will Rock You*', *Independent on Sunday*, 19 May 2002, reprinted in *Theatre Record* 22, no. 10 (2002): 591.

52. Ibid.

53. Michael Coveney, 'Review: *We Will Rock You*', *Daily Mail*, 15 May 2002, reprinted in *Theatre Record* 22, no. 10 (2002):613–614; here: 613.

54. Elton and Queen, 'We Will Rock You', 20.

55. Meisel, 'Review: We Will Rock You'.

56. Dave Marsh, 'It's Like That: Rock 'n' Roll on the Home Front', in *The First Rock 'n' Roll Confidential Report*, ed. Dave Marsh and the editors of *Rock 'n' Roll Confidential* (New York: Pantheon Books, 1985), 12–33; here: 12.

57. Ibid, 31.

58. Dave Marsh, 'Review: *Jazz*', *Rolling Stone*, 8 February 1979, https://www.rollingstone.com/music/music-album-reviews/jazz-188987/, accessed 21 July 2019.
59. Reynolds, Shock and Awe, 470.
60. As the blogger and academic Conrad Brunstrom has pointed out, it is difficult to imagine a band less like Queen than Madness, although they also had a sense of humour, as well as their own songbook show, *Our House* (2002). Conrad Brunstrom, '*Bohemian Rhapsody* Reviewed', 28 October 2018, https://conradbrunstrom.wordpress.com/2018/10/29/bohemian-rhapsody-reviewed-nothing-really-matters-at-all/, accessed 22 July 2019.)
61. Mercury had a series of very public relationships with women and often said in interviews that he was 'Persian'. It says something about the ambiguity of the glam rock era that it enabled the concealment of both Freddie Mercury's gayness and David Bowie's heterosexuality.
62. Susan Sontag, 'Notes on "Camp"', in Against Interpretation (London: Eyre & Spottiswoode, 1967), 275–292; here: 277.
63. Ben Marshall, 'Cum On, Feel the Noize', *Guardian*, 23 December 1999, https://www.theguardian.com/uk/1999/dec/23/christmas.tvandradioarts, accessed 29 September 2019.
64. Irwin and McLear, *The Mojo Collection*, 368.

## BIBLIOGRAPHY

Brunstrom, Conrad. '*Bohemian Rhapsody* Reviewed', 28 October 2018, https://conradbrunstrom.wordpress.com/2018/10/29/bohemian-rhapsody-reviewed-nothing-really-matters-at-all/, accessed 22 July 2019.

Coveney, Michael. Review of *We Will Rock You*. *Daily Mail*, 15 May 2002. Reprinted in *Theatre Record* 22, no. 10 (2002): 613–614.

Curtis, Richard. *Four Weddings and a Funeral*. London: Corgi, 1994.

Eco, Umberto. *Reflections on 'The Name of the Rose'*. Translated by William Weaver. London: Secker & Warburg, 1985.

Elton, Ben. 'Letter to My Younger Self'. *Big Issue*, 2 July 2018, https://www.bigissue.com/interviews/ben-elton-i-was-never-able-to-say-goodbye-to-rik-mayall/, accessed 21 July 2019.

Elton, Ben. *Silly Cow*. London: Samuel French, 1991.

Elton, Ben, and Queen. 'We Will Rock You'. Typescript, 5 October 2002. British Library Manuscripts Collection, MPS 9966, 2002.

Gerard, Jeremy. 'Review: *Starlight Express*'. *Variety*, 5 June 1995, https://variety.com/1995/legit/reviews/starlight-express-1200442013/, accessed 15 July 2019.

Irwin, Steve, and Colin McLear, eds. *The Mojo Collection: The Ultimate Music Companion*. 3rd ed. Edinburgh: Canongate, 2003.

Lloyd Webber, Andrew. *Unmasked: A Memoir*. London: Harper Collins, 2018.

Mandelbaum, Ken. *Not since 'Carrie': Forty Years of Broadway Musical Flops*. New York: St. Martin's Press, 1991.

Marshall, Ben. 'Cum On, Feel the Noize'. *The Guardian*, 23 December 1999, https://www.theguardian.com/uk/1999/dec/23/christmas.tvandradioarts, accessed 29 September 2019.

Marsh, Dave. 'Review: *Jazz*', *Rolling Stone*, 8 February 1979, https://www.rollingstone.com/music/music-album-reviews/jazz-188987/, accessed 21 July 2019.

Marsh, Dave. 'It's Like That: Rock 'n' Roll on the Home Front'. In *The First Rock 'n' Roll Confidential Report*, edited by Dave Marsh and the editors of *Rock' n' Roll Confidential*, 12–33. New York: Pantheon Books, 1985.

448 DAVID COTTIS

Meisel, Myron. 'Review: *We Will Rock You*'. *The Hollywood Reporter*, 21 July 2014, https://www.hollywoodreporter.com/review/we-will-rock-you-theater-720064, accessed 21 July 2019.

Mordden, Ethan. *The Happiest Corpse I've Ever Seen: The Last Twenty-five years of the Broadway Musical*. New York: Palgrave Macmillan, 2005.

Morley, Sheridan, 'Review: *Starlight Express*'. *Punch*, 4 April 1984. Reprinted in *London Theatre Record* 4, no. 7 (1984): 239.

Mulholland, Garry. *Popcorn: Fifty Years of Rock 'n' Roll Movies*. London: Orion, 2010.

Nunn, Trevor. 'Follies and Grandeur'. Programme note, *Starlight Express* programme, 4–5. London: RUG, 1984.

Reynolds, Simon. *Shock and Awe: Glam Rock and Its Legacy, from the Seventies to the Twenty-first Century*. London: Faber & Faber, 2016.

Rich, Frank. 'Review: *Starlight Express*'. *New York Times*, 16 March 1987, https://www.nytimes.com/1987/03/16/theater/stage-andrew-lloyd-webber-s-starlight-express.html, accessed 15 July 2019.

Rushdie, Salman. *The Ground Beneath Her Feet*. London: Jonathan Cape, 1999.

Shulman, Milton. 'Review: *Starlight Express*'. *London Evening Standard*, 28 March 1984. Reprinted in *London Theatre Record* 4, no. 7 (1984): 237.

Sontag, Susan. 'Notes on "Camp"'. In Susan Sontag, *against Interpretation*, 275–292. London: Eyre & Spottiswoode, 1967.

Spencer, Charles. 'Review: *We Will Rock You*'. *Daily Telegraph*, 15 May 2002. Reprinted in *Theatre Record* 22, no. 10 (2002): 615.

Steyn, Mark. *Broadway Babies Say Goodnight: Musicals Then and Now*. London: Faber & Faber, 1997.

Stilgoe, Richard, and Andrew Lloyd Webber. 'Starlight Express'. Typescript. British Library Manuscript Collection, MPS 2437, 1984.

Street-Porter, Janet. 'Review: *We Will Rock You*'. *Independent on Sunday*, 19 May 2002. Reprinted in *Theatre Record* 22, no. 10 (2002): 591.

Tinker, Jack. 'Review: *Starlight Express*'. *Daily Mail*, 28 March 1984. Reprinted in *London Theatre Record* 4, no. 7 (1984): 234.

Young, Toby. 'Review: *We Will Rock You*'. *Spectator*, 25 March 2002. Reprinted in *Theatre Record* 22, no. 10 (2002): 618.

# PART VI

# POPULAR IN GERMANY/ AUSTRIA?

CHAPTER 16

......................................................

# KURT WEILL'S AMERICAN WORKS IN TWENTY-FIRST-CENTURY GERMANY

......................................................

JUDITH WIEMERS

We want popular art, which truly speaks to the masses and simultaneously offers critical ideas and food for thought. This is, by the way, not a new endeavour.

Kurt Weill, 1936[1]

THE reception of Kurt Weill's American works in twenty-first-century Germany is entangled with the nation's complicated relationship with its own history, and with those artists that it lost to North American society and culture.[2] Its conflicted view of Weill, who escaped Nazi Germany and identified as American long before being granted citizenship, manifests in the German treatment and reception of his works written for the American musical stage. Weill's aspirations to create 'the' genuine American opera and his embrace of the parameters of American cultural life have presented problems to German artistic directors and audiences. These problems, which are intimately related to both immanent elements and structural principles of the German theatrical system, will be considered when mapping twenty-first-century German reception history. Despite these challenges, Weill's *Johnny Johnson* (1936), *The Eternal Road* (1937), *Lady in the Dark* (1941), *One Touch of Venus* (1943), *Firebrand of Florence* (1944), *Street Scene* (1947), *Down in the Valley* (1948), *Love Life* (1948), and *Tom Sawyer and Huckleberry Finn* (1950, unfinished) have increasingly attracted interest through numerous recent German productions. Weill's *Knickerbocker Holiday* (1938) and *Lost in the Stars* (1949) have not been performed in Germany for several decades and will not be considered in this chapter.[3]

# JUST ONE WEILL

In 1932 Weill voiced his conviction that the solution to the 'opera crisis' of the early twentieth century must be the 'courageous' realisation of productions which 'allow the theatre director to balance his budget while maintaining the highest artistic aspirations.'[4] Weill's writings of the late 1920s and 1930s repeatedly address the role of opera in modern society and its problematic dependence on state subsidy in the German *Stadttheater* system.[5] In the 'turbulent times' of the early 1930s, Weill called for a reform that allowed opera to move away from the depiction of 'random love relationships, horror stories from the Renaissance era, or family feuds'.[6] Instead, he believed strongly in opera's duty not only to respond to the 'big themes of our times', but also to adapt to the realities of the contemporary entertainment industry and its audiences.[7] His *Threepenny Opera*, he argued, was the first work of its kind to 'break into the consumer market' and 'reach an audience that [ ... ] would have denied our ability to attract listeners from beyond the realm of opera goers.'[8] Weill was of course not alone in his endeavour to move opera away from the *l'art pour l'art* ideal and make it accessible to a broader audience demographic, not only in the genre's choice of themes, but also in its 'simplified means of musical expression'.[9] The question of how lastingly successful the attempts to reform the established dramaturgy and formal composition of the nineteenth-century operatic canon ultimately were is an altogether different matter. What Weill's writings highlight, however, is a certain consistency in ambition with his later American stage works. Just like his colleague Paul Hindemith, Weill was an ambassador for writing *Gebrauchsmusik*, 'usable' music designed for consumption by a live audience. In 1927 he wrote:

> There is a clear divide between those musicians who work on the solution to aesthetic problems solitarily while harbouring a deep contempt for the audience, and those who seek artistic connection with an audience because they understand that beyond the artistic vision, the development of a work of art must also be driven by a collective social component.[10]

Weill reinforced this ambition, relating to both the form and functionality of music within a given societal context, throughout his career. This serves as only one reminder that the many biographical and even musicological accounts of Weill's 'split' compositional history—the neat divide into a European and an American oeuvre—are too simple, and potentially misguided.

However, an overview of the German reception of Weill's American works can hardly ignore nor completely discount the discourse that contrasts the avant-garde, 'authentic' Weill during his Berlin years with the 'commercially minded' Weill in New York. These very simplifications have informed much of Weill's reception history not only in postwar Germany but also in America, and to some extent continue to do so. To investigate and document the origins and persistent repetitions of these misconceptions in full would be

FIG. 16.1 A 1933 portrait of composer Kurt Weill (1900–1950). Photographer unknown; image provided by the editors.

laborious. It suffices here to point to some of the key sources upholding the claim of the 'two Kurt Weills'. In the English-speaking world, the Weill biographers Virgil Thomas and Ronald Taylor in particular were responsible for calling attention to the perceived aesthetic shift, with both authors initially pinpointing the composer's geographical relocation as a trigger for a radically changed artistic outlook and then decrying the 'American Weill' as uncompromisingly commercial.[11] As Thomas put it bluntly: 'After Weill came to live in America, he ceased to work as a modernist.'[12] David Drew, an avid admirer of Weill, cemented what Kim Kowalke has called the 'critical construct' of the divided composer in his Weill entry in *The Grove Dictionary of Music and Musicians*.[13] Not only does Drew title a subsection 'The Two Weills', but he even more figuratively speaks of the composer as being 'reborn' with his première of *One Touch of Venus*.[14] In Germany, it was Theodor Adorno who transformed Weill reception. The impact of his much-quoted obituary in the *Frankfurter Rundschau* has been described retrospectively as 'destructive' and 'unreasonable'.[15] While speaking highly of Weill's early achievements, Adorno discredited the composer's work for the American stage in one fell swoop. His verdict on Weill as retaining 'little of the surrealistic' and 'becoming a Broadway composer modelled on Cole Porter', who 'talked as if concession to the commercial field were no concession', amounts to a defamatory obliteration of a meaningful and often successful stage in Weill's career.[16] Several authors have argued that Adorno had neither detailed knowledge of Weill's later works nor any real insight into the artistic practices on Broadway and the standards required to 'make it' there.[17] Nonetheless, Adorno's words carried the weight of authority for several generations: some of his sentiments still reverberate through today's German press, with newspapers regularly citing Weill's work for the Berlin stages as his more 'worthy' artistic contributions.

## SPEAKING TO THE MASSES

The dichotomous polarity between the 'modernist' European Weill and 'popular' American Weill ignores two additional important points that had a lasting impact on twenty-first-century reception; first, the popular success of the Weill-Brecht collaborations in the late 1920s and 1930s, and secondly, an entire generation's fascination with American culture and society in Weimar Germany and beyond. As Stephen Hinton has demonstrated, *The Threepenny Opera* was received ambiguously on its opening night in August 1928 but soon turned into the must-see theatrical event of the season. In its first year it saw fifty new productions, and subsequently became an international phenomenon within a couple of seasons.[18] Although Brecht puritanically claimed that the popularity of the piece was unintended and based entirely on its tuneful songs and romantic plot rather than on his social critique, its commercial success cannot have been entirely unexpected, or even unwanted.[19] After all, the collaborators had already established a certain reputation in Berlin's cultural scene and for *The Threepenny Opera* used well-known and distinguished creative personnel who were bound to attract the attention of critics and punters alike.[20] None of Weill's American works were comparable box-office successes, nor are they likely to ever challenge the dominance of *The Threepenny Opera* or *Rise and Fall of the City of Mahagonny* as Weill's most-produced theatre compositions. The first productions of his *Street Scene*, *Love Life*, and *The Firebrand of Florence* had all been financial flops, leaving Weill desperate for commercial success.[21]

It could be argued that the popular appeal of Weill's melodies was exactly what can be considered avant-garde in the context of operatic practice. After all, in his own words, it was only 'the comprehensible', 'simplified' use of melody in *The Threepenny Opera* that brought opera back to its 'primitive' roots and in turn allowed the creation of a new genre of musical theatre.[22] Of course, Weill's own accounts of opera composition must always be considered attempts to create a public image of compositional 'worthiness', as Nils Grosch has convincingly argued.[23] However, the themes that Weill concerned himself with in the late 1920s regarding both the form and the scope of musical theatre were not at all dissimilar to his reflections in the United States.[24] After the première of *Street Scene*, he intimated that he had 'continuously tried to solve [ ... ] the form-problems from every angle.'[25] Weill's sketches for a talk entitled 'What Is Musical Theatre?' and his article 'The Future of Opera in America' reveal what the composer himself supposedly felt about his engagement with the American entertainment industry: his words paint a picture not of an adaptation to a foreign concept of theatre practice, but of the discovery of a system that naturally suited his ideas. America offers, he argued, 'enormous fields [i.e. potential] for musical theatre'.[26]

# WEILL AND AMERICANISATION

The perceived caesura in Weill's compositional trajectory and its continuous effect on his reception can be further challenged when considering the intense engagement with American culture in Germany following World War I. The advent of public broadcasting, burgeoning mass media, and technological advances in film production enabled an unprecedentedly broad access to American music, cinema, and fashion in the early 1920s. So strong was the influence that the phenomenon was swiftly labelled 'cultural Americanisation'.[27]

The artistic inspiration drawn from African American musical idioms and their associated dances, all subsumed under the buzzword 'jazz', subverted the rigid demarcations of German 'E' (*ernst*, serious) and 'U' (*unterhaltend*, entertaining) music and sparked much debate among cultural critics. It was not only aesthetics, however, that caused a stir. The principles of America's entertainment industry and the entanglement of its various branches with the commercial sector simultaneously caused concern for the sacrosanct identity of 'independent' art and hopes for the democratisation of elitist culture.[28]

Like most of his contemporaries, Weill was deeply affected by the sounds of jazz and actively experimented with its instrumentation and harmonic language in his early stage works.[29] Adorno's implicit accusation of Weill's having lowered his standard to conform with Tin Pan Alley composers as soon as he hit American ground distorts the composer's much more complex engagement with American musical idioms earlier in his career. George Gershwin—one of the most frequent references in the reception of Weill's American works—was a monumental influence on many of the most prolific stage composers of the Weimar Republic, such as Paul Abraham and Emmerich Kálmán.[30] Gershwin's compositions were widely available on recordings and as sheet music, and his *Rhapsody in Blue* featured prominently in one of the most popular American sound films of the era, *King of Jazz* (1930), which was received enthusiastically in Germany.[31] The film's main star, the band-leader Paul Whiteman, was recognised as the inaugurator of so-called symphonic, even 'cultivated' jazz and as such served as a typical reference in German contemporary writing. So too did Cole Porter, whom Adorno later mentioned disparagingly in his obituary, and whose songs were popular in the German market throughout the Weimar Republic and beyond. It can be argued, therefore, that the German frame of reference in the reception of Weill's American works has always been determined (and perhaps limited) by the specific experience and consumption of what was available as 'American culture' at any given time. While many contemporary reviewers still accuse Weill of developing a style that is considered 'too American' in character, meaning that it is popular, accessible, and/or melodious, the reverse does also creep in. Christoph Zimmermann, writing on the German opera scene for the British magazine *Opera*, claims that 'one cannot deny that his [American] musical idiom was acquired, not inborn'—as if musical style were not always acquired, and as if culture could indeed be 'inborn'.[32]

Beyond his experiments with American jazz, Weill was interested in the ways that music was embedded in American types of public entertainment, in its functionality on both stage and screen. Like many of his German colleagues, he also remained critical of the seemingly uncompromising capitalism of America's entertainment industry. In 1937, two years after his arrival in New York, he wrote: 'I don't want to make the same mistake as so many others: spending all my money, then having to take on another job immediately, and ultimately becoming a slave of Hollywood.'[33]

While the creation of musical theatre with a social conscience was certainly a concern that Weill shared with Brecht, and later with his other collaborators, the writers Elmer Rice and Maxwell Anderson, it seems that his primary aim was to foster an accessible stage genre in which music moved away from naturalism and mere illustration and instead developed a meaningful dramaturgical purpose.[34] By its very nature, this type of musical theatre would have to be flexible enough to adapt to changing audience expectations and new socio-political contexts—something that the German *Stadttheater*, with its sluggish bureaucratic processes and institutionalised conservatism, could evidently not address. In this respect Weill's endeavours aligned with the booming sound-film industry, which was strongly driven by popular demand and had to react quickly to social change. Weill thought it an art form with great potential and throughout his life harboured the ambition to create the genre of a 'film-opera'.[35]

Weill's conviction that there was, 'in all its variations, just one art', with 'the basic principles always the same', made him less dogmatic than some of his colleagues, for example Arnold Schoenberg and his commitment to *l'art pour l'art*. It explains Weill's aversion to artistic practices that were governed by institutionalised rules rather than by the demands of the work and its audience.[36] His comments on both German opera houses and the New York Metropolitan Opera offer testimony to this.[37] Weill's efforts to break with opera conventions was recognised in contemporary criticism. In 1932 Kurt London described the première of Weill's *Bürgschaft* as a 'turning point in the art of opera composition'. He continues to praise Weill's 'strange combination of didactic play [*Lehrstück*], oratorio, and number opera [*Nummernoper*], of Bachian polyphony, lucid baroque, and sublimated jazz', as a 'singular work of art'. He concludes: 'This music is modern and can be understood even by uneducated listeners.'[38] One year later, with the beginning of Nazi rule, Weill left Germany and, after brief but busy periods in London and Paris, re-established his career in New York.[39] Unlike many of his high-profile emigrant colleagues, such as Brecht, the composers Paul Abraham and Paul Dessau, the screenwriter Paul Liebmann, and the actress Lilian Harvey, whose hopes for a continuation of their German careers remained unfulfilled or who faced personal unhappiness in exile, Weill seemed to take well to both the new language and the American conception of art and entertainment. Over the next fifteen years, until his untimely death in April 1950, Weill composed more than a dozen works for the American musical stage, and it should come as no surprise that he adapted his pieces as rigorously as possible to what he believed were the requirements of the sector, the spectrum of theatrical genres, and the demands of the American audience.

# Twenty-first-Century German reception

The gradual German discovery of Weill's American oeuvre since the 1950s has presented theatres and their audiences with problems and in certain ways continues to do so. Some of these are inherent in the works themselves, others reflect the conventions and limitations of the German opera industry, and still others are a consequence of lingering prejudice. The years since the new millennium have seen some bold programming, and much has been done to re-establish Weill in his country of origin.

However, even after seventy years, the idea of Weill as an American composer has not yet been normalised, with the consequence that his American works are still not fully integrated into the repertoire. (Table 16.1) Often, even the more successful original works appear as novelties when the theatrical seasons are programmed in Germany. Recent press materials reveal that many critics spend considerable editorial space on critiquing the works themselves rather than reviewing the interpretation of a specific production—a treatment usually reserved for newly composed music before it has become canonical. All of Weill's American works are handled this way, even the operatic *Street Scene*, which has possibly proved the most viable for the German opera and theatre scene.[40] Although the educational aspect of this approach is potentially useful, it sometimes subverts the efforts of opening audiences' minds to these works by reinforcing some of the older prejudices disseminated by Adorno and like-minded critics. In 1955 Hans Heinz Stuckenschmidt claimed that in *Street Scene*, '[S]ong has become elegant and sweet. Three dollars are, after all, less artistically valuable than three pennies [a reference to *The Threepenny Opera*].'[41] Compare this to a review of the 2019 Oper Köln (Cologne Opera) production: the *Kölner Stadtanzeiger*, while lauding the company for 'introducing this barely known work', concludes that in *Street Scene*, the social critique of *The Threepenny Opera* has been 'tailored to suit Broadway, just like Weill himself after his emigration—motivated by survival instinct and a readiness to conform.'[42] An analogy that seems to have been drawn here is one between accessibility and supposed lack of quality, a point not further substantiated in the article. Weill's 'conforming' to his American audience equally is portrayed as something that is, a priori, objectionable. The *Aachener Zeitung* dismissed both work and the production, which 'could not dispel the reservations' about the piece. Pedro Obiera argues that Weill's endeavour to create a specific type of American opera was 'not particularly successful', for which failure he blamed the 'muddled' stylistic mix of 'spiritual, revue, dance, opera and the broad symphonic sounds of film'. He further describes the social criticism as 'attenuated by the music.'[43] These statements, while not reflecting the majority of recent journalistic writing, seem to regurgitate Adorno's approach more or less uncritically, and using a

## Table 16.1 Productions of Kurt Weill's American stage works in Germany since 2000

| Work | Year | Theatre |
| --- | --- | --- |
| *Johnny Johnson* (1936) | 2010 | Kurt Weill Fest, Anhaltisches Theater Dessau |
| *The Eternal Road* (*Die Verheißung*, 1937) | 2013 | Kurt Weill Fest, Anhaltisches Theater Dessau (concert performance) |
| *Lady in the Dark* (1941) | 2011 | Staatsoper Hannover |
| | 2014 | Staatstheater Mainz |
| *One Touch of Venus* (*Ein Hauch von Venus*, 1943) | 2010 | Kurt Weill Fest, Anhaltisches Theater Dessau |
| | 2011 | Oper Leipzig (concert performance) |
| | 2019 | Staatsoperette Dresden |
| *The Firebrand of Florence* (1944) | 2005 | Kurt Weill Fest, Anhaltisches Theater Dessau (semi-staged concert) |
| | 2013 | Staatsoperette Dresden |
| *Street Scene* (1947) | 2002 | Theater Aachen |
| | 2004 | Kurt Weill Fest, Anhaltisches Theater Dessau |
| | 2009 | Theater Hagen |
| | 2012 | Musiktheater im Revier Gelsenkirchen |
| | 2014 | Staatsoper Hannover |
| | 2016 | Stadttheater Pforzheim |
| | 2018 | Theater Münster |
| | 2019 | Oper Köln |
| *Down in the Valley* (1948) | 2007 | Kurt Weill Fest, Anhaltisches Theater Dessau |
| *Love Life* (1948) | 2017 | Theater Freiburg |
| *Tom Sawyer and Huckleberry Finn* (1950, unfinished) | 2014 | Deutsches Theater Göttingen |
| | 2016 | Landestheater Detmold |

similarly dismissive tone. However, although stylistic eclecticism, as mentioned here, cannot be rated as a marker of poor compositional quality per se, the critics' concerns about how to identify which genre the work belongs to deserves special attention, as does the reference to the allegedly popular Broadway musical idiom.

# THE PROBLEM WITH GENRE

Premièring in early 1947, *Street Scene* is based on the 1929 drama of the same name by the Pulitzer Prize winner Elmer Rice, who also adapted his original text for Weill's purposes. The lyrics were written by the poet Langston Hughes. The narrative revolves around the residents of a New York tenement building—their worries, their conflicts, and their cultural diversity. The piece was a notable success in New York, and Weill had high hopes that it would become his most respected work. He thought of *Street Scene* as the culmination of his efforts to create the prototype of the 'American opera' in its ambitious musical dramatisation, broad appeal, and liberation from the confines of opera as an institution. He saw all elements of musical theatre effectively and meaningfully combined: the 'triple threat' of song, speech, and dance.[44] As much as *Street Scene* fulfilled Weill's idealistic views on form and musical function, according to Gisela Maria Schubert,[45] it has caused 'headaches' for its German reception ever since its Düsseldorf premiere in 1955. A main point of puzzlement and criticism is its lack of a unifying musical style, such that it resists simple genre classification. *Street Scene* has always defied categorisation, having first been billed as a 'dramatic musical'—surely with marketing goals in mind—and only later as an 'American opera'.[46] As Schubert has demonstrated, the German press has always grappled with its genre categorisation, offering a jumble of alternative suggestions, such as 'tragische Operette' ('tragic operetta'), 'Musical-Oper' ('musical-opera'), 'Musical', 'Musical Play', and—in reference to Gershwin's 'folk opera' *Porgy and Bess*—'Volksoper' and 'amerikanische Volksoper' ('American folk opera').[47] In recent years the variety of terms has decreased, with most sources using either 'Oper',[48] 'Broadway Oper',[49] or variations on the work's official identifications as 'amerikanische Oper',[50] 'American opera',[51] and the earlier 'dramatisches Musical'.[52] Other choices include 'sozialkritisches Musical' ('musical of social criticism')[53] and the more vague 'Musiktheater-Experiment' ('experiment in music theatre'),[54] 'Bühnenwerk' ('stage work'),[55] and 'Nummernoper' ('number opera').[56]

While other American Weill pieces that have made it into German season programming can be more easily identified in terms of genre, *Street Scene* is not the only piece to invite an assortment of generic categories.[57] Weill's *One Touch of Venus* (1943), which qualifies as his greatest commercial and critical Broadway success, with a respectable first run of 567 performances, is rarely performed in Germany to this day but in summer 2019 was given an ambitious production at the Staatsoperette Dresden.[58] Its reception was mostly lukewarm, with critics referring to the piece either as a 'musical',[59] a 'revue',[60] or a 'musical comedy'.[61] Then there is the idiosyncratic *Love Life*, which did not première in Germany until 2017. Giselher Schubert argues that with *Love Life* and its depiction of a how a couple's marriage would mirror 150 years of American history, Weill created the genre of the concept musical. Owing to its episodic character, it had been labelled by the publisher as a 'vaudeville'—a choice replicated by most reviewers. The exception is *Opernwelt*, which additionally uses the more appropriate 'pasticcio'.[62] While *Lady in the Dark* (1941) is regularly labelled a 'musical' (in agreement with its official title), critics make sure to note its musically diverse score, which 'breathes the spirit of opera and Singspiel' and 'oscillates between Broadway song, modern classical music, and a touch of *Threepenny Opera*.'[63] One review opines that its extraordinarily large proportion of dialogue actually renders the piece a 'play with music'.[64] The broadsheet *Die Welt* describes the work's form as 'a clever play, into which songs and dance numbers have been integrated, like mini-operas'.[65] The *Süddeutsche Zeitung*, in reference to the Hannover production in 2011, calls it a 'crazy experiment of form and an amalgam of classic Broadway melody, the harmonics of the Berlin Weill, and verismo'.[66] It may not come as a surprise that many reviewers reference operas rather than pieces from the spectrum of operetta and musical comedy when evaluating Weill's scores, with Puccini the most frequent point of comparison.[67]

The ongoing discourse about genre is linked to Weill's stylistic diversity. While some critics interpret his compositional eclecticism as an advantage, others decry it as arbitrary, and confusing. The *Frankfurter Allgemeine Zeitung* describes the 'brazen mixture of styles' in *Street Scene* as its main attraction: 'an ingenious melting pot of allusions, borrowings, quotes and plagiarisms'.[68] The *Pforzheimer Zeitung* views the score as a 'sometimes disturbing, but always fascinating mix', which the critic interprets as the result of the integration of Weill's European heritage with his American experience.[69]

# CHALLENGES FOR GERMAN CULTURAL INSTITUTIONS

Occasionally, Weill's stylistic eclecticism is portrayed in the press as presenting difficulties for both the singers and the orchestras. The magazine *Opernwelt* alleges that '[i]t is exactly this seemingly untroubled plundering of music history, the carefreeness of these pieces, that its interpreters, especially on German stages, find challenging'.[70] The *Online Merker* highlights the fact that the Gürzenich Orchester, playing for the Cologne production of *Street Scene*, must convincingly balance 'operetta sentiment and bel canto' and 'even present itself as jazzy'.[71]

The reason genre ambiguity presents 'challenges' to performers is embedded in the German opera industry and its respective institutions. Depending on an opera house's specific profile, meaning its outlook on repertoire, a work such as *Street Scene* can adopt various 'identities'. At a revered institution such as the Dresden Semperoper, which traditionally programmes well-established core operatic repertoire on its main stage, the 2011 production of *Street Scene* was treated as 'große Oper' ('grand opera'), in the words of the *Frankfurter Allgemeine Zeitung*. This means that 'the luxurious sounds of the Sächsische Staatskapelle, with Jonathan Darlington conducting neatly', made the score sound 'anodyne' and 'too polite', smoothing over its contrasts and edges.[72] The staging is described as similarly stiff, 'because it is afraid of kitsch on the one hand, but only offers very mild social critique on the other'.[73] Commenting on the *Street Scene* at the Musiktheater im Revier in Gelsenkirchen, Elisabeth Höving writes that the Neue Philharmonie Westfalen orchestra 'tried its best' to bring the 'melting pot of big opera and swinging Broadway-sound' to life, but ultimately without being able to create 'diverting entertainment'.[74] *Street Scene* at the Theater Hagen was criticised in two papers for its 'uncontoured', 'overly powerful' sound from the pit.[75]

Other reviews are much more positive about the efforts of the opera and radio orchestras tackling the Weill scores. The MDR radio orchestra, playing a semi-staged version of *The Firebrand of Florence* in Dessau, allegedly did so with 'exuberant precision' (*Frankfurter Allgemeine Zeitung*), and the orchestra at Staatsoperette Dresden reportedly 'waltzed and grooved' with 'verve' when playing *One Touch of Venus*.[76] Many reviews, however, are mostly dispassionate when it comes to orchestral performance; offering mild praise and remarking—not without sympathy—on a certain '*Stadttheater* sedateness', which must be shaken off for an engaging performance.[77]

It is not only the orchestras that are criticised for their inability to create a convincing 'American' sound. Highlighted frequently is the issue of casting, correlating with the difficulties posed by genre ambiguity. Several critics observe that in terms of casting requirements, Weill's American pieces neither fit readily into the concept of the German *Sprechtheater* (spoken theatre), nor do they suit the artistic convention of the country's opera companies. Commenting on a cast of opera singers in the *Street Scene* production in Pforzheim, a local newspaper writes that 'the score demands extraordinary versatility from the singers', while the *Kurt Weill Newsletter* draws similar conclusions for a production of *Lady in the Dark* at the Staatstheater in Mainz, when suggesting that 'the roster of German state theatres seldom includes performers who specialise in musicals, so nearly all of the roles are cast here with actors, and the quality of the singing does not generally match that of the acting.'[78]

Reviewing the same production, *Die deutsche Bühne* states that even 'most of the classically trained singers don't hit the right idiom.' This is, the author continues, 'not an issue specific to Mainz: in German performances of musical theatre, performers time and time again revert to operatic or operetta-style singing.'[79] Reviewers make a crucial point here. With musicals booming on German stages only since the 1990s and specialised training still rare, the pool of suitable professional performers of American-style musical comedy is relatively small, albeit growing. Many German city and regional theatres have a so-called *Dreisparten* approach, meaning they programme drama, dance, and *Musiktheater*, which is divided further into opera, operetta, and musical. Most companies running this model have very few, if any, specialised musical theatre performers and usually recruit from the ranks of ensemble singers with operatic training. This brings us back to Weill's early misgivings about the Berlin-based Kroll Opera (which had refused to programme *Mahagonny*) and the German state-subsidised *Stadttheater* system in general.[80] The composer's reservations might have motivated him to write a letter to his wife, Lotte Lenya, in 1950, stating his opposition to his the performance of *One Touch of Venus* in Germany at that time: 'From all I know about the present status of the German theatres, my impression is that they are in no way equipped to do justice to a piece like *Venus*, and a bad production would do a lot of harm to me. My European reputation is worth more to me than the negligible amount of money I can make with this production.'[81] Weill may be referring to the devastating effects of World War II on the theatre infrastructure here, but this comment most likely was also informed by his general concerns about German opera houses.

The difficult relationship between the institutional opera house and Weill's American stage-works does not end with the challenges facing the musicians and the performers. Weill's masterful orchestrations require major orchestral forces as well as unusually large casts—for example, *Street Scene* requires over thirty soloists. Other than the economically robust mid- to large-sized houses, very few companies could tackle such an undertaking logistically, let alone financially. When huge capital investment is involved, potential risks need to be minimised. Concerns about jeopardising audience loyalty, box-office failure, and fragile public funding streams can at times lead to productions that opt for 'safety first'. As several critics have observed, this may not be the best approach to Weill's American works.

Weill's concerns about a German *One Touch of Venus* were not entirely unfounded. A variation of the Pygmalion story, it contains some of his most beloved songs, yet it also requires an outstanding, charismatic leading lady as well as a ballet company and a large orchestra. In his review of *One Touch of Venus* at the Kurt Weill Fest in 2010, Kevin Clarke, director of the Operetta Research Centre, opens with a plea for the qualities of the piece, describing its songs as 'wonderful', its ballet scene as 'terrific', and its lyrics as 'funny'.[82] His verdict on the realisation by the director Klaus Seiffert, the conductor James Holmes, and the designer Imme Kache, in contrast, is cutting. Their 'frumpy' approach, with 'no sign of glamour' in its décor and no apparent feeling for the topical undercurrents of the original—especially its discussions of gender struggles and the inviolability of the freedom of art—not only rendered this production a 'missed opportunity', but in Clarke's eyes also did lasting harm to the German reputation of the musical as a genre. Instead of attracting new audiences, it 'unnecessarily confirms all the prejudices'. As a main contributing factor to this unfavourable impression, Clarke pinpoints casting. Too many singers, he suggests, failed to create a 'musical idiom'. The only scenes that he described as 'truly impactful' were those performed by the students of the musical branch at Berlin's Akademie der Künste. 'It is an enigma to me', he says, 'why the company didn't engage these students—some of them winners of the Bundeswettbewerb Gesang—in the main roles.'[83] Clarke is not the only one who recommends stronger involvement of students with specialised training. Wolfgang Jansen comes to the same conclusion in his review of the same production. The involvement of the students of the Munich-based Theaterakademie August Everding in the production of *Street Scene* in Gelsenkirchen equally received praise in the press.[84] An overarching issue that emerges from recent reviews is that of the place of Weill's American works within the context of the producing institutions and their ensembles. When a piece does not sit comfortably in one of the genres an opera house or theatre has chosen as its remit, it presents problems in terms of the tailored expertise of the institution's staff and ensemble. The strict classification into 'serious' and 'entertaining' stage genres and their respective associated training arguably does a disservice to many works that consciously or unwittingly transcend these often arbitrary boundaries.

# The Involvement of the Kurt Weill Foundation

When it comes to choosing the cast and creative teams, the role of the New York–based Kurt Weill Foundation (KWF) is worth mentioning. Run by the world's leading Weill scholars, the foundation is reputedly strict with adaptations of the original materials and regularly demands a degree of creative control over productions. The KWF's involvement ranges from the choice of translators, conductors, and individual performers to its insistence on *Modellinszenierungen* (model productions): stagings that prescribe certain choreographies or sets, as well as production aesthetics, as is common practice for many Broadway musicals.[85] It also actively commissions new productions. Its championing of Weill's American works has undoubtedly increased interest, with a newly adapted version of *The Eternal Road*—presented at the 2013 Kurt Weill Fest in Dessau as an oratorio, with a running time of two hours—as a recent, impressive example of the foundation's tireless promotion of underrepresented pieces.[86] The foundation's omnipresence has, however, also evoked criticism. It is again Kevin Clarke who suggests that its intentions can have a stifling effect, 'stultifying any innovation' in practice. His criticism targets the organisation's insistence on a creative team and performer (Ute Gferer) for the *Venus* at Dessau.[87] A similar observation was offered by the *Mitteldeutsche Zeitung*, which noted that the piece had been treated with 'conservatory care' rather than having been realised with an innovative and possibly more engaging approach.[88]

Most other reviews that voice concern about the foundation's power do so with regard to the German translations of libretti and textbooks. The *Süddeutsche Zeitung* speaks of the Semperoper Dresden's being 'at the mercy' of Stefan Troßbach's approved translation, which was further criticised in the context of several other German productions (in Gelsenkirchen and Münster).[89] In 2013 the European premiere of a fully staged production of *The Firebrand of Florence* at the Staatsoperette Dresden elicited dismissive verdicts on the translation of the experienced Weill translator Roman Hinze. Hinze had been praised for his 'pleasantly unpretentious' translation of *Lady in the Dark*, as the *Süddeutsche Zeitung* remarked, but fared less well with his newly commissioned German *Firebrand*.[90] The *Neue Musikzeitung* slates this version as 'laboured', with forced rhymes ('In Firenze/gibt's Feste und Tänze' ['In Florence/there are celebrations and dances']; *Pamplemusen—Busen'* [grapefruits—bosoms]) and awkward wordplay.[91] The criticism is repeated in several other reviews, with *Die Welt* clarifying that 'this is not the smut found on the *Playboy* joke page, but precisely Roman Hinze's German translations of the reputable Ira Gershwin'.[92] Hinze's version of *One Touch of Venus* was also attacked when the piece was performed in 2019 at the Staatsoperette Dresden.[93] At the other end of the spectrum is a translation approved by the KWF that contributed significantly to the extraordinary critical and popular success of the Freiburg production of *Love Life* in 2017. In his translation of Alan Jay Lerner's original, the dramaturge Rüdiger Bering 'succeeded in striking a tone reminiscent of the great song and operetta lyricists of the German and Viennese interwar years, such as Marcellus Schiffer and Fritz Löhner-Beda', a critic noted.[94] Where translations are concerned, it is impossible to ascertain how much knowledge critics have of the original libretti or original-language recordings; however, direct comparisons between lines of the English and German texts suggest good familiarity at least.

## STAGING TRENDS

The difficulty of translating not just Weill's American oeuvre, but operetta and musical theatre in general, is testament to the strong ties of these genres with contemporary culture and specific socio-political contexts. Faced with the task of translating *One Touch of Venus* into German, Richard Weihe comments that its dialogue 'contains more referential than semantic content' and concludes: 'If only one could translate culture rather than merely language.'[95] His attempt to 'update' the musical by transferring its plot to Berlin in the early 2000s was vetoed by the KWF, which insisted on 'faithfulness to the original'.[96] The question of how to make Weill's American works accessible to German audiences continuously occupies critics' minds. Time and time again, reviews complain about the American 'kitsch' in these pieces, their (as it were) alien identities as popular Broadway shows, seemingly incompatible with internalised German values of art for art's sake.[97] They are usually contrasted with *The Threepenny Opera* and *Mahagonny* as examples of 'truly' experimental works with strong social messages. In 1948 *Die Welt* wrote about *Knickerbocker Holiday* that 'it is a type of modern American theatre that is not particularly compatible with German mentality.'[98] There are still critics who seem to be guided mostly by perceived notions about Broadway and its effects on Weill when cooking up phrases such as Jens Frederiksen's verdict on *A Lady in the Dark*: 'a confetti-coloured entertainment commodity: nice, sometimes cheeky but in general disappointingly sentimental and psychologically thin. [ ... ] There is nothing left of the sass of the Weill/Brecht collaborations.'[99] Increasingly, however, critics call out directors and producers, instead of blaming the writers, for contemporary productions that lack critical bite and fail to address the underlying political themes. As early as 2012 the *Dreigroschenheft* diagnosed a new age of Weill popularity in Germany. Commenting on *Street Scene*, a piece that was arguably written as a study on social milieu, Andreas Hauff argues that 'we can finally understand the theme of multiculturalism'.[100] His remark has only gained in relevance in subsequent years. The migrant crisis, at its most acute in the years around 2015 but remaining a continuous challenge, occupies the collective European psyche. In Germany, which housed 1.9 million refugees by December 2022, local communities are deeply affected by the responsibilities of integrating and educating newcomers; meanwhile the government struggles with the rise of far-right movements, which have used the crisis to further their fundamentally racist ideology.[101] In this context, several journalists have recently commented that the engagement with the themes of cultural prejudice, exploitation, and poverty in *Street Scene* is not radical enough in contemporary productions.

Most stagings replicate the tenement block, either as a façade standing upright (such as Dick Bird's design at Cologne) or lying on the floor with a giant mirror 'projecting' the actions into the audience (the stage design by Rifail Ajdarpasic at Theater Münster). One newspaper calls the Cologne version, which retained the visual association with 1930s New York, 'too innocent, picturesque, traditional'.[102] In Gelsenkirchen, the direction of Gil Mehmert was described as 'old fashioned [and] indecisive', whereas in the student production in Munich there was 'no trace of the New York slums—even the [trash] bins are sparkling clean. We don't see a critical view of a difficult milieu but a lively, light-hearted soap'.[103] For the Hannover production—one of the best-received of recent years—the director Bernd Mottl chose a gymnasium with camp beds as the claustrophobic space shared by people of different social and cultural backgrounds. It is reminiscent of both emergency shelters used in natural disasters and refugees' makeshift accommodations. In Dresden the performance was embedded in the context of the exhibition Verstummte Stimmen (Silenced Voices), which commemorated artists persecuted during the era of National Socialism. This connection especially made the production's overly cautious approach, criticised in several reviews, questionable.

The *Frankfurter Allgemeine Zeitung* is among the very few media outlets to highlight the parallels between Weill's German and American works, stating that *Street Scene* combines 'the old critical view on capitalism' and 'a life-long love of the world of entertainment', combined in a more 'complex' score than a first impression might suggest. Accordingly, the concluding evaluation of Bettina Bruinier's 'uninspired' direction was unfavourable. 'In this country', writes Julia Spinola, 'the boundaries between high artistic standards and entertainment seem often insurmountable'.[104] Other authors and critics also lament that directors don't dig deep enough but instead readily reproduce musical theatre clichés. The productions at the Staatsoperette Dresden, a theatre which deserves credit for regularly choosing to present obscure material, are often accused of offering simplistic, comfortable readings. *One Touch of Venus*, presented as *Ein Hauch von Venus*, was reportedly performed satisfactorily by the house orchestra but was deemed superficial and flat in its direction. For the *Dresdner Neueste Nachrichten*, the production's failure to assume a position on the piece's gender issues was unforgivable: 'Modifying the plot would have added a lot of humour. After all, there is some good comedy in its lyrics, which remains unmined here.' The verdict was scathing: '[T]here shouldn't be stagings like this anymore'.[105] The *Sächsische Zeitung* emphasised the plot's potential for 'contemporary relevance', highlighting its discussions of a woman's role in a patriarchal society and the negotiations between personal freedom and economic security. These 'stories, that sleep underneath the surface and could give the work some depth, have not been awakened', the newspaper concludes. Under the direction of Matthias Davids, *One Touch of Venus* is described as a 'light comedy', with some of the jokes—such as Anatole brandishing a knife—'on the cusp of tastelessness'.[106]

When bringing *The Firebrand of Florence* to Dresden in 2013, the Staatsoperette was surely aware of the work's difficult performance history in America. Its plot, revolving

FIG. 16.2 Scene from the 2014 Hannover production of *Street Scene* with soloist Ania Vegry. Photo: Thomas Jauk, courtesy of the photographer.

around the Italian anarchist artist Cellini, was too un-American, its genre identity as European-style operetta controversial towards the end of World War II.[107] In Dresden, the reservations about the work could not be eliminated. The general impression was, once again, that direction and the ensemble's performance alike failed do justice to either the score or the book. Although the costumes and stage design were 'opulent', with the ballet in Renaissance dress and the leading lady's 'Marlene Dietrich look', the direction exhausted the use of cheap comedy tricks, with 'every gag being overplayed'.[108]

Two examples of successful rediscoveries are Weill's unfinished *Tom Sawyer and Huckleberry Finn* and the German première of *Love Life*. Weill was in the midst of adapting Mark Twain's famous novel when he died prematurely in 1950. The work survives as a fragment, with only five completed songs. In the early 2010s the German publisher Felix Bloch Erben and the KWF commissioned John von Düffel to write a new book, which was combined with the existing music and other Weill songs from his

FIG. 16.3 Scene from the 2017 German première of *Love Life* (1948) at the Theater Freiburg. Photo: Birgit Hupfelt, courtesy of the photographer.

American period to create a new work suitable for children.[109] The piece, which offers a critical perspective on segregation in American society, premiered in Göttingen and Basel in 2014 and was produced again in 2016 at the Landestheater Detmold. There the score was performed in arrangements by Wolfgang Böhmer, and the press remarked upon the score's 'sound panopticon' and praised the 'whimsical characters, slapstick comedy, macabre humour, and clever wordplay.'[110]

The production of *Love Life* in Freiburg was truly a surprise hit. It embraced the referentiality of the original by playing with the ideas and concepts Germans have of American culture and its icons. Audiences saw a dance routine modelled on the films of Ginger Rogers and Fred Astaire, a character dressed as Groucho Marx, and evocations of some of Hollywood's biggest successes—*Modern Times* (1936), *Gone with the Wind* (1939), *Casablanca* (1943)—projected as film sequences on a cyclorama. The press not only enthused about the visual feast, but also recognised the work's undercurrents of surprisingly modern thought, which include 'women's rights, equality, and criticism of capitalism.'[111] The reviewer Andreas Hauff came to the conclusion that '[u]pon closer inspection, *The Threepenny Opera* is much more entertaining than one might have thought, and *Love Life* contains more social critique than one might expect.'[112]

# CONCLUSION

In German-language countries, well-crafted, popular operetta of the so-called silver age has seen a comeback, with ambitious productions in recent years spearheaded by Barrie Kosky's sharp, frivolous interpretations of Paul Abraham and Oscar Straus pieces. The director has included an evening of Weill's American songs in the 2019–2020 season at the Komische Oper in Berlin, with the blurb in the season brochure assuring us that Weill's compositions for the American theatre 'are no less revolutionary than those he wrote in Germany'. Kosky's programming, which is decidedly unapologetic about its transgressing of the still-established boundaries between 'E' and 'U' music, has found many admirers. Inclusive concepts such as Kosky's question traditional views of the operatic canon, and of perceptions of what should be included in it and what should not. This development is encouraging and gives reason for hope that eventually artistic directors and theatre critics will fully overcome the idea of the two Kurt Weills, one belonging to 'us' and one belonging to 'them'. Especially in the composer's native country, his American works deserve more than 'conservatory care' or a mere reproduction of worn-out musical theatre clichés. The German theatre and opera sector receives a level of public funding that is unmatched in Europe and elsewhere. With the subsidy comes a *Bildungsauftrag* (mandate to educate)—a responsibility to widen the repertoire and enable access to neglected works and their composers. There is still great potential for subsidised venues of diverse sizes and remits to respond to Weill's American oeuvre with innovative and brave readings, critical rigour, and, of course, joy.

## NOTES

The author would like to thank David Stein and Elmar Juchem at the Kurt Weill Foundation, JÜrgen Hartmann at the publisher Musik und Bühne, Heiko Cullmann at Concord Theatricals (previously at Staatsoperette), as well as the Theater Hagen and the Staatsoper Hannover for providing press materials and other documents.

1. Kurt Weill, 'What Is Musical Theatre?', unpublished typescript, 1936, archived at the Yale University Music Library, provided as a scan by the Kurt Weill Foundation.
2. In 1955 Hans Heinz Stuckenschmidt admitted that 'of all German musicians that emigrated after 1933, Kurt Weill has eluded us the most.' Quoted in Gisela Maria Schubert, 'Ein Weg, seinen Ruf zu verlieren? Zur deutschen Rezeption von Kurt Weills *Street Scene*', in *Die Rezeption des Broadwaymusicals in Deutschland*, ed. Nils Grosch and Elmar Juchem, Veröffentlichungen der Kurt-Weill-Gesellschaft (Dessau: Waxman, 2012), 104.
3. Information provided by the German publisher of these works, Musik & Bühne.
4. Kurt Weill, 'Gibt es eine Krise in der Oper?', *Neues Wiener Journal* (April 1932), reprinted in *Kurt Weill: Musik und musikalisches Theater; Gesammelte Schriften*, ed. Stephen Hinton, Jürgen Schebera, and Elmar Juchem (Mainz: Schott, 2000), 137.
5. German theatres or opera houses with permanent ensembles and regular performance schedules typically receive major subsidy from public funds, either administered by the city or federal states of residence (*Stadttheater* vs. *Staatstheater*). A third type is the *Landestheater*. Companies of this category are funded by their federal states of residence but are required to perform more than 50 percent of their season on smaller regional stages.
6. Weill, 'Gibt es eine Krise in der Oper?'
7. See e.g. 'Bekenntnis zur Oper', programme for *Der Protagonist*, March 1926, reprinted in *Kurt Weill: Musik und musikalisches Theater; Gesammelte Schriften*, ed. Stephen Hinton, Jürgen Schebera, and Elmar Juchem (Mainz: Schott, 2000), 45–49.
8. Kurt Weill, 'Korrespondenz über *Dreigroschenoper*', *Anbruch* 11 (January 1929): 24–25, reprinted in *Kurt Weill: Ein Leben in Bildern und Dokumenten*, ed. David Farneth, Elmar Juchem, and Dave Stein (Berlin: Ullstein, 2000), 98.
9. Ibid. Weill was deeply influenced by his teacher Ferruccio Busoni and his experiments with musical theatre. For more details, see Stephen Hinton, *Weill's Musical Theatre: Stages of Reform* (Berkeley and Los Angeles: University of California Press, 2012), 37–65.
10. Kurt Weill, 'Verschiebungen in der musikalischen Produktion', *Berliner Tageblatt*, 1 October 1927, reprinted in *Kurt Weill: Musik und musikalisches Theater; Gesammelte Schriften*, ed. Stephen Hinton, Jürgen Schebera, and Elmar Juchem (Mainz: Schott, 2000), 61. This and the following quotations have been translated by the author.
11. Ronald Taylor, *Kurt Weill: Composer in a Divided World* (New York: Simon & Schuster, 1991), 304–306.
12. Virgil Thomson, 'Kurt Weill Concert', *New York Herald Tribune* (February 1951), quoted in Kim Kowalke, 'Kurt Weill, Modernism, and Popular Culture: Öffentlichkeit als Stil', *Modernism/Modernity* 2, no. 1 (January 1995): 28.
13. David Drew, 'Kurt Weill', in *The New Grove Dictionary of Music and Musicians*, ed. Stanley Sadie (London: MacMillan, 1980), 20:307.
14. Ibid.
15. David Drew, 'Reflections of the Last Years: *Der Kuhhandel* as a Key Work', in *A New Orpheus: Essays on Kurt Weill*, ed. Kim H. Kowalke (New Haven, CT: Yale University Press, 1986), 218; and Gisela Maria Schubert, 'Ein Weg, seinen Ruf zu verlieren?', 102. The original article by Adorno is reprinted in *Kurt Weill: Ein Leben in Bildern und Dokumenten*, ed. David Farneth, Elmar Juchem, and Dave Stein (Berlin: Ullstein, 2000), 286. David Drew has translated the complete article into English; see Drew, 'Reflections of the Last Years', 218–219.
16. Drew, 'Reflections of the Last Years', 218–219.
17. Gisela Maria Schubert, 'Ein Weg, seinen Ruf zu verlieren?', 102–103.

18. Stephen Hinton, 'The Première and After', in *Kurt Weill: The Threepenny Opera*, ed. Stephen Hinton, Cambridge Opera Handbooks (Cambridge: Cambridge University Press, 1990), 50–55.

19. Brecht revealed this in an interview from ca. 1933, which survives as an undated document in the Bertolt Brecht Archive, Archiv der Akademie der Künste, BBA 461/93. Quoted in Kim H. Kowalke, 'The Threepenny Opera in America', in *Kurt Weill: The Threepenny Opera*, ed. Stephen Hinton, Cambridge Opera Handbooks (Cambridge: Cambridge University Press, 1990), 78.

20. These included the film and theatre director Erich Engels, the composer Theo Mackeben as conductor, and the scenographer Caspar Neher.

21. Elmar Juchem, *Kurt Weill und Maxwell Anderson: Neue Wege zu einem amerikanischen Musiktheater, 1938–1950*, Veröffentlichungen der Kurt-Weill-Gesellschaft Dessau 4 (Stuttgart: Metzler Verlag, 2000), 86.

22. Weill, 'Korrespondenz über Dreigroschenoper'.

23. Nils Grosch, 'Oper als Strategie der kompositorischen Selbstinszenierung und Wertbegriff: *Street Scene* (1946) und *West Side Story* (1957)', in *In Search of the Great American Opera: Tendenzen des amerikanischen Musiktheaters*, ed. Fréderic Döhl and Gregor Herzfeld (Münster: Waxmann, 2016), 101–112.

24. Stephen Hinton draws a connection between Busoni's concept of *Urform* and Weill's continued engagement with the problem of form. See Hinton, 'Weill's Musical Theatre', 48.

25. Undated typescript, used without title in the liner notes to the original cast album of *Street Scene*, quoted in ibid.

26. Weill, 'What Is Musical Theatre?'

27. See, for example, Ursula Säkel, *Der US-Film in der Weimarer Republik: Ein Medium der 'Amerikanisierung'?* (Paderborn: Schöningh Verlag, 2008), 27–35.

28. Kaspar Maase, *Grenzenloses Vergnügen: Der Aufstieg der Massenkultur 1850–1970* (Frankfurt am Main: Fischer, 2007), 115–173, provides a good overview of the dawn of mass culture and 'cultural Americanisation' in Germany.

29. He also commented on the influence of jazz on composition in his 'Notiz zum Jazz', *Monatsschrift für moderne Musik* 9 (March 1929): 138. Reprinted in *Kurt Weill: Musik und musikalisches Theater; Gesammelte Schriften*, ed. Stephen Hinton, Jürgen Schebera, and Elmar Juchem (Mainz: Schott, 2000), 82–83.

30. See, for example, Kevin Clarke, *Im Himmel tanzt auch schon die Jazzband: Emmerich Kalman und die transatlantische Operette* (Neumünster: Bockel Verlag, 2007), 19 and 128–129. Edward Latham wrote that the 'influence of Gershwin on Weill cannot be overestimated'. (Edward Latham, *Tonality as Drama: Closure and Interruption in Four Twentieth-century American Operas* [Denton: University of North Texas Press, 2008], 139–164.

31. Film reviews include Kurt London, *Der Film* 42, 18 October 1930; and *Film-Kurier* 245, 16 October 1930.

32. Christoph Zimmermann, *Opera* (January 2010).

33. David Farneth, Elmar Juchem, and Dave Stein, eds., *Kurt Weill: Ein Leben in Bildern und Dokumenten* (Berlin: Ullstein, 2000), 194.

34. See the quote at the very beginning of this chapter.

35. See Lotte H. Eisner, 'Musikalische Illustration oder Filmmusik?', *Film-Kurier*, 13 October 1927; and Stephen Hinton, *Weill's Musical Theatre*, 321–350.

36. Quoted in ibid.

37. Weill, 'What Is Musical Theatre?'

38. Kurt London, 'Weill-Neher's *Bürgschaft*', *Der Film* 11 (12 March 1932).

39. For a detailed insight into Weill's French years and his engagement with French music, see Andreas Eichborn, ed., *Kurt Weill und Frankreich* (Münster: Waxman, 2014).

40. Since 2000 it has seen at least nine new German productions. See www.operabase.com, acessed 10 August 2019.

41. Gisela Maria Schubert, 'Ein Weg, seinen Ruf zu verlieren?', 96.

42. Markus Schwering, *Kölner Stadtanzeiger*, 29 April 2019.

43. Pedro Obiera, *Aachener Zeitung*, 29 April 2019.

44. Kurt Weill, 'Über meine Tätigkeit seit 1933' and 'Zwei Träume werden wahr' ('Two Dreams Coming True'), undated typescripts, reprinted in *Kurt Weill: Musik und musikalisches Theater; Gesammelte Schriften*, ed. Stephen Hinton, Jürgen Schebera, and Elmar Juchem (Mainz: Schott, 2000), 202 and 183.

45. Gisela Maria Schubert, 'Ein Weg, seinen Ruf zu verlieren?', 95.

46. See Grosch, 'Oper als Strategie', 102–110.

47. Gisela Maria Schubert, 'Ein Weg, seinen Ruf zu verlieren?', 99.

48. Christoph Zimmermann, *Online Merker*, 29 April 2019; Bernhard Hartmann, *Generalanzeiger Bonn*, 30 April 2019; and Jutta Rinas, *Hannoversche Allgemeine Zeitung*, 4 November 2013.

49. Elisabeth Höving, *Der Westen*, 24 September 2012; and Albrecht Dümling, *Frankfurter Allgemeine Zeitung*, 14 March 2000.

50. Thomas Hilgemeier, *Theater Pur—theaterpur.net*, 4 October 2012; and Marieluise Jeitschko, *Giessener Allgemeine Zeitung*, 9 September 2009; and Robert Braunmüller, *Abendzeitung München*, 15 February 2011.

51. Marie Stapel, *Terzwerk—terzwerk.de*, 25 December 2008.

52. Deborrah Triantafyllidis, *Stadtspiegel Gelsenkirchen*, 3 October 2012.

53. Hannes S. Macher, *Donaukurier*, 14 February 2011.

54. Werner Häußner, *Online Merker*, 9 January 2019.

55. Stefan Drees, *Klassik.com*, 7 September 2009.

56. Georg-Friedrich Kühn, *Deutschland Radio Kultur—Dradio.de*, broadcast, 20 June 2011.

57. According to Giselher Schubert, *The Firebrand of Florence* is an 'operetta', *One Touch of Venus* a 'conventional musical', *Street Scene* an 'American opera', *Love Life* a 'concept musical', and *Lost in the Stars* a 'musical tragedy'. Giselher Schubert, 'Der angepasste Komponist, Kurt Weill in der Fremde', in '*. . . wie es uns gefällt': Kurt Weill, 'The Firebrand of Florence'; Eine Werkmonografie in Texten und Dokumenten*, ed. Heiko Cullmann and Michael Heinemann (Dresden: Staatsoperette, 2014), 85.

58. Michael Baumgartner, 'Kurt Weills *One Touch of Venus* in Deutschland', in *Die Rezeption des Broadwaymusicals in Deutschland*, ed. Nils Grosch and Elmar Juchem, Veröffentlichungen der Kurt-Weill-Gesellschaft (Dessau: Waxman, 2012), 109.

59. Roland Dippel, *nmz—Neue Musikzeitung online*, 27 June 2019.

60. Jens Daniel Schubert, *Sächsische Zeitung*, 24 June 2019.

61. Boris Gruhl, *mdr.de*, 23 June 2019.

62. Alexander Dick, *Opernwelt*, February 2018.

63. Bernhard Uske, *Frankfurter Rundschau*, 19 May 2014; and Rainer Nolden, *Die deutsche Bühne online*, 19 May 2014.

64. Benedikt Stegemann, *Frankfurter Allgemeine Zeitung*, 19 May 2014.

65. Manuel Brug, *Die Welt*, 17 October 2011.

66. Egbert Tholl, *Süddeutsche Zeitung*, 17 October 2011.

67. The German reception of the Broadway musical has been troubled since the first works began to appear on German repertory lists after World War II. The reluctance with which art critics began to approach a genre that felt 'foreign' in style and thematic outlook was mirrored in academic musicological writing and university teaching, which for several decades ignored or even dismissed the musical as unworthy of scholarly scrutiny. Even in the 2000s, art critics are much more comfortable with referencing the established repertoire of opera and theatre when reviewing musicals. Despite a veritable boom in musicals commencing in the 1980s, familiarity with the canon of Broadway musicals seems still limited. For more information, see, for example, Nils Grosch and Elmar Juchem, eds., *Die Rezeption des Broadwaymusicals in Deutschland*, Veröffentlichungen der Kurt-Weill-Gesellschaft (Dessau: Waxman, 2012).
68. Eleonore Büning, *Frankfurter Allgemeine Zeitung*, 12 March 2004.
69. Rainer Wolff, *Pforzheimer Zeitung*, 25 January 2016.
70. Albrecht Thiemann, *Opernwelt*, August 2011.
71. Christoph Zimmermann, *Online Merker*, 29 April 2019.
72. Julia Spinola, *Frankfurter Allgemeine Zeitung*, 22 June 2011.
73. Ibid.
74. Elisabeth Höving, *Der Westen*, 29 September 2012.
75. Monika Klein, *Rheinische Post*, 1-2 May 2010; and Gerhard Bauer, *Leverkusener Anzeiger*, 29 April 2010. Several other reviews, however, highlighted the 'nuanced' musical direction of conductor Ludwig—for instance, Stefan Drees, *Klassik.com*, 7 September 2009, and Martin Schrahn, *Westdeutsche Allgemeine Zeitung*, 6 September 2009.
76. Isabel Herfeld, *Frankfurter Allgemeine Zeitung*, 12 March 2005; and Christian Schmidt, *Freie Presse Chemnitz*, 24 June 2019.
77. Manuel Brug, *Die Welt*, 17 October 2011. The expression used by Brug may refer on the one hand to the lack of experience of many opera orchestras when playing scores from the musical theatre spectrum, and on the other to general working conditions in the German *Stadttheater* system. In the latter case, reasons for the 'sedateness' he claims to have detected could be twofold: first, theatres subsidised by local municipalities perform a great variety of repertoire throughout the year, with a break only between seasons in the summer. The lack of energy he hears may therefore stem from weariness. Secondly, if the pit sounds tired, that may be because of the stable work conditions and strong union protections enjoyed by opera orchestras and choruses. Many singers and instrumental players work on the same position until retirement age and are arguably prone to lose some of their pizzazz along the way.
78. Rainer Wolff, *Pforzheimer Zeitung*, 25 January 2016; and Gisela Maria Schubert, *Kurt Weill Newsletter* 2, no. 32 (June 2014).
79. Rainer Nolden, *Deutsche Bühne online*, 19 May 2014.
80. For a detailed account of this case, see John Rockwell, 'Kurt Weill's Operatic Reform and Its Context', in *A New Orpheus: Essays on Kurt Weill*, ed. Kim H. Kowalke (New Haven, CT: Yale University Press, 1986), pp. 51–61.
81. Kurt Weill, letter to to Lotte Lenya, 7 January1950, quoted in Juchem, *Kurt Weill und Maxwell Anderson*, p. 126.
82. Kevin Clarke, *Klassik.com*, 5 March 2011.
83. Ibid. Bundeswettbewerb Gesang is an annual German singing competition, which specialises in musicals and chanson every second year. The competition, which recruits candidates from all over Germany, is funded by the mayor of Berlin, the federal government, and several trusts and foundations.

84. Karsten Mark, *Ruhr-Nachrichten*, 23 September 2012.

85. Georg-Friedrich Kühn, *Deutschland Radio Kultur—Dradio.de*. broadcast, 20 June 2011.

86. The work, by Weill and Franz Werfel, was originally performed in New York under the direction of Max Reinhardt. Other recent discoveries presented at the Kurt Weill Fest were *Johnny Johnson* (2002) and, in 2007, *Down in the Valley*. Since then, neither of these pieces has been presented in a full production.

87. Kevin Clarke, *Klassik.com*, 5 March 2011.

88. Andreas Hillger, *Mitteldeusche Zeitung*, 7 March 2010.

89. Elisabeth Höving, *Der Westen*, 24 September 2012; Werner Häußner, *Online Merker*, 9 January 2019; Egbert Tholl, *Süddeutsche Zeitung*, 26 June 2011; and Albrecht Thiemann, *Opernwelt*, August 2011.

90. Egbert Tholl, *Süddeutsche Zeitung*, 17 Octobber 2011.

91. Michael Ernst, *nmz—Neue Musikzeitung online*, 27 October 2013.

92. Manuel Brug, *Die Welt*, 4 November 2013.

93. Christian Schmidt, *Freie Presse Chemnitz*, 24 June 2019.

94. Andreas Hauff, *nmz—Neue Musikzeitung online*, 2 February 2018.

95. Weihe, email to Michael Baumgartner, 19 January 2008, quoted in Baumgartner, 'Kurt Weills *One Touch of Venus* in Deutschland', 120.

96. Ibid.

97. Markus Schwering, *Kölner Stadtanzeiger*, 29 April 2019.

98. *Die Welt*, 27 November 1948, quoted in Juchem, *Kurt Weill und Maxwell Anderson*, 26.

99. Jens Frederiksen, *Allgemeine Zeitung—Rhein-Main Presse*, 19 May 2014.

100. Andreas Hauff, *Dreigroschenheft*, January 2012.

101. Statistic from https://mediendienst-integration.de/migration/flucht-asyl/zahl-der-fluec htlinge.html, accessed 02 July 2023.

102. Markus Schwering, *Kölner Stadtanzeiger*, 29 April 2019.

103. Hannes S. Macher, *Donaukurier*, 14 February 2011.

104. Julia Spinola, *Frankfurter Allgemeine Zeitung*, 22 June 2011.

105. Rico Stehfest, *Dresdner Neueste Nachrichten*, 24 June 2019.

106. Christian Schmidt, *Freie Presse Chemnitz*, 24 June 2019.

107. For a detailed overview of the American and early German reception history, see Walter Schmitz, 'Vermiedene Apokalypse, enttäuschter Amerikanismus: Zu Misserfolg und Nicht-Rezeption von Kurt Weills *The Firebrand of Florence*', in '*. . . wie es uns gefällt': Kurt Weill, 'The Firebrand of Florence'; Eine Werkmonografie in Texten und Dokumenten*, ed. Heiko Cullmann and Michael Heinemann (Dresden: Staatsoperette, 2014), 93–120.

108. Jens Daniel Schubert, *Sächsische Zeitung*, 28 October 2013.

109. www.felix-bloch-erben.de/tom_sawyer_und_huckleberry_finn, accessed 19 August 2019.

110. Ilse Franz-Nevermann, *Lippische Landeszeitung*, 20 March 2016.

111. Alexander Dick, *Badische Zeitung*, 11 December2017; and Gerd Rudiger, *Neue Zürcher Zeitung*, 11 December 2017.

112. Andreas Hauff, *nmz—Neue Musikzeitung online*, 2 February 2018.

## BIBLIOGRAPHY

Baumgartner, Michael. 'Kurt Weill's *One Touch of Venus* in Deutschland'. In *Die Rezeption des Broadwaymusicals in Deutschland*, edited by Nils Grosch and Elmar Juchem, 109–132. Veröffentlichungen der Kurt-Weill-Gesellschaft. Münster: Waxman, 2012.

Clarke, Kevin. *Im Himmel tanzt auch schon die Jazzband: Emmerich Kalman und die transatlantische Operette*. Neumünster: Bockel Verlag, 2007.

Cullmann, Heiko, Michael Heinemann, and Staatsoperette Dresden, eds. '... *wie es uns gefällt': Kurt Weill, 'The Firebrand of Florence'; Eine Werkmonografie in Texten und Dokumenten*. Dresden: Thelem, 2014.

Drew, David. 'Kurt Weill'. In *The New Grove Dictionary of Music and Musicians*, edited by Stanley Sadie, 20:300–310. London: MacMillan, 1980.

Drew, David. 'Reflections of the Last Years: *Der Kuhhandel* as a Key Work'. In *A New Orpheus: Essays on Kurt Weill*, edited by Kim Kowalke, 217–267. New Haven, CT: Yale University Press, 1986.

Eichborn, Andreas, ed. *Kurt Weill und Frankreich*. Münster: Waxman, 2014.

Farneth, David, Elmar Juchem, and Dave Stein, eds. *Kurt Weill: Ein Leben in Bildern und Dokumenten*. Berlin: Ullstein, 2000.

Grosch, Nils. 'Oper als Strategie der kompositorischen Selbstinszenierung und Wertbegriff: *Street Scene* (1946) und *West Side Story* (1957)'. In *In Search of the Great American Opera: Tendenzen des amerikanischen Musiktheaters*, edited by Fréderic Döhl and Gregor Herzfeld, 101–112. Münster: Waxmann, 2016.

Grosch, Nils, and Elmar Juchem, eds. *Die Rezeption des Broadwaymusicals in Deutschland*. Veröffentlichungen der Kurt-Weill-Gesellschaft. Dessau: Waxman, 2012.

Hinton, Stephen. *Weill's Musical Theatre: Stages of Reform*. Los Angeles: University of California Press, 2012.

Hinton, Stephen, Jürgen Schebera, and Elmar Juchem, eds. *Kurt Weill: Musik und musikalisches Theater; Gesammelte Schriften*. Mainz: Schott, 2000.

Hinton, Stephen. 'The `Première and After'. In *Kurt Weill: The Threepenny Opera*, edited by Stephen Hinton, 50–77. Cambridge Opera Handbooks. Cambridge: Cambridge University Press, 1990.

Juchem, Elmar. *Kurt Weill und Maxwell Anderson: Neue Wege zu einem amerikanischen Musiktheater, 1938–1950*. Veröffentlichungen der Kurt-Weill-Gesellschaft Dessau 4. Stuttgart: Metzler Verlag, 2000.

Kowalke, Kim. 'Kurt Weill, Modernism, and Popular Culture: Öffentlichkeit als Stil'. *Modernism/Modernity* 1, no. 2 (1995): 27–58.

Kowalke, Kim H. 'The *Threepenny Opera* in America'. In *Kurt Weill: The Threepenny Opera*, edited by Stephen Hinton, 78–119. Cambridge Opera Handbooks. Cambridge: Cambridge University Press, 1990.

Kowalke, Kim H., ed. *A New Orpheus: Essays on Kurt Weill*. New Haven, CT: Yale University Press, 1986.

Latham, Edward. *Tonality as Drama: Closure and Interruption in Four Twentieth-Century American Operas*. Denton: University of North Texas Press, 2008.

Maase, Kaspar. *Grenzenloses Vergnügen: Der Aufstieg der Massenkultur 1850–1970*. Frankfurt am Main: Fischer, 2007.

Rockwell, John. 'Kurt Weill's Operatic Reform and Its Context'. In *A New Orpheus: Essays on Kurt Weill*, edited by Kim H. Kowalke, 51–59. New Haven, CT: Yale University Press, 1986.

Säkel, Ursula. *Der US-Film in der Weimarer Republik: Ein Medium der 'Amerikanisierung'?* Paderborn: Schöningh Verlag, 2008.

Schmitz, Walter. 'Vermiedene Apokalypse, enttäuschter Amerikanismus: Zu Misserfolg und Nicht-Rezeption von Kurt Weills *The Firebrand of Florence*'. In '... *wie es uns gefällt': Kurt Weill, 'The Firebrand of Florence': Eine Werkmonografie in Texten und Dokumenten*, edited by Heiko Cullmann, Michael Heinemann, and Staatsoperette Dresden, 93–120. Dresden: Thelem, 2014.

Schubert, Gisela Maria. 'Ein Weg, seinen Ruf zu verlieren? Zur deutschen Rezeption von Kurt Weills *Street Scene*'. In *Die Rezeption des Broadwaymusicals in Deutschland*, edited by Nils Grosch and Elmar Juchem, 95–108. Veröffentlichungen der Kurt-Weill-Gesellschaft. Dessau: Waxman, 2012.

Schubert, Giselher. 'Der angepasste Komponist: Kurt Weill in der Fremde'. In ' ... *wie es uns gefällt': Kurt Weill, 'The Firebrand of Florence'; Eine Werkmonografie in Texten und Dokumenten*, edited by Heiko Cullmann, Michael Heinemann, and Staatsoperette Dresden, 73–92. Dresden: Thelem, 2014.

Taylor, Robert. *Kurt Weill: Composer in a Divided World*. New York: Simon & Schuster, 1991.

Weill, Kurt. 'What Is Musical Theatre?'. Typescript, 1936. Yale University Music Library Archive.

Weill, Kurt. 'Gibt es eine Krise in der Oper?' In *Kurt Weill: Musik und musikalisches Theater; Gesammelte Schriften*, edited by Stephen Hinton, Jürgen Schebera, and Elmar Juchem, 137–138. Mainz: Schott, 2000. Originally published in April 1932.

Weill, Kurt. 'Notiz zum Jazz'. *Monatsschrift für moderne Musik* 11, no. 9 (March 1929): 138.

Weill, Kurt. 'Korrespondenz über Dreigroschenoper'. In *Kurt Weill: Ein Leben in Bildern und Dokumenten*, edited by David Farneth, Elmar Juchem, and Dave Stein, 98. Berlin: Ullstein, 2000. Originally published in January 1929.

Weill, Kurt. 'Verschiebungen in der musikalischen Produktion'. In *Kurt Weill: Musik und musikalisches Theater; Gesammelte Schriften*, edited by Stephen Hinton, Jürgen Schebera, and Elmar Juchem, 61. Mainz: Schott, 2000. Originally published in October 1927.

Weill, Kurt. 'Verschiebungen in der musikalischen Produktion'. *Berliner Tageblatt*, October 1927. Reprinted in *Kurt Weill: Musik und musikalisches Theater; Gesammelte Schriften*, edited by Stephen Hinton, Jürgen Schebera, and Elmar Juchem, 61–64. Mainz: Schott, 2000.

Weill, Kurt. 'Bekenntnis zur Oper', program for *Der Protagonist*. In *Kurt Weill: Musik und musikalisches Theater; Gesammelte Schriften*, edited by Stephen Hinton, Jürgen Schebera, and Elmar Juchem, 45–49. Mainz: Schott, 2000. Originally published in March 1926.

Weill, Kurt. 'Über meine Tätigkeit seit 1933', undated typescript. In *Kurt Weill: Musik und musikalisches Theater; Gesammelte Schriften*, edited by Stephen Hinton, Jürgen Schebera, and Elmar Juchem, 202. Mainz: Schott, 2000. 202.

Weill, Kurt. 'Zwei Träume werden wahr', undated typescript. In *Kurt Weill: Musik und musikalisches Theater; Gesammelte Schriften*, edited by Stephen Hinton, Jürgen Schebera, and Elmar Juchem, 182–184. Mainz: Schott, 2000.

## Archives and Collections

Kurt Weill Foundation New York
Online Archive Frankfurter Allgemeine Zeitung
Süddeutsche Zeitung Archiv
Musik und Bühne Press Collection
Press reviews from Staatsoper Hannover, Theater Hagen, Staatsoperette Dresden

## Press Articles and Radio Features

Bauer, Gerhard. *Leverkusener Anzeiger*, 29 April 2010.

Braunmüller, Robert. *Abendzeitung München*, 15 February 2011.
Brug, Manuel. *Die Welt*, 4 November 2013.
Brug, Manuel. *Die Welt*, 17 October 2011.
Büning, Eleonore. *Frankfurter Allgemeine Zeitung*, 12 March 2004.
Clarke, Kevin. *Klassik.com*, 5 March 2011.
Dick, Alexander. *Opernwelt*, February 2018.
Dick, Alexander. *Badische Zeitung*, 11 December 2017.
Dippel, Roland. *nmz—Neue Musikzeitung online*, 27 June 2019.
Drees, Stefan. *Klassik.com*, 7 September 2009.
Dümling, Albrecht. *Frankfurter Allgemeine Zeitung*, 14 March 2000.
Ernst, Michael. *nmz—Neue Musikzeitung online*, 27 October 2013.
*Film-Kurier* 245, 16 October 1930.
Franz-Nevermann, Ilse. *Lippische Landeszeitung*, 20 March 2016.
Frederiksen, Jens. *Allgemeine Zeitung—Rein-Main Presse*, 19 May 2014.
Hartmann, Bernhard. *Generalanzeiger Bonn*, 30 April 2019.
Hauff, Andreas. *nmz—Neue Musikzeitung online*, 2 February 2018.
Herfeld, Isabel. *Frankfurter Allgemeine Zeitung*, 12 March 2005.
Klein, Monika. *Rheinische Post*, 1–2 May 2010.
Gruhl, Boris. *mdr.de*, 23 June 2019.
Häußner, Werner. *Online Merker*, 11 January 2019.
Hilgemeier, Thomas. *Theater Pur—theaterpur.net*, 4 October 2012.
Hillger, Andreas. *Mitteldeusche Zeitung*, 7 March 2010.
Höving, Elisabeth. *Der Westen*, 24 September 2012.
Jeitschko, Marieluise. *Giessener Allgemeine Zeitung*, 9 September 2009.
Kühn, Georg-Friedrich. *Deutschland Radio Kultur—Dradio.de*. Broadcast, 20 June 2011.
London, Kurt. 'Weill—Nehers "Bürgschaft"', *Der Film* 11, 12 March 1932, p. 5.
London, Kurt. *Der Film* 42, 18 October 1930, p. 3.
Macher, Hannes S. *Donaukurier*, 14 February 2011.
Mark, Karsten. *Ruhr-Nachrichten*, 23 September 2012.
Nolden, Rainer. *Deutsche Bühne online*, 19 May 2014.
Obiera, Pedro. *Aachener Zeitung*, 29 April 2019.
Rinas, Jutta. *Hannoversche Allgemeine Zeitung*, 4 November 2013.
Rudiger, Gerd. *Neue Zürcher Zeitung*, 11 December 2017.
Schmidt, Christian. *Freie Presse Chemnitz*, 24 June 2019.
Schrahn, Martin. *Westdeutsche Allgemeine Zeitung*, 6 September 2009.
Schubert, Jens Daniel. *Sächsische Zeitung*, 24 June 2019.
Schubert, Jens Daniel. *Sächsische Zeitung*, 28 October 2013.
Schwering, Markus. *Kölner Stadtanzeiger*, 29 April 2019.
Spinola, Julia. *Frankfurter Allgemeine Zeitung*, 22 June 2011.
Stapel, Marie. *Terzwerk—terzwerk.de*, 25 December 2008.
Stegemann, Benedikt. *Frankfurter Allgemeine Zeitung*, 19 May 2014.
Stehfest, Rico. *Dresdner Neueste Nachrichten*, 24 June 2019.
Thiemann, Albrecht. *Opernwelt*, August 2011.
Tholl, Egbert. *Süddeutsche Zeitung*, 17 October 2011.
Tholl, Egbert. *Süddeutsche Zeitung*, 26 June 2011.
Triantafyllidis, Deborrah. *Stadtspiegel Gelsenkirchen*, 3 October 2012.
Uske, Bernhard. *Frankfurter Rundschau*, 19 May 2014.

Wolff, Rainer. *Pforzheimer Zeitung*, 25 January 2016.
Zimmermann, Christoph. *Online Merker*, 29 April 2019.
Zimmermann, Christoph. *Opera*, January 2010.
Zimmermann, Christoph. *Online Merker*, 29 April 2019.

## Websites

www.felix-bloch-erben.de/tom_sawyer_und_huckleberry_finn, accessed 19 August 2019.
www.operabase.com, accessed 10 August 2019.
https://mediendienst-integration.de/migration/flucht-asyl/zahl-der-fluechtlinge.html,
    accessed 24 August 2019.
https://www.sueddeutsche.de/archiv, accessed 1 August 2019.
https://fazarchiv.faz.net, accessed 5 August 2019.
www.klassik.com, accessed 18 August 2019.

CHAPTER 17

# 'EV'RY HOTSY TOTSY NAZI STAND AND CHEER'

## *Cultural Sensitivity to Musicals about the Third Reich*

NILS GROSCH AND SUSANNE SCHEIBLHOFER

## INTRODUCTION

'THE Holocaust is not a topic that can be turned into a musical', Buddy Elias asserted in 2008 on the occasion of the production of *El diario de Ana Frank: Un canto a la vida* (*The Diary of Anne Frank: A Song to Life*) at Madrid's Calderón theatre, a musical produced and authored by the playwright Rafael Alvero and the composer José Luis Tierno.[1] Elias, a Swiss actor and a cousin of the Holocaust victim Anne Frank, who had been murdered in the concentration camp Bergen-Belsen in 1945, did not criticise the show directly. Rather, he emphasised the incompatibility of the genre of the commercial musical theatre itself with the topic: 'It is impossible! The life of Anne Frank and the Holocaust as a merry night with song and dance'.[2] The German-language press—though divided in its evaluation of the musical—observed the Madrid production closely, basically adapting this argumentation by lamenting that a musical about Anne Frank is 'hardly bearable'.[3] This common misconception that serious topics have no place in musical theatre lingers among people unfamiliar with the genre's history despite such successful shows as *West Side Story* (1957) or *Sweeney Todd* (1979), which prove that the genre is not restricted to musical comedies in the style of *Kiss Me, Kate* (1948) and *Hello, Dolly!* (1964).

In 2014, when Leon de Winter and Jessica Durlacher's production *Anne*, a Dutch musical about the diary and the life of Anne Frank, premiered at the newly built Amsterdam Theatre, German reviewers still questioned the topic's aptness for a genre located 'closer to *The Lion King*' or 'commercial musicals' than 'theatre with an educational mandate' (*Theater mit Bildungsauftrag*).[4] In fact, other works that try to depict the Shoah in serious, dramatic works, as Joshua Sobol did with *Ghetto* (1984), which takes place in the Vilna ghetto, or Shuki Levy, David Goldsmith, and Glenn Berenbeim attempted with

*Imagine This* (2007), set in the Warsaw ghetto, turn out to generate global interest. *Ghetto*, which is a play with songs,[5] garnered international attention, with acclaimed productions in Berlin, London, and New York.

Whereas in the field of drama and opera, elements of the Holocaust and Third Reich have been omnipresent in American as well as European theatres since the 1950s, be it in the play's text or mise-en-scène, the commercial musical theatre, owing to the aforementioned stereotypical misconception of the genre, is presumed to be incapable of addressing profoundly serious topics.[6] Of course, this position, and the careless application of the word 'kitsch' which often goes along with it, reveal more about the critics' attitudes towards the musical as a genre of production and towards popular culture in general than about the artistic structure and aesthetic value of the show at hand.[7] On the other hand, as a critical stance it testifies to a rather fraught understanding of *Vergangenheitsbewältigung*, the coming to terms with the Nazi past, only allowing that aspect of German history to be discussed in more highbrow artistic genres, thus neglecting the mass communicative potential of popular culture to address important issues.

Rather than joining this specious debate, we concentrate on four works whose plots steer clear of depicting the Holocaust for the most part, yet focus on portrayals of Nazi Germany as well as German and Austrian Nazis. We ask how these shows engage with Nazism, how they represent dangerous characters and situations, and how they manage to use the theatrical fabric of the popular musical to renegotiate a terrifying and shameful chapter of the past. A key aspect of our analysis is how the productions frame the Nazi elements and figures and whether they manage to de-demonise them—and de-demonising is of course a prime characteristic of comedy—without minimising the severity of issues that may be the most serious conceivable. Because *Schweyk*, *The Sound of Music*, *Cabaret*, and *The Producers* confront Germans and Austrians with a historical calamity that is still mortifying and deeply troubling for them, the critical reaction and audience responses in both countries are of particular interest for this chapter.

## SCHWEYK IN NAZI LAND, 1943–1957

As early as 1957, the reviews of Bertolt Brecht and Hanns Eisler's comedy *Schweyk im Zweiten Weltkrieg* (*Schweyk in the Second World War*),[8] the staging of which represented Adolf Hitler and Hermann Göring as oversized, larger-than-life figures, triggered similar arguments to the objections raised regarding the more recent Anne Frank musicals. 'Hitler's Germany was not a state of operettas,[9] the Polish press polemicised after the first night of the Warsaw world première in 1957, while Joachim Kaiser, an influential literary critic in West Germany, stated after the German première of the musical at the Frankfurt municipal theatre: 'If the SS is an object of entertainment, then it is not the SS anymore. If it cannot scare Schweyk, the horror is not perceptible anymore. This is historically implausible.'[10]

FIG. 17.1 Bill Patterson as Schweyk and James Carter as Hitler in the 1982 London production of *Schweyk in the Second World War*, directed by Richard Eyre at the National Theatre. Photo: John Haynes/Performing Arts Images © ArenaPal.

In fact, *Schweyk im Zweiten Weltkrieg* had been conceived as a theatre production in the tradition of the satirical musical as it was understood in the 1930s and 1940s, before the term 'musical play' replaced the much older 'musical comedy'.[11] Weill perceived the genre as a diverse field for innovative 'collaboration between playwright and composer', as 'musical comedy that seeks to be both intellectual and undemanding,'[12] and formed some of his major Broadway shows, such as *Lady in the Dark*, *One Touch of Venus*, and *Love Life* in the generic traditions typified by the shows of the Gershwins and Porter. Even if Brecht molded his script according to the satirical style and form of certain comic Broadway musicals, the musical comedy genre not only deployed light-hearted comic formulae but also utilised a full panoply of the industrial and generic conventions through which it had been able to address a wide range of subjects. Thus, even as late as the 1950s, Leonard Bernstein identified the yet-to-be written *West Side Story* as a 'musical that tells a tragic story in musical comedy terms, using only musical comedy techniques'.[13]

Based on a Czech novel, which was dramatised as a comedy first in interwar Berlin and then in New York, *Schweyk* was composed in the German Democratic Republic and premiered in Warsaw; later it was revived all over Europe (with spectacular productions in Frankfurt, Lyon, and at the National Theatre in London). With that in mind, *Schweyk* can be regarded as a 'global musical'. The composer Kurt Weill had as early as the late 1920s expressed a keen interest in adapting Jaroslav Hašek's 1921 novel *Osudy dobrého vojáka Švejka za světové války* (*The Good Soldier Schwejk and his Fortunes in the World War*) into a popular opera. Back then, Weill found himself in the middle of European— and especially Berlin's—theatrical reforms, which developed multilayered, Broadway-like structures of commercial stage production.[14] To Weill, the figure of Schwejk was an ideal vehicle through which 'to demonstrate the fantastic mistake of war'.[15]

Although he was closely collaborating with Brecht during those years on other works, he initially withheld his plan for a popular opera about Schwejk from his colleague while discussing the idea with his publisher, Universal-Edition (UE), in Vienna. UE negotiated with a Czech lawyer in order to obtain the permission from Hašek's widow for a musical adaptation by Weill.[16] Nevertheless, in those years Weill pondered whether to write the book jointly with Brecht. Because of other projects and Weill's forced emigration from Germany in 1933, a Schwejk project with Brecht did not materialise, although both artists carried the idea with them on their different paths into exile.[17]

Almost a decade later, in 1942, the contact between Brecht, who by then lived in California, and Weill, who had in the meantime achieved the status of an industry insider on Broadway, was renewed. The project of *Schwejk* popped up again, now as a political comedy to be produced on Broadway in the tradition of popular anti-Nazi comedies. In order to come up with a concept for the production, Brecht visited Weill in his home in New City, N.Y. in May 1943. Here the two developed an initial outline of the plot, the 'Schweyk-Fabel', allegedly written by Brecht on Weill's typewriter.[18] Schwejk's name was Americanised to Schweyk, the plot was relocated to World War II, and Hitler and other Nazi politicians were turned into stage characters.

Back in Hollywood, Brecht immediately drafted the book for *Schweyk im Zweiten Weltkrieg*; the English-language working title was *Schweyk in Naziland*. The latter linked *Schweyk* with a broad repertoire of anti-Nazi works in US popular culture, such as Charlie Chaplin's film comedy *The Great Dictator* (1940) and Walt Disney's animated short film *Der Fuehrer's Face* (1943), to name only two of the most popular. The Oscar-winning cartoon had originally been titled *Donald Duck in Nutzi Land*, which might even have inspired the English title for *Schweyk*. Both *Schweyk* and *Der Fuehrer's Face* presented caricatures of Hitler, Göring, Goebbels, and Himmler, while Disney and the Weill-Brecht team made their popular comic heroes Donald Duck and Schwejk, respectively, representatives of the 'common man' in Hitler's army. In the same year, Weill, along with Ira Gershwin, started writing the score for *Where Do We Go from Here?* (Twentieth Century-Fox, 1945), a pastiche-driven musical film with strong anti-Nazi elements.

Although the first script of *Schweyk* was never considered final by either Brecht or Weill—especially because it was written in German and thus still had to be reconceived in English—this text, after many mostly minor revisions by Brecht, was the basis of what was published later as a 'play in three acts', a misleading genre attribution for the draft of a musical.

It was only in 1957, after the death of both Weill and Brecht, that Hanns Eisler began to work on his musical version of *Schweyk* in Europe, which became quite a success. It is important to remember the genesis of the work, because the 1943 version, as provisional as it was, already indicated many ideas of a musical dramaturgy conceived with a Broadway production in mind. The musical material of the whole show is clearly separated into two groups: Threaded through the entire plot, there are eleven self-contained songs, most of them performed by the lower-class characters, especially Anna and Schweyk, in a popular pub called the Kelch (which translates as 'chalice'). The other group of musical numbers comprises the prelude and the two interludes located between the acts. They take place in 'higher regions' ('höhere Regionen'), and stage Hitler, Göring, Goebbels, and Himmler as literally larger-than-life Nazi caricatures. Both groups of musical numbers offer manifold musical indications that showcase the musical fantasy of both authors and give an idea of what Weill might have planned to compose and what, to at least some extent, was eventually realised by Eisler under quite different circumstances.

The works of the 'higher regions' are composed in quite a different style than the pub songs. They employ long, metrically irregular verses—although all rhyme—which call for a prosaic, even operatic form of musical setting. The songs in the Kelch, on the other hand, have regular, short verses and double or crossed rhymes that demand a popular song style of composition. Many of the lyrics have intertextual references or even compositions in the form of musical pastiches. Thus, the 'Kälbermarsch' ('March of the Calves'), as a parodying contrafactum of the well-known Nazi hymn the 'Horst-Wessel-Lied', suggests a musical reference to this compositional model. Also very obvious is the use of the 'Moldova' theme from Bedřich Smetana's symphonic poem *Má vlast* in the 'Lied von der Moldau' ('Moldova Song'), as Eisler realised it in his powerful 1957 composition of the song, which was a central musical moment of the whole show (in 1972, the song was impressively interpreted by Zarah Leander). The book even asks for an (unchanged) presentation of 'Heinrich schlief bei seiner Neuvermählten' ('Heinrich Slept beside His New Bride'), a popular ballad written by a German folk lyricist in 1779 and popularised as a *Bänkellied* (broadside ballad) during the 19th century.

Thus the lyrics, filled with intertextual references, open up opportunities for an alienating musical pastiche, a dramaturgical technique that had already been central for the epic theatre in Weill's and Brecht's collaborative stage works before 1933—such as, for instance, *Mahagonny* or *The Threepenny Opera*.[19] This is also true for the 'higher region' interludes, including the satire of the Nazi politicians. Because they are conceptualised by their lyrics and formal framing as being on a completely different level dramaturgically, Eisler designed these characters' voices to be operatic and to compose the rogues' music in a dodecaphonic manner as 'musical prose',[20] with quotations from Richard Wagner's *Tristan und Isolde*—references that created a remarkable contrast to the popular attitude of the songs. But also the reverse musical solution could be imagined: In his 1931 opera *Die Bürgschaft* (*The Pledge*), Weill portrayed the villains as creditors, highwaymen, blackmailers, and agents, who in this show became the engine of a kind of fascist revolution and were musically characterised by popular dance–style music such as the tango and the foxtrot. This enables him to dramatise the seductiveness of their characters.

In the film *Where Do We Go From Here?*, there is a certain Nazi element to the musical caricature of the eighteenth-century Hessian soldiers in the American Revolutionary War. Here, the disguised Nazis sing a comic *Ländler*, 'The Song of the Rhineland'. Ira Gershwin's lyrics caricature the Germans in clichés and stereotypes, for example those coming from Third Reich role models of masculinity ('each man is a fighter, a lover und so weiter'), while the claim of superiority at the same time is undermined and ridiculed by the awkward English ('the beer is beerier, and the soup superior [ … ] what yours is minier'; but also, 'no other land is for us'). Weill's score, a juxtaposition of *Ländler* and waltz elements, characterises the Germans as clumsy and awkward, with a display of polymodal and polyrhythmic elements in the beginning and interlude parts: overlapping F major accompaniment with G-flat major arpeggios in a duple-against-triple (6/8) meter.[21]

On the dramaturgical level, the alienation effect is achieved by the sinister nature of the Hessian colonel, originated by Herman Bing, who sings most of the song. His hilarious and cheerful performance is in complete opposition to his aim of executing the film's American protagonist, Bill, a contradiction that reduces neither the comic effect nor the anxiety his character generates. In this way the colonel is depicted paradoxically—an early precursor of the Emcee in *Cabaret*. Thus, it is easy to imagine that Weill had a similar plan for the SS representatives or the 'higher regions' in *Schweyk*, which would have savagely mocked the Nazis in order to de-demonise them without downplaying the threat they represent.

Irony, alienation, and comic effects would have been strongly associated (by means of music) with these villains in the story. On the other hand, the working-class protagonist, Anna Kopecka, the owner of the pub, is rendered in all her seriousness in Eisler's (and of course Brecht's) shaping of 'Das Lied von der Moldau'. This is also true for Weill's sole composition for *Schweyk*, 'Das Lied vom Soldatenweib' ('The Song about the Soldier's Wife', composed in 1942–43), which was also conceived with Anna Kopecka in mind.[22]

An important indication of the musical dramaturgy, laid out as early as the first *Schweyk* draft, is the inclusion of a mechanical instrument for music reproduction—a calliope or, in earlier versions, a player-piano.[23] This provides the opportunity to situate music on different levels as it comes from different sources as well as to mark music that is mechanically reproduced as mass-mediated, for instance, popular music. Weill had experimented with the kind of multilayered musical dramaturgy offered by mechanical reproduction before: In his 1928 one-act opera *Der Zar lässt sich photographieren* (*The Czar Has His Photograph Taken*), a gramophone played the 'Tango Angèle'; in *Aufstieg und Fall der Stadt Mahagonny* (*Rise and Fall of the City of Mahagonny*, 1930) a player-piano reproduced Tekla Bądarzewska-Baranowska's *A Maiden's Prayer*; and in 1947, during *Street Scene*'s opening scene, we hear music played by an on-stage radio. In all of these examples, the music reproduced on a diegetic layer is structurally interwoven with the music sung by the actors and played in the pit.

In his 1957 *Schweyk*, Eisler drew on this conceptual basis developed by Weill and Brecht when he utilised the player-piano for the accompaniment of almost all of the songs which were sung in the Kelch pub. It was, in Eisler's words, 'admittedly, in contrast to the "higher" music, as a means of low entertainment', thus separating them, the 'lower' songs, strictly from the music in the 'higher regions', a 'distorted opera' with levels of 'alienating music, mercilessness, [and] evil revelation',[24] which were accompanied by the pit orchestra.

It is quite remarkable that, in order to include the serious subject of Nazism in a popular genre, the form of the piece as drafted by Brecht and Weill during their concept meeting in 1943 already reveals a two-layer dramaturgy, which marks the 'singing Nazis' by means of alienation, parody, and irony, whilst the group of characters representing the 'common man' is linked to quotidian music reproduction and reception by means of mass-media instruments in a public place—a decision that made it possible to mark the latter group's seriousness. This double-layer dramaturgy, which dramaturgically separates the higher regions from the rest of the plot, was used again much later for musicals which dealt with Nazi Germany, especially *Cabaret*.

## *THE SOUND OF MUSIC* (1959)

When Howard Lindsay and Russel Crouse adapted the movie *Die Trapp Familie* (*The Trapp Family*, 1956) into a book for the new Rodgers and Hammerstein musical *The Sound of Music*, they encountered a problem. True to its generic nature as a *Heimatfilm*, the German original eschewed the depiction of Nazism and the Holocaust entirely, even though the plot was set around the time of the *Anschluss*—the 1938 annexation of Austria by Nazi Germany. It loosely follows the life story of Maria Augusta von Trapp, who was dispatched by her convent as a governess for the retired Austrian navy captain Georg von Trapp's children and ended up marrying their father. When the Nazis tried to impress Captain von Trapp into Hitler's navy after the *Anschluss*, the family left Austria for the United States, where they launched a successful career as the Trapp Family Singers.[25] Lindsay and Crouse kept the love story at the centre of the plot but also wanted to convey for New York audiences the sinister machinations of the Nazis.

Initially an overwhelming visual presence of Nazism was planned on-stage in *The Sound of Music* to demonstrate the ubiquitous threat of the authoritarian regime. Early drafts of the script contain scenes in which Nazi symbols and paraphernalia, such as swastikas, Nazi salutes, the Gestapo, and storm troopers, are featured prominently. At one point, act 2 opened with a love duet between Fräulein Maria and the Captain against a mountain backdrop of bonfires arranged in the form of swastikas.[26] During the Boston try-out, however, the creative team decided to relegate the Nazis to the sidelines in order to avoid being criticised for 'melodramatic' staging. The composer, Richard Rodgers, fell back on the old saying that 'less is more' when he reasoned that '[h]aving them offstage exerts more pressure on the situation than seeing them did'.[27] The original depiction of Nazism in the early scripts, however, provides insight into what imagery New York audiences were most likely to associate with Nazism in 1959.

Since *The Sound of Music* was devised as a family show from the beginning, Lindsay and Crouse probably considered the Holocaust and other Nazi crimes against humanity to be unsuitable topics for young viewers. Even though they introduced new characters, such as the impresario Max Detweiler, Captain von Trapp's friend, and Rolf Gruber, a telegram messenger and the love interest of the Captain's oldest daughter, into the plot of the musical, the creators chose to not make them Jewish. Instead, as the story unfolds, they turn from passive Nazi sympathisers into active collaborators. After the annexation, Rolf enlists in the SS and Detweiler rises through the political ranks, organising a music festival in Salzburg for which he promptly signs up the Trapp children as a demonstration to the new regime, a gesture of goodwill so to speak. As a result of this choice, the conflict between the Trapp family and the Nazi aggressors is reduced to the legal question of the annexation of Austria by its more powerful neighbour, thereby avoiding any reference in the original Broadway production to the atrocities committed by the Nazis.

Overall, *The Sound of Music* paints the political world in which the good Trapp family is pitted against the evil Nazis in black and white, leaving very little room for moral ambiguity. What there is, is expressed by von Trapp's fiancée, Elsa Schraeder, and by Max, collaborators with the new regime, who implore the Captain to come to terms with the imminent *Anschluss* in 'No Way to Stop It' (act 2, scene 1). This song is an attempt by Rodgers and Oscar Hammerstein to express these characters' sophisticated esprit. It places the trio at the centre of the universe, in which 'A crazy planet full of crazy people/ Is somersaulting all around the sky', albeit 'at a cock-eyed angle'.[28] According to Stacy Wolf, the melodic line of Rodgers's music imitates the circular motion suggested by Hammerstein's lyrics,[29] while the continuously changing rhythmic accompaniment creates unrest. The show reveals Captain von Trapp literally marching to the beat of a different drum than Elsa and Max because he uses a guitar not only to accompany the song but to voice his protest. Ultimately, however, 'No Way to Stop It' is more about each character's personality than politics, exposing the fine line between self-preservation and profiteering.

In previous versions of the song, however, Hammerstein considered a stronger political tone in his lyrics. Most notably, when the song was still titled 'Play Safe!' in July 1959, he addressed the brutality of the Nazi regime directly.[30] Using cynicism, he had Elsa and Max conjure up imagery of firing squads and concentration camps while they laid out the consequences for the Captain if he continued to fight the Nazis. Since Hammerstein also put Yiddish words, such as 'schlepper' and 'schnook', into Max Detweiler's mouth in this early version, he may have briefly considered making this character Jewish. Because the musical still had overt political overtones at the time, both deliberations might have fit in with the show's intended trajectory.

With the exception of Rolf, the Nazi characters, such as Franz the butler, Herr Zeller, and Admiral von Schreiber, remain stereotyped and underdeveloped, since they were meant to be somewhat dehumanised as a result of their political affiliations. Their lines are few and far between, and until halfway through act 2 neither Herr Zeller nor Rolf intervenes in shaping the plot directly. These two characters, in particular, are portrayed as power-hungry men with inferiority complexes who utilise their Nazi Party membership to hold sway over Captain von Trapp, an aristocrat who occupies a position superior to both. Their pettiness contrasts starkly with the Captain's noble stoicism. Most importantly, the Nazis in *The Sound of Music* are confined to smaller speaking roles. Since they have no songs, they cannot harness the symbolic value and affect of music in the same way the von Trapp family does. Thus, Rodgers and Hammerstein's utilisation of music as a line of demarcation between good and evil creates an effect parallel to Brecht and Weill's double-layer dramaturgy in *Schweyk*. The idea of music as the sole prerogative of goodness goes as far back as the twelfth-century abbess, visionary, composer, poet, and mystic Hildegard von Bingen's liturgical play *Ordo Virtutum*, in which the devil is isolated from the rest of the cast because he cannot sing. When Fräulein Maria joins the Trapp family, the household is run with a military efficiency bordering on fascism. She uses the power of music to liberate the children and reconnect them with their father, transforming the broken home into a whole family again right before the audience's eyes. Conversely, Rolf stops singing when he becomes a Nazi in act 2, so Maria takes over his part in the reprise of 'Sixteen, Going on Seventeen', his previous love duet with Liesl.

With harmony in his life and family restored, the Captain is able to stand up to the Nazis when the time comes. First, he uses his participation in the Kaltzberg Festival—an enterprise he had up till then strongly opposed—as an excuse to delay Admiral von Schreiber's orders to report to duty immediately. Second, he turns his performance of 'Edelweiss' into a politically charged protest song.[31] Third, the family takes advantage of their performance of 'So Long, Farewell' to get a head start in their escape from the Nazis, as they leave the stage one by one in accordance with the song's blocking. In a way, music becomes a weapon of empowerment for the Captain in *The Sound of Music*, allowing him to keep the upper hand in avoiding the demands of the Nazis.

Since its Broadway première, international productions of *The Sound of Music* have increasingly emphasised the political context of the plot. During their lifetime, Rodgers and Hammerstein opposed German-speaking productions of their works, which explains the comparative obscurity of the musical in Germany and Austria even as it became an international hit.[32] One aspect of this poor reception was also the box-office fiasco in the German-speaking world of the 1965 movie adaptation, which (not adjusted for inflation) made more money in the United States than had any other Hollywood movie up to that time.[33] When the stage musical was finally performed for the first time in Salzburg, the von Trapp family's hometown, the 2010 production situated the plot in an overtly Nazi context. The show opened with a flashback from Rolf's perspective as sirens blasted through the auditorium, simulating an air strike. Most notably, the Salzburg production introduced Jews into the musical when it had them scrub the streets during the nun's 'Hallelujah' chorus. Clips from the *Wochenschau* (the German newsreel), stylised swastikas, and portraits of Hitler rounded off this critically engaging adaptation. In contrast, Susan H. Schulman's Broadway revival in 1998 'introduces Nazism a little bit at a time, as it was introduced in Salzburg, very insidiously, like bacteria—one little flag, then it grows and grows'.[34] She used oversized Nazi flags and swastika armbands to ground the plot in historical reality. These grimmer versions of *The Sound of Music* would not have been possible without John Kander and Fred Ebb's 1966 hit *Cabaret*, which introduced a darker and more savagely ironic tone into Broadway musicals.

# *CABARET* (1966)

The racial tensions across the United States during the early 1960s inspired the director-producer Hal Prince and the author Joe Masteroff to develop John van Druten's play *I Am a Camera*, based on Christopher Isherwood's *The Berlin Stories*, into a Broadway musical and turn the Nazi anti-Semitism of 1930s Berlin into a metaphor for white supremacism in 1960s United States. Just as the characters in *Cabaret* have to navigate hedonistic pleasures and social responsibilities in the face of rising fascism, so too the musical's middle-class audience members were expected to confront their own role in the racism that sparked the civil rights movement. For this to work, *Cabaret* took a much subtler approach to representing Nazi characters than *The Sound of Music* had, which vilifies the Nazis before the first one even sets foot on stage.

In *Cabaret*, the Nazis are three-dimensional characters whom people in the audience might initially relate to. Neither Ernst Ludwig nor Fräulein Kost is introduced as in any way morally culpable. Even though Fräulein Kost annoys Fräulein Schneider because she makes ends meet as a prostitute in the latter's boarding-house, her sassy comebacks to the straightlaced landlady make audiences laugh. And despite his morally dubious attitude, Ernst endears himself to audiences easily with his charming behaviour towards a stranger on the train as he helps Cliff find his way in Berlin. There is nothing menacing about them, which makes the revelation at the end of act 1 that both are staunch Nazis all the more powerful. After all, evil is at its most effective when it comes in the form of seeming politeness on the part of self-righteous 'citizens'.

In contrast to *The Sound of Music*, *Cabaret* stages a big revelation scene, in which music is used as an ethnic marker to expose Herr Schultz's Jewish cultural background and to rally the Nazis. At his engagement party, Herr Schulz entertains his guests with a Yiddish song called 'Meeskite', designed to make the guests laugh. Feeling personally affronted, Ernst Ludwig threatens to leave and advises Fräulein Schneider against marrying a Jew. Fräulein Kost steps in and sings the anthemic and sinister 'Tomorrow Belongs to Me'. Moved by the words and music, Ernst Ludwig joins in, and soon all the other party guests follow suit—with the exception of Sally Bowles, Cliff Bradshaw, Herr Schultz, and Fräulein Schneider. This first reprise of the song, which was introduced a few scenes earlier by a group of waiters as some kind of folk tune, demonstrates the infectious power of music as the Nazis identify themselves and unite in singing together. The curtain falls after this performance, leaving audiences to ponder the implications of the events for the action ahead.

Some directors in Germany and Austria took the chilling effects of the act 1 finale one step further by capitalising on either country's Nazi past. In the 1996 production at the Messepalast in Vienna, the theatre audience became patrons at the fictitious Kit Kat Klub with table service. Director Meret Barz planted extras in the audience who rose from their seats and sang along to the German version 'Der morgige Tag ist mein' with the performers on stage. Kander's melodic contour is nearly identical to the first eight bars of Heinrich Silcher's 'Lorelei'—a nineteenth-century German art song that many Viennese audience members would have recognized as a popular German folk tune and associated with Nazi propaganda.[35] Thus, the plants in the audience created the impression that the spirit on stage caught on with the audience and encouraged closeted Nazis to out themselves. In a similar but completely independent move four years later, director Jens Schmidl positioned 30–35 choristers strategically in the auditorium of the Theater Freiburg and had them join little by little in 'Der morgige Tag ist mein'. Schmidl recalls that the members of the opera ensemble had to be coaxed into participating in this 2001 production of *Cabaret*: 'What also comes into play in this scene is that they were virtually scared. Of course, one could say that we're only acting but they're acting without protection. They don't have the apron stage but the actual problem that they could be sitting next to a victim of Nazism without knowing and stand up and play their part and the victim flips out.'[36] Although Schmidl did not conceive of this moment with Brecht in mind, he zeroed in on the dialectic between passive and active consumption among theatre-goers, who chose, rather shocked, to watch the plants in the audience rise and sing along one by one over trying to put an end to it.

'Tomorrow Belongs to Me' thus follows a similar dramaturgical trajectory to 'Edelweiss' in *The Sound of Music*, although to opposite effect. Both songs pass themselves off as folk tunes initially but become recontextualised as political songs through performative circumstances, such as narrative cues and visual signifiers. To invoke pastoral values, they use nature imagery in the lyrics and simple accompaniment: the guitar in 'Edelweiss', and none at all in 'Tomorrow Belongs to Me', which is sung a cappella. The latter's reprise at the engagement party, however, is accompanied by the accordion. Each instrument allows the singer to accompany himself (the Captain) or herself (Fräulein Kost). While the skips and leaps in the melodic line of 'Edelweiss' are not found frequently in German folk music, the stepwise motion in 'Tomorrow Belongs to Me' fits the genre. Whereas in *The Sound of Music* the folk idiom is ascribed an immaculate status, untainted with sinister Nazi ideology, *Cabaret* demonstrates how political systems can appropriate popular cultural goods to bolster their agendas. Both examples are a testament to the expressive force of music, which has led audiences to create myths that regard them as true folk songs or, in the case of 'Tomorrow Belongs to Me', as a genuine Nazi hymn.[37]

*Cabaret* is a departure from the conventional book musical format, which had been perfected by Rodgers and Hammerstein between *Oklahoma!* (1943) and *The Sound of Music*.[38] Although the love stories between the two couples—Sally and Cliff, Fräulein Schneider and Herr Schultz—still unfold in traditional book scenes, a new mode emerges in the loosely connected cabaret numbers, which are held together by mise-en-scène rather than narrative. Originally they were planned to appear in a self-contained sequence in the middle of the show—a show within a show, similar to what 'Springtime for Hitler' would become for *The Producers*. Joel Grey, who created the role of the Emcee in 1966, reported: 'But by the time rehearsals began, they decided to break up the numbers and spread them throughout the show in such a way that the cabaret numbers became reflections about what was happening in the story'.[39] Now interspersed throughout Masteroff's book, they disrupt the linear narrative which had shaped the dramaturgy of the book musical, forcing the audience to switch back and forth between the sombre reality of Fräulein Schneider's boarding-house and the phantasmagorical world of the nightclub. Dramaturgically, *Cabaret* is closer to *Schweyk* than to *The Sound of Music*, since the cabaret numbers function similarly to the interludes in the 'higher regions'. Thus emerged *Cabaret*'s characteristic double-layer dramaturgy,[40] which would come to typify certain kinds of 'concept' musicals.

The split between the two worlds is reflected in the score, too. For the Kit Kat Klub, Fred Ebb and John Kander wrote highly energetic songs featuring lewd lyrics, jaunty rhythms, sexy vamps, campy humour, and an overall unpolished sound, such as in 'The Telephone Song', 'Don't Tell Mama!', or 'Cabaret'. The orchestrations by Don Walker emphasise the honky-tonk nature of the jazzy cabaret numbers via the muted brass and frantic drumrolls frequently produced by the Kit Kat Klub's onstage band. At the same time, Walker used a second orchestra geared towards a more traditional sound for the book scenes.[41] The music in these scenes ranges from light-hearted love duets with lively rhythms, such as 'Perfectly Marvellous' or 'It Couldn't Please Me More', to the more pensive 'So What' and emotionally urgent 'What Would You Do?', in which Kander evoked Weill's style. He wrote the last two specifically for Weill's widow, Lotte Lenya, who played Fräulein Schneider in the original Broadway production. Kander brings all those different elements together in his pastiche score to capture the sounds of Berlin in the 1930s.

*Cabaret*'s original Broadway staging accommodated the different worlds as well. The main stage was occupied by either Boris Aronson's sparse set for the seedy Kit Kat Klub or the run-down interior of Fräulein Schneider's boarding-house. Using a glittering slashed curtain, however, the lighting designer, Jean Rosenthal, separated the apron from the rest of the stage.[42] Hal Prince dubbed this area 'limbo', a place between the two worlds upstage that '[links the characters'] unconventional sexuality, money problems, and political cowardice to Berlin's general moral collapse'.[43] It is the domain of the Emcee, where he draws the audience into his world with 'Willkommen' and frequently comments on the book scenes with songs, such as 'Two Ladies', 'The Money Song', or 'If You Could See Her'.

The most powerful of the instances, when the Emcee breaks the fourth wall to engage with the audience, is 'If You Could See Her'. He dances a grotesque foxtrot with a gorilla, touting the virtues and talents of the primate. He reels the audience in with uproarious laughter until he delivers the final blow: 'If you could see her through my eyes/She wouldn't look Jewish at all'[44]. All at once the anti-Semitic point of the song is revealed, and the audience is left to grapple with their complicity, for the Aronson's large trapezoid mirror, mounted to the fly tower, makes it impossible for any spectator to blend into the anonymity of the audience. The mirror first reflected the audience members' enjoyment; now it exacerbates their discomfort over having been caught applauding a pervasive prejudice. Using classic alienation strategies, such as the mirror and the breaking of the fourth wall, this scene seems to come directly out of Brecht's playbook on epic theatre.

During *Cabaret*'s original runs on Broadway and in the West End, however, the show's creators caved to pressure from the Jewish League and changed the line from 'She wouldn't look Jewish at all' to 'She isn't a Meeskite at all', although Joel Grey would slip in the original wording on Broadway whenever he thought he could get away with it. In subsequent revivals, however, *Cabaret* returned to the anti-Semitic punchline. Not so in Austria, where the line would have probably ruffled too many feathers. In 1970 Rolf Kutschera stayed true to the original production and substituted the German equivalent 'Miesnick' for 'Meeskite' in the German-speaking première at the Theater an der Wien. Twenty years later, however, Meret Barz interpreted the meaning of the scene differently. Here, the Emcee did not dance with a gorilla but carried a young girl in his arms during the song. It is suggested that she was shot by the Gestapo, and the Emcee mourns her death. In this version, the song takes on a very somber note and consequentially foregoes the anti-Semitic punchline as well. The song ends with the line 'Säht ihr sie mit meinen Augen/Dann säht ihr mein Mädchen ist schön' ('If you could see her through my eyes,/You'd see that my girl is beautiful').

'If You Could See Her' is a commentary on the preceding book scene, in which Fräulein Schneider calls off her engagement to Herr Schultz because he is Jewish. After the party, anti-Semitism invades everyone's lives; not even the Kit Kat Klub is safe from Nazism anymore. Herr Schultz moves out of the boarding-house after his breakup with Fräulein Schneider. Ever the pragmatist, she surrenders to the rising power of the Nazis, sacrificing her happiness for her livelihood. It is a different kind of collaboration from that of Max and Elsa in *The Sound of Music*, one that is born out of desperation and expedience rather than opportunism and convenience. When Cliff confronts her about her choice, she replies in song, 'What Would You Do?'

The limited range of 'What Would You Do?'s melody reflects the limited options at her disposal. The narrow confines of Fräulein Schneider's world, which is essentially reduced to the boarding-house she runs, leave her no choice other than to co-operate with the Nazis unless she wants to lose her sole means of survival. The persistent rhythmic ostinato in the song's accompaniment evokes not only Fräulein Schneider's ticking clock, running out of time, but also the relentless force of the Nazi threat.[45] The strong presence of dissonances, such as the tritone in the opening measures and the raised fourth degree on 'time' and 'clock', signal the loss of her harmonious life. Each time she sings 'What would you do?', the word 'you' is emphasised by either a raised second or raised sixth degree. It seems as if she is really addressing the audience here, although she sings the song to Cliff and Sally.

In this sense, 'What Would You Do?' parallels the song 'Cabaret' on the surface level, which poses a direct question to the audience a few scenes later: 'What good is sitting alone in your room?'[46] Fräulein Schneider's self-criticism is drowned out by Sally's triumphant return to the Kit Kat Klub. The opening line of 'Cabaret' is a rhetorical question, as Sally tells the audience to 'come to the cabaret'.[47] She does not heed Fräulein Schneider's cautionary tale and chooses hedonistic pleasures over moral culpability. The audience, which enjoys Sally's rousing swan song, becomes complicit again.

Overall, the German-speaking reception history of Cabaret has been more successful than that of The Sound of Music, although it had obstacles to overcome in the beginning, too. When Rolf Kutschera brought Cabaret to Vienna in order to challenge his audiences intellectually, he was aware of the financial risks.[48] Cabaret closed at the Theater an der Wien after only fifty-nine performances, and Kutschera concluded:

> [T]he theme of 'CABARET' is too modern for our audience and too serious to be taken as a musical play. It is interesting to observe: People over fifty who have seen that time, also in Austria, refuse the theme. Young people, up to thirty and thirtyfive [sic], accept the show, the sophistication, the wit and the esprit it offers and are not offended by the theme, for what they know of that time is only what their parents told them, and that is to a great extent very subjective. On the contrary, the young people's reaction to the theme is very positive.[49]

The musical did not fare much better in West-Germany during the 1970s.[50]

By contrast, Cabaret was received more favorably by critics and audiences in East Germany, although the première at the Staatsoperette Dresden did not escape controversy. Maja-Rosewith Riemer, who played Sally in that first GDR production, recalled in a phone conversation the political and economic obstacles that had to be overcome.[51] The stage rights had to be paid in Westmark, the currency of West Germany, and it was no small feat for the run-down Dresden theatre to persuade the GDR officials to pay the steep licensing fees from their limited budget of Western money; but in turn the theatre agency strongly advocated the East German première. Riemer remembered they even had to start rehearsals before the license was secured,[52] but in the end the theatre's impresario, Fritz Steiner, managed to convince the political officials of the enterprise, and Cabaret opened on 18 January 1976 at the Staatsoperette Dresden.[53] Although Gottfried Schmiedel, of the Sächsisches Tagesblatt, sided with his Viennese colleagues when he called the show too sentimental and superficial and criticised it for its makeshift dramaturgical concept,[54] the Sächsische Neueste Nachrichten, the Union, and the Stimme der DDR praised Cabaret for its departure from standard Broadway fare,[55] realistic depiction,[56] and brave ending,[57] respectively. Riemer vehemently countered speculations that Cabaret was more popular in East Germany because the GDR had essentially absolved itself from any involvement in Nazi crimes, which the East German government had deemed a direct result of Western capitalism, and saw as the sole responsibility of West Germany: 'We were Nazis, too! The audience is not that stupid—they grasp that.'[58]

The tide turned for *Cabaret* in West Germany in the theatrical season of 1986–1987 with two groundbreaking productions: the Düsseldorfer Schauspielhaus presented a

FIG. 17.2 A twenty-three-year old Ute Lemper as Sally Bowles performs 'Don't Tell Mama!' in *Cabaret*. The 1986 production was directed by Jérôme Savary and played at the Schauspielhaus Düsseldorf before moving to the Théâtre Mogador in Paris. Photo © Ullstein Bild.

production by Jérôme Savary before it went on to Paris, and Helmut Baumann staged his own version at the Theater des Westens in Berlin. Savary's Kit Kat Klub was 'a tick too chic' for a third-rate nightclub[59] but it launched the career of Ute Lemper, who played Sally Bowles. Baumann managed a casting coup similar to the one Hal Prince had achieved with Lenya when he landed Hildegard Knef in the role of Fräulein Schneider.[60] Both Savary and Baumann sought to confront German audiences with their political past using Nazi symbols. In Savary's version, 'what appears to be at first a red curtain turns out to be a stage-filling Nazi banner',[61] and Baumann shoves an oversized lollipop with a swastika on it into the Emcee's hand.[62]

The matter of whether or not Nazism can be staged in *The Sound of Music* becomes a question of *how* Nazism can be staged in *Cabaret*. Prince went for a realistic depiction of how the Nazis came to power, portraying a nuanced world of flawed characters whose goal is to survive in hard times. Fräulein Schneider's earlier political naïvety gives way to her pragmatic decision to sacrifice marital happiness in order to escape Nazi persecution; this, Herr Schultz's inability to face reality, and Sally Bowles's blind ignorance of politics symbolically enable the Nazis' rise to power. The only one ready to take a stand against evil is Cliff, but he is distracted by his romance with Sally and in the end decides to leave Berlin and leave the fight to the Germans. They are all collaborators and victims simultaneously.

It was during the initial run of *Cabaret* that the movie *The Producers* was conceived, shot, and released. The two works shared an attitude that encouraged use of 'the symbolism of Nazi Germany to critique American society from a liberal perspective'[63].

## *THE PRODUCERS*

The musical *The Producers*,[64] composed and co-adapted by Mel Brooks together with Thomas Meehan from his own 1967 film comedy, was a huge hit on Broadway, where it premiered at the St. James Theatre in 2001, running for over 2,500 performances before starting a national tour as well as a series of productions in London, Buenos Aires, Mexico City, Vienna, Berlin, and other cities throughout the first decade of the new millennium. *The Producers* is a backstage story about two fraudulent Broadway producers, Max Bialystok and Leo Bloom, who fail in their cunning plan to produce a surefire flop by overselling investors' shares. In order to make their production a guaranteed fiasco, they search for the worst play ever written and come across a script entitled *Springtime for Hitler: A Gay Romp with Adolf and Eva at Berchtesgaden*. 'Springtime for Hitler' is a fifteen-minute revue sequence that functions as a self-contained show within the theatrical plot.

The National Socialist subject is introduced through the fictitious theatrical libretto for 'Springtime for Hitler', which provides the plot for the show within the show, as well as through that book's fictitious author, the escaped German National Socialist Franz Liebkind. He has two songs in the frame story that are integrated as diegetic numbers. The first is 'Der Guten Tag Hop-Clop', a parody of a Ländler with corrupt Bavarian *Schuhplattler* (a popular folk dance, usually performed by male dancers in the alpine region, who pat their thighs and the soles of their shoes with their flat hands) and *Watschentanz* elements. Liebkind sings it for Bloom and Bialystok while trying to make them dance along. *Watschentanz* (slap dance) elements had already been seen on Broadway in Eric Charell's 1936 New York production of his 1930 Berlin show *White Horse Inn*, but they were also used ironically in Bob Fosse's 1972 film version of *Cabaret*, where they are cross-cut with some Nazi villains' brutal bludgeoning of an unwelcome Jewish nightclub customer. In *The Producers*, the *Schuhplattler* in 'Der Guten Tag Hop-Clop', with its association with a somewhat aggressive masculine competition/fighting dance, allows Liebkind to demonstrate his camp hypermasculinity by hitting Bloom and Bialystok while singing some pseudo-German nonsense lyrics.

His second song, 'Haben Sie Gehört das Deutsche Band?', on the other hand, is presented during his auditions for the role of Hitler. Through his performance of that song, Liebkind, who is present as a part of the production team, unintentionally wins the part. Originally, Franz spontaneously entered the stage just to demonstrate how the song should properly be sung; thus, the focus lies on questions of style and performance.

It is notable that Brooks here refers to the tradition of German bands, a conventional marker of Germanness in the popular American imagination. From the eighteenth century on, small bands coming from Germany, mostly wind bands playing the popular repertoire of their time, toured from Western Europe, mostly via England, to the Americas and onwards to Australia. Those bands marked a specific musical style, often non-professional, and their appearance was widely accepted as an aspect of urban street culture in England, the United States, and other countries. They gave the players a reliable income, at least until World War II.[65] So while 'Haben Sie Gehört das Deutsche Band?' alludes neither to a living German musical tradition nor to a practice common in Nazi Germany, this reference invokes a stereotype of Germanness derived from the collective memory of New York popular culture.[66] Indeed, this is the intertextual strategy that typifies the musical pastiches of *The Producers*.

Apart from the martial style of the marcato and fortissimo chords of the first four measures and some bars before the finish of the song, which match Franz's clipped and shouty, Hitlerian way of speaking (for example in his commands to the musical accompanist, who responds with a Hitler salute), the song is musically a charming syncopated foxtrot. It pastiches a 1930s musical-comedy soft-shoe and features a smooth, saxophone-dominated sound texture, soft, jazzy harmonies with an emphasis on the first and second steps (D major–E minor), and foxtrot-like syncopations used as fills on the long notes and rests of Franz's singing. The comic effect in his presentation is derived especially from the smooth and bouncy nature of the song, along with its charming choreography, redolent of Broadway musical comedy and vaudeville, incongruously juxtaposed against the loud and vigorous introduction as well as the rude Nazi thug who presents it.

This humour, built on the contradiction between style and content, returns in the subsequent revue entitled 'Springtime for Hitler', which presents the inner plot of the show of the same name. Brooks had already composed it for his 1967 film comedy *The Producers*, keeping most of its musical and formal structure intact in the 2001 theatre adaptation (and the 2005 film adaptation of the Broadway show). This production number is introduced by a pseudo-folkloric song presented by a group wearing dirndls and lederhosen. It is followed by a parody spoofing the Ziegfeld Follies girls' introductory number with a presentation of elaborate dresses and costumes. While the girls descend the revue stairs, a bright-voiced tenor soloist in a stylised Nazi uniform extols the 'Springtime for Hitler' in a widely swinging melody (starting with an octave on the word 'springtime')—a revue routine reminiscent of classical Broadway revues or Follies productions—as, for example, in the introduction number 'Time Marches On', composed by Vernon Duke and Ira Gershwin, or as a pastiche in Stephen Sondheim's 'Beautiful Girls' in *Follies* (1971). Even though the costumes in *The Producers* feature clichéd German symbols, such as giant pretzels, sausages, beer mugs, and the like, the compositional style and stage presentation remain in the tradition of the Broadway revue.

It is remarkable that in this sequence we find a dramaturgical paradox between the frame plot and the presentation of artistic perfection. Although 'Springtime' should present the least talented cast to assure that the show will flop, what we see may be in bad taste, but it is utterly professional—the performers have great voices, the choreography is offensive but brilliant, and the dancers are always in sync. The exhibited perfection of performance, even if in dissonance with the narrative, can be read as the necessary

FIG. 17.3 'Springtime for Hitler' from the 2009 Berlin production of *The Producers*. Photo © Ullstein Bild.

vehicle for the elaboration of camp in this scene. Described by Susan Sontag as an aestheticism that is represented 'not in terms of beauty but in terms of the degree of artifice, of stylization',[67] camp emphasises style over content.

In the 1967 film version, this number is followed by sketches consisting of dialogue and songs performed by a character named LSD, a gay hippie who plays Hitler singing a blues number in the inner plot. The 2001 show drops these elements and sticks to the revue aesthetics. Thus, what follows is the song 'Heil Myself', delivered by Hitler himself.

This scene, which spoofs Judy Garland's concluding stage routine (sitting on the edge of the stage while singing 'Over the Rainbow'), is the epitome of the camp aesthetic of *The Producers*. Since the role of Hitler is spontaneously taken over by the flamboyantly camp director of the show within the show, Roger de Bris, after Liebkind breaks his leg just before the opening, the character is no longer arrogant and 'butch', as conceived by Liebkind, but gay in the most stereotypical sense of the word, thereby living up to Roger's punning motto (in his song 'Keep It Gay!') that all musicals should be 'gay'.

In the 2005 screen musical, the audience members' reactions change during this number, as now the show is mistakenly interpreted as comic and construed as a double entendre. 'Heil Myself' is the number which convinces the audience of the ironic inclination of 'Springtime', and whereas people left the theatre in disgust during the previous revue number, the audience now laughs and applauds. When the patrons return to their seats because they want to see de Bris's camp delivery of the lyrics, their content is no longer offensive. Thus the producers' calculated plan to produce a genuine flop fails.

Similar to how it is used in Fosse's film version of *Cabaret* (1972), in the film versions of *The Producers* the fictive audience of the show and its response to the performance onstage are crucial to the development of the plot (Springtime as a success instead of a flop). Thus, without this additional element, in the stage versions of *The Producers* and *Cabaret* the reaction of the 'real' audience in the stalls matters tremendously: It is we who have to understand the metadramatic meaning of the (planned) offensiveness of the first part in 'Springtime' and the (unintentend) irony in the performance of 'Heil Myself' without necessarily reacting the same way as the audience does in the movie. Similarly, the real audience has a chance to be shocked (and laugh at the same time) in Fosse's *Cabaret*, where the staged audience laughs about the Emcee's racist punchline after 'If you could see her through my eyes'.[68]

Unlike the staged audience in the film versions of *The Producers*, however, the theatre audiences in Vienna (2008) and Berlin (2009)—where the stage musical had its Austrian and German premières, respectively—likely knew what they were getting themselves into when they purchased their tickets, for in their coverage ahead of each opening the German-speaking press expounded at length about the moral question of whether or not one is allowed to laugh about Hitler.[69] Still, night after night the real audience of *The Producers* becomes as complicit in the success of Springtime, when they cheer and applaud the offensive revue, as they do when they laugh at the Emcee's love song to a supposedly 'Jewish' gorilla in *Cabaret*.

The mise-en-scène of the 'Springtime' sequence in Brooks's 1967 film had piled on all the stylistic (visual, musical, and choreographic) elements of camp; in the stage version, these come back with a vengeance throughout the evening.[70] It juxtaposes the heavy use of German stereotypes and Nazi clichés and even parodies stage representations of war, with its musical and visual reference to Florence Ziegfeld's shows from the 1900s to 1920s as well as Busby Berkeley's movie *42nd Street* from 1933 and the 1980 Broadway stage version of that film.

By framing the sinister Nazi elements with the kitschy showbiz glitter of a revue or musical comedy, Brooks takes the self-referential camp up a notch from *Cabaret*, which has a different kind of camp, being darker and sleazier while its ironic staging makes the milieu of both the Emcee and Sally Bowles seem more decadent. In a similar fashion to the Ziegfeld parody in *The Producers*, *Cabaret* featured in Hal Prince's original production and its 1986 revival a poor man's version of a Follies routine, when the Emcee had the cabaret girls parade around the stage dressed up as currencies (à la Miss French Franc, Miss American Buck, or Brünhilde, Miss German Mark). Over the years international productions have emphasised the camp aspects of *Cabaret*, especially the overtly sexualized decadence of Sam Mendes's 1993 revival, paving the way for the over-the-top treatment of camp in *The Producers*.

Whereas *Cabaret* constantly tries to ironise the camp elements, which are confined to the Kit Kat Klub; even in the book scenes, the characters in *The Producers* embrace it wholeheartedly. It is lighter, self-referential, all-pervasive—and in 'Springtime' the 'swastika' choreography seems technically sophisticated in comparison to *Cabaret*'s crude goose-stepping kick-line at the start of act 2. Whereas there is an underlying threat or menace, or at least debauchery, in the camp mockery of kitsch in *Cabaret*, in *The Producers* it is delightfully disarming.

*The Producers'* songs are quite homogeneously composed in the style, orchestra sound, and AABA form of classical musical comedy and American revue songs. They include traditional show business elements as well as musical elements taken from American vaudeville and revue, African American popular music, and Jewish traditions.[71] *The Producers* stages the contrast of form and content resulting from its camp transformation of (pseudo-)German and Nazi symbols as 'a victory of "style" over "content", "aesthetics" over "morality", of irony over tragedy'.[72] This form of multilayered representation turns out to be the main vehicle for defusing the demonic aura of the otherwise scary figures, and, in this case, also the symbols of Nazi evil.[73]

It is remarkable that after its Vienna première at the Ronacher Theater in 2008, German-language reviews again focused on the question of whether it is legitimate to ridicule Hitler. 'As far as their compatriot Adolf Hitler and National Socialism are concerned, the Austrians cannot take a joke'[74], the *Jüdische Allgemeine Zeitung* commented on the Austrian reception of *The Producers*. The Berlin production, in contrast, succeeded, probably because it was framed and marketed aggressively with a direct reference to the show's play with corrupted Nazi imagery: The front of the Admiralspalast theatre was decorated with pseudo-swastika flags that replaced the Nazi symbol with a black pretzel. This imagery was widely accepted as an ironic provocation.[75] Here, reviews and TV presentation, as in the series *Schmidt & Pocher*,[76] reacted affirmatively, but without the Jewish or the aggressive political reading that had dominated the reception of its initial Broadway production.

In New York the musical had been mostly been perceived as a triumphant 'victory over Hitler'.[77] This constitutes quite a different interpretation of the initial question regarding the inclusion of Nazis in musical comedy. In a genre created predominantly by Jewish authors (to recall only the authors referenced in this essay: Weill, Eisler, Rodgers and Hammerstein, Kander and Ebb, and Brooks), the question of whether it is legitimate to use Nazi protagonists and symbols in entertainment perhaps transforms into a vindication of the agency and empowerment entailed in laughing at one's enemies.

## NOTES

1. 'Der Holocaust ist kein Thema, aus dem man ein Musical machen kann'. 'Streit um ein Musical zu Anne Frank', *Die Welt*, 18 February 2008, https://www.welt.de/kultur/article 1689181/Streit-um-ein-Musical-zu-Anne-Frank.html, accessed 10 January 2020.
2. 'Es ist unmöglich! Das Leben der Anne Frank und der Holocaust als lustiger Abend mit Gesang und Tanz'. Reiner Wandler, 'Anne-Frank-Tagebuch als Musical', *TAZ*, 12 February 2008, https://taz.de/Anne-Frank-Tagebuch-als-Musical/!5186857/, accessed 10 January 2020.
3. 'Doch ist es eben dieser Kitsch von Liebesgeschichtchen und süßlichem Latinopop, der es schwer macht, das Tagebuch der Anne Frank als Musical zu ertragen'. Annekatrin Lammers, 'Kritik zu *Anne Frank: The Musical*', *ARD Nachtmagazin*, broadcast 29 February 2008.
4. Marie Gamillscheg, 'Anne Frank, jetzt auch mit Snack-Box', *Die Welt*, 8 May 2014, https://www.welt.de/kultur/article127747424/Anne-Frank-jetzt-auch-mit-Snack-Box.html, accessed 10 January 2020.
5. Joshua Sobol, *'Ghetto': In a Version by David Lan with Lyrics Translated and Music Arranged by Jeremy Sams* (London: Nick Hern Books, 1989). The play was first staged by one of Germany's most prominent directors, Peter Zadek, in a German-Israeli co-production that featured many of Germany's most famous actors, including Michael Degen, Ulrich Tukur, and Hannes Jaenicke, as well as several high-profile Israeli artists such as Esther Ofarim and Giora Feidman.
6. Jessica Hillman-McCord, *Echoes of the Holocaust on the American Musical Stage* (Jefferson, NC: McFarland, 2012), 1–2. For more information on this discussion surrounding the premieres of *Sound of Music*, *Cabaret*, and *The Producers* in Vienna, please see Susanne Scheiblhofer, 'Confronting the Past through Popular Musical Theatre: The Effects of Austrian Postwar Cultural Policies on the Reception History of Musicals', 'Austrian Music Studies: Topics, Perspectives, Concepts', special issue, *Musicologica Austriaca: Journal for Austrian Music Studies* (April 13, 2023), https://www.musau.org/parts/neue-article-page/view/146, accessed July 5th, 2023.
7. Nils Grosch and Carolin Stahrenberg, 'Nationaler "Kitsch" als ästhetisches Problem im populären Musiktheater', in *Kitsch und Nation: Zur kulturellen Modellierung eines polemischen Begriffs*, edited by Kathrin Ackermann und Christopher F. Laferl (Bielefeld: Transcript, 2016), 163–183.

8. The draft libretto was later published in Brecht's complete works; see Bertolt Brecht, *Werke*, vol. 7, Stücke 7 (Frankfurt, 1991), 181–257, 416–452. Eisler's 1957 composition can be found in Hanns Eisler, *Bühnenmusik zu 'Schweyk im zweiten Weltkrieg' von Bertolt Brecht*, Lieder und Kantaten 8 (Leipzig: Breitkopf & Härtel, 1964).

9. 'Hitler-Deutschland war kein Operettenstaat'. 'Braver Schweyk', *Der Spiegel* 13, no. 57 (27 March 1957), https://www.spiegel.de/spiegel/print/d-41120961.html, accessed 10 January 2020.

10. 'Wenn die SS Gegenstand der Unterhaltung ist, dann ist es nicht mehr die SS. Schweyk hat vor ihr keine Angst, das Furchtbare ist nicht mehr zu spüren. Das ist historisch unglaubwürdig'. Quoted in Ellen Gerdeman-Klein, 'The Dramaturgical Integration of Text and Music in Brecht's *Schweyk im Zweiten Weltkrieg*' (PhD diss., University of Illinois Urbana-Champaign, 1995), 201.

11. Hammerstein's term 'musical play' diversified the generic field of the commercially produced stage work that combined song, music, dance, dialogue, plot, and scenography as authored by the Gershwins, Kern, Rodgers and Hart, as well as Porter, among others.

12. Kurt Weill, 'Was ist musikalisches Theater? (Notate für einen Vortrag)', in *Musik und musikalisches Theater: Gesammelte Schriften; Mit einer Auswahl von Gesprächen und Interviews*, edited by Stephen Hinton and Jürgen Schebera (Mainz: Schott, 2000), 144–148.

13. Leonard Bernstein, excerpts from Bernstein's *West Side Log*, 1957, www.westsidestory.com/notes-and-letters, accessed 20 May 2020.

14. Nils Grosch, 'Kurt Weill, *Mahagonny* and the Commercialization of Berlin Musical Theatre in the Weimar Republic', in *Beyond Glitter and Doom: The Contingency of the Weimar Republic*, edited by Jochen Hung, Godela Weiss-Sussex, and Geoff Wilkes (Munich: Iudicium Verlag, 2012), 192–208; and Nils Grosch, 'Zur medialen Dramaturgie des populären Musiktheaters in der Weimarer Republik', in *Populärkultur, Massenmedien und Avantgarde 1919–1933*, edited by Jessica Nitsche and Nadine Werne (Munich: Wilhelm Fink, 2012), 239–250.

15. '[D]en fantastischen Irrtum des Krieges aufzuzeigen'. This is how Weill explained it to the Universal Edition A.G. Nils Grosch, ed., *Kurt Weill: Briefwechsel mit der Universal Edition Wien* (Stuttgart: Metzler, 2002), 203f.

16. Nils Grosch, 'Schweyk—ohne Weill? Zu einem späten Projekt des Teams Brecht/Weill', in *Musik-Kontexte: Festschrift für Hanns-Werner Heister*, edited by Thomas Phelps and Wieland Reich (Münster: MV-Wissenschaft, 2011), 304–313.

17. '[A]n einer einzelnen humoristischen Figur den phantastischen Irrtum des Krieges aufzuzeigen', quoted in Nils Grosch, 'Weill, Eisler und die musikalische Dramaturgie in *Schweyk*', in *De Hašek à Brecht: Fortune de la figure de Chvéïk en Europe*, ed. Marie-Odile Thirouin, special issue, *Cahiers de l'ILCEA* 8 (Grenoble: Institut des Langues et Cultures d'Europe et d'Amérique, 2006), 153–66.

18. Bertolt Brecht, 'Die *Schweyk*-Fabel', in *Materialien zu Bertolt Brechts 'Schweyk im Zweiten Weltkrieg'*, ed. Herbert Knust (Frankfurt: Suhrkamp, 1974), 157–165.

19. *Mahagonny* refers to a group of work forms that materialised in at least five versions: the 1927 twenty-five minute *Songspiel Mahagonny*'; the 1930 full-length opera *Aufstieg und Fall der Stadt Mahagonny* (published by Universal Edition); the 1931 Berlin version arranged by Weill and others for a commercial production in the Theater am Kurfürstendamm; the 1932 Vienna version arranged by Hans Heinsheimer, permitted by Weill for a commercial production in the Raimund Theater; and the 1932 Paris version of the 1927 *Songspiel*. The last three are all lost.

20. In dodecaphonic music, the term 'musical prose' is primarily used to describe 'the metrical and syntactical moment of asymmetrical subdivision of musical phrases'; see Hermann Danuser, 'Musikalische Prosa' in *Die Musik in Geschichte und Gegenwart*, Sachteil 6, ed. Ludwig Finscher (Kassel: Bärenreiter, and Stuttgart: Metzler, 1997), 857–866, here: 855.

21. Kurt Weill [and Ira Gershwin], 'The Song of the Rhineland: From the Film *Where Do We Go from Here?* Sheet Music' (New York: Chappell, 1945).

22. Nils Grosch, '"Vom Weib des Nazisoldaten": Musik, Propaganda, und Aufführung eines Brecht-Songs', in *Lied und populäre Kultur/Song and Popular Culture* 50/51, ed. Max Matter and Tobias Widmaier (Münster: Waxmann, 2005–2006), 137–161.

23. As indicated in the draft libretto; see Brecht, *Werke*, 182 and 436.

24. 'Die Lieder auf der Bühne gesungen und vom elektrischen Klavier [ ... ] [begleitet]. Sie bekennt sich, zum Unterschied von der hohen Musik, als niedriges Genußmittel'; 'distanzierende Musik, erbarmungslos, böse Enthüllung'. Hanns Eisler, '*Schweyk* und der deutsche Militarismus: Interview with André Gisselbrecht, 11 October 1961', in special issue on Hanns Eisler, *Sinn und Form* (1964): 271–275.

25. Laurence Maslon, *The Sound of Music Companion* (New York: Simon & Schuster, 2007).

26. Howard Lindsay, Russel Crouse, and Oscar Hammerstein II, 'The Sound of Music', script draft, 27 May 1959, Library of Congress, Music Division, Oscar Hammerstein II Collection, Box 49, Folder 6: 2-1-11–2-1-12.

27. Seymour Peck, 'They Made *The Sound of Music*: About Those Who Helped Make *The Sound of Music*', *New York Times*, 15 November 1959, 3.

28. Howard Lindsay and Russel Crouse, *The Sound of Music. A New Musical Play* (New York: Random House, 1960), 104.

29. Stacy Wolf, *A Problem like Maria: Gender and Sexuality in the American Musical* (Ann Arbor: University of Michigan Press, 2002), 219.

30. Oscar Hammerstein II, 'Play Safe!', Library of Congress, Music Division, Oscar Hammerstein II Collection, Box 48, Folder 6-7: 2-1-11–2-1-12.

31. For the political symbolism of this song, especially as an American metaphor for the *Opferthese* (the myth that Austria was Nazi Germany's victim rather than a proactive agent in World War II), see Carolin Stahrenberg, 'Rodgers and Hammerstein's "Edelweiß": Hymne der (österreichischen) Unschuld?', in *Salzburgs Hymnen von 1816 bis heute*, ed. Thomas Hochradner and Julia Lienbacher (Vienna: 2017), 157–166.

32. For further discussion of this decision, see Susanne Scheiblhofer, 'The Singing Nazi: Representations of National Socialism in Broadway Musicals' (PhD diss., University of Oregon, 2014), 93–100.

33. For more information on *The Sound of Music* in Austria, see Christian Strasser, '*The Sound of Music*: Ein unbekannter Welterfolg', in '*The Sound of Music*': *Zwischen Mythos und Marketing*, ed. Ulrike Kammerhofer-Aggermann, Alexander G. Keul, and Andrea Weiss (Salzburg: Salzburger Landesinstitut für Volkskunde, 2000), 267–295.

34. Mervy Rothstein, 'In Three Revivals, the Goose Stepping Is Louder', *New York Times*, 8 March 1998, 4.

35. For more information on the relationship between 'Tomorrow Belongs to Me' and the 'Lorelei' see Susanne Scheiblhofer '"Tomorrow Belongs to Me": The Journey of a Show Tune from Broadway to Rechtsrock', *Studies in Musical Theatre* 11, no. 1 (March 2017): 5–22, https://doi.org/10.1386/smt.11.1.5_1, accessed 1 October 2020.

36. Jens Schmidl, Zoom Conversation with Susanne Scheiblhofer, 19 February 2021: 'Was auch für die Szene natürlich eine Rolle spielte, dass die natürlich auch praktisch Angst hatten.

'EV'RY HOTSY TOTSY NAZI STAND AND CHEER' 501

Also kann man sagen, wir spielen das nur, aber sie spielen das ohne Schutz. Sie haben eben nicht die Rampe, sondern sie haben schon das Problem, dass da – also sie können ja jetzt neben irgendeinem Opfer des Nationalsozialismus sitzen und es nicht wissen und stehen daneben auf und spielen die Rolle und der flippt total aus.'

37. Scheiblhofer, "'Tomorrow Belongs to Me".
38. For more information on how Rodgers and Hammerstein perfected the book musical, see Geoffrey Block, *Richard Rodgers* (New Haven, CT: Yale University Press, 2003).
39. Quoted in Myrna Katz Frommer and Harvey Frommer, *It Happened on Broadway: An Oral History of the Great White Way* (New York: Houghton Mifflin Harcourt, 1998), 181.
40. See Nicholas G. Rinaldi, 'Music as Mediator: A Description of the Process of Concept Development in the Musical *Cabaret* (PhD diss., Ohio State University, 1982), 23–88.
41. Steven Suskin, *The Sound of Broadway Music: A Book of Orchestrators and Orchestrations* (New York: Oxford University Press, 2009), 223.
42. For background information on the set and lighting design of *Cabaret*, see Keith Garebian, *The Making of Cabaret* (New York: Oxford University Press, 2011), 38–49.
43. Foster Hirsch, *Harold Prince and the American Musical Theatre*, expanded and rev. ed. (New York: Applause, 2005), 61.
44. Joe Masteroff and Fred Ebb, *Harold Prince's 'Cabaret'* (New York: Random House, 1967), 93.
45. John Kander, Fred Ebb, and Joe Masteroff, *Cabaret*, Vocal Score (New York: Times Square Music Publications, 1968), 171–176.
46. Ibid., 182.
47. Ibid., 183.
48. Rolf Kutschera, personal correspondence with Hal Prince, 2 March 1970, New York Public Library for the Performing Arts, Hal Prince Papers, Box 4.
49. Rolf Kutschera, personal correspondence with Fred Ebb, 16 December 1970, New York Public Library for the Performing Arts, Fred Ebb Papers, Box 11.
50. Friedbert Streller, 'Cabaret als zeitkritisches Kabarett', *Süddeutsche Zeitung*, 23 January 1976. This and the following newspaper reviews of *Cabaret* have been archived by the New York Public Library for the Performing Arts without page numbers.
51. Maja-Rosewith Riemer, phone conversation with Susanne Scheiblhofer, 4 May 2015.
52. Ibid.
53. 'Eine, die damals dabei war', *Morgenpost*, 18 October 2011.
54. Gottfried Schmiedel, 'Faschistische Vergangenheit aus Broadway-Sicht', *Sächsisches Tageblatt* 1976, New York Public Library for the Performing Arts, Hal Prince Papers, Box 4.
55. H. W. F., 'Cabaret auf der Bühne', *Sächsische Neueste Nachrichten*, 20 January 1976.
56. Ingo Zimmermann, 'Leichte Muse—Apokalyptisch', *Union*, 21 January 1976.
57. Horst Heitzenröther, 'Cabaret—DDR-Erstaufführung des Musicals an der Staatsoperette Dresden', in *Kulturspiegel*, Stimme der DDR, broadcast 21 January 1976.
58. 'Nazis waren wir auch! So blöd ist das Publikum nicht—die begreifen das schon'; Riemer, phone conversation.
59. Gerhard Knopf, 'Einen Tick zu Chic', *Das Musical*, February 1987, 14.
60. Hildegard Knef (1925–2002) was the first female German movie star after the end of World War II to be invited to Hollywood. She was also the first of only three German actresses ever to play the lead in a Broadway musical: she appeared, billed as Hildegarde Neff, in Cole Porter's 1955 *Silk Stockings*. (The other two are Ute Lemper and Anna Montanaro, both of whom played Velma Kelly in the revival of *Chicago*.) In addition to being a

celebrated actress, Knef was also an accomplished chanteuse, songwriter, and bestselling author; as a result of her many talents, hers remained a household name in Germany for more than five decades.

61. Knopf, 'Einen Tick zu Chic', 14.

62. D. Plögert and M. Barricelli, 'Willkommen, Hilde! Großes Staraufgebot bei *Cabaret* im Theater des Westens', *Das Musical*, October 1987, 18.

63. Kirsten Fermaglich, 'Mel Brooks' *The Producers*: Tracing American Jewish Culture through Comedy, 1967–2007', *American Studies* 48, no. 4 (2007): 59–87.

64. See Mel Brooks and Thomas Meehan, *The Producers: The Book, Lyrics, and Story behind the Biggest Hit in Broadway History* (New York: Round Table Press/Miramax, 2000), and Mel Brooks and Thomas Meehan, *The Producers: Piano/Vocal Highlights* (Milwaukee, WI: Hal Leonard, 2000).

65. See Tobias Widmaier, "'Listen to the German Band". Straßenkapellen aus Deutschland als Thema amerikanischer Songs 1872–1932', in *Lied und populäre Kultur/Song and Popular Culture*, Jahrbuch des Deutschen Volksliedarchivs Freiburg 55 (Münster: Waxmann, 2010), 77–99. In Disney's *The Fuhrer's Face*, a German band is caricatured both visually and aurally, which is just one example of how those musicians have been depicted for decades. Tobias Widmaier, "'Does Dot Leedle German Band Make Music or Noise?" Deutsche Straßenmusikkapellen in London und New York 1850–1914', in *Populäre Musik in der urbanen Klanglandschaft: Kulturgeschichtliche Perspektiven*, ed. Tobias Widmaier and Nils Grosch (Münster: Waxmann, 2014), 65–73.)

66. 'Does Dot Little German Band Make Music or Noise? If Musik, Goot! If Noise, "Raus mit the Oompah Peddlars"', *Chicago Daily Tribune*, 2 July 1911, B3.

67. Susan Sontag, 'Notes on "Camp"', in *Camp: Queer Aesthetics and the Performing Subject: A Reader*, ed. Fabio Cleto (Edinburgh, 1999): 53–65; here: 53. Originally published in 1964.

68. For the encapsulated communicative situation including a staged or imagined audience in concept musicals, see Nils Grosch, "'That's the Alienation Effect": Verfremdung und Song im Concept Musical', in *Verfremdungen: Ein Phänomen Bertolt Brechts in der Musik*, ed. Jürgenn Hillesheim (Freiburg im Breisgau: Rombach, 2013), 317–333.

69. To give but two examples: David Crossland, 'It's Springtime for Hitler in Berlin: *The Producers* Debuts in Germany', *Spiegel Online*, 4 September 2009, http://www.spiegel.de/international/zeitgeist/the-producers-debuts-in-germany-it-s-springtime-for-hitler-in-berlin-a-617987.html, accessed 12 January 2016; and Peter Strasser, 'Hitlerspaß und Hitlerernst', *Kleine Zeitung*, 16 March 2008, 108.

70. Susan Gubar, 'Racial Camp in *The Producers* and *Bamboozled*', *Film Quarterly* 60, no. 2 (2006): 26–37.

71. For the musical elements in *The Producers* and their historical heritage, see Katherine Baber, "'The Jew Who Buried Hitler": Music and Identity in Mel Brooks' *The Producers*', *Institute for Studies in American Music Newsletter* 35, no. 2 (2006): 6–8.

72. Sontag, 'Notes on "Camp"', 62.

73. For a more in-depth discussion of the correlations between fascism and homosexuality, see Fermaglich, 'Mel Brooks' *The Producers*: Tracing American Jewish Culture', 59–87.

74. Christian Höller, 'Der Führer in Wien: *The Producers*; Mel Brooks' Nazimusical wird erstmals deutsch aufgeführt—und die Österreicher tun sich schwer,' *Jüdische Allgemeine*, 17 July 2008, https://www.juedische-allgemeine.de/allgemein/der-fuehrer-in-wien/, accessed 20 January 2020.

## 'EV'RY HOTSY TOTSY NAZI STAND AND CHEER'    503

75. 'Admiralspalast provoziert mit Brezel-Fahne', *Berliner Morgenpost*, 9 April 2009, https://www.morgenpost.de/berlin/article104133905/Admiralspalast-provoziert-mit-Brezel-Fahne.html, accessed 20 January 2020.
76. Harald Schmidt and Oliver Pocher, *Schmidt & Pocher*, ARD, 2 April 2009, https://www.youtube.com/watch?v=hH-SeX3nO9s, accessed 1 June 2020.
77. For this reading and the reception of the three versions of *The Producers*, see Fermaglich, 'Mel Brooks' *The Producers*: Tracing American Jewish Culture'.

## BIBLIOGRAPHY

Note: All the reviews of *Cabaret* listed below are archived without page numbers at the New York Public Library for the Performing Arts, Hal Prince Papers, Box 4.

'Admiralspalast provoziert mit Brezel-Fahne'. *Berliner Morgenpost*, 9 April 2009, https://www.morgenpost.de/berlin/article104133905/Admiralspalast-provoziert-mit-Brezel-Fahne.html, accessed 1 June 2020.

Baber, Katherine. '"The Jew who Buried Hitler": Music and Identity in Mel Brooks' *The Producers*'. *Institute for Studies in American Music Newsletter* 35, no. 2 (2006): 6–8.

Bernstein, Leonard. 'Excerpts from Bernstein's *West Side* Log', 1957, www.westsidestory.com/notes-and-letters, accessed 20 May 2020.

Block, Geoffrey. *Richard Rodgers*. New Haven, CT: Yale University Press, 2003.

'Braver Schweyk'. *Der Spiegel*, 27 March 1957. https://www.spiegel.de/spiegel/print/d-41120961.html, accessed 10 January 2020.

Brecht, Bertolt. 'Die *Schweyk*-Fabel'. In *Materialien zu Bertolt Brechts 'Schweyk im Zweiten Weltkrieg'*, edited by Herbert Knust, 157–166. Frankfurt: Suhrkamp, 1974.

Brecht, Bertolt. *Werke*. Vol. 7, Stücke 7. Frankfurt: Suhrkamp, 1991.

Brooks, Mel, and Thomas Meehan. *The Producers: Piano/Vocal Highlights*. Milwaukee, WI: Hal Leonard, 2001.

Brooks, Mel, and Thomas Meehan. *'The Producers': The Book, Lyrics, and Story behind the Biggest Hit in Broadway History*. New York: Round Table Press/Miramax, 2001.

Danuser, Hermann. 'Musikalische Prosa'. In *Die Musik in Geschichte und Gegenwart*, Sachteil 6, edited by Ludwig Finscher, 857–866. Kassel: Bärenreiter and Stuttgart: Metzler, 1997.

'Does Dot Little German Band Make Music or Noise? If Musik, Goot! If Noise, "Raus mit the Oompah Peddlars"'. *Chicago Daily Tribune*. 2 July 1911.

'Eine, die damals dabei war'. *Morgenpost*, 18 October 2011.

Eisler, Hanns. '*Schweyk* und der deutsche Militarismus: Interview conducted by André Gisselbrecht, 11 November 1961'. In special issue on Hanns Eisler, *Sinn und Form*, 271–275. Berlin, 1964.

Eisler, Hanns. *Bühnenmusik zu 'Schweyk im zweiten Weltkrieg' von Bertolt Brecht*. Lieder und Kantaten 8. Leipzig: Breitkopf & Härtel, 1964.

Fermaglich, Kirsten. 'Mel Brooks' *The Producers*: Tracing American Jewish Culture through Comedy, 1967–2007'. *American Studies* 48, no. 4 (2007): 59–87.

Gamillscheg, Marie. 'Anne Frank, jetzt auch mit Snack-Box'. *Die Welt*, 8 May 2014, https://www.welt.de/kultur/article127747424/Anne-Frank-jetzt-auch-mit-Snack-Box.html, accessed 10 January 2020.

Garebian, Keith. *The Making of 'Cabaret'*. Oxford and New York: Oxford University Press, 2011.

Gerdeman-Klein, Ellen. 'The Dramaturgical Integration of Text and Music in Brecht's *Schweyk im Zweiten Weltkrieg*'. PhD diss., University of Illinois Urbana-Champaign, 1995.

Grosch, Nils, ed. *Kurt Weill: Briefwechsel mit der Universal Edition Wien*. Stuttgart: Metzler, 2002.

Grosch, Nils. 'Kurt Weill, *Mahagonny* and the Commercialization of Berlin Musical Theatre in the Weimar Republic'. In *Beyond Glitter and Doom: The Contingency of the Weimar Republic*, edited by Jochen Hung, Godela Weiss-Sussex, and Geoff Wilkes, 192–208. Munich: Iudicium Verlag, 2012.

Grosch, Nils. '*Schweyk*—ohne Weill? Zu einem späten Projekt des Teams Brecht/Weill'. In *Musik-Kontexte: Festschrift für Hanns-Werner Heister*, edited by Thomas Phleps and Wieland Reich, 304–313. Münster: MV-Wissenschaft, 2011.

Grosch, Nils. '"That's the Alienation Effect": Verfremdung und Song im Concept Musical'. In *Verfremdungen: Ein Phänomen Bertolt Brechts in der Musik*, edited by Jürgen Hillesheim, 317–333. Freiburg im Breisgau: Rombach, 2013.

Grosch, Nils. '"Vom Weib des Nazisoldaten": Musik, Propaganda, und Aufführung eines Brecht-Songs'. In *Lied und populäre Kultur/Song and Popular Culture: Jahrbuch des Deutschen Volksliedarchivs Freiburg*, 50–51 (2005–2006): 137–161.

Grosch, Nils. 'Weill, Eisler und die musikalische Dramaturgie in *Schweyk*'. In *De Hašek a Brecht: Fortune de la figure de Chveik en Europe*, edited by Marie-Odile Thirouin, 153–166. Special issue, *Cahiers de l'ILCEA* 8. Grenoble: Institut des Langues et Cultures d'Europe et d'Amérique, 2006.

Grosch, Nils, 'Zur medialen Dramaturgie des populären Musiktheaters in der Weimarer Republik'. In *Populärkultur, Massenmedien und Avantgarde 1919–1933*, edited by Jessica Nitsche and Nadine Werner, 239–250. Munich: Wilhelm Fink, 2012.

Grosch, Nils, and Carolin Stahrenberg. 'Nationaler "Kitsch" als ästhetisches Problem im populären Musiktheater'. In *Kitsch und Nation: Zur kulturellen Modellierung eines polemischen Begriffs*, edited by Kathrin Ackermann und Christopher F. Laferl, 163–183. Edition Kulturwissenschaft 60. Bielefeld: Transcript, 2016.

Gubar, Susan. 'Racial Camp in *The Producers* and *Bamboozled*'. *Film Quarterly* 60, no. 2 (2006): 26–37.

Hammerstein, Oscar. Play Safe! Library of Congress, Music Division, Oscar Hammerstein II Collection, Box 48, Folder 6-7: 2-1-11–2-1-12.

Heitzenröther, Horst. '*Cabaret*: DDR-Erstaufführung des Musicals an der Staatsoperette Dresden'. In *Kulturspiegel*, Stimme der DDR, broadcast 21 January 1976.

Hillman-McCord, Jessica. *Echoes of the Holocaust on the American Musical Stage*. Jefferson, NC: McFarland, 2012.

Hirsch, Foster. *Harold Prince and the American Musical Theatre*. Expanded and revised ed. New York: Applause, 2005.

Höller, Christian. 'Der Führer in Wien: *The Producers*, Mel Brooks' Nazimusical wird erstmals deutsch aufgeführt—und die Österreicher tun sich schwer'. *Jüdische Allgemeine*, 17 July 2008, https://www.juedische-allgemeine.de/allgemein/der-fuehrer-in-wien/?q=the%20producers, accessed 1 June 2020.

H. W. F. '*Cabaret* auf der Bühne'. *Sächsische Neueste Nachrichten*, 20 January 1976.

Kander, John, Fred Ebb, and Joe Masteroff. *Cabaret*. Vocal Score. New York: Times Square Music Publications, 1968.

Katz Frommer, Myrna Frommer, and Harvey Frommer. *It Happened on Broadway: An Oral History of the Great White Way*. New York: Houghton Mifflin Harcourt, 1998.

Knopf, Gerhard. 'Einen Tick zu Chic'. *Das Musical*, February 1987, 14.

Lammers, Annekatrin. 'Kritik zu *Anne Frank: The Musical*'. *ARD Nachtmagazin*, 29 February 2008.

Lindsay, Howard, and Russel Crouse. *The Sound of Music: A New Musical Play*. New York: Random House, 1960.

Lindsay, Howard, Russel Crouse, and Oscar Hammerstein II. 'The Sound of Music'. Script draft, 27 May 1959. Library of Congress, Music Division, Oscar Hammerstein II Collection, Box 49, Folder 6: 2-1-11–2-1-12.

Maslon, Laurence. *The Sound of Music Companion*. New York: Simon & Schuster, 2007.

Masteroff, Joe, and Fred Ebb. *Harold Prince's Cabaret*. New York: Random House, 1967.

Peck, Seymour. 'They Made *The Sound of Music*: About Those Who Helped Make *The Sound of Music*'. *New York Times*, 15 November 1959, 3.

Plögert, D., and M. Barricelli. 'Willkommen, Hilde! Großes Staraufgebot bei *Cabaret* im Theater des Westens'. *Das Musical*, October 1987, 18–19.

Rinaldi, Nicholas G. 'Music as Mediator: A Description of the Process of Concept Development in the Musical *Cabaret*'. PhD diss., Ohio State University, 1982.

Rothstein, Mervy. 'In Three Revivals, the Goose Stepping Is Louder'. *New York Times*, 8 March 1998, 4.

Scheiblhofer, Susanne. 'Confronting the Past through Popular Musical Theatre: The Effects of Austrian Postwar Cultural Policies on the Reception History of Musicals', 'Austrian Music Studies: Topics, Perspectives, Concepts', special issue, *Musicologica Austriaca: Journal for Austrian Music Studies* (April 13, 2023), https:// www.musau.org/ parts/ neue- arti cle- page/ view/ 146, accessed July 5th, 2023

Scheiblhofer, Susanne. '"Tomorrow Belongs to Me": The Journey of a Show Tune from Broadway to Rechtsrock'. *Studies in Musical Theatre* 11, no. 1 (March 2017): 5–22, https://doi. org/10.1386/smt.11.1.5_1, accessed 10 January 2020.

Scheiblhofer, Susanne. 'The Singing Nazi: Representations of National Socialism in Broadway Musicals'. PhD diss., University of Oregon, 2014.

Schmiedel, Gottfried. 'Faschistische Vergangenheit aus Broadway-Sicht.' *Sächsisches Tagesblatt* 1976.

Sobol, Joshua. *'Ghetto': In a Version by David Lan with Lyrics Translated and Music Arranged by Jeremy Sams*. London: Nick Hern Books, 1989.

Sontag, Susan. 'Notes on "Camp"'. In *Camp: Queer Aesthetics and the Performing Subject; A Reader*, edited by Fabio Cleto, 53–65. Edinburgh: Edinburgh University Press 1999. Originally published in 1964.

Stahrenberg, Carolin. 'Rodgers und Hammerstein's "Edelweiß": Hymne der (österreichischen) Unschuld?' In *Salzburgs Hymnen von 1816 bis heute*, edited by Thomas Hochradner and Julia Lienbacher, 157–166. Vienna: LIT, 2017.

Strasser, Christian. '*The Sound of Music*: Ein unbekannter Welterfolg'. In *'The Sound of Music': Zwischen Mythos und Marketing*, edited by Ulrike Kammerhofer-Aggermann and Alexander G. Keul, 267–295. Salzburg: Salzburger Landesinstitut für Volkskunde, 2000.

'Streit um ein Musical zu Anne Frank'. *Die Welt*, 18 February 2008. https://www.welt.de/kultur/ article1689181/Streit-um-ein-Musical-zu-Anne-Frank.html, accessed 10 January 2020.

Streller, Friedbert. '*Cabaret* als zeitkritisches Kabarett'. *Süddeutsche Zeitung*, 23 January 1976.

Suskin, Steven. *The Sound of Broadway Music: A Book of Orchestrators and Orchestrations*. Oxford and New York: Oxford University Press, 2009.

Wandler, Reiner. 'Anne-Frank-Tagebuch als Musical'. *TAZ*, 12 February 2008, https://taz.de/Anne-Frank-Tagebuch-als-Musical/!5186857/, accessed 10 January 2020.

Weill, Kurt. 'Was ist musikalisches Theater? [Notate für einen Vortrag]'. In *Musik und musikalisches Theater: Gesammelte Schriften; Mit einer Auswahl von Gesprächen und Interviews*, edited by Stephen Hinton and Jürgen Schebera, 114–148. Mainz: Schott, 2000.

Weill, Kurt, [and Ira Gershwin]. 'The Song of the Rhineland: From the Film *Where Do We Go from Here?* Sheet Music.' New York: Chappell, 1945.

Widmaier, Tobias. '"Does Dot Leedle German Band Make Music or Noise?" Deutsche Straßenmusikkapellen in London und New York 1850–1914'. In *Populäre Musik in der urbanen Klanglandschaft: Kulturgeschichtliche Perspektiven*, edited by Tobias Widmaier and Nils Grosch, 65–73. Münster: Waxmann, 2014.

Widmaier, Tobias. '"Listen to the German Band": Straßenkapellen aus Deutschland als Thema amerikanischer Songs 1872–1932'. *Lied und populäre Kultur/Song and Popular Culture: Jahrbuch des Deutschen Volksliedarchivs Freiburg* 55 (2010): 77–99.

Wolf, Stacy. *A Problem like Maria: Gender and Sexuality in the American Musical*. Ann Arbor: University of Michigan Press, 2002.

Zimmermann, Ingo. 'Leichte Muse-Apokalyptisch'. *Union*, 21 January 1976.

CHAPTER 18

# BETWEEN *STARLIGHT EXPRESS* AND *MY FAIR LADY*, FRANK WILDHORN AND MARTIN LINGNAU

## Musicals in Contemporary German-Language Theatre

FRÉDÉRIC DÖHL

## INTRODUCTION: THE ROLE OF MUSICALS IN CONTEMPORARY GERMAN-LANGUAGE THEATRE

AT the end of a period of development initiated by the Austrian première in Vienna (1983) and the German première in Hamburg (1986) of *Cats*—using different German translations—the current situation of the musical as a genre in German-speaking Europe can be best summed up by a slogan used recently in British politics: 'strong and stable'. The general quality of productions, performers, and directors has risen significantly since the 1980s, supported by the introduction of some specialist study programmes at institutions of higher education. Production teams have become more experienced, too. According to the annual statistics of the Deutscher Bühnenverein (German Stage Association), twice as many theatres produce musicals today as at the time of *Cats*,[1] and the repertoire has tripled during the last three and a half decades.[2] Supported by these developments, musicals nowadays are mostly produced at a solid professional level; the genre is institutionally consolidated and has a robust, well-organised fan base.[3] Overall, musical theatre is a success story in the German-language market—however, with some qualifications, reservations, and specific points of note.

This essay offers an introduction to the German-language musical theatre market in Germany, Austria, and northern Switzerland for Anglophone musicals. Beyond the

United States and the United Kingdom, the German-language theatre scene is the third-biggest market for popular musical theatre in the world.[4] The chapter is mainly focused on the present-day situation, with a special emphasis on repertoire.[5] Present-day means as of season 2019/20—until covid closed theatres in March 2020.

To understand the impact of the covid pandemic that followed, one only must compare the numbers of productions of the most-produced musicals in German-language theatres since the mid-1990s (Table 18.2) in the last full season before (2018/19) and the first full season in the age of covid (2020/21) (see Table 18.1).

Selected additional information regarding the highly inconsistent era of the covid pandemic is given here and there in the following, too, up to the German-language premiere of *Hamilton* in Hamburg in October 2022. However, focus lies on the pre-pandemic configuration of the domestic market. The story of the stage musical in Central Europe since March 2022 is quite a different story to tell. Furthermore, if any trends from the covid years from a reduced schedule of productions to changed emphases and priorities in the repertoire to the extended presence of official (non-bootleg) audio-visual representations of stage musicals on the web will be of lasting nature, remains to be seen. As of now, at least, it is to be expected that the domestic market more or less will return to its pre-covid structures, proportions, and specifics after the pandemic as introduced in this essay, not least because of the key, stabilizing role of the public, subsidized theatre sector here and the substantial state support that private theatres received, too.[6] Having said that, as of October 2022 many potentially far-reaching factors of uncertainty remain in force and have newly joined in, respectively, from the reluctance of significant parts of the traditional target audiences for musicals to return to the theatres for security reasons to the energy cost crisis as result of the Russian invasion in Ukraine in February 2022.

Compiling a statistically sound overview of the German, Austrian, and Swiss theatre scene regarding musicals is complicated: on the hand, studies by Wolfgang Jansen (2008), Jonas Menze (2018), and Thomas Siedhoff (2007 and 2018) concerning the domestic production of original German-language musicals proffer an in-depth introduction to the domestic production of musicals in German, the local scene. and its main protagonists.[7] This scholarship is accompanied and complemented by:

- the aforementioned annual performance statistics of the Deutscher Bühnenverein;
- the lists of winners and nominees of the annual Deutscher Musical Theater Preis (German Musical Theatre Prize), which has been awarded since 2014;
- the holdings of the Deutsches Musicalarchiv (German Archive for Musical Theatre) in Freiburg;
- the holdings of the Deutsches Musikarchiv (German Music Archive) of the German National Library in Leipzig (especially cast recordings and sheet music);
- several specialised print media (e.g., *Musicals: Das Musicalmagazin*, bi-monthly, since 1986) and websites;
- the websites of (and personal exchange with) major publishing houses holding the performance rights to important musicals; and

**Table 18.1 Top 12 of most–produced musicals in German–language theatres, 2018/19 and 2020/21**

| Theatrical Season | Most-produced Musicals in Order of Ranking – Number of Annual Productions | | | | | | | | | | | |
|---|---|---|---|---|---|---|---|---|---|---|---|---|
| | 1.<br>My<br>Fair<br>Lady<br>(1956) | 2.<br>Fiddler<br>on the<br>Roof<br>(1964) | 3.<br>Cabaret<br>(1966) | 4.<br>The<br>Rocky<br>Horror<br>Show<br>(1975) | 5.<br>Heute<br>Abend:<br>Lola<br>Blau<br>(1971) | 6.<br>West<br>Side<br>Story<br>(1957) | 7.<br>Kiss<br>Me,<br>Kate<br>(1948) | 8.<br>Little<br>Shop of<br>Horrors<br>(1982) | 9.<br>Evita<br>(1978) | 10.<br>Sekretärin-<br>nen (1995) | 11.<br>La<br>Cage<br>aux<br>Folles<br>(1983) | 12.<br>Jesus<br>Christ<br>Superstar<br>(1971) |
| 2018–19 | 15 | 5 | 12 | 7 | 3 | 6 | 9 | 3 | 3 | 2 | 3 | 6 |
| 2020–21 | 1 | 2 | 5 | 0 | 5 | 2 | 2 | 3 | 2 | 0 | 0 | 1 |

Source: Annual Statistics of the Deutsche Bühnenverein (productions by theatre; additional guest touring productions in public theatres are included occasionally but not systematically in these statistics)

- the websites of (and personal exchange with) theatres producing musicals.[8]

Compared to the fairly complete and coherent statistics of the subsidised professional theatres, which have been recorded and published each season for decades now mainly by the Deutscher Bühnenverein, the accessible data for some important private producers of musicals (including the largest, Stage Entertainment) is incomplete and less carefully differentiated. At the same time, amateur and student productions tend not to show up in the statistics and are challenging to compile, yet they are important to bear in mind (for example, Stephen Sondheim's *Anyone Can Whistle* and *Merrily We Roll Along* have only been performed in those sectors of German-language theatre market, as have major contemporary pieces such as Jason Robert Brown's *Parade*). However, with some caution a fair approximation of a reliable overall picture is possible, especially regarding repertoire.[9]

As a starting point, the present-day situation of musicals in the German-language market (where Germany is closely interconnected with Austria and northern Switzerland) can be summed up as follows: there is a stable two-tier local system now of both private theatres (mostly metropolitan and Broadway-style) and public theatres (mostly mid-sized, provincial, subsidised by states and municipalities, non-profit, and repertory-oriented), both of which regularly produce musicals. Some touring companies and a few summer festivals (like Bad Hersfeld and Tecklenburg) complete the picture. However, public theatres, especially the prestigious large metropolitan opera houses, still rarely schedule musicals (other than touring productions during the summer recess), occasional exceptions such as the Komische Oper in Berlin notwithstanding.

In total, there are about eight hundred professional theatre stages in Germany alone today, of which about a quarter are run privately. Some private and public institutions run several stages in parallel. Many public theatres are multipurpose venues (*Mehrspartenhaus*) which produce musicals in addition to opera, operetta, ballet, straight plays, and avant-garde performance theatre. However, there is hardly any major public theatre in the German-language market focused primarily on musicals. From the 1960s to the 1990s, the now privatised Theater des Westens in Berlin offered major productions, including *My Fair Lady* (1961), *La Cage aux Folles* (1985), and *Porgy and Bess* (1988), the first two of which were German premières. And as of today, the Staatsoperette Dresden, funded by the city of Dresden, is highly invested in musicals, having been the first to stage such works as Andrew Lloyd Webber's *Aspects of Love* (1997) and Stephen Sondheim's *Passion* (2011). In Austria there is the unique case of the Vereinigte Bühnen Wien in Vienna, a company of three theatres which are mainly owned by the city of Vienna; two of these (the Raimund Theater and the Ronacher Theater, respectively[10]) focus on musicals, with a repertoire and programming style similar to that of the large private theatre companies in Germany. But these institutions are exceptions in the public theatre sector. Usually musicals get integrated into a mixed programme.

FIG. 18.1 Eliza at the races; scene from the first German production of *My Fair Lady*, staged in 1961 at the Theater des Westens, Berlin. To this day, the Lerner and Loewe classic remains by far the most often staged Anglophone musical in Germany. *At the centre, left to right*: Friedrich Schönfeld (Colonel Pickering), Paul Hubschmid (Henry Higgins), Karin Hübner (Eliza Doolittle), and Rex Gildo (Freddy Eynsford-Hill). Photo: Harry Croner/Ullstein Bild © Getty Images.

A typical example is the repertoire of the Theater Dortmund, the municipal theatre of Germany's ninth largest city. It is a classic multipurpose venue that presents opera, musicals, operettas, ballets, orchestral concerts, and straight plays, as well as youth and children's theatre.[11] Theater Dortmund produces one musical per season, and its repertoire during the last ten seasons reads as a paradigm of the German-language subsidised theatre scene: *Jekyll and Hyde* (2019–2020), *West Side Story* (2018–2019), *Hairspray* (2017–2018), *Sunset Boulevard* (2016–2017), *Kiss Me, Kate* (2015–2016), *Jesus Christ Superstar* (2014–2015), *Fiddler on the Roof* (2013–2014), *Funny Girl* (2012–2013), *The Full Monty* (2011–2012), and *Sekretärinnen* (2010–2011). This is a typical mix for subsidised venues that perform musicals on a regular basis: one rarely produced classic (*Funny Girl*), two contemporary musicals with extra name recognition from the movies (*The Full Monty* and *Hairspray*) and, as safe choices, one original German-language hit (*Sekretärinnen*) and six imports with an excellent standing and a reputation for high production values in the German-speaking market. In addition, a few additional works of popular musical theatre, such as the German-language classics *Das Weiße Rößl* (*White Horse Inn*, 1930) and *Linie 1* (*Line 1*, 1986), were produced by other departments of the playhouse, covering operetta and youth theatre, respectively.

The two most important private companies for musicals in Germany are currently the aforementioned Stage Entertainment (with fourteen private theatres in Berlin, Essen, Hamburg, Munich, Oberhausen, and Stuttgart[12]) and Mehr-BB Entertainment (with five theatres in Berlin, Bochum, Cologne, Dusseldorf, and Hamburg, as well as touring productions; owned since 2018 by the Ambassador Theatre Group, United Kingdom). The most active off-Broadway-size producer is Schmidt Theater in Hamburg, which runs three St Pauli–based venues, Schmidtchen (200 seats), Schmidt Theater (423 seats), and Schmidts Tivoli (620 seats). In stark contrast to the public theatre, private theatres and private touring production companies prefer a run-based approach, either open-ended or limited. Both segments of the private sector charge average ticket prices of around €100; in contrast, tickets for the highly subsidised public theatres are much cheaper and can regularly be obtained for a third of that, as is also the case with important smaller private producers of original musicals such as the Schmidt Theater in Hamburg or the Neuköllner Oper in Berlin.

Since the mid-2000s, the statistics of the Deutscher Bühnenverein has every season reported 2,000,000–2,500,000 million visitors attending musicals in Germany alone, plus some 300,000 more in Austria and northern Switzerland. This figure includes significant numbers from important private producers, such as Mehr-BB Entertainment (about 400,000 visitors annually just for *Starlight Express* in Bochum) and Schmidt Theater (about 130,000 visitors annually just for *Heiße Ecke* [*Hot Corner*, 2003] in Hamburg).[13] However, the market leader, Stage Entertainment, is not included: it announced an additional 3.3 million tickets sold for its fourteen private theatres in 2017–2018. The most important Austrian producer, Vereinigte Bühnen Wien, has to be added as well, with about half a million visitors for musicals annually announced in its last published business report of 2021. Based on these figures, the size of the combined overall audience in German-language theatres for the musical as a genre adds up to an estimated 6 million theatre-goers per season (plus audiences for regular touring venues for musicals, such as the Admiralspalast in Berlin) which amounts to about 70 percent of West End audiences (approximately 9.5 million) and about 40 percent of Broadway audiences (approximately 15 million) for musicals.[14]

Usually between 220 and 270 musicals (excluding musicals primarily for and with children) are staged each season for this target audience in private and public German theatres, plus some thirty more in Austria and northern Switzerland.[15] In most seasons, only *My Fair Lady* reaches double-digit numbers of productions. In general, the market is quite diverse: between 100 and 150 different works are produced.[16] For 2017–2018, 141 different stages from all over the country reported the production of at least one musical to the Deutscher Bühnenverein (plus an additional fourteen for Austria and northern Switzerland).[17] Stage Entertainment ran an additional fourteen venues, and Vereinigte Bühnen Wien another two. In total, that adds up to 171 performance spaces for musicals,[18] more than for opera.[19] Every season between 2,000 and 2,500 performances of musicals take place in the public theatre sector alone.[20] Combined with the programming in most private theatres, which normally is organised around runs, either open-ended or limited, of a specific work, the total number of single performances of musicals per season adds up to about 8,000—again, higher than that of opera.[21]

Usually, about 5 percent of the musicals recorded each season by the Deutscher Bühnenverein are first productions of imported shows (2016–2017: 11 of 235), and another 5 percent are first productions of originals (2016–2017: 15 of 235). Altogether German-language and world premières thus account for about 10 percent of all music theatre productions. Thus, about twenty-five to thirty new musicals are staged in Germany alone each season, with Berlin, Hamburg, and Vienna being the hot spots for new works. The numbers for new works go up to about forty when Austria and northern Switzerland are included and when additional sources beyond the annual statistics of the Deutscher Bühnenverein are consulted.[22]

Nonetheless, these figures are evidence that no matter which data one uses, the ratio of new works to revivals is quite different from that on Broadway, where that relationship is two to one. To note, among the 101 works produced in the last twenty years by Stage Entertainment, the largest private producer of musicals operating in Germany since the millennium, are a mere six German originals, three jukebox musicals, and three 'screen-to-stage transfers' based on well-known German movies—*Ich war noch niemals in New York* (*I Have Never Been to New York*, 2007), *Ich will Spass!* (*I Want Fun!*, 2008), *Hinterm Horizont* (*Beyond the Horizon*, 2011), *Der Schuh des Manitu* (*The Shoe of Manitou*, 2008), *Das Wunder von Bern* (*The Miracle of Bern*, 2014), and *Fack Ju Göhte* (*Suck Me Shakespeer*, 2018), respectively.[23] The Vereinigte Bühnen Wien, Austria's main producer, originated fourteen musicals in thirty years, from *Freudiana* (1990) and *Elisabeth* (1992) to *Schikaneder* (2016) and *I Am from Austria* (2017); these world premières also include such domestically well-known works as *Tanz der Vampire* (*Dance of the Vampires*, 1997), *Mozart!* (1999), and *Rebecca* (2006).[24] Additionally, there are a few smaller private producers which specialise in devising new works, such as the Schmidt Theater in Hamburg (*Swinging St. Pauli*, 2001; *Heiße Ecke*, 2003; *Villa Sonnenschein* [*The Mansion of Sunshine*, 2005]; *Die Königs vom Kiez* [*The Kings of the Hood*, 2013]; and *Cindy Reller*, 2016) and the Neuköllner Oper in Berlin (*Das Wunder von Neukölln* [*The Miracle of Neukölln*, 1998]; and *Stella: Das blonde Gespenst vom Kurfürstendamm* [*Stella: The Blond Ghost of Kurfürstendamm*, 2016]). Yet overall, despite these activities, the creation of original musicals still plays a subordinate role in the German-language market, especially outside the area of theatre for and with children.

Taking all this information into account, there is a crucial point to be made that still goes widely unrecognised in German-language scholarship and music journalism: musicals do not merely constitute a vital part of contemporary music theatre in the three German-language countries, they actually predominate when it comes to contemporary (more properly, post-1945) music theatre (musicals, operas, operettas, ballets, avant-garde performance theatre productions, etc.).[25] In spite of this statistical fact, the German cultural discourse still centres mostly on the field of opera as the most prestigious of theatrical genres involving music.

In the 2016–2017 season, for example, the top-ten list of the highest number of productions (led by *My Fair Lady* with 23), most performances (led by *Starlight Express* in Bochum with 375), and total attendance (again headed by *Starlight Express* with 416,566) includes only musicals.[26] Additionally, the top ten for total performances of works which premièred that season include only two non-musicals: two chamber operas by Massimiliano Matesic and Arash Safaian, respectively. The rest are homegrown original musicals. In the most recently published data for 2017–2018, the results are similar: the top ten lists for total productions (again: *My Fair Lady* with 18), total performances (as before: *Starlight Express* with 361), and total attendance (once again *Starlight Express* with 406,493) are all completely dominated by musicals; for the second year in a row, the top ten for total performances of individual works to have premiered that season again features only two non-musicals: works by Ruedi Häusermann and Marc Sambola, respectively.

This point can be further emphasised: musicals also draw disproportionately bigger audiences in comparison to all other areas of music theatre. For years now, about 20 percent of all productions dedicated to music theatre of any kind in private and public venues in Germany recorded by the Deutscher Bühnenverein were musicals, yet these productions attracted 35 percent of the recorded overall attendance for this form of performance.[27] One key factor here is that in public theatre musicals generate about 85 percent average attendance, or about 10 percent more than opera. The numbers may be seen in an even more favorable light when one limits the statistics to post-1945 works.[28] Thus, the share of musicals when it comes to attendance at any kind of contemporary music theatre of any type in German-language venues nowadays equals 85–90 percent during a typical season.[29] At the same time, musicals account for about 60 percent of all productions of contemporary (post-1945) works for music theatre of any kind.[30] In comparison, although fifty-five to sixty-five new operas première each season in subsidised opera houses, double the number of musicals premièred in German-language theatres, no piece composed after Puccini's *Turandot* (1924) reaches the annual top twenty of the most-performed operas.

So in stark contrast to domestic cultural politics—public funding and academic as well as journalistic music criticism are all entirely focused on classical and avant-garde works[31]—for general audiences, contemporary music theatre in German-language performance venues means first and foremost musicals. These are what is actually seen.

# Centres of Gravity in the Imported Repertoire

This diagnosis inevitably leads to a follow-up question: What kinds of post-1945 musicals are frequented by these large audiences in Germany, Austria, and northern Switzerland?

The first observation to be made is an important one: no matter whether the work is domestic or imported, what is performed is presented in German. That means that imports get translated, just like movies and TV series or books and straight plays. However, this convention stands in stark contrast to that regarding opera, where only specialised houses still do translations on a regular basis. In contrast, musicals have only recently been shown in English. Yet even in those cases, it is typically only the songs which are not done in German-language. All-English-language productions usually only occur in high-profile touring productions or in all-English-language theatres.

On the one hand, this approach generates an environment which is especially challenging for presenting the work of sophisticated Anglophone lyricists, Stephen Sondheim in particular, since the time set aside for the translation generally is as short, and the funding provided for it as low, as possible.[32] On the other hand, this performance tradition also has created additional problems for the reception of the musical as a genre in the German-language market during the extended period since the arrival of *Cats* in the mid-1980s, when predominantly Anglophone performers or other non-native speakers were used in German-language theaters, especially in the private sector.[33] For a long time those performers were the producers' first choice because they were simply better by all professional standards, not least because there were few or no local training facilities for musical theatre, and these performers still play a significant role in German-language musical productions as of today. Yet these foreign performers tended too often to lack the ability to sing accurately in German without a noticeable accent. Those two problems reinforced each other: otherwise excellent performances were regularly undermined by the bad enunciation of unsatisfactory translations, as I know from personal experience of German-language productions of American and British musicals in the 1990s and early 2000s, from *Starlight Express* to *Rent* and *Jekyll and Hyde*. This led at best to underwhelming results, at worst to absurd ones close to caricatures, undercutting the strengths of the genre.

At the same time, however, musicals as a genre have been popularised, especially from *Cats* onwards, as a form of full-blown, aesthetically ambitious music theatre that has a scope beyond the elite culture of opera while at the same time addressing contemporary topics and trends of popular culture. In this framework, the use of the German language was one key factor to support a strategy of outreach to attract new audiences for music theatre. For better or worse, it stuck. It is still the default position today that a musical is performed in German unless advertised differently. That is true for both private and public theatres. The introduction of higher-education programmes for German-language performers at several music schools since the 1990s, as well as the current trend towards creating more careful translations of such important lyricists as Sondheim, has helped to soften the aforementioned side effects.[34]

Although the two ends of the spectrum are joined in the norm of producing only German-language musicals, the development of that stable two-tier local system of private and public theatres has led to two quite different ecologies in many other respects. A very few works, such as *West Side Story*, are done for both markets (although never in direct competition with each other; the alternation of licensing is the norm for the import of Anglophone originals to the German-language market). Sometimes works with underwhelming runs in private theatres, such as *Sunset Boulevard* and *Jekyll and Hyde*, find a healthy afterlife in public theatre in slimmed-down, less costly productions licensed outside the original franchise model (requiring original sets, costumes, lighting, direction, etc.). Today there are even co-productions, such as the recent screen-to-stage transfer *Ghost* (*Nachricht von Sam*, 2017), of the private Stage Entertainment and the public Landestheater Linz of Austria.[35] Yet overall, the repertoires of private theatres and public theatres do not overlap. There is constant exchange between private and public theatres regarding many aspects of production, such as performers and others, but when it comes to repertoire, the German-language theatre is a market with two completely distinct sectors.

In public theatres, today's repertoire is dominated by Anglo-American imports, mostly older, post-1945, pre-1990 musicals, headed by *My Fair Lady*, *Fiddler on the Roof* (*Anatevka*), and *Cabaret* (see Table 18.2). The subsidised sector prefers more traditional narrative storylines (compared to, for instance, 'concept musicals'), with dance generally not at the forefront of the selected shows (apart from *West Side Story*). 'European' plots are favoured over 'American' ones (again, apart from *West Side Story*).

This focus on a traditional, non-contemporary repertoire and its characteristics becomes evident both when comparing multiple seasons (see Table 18.2), which shows the results of adding up the years 1994–1995 to 2017–2018), and contrasting two recent seasons (see Table 18.3):

The predominant approach of most public theatres to programming is to stage older, well-known, tested shows; however, this is neither surprising nor specific to the musical as a genre. It is the same approach in the public sector with opera and, to a slightly lesser extent, straight plays. Yet, regarding musicals, this is not so much a consequence of director's theatre which in German-language theatre remains de rigeur in the field of both opera and straight plays, but rather a reflection of the pressure to control extra costs. These include such significant factors as licensing fees and the need to hire specialised musicians and performers to augment the classical music–orientated permanent ensembles and orchestras, especially since the subsidised production system is not organised around open-ended runs. Among the fifty most-performed operas during the season 2018–2019—by far the biggest market for opera in the world—only seven works were still protected by copyright (four of these were by Richard Strauss, whose work entered the public domain in 2020). This clearly indicates the importance of cost control when scheduling the repertoire.[36]

In addition, none of the most often performed shows in subsidised houses requires expensive stage design or state-of-the-art technical equipment. Shows such as *Starlight Express*, *The Lion King*, *Titanic*, *Tarzan*, *Wicked*, and *Mary Poppins* tend to go to the private sector, where an elaborate production style is expected by fans who were first introduced to the genre through the megamusicals of the 1980s and 1990s: those people want to see their considerable ticket investment reflected in the look of a show. At the same time, such technically challenging productions are also much better suited to an

**Table 18.2 Top Twelve of Most-Produced Musicals in German-Language Theatres, 1994/95–2020/21**

| Theatrical Season | 1. My Fair Lady (1956) | 2. Fiddler on the Roof (1964) | 3. Cabaret (1966) | 4. The Rocky Horror Show (1975) | 5. Heute Abend: Lola Blau (1971) | 6. West Side Story (1957) | 7. Kiss Me, Kate (1948) | 8. Little Shop of Horrors (1982) | 9. Evita (1978) | 10. Sekretä-rinnen (1995) | 11. La Cage aux Folles (1983) | 12. Jesus Christ Superstar (1971) |
|---|---|---|---|---|---|---|---|---|---|---|---|---|
| 1994/95 | 21 | 21 | 16 | 12 | 14 | 18 | 7 | 15 | 7 | 0 | 11 | 2 |
| 1995/96 | 22 | 17 | 10 | 14 | 12 | 22 | 13 | 8 | 11 | 0 | 9 | 0 |
| 1996/97 | 19 | 20 | 7 | 14 | 10 | 16 | 5 | 8 | 4 | 1 | 7 | 0 |
| 1997/98 | 22 | 14 | 8 | 14 | 13 | 14 | 7 | 10 | 7 | 2 | 14 | 3 |
| 1998/99 | 22 | 15 | 5 | 16 | 7 | 16 | 5 | 11 | 6 | 5 | 8 | 3 |
| 1999/00 | 21 | 7 | 9 | 16 | 14 | 12 | 10 | 4 | 11 | 6 | 7 | 0 |
| 2000/01 | 18 | 8 | 9 | 8 | 9 | 11 | 6 | 4 | 14 | 15 | 4 | 5 |
| 2001/02 | 21 | 6 | 14 | 10 | 10 | 12 | 11 | 4 | 12 | 14 | 5 | 10 |
| 2002/03 | 16 | 12 | 12 | 8 | 9 | 7 | 6 | 6 | 4 | 18 | 4 | 9 |
| 2003/04 | 21 | 12 | 9 | 9 | 12 | 9 | 10 | 6 | 2 | 18 | 4 | 9 |
| 2004/05 | 16 | 14 | 14 | 10 | 11 | 3 | 4 | 6 | 4 | 18 | 4 | 11 |
| 2005/06 | 12 | 11 | 11 | 6 | 10 | 0 | 11 | 6 | 8 | 12 | 6 | 11 |
| 2006/07 | 8 | 14 | 5 | 4 | 10 | 0 | 9 | 8 | 4 | 9 | 8 | 10 |
| 2007/08 | 16 | 7 | 7 | 2 | 9 | 1 | 9 | 11 | 5 | 6 | 5 | 14 |
| 2008/09 | 21 | 4 | 11 | 0 | 4 | 5 | 4 | 8 | 6 | 4 | 3 | 9 |
| 2009/10 | 25 | 9 | 9 | 1 | 3 | 8 | 6 | 7 | 9 | 3 | 3 | 7 |

(*continued*)

**Table 18.2 Continued**

| Theatrical Season | 1. My Fair Lady (1956) | 2. Fiddler on the Roof (1964) | 3. Cabaret (1966) | 4. The Rocky Horror Show (1975) | 5. Heute Abend: Lola Blau (1971) | 6. West Side Story (1957) | 7. Kiss Me, Kate (1948) | 8. Little Shop of Horrors (1982) | 9. Evita (1978) | 10. Sekretä-rinnen (1995) | 11. La Cage aux Folles (1983) | 12. Jesus Christ Superstar (1971) |
|---|---|---|---|---|---|---|---|---|---|---|---|---|
| 2010/11 | 27 | 10 | 10 | 10 | 4 | 7 | 4 | 6 | 3 | 4 | 2 | 3 |
| 2011/12 | 29 | 9 | 10 | 9 | 6 | 7 | 4 | 9 | 4 | 6 | 6 | 1 |
| 2012/13 | 21 | 11 | 10 | 13 | 10 | 4 | 9 | 7 | 10 | 3 | 6 | 2 |
| 2013/14 | 27 | 12 | 7 | 13 | 7 | 5 | 7 | 5 | 8 | 4 | 4 | 5 |
| 2014/15 | 21 | 9 | 12 | 12 | 7 | 9 | 3 | 6 | 4 | 7 | 9 | 5 |
| 2015/16 | 21 | 8 | 8 | 7 | 9 | 9 | 9 | 7 | 6 | 2 | 7 | 6 |
| 2016/17 | 23 | 11 | 5 | 9 | 8 | 8 | 3 | 4 | 7 | 2 | 3 | 4 |
| 2017/18 | 18 | 7 | 9 | 6 | 4 | 7 | 3 | 2 | 2 | 2 | 7 | 6 |
| 2018/19 | 15 | 5 | 12 | 7 | 3 | 6 | 9 | 3 | 3 | 2 | 3 | 6 |
| 2019/20 | 12 | 3 | 13 | 5 | 7 | 3 | 2 | 2 | 2 | 1 | 1 | 1 |
| 2020/21 | 1 | 2 | 5 | 0 | 5 | 2 | 2 | 3 | 2 | 0 | 0 | 1 |
| sum total | 516 | 278 | 257 | 235 | 227 | 221 | 178 | 176 | 165 | 164 | 150 | 145 |

Source: Annual Statistics of the Deutsche Bühnenverein (productions by theatre; additional guest touring productions in public theatres are included occasionally but not systematically in these statistics)

**Table 18.3  Top Fourteen Most-Produced Musicals in German-Language Theatres, 2016–2017 and 2017–2018 Seasons**

| Overall ranking | Title | Productions 2016–2017 | Productions 2017–2018 |
|---|---|---|---|
| 1. | *My Fair Lady* (1956) | 23 | 18 |
| 2. | *Anatevka* (*Fiddler on the Roof*, 1964) | 11 | 7 |
| 3. | *The Rocky Horror Show* (1973) | 9 | 6 |
| 4. | *Heute Abend: Lola Blau* (1971) | 8 | 4 |
| 4. | *West Side Story* (1957) | 8 | 7 |
| 6. | *Evita* (1978) | 7 | 2 |
| 6. | *Struwwelpeter* (*Shockheaded Peter*, 1998) | 7 | 6 |
| 6. | *Monthy Python's Spamalot* (2005) | 7 | 7 |
| 9. | *Cabaret* (1966) | 5 | 9 |
| 10 | *Little Shop of Horrors* (1982) | 4 | 2 |
| 10. | *Jesus Christ Superstar* (1971) | 4 | 6 |
| 10. | *The Addams Family* (2010) | 4 | 3 |
| 10. | *Non(n)sens* (*Nunsense*, 1985) | 4 | 3 |
| 10. | *Some Like It Hot* (1972) | 4 | 2 |

Source: Annual Statistics of the Deutsche Bühnenverein (productions by theatre; additional guest touring productions in public theatres are included occasionally but not systematically in these statistics)

open-ended or at least longer limited run where the stage design and technical facilities do not need to be replaced almost daily.[37]

The educational mandate (*Bildungsauftrag*) of the public theatre sector, which is a prerequisite of public funding, is an additional factor when it comes to deciding on the repertoire in subsidised houses: the musicals most often scheduled all have a degree of perceived artistic status, with verified genre classics such as *My Fair Lady*, *Fiddler on the Roof*, *Cabaret*, *West Side Story* and *Kiss Me, Kate* among the top eight. Many of the top shows—including the most-produced domestic work, the Nazi refugee drama *Heute Abend: Lola Blau*—feature socially ambitious themes. However, more important, in the subsidised municipal theatre the standard musical theatre repertoire is expected to generate revenue by achieving high attendance figures, the actual or at least predominant reason in most houses for presenting popular musical theatre as part of its mix of genres. This is evident not just from the top twelve's lighter works, such as *The Rocky Horror Show*, *Little Shop of Horrors*, the revue *Sekretärinnen*, and *La Cage Aux Folles*, all of which have cult followings, or from more recent hits such as *Monty Python's Spamalot*, *The Addams Family*, or *Nunsense*, but also from the constantly high production numbers of pieces that are clearly sold on name recognition, such as the few Lloyd Webber hits which are licensed to the public theatre: *Evita, Jesus Christ Superstar*, and *Sunset Boulevard*.

Moreover, if education were actually the chief remit—for example, the representation of social problems of the local community or the targeting of those age groups which are not yet well represented in the audience profile of the respective theatre—it would be paramount to invest in the production of shows that are much closer to today's popular culture. Nonetheless, this happens only occasionally, such as with *Spring Awakening* (twenty-six recorded productions since 2008–2009) and *Next to Normal* (fifteen recorded professional and amateur productions since 2013–2014). But then, the former is based on a well-known German-language original by Frank Wedekind, while the latter requires only six actor/singers and six instrumentalists and can be done with relatively simple scenography, allowing it to fall squarely into the category of low-cost musicals, which are preferred by the cash-strapped subsidised sector—as does another popular small-scale choice, Jason Robert Brown's *The Last Five Years* (9 productions in seasons 2018/19–2020/21 alone).

The approaches and repertoires of private theatres are significantly different. The private sector is dominated by Anglo-American imports too, but mainly musicals from the 1980s and after, with an obvious emphasis on contemporary works imported relatively close to their successful Broadway and West End runs. The oldest work offered by today's market leader Stage Entertainment is *Cats*, which had its world première in 1981.

Public theatres began early on to integrate musicals into their repertory-oriented programming, offering between ten and twenty performances per season of any individual piece. By contrast, today's private theatre scene for musicals whose key players, including Vereinigte Bühnen Wien (founded 1987), Stella (1988–2002), Schmidt Theater (founded 1988), and Stage Entertainment (founded 2000), all entered the market only after *Cats* had its first German-language production in 1983. At first they tried to follow the Broadway/West End model of open-ended runs. There have indeed been some exceptionally long runs in German-language theatres, such as those of *Starlight Express* (Bochum, since 1988), *The Lion King* (Hamburg, since 2001), *Heiße Ecke* (Hamburg, since 2003), *Cats* (Hamburg, 1986–2001), *The Phantom of the Opera* (Hamburg, 1990–2001), *Buddy: The Buddy Holly Story* (Hamburg, 1994–2001), *Miss Saigon* (Stuttgart, 1994–1999), *Mamma Mia!* (Hamburg, 2002–2007), *We Will Rock You* (Cologne, 2004–2008), *Tarzan* (Hamburg, 2008–2013), and *Hinterm Horizont* (Berlin, 2011–2016).

However, there are few cases as successful as these in the private sector. Ranging from *Rent* to *Wicked* and *Kinky Boots*, the list of disappointments is much longer. The reasons major American or British hits attempted but were unable to conquer the German-language market as they did at home are diverse and not always clear. *Wicked*, for instance, did not leave much of an impression, despite being close in musical style and in its emphasis on luxurious stage design to the megamusicals which had been successful earlier, because *The Wizard of Oz* is the show's main reference point but is not universally known in German-speaking countries, as it is in English-speaking culture. *Rent* also never came close to the success it had in New York, where Jonathan Larsen's untimely death had contributed a tragic aura to the original production context. These circumstances played no part in the show's reception a few years later in Germany, and it did not help that the public was by 1999 becoming less concerned with HIV/AIDS as a theme. The Dusseldorf staging is also a key example of a production that fared badly because of the actors' poor spoken German.[38] On the other hand, the case of *Kinky Boots* is more difficult to comprehend: it had an underwhelming run even though *La Cages aux Folles* was one of the most widely produced works in the German-language market; the composer, Cindy Lauper, was a well-known pop artist; LGTBQ-friendly Hamburg was (besides Berlin and Cologne) the most appropriate location for its subject matter of drag queens; and attendees reported an enthusiastic audience reaction.

Be that as it may, open-ended runs soon turned out to be an especially risky strategy for private theatre in the German-language market. As a consequence, the German situation has changed since the 1990s: whereas private producers used to aim for an open-ended run of multiple years in one place, they now tend to plan limited shorter runs—between several months and two years—with changes of location planned in advance and more frequent returns of the same production as the preferable and economically more viable concept. The guiding idea behind this approach is to keep interest in and demand for successful pieces high through coordinated breaks and returns, supported by the pre-announcement that runs are strictly limited. As a typical example, *Tanz der Vampire* played several times in Vienna where it originated at the Vereinigte Bühnen Wien (1997–2000, 2009–2011, and 2017–2018), with runs in major private houses in between, in this case by Stage Entertainment in Stuttgart (2000–2003 and 2010–2011), Hamburg (2003–2006), Berlin (2006–2008 and 2011–2013), and Oberhausen (2008–2010), as well as a touring production (2016–2019) that again played even shorter periods in Berlin, Munich, Stuttgart, Hamburg, Cologne, and Berlin. That formula is key to the approach especially of Stage Entertainment. As *Tanz der Vampire* demonstrates, this approach can work: in 2018 this show was the domestic musical most beloved by German-speaking audiences.[39]

Yet, once again, it must be recognised that the list of success stories as impressive as that of *Tanz der Vampire* is short. To stage musicals within the general economic framework of non-subsidised private theatres is no less a risk in Germany than it is on Broadway, where eight out of every ten productions loses money.[40] That is why there are no longer many private Broadway- and off-Broadway-type companies focused on producing musicals in the German-language theatre; this is very different from the situation in the 1990s, when the boom of popular musical theatre produced a goldrush sensibility.[41]

As the data shows, *My Fair Lady* is by far the most widely produced import in public theatres, while for decades now *Heute Abend: Lola Blau*, by the legendary Austrian cabaret singer-songwriter Georg Kreisler—a cabaret-like piece for only one actress and piano accompaniment that can be produced basically everywhere—has held on to its position as the most regularly produced domestic original. In the private sector, the aforementioned long runs of *Starlight Express* and *The Lion King* have set the high-water marks for imports: *Heiße Ecke* the one for domestic originals, with *Tanz der Vampire* remaining especially popular among genre fans and *Elisabeth* (1992) still being celebrated as the first domestic original to reach the professional standards of Broadway and West End, thus achieving a certain status while also succeeding commercially.

The benchmark regarding cultural impact on the German-language market, however, is still Andrew Lloyd Webber's *Cats*. It is important to acknowledge this domestic watershed moment for what it was, because it still shapes the general perception and expectations of the public in Germany, Austria, and northern Switzerland with respect to what a musical is and consequently to some extent also determines the particular constitution of the repertoire and what might succeed in the market. With the première of *Cats* (1986) in Hamburg (in the wake of the triumphant first continental production in Vienna, 1983–1990), which was followed soon after by both the composer's *Starlight Express* (1988) and *The Phantom of the Opera* (1990, again retracing the trailblazing path of a Viennese production, 1988–1993), the landscape for popular musical theatre changed significantly in Germany, Austria, and northern Switzerland.[42]

For many, this seminal moment was a revelation, initiating a dynamic that has led to what remains over thirty-five years later a lively and diverse domestic scene. Since *Cats*, the interest of subsidised theatres in the genre has increased significantly, and over the years both the private and public sectors have increased in diversity and at times aesthetic competence. Mainstays of the present-day repertoire such as Frank Wildhorn and Martin Lingnau to this day follow in their preferred soundscape of mainstream popular music, heavy on synthesisers, and a 1980s rock aesthetic, which introduced German audiences to the notion of what constitutes the genre.

It should not therefore come as a surprise that Lloyd Webber's *Starlight Express*, after a run of more than thirty years, remains an audience favourite, drawing about 400,000 visitors each season, while *Sunset Boulevard* has been accumulating productions in public theatres as if it were a classic (see Table 18.4), since the show's performing rights finally became available for public theatres during the 2010–2011 season (amongst other things, as a vehicle for older domestic star performers of the genre, such as Pia Douwes), while *Jesus Christ Superstar* and *Evita* are constantly in the top twelve of most-performed pieces in the repertoire of public theatres. When it comes to musicals, Andrew Lloyd Webber still has the greatest name recognition in the German-language market in both the private and public theatre sectors. His name usually tops the annual lists of productions, performances, and attendance for musicals of the Deutscher Bühnenverein, being on equal footing in terms of attendance figures with Mozart and Verdi in the field of music theatre broadly speaking. Lloyd Webber's work is the main reason it is appropriate to speak of a focus on Anglophone and not just American repertoire in the German-language market.

In this context it is instructive to compare how the works of Stephen Sondheim, arguably the key proponent of musicals as an art form since the 1970s, have fared in English- and German-language theatre, respectively. The progenitor of many of today's most ambitious writers, Sondheim and his oeuvre have become a fixture in Anglo-American music theatre. Although most of his shows lost money in their original productions, several of his works have been consistently revived not just in regional theatre but

## Table 18.4 Productions of *Sunset Boulevard* in Germany, Austria, and German-Speaking Switzerland

| Theatrical season of premiere | Number of new productions per season | Town/Festival |
| --- | --- | --- |
| 1995/96 | 1 | Niedernhausen (privately run theatre; 992 performances) |
| 2010/11 | 2 | Magdeburg // Bad Hersfeld |
| 2012/13 | 3 | Braunschweig // Klagenfurt // Hof |
| 2013/14 | 5 | Coburg // Lüneburg // Pforzheim // Tecklenburg // Würzburg |
| 2014/15 | 7 | Bielefeld // Döbeln // Freiberg // Fürth // Halberstadt/Quedlinburg // Schleswig // Titisee-Neustadt |
| 2015/16 | 3 | Ettlingen // Rendsburg // Röttingen |
| 2016/17 | 3 | Dortmund // Lübeck // Bad Vilbel |
| 2017/18 | 3 | Altenburg/Gera // Bonn // Trier |
| 2018/19 | 2 | Bremerhaven // Görlitz-Zittau |
| 2019/20 | 3 | Baden // Kaiserslautern // Mönchengladbach |
| 2020/21 | 1 | Koblenz |
| 2021/22 | 2 | Kiel // Krefeld |
| 2022/23 | 1 | Heidelberg |

Source: Annual statistics of the Deutscher Bühnenverein; data for 2021–2022 and 2022–2023 provided by musicalzentrale.de

since 2000 also in regular major productions in both New York and London, winning eight Olivier Awards for Best Musical Revival (plus six more nominations) and three Tony Awards for Best Revival of a Musical (plus eleven more nominations) along the way.[43] While theatres are being renamed in Sondheim's honor both on Broadway (2010) and in the West End (2019) and a notable academic interest has developed since around 1990,[44] in Germany, Austria, and Switzerland Sondheim is still not a household name: his shows are not performed on a regular basis even in the subsidised sector (see Table 18.5), and his work is only rarely taught in higher education. When I asked about a hundred students from musicology, film studies, theatre studies, and literature studies in my lecture course on the history of musicals during the summer term of 2019 at the Freie Universität Berlin whether they were familiar with his name and body of work, only a quarter of them raised their hands—in a roomful of people who were at least interested in this genre of musical theatre. In my course on Sondheim during the winter term of 2019–2020 at the same institution, only one of the twenty-six students who participated was a fan and had extensive knowledge of his body of work; the rest had chosen the course out of a more general curiosity, mainly about the recent movie adaptations of *Sweeney Todd* and *Into the Woods*.

# 524 FRÉDÉRIC DÖHL

**Table 18.5 Recent Productions of Stephen Sondheim Musicals in German-Language Theatres, 1999–2000 Season to 2019–2020 Season[71]**

| Musical | No. of productions | No. of performances | Date of first production | Town/theatre of first production |
|---|---|---|---|---|
| *Saturday Night* (1954) | – | – | – | – |
| *West Side Story* (1957) | 68 | 2,216 [i] | 25 February 1968 | Vienna; Volkstheater |
| *Gypsy* (1959) | 5 | 52 | 09 March 1979 | Münster; Städtische Bühnen |
| *A Funny Thing Happened on the Way to the Forum/ Zustände wie im alten Rom // Toll trieben es die alten Römer* (1962) | 7 | 85 | 24 February 1972 | Berlin; Theater im Reichskabinett |
| *Anyone Can Whistle* (1964) | 1 | 2 | 10 February 2012 | Berlin; Ufa-Fabrik |
| *Do I Hear a Waltz* (1965) | – | – | – | – |
| *Company* (1970) | 8 | 92 | 06 January 1973 | Düsseldorf; Schauspielhaus |
| *Follies* (1971) | 1 | 17 | 27/09/1991 | Berlin; Theater des Westens |
| *A Little Night Music/ Das Lächeln einer Sommernacht* (1973) | 10 | 124 | 24 February 1975 | Vienna; Theater an der Wien |
| *The Frogs* (1974) | – | – | – | – |
| *Pacific Overtures* (1976) | – | – | – | – |
| *Sweeney Todd, the Demon Barber of Fleet Street/Sweeney Todd, der Teufelsbarbier der Fleet Street* (1979) | 36 | 608 | 11 April 1985 | Freiburg im Breisgau; Städtische Bühnen |
| *Merrily We Roll Along/ Gestern ist vorbei* (1981) | 1 | 8 | 26 June 2003 | Essen; Folkwang University of the Arts |
| *Sunday in the Park with George/Sonntags im Park mit George* (1984) | 1 | 7 | 30 September 1989 | Kaiserslautern; Pfalztheater |
| *Into the Woods/Ab in den Wald* (1987) | 15 | 235 | 31 March 1990 | Heilbronn; Theater Heilbronn |
| *Assassins/Attentäter* (1990) | 3 | 44 | 31 March 1993 | Heilbronn; Theater Heilbronn |
| *Passion* (1994) | 1 | 18 | 28 January 2011 | Dresden; Staatsoperette |
| *Road Show* (2008) | – | – | – | – |

[i] plus additional touring productions

Many of Sondheim's musicals have not been performed at all (*Saturday Night, Do I Hear a Waltz?, The Frogs, Pacific Overtures*, and *Road Show*) in German-speaking countries, some only in small-scale amateur or student productions (*Anyone Can Whistle* and *Merrily We Roll Along*) or merely sporadically (*Gypsy, Follies, Sunday in the Park with George, Assassins*, and *Passion*). With forty productions as a group since the turn of the century, *A Funny Thing Happened on the Way to the Forum, Company, A Little Night Music*, and *Into the Woods* are at the forefront. However, each one of them has only achieved combined production figures that works like *My Fair Lady, Fiddler on the Roof*, or *Cabaret* attain every season. Excluding *West Side Story*, which is promoted in the German-speaking world on the basis of Leonard Bernstein's extraordinary fame as a classical musician, the only true exception is *Sweeney Todd*, with forty-two productions (see Table 18.6).

Here, a contributing factor seems to be the name recognition achieved since Tim Burton's popular movie version of 2007. After all, it was not just thirty-sixth on the list of highest-grossing movies worldwide in 2007,[45] it was also seen by almost half a million German cinema-goers in 2008.[46] On the one hand, the film ranks only sixty-fifth on the annual chart of best-attended movies in Germany that season, yet on the other hand this puts the overall audience for the film version of *Sweeney Todd* on an equal footing with those of the best-attended stage musicals of that season—*The Lion King, Tarzan, Dance of the Vampires, Starlight Express*, and *We Will Rock You*[47]—which may well have influenced the programming decisions of German-language public theatres.

Still, the numbers presented above might also be interpreted differently. Interestingly, his German-language publisher today regards Sondheim's body of work as well established in the repertoire.[48] On the publisher's website there is even talk of a 'Sondheim boom', explicitly fighting (while involuntarily confirming und perpetuating) the tired cliché of Sondheim as 'box office poison'.[49] It is true that the numbers have increased considerably. During the 1980s, the records of the Deutscher Bühnenverein would hardly have allowed one to speak of Sondheim reception: one single production of *Sweeney Todd* (nineteen performances, with a total of 14,440 attendees) in 1983–1984, one *Company* (twenty-six performances, with a total of 19,147 attendees), and one *A Little Night Music* (eleven performances, with a total of 7,440 attendees) in 1985–1986, one *A Little Night Music* (six performances, with a total of 3,783 attendees) in 1986–1987, and finally the aforementioned German-language premières of *Sunday in the Park with George* (seventeen performances, with a total of 8,857 attendees) and *Into the Woods* (twenty-one performances, with a total of 14,450 attendees) during the 1989–1990 season. That's all. While 'boom' might be too strong a word to use even today, some of Sondheim's works are indeed currently staged more often than in the past, although only in subsidised houses, so there are indeed signs of a turnaround.

At the same time, however, most major public theatres that do music theatre, especially those focused on opera in major cities, typically still do not produce musicals at all, beyond occasional guest productions during the summer recess. And if they do, the standard maximum is one musical per season, as at the aforementioned Theater Dortmund. Very few public theatres, among them Vereinigte Bühnen Wien and Staatsoperette Dresden, have become specialised in musicals and prioritise them in their

## Table 18.6 Productions of *Sweeney Todd* in German–Language Theatres since 1999/2000[72]

| Theatrical Season | Town/Festival | No. of Performances |
| --- | --- | --- |
| 1999/2000 | Mannheim | 22 |
| | Osnabrück | 17 |
| 2000/2001 | Annaberg | 4 (+ 9 the following season) |
| 2001/2002 | Mainz | 20 |
| 2002/2003 | Schleswig | 13 |
| | Plauen-Zwickau | 12 (+4 the following season) |
| 2003/2004 | Graz | 16 |
| | Neustrelitz | 4 |
| 2004/2005 | Berlin | 18 |
| 2006/2007 | Ulm | 19 |
| 2007/2008 | Hagen | 16 |
| 2008/2009 | Linz | 23 |
| | München | 13 (+ 9 the following season) |
| 2009/2010 | Coburg | 12 (+ 3 the following season) |
| | Klagenfurt | 24 |
| | Koblenz | 17 |
| 2012/2013 | Ettlingen | 26 |
| | Hildesheim | 12 |
| | Magdeburg | 10 (+ 9 the following season) |
| 2013/2014 | Eggenfelden | 9 |
| | Görlitz-Zittau | 7 |
| | Vienna | 14 (+ 22 the following seasons) |
| 2014/2015 | Pforzheim | 12 |
| 2015/2016 | Freiburg | 17 |
| | Luzern | 18 |
| | Trier | 9 |
| 2016/2017 | Braunschweig | 13 |
| | Oldenburg | 16 (+ 2 the following season) |
| 2017/2018 | Halle | 9 |
| | Kaiserslautern | 9 |
| | Heilbronn | 4 |
| | Vienna | 4 |
| 2018/2019 | Kiel | 16 |
| | Zürich | 12 |
| 2019/2020 | Biel | 16 |
| | Frankfurt a.M. | 92 |
| 2020/2021 | Hannover | 5 |
| | Leipzig | 8 (+ 6 the following season) |
| 2021/2022 | Aachen | 10 |
| | Erfurt | 9 |
| | Innsbruck | 13 |
| 2022/2023 | Mainz | 8 |

repertoire. So, although the production numbers for Sondheim are better now than in the 1980s, when *Cats* changed the situation for the genre in German-speaking countries, the short lists of German-language Sondheim productions compiled in the tables above indicate that the theatre system in these three European countries still exhibits notable resistance to comprehending the potential of musical theatre as an artistically challenging and dramaturgically ambitious form of music theatre. Even *Sweeney Todd* is produced mostly in mid-sized provincial theatres (see Table 18.6).

This assumption is reinforced by another fact. In contrast to other contemporary scores of Broadway musicals with a challenging social or psychological content, such as *Caroline, or Change* (Broadway-premiere: 2004), *The Color Purple* (2005), *Spring Awakening* (2006), *In the Heights* (2008), *Next to Normal* (2009), *The Scottsboro Boys* (2010), *Fun Home* (2015), *Hamilton* (2015), *Dear Evan Hansen* (2016), and *Hadestown* (2019), all of Sondheim's mature works are available in orchestrations for mostly classical instrumentation: *Pacific Overtures, Merrily We Roll Along, Sunday in the Park with George, Into the Woods, Assassins*, and *Passion* only request an additional synthesiser/keyboard player, while *Company* and *Assassins* require an additional guitar player.[50] Therefore they could be performed satisfactorily by staff players of the standing theatre orchestras still common in subsidised German-language music theatres. Moreover, Sondheim's musicals do not need expensive, elaborate stage designs or technical equipment and were originally staged by artists such as like Harold Prince and James Lapine, who could be said to represent the kind of *Regietheater* (director's theatre) favoured in German-speaking countries. Nonetheless, Sondheim's reception remains limited even in the public theatre, as are other more recent 'symphonic' scores: *Titanic* (1997), *Ragtime* (1998), *Parade* (1998), and *The Light in the Piazza* (2005). The same applies to many of the modern musicals which are theatrically, socially and/or psychologically extremely ambitious (e.g. *Caroline, or Change, The Scottsboro Boys*, and *Fun Home*).

At the same time, while the ambitious musicals of Sondheim and 'Sondheim's Children',[51] from Jonathan Larson, Jason Robert Brown, and Jeanine Tesori to Michael John LaChiusa, Robert Lopez, Tom Kitt, and Lin-Manuel Miranda, only slowly gain ground or are still awaiting their first production, other composers such as Frank Wildhorn are able to succeed disproportionally in the German-language market (see Table 18.7). Wildhorn does so not only by staying true to the aesthetics of the 1990s musical theatre boom in Europe, but also by selecting topics that respond to and correspond with the aforementioned paradigms of local or regional title recognition.

With these numbers, in stark contrast to Sondheim, Wildhorn consistently appears in the top ten of the most-produced composers in the annual statistics of the Deutscher Bühnenverein. For example, in 2014–2015, 2015–2016, and 2017–2018 he ranked fifth (with ten, nine, and seven productions, respectively), while in 2016–2017 he held the seventh position, based on six productions. In the top ten, Wildhorn competes with other regulars such as Andrew Lloyd Webber, Frederick Loewe, Cole Porter, Leonard Bernstein, Jerry Herman, Jerry Bock, and John Kander. It has to be noted, however, that only Lloyd Webber's entry regularly includes songs from the production of multiple works. The other composers are, like Wildhorn, mainly represented by one major hit.

However, taking into account these specifics of the domestic market since the Hamburg première of *Cats* in 1986, it is not surprising to see musicals such as Wildhorn's

FIG. 18.2 Scene from the 2019 production of *Sunday in the Park with George* at the Landesbühne Sachsen in Radebeul, starring Veronika Hörmann as Dot and Tobias Bieri as George. Sondheim's 1984 musical is rarely staged in German-speaking countries. Photo: Pawel Sosnowski, courtesy of the Landesbühne Sachsen, Radebeul.

*Jekyll and Hyde* and, to a lesser extent, *The Scarlet Pimpernel* and *Dracula* succeed, because they fit in with the perception of what constitutes a typical contemporary musical. This understanding was formed in relation to the composer of *Cats*, and thus these musicals are a logical choice for the repertoire of German-language theatres, whose comprehension of what constitutes a modern musical was mainly influenced by Lloyd Webber (and to a lesser extent Claude-Michel Schönberg), whereas, for instance, Sondheim's canonical musicals (with the exceptions of *West Side Story* and to a lesser extent *Sweeney Todd*), in spite of gaining the highest critical and academic prestige in the United States and the United Kingdom, do not.

About a decade ago Wildhorn even seemed to be on the verge of challenging the seminal status of his British colleague to become the 'new Lloyd Webber' with solid productions numbers and several world premières in Central Europe in short succession.[52] That promise was not fulfilled. A key factor seems to be that even fans sympathetic to his style and output lament that his works are too predictable and too focused on solo ballads, which are effective in themselves but slow down the action significantly; simply put, his shows are described as too boring in theatrical terms.[53] However, currently musicals such as *Sweeney Todd*, *Sunset Boulevard*, and *Jekyll and Hyde* achieve a comparable number of productions, and that is quite an accomplishment for Wildhorn. Yet, it feels as though Wildhorn has recognised that his formula has run out of steam

## Table 18.7 Productions of Musicals by Frank Wildhorn in German-Language Theatres[73]

| Work | Theatrical Season | Productions | Number of Performances |
|---|---|---|---|
| Jekyll & Hyde (1997) | 2001/02 | Vienna | 192 (+ 205 and 98 the following seasons) |
| | 2003/04 | Cologne | 150 (+ 187 the following season) |
| | 2006/07 | Chemnitz* | 16 |
| | | Tecklenburg Festival | 20 |
| | | Chemnitz | 12 |
| | | Saarbrücken | 25 |
| | 2007/08 | Bad Hersfeld Festival | 26 |
| | | Bad Vilbel Festival | 27 |
| | | Bielefeld* | 27 |
| | | Dresden* | 15 |
| | 2008/09 | Bremerhaven* | 23 |
| | | Coburg* | 22 |
| | | Dresden* | 13 (+ 9 and 7 the following seasons) |
| | | Lüneburg* | 20 |
| | | Magdeburg* | 7 (+ 8 and 8 the following seasons) |
| | 2009/10 | Cottbus* | 11 (+ 9 and 5 the following seasons) |
| | | Hagen* | 18 |
| | | Lübeck* | 16 |
| | | Nordhausen* | 10 (+ 3 the next season) |
| | | Regensburg* | 11 (+ 8 the next season) |
| | 2010/11[i] | Leipzig* | 16 (+ 36 over the following five seasons) |
| | | Pforzheim* | 16 |
| | 2011/12 | Hof* | 19 |
| | 2013/14 | Kassel* | 23 |
| | | Innsbruck* | 15 |
| | 2014/15 | Eggenfelden* | 6 |
| | | Gera* | 10 (+ 14 the following season) |
| | 2015/16 | Baden near Vienna | 10 |
| | | Greifswald/Stralsund* | 6 (+ 10 the following season) |
| | | Lahnstein* | 12 |
| | | Osnabrück* | 13 (+ 6 the following season) |
| | | Würzburg* | 24 |
| | | Zwingenberg am Neckar* | 6 |
| | 2016/17 | Trier* | 10 |
| | 2017/18 | Frankfurt am Main | 95 |
| | | Freiberg* | 8 (+ 14 the following seasons) |
| | | Schwerin* | 15 (+ 12 the following seasons) |
| | 2018/19 | Halberstadt* | 4 (+ 6 the following season) |

(*continued*)

## Table 18.7 Continued

| Work | Theatrical Season | Productions | Number of Performances |
|---|---|---|---|
| | 2019/20 | Dortmund* | 20 |
| | 2021/22 | Merzig* | 7 |
| | 2022/23 | Brandenburg | 7 |
| The Scarlet Pimpernel (1997) | 2002/03 | Halle* | 10 (+ 27 the following seasons) |
| | 2002/03 | Clingenburg Festival | (?) |
| | | Halle | (?) |
| | 2007/08 | Baden near Vienna | (?) |
| | | Ettlingen Festival | 27 |
| | | Staatz Festival | (?) |
| | 2008/09 | Baden near Vienna | 15 |
| | | Bremerhaven* | 18 |
| | 2009/10 | Bielefeld* | 9 (+ 12 the following season) |
| | 2010/11 | Schwäbisch Gmünd | (?) |
| | 2016/17 | Chemnitz* | 15 |
| Dracula (2004) | 2004/05 | St. Gallen* | 20 (+ 14 the following season) |
| | 2006/07 | Graz (Summer Festival) | (?) |
| | 2011/12 | Radebeul* | 10 (+ at least 19 the following seasons) |
| | | Thale | (?) |
| | 2012/13 | Lüneburg* | 17 |
| | | Munich* | 10 |
| | | Pforzheim* | 23 (+ 16 the following seasons) |
| | | Röttingen Franken Festival | 13 |
| | 2013/14 | Rendsburg/Schleswig* | 19 |
| | 2014/15 | Clingenburg Festival | 22 |
| | 2015/16 | Hildesheim* | 16 |
| | | Leipzig* | 12 (+ 11 the following seasons) |
| | 2016/17 | Bremerhaven* | 20 |
| | | Nordhausen* | 10 (+ 9 the following seasons) |
| | 2017/18 | Detmold* | 21 |
| | 2020/21 | Greifswald/Stralsund* | 6 |
| | | Ulm* | 23 |
| | 2021/22 | Wien | (?) |
| | 2022/23 | Halberstadt* | 4 |
| | | Munich* | 26 |
| Rudolf – The Last Kiss (2006 [Budapest]) | 2008/09 | Vienna | 117 (+ 93 the following season) |

**Table 18.7 Continued**

| Work | Theatrical Season | Productions | Number of Performances |
|---|---|---|---|
| The Count of Monte Christo (2009 [St. Gallen]) | 2008/09 | St. Gallen* | 20 (+ 23 over the following seasons) |
| | 2011/12 | Leipzig* | 22 (+ 34 over the following seasons) |
| | 2012/13 | Tecklenburg Festival | 18 |
| | 2014/15 | Röttingen Franken Festival | 13 |
| | 2018/19 | Staatz Festival | (?) |
| | 2019/20 | Bremerhaven* | 16 |
| | | Freiberg* | (?) |
| | 2022/23 | Meiningen* | 13 |
| Bonnie and Clyde (2011) | 2014/15 | Bielefeld* | 25 |
| | 2016/17 | Trier* | 13 |
| | 2017/18 | Baden near Vienna | 12 |
| | 2018/19 | Lüneburg* | 16 |
| Artus – Exacalibur (2014 [St. Gallen]) | 2013/14 | St. Gallen* | 14 (+ 28 over the following two seasons) |
| | 2015/16 | Tecklenburg Festival | (?) |
| | | Staatz Festival | (?) |
| | 2018/19 | Zwingenberg Festival | 7 |
| | 2021/22 | Theater unter den Kuppeln Festival | (?) |

\* = Subsidised theatre; if not otherwise noted, festivals are also partly subsidised

ˡ there was also a touring production that season starting in Titisee-Neustadt, with eighty-four performances

in Central Europe. He has moved on, with his latest musicals receiving their world premières in Asia: *Death Note* (Tokyo, 2015), *Mata Hari* (Seoul, 2016), and *The Man Who Laughs* (Seoul, 2018).

# DOMESTIC PRODUCTION

Overall, the musical as a genre still lacks academic, journalistic, and general cultural prestige in Germany, Austria and Switzerland.[54] This is especially true when it comes to homegrown musicals.

The general divide between the Anglophone and the German-language markets in terms of the genre's artistic recognition becomes clearer when one takes into account that major 'serious' actors, from Glenn Close and Judi Dench to Jake Gyllenhaal and Ewan McGregor, perform in musicals in the United States and the United Kingdom, while the biggest star in the domestic market with cross-cultural prominence is at

FIG. 18.3 Ethan Freeman as the eponymous character(s) in the 1999 German première of *Jekyll and Hyde* at the Musical-Theater Bremen. Frank Wildhorn's 1997 musical remains a perennial on stages in both Germany and Austria. Photo: Peter Bischoff © Getty Images.

best a minor one: Alexander Klaws, who won the German version of *American Idol* (*Deutschland sucht den Superstar*, or *DSDS*) in 2002–2003 (with Uwe Kröger being the performer with arguably the biggest reputation within the genre). It still seems to be impossible for an actor or actress of serious standing to be cast in a musical—with only one exception: *Die Dreigroschenoper* (*The Threepenny Opera*, 1928), which, tellingly, is classified as an opera in the German-language statistics.

An example from my time as a trainee on the production of *Das Mädchen Rosemarie* (*The Girl Rosemarie*) at Capitol Theater Düsseldorf may serve as an illustration of the general lack of interest in the art form and its subtleties still common among cultural commentators. The musical, written by Heribert Feckler and Dirk Witthuhn, dramatises a famous scandal in postwar Frankfurt involving the death of a high-class prostitute named Rosemarie Nitribitt. The eponymous protagonist was played by Anna Montanaro,[55] who starred as Velma Kelly in *Chicago* both on Broadway and in the West End. One of Germany's leading newspapers, the *Frankfurter Allgemeine Zeitung*, published a detailed report on the show's world première on 21 January 2004, yet discussed the score, parts of which are excellent, in all of one line.[56] They only cared about the infamous historic local scandal on which this musical is based.

Regarding this general lack of academic, journalistic, and general cultural prestige, several factors come into play, starting with an all-encompassing lack of basic knowledge about the genre: many artistically important contemporary musicals have not yet been produced on the German-language stage or are mounted only occasionally. There is also still a general distrust of products from the American culture industry, which was first articulated after World War II by such influential cultural commentators as the philosophers Theodor Adorno and Max Horkheimer and is still widespread, especially among intellectuals.[57] This is amplified by a disregard of the qualities of entertainment, which adorn even the works of daring and progressive writers of musicals like Sondheim. The actual lack of quality in both productions and performances when compared to Broadway and West End standards is also a contributing element. Although this gap has been noticeably reduced since the 1990s, despite all efforts it has not yet been closed in most contexts. This factor perpetuates a challenging situation, as it consistently leads to unfavourable comparisons with opera, often presented in the same towns or even on the same subsidised theatre stages and offering many of the best productions in the world with classical music's finest performers. Musicals are still rarely produced at the same level of excellence. In New York or London, the situation is virtually the opposite, with far more money spent, for example, on the scenographic design of musicals by the greatest designers of the Anglophone stage than on opera sets, while renowned directors such as Mathew Warchus, Richard Eyre, and Trevor Nunn moved regularly from Shakespeare and the classics of world drama to musicals, and others, such as Harold Prince, Richard Jones, and Francesca Zambello worked with equal facility in opera and musical theatre. In German-language theatre, Harry Kupfer is a rare exception in this regard, having directed, among others, the world premières of *Elisabeth* (1992) and *Mozart!* (1999) in addition to his work in opera.

Yet, most of all, the reputation of the musical suffers from not achieving any international resonance with its domestic production in the markets that count the most regarding prestige, in this case London and New York. Negative factors at play here reinforce one another. A lack of opportunities for first-class education and limited working conditions for creators of musicals go hand in hand and slow down any significant development of the German-language musical as product for export: there has not been one single musical of German-language origin written since World War II which has succeeded on Broadway or in the West End. At home, none has been able to draw attention, elicit respect, and encourage financial investment in the genre beyond the (still narrow) realms of the genre and its few main protagonists, producers as well as writers. Compare this lack of top-notch success to, for example, the significant effects German-speaking actors (such as Maximilian Schell and Christoph Waltz) and directors (such as Volker Schlöndorff, Caroline Link, and Florian Henckel von Donnersmarck) winning an Academy Award, or music acts (such as the Scorpions and Rammstein) having hits in the US charts and succeeding on the international touring circuit, or writers winning the Noble Prize for Literature (such as Günter Grass, Elfriede Jelinek, and Herta Müller), respectively, have had on the domestic cultural discourse. It matters. And it is missing here. The occasional yet continuous success that German-language musicals such as *Linie 1* and *Elisabeth* find abroad, especially in the major Asian markets of South Korea and Japan, has of course been noticed and welcomed by its authors and producers. However, justified or not, when it comes to musicals, from a German perspective, the gold standard is to make it in New York or London. This is not just evident from the domestic reputation of one performer, Ute Lemper, to fulfill such an aspiration when she starred as Velma Kelly in the celebrated revival of *Chicago*, first in London (winning the 1998 Laurence Olivier Award for Best Actress in a Musical) and then in New York. It is also part of every fan forum debate. Even a New York misfire such as *Tanz der Vampire* usually gets tagged as 'did run on Broadway' as a seal of both approval and quality in domestic circles. Overall, the domestic situation is not much different in this regard compared to having a shot at the U. S. regional theatre market: you need to make it on Broadway (or at least off-Broadway) first.[58] And the German-language musical is not there yet.

That being said, domestic originals do indeed play a role in the local market alongside imports, of course, and they do so in both private and public theatres. The most important domestic composer of musicals, Martin Lingnau, belongs to a category similar to that of Wildhorn, although his oeuvre is a bit more versatile. Lingnau has created shows such as the aforementioned *Swinging St. Pauli* (2001), *Heiße Ecke* (2003), *Villa Sonnenschein* (2005), *Der Schuh des Manitu* (2008), *Die Königs vom Kiez* (2013), *Das Wunder von Bern* (2014), and *Cindy Reller* (2016), mainly writing for the private Schmidt Theater in Hamburg, with its three medium-sized stages. Yet he has also worked for the much larger theatres of the Hamburg-based Stage Entertainment.[59] Lingnau also wrote children's musicals: *Die 13½ Leben des Käpt'n Blaubär* (*The 13½ Lives of Captain Bluebear*, 2006) and *Der Räuber Hotzenplotz* (*The Robber Hotzenplotz*, 2011), based on very well-known German children books by Walter Moers and Otfried Preußler respectively. Lingnau's style can be best descripted as a mixture of mainstream rock, period pastiche, and German *Schlager*, a particular form of easy listening that developed after 1945. His style is effective, straightforward, and professional, yet it lacks the ambition and sophistication, the adventurousness and catchiness of leading contemporary Anglophone artists, as is proved by listening to the original cast albums (available on, for example, Spotify).

However, Lingnau's pieces accrue major performance figures and attract large audiences. For example, in 2015–2016 his works reached positions three (*Das Wunder von Bern*: 420), seven (*Heiße Ecke*: 318) and thirteen (*Die Königs vom Kiez*: 189), while in 2016–2017 his works ranked second (*Heiße Ecke*: 291), fifth (*Cindy Reller*: 167), and fourteenth (*Die Königs vom Kiez*: 69) in the annual top twenty of the most-performed musicals in German-language theatres, with *Heiße Ecke* being seen by 153,914 and 136,096 people, respectively. They basically succeed on the one hand via title recognition of the source material (either famous children's books such as *Die 13½ Leben des Käpt'n Blaubär* [1999] and *Der Räuber Hotzenplotz* [1962]; regional legends such as *Der kleine Störtebeker* [*The Little Störtebeker*, 2014]; or popular German movies such as *Der Schuh des Manitu* and *Das Wunder von Bern*). On the other hand, they incorporate decidedly local topics customised to their original performance venue and thus offer entertainment for tourists (e.g. his 'St.-Pauli-musicals' for the St Pauli–based Schmidt Theater in Hamburg: *Swinging St. Pauli, Heiße Ecke, Die Königs vom Kiez*, and *Cindy Reller*).

Title recognition is key to understanding the domestic productions for the German-language market. Musicals have to sell tickets, not just in commercial theatres but also in subsidised theatres, where their consistently higher attendance rate generates revenue that is widely used to co-finance other projects in opera and contemporary avant-garde music theatre with less audience appeal and/or massive costs. Title recognition has evolved as the dominant strategy; it lies behind the establishment of a small, constantly revived core repertoire in both subsidised and commercial theatre. It is behind the aforementioned projects of original German-language jukebox musicals, the screen-to-stage transfers by producers such as Stage Entertainment and the historical and literary subjects favoured by the Vereinigte Bühnen Wien or Frank Wildhorn. It also accounts for Lingnau's oeuvre, commissioned by subsidised and both small- and large-scale private theatres.

In this regard Lingnau is paradigmatic. The creation of musicals about local protagonists and places that strive mainly to succeed in their own region and/or musicals about subjects with title recognition is paramount to the German-language theatre when it comes to the production of home-grown originals.[60] Other German-language musicals of the 2010s in the same vein covered historical topics such as the Berlin Wall (*Hinterm Horizont*, Berlin, 2011) and the World Cup triumph of 1954 (*Das Wunder von Bern*, Hamburg, 2014), or dealt with historical personalities. The latter include Frederick the Great (*Friedrich: Mythos und Tragödie* [*Frederick: Myth and Tragedy*, Potsdam, 2012]); William Tell (*Tell*, Walenstadt, Switzerland, 2012); Johann Joseph Schickeneder, alias Emanuel Schikaneder (*Schikaneder*, Vienna, 2016) and Martin Luther (*Luther: Rebell Gottes* [*Luther: God's Rebel*, Fürth, 2017]). Other pieces are centred on certain locations, referencing for example the Sonnenallee and the Kurfürstendamm, both well-known streets and socio-cultural milieus in Berlin (*Sonnenallee*, Schwerin, 2014; and *Stella: Das Gespenst vom Kurfürstendamm*, 2016). Title recognition and/or local plot context are paramount. It seems that the combination of both factors in the 1992 success of *Elisabeth*, the musical about the Austrian-Hungarian empress, established a blueprint for the 'Austrification' (and its German and Swiss equivalents) of the genre. The domination of this approach in the German-language theatre is mirrored by the lack of interest in Anglophone musicals with pronounced American or British settings. There is only one major exception from this rule: *West Side Story*, mainly because of the reputations of Bernstein and Shakespeare. It will be interesting to see if domestic premieres such as Lin-Manuel Miranda's *Hamilton* (2022 in Hamburg) or Sting's *The Last Ship* (2021 in Koblenz) will be able to challenge that well-established pattern.

Lingnau's oeuvre shows, furthermore, that writing musicals based on popular culture for children and young adults, such as *Wicked* or *Matilda*, is also a regular artistic endeavour in German-language theatre. However, in this context it is once more important to adapt works that are widely known in Germany, Austria, and Switzerland. That is why *Shockheaded Peter* is a success—after all, it is based on a famous nineteenth-century

German-language original, Heinrich Hoffmann's 1844 *Der Struwwelpeter*—where more renowned Anglophone shows struggle to find an audience. Although not completely unheard of, *The Wizard of Oz* and the books of Roald Dahl and their movie adaptations do not have the same purchase in the popular culture of German-speaking Europe.

Lingnau and Wildhorn are not the only contemporary writers of musicals who have succeeded with new works in the German-language market. Wolfgang Böhmer, Frank Nimsgern, Sylvester Levay (who is Hungarian), Marc Schubring, Frank Wittenbrink, and Thomas Zaufke are other well-established composers, while Michael Kunze, Peter Lund, and Heiko Wohlgemuth have made a name for themselves as book writers and lyricists. Regarding authors of domestic musicals, however, there is no household name who has achieved the sort of public recognition in the general cultural consciousness as Andrew Lloyd Webber has since 1990.

But what are the odds for new artists to succeed, and where should they come from? First and foremost, quality is key; but how can it be judged, and in what way can it be achieved? In this context, one has to remember that there are only two musicals from the 1970s and 1980s that have been able to establish themselves in the local repertoire as long-term successes:[61] Georg Kreisler's aforementioned *Heute Abend: Lola Blau* (1971) and Birger Heymann and Volker Ludwig's *Linie 1* (*Line 1*, 1986). Kreisler, himself a renowned cabaret writer, singer, and pianist, conceived his work for his wife, Topsy Küppers, herself a cabaret performer.[62] Heymann and Ludwig's work was written for the children and youth playhouse GRIPS-Theater in Berlin (founded and run by Ludwig from 1969 until 2017).[63] For a long time these two shows exemplified successful German-language originals, suggesting that there is not much experience and only a few models to build on.

Furthermore, one has to remember that in German-speaking countries, there are still no training opportunities for composers, lyricists, or book writers of musicals at any of their prestigious, world-class higher-education institutions for music and theater, not to mention programmes with the track record of the ASCAP Foundation Musical Theater Workshop or the BMI Lehman Engel Musical Theater Workshop.[64] Even someone like Martin Lingnau is basically an autodidact who had some private teaching and later attended a minor study programme for popular music at Hamburg's School of Music and Theatre, yet basically learned on the job, having worked in the theatre since his youth.[65] Franz Wittenbrink gained the knowledge he later applied as a writer of scenic song plays and revues like *Sekretärinnen* (ninth overall in public theatres, 1994, 1995, 2017, and 2018) as a member of the famous boys' and young men's choir Regensburger Domspatzen and in pop bands. He started writing such pieces when working as musical director for straight theatres, such as the famous Hamburger Schauspielhaus (there during the seasons 1993–1994 to 1999–2000).[66] Consequently, in the field of musical theatre writing, lateral career changes and autodidactic education are the norm. That might be a contributing factor to the rarity of bold dramaturgical ideas such as turning death into an active protagonist in *Elisabeth*. Half a century after the birth of the 'concept musical', conventional storytelling and revue-formats still prevail.

But working conditions are just as important as education when it comes to the quality of original shows. The widespread disrespect of musical theatre in the cultural discourse of academics, journalists, and the general public is mirrored by a lack of financial investment for developing ambitious musicals; as a result, these are usually created under enormous time pressure. The development of a Broadway show takes several years, accompanied by a demanding workshop and try-out process. In the same time that someone as extraordinarily productive as Jeanine Tesori opened five musicals on and off Broadway in New York (*Thoroughly Modern Millie*, 2002; *Caroline, or Change*, 2004; *Shrek*, 2008; *Fun Home*, 2015; and *Soft Power*, 2019, as well as the 2014 Broadway production of *Violet*, 1997), Martin Lingnau premiered three times as many works: since *Swinging St. Pauli* (2001), he has composed no fewer than seventeen musicals.

These numbers are absolutely typical. Marc Schubring, another well-established writer of musicals (who participated in the BMI Lehman Engel Musical Theater Workshop), completed fifteen musicals in twelve years, besides writing music for films and plays. The body of work of such artists as Frank Nimsgern and Peter Lund is of similar size. Even including *The Frogs* (1974), Sondheim in his immensely productive 'mature' period, that is, the twenty-five years between *Company* (1970) and *Passion* (1994), produced only eleven shows. On the one hand, these figures show an impressive output and work ethic on the part of key protagonists of today's German-language musical. On the other hand, it becomes evident that neither the commercial nor the subsidised German-language theatre sector cares enough (or is daring enough) to invest properly in the painstaking developmental process for musicals or to demand the same originality they do of opera. It is not surprising that many of the most successful domestic originals from the 1970s, 1980s, and 1990s—*Heute Abend: Lola Blau*, *Linie 1*, and *Sekretärinnen*—are actual revues or at least predominantly revue-like in structure.

Because of the working conditions outlined above, it can come as no surprise that the domestic production is dominated by solid yet unimaginative works, whereas aesthetically ambitious offerings that receive a notable amount of productions, like the musical play *The Black Rider* by Tom Waits, William Burroughs, and Robert Wilson, which is based on the same source material as Carl Maria von Weber's Romantic opera *Der Freischütz* and which received its world première in 1990 at Hamburg's famous Thalia-Theater, are the exception.[67] So it might not just be uninformed cultural snobbery regarding musical theatre as a genre that causes academics, critics, artistic directors, and fans to find original indigenous musicals underwhelming when compared to the classic shows that prevail in the repertoire or those which can be seen in New York and London. Yet how can accomplished authors emerge and establish themselves if in reality they have to produce musicals as if they were working on an assembly line?[68]

Nonetheless, what German-language musical theatre is waiting for first and foremost is a unique domestic voice in the vein of Robert Lopez, Lin-Manuel Miranda, or Benj Pasek and Justin Paul, who might elevate the homegrown musical to the next level of contemporary aesthetics, mainstream popular cultural relevance,[69] and international recognition. What is needed is the one individual or songwriting team that does not just produce solid works like *Linie 1*, *Sekretärinnen*, *Elisabeth*, or *Heiße Ecke*—to list but a few major domestic success stories since the 1980s—but that conceive the next *Threepenny Opera* (1928) or *White Horse Inn* (1930) for the upcoming next Roaring Twenties: works that bring back a time when homegrown musical theatre still had resonance, even in the West End and on Broadway.[70]

Yet until this next step is taken here, too, despite its important role in today's music theatre repertoire in its own region, musical as a genre still feels largely like a cultural import not yet fully assimilated and integrated into the local cultural DNA. More important, the genre will be treated that way until the next *Threepenny Opera* is written. For now at least, arguably the most important challenge for the future of the genre in the German-language market lies in the fact that until now, even the best original home-grown musicals lack the aesthetic highs, excitement, and general cultural resonance of the best Anglophone musicals.

Of course, under the overall circumstances I have described, it would be a tremendous stroke of luck if another Kurt Weill came along, a first-class composer from the realm of either classical or popular music, to team up with a first-class playwright such as Bertolt Brecht—and, like Brecht, not reared in popular (musical) theatre—and if those two were able to write a true masterpiece of popular musical theatre. Considering all of the above, it seems a bit unfair to judge the quality of indigenous musicals too harshly.

What is needed today is a work that does for the reputation of the genre at home and of the German-language musical abroad what *Cats* did nearly forty years ago for contemporary British and American musicals in continental Europe: namely, bring about a watershed moment which creates a new dynamic. Without such a show, there is not much of a chance to catch up with the latest developments of the Anglophone musical and thus to increase the academic, journalistic, and general cultural respectability of the genre as a whole. But more than that, as long as musical theatre has no prestige to speak of in Germany, Austria, and Switzerland, most of the budget in the public sector for the development of new works will remain reserved for opera.

Admittedly, it is far from certain that such a change of priorities will bring about something exciting with a lasting effect; the lack of experience when it comes to developing successful new musicals (with the Vereinigte Bühnen Wien as a rare exception), may still result in artistic failure. Nonetheless, the current situation feels like a wasted opportunity, considering the strength of public financial support for music theatre in general in German-speaking countries and the impact non-profit or only partly publicly funded theatre companies in the last few decades have had elsewhere on musical theatre: after all, it was organisations like the Public Theater, Playwrights Horizons, Roundabout Theater, and Second Stage Theater in New York and the Royal Shakespeare Company in the UK which supported the development of such notable musicals as *A Chorus Line*, *Sunday in the Park with George*, *Matilda*, and *Hamilton* and guided these groundbreaking shows to completion. The progress on all fronts since the Austrian and German premières of *Cats* and the richness and strength especially of the public theatre sector here should be enough to provide a basis for such a development.

## NOTES

1. In 2017–2018, 155 out of 464 theatres in Germany, Austria and Switzerland staged a musical, compared to 73 (out of 308) in 1983–1984, 72 (384) in 1987–1988, 99 (399) in 1989–1990, and then 135 (468) in 1991–1992 (the first theatrical season after reunification). These figures were compiled by the Deutscher Bühnenverein, whose annual statistics are incomplete but nonetheless extensive. Musicals were also produced in the German Democratic Republic (GDR), see Jansen, Wolfgang. "'Bringt es uns weiter?' Zur Rezeption des Musicals in der DDR'. In *Die Rezeption des Broadwaymusicals in Deutschland*, ed. Nils Grosch and Elmar Juchem, 133–157. Münster: Waxmann, 2012. Thus, the significant increase of theatres producing musicals after 1989–1990 is not just a consequence of the success of *Cats* and the boom it created but also to the reunification which led to East German theatres becoming part of the statistics.

2. 145 works produced in Germany, Austria and Switzerland in 2017–2018 compared to 41 in 1983–1984, 78 in 1991–1992, and then 132 in 2001–2002, according to the annual statistics of the Deutscher Bühnenverein.

3. See for instance fan-run websites like https://musicalzentrale.de, http://kulturpoebel.de, and http://www.musicalspot.de. All websites were accessed 5 June 2019.

4. See Wolfgang Jansen. *Cats & Co.: Geschichte des Musicals im deutschsprachigen Theater* (Leipzig: Henschel, 2008), 243; Jürgen Schmude and Philipp Namberger, 'Musicals als tourismuswissenschaftlicher Forschungsgegenstand: Grundsätzliche Überlegungen und Marktsituation in Deutschland im Jahr 2012', in *Kulturtourismus zu Beginn des 21. Jahrhunderts*, ed. Heinz-Dieter Quack and Kristiane Klemm (Munich: Oldenbourg, 2013), 255–264; here: 255.

5. I have explored the specifics of the present two-tier local scene with regard to decentralisation, cultural politics, economics, audiences, production standards, higher education, etc., elsewhere. That essay also introduces the main companies, venues, and creatives of the homegrown musical. See Frédéric Döhl, 'The Third Biggest Market: Musical Theatre in Germany since 1990', in *The Routledge Companion to the Contemporary Musical*, ed. Jessica Sternfeld and Elizabeth L. Wollman (New York: Routledge, 2020), 427–436.

6. See the programs for theatres by the federal government as part of its overall supports program for culture called "Neustart Kultur" ("Fresh Start for Culture"), https://www.bundesregierung.de/breg-de/bundesregierung/bundeskanzleramt/staatsministerin-fuer-kultur-und-medien/kultur/neustart-kultur-1772990.

7. See Thomas Siedhoff. *Handbuch des Musicals* (Mainz: Schott, 2007); Jansen, *Cats & Co.*; Jonas Menze, *Musical Backstages: Die Rahmenbedingungen und Produktionsprozesse des deutschsprachigen Musicals* (Münster: Waxmann, 2018); and Thomas Siedhoff, *Deutsch(sprachig)es Musical* (Freiburg im Breisgau: ZPKM, 2018), https://freidok.uni-freiburg.de/data/14628, accessed 5 June 2019. For the years before the première of *Cats* in 1986, see also Wolfgang Jansen, "'I've Grown Accustomed … '": Das Musical kommt nach Deutschland, 1945–1960', in *Die Rezeption des Broadwaymusicals in Deutschland*, ed. Nils Grosch and Elmar Juchem (Münster: Waxmann, 2012), 21–42; Thomas Siedhoff, 'Aufstieg, Fall und Emanzipation des deutschen Musicals', in ibid., 43–60; and Wolfgang Jansen, 'Operette oder Musical? Zum populären Musiktheater der DDR in den Jahren 1949 bis 1964', *Lied und populäre Kultur/Song and Popular Culture: Jahrbuch des Zentrums für populäre Kultur und Musik* 60–61 (2015–2016): 383–399.

8. See https://www.deutschemusicalakademie.de/deutscher-musical-theater-preis/deutscher-musical-theater-preis-2019/; http://www.buehnenverein.de/de/publikationen-und-statisti ken/statistiken/werkstatistik.html; http://www.deutsches-musicalarchiv.de/; https://www.dnb.de/DE/Ueber-uns/DMA/dma_node.html; http://www.musicals-magazin.de; https://musicalzentrale.de/; http://kulturpoebel.de; https://unitedmusicals.de/; https://maybemusi cal.com; and https://www.musicalspot.de; https://www.musical1.de.

9. All data in this essay are taken from the following sources if not noted otherwise: Arnold Jacobshagen, *Musiktheater, Musiktheater*, 2018, http://www.miz.org/static_de/themen portale/einfuehrungstexte_pdf/03_KonzerteMusiktheater/jacobshagen.pdf, accessed 18 August 2019; Deutsches Musikinformationszentrum/MIZ (ed.), *Ur- und Erstaufführungen der Musiktheater in Deutschland*, 2015, http://www.miz.org/downloads/statistik/80/stat istik80.pdf, accessed 5 June 2019; Deutsches Musikinformationszentrum/MIZ (ed.)., *Musicals mit den meisten Aufführungen in Deutschland*, 2018, http://www.miz.org/downlo ads/statistik/75/75_Musicals_mit_den_meisten_Auffuehrungen_in_Deutschland.pdf, accessed 5 June 2019; Statista, *Dossier Musical*, 2019, https://de.statista.com/statistik/stu die/id/56556/dokument/musicals/, accessed 7 July 2019; and the annual statistics of the Deutscher Bühnenverein (German Stage Association), called *Werkstatistik*.

10. An important venue for the productions of musicals, both of imports (i.e., the German-language premières of *Cats*, 1983, and *The Phantom of the Opera*, 1988) and of originals (esp. *Elisabeth*, 1992, and *Mozart!*, 1999) in the 1980s and 1990s, the third theatre of the original group, the Theater an der Wien, went back to staging only opera in the mid-2000s.

11. See Theater Dortmund, https://www.theaterdo.de/spielplan/alle-sparten/, accessed 15 October 2019.

12. See also chap. 9 of the volume about stage entertainment, by Jonas Menze.

13. *Heiße Ecke* is a work about a sausage stand in Hamburg's notorious entertainment quarter, St. Pauli. Four actors and five actresses play about fifty roles of everyday people that pass the sausage stand and interact with its personal and each other over the course of twenty-four hours. The work aims to depict the special atmosphere and character of this part of Hamburg. *Heiße Ecke* is scored for an eight-piece band and lasts about three hours (including intermission); it opened on 16 September 2003 in Schmidts Tivoli, Hamburg. For additional information about the work, see the websites of the show's producer and publisher: Schmidt Hamburg Theater Reeperbahn, https://www.tivoli.de/programm-tickets/heisse-ecke/, accessed 5 June 2019; and Hartmann und Stauffacher Verlag. https://www.hsverlag.com/werke/detail/t6543, accessed 5 June 2019.

14. See Statista, *Dossier Musical*; UK Theatre, *2018 Sales Data Report*, 2019. https://ukthea tre.org/theatre-industry/news/2018-sales-data-released-uk-theatre-and-society-of-london-theatre/, accessed 7 July 2019; WhatsOnStage, *Box-Office Figures Show London's West End Drew Revenue of £765 million in 2018*, 2019, https://www.whatsonstage.com/lon don-theatre/news/box-office-figures-london-west-end-solt-2018_48370.html, accessed 7 July 2019; Society of London Theatre, *Musicals Drive Record London Theatre Attendance in 2018*, 2019, https://www.londontheatre.co.uk/theatre-news/news/musicals-drive-rec ord-london-theatre-attendance-in-2018, accessed 7 July 2019; and The Broadway League, *Broadway Season Statistics*, 2019, https://www.broadwayleague.com/research/statistics-broadway-nyc/, accessed 7 July 2019.

15. According to the annual statistics of the Deutscher Bühnenverein, in 2017–2018 German theatres staged 242 musicals (272 when one includes Austria and northern Switzerland).

In 2016–2017, there were 235 (269) productions. The following figures are also all based on this source.

16. In 2017–2018, Germany staged 128 different musicals; when including Austria and northern Switzerland, the number rises to 145. This represents a slight increase over the previous season (2016–2017), which saw 118/140 premières.

17. In the previous season (2016–2017), 135 German theatres staged a musical, as did 16 venues in Austria and northern Switzerland.

18. In 2016–2017, there were 151 performance spaces dedicated to musical theatre.

19. In 2017–2018, 113 theatres in Germany, plus 20 in Austria and northern Switzerland, staged operas, down from 122 German stages and another 24 venues in the other two countries in 2016–2017.

20. The exact number for 2016–2017 is 2,331 performances.

21. In 2015–2016, there were 6,795 opera performances in German-speaking countries. See Jacobshagen, *Musiktheater*. This is by far the highest productivity rate for opera in the world. The United States ranked second, with 1,657, and the UK seventh, with 989 performances.

22. See Menze, *Musical Backstages*, 83.

23. See Stage Entertainment, https://www.stage-entertainment.de/unternehmen/ueber-stage/ueber-stage.html; and https://www.stage-entertainment.de/landingpages/backst age/eigenproduktionen/eigenproduktionen.html#news_teaser_1-108243, both accessed 7 July 2019.

24. The other world premières included *Wake Up* (2002), *Barbarella* (2004), *Die Weberischen* (*The Webers*, 2006, about Mozart's wife and her family), *Die Habsburgischen* (*The House of Habsburg*, 2007), *Rudolf* (2009), *Woyzeck & The Tiger Lillies* (2011), and *Der Besuch der alten Dame* (*The Visit*, 2014).

25. This is evidenced by the very small number of courses on musical theatre at higher education institutions in German-speaking countries, as listed annually by the academic journal *Die Musikforschung* of the German Musicological Society (GfM).

26. Overall, the Bochum *Starlight Express* has reached more than 12,000 performances and attracted 17 million viewers since 1988. Any production running for such a long time has to deal with varying interest from the audience, and the rollerskate musical is no exception: in 2015–2016 it had 441,623 visitors (during its 375 performances), whereas in previous years the numbers were as follows: 2010–2011: 424,040 (371); 2007–2008: 413,122 (371); and 2006–2007: 444,000 (362). See Jacobshagen, *Musiktheater 2019*; plus the archived older versions 2005 to 2018 of the same article at http://www.miz.org/fachbeitraege_archiv. html, accessed 18 August 2019. The fluctuation in numbers can be explained in a variety of ways. First, over the years, the different owners of the production executed different strategies. For example, they reduced the total amount of annual performances from 420 (as was typical around the millennium) to around 370 today. Secondly, *Starlight Express* has been reworked substantially over the years, incorporating new songs, a new stage design and special effects, new choreography, changes in the lyrics, and even in characters. For example, new songs were introduced in 2002, 2008, and 2013. In 2006 new characters singing hip-hop were added, and in 2018 there was a general overhaul to celebrate the show's thirtieth anniversary. See Anna Seifert, 'Nachgedacht: 30 Jahre *Starlight Express*; Ein Kommentar zur Neugestaltung des Musicals', *kulturpoebel.de*, 20 February 2019, http://kulturpoebel.de/2019/02/nachgedacht-30-jahre-starlight-express-ein-kommen tar-zur-neugestaltung-des-musicals/, accessed 5 July 2019. Another factor is the constant

542 FRÉDÉRIC DÖHL

reorganising of ticketing, especially ticket packages for groups and families as well as cheaper tickets for weekdays. Since key data such as licencing costs and running costs are not published, the break-even point for this production is difficult to calculate. Yet, the aforementioned steps seem to secure enough continuous interest to keep the show profitable, even with an average attendance of around 70 percent at its Bochum home (which seats 1,650).

27. For instance, in 2016–2017 about 18 percent of the 1,282 German productions in private and subsidised venues dedicated to music theatre recorded by the Deutscher Bühnenverein were musicals, yet these 235 productions attracted 35 percent of the recorded overall attendance to music theatre of any kind (2,367,845 out of 6,834,627 theatre-goers. Out of these 2,367,845 theatre-goers, 1,445,866 visited a subsidised theatre. The following season (2017–2018), the number of people paying to see a musical dropped slightly to 2,348,289.

28. Anglo-American musicals dating from before 1945 are rarely produced in Germany, Austria, or Switzerland. In 2016–2017 only three of these works were staged, including Cole Porter's *Anything Goes* (1934), which was seen by 19,556 people.

29. These numbers and proportions are typical: 63 percent of the productions in 2017–2018 (242 out of 386) had an audience share of 88 percent, while for 2015–2016 and 2014–2015 the numbers are 63 percent and 62 percent of productions (or 248 out of 391 and 247 out of 298) attracted 87 percent and 88 percent of the overall audience.

30. In 2017–2018 they accounted for 240 out of 384 productions; the figures for the previous years are similar (2016–2017: 232 out of 390 productions; 2015–2016: 248 out of 391).

31. When it comes to reviewing musical theatre, no German-language media outlet has the prestige and influence of the *New York Times* and its main theatre critics, such as Brooks Atkinson, Clive Barnes, Walter Kerr, Frank Rich, and Ben Brantley. In general, only the local media comment on musicals. There is also a sizeable lack of academic literature compared to the United States and the United Kingdom, a gap that has only widened since 2000. Basically, German, Austrian, and Swiss research into the genre is still undertaken by only a small group of enthusiasts. Courses on musical theatre at German-language institutions of higher education are still rare, other than a few programmes at training facilities for performers. See again the annual list of courses compiled by the academic journal *Die Musikforschung*.

32. See Olaf Jubin, 'Lost in Translation? Die Werke Stephen Sondheims und ihre Rezeption auf dem deutschsprachigen Musicalmarkt', in *Die Rezeption des Broadwaymusicals in Deutschland*, ed. Nils Grosch and Elmar Juchem (Münster: Waxmann, 2012), 177–201.

33. For the German-language market, foreign performers from non-English-speaking countries, such as the Dutch Pia Douwes and Willemijn Verkaik (both of whom became famous stars) have been of major importance.

34. Jansen. *Cats & Co.*, 221f. As of 2023, some excellent higher-education institutions run study programmes for musical theatre performers, including for instance the University of Arts, Berlin; the Folkwang-University Essen; and the Bavarian Theatre Academy August Everding, Munich. New translations of Sondheim's *Follies* (by Martin G. Berger) and *Sunday in the Park with George* (by Robin Kulisch) were to open during the 2019–2020 season in subsidised theatres in Dresden and Radebeul. Roman Hinze provided the German-language version of *Passion* (for its first German-language staging 2011 in Dresden), and in 2019 there will be new German translations of both *A Funny Thing Happened on the Way to the Forum* and *Sweeney Todd* (by Wilfried Steiner). Martin G. Berger also translated *Anyone Can Whistle* for the first time; this version still awaits its

German-language première. See Sondheim's German publisher, Musik und Bühne Verlagsgesellschaft mbH, https://www.musikundbuehne.de/nc/stuecksuche.html, accessed 15 October 2019.

35. See Landestheater Linz, https://www.landestheater-linz.at/stuecke/detail?k=16104&s=2016/17, accessed 5 June 2019.

36. These seven operas are: Kurt Weill's *The Threepenny Opera* (ranked 17th, 68 performances/5 productions), Leonard Ever's *Gold* (23rd, 51/6, an opera for children), Richard Strauss's *Ariadne auf Naxos* (24th, 50/8), *Salome* (28th, 46/10) and *Der Rosenkavalier* (35th, 36/7), Wolfgang Mitterer's *Schneewittchen* (42nd, 35/2, an opera for childrend six years old and up), and Richard Strauss's *Elektra* (46th, 33/10). See Operabase, https://www.operabase.com, accessed 15 October 2019.

37. When this kind of show becomes available for subsidised theatres, as *Les Misérables* did several years ago, the license includes reduced production requirements while also freeing up the production to individual interpretations as preferred by Regietheater (director's theatre).

38. See Siedhoff, *Handbuch des Musicals*, 489.

39. This was the result of a poll by the website Musical1.de, which covered eighteen categories and had a response of 250,000 votes (see Musical1, https://www.musical1.de/wahlen/, accessed 18 June 2019). In the category 'Long Run', two productions of the show, running at that time in Cologne and Vienna, respectively, ranked first and second (with 18 percent and 11 percent), while also topping categories like 'Best Musical Song'. 'Best Costumes', 'Best Stage Design', and 'Best Choreography'. However, a rewritten version of *Dance of the Vampires* was a notorious Broadway flop in 2002–2003.

40. There is a lack of official data regarding the investment, licencing costs, gross, and break-even point for shows produced by commercial theatre companies in Germany. However, taking into account how few larger companies there are in the private musical theatre sector and the high number of works they produce (Stage Entertainment has offered 101 works in less than 20 years), the economic risks and success rate seems to be of a similar scale compared to Broadway, the main difference being that in New York the cost of running a production are much higher and the costs of developing new works seem to be lower.

41. Jansen, *Cats & Co.*, 179–239.

42. Jacobshagen, *Musiktheater 2013*, 12; Werner Heinrichs, 'Kulturbetrieb', in *Glossar Kulturmanagement*, ed. Verena Lewinski-Reuter and Stefan Lüddemann (Wiesbaden: VS Verlag für Sozialwissenschaften, 2011), 131–137; here: 131; and Schmude and Namberger, *Musicals als tourismuswissenschaftlicher Forschungsgegenstand*, 256.

43. In 2010, there was also the metamusical/revue *Sondheim on Sondheim*.

44. For an overview, see Robert Gordon, 'Sondheim Scholarship: An Overview', *Studies in Musical Theatre* 13, no. 2 (2019): 197–204.

45. Box Office Mojo by IMDbPro, https://www.boxofficemojo.com/yearly/chart/?view2=worldwide&yr=2007&p=.htm, accessed 5 May 2019. For more about the movie adaptation, see David Thomson, 'Attending the Tale of *Sweeney Todd*: The Stage Musical and Tim Burton's Film Version', in *The Oxford Handbook of Sondheim Studies*, ed. Robert Gordon (New York and Oxford: Oxford University Press, 2014), 296–305; and Tim Stephenson, 'The Ethical Exculpation of Moral Turpitude: Representations of Violence and Death in *Sweeney Todd* and *Into the Woods*', in *Twenty-first Century Musicals: From Stage to Screen*, ed. George Rodosthenous (London and New York: Routledge, 2017), 164–180.

46. Wulfmansworld.com, https://wulfmansworld.com/Die_besten_Filme/Kinocharts/Kinoc harts_2008_-_Plaetze_61-70.htm, accessed 19 June 2019; and Inside Kino, http://www.ins idekino.com/DJahr/D2008.htm, accessed 19 June 2019.
47. Jacobshagen, *Musiktheater 2010*.
48. Email to the author, 15 October 2019.
49. Musik und Bühne Verlagsgesellschaft mbH, https://www.musikundbuehne.de/aktuel les/aktuelles-detailansicht.html?tx_news_pi1%5Bnews%5D=918&tx_news_pi1%5Bcon troller%5D=News&tx_news_pi1%5Baction%5D=detail&cHash=fc644336b827821b4b639 9d41434495c, accessed 15 October 2019.
50. Musik und Bühne Verlagsgesellschaft mbH, https://www.musikundbuehne.de/nc/stue cksuche.html, accessed 15 October 2019.
51. Larry Stempel, *Showtime: A History of the Broadway Musical Theatre* (New York: Norton, 2010), 668.
52. Jubin. *Lost in Translation?*, 198f.
53. Nadine Jobst, 'How to Be a Legend: Frank Wildhorn', 11 August 2016, http://kulturpoebel. de/2016/08/how-to-be-a-legend-frank-wildhorn/, accessed 15 August 2019.
54. See Nils Grosch, 'Zwischen Ignoranz und Kulturkritik: Das Musical in der Rezeption durch die deutschsprachigen Wissenschaften', in *Die Rezeption des Broadwaymusicals in Deutschland*, ed. Nils Grosch and Elmar Juchem (Münster: Waxmann, 2012), 9–19.
55. After Hildegard Knef, who—billed as Hildegarde Neff—starred in *Silk Stockings* (1955), and Ute Lemper, who replaced Bebe Neuwirth as Velma Kelly in the revival of *Chicago*, Anna Montanaro was only the third German actress to perform on Broadway.
56. Wolfgang Sandner, 'Das Mädchen und der Tot', *Frankfurter Allgemeine Zeitung*, 23 January 2004, 33.
57. This factor seems to be of special importance for the very limited reception of Rodgers and Hammerstein in German-speaking countries; see Elmar Juchem, 'Der Inbegriff greift nicht. Zur eingeschränkten Wahrnehmung von Rodgers & Hammerstein in Deutschland', in *Die Rezeption des Broadwaymusicals in Deutschland*, ed. Nils Grosch and Elmar Juchem (Münster: Waxmann, 2012), 61–76.
58. See Stacy Wolf, *Beyond Broadway: The Pleasure and Promise of Musical Theatre across America* (London and New York: Oxford University Press, 2020), 7.
59. *Der Schuh des Manitu* ran at the Theater des Westens (Berlin), which seats 1,611, while *Das Wunder von Bern* was shown at the Theater an der Elbe (Hamburg), which has 1,850 seats. The reception for both, however, was mixed at best. See Jonas Menze, '*Der Schuh des Manitu*: Zum Einfluß des Broadway-Megamusicals auf die deutsche Musical-Landschaft', in *Die Rezeption des Broadwaymusicals in Deutschland*, ed. Nils Grosch and Elmar Juchem (Münster: Waxmann, 2012), 203–216, here 215f.
60. See Menze, *Musical Backstages*; and Siedhoff, *Deutsch(sprachig)es Musical*.
61. In this context, see the list of all German-language musicals, which premiered between the end of World World II and the early 1990s as compiled in Wolfgang Jansen, 'Chronik: Werke des unterhaltenden Musiktheaters im deutschsprachigen Theaters, 1945–1990', in *Die Rezeption des Broadwaymusicals in Deutschland*, ed. Nils Grosch and Elmar Juchem (Münster: Waxmann, 2012), 217–256.
62. See Frédéric Döhl, 'Broadway-Rezeption im Kammerformat: Georg Kreislers *Heute Abend: Lola Blau*', in *Die Rezeption des Broadwaymusicals in Deutschland*, ed. Nils Grosch and Elmar Juchem (Münster: Waxmann, 2012), 159–176.

63. Similar to Wittenbrink's *Sekretärinnen*, *Linie 1* is more like a revue in format, although it has an original score. The reference is to the old subway line 1, which ran through West Berlin; this is where all the action is set. The strength of the piece lies in how it captures the flavour of 1980s West-Berlin. For more details see Siedhoff, *Aufstieg, Fall und Emanzipation des deutschen Musicals*, 57; and Siedhoff, *Deutsch(sprachig)es Musical*.

64. In Britain, there is a master of arts for musical theatre writers/composers at Goldsmiths, University of London; Mercury Musical Developments offers some courses for fledgling professionals, and there are some private courses on musical theatre composition and lyric writing; Musical Theatre Network hosts a biennial showcase for new musical theatre writers; and Perfect Pitch offers to develop selected new musicals annually.

65. See Sylke Wohlschiess, 'Interview mit Martin Lingnau', April 2017, https://www.musi calspot.de/martin-lingnau-04-2017-musik-addiert-was-man-nicht-sieht, accessed 17 October 2019.

66. See Barbara Hornberger, 'Der Wittenbrinkabend: Musikalisches Theater zwischen Pop und Postdramatik', *Lied und populäre Kultur/Song and Popular Culture: Jahrbuch des Deutschen Volksliedarchivs Freiburg* 58 (2013): 173–205.

67. See Gregor Herzfeld, 'Zur Romantikrezeption in *The Black Rider* von William Burroughs, Robert Wilson und Tom Waits', in *Die Schaubühne in der Epoche des Freischütz: Theater und Musiktheater der Romantik; Vorträge des Salzburger Symposions 2007*, ed. Jürgen Kühnel, Ulrich Müller, and Oswald Panagl (Salzburg: Mueller-Speiser, 2009), 330–343.

68. Menze, *Musical Backstages*, 226–233 and 251–259. Menze interviewed the subjects of this article regarding their experiences, motivations, and strategies while working in the German-language market.

69. The original Broadway cast recordings of *The Book of Mormon*, *Hamilton*, and *Dear Evan Hansen* all became Top 20 albums in the US *Billboard* charts.

70. See, for instance, William Farina, *The German Cabaret Legacy in American Popular Music* (Jefferson, NC: McFarland, 2013); Len Platt, Tobias Becker, and David Linton (eds.), *Popular Musical Theatre in London and Berlin, 1890 to 1939* (Cambridge: Cambridge University Press, 2014); Tobias Becker, *Inszenierte Moderne: Populäres Theater in Berlin und London, 1880–1930* (Munich: Oldenbourg, 2014); Frédéric Döhl, 'Zur Figur des Produzenten im Spiegel von Urheberrecht und Musiktheatergeschichtsschreibung: Erik Charell und das *Weiße Rößl*', in '*Im weißen Rößl*': *Kulturgeschichtliche Perspektiven*, ed. Nils Grosch and Carolin Stahrenberg (Münster: Waxmann, 2016), 43–50; Derek B. Scott, *German Operetta on Broadway and in the West End, 1900–1940* (Cambridge: Cambridge University Press, 2019); and Anastasia Belina and Derek B. Scott (eds.), *The Cambridge Companion to Operetta* (Cambridge: Cambridge University Press, 2020). For in-depth case studies, see Stephen Hinton (ed.), *Kurt Weill: The Threepenny Opera* (Cambridge: Cambridge University Press, 1990); Anton Mayer, *Franz Lehár: Die Lustige Witwe; Der Ernst der leichten Muse* (Vienna: Ed. Steinbauer, 2015); Ulrich Tadday (ed.), '*Im weißen Rößl*: *Zwischen Kommerz und Kunst* (Munich: text + kritik, 2006); and Nils Grosch and Carolin Stahrenberg (eds.), '*Im weißen Rößl*': *Kulturgeschichtliche Perspektiven* (Münster: Waxmann, 2016).

71. The table is based on statistics by the Deutscher Bühnenverein (up to 2017–2018), with additional information from Musicalzentrale, https://musicalzentrale.de, accessed 5 June 2019; United Musicals, https://unitedmusicals.de/, accessed 5 June 2019; and Siedhoff, *Handbuch des Musicals*. The musical *Marry Me a Little* (1980), featuring material cut

546     FRÉDÉRIC DÖHL

from earlier Sondheim projects, has been produced several times in German-language theatres, too. Its local première was on 25 September 1991 in the Thüringer Landestheater, Rudolfstadt.

72. For sources, see n. 44.
73. For sources, see n. 44.

## BIBLIOGRAPHY

Becker, Tobias. *Inszenierte Moderne: Populäres Theater in Berlin und London, 1880–1930*. Munich: Oldenbourg, 2014.

Belina, Anastasia, and Derek B. Scott, eds. *The Cambridge Companion to Operetta*. Cambridge: Cambridge University Press, 2020.

Box Office Mojo by IMDbPro. https://www.boxofficemojo.com/yearly/chart/?view2=worldw ide&yr=2007&p=.htm, accessed 5 May 2019.

The Broadway League. *Broadway Season Statistics*. New York, 2019, https://www.broadwaylea gue.com/research/statistics-broadway-nyc/, accessed 7 July 2019.

Deutscher Bühnenverein. http://www.buehnenverein.de/de/publikationen-und-statistiken/ statistiken/werkstatistik.html, accessed 5 June 2019.

Deutsche Musical Akademie. https://www.deutschemusicalakademie.de/deutscher-musical-theater-preis/deutscher-musical-theater-preis-2019/, accessed 5 June 2019.

Deutsches Musicalarchiv. http://www.deutsches-musicalarchiv.de/, accessed 5 June 2019.

Deutsches Musikinformationszentrum/MIZ, ed. 'Ur- und Erstaufführungen der Musiktheater in Deutschland', 2015, http://www.miz.org/downloads/statistik/80/statistik80.pdf, accessed 5 June 2019.

Deutsches Musikinformationszentrum/MIZ, ed. 'Musicals mit den meisten Aufführungen in Deutschland', 2018, http://www.miz.org/downloads/statistik/75/75_Musicals_mit_den_ meisten_Auffuehrungen_in_Deutschland.pdf, accessed 5 June 2019.

Deutsche Nationalbibliothek. https://www.dnb.de/DE/Ueber-uns/DMA/dma_node.html, accessed 5 June 2019.

Döhl, Frédéric. 'Broadway-Rezeption im Kammerformat: Georg Kreislers *Heute Abend: Lola Blau*'. In *Die Rezeption des Broadwaymusicals in Deutschland*, edited by Nils Grosch and Elmar Juchem, 159–176. Münster: Waxmann, 2012.

Döhl, Frédéric. 'Zur Figur des Produzenten im Spiegel von Urheberrecht und Musikt heatergeschichtsschreibung: Erik Charell und das *Weiße Rößl*'. In *'Im weißen Rößl': Kulturgeschichtliche Perspektiven*, edited by Nils Grosch and Carolin Stahrenberg, 43–50. Münster: Waxmann, 2016.

Döhl, Frédéric. 'The Third Biggest Market: Musical Theatre in Germany since 1990'. In *The Routledge Companion to the Contemporary Musical*, edited by Jessica Sternfeld and Elizabeth L. Wollman, 427–436. New York: Routledge, 2020.

Farina, William. *The German Cabaret Legacy in American Popular Music*. Jefferson, NC: McFarland, 2013.

Gordon, Robert. 'Sondheim Scholarship: An Overview'. *Studies in Musical Theatre* 13, no. 2 (2019): 197–204.

Grosch, Nils. 'Zwischen Ignoranz und Kulturkritik: Das Musical in der Rezeption durch die deutschsprachigen Wissenschaften'. In *Die Rezeption des Broadwaymusicals in Deutschland*, edited by Nils Grosch and Elmar Juchem, 9–19. Münster: Waxmann, 2012.

Grosch, Nils, and Carolin Stahrenberg, eds. 'Im weißen Rößl': Kulturgeschichtliche Perspektiven, Münster: Waxmann, 2016.

Hartmann & Stauffacher Verlag. https://www.hsverlag.com/werke/detail/t6543, accessed 5 June 2019.

Heinrichs, Werner. 'Kulturbetrieb'. In Glossar Kulturmanagement, edited by Verena Lewinski-Reuter and Stefan Lüddemann, 131–137. Wiesbaden: VS Verlag für Sozialwissenschaften, 2011.

Herzfeld, Gregor. 'Zur Romantikrezeption in The Black Rider von William Burroughs, Robert Wilson und Tom Waits'. In Die Schaubühne in der Epoche des 'Freischütz': Theater und Musiktheater der Romantik; Vorträge des Salzburger Symposions 2007, edited by Jürgen Kühnel, Ulrich Müller, and Oswald Panagl, 330–343. Salzburg: Mueller-Speiser, 2009.

Hinton, Stephen, ed. Kurt Weill. The Threepenny Opera. Cambridge: Cambridge University Press, 1990.

Hornberger, Barbara. 'Der Wittenbrinkabend: Musikalisches Theater zwischen Pop und Postdramatik'. Lied und populäre Kultur 58 (2013): 173–205.

Inside Kino. http://www.insidekino.com/DJahr/D2008.htm, accessed 19 June 2019.

Jacobshagen, Arnold. 'Musiktheater (April 2005)', 2005, http://www.miz.org/static_de/themenportale/einfuehrungstexte_pdf/archiv/jacobshagen_musiktheater_2005.pdf, accessed 18 August 2019.

Jacobshagen, Arnold. 'Musiktheater (December 2012)', 2013, http://www.miz.org/static_de/themenportale/einfuehrungstexte_pdf/archiv/jacobshagen_musiktheater_2012.pdf, accessed 18 August 2019.

Jacobshagen, Arnold. 'Musiktheater (July 2007)', 2007, http://www.miz.org/static_de/themenportale/einfuehrungstexte_pdf/archiv/jacobshagen_musiktheater_2007.pdf, accessed 18 August 2019.

Jacobshagen, Arnold. 'Musiktheater (June 2010)', 2010. http://www.miz.org/static_de/themenportale/einfuehrungstexte_pdf/archiv/jacobshagen_musiktheater_2010.pdf, accessed 18 August 2019.

Jacobshagen, Arnold. 'Musiktheater (June 2018)', 2018, http://www.miz.org/static_de/themenportale/einfuehrungstexte_pdf/archiv/jacobshagen_musiktheater_2018.pdf, accessed 18 August 2019.

Jacobshagen, Arnold. 'Musiktheater, Musiktheater (March 2019)', 2019, http://www.miz.org/static_de/themenportale/einfuehrungstexte_pdf/03_KonzerteMusiktheater/jacobshagen.pdf, accessed 18 August 2019.

Jansen, Wolfgang. Cats & Co.: Geschichte des Musicals im deutschsprachigen Theater. Leipzig: Henschel, 2008.

Jansen, Wolfgang. "'I've Grown Accustomed… ': Das Musical kommt nach Deutschland, 1945–1960'. In Die Rezeption des Broadwaymusicals in Deutschland, edited by Nils Grosch and Elmar Juchem, 21–42. Münster: Waxmann, 2012.

Jansen, Wolfgang. "'Bringt es uns weiter?" Zur Rezeption des Musicals in der DDR'. In Die Rezeption des Broadwaymusicals in Deutschland, edited by Nils Grosch and Elmar Juchem, 133–157. Münster: Waxmann, 2012.

Jansen, Wolfgang. 'Chronik: Werke des unterhaltenden Musiktheaters im deutschsprachigen Theaters, 1945–1990'. In Die Rezeption des Broadwaymusicals in Deutschland, edited by Nils Grosch and Elmar Juchem, 217–256. Münster: Waxmann, 2012.

Jansen, Wolfgang. 'Operette oder Musical? Zum populären Musiktheater der DDR in den Jahren 1949 bis 1964'. Lied und populäre Kultur/Song and Popular Culture: Jahrbuch des Zentrums für populäre Kultur und Musik 60–61 (2016): 383–399.

Jobst, Nadine. 'How to Be a Legend: Frank Wildhorn', 11 August 2016, http://kulturpoebel.de/2016/08/how-to-be-a-legend-frank-wildhorn/, accessed 15 August 2019.

Jubin, Olaf. 'Lost in Translation? Die Werke Stephen Sondheims und ihre Rezeption auf dem deutschsprachigen Musicalmarkt'. In *Die Rezeption des Broadwaymusicals in Deutschland*, edited by Nils Grosch and Elmar Juchem, 177–201. Münster: Waxmann, 2012.

Juchem, Elmar. 'Der Inbegriff greift nicht. Zur eingeschränkten Wahrnehmung von Rodgers & Hammerstein in Deutschland'. In *Die Rezeption des Broadwaymusicals in Deutschland*, edited by Nils Grosch/Elmar Juchem, 61–76. Münster: Waxmann, 2012.

Kulturpoebel. http://kulturpoebel.de, accessed 5 June 2019 (offline 14 March 2020).

Landestheater Linz. https://www.landestheater-linz.at/stuecke/detail?k=16104&s=2016/17, accessed 5 June 2019.

Maybe Musical. https://maybemusical.com, accessed 5 June 2019.

Mayer, Anton. *Franz Lehár: Die Lustige Witwe; Der Ernst der leichten Muse*. Vienna: Ed. Steinbauer, 2015.

Menze, Jonas. '*Der Schuh des Manitu*: Zum Einfluß des Broadway-Megamusicals auf die deutsche Musical-Landschaft'. In *Die Rezeption des Broadwaymusicals in Deutschland*, edited by Nils Grosch and Elmar Juchem, 203–2016. Münster: Waxmann, 2012.

Menze, Jonas. *Musical Backstages: Die Rahmenbedingungen und Produktionsprozesse des deutschsprachigen Musicals*. Münster: Waxmann, 2018.

Musical1. https://www.musical1.de, accessed 5 June 2019.

Musicals. Das Musicalmagazin. http://www.musicals-magazin.de, accessed 5 June 2019.

Musicalspot. http://www.musicalspot.de, accessed 5 June 2019.

Musicalzentrale. https://musicalzentrale.de, accessed 5 June 2019.

Musik und Bühne Verlagsgesellschaft mbH. https://www.musikundbuehne.de/nc/stuecksuche.html, accessed 15 October 2019.

Operabase. https://www.operabase.com, accessed 15 October 2019.

Platt, Len, Tobias /Becker, and David Linton, eds. *Popular Musical Theatre in London and Berlin, 1890 to 1939*. Cambridge: Cambridge University Press, 2014.

Sandner, Wolfgang. 'Das Mädchen und der Tot'. *Frankfurter Allgemeine Zeitung*, Daily Newspaper. 23 January 2004: 33.

Scott, Derek B. *German Operetta on Broadway and in the West End, 1900–1940*. Cambridge: Cambridge University Press, 2019.

Schmidt Hamburg Theater Reeperbahn. https://www.tivoli.de/programm-tickets/heisse-ecke/, accessed 5 June 2019.

Schmude, Jürgen/Namberger, Philipp. 'Musicals als tourismuswissenschaftlicher Forschungsgegenstand: Grundsätzliche Überlegungen und Marktsituation in Deutschland im Jahr 2012'. In *Kulturtourismus zu Beginn des 21. Jahrhunderts*, edited by Heinz-Dieter Quack and Kristiane Klemm, 255–264. Munich: Oldenbourg, 2013.

Seifert, Anna. 'Nachgedacht: 30 Jahre *Starlight Express*; Ein Kommentar zur Neugestaltung des Musicals'. *kulturpoebel.de*, 20 February 2019, http://kulturpoebel.de/2019/02/nachgedacht-30-jahre-starlight-express-ein-kommentar-zur-neugestaltung-des-musicals/, accessed 5 July 2019.

Siedhoff, Thomas. *Handbuch des Musicals*. Mainz: Schott, 2007.

Siedhoff, Thomas. 'Aufstieg, Fall und Emanzipation des deutschen Musicals'. In *Die Rezeption des Broadwaymusicals in Deutschland*, edited by Nils Grosch and Elmar Juchem, 43–60. Münster: Waxmann, 2012.

Siedhoff, Thomas. *Deutsch(sprachig)es Musical*. Freiburg im Breisgau: ZPKM, 2018. https://frei dok.uni-freiburg.de/data/14628, accessed 5 June 2019.

Society of London Theatre. 'Musicals Drive Record London Theatre Attendance in 2018', 2019, https://www.londontheatre.co.uk/theatre-news/news/musicals-drive-record-london-thea tre-attendance-in-2018, accessed 7 July 2019.

Stage Entertainment. https://www.stage-entertainment.de/, accessed 7 July 2019.

Statista. 'Dossier Musical', 2019, https://de.statista.com/statistik/studie/id/56556/dokument/ musicals/, accessed 7 July 2019.

Stempel, Larry. *Showtime. A History of the Broadway Musical Theatre*. New York: Norton, 2010.

Stephenson, Tim. 'The Ethical Exculpation of Moral Turpitude: Representations of Violence and Death in *Sweeney Todd* and *Into the Woods*'. In *Twenty-first Century Musicals: From Stage to Screen*, edited by George Rodosthenous, 164–180. London and New York: Routledge, 2017.

Tadday, Ulrich, ed. 'Im weißen Rößl': Zwischen Kommerz und *Kunst*. München: text + kritik, 2006.

Theater Dortmund. https://www.theaterdo.de/spielplan/alle-sparten/, accessed 15 October 2019.

Thomson, David. 'Attending the Tale of *Sweeney Todd*: The Stage Musical and Tim Burton's Film Version'. In *The Oxford Handbook of Sondheim Studies*, edited by Robert Gordon, 296–305. New York and Oxford: Oxford University Press, 2014.

UK Theatre. '2018 Sales Data Report', 2019, https://uktheatre.org/theatre-industry/news/2018-sales-data-released-uk-theatre-and-society-of-london-theatre/, accessed 7 July 2019.

United Musicals. https://unitedmusicals.de/, accessed 5 June 2019.

WhatsOnStage. 'Box-office Figures Show London's West End Drew Revenue of £765 million in 2018', 2019, https://www.whatsonstage.com/london-theatre/news/box-office-figures-lon don-west-end-solt-2018_48370.html, accessed 7 July 2019.

Wohlschiess, Sylke. 'Interview mit Martin Lingnau', April 2017, https://www.musicalspot.de/ martin-lingnau-04-2017-musik-addiert-was-man-nicht-sieht, accessed 17 October 2019.

Wolf, Stacy. *Beyond Broadway: The Pleasure and Promise of Musical Theatre across America*. London and New York: Oxford University Press, 2020.

Wulfmansworld.com. https://wulfmansworld.com/Die_besten_Filme/Kinocharts/Kinochart s_2008_-_Plaetze_61-70.htm, accessed 19 June 2019.

# PART VII

## POPULAR IN EAST ASIA

# CHAPTER 19

······································································

# THE DREAM MACHINE

*Takarazuka, Japan's All-Female Musical Theatre
Extravaganza*

······································································

## BUD COLEMAN

OF the many facts about Takarazuka that are unique and surprising (to non-Japanese) is that this theatre company was created not by a performer or writer, but rather by the owner of a transportation company. When the Minoo Arima Electric Tramway Company opened a new line in 1910 from Osaka to the town of Takarazuka, twenty-five kilometers away, the number of passengers was not meeting expectations, so Ichizo Kobayashi created the Paradise Hot Spring to draw customers. But with many *onsen* (hot springs) in Japan, Kobayashi needed to come up with something else to distinguish this location. Taking note of the popularity of Western music in Japan, Kobayashi created an all-girl choir to perform in his Paradise Theatre, which opened in 1914. Kobayashi was a visionary, but he was not the first to come up with this idea: the Tokyo department stores Mitsukoshi and Shirokiya had created children's musical groups (boys at Mitsukoshi and girls at Shirokiya) around 1910 which performed at their stores in Tokyo and Osaka with the intention of luring customers.

Reasoning that girls would learn faster than boys (and require less remuneration), Kobayashi went about creating a repertoire of operetta and contemporary popular music. Starting with seventeen young women, all under the age of fifteen, for his first troupe, Kobayashi first adapted tales from Nô, Kyogen, and Kabuki, but the revues were most popular when they veered towards fairy tales. Incorporating Western music and dance genres, Kobayashi had created a uniquely Japanese family entertainment: fairy-tale operas performed to Western music with all-female casts.[1] Originally called the Takarazuka Girls' Opera Training Association, the young women—many from well-placed families—were performing under stage names (*geimei*), created at first by Kobayashi himself. The use of stage names continues to this day; some women, when they leave the company, will continue to perform under that name, since that is how they are known professionally. The choice of Takarazuka's remote location proved prescient:

it was far removed from the entertainment districts in Tokyo and Osaka, where the professional standards were undoubtedly higher, and those big-city shows had a reputation for ribald and mature entertainment options. Constantly inventing ways to validate the respectability of his enterprise, Kobayashi created a motto for Takarazuka: *kiyoku, tadashiku, utsukushiku*, which is variously translated as 'purely, righteously, beautifully',[2] 'Pure Righteous Beautiful',[3] 'purely, righteously, gracefully',[4] or 'Modesty, Fairness, and Grace'.[5]

Women in Japan had returned to the stage as actresses (*joyu*) late in the nineteenth century but were often publicly denounced as 'defiled women'.[6] According to Jennifer Robertson, 'Theatre critics proclaimed the newly coined term *joyu*, with its connotations of superiority and excellence (*yu*), preferable to the older term *onnayakusha*, with its historic[al] connotations of itinerant actresses associated with unlicensed prostitution'.[7] Because much Western popular music features heterosexual love duets, Kobayashi would dress some of his youthful performers in male-gendered costumes so that the songs could be performed 'realistically'. Tellingly, Kobayashi did not use the term *onnayaku* (woman-role player) to define his performers playing female characters; rather, he chose to label them *musumeyaku* (daughter-role player). For audiences, the word '*musumeyaku*' 'connoted filial piety, youthfulness, pedigree, virginity, and an unmarried actress'.[8] Although Kobayashi considered the Takarazuka male-role players (*otokoyaku*) to be a parallel to the female-role actors (*onnagata*) in Kabuki, he was careful to distinguish them linguistically. In Japanese culture, the *onnagata* is considered a model (*kata*) of female (*onna*) gender, while the *otokoyaku* connotes 'serviceability and dutifulness'; so the Takarazuka male-role players showcase masculinity as part of their theatrical duty, not as a model for men to emulate.[9]

Kobayashi was of the opinion that Kabuki was already disconnected from ordinary people, so he sought to create a wholesome entertainment—newly renamed the Takarazuka Singing Corps—for the entire family, a product which would be financially and culturally accessible. Painfully aware of the seedy reputation of the adjacent Takarazuka Spa (where male patrons might hire a geisha for sex), he advertised that his performers were musicians, rather than actresses, as the former had more prestige.[10] Within a year Kobayashi's experiment paid off, with the newly branded Takarazuka Girls' Opera Training Company drawing over a thousand people a day to the hot spring. The Paradise Theatre quickly became inadequate, so the company bought a 1,500-seat theatre in Osaka, dismantled it, and rebuilt it in Takarazuka in 1920. Word of this unique entertainment spread so quickly that only five years after its creation, Takarazuka was performing at the Imperial Theatre in Tokyo to two thousand people a day.

## The Takarazuka Music School

Because adult Japanese woman were expected to be married and taking care of a family, Kobayashi demanded his performers quit the company once they decided to wed.

To improve stylistic consistency and make the company appear more respectable, he founded the Takarazuka Music School in 1919, acting as its first principal. As much finishing school as musical theatre conservatory, the young women took classes not only in voice and dance, but also in sewing, English, and etiquette. After a year of instruction, the graduates began performing with the company; the school inaugurated a two-year program in 1922. The only performers in the company were and still are graduates of the school. Later, in order to make more room for instruction in voice, dance, and acting, the classes in sewing, English, and etiquette were dropped from the curriculum.

The Takarazuka Music School now accepts auditions from thousands of young women each year between the ages of fourteen and eighteen. During the twentieth century, the School's instruction (and discipline) became notoriously rigorous: an English-language documentary made in 1994 is obsessed with the fact that the first-year students clean the school. In 1994 only one in forty-six applicants was admitted to the school.[11] Even in the twenty-first century, discipline in a regular Japanese classroom looks nothing like the freedom seen in a Western classroom. And in a culture which values conformity more than individualism, it makes sense that this two-year conservatory program is focused on creating a unified ensemble out of the fifty women in each cohort. There are numerous specialty prep schools which some applicants pay for in order to improve their technique so as to better their chances of passing the audition.

When graduates of the Takarazuka Music School join the company—which they all do—they are still referred to as *seito* (students); indeed, when they leave the company they are said to have 'graduated'. Approximately half of the performers 'graduate' (retire) by their sixth year;[12] however, otokoyaku in particular may stay with the company for fifteen years, or more. The relatively short tenure with the company and the constant influx of young alumnae from the Takarazuka Music School keeps the average age of a Takarazuka performer down to around twenty-two. Seemingly in line with Kobayashi's stated goal to produce 'graduates' who would become good wives and mothers, only a small percentage of the performers stay with the company into their forties, fifties, and sixties. And, especially after World War II, many of the performers left Takarazuka not to get married, but rather to pursue careers in theatre, television, and/or film.

# THE 1920S AND 1930S

What Kobayashi didn't know about the entertainment industry, he more than made up for with his business acumen. After a fourteen-year career as an executive director of Mitsui Bank, he created his railroad company in 1907. Subsequently, he started a professional baseball team (now the Orix Buffaloes), ran a diesel-truck manufacturing company, and held various government posts, all the while overseeing the expansion of the Hankyu Corporation into a behemoth conglomerate that includes railways, department stores, film, television, radio, hotels, bus and taxi fleets, and, of course, Takarazuka. When he established the Takarazuka Music School in 1919, parents did not pay tuition for instruction; rather, their daughters were paid very well, the equivalent salary of a middle-ranking salary man.[13] The reason for Kobayashi's insistence on calling women in the school and the company 'students' was not only to distance them from any negative association of women as professional performers—it was also a shrewd business move. Until World War II, a licence was mandatory for professional actors, so Kobayashi avoided licence fees by branding everything Takarazuka did as educational: the rehearsal rooms are called classrooms (*kyoshitsu*), writer-directors are referred to as teachers (*sensei*), and when he divided the acting company in smaller units, they were given school class names (Flower Class, Moon Class, etc.). Takarazuka's non-taxable status was not questioned until 1935, when local authorities accused the company of tax evasion. Payments to trainees at the Takarazuka Music School were abolished in 1936; the pre-war actors' licensing system was revoked during World War II. Nevertheless, the company still refers to its performers as students and celebrates their quasi-amateur status as part of the allure of the acting company.[14]

The growing popularity of the company motivated Kobayashi in 1921 to create two troupes, Moon and Flower (Snow was added in 1924), so that one troupe could be rehearsing while the other was performing. When the Paradise Theatre burned down in 1923, the Takarazuka Grand Theatre replaced it; seating 3,000 patrons, this state-of-the-art proscenium-arch structure served the company until 1992. Takarazuka started to perform in Tokyo in 1918 and by 1925 was performing year-round in both Tokyo and Takarazuka, the later the home of Hankyu's newly created amusement park, the Takarazuka Luna Park. The company's popularity allowed it to build its own theatre in Tokyo in 1934, in Hibiya, close to the financial district of Marunouchi and the haute couture haunts of Ginza.

As the principal architect of everything that is Takarazuka, Kobayashi never lost sight of his original goal of creating an entertainment troupe to drive up business on his railroad. Not bound by the fixed repertoire of Nô, bunraku, and Kabuki, he would send staff abroad to bring back ideas. Tatsuya Kishida created *Mon Paris* (1927) after studying overseas. This work set up a convention that is usually still observed today: a long narrative piece followed by a musical revue after intermission. *Mon Paris* also introduced the line dance to Japan and featured the debut of the now-famous grand staircase (*ookaidan*), which appears in the revue's finale (originally sixteen steps, it now comprises twenty-six steps, which stretch the entire width of the stage, 48 feet). *Mon Paris*'s popularity not only inspired numerous other French-influenced revues, performers in the company now began to be called 'Takarasiennes'.

The 1930s saw the consolidation of many features which helped define Takarazuka for the rest of the century. While the convention of having some of the women appear as male characters in the revues began at the outset, it was not until the early 1930s that some women began to appear exclusively as otokoyaku; they eventually became more popular than the musumeyaku. The otokoyaku cast in the show *Bouquet d'Amour* (1932) were the first women in Japan to cut their hair short, which meant they were immediately recognisable outside of the confines of the theatre; this no doubt increased the allure of the otokoyaku, as they were no longer 'normal' Japanese women on the street.

The 'silver bridge' (*ginkyo*), a walkway in front of the orchestra pit, was first constructed for *Rose Paris* (1931). Analogous to the *hashigakari* in Nô and the *hanamachi* in Kabuki, this architectural element gave the Takarazuka fans a unique way to get physically close to their beloved star performers. In 1934 Tomo no Kai, the official Takarazuka fan club, was established, inspiring the creation of dozens of unofficial fan clubs, most of them dedicated to a single performer. By the 1980s the 'unofficial' fan culture would grow beyond anything Kobayashi could have imagined, with thousands of fans promoting his company, its stars, and its ideals ('modesty, fairness, and grace').

## Takarazuka post-Kobayashi

Just as the Folies Bergère has subtly morphed since it began performing in 1872, so too has Takarazuka. Most of Kobayashi's instincts in initially shaping the company were very popular with patrons, with one major exception. In the fifth year of the company's existence, Kobayashi hired ten male performers to perform as the 'Male Senka' (aka 'Male Speciality'); audiences were not attracted to this innovation, so the unit was disbanded after only ten months. Before he died in 1957, Kobayashi tried again to entice audiences to support the inclusion of cisgender male performers in the company. Twelve men were hired in 1952, but the organisation bowed to fan pressure, and they were released from their contracts in 1954.[15] Not only did fans not approve of the new personnel, but the pupils and their parents pushed aggressively to exclude them from the school. The sociologist Tsuganezawa Toshihiro claims that 'not a single member of the Girls' Opera Company wished to make a lifelong career as a performing artist if it meant collaborating with boys'.[16]

The hundred-plus-year history of this all-female entertainment company has challenged Western observers to explain the continued popularity of the otokoyaku, especially given changes in the perception of women, sexual preference, gender identity, gender expression, and feminism over the twentieth and twenty-first centuries. The performance of masculinity by a Takarasinee is not conventional drag, where the intent is to pass; nor is it a camp performance, where the performer and audience share a knowing wink at the artifice. Rather than trying to look like men, the otokoyaku simultaneously presents both traditional male and female visual codes: to emphasise their height, otokoyaku typically wear tight, high-waisted trousers and dainty boots with a heel. While the otokoyaku may thicken their eyebrows and add facial hair, they also don fake eyelashes and apply eyeshadow. The goal is not verisimilitude, but rather the creation of an 'ideal man' (*risoteki na dansei*). This professed aim is confounded by the otokoyaku's performance offstage. When the otokoyaku greets her fans before and after a performance, they usually wear a street version of their stage androgyny: pants, lots of makeup, a hat worn at a rakish angle, and/or their short hair sculpted in an elaborately moussed creation. Writing in 1987, Zeke Berlin considered this creation to be a 'third gender',[17] as most otokoyaku performers stick to the Takarazuka script of creating

FIG. 19.1 A performance by Takarazuka's Flower Troupe in 1963. Photographer unknown; image provided by the editors.

an idealised portrait of masculinity. In *The Art of Seduction* (2003), Robert Greene unpacks the allure of this gender hybridity: '[Androgynous individuals] excite us because they cannot be categorised, and hint at a freedom we want for ourselves. They play with masculinity and femininity; they fashion their own physical image, which is always startling.'[18]

Many cultural historians attempt to explain Takarazuka in comparison to the better-known Japanese art form of Kabuki. In Kabuki, the adult men who perform female roles are called *onnagata*, which translates as 'female role specialist' (Griffith),[19] not 'female impersonator'. As the twentieth century's most famous onnagata, Bandō Tamasaburō, explained in 1995, 'I act a woman with the eyes and feelings of a man; like a man painting the portrait of a woman.... I gather up knowledge by watching: this is how they react, this is how they place their hand on their hair. I gather up this type of material and transform it.'[20] While men have been writing, painting, and performing their idealisation of women for centuries, Takarazuka appears as that rare phenomenon, a female-authored view of 'maleness'. But as Jennifer Robertson points out, 'The Revue claims to sell dreams; the fans claim that Takarazuka is a bouquet of dreams, [and] the Takarasiennes claim that they protect their fans' dreams.'[21] Just as the female characters created by the onnagata in Kabuki are celebrated because they are not real, so too are the male characters in Takarazuka. When an American director was hired to stage the

1968 Takarazuka production of *West Side Story*, he made it clear that the male characters were to have no false eyelashes and no heavy eye makeup. Fans were not happy with this change in the otokoyaku's appearance, so once the director left Japan, the eyelashes and makeup returned.[22]

When the first young women were hired in 1914 to perform in the Paradise Theatre, they unknowingly shook up traditional gender expectations for Japanese women. Although women did work in turn-of-the-century Japan, it was usually as part of a family business or farm. Other than geishas, respectable women did not work outside the family. As Takarazuka became more popular, performing for the company became a full-time job. The company's audience grew and changed (especially after World War II) to predominantly female (90 percent during the 1970s, 1980s, and 1990s); with a hundred women on-stage and thousands of women in the audience, it seems logical to view Takarazuka as finding a new purpose as the feminist movement grew. However, Lorie Brau contends that 'Takarazuka is not only *not* feminist, but almost reactionary in its views of women'.[23] Regardless of the source material, once staged, all the narratives take on a dreamy quality much closer to Anita Bryant than to Gloria Steinem. That said, especially given that otokoyaku are more popular with fans than are musumeyaku, there are undoubtedly women in the audience who derive pleasure, if not a sense of empowerment, from watching women perform masculinity. Like its fellow performing arts Nô, Kabuki, and bunraku, Takarazuka completely blows out of the water any theory that gender is purely genetic. In a country with persistent and oppressive gender roles, Takarazuka represents an escape by creating an alternative world full of beauty, with lush orchestrations, stunning costumes, captivating stories, and no cisgender men on-stage.

## *SAYONARA*

For many mid-century Americans, it is possible their one and only glimpse of Takarazuka was via James A. Michener's novel *Sayonara* (1954) and its subsequent 1957 film adaptation, starring Marlon Brando, Red Buttons, Miyoshi Umeki, and Miiko Taka. The company is seen through the eyes of Air Force Major Lloyd Gruver, who is stationed in Osaka during the Korean War. Gruver's lack of commitment to his American girlfriend, Eileen, is in contrast to his feelings for Hana-ogi, a star of the Takarazuka-type company. The affair is doubly doomed: Takarazuka expressly prohibits casual dating (i.e. any relationships not seriously directed towards marriage), and US military personnel are forbidden to take Japanese wives to America. Despite these restrictions, Marine Captain Mike Bailey and Air Force Airman Joe Kelly are dating Japanese women; Kelly is willing to give up his US citizenship if he is not allowed to live with his Japanese bride in America. While the novel and film traffic in exoticism and the orientalist trope that Japanese women make great wives, it does address the racism of US military policy and provides a brief glimpse into the world of Takarazuka. Called the Matsuabashi Girls Revue in the film, the performance sequences were actually those of the Shochiku

FIG. 19.2 Scene featuring the Matsuabashi Girls Revue (modelled after Takarazuka) from the 1957 film *Sayonara*, directed by Joshua Logan. The movie starred Marlon Brando (*front*) and Miiko Taya (*centre, with arms outstretched*). Production still provided by the editors.

Kagekidan Girls Revue (Shochiku Kageki Dan, aka SKD), a rival all-female revue troupe (1928–1996) based in Tokyo.[24] In the film, we see snippets of Hana-ogi performing male and female roles (mainly female), so that there is no doubt about Gruver's heterosexual desire. The film's brief performance clips focus on the female character performers; the choreography is rudimentary, and the scale and production values are a shadow of what would define Takarazuka in the late twentieth century.

## Repertoire

As with any entertainment company which caters to a popular audience, Takarazuka has made changes over the decades in order to continue attracting audiences to its dream factory. Beginning with *Mon Paris* in 1927, they started to import stories from Europe. Other European and American titles produced that were adapted by Takarazuka include

FIG. 19.3 Scene from the 2009 Takarazuka production of *Elisabeth*, performed by the Moon Troupe and featuring Asumi Rio as Death and Ranno Hana as Elisabeth. Photographer unknown; image provided by the editors.

*Oklahoma!, Carousel, South Pacific, Guys and Dolls, Show Boat, Me and My Girl, Flower Drum Song, Grand Hotel, One Touch of Venus, Singin' in the Rain, Top Hat, On the Town, Anastasia, Elisabeth, Roméo et Juliette, I Am from Austria*, and *Mozart, l'Opéra Rock*. One thing that has not changed much over the decades is the performance style. Many interviews with the stars delve into their process of creating a character, which sounds very much like the Stanislavski school of psychological realism, as though the goal were to conjure up realism in the artificial world of the stage. Takarazuka, on the other hand, fully rejects any semblance of realism or naturalism, gleefully creating worlds and characters that never existed.

The action of one of their classics, *The Rose of Versailles*, is set in France but is based on a Japanese manga of the same name, written by Riyoko Ikeda, that was serialised in 1972. *The Rose of Versailles* has become a media empire unto itself. In 1979 a forty-episode animated television series was broadcast; it was published as a ten-volume book in 1982 and has been made into at least four feature films.[25]

Taking place during and after the French Revolution, *The Rose of Versailles* focuses on Oscar, the youngest of six daughters. In his despair over not having a son, General Jarjayes raises Oscar as a boy. With training in combat, horsemanship, and fencing, Oscar often practices with André Grandier, the grandson of Oscar's nanny. As the children grow older, they fall in love (André knows Oscar's true identity). Oscar becomes commander of the Royal Guard and is responsible for the safety of Marie Antoinette. At the onset of the French Revolution, when Oscar sees the royal troupes firing on common citizens, she moves her support to the insurgents. André and Oscar declare their love for one another, but in the next battle André is shot and Oscar is gravely wounded. As the monarchy surrenders, Oscar dies, knowing she found her true love, albeit briefly, while fighting on the side of right. As is often the case in Shakespeare, a woman can have agency and earn the respect of others for their leadership and bravery, but they must dress and act like a man to do so.

The Takarazuka stage version, by Shinji Ueda, is the troupe's most popular show: all four troupes performed it between 1974 and 1978, attracting an audience of 1.6 million.[26] When the musical was revived in 1989, it drew an audience of 2.1 million. As Ikeda continued to write sequels and side stories to the original *The Rose of Versailles*, she also created three new scenarios, which were staged by Takarazuka in 2008.

# FAN CULTURE

Writing for the *New Yorker* in 1992, Ingrid Sischy persuasively argued that not only is there 'no equivalent to this theatre in America', '[w]e have no stars like Takarazuka's in America'.[27] Sischy is not talking about the talent or charisma of the performers, but rather the Takarazuka fan culture, which creates a unique relationship between performer and fan and also influences the actual performance. Each of the current five 'regular' troupes has its own hierarchy of stars; a sixth group (*Senka*) is made up of senior members of the company who are jobbed out to one of the other five troupes as needed. While the company itself does not run the fan clubs for individual stars—that is done by volunteers—these are sophisticated networks which do much more than provide a website with photos of the star and a list of upcoming appearances. Membership in the fan club might require not only a membership fee but also a commitment to see a minimum number of performances a year. Not only do fan club members pledge to see a certain number of performances a year by their star, they also pledge to participate in the post-show ritual.

Although Takarazuka performs eight performances a week, like a standard run on Broadway or the West End, double show days are not on the weekend but during the week. Performance times vary: curtain is typically at 11 A.M., 1 P.M., or 3 P.M., with a rare evening performance at 6 P.M. Because the audience is mostly women, performance times are geared to a typical housewife's schedule. Once the kids and breadwinner husband are out of the house, she has time to clean, go to the theatre, and be home in time to prepare dinner before any of her charges have returned. It is worth noting that the performance times of traditional musicals in Japan do not always adhere to a Broadway–West End performance schedule. For example, Shiki, the biggest producer of Western musicals in Japan, will often run a production such as *The Lion King* with five matinees a week and two evening performances.

Six times a week, after the last Takarazuka performance of the day, the fan clubs will wait patiently for about an hour to see their star come out of the stage door. In the street outside of both the Tokyo and the Takarazuka theatres, the fans—all female—arrange themselves on both sides of the street in order of the star's status. There are typically fifteen to thirty women in each cluster, easily identifiable, since each fan club member wears something distinctive—identical scarves, sweaters, jackets, or flannel shirts. When the star comes out of the stage door, she is always accompanied by an assistant, who carries her shopping bags, flowers, and other items; her fan club quickly organise themselves in straight rows, and the women in the front row kneel so that the women behind her can see the star. Just as discipline is a defining feature of the Takarazuka Music School, so too is the fan club audience with their star. While the women in the fan club are visibly moved to be in such close proximity to the object of their affection, there is no screaming, nor any attempts to touch the performer. Decorum rules the day as the star, exuding elegance and self-confident modesty, glides to maintain a respectable distance from her fan club. A leader from the fan club usually presents a small gift or card to the performer and perhaps says a couple of words to praise the actor on her performance that day and to thank her for the privilege of this personal encounter. The star might not even speak but just basks in the adoration of her fans and concludes the brief encounter with a bow. Since there are often twenty different fan clubs lined up on both sides of the street, the stars time their exits from the theatre so that there is typically only one star on the street at a time. After a star has left her fan club, they might wait on the street until all the stars have exited to show respect to the other stars and their fan clubs.

It is worth remembering that half of each cohort of performers 'graduate' by their sixth year, and while the otokoyaku tend to stay longer, most of them have left the company after fifteen years of performing. Fans of any performer or athlete know that this person is mortal and won't be around forever, but the ticking clock that is the world of Takarazuka adds a very real urgency to each performance by a star: will this be her last? Most actors in Takarazuka have a career trajectory more like that of a gymnast or ice skater and age out of the profession in their early twenties. Fans respond to this reality in different ways: some women may belong to more than one fan club, while other fans stay loyal to their star long after she has left the company.

The pressures on popular performers around the world are unquestionably intense, and many have difficulty being constantly in the public spotlight. Stories of temper tantrums, substance abuse, brushes with the law, questionable romantic liaisons, and the like fill news outlets and social media threads, since their followers seemingly want to elevate their object and at the same time relish their personal failures, as this makes them more human. The world of Takarazuka is radically different; it is indeed a dream factory. Because all the women in the company are unmarried and ostensibly virgins, the publicity machine around Takarazuka is all about 'modesty, fairness, and grace', which is aided by the fact that Japan's tabloid culture is not mainstream. Since every Takarazuka musical plot contains a heterosexual love story and one musical number after another features male and female characters in various romantic scenarios, there is no whiff of sexual ambiguity in terms of desire. Contributions to fan magazines and websites perpetuate this adherence to romance over sexuality. One poem in the fan magazine *Kegeki* to the otokoyaku star Tsuugi Miyuki reads: 'Are you a man or a woman? It doesn't matter. I didn't love you as a person but as I would love time or the wind. . . . Ah, if only you were a doll, I could touch you'.[28]

Both within and outside of Japan, much of what is written about the Takarazuka fan culture is condescending and negative. Writing in 1992, Henry Jenkins explains in 'Textual Poachers', the pernicious stereotype of a fan is that of a 'basement-dwelling virginal dweeb', a social misfit whose stunted emotional life finds meaning only by living vicariously through others. Jenkins, on the other hand, sees fandom as 'a source of creativity and expression for massive numbers of people who would otherwise be excluded from the commercial sector'.[29] Obviously, the level of engagement varies widely amongst Takarazuka fan club members, but the possibilities for participation are endless: fanzines, fan fiction, re-edited performances, tribute videos, visual art, mixed tapes, cosplay (fan-made costumes), and so on. One of the challenges of writing about fandom is our own myopic viewpoint, which views our own likes and passions—our own fandoms—as reasonable, adorable quirks and everyone else's as pathetic obsessions.

Since the founding of Takarazuka, the company machine has created novel ways not only to advertise the company but also to facilitate fan engagement. Takarazuka scripts began to be published in 1916, enabling enthusiasts both to read the librettos and to rehearse or even stage their own version of a scene.[30] Official fan-orientated magazines— *Kageki* (*Opera*), founded in 1918, and *Takarazuka gurafu* (*Takarazuka Graphic*), founded in 1936—both of which are still published today—include photos, interviews, articles, and illustrations to give fans more access to their stars. In 1928, when gramophone records went on sale, not only did they feature singles and full studio sessions with Takarazuka performers, but some later LPs were recorded live so that the listener could hear applause as well as the voices of fans who called out the names of stars on their entrances and exits. Cassette tapes and later CDs were available in karaoke versions so fans could sing on their own. Fan culture went more public when *Takarazuka fan kontesuto* (*Takarazuka Fan Contest*) hit the radio in 1955. Takarazuka fans and aspiring Takarasiennes could sing Takarazuka songs and perform scenes with Takarazuka stars and then get feedback from a revue musical director and writer. This popular program stayed on the air until 1974.

In the twenty-first century, fans have not only created unofficial postings on Facebook, Twitter, Instagram, and other social media sites, but many also subscrib to the satellite television channel Takarazuka Sky Stage. Created in 2002, they broadcast performances as well as interviews with the performers and behind-the-scenes stories about current and upcoming productions. Live broadcasts of selected performances are occasionally available in movie theatres throughout Japan. Of course, official Takarazuka merchandise is available 24/7 online and in person at five brick-and-mortar shops in Japan.

# Takarazuka in Perfomance: The Dream Machine

Ingrid Sischy, in her 1992 *New Yorker* article, recalls seeing the company perform in Radio City Music Hall in 1989; it had begun touring internationally in 1938. Although the performance contained the standard elements of Takarazuka, a 'surreal mixture of East and West' singing, acting, and dancing, Sischy notes that 'although the audience consisted primarily of Japanese, I didn't notice that they were getting any special kicks. There was no real sense of excitement in the air—or on stage for that matter'.[31]

I had the same reaction when I saw Takarazuka perform in London in 1994: the eye-popping costumes (including jackets Liberace would have been proud to wear), lavish sets, lush orchestrations, vibrant makeup, and even the enormous mirror ball which twirled overhead in the finale were all present, but the energy in the auditorium did not match what I experienced in Tokyo. There, the fans *made* the performance, not just with their applause and calling out the names of their beloved stars, but with their attention.

Every Takarazuka performance ends with a musical revue where the actors perform directly to the audience, breaking the fourth wall. Yamazaki Masakazu theorises the Japanese perception of the 'I and thou' principle as one of the reasons for their unbroken love of the theatre over the centuries. Lorie Brau continues this analysis to suggest that the Takarazuka fan is not only 'perceived by the eye/I of the' performer, but also 'affirmed by the other': 'Because she [the otokoyaku] is really a woman and not a man (who may be perceived as the oppressor, or at least the suppressor), because she is—underneath her role—the same as the female spectator, she affirms her'.[32] Clearly, the chemistry continues to work as 2.6 million people a year see a performance by the Takarazuka Revue in Takarazuka, Tokyo, and on tour.

When I first saw the troupe in performance in 1986, I had little knowledge of the company. Entering the lavish 2,000-seat Tokyo Takarazuka Theatre, I was seated with two

FIG. 19.4 The Takarazuka Revue Company performing in October 1989 at New York's Radio City Musical Hall. Photographer unknown; image provided by the editors.

dozen other men who had purchased a single ticket. We were completely surrounded by the women in the audience.[33] The musical I watched was a Technicolor pastiche of every performing arts genre that exists—Broadway musical, Las Vegas revue, Busby Berkeley extravaganza, film noir, show choir, ballet, jazz, modern dance, and with a hundred performers on-stage—on a scale I had never witnessed before. After intermission, the musical revue expanded this multi-cultural aesthetic with songs sung in English and Japanese and embracing even more musical theatre genres. But the best was yet to come. During a blackout, a Japanese voice made an announcement that sent the audience into a frenzy. As the curtain opened onto an enormous silver staircase that stretched from wing to wing and seemed to be two stories tall, one solitary performer, a retiring otokoyaku, impeccably dressed in an elegant black tuxedo with brilliantined jet-black hair, began a slow descent down the stairs. While all the women I had seen that afternoon were undeniably talented and the entire production had a slick polish, nothing prepared me for the Marlene Dietrich–Katharine Hepburn–Grace Jones vision in front of me. As the otokoyaku descended the stairs, he didn't sing, dance, or even talk. He took in the room with a smoldering gaze, and with a precision honed over decades on the Takarazuka stage, he slid one hand nonchalantly into his pants pocket. The crowd was beside themselves; more than once I thought, this is what it must have been like to see Frank Sinatra in performance in his mature years. Indeed, the Chairman of the Board in front of me could have taught Ol' Blue Eyes some tricks. After what seemed like a fifteen-minute stroll down the staircase, the star was now on the stage floor and with one gesture silenced the audience. When he began to sing, it was a master class in what it means to be a crooner. I don't think this Mel Tormé had a cigar or a tumbler of whiskey in his hand, but he immediately conjured up a smokey little bar where Humphrey Bogart would love to hang out.

Yes, Takarazuka is the creation of a male-dominated corporation whose glossy commercialism can make Disney look like amateurs; but witnessing an otokoyaku at the peak of her powers made all the contradictions of Takarazuka meaningless. The stage presence of this otokoyaku was epic, as was the power the audience transferred to her. The otokoyaku rewarded the audience's devotion and adoration with bedroom eyes and a swagger that triggered a tsunami of desire, admiration, and gratitude.

I could see women in the audience covering their mouths with their hands to suppress cries or shouts so not as to interrupt this farewell performance. I don't believe this otokoyaku had appeared earlier in the performance, I don't know her stage name, and I didn't know I was witnessing her 'graduation' from the company, but this I did know: I was in the presence of a *star*.

## Notes

1. Leonie R. Strickland, *Gender Gymnastics: Performing and Consuming Japan's Takarazuka Revue* (Victoria, Australia: Trans Pacific Press, 2008), 26.
2. Ibid., 32.
3. Ian Buruma, *Behind the Mask: On Sexual Demons, Sacred Mothers, Transvestites, Gangsters and Other Japanese Cultural Heroes* (New York: Pantheon Books, 1984), 113.
4. Makiko Yamanashi, 'Revue as a Liminal Theatre Genre' (PhD thesis, University of Trier, Fachbereich II, 2019), 151.
5. Ingrid Sischy, 'Onward and Upward with the Arts: Selling Dreams', *New Yorker*, 2 September 1992, 89.
6. Quoted in Jennifer Robertson, 'The "Magic If": Conflicting Performances of Gender in the Takarazuka Revue of Japan', in *Gender in Performance: The Presentation of Difference in the Performing Arts*, ed. Laurence Senelick (Hanover, NH: University Press of New England, 1992), 48.
7. Ibid..
8. Ibid.
9. Ibid., 14.
10. Strickland, *Gender Gymnastics*, 23.
11. Ibid., 47.
12. Lorie Brau, 'The Women's Theatre of Takarazuka', *TDR* 34, no. 1 (1990): 84.
13. Strickland, *Gender Gymnastics*, 27.
14. Ibid., 29.
15. A 2007 Japanese musical by Atsuhiko Naakajima, *Takarazuka Boys*, tells the story of this failed experiment. Professional productions of this musical toured Japan throughout 2018.
16. Quoted in Strickland, *Gender Gymnastics*, 29.
17. Quoted in Brau, 'Women's Theatre', 86.
18. Quoted in ibid.

# 568    BUD COLEMAN

19. Paul Griffith, 'Kabuki: Where Are the Women?', *Japan Forward*, 13 January 2018, n. pag.
20. Quoted in ibid.
21. Ibid.
22. Brau, 'Women's Theatre', 86.
23. Ibid., 80; emphasis in the original.
24. Yet another rival company was based in Osaka: the Osaka Shochiku Kagekidan.
25. *The Rose of Versailles* was the first manga to be translated into English, and it is currently the fourteenth all-time best-selling manga aimed at teenage girls, with fifteen million volumes sold worldwide.
26. Over the decades, as Takarazuka expanded its activities, the number of troupes has increased; currently there are five: *hana-gumi* (the Flower Troupe), *tsuki-gumi* (the Moon Troupe), *yuki-gumi* (the Snow Troupe), *hoshi-gumi* (the Star Troupe), and *sora-gumi* (the Cosmos Troupe).
27. Sischy, 'Onward', 85.
28. Quoted in Brau, 'Women's Theatre', 88–89.
29. Quoted in Michael Schulman, 'The Force Is With Them', *New Yorker*, 16 September 2019, 28.
30. Strickland, *Gender Gymnastics*, 56.
31. Sischy, 'Onward', 85.
32. Brau, 'Women's Theatre', 90; emphasis in the original.
33. Takarazuka no longer segregates solo male audience members, but in a city with women-only subway cars, it is not surprising that female patrons in the 1980s did not want their 'dream' trip to Takarazuka to be spoiled by sitting next to an unknown man.

## BIBLIOGRAPHY

Berlin, Zeke. 'The Takarazuka Touch'. *Asian Theatre Journal* 8, no. 1 (1991): 35–47.
Brau, Lorie. 'The Women's Theatre of Takarazuka'. *TDR* 34, no. 1 (1990): 79–95.
Deutsch, Lauren. 'Takarazuka Revue: Japanese All-Female Musical Theatre Troupe', 7 December 2016, thetheatretimes.com/takarazuka-review-japanese-female-musical-theater-troupe/, accessed 29 December 2019.
Buruma, Ian. *Behind the Mask: On Sexual Demons, Sacred Mothers, Transvestites, Gangsters, and Other Japanese Cultural Heroes*. New York: Pantheon Books, 1984.
Griffith, Paul. 'Kabuki: Where Are the Women?', *Japan Forward*, 13 January 2018, https://japan-forward.com/kabuki-where-are-the-women/, accessed 4 Jan. 2020.
Longinotto, Kim, and Jano Williams, dirs. *Dream Girls*. Documentary. 50 minutes. Produced by Jano Williams. A Twentieth Century Vixen (UK) production, released by Women Make Movies, 1994.
Robertson, Jennifer. 'The "Magic If": Conflicting Performances of Gender in the Takarazuka Revue of Japan'. In *Gender in Performance: The Presentation of Difference in the Performing Arts*, edited by Laurence Senelick, 46–67. Hanover, NH: University Press of New England, 1992.
Robertson, Jennifer. *Takarazuka: Sexual Politics and Popular Culture in Modern Japan*. Berkeley and Los Angeles: University of California Press, 1998.
Schulman, Michael. 'The Force Is With Them'. *New Yorker*, 16 September 2019, 26–31.

Sischy, Ingrid. 'Onward and Upward with the Arts: Selling Dreams'. *New Yorker*, 28 September 1992, 84–103.

Strickland, Leonie R. *Gender Gymnastics: Performing and Consuming Japan's Takarazuka Revue*. Victoria, Australia: Trans Pacific Press, 2008.

Yamanashi, Makiko. 'Revue as a Liminal Theatre Genre'. PhD thesis, University of Trier, Fachbereich II, 2019, https://ubt.opus.hbz-nrw.de/opus45-ubtr/frontdoor/deliver/index/docId/1241/file/Trier+PhD+Makiko+Yamanashi+2019+publication.pdf, accessed 5 November 2019.

CHAPTER 20

# THE DEVELOPMENT PROCESS AND CHARACTERISTICS OF THE SOUTH KOREAN MUSICAL MARKET

### YONGMIN KWON, HYEYOUNG RA, AND KANGJOO CHO

## INTRODUCTION

MUSICALS are a blend of every art form and are most characteristic of modern culture, emphasising not only contemporary values but also elements of mass entertainment. In Korea, musicals make up approximately 55 percent of the performing arts market.[1] First developed in the 1960s, Korea's musical industry has experienced a 15 percent growth per annum since the early 2000s, when the market size was $16.67 billion. This chapter examines the Korean musical market in three sections. The first section delineates the history of Korean musicals to identify how unique characteristics have formed in the historical context. The second examines the current status of the Korean musical market by assessing various recent statistics and estimating the market size in order to determine which phenomena require attention in 2020. The third investigates features recognisable as unique to Korea and considers the prospects and limits of the Korean musical market.

## THE HISTORY OF KOREAN MUSICAL THEATRE

The development of musical theatre as an art form dates back over a century. The musical is comprised of elements from Western European Baroque and grand opera, comic opera, operetta, minstrel shows, burlesque, and vaudeville. Despite its short history, Korean musicals have advanced more spectacularly than any other performing-arts genre. Starting in the 1960s, the market attained a size of $333 million by the 2000s. Today, large-scale musical productions licensed from the United Kingdom, and the

United States, France, Germany, and Austria are being introduced in Korea, with original musicals also being performed in small theatres. Moreover, the diversification of musical and dramatic content and regular casting of K-pop stars promote ticketing not only among Korean fans but also from overseas fan bases.

For many years since the 1960s, musicals were deemed a genre alien to Korean sensibilities, regarded mostly as special events experienced as part of a trip to Broadway or the West End. There was no real market for musicals in Korea during this period, hence there were almost no theatres, actors, staff, or educational courses specialising in them. Then, in 2001, *The Phantom of the Opera* (which played from December 2001 to June 2002), produced with an investment of $8.33 million (approximately KRW 15 billion), amassed 240,000 spectators over the course of seven months and 244 performances, earning $16 million in sales and $1.67 million in net profit. This served as a testament to the commercial potential of musicals in Korea and heralded the swift growth of the market.

As mentioned, the Korean musical market has grown rapidly, and today characteristics unique to Korea can be perceived. This section divides the developmental process into four stages to study the attributes of each stage. Korean researchers who have studied the industrialisation of Korean musicals divide it into three stages: pre-industrialisation (1960s–1980s), early industrialisation (late 1980s–2000), and industrial expansion (post-2000).[2] Although we adhere to that division, we also add an introductory phase.

The chief elements of a musical are music, singing, acting, and dance.[3] Prior to the 1960s, when musicals in their modern sense were introduced in Korea, there were traditional performances that shared formal aspects with musicals, though they are stylistically distinct: *pansori*,[4] *changgeuk*,[5] and *akgeuk*. Pansori is a performative art form that emerged from the lower classes as a grassroots art and saw its heyday in the nineteenth century after becoming popular among the upper classes in the eighteenth century. In the twentieth century, pansori evolved into *changgeuk*, as it began to be performed in theatres. Whereas pansori is performed solo, changgeuk is characterised by its dialogical dramatisation, division of roles, presentation on a theatre stage, and abridged duration.[6] Changgeuk failed to put down roots and soon faded owing to Korea's loss of national sovereignty, the popularisation of melodramas, and amateurish performances by the actors.

*Akgeuk* is an art form that was conceived in the 1930s and remained in fashion until the 1950s. Composed of spoken lines, gestures, songs, dances, and background music, akgeuk is similar in structure to contemporary musicals except that music doesn't play a significant part in its narrative. Akgeuk sought commercialisation, providing a wider platform for Korean playwrights and composers and giving birth to many of the star actors and singers who are widely celebrated to this day. In the stage leading up to the introduction of musicals, various performances akin to contemporary musicals were staged in Korea until the scene took an unexpected turn with Japanese colonial rule, liberation, and national division. After Korea's liberation, musicals were introduced as a result of American influence. American culture spread spontaneously with the stationing of US troops in Korea, and a wave of classic film musicals flooded in during the 1950s. These films inspired many akgeuk performers to team up as show troupes specialising in American-style shows and music. The post-liberation attempts to identify and work with elements of musicals found in traditional performances and pick up elements of foreign musicals led to the birth of Korean musicals.

With the foundation of musicals established, the musical that marked the full-fledged beginning of the industrial preparation stage (1960s–1980s) was *Sweet, Come to Me Stealthily* (1966) by the Yegrin Musical Theatre (Yegrin Akdan);[7] the narrative is based on the classic novel *Baebijangjeon*. *Sweet, Come to Me Stealthily* was performed a total of five times on 26–30 October 1966 at the Seoul Civic Center (now the Sejong Center for the Performing Arts). Because at the time there were no actors trained in musicals, popular stars from each field of the performing arts—singers, entertainers, actors, and dancers—were deployed to stage the piece, generating an explosive response.[8]

Established with a political motive in reaction to North Korea's Sea of Blood Theatrical Troupe (Pibada Geukdan), Yegrin Musical Theatre aimed to produce original musicals incorporating Korean themes, music, and dance. After the success of *Sweet, Come to Me Stealthily*, the theatre went on to produce other original musicals, such as *Kkonnimi Kkonnimi* (1967), *Dae Chunhyang-Jeon* (1968), *Badayeo Malhara* (1971), *Hwaryeohan Sanha* (1971), and *Jongiyeo Ullyeora* (1972). The theatre performed continuously through its transition into the National Music and Dance Company (1974), then into the National Yegrin Musical Company (1976), and finally into the Seoul Music and Dance Company (1977).[9]

While public theatre groups continued to perform original musicals, private theatre companies staged a number of works from a variety of musical traditions. The Drama Center performed *Porgy and Bess* (1966), and the Shilhum Theater Group performed *Man of La Mancha* (1967) with piano accompaniment at the National Theater of Korea in Myeong-dong, starring the pop sensation Jo Young-nam; it amassed some 4,700 viewers. The Hyundai Theatre Company commenced consistent, systematic production of large-scale shows in the 1970s, demonstrating the musical's potential for industrialisation. The company mostly put on adapted versions of western musicals such as *Piaf* (1977), *Peter Pan* (1979), *Jesus Christ Superstar* (1980), *The Sound of Music* (1981), *Evita* (1981), *Snow White and the Seven Dwarfs* (1982), *Fiddler on the Roof* (1982), *Oliver!* (1983), *West Side Story* (1987), and *Les Misérables* (1988).

In the early stage of its industrialisation (late 1980s–2000), Korea's musical theatre developed diligently, having identified a local demand for musicals through adapted British and American ones. This period was marked by such changes as Korea's entry into the Universal Copyright Convention; the birth of production companies specialising in musicals; the coexistence of directly imported, jointly produced, licensed, and original musicals; large corporate firms' entry into and exit from the musical market; and the flow of large amounts of capital into the performing arts industry. The adapted musicals of the 1980s were strictly illegal reproductions of Anglo-American musicals, and issues regarding the quality of their music, stage design, and dance were ever-present. As they imitated Western musicals, Korean musical producers were honing their production

FIG. 20.1 Scene from the finale of *Sweet, Come to Me Stealthily* (1966); excerpts from the show performed on Korean Television in 1967. Photo © KTV.

techniques and accumulating know-how in order to improve output; but simple reproduction had its limits, and it was not sufficient to enhance the overall quality of Korean musicals. The lag in progress was technically rooted in financial problems tied to the running of a theatre company. At the time, theatre companies operated mostly under a group system (*donginje*),[10] so to pay expensive royalties to import well-produced foreign musicals was not an option. On the other hand, as the era of the cultural globalisation arrived, the Korean performing arts industry also reached a point where a change in its perception of copyright was urgently demanded.

Korea joined the Universal Copyright Convention in 1987 and the Berne Convention in 1996, agreeing to full royalty payments.[11] Nonetheless, theatre companies operating under the group system still struggled to pay royalties, a problem that was only resolved once theatre companies specialising in musicals emerged and replaced the group system with a producer system.[12] With the adoption of the producer system, the performing arts industry chose in the 1990s to develop in a way that was completely different from the 1980s. It became difficult for musical companies run under the group system to sustain their practices, so instead of licensing foreign musicals, most of them turned to original or children's musicals.

During the 1990s large corporations began entering the musical theatre scene. As the market grew and performing arts came to be recognised as a cultural commodity, large enterprises that used to contribute to the industry through sponsorship or the building of small theatres recognised how lucrative the practice of producing musicals and other performances themselves could be.[13] Once capitalist conglomerates and media networks began to see the potential of the musical theatre market, the industry saw an influx of capital, so production and marketing became more specialised. This change enabled the production of large-scale musicals, which in turn enabled the rapid growth of the industry in the 2000s. However, in spite of the positive effects, such as growth of the market and specialisation of production, there was a downside to the entry of large capital into the musical scene. First, strong competition among production companies, thanks to productions focused entirely on famous imported or licensed musicals, brought excessive increases in production costs and thus ticket prices. Secondly, as profit-hungry companies and investors entered Korea's underdeveloped system and infrastructure of human and material resources, the performing arts market was further destabilised.

In the 2000s the musical market exploded with productions of large-scale musicals made possible by the capital and expertise procured in the 1990s. In this stage of industrial growth, the musical theatre industry made tremendous strides, officially being recognised as a significant part of the cultural industry. As mentioned above, the musical that signalled this growth was the Korean première of *The Phantom of the Opera* in 2001. This production instantly boosted the size of the musical theatre market, valued at US$16.67 million, to US$33.34 million—a result significant enough to prove that the musical theatre industry was a realm where the 'economy of scale' applied.

The huge success of the Andrew Lloyd Webber show led to the introduction of a series of large-scale, long-running musicals such as *Cats, Mamma Mia!, Beauty and the Beast*, and *Jekyll and Hyde*—a shift that set a trend in the Korean musical theatre industry. What made those productions possible was the increase in investment that followed *The Phantom of the Opera*. Elaborately staged licensed musicals achieved a high level of success during this period, which meant high returns on investment. Musicals were also attractive for investors, since they often only needed two or three months from investment to return. Apart from those by corporations, investments in the 2000s took the form of various types of funds, such as private equity funds, which were popular in the mid-2000s.[14] Private equity funds grew larger following the Aida Fund, the first musical fund launched by Hana Bank in 2004. For instance, IMM Investment created a fund of $9 million for Cirque de Soleil's *Quidam*, the largest investment for a single show to date. In 2007, the Performing Arts Investment Association Fund was established as a 'fund of funds'.[15] Money raised in the form of private equity funds and 'fund of funds' amounted to $50 million by 2007, so increasing investment soon brought quantitative growth to the musical market. According to the cultural arts yearbook published by the Arts Council Korea, a total of 58 musicals were performed in Seoul in 2000, and that number grew exponentially to 89 in 2005, 137 in 2006, 203 in 2007, and 256 by 2008. But the quantitative growth was attributed to increased investment specifically in large-scale licensed musicals. It was only natural—considering the nature of the funds operated to generate profit—that investment in large-scale, licensed (and hence pre-tested) musicals was prioritised.

Observing the development of Korea's musical industry, it is still not clear whether the market has entered a stage of industrial maturity. This uncertainty results from a set of unique factors.

(a) The first factor is the successful establishment of professional musical groups that have adopted the producer system in place of the group system. Up until the 1990s, the main operating method employed by theatre companies in the Korean performing arts scene was the group system. The group system was initially run in such a way that all members of the company shared equal rights and responsibilities, so as to create an environment for the actors to pursue acting as a professional career; but with advances in the production environment, it became difficult for them to focus on acting alone. This led to the emergence in the 1990s of professional musical groups operating under the producer system. With the advent of professional musical companies, overseas musicals began to be legitimately imported and performed, which soon enabled musical production to be specialised. Working with overseas artists using advanced production techniques ultimately enhanced the quality of production in Korea. These advances are what drove the success in 1996 of the original musical *The Last Empress*, produced by the musical production company Acom.

(b) The second factor is the proliferation of theatres dedicated to musicals. As a series of large-scale licensed musicals became hits in the 2000s and revenues from long-running shows surged, theatres dedicated exclusively to musicals began to open. This in turn enabled longer runs of large-scale musicals, but most of these theatres are still leased only to large-scale licensed musicals with high potential returns, leaving original and small- and medium-scale shows struggling to rent a theatre. Even with numerous musical theatres opening up, a cluster of theatres, such as that found on Broadway or the West End, has failed to emerge,[16] and owing to the limited number of theatres, most of the shows have short-term rather than open runs, which is one of the reasons for the general increase in production costs.

(c) The third factor is that licensed musicals have been dominating the Korean musical market, thanks largely to the huge success of *The Phantom of the Opera* in 2001. Having confirmed the profitability of the musical industry, large enterprises and investors began investing in the musical theatre industry, which thrived from then on. Big investors preferred to invest in licensed musicals from overseas to reduce volatility, and as a result, such shows came to monopolise the market. This significantly improved the quality of musical productions over those of the past, when illegal reproductions were prevalent, and ensured quality experiences for audiences. Nevertheless, more successful original musicals need to be originated for the Korean musical industry to enter a stage of maturity. A number of original musicals, such as *Nanta* (1997) and *Jump* (2003), have been successes. Produced from their very conception with overseas performances in mind, these works have managed to achieve long runs abroad after winning recognition at the Edinburgh Fringe Festival. Both are still performed in updated versions and are recognised as model examples of original Korean musicals that managed to expand overseas. Nevertheless, whereas *Nanta* and *Jump* have neither book nor lyrics, other original Korean musicals have to overcome a language barrier before they can compete with Broadway or West End shows. Thus, it seems the Korean musical market will continue to be dominated by licensed musicals for the foreseeable future.

(d) The fourth factor is the popularisation of celebrity marketing. More and more celebrities—mostly professional singers, actors (in both film and TV series), and comedians—are cast in musicals, and the K-pop stars who have been leading the recent K-pop boom have also been actively participating in musicals, for a number of reasons. To begin with, there is the tendency of production companies to cast celebrities as a way to reduce the risk of producing large-scale musicals and to achieve greater returns. These celebrities also aim to mitigate the uncertainty of their careers through appearing in musicals. The basic elements of a musical are singing, dancing, and acting, and performing a leading role in a musical is an excellent opportunity for K-pop stars to demonstrate their talent. Lastly, with the Korean musical market reaching a point of saturation, producers are choosing celebrity marketing to ease their way into overseas markets; in fact, the number of foreigners visiting Korea to see musicals starring K-pop stars has increased. Celebrity marketing reduces the uncertainty of audience responses and has a positive impact on the overseas foray of Korean musicals, but this is a double-edged sword. The salaries of some of the stars account for a significant portion of the production budget, resulting in higher ticket prices. In addition, because of the stars' busy schedules, it has become the practice to cast multiple actors in one role. The rise in ticket prices significantly hinders the expansion of the musical theatre scene, and because the genre relies heavily on teamwork, the system faces criticism that the casting of multiple actors prevents proper immersion into the roles and undermines the overall quality of the audience experience.

(e) The fifth factor is the formation of a pool of superfans. A unique cultural phenomenon has emerged—audiences loyal to musicals to the level of addiction. These superfans attend the same show numerous times and actively involve themselves in the musical industry to play the role of an alternative group of critics. In this context it should be pointed out that the musical market at large seemingly has failed to secure diverse audiences. According to surveys, theatre-goers of the genre are chiefly women in their twenties and thirties; they constitute a pool of aficionados who attend shows repeatedly. The surveys show that although the Korean musical market has experienced quantitative growth, that growth hasn't taken the form of an expansion based on an influx of new consumers. The practise of double and triple casting, resulting from the increase in celebrity casting mentioned above, is creating more and more 'revolving audiences' who attend the same shows more than once.[17] Thus, a growing number of Korean viewers are attending the same shows over and over until they have seen all the combinations of actors; a term has even developed that translates as 'checking off the whole cast'. The industry is already coming up with marketing plans that cater to these superfans, and this cycle is gradually culminating in a market led by the taste of a small group of consumers. Moreover, the increase in ticket prices due to the growing scale of musicals (and their increased production costs) raises a barrier to new consumers looking to enter the market.

This sums up the developmental process of Korean musicals and some of the market's characteristics, revealed in its historical context. It is true that the Korean musical theatre industry has significantly extended its boundaries and harbours further potential. However, there are issues—the high reliance on overseas licensed musicals, celebrity casting, and a narrow audience base—that make it difficult to claim that the industry has reached full maturity.

# THE STATUS OF THE KOREAN MUSICAL THEATRE INDUSTRY

As of April 2020, no official data is available to estimate accurately the size of the Korean musical market. Only three reliable sources help us to grasp its scale. The first is a conjecture of market size based on the sales data provided by Interpark ENT. This data, available up to 2015, is considered the most accurate when it comes to reflecting the actual status of the Korean musical theatre industry. Because Interpark ENT is estimated to hold about a 60 percent share of the ticketing market for musical performances, their data was used in calculating the total size of the market. According to the *Factual Survey on Musicals 2015*, published by Korea Arts Management Service (KAMS), which is based on this data, the size of the Korean musical market is estimated to have doubled in size, from $134,833,000 in 2010 to $271,613,000 in 2014 (Table 20.1).

The second source deals with the scale of the musical theatre performances, estimated through the annual Factual Survey on Performing Arts, published by KAMS, a national statistic that provides a reliable time-series analysis. Table 20.2 summarises the scale of shows performed in Korea since 2010. It is evident that between 2010 and 2014, the number of musical performances, the performance runs, the number of times they were performed, and the number of attendees have grown remarkably. But from 2014 to 2018 the numbers were stagnant, with minimal upticks and downticks, and the number of attendees stalled around twelve to thirteen million.

**Table 20.1  Estimated Size of the Korean Musical Market (2010–2014)**

| Year | 2010 | 2011 | 2012 | 2013 | 2014 | Average annual growth rate |
|---|---|---|---|---|---|---|
| Estimated size of the Korean musical market (unit: $1,000) | 134,833 | 181,875 | 230,694 | 251,528 | 271,613 | 19.1% |

Source: *Factual Survey on Musicals 2015* (Seoul: KAMS, 2015).

Note: The numbers are estimates based on the musical ticket sales data provided by Interpark ENT.

**Table 20.2  Scale of Korean Musical Theatre Performances (2010–2018)**

| Year | No. Performance venues | Performance halls | No. of productions Total | Avg. | Performance periods (days) Total | Avg. | No. of times performed Total | Avg. | No. of attendees Total | Avg. | % of paying audience |
|---|---|---|---|---|---|---|---|---|---|---|---|
| 2010 | 820 | 1,021 | 2,892 | 2.8 | 18,314 | 17.9 | 25,486 | 25.0 | 6,782,098 | 6,642.6 | — |
| 2011 | 868 | 1,093 | 3,790 | 3.5 | 25,283 | 23.1 | 41,436 | 37.9 | 10,122,212 | 9,260.9 | — |
| 2012 | 944 | 1,188 | 4,462 | 3.8 | 29,166 | 24.6 | 42,881 | 36.1 | 11,532,900 | 9,707.8 | — |
| 2013 | 984 | 1,227 | 5,255 | 4.3 | 30,425 | 24.8 | 57,027 | 46.5 | 12,810,939 | 10,440.9 | — |
| 2014 | 1,034 | 1,280 | 7,292 | 5.7 | 35,452 | 27.7 | 56,949 | 44.5 | 12,659,367 | 9,890.1 | — |
| 2015 | 1,026 | 1,290 | 4,799 | 3.7 | 32,467 | 25.2 | 50,996 | 39.5 | 13,142,618 | 10,188.1 | 51.3 |
| 2016 | 992 | 1,268 | 5,205 | 4.1 | 30,152 | 23.8 | 47,074 | 37.1 | 12,472,150 | 9,836.0 | 56.9 |
| 2017 | 1,019 | 1,323 | 5,401 | 4.1 | 36,232 | 27.4 | 60,809 | 46.0 | 13,238,845 | 10,006.7 | 48.6 |
| 2018 | 1,029 | 1,324 | 4,879 | 3.7 | 33,980 | 25.7 | 52,986 | 40.0 | 13,595,834 | 10,268.8 | 51.9 |

Source: Factual Survey on Performing Arts by KAMS (yearly data).

Note: The Factual Survey on Performing Arts is statistical data managed as part of the national statistics attained through surveys of performance facilities and groups. The items, subjects, and scope of this research differ from those of the KOPIS (to be discussed below); therefore, a simple comparison of the two is invalid. The Factual Survey on Performing Arts includes free performances as part of their research subject, and therefore the numbers of performances and performance period generally appear higher than those researched by KOPIS.

## Table 20.3 Size of the Korean Musical Market Estimated by KOPIS (July 2019–March 2020)

| Genre | Productions produced | | Productions staged | | Times performed | | Sales | | Tickets | |
|---|---|---|---|---|---|---|---|---|---|---|
| | No. | % | No. | % | No. | % | S$1,000 | % | No. | % |
| All | 7,574 | 100 | 7,331 | 100 | 67,559 | 100 | 204,711 | 100 | 7,581,595 | 100 |
| Musicals | 1,798 | 23.7 | 1,712 | 23.4 | 26,633 | 39.4 | 157,130 | 76.8 | 4,139,926 | 54.6 |
| Plays | 1,459 | 19.3 | 1,343 | 18.3 | 34,459 | 51.0 | 19,913 | 9.7 | 1,544,329 | 20.4 |
| Classical Concerts | 2,853 | 37.7 | 2,835 | 38.7 | 3,095 | 4.6 | 14,166 | 6.9 | 1,058,184 | 14.0 |
| Operas | 191 | 2.5 | 191 | 2.6 | 314 | 0.5 | 3,056 | 1.5 | 151,996 | 2.0 |
| Dance | 439 | 5.8 | 433 | 5.9 | 1,061 | 1.6 | 8,185 | 4.0 | 351,937 | 4.6 |
| Gugak | 406 | 5.4 | 395 | 5.4 | 1,045 | 1.5 | 892 | 0.4 | 166,987 | 2.2 |
| Integrated | 428 | 5.7 | 422 | 5.8 | 952 | 1.4 | 1,368 | 0.7 | 168,236 | 2.2 |

Source: KOPIS, http://www.kopis.or.kr, accessed 15 April 2020.

Note: KOPIS only shows records of electronically purchased tickets (excluding on-site purchases and phone reservations). The use of the KOPIS system was mandated on 25 June 2019.

The third source is the Korean Ministry of Culture, Sports and Tourism, which revised the Performance Act in December 2018 to investigate the state of the performing arts industry and mandated an update of performing-arts ticket-sales data on the Korea Performing Arts Box Office Information System (KOPIS). KOPIS provides accurate and reliable information and statistical data by aggregating scattered information on ticket purchases and cancellations.As of April 2020, the size of the Korean musical market estimated based on the number of issued tickets registered on KOPIS (during the nine months from July 2019 to March 2020) is $157,130,000 (Table 20.3). If we convert the nine-month data into an annual scale, this hints at an actual market size of about $209,507,000. Taking into account the COVID-19 pandemic, which damaged Korea's performance market from January to April 2020, this year's musical market size is estimated to be around $250,000,000–333,330,000, which corroborates the hypothesis that the market has become relatively static in comparison to 2014, when the size was US$271,613,000 million (see again Table 20.1).

Even though the three estimates given above were arrived at by disparate methods, what seems undeniable is that the growth rate of the Korean musical market has slowed since 2023. The reason for this stagnation is, as mentioned earlier, its limits in securing a diverse pool of audiences. The main problem is the revolving audience—those repeat attendees who return to see the same show a number of times.[18] Just how many times do these revolving audiences return to the same show? In October 2015 The Musical, a Korean journal dedicated to musicals, attempted to draw up quantitative statistics regarding performing arts superfans. Their survey showed that, on average, superfans

## Table 20.4 Quantitative Statistics and Tendencies of Performing Arts Superfans

| Criteria | General attendees | Fans | Superfans | Aficionados |
|---|---|---|---|---|
| Average annual attendances | 7.02 | 25.94 | 59.41 | 118.87 |
| Average annual no. of shows attended | 5.53 | 11.9 | 22.12 | 40.05 |
| Rate of repeat attendance | 16% | 43% | 56% | 64% |
| Average no. of shows repeat-attended | 0.5 | 2.3 | 5.06 | 7.73 |
| Average no. of repeat attendances per show | 2.55 | 4.3 | 5.45 | 11.52 |

Source: Park Byeong-seon, 'Statistics on Performing Arts Enthusiasts', *Musical* 145 (October 2015), https://www.themusical.co.kr/Pick/Detail?enc_num=HQ1uEPMMLENeNg4fzLpz5Q%3D%3D, accessed 10 April 2020.

attended shows 59.41 times a year and repeat-attended 5.06 shows, seeing each of those shows 5.45 times. The survey also showed that most of the superfans were women in their twenties and thirties, who tend to attend alone (Table 20.4).

Looking at the status of consumption in the Korean musical theatre industry, it is evident that the market is heavily dependent on superfans and aficionados. Table 20.5 shows that 80.6 percent of all musical theatre–goers are women and that 66.3 percent are in their twenties or thirties. Women make up 72.9 percent of all theatre-goers, a very high percentage considering that the percentages of attendees of classical concerts and operas in their twenties and thirties are 52.1 percent and 44.6 percent respectively. The percentage of solo attendees of musicals is 22.5 percent, also higher than that of plays (22.3 percent), classical concerts (16.3 percent), and opera (11.2 percent).

The fast and concentrated growth of the Korean musical theatre market (in terms of sales) cannot be explained without acknowledging that the genre, in contrast to other performance forms, was invigorated on a nationwide level. Table 20.6 shows that musicals top other genres in terms of number of shows and ticket sales in regions outside the capital and other major cities. In 2018 alone, the musicals staged in such regions accounted for 52.2 percent of all musicals and 20.3 percent of all musical ticket sales. Among the reasons that musicals proliferated in non-capital regions was that mid-size theatres with seating capacities of 300–1,000 were built across the nation, helping secure commercial viability.

## ATTRIBUTES OF THE KOREAN MUSICAL THEATRE INDUSTRY AND ITS PROSPECTS

Having established the historical context and examined the status of the Korean musical theatre market, it has become clear that the industry is characterised by growth centring

**Table 20.5 Ticket Sales by Genre (2018)**

| Genre | Gender | | Age group | | | | | Solo attendees | |
|---|---|---|---|---|---|---|---|---|---|
| | Female | Male | Teens and under | 20s | 30s | 40s | 50s and Over | Total no. of tickets sold | % of solo attendees |
| All | 2,880,007 (78.4) | 793,021 (21.6) | 73,974 (2.2) | 881,293 (26.2) | 1,415,163 (42.1) | 788,395 (23.4) | 206,129 (6.1) | 4,085,163 (100.0) | 872,186 (21.4) |
| Musicals | 2,081,929 (80.6) | 502,418 (19.4) | 48,906 (2.1) | 518,199 (22.0) | 1,089,086 (46.3) | 571,532 (24.3) | 124,680 (5.3) | 2,709,969 (100.0) | 608,915 (22.5) |
| Plays | 562,305 (72.9) | 208,821 (27.1) | 20,639 (2.8) | 309,056 (42.2) | 232,651 (31.8) | 120,199 (16.4) | 49,486 (6.8) | 844,132 (100.0) | 188,045 (22.3) |
| Classical Concerts | 128,304 (70.9) | 52,599 (19.1) | 2,794 (1.7) | 31,377 (19.2) | 53,778 (32.9) | 55,748 (34.1) | 19,716 (12.1) | 272,987 (100.0) | 44,497 (16.3) |
| Operas | 18,981 (72.5) | 7,202 (27.5) | 471 (2.0) | 4,186 (18.0) | 6,189 (26.6) | 8,794 (37.8) | 3,624 (15.6) | 58,026 (100.0) | 6,515 (11.2) |
| Dance | 62,691 (78.2) | 17,444 (21.8) | 872 (1.1) | 15,103 (19.0) | 29,490 (37.1) | 27,298 (34.3) | 6,736 (8.5) | 128,684 (100.0) | 21,167 (16.4) |
| Gugak | 25,797 (85.0) | 4,537 (15.0) | 292 (2.0) | 3,372 (23.5) | 3,969 (27.7) | 4,824 (33.6) | 1,887 (13.2) | 71,365 (100.0) | 3,047 (4.3) |

Source: KAMS, *2018 Performing Arts Consumption Report* (Seoul: KAMS, 2018), 47–48.

Note 1: The numbers are based on online (web and mobile) and non-free performance ticket sales data collected via KOPIS and major ticketing sites. The numbers do not reflect on the market as a whole as on-site purchases, phone reservations, and purchases via social commerce are excluded from the count.

Note 2: The purchases by each gender and age group and solo attendees do not add up to the total number of tickets sold because certain purchase details were inaccessible.

## Table 20.6 Number of Shows and Ticket Sales in Each Region by Genre (2018)

| | No. of shows | | | | | No. of tickets sold | | | | |
| | | Capital region | | Non-capital regions | | | Capital region | | Non-capital regions | |
| Genre | Total | No. | % | No. | % | Total | No. | % | No. | % |
|---|---|---|---|---|---|---|---|---|---|---|
| All | 8,668 | 5,902 | 68.1 | 2,766 | 31.9 | 4,085,163 | 3,353,411 | 82.1 | 731,752 | 17.9 |
| Musicals | 2,356 | 1,126 | 47.8 | 1,230 | 52.2 | 2,709,969 | 2,159,252 | 79.7 | 550,717 | 20.3 |
| Plays | 1,873 | 1,279 | 68.3 | 594 | 31.7 | 844,132 | 750,464 | 88.9 | 93,668 | 11.1 |
| Classical Concerts | 3,329 | 2,628 | 78.9 | 701 | 21.1 | 272,987 | 220,344 | 80.7 | 52,643 | 19.3 |
| Operas | 211 | 126 | 59.7 | 85 | 40.3 | 58,026 | 46,915 | 80.9 | 11,111 | 19.1 |
| Dance | 412 | 345 | 83.7 | 67 | 16.3 | 128,684 | 109,353 | 85.0 | 19,331 | 15.0 |
| Gugak | 487 | 398 | 81.7 | 89 | 18.3 | 71,365 | 67,083 | 94.0 | 4,282 | 6.0 |

Source: KAMS, *2018 Performing Arts Consumption Report* (Seoul: KAMS, 2018), 55–56.

on large-scale licensed musicals. Beginning in the 2000s, however, productions with high budgets showed new tendencies. Influenced by a shift in the structure of the surrounding cultural industries, the musical theatre industry improved its profit strategies as large corporate entities entered the market.

The Korean government promoted revitalisation of the cultural industries in the 1990s, and large corporations and media companies that had previously been barred entered the industry, propelling vertical and horizontal mergers of related industries and maximising profitability through large-scale productions and reinforcement of their PR and marketing divisions.[19] This way their production divisions could raise production funds and create profit by securing a stable distribution network, while their distribution divisions created added value through one-source, multi-use (OSMU) opportunities and the window effect created by 'killer content'. This phenomenon was seen throughout the film, game, music, media, and performance industries, and corporate monopolisation also affected the musical theatre ecosystem. CJ E&M, one of Korea's representative media companies, is growing into an absolute powerhouse in the content production and distribution sectors, expanding its reach to film, music, performance, animation, conventions, advertising, broadcasting, and home shopping while also wielding a great deal of power over the musical theatre industry. Looking at Interpark's annual list of the top fifty musicals with the highest sales from 2011 to 2017, CJ ENM produced a total of sixty-two musicals during these seven years, which is thirty-one more than EMK. The latter ranked second for producing 27 percent of all musicals staged by the top ten production companies. On the other hand, out of the fifty-one musicals offered by CJ EN (excluding co-produced works), only ten or so were original musicals produced entirely domestically, attesting to the company's concentration on licensing foreign works.

The establishment of large musical theatres also served as one of the reasons for the prioritisation of licensed musicals. Numerous theatres with seating capacities exceeding 1,000 were built after 2011 specifically to house musicals, and these venues favoured well-known licensed musicals with short runs, which generate large revenues. Among a total of eighty-seven licensed musicals staged in 2014, sixty (69 percent) were short-term shows with a performance run of fewer than thirty-one days, and approximately 84 percent were staged at large-scale theatres with more than 1,000 seats. Under these circumstances, production companies gave priority to licensed musicals, which come pre-tested in terms of 'quality' and commercial success, because they are less risky investments compared to original musicals; they are also cost-effective in that the script and music already exist, drastically curtailing the overall production costs.

Licensed musicals certainly enhanced the Korean musical industry, promoting audience growth as well as public attention, but they ultimately culminated in quantitative rather than qualitative growth, a rise in royalties, and a structure centred around investment return. This structure also has to do with another prominent aspect of the industry: its increased dependence on celebrity ('idol') casting, referred to earlier. Celebrity casting and marketing are strategies used everywhere in the world, but the rush of K-pop stars into the Korean musical scene in the late 2000s was a specific consequence of the coinciding interests of production companies and the stars themselves. To understand the culture of idol casting prominent in the Korean musical scene, it is important to understand the background from which these idols emerged.

What is distinctive about the Korean music industry is that independent production companies have developed a specialised production system. Production companies were founded in the 1980s, when record labels required certain services, as a way into the industry for those producers who could not sign musicians and produce albums. As the demand for domestic pop music grew around broadcasting networks following Korea's entry into the Universal Copyright Convention in 1987, production companies began concentrating on their roles as management companies, generating profit by booking television appearances for their talents. In the 1990s idol groups began to be produced by large entertainment/management companies. SM Entertainment was the first to camp-train ordinary teenage boys and lead them to overnight stardom. This is how the five-member boy band H.O.T. was created in 1996, which marked the beginning of the Korean idol group legacy.[20] The term 'idol' refers generally to celebrities popular among teenagers and youths, but in Korea it refers specifically to those teen performers who have débuted as members of K-pop groups trained under the idol system—a training system run by entertainment companies through which prospective K-pop stars are selected, grouped, and launched with meticulously produced music and image concepts.

The reason entertainment companies operate an idol system is obviously to incubate stars and generate profit. The trainees undergo training processes that last anywhere from three months to six or seven years and an average of two to three years until their début, during which time they learn to sing, act, dance, and even speak foreign languages in case of overseas ventures. The fact that entertainment companies are willing to assume the increased responsibility associated with idol selection, education, and début indicates that these types of companies will not only grow in scale but also into more than simple entertainment/management companies, eventually merging or intimately interacting with the pop-culture and media industries.[21] Not only does casting idols for large-scale musicals simply work as celebrity marketing, lead to ticket sales, and meet the commercial needs of the musical theatre production companies, but it also guarantees publicity and income for idols in their spare time between short album promotion cycles, and these mutual benefits ultimately encourage the practice.

There have been cases in the past where celebrities such as singers and actors were featured in musicals, but the casting of idol group members increased greatly in the late 2000s. The pool of musical theatre actors with ticket-selling power has always been small, and as competition intensified, production companies turned to idol casting to heighten recognition and secure a competitive edge. From a musical theatre producer's perspective, idols already have the capacity to perform musicals owing to their lengthy training in singing, acting, and dancing, and their successful launch and continued popularity in the competitive idol market vouch for their persistence and professionalism, which makes idol casting less risky than casting emerging musical actors.

This is not to say that idols were welcomed by the musical industry from the very beginning. Idols first began venturing into the musical field in the early 2000s. Members of S.E.S. and Fin.K.L—the top two girl groups at the time—could be seen as the first generation of K-pop stars to venture into the field. Starring in the musical *Peppermint* in 2003, Bada, a member of S.E.S., became the first idol to transition into a musical theatre actor, followed by Ock Joo-hyun, who won the lead role in the musical *Disney's Aida* with her audition in 2005; twelve years later she performed the villainous Mrs Danvers in the 'drama musical' *Rebecca*.[22] These are successful cases in which former idols transitioned into musical theatre actors, but musical fans at the time were resistant towards celebrity casting and favoured shows starring professional actors. The two idol members both turned to musicals after their solo début following the disbanding of their groups in 2002, which differs from recent idols' pattern of entry into the musical theatre scene.

In 2008 a total of twelve idol group members débuted on musical stages. From an entertainment company's standpoint, their artists' venture into the musical scene is advantageous in that they can make use of the free time in between album releases and sustain publicity, and from the artists' point of view, musicals are opportunities to cultivate and flaunt their individual talents outside of their groups. It was then that some entertainment companies took the initiative of diving into the musical theatre business themselves.[23] SM Entertainment established the subsidiary company SM Art Company and licensed the musical *Xanadu*, starring members of their boy group Super Junior. Also interested in musical production, YG Entertainment formed a strategic alliance with Seol and Company, which had led *The Phantom of the Opera* and *Cats* to success, also casting members of their boy group Big Bang for *Rain Shower* (2012) and *Cats*. Thus, two

FIG. 20.2 The housekeeper, Mrs Danvers (Ock Joohyun), tempts the second Mrs de Winter (Lee Ji Hye) to commit suicide. Scene from the 2017 Korean production of *Rebecca*. Photo © EMK Musical Company.

of Korea's largest entertainment companies jumped into the musical theatre business, partly because the industry had reached its prime, with heightened public recognition as well as investment, and partly because the companies calculated that their idol incubation system had leverage in the performing arts field. These companies sought to create sustainable revenue from self-produced musicals featuring their own music content and talents. Nevertheless, as their musicals continued to underwhelm audiences, even with members of the then extremely popular idol groups Super Junior, Girls' Generation, and Big Bang as the stars, they failed to establish a successful model for entertainment companies entering the musical market.

The year 2010 was when the musical scene saw a successful case of idol casting, which served as momentum towards increasing the tendency. In that year a total of nineteen idol group members performed in musicals—more than double the number who had done so in 2009. The reason there were fewer idols expanding into the musical scene in 2009 was in part that the market was in recession following the overall economic downturn, and in part that the entertainment companies that had been involved in musical production in 2008 stopped producing anything substantial. The atmosphere changed with the successful début of Kim Jun-su, former member of TVXQ!, in the lead role of the musical *Mozart!* His drawing power proved to surpass that of Cho Seung-woo, a musical star who had been breaking his own records of sold-out performances.[24] Kim's success demonstrated the power of fandom and made production companies turn their

FIG. 20.3 In 2010 the K-pop superstar Kim Jun-su performed the title role of the 'drama musical' *Mozart!* (1999), sparking record ticket sales. Photo © EMK Musical Company.

eyes towards and actively solicit idol group members in the hopes of creating the next Kim Jun-su.

Since 2010 members of the hottest idol groups in the music scene, including U-Know Yunho from TVXQ!, Onew from SHINee, and Taeyeon from Girls' Generation, have been cast in musicals. As part of the trend, shows even appeared composed almost entirely of idol casts. More and more works came to involve or centre on idols as a strategy to attract both Korean and overseas fans. This marked the introduction of *Hallyu* star marketing to the musical theatre industry. In 2010 the share of foreign attendees of *Mozart!*, starring Kim Jun-su, was 16 percent, and that of *Jack the Ripper*, starring Sungmin from Super Junior, was 10 percent. Casting Hallyu stars–that is, stars from the so-called Korean wave',[25] became essential to musicals' overseas expansion, especially to Japan, where the impact of Hallyu was the greatest. Featuring several idols and celebrities was also how *The Three Musketeers* achieved a huge success when staged in Japan in 2013.

As entertainment companies viewed the main source of their management revenue shifting from album sales to musical theatre performances, they began to pay more and more attention to the field.

Idol casting continued to prevail following a series of success stories, and even though there has not been a ground-breaking success since then, the musical scene is still showing growing dependence on idols. Cases of idol casting increased from 24 in 2012 to 34 in 2013, then to 53 in 2014. Around this time, entertainment companies also returned to the ever-growing musical theatre industry.[26] As Hallyu opened the doors to overseas markets for musicals, SM Entertainment founded a subsidiary company, SM Culture & Contents, and presented musicals such as *Singin' in the Rain*, featuring a number of in-house artists, including members of Super Junior, EXO, and Girls' Generation, to draw

## Table 20.7 SM Entertainment's Revenue Structure, 2015

| Division | Revenue type | Revenue source | Overseas/ domestic | Revenue (US$1,000) | Weight to total (%) | |
|---|---|---|---|---|---|---|
| Music production | Album sales | Physical albums | Overseas | 6,864 | 4.2 | 21.8 |
| | | | Domestic | 28,583 | 17.5 | |
| | | Downloads/ streaming | Overseas | 5,107 | 3.1 | 8.5 |
| | | | Domestic | 8,688 | 5.3 | |
| Talent management | Talent fees | Performance | Overseas | 40,533 | 24.9 | 34.1 |
| | | | Domestic | 14,933 | 9.2 | |
| | | Commercials | Overseas | 3,379 | 2.1 | 13.6 |
| | | | Domestic | 18,849 | 11.6 | |
| | | Sittings, etc. | Overseas | 19,099 | 11.7 | 22.1 |
| | | | Domestic | 16,837 | 10.3 | |
| Total | | | Overseas Total | 74,899 | 46.0 | |
| | | | Domestic total | 87,889 | 54.0 | |
| | | | Total | 162,872 | 100.0 | |

Source: J. H. Lee, *A Theory of Idol Commodity: Focusing on the Commodity Form and Labor Process of the Idol Industry* (master's Thesis, Graduate School of Communication of Media Studies, Sogang University, 2016), 15.

public attention (Table 20.7). Kim Jun-su's company officially entered the musical theatre business with the continued success of his musicals, launching CJeS Culture and producing *Death Note: The Musical* (2015), which received favourable reviews for both the quality and the popularity of the work.

As we have seen, production and entertainment companies sought to utilise the advantage idols have in the musical theatre industry, and idols sought to develop their careers and gain a foothold in the growing market for musicals. Some say that the promotional effect and ticket-selling power associated with idol casting aren't as strong as they used to be, since musicals starring idols have become common; but idol casting is still a major factor in the production and distribution of musicals in that they attract media attention.[27] Production companies hope to produce quality works that will succeed with idols as the catalysts, but not all musicals starring idols are successful. It also has to be pointed out that it can set a high entry barrier for new audiences, because idol casting pumps up production costs and therefore ticket prices. In addition, there is the issue of incompatibility between idols and traditional musical theatre actors over the discrepancy in their performance fees and the resentment felt by actors trained for musical theatre in regard to idols filling up lead roles without auditioning. There have been actual cases in which idols with busy schedules hindered rehearsals and run-throughs, making it difficult for the crew to bond. Idol casting has also encouraged the problematic practice of multiple casting. On the flip side, of course, sometimes other actors cast in the same roles as popular idols have moved into the spotlight.[28] Some believe that idols are contributing to the popularisation of musicals and that these problems should be considered simply an aspect of the developmental process.

# CONCLUSION

The Korean musical theatre industry has seen such rapid growth since the 2000s that it is ranked fourth in the world, after the United States, the United Kingdom, and Germany, in terms of market size. The portion taken up by musicals in the Korean performing arts industry is also significant. They account for approximately 55 percent of all paying audiences in the industry, and whereas plays generate an average of $13,000 in ticket revenue, musicals generate an average of $109,000.[29] What is dubious, however, is whether the quantitative growth of musicals has culminated in the qualitative growth of the musical theatre ecosystem.

On the one hand, there is the side effect of increased dependency on short-term, large-scale licensed musicals and idol casting. Licensed musicals with high returns have boosted the size of the musical market and consumer demand, but in the long run they have weakened the make-up of the industry. The short-term, success-driven market has reduced investment in original musicals, thereby diminishing the diversity of musicals and leaving production companies, other than a handful of large enterprises, struggling. Oral contracts remain covertly prevalent in the industry, and some companies have been known to shut down their businesses after failing to make payments, then reopen under another name.

There are structural limitations to musical consumption as well. Even though the number of musical theatre-goers has increased, the main consumer pool is fixed, composed of 'revolving audiences' who are musical or idol superfans. Major consumption by women with high socioeconomic status and devoted fans is causing the strange phenomenon of one viewer attending one show up to 120 times, pointing to the fact that licensed and celebrity-centred musical production is not useful in generating fresh audience pools. The rising production costs and higher ticket prices resulting from celebrity casting also impedes the influx of new audiences.

For these reasons, the Korean musical theatre industry has foreseen the limits of the domestic market and is directing its efforts to overseas ventures. Hallyu may be an opportunity for the musical theatre industry, but overseas tours of large-scale shows often have to deal with technical difficulties, Hallyu marketing alone won't be enough to guarantee the competitive edge necessary for sustainable growth. Hallyu and idol casting as a strategy for overseas expansion will continue. But the industry must bear in mind that prolonged reliance on idol casting will increase star salaries, and that in turn will make it difficult for the industry to escape the distorted cost structure of production, jeopardising it in the long run. This is why the core sector of content development dedicated to production of high-quality original musicals has to be revived. Fortunately, the response to large-scale original musicals such as *The Man Who Laughs* (2018) and *Xcalibur* (2019) by both critics and audiences was positive, and small- and medium-scale original musicals are consistently making qualitative improvements. *Red Book*, produced in 2016 with support from the Performing Arts Creation Chamber of Arts Council Korea, is rewriting the history of original musicals, garnering high ticket sales and an audience rating of 9.7.[30]

Whilst the Korean musical industry is growing rapidly and consistently, it is also in transition. Competition among domestic companies has already intensified to the point of undermining the profitability of the licensing strategy, and although licensed musicals that have been hits in the past are still popular, new works and a more varied audience base need to be developed for further growth of the market. It is time for the Korean musical industry to reform its foundation and strengthen its internal stability.

## NOTES

1. Lim Dong Geun, 'The Domestic Performance Market Has Grown for Two Consecutive Years', *Yonhap News Agency*, 30 December 2019, https://www.yna.co.kr/view/AKR201912 30053100005, accessed 20 July 2020.
2. W. G. Choi and B. J. Yim, 'A Study on the Industrial History and Development of the Musical Theatre in Korea', *Review of Business History* 30, no. 3 (2015): 35–56; here: 37–42.
3. Musicals are also widely referred to as 'song and dance' because they mix instrumental music, singing, drama, dynamic dance moves, and stage mechanisms; they also interact with the audience.

4. *Pansori* is a form of Korean combination of traditional music and play, introduced in the seventeenth century. It is characterised by a *sorikkun* who narrates the story through singing, speaking, and gesturing to the rhythm played by *gosu*.

5. Derived from *pansori*, *changguek* is a genre of Korean theatre performed by a group of singers who led the narrative through pansori-infused acting.

6. *Chunghyang-ga*, one of the famous *madang* (song cycle) of pansori, for example, consists of a narrative that can last up to eight and a half hours.

7. Yegrin Musical Theatre was launched by the founder of the Korean Central Intelligence Agency, Kim Jong-pil, in 1961. After seeing how grand and fancy a North Korean opera could be, Kim organised and fostered a rival theatre group, which he sponsored by establishing and running a sponsors' association consisting of thirty financial magnates. After a series of six dissolutions and re-foundations, the group now performs under the name Seoul Metropolitan Musical Theatre.

8. *Sweet, Come to Me Stealthily* was also produced as a sound recording, and the eponymous theme song, performed by Patti Kim, a popular singer at the time, was a huge hit.

9. Works performed by the National Music and Dance Company include *Sijipganeun Nal* (1974), *Sangnoksu* (1975), and *Taeyangcheoreom* (1976). The National Yegrin Musical Company staged *Ireon Saram* (1977) and *Sijipganeun Nal* (1977), while the Seoul Music and Dance Company scheduled *Dalbin Nageune* (1978), *Urideurui Chukje* (1981), *Sarangeun Murirang Tago* (1983), *Porgy and Bess* (1984), *Jibung Wiui Bailollin* (1985), *Yongi Narisya* (1988), *Gohyangui Mindeulle* (1990), *Chumchuneun Dosi* (1994), and *Gando Arirang* (1995).

10. The group system (*donginje*) refers to the operational system in which all the members of a theatre company equally share both rights and responsibilities, which makes everyone both producers and managers of the company.

11. An international agreement governing copyright, the Berne Convention was first signed by ten countries—Switzerland, Germany, Belgium, Spain, France, Italy, Great Britain, Haiti, Liberia, and Tunisia—on 9 September 1886 to protect the copyrights of literary and artistic works; as of 2023, more than 150 nations have signed it.

12. Prime examples are Acom, Seensee Company, Hwan Performance, and Seoul Musical Company.

13. The nature of corporate participation had previously supported the arts and was more orientated towards social benefits than investment.

14. A private equity fund is a fund that invests the equities of a small group of privately recruited investors.

15. A 'fund of funds' is a pooled investment fund that invests in different underlying portfolios of other funds rather than directly in enterprises, to reduce risk.

16. An example of such a clustered area would be Daehangno, but the area comprises mostly small theatres rather than theatres dedicated to musicals.

17. The term 'revolving audiences' refers to those who return to see the same show over and over again; the phrase likens them to revolving doors.

18. According to research, approximately 6 percent (38,000) of all musical goers in 2018 were repeat attendees, and one out of ten repeat attendees see one show more than ten times. The most number of times a repeat attendee saw a single show was 120. Lee Wu-jin, *Magazine PlayDB*, http://m.playdb.co.kr/MobileMagazine/ListicleDetail?magazineno= 2955&subcategory=067005, accessed 10 April 2018.

19. Technological advances enabled access to various types of content, such as films, music, and games, through a single device, which leads to an expanded user pool and more possibilities for profit generation for the cultural content industry. The integration of digital environments has also increased the potential window effect and OSMU opportunities of creating numerous pieces of content using a single source.

20. Lee Sooman, the founder of Korea's largest entertainment company, SM Entertainment, mentioned that he adopted the artist training system after learning that the singer Kim Wansun, who took the 1980s by storm, had three years of intensive training before making her début.

21. As the idol system continues to develop, the cost of concept planning, production, and marketing inevitably increases. For example, in addition to a training period, at least one or two years are invested in concept development and preparation for the début. The companies accrue copious cost for record production, costume fees, and marketing expenses, not to mention invisible costs such as labor fees that go into managing the artists. The size of investment that goes into producing one idol is estimated to range from KRW 2–3billion (Cho Eun Byul, '3 Billion Idol vs Misari Singer ', *No Cut News*, 22 June 2012, https://www.yna.co.kr/view/MYH20171221004300038, accessed 10 May 2020) to 3–5 billion (Baek Gil Hyun, 'Stay Strong to Be a Star: Sick Children in Competition', *Yeonhap News*, 21 December 2017, https://www.nocutnews.co.kr/news/4264264, accessed 10 May 2020).

22. For more information on *Rebecca* (2006), see chap. 26.

23. Making close to 30 percent growth every year since 2002, the Korean musical market was showing the steepest growth at this time, with an unprecedented market size of KRW 100 billion.

24. Kim Jun-su's first musical, *Mozart!* (2010), filled all of the 45,000 available seats for every one of its fifteen performances. This success was followed by *Tears of Heaven* (2011), which was another smash hit, selling every single one of its 30,200 tickets for its run of twenty performances, making Kim the new blue chip of the market. For more information on *Mozart!* see chap. 26.

25. *Hallyu* refers to the craze for Korean pop culture that began in Asia in the 1990s. With the establishment of diplomatic ties with China in 1992, Korean popular music (e.g. H.O.T.) began to gain popularity among Chinese youth, and the term *Hallyu* was introduced. The popular culture craze, involving pop music, dramas, and movies, later expanded to Southeast Asia. Now the Korean Wave culture craze is used to greatly expand Korean traditional culture, food, literature, and Korean-language learning; https://www.factsabo utkorea.go.kr/bbs/view.do?bbs_id=BBSMSTR_000000000311&nttId=NI_0000000000 0004143, accessed 28 May 2020.

26. Park Byung-Sung, 'Evolution of Star Casting-Flow of Idol Casting', *Musical* 146 (2015): 11, https://www.themusical.co.kr/Magazine/Detail?num=2625, accessed 20 July 2020.

27. When an idol goes on TV to promote the musical in which they have been cast, the impact is greater than that of standard advertising.

28. A representative case is *Hedwig*. After being double cast with Cho Seung-woo, the actor Oh Man-seok was newly recognised for his acting skills. This shows that double casting isn't so much a problem in and of itself, and some argue that professional musical actors should focus on honing their skills before criticising this phenomenon; see the discussion at www.themusical.co.kr, accessed 20 May 2020.

29. Ministry of Culture, Sports and Tourism and Korean Arts Management Service, *2018 Performing Arts Survey* (Seoul: Ministry of Culture, 2019), 265; Lim Dong Geun, 'The Domestic Performance Market Has Grown'.
30. Lee Ji-young, 'What Did Audiences in Their 20s and 30s Say Was the Key to *Red Book*'s Success?', *JoongAng Ilbo*, 5 April 2018, https://news.joins.com/article/22510013 accessed 10 April 2020.

## BIBLIOGRAPHY

Baek, S. M. 'The Effect of Musical Performers on Musical Awareness and Ticket Sales—Focusing on Musical Maniacs.' Master's thesis, Chung-Ang University, 2014.

Choi, S. Y. 'A Study on Aspects of the Performance of Musical Theatre in Korea from 1990 to 2000.' *Journal of Korean Theatre Studies Association* 29 (2006): 263–291.

Choi, W. G., and B. J. Yim. 'A Study on the Industrial History and Development of the Musical Theatre in Korea.' *Review of Business History* 30, no. 3(2015): 35–56.

Chun, B. J., and M. J. Yoon. 'Strategy of Korean Musical Industry under Market Uncertainty.' *Korean Association of Arts Management* 17 (2010): 111–139.

Geun, Lim Dong. 'The Domestic Performance Market Has Grown for Two Consecutive Years', *Yonhap News Agency*, 30 December 2019, https://www.yna.co.kr/view/AKR20191230053100 005, accessed 20 July 2020.

Hong, S. H., and J. W. Jung. 'A Study on the State and Development of the Korean Musical Market.' *Media & Performing Arts* 10, no. 2 (2015): 119–145. https://www.themusical.co.kr/

Hur, E. Y. *A Study on the Supporting Policy for Oversea Expansion of Performance: Focused on Musicals.* Seoul: Korea Culture & Tourism Institute, 2013.

Jee, S. W., and I. H. Cho. 'A Study on the Development Strategy of Korean Musical work: Based on Musical Work Planning Strategy.' *Journal of the Korea Entertainment Industry Association* 8, no. 3 (2014): 231–239.

Jeong, E. M. 'Study on Unfair Practices in Musical Production and Distribution.' *Journal of Culture Industry* 18, no. 1 (2018): 73–84.

Kim, Y. A. 'Future Challenges for Korean Musicals Improved under the Influence of Broadway.' *Humanities Contents* 10 (2007): 363–382.

Lee, J. H. 'A Theory of Idol Commodity: Focusing on the Commodity Form and Labor Process of the Idol Industry.' Master's thesis, Sogang University, 2016.

Lee, J. H., and G. E. Chung. 'A Study on the Development Status and Change of Korean Musical Industry.' *Journal of Culture Industry* 13 (2013): 43–53.

Lim, C. M. 'The Analysis of the Structure and Changing Trends of Production Budget of Large-Theater Musicals in Korea: Based on Musical Productions Presented during the Decade of 2008–2017.' PhD diss., Sungkyunkwan University, 2019.

Ministry of Culture, Sports and Tourism and Korean Arts Management Service. *2018 Performing Arts Survey.* Seoul: Ministry of Culture, 2019.

Park, B. S. 'A Study on the Industrialization of Licensed Musicals in the 2000s.' Master's thesis, Korea National University of Arts, 2015.

Park, Byung-Sung. 'Evolution of Star Casting—Flow of Idol Casting.' *Musical* 146 (2015): 11, https://www.themusical.co.kr/Magazine/Detail?num=2625, accessed 20 July 2020.

Park, H. J., and Great Root Woods. 'Current Status and Characteristics of Licensed Musicals in Korea.' *Humanities Contents* 40 (2016): 253–269.

Ra, H. Y. 'Study on Integration Movement and Locational Characteristic of Cultural Contents Industries'. *Journal of Culture Industry* 11, no. 3 (2011): 81–98.

Shin, H. S. 'A Study on the Market Segmentation of Musical's Audience—Focused on University Student Audience'. Master's thesis, Sookmyung Women's University, 2005.

Song, K. O. 'Analysis of Musical Consumer's Motives for Viewing the Musicals by Using the "Q" Methodology'. Master's thesis. Department of Mass Communication, Graduate School of Yonsei University, 2007.

You, I. K. 'The Growth Momentum and Issues of Musical Industrialization in Korea: Focused on the Hyundai Art Theater, the Lotte World Art Theater and the Samsung Visual Arts Foundation'. *Research of Performance Art and Culture* 21 (2010): 403–447.

# CHAPTER 21

.............

# THE PATH AND DEVELOPMENT OF THE CHINESE MUSICAL

.............

## CAI FANGTIAN

MUSICALS are just one of the many products that have been imported since China instituted its 'open and reform' policy in December 1978 and have appeared on Chinese stages for about three decades. During this period, many Chinese theatre professionals have tried various means to cultivate and promote the creation and production of this genre of performing art that is new to China. Currently, musicals in China mainly fall into three types: Western musicals with their own casts in the original languages, Chinese-language versions of Western musicals performed by local casts and original Chinese musicals.[1] It is estimated that in the year 2018 alone, there were about eleven Western musicals, including *Cats* [猫 4th ed.], *Romeo and Juliet* [罗密欧与朱丽叶 4th ed.], *Kinky Boots* [长靴皇后4th ed.], *Chicago* [芝加哥4th ed.], *Gone with the Wind* [飘4th ed.], and *Les Miserables* [悲惨世界4th ed.]; twelve Chinese-language replicas of Western musicals, including *The Lion King* [狮子王4th ed.], *Mamma Mia!* [妈妈咪呀4th ed.], *Cinderella* [灰姑娘4th ed.], and *The Sound of Music* [音乐之声4th ed.]; and more than fifteen original Chinese musicals that premièred that year, including *Journey under the Midnight Sun* [白夜行4th ed.], *Love of the White Snake* [白蛇传4th ed.], and *The Rainbow of Time* [时光电影院4th ed.]. Of these three types, the first two are far more successful than the last in terms of box office. Generally speaking, the size of the musical theatre audience in China is still small, and the current situation of musical development in China is far from satisfactory. Most original Chinese musicals run for a relatively short time, and there has not been a sustainable and profitable mode of musical productions in China so far. In the following chapter, the author will chiefly consider the spread and influence of Western musicals in China, the problems facing the development of original Chinese musicals, and the education of professionals in musical theatre departments in academies and universities in China.

FIG. 21.1 K-pop star Bada as Scarlett O'Hara in the musical version of *Gone with the Wind*, one of eleven Western musicals imported to China in 2018 in their original language and with their original cast. Photo: Yonhap/Newcom © Alamy Stock Photo.

## THE WESTERN MUSICAL IN CHINA SINCE THE 1980S

In the 1980s many Chinese intellectuals were able to travel abroad, where they were exposed to Western trends in art and culture. They brought home with them new ideas and practices, including musical theatre. It was thus that China got a look at its first Western musical: *The Music Man*; it premièred at the Beijing Tiaoqiao Performing Arts Centre on 9 August 1987. The audience was entranced by this new theatrical performance, and the production team was excited and hopeful about the musical's prospects in China. Lou Naiming, who participated in the show's Chinese production, recalled his theatre-going days in the United States in the late 1980s, when during a brief span he managed to watch more than fifty plays, among them more than twenty musicals.[2] The prosperity of the Broadway musical scene provided a great incentive for Chinese theatre professionals.

The performance of *The Music Man* [乐器推销员 4th ed.] was followed by *The Fantasticks* [异想天开 4th ed.], which made its début at the National Palace Theatre in Beijing the next day. These two musicals were brought to China as part of a cultural exchange program coordinated by the China Theatre Association, the China National

Opera House, and the Eugene O'Neill Theater Center in Waterford, Connecticut. In order to provide the Chinese audience with a better understanding and appreciation of these two musicals, the dialogue was translated into Chinese, and both musicals were performed by Chinese actors and actresses from the China National Opera, a state-run opera company based in Beijing that was operated by the Chinese Ministry of Culture. These two musicals were co-directed by Chinese and American directors, headed by George White, back then the artistic director of the Eugene O'Neill Theater Center. After its première in Beijing, *The Fantasticks* managed to tour to Jiangsu and Zhejiang provinces—probably the first musical tour of its kind in China. These two works thus became a milestone and marked the beginning of a wave of adaptations of Western musicals in the country.

During the 1980s and 1990s Western musicals were mainly adapted into Chinese and performed in Mandarin by Chinese actors and actresses. In the new millennium, co-operation between China and Western countries in the field of artistic creation intensified, and the Chinese theatre market offered greater potential to the outside world. From then on Chinese audiences were able to enjoy live performances of Western musicals in China.

On 22 June 2002 the original production of *Les Misérables* made its Chinese première at the Shanghai Grand Theatre. It was an icebreaker and ushered in the second wave of Western musicals in China. For the first time in history, the Chinese audience was able to enjoy a Western musical with its original cast without having to travel abroad. The mastermind behind this grand project was Qian Shijin, at the time the artistic director of the Shanghai Grand Theatre. In 1988 Qian saw his first Broadway show: the West End musical *Les Misérables*; he was so impressed that he made up his mind to import the show to China and worked for more than a decade on bringing his plan to fruition. In order to keep the performance as faithful as possible to its original production in the West End, all props—more than ninety tons' worth—were flown to Shanghai before the show. The performance of *Les Misérables* was an iconic moment, providing an eye-opener for Shanghai audiences. By its fourth performance, all forty thousand tickets had been sold, and for its last performance the theatre even sold fifty-two standing-room-only tickets, an unprecedented phenomenon.[3] *Les Misérables* was indeed a landmark in the performing history of Western musicals in China. To this day it is one of the most sought-after Western musicals in the country. Productions of other Western musicals followed, flooding into China.

In 2003 *Cats* made its Chinese première at the same theatre in Shanghai, followed by *The Sound of Music* in 2004, *The Phantom of the Opera* [歌剧魅影4th ed.] in 2005, *The Lion King* in 2006, *Mamma Mia!* in 2007, *Hairspray* [发胶星梦4th ed.] in 2008, and *High School Musical on Stage* [歌舞青春4th ed.] in 2009. These shows were performed in English with Chinese subtitles, enabling the audiences to keep up with the happenings on the stage and be more engaged. Most of these musicals had comparatively long runs. *Cats* ran for fifty-three performances and *The Sound of Music* for thirty-five, while *Phantom* had a hundred performances in three months. *The Phantom of the Opera* set numerous records in the history of theatrical performance in China. According to a news report on the Shanghai government website, it is estimated that more than 170,000 people watched the show that year.[4] Given this enthusiastic response, the Shanghai Grand Theatre vowed to bring in at least one Western musical a year for Chinese audiences, which they did. Its vision encompassed not just Broadway and West End musicals, but musicals from around the world. For example, on 22 January 2003 it brought in the French musical production *Notre Dame de Paris* [钟楼怪人 4th ed.].

Cameron Mackintosh, the famous British producer, also had a vision of the development of Western musicals in China. In 2007 Mackintosh set up a joint venture with China's biggest performing arts agency, China Arts and Entertainment Group (CAEG), which is affiliated with the Ministry of Culture, to bring more classic Western musicals to China. Mackintosh believed that he would bring about a revolution in China by introducing the Chinese versions of his most successful musicals.

This is the context in which *42nd Street* [第42街 4th ed.] was brought to China. It had its Chinese première in Beijing on 13 November 2007 and had eight performances at the Beijing Exhibition Centre Theatre. It later toured to five other cities in China: Shanghai, Hangzhou, Nanjing, Ningbo, and Hefei. One innovation made by *42nd Street* in China was to incorporate certain local elements into each performance. For example, when performed in Nanjing, a performer cleverly used a song called 'Jasmine Flower' in one of her numbers. This song originated from Nanjing in Jiangsu province and is probably the most famous folk song in China. The audience immediately sang along, and thus an emotional connection was made between performers and the theatre-goers. So successful was *42nd Street* that it started a craze in China for tap dance. Another sensational success was the Chinese version of *Mamma Mia!*, which premièred at the Shanghai Grand Theatre on 11 July 2011 and closed on 18 January 2012 at the Shanghai Cultural Square. It was estimated to have been seen by 250,000 people in a total of 190 performances.[5] On 27 July 2019 the Chinese-language version of *Mamma Mia!* played its five hundredth performance at the Shanghai Grand Theatre.

One of the problems for Western musicals in China, both musicals in their original languages and the Chinese versions, is the limited audience. Chinese audiences are dealing with not just a language barrier but also with the incomprehensibility of subject matter heavily loaded with foreign cultural and social implications. Western musicals will always play an important role in the development of the Chinese musical theatre industry; however, there is a huge gap in the Chinese market when it comes to original Chinese musicals.

The introduction of Western musicals in China has been inspirational since the 1980s; it has largely stimulated and influenced the creation and production of original Chinese musicals. Through cooperation with experienced professionals from the West, Chinese professionals are able to learn the ropes of musical theatre production and have recently grown more familiar with the process of originating musicals. Meanwhile, Chinese theatre practitioners have started to crave the creation of Chinese musicals that tell the stories or depict the lives of local Chinese people, stories that are culturally and emotionally closer to the Chinese audience.

# The Gestation of Original Chinese Musicals

Before the live performance of *The Music Man* and *The Fantasticks*, Chinese theatre professionals had already started to create Chinese musicals by imitating Western musicals. The first original Chinese musical was called *We Young People Nowadays* [我们现在的年轻人 4th ed.]. Written by Sheng Heyu, Wang Dangping, and Liu Zhengqiu, it was performed in 1982 through a collaboration between the China National Opera House in Beijing and the Xiang Tan Opera House in Hunan province. The early 1980s was a vibrant time in China. After a long period of isolation, the country ended the ten-year Cultural Revolution, opened its doors to the outside world, and entered into a phase of reformation. Culturally speaking, owing to a publishing boom that occurred at the time, a large body of modern Western philosophy and literature was translated into Chinese and published, which greatly influenced art and literature in China. Economically speaking, individuals or groups were allowed to manage enterprises through contracts, and private enterprises were allowed to coexist with state-owned enterprises in the market. With the goal of improving production efficiency, urban industries began to undergo reforms.

This is the context in which the narrative of *We Young People Nowadays* takes place. Problems are beginning to arise in factories that are coping with societal changes in the new China. Faced with technological evolution, two generations of workers find themselves on opposing sides, which constitutes the major dramatic conflict of the musical. At the time it was popular among young people, because they found trendy elements on-stage, such as disco and jeans. Also, the style of music was a fusion of Chinese folk music with Western pop music.[6] As the first attempt at making an original Chinese musical, it was not a bad beginning. The creators tried to capture the zeitgeist of the 1980s— a spirit of curiosity, hard work, and resilience in the face of challenges.

Another influential original musical of the time was *Heart of Scent* [芳草心 4th ed.], written by Xiang Tong, He Zhaohua, Wang Zujie, and Zhang Zhuoya. It was adapted from a 1982 Chinese play called *True Feeling and False Intention* [真情与假意 4th ed.]. *Heart of Scent* was first performed in 1983 in Nanjing. The musical follows the plot of the play, the story of which can be traced back to the local Chinese traditional Suzhou pingtan opera. The musical depicts the twisted relationship between a young man and a pair of identical twin sisters, one of whom is gentle and kind, while the other is selfish and cold-hearted. The musical was created in only four months, the music alone taking about two months. There were altogether twenty-one songs and ten pieces of underscored theme music, some of which became big hits after the performance. For example, the song 'Little Grass' was probably one of the most popular songs in China in the 1980s. This musical was critically acclaimed for various reasons: much praise went to its music because it incorporated many elements of local Chinese folk music.

FIG. 21.2 Rodgers & Hammerstein's *The Sound of Music* is also popular in China where it was staged several times (1998, 2004 and 2018). Image from the first Chinese language production, starring Cheng Fangyuan (成方圆) as Maria; it opened on January 17, 1998, at the Beijing Poly Theatre. Photo: Li Yan, courtesy of the photographer.

Premièring in 1985, *An Accident of Love* [搭错车 4th ed.] was the most successful original Chinese musical of the 1980s. It was produced by the Shenyang Opera Troupe, written by Chen Yuhang, and directed by Wang Yansong. It ran for 1,025 performances and toured to seventeen provinces, covering eighty-six cities in China in about ten years—a record for performances of musicals.[7] *An Accident of Love* was adapted from a 1983 Taiwanese movie called *Papa, Can You Hear Me Sing?*, which tells the story of an orphan girl named Mei and her mute foster father, a bottle recycler, showing how the family copes when Mei achieves great personal success as a singer. Since its première, *An Accident of Love* has been one of the most often revived musicals in the country. Although it was often criticised for its poor structure and slow pace in the first half, what it lacked in structure was compensated for by its popular musical numbers.

Many other Chinese musicals were created after that, though few were as influential as the ones I have discussed. According to Zhou Yingchen, about forty Chinese musicals were created in the 1980s and 1990s.[8] It was a time when most Chinese theatre professionals were still exploring and experimenting with the form and content of musical theatre. One thing that they realised after a series of musical productions was that Chinese audiences reacted more enthusiastically to local content—to stories, people, and events that they know about—which led theatre professionals to address subjects that were familiar to the audience. At that time in China, most theatre-goers were either theatre professionals or intellectuals. However, turning to Chinese classics and traditional culture for inspiration was a new creative trend. Between 2005 and 2015 about sixty original Chinese musicals were adapted from traditional Chinese stories or classic movies featuring historical or fictional figures that are well-known among the Chinese.

For example, the musical *Visitors on the Icy Mountain[冰山上的来客 4th ed.]* was adapted from the 1963 Chinese film of the same name; it featured the stories of People's Liberation Army soldiers and their work in the 1950s in China's vast northwest. Written by Yi Ming and Lei and produced by Xinjiang Opera Theatre in 2005, it appealed to the memories of an older audience. The musical *Zhou Xuan [周璇 4th ed.]*, which also premièred in 2005, is based on the story of the iconic Shanghai singer and film superstar Zhou Xuan, presenting her life story from the 1920s till her death in 1957 and including many of her songs that are still popular today. Another musical, whose main character is a prestigious Chinese singer, was the 2011 production *Falling in Love with Teresa Teng [爱上邓丽君 4th ed.]*. It centered upon the famous singer Teresa Teng and her mother, depicting the love stories of two generations of women during a turbulent time in Chinese history.

*Raise the Red Lantern[大红灯笼高高挂 4th ed.]*, which premiered in 2013, took its name from the Chinese film director Zhang Yimou's 1991 award-winning film of the same title, which examined the conflicted lives and tragic fates of the wives in a large feudal family. Both were based on the book *Raise the Red Lantern* by the Chinese writer Su Tong, which was translated and published in English in 1993. Its Chinese title, *Qi Qie Cheng Qun [妻妾成群 4th ed.]*, literally means 'Wives and Concubines'. The musical *Raise the Red Lantern* was written by Peng Feng, composed by Lao Zai, choreographed by Jiang Jinjin, and directed by Zhou Yingchen. The choreography of the musical showcased the combination of traditional Chinese folk dance and contemporary dance. For example, the show employed water sleeves—the long white silk sleeves attached to the cuffs of the traditional costumes worn by the female characters in Chinese opera. Obviously the creators were attempting to combine tradition and modernity. Though there were some highlights in the performance, it was not well received. The narrative structure was fragmented, so at the beginning of each scene a plot summary of it would appear on a screen so that the audience could keep up with the action on the stage. The story was loosely constructed, consisting of pieces that highlighted the dancing and singing.

Also directed by Zhou Yingchen, the musical *Cao Xueqin [曹雪芹 4th ed.]* was performed for the first time in 2013. Written by Kuang Da and composed by Zhou Xueshi, the show was created to commemorate the 250th anniversary of the death of the great Chinese writer Cao Xueqin. Its main character, Cao Xueqin, is the author of *A Dream of Red Mansions [红楼梦 4th ed.]*, which belongs to China's canonic Four Great Masterpieces.[9] The musical was named after this great and mysterious author, who has the largest reader base in China. In *Cao Xueqin* the show's creators incorporated elements from classic Chinese opera, such as traditional costumes and folk music. Though the lighting, stage design, and costumes were nicely presented, the show was criticised for its poor narrative techniques and story structure.

Another musical that was based on a well-known literary classic, this one by the Chinese writer Eileen Chang, is *Half a Lifelong Romance [半生缘 4th ed.]*. The musical, which centres upon the destiny of two doomed lovers, Shen Shijun and Gu Manzhen, premièred in January 2005 at the National Theatre of China. *Half a Lifelong Romance* is one of the most adapted classics in China. Before the musical, it had already been turned into a film titled *Eighteen Springs* by the award-winning Hong Kong director Ann Hui in 1997. In 2002 and 2017 it was made into a TV series.

# The Problems with Original Chinese Musicals and the Steps Taken to Overcome Them

These Chinese musicals drew a certain degree of attention from critics and the audience, not least because of problems with their construction. The structure of these musicals still followed that of playwriting. Wei Ming, one of the early researchers and practitioners of Chinese musicals, commented that the script of *Heart of Scent* read like 'a play with songs.'[10] In other words, the songs and the story lacked an internal dramaturgical connection.

Take *An Accident of Love*, for example. Many critics believed that the success of the musical was due in great measure to the popularity of the original soundtrack of the Taiwanese movie on which it was based,[11] since the film was an award-winning hit. Prior to the creation of the musical, the songs featured in the film had already been extremely popular in China for more than a decade. This jukebox musical was a nostalgic memory for most people—as it was a collage of various popular songs and elements that the audience members were familiar with.

The same can be said about *Half a Lifelong Romance*. In this musical, the female protagonist was played by Rene Liu, a Taiwanese pop singer who had a successful career in mainland China. Not long before the musical premièred, the star had completed a successful concert tour in China. It is interesting to note that during its promotion, one of its selling points was that in the musical the audience would be able to hear four brand-new songs that weren't included in any of the singer's previous albums and that these songs would be performed for the first time in the musical. In fact, this mode of promotion worked well. When tickets for *Half a Lifelong Romance* went on sale, the lower-priced ones were immediately sold out, which was unusual for original Chinese productions. The production of Chinese musicals has long followed this pattern, which relies on the popularity of certain works and pop stars because they provide a safety net for musical creators. But this has greatly compromised the healthy development and maturity of the Chinese musical. Though Western musical writers and producers experience more or less the same commercial pressures these days, they are able to rely on a fully developed, mature musical creation system and audience; these elements have yet to be cultivated in China. Compared with their Western counterparts, Chinese musical creators are still finding their way.

Though a large number of Chinese musicals were produced in the first two decades since the introduction of the genre to China, the number has been decreasing since the start of the new millennium. In the 2002 only four original musicals were produced; in 2003 that number was only three, and 2004 saw the premières of just four original Chinese musicals. In both 2007 and 2009 only two new musicals premièred. The number would be even less if it were not for the fact that some of these musicals were commissioned by the central or local government for specific occasions. The decline in the number of original musicals produced during this period may be attributed to three main factors. First, more Western musicals were brought to China during that time; secondly, the number of Chinese versions of Western musicals also increased; and thirdly, the ability to write and produce original musicals was lagging because of the industry's failure to recognise that specialised training in musicals was needed for it to become a viable art form in China.

Meanwhile, the authors and producers of Chinese musicals realised that they should try to cultivate bigger Chinese audiences by improving their techniques and methods of creation. Evidence shows that localisation is one of the keys to attracting a larger audience. Instead of offering a mere imitation of the form and content of Western musicals, Chinese professionals started to cultivate forms and techniques derived from traditional Chinese dance, music, opera, and so on. In terms of their subject matter, they started to embrace the changes and problems of the first decade of the twenty-first century, when the country was put on a fast track toward technological and economic development.

One of the most successful examples of an original Chinese musical that went through the process of localisation was *The Piano in the Factory* [钢的琴 4th ed.], which premièred on 24 October 2012 at the Dongguan Yulan Theatre in the province of Guangdong. The musical was written by the Chinese composer San Bao and the playwright Guan Shan and addressed what was at the time a heated topic: laid-off workers. It was produced soon after the award-winning film, written by the same author, released in 2011. Chen Guilin is a laid-off worker in a state-owned steel factory; now he is barely making ends meet performing in a small band in the same factory. His wife, Xiaoju, runs off with a wealthy businessman and wants not only a divorce but also custody of their daughter. The girl loves her father, but she also loves playing the piano. She tells him that she would prefer to stay with him if he can give her a piano. Of course, Chen cannot afford such an instrument, but he doesn't want to lose his daughter. In the end, he and his co-workers collect scrap metal from the factory and built a piano from scratch out of steel. In the finale, his daughter sits at the 'steel piano', which has a steel exterior but has been remodelled from an actual grand piano with a real keyboard, and plays for her father and all the other workers who helped make her dream a reality.

The musical was warmly received on its première and went on to celebrate more than six hundred performances. The musical is set in the eastern part of China, which was greatly influenced by Russian culture in the 1950s, so the composer cleverly incorporates popular Russian songs that Chinese audiences were familiar with, while also including

FIG. 21.3  Fig 3 Scene from the 2014 production of *Falling in Love with Teresa Teng*. The eponymous character was played by Wang Jing. Photo: Li Yan, courtesy of the photographer.

a great deal of local folk music. In addition, its subject matter was quite pertinent for the audience. For the first time a theatre audience was able to examine the challenging living conditions of factory workers and their limited financial means of solving family problems. The show offered a realistic presentation of the state-owned factories in the eastern provincial cities of China, which provoked a sense of nostalgia among a large number of spectators. Thanks to its successful localisation, *The Piano in the Factory* was able to present an identifiable local milieu and audience-appropriate cultural markers.

Localisation provides a possible solution for the Chinese musical to find a way out of its current predicament. Chinese theatre professionals are now more willing to look into existing Chinese art forms and cultural heritage for inspiration. In one of his visits to China in the 1990s, Keita Asari, the founder of Shiki Theatre Company, commented after watching a performance of the Chinese traditional opera *The White-Haired Girl* [白毛女 4th ed.] that China had always had a great tradition of musical performance. This was one of the many operas created during the 1940s depicting the hard lives of Chinese peasants before the foundation of the People's Republic of China.[12] According to Asari, it would be of great value for the development of the Chinese musical if theatre professionals could find a way to incorporate traditional Chinese opera into the creation of contemporary musicals.

In fact, Chinese audiences have long been familiar with traditional Chinese opera, which achieves its desired theatrical effects by combining singing, dancing, and acting, much like Western musicals. Currently there are more than three hundred kinds of local operas nationwide; some can be traced back a thousand years. For a long time it was the most popular form of entertainment in the country. However, on the traditional Chinese stage, every move, every gesture, and every melody must adhere strictly to set formulas, and the genre tolerates few changes. The subject matters it treats have also become old-fashioned in the eyes of contemporary audiences. As a result, in recent years Chinese traditional opera has lost its grip on China's younger generations. Unable to make a living from the take at the box office, many traditional opera companies are reduced to depending financially on either central or local governments. Western musicals, on the other hand, are full of life and are constantly renewing themselves in performance. They are thus more attractive to the younger generation and have a better market potential in China.

The localisation of the Chinese musical would inevitably involve the deployment of certain elements from traditional Chinese opera, local folk music, dance, costumes, and the like. After all, traditional Chinese opera has been on Chinese stages for more than a thousand years and can attract audiences even in the most remote parts of the country. The musical, however, was introduced to China a comparatively short while ago and has made its mark only in the cosmopolitan environment of large cities. The success of Chinese opera throughout the entire country suggests that it will be possible to cultivate a large audience base in China for musical theatre. It is to be hoped that Chinese writers and producers will be able to deploy the narrative techniques used by their Western counterparts and improve their ability to tell good stories based on local content and inspiration.

# Musical Education in China

Looking back, the 1980s and 1990s were not only an important time for the introduction and development of musicals in China, they were also an essential period of musical education in China. In May 1988 the National Musical Seminar, the first of its kind, was held in Shanghai. Theatre professionals, theorists, and practitioners from all over the country gathered to talk about their understanding of musical theatre and the creation of musicals. They were eager to put this new genre of theatrical art into clearer perspective after almost a decade of exploration and practice and aimed at clarifying the definition of the musical and identifying its differences from Western opera and traditional Chinese opera. This seminar marked the acceptance of the musical as a subject of study in the academic world.

It was during these two decades that musical theatre as a field of study began at a number of colleges and universities in China. The Central Academy of Drama was among the forerunners in the introduction of musical theatre education in China. Early in 1992 the Central Academy set up its musical theatre group, consisting of teachers from the Acting Department and the Directing Department. Since then courses on music theory and the practice of music have been included in the curriculum of the Acting Department. Students started to learn how to perform musical theatre by rehearsing scenes from the Broadway musical *West Side Story* [西区故事 *4 th ed.*]. According to Liu Hongmei, the current director of the Central Academy's Department of Musical Theatre and one of the earliest members of the musical theatre group, students from the university rehearsed ten scenes from the 1957 classic. Both students and teachers were passionate about the learning and teaching of the performance of musicals. In 2012 this small theatre group became the Department of Musical Theatre.

The teaching of musicals in colleges involved detailed study of Western musicals. At this time in China, the main method of teaching music was through imitation, as it had once been in many Western universities and conservatories. As early as the summer of 1988, students in the Acting Department of the Shanghai Theatre Academy rehearsed and performed the Chinese-language version of *My Fair Lady* [窈窕淑女 *4 th ed*] as their graduation showcase. This caused a great sensation. Although the Shanghai Theatre Academy did not establish a musical theatre department, it set up a musical center within the Acting Department in 2005. It is worth mentioning that Wang Luoyong, a 1985 alumni of the Shanghai Theatre Academy who later studied in the Department of Drama and Performance at Boston University, became the first Chinese actor to appear as a lead in *Miss Saigon* [西贡小姐 *4 th ed*] on Broadway. In 2001 Wang Luoyong returned to the Shanghai Theatre Academy and started teaching in the Acting Department as a guest professor.

Besides *West Side Story*, in the 1990s students at the Central Academy of Drama also adapted and rehearsed other Broadway musicals, such as *Fame* [名扬四海 *4 th ed*] and *Crazy for You* [为你疯狂 *4 th ed*]. During this time the eagerness and passion for musicals led teachers and students to seek out means to learn about and practice this new theatre genre. In the early 1990s the Central Academy of Drama established a co-operative venture with the Shiki Theatre Company, the most successful musical theatre company in Japan. A few teachers and students were sent abroad to work as practitioners in in Shiki, which has a lot of experience with successfully adapting Western musicals and localising them for Japanese audiences. Keita Asari, the artistic director and founder of the company, was invited to visit the Central Academy more than once in the 1990s to work with its teachers and students.

Colleges and universities in Beijing and Shanghai pioneered the localisation and performance of Western musicals in Mandarin. Mechanistic copies of Western musicals presented a barrier to Chinese audiences. Although these Western musicals had been translated into Chinese, their content and subject matter, themes and dialogue, even some of the dramatic conflicts were emotionally and culturally alien to a Chinese audience. In order to build a closer relationship with the audience, the Broadway musicals performed in China underwent a series of changes. Not only were they translated into Chinese, but their contents, settings, and characters were adapted so that they would strike a sense of familiarity with the audience. Take *Fame*, for example: characters such as Tyrone Jackson and Miss Esther Sherman were changed to Asian ones, and the names of famous stars and athletes that appeared in the original were changed to those of local celebrities. Generally speaking, the process of localisation involved the script, music, character, and dance.

Besides rehearsing Chinese-language versions of Western musicals, musical theatre departments in China also tried to create original musicals. In 2011 the Department of Musical Theatre of the Central Academy of Drama created a musical called *The Family [家 4 th ed]*, which was based on a work by the famous Chinese writer Ba Jin. *The Family* tells the story of a large family in feudal China. Written by Chen Xiaoling, composed by Dai Jingsong, and directed by Liu Hongmei, the musical went through four phases of creation, and its length kept expanding until eventually, by 2016, a fifty-minute performance had grown to a full two-hour stage production. In 2017 this production was made into a film musical, directed by Liu Hongmei and starring the students and teachers from the Central Academy's Department of Musical Theatre. The film was shown in cinemas nationwide in 2018 and the same year was entered in a number of foreign film festivals, including the Miami International Film Festival in the United States and the China-EU Film Festival in Brussels, Belgium.

By 2014 thirteen institutions of higher education in China—the Central Academy of Drama, the Beijing Dance Academy, the Shanghai Theatre Academy, the Nanjing University of Arts, the Communication University of Zhejiang, the Sichuan Normal University, the Shangdong University of Arts, the Shanghai Conservatory of Music, the Wuhan Conservatory of Music, the Shenyang Conservatory of Music, the Xinghai Conservatory of Music, the Tianjin Conservatory of Music, and the Sichuan Conservatory of Music—had set up musical theatre departments.[13] Of these universities, only a few—for example, the Central Academy of Drama and the Beijing Dance Academy—have set up independent musical theatre departments; most attach the teaching and practice of musical theatre to other departments. It is estimated that there are more than twenty institutions of higher education that teach musical theatre today; however, considering that there are more than two thousand institutions of higher education in China, this is still a small number.

One problem with musical theatre pedagogy in China is that curricula lean too heavily on training in performance—dancing, singing, and acting. Education in writing for musical theatre lags far behind, as does the teaching of musical production. One possible reason for this might be that in China most musical theatre departments are part of either a music or a dance academy. Musical theatre, generally speaking, has been considered a showcase for and an indication of these academies' individual strengths, demonstrating the talent of their students and the polish of their training. Students from musical theatre departments in a dance academy often do better in dancing, while those from a music academy excel in singing, and so on. One of the challenges for musical theatre education is to establish more efficient ways to incorporate the training of all these musical theatre skill sets in colleges and universities throughout China. After all, music departments in colleges and universities in China shoulder the chief responsibility for the cultivation of musical talent in the country.

# CONCLUSION

Besides training musical performers to excel in singing, dancing, and acting, it is crucial to cultivate talented producers and skilled stage managers; up to now these have been the weak links of the Chinese theatre industry. Musical theatre education as well as modern theatre education in general is just beginning in China, and the industry has yet to acquire efficient production methods and pedagogical approaches to the cultivation of skilled professionals. Increased co-operation with experienced Western musical theatre professionals will hopefully help accelerate the future development of Chinese musicals. In the recent past China has witnessed rapid growth in its entertainment industry. With higher incomes, Chinese people are more willing to spend money in cinemas and theatres. According to data released by the China Film Administration, in 2018 the total box-office returns for Chinese films in China surpassed sixty billion Chinese yuan.[14] There is reason for optimistic expectations of a similar increase in the pace of the theatre industry's growth. At the moment, an extremely large group of theatre-goers is being cultivated, drawn chiefly from college and university students nationwide.

Xu Xiaozhong, the former president of the Central Academy of Drama, who has been promoting musical education for years, believes that the development of musical theatre in China still 'limps along'.[15] The problems that Chinese musical professionals are dealing with are complicated and unprecedented, especially within a context of the competing forces of globalisation and localisation. Compared with the highly developed musical industry on Broadway and in the West End, the musical industry in China has yet to assume a distinctive shape. Lacking a common understanding of what a 'good' Chinese musical might be, the quality of musical productions in China is not all it should be: the musical has not yet developed a suitable cultural model. It is crucial that the Chinese musical forge its own unique artistic identity. So far, there have been no appropriate standards or criteria to evaluate Chinese musicals or establish their goals.

More than thirty years have passed since the introduction of the musical in China, yet for most theatre professionals the definition of what constitutes a Chinese musical remains vague: they are still exploring its possibilities and boundaries as a genre. Moving between various forms and subjects, most Chinese practitioners are currently restricted to moulding and remoulding the musicals in their heads. Platforms for communication and exchanges of musical experience and practice have yet to be constructed in the country. It has always been held that China has the largest market potential for musicals in the world; however, at the moment this potential is more a fantasy than a reality for theatre professionals. So far no awards have been established that recognise excellence in musical theatre in China. The time has now surely arrived for Chinese practitioners of the musical to establish certain guidelines and to join their efforts towards the development of a musical theatre industry in the country in order to create more Chinese musicals with appealing stories and qualities that are entertaining in the context of Chinese culture.

## NOTES

1. Chen Gan陈刚, '中国音乐剧产业为何难见春光', in *The Study of Education and Creation for Chinese Musicals*, ed. Liao Xianghong 廖向红 and Zhang Yin张殷, 4th ed. (Beijing: Culture Art Publishing House, 2013), 34.
2. Wei Ming, *Essays on China's Opera and Musicals* (Beijing: China Federation of Literary and Art Circles Press, 2010), 233–240
3. Documentary clip of *Les Misérables* in Shanghai, 2002, https://www.youtube.com/watch?v=Yv6pzXfZ1mw, accessed 20 January 2020.
4. http://www.shanghai.gov.cn/nw2/nw2314/nw2315/nw5827/u21aw102165.html, accessed 20 January 2020.
5. http://ent.sina.com.cn/j/2012-01-20/19093539580.html, accessed 20 January 2020.
6. Ma Haixing马海星, '看歌剧现在的年轻人', *People's Music*人民音乐9 (1982): 23–24.
7. Fu Lei 付磊, 中国音乐剧发展历程与现状研究 (Chengdu: Sichuan University Press, 2017), 75.
8. Zhou Yingchen 周映辰. 全球化时代的中国音乐剧 (Beijing: Peking University Press, 2016), 36.
9. The 'Four Great Masterpieces' include the classic Chinese works *Three Kingdoms* (written by Luo Guanzhong); *Water Margin: Outlaws of the Marsh* (Shi Naiyu), *Journey to the West* (Wu Chengen), and *A Dream of Red Mansions* (Cao Xueqin).
10. Ming, *Essays on China's Opera and Musicals*, 246.
11. Yingchen, 36.
12. Ming, *Essays on China's Opera and Musicals*, 262.
13. Yingchen, 54.
14. http://www.xinhuanet.com/2018-12/31/c_1123931741.htm,, accessed 20 January 2020.
15. Xu Xiaozhong徐晓钟, '音乐剧的一次近距离的赏析和建构文化产业格局的一次勇敢的尝试', in *The Study of Education and Creation for Chinese Musicals*, ed. Liao Xianghong 廖向红 and Zhang Yin张殷, 4th ed. (Beijing: Culture Art Publishing House, 2013), 15.

## APPENDIXES

I. Chinese Musicals and Their English Translations

《我们现在的年轻人》 *We Young People Nowadays*

《芳草心》 *Heart of Scent*

《真情与假意》 *True Feeling and False Intention*

《搭错车》 *An Accident of Love*

《冰山上的来客》 *Visitors on the Icy Mountain*

《周璇》 *Zhou Xuan*

《爱上邓丽君》 *Falling in Love with Teresa Teng*

《大红灯笼高高挂》 *Raise the Red Lanterns*

《曹雪芹》 *Cao Xueqin*

《半生缘》 *Half a Lifelong Romance*

《钢的琴》 *The Piano in the Factory*

《白毛女》 *The White-Haired Girl*

《家》 *The Family*

《白夜行》 *Journey under the Midnight Sun*

《白蛇惊变》 *Love of the White Snake*

《时光电影院》 *The Rainbow of Time*

《妻妾成群》 *Qi Qie Cheng Qun*

II. Names of Colleges and Universities in Chinese and English

中央戏剧学院 Central Academy of Drama

上海戏剧学院 Shanghai Theatre Academy

北京舞蹈学院 Beijing Dance Academy

上海音乐学院 Shanghai Conservatory of Music

南京艺术学院 Nanjing University of Arts

武汉音乐学院演艺学院 Wuhan Conservatory of Music

沈阳音乐学院 Shenyang Conservatory of Music

星海音乐学院 Xinghai Conservatory of Music

天津音乐学院 Tianjin Conservatory of Music

四川音乐学院 Sichuan Conservatory of Music

浙江传媒学院 Communication University of Zhejiang

四川师范大学 Sichuan Normal University

山东艺术学院 Shangdong University of Arts

III. Chinese Theatres and Their English Translations

中央歌剧院 China National Opera House

上海大剧院 Shanghai Grand Theatre

上海歌剧院 Shanghai Opera House

国家话剧院 National Theatre of China

中国歌剧舞剧院 Chinese Opera and Dance Theatre

新疆歌剧院 Xinjiang Opera Theatre

北京天桥剧院 Beijing Tiaoqiao Performing Arts Center

广东东莞玉兰大剧院 Dongguan Yulan Theatre

## Bibliography

Lei, Fu 付磊. 中国音乐剧发展历程与现状研究. Chengdu: Sichuan University Press.

Liao Xianghong 廖向红, 2017.

Ming, Wei. *Essays on China's Opera and Musicals*. Beijing: China Federation of Literary and Art Circles Press, 2010.

Shuo, Wen. *The Modern History of Musicals in China*. Vol. 2. Beijing: Xiyuan Publishing House, 2012.

Yin, Zhang 张殷, ed. *The Study of Education and Creation for Chinese Musicals Fourth*. Beijing: Culture Art Publishing House, 2013.

Yingchen, Zhou 周映辰. 全球化时代的中国音乐剧. Beijing: Peking University Press, 2016.

# PART VIII

## SONDHEIM ABROAD

CHAPTER 22

# *A LITTLE NIGHT MUSIC* IN SWEDEN

### RENATE STRIDH

## Preamble: Stephen Sondheim in Sweden

ALL foreign musicals produced in Sweden are translated and performed in Swedish, and the musicals of Stephen Sondheim are no exception[1]. However, his musicals are not produced very frequently in Sweden. His works are loved and respected by musical theatre aficionados, but they are not enough of an audience magnet to warrant staging them at the larger commercial venues, such as Cirkus, Oscarsteatern[2], Chinateatern, and Göta Lejon in Stockholm. If Sondheim musicals are scheduled at all, it is by subsidised theatres.

Although several of his shows—like *Follies*, *Pacific Overtures*, *Merrily We Roll Along*, and *Sunday in the Park with George*—are still awaiting their Swedish premières, some of the artist's most celebrated works have been seen in Sweden only once or twice; they include *A Funny Thing Happened on the Way to the Forum* (Ideonteatern, Stockholm, 1965; and Östgötateatern, 2001), *Company* (Stora Teatern, 1971), *Assassins* (Södra Teatern, Stockholm, 2013), and *Passion* (a co-production of Smålands Musik och Teater, Jönköping, 2016; and Norrlandsoperan, Umeå, 2017). *Into the Woods* has been performed five times,[3] and *Sweeney Todd, the Demon Barber of Fleet Street* has had at least six productions.[4] Not surprisingly, the one show that has fared slightly better is *A Little Night Music*, with its strong connection to Swedish culture.

The situation is a little different in musical theatre colleges and other schools that train future musical theatre actors,[5] where the works of Sondheim—especially such pieces as *Company*, *Into the Woods*, *A Little Night Music*, *Sweeney Todd*, and *Assassins*—are often studied and performed. On rare occasions, staff and students also turn to *A Funny Thing*, *Merrily We Roll Along*, or *Sunday in the Park with George*.

# Introduction: *A Little Night Music* Comes 'Home'

No other Swedish film director is as famous around the world as Ingmar Bergman: three of his movies won the Oscar for Best Foreign Language Film (*The Virgin Spring*, 1960; *Through a Glass Darkly*, 1961; and *Fanny and Alexander*, 1983), and his oeuvre has influenced filmmakers from various generations and parts of the world. However, his reputation as an auteur who doesn't shy away from the darkest of subjects often overshadows the fact that he was in addition a brilliant writer and director of comedy, as is attested by his 1955 masterwork *Smiles of a Summer Night*.

When this bittersweet romantic roundelay was adapted in the early 1970s by Stephen Sondheim, Harold Prince, and the librettist Hugh Wheeler, the musical version, *A Little Night Music*, not only won five Tony Awards and gave the composer-lyricist his biggest hit in the wistful ballad 'Send in the Clowns', but it also 'made a comfortable profit for its backers. It was cited as an example of the way in which art and commercialism could co-exist on Broadway.'[6]

This chapter will gauge the musical's reception when it was performed in the country in which it takes place: were the Sweden and the Swedes depicted in the musical recognisable, or did the critics feel something was lost in the cultural translation? And how has the understanding of and attitude towards Stephen Sondheim's work in particular and musical theatre in general changed in Sweden since 1973?

# The Source Material: *Sommarnattens leende* (1955)

Both Ingmar Bergman and Stephen Sondheim are nowadays considered innovators and giants in their respective artistic fields, but in the middle of the 1950s Bergman films such as *Gycklarnas afton* (*Sawdust and Tinsel*, 1953) and *Kvinnodröm* (*Dreams*, 1955), both produced by Sandrews Studio, had been financial or artistic failures. Carl Anders Dymling, the boss at the big film studio Svensk Filmindustri, who had employed the young Bergman as a screenwriter in 1943, reluctantly welcomed him back to the studio, as the director later remembered:

> When it came to *Sommarnattens leende* [*Smiles of a Summer Night*], it was about me needing to have a hit again. Then *Kvinnodröm* had gone to hell and I was to reunite with Svensk Filmindustri. It was one of the darkest times of my life. I was directing in Malmö since a couple of years and the Harriet era was over,[7] and I had promised Carl Anders Dymling that the next film would not be a tragedy. He had implied that if it

ended up being a serious piece, there would hardly be any point in my hoping for a film this summer. I needed money, so I thought it wisest to do a comedy.[8]

Bergman had had a few years of artistic triumphs at Malmö Stadsteater, where he had the freedom to direct whatever he wanted. In 1954 he directed Franz Lehár's *The Merry Widow*, which inspired him to write a light sex comedy. In his notebook he described his plans for the new film:

> The men are potent and the women are particularly willing! Love is not a heavy duty or a little unpleasantness to be done with as fast as possible two times a week. Love is a pleasure a pastime a serious activity that requires fantasy and inventiveness. (I decided today that this film is going to be a play a comedy first, and that I will make a hell of a lot of money off it.)[9]

*Sommarnattens leende* opened in Swedish cinemas in December 1955. The film had been expensive to make and would need a Swedish audience of at least 1.3 million to break even.[10] It did indeed turn out to be the commercial success the studio wanted.[11] The comedy was for the most part well received, but it also triggered a few harsh reactions from the cultural establishment. The film critic Hanserik Hjertén even accused Bergman of making pornography.[12] When Bergman got an award for best Swedish film of 1955, he was criticised by the author Olof Lagercrantz: 'A pimply youth's poor fantasy, an immature heart's dirty dreams, a limitless contempt for artistic and human truth are the powers that created this "comedy". I am ashamed to have seen it.'[13] At the 1956 Cannes Film Festival *Smiles of a Summer Night* received the Prix de l'humour poétique,[14] which gave Bergman's international career a major boost. Bergman told Mikael Timm: '*Sommarnattens leende* was the turning point. After that [film] I was totally independent. I have been completely free [ ... ] have been able to do exactly what I have wanted. No-one dared say anything, no-one interfered.'[15]

# SONDHEIM, PRINCE, BERGMAN, AND *A LITTLE NIGHT MUSIC*

The first two collaborations between the composer-lyricist Stephen Sondheim and the director-producer Harold Prince, *Company* and *Follies*, opened on Broadway in 1970 and 1971, respectively. Yet *Follies* lost all the backers' money,[16] so, after failing financially the two artists needed a hit. Prince remembered:

> In 1957, right after *West Side Story* opened, Sondheim and I talked about doing a kind of court masque, a chamber opera: elegant, probably about sex, a gavotte in which couples interchange, suffering mightily in elegant country homes, wearing elegant clothes.[17]

FIG. 22.1 The dinner scene from Ingmar Bergman's 1955 classic film comedy *Sommarnattens leende* (*Smiles of a Summer Night*). *Foreground, left to right*: Margit Carlqvist (Countess Malcolm), Gunnar Björnstrand (Fredrik Egerman), Ulla Jacobsson (Anne Egerman), and Björn Bjelfvenstam (Henrik Egerman). *Background, centre*: Harriet Andersson as the maid, Petra. Production still provided by the editors.

They revived that idea together with the librettist Hugh Wheeler and looked at a few screenplays that seemed to fit their aims before choosing *Smiles of a Summer Night* and contacting Bergman through his lawyer:[18] 'The purpose was to assure [Bergman] that we did not intend a literal translation of his screenplay. It was to be *suggested by*, rather than *adapted from*. Apparently, this appealed to him. [ . . . ]'.[19]

By 1971 Ingmar Bergman had made *The Seventh Seal*, *Wild Strawberries*, *The Virgin Spring*, and *Persona*, all of which augmented his international position as an auteur. He had also continued to direct plays, not only at Malmö Stadsteater, but, since 1961, at the prestigious Royal Dramatic Theatre in Stockholm—classics by Molière, Chekhov, Ibsen, Strindberg, and Büchner, a few of his own works, and plays by such twentieth-century playwrights as Albee, Pirandello, and Weiss.[20]

On 7 December 1971 Sondheim and Prince got the go-ahead from Bergman. Sondheim later recalled: 'He granted us the rights, withholding only the title, a restriction that I welcomed, since I already had a title I wanted to use: *A Little Night Music*'.[21] The show, with music and lyrics by Sondheim and book by Hugh Wheeler, opened on Broadway on 25 February 1973. Meanwhile Bergman was busy working on a screenplay, rewriting *The Merry Widow*, in which he wanted Barbra Streisand to star in the title role. A year after *A Little Night Music* opened, Bergman approached Sondheim and asked him to both write the English lyrics for the project and help Bergman with the English-language script.[22] However, the director abandoned the project altogether later that spring.[23]

# THE LYRIC REPERTOIRE AT STORA TEATERN

*A Little Night Music* had its European première on 11 January 1974 in Gothenburg, Sweden's second-largest city, at Stora Teatern. This theatre was dedicated to the performance of lyric repertoire;[24] it used the term 'musical' (often pronounced the English way) for the first time in the 1960–1961 season, but when it first revived *Show Boat* in 1965,[25] that work was still labelled an 'American operetta'. (More recently the term 'musical' has been replaced by 'musikal', with the spelling and pronunciation now in Swedish.)

When *A Little Night Music* opened at Stora Teatern in 1974, it was thus before an audience that had a great fondness for operetta, but that also had had the opportunity to see a number of foreign (mostly American) musicals: *Kiss Me, Kate* (1962–1963 season), *Show Boat* (1954–1955 and 1964–1965), *Annie Get Your Gun* (1957–1958, 1966–1967, and 1967–1968), *Fiddler on the Roof* (1967–1968, 1968–1969, 1970–1971, and 1971–72), *Cabaret* (1968–1969), *Zorba* (1969–1970), *Celebration* (1970–1971), and *Company* (1971–72). Ola Nilsson, the musical director at Stora Teatern, is said to have been American musical theatre's greatest promoter and enthusiast in the 1960s and the early 1970s.[26] Nilsson regularly travelled to Broadway and saw new productions as early as possible. It was on his initiative that Stora Teatern produced *Company* as early as 1971, opening on 22 September.

The intended number of performances in the main musical repertoire ranged from forty-eight to sixty-two. *Fiddler on the Roof* surpassed that number in its first run, with seventy performances. *Company*, however, received mostly harsh reviews and met with a negative response from the audience, so it was taken out of the repertoire after only sixteen performances and *Fiddler on the Roof* was put back in for a fourth run. In an article which tried to analyse what had caused *Company* to fail, the theatre's artistic director, Folke Abenius, was quoted as having said in the spring before the show's Gothenburg opening: 'We will try to replace the many American musicals with plays that are closer to us.'[27] The reporter agreed with Abenius, and concluded that 'most of what is written in America today is not worth performing', betraying a pronounced hostility towards American and possibly other foreign musicals.

Stora Teatern produced no musicals at all in the 1972–1973 season, and *A Little Night Music* was their only musical during the following season. It seemed a much better choice than *Company*: it was undoubtedly a material 'closer to us', with a far more traditional narrative structure and form of presentation, despite the creative use of the

*Liebeslieder*; in short, it was much closer to what an operetta audience might feel at home with.

After *A Little Night Music*, the number of new American musicals in the repertoire decreased significantly; the main reason for this may have been the sudden death of Nilsson in December 1973, at the age of thirty-eight.

## The First Production of the Show: *A Little Night Music* in Gothenburg, 1974

The first Swedish staging of Sondheim's musical had forty-seven performances, a normal run at Stora Teatern around this time.[28] The translation into Swedish was by the lyricist and entertainment writer Björn Barlach. The production was directed by Herman Ahlsell, who had performed in six plays directed by Bergman at Göteborgs Stadsteater between 1946 and 1950.[29] In 1949 Ahlsell began to focus more and more on directing, working both with plays and musical theatre. Before directing *A Little Night Music*, he had directed Danish, British, Swedish, and German musical theatre, often of the more satirical or political kind. The only American musical on his résumé was *Zorba*, which he directed at Stora Teatern in 1970.[30] *A Little Night Music*'s cast consisted mainly of members of Stora Teatern's lyric ensemble; Gun Andras, who played Desirée, was the only performer marked 'guest' in the cast list of the programme.[31]

FIG. 22.2  The act 1 finale from the 1974 Swedish première of *A Little Night Music* at Stora Teatern in Göteborg. Photo courtesy of Göteborgs Stadsmuseum.

The artistic impetus behind the production and the reception of the show can best be reconstructed from records at the theatre and in local archives, including newspaper articles, reviews, and the theatre programme. In the reporting leading up to opening night, the newspapers all focused on the director Herman Ahlsell's claim that he planned to stay loyal to the Bergman film: 'We entirely aim to do a production that will follow the film and by that I mean that we are using the author's—meaning Bergman's—viewpoints without modifying them in any way or changing them for our own purposes.'[32] To the readers of *Göteborgs-Posten* Ahlsell announced his intention in a similar fashion: 'I have no other ambitions with *Sommarnattens leende* than to do the author, Ingemar [*sic*] Bergman, justice. We play in his spirit without any of the attitudes or twists that are in fashion right now and without adding aspects that don't exist [in the material].'[33]

It is clear from these pronouncements that the production's loyalty was first and foremost to Bergman, not to Sondheim and Wheeler. The director also emphasised that he had not seen the production on Broadway, 'which I know [the directors] have, both in Malmö and Norrköping',[34] where the musical was scheduled to open a few weeks later in January and February 1974 respectively.

The stage manager's copy of the 1974 script reveals that although only minor changes were made to the (translation of the) dialogue, some songs had been shortened or completely cut, for example 'Now/Later/Soon', 'Liaisons', 'In Praise of Women', and 'Every Day a Little Death'.[35] Considering that Storan is a lyric theatre and that therefore its strengths should lie in performing music, it is a surprising discovery.

In another preview article, Nils Andersson delivered a harsh judgement on *A Little Night Music* as performed on Broadway: 'Viewed through Swedish—and quite critical—eyes, it turned out badly, lame, without lift, without excitement.'[36] The reporter predicted that the New York production would not work well in Sweden, but that maybe a tough Swedish overhaul could produce 'a better-tasting brew'.[37]

Andersson's article reveals (yet again) an underlying negative opinion of the commercial American musical among Swedish journalists and in the Swedish theatrical community. The artistic director of the theatre, Folke Abenius, was quoted as saying: 'The reviews [for *A Little Night Music* in New York] were so exceptionally glowing, and suggested a quality [ . . . ] that is unusual in cases like these'.[38] The same article ends: 'But Ingmar Bergman has never seen his film re-made into an Americanised musical.[39] No one knows what he actually thinks about that.' It is the term 'Americanised musical' (instead of just 'American musical') that offers a clue as to the distance some homegrown journalists perceived to lie between Sweden's lyric theatre and America's strictly-for-profit stage.

# REVIEWS FOR THE GOTHENBURG PRODUCTION

The critical response to the first Swedish staging of *A Little Night Music* in seven daily newspapers provides insight into several intriguing aspects of the production.[40] Apart from the general reaction of the reviewers to Sondheim and Wheeler's version of the Bergman film, the articles also reveal that some of their authors responded to the setting of the musical, pondering whether the musical version had captured it convincingly. Critics commented on the change of title, which replaced Bergman's with a reference to a chamber work by Mozart. It would seem it was not commonly known that it was indeed Bergman who had withheld the use of the film's title, or that substantial cuts had been made to the songs.

Alf Thoor's review in *Expressen* began: 'What should the child be named? In the Stora Teatern programme it says: *A Little Night Music*. Directly from the American original. [ ... ] We cannot go around saying that, no matter how much the rights holders in New York would like us to. In Swedish only one name is possible: *Sommarnattens leende*.'[41] The critic praised the wittiness of the material and Sondheim's superior craft. The combination of Bergman, who had 'operetta in his blood' when he wrote the film,[42] with Sondheim, Wheeler, and Prince, who were right to see the hidden musical in the 1955 comedy, has resulted in 'something so unthinkable as an intelligent operetta'.[43] Thoor liked the musical itself but was not pleased with either the direction or the acting style of the Gothenburg production. To him it was too heavy, lacked sensuality, and seemed mired in the over-explicitness of old operetta. He believed neither the director nor the cast were right or ready for this kind of material, but there was hope: 'The right production, and we will love it.'[44]

Sune Hofsten from *Göteborgs-Tidningen* was less enthusiastic and pondered:

> How might a couple of American musical theatre manufacturers understand Bergman's mockery of nobility and officers in Sweden *annodazumal*?[45] Can the genuine Swedish midsummer night mood be interpreted in music à la Broadway? These fears unfortunately were partly confirmed. The music often feels contour-less and indifferent and functions as some kind of filler. It does not further the dramatic plot.[46]

Tellingly, the review in *Arbetet* was headlined: 'A chilly summer night without Bergman's smile'.[47] There Tony Kaplan stated that the work was 'not at all a bad musical' and mainly critiqued the directing, casting and acting: '[T]his waltz musical is rather a play for a dramatic theatre than material for a purely lyric ensemble. [ ... ] The film was funny. The way it is presented now, the musical is boring.'[48] Kaplan also lauded what he found to be the most 'Swedish' moment in the show: Petra and Frid making love to each other (to the point of bruising) to the sound of an accordion.[49] In *Göteborgs-Posten* Åke Perlström was generally positive about the musical, appreciating the difference between the old European operettas and the complexity of the music as well as the dramatic depth of *A Little Night Music*.[50]

Ulla-Britt Edberg, the critic in *Svenska Dagbladet*, found the production slow as well as 'a little tame and lame'[51]; she complained that there was not much 'Bergmanian' to this production: as it lacked the film's lustre, which according to Edberg was the fault of neither the length of the show (more than three hours) nor Sondheim's extravagantly skilful music.

Bengt Jahnsson in *Dagens Nyheter* described Sondheim as very knowledgeable about the commercial aspects of musical theatre, since he was behind such Broadway hits as *Follies* [*sic*] and *Company*.[52] His review focuses on how the director had misunderstood or failed to convey what part of the story is told in the music. According to Jahnsson, in his efforts to be true to the film, Ahlsell turned it into a play, instead of directing the musical at hand. Sondheim, however, was praised for having honoured Bergman's 'morality'.[53]

The review in *Aftonbladet* by Jurgen Schildt stated that both Sondheim and Ahlsell had let Bergman down,[54] with the music not adding anything of substance or beauty and the direction failing to embrace all the lust and heat: 'The sexual temperature at Storan is alarmingly low'.[55] Only two of these seven critics demanded that the musical be called *Sommarnattens leende*,[56] and they were also the most complimentary about the musical. Perhaps they viewed it as an honour to grant the musical the film's title, instead of respecting the one given to the work by Sondheim.

After the hostile reactions in the press to the production of *Company* and the rather negative attitudes towards the American musical in general expressed in some of the articles published before *Night Music* opened, it is surprising to find that the critics actually had more objections to how the production was directed and performed than to the musical adaptation itself. There were also few in-depth comments on the film's or the show's 'Swedishness'. More references were made to the film's qualities as a comedy or a 'roundelay' as well as to Bergman's playful homage to European theatre history and to his own work for the stage: 'It was as if Bergman in this film aired all of the stored and more lightweight parts of his theatrical experience, with fragments of Anouilh, Schnitzler, Feydeau, marionettes, the intrigues of rococo, not to forget the steaming atmosphere of *Miss Julie*'.[57]

## THE SECOND PRODUCTION OF THE SHOW: *A LITTLE NIGHT MUSIC* IN MALMÖ, 1974

*A Little Night Music* opened on 1 February 1974 in Malmö, Sweden's third-largest city. It was produced by Malmö Stadsteater (Malmö City Theatre), which was later divided into the lyric Malmö Opera and the dramatic Malmö Stadsteater. Before that division in the early 1990s, the theatre produced all genres: plays, opera, operettas, and musicals, as well as ballet and dance. Bergman himself directed at Malmö Stadsteater for the first time in 1945 and was permanently employed as director and artistic advisor there from 1952 to 1958, staging, among other works, Franz Lehár's operetta *The Merry Widow* in 1954.

*A Little Night Music* was performed on the main stage, which has an auditorium of just over 1,500 seats—similar in size to the Shubert Theatre, where *Night Music* opened on Broadway. The Malmö production had a run of twenty-nine performances—fewer than *My Fair Lady* (sixty-seven performances, 1971–1972 season), *Annie Get Your Gun* (fifty-four performances, 1972–1973 season), *Kiss Me, Kate* (thirty-six performances, 1974–1975 season), and *Czardasfurstinnan* (*The Gipsy Princess*, by Kalmàn; sixty-eight performances, 1975–1976 season). To be fair, these are of course all older and more established shows.

*A Little Night Music* in Malmö was directed by the Vienna-born Josef Halfen and used the same translation as Gothenburg did. The cast was a mix of lyric and dramatic actors, which was standard operating procedure for Malmö Stadsteater.[58] Dagny Lind, who portrayed Madame Armfeldt, had acted in fifteen of Bergman's theatre productions and had been part of his early ensembles at Helsingborgs Stadsteater in the 1940s and Malmö in the 1950s.[59]

Three weeks before opening night of the Malmö *A Little Night Music*, the director, Josef Halfen, was quoted in *Dagens Nyheter*: 'We don't take any special 'approach' [to the material]. What we are trying to convey is the story. I think the Americans in their adaptation have been so true to Ingmar Bergman's original ideas that it all feels truly genuine, even though they of course see Sweden as a somewhat exotic country.'[60] Sven Tollin, the marketing director at Stadsteatern, declared that they were going to use both titles for the production, since '[we] have slightly more right to the Swedish title. Ingmar Bergman worked here when he wrote his screenplay and the film was shot at Jordberga [castle] outside of Malmö.'[61] In addition, the Malmö production enlisted the costume designer Mago, who had created the outfits for the Bergman film—presumably to give the production more of a Bergman flavour and thus display greater fidelity to the film.

The reviews of the second Swedish production were just as divided as those for the show's première in Gothenburg, even though the critics at least seemed to agree that the women of the cast outshone the men. Again, very few of the notices comment on how the show managed to capture its Swedish setting. Carlhåkan Larsén in *Sydsvenska Dagbladet* was an exception: 'Mago's costumes are naturally extravagant, fancy, turn-of-the-century in Skåne. But unfortunately, Stig Nelson's set design does not capture the most moving nuances of the Nordic summer night. Birch trees, for example, can of course be designed in stylised form, but they need not look as if they were shrouded in spider-webs or dust rags. That is not poetic.'[62] His colleague Jan Richter, writing in *Expressen*, found the Malmö production gentler and more emotionally expressive than the one in Gothenburg but objected that Bergman's dialogue had lost much of its wit and suggestiveness on its way to Broadway. Moreover, the production was 'slow, so slow'.[63]

'*A Little Night Music* underlines how phenomenally good the film was—and is. Turning it into a musical has not added any extra dimensions,'[64] wrote Sven Malm in *Svenska Dagbladet*. While he attested that Sondheim's music is 'good and beautiful and grows on you', Malm was not too taken with the staging as a whole: 'This production has neither excitement nor vitality.' Carlhåkan Larsén, the critic in *Sydsvenska Dagbladet*, appreciated that this was a different kind of musical: '*A Little Night Music*—we Swedes would probably want to call it *Sommarnattens leende*—doesn't need a chorus dressed for a party, ballet, prodigious showmanship, or showstoppers. That description is meant as a positive.'[65] But in Larsén's view, the production lacked atmosphere, since the set design couldn't suggest the proper mood and colour of the Nordic summer night.

# The Third Production of the Show: *A Little Night Music* in Norrköping/ Linköping, 1974

The third production of *A Little Night Music* opened on 26 February 1974 at Stadsteatern Norrköping-Linköping, a city theatre which serves two cities in the region of Östergötland. Its ensemble is made up mainly of dramatic actors, but the theatre has a long tradition of producing musicals as well. Classic shows such as *Cabaret* (1969, Norrköping) and *Chicago* (1976, Norrköping; European première)[66] had their Swedish, Nordic or European première here, as later on did the musicals *The Scarlet Pimpernel* (2007, Linköping), *The Addams Family* (2012, Norrköping) and *Come From Away* (2020, Norrköping).

The theatre in Norrköping has an auditorium of approximately six hundred seats, the one in Linköping a third fewer (four hundred seats). *A Little Night Music* ran in Norrköping for twenty-two performances and was shown twenty-eight times in Linköping.[67] Torsten Sjöholm, an actor and director engaged at the theatre since 1960, directed. Again, Barlach's translation was used, but it was slightly rewritten.[68] The songlist in the programme indicates that no whole songs were cut.[69] It should be noted that for this production, the story was updated from 1901 to 1908–1910, because according to the costume designer, Ulrika Friberger, 'the fashion from those years is so gratifying to display on a stage'.[70]

The reviews for the third Swedish production were just as varied as the reviews had been for Gothenburg and Malmö. The novelty of the Bergman film's having been turned into an American musical seems to have worn off, though. The wilful attitude towards the two titles continued: the theatre programme had *A Little Night Music* on the cover, but put 'efter Ingmar Bergmans film *Sommarnattens Leende*' on the credits page, in almost as large a font as the English title.[71] This of course contributed to the confusion around the title; one critic refused to use the English title, so in total two reviews used *Sommarnattens leende*, two reviews referred to the production as some variation of *A Little Night Music* (*Sommarnattens leende*)—as it is still called on the theatre's website[72]—and three reviews referred to it only as *A Little Night Music*.

Alf Thoor, writing in *Expressen*, once again opened his review with a diatribe against American (commercial) culture:

> The international musical theatre industry has its customary sales methods. That is why three Swedish theatres right now have the title *A Little Night Music* on their posters [ ... ] In addition, the words are displayed there in the same curlicued writing—*logotype*—because that's how it's done: it's supposed to accompany us until an unsurpassable dazzling super-ensemble (with Liza Minnelli—want to bet?) has the final say in a movie version. [ ... ] That is how it is done, and that's kind of sad, because the tricks of the trade seem so routine: it's a machine we see.[73]

Thor had his own view regarding the title while being ambivalent about the show's Swedishness: 'In Swedish we now say *Sommarnattens leende* and no one will be able to stop us, because we won't find a more Swedish musical anytime soon. Here Stephen Sondheim and Hugh Wheeler have, with the aid of Bergman's film as source material, succeeded in transforming Sweden into something that to foreigners seem as incomprehensible and wacky as the duchies of the Viennese operetta do to us.'

Carl-Gunnar Åhlén in *Svenska Dagbladet* was very unhappy with Wheeler's [*sic*] lyrics, which he found too sophisticated.[74] He also thought the music 'lacking substance' and the musical 'uninteresting and clichéd'.[75] To Åhlén, Bergman's film is all too complete, but neither the music nor Wheeler's book can compensate for what was lost when it came to the portrayal of characters and milieu; his most positive remark was that the production had a generally friendly, unassuming tone and now and then was harmlessly entertaining.[76]

Bengt Jahnsson, writing in *Dagens Nyheter*, finally approved of a production of *A Little Night Music*: 'For the first time the complex piece of art this actually is has been recreated. Not even Broadway succeeded in doing that. This production is melancholy and sensuous, ironic and burlesque.'[77] Jahnsson applauded the fact that set designers Ulrika Friberger and Tyr Martin ignored the usual birch trees and instead created a dreamy, abstract set that hints more at a middle-aged September than a youthful August, while director Sjöholm got credit for focusing solely on the musical and not minding the film.[78]

The singing actors in Norrköping did not satisfy Åke Brandel of *Aftonbladet*, but he found the systematic (sexual) liberation and infidelity appealing.[79] Brandel noted that not only the world but Sweden, too, had gotten a musical to be happy about: being based on the Bergman film, the show had first-rate source material—a rarity in operetta and musical theatre.[80] He also remarked that Sondheim had refrained from giving the music any Nordic touch but had instead written 'international music', which Brandel perceived as fresh and edgy.[81]

The critic Arne Malmberg, writing in the local newspaper *Norrköpings Tidning*, found the abstract set design confusing, saying it was 'cold and poor in emotion. The summer is completely lost. The audience doesn't know if it's winter or summer, indoors or outdoors.'[82] He declared: 'God help me, but the thought hit me that some whining from an accordion and a substantial haystack in the burlesque love scene with the servants perhaps would have rescued the identity. We Swedes have our symbols, and they are deeply rooted.'[83] He added: 'In this circumstance it feels like a misfortune to remember Bergman's film, with its summer-night charm and erotic pulse.'[84] Nils A. Hertz in *Folkbladet Östgöten* had a different approach to the production: 'You would do best to firstly detach from any possibly lingering memories of the Bergman film and accept the musical as an [artistic] work in its own right.'[85]

What is it that Bergman's film has which, for the critics of the first three productions of *A Little Night Music*, is undeniably Swedish? It is not the nobility duelling in country estates, nor the witty, erotic repartee. It is the mythical and magical summer night itself. In Sweden, the celebration of the pagan feast Midsummer's Eve has an almost sacred status. It occurs on the Friday closest to the summer solstice, when the night never gets completely dark. Throughout history it has been the one true folk feast, since it is the only pagan holiday that was never converted into a Christian holiday. It is celebrated all day and all night, mostly outdoors, by Swedes of all ages, often dressed in white clothes, with games, songs, violin and accordion music, food, and alcohol. This feast still vividly uses ancient myths and traditions: the erection of the maypole, decorated with flowers and leaves, popularly but incorrectly believed to be an old pagan (phallic) ritual used to stimulate fertility. And if you collect seven types of flowers and place them under your pillow during Midsummer Night, you will dream of your intended.

Although the night in *Sommarnattens leende* is not Midsummer Night, the bright night portrayed there—amplified by Sondheim in the second-act quintets in *A Little Night Music*—instantly triggers associations to that specific night: the shimmer of the white night, the myths, the sense that the membrane between the rational world and the magical is especially thin.

# The Only Commercial Production of the Show: Stockholm, 1978

Just as in many other countries, musical theatre in Sweden is both a commercial genre, providing large audiences with entertainment, and—on the best of occasions—an artistic endeavour, especially when it is being produced by subsidised venues. Nearly all productions of *A Little Night Music* in Sweden have been scheduled in theatres or opera houses supported by state or regional funds. The one exception was the 1978 staging in Stockholm. It was financed by the commercial producer Olle Kinch, who had previously produced comedy and shows like *Oh, Calcutta!* (which opened in June of 1971) and *Godspell* (opening in the autumn of 1973). In 1978 he finally bought a theatre of his own, Folkan, and chose *A Little Night Music* as its first production. This time the show was called *Sommarnattens Leende*, the title announced in a large font on the front page of the program, with *A little night music* written underneath in smaller font (and in lower case). Kinch chose Stig Olin, head of entertainment at the Swedish Radio, to direct. He also commissioned a new translation from Beppe Wolgers. Once again, Mago created the costumes, but this time he was also the set designer.

Commercial producers are of course under heavy pressure to sell tickets, and Kinch's undertaking betrays signs of calculatedly stimulating the curiosity of both the audience and the press while at the same time promising to satisfy the capital's appetite for glamorous entertainment: for example, the impresario had cast Zarah Leander in the role of Madame Armfeldt, a role she had played three years earlier in Vienna. This casting was artistically sound, but it probably was first and foremost intended to spark attention before opening night, since Leander carried with her an air of mythical Middle European worlds and controversial liaisons—she had been one of the biggest movie stars in Nazi Germany before and during World War II. In joining this production, Leander also returned to Folkan, forty-eight years after she had first appeared there.[86]

There are clear signs that this production preferred dialogue from the film to Hugh Wheeler's. In the programme,[87] one of the first texts states that Madame Armfeldt explains the three smiles of the summer night with Frid's lines from the film,[88] not the lines given to her by Wheeler in the musical. In the same publication, Beppe Wolgers clarified his approach to the material:

> Surely Stephen Sondheim and Hugh Wheeler have crafted a nice adaptation for their audience in their country, when they made the American summer night smile. But after all I think the summer night smiles in Swedish. At least for me. And probably for the many others in this country, that ever have been in love on a temperate Nordic July night. [ ... ] That is why, as best I could, I have tried to draw close to the original. [ ... ] I think Ingmar Bergman's original screenplay' dialogue and plot are delicate and psychologically correct for this romantic comedy.'[89]

Wolgers goes on to claim that he has been true to Sondheim in translating the lyrics.[90] Kinch must also have requested the insertion of the song 'I Remember' from Sondheim's 1966 television musical *Evening Primrose*, to provide Zarah Leander with a number in the second act.[91] Kinch made sure the rest of the cast, too, was as star-studded as possible: Jan Malmsjö, an established musical theatre actor, played Fredrik Egerman, while Ulla Sallert, a star of the genre since 1944 and most famous for her Eliza in the first Swedish production of *My Fair Lady* (1959), played Desirée.[92]

Articles written after the press conference in January 1978 list the line-up of stars, reporting that this production was going to be 'lighter and more fun' than the production in London,[93] and that Bergman might have directed but for a prior engagement as director of Strindberg's *The Dance of Death* at The Royal Dramatic Theatre.[94] The headlines read, for example, 'Leander, Sallert and Malmsjö: Star ensemble at New Folkan',[95] 'Zarah Leander at Folkan again',[96] 'Seven stars at the new Folkan',[97] and 'Star explosion'.[98] For the press it was more important to mention the rave reviews on Broadway than to discuss the authors. Later articles compared the casts of the film and stage versions,[99] described how expensive the production was, and noted the lack of success of the previous Swedish productions.[100]

*Sommarnattens Leende* at Folkan opened on 14 September 1978 and ran for 140 performances, closing on 18 February 1979. In the late 1970s it was the norm for commercial theatres to perform six or seven shows per week.[101] Folkan was a seven-hundred-seat theatre, and according to Kinch, the show needed to sell 80 percent of the seats to break even. However, the show could not compete with the concurrent commercial staging of *My Fair Lady* at Oscarsteatern, produced by Kinch's chief rival, Sandrews, as the Lerner and Loewe classic ran for two seasons, achieving 385 performances between 1977 and 1979.

# Reviews for the Stockholm Production

Because twentieth-century musical theatre developed in commercial contexts in Europe and the United States it has often been viewed as artistically inferior to spoken drama and opera. In some Swedish newspapers there is a clear division between 'art' and 'entertainment' sections, so when reviewing the 1978 *A Little Night Music*, the evening papers *Aftonbladet* and *Expressen* relegated the show to the entertainment pages. In contrast, the morning papers *Dagens Nyheter*, *Svenska Dagbladet*, *Sydsvenska Dagbladet*, and *Göteborgs-Posten* published reviews in the 'arts' pages, under 'première' or 'theatre' rubrics.[102]

*Aftonbladet* dedicated one whole page to covering the opening night. The review by Allan Fagerström took up only one column out of six;[103] a photo of Leander during the curtain call, under the headline 'ZARAH!', occupied the top half of the page, while the bottom half was dedicated to an article about the actor's emotional performance, audience reactions, and her comments and behaviour after the show, plus a photo of Leander being courted by a kneeling Mago.[104] Fagerström declared that he was reluctant 'to say anything that can be perceived as negative' but still pointed out that the director, Stig Olin, had turned the musical into an operetta: 'There is a difference—an enormous one—between these two art forms. [ ... ] An operetta is a textually artificial comedy [built] around fantastic melodies. A musical is a play that needs the melody to give the text its completed meaning.' Although this implied that Fagerström respected musicals as a genre, he didn't mention Sondheim or Wheeler once in his report.

Lasse Bergström's review in *Expressen* was mostly nuanced and positive, acknowledging 'young' Sondheim's musical talent and praising Ulla Sallert's interpretation of the musical's only hit song.[105] The critic compared the actors to their counterparts in the Bergman film and was satisfied with their performances. All in all, he concluded that Sondheim's musical withstood close comparison to the witty and sophisticated original.

At this time, musicals in Stockholm were—with rare exceptions—produced only by commercial theatres. Leif Zern in *Dagens Nyheter* questioned this situation and praised the way the music was performed at Folkan:

> Musically this production surpasses most of what one has been able to see these past few years in Stockholm. That already is a small sensation, considering that neither the [Royal] Opera nor Oscarsteatern consider themselves obliged to take any artistic responsibility for the lighter musical theatre genre.[106]

For the critic, the most incomprehensible aspect of the production was the world Mago and Olin presented:

> But what I don't understand is where this happens? In what society? Among what people and for what people? The big mistake, I think, is within Mago's set design

and costumes, that places this story in a no-man's-land of the upper class that only exists in the imagination of theatre. [... I]t stands in the way of every attempt to give the play a connection to reality. Sure, Bergman's story is a crossbreed of Shakespeare and Anouilh. [ ... ] But at the same time *Sommarnattens leende* is among the most Swedish one can imagine, with its summer-night mystique and its bursting small-town idyll. [ ... ] At Folkan there is nothing of this, nothing of the erotic atmosphere, of the conflict and anguish that is the essence of the film.'[107]

The various newspaper articles offer evidence that Kinch was not interested in the artistic innovations of Sondheim, Wheeler, and Prince. Since he hoped for a decent return for his backers, he was mainly interested in finding a proper vehicle for Zarah Leander and the rest of his stars, one that could lure an audience from the appropriate economic demographic to his theatre. But despite Kinch's obvious commercial interests, Zern attests that it did serve one important purpose:

It is, despite it all, extremely important that Folkan demonstrates that it is possible to make good and entertaining musical theatre even in Stockholm. That it is a commercial theatre which mounts the project in a blaze of publicity and celebrates it with champagne is not, in my view, anything to moralise over. At least not as long as our state- and city-appointed culture politicians refuse to engage in the matter.[108]

# Development of Musical Theatre in Sweden, 1978–1997

By 1997 Bergman had reached the pinnacle of his career. His film *Fanny och Alexander* (1983) was a great success both nationally and internationally and received four Academy Awards, as well as several other international accolades.[109] He had unique cultural status and power in Sweden.[110] Bergman returned to Dramaten (the Royal Dramatic Theatre in Stockholm) in 1984 and directed an eclectic range of plays there: *Markisinnan de Sade* (*Madame de Sade*, 1992), *Misantropen* (*The Misanthrope*, 1995), and *Backanterna* (*The Bacchae*, 1996); several of these productions toured to other European countries and the United States.

Sondheim had worked his way to a similar position by 1997. He had written all his major works and enjoyed a revered position as innovator of the genre. However, the only Sondheim musicals that had been produced professionally in Sweden in the previous two decades were *Sweeney Todd* and *Into the Woods*.[111]

The two decades since 1978 had reshaped the musical theatre landscape in Sweden. The genre enjoyed greater popularity; theatres which earlier had produced various forms of entertainment, such as operettas, revues, or musicals, now more and more exclusively focused on the latter. Subsidised theatres that had not produced musical theatre started to incorporate the genre into their repertoire.[112]

The movie *Fame* had its Swedish cinema release in 1980, and the TV series started to air in October 1982 on one of Swedish television's two broadcast channels. This exposed a new generation to the appeal of musical theatre. Sweden's first school to train musical theatre artists, Balettakademien in Gothenburg, opened in the autumn of 1983. In 1992 Artisten, in Gothenburg, started what was to become Sweden's first government-funded musical theatre college. The interest awakened in a young audience generated a succession of productions which were aimed at this demographic, especially at Chinateatern in Stockholm: *Cats* (the 1987–1988 and 1988–1989 seasons), *West Side Story* (the 1988–1989 and 1989–1990 seasons), *Grease* (the 1991–1992 season), *Fame* (the 1992–1993 and 1993–1994 seasons), and *Hair* (the 1994–1995 season), showcasing a new generation of (seemingly) triple-threat artists. The Lloyd Webber and Mackintosh hit musicals conquered the world, with *The Phantom of the Opera* opening in 1989 at Stockholm's Oscarsteatern, where it ran for an unprecedented six years and 1,173 performances. *Les Misérables* premiered one year later at Cirkus in Stockholm and lasted 275 performances.

This musical theatre boom also came about because directors, artistic directors, performers, composers, and writers were there to champion the genre, suggesting lesser-known titles, to bring the genre to new stages and to write new, Swedish musicals. *Kristina från Duvemåla*, written by Björn Ulvaeus and Benny Andersson from ABBA together with the director Lars Rudolfsson, was the most successful example of new musicals 'closer to us.'[113]

## The National Tour: *Sommarnattens Leende, 1997–1998*

The fifth Swedish production of *A Little Night Music* was produced by Riksteatern, the subsidised national touring theatre. Riksteatern was founded in 1933 and is financed and owned by over 230 local economic (theatre) associations throughout Sweden. Its goal is to promote and produce quality theatre outside the major cities. This time the musical was called *Sommarnattens leende*; it was helmed by Benny Fredriksson, who was a novice at directing musical theatre. Berit Anmar, the dramaturge at Riksteatern since 1967, emphasised in the programme: 'It is an old dream that has been realised. For 20 years I have fought for us to do this—now all the pieces of the puzzle have finally fallen into place!'[114] Still, the production did not have the capacity to cast a full *Liebeslieder* quintet; rather, it had one designated female and one male artist, who sung those parts together with other members of the cast. The set design was a tour-friendly abstract space, the costume design more modern than traditional.

This *Sommarnattens leende* opened on 24 October 1997 at Skövde Teater, travelled all over Sweden, and had two short runs at Södra Teatern in Stockholm. In total it had fifty-seven performances and played to an average attendance of 294 persons.[115] Since the production had a cast of twelve and an orchestra of ten, it is fair to assume that it played

FIG. 22.3 The ensemble of the Riksteatern production of *A Little Night Music*, which toured Sweden in 1997–1998 under the title *Sommarnattens leende*. Photograph by Joakim Strömholm, courtesy of the photographer.

the large and medium-sized stages available to Riksteatern. Those attendance figures must be considered well below expectations.

In newspaper articles before the opening nights in Skövde and Stockholm, the director, Fredriksson, assured readers that although he had moved the story to a 'flexible present time',[116] he nonetheless remained loyal to Bergman and Sondheim: 'I haven't cut a single line nor removed a single note. But I might be doing the musical [in a way that ensures that it] does not look the way it has before.'[117] There were indeed changes, though. The last page of the script, for example, lacks Fredrik and Desirée's short dialogue about playing Hedda Gabbler in Helsingborg as well as the two first lines of Fredrika and Madame Armfeldt. On the other hand, the latter was given Frid's line from the film about the third smile of the summer night, meaning that the last line in this production was not Wheeler's, but Bergman's. Because it used Beppe Wolgers's translation, made for Folkan in 1978, there might already have been substantial changes to the dialogue. Fredriksson added the cut songs 'Silly People' and 'My Husband the Pig' and commissioned Gerhard Hoberstorfer and Eva Carlberg to translate them, in addition to retranslating 'In Praise of Women' and 'Perpetual Anticipation'.[118]

The notices for this production suffered many of the by now familiar reproaches,[119] revealing the critics to be still preoccupied with the same elements. While praising some of

FIG. 22.4 In his rivalry with Fredrik Egerman (Anders Beckman, *left*), Carl-Magnus (Richard Carlsohn, *right*) goes for the jugular. Scene from the 1997 touring production of *A Little Night Music*. Photograph by Joakim Strömholm, courtesy of the photographer.

the actors, they accused the director of failing to find the 'soul' of the show, so that it had neither style nor flow. A number of reviewers again questioned the notion of turning the film into a musical, while others continued to emphasise the merits of Sondheim and Wheeler's work. What had undeniably changed since 1978 was Sondheim's status. None of the 1997 articles or reviews mentions Harold Prince, and the few that mention Wheeler do not attach any artistic value to his name—they merely state that he wrote the libretto. Sondheim, on the other hand, is brought centre stage, appreciated for his skills and recognised as an artist.

Fredriksson's conversion to a 'flexible present time' was not well received. Leif Zern in *Dagens Nyheter* was typical: he declared this modern take 'so misguided that the whole show seems to take place in an even more distant land: [the land of] platitudes.'[120] Zern then elaborates: 'First of all, I don't understand how these broads in plastic miniskirts have ended up in Bergman's and Sondheim's romantic comedy, where shy emotions play with the double-layer veil of seduction. [ . . . ] Second of all, we have seen this type of plastic sensuality too often for it to work anymore. It is as dead as the parrot in the Monty Python sketch.'[121] So while Sondheim was respected as an artist, the poor reviews of the production help explain why it did not do very well.

# Development and Status of Musical Theatre in Sweden, 1998–2023

How we consume music, books, television, and films has changed significantly in the twenty-first century. More than ever, commercial theatres need to deliver what appeals to a modern audience. The winning formula seems to be a combination of nostalgia and novelty, such as screen-to-stage transfers, jukebox musicals, and classic musicals cast with stars from different areas. In the Swedish cities where commercial and subsidised theatres coexist, the latter are often criticised for producing musicals that are too commercial, giving them an unfair advantage over their competition.[122]

Still, in the last few decades, new forms of musical theatre have developed in Sweden: there are fringe productions of less commercial titles, and new musicals are being written for both commercial and subsidised stages. The latter often explore Swedish themes, characters and source material, for example *Så som i himmelen* (*As It Is in Heaven*, 2018), based on the Oscar-nominated 2004 film with the same title, and *Camera: The Ingrid Bergman Musical* (2020). A couple of jukebox musicals with Swedish origins have successfully been written for the international market: *Mamma Mia!* (1999, London) and *& Juliet* (2019, London). But the reality is still that there is not a large enough audience in Sweden to sustain productions of non-commercial musicals, such as those by, for instance, Sondheim, Adam Guettel, or Michael John LaChiusa.

Musical theatre remains a minor genre in Sweden, its few productions vastly outnumbered by 'regular' dramatic plays. This results in musicals' being defined by and compared to straight theatre, with the latter considered the norm as 'art' and having a far higher status than musical theatre in the cultural hierarchy. Thus, the musical, with its roots in Anglophone commercial theatre, is denigrated as 'entertainment', which is equated with escapism. It is seen as a cultural undertaking that doesn't demand anything of its audience but is simply there to reassure and divert. 'Art', on the other hand, is often defined as having the nobler purpose of challenging theatre-goers, of showing us what and how we are and demanding us to scrutinise the state of things, the state of us.

Anglophone musicals produced in Sweden are—perhaps unconsciously—arranged in a certain hierarchy. For example, a musical with a strong European connection, often through its source material, has higher status than a musical that could be labelled 'American'.[123] A musical whose theme and conflict occur within the private or familial sphere is often held in lower regard than one in which the conflict is with society at large. When these musicals are staged, they sometimes still 'ascend' or 'descend' in the hierarchy, depending on which Swedish theatre is behind the production, with the subsidised theatres and opera houses of course being granted higher status than the commercial ones.[124] This unofficial ranking also extends to artists working in the field: a theatre director with a background primarily in 'art' and text-based drama often has higher status than a director who specialises in commercial disciplines such as musical theatre, show choreography, or popular music. Sometimes it seems that a production where the director, choreographer, designer, or theatre has applied their unique artistic interpretation to a musical is more prestigious than a traditionally mounted production. The many examples of cuts and changes to the *Night Music* libretto is one of the ways this hierarchy manifests itself.

On the bright side, the rules of these different hierarchies are changing slowly on all fronts, thanks to American and European writers and producers redefining the genre, and Swedish writers, directors, and producers finding new ways to influence and develop it.

## The Second Production in the Capital: *Sommarnattens leende—A Little Night Music*, 2010

Bergman died in 2007. Through his career he wrote and/or directed 77 films and television series and 171 theatre productions.[125] Leif Zern described Sweden's relationship to Bergman:

> Whether he wanted it or not, his life's work runs parallel to *folkhemmet*.[126] [ ... ] No artist in Sweden comes close to the position Ingmar Bergman has achieved in both [fields]. He is our greatest film celebrity after Greta Garbo, for decades much more popular internationally than in his homeland, where he—all throughout his career— has been the object of a persistent love-hate relationship. Loved by the common man is the last thing he has been. [ ... ] The role he has played cannot be measured in popularity. It runs deeper than that; it is symbolic: sometimes he has shown what we want to see, sometimes what we most of all fear to learn about ourselves.'[127]

After his death Bergman was once again, towards the end of the decade of the 2000s, the centre of cultural attention: new books about every single aspect of his work and life were being published, and some of his films and television series were adapted to the stage. The Royal Dramatic Theatre in Stockholm arranged the first Ingmar Bergman International Theatre Festival in the early summer of 2009. Thus, by 2010, when Sondheim's musical was seen once more in Sweden's biggest city, Bergman himself seemed to be a stronger trademark than his individual films. This time *A Little Night Music* was staged at Stockholms Stadsteater, a large subsidised repertoire theatre with multiple stages. Directed by Tobias Theorell, the production was called *Sommarnattens leende—A Little Night Music*, with both titles in the same size font. Magdalena Åberg's colourful and playful set design, interpreting the minimalist and maximalist possibilities of a theatre, contrasted her more traditional costume design for the principals with the *Liebeslieders* as dusty, confused opera ghosts. Although it is customary for musicals here to run for eighty to a hundred performances, the production played only twenty-five times, notwithstanding the good level of attendance per performance.

FIG. 22.5 Scene from the 2010 production of *A Little Night Music* at the Stockholms Stadsteater, the second staging of the musical in the Swedish capital. Photo: Petra Hellberg, courtesy of the Kulturhuset Stadteaterns arkiv.

This production utilised the 1978 Beppe Wolgers translation.[128] It is remarkable how much of the dialogue was taken verbatim from the screenplay. Most of Wheeler's dialogue in the first act was replaced by Bergman's, as were aspects of the structure.[129] Substantial changes were also made to the first half of the second act,[130] while Madame Armfeldt's description of the wine's special properties were taken word for word from the film.[131] It is not clear if all of these changes had already been made in 1978 or if some of them were introduced in the 1997 or 2010 production.[132] Yet there are clear signs that the 2010 libretto was not faithful to the 1978 version: there were slight changes to the Swedish lyrics,[133] and the song 'I Remember', which was added for Zarah Leander in 1978, was cut, as was indeed a section of 'Liaisons'. 'Silly People,' however, remained. The 2010 production also changed the ending: it presented Madame Armfeldt's explanation of the third smile as a voice-over before Desirée and Fredrik's last scene and restored Desirée's lines about having to perform Hedda in Helsingborg. The audience did not witness Madame Armfeldt's death.

All these cuts, changes, and dramaturgical restructurings—whether made in 1978, 1997, or 2010—indicate that the people who initiated and agreed to them hold Bergman's script in higher regard than Hugh Wheeler's. Whether that opinion is motivated by the belief that the Swedish work is of better quality than the American version or by the idea that the (artistic) film deserves more respect than the (commercial) musical can only be answered by the individuals involved in the alterations.[134]

Stadsteatern was not overly concerned with the film's local flavour; in fact, the Swedish playwright and actor Staffan Göthe concluded in the programme that the world of *Sommarnattens leende* is not at all a Swedish one, but rather the theatrical world of European operettas and French comedies: 'It is a magical theatreland that Bergman has borrowed and created, a fantasy-Sweden further exoticised and Broadway-fied in Wheeler/Sondheim's three-quarter-time musical'.[135]

Five days before opening night, the morning newspaper *Dagens Nyheter* published a two-page essay titled 'Sondheim Put the Knife in the Whipped Cream of Musical Theatre',[136] referring to Harold Prince's famous description of the show as 'whipped cream with knives'.[137] Its chief rival, *Svenska Dagbladet*, published an essay that also highlighted Sondheim's upcoming eightieth birthday.[138]

Yet despite the focus on Sondheim in these two features, he was not given much attention by the critics who reviewed the production. The national newspapers treated him as a given, commenting briefly but positively on his music. The local newspapers merely introduced him ('American composer') and then went on to describe his music in one word or complain about it.[139] Instead, several of the 2010 reviews had much to say about Bergman, possibly because of his recent death. The director's work was a sounding board in most of the notices. For example, Ingegärd Waaranperä in *Dagens Nyheter* declared that she was not a Bergman enthusiast and did not like the film.[140] She then drew attention to the carillon roundelay—one of the film's visual motifs—and observed that the actor playing Malcolm seemed to parody the actor (Jarl Kulle) who originated the part in the film. Sara Jangfeldt, the actor playing Petra, in Waaranperä's eyes embodied the true spirit of Bergman, while the musical used at least one typical Bergman trait—that of the travelling troupe of actors (in the quintet). Bo Löfvendahl in *Svenska Dagbladet* missed the erotic charge that had been promised but found it 'in Sara Jangfeldt as the maid Petra, with Harriet Andersson–like wiggling hips.'[141]

Obviously unfamiliar with the original 1973 libretto and thus unaware that the Swedish version was significally changed, several of the critics commented on the play's text being so similar to Bergman's script. Curt Bladh in *Sundsvalls Tidning* opined: 'Wheeler has been wise enough to rely on the film; the story follows it faithfully, [and] many of the lines are transferred verbatim from film to stage. That saves it all and would have worked as a play.'[142] He also muses: 'It is beautiful, very entertaining, elegant and [ ... ] actually a very un-Swedish comedy.'[143] Lisa Berg Ortman in *Norrköpings Tidningar* questioned 'why Stadsteatern has chosen to do this night music. The play is passé and has nothing to say.'[144] Critics also found the production 'antiquated' and having a 'deplorable view of women'.[145]

# The 1955 Film Still Looms Large

An article published in *Dagens Nyheter* prior to the 2010 opening night illustrates the hierarchical aesthetics outlined earlier.[146] It points out that the suggestion to produce *A Little Night Music* at Stockholms Stadsteater came from the artistic director Benny Fredriksson, who directed the 1997 production. The feature assures the readers that the film's dialogue is largely intact in Sondheim's 'version' and that most of the classic lines are in the show; *A Little Night Music* is described as 'too good for its genre'.[147] Bergman's comedy was a great commercial success, which may be one reason the publicity constantly compared the film and stage versions. The 1955 film still cast a long shadow in 2010: the *Dagens Nyheter* article compared the two, with photos of the nine screen actors beside those of the corresponding stage performers, all in make-up and costume. There were photo pairings of the film and stage actors in four to eight of the prominent roles prior to the Gothenburg,[148] Stockholm 1978,[149] and Stockholm 2010 openings.[150] One article refers to the stage performers 'playing' or 'doing' the film actors, for instance, 'Grynet Molvig "plays" Harriet Andersson'.[151]

The success of each stage performer is judged by reviewers according to how well they recreate the screen actor's performance—almost always to the stage actor's disadvantage. In the second Stockholm production, despite its modern and expressive set design, actors' hair and make-up was apparently designed to evoke the film actors, Count Malcolm in the stage version even adopting the identical accent that Jarl Kulle gave the film character:

> In the stage production the roles allude to the film's characters and wink frequently at their movie shadows; Andreas Kundler is some of the time a very funny copy of Jarl Kulle's Count Malcolm, just as Yvonne Lombard does an excellent Naima Wistrand's [*sic*] Madame Armfeldt.[152]

The directorial decision to imitate the film characterisations was strongly criticised by some reviewers.[153]

# THE SECOND PRODUCTION IN MALMÖ: *SOMMARNATTENS LEENDE*, 2013

The Malmö Opera (previously Malmö Stadsteater) is the only Swedish theatre to produce *A Little Night Music* twice, but the later production was given the Swedish title. Despite its name, Malmö Opera is not a traditional opera house:[154] its repertoire comprises opera, musical theatre, the occasional operetta, and concerts. Its large auditorium of 1,511 seats can be reduced in size to fit the production. The 2013 *Sommarnattens leende* had a run of twenty performances in an adjusted auditorium that seated 1,100. Although well received by audiences, it sold just over 50 percent of the theatre's seats.[155] For the 2013 production a new translation was commissioned from Erik Fägerborn,[156] making this the third Swedish translation of the show.[157] This time the translator and the producing theatre stayed true to Sondheim, Wheeler, and Prince.

The 2013 *Sommarnattens leende* was directed by Dennis Sandin, another musical theatre novice.[158] The set design, by Nina Fransson, was non-traditional: a gigantic wood-coloured parcel tied with a red ribbon was opened to reveal a set with a flat-packed feel to it (what could be more Swedish than that?), which unfolded to form the city silhouette in the first act and the mansion and park of Madame Armfeldt in the second. Just as in the Stockholm 2010 production, the playful set design contrasted with traditional costumes for the principal characters. Musically the production was lush and included a full opera orchestra. The first-generation actors with musical theatre training were now nearing middle age, so even the roles of Fredrik and Carl-Magnus could be cast from among their ranks (Christer Nerfont and Daniel Engman, respectively). Except for the opera singer Kerstin Meyer as Madame Armfeldt, the whole cast had a background in musical theatre or in a combination of musical theatre and opera.

The particular focus on the artistic style and demands of Sondheim's piece in the new translation and the casting was not highlighted in the theatre programme, however: the artistic director, Bengt Hall, proudly welcomed the audience with a text focusing on Bergman and his relationship with the city and the theatre.[159] The programme had three editorial contributions, two of which focused mostly on the Swedish icon.[160]

The doubts expressed by reviewers of earlier productions of A Little Night Music are mostly absent from the 2013 reviews. These notices reflect a sense of confidence in Sondheim's creation of a compelling piece of musical theatre suggested by the film, and that Malmö Opera is its natural producer. The most common criticisms concerned the performers' lack of acting skills and Sandin's inadequate handling of the dialogue scenes. Carlhåkan Larsén's review in Sydsvenskan began: 'Have you seen the Bergman film Sommarnattens leende? Forget it. The musical is something different, apart from its having the same story, as Ingmar Bergman himself said. The transformation is mainly due to Stephen Sondheim, the most respected creator of musicals, even if he is not the most popular.'[161] Larsén ended his review with: 'The production gives the audience elegant musical art without Eurovision Song Contest hysteria, cultivated and piquant entertainment without vulgarity. A smile of a winter evening.'[162]

Johanna Paulsson in Dagens Nyheter called the production a 'Sondheim sensation, rich in both nuance and elegance'.[163] The Broadway stalwart was also evoked by the critic in Svenska Dagbladet, Bo Löfvendahl: 'Erik Fägerborn's new translation also brings to the lyrics an elegant Sondheim-ness.'[164] Yet again the film is unavoidable, as the reviewer continues: 'Gunilla Backman [as Desirée] demonstrates what a great artist she is, just as elusively majestic as Eva Dahlbeck in Bergman's film.'[165]

# CONCLUSION

Over the course of these seven productions of A Little Night Music from 1974 to 2013, Bergman's and Sondheim's artistic reputations seem to rise and fall according to changes in cultural fashion.

Sondheim wanted actors rather than singers to perform A Little Night Music, but he did not have Scandinavian performers in mind, as he created the musical in a rather different artistic milieu. I dare say that the Swedish temperament is closer to that of

Henrik Egerman than that of Desirée Armfeldt, and thus Swedish actors seem to feel more at home in dramatic musicals than in extroverted and witty ones. This is of course a generalisation, which has varied over time with the decline of operetta and revue as well as the rise of musical theatre schools. But as a national temperament, it prevails. As much as the critics complained about not getting enough lightness and esprit in these productions, they nevertheless praised the various actresses portraying Desirée for their interpretations of 'Send in the Clowns'—moving, mature, and free from sentimentality. In these performances the national temperament appeared to match the tone of the (American) material.

With its linear plot, *A Little Night Music* might be mistaken for a conventional musical, an uncomplicated romantic comedy. I would argue it is instead one of Sondheim's most complex to perform or direct. Sondheim's score has been labelled 'difficult to sing', 'sophisticated', and even 'sadistic' by Swedish critics. What it demands from its cast is a different set of triple-threat skills: the cast needs to master that music as well as evoking the 'whipped cream' and 'the knives'.

Did something Swedish disappear when Sondheim, Wheeler, and Prince created their musical 'suggested by Ingmar Bergman's film'? For the most part not, since the film already has an air of French comedy and Middle European operetta. Yes, Sweden is a kingdom with a royal family, counts, and dukes, but most Swedes find it easier to identify with maids, coachmen, and farmhands. By making Madame Armfeldt the observer and a master of ceremonies of sorts and by relegating Frid completely to the sidelines, Sondheim and Wheeler lost 'us' one of our representatives on-stage, and our chance to observe, envy, and finally smile at the upper classes. Furthermore, excising the folkloric connotations of the wine served at the country weekend deprives the story of something that unconsciously connects to the myths of the Swedish Midsummer.

Was a certain undeniable Swedishness preserved or even strengthened in *A Little Night Music*? To judge from the consistent praise heaped by the local critics on the character and the different Swedish actresses portraying her, the source of that Swedishness seems to be Petra. Sondheim's maid was just as recognisable as Bergman's: the independent, genuine, sexually liberated young woman, free because she is not restricted by conventions. It is a vision, not necessary a reality, but it connects us backwards to our historic struggles and forward into *folkhemmet*. Sondheim and Wheeler also made sure to celebrate the light—the perpetual, magical twilight of the Swedish summer night, for instance in the song 'Nightwaltz (The Sun Won't Set)'. What was lost in translation in the Sondheim musical when it arrived on Swedish stages seemed to be Bergman's wit and acidic lightness—so well preserved by the American songwriter in his score—as well as the seething lust, barely contained by buttons and corsets. Reviewers also found the actors inadequate as singers or vice versa, while they observed theatre directors getting lost in attempting to respect the music while remaining loyal to Bergman's dramaturgy. Through these seven productions there have been instances when creatives or critics seemed to be rushing to Bergman's defence against menacing foreign powers, but also instances when critics reprimanded Swedish productions for not living up to (the critics' perception of) Sondheim's artistic standards.

Clearly, finding the perfect balance between the American composer-lyricist and the Swedish filmmaker has proven difficult in the latter's home country—even though it seems Bergman never saw them as competitors. Sondheim, in *Finishing the Hat*, tells the story of going to meet Bergman at his hotel suite the night after the Swedish director had seen *A Little Night Music* on Broadway. Sondheim, anxious to hear the verdict before even considering working with Bergman on *The Merry Widow*, babbled on, but Bergman graciously cut him off: 'No, no, Mr Sondheim, please. I enjoyed the evening very much. Your piece has nothing to do with my movie, it merely has the same story.' Sondheim recalls: 'I thought: only someone with that understanding and generosity would realize, much less say, such a thing. And then came the kicker: "After all," [Bergman] added, "we all eat from the same cake." '[166]

## Notes

1. There are two specific exceptions to the rule of translating musical theatre in Sweden: The most common is the use of diegetic pop songs in jukebox musicals and the rarely used is when an opera house decides to perform a musical in its original language.
2. Most names of theatres and newspapers are in definite form in Swedish, shown through the end "n" of the name. I have chosen to keep the Swedish names through this chapter, so as not to create a double definite form through the addition of "the" in front of the name.
3. *Into the Woods* has been produced at Wermland Opera, Karlstad, 1990–1991; Lillan (the smaller stage connected to Storan, focusing on children's and youths' repertoire), Gothenburg, 1991–1992; Malmö Stadsteater, 1991–1992; Södra Teatern, Stockholm, 1998; and Norrlandsoperan, Umeå, 2001.
4. *Sweeney Todd* has been produced at Wermland Opera, Karlstad, 1985–1986, 1989, and 2008; Lillan, Gothenburg, 1988–1989; Malmö Stadsteater, 1991; and Stockholms Stadsteater, 2013–2014. The Gothenburg Opera did a semi-staged production with English artists, performed in English, for a short run in 2008 and The Royal Swedish Opera in Stockholm did a full production, in English, in 2023. Sondheim productions in Sweden have often come about because of these aficionados or knowledgeable enthusiasts. When Staffan Aspegren was the artistic director at Lillan in Gothenburg, he programmed both *Into the Woods* and *Sweeney Todd*, directing them there and in Malmö. In 2013 he directed *Assassins*, and as artistic director at Smålands Musik & Teater he programmed a production of *Passion* that opened in 2016.
5. For example Högskolan för Scen och Musik, Göteborg; Balettakademien, Göteborg; Performing Arts School, Göteborg; Stockholm Musikalartist Utbildning; and Musikalakademien, Umeå.
6. Meryle Secrest, *Stephen Sondheim: A Life* (London: Bloomsbury, 1999), 258.
7. Bergman refers here to his affair with the actress Harriet Andersson, star of several of his movies.
8. Ingmar Bergman, quoted in Stig Björkman, Torsten Manns, and Jonas Sima (eds.), *Bergman om Bergman* (Stockholm: Norstedts, 1970), https://www.ingmarbergman.se/verk/sommarnattens-leende, accessed 20 April 2020. Translations of these and all other quotations are by the author.

9. Bergman, handwritten note, November 1954, quoted in Mikael Timm, *Lusten och dämonerna Boken om Bergman* (Stockholm: Norstedts, 2008), 246.
10. Anders Edström, 'Om Ingmar Bergman och *Sommarnattens leende* och Malmö Stadsteater', *A Little Night Music*, programme, 1974, Malmö Stadsteater, Malmö, 25.
11. Svenska Filminstitutet (The Swedish Film Institute) only offers Swedish box-office figures for national and international films that opened in Swedish cinemas in 1965 and later; https://www.filminstitutet.se/sv/fa-kunskap-om-film/analys-och-statistik/biografstatistik/. Distribution to foreign cinemas added to the sales figures. The film is described as successful when written about, for example, in Timm, *Lusten och dämonerna Boken om Bergman*, 253.
12. Ibid., 250.
13. Ibid., 247.
14. This prize was only given out in 1956; it seems to have been tailored to Bergman's film.
15. Timm, *Lusten och dämonerna Boken om Bergman*, 253.
16. Secrest, *Stephen Sondheim: A Life*, 219.
17. Harold Prince, *Sense of Occasion* (Milwaukee: Applause Theatre & Cinema Books, 2017), 171.
18. The screenplays mentioned by Prince are *Ring Round the Moon* by Jean Anouilh, *Rules of the Game* by Jean Renoir, and *Smiles of a Summer Night* (ibid., 171).
19. Ibid., 172.
20. Since Sondheim and Prince also had looked at a screenplay by Anouilh, it is worth noting that Bergman in the 1940s had directed two of Jean Anouilh's plays: *Tjuvarnas bal* (*Le Bal de voleurs*) in 1948 and *En vildfågel* (*La Sauvage*) in 1949, both at Göteborgs Stadsteater (Gothenburg City Theatre).
21. Stephen Sondheim, *Finishing the Hat: Collected Lyrics (1954–1981), with attendant Comments, Principles, Heresies, Grudges, Whines, and Anecdotes* (New York: Virgin Books, 2010), 252.
22. Ibid., 282–283.
23. On the Saturday before Easter 1974 Bergman wrote in his workbook: 'Now I have liquidated *The Merry Widow* and I must say it was with great relief I terminated the difficult lady.' Ingmar Bergman, *Arbetsboken 1955–1974* (Stockholm: Norstedts, 2018), 380.
24. For more details about the repertoire up to 1975, see http://www.diva-portal.org/smash/get/diva2:636905/FULLTEXT02, 208–252, accessed 20 February 2020.
25. The theatre first performed the Kern/Hammerstein show in its 1943–1944 season.
26. This was how several people who worked at the theatre in the early 1970s described him to me.
27. Lars Åhrén, 'Hur kunde *Company* slå så fel?', *GT*, 6 October 1971. All articles and reviews on Stora Teatern in the 1970s and the 1974 Gothenburg production are archived (without page numbers) at Faktarummet, Göteborgs Stadsmuseum.
28. I have not been able to find information on how this production (or any of the previous productions) fared at the box office. It is also difficult to find any records of how the audience reacted to the productions. In a conversation with Monica Lundberg, property mistress for *A Little Night Music* at Storan, she described the production as having done well at the box office and having been appreciated by the audience.
29. See https://www.ingmarbergman.se/en/productions/theater/göteborgs-stadsteater, accessed 3 May 2021.

30. *A Little Night Music*, programme, Stora Teatern, Stockholm, 1974, 6. Musikbiblioteket, GöteborgsOperan.
31. Ibid., 4.
32. Christer Tovesson, 'Sex dagar kvar till urpremiären: *Sommarnattens Leende* i ny form', *Arbetet*, 5 January 1974.
33. Britt Larsson, 'Jag vill bara göra Ingmar Bergman rättvisa', *Göteborgs-Posten*, 5 January 1974. What Ahlsell probably also refers to are artistic and political theatre trends at that time, leading to a "new" experimental theatre style where *Company* would fit in well. The failure of that production indicated that the audience at Stora Teatern was not interested in that type of musical theatre.
34. Nils Andersson, '*Sommarnattens leende*', *Arbetet*, 8 January 1974.
35. *A Little Night Music*, script, Stora Teatern, Gothenburg, 1974. Musikbiblioteket, GöteborgsOperan.
36. Andersson, '*Sommarnattens leende*'.
37. Ibid.
38. Pia Gadd, 'Sommarnatten ler igen', *Expressen*, January 10, 1974
39. Albenius may be mistaken here. Hal Prince claims that Bergman saw the show 'early in its run' which would be before January 1974 (Prince, *Sense of Occasion*, 180). However, according to Sondheim, Bergman saw the show after having approached Sondheim about writing the lyrics for *The Merry Widow*, a year into the run, i.e. after the musical's Swedish première (Sondheim, *Finishing the Hat*, 282).
40. How many and which newspapers write about and review local productions varies from town to town. Standard practice is to have a couple of reviews in local or regional newspapers, along with one or more of the four national newspapers: *Dagens Nyheter*, *Svenska Dagbladet*, *Expressen*, and *Aftonbladet*. Also highly variable is the number of notices to be found in the various archives and libraries, which explains why not all productions seem to have received the same amount of critical attention. The seven newspapers that reviewed *A Little Night Music* were *Expressen*, *Göteborgs-Tidningen*, *Arbetet*, *Göteborgs-Posten*, *Svenska Dagbladet*, *Dagens Nyheter*, and *Aftonbladet*.
41. Alf Thoor, 'Den blir en farsot', *Expressen*, 12 January 1974.
42. Ibid.
43. Ibid.
44. Ibid.
45. A German word meaning 'from way back when'.
46. Sune Hofsten, 'Lysande komedi—men valhänt som musical', *Göteborgs-Tidningen*, 12 January 1974.
47. Tony Kaplan, 'En kylig sommarnatt utan Bergmans leende', *Arbetet*, 12 January 1974.
48. Ibid.
49. This comment indicates that incidental music performed on an accordion was added. The accordion is a typical workers' instrument and as such strongly connected with Swedish folk music, accompanying dances outdoors and in barns.
50. Åke Perlström, 'Valsernas återkomst', *Göteborgs-Posten*, 12 January 1974.
51. Ulla-Britt Edberg, 'Skicklig men tam musical', *Svenska Dagbladet*, 12 January 1974.
52. Bengt Jahnsson, 'Storans *Sommarnatt* saknar entusiasmen', *Dagens Nyheter*, 12 January 1974. The comment shows that Jahnsson was not very knowledgeable about Sondheim—probably the least commercial of all Broadway composers—or his shows' (lack of) financial success.

53. Ibid.
54. Jurgen Schildt, 'Vart tog vinet vägen?', *Aftonbladet*, 12 January 1974.
55. Ibid.
56. These were the critics of *Expressen* and *Arbetet*.
57. Schildt, 'Vart tog vinet vägen?'
58. Henrik Sjögren, *Konst & nöje* (Malmö: Bra Böcker AB & Malmö Musik och Teater AB, 1994), 227.
59. See https://www.ingmarbergman.se/en/productions/theater, accessed 2 May 2021.
60. Claes Sturm, 'Malmö: Utan särskilda konstgrepp', *Dagens Nyheter*, 6 January 1974. All articles and reviews on the 1974 Malmö production are from Musik- och teaterbiblioteket, Musikverket, Stockholm, where they have been archived without page numbers.
61. Quoted in ibid.
62. Carlhåkan Larsén, 'Sommarnatt med stilfullt småleende', *Sydsvenska Dagbladet*, 2 February 1974.
63. Jan Richter, 'Kvinnoseger', *Expressen*, 2 February 1974.
64. Sven Malm, 'Kvinnorna var bäst', *Svenska Dagbladet*, 2 February 1974.
65. Larsén, 'Sommarnatt med stilfullt småleende'.
66. Bengt Haslum, *Operett och musical* (Stockholm: Sveriges Radios förlag, 1979), 230.
67. I have not found any records of how many people attended these performances.
68. Bengt Jahnsson, 'A Little Night Music: I Norrköping blev musicalen ypperlig', *Dagens Nyheter*, 28 February 1974. Musik- och teaterbiblioteket, Musikverket, Stockholm.
69. *A Little Night Music*, programme, Stadsteatern Norrköping-Linköping, Norrköping, 1974, 17.
70. Anna Greta Ståhle, 'Norrköping: Tiden flyttad till 1908', *Dagens Nyheter*, 6 January 1974. Musik- och teaterbiblioteket, Musikverket, Stockholm.
71. *A Little Night Music*, programme, Norrköping Stadsteatern, Norrköping-Linköping, 1974, 1. Stadsarkivet Norrköping.
72. See https://ostgotateatern.wordpress.com/category/nar/1970-tal/repertoar-1973-74/, accessed 20 April 2020. Nowadays the venue is called Östgötateatern.
73. Alf Thoor, 'Norrköping lyfter sig i håret—igen!', *Expressen*, 27 February 1974. Musik- och teaterbiblioteket, Musikverket, Stockholm.
74. Carl-Gunnar Åhlén, 'Vänligt men vagt', *Svenska Dagbladet*, 28 February 1974. Musik- och teaterbiblioteket, Musikverket, Stockholm.
75. Ibid.
76. Ibid.
77. Jahnsson, 'A Little Night Music: I Norrköping blev musicalen ypperlig'.
78. Ibid.
79. Åke Brandel, 'Sommarnatten i Norrköping: Stockholm behöver också föreställningen', *Aftonbladet*, 27 February 1974. Musik- och teaterbiblioteket, Musikverket, Stockholm.
80. Ibid.
81. Ibid.
82. Arne Malmberg, 'Sommarnatt utan leende i Norrköping', *Norrköpings Tidning*, 27 February 1974. Stadsarkivet, Norrköping.
83. Ibid.
84. Ibid.
85. Nils A. Hertz, 'Färg- och klangskön musicalföreställning', *Folkbladet Östgöten*, 27 February 1974. Stadsarkivet, Norrköping.

86. *Sommarnattens Leende*, programme, Folkan, Stockholm, 1978, 4. Musik- och teaterbiblioteket, Musikverket, Stockholm; part of the collection of documents donated by Mago.
87. Ibid.
88. Ingmar Bergman, *Sommarnattens leende* (Stockholm: Norstedts, 2018), 79, 90, and 93.
89. *Sommarnattens Leende*, programme, Folkan, Stockholm, 1978, 20.
90. The script from this production has not been preserved in any library or archive. Commercial theatres did not routinely donate scripts, programmes, photos, or other production materials to archives or libraries.
91. The song was included in the song list of the programme. This addition was mentioned, for example, in the review in *Expressen*. None of the critics raised any objections to this addition.
92. Sallert had proved her international star quality when she appeared in *Ben Franklin in Paris* on Broadway in 1964. See https://www.ibdb.com/broadway-production/ben-frank lin-in-paris-2827#OpeningNightCast, accessed 12 April 2020.
93. Elisabeth Sörenson, 'Zarah Leander på Folkan igen', *Svenska Dagbladet*, 14 January 1978. All articles and reviews on the 1978 Stockholm production are from the Musik- och teaterbiblioteket, Musikverket, Stockholm.
94. Bergman was arrested on 30 January 1976 while rehearsing *The Dance of Death* at the Dramaten and accused of tax evasion. The charges were later dropped, and Bergman left Sweden for Munich, vowing never to work in his home country again. It would have been quite a coup if Kinch had managed to persuade Bergman to return home to direct *Sommarnattens leende*. Whether there were plans to resume work on *The Dance of Death* or not, Bergman didn't direct at Dramaten until *King Lear* in 1984. See, for example, 'Bergman Says He Will No Longer Live in Sweden', *New York Times*, 23 April 1976, 76. See https://www.ingmarbergman.se/en/productions/theater/dramaten, accessed 2 May 2021.
95. Alf Halldin, 'Leander, Sallert och Malmsjö: Stjärnensemble på Nya Folkan', *Göteborgs-Posten*, 14 January 1978
96. Sörenson, 'Zarah Leander på Folkan igen'.
97. Lars Weck, 'Sju stjärnor på nya Folkan', *Dagens Nyheter*, 14 January 1978.
98. Tony Kaplan, 'Stjärnsmäll', *Arbetet*, 14 January 1978.
99. Björn Vinberg, 'Molvig = Andersson, Sallert = Dahlbeck', *Expressen*, 9 September 1978.
100. Tony Kaplan, 'Show för miljonen!', *Arbetet*, 11 September 1978.
101. In the past twenty years the number of performances per week in commercial theatres has diminished to four or five, concentrated over the weekend. Only the most popular productions still manage to do six performances per week.
102. Erik Näslund, 'Doftlös sommarnatt', *Sydsvenska Dagbladet*, 16 September 1978; Alf Halldin, 'Ingen fullträff på Folkan', *Göteborgs-Posten*, 16 September 1978; and Åke Janzon, 'En aning konventionellt men vackert och vårdat ..', *Svenska Dagbladet*, 16 September 1978.
103. Allan Fagerström, 'Djävlar! säger hon. Det räcker', *Aftonbladet*, 15 September 1978.
104. Tomas Sjöman, 'Här hyllas hon efter sin svåraste premiär', *Aftonbladet*, 15 September 1978.
105. Lasse Bergström, 'ZARAH I CENTRUM!—en lysande kväll', *Expressen*, 15 September 1978.
106. Leif Zern, 'Musikfest i *Sommarnatten*', *Dagens Nyheter*, 16 September 1978.
107. Ibid.

108. Ibid.

109. https://www.imdb.com/title/tt0083922/awards?ref_=tt_awd, accessed 2 May 2021.

110. See, for example, 'Makten och härligheten' ('The Power and the Glory'), episode 4 of the television documentary *Bergman—ett liv i fyra akter* (2018), directed by Jane Magnusson.

111. It is worth noting that the first Swedish production of the 1979 'musical thriller' was directed by Christopher Bond; it was produced by Musikteatern i Värmland, Karlstad, 1985. The company was later renamed Wermland Opera.

112. For example, the Stockholms Stadsteater started with musical productions on their outdoor summer stages in 1984, 1985, 1987, and 1990, and then programmed musical theatre for the main stage, starting with *City of Angels* in 1993; see Claes Englund (ed.), *Teaterårsboken 1982–1993* (Jönköping: Riksteatern, 1982–1993).

113. For more information on *Kristina från Duvemåla*, see chap. 27.

114. *Sommarnattens leende*, programme, Riksteatern, Stockholm, 1997, 17.

115. Claes Englund (ed.), *Teaterårsboken 1998* (Jönköping: Riksteatern, 1998), 102.

116. Marcus Boldemann, '*Sommarnattens leende*: Stephen Sondheims bitterljuva musikal här', *Dagens Nyheter*, 24 October 1997. All articles on and reviews of the 1997 production are from the Musik- och teaterbiblioteket, Musikverket, Stockholm.

117. Kristina Torell, 'Sommarnatt av riksintresse', *Göteborgs-Posten*, 22 October 1997.

118. Either Fredriksson was not satisfied with the quality of Wolgers's original translation, or these two songs had been cut from the 1978 script. However, according to the programme, 'Silly People' had been added to the 1978 commercial production. *A Little Night Music*, programme, Folkan, Stockholm, 1978, 9. Teatermuseet, Malmö.

119. In *Svenska Dagbladet, Dagens Nyheter, Göteborgs-Posten*, and *Sydsvenska Dagbladet*.

120. Leif Zern, 'Sommarnatt utan leende', *Dagens Nyheter*, 2 November 1997.

121. Ibid.

122. There are certain exceptions: Malmö Opera and the Gothenburg Opera regularly tour smaller productions of often lesser-known titles in their regions, while Stockholms Stadsteater and Wermland Opera occasionally produce musicals on their smaller stages. Östgötateatern continue to combine classics with new titles in their musical theatre repertoire, such as *Come From Away* (2020–2021 season) and *Waitress* (2023–2024 season). Riksteatern, however, no longer regularly includes musical theatre as part of their repertoire, and Folkan went out of business in 2001; the building has since been demolished. And a title such as *Wicked*, by many considered to belong to the commercial musicals, is scheduled to open at the subsidised GöteborgsOperan in the 2023–2024 season.

123. I imagine in the United States this ranking applies to Rodgers and Hammerstein musicals such as *Oklahoma!*: the material 'close to us' is likely to be placed higher in the American hierarchy than is European operetta.

124. It is possible to visualise these positions and how they change by using Pierre Bourdieu's map of cultural tastes; see Pierre Bourdieu, *Kultursociologiska texter* (Stockholm: Brutus Östlings Bokförlag Symposion, 1993), 290–291.

125. See https://www.ingmarbergman.se/verk, accessed 15 April 2020.

126. *Folkhemmet* ('the people's home') is a poetic name for the Swedish welfare state. It is a political concept introduced by Swedish Social Democratic prime minister Per Albin Hansson in 1928. The *folkhem* vision is based on the understanding that the entire society ought to be like a family, where everybody contributes, but also where everybody looks after one another. The Swedish Social Democrats' successes in the postwar period is often explained by the fact that the party managed to motivate major social reforms

A LITTLE NIGHT MUSIC IN SWEDEN   645

(for example, free health care, free education at all levels, free childcare, and unemployment benefits) with the idea of the *folkhem* and defining them as a joint endeavour of the national family; https://en.wikipedia.org/wiki/Folkhemmet, accessed 3 May 2020.

127. Leif Zern, *Se Bergman* (1993; Stockholm: Natur & Kultur, 2018), 15.

128. *Sommarnattens leende—A little night music*, script, Stockholms Stadsteater, Stockholm, 2010. Referens- och forskningsbiblioteket, Kulturhuset Stadsteatern, Stockholm.

129. This includes changing Madame Armfeldt's explanation of the three smiles to Frid's, prolonging Desirée's speech in the play-within-the-play, substituting almost the entire Desirée/Fredrik/Carl-Magnus dialogue in scene 4, and adding the film scene where Anne torments Henrik; see Bergman, *Sommarnattens leende*, 56–57 and 67.

130. Among the additions are the dialogue between Frid and Petra, a scene between Charlotte and Desirée (which was given to Charlotte and Anne instead), and Count Malcolm's long speech at the dinner about conquering women; see Bergman, *Sommarnattens leende*, 67 and 70.

131. 'A legend says that this wine is pressed from grapes whose juices emerge like drops of blood on the bright skin. [ ... ] Furthermore, it is recounted that into every vat that has been filled with this wine was added a drop of milk from a first-time mother's plump breast and a drop of semen from a young stallion. This sap gives the wine a secret arousing power, and whoever drinks of it must drink it on their own risk and responsibility.' Ibid., 70.

132. It is safe to assume that, since both the 1997 and 2010 productions had a dramaturge connected to the production, they did at least consult the original Wheeler/Sondheim libretto.

133. Wolgers's 1978 translation of 'Send in the Clowns' had the title 'Ta in en clown', whereas the 2010 production used 'Ge mig en clown'.

134. Artistic directors and directors who think Bergman's screenplay is better nowadays have the choice of staging a direct stage adaptation, just as Romateatern did in 2018; see http://romateatern.se/om-teatern#tidigare, accessed 4 May 2020.

135. Staffan Göthe, 'Det rosa och det svarta', in *Sommarnattens leende – A little night music*, programme, Stockholms Stadsteater, Stockholm, 2010. Referens- och forskningsbiblioteket, Kulturhuset Stadsteatern, Stockholm.

136. Sara Norling, 'Sondheim satte kniven i musikalgrädden', *Dagens Nyheter*, 14 February 2010.

137. Quoted in Craig Zadan, *Sondheim & Co.* (London: Pavilion, 1987), 182.

138. Ulricha Johnson, 'Musikalmästare med smak för dissonanser', *Svenska Dagbladet*, 26 February 2010. Johnson is also one of Sweden's most noted Sondheim translators, having translated *A Funny Thing Happened on the Way to the Forum*, *Company*, *Into the Woods*, *Assassins*, and *Passion*.

139. In this context, it is important to remember that Stockholm had not seen many productions of Sondheim musicals, if one doesn't include *West Side Story*. *A Funny Thing Happened on the Way to the Forum* in 1965 did not cause a tidal wave of Sondheim. *A Little Night Music* in 1978 was never promoted to audiences as a Sondheim musical, while the 1997 production only had a small number of Stockholm performances as part of its national tour. Finally, *Into the Woods* in 1998 was more of a fringe production, initiated by musical theatre actors, and had fewer than ten performances at Södra Teatern. It was not until 2013 that Stockholms Stadsteater produced *Sweeney Todd*, also directed by Theorell.

140. Ingegärd Waaranperä, 'En sommarnatt i Bergmans anda', *Dagens Nyheter*, 21 February 2010. All articles and reviews on the 2010 Stockholm production are archived at Referens- och forskningsbiblioteket, Kulturhuset Stadsteatern, Stockholm.

141. Bo Löfvendahl, 'Leendet lyfts av kören', *Svenska Dagbladet*, 21 February 2010.

142. Curt Bladh, 'Filmtrogen hyllning till Bergman', *Sundsvalls Tidning*, 21 February 2010.

143. Ibid.

144. Lisa Berg Ortman, 'Scenografin det enda som är sevärt', *Norrköpings Tidningar*, 22 February 2010.

145. "Antiquated": Waaranperä, 'En sommarnatt i Bergmans anda'; "deplorable view": Ortman, 'Scenografin det enda som är sevärt'.

146. Calle Pauli, 'Sommarnatten ler igen', *Dagens Nyheter*, 9 February 2010; in this article the director, Theorell, is quoted as stating that he 'never before had an intention to work in musical theatre.'

147. Ibid.

148. Gadd, 'Sommarnatten ler igen'.

149. Björn Vinberg, 'Molvig = Andersson Sallert = Dahlbeck', *Expressen*, September 9, 1978.

150. Pauli, 'Sommarnatten ler igen'.

151. Vinberg, 'Molvig = Andersson Sallert = Dahlbeck'.

152. Marita Jonsson, 'Sommarnattens leende i rykande snöstorm', *Gotlands Tidningar*, February 26, 2010.

153. '[I]t is definitely a directing mistake to place Jarl Kulle's heavy parade uniform on the shoulders of the inexperienced Andreas Kundler.' Lena S. Karlsson, 'Lagercrantzska uttalanden uteblir i djärv satsning', *Tidningen Kulturen*, 3 March 2010.

154. After the division of the theatre in the 1990s, it was renamed Malmö Opera och Musikteater. The name was shortened to Malmö Opera in 2008.

155. What importance does the Malmö Opera assign to the 2013 production, compared to other productions? The commemorative publication *Opera! Musikal! Konsert! Malmö Opera och Musikteater 1994–2019*, commissioned by the opera house to celebrate its first twenty-five years, provides one possible answer. In it, the gestation of *Kristina från Duvemåla* (which features on the book's cover) is told over seventeen pages, whereas *Sommarnattens leende* is only mentioned once, in the repertoire list.

156. Erik Fägerborn has translated such Sondheim works as *Sunday in the Park with George*, *Assassins*, *Merrily We Roll Along*, *Marry Me a Little*, and *West Side Story* and has directed eight Sondheim productions, including *Into the Woods* at Södra Teatern, 1998; see http://www.fagerborn.com/, accessed 4 May 2020.

157. A new translation is sometimes commissioned by the theatre, especially if the existing translation is found to be dated or if a different understanding of the work has emerged.

158. If we choose to categorise *The Threepenny Opera* as 'music theatre' as opposed to 'musical theatre', as is customary in continental Europe.

159. Bengt Hall, 'Kära publik', in *Sommarnattens leende*, programme, Malmö Opera, Malmö, 2013, 5. Marknadsavdelningen, Malmö Opera.

160. Timm, 'Skicka in skådespelarna', in *Sommarnattens leende*, programme, Malmö Opera, Malmö, 2013, 20–23; Marknadsavdelningen, Malmö Opera. Jan Richter, 'Tacka France för det!', in *Sommarnattens leende*, programme, Malmö Opera, Malmö, 2013, 32–33; Marknadsavdelningen, Malmö Opera.

161. Carlhåkan Larsén, 'Shakespearsaga i leksaksland', *Sydsvenskan*, 4 February 2013. All reviews of the 2013 Malmö production are from Marknadsavdelningen, Malmö Opera.

162. Ibid.
163. Johanna Paulsson, 'Lysande elegant kärlekskarusell', *Dagens Nyheter*, 4 February 2013.
164. Bo Löfvendahl, 'Respektlös lätthet i sommarnatten', *Svenska Dagbladet*, 4 February 2013.
165. Ibid.
166. Sondheim, *Finishing the Hat*, 282.


## BIBLIOGRAPHY

Please note that the theatre programmes, scripts and reviews referenced in this chapter are archived (the latter without page numbers) in the following institutions:

- Göteborg/Gothenburg: Faktarummet, Göteborgs Stadsmuseum; Musikbiblioteket, GöteborgsOperan
- Stockholm: Musik- och teaterbiblioteket, Musikverket; Referens- och forskningsbibliioteket, Kulturhuset Stadsteatern
- Malmö: Teatermuseet; Marknadsavdelningen, Malmö Opera
- Norrköping: Stadsarkivet Norrköping

Bergman, Ingmar. *Sommarnattens leende*. Stockholm: Norstedts, 2018.

Bergman, Ingmar. *Arbetsboken 1955–1974*. Foreword by Dorthe Nors. Stockholm: Norstedts, 2018.

Bourdieu, Pierre. *Kultursociologiska texter*. Stockholm: Brutus Östlings Bokförlag Symposion, 1993.

Haslum, Bengt. *Operett och musical*. Stockholm, Sveriges Radios förlag, 1979.

Prince, Harold. *Sense of Occasion*. Milwaukee, WI: Applause Theatre & Cinema Books, 2017.

Secrest, Meryle. *Stephen Sondheim: A Life*. London: Bloomsbury, 1999.

Shargel, Raphael, ed. *Ingmar Bergman Interviews*. Jackson: University Press of Mississippi, 2007.
Sondheim, Stephen. *Finishing the Hat: Collected Lyrics (1954–1981), with attendant Comments, Principles, Heresies, Grudges, Whines, and Anecdotes*. New York: Virgin Books, 2010.

Sondheim, Stephen, and Hugh Wheeler. *A Little Night Music*. New York: Applause Theatre & Cinema Books, 1991.

Taylor, Millie, and Dominic Symonds. *Studying Musical Theatre: Theory and Practice*. London: Palgrave Macmillan, 2014.

Timm, Mikael. *Lusten och dämonerna Boken om Bergman*. Stockholm: Norstedts, 2008.

Zadan, Craig. *Sondheim & Co*. London: Pavilion, 1987.

Zern, Leif. *Se Bergman*. 1933. Stockholm: Natur & Kultur, 2018.

# CHAPTER 23

## *PACIFIC OVERTURES*

### *Varied Perspectives*

GARY PERLMAN

## Bringing Japan to Japan

The idea of a Tokyo production of *Pacific Overtures*, the 1976 musical oddity about the American-driven opening of isolationist Japan in the nineteenth century, has a rather dizzying feel: a Japanese production of an American musical about the Japanese re-action to the arrival of Americans in Japan.[1] This is not like bringing a Japanese *Pearl Harbor Memories* to Honolulu, but it is true that the momentous changes that Commodore Perry's arrival helped foment, a quaint tale for most foreigners, are a vital part of the Japanese national identity. Indeed, many of the events and characters portrayed in the show—Japan's self-imposed isolation from the world, Manjiro, the Tokugawa shogunate, the Meiji Restoration and its consequences—are as familiar to any Japanese schoolchild as George Washington and the Revolutionary War are to Americans.

Even so, because the show was written by Americans for American audiences, the change in perspective made a Japanese production a challenge in some unexpected ways. Amon Miyamoto's radical Japanese-language rethink at Tokyo's New National Theatre nearly a quarter of a century later in October 2000, shed new light on the show and proved an unquestioned critical and popular triumph for the show's com-poser, Stephen Sondheim, and book writer, John Weidman, who attended the final performances. Sondheim declared it 'sensational', while Weidman remarked: 'I feel Miyamoto-san's choices delivered the intention of the show more successfully than it has ever been delivered before. Indeed, it is hard to imagine a more sensitive interpreta-tion of what Hal [the original director, Harold Prince], Steve and I intended.'[2] The suc-cess of the one-month run prompted a revival two years later at the same theatre and again in 2011 at the Kanagawa Arts Theatre in Yokohama, where Miyamoto was serving as artistic director. The original Japanese production travelled to Washington, DC and New York's Lincoln Center in 2002, and, in a nice reversal, was recreated by the director

FIG. 23.1 Stephen Sondheim and John Weidman in front of the marquee for the 1984 off-Broadway revival of their 1976 musical *Pacific Overtures*. Photo: Marty Reichenthal, provided by the editors.

in English two years later on Broadway, where it received a Tony Award nomination for Best Musical Revival.

Yet how did the Japanese themselves view the show, and how did they react to both its text and the production? These important questions will be considered in the following essay.

## The Show's Gestation and Original Reception

Sondheim has spoken of seeing a three-panelled Japanese screen in New York's Metropolitan Museum of Art as part of his research for the show. He recalls that he was overwhelmed by the near blankness of the middle and right panels, reflecting what he saw as Japanese minimalism, and cites this as a prime inspiration for his work on the musical.[3]

It is worth noting that formal screens were often created as backdrops for dignitaries, designed with densely painted outsides and mostly blank middle sections so that the sitter would be highlighted and not obscure the work. If that is the case here, what Sondheim saw as an empty space would in fact be where a high-ranking person would sit. That is, the screen was not simply decoration but a functional object, and the space was not blank—it was simply missing the human as the final piece, like a lyric without the music.

That's essentially how Westerners view *Pacific Overtures*. Without a knowledge of the circumstances behind Perry's mission or the crumbling structure of Japan's shogunate (military government), audiences see only a limited picture of the whole. Differing readings of musicals among cultures are hardly rare; *My Fair Lady*, for example, seen by the British as an archetypal study of class, is to US viewers a typical American success story where even a flower girl can become a princess (metaphorically speaking) if she works hard enough. Still, Japan's starkly different history and relation to the West make for an especially enlightening comparison when considering the reception of the 1976 show.

Even within Sondheim's extraordinary oeuvre, which encompasses shows about crushed illusions (*Follies*, 1971), cannibalism (*Sweeney Todd*, 1979), and presidential assassins (*Assassins*, 1990), *Pacific Overtures* stands out for the eclectic choice and treatment of its topic. The show was not originally conceived as a musical: Weidman, drawing on his studies in East Asian history at Harvard, had written a play about America's incursion into Japan. It was the legendary director Harold Prince who suggested portraying the story from the Japanese perspective and, to Weidman's surprise, envisaged it as a musical. He then convinced a reluctant Sondheim to go along.[4] The major characters are all Japanese, with Westerners limited largely to brief appearances in the songs. Sondheim describes the show as 'historical narrative as written by a Japanese who's seen a lot of American musicals'.[5] Sondheim's score strives to reflect this with a less-is-more style in both music and lyrics to approximate a traditional Japanese sound and sensibility, attempting to 'infuse the lyrics with the evocative simplicity of haiku'.[6] Most strikingly, Prince employed a daring Kabuki-inspired approach to highlight the 'otherness' of the East: he used an all-male cast with white painted faces and exaggerated acting styles, while the set emphasised what the director saw as the flatness of Kabuki theatre, spreading the action across the length of the stage.

It was a highly inventive if commercially risky production of a type that is probably no longer possible under Broadway's current economic regime. Failing to find public favour in the shadow of that year's megahit *A Chorus Line*, the show closed after only 193 performances, the shortest run of the four Prince-Sondheim collaborations up to that time and the first not to win a Tony Award for Best Musical. Tellingly, John Simon wrote years later that for him a basic problem with the show was that '[t]he opening up of Japan is not a topic that elicits potent echoes in our psyche'.[7] That was obviously not a problem for the Tokyo production.

The show's story derives from an historical incident, the uninvited arrival of US Admiral Matthew Perry off the shores of modern-day Tokyo in 1853. Perry was on an official mission to pry open an isolationist Japan to trade, whether Japan wanted this or not. Japan's capitulation and the signing of a formal trade treaty the next year opened the floodgates for other Western nations, followed in rapid order by civil war, the toppling of the government, a wholesale upheaval of society, and a headlong plunge into the modern era, all of which is touched upon in the span of this remarkable musical.

The story begins with the arrival of a number of massive American warships, 'four black dragons', on Japanese shores, sending the government into a frenzy. Kayama, a minor official initially tasked with getting rid of the frightening invaders, has enlisted the help of Manjiro, an English-speaking fisherman who, having lived for some time in America after his rescue at sea by US sailors, had been imprisoned back in Japan for dealing with foreigners. Though he fails in his mission, Kayama becomes increasingly enamoured of the Western lifestyle after the rise of the new government, while Manjiro despairs at what is being lost. Their relationship and Japanese history move relentlessly in a direction neither envisaged.

Despite the Japanese setting, reviews through the years suggest that Americans look upon the show largely as a comment on themselves. In their minds, the point of the show, coming in the wake of America's withdrawal from Vietnam, was the inadvertent consequences of intervention into the political affairs of other nations. The *New York Times*, discussing a later Chicago revival, saw the musical's theme as 'the West's reckless insinuation of itself into the affairs of the other hemisphere' and the dangers of 'the superimposition of one culture on another, however well intended'.[8] In this context, the review noted a connection with the American involvement in Afghanistan, which was just getting under way.

# PACIFIC OVERTURES IN TOKYO

The Japanese production got its start when Miyamoto, who had made his name with his lively take on classic American musicals, was approached by Tokyo's New National Theatre to direct a musical of his choice. Miyamoto had been interested in *Pacific Overtures* ever since he saw a broadcast on Japanese television in 1976 of the original Broadway production, filmed by the Coca-Cola Company as a gift to Japan to commemorate America's bicentennial.[9] Seen largely as a curiosity, the show was never rebroadcast and was not considered commercially viable for a local staging given its unusual structure, especially the Kabuki-inspired format. It quickly faded from memory. Miyamoto, an unabashed Sondheim fan, saw the New National Theatre's offer as his perfect chance. With the theatre's enthusiastic backing, he took a look at the forgotten musical and spent the next year and a half developing it, including much back and forth with the creators over proposed changes.

Sondheim was not unknown in Japan, but the occasional productions of his shows, from *Company* and *Sweeney Todd* to such unlikely candidates as *Do I Hear a Waltz?*, had made little impact. His fame derived almost entirely from his work as lyricist for *West Side Story*, a seminal show that helped spark Japan's enduring musical boom upon its first Japanese-language performance in the 1960s. He was honoured in 2000 with Japan's prestigious Praemium Imperiale, often described as the 'Nobel Prize of the Arts', but that was connected largely with *West Side Story* and his fame in the West; the obscure *Pacific Overtures* was not even mentioned, though a small photo of the show does appear inconspicuously on the website.[10] In an uncanny coincidence, the award ceremony was held toward the end of *Pacific Overtures*' brief Tokyo run. Taking advantage of the fortuitous timing, Sondheim brought Weidman along to Japan to catch the show.

Notwithstanding the mid-1970s television broadcast, for the vast majority of the Tokyo audience the Japanese-language production represented their first experience with the show. As opposed to the America-centric view of Broadway audiences, Japanese theatregoers tended to see the musical as a comment on the peculiarities of their own society, with Perry's sudden appearance serving largely as a catalyst for changes that they considered inevitable over the long run. Their Japan was not a victim but very much the protagonist. Of course, they were seeing the incident within a much broader context.

For nearly 250 years the shoguns, Japan's military dictators, had artificially prevented change due to a perceived threat from foreigners by simply shutting off the island nation from the rest of the world. The rising interest that the public had shown in the West, beginning with the arrival of the Portuguese in the sixteenth century was decisively suppressed: Japanese were expressly forbidden from leaving the country, outsiders were not allowed into the nation, and foreign trade was restricted to limited exchange with the Dutch and Chinese on a small man-made island off the distant southern city of Nagasaki. The general peace associated with the period was imposed by considerable force from the centre. By the nineteenth century, the regime was coming under threat from mounting internal dissent, mainly from the country's southwest, and the arrival of Perry's 'Black Ship' was in some ways the excuse that the rebels had been waiting for. The subsequent opening of the country was as dramatic as it was only because the leaders had kept the lid on for so long; any contact with the rest of the world was bound to be a shock, as Japan could no longer open itself up in any organic way.

This is the perspective from which Japanese audiences approach the musical. The focus for them is not the rights and wrongs of the American incursion as such. They would not subscribe to the belief that the Americans were attempting to impose their culture on Japan; it was the abiding curiosity among the Japanese for things foreign that the shogunate had been so determined to repress in the first place. In their minds, America is neither to be blamed nor credited for developments that are rooted deep in Japan's history and psyche. For instance, the government's strong aversion to change of any kind unless compelled by outside pressure, so deftly portrayed in the musical, is a characteristic that remains much commented upon today.

One of the charges commonly levelled against the musical in the United States is that the characters often seem little more than symbolic representations of ideas rather than flesh-and-blood figures. This was much ameliorated in Tokyo by the fact that such roles as the fisherman Manjiro (known in Japan as 'John Manjiro') and Emperor Meiji are well-known historical figures and thus immediately recognisable to Japanese audiences. While this does not preclude the need to develop the characters within the context of the show itself, the roles do come with built-in personalities that make any such weaknesses less apparent, similar to *Hamilton*'s reliance on Westerners' familiarity with individuals such as Thomas Jefferson and King George III. In this sense, Weidman's book perhaps comes off even better in Japanese than in the original English.

## THE PHYSICAL STAGING

Miyamoto sought in his production to highlight the distinction between the Japanese ('us') and the rest of the world ('them'). His approach was suggested in the poster art: as opposed to the American logo featuring a vigorous Kabuki-esque figure, the Tokyo advertising reproduced a realistic (and none too flattering) rendering of Commodore Perry by a nineteenth-century Japanese artist.

A visible metaphor for this division was established in the very structure of the set. The stage was a square platform surrounded on three sides by water, looking very much like the island 'floating in the middle of the sea' described in the opening number.[11] The stage was framed by two giant *torii*, the large crossbar-like structures that mark the entrance to shrines, thus suggesting the sacred nature of Japan. In the back was a wooden lattice frame with doors in the centre that opened to reveal two more sliding doors, which were used for scenes such as those with the emperor. This gave a feeling of multiple layers, of another world within. Screens were also introduced, in extremely inventive ways, for many other scenes. During the first act, before the nation was 'violated', Japanese characters all remained within the confines of the stage proper, an effective symbol of the nation's isolation.

In contrast, the *hanamichi*, the walkway extending to the back of the theatre, represented the sea and more generally the world outside. The Black Ship never appeared as it did so memorably in Boris Aronson's Tony-winning design, remaining an abstract presence, and foreigners initially stayed exclusively on the hanamichi. Thus, the hanamichi was used not just for entrances and exits, as in Prince's concept, but for entire scenes involving the foreigners, who delivered their lines essentially from the middle of the audience. This gave an otherworldly quality to the foreign invaders and added a three-dimensional aspect to the show, pulling the audience into the action. In the real payoff, it heightened the drama significantly in moments when the gap was breached, such as Kayama's venture onto the hanamichi to confront the Black Ship as well as the eventual entrance of foreigners onto Japanese soil. The invasion of the foreign ambassadors in 'Please Hello' put an end to the divide, with foreigners and Japanese alike appearing subsequently on both sides of the footlights.

More strikingly, the director abandoned the distinctive Kabuki style of the original production for a more naturalistic approach. He reasoned that, for one thing, Japanese audiences do not see Japan as particularly exotic—even the nineteenth-century setting is standard fare for television samurai dramas. Moreover, because Kabuki is a well-entrenched art form in Japan, expectant audiences might hold acting and production standards to levels that ordinary musical actors could not hope to meet (Miyamoto himself was raised next door to one of Tokyo's major Kabuki theatres). In any event, a Kabuki version would have required an entirely different style of acting and language that would have been more alienating than enlightening.

Thus, the Japanese scenes were generally acted, spoken, and costumed in a fairly standard manner, as a kind of costume drama. The Reciter was portrayed in *rokyoku* style, a form of traditional storytelling. The role was played in fact by a well-known rokyoku comedian, Takeharu Kunimoto, who was able to interpolate some of the tricks of his trade, using a specific singing style and the three-stringed shamisen, in a way that made the role completely his own. Overall, the Reciter played a more dynamic and physical role than the stationary narrator in Prince's version, adopting an ironic stance rather than the angrier approach of the original. The rest of the cast played their roles as was appropriate.

In the impressive opening scene, the cast, all dressed in nondescript black outfits, appeared slowly on stage as a figure clad in a loincloth beat a *taiko* drum. As the Reciter took over, they gradually rose and disappeared before reappearing in their costumes behind moving screens. The director thus established immediately the abstract feel of the overall piece as the Reciter told the story, even as the individual scenes themselves were presented realistically. In another example, 'There Is No Other Way' was not danced as in the original but intricately staged to the music as Kayama and his wife slowly prepared for his journey in a natural yet highly evocative manner. In 'Four Black Dragons', the actors again played their roles straight but were backed by an innovative use of wooden screens, which almost became characters on their own: unseen actors not only slid them across the stage but brought them forward, turned them on their sides, and wove them in to accent the music and action on stage. The director's own favourite point in the show was 'Someone in a Tree', with its simultaneous representation onstage of past and present. He interpolated this idea into other moments, such as introducing Tamate as a ghostly vision in the early stanzas of 'A Bowler Hat'.

The general presentation was straightforward; the sets were clean and spare, and even the exquisite costumes were generally rendered in subdued tones, mainly white for lords and high officials, blue for the townspeople, and black for foreigners. The show's austere look, inspired more by aristocratic Noh theatre than by populist Kabuki, actually brought out the humour in an effective manner. Miyamoto is an old hand at comedy and made the most of his opportunities here.

Having ditched the Kabuki style, Miyamoto also abandoned the concept of an all-male cast, employing women for the more serious female roles such as Kayama's wife, Tamate.

FIG. 23.2 The foreigners arrive in Japan: the musical number 'The Advantages of Floating in the Middle of the Sea' in the 2002 Tokyo production of *Pacific Overtures*, the first revival of Amon Miyamoto's celebrated 2000 staging. Photo: Masahiko Yako, courtesy of the New National Theatre Tokyo.

This changed the dynamics of such scenes as 'Welcome to Kanagawa', which in Tokyo used only two men in drag along with three women. Local audiences were also deprived of the sudden jolt in the original production when women suddenly appeared on stage in the final number, 'Next'. Worse, many women in the audience expressed offence at what they felt were stereotypically weak female characterisations, especially Tamate's Butterfly-like suicide and the 'Pretty Lady' sequence.[12] The use of men in these roles, as in Kabuki, would have injected a layer of fantasy that might have made such scenes easier to accept. Still, this also involves questions of modern women's image of themselves, which is a matter for another essay. (It should be remembered here that the director, while Japanese, is also male.)

Miyamoto had his real fun with the foreign characters in the show. As opposed to the authentic costumes and look of the Japanese characters, the foreigners wore frightening half-face masks with huge noses and wild wigs, resembling the contemporary drawing used for the poster art. As that drawing suggests, foreigners must have been perceived as monsters, and the production shows this very humorously. Miyamoto gave Commodore Perry this same look rather than attempting to recreate the lion-like Kabuki figure of the original script, making him into an awesome seven-foot figure. The director further preserved the Japanese/foreign divide by having the American characters on the Black

FIG. 23.3 The Japanese director Miyamoto opted for an austere design that featured costumes in subdued tones, with white for lords and high officials while the townspeople were clad in blue. Scene from the 2002 Tokyo production. Photo: Masahiko Yako, courtesy of New National Theatre Tokyo.

Ship speak English as per the original script, a foreign language for the audience as well as the characters. Manjiro interprets back into Japanese for Kayama—and, therefore, the audience—which actually makes more sense than the original version. Miyamoto gets terrific mileage out of this at the end of the scene: when the Americans threaten in English to 'blast [Japan] off face of earth', Manjiro is speechless for a moment, leaving the expectant Kayama and the audience hanging before he interprets the remark. This adds a wonderful comic touch that would be difficult to convey in an English-language production.

With the lion gone, Miyamoto cut the Lion Dance at the end of the first act, a major change that jettisoned much of the music and reworked the scene (with the authors' permission, it should be noted) so that the foreigners were back on the hanamichi and the entire Japanese cast gathered on the stage. The invaders then scream, somewhat histrionically, 'Remember America!', followed by an immediate blackout, bringing the first act to a dramatic close.

The subsequent arrival of foreigners in 'Please Hello', when the various admirals bounded from the hanamichi into 'Japan', was performed with appropriate broadness of touch and very humorously. The various foreigners all had the same frightening masks as the Americans, with only different-coloured wigs to distinguish them. They had Lord

FIG. 23.4 'Please Hello', the opening number of act 2, in the 2011 Kanagawa revival of Miyamoto's production. Photo: Akihito Abe, courtesy of Kanagawa Arts Theatre (KAAT).

Abe sign not documents but large national flags that they carried in with them, an interesting variation that again shows the stylised nature of the foreign scenes versus the more realistic Japanese scenes.

By contrast with the lovely and historically accurate Japanese costumes, some curious choices were made when it came to the foreign costumes. Rather than using the various uniforms of the nations represented, the show's costume designer, Emi Wada (an Academy Award–winner for Akira Kurosawa's *Ran*, 1985), dressed all the ambassadors in the same undefined outfits—a more unified approach presumably intended to play down the differences among the various foreigners in order to preserve the stress on the Japanese/foreigner gap. However, the Russian ambassador's repeated warnings not to touch his coat are much funnier when he is wearing mink rather than a normal jacket (he had only a thin furry thread running down the front), and the Dutch ambassador, oddly, wore normal shoes even as he refers specifically to his wooden clogs. Less forgivable was 'A Bowler Hat', when Kayama refers to a cutaway even as he holds a regular suit jacket. Since the Western items referred to in this scene are highly symbolic of the great changes in Japanese society at the time, it may have been wiser to stick to the real thing.

All in all, Miyamoto's confident production worked superbly for Japanese audiences, playing ingeniously on their familiarity with the Black Ship incident. The initial isolation of the Japanese was splendidly evoked, giving great power—and, in the end, poignancy—to the nation's chaotic emergence into the modern world. Additionally, the choreographed movement in such scenes as 'Four Black Dragons' and 'Pretty Lady' made skilful use of screens and the small stage, being wonderfully integrated into the story. Sondheim and Weidman felt that the understated quality of the set, costumes, lighting, and direction itself enhanced the narrative and songs, making the show, according to Sondheim, 'much funnier than the Broadway version'.[13] Miyamoto proved definitively that the show could stand on its own without the Kabuki elements that defined the original production.

## Miyamoto's Handling of Historical and Cultural Inaccuracies

There were certain elements in the script that were strange or unclear to Japanese audiences, though Miyamoto was able to negotiate the staging around most of these. For instance, he simply excised the sumo wrestlers, who would not have played any part in the shogun's household or politics. Also, in the original script, the procession in the opening scene introduces the emperor first, followed by the shogun and then the feudal lords. Miyamoto reversed the order to present the emperor last, for reasons of respect enshrined in Japanese tradition. Although this unfortunately goes against the music, it is a logical choice given the expectations of the audience, not to mention the continued presence of an emperor in Japan today (Meiji's great-grandson when the Japanese production was mounted).

However, other difficulties inherent in the text proved impossible to resolve satisfactorily. The shogun's murder in 'Chrysanthemum Tea' was already considered pretty farfetched even for a fictional treatment, but worse, the idea of Lord Abe taking over as shogun would be akin to the UK prime minister's taking the crown after the death of the sovereign. As audiences were well aware, the shogun would be chosen strictly from the ruling Tokugawa family. Faced with this clear impossibility, the translator suggested making Abe a representative of the shogun. Miyamoto, however, made a deliberate choice in this case to retain the original script. Interestingly, he felt that an obvious fabrication of this scale would help audiences see the overall musical as an invention, allowing them to accept other historical inaccuracies more readily.[14]

Another problematic case was Tamate's suicide, which puzzled many viewers. They saw no clear reason for an action so desperate. Had she borne her worries stoically and waited patiently for her husband to return, she would have painted a sympathetic and indeed more 'Japanese' picture (as seen by the Japanese). Then, if he had failed in his mission, her suicide might have been understandable. As it was, her death seemed to come from nowhere.

Still more troublesome was the portrayal of Manjiro. Audiences could forgive as dramatic licence the concept of Manjiro as an intermediary with the Americans—though the real Manjiro, suspected initially as a spy after his return from the United States, was never allowed anywhere near the invaders. The real problem was his transformation from a fisherman to a samurai, which was lacking in verisimilitude in the form presented here. (The actual Manjiro served honourably in the Meiji government after the demise of the shogunate and lived a long peaceful life. Incidentally, prior to the production, the producers visited Manjiro's descendants, bowing and bearing gifts to apologise for the show's treatment of their ancestor.[15]) Local audiences were aware that social boundaries in feudal Japan were not crossed quite so easily in terms of either actual rank or sensibility; even if Manjiro was accorded samurai status in name, which appears to be true, the idea of a fisherman turned killer brought the portrait at times close to caricature. It doesn't help that the Japanese have an image of Manjiro as a Westernised character— indeed, Japan's first international figure—rather than a rabid samurai.

Miyamoto's approach to the issue illustrates his meticulous concern for detail in realising his overall vision. First, against the explicit directions of the script, Manjiro, glancing into Kayama's home, becomes aware of Tamate's suicide. Miyamoto felt that this would set off doubts in Manjiro's mind about whether the involvement of foreigners in Japan is really for the best.[16] Later, when Manjiro is granted the status of samurai, he did not immediately change into the appropriate clothes as on Broadway, because this was felt to be too sudden. Similarly, during 'A Bowler Hat', he does not perform the refined art of the tea ceremony indicated by the script, but rather stares blankly at the sword placed in front of him as if contemplating the meaning of his new position. It is only then that he changes outfits, accepting gradually, if reluctantly, his new role, thereby offering a nice contrast with Kayama, who changes into Western clothing in the same scene.

A more substantial change concerned Manjiro's final confrontation with Kayama. In the original production, Manjiro, having taken the side of the anti-Western forces, attacked and killed Kayama with a sword. Given the fact that Kayama had earlier saved his life, this had a false feel to it in a country where loyalty is valued above all. In the Tokyo production, it was Kayama who challenged first, and not with a sword but a gun, a symbol of his Westernisation. Manjiro thus took up the challenge only in defence, which avoided the problematic image of the sword-happy samurai. When he told Kayama to 'draw your sword as a samurai', he was telling him to put away his gun, effectively challenging Kayama's very identity as a Japanese. Despite the unlikely picture for audiences of Manjiro as assassin, the scene rang psychologically true. It would not be surprising if this were to be introduced into future versions of the show as the definitive interpretation of the scene.

As opposed to these problematic elements, the Japanese language and perspective added immeasurably to several scenes that might not be replayable elsewhere. The humorous confrontation between Kayama/Manjiro and the Americans on the Black Ship has already been mentioned. In another splendid example, the metaphorical story told to the emperor about Korea was done in the tradition of ancient *kyogen* comedy in an exceptionally well-written and beautifully choreographed scene. Miyamoto was able to take advantage of a certain level of knowledge here regarding kyogen conventions and language. Similarly, the rokyoku tradition involves a certain way of singing and narrating that was perfectly adapted to the show's requirements. More generally, the audience's familiarity with the history permits many short cuts. The mere mention of Emperor Meiji, for instance, immediately evokes images both of Japan's rapid modernisation and the growing dominance of the military in that era, affecting the director's choices in the final scene.

The most crucial change to the show came with a startling addition by Miyamoto during the final song, 'Next'. The song began as in the original production, but as the Japan of the story hurtled forward in its modernisation and the music intensified, the performers, dressed in black as in the show's opening scene, appeared on the stage with rifles in hand, representing the militarisation that eventually carried Japan into World War II. Commodore Perry then makes an ominous appearance, walking slowly and deliberately down the hanamichi towards the stage. He was the same monstrous giant as in the end of the first act, but his eyes this time were two bright lights. When he reached the end, facing down the guns that were now pointed at him, the stage suddenly exploded in a bright flash of light, with the torii toppling and people onstage collapsing in death; this represented the explosion of the atomic bomb in 1945, a moment in Japanese history as pivotal and symbolic as the arrival of the Black Ship.

It was an addition that felt necessary and was brilliantly realised, singled out by Sondheim as 'the most powerful five minutes in the show'.[17] The composer noted that the original production was criticised severely for leaving out World War II, which wasn't the initial intention: he had originally conceived 'Next' as a series of images that would cover Japan's entire history from the Meiji era to the present, including the war and the atomic bomb. Ultimately the creators discarded this as unwieldy. (Weidman recalled wryly that the first question asked by numerous viewers after the Broadway opening in 1976 was 'What happened to Pearl Harbor?' They were essentially accusing the musical of letting the Japanese off too easily, thus displaying their own fundamental misunderstanding of what the show is about.[18])

The Japanese, of course, knowing full well the tragic course of their history in the first half of the century, did not need to have such things spelled out and could therefore appreciate the scene in the larger context of their own relentless pursuit of progress. The characters at this point rise slowly and move back into the number, but the lingering image of the bomb makes clear the price that Japan has had to pay for its journey into the present. The performers subsequently shed their jackets to reveal black tank tops, and the pace gradually picked up to a powerful crescendo. The narration within the song, which included updated references to cell phones and the internet, was dominated by an unbroken recital of numbers—dates, sales figures, production volumes, share prices—while the images of numbers were flashed onto the set. This was Miyamoto's own comment on Japan's race for economic pre-eminence in the postwar era. It was a marvellously accomplished number.

## The Musical's Reception in Tokyo

Weidman's book played remarkably well in Japanese, even out of its Kabuki context. The progression of the story, relationships between the characters, and overall tone of the show, with the significant exceptions mentioned above, fit smoothly into a Japanese context. This was helped as well by the brilliant directorial vision of Miyamoto, who made certain adjustments to fit his audience's understanding and perception. To an extent, the reception of the book was affected by the awareness that this was a Western creation. For example, whatever the feelings towards Manjiro's presentation, which might have been rejected in a Japanese work, audiences could appreciate the idea of a character who becomes more Japanese in spite of (or because of) his knowledge of the West, as opposed to the gradual Westernisation of the very Japanese Kayama.

Sondheim's music, removed from the familiar context of its English lyrics, was cast in a notably new and unexpected light. The orchestra had only seven pieces and two percussionists yet sounded absolutely thrilling. The music itself is neither Japanese nor pretending to be so, but the composer has found an idiom that wonderfully suits the Japanese sensibility, combining the pentatonic scale of Japanese music with the sound of the Spanish composer Manuel de Falla for an exotic East-West blend in a minor key.[19] The limited range of the music, without showy leaps up the scale or belting endings, fits precisely the Japanese fondness for more controlled emotions, giving the lyrics a perfect underpinning. The opening number worked exceptionally well with the rokyoku style of narration, crucial for laying the groundwork for audiences expecting a 'Broadway' sound. Other standouts included 'There Is No Other Way' and 'Chrysanthemum Tea', which sounded almost as they had been composed for the Japanese lyrics. The more melodious 'Pretty Lady' and 'Next' convey nicely the ambience of Japan's increasing Westernisation after the restrained sounds that have preceded them. If the Japanese production did anything, it highlighted the genius of the music as an integral part of the drama.

The lyrics were superbly translated by Kuni Hashimoto. This is an impressive feat considering the complexities of the Japanese language, encompassing nineteenth-century court dialogue, kyogen theatre, traditional poetry, and more, which have to sound fairly authentic yet still understandable to Japanese ears. Particularly impressive was 'Chrysanthemum Tea', which, sung by the mother of the shogun, needed to be in a very specific idiom while still dealing with the intricate word play of the English lyrics. The result remarkably resolved these issues. As it turns out, Hashimoto says that such densely worded songs were actually easier than the sparer sound of, for instance, 'A Bowler Hat', which he cites as the biggest single challenge.[20] Another enjoyable number was 'There Is No Other Way', whose title was translated interestingly as 'The Bird Waiting for [Someone's] Return'. Sondheim gave special praise to 'Welcome to Kanagawa', a number that he said had never worked in the United States because of an overly intricate rhyme scheme (he has called it 'the most annoyingly problematic song I've ever written').[21] He sensed from the enthusiastic audience reaction in Tokyo that the intended humour was finally getting across.[22]

The Japanese, known for their perverse interest in how the world views them, responded with vocal enthusiasm to the production as a whole, especially the second act. Musically, the comic numbers 'Welcome to Kanagawa' and 'Please Hello' were big crowd-pleasers, expertly translated and inventively staged (including a novel use of ropes by prostitutes in the former that is best not described). Most popular seemed to be the 'Bowler Hat' sequence, which appeared to strike a particular chord with its depiction of a world in gradual but inexorable transition. The final moments of the show, when Kayama and his wife reappear quietly in a moving reminder of what has been lost, were also considered supremely effective.

At the same time, there was a subtle shift in the show's theme. Miyamoto cannot be said to have ignored America's role entirely: among other touches, he created a striking tour de force involving the American flag as a symbol of US assertiveness, rewrote the first-act ending to heighten the American threat, and inserted a curious reference to Iraq, in which the United States (but not Japan) was deeply involved at the time. This undoubtedly attracted the attention of American viewers when the show moved to Broadway, where more than one reviewer noted the 'timeliness' of the show',[23] and may very well reflect the intentions of the show's creators.

## CONCLUSION

For Japanese audiences, the show is a timeless re-examination of their own past and present—notably, whether it is desirable or possible forcibly to prevent the natural flow of history, even for the sake of apparent stability. That is, in their minds the musical is concerned less with the perils of progress than with its inevitability; it is a warning not against change but against a refusal to change, an issue still relevant in that conservative country. The question then becomes how best to adapt one's traditions to a changing world. In this sense, the show interestingly brings to mind another Harold Prince show about tradition and change, *Fiddler on the Roof*, whose Japanese-language version has been enormously popular for decades.

The perspective of the show was thus entirely different in the eyes of its subject, the Japanese people, whose perception of Japan's experience with US intervention— including America's postwar occupation of their country—has not been altogether negative. (A Japanese friend, asked why Commodore Perry bullied himself into Edo when he could have simply sailed a bit further down to Nagasaki, where the shogun was already allowing limited foreign trade, shrugged and said, 'Because he was American.') Even as Americans prefer to think of themselves as the centre of events in Japan as elsewhere, it is helpful to recall the first-act song 'Someone in a Tree', the mini-*Rashomon* in which several characters provide vastly different accounts of a single event according to their varied perspectives. That may be the show's real lesson.

## NOTES

1. The author would like to acknowledge the help of Timon Screech, professor of art history at the School of Oriental and African Studies (SOAS), University of London, for his advice on certain aspects of this essay. Parts of this chapter were previously published in the *Sondheim Review*. The author and editors wish to thank Rick Pender for permission to reuse the material.
2. Quoted in Gary Perlman, 'Sondheim and Weidman Praise the Production', *Sondheim Review* 7, no. 3 (2001): 11. Weidman emphasised Prince's vital contribution: he stresses that 'Hal was one of the essential creators of *Pacific Overtures*, and it would not have existed to be re-imagined by another director without his seminal ideas and inspiration', adding, 'Hal's production made theatrical sense in New York in 1976, and Miyamoto's production made theatrical sense in Tokyo in 2000.'
3. Stephen Sondheim, *Finishing the Hat: Collected Lyrics (1954–1981), with Attendant Comments, Principles, Heresies, Grudges, Whines, and Anecdotes* (New York: Virgin Books, 2010), 304.
4. Carol Ilson, *Harold Prince: A Director's Journey* (New York: Limelight Editions, 2004), 227–229.
5. Sondheim, *Finishing the Hat*, 323.
6. Ibid, 304.
7. John Simon, 'The Singing Samurai', *New York Magazine*, 2 December 2004, https://nymag.com/nymetro/arts/theater/reviews/10600/, accessed 10 March 2020.
8. Bruce Weber, 'Critic's Notebook: Sondheim's Kabuki Hybrid May Have Found Its Moment', *New York Times*, 26 November 2001, E1.
9. Harold Prince, *Sense of Occasion* (New York: Applause Books, 2017), 212.
10. 'Stephen Sondheim', https://www.praemiumimperiale.org/en/laureate-en/laureates-en/sond-en, accessed 10 March 2020.
11. Sondheim, *Finishing the Hat*, 305.
12. These opinions were voiced by various members of the audience who communicated with me at the performance.
13. Quoted in Perlman, 'Sondheim and Weidman Praise the Production'.
14. Amon Miyamoto, interview with the director, 9 October 2000.
15. Ibid.
16. Ibid.
17. Quoted in Perlman, 'Sondheim and Weidman Praise the Production'.
18. Miyamoto, interview.
19. Ilson, *Harold Prince*, 233–235.

20. Miyamoto, interview.
21. Sondheim, *Finishing the Hat*, 316.
22. Perlman, 'Sondheim and Weidman Praise the Production'.
23. See e.g. Jeremy McCarter, 'Made in Japan (& America, & Japan . . .)', *New York Sun*, 3 December 2004, https://www.nysun.com/arts/made-in-japan-america-japan/5763/, accessed 10 March 2020; and Elyse Sommer, 'A Curtain Up Review: *Pacific Overtures*', *Curtain Up: The Internet Theater Magazine of Reviews, Features, Annotated Listings*, 2004, www.curtai nup.com/pacificovertures2004.html, accessed 10 March 2020.

## BIBLIOGRAPHY

Ilson, Carol. *Harold Prince: A Director's Journey*. New York: Limelight Editions, 2004.

McCarter, Jeremy. 'Made in Japan (& America, & Japan . . .)'. *New York Sun*, 3 December 2004, https://www.nysun.com/arts/made-in-japan-america-japan/5763/, accessed 10 March 2020.

Miyamoto, Amon. Interview with the director, 9 October 2000.

Perlman, Gary. 'A New *Overtures* Coming to Broadway'. *Sondheim Review* 10, no. 3 (2004): 10–11.

Perlman, Gary. '*Pacific Overtures* Is a Triumph in Japan'. *Sondheim Review* 7, no. 3 (2001): 6–10.

Perlman, Gary. '*Pacific Overtures*: Varying Perspectives'. *Sondheim Review* 11, no. 4 (2005): 26–27.

Perlman, Gary. 'Sondheim and Weidman Praise the Production'. *Sondheim Review* 7, no. 3 (2001): 11.

Perlman, Gary. 'Translating Sondheim'. *Sondheim Review* 8, no. 1 (2001): 29–31.

Prince, Harold. *Sense of Occasion*. New York: Applause Books, 2017.

Simon, John. 'The Singing Samurai'. *New York Magazine*, 2 December 2004, https://nymag.com/nymetro/arts/theater/reviews/10600/, accessed 10 March 2020.

Sommer, Elyse. 'A *Curtain Up* Review: *Pacific Overtures*'. *Curtain Up: The Internet Theater Magazine of Reviews, Features, Annotated Listings*, 2004, www.curtainup.com/pacificovertu res2004.html, accessed 10 March 2020.

Sondheim, Stephen. *Finishing the Hat: Collected Lyrics (1954–1981), with Attendant Comments, Principles, Heresies, Grudges, Whines, and Anecdotes*. New York: Virgin Books, 2010.

'Stephen Sondheim'. https://www.praemiumimperiale.org/en/laureate-en/laureates-en/sond-en, accessed 10 March 2020.

Weber, Bruce. 'Critic's Notebook: Sondheim's Kabuki Hybrid May Have Found Its Moment'. *New York Times*, 26 November 2001, E1.

# CHAPTER 24

## FROM FLEET STREET TO BROADWAY AND BACK

*Stages in the Career of Sweeney Todd*

### ROBERT LAWSON-PEEBLES

## PROLOGUE

THE first vocal line of Stephen Sondheim's 'musical thriller' demands that we 'attend the tale of Sweeney Todd'.[1] It is a lurid tale of a barber who developed a highly successful business model that involved a tilting chair, a willing pâtissière who baked the choicer cuts from his victims into pies, and a church crypt for the inedible bits. Some supposed 'facts' of Todd's life were sifted 'from amidst the fiction' by Peter Haining, whose obituary confirms that he was a gourmet chronicler of the gruesome.[2] Haining asserted that Todd was born in London in 1756 and began his bloody career in 1784. He was apprehended in 1801 after disposing of a large number of customers and was executed in January 1802. Robert Mack's scholarly monograph *The Wonderful and Surprising History of Sweeney Todd*, written with some input from Sondheim, showed that those 'facts' were completely false. Todd never existed. Nevertheless, he can be found in the pages of the *Oxford Dictionary of National Biography*.[3] The mission of the *ODNB* is to be 'the national record of men and women who have shaped British history and culture, worldwide, from the Romans to the 21st century', and it is overwhelmingly devoted to figures that can be historically verified.[4]

Todd's heterodox inclusion in the *ODNB* is, I suggest, a tribute to a symbolic economy that is constructed through an interaction of time with place. The place is precisely located. Fleet Street runs for one-third of a mile from Temple Bar, at the boundary of the Cities of Westminster and London, eastwards to Ludgate Circus. The street's name and limits are the only constants. The changes to its buildings and its surroundings provide the indices to the character of Todd, who is transformed from an archetype of a local gangster first to a comic villain and then to a demonic icon. The tale of Todd is mutable and multilayered; yet beneath each layer may be detected spectral shapes, inherited penumbrae, creating a relationship between present and past that resembles a network rather than a simple dialogue. Sondheim's *Todd* is both a late addition to, and summative of, that network, fashioning from it an urban myth that requires our close attention. Sondheim's *Todd* is therefore a more densely woven text than it appears at first sight.

This essay asks three questions: why Sweeney Todd was created, why he became inextricably associated with Fleet Street, and how Sondheim nevertheless transformed him into a global figure. The first part of this essay is therefore devoted to an account of the conditions of Fleet Street that gave rise to Sweeney Todd before attempting to uncover a complex web, not only of individual stage and film productions, but also of physical environments, styles of appearance, communal memories, the marketing of meat, and the technology of barbering. The essay extends Jacky Bratton's concept of the 'intertheatrical' to what might be called the 'extratheatrical'. According to Bratton:

> An intertheatrical reading goes beyond the written. It seeks to articulate a mesh of connections between all kinds of theatre texts, and between texts and their users. It posits that all entertainments [ . . . ] are more or less interdependent. They are uttered in a language, shared by successive generations, which includes not only speech and the systems of the stage—scenery, costume, lighting, and so forth—but also genres, conventions and, very importantly, memory.

The starting point for Bratton's intertheatrical analysis is the playbill, examined in its entirety as part of the audience's 'personal experience of theatre'.[5] I will be looking at the playbills for Todd's first appearance on the stage, in 1847, and for Sondheim's first 1979 Broadway production of *Sweeney Todd*, and also questions of stage machinery, accounts of audience reactions, and the sites of the theatres where productions were staged.

An extratheatrical analysis adds a further dimension. It relates the audience's experience within the theatre to the concerns of everyday life outside the theatre. I will argue that Fleet Street is as essential to *Sweeney Todd* as, say, the woods are to *Little Red Riding Hood* and a motel is to *Psycho*. The difference between *Todd* and those texts is that *Todd* relies on a specific environment. This essay therefore begins as an example of local history, or—to put it more informally—as a ghost hunter's street map.

## THE CREATION OF THE FLEET STREET
## VILLAIN, 1846

Sweeney Todd made his debut on 21 November 1846 in the opening episode of a penny dreadful titled *The String of Pearls*. The title of the text subordinates him, and in a carefully crafted opening sentence, the narrator delineates the scene before allowing him to enter:

FROM FLEET STREET TO BROADWAY: *SWEENEY TODD* 667

> Before Fleet-street had reached its present importance, and when George III was young, and the two figures who used to strike the chimes at old St Dunstan's church were in all their glory—being a great impediment to errand-boys on their progress, and a matter of gaping curiosity to country people—there stood close to the sacred edifice a small barber's shop, which was kept by a man of the name of Sweeney Todd.[6]

The sentence creates the matrix of the fiction by means of a linked set of contrasts, between sacred and profane, country and city, and past and present. It focuses on the old church of St Dunstan-in-the-West (to give it its formal title). One notable feature of the old church was the clock, superintended by automatons that struck each quarter-hour. It was constructed in 1671, five years after St Dunstan's narrowly escaped the Great Fire of London. The automatons may represent Gog and Magog (in Revelation 20:8–15); if so, they reflect on one apocalypse and may presage another.

The clock is the clearest marker of change, for two reasons. First, it was notable in its absence at the time that *The String of Pearls* was published serially, from November 1846 to March 1847.[7] The old church had been demolished in 1829, and the clock was bought by the Marquess of Hertford and installed at his house in Regent's Park. It was not returned to St Dunstan's until 1935, by the press baron Lord Rothermere.[8] It is still there, a prominent feature in Fleet Street. Secondly, although the narrator's grasp of national history is rather casual, the temporal structure of the narrative is precise. The action begins at 6:45 P.M. on Tuesday, 19 August 1785, and the progress of Todd's murderous career is marked by repeated references to the clock.[9] The opening sentence, therefore, does not create that formulaic beginning of a folk or fairy tale, 'once upon a time'. Instead, we are witness here to an account of local history, in which a demarcated earlier period is examined for the lessons it may teach.

Temporal precision within the narrative is matched by geographical precision. Todd's shop can be located with some accuracy, on the north side of Fleet Street, towards its western end, and a few paces away from Mrs Lovett's pie shop, round the corner in Bell Yard. Peter Haining, as ever, went further, insisting that the shop was at 186 Fleet Street, alongside St Dunstan's Church.[10] The narrative is not quite so precise, but an examination of *Reynolds's Map of London* (1847) shows that the narrator had a detailed knowledge of an area of approximately one mile surrounding Fleet Street.[11] The narrative is also clearly aware of the developments that led to the 'present importance' of Fleet Street. The demolition of the old St Dunstan's church was part of a program of extensive rebuilding in the area. Before 1829, traffic along Fleet Street had to avoid St Dunstan's 'market', a collection of 'rude open sheds' leaning against the walls of the original 'dilapidated' church. In order to widen Fleet Street by some thirty feet, the new church was built partly over the burial ground at its north face. The sheds gave way to 'commodious and elegantly glazed shops', and with the consecration of the new church in 1833, Fleet Street began to take on the aspect that it bears today.[12] Reconstruction inevitably involved excavation. Walter Thornbury, a colleague of Charles Dickens, recognised that 'every street and alley' was 'haunted by memories of the past'. So he took care to record the evidence before it was obliterated by the builder's sledgehammer.[13]

*The String of Pearls* anticipates Thornbury, structuring its narrative as archaeology. A reference to Fleet Market, 'then in all its glory' with 'all sorts of filth enough to produce a pestilence within the city of London', acts as a pungent reminder of the area before it was modernised.[14] In 1737 Fleet Market had been built above the River which gave Fleet Street its name. It was removed in 1829 to make way for Farringdon Street.

The Fleet River had once been a fast-flowing, sweet-water tributary of the Thames. By the eighteenth century it had become an open sewer swiftly carrying effluent into the river. A coroner's inquest in 1835 recorded that the 'Great Fleet Ditch Sewer', as it was then known, had become so dilapidated that it 'was not only dangerous, as open to accidents, but fearful, as affording facilities for the commission of murder with impunity'. In 1839 a doctor gave details of the dangers. Alongside the Ditch 'almost every house is the lowest and most infamous brothel'. Thirteen-year-old girls lured punters into the houses. They were robbed and murdered by 'bullies' (pimps) and thrown into the Ditch, to be 'discharged at a considerable distance into the Thames, without the slightest chance of discovery'.[15] Over the next six years the Fleet Ditch was completely enclosed and the area rebuilt, exposing more iniquities of the past: in 1844 workmen stumbled upon the hideout of the criminal Jonathan Wild (1682/3–1725). The house was on the Fleet Street side of the Ditch:

> Its dark closets, trap doors, sliding panels, secret recesses and hiding places, no doubt rendered it one of the most secure places for robbery and murder. [ ... ] A skull and numerous human bones have been found in the cellars.

*The Times* reported that the discovery of this squalid refuge caused 'the greatest excitement'.[16]

London had become, in Jerry White's words, 'a city of paradox', with modern commercial streets just a few steps away from the most toxic areas.[17] In 1850, for instance, William Hepworth Dixon described a walk, starting at the notorious Newgate prison, just a few yards from where Farringdon Street joined Fleet Street. Dixon praised newly built streets like Bridge Street, which continued Farringdon Street southwards to the river. But just north of Farringdon Street was the unhappily-named Field Lane, which ran from Holborn Hill to Saffron Hill:

> The stench is awful. Along the middle of the narrow lane runs a gutter, into which every sort of poisonous liquid is poured. This thoroughfare is entirely occupied by receivers of stolen goods [ ... ]. Here you may *re*-purchase your own hat, boots, or umbrella...

Smithfield Market was another of Dixon's sites 'of low vice, of filth, fever, and crime'.[18] In that same year, 1850, Dickens wrote that the Market was an 'odious spot, associated with cruelty, fanaticism, wickedness and torture', with maddened animals running amok through the streets.[19] The most vivid portrait of Smithfield was written in 1843 by T. J. Maslen, a retired army officer. He was shocked by the 'cruelty, filth, effluvia, pestilence,

# FROM FLEET STREET TO BROADWAY: *SWEENEY TODD*    669

impiety, horrid language, danger, disgusting and shuddering sights, and every obnoxious item that can be imagined'. The butchers' shops presented

> the gory sight of hundreds of beings hanging with their heads downwards, and their throats cut; scores of noble heads staring with their sightless glazed eyes, and long rows of headless trunks, inundating the foot pavement with rivers of blood, at which I have seen living animals stop to smell and give an awful shudder, as if the crimson gore possessed a tongue that revealed to their instinct a murderous secret.[20]

Smithfield is portrayed as a sink of iniquity, and Maslen rubs the reader's nose in it. Maslen recognises that crime and disease share the same language and compulsions. Assembling a picture that combines physical violence with moral decay, he reverses the normal distinction between the human and the animal. Animals, it seems, care about their kind and discriminate about their dinner.

This account of the Fleet Street area as the nexus of cloaca, crime, and suspect food has been taken from contemporary published documents.[21] We have those documents thanks to the expansion of the printing industry for which the street is now best remembered. Technological developments and the growth of literacy prompted a vast increase in books, magazines and newspapers. Until Fleet Street itself became the epicentre of mass publishing, 'polite letters' (as the genre has sometimes been called) had been symbolised by Dr Johnson's house, just north in Gough Square; while the law was represented by the Temple to the south. By 1846 Fleet Street had become both the producer and the subject of popular reading.[22] Two examples confirm that vivid, controversial material could be found almost on the publishers' doorsteps. Dickens' *Oliver Twist*, published serially between 1837 and 1839, made Saffron Hill the turf of Fagin's gang. The enthusiastic response to *Oliver Twist* was outdone by the 'craze' following the serial publication in 1839 of W. H. Ainsworth's *Jack Sheppard*, 'generating a great wave of pamphlets and abridgments, plays and street shows, prints and cartoons, and related baubles and souvenirs'. Walter Thornbury lamented that Ainsworth had 'mischievously immortalised' Sheppard as the 'hero of modern thieves'.[23] Little wonder that the discovery of Jonathan Wild's hideout created a sensation. He had been Sheppard's erstwhile boss and his betrayer. Here was further evidence of the ghostly presence of the eighteenth century: John Gay's *The Beggar's Opera* brought to life. *The Beggar's Opera*, drawing on the exploits of Jonathan Wild, depicted London in 1728 as the metropolis of vice. *Oliver Twist* and *Jack Sheppard* added modern local colour to that portrayal.

*The String of Pearls* was one of a number of grisly tales that, because they were published in an office just south of Fleet Street, came to be known as 'Salisbury Square fictions'. The tale used a local scandal as a vehicle to explore a widespread taboo. The contours of the narrative, I suggest, are to be found in the images of Fleet Street and its immediate surroundings. The clubs of Gog and Magog, striking St Dunstan's bell, herald Lieutenant Thornhill's decision to get a shave. Thornhill's 'noble-looking' (and nobly named) dog, Hector, having 'sniffed the air' of Todd's shop, takes a singular dislike to the barber; but to no avail, for Thornhill is 'polished off' by Todd. By using a phrase that would become famous, Todd cloaks the murder in the language of refinement. Yet Hector instinctively senses Todd's 'murderous secret' (in Maslen's words) and tries hard to reveal it. So Todd has to kill 'that melancholy but faithful animal'.

Trying to sell Thornhill's string of pearls, Todd comes into conflict with a nearby den of thieves. He has stored the other items he has acquired from his victims, the common currency of street theft—'hats, [ . . . ] walking-sticks, umbrellas, watches and rings'—because the retail side of his consortium, Mrs. Lovett's pie shop, is doing great business. In stark contrast to the 'horrible effluvia' of that 'charnel house', St Dunstan's, the shop impregnates the air 'with a rich and savoury vapour'. Lawyers from the nearby Inns of Court neglect their business to enjoy her 'golopshious' pies. But one member of the legal profession is not to be put off the scent. He is Sir Richard Blunt, the local magistrate; Blunt traps Todd by adopting the persona and dialect of a wealthy country drover who has sold his beasts at Smithfield. The secrets of the tilting chair and the noxious crypt are revealed, and Todd swings for it outside Newgate.[24]

In addition to neighbourhood crime, food standards, and animal welfare, the tale raises issues about mercantilism, the treatment of the young, religious quackery, the abuse of asylums, and the problems of urbanisation. As its full title—*The String of Pearls: A Romance*—indicates, these issues are interwoven with a sentimental plot. At the close of the narrative, the young lovers, Mark Ingestrie and Johanna Oakley, have survived many vicissitudes to live 'long and happily together'.[25] With one exception, *The String of Pearls* is a conventional example of early Victorian fiction, of which the most accomplished, influential, and well-known practitioner is Dickens. That exception is the character of Sweeney Todd. He may be a Londoner, but he is marked as an outsider by his first name, Sweeney (possibly Irish), by his 'disagreeable kind of unmirthful laugh', and by his appearance:

> The barber himself was a long, low-jointed, ill-put-together sort of fellow, with an immense mouth, and such huge hands and feet, that he was, in his way, quite a natural curiosity; and what was more wonderful, considering his trade, there was never seen such a head of hair as Sweeney Todd's. We know not what to compare it to: probably it came nearest to [ . . . ] the appearance of a thickset hedge, in which a quantity of small wire had got entangled. In truth, it was a most terrific head of hair; and as Sweeney Todd kept all his combs in it—some said his scissors likewise—when he put his head out of the shop-door to see what sort of weather it was, he might have been mistaken for some Indian warrior with a very remarkable head-dress.[26]

The compound adjective 'ill-put-together' gives us the clue. Sweeney Todd was not born but made. He is as much a creation as the monster in Mary Shelley's *Frankenstein*, that brute whose 'unearthly ugliness rendered it almost too horrible for human eyes'.[27]

*Frankenstein*, published in 1818, is an allegory of the French Revolution, with the monstrous creation wreaking violence on its makers.[28] The Reign of Terror continued to resonate over the next three decades, for widespread and systematic violence, initiated by the storming of the Bastille, had not waned with the passage of time. In *The*

French Revolution (1837), Thomas Carlyle described a trajectory which inevitably led to self-destruction; and in 1841 he asserted that the 'reigns of terror, horrors of French Revolution' were no mere 'transitory' events, but integral to contemporary life.[29] In 1838 another account of the Revolution attributed to Rousseau a statement that has since become commonplace: 'When the people shall have nothing more to eat, they will eat the rich'.[30]

*The String of Pearls* added to the debate about the Terror. One of its sources was the 'Terrific Story of the Rue de la Harpe in Paris', first published in 1822, involving a barber, a pastry cook, a wealthy country dweller, and a dog that refused to 'desert his post'.[31] *The String of Pearls* turned Sweeney into an engineer of violence, with his tilting chair a utilitarian version of that symbol of the Reign of Terror, the guillotine, once described as 'the modern beheading machine' of Paris.[32] The narrator's description of Sweeney's hairstyle is by no means adventitious: rather, it is the first indicator of his attitude to violence. 'Terrific' was at that time a pejorative term, cognate with 'terror', and in this case, with the Reign of Terror. And in Fleet Street, with its blood-soaked environment, Sweeney found his natural milieu.

## THE FLEET STREET VILLAIN AND BRITISH POPULAR STAGE, 1847–1969

The French Revolution created a theme in early Victorian life and a mode of expression in the dramaturgy of melodrama.[33] A key moment for my purposes occurred even before the last instalments of *The String of Pearls* had appeared in print. On 1 March 1847 Sweeney Todd made his first appearance on-stage, at the Britannia Theatre, Hoxton. Opened in 1841 as a music hall, the Britannia was revitalised in 1843 by the Theatre Regulation Act—which allowed local authorities to grant licences—and by the arrival of an acting manager and stock dramatist, George Dibdin Pitt (1799–1855). Pitt was apparently able to produce work, from inception to production, within four days, yet the staging was of sufficient quality to attract the attention of the theatre journals, and then the major newspapers.[34] The draft script submitted to the Lord Chancellor's Office bears evidence both of hasty composition and of dramaturgical skill in reducing a lengthy and convoluted plot to a two-act drama lasting around one and a half hours.[35]

*The String of Pearls* already had some of the characteristics of melodrama, with its two-dimensional characters, moral absolutes expressed in hyperbole, and an emotional rhythm of cliffhangers demanded by serial publication. Pitt enhanced that rhythm by the use of (unfortunately unspecified) music cues; he added tableaux and choreography and made full use of the machinery of the Victorian stage. For instance, he replaced Todd's tilting chair with a 'Vampire Trap', through which Thornhill made a spontaneous exit. Pitt combined the characters of Thornhill and Ingestrie. Thornhill is only injured and makes a transient appearance, 'bleeding and pale', before 'exiting a la Banquo'.[36]

Although trained animals were a feature of nineteenth-century theatre, Pitt cast Hector as a young Black mute, making him proactive in saving Thornhill and indicting Todd.

The playbill of *The String of Pearls* notes that the setting is 'in the Olden Time', but the drama itself proceeds as if it is in the present. Pitt's dramatisation retained the title of the serial and the outlines of its main plot, assuming that the audience would be familiar with 'the much admired Tale' from which it is 'taken'. It was now subtitled *The Fiend of Fleet Street!*—a change no doubt designed to give a frisson to the audience, for the play-bill claimed that the story was 'founded on fact', and the Britannia was just two miles northeast of Fleet Street.[37] When a 'theatrical scene-painter', Thomas Erle, saw a pro-duction at the Britannia (probably around 1860), he noted: 'Dramatic impressions are so strong with me that I should not go out of my way to get my hair cut in Fleet Street just at present'.[38]

A haircut, but not a shave. Sweeney Todd was not yet famous for shaving his customers. Although in the 1847 script Todd threatens to cut the throat of his appren-tice, Tobias, 'from ear to ear', there is no sign of a razor. Knife crime was common in London; so Erle remarked that Todd dispatched his customers 'in a mere business-like way by a commonplace dab with a knife'. 'The butchering process' was offstage, confined instead to Erle's vivid professional imagination.[39]

In 1862 Frederick Hazelton rewrote the drama for performance at the Bower Theatre, Upper Marsh, Lambeth (close to Waterloo Station) under the new title of *Sweeney Todd: The Barber of Fleet Street*. Todd's promotion to eponymous status was accompanied by an increase in the melodramatic depiction of villainy. For the first time on the stage, Todd wields the cut-throat razor with which he has since become so closely associ-ated, and the drama closes with 'red fire' and a general conflagration as Todd slashes Mrs Lovett's throat.[40] This is another stage in the career of Todd: an increment of horror accompanied by a decline in realism.

The presentation of Todd changed again in 1883, when *Sweeney Todd* was included in John Dicks's edition of plays. Black comedy was added to the melodramatic spectacle of villainy. In part, this involved a return to the 1846 narrative, with Todd recovering both his chair, now on a 'revolving trap', and his felonious snigger:

> Sweeney (*Chuckling aside, and whetting his razor on his hand*)
> I shall have to polish him off. Ha ha ha! Heugh!
> Mark   What the devil noise was that?
> Sweeney  It was only me. I laughed.[41]

But the temporal and geographical precision that marked the 1846 narrative had been lost. The conditions of Fleet Street, which had played a large part in the initial creation of Todd, no longer existed. The improvements that William Hepworth Dixon noted during his walk had continued until the area was transformed. By 1868 the sewers had been developed into a comprehensive underground system, directing the outfalls into the Thames beyond the city limits.[42] When the new Smithfield Market was opened in 1868, Walter Thornbury wrote a lavish description praising the well-designed and sanitary building. Finally, in 1879, Dickens's son, Charles Jr., celebrated Fleet Street as the centre for 'some of the greatest newspapers in the world'.[43] By the 1880s the centre of disrepute had moved more than two miles eastwards, to Whitechapel; and in 1888 that 'dense cultural grid' (to use Judith Walkowitz's apt phrase) produced its demonic figure in the shape of Jack the Ripper.[44]

With no local evidence to authenticate his nefarious activities, the 1883 Dicks edition began Todd's metamorphosis to a comic villain. The best-known presentation of this role is the 1936 film *Sweeney Todd: The Demon Barber of Fleet Street*, with Tod Slaughter (as Jeffrey Richards puts it) 'in his element, gleeful in his villainy, leering, cackling, eye-rolling, hand-rubbing, revelling in lechery and murder'.[45] The film is organised into two narratives. The embedded narrative is staged as an early Victorian costume drama. The arrival of a beadle, to place an orphan with Todd, confirms both the setting and *Oliver Twist* as a supplementary source. A racialised interlude in a studio-bound African jungle, somewhere near the Cape of Good Hope, extends the geographical reach of the tale to reveal the source of the pearls. A series of signs, including the tilting chair and a visual gag about Mrs Lovett's pies, presumes the audience's foreknowledge of the embedded narrative.

The brief framing narrative contains the only location shots in the film and links the story-within-the-story to a present-day Fleet Street, with its modern street furniture and busy traffic. This narrative introduces us to a passer-by who innocently chooses 'Sweeney Todd Ladies' & Gents' Hairdressers' although there is an alternative clearly visible three doors away. The present proprietor begins the tale, and a lap dissolve takes us from the lathered face of the customer to the street scene outside the Boar's Head pub a century earlier. Another lap dissolve at the conclusion of the embedded narrative returns us to the still-lathered face, which registers increasing alarm as the hairdresser lovingly strops his razor and reveals that a pie shop still operates next door. This is too much for the customer, who is last seen fleeing towards St Paul's in pursuit of a double-decker bus.[46]

A year earlier, in 1935, Stanley Holloway (1890–1982), best known as Alfred P. Doolittle in *My Fair Lady*, added 'Sweeney Todd, the Barber' to his collection of monologues. He began the collection in 1929 with a supposed encounter between the Duke of Wellington and a Yorkshire private soldier, Sam Small ('Sam, Pick Oop Tha' Musket'). In contrast to the 1936 film, Holloway makes no bones, as it were, about the provenance of the Mrs Lovett's meat:

> She made her living by selling pies,
> Her meat pies were a treat,
> Chock full of meat and such a size
> 'Cos she was getting the meat from
> Mr Sweeney Todd, the Barber,
> Ba Goom, he were better than a play
> Sweeney Todd, the Barber
> 'I'll polish them off', he used to say.

And many's the poor young orphan lad
'Ad the first square meal he'd ever had—
A hot meat pie, made out of his Dad,
From Sweeney Todd, the Barber.[47]

With Holloway's monologue Sweeney Todd joins a select group of vernacular icons that includes "'Arold with an eye-full of arrow' (in the Battle of Hastings, recounted as a football match), Anne Boleyn, 'With Her Head Tucked Underneath Her Arm'. and Holloway's distant ancestor, Uncle George, who claimed to have slain the dragon.

The versions of Sweeney Todd by Tod Slaughter and Stanley Holloway confirm that the villain had been absorbed into the tradition of British comic theatre, a tradition extended when the Pitt edition was rewritten for repertory in Birmingham, in 1962, and Dundee, in 1969.[48] However, reviews of two 1959 productions, appearing in the Times on the same day, suggested that Sweeney Todd occupied an equivocal space in the comic tradition. A ballet, choreographed by John Cranko and with music by Malcolm Arnold, 'draws enthusiastically on music-hall dance routines' and contains 'much knock-about comedy'. But a musical version, written for the Christmas season at the Lyric Theatre, Hammersmith, seemingly went too far. The reviewer felt that, lacking the grim early Victorian context of the original, 'this story too easily takes on the meaningless absurdity of a pantomime story'.[49] The Times reviews highlighted issues of congruity between theme and presentation that would trouble the versions by Christopher Bond and Stephen Sondheim.

# Todd's Global Ambitions, 1973–1979

The Scots journalist James Naughtie got a dusty answer when, in December 2003, he asked Sondheim if he found it 'exciting in a cultural way' to see Sweeney Todd at the Royal Opera House, Covent Garden, 'round the Corner from Fleet Street'. Sondheim replied: 'Its main reference in this country is to newspapers, right? [ ... ] I'm afraid that to me, coming from New York, it really means nothing at all'.[50] Sondheim's prickly response may be chalked up to his chagrin at the failure of the first British production of 'my love letter to London', as he—perhaps wryly—called his version of the Demon Barber,[51] in 1980 at the Theatre Royal Drury Lane. Certainly, Sondheim thought that 'all these earlier Sweeney Todd plays were very boring and essentially over-written one-act dramas'.[52]

The major source for Sondheim's 'love letter to London' was a text that transformed Sweeney's villainy yet again. Christopher Bond believed that 'the Blood Tubs and Music Halls of the nineteenth century were the last example of a truly populist theater in England', but that most of the melodramas had been 'carelessly and unimaginatively put together'.[53] So he spent part of his career rewriting them. Bond's production of Sweeney Todd: The Demon Barber of Fleet Street aimed to make melodrama 'acceptable

FROM FLEET STREET TO BROADWAY: *SWEENEY TODD*    675

to a modern audience', with 'characters that are large but real, and situations that, given a mad world not unlike our own, are believable'. To achieve this aim he used the original 1846–1847 narrative for the Fleet Street setting, the 1862 Hazelton version for his title as well as the cut-throat razor, and Pitt's dramatisation, particularly in the 1883 John Dicks edition, with its revolving chair. Bond's 'Author's Note' to the published version of the play showed that he 'borrowed' from a wider range of sources, including Renaissance drama, Alexandre Dumas's *The Count of Monte Cristo* (1844), and street market vernacular. He also drew, unacknowledged, on the novels of Dickens, particularly *Bleak House* (1853) and *Great Expectations* (1860).

These sources prompted Bond to change *Sweeney Todd* into a revenge tragedy in which an ordinary family is destroyed by a corrupt and oppressive hierarchical society. The judiciary is represented by the sadomasochistic Judge Turpin, ironically named after the highwayman executed in 1739 for illegal dealings in horseflesh. Bond's Turpin deals in human flesh, and he has the barber transported to Australia on a false charge to allow unhindered access to his wife and daughter. Alfredo Pirelli is the lower-class parallel to Turpin, a quack threatening to peach on the barber, knowing that he has returned illegally (like Magwitch in *Great Expectations*) and adopted the pseudonym of Todd. Mrs Lovett lies to Todd about the death of his wife in order to create a sexual as well as a business relationship. The disposal of Pirelli begins a cavalcade of throat-slashing and pie-making, ending when the apprentice Tobias, prematurely aged by the trauma, murders Todd. The revenge tragedy has run its course, barely leaving space for the romance closure, with the young sailor (now given the surname of Hope) and Johanna promising to marry and sail away, leaving 'this evil town far, far behind'.[54]

The plot is elegant and tightly structured, but it inevitably rests on an anachronistic treatment of Fleet Street. The note on the Cast Page, that the date is the 'early nineteenth century', is confirmed by the third scene, set in 'St Dunstan's Market Place', returning the street to its condition before 1829 in order to accommodate the public shaving competition between Todd and Pirelli. However, the depiction of corrupt law officers in the play reflects Dickens's attacks on the English legal system, begun in *The Pickwick Papers* (1836) and reaching its definitive indictment in *Bleak House*. The interwoven images of the law and fog in the splenetic first five paragraphs of *Bleak House* reach a climax with the image of Temple Bar, Christopher Wren's ceremonial gate to the City of London at the western end of Fleet Street.[55]

Like many of the more innovative ventures in British musical theatre, Bond's *Sweeney Todd* was influenced by *Die Dreigroschenoper* (1928), the modernisation of *The Beggar's Opera* by Brecht and Weill.[56] It was produced in a sympathetic forum, at the Theatre Workshop, a repertory company at the Theatre Royal, Stratford East. Yet the problem of presenting the subject matter can be seen in two reviews. Irving Wardle reported on 'a rough-and-ready, low-budget affair', with 'scratch costumes, two-piece orchestra, and blundering lighting'. But 'no expense [ ... ] has been spared on Sweeney's chair which flushes the victims away like a regal water-closet'.

Wardle noted that the play changed register at the end of act 1. Up till then, Todd murdered either out of necessity (Pirelli) or for revenge (the attempt on Turpin). But when the judge escapes the razor, Todd 'discovers his taste for blood', turning his thirst for vengeance into a massacre. Henceforth Bond 'lays on the horrors with a shovel'. The body count increases greatly, which solves Mrs Lovett's supply problem: previously, the price of meat in hard times had prompted her to seek out neighbourhood pets, but now there are 'queues in Fleet Street gorging themselves on human flesh'.[57] In such an environment humour arises from street-corner vernacular—and from audience participation, encouraged by the Theatre Workshop ethos. 'Don't sit in the chair!' was one popular interjection.[58] It turned gory drama into pantomime and converted the second reviewer, Harold Hobson. He wrote that 'a responsive and witty audience [filled] the theatre with infectious jollity', a comment that Theatre Workshop used in its advertisements.[59]

The ambivalence inherent in the production conditioned Sondheim's attitude to it. He expected Grand Guignol; instead, he found himself watching 'this charming melodrama'.[60] Charming? In the warmly collaborative environment of Theatre Workshop, *Sweeney Todd* may have seemed more charming than the theatre of horror that was Grand Guignol. Named after a small theatre in the Pigalle district of Paris, Grand Guignol was popular in the years before World War I. The theatre provided 'an emotional rollercoaster', alternating farce with bloodletting so realistic 'that audiences would flee the auditorium or lose consciousness'.[61] Grand Guignol was performed in London after the war at the Little Theatre (an avant-garde theatre in a converted bank near the Strand), but the activities of the censor and the departure of its leading actress, Sybil Thorndyke, ended productions after just two years.[62] Then the cinema quickly colonised the spectacle of violence with such films as Buñuel's *Un Chien andalou* (1929). Grand Guignol went into decline until, when Sondheim saw it in Paris in the 1960s, 'it was just red tomato sauce and a lot of people in terrible make-up overacting'.[63]

# Modern Psychology and Modernist Music

Sondheim's persistent, if unsatisfied, interest in Grand Guignol prompted a major change to Bond's plot. He (and his 'unsung collaborator', Hugh Wheeler) felt it was 'weakest' at the close of act 1, where Turpin escapes Todd's razor and Todd decides 'to pass the time in practise on less honoured throats'. This sounded too casual; instead, they wished 'to motivate Todd from wanting to kill one man to wanting to kill all men'.[64] After the 1883 Dicks edition, there was nothing in the British tales of comic villainy to encompass the psychology of mass murder. So Sondheim and Wheeler looked elsewhere. Steve Swayne has shown that Sondheim's style was a 'generous assimilation of a given tradition',[65] and the tradition to which they turned had begun a century or so before they wrote *Sweeney Todd*, and which included but also transcended modernism.[66]

The clue is in the title of the song marking Todd's transformation, 'Epiphany'.[67] Between 1900 and 1904 James Joyce wrote a series of 'Epiphanies', defining them as moments of 'sudden spiritual manifestation' and thus releasing the term from its place in the Christian calendar in order to describe profound psychological insight.[68] Virginia Woolf later suggested that modern fiction should take an interest in 'the dark places of psychology'.[69] Woolf and Joyce were early practitioners of the art of narrating introspection, creating a syntax suited to the revelatory non-rational ebb and flow of intense subjective experience.

The comparable examination of the 'dark places' of subjectivity in music could be said to begin with the first chord of the Prelude to Wagner's *Tristan und Isolde* (1865). The opera's hours of deferred consummation were enabled by a complex harmonic structure that was then transformed by Schoenberg into his 1909 monodrama *Erwartung*—a more neurotic, if briefer, exercise in atonal frustration.[70] Schoenberg's foremost American acolyte was Milton Babbitt, and when Sondheim studied with Babbitt he wondered about learning twelve-tone technique. Babbitt, who believed that Schoenberg's system had created an entirely separate musical language, thoughtfully responded (perhaps with the *Tristan* chord in mind) that there was no point in that until Sondheim had 'exhausted' the resources of tonality. So Sondheim became, as he put it, Babbitt's 'maverick, his one student who went into the popular arts armed with all his serious artillery'.[71] Suitably kitted out, Sondheim raided the resources of Alban Berg, Benjamin Britten, and, through Bernard Herrmann, Liszt and Wagner.

Part of Babbitt's arsenal was the ability to 'manage time'.[72] In *Sweeney Todd* Sondheim managed time with particular formal rigour, creating a tight dramatic and musical structure, with parallels between the two acts.[73] Critics have suggested that *Sweeney Todd* marked a shift in Sondheim's work towards the status of opera, although he has taken care to distance it from conventional definitions of the genre.[74] Nevertheless, the work owes a debt to two operas which portray the plight of an antihero: Berg's *Wozzeck* (1922) and Britten's *Peter Grimes* (1945).

Like *Sweeney Todd*, *Wozzeck* portrays an oppressive and corrupt class-based society which turns its eponymous character, a sensitive yet simple man, into a sociopath. Furthermore, Berg, like Sondheim, acted as his own dramaturge. It enabled him to underpin the music and drama with a formal structure so tightly conceived that it was summarised by a chart, distributed in 1923 to critics with the vocal score. *Wozzeck* was a 'paradoxical fusion of technical calculation and emotional spontaneity', creating a structure that conveyed the impact of an indifferent universe on an individual sensibility.[75]

In contrast, the influence of *Peter Grimes* on *Sweeney Todd* has more to do with characterisation than with structure. Grimes is a more complex character than Wozzeck, his reputation for ill-treating his apprentices making him both alienated from and representative of his community. As Britten remarked in a 1948 interview: 'The more vicious the society, the more vicious the individual'.[76] Like Wozzeck, Britten's Grimes is a sensitive man, yet his drive to achieve acceptance through commercial success leads to the death of another apprentice and the outrage of the citizens of the Borough. In act 3, scene 2 of *Peter Grimes*, the protagonist's name becomes both the rallying cry of the vengeful hunt and the symbol of Grimes's acceptance of a fate that, like Wozzeck's, would culminate in drowning.[77]

In 1945 the fifteen-year-old Sondheim wrote to Bernard Herrmann praising the 'Concerto Macabre' from *Hangover Square*. He had seen the film twice in order to memorise the first eight bars of Herrmann's music, 'glimpsed briefly on Laird Cregar's piano'.[78] They accompany the title sequence, with diabolical augmented fourths played in the left hand of the piano (G to C-sharp) suggesting the mental instability of its 'composer', George Harvey Bone, acted by Cregar. In a letter to the *New York Times* published soon after the release of *Hangover Square*, Herrmann argued that 'music on the screen can seek out and intensify the inner thoughts of the characters'.[79] In *Hangover Square*, Herrmann (working with the director, John Brahm) goes further, employing both music and the paramusical instrumentally. This becomes clear when comparing *Hangover Square* with its source text. Patrick Hamilton's 1941 novel describes a monitory 'snap' in Bone's head as a 'break in the sound-track, that sudden burst into a new, silent world'; that 'snap' signals his schizophrenia and triggers his homicidal intentions.[80] In the film, Herrmann and Brahm reverse the sonic direction of psychosis, from silence into sound. Bone knocks over four stringed instruments, their collapse precipitating whistling screeches unbecoming of a quartet. These, followed by a sequence of underscored augmented fourths, induce Bone to commit murder. After incinerating the body (it is, conveniently, Guy Fawkes Night), Bone returns home and, glancing at the manuscript, plays the opening bars of the concerto.[81]

In 1997 Sondheim used the key term 'epiphany' to describe his brief glimpse of the manuscript of 'Bone's' and his later wish to 'pay homage' to Herrmann with *Sweeney Todd*.[82] The composer's musical language was particularly useful to Sondheim because it allowed him to follow Babbitt's advice and explore the limits of tonality. Herrmann's unconventional orchestration and use of *moto perpetuo* and *ostinato* figures represents a significant development from the prevailing model of film scoring in 1940s Hollywood, adapted from Wagner's theory of integrated music-drama.[83] Herrmann could improve on Wagner whenever Hitchcock required it, as in *Vertigo* (1958), where the music of *Tristan und Isolde* is ironically recomposed as a motif for necrophilia. In the *Concerto macabre*, Herrmann employs instead the daemonic signifiers to be found in the later piano music of Franz Liszt. Liszt's experiments in tonality were more daring than those of Wagner, with the *Bagatelle ohne Tonart* perhaps the boldest exploration of tonal syntax without entirely rejecting it.[84] Herrmann took those experiments further, refusing to resolve minor and major chords within a harmonic framework, thereby creating a rhetoric of disquiet and unsettling the audience.[85] This rhetoric is apparent in much of Herrmann's work for Hitchcock, and for those directors inspired by the British master of the macabre.[86]

In a 1964 BBC interview, Hitchcock talked of a universal 'fright complex' learned in childhood, citing *Little Red Riding Hood*.[87] Hitchcock therefore locates the origin of the thriller in the folk tale, first recorded by Charles Perrault (1697) and then by the Brothers Grimm (1812).[88] Sondheim created a similar genealogy in his 'Author's Note' to the playbill of the original 1979 production at the Uris Theatre on Broadway:

FROM FLEET STREET TO BROADWAY: *SWEENEY TODD* 679

[F]or more than a century in England [Todd] has become a household word. 'Sweeney Todd will get you if you don't watch out' has been more than enough to send countless thousands of recalcitrant children scurrying to finish their porridge or to jump into bed on time. However, it is not only the children who are haunted by Sweeney Todd. He is the demon, the half-admitted shadowy lodger, who lurks in the back of all our minds. Not a barber to be trifled with.[89]

This sounds more like a Hitchcock pastiche than a genuine English parental admonition. The fairy tale genre would be re-evaluated at greater length in *Into the Woods* (1987).[90] Here it is part of an adversarial imagery for Todd, both more complex and universal than the black comedy of a Stanley Holloway monologue. The reference to the lodger, adopted from Bond's script, turns Mrs Lovett into Todd's landlady, and Todd into a protagonist more dangerous than Wozzeck or Peter Grimes.

## THE SOCIAL GEOGRAPHY OF *SWEENEY TODD*

By referring to the lodger, Sondheim the cinephile is summoning the ghost of Laird Cregar. Before *Hangover Square*, Cregar had starred in *The Lodger* (1944), also directed by John Brahm. That film was based on a novel by Marie Belloc Lowndes, published in 1913 in response to the Jack the Ripper murders that had been committed some twenty-five years earlier. Hitchcock had directed a silent version of *The Lodger* in 1926, but the casting of the matinee idol Ivor Novello as protagonist indicated that this was a Hitchcock play on mistaken identity. From Cregar's first emergence out of the swirling London fog, swathed in a black Ulster coat and bowler hat, it is clear that there is no mistake this time. Low-angle shots magnify Cregar's bulk, looming over his hosts, and emphasise his pasty face and proptotic eyes. This is the face of the psychopathic male, established by Peter Lorre in Fritz Lang's *M* (1931). As Lang had written in 1926, 'the rediscovery of the human face' was a gift bestowed by film.

By the time *M* was released, two events had helped shape the public's awareness of psychopathy: the Berlin première of *Wozzeck* and the trial of the serial child murderer Peter Kürten, 'the Vampire of Düsseldorf', who admired Jack the Ripper.[91] *M* therefore begins with a children's elimination song (of a bogeyman who will chop you into small pieces) and reaches its climax in Lorre's bravura study in derangement before a kangaroo court of criminals. The film critic Thomas Elsaesser has argued that the connection between Weimar cinema and Hollywood is complex and multipolar, but one shared image is the face of the compulsive murderer.[92] In *The Lodger*, Laird Cregar portrays a pathologist who takes his work home at night. The film was a success, and 20th Century-Fox demanded a repeat in *Hangover Square*. Preferring to be a romantic lead rather than a hulking psychopath, Cregar reluctantly took the part, then went on a crash diet, suffered a heart attack, and died before *Hangover Square* was released.[93]

680    ROBERT LAWSON-PEEBLES

Sondheim's use of European and American sources changed the tale of Sweeney from a hoary British joke into a portent of widespread doom.[94] *Hangover Square* taught Sondheim

> that in order to scare people [ ... ] the only way you can do it [ ... ] is to keep music going all the time. That's the principle of suspense sequences in movies. And Bernard Herrmann was a master in that field. So *Sweeney Todd* not only has a lot of singing, it has a lot of underscoring. It's *infused* with music, to keep the audience in a state of tension.[95]

Sondheim praised John Williams's use of double basses at the start of Steven Spielberg's *Jaws* (1975): it is music that 'scares the hell out of you'. This is the aim of the Organ Prelude that begins *Sweeney Todd*. Sondheim noted that the opening chords of the Prelude are based on the *Kyrie eleison* of the Catholic mass, but dissonances suggest that there is no mercy, and a paramusical whistling screech, adapted from *Hangover Square*, brings the Prelude to a startling premature close.[96] The Prologue turns the screw further, with ostinato strings later counterpointed against short, dissonant wind phrases. Those well-known first six words, quoted at the start of this chapter, insist on the didactic nature of the folk tale, and Sondheim, with his lyricist's attention to detail, notes that 'the alliteration on the first, second and fourth accented beats of 'Attend the tale of Sweeney Todd' [ ... ] gives the line a sinister feeling, especially with the sepulchral accompaniment that rumbles underneath it'.[97] The Prologue reaches a crescendo as the company repeat the name of Sweeney, not in vengeance (as in Benjamin Britten's *Peter Grimes*) but as an invocation of the grave. It ends with the dental plosives that spatter Todd's turf. Despite Sondheim's claim that Fleet Street 'means nothing', his sonic acuity ensures that Fleet Street and its protagonist are fatally linked (No. 1, pp. 4–18). The Prologue provides us with some fine instances of 'melopoetic integration' (to use Stephen Banfield's phrase): of meaning created by the intimate relationship of sound and word.[98]

*Sweeney Todd* is saturated with the familiar in both music and street sounds. The debt, again, is to *Hangover Square*, which opens to Cockney merrymaking around a barrel organ. Sondheim was also indebted to DuBose Heyward, whose vernacular lyrics in *Porgy and Bess* represented 'the high-water mark in musical theater'.[99] The arrival of morning in *Porgy and Bess* (act 2, scene 3) is marked by the sound of bells and the parlando calls of street vendors (a passage recalled at the beginning of the 1956 Presley vehicle *King Creole*). In *Sweeney Todd*, Sondheim ventured into London vernacular, creating 'an amalgam of pure invention, authentic Cockney, American slang and universal poetry'.[100]

Bells are both universal paramusical signifiers and site-specific objects. Stephen Banfield has shown that Sondheim follows Liszt and Rachmaninoff (among others) in making extensive use of bells, and of the *Dies irae*, 'the symbol of doom'.[101] The bells of St Dunstan's may be absent from Fleet Street, but 'Oranges and Lemons', the well-known nursery rhyme, names many other London bells (before turning into an elimination song related to the one in Lang's *M*). Noël Coward used both the traditional street cries

FIG. 24.1 'Attend the tale of Sweeney Todd': the ensemble of the celebrated 1993 production of Sondheim's musical at the National Theatre. It was directed by Declan Donnellan and starred Julia McKenzie and Alun Armstrong (*fourth and fifth from left*) as well as Adrian Lester (*far right*) as Anthony. Photo: Alastair Muir, courtesy of the photographer.

of London and the sound of bells in his response to the Blitz, 'London Pride': 'Cockney feet mark the beat of history./Every street pins a memory down'.[102] As Anthony and Todd arrive they are anchored in London by bells. Bells are prominent in 'No Place like London', and Anthony's hymn to the city imitates change-ringing. But this is no longer home to Todd. His loathing is first suggested when he flattens Anthony's G-natural (on 'London') by a semitone and is confirmed when he reviles the city as 'a great black pit' inhabited by 'the vermin of the world' (No. 2, pp. 19–27).

The second line of the Prologue warns us about Todd: 'His skin was pale and his eye was odd' (No. 1, p. 4). Three characters act as foils to Todd's singularity. Anthony, as befits his surname, is initially stereotyped as a 'jolly Jack Tar'.[103] Pirelli seems—again at first sight—to have wandered in from a Rossini opera. But it is Mrs Lovett who most diverges from her stereotypical name. Todd's landlady is more manipulative than the poor-but-honest skivvy of Lowndes's novel, or the shabby-genteel housewife of Brahm's film. Her first song, 'The Worst Pies in London', is a typically energetic Cockney lament that 'times is hard' (No. 3, pp. 34–40). Hints that she is looking for a partner to alleviate her troubles are confirmed in her second song, 'Poor Thing' (No. 4, pp. 41–51). Sondheim compared the song to Poe's 1843 short story 'The Tell-Tale Heart', noting that with 'a calculated regularity of rhythm and rhyme' she goads Todd into a self-revelatory fury.[104] The duet, 'My

Friends' (No. 5, pp. 51–57) gives the first sign that her choice will prove fatal, for Todd is attached only to his razors. His pathological tendencies are fully realised in 'Epiphany' (No. 17, pp.170–179), when Mrs Lovett's attempt to calm him is quickly silenced by a rage that transforms his desire for revenge into wholesale butchery. It is here that Sondheim puts into practice everything he had learned from Babbitt and Herrmann about the tonal and rhythmic resources necessary for the full expression of Todd's onset of madness. Sondheim's description of his method is almost disarmingly nonchalant:

> To demonstrate musically that his mind is cracking I switched between violent and lyrical passages, and had rapid rhythmic shifts, from quick to slow. His murderous vengeance announced to a chugging engine-like theme (the *Dies Irae* disguised) alternates with a keening threnody for his wife and daughter.[105]

An oxymoron, controlled mayhem, may be the only way to describe the resulting three minutes of 'Epiphany'. The song is a test of virtuoso singing. In Jonathan Tunick's inspired orchestration, the string-supported laments for Todd's family are interrupted by the spectacular tumult of his raving, driven by brass, punctuated by percussion, and reminiscent of *The Rite of Spring*. Todd's rage increases with a reprise of his hostility to London and reaches its height at the close of 'Epiphany', where grief over the loss of his family is overcome by a lust for life created by his demonic new sense of purpose. Todd's closing sustained fortissimo F-natural (on 'joy'), unlike the normal climax to an aria, is confronted in the orchestra by unresolved clotted discords (No. 17, pp. 70–79). Todd places himself musically in the position of Milton's Satan: 'onely in destroying I finde ease/To my relentless thoughts'.[106]

'That's all very well, dear': not the Almighty's response to his dark angel, but Mrs Lovett's pragmatic put-down of Todd's satanic exuberance. Her interjection initiates a volte-face that Sondheim learned from Grand Guignol rather than from the 'charming' Theatre Workshop production. The close of act 1 of Bond's script presented the new meat-supply agreement as a brief exchange, with the partners in crime promptly collapsing in a fit of giggles. In contrast, Sondheim constructed 'A Little Priest' as an extended repartee, set to a waltz.[107] The particular qualities of this waltz can be highlighted by a brief comparison. 'By Strauss' was originally a dotty experiment by the Gershwin brothers, becoming their sole contribution to an ephemeral 1936 revue directed by Vincente Minnelli. Minnelli revived the song for his 1951 Gershwin vehicle *An American in Paris*, now including a quotation from Johann Strauss's *Tales from the Vienna Woods*. Sung by Georges Guétary with slapstick assistance from Gene Kelly and Oscar Levant, the trio recruit the plump *patronne* of the café and an elderly flower seller, restructuring the spoof into a joyous ensemble dance that collects an appreciative audience. This Franco-American celebration of Vienna can be summed up by the couplet in the refrain: 'It laughs, it sings! The world is in rhyme/Swinging to three-quarter time'.[108]

As 'A Little Priest' accelerates into full swing, Todd's vocal line alludes rhythmically to Ira Gershwin's refrain before creating imagery different from the jollity of 'By Strauss':

FIG. 24.2 Sweeney Todd has a frightening 'Epiphany'; a perturbed Mrs Lovett looks on. Scene from the 2012 London revival, starring Michael Ball and Imelda Staunton, directed by Jonathan Kent. Photo © Donald Cooper/Photostage.

> How choice! How rare!
> For what's the sound of the world out there?
> Those crunching noises pervading the air?
> It's man devouring man my dear [ . . . ] (No. 18, pp. 184–186)

Sondheim's three-quarter time is no celebration of a world 'in rhyme'. The genial music of the Strauss family is hardly grist to Mrs Lovett's meat grinder. Sondheim's waltz therefore originates several hundred miles and half a century from the 'Mittel Europa' hymned by Guétary in Ira Gershwin's revised lyrics. When Todd at last grasps Mrs Lovett's 'bright idea', a rumble in the bassoons indicates that the ensuing waltz is indebted to Ravel's *La Valse* (1920). Ravel described his composition as 'a fantastic, fatal whirling', an ironic reflection on the elegant Viennese tradition from the perspective of the carnage of World War I. Sondheim and Tunick first drew on *La Valse* to open *Follies*.[109] In *Sweeney*, at the close of act 1, the counterpoint of the 3/4 time and the complex, turbulent, orchestration of *La Valse* is used as a structural model for Todd and Lovett's newly achieved but fragile unity of homicidal purpose, their choreography interrupted by outbursts of hilarity and ferocity.[110] Their patter, replete with gallows humour, lists some of those vocations which might be suitable for their oven before they decide that cannibalism, like death, is a great leveller: 'We'll not discriminate great from small./No, we'll serve anyone, And to anyone at all' (No. 18, pp. 210–212). In bringing the waltz to a close, the Todd-Lovett business plan turns the Brechtian dialectic of 'who gets eaten and who gets to eat' (No. 18, p. 202) into an egalitarian exercise.[111]

The closely knit structure that Sondheim adapted from Bond's script becomes evident in act 2. In the complex, multifaceted opening number, 'God, That's Good', Mrs Lovett's business is announced by chiming bells. Her shop is so successful that Todd is presented with difficulties of supply, even with his efficient new chair, which tilts rather than revolves. The chair completes Todd's murderous apparatus. The words of his song—'Is that a chair fit for a king'—bring to mind the 'beheading machine' of the Reign of Terror, and its lovely melody recalls the serenade to the razors in 'My Friends' in act 1.[112]

The predatory dimensions of evil are manifested in two habitués of Fleet Street who played smaller roles in act 1. Toby adapts his fanfaronade from the one he gave as Pirelli's barker in act 1 (No. 9), with words praising Mrs Lovett's 'ambrosial' pies rather than Pirelli's evil-smelling elixir (No. 19, pp. 213–216). The second character is the Beggar Woman. In act 1, Sondheim signals her importance to the plot by weaving her motifs into the musical tapestry, beginning with the anticipation in the Organ Prelude of her cry for alms. Her two interventions in act 1 remind Todd of the 'ghostly shadows' which haunt 'these once-familiar streets' and warn Anthony of the punishment awaiting those who 'go trespassing' on 'the great Judge Turpin's' domain.[113] In act 2 the Beggar Woman's warnings become more urgent and less specific. Interpreting the smoke from Mrs Lovett's bakehouse oven as a sign of the fires of hell, she cries an alarm that is taken up by the inmates of Fogg's insane asylum (No. 26).

In contrast to their street music, both Tobias and the Beggar Woman sing the most intimate of songs, the lullaby, but with its therapeutic value darkened by foreboding, derived from Auden's well-known 'Lullaby', where 'the grave/Proves the child ephemeral'.[114] The status of 'Not While I'm Around' (No. 23) is disguised because it is sung by Tobias to his 'mum', Mrs Lovett. Its beautiful assurance of loving guardianship is clearer when treated as a discrete song, for instance by Barbra Streisand.[115] Within its dramaturgical context and assisted by Tunick's orchestration, Toby's song reveals more troubling emotions.[116]

The second, untitled, lullaby is sung by the Beggar Woman to an imaginary infant. It stands out as a simple but poignant reminder of loss in the complex and vivid assemblage of voices in the two-part 'Searching' (No. 27A, pp. 338–339). Sondheim extended it for the 1980 London production (No.27A Insert, pp. 390–395), set in 6/8 time to suggest a cradle lullaby. Its lyrics contain hints of the tale of Cinderella, and the repeated phrase 'home again' is a poignant reminder of the Beggar Woman's first encounter with Todd, shortly after his return to Fleet Street.[117] The melody of the lullaby is adapted from the latter part of 'Poor Thing', Mrs Lovett's song in act 1; and its organisation, beginning with a minuet and ending with Todd's tormented interruption, confirms the link between Mrs Lovett's sly narrative and its disastrous consequences.

Sondheim was uncertain of the value of the extended lullaby, placing it as an option in the appendix to the score. Banfield disagrees, arguing that the lullaby is an important indicator of the direction of Sondheim's work towards more universal forms of expression; and Sondheim's 'Author's Note' to the 1979 playbill (quoted earlier) confirms this.[118]

FROM FLEET STREET TO BROADWAY: *SWEENEY TODD*    685

Like the fairy tales to which they are related, the two lullabies anticipate *Into the Woods* by upsetting the conventional relationship between adults and their young. The lullabies also perform multiple tasks in *Sweeney Todd*. They express the emotions of their singers, victims of a system of oppression that is very precisely located in 'Fleet street and environs', as the Cast Page puts it.[119] At the same time they deploy their generic function as part of a universal didactic mythology. Finally, they act as triggers for action, while exposing the diverging vectors of ambition pursued by Todd and Mrs Lovett.

The dynamic contrasts of 'God, That's Good' present the first musical signs of the cracks in the unity they seemed to have achieved in 'A Little Priest'. It becomes more apparent in the numbers that follow. The strict allegretto tempo of Todd's part in the quartet, 'Johanna' (No. 20), prompts him to synchronise the affectionate song to his daughter with the slaughter of his customers. In 'By the Sea' (No. 21) Todd responds absent-mindedly both to Mrs Lovett's landlady-like pretensions to a seaside guest house and her increasingly overt sexual overtures. Todd's monomania resurfaces when he betrays Anthony, the man who saved his life, to the Judge (No. 22A), which results in the murder of the Beggar Woman. In the dénouement, Mrs Lovett sings her self-justification to the melody that created the lie, 'Poor Thing'. Her frantic ad-lib gabble shows that she is still driven by the pleasure principle; but now Todd has another outcome in mind as he waltzes her towards the oven in a reprise of 'A Little Priest'. To paraphrase Ravel, the 'whirling' is fatal for Mrs Lovett; but, unlike the juddering explosion that completes *La Valse*, slamming the oven door leaves the dance unresolved and still does not bring closure for Todd. His lament for Lucy, first heard in 'No Place like London', is interrupted by Toby. He executes Todd to one of the oldest English nursery rhymes, 'Pat-a-cake, pat-a-cake, baker's man', leaving the final rendering of the 'Ballad' to draw the moral conclusion: 'To seek revenge may lead to hell,/But everyone does it, and seldom as well [ ... ]/ As Sweeney Todd/The Demon Barber of Fleet Street'.[120]

# The Journey of *Sweeney Todd* from 1979 to the Present

*Sweeney Todd* was first staged in March 1979 at the Uris Theatre (now the Gershwin) on Broadway. Hal Prince's production matched the scale of the 1,933-seat auditorium, with the primitive square shed of the Todd-Lovett enterprise overawed by the rusting stairwells and gantries that once had been a Rhode Island iron foundry. The contrast in scale reflected the diverging interests of Prince and Sondheim. Prince recalled that he got the inspiration for the set after touring the Dublin prison which memorialised republicans such as Michael Collins. The set resembled a Foucauldian critique of the power relations inherent in imperialism and industrialism, dwarfing Len Cariou (Todd) and Angela Lansbury (Mrs Lovett) and preventing them from fully expressing the evil energies central to their roles.[121]

The members of the company could not encompass Sondheim's heteroglossic experiments and instead voiced a simple transatlantic parody of London vernacular.[122] The result, in Robert Gordon's opinion, 'seemed like a didactic and pretentious charade about the horrors of street crime in New York'. Gordon was more impressed with the London production, which opened in July 1980 at the Theatre Royal. With a stage and actors close to Todd's home turf, the 'Drury Lane production captured the Brechtian insouciance and cynicism' that Sondheim had adopted from Bond. Denis Quilley and Sheila Hancock acted with greater depth and range than Cariou and Lansbury, conveying 'a more genuine sense of the macabre'.[123]

The reviews, on both sides of the Atlantic, were divided. Although the original staging received a clutch of awards, some critics regarded *Sweeney Todd* as a vapid exercise in bad taste. The most negative review, by James Fenton, dismissed the work as 'a tissue of bullshit' that lacked the crude realism of Victorian melodrama. Although Prince's production was expensively mounted, it was different in kind from the big-budget revivals, such as *The Sound of Music*, that at that time were attracting large audiences. After the London production closed prematurely, Sheila Hancock called *Sweeney Todd* 'the most awarded flop in the history of theatre'.[124]

Fenton's vitriolic response was the result of a category error, because *Sweeney Todd* is not a modish rehash of Victorian shock-horror.[125] Sondheim had transformed Bond's vengeful barber into a vehicle for examining the origins and calamitous results of psychopathy. Michael Billington gave a more prescient estimate of *Sweeney Todd* when he declared it 'one of the two (*My Fair Lady* being the other) durable works of popular musical theatre written in my lifetime'.[126]

Billington has been proven right. *Sweeney Todd* has appeared in many different forms on a vast range of arenas. It was resuscitated by Christopher Bond, first at the Liverpool Playhouse in 1982 and then in 1985 at the tiny Half Moon Theatre in London's Mile End Road, quite close to the tale's setting.[127] Two acclaimed British productions have been mounted by directors with a classical theatre background. The National Theatre's 1993 chamber production displayed the starkly minimalist aesthetic developed by Declan Donnellan in his innovative productions of Shakespeare and European classics.[128] Michael Ball and Imelda Staunton deftly counterpointed comedy and horror in Jonathan Kent's 2011 production at the Chichester Festival Theatre; it transferred to the West End the following year.[129]

Following an innovative production in 1984 by the Houston Grand Opera, *Sweeney Todd* has also been seen in opera and concert venues. Bryn Terfel brought Wagnerian heft to his performance of Todd, first seen at the Chicago Lyric Opera in 2002, then in a 2007 concert performance at London's Royal Festival Hall, and most recently in a semi-staged production with Emma Thompson—first at Lincoln Center, New York, in 2014, and with the English National Opera in 2019.[130] It has been performed by actor-musicians in a pared-down production by John Doyle that travelled from the tiny Watermill Theatre in Berkshire (2004) to the West End (2005) before transferring to Broadway with Patti LuPone and Michael Cerveris (2006).[131] Tim Burton filmed

FIG. 24.3 The urban legend returns to his place of origin: scene from the first London staging of *Sweeney Todd, the Demon Barber of Fleet Street*. The 1980 production at Theatre Royal Drury Lane starred Dennis Quilley and Sheila Hancock. Photo © Donald Cooper/Photostage.

*Sweeney Todd* in 2007, with techniques learned from directors such as Fritz Lang, and St Dunstan's Market resembling the rebuilt Smithfield.

But perhaps *Sweeney Todd* was most purely incarnated in two modest London productions. In 1991 Pimlico Opera developed a production in Wormwood Scrubs prison, with a chorus drawn from its inmates and staff. Pimlico Opera then went on tour, but without its partners in crime.[132] In 2014 the Tooting Arts Club production took place in the cramped conditions of London's oldest pie-and-mash shop, with the thirty-two members of the audience splashed by Pirelli's elixir and threatened by Todd's razor. In 2017 the Club returned *Sweeney Todd* to New York, but to the off-Broadway Barrow Street Theatre, where a limited arena still maintained the 'pressure-cooker' atmosphere of the original site.[133] Pie-and-mash shops are no longer to be found in Fleet Street or

# 688   ROBERT LAWSON-PEEBLES

Bell Yard; they have followed their working-class clientele out of central London.[134] But the aura of Fleet Street continues to permeate Sondheim's 'musical thriller'.

## Acknowledgements

This essay has been written with the lasting memory of my first shocked encounter with *Sweeney Todd* on Broadway in 1979. I am grateful to my former colleague Robert Mack, for the years of shared appreciation of Sondheim's work; to Robert Gordon and Olaf Jubin for their constructive editing and considerate patience during a difficult time; and to Jenny Wigram for her advice and support.

## Notes

1. Stephen Sondheim and Hugh Wheeler, *Sweeney Todd: The Demon Barber of Fleet Street* (London: Nick Hern Books, 1991), 1.
2. Peter Haining, *Sweeney Todd: The Real Story of the Demon Barber of Fleet Street* (London: Robson, 1998), x. https://www.independent.co.uk/news/obituaries/peter-haining-anthologist-of-strange-horrid-tales-760724.html, accessed 27 May 2019.
3. Robert L. Mack, *The Wonderful and Surprising History of Sweeney Todd: The Life and Times of an Urban Legend* (London: Continuum, 2007), ix, 79–82, 156–158; Matthew Kilburn, 'Sweeney Todd (*called* the Demon Barber of Fleet Street)', in *Oxford Dictionary of National Biography* (Oxford and New York: Oxford University Press, 2003), 54:887–888.
4. See https://www.oxforddnb.com/page/about, accessed 21 March 2019.
5. Jacky Bratton, *New Readings in Theatre History* (Cambridge: Cambridge University Press, 2003), 37–40.
6. Robert L. Mack, ed., *Sweeney Todd: The Demon Barber of Fleet Street* (Oxford and New York: Oxford University Press, 2007), 3.
7. The authorship of the fiction is still uncertain. See Dick Collins, 'Introduction', in *Sweeney Todd*, 2nd ed. (Ware: Wordsworth Editions, 2010), vi–xix.
8. Ben Weinreb and Christopher Hibbert, eds., *The London Encyclopaedia* (London: Macmillan, 1983), 703–705.
9. Mack, *Sweeney Todd*, 283–284, 286–287; Mack, *The Wonderful and Surprising History*, 89–94.
10. Haining, *Sweeney Todd*, 48.
11. See http://www.bl.uk/onlinegallery/onlineex/maps/uk/004879221.html, accessed 15 June 2019. A sketch of the area can be found in Mack, ed., *Sweeney Todd*, xxxviii.
12. *Gentleman's Magazine* 102 (October 1832): 297–298; George Godwin, *The Churches of London* (London: C. Tilt, 1838), 1:1–14 and Plate. (The pagination is separately numbered for each church.) The changes to London are discussed in Alison O'Byrne, '"Unceasing Bustle and Traffic": Print Culture and Metropolitan Spaces in the 1830s', *Yearbook of English Studies* 48 (2018): 171–198; an 1842 lithograph of the widened Fleet Street near the new church is reproduced on page 195.
13. Walter Thornbury, *Haunted London* (London: Hurst & Blackett, 1865), v.
14. Mack, ed., *Sweeney Todd*, 163, 293.

15. 'Coroner's Inquest', *Weekly True Sun*, 2 August 1835, 807; and Michael Ryan, *Prostitution in London, with a Comparative View of That of Paris and New York* (London: H. Bailliere, 1839), 176–177.

16. *Times*, 31 July 1844, 3; and 6 August 1844, 8.

17. Jerry White, *London in the Nineteenth Century: A Human Awful Wonder of God* (London: Jonathan Cape, 2007), 3.

18. William Hepworth Dixon, *The London Prisons [ . . . ]* (London: Jackson & Walford, 1850), 226–227; emphasis in the original.

19. Charles Dickens, with W. H. Wills, 'The Heart of Mid-London', *Household Words*, 4 May 1850, reprinted in *The Uncollected Writings of Charles Dickens*, vol. 1, ed. Harry Stone (1968; London: Allen Lane, Penguin Press, 1969), 110–111.

20. T. J. Maslen, *Suggestions for the Improvement of Our Towns and Houses* (London: Smith, Elder, 1843), 16.

21. For further discussion of the history of Fleet Street, see Jerry White, 'Fleet Street: City of Words', in *London in the Nineteenth Century*, 225–253; Sally Powell, 'Black Markets and Cadaverous Pies: The Corpse, Urban Trade and Industrial Consumption in the Penny Blood', in *Victorian Crime, Madness and Sensation*, edited by Andrew Maunder and Grace Moore (Aldershot: Ashgate, 2004), 45–58; and Rosalind Crone, 'Selling Sweeney Todd to the Masses', in *Violent Victorians: Popular Entertainment in Nineteenth-Century London* (Manchester: Manchester University Press, 2012), 160–208.

22. Louis James, *Fiction for the Working Man, 1830–1850: A Study of the Literature Produced for the Working Classes in Early Victorian Urban England* (1963; Harmondsworth: Penguin, 1974).

23. Matthew Buckley, 'Sensations of Celebrity: "Jack Sheppard" and the Mass Audience', *Victorian Studies* 44, no. 3 (2002): 426; Walter Thornbury, *Old and New London: A Narrative of Its History, Its People and Its Places*, vol. 2 (London: Cassell, Petter & Galpin, 1873–1874), 459.

24. Mack, ed., *Sweeney Todd*, 6–7, 24, 29, 50, 54, 93, 150, 153, 267, 274–277, 279, 281.

25. Ibid., 282.

26. Ibid., 4. For speculation about his first name, see ibid., 284.

27. Mary Shelley, *Frankenstein, or The Modern Prometheus*, ed. J. Paul Hunter (1818; New York: W. W. Norton, 1996), 34.

28. Ronald Paulson, *Representations of Revolution (1789–1820)* (New Haven, CT: Yale University Press, 1983), 239–247.

29. Thomas Carlyle, *The French Revolution: A History*, vol. 2, ed. K. J. Fielding and David Sorensen (1837; Oxford and New York: Oxford University Press, 1989), 329; Thomas Carlyle, *On Heroes, Hero-Worship, and the Heroic in History*, introduction by Michael K. Goldberg (1841; Berkeley and Los Angeles: University of California Press, 1993), 173.

30. M. A. Thiers, *The History of the French Revolution*, trans. Frederick Schobel, vol. 3 (London: Richard Bentley, 1838), 210; italics in the original.

31. 'B', 'Terrific Story of the Rue de la Harpe', *Tickler Magazine* 4, no. 2 (1 February 1822); reprinted in *The Tell-Tale* (London: Caxton Press, [1824]), columns 509–512. Mack, *The Wonderful and Surprising History*, 159–161, reprints most of the communication from 'B'.

32. Anon., *Massacre of the French King! View of la Guillotine; or, Modern Beheading Machine, at Paris* (London: William Lane, [1793]).

33. Peter Brooks, *The Melodramatic Imagination*, 2nd ed. (New Haven, CT: Yale University Press, 1995), 14–15.

34. Michael R. Booth, *Theatre in the Victorian Age* (Cambridge: Cambridge University Press, 1991), 6, 145–146; Michael Kilgarriff, *The Golden Age of Melodrama* (London: Wolfe, 1974), 238–241; and Dwayne Brenna, *George Dibdin Pitt: His Life and Work* (PhD diss., Royal Holloway, University of London, 2000), 45–49.

35. The script, together with the playbill and critical commentary, is reprinted in Sharon Aronofsky Weltman, *Nineteenth Century Theatre & Film* 38, no. 1 (2011): 1–85.

36. George Dibdin Pitt, *The String of Pearls*, ed. Sharon Arononfsky Weltman, *Nineteenth Century Theatre & Film* 38, no. 1 (2011): 37, 53. On the 'Vampire Trap' and other techniques of Victorian staging, see Booth, *Theatre in the Victorian Age*, 70–94. Banquo's ghost makes his non-committal appearance in act 4 of *Macbeth*.

37. Playbill, 1 March 1847, reprinted in Weltman, *Nineteenth Century Theatre & Film* 38, no. 1 (2011): 25–26.

38. [Thomas William Erle], *Letters from a Theatrical Scene-Painter*, 2nd ser. (London: Printed by J. Chisman, 1862), 39.

39. Pitt, *The String of Pearls*, ed. Weltman, 34; and [Erle], *Letters*, 31–32.

40. Frederick Hazelton, *Sweeney Todd: The Barber of Fleet Street: or, The String of Pearls* (London: Samuel French, 1862), 35. On red fire and other lighting effects, see Booth, *Theatre in the Victorian Age*, 90.

41. George Dibdin Pitt, *Sweeney Todd* (London: Dicks' Standard Plays no. 499, [1883]), 3. For a detailed account of the changes between the 1847 and 1883 dramas, see Sarah A. Winter, "'His Knife and Hands Bloody": Sweeney Todd's Journey from Page to Stage—Melodrama, Adaptation and the Original 1847 Manuscript', *Journal of Adaptation in Film & Performance* 8, no. 3 (2015): 233–247.

42. Paul Dobraszczyk, *Into the Belly of the Beast: Exploring London's Victorian Sewers* (Reading: Spire Books, 2009); Stephen Halliday, *The Great Stink of London: Sir Joseph Bazalgette and the Cleansing of the Victorian Metropolis* (Stroud: Sutton, 1999).

43. Thornbury, *Old and New London*, 491–496; and Charles Dickens, Jr., *Dictionary of London* (London: Charles Dickens, 1879), 102.

44. Judith R. Walkowitz, *City of Dreadful Delight: Narratives of Sexual Danger in Late-Victorian London* (London: Virago Press, 1992), 5.

45. Jeffrey Richards, 'Tod Slaughter and the Cinema of Excess', in *The Unknown 1930s: An Alternative History of the British Cinema 1929–1939*, ed. Jeffrey Richards (London: I. B. Tauris, 1998), 150.

46. *Sweeney Todd: The Demon Barber of Fleet Street*, dir. George King, George King Productions, 1936, DVD, Odeon Entertainment ODNF127, 2006.

47. Stanley Holloway, *The Stanley Holloway Monologues*, ed. Michael Marshall (London: Elm Tree Books, 1979), 79–81.

48. Brian J. Burton, *Sweeney Todd the Barber: A Melodrama* (1962; London: French, 1984); and Austin Rosser, *Sweeney Todd: A Victorian Melodrama* (London: French, 1971).

49. 'Cranko's New Ballet' and 'Demon Barber with Music', *Times*, 11 December 1959, 16.

50. James Naughtie, 'Sharp Operator', *Times*, 20 December 2003, 18–19.

51. Sarah Crompton, 'Cut-throat Business', *Daily Telegraph*, 20 July 2004, 17; and Stephen Sondheim, *Finishing the Hat: Collected Lyrics (1954–1981), with Attendant Comments, Principles, Heresies, Grudges, Whines and Anecdotes* (New York: Alfred A. Knopf, 2011), 332, 376.

## FROM FLEET STREET TO BROADWAY: *SWEENEY TODD* 691

52. Stephen Sondheim, 'Larger than Life: Reflections on Melodrama and *Sweeney Todd*', in *Melodrama*, ed. Daniel Charles Gerould (New York: New York Literary Forum, 1980), 3–15; here: 5.

53. Christopher Bond, 'The Theater of Pyramids (and a Camel)', in *Melodrama*, ed. Daniel Charles Gerould (New York: New York Literary Forum, 1980), 15–18; here: 15, 17.

54. C. G. Bond, *Sweeney Todd* (London: Samuel French, 1974), 'Author's Note', cast page, and 9, 45, 76.

55. Charles Dickens, *Bleak House*, ed. Norman Page (1853; Harmondsworth: Penguin Books, 1971), 49–50. The gate was replaced in 1880 by the Temple Bar Memorial, in front of the imposing Gothic structure of the Royal Courts of Justice, completed in 1882. The building is the embodiment of the Supreme Court of Judicature Act of 1873, which unified eight separate courts of justice. Its eastern edge overlooks Bell Yard, the site of Mrs Lovett's Pie Shop. Dickens, had he lived (he died in 1870), would have been disconcerted by the contrast.

56. See Robert Lawson-Peebles, 'The Beggar's Legacy: Playing with Music and Drama, 1920–2003', in *The Oxford Handbook of the British Musical*, ed. Robert Gordon and Olaf Jubin (Oxford and New York: Oxford University Press, 2016), 585–611; and 'From Macheath to Mackie Messer and Mack the Knife: Transatlantic Transformations of *The Beggar's Opera*, 1920–1956', *Symbiosis* 22, no. 1 (2018): 3–28.

57. Irving Wardle, 'Sweeney Todd', *Times*, 3 May 1973, 7.

58. Maxwell Shaw, introduction to Bond, *Sweeney Todd*, n.p.

59. Harold Hobson, 'Happy Days', *Sunday Times*, 6 May 1973, 38.

60. Sondheim, quoted in Meryle Secrest, *Stephen Sondheim: A Life* (London: Bloomsbury, 1998), 289–290.

61. Richard J. Hand and Michael Wilson, *Grand-Guignol: The French Theatre of Horror* (Exeter: University of Exeter Press, 2002), 11–12.

62. Richard J. Hand and Michael Wilson, *London's Grand Guignol and the Theatre of Horror* (Exeter: University of Exeter Press, 2007), 75.

63. Hand and Wilson, *Grand-Guignol*, 76; Sondheim, 'Larger than Life', 4.

64. Sondheim, *Finishing the Hat*, v, 355; Bond, *Sweeney Todd*, 35; Foster Hirsch, *Harold Prince and the American Musical Theatre* (Cambridge: Cambridge University Press, 1989), 125.

65. Steve Swayne, *How Sondheim Found His Sound* (Ann Arbor: University of Michigan Press, 2007), 3–4.

66. The discussion of modernist music which follows has been influenced by the revisionary work of Peter Franklin. Particularly relevant is Peter Franklin, *Seeing through Music: Gender and Modernism in Classic Hollywood Film Scores* (Oxford and New York: Oxford University Press, 2011), 12–17, 138–167.

67. Stephen Sondheim, *Sweeney Todd: The Demon Barber of Fleet Street*, vocal score (New York: Rilting Music, 1981), No. 17, 'Epiphany', 170–179.

68. Robert Scholes and Florence L. Walzl, 'The Epiphanies of Joyce', *PMLA* 82 (1967):152–154; and James Joyce, *Stephen Hero* (London: Jonathan Cape, 1956), 216.

69. Virginia Woolf, 'Modern Fiction', in *The Common Reader*, 1st ser., ed. Andrew McNeillie (1925; London: Hogarth Press, 1984), 152.

70. On the connection between Wagner and Schoenberg, see John Deathridge, *Wagner Beyond Good and Evil* (Berkeley and Los Angeles: University of California Press, 2008), 114–115, 236.

71. James Lipton, 'Stephen Sondheim: The Art of the Musical', *Paris Review* 39 (Spring 1997): 264; and Anthony Tommasini, 'Finding Still More Life in a "Dead" Idiom', *New York Times*,

6 October 1996, sec. 2, 39. For Babbitt's robust view on the distinction between tonality and the twelve-tone system, see Milton Babbitt, 'Contemporary Music Composition and Music Theory as Contemporary Intellectual History', in *The Collected Essays of Milton Babbitt*, ed. Stephen Peles, Stephen Dembski, Andrew Mead, and Joseph N. Straus (Princeton, NJ: Princeton University Press, 2003), 270–307.

72. Lipton, 'Stephen Sondheim: The Art of the Musical', 264.

73. Stephen Banfield, *Sondheim's Broadway Musicals* (Ann Arbor: University of Michigan Press, 1993), 287–292; and Millie Taylor, '*Sweeney Todd*: From Melodrama to Musical Tragedy', in *The Oxford Handbook of Sondheim Studies*, ed. Robert Gordon (Oxford and New York: Oxford University Press, 2014), 342–344.

74. Banfield, *Sondheim's Broadway Musicals*, 287–291, summarises the discussion about Sondheim and opera.

75. Douglas Jarman, *Alban Berg: 'Wozzeck'* (Cambridge: Cambridge University Press, 1989), 41–45, 21. See also Swayne, *How Sondheim Found His Sound*, 38–39.

76. Britten, quoted in Philip Brett, *Music and Sexuality in Britten: Selected Essays*, ed. George E. Haggerty (Berkeley and Los Angeles: University of California Press, 2006), 38. On the influence of *Wozzeck* on the composition of *Peter Grimes*, see Paul Kildea, 'Benjamin Britten: Inventing English Expressionism?', *University of Toronto Quarterly* 74 (2005): 657–660.

77. Further comparison between the conclusions of *Peter Grimes* and *Sweeney Todd* may be found in Banfield, *Sondheim's Broadway Musicals*, 290, and Swayne, *How Sondheim Found His Sound*, 38.

78. Sondheim, 1986, letter to Steven C. Smith, quoted in Smith, *A Heart at Fire's Center: The Life and Music of Bernard Herrmann* (1991; Berkeley and Los Angeles: University of California Press, 2002), 119.

79. Bernard Herrmann, 'Music in Films', *New York Times*, 24 June 1945, 27.

80. Patrick Hamilton, *Hangover Square* (1941; London: Penguin, 2001), 17.

81. Analyses of *Hangover Square* can be found in Claudia Gorbman, *Unheard Melodies: Narrative Film Music* (London: British Film Institute, 1987), 151–161; Lloyd Whitesell, 'Concerto Macabre', *Musical Quarterly* 88 (2005): 167–203; and Stephen Banfield, 'Sondheim's Genius', in *The Oxford Handbook of Sondheim Studies*, ed. Robert Gordon (Oxford and New York: Oxford University Press, 2014), 16–19.

82. Lipton, 'Stephen Sondheim: The Art of the Musical', 273–274. Sondheim elaborates on the 'epiphany' in *Finishing the Hat*, 331–332.

83. Graham Bruce, *Bernard Herrmann: Film Music and Narrative* (Ann Arbor: UMI Research Press, 1985), 5–9.

84. James M. Baker, 'The Limits of Tonality in the Late Music of Franz Liszt', *Journal of Music Theory* 34, no. 2 (1990): 145–173.

85. Craig M. McGill, 'Sondheim's Use of the "Herrmann Chord" in *Sweeney Todd*', *Studies in Musical Theatre* 6, no. 3 (2012): 291–312. The first eight bars of Bone's Concerto are reproduced on page 294.

86. See Jack Sullivan, *Hitchcock's Music* (New Haven, CT: Yale University Press, 2006), 183–213, 222–289; and Royal S. Brown, 'Herrmann, Hitchcock, and the Music of the Irrational', in *Overtones and Undertones: Reading Film Music* (Berkeley and Los Angeles: University of California Press, 1994), 148–174. A particularly ominous example of Herrmann's work is in *Cape Fear* (1962), a revenge thriller directed by J. Lee Thompson in homage to Hitchcock, who had been involved in the film's early stages. The contemporary

Universal Studios fanfare is replaced by Herrmann's four-note figure, played on the horns three times, each ending with a diabolic augmented fourth (this time B-flat to E). Tremolo violins play a contrary-motion chromatic scale against bass strings as jagged credits appear over location shots of a Southern town, while Robert Mitchum heads directly for the courthouse, barely heeding the busy traffic. This is a man on a mission, and Herrmann's music tells the audience that the mission is evil. *Cape Fear*, dir. J. Lee Thompson (Universal Studios, 1961). DVD Universal 820 018 5, 2003. Indeed, that initial four-note figure was so striking that when Martin Scorsese (also inspired by Hitchcock) remade *Cape Fear* in 1991, Elmer Bernstein kept it unchanged in the title sequence and then reorchestrated it for key moments in the film, turning the figure into a spine-chilling motif. See Elmer Bernstein, interview, 'The Making of the 1991 *Cape Fear*', *Cape Fear*, dir. Martin Scorsese, Universal Studios, 1991, DVD, Universal 820 396 9, 2003.

87. 'Huw Weldon Meets Alfred Hitchcock', Monitor BBC, broadcast 5 May 1964, https://www.youtube.com/watch?v=c9PO-767D8I, accessed 12 February 2020.

88. On the relation of *Little Red Riding Hood* to cannibalism, see Joyce Thomas, *Inside the Wolf's Belly: Aspects of the Fairy Tale* (Sheffield: Sheffield Academic Press, 1989), 50–51, 76-77, 115–116; and Mack, *The Wonderful and Surprising History*, 51–52, 69.

89. Playbill for *Sweeney Todd: The Demon Barber of Fleet Street* (New York: American Theatre Press, July 1979), [18].

90. Olaf Jubin, *Sondheim and Lapine's 'Into the Woods'* (London: Routledge, 2017).

91. Fritz Lang, 'The Future of the Feature Film in Germany' (1926), in *The Weimar Republic Sourcebook*, ed. Anton Kaes, Martin Jay, and Edward Dimendberg (Berkeley and Los Angeles: University of California Press, 1994), 622–623; and Anton Kaes, *M* (London: British Film Institute, 2001), 29, 72–73.

92. Thomas Elsaesser, *Weimar Cinema and After: Germany's Historical Imaginary* (London: Routledge, 2000), 425–426.

93. *New York Times*, 10 December 1944, 54.

94. The analysis of *Sweeney Todd* that follows focuses on Todd and Mrs Lovett. For fuller analyses of the 'musical thriller', see Banfield, *Sondheim's Broadway Musicals*, 281–310; Joanne Gordon, *Art Isn't Easy: The Theater of Stephen Sondheim* (New York: Da Capo Press, 1992), 207–254; Raymond Knapp, *The American Musical and the Performance of Personal Identity* (Princeton, NJ: Princeton University Press, 2006), 331–342; Robert L. McLaughlin, *Stephen Sondheim and the Reinvention of the American Musical* (Jackson: University Press of Mississippi, 2016), 119–133; Taylor, '*Sweeney Todd*', 335–349; and Aaron C. Thomas, *Sondheim and Wheeler's 'Sweeney Todd'* (London: Routledge, 2018).

95. Lipton, 'Stephen Sondheim: The Art of the Musical', 273–274; emphasis in the original.

96. Sondheim, interview with Foster Hirsch, in Hirsch, *Harold Prince*, 123; Sondheim, *Sweeney Todd*, vocal score, Prelude, 1–3. Future references to this text will be given in parentheses.

97. Sondheim, *Finishing the Hat*, 333.

98. Stephen Banfield, 'Sondheim and the Art That Has No Name', in *Approaches to the American Musical*, ed. Robert Lawson-Peebles (Exeter: University of Exeter Press, 1996), 139.

99. Sondheim, *Finishing the Hat*, xx.

100. Ibid., 334.

101. Banfield, *Sondheim's Broadway Musicals*, 293–300. Edgar Allan Poe's 1848 onomatopoetic experiment about the psychological functions of bells was transformed by the Russian

symbolist Konstantin Bal'mont into a meditation on Poe's ill-fated life; then it was linked to the *Dies irae* in Rachmaninoff's 1912 choral symphony *The Bells*.

102. *London Pride: A Celebration of London in Song*, Catherine Bott (soprano), David Owen Norris (piano), CD, Hyperion, CDA67457, 2004.

103. 'Jolly Jack Tar' was an affectionate name for a seaman, the surname adopted from their practice of tarring their clothes to waterproof them. The name appears in English folk songs and in Gilbert and Sullivan's 1878 operetta, *H.M.S. Pinafore*.

104. Sondheim, *Finishing the Hat*, 340.

105. Hirsch, *Harold Prince*, 125.

106. *Paradise Lost* IX, 149–150, in *The Poetical Works of John Milton*, ed. Helen Darbishire (London: Oxford University Press, 1958), 185.

107. Bond, *Sweeney Todd*, 36; and Sondheim, *Finishing the Hat*, 361.

108. Ira Gershwin, 'By Strauss', in *Lyrics on Several Occasions* (London: Omnibus Press, 1978), 169–171; and *An American in Paris*, dir. Vincente Minnelli, MGM, 1951, DVD, Warner Home Video Z5 5627395.

109. Arbie Orenstein, ed., *A Ravel Reader* (New York: Columbia University Press, 1990), 32; see also Robert Lawson-Peebles, '*Follies*: Musical Pastiche and Cultural Archaeology', in *The Oxford Handbook of Sondheim Studies*, ed. Robert Gordon (Oxford and New York: Oxford University Press, 2014), 384–403; and George Benjamin, 'Last Dance', *Musical Times* 135 (1994): 432–435.

110. See Alfred Mollin, 'Mayhem and Morality in *Sweeney Todd*', *American Music* 9 (1991): 410–412.

111. On Brecht, see Thomas, *Sondheim and Wheeler's 'Sweeney Todd'*, 59–60; and Gordon, *Art Isn't Easy*, 345 n. 9.

112. The *mezzo-piano dolce* marking of Todd's song contrasts with the increasingly strident feasting in Mrs Lovett's beer garden, which ends with the customers, in unison, chanting an ecstatic *fortissississimo*. The title and refrain of 'God, That's Good' alludes to Psalm 100 ('Make a joyful noise unto the Lord'), confirming that the communal consumption of human flesh is a diabolic celebration (No. 19, 213–216, 229–230, 233–234).

113. On both occasions she offers her body, cruder instances of the pervasive economics of sex. Sondheim and Wheeler, *Sweeney Todd*, 9, 25; see also Thomas, *Sondheim and Wheeler's 'Sweeney Todd'*, 32–35, 51–54.

114. W. H. Auden, *Selected Poems* (London: Faber & Faber, 1968), 24. Sondheim may have encountered Auden's work through Bernstein and Britten.

115. Barbra Streisand, *The Broadway Album*, CD, Columbia, CK 40092, 1985.

116. Toby sings his touching declaration, supported by rocking harp notes, amidst an atmosphere of growing fear. Mrs Lovett's response is undermined by acid violin phrases. The lullaby leads, ironically, to the confinement of Toby to the bakehouse, where he finally makes good on his promise of retribution by killing Todd.

117. Sondheim and Wheeler, *Sweeney Todd*, 143–144.

118. Sondheim, *Finishing the Hat*, 372–373; and Banfield, *Sondheim's Broadway Musicals*, 309–310. The extended version of the Beggar Woman's lullaby may be heard on the recording of the New York Philharmonic semi-staged production of 2000, starring George Hearn and Patti LuPone, which was conducted by Andrew Litton. *Sweeney Todd Live at the New York Philharmonic*, 2 CDs, New York Philharmonic Special Editions, NYP 2001–2002, 2000.

119. Sondheim and Wheeler, *Sweeney Todd*, Cast Page, n.p.

120. Ibid., 152, 156.

121. Hirsch, *Harold Prince*, 120; Sondheim, 'Larger than Life', 10. An illustrated account of the development of the 1979 production is in Craig Zadan, *Sondheim & Co.*, 2nd ed. (New York: Harper & Row, 1989), 242–261.
122. *Sweeney Todd: The Demon Barber of Fleet Street*, original Broadway cast, 2CDs, RCA, 3379-2-RC, 1979. The production was filmed on tour in Los Angeles, with George Hearn replacing Cariou. *Sweeney Todd: The Demon Barber of Fleet Street*, dir. Terry Hughes, 1982. DVD, Warner Home Video, Z1 T 6750, 1982.
123. Personal communication with Robert Gordon, 23 June 2020.
124. James Fenton, 'The Barberous Crimes of Sondheim and Prince', *Sunday Times*, 6 July 1980, 40; Anon., '"Flop" Wins Award for Best New Musical', *Times*, 21 January 1981, 16. For a summary of the reviews, see Thomas, *Sondheim and Wheeler's 'Sweeney Todd'*, 12–14.
125. Kenneth Gosling, '£1m bookings for *Sound of Music*', *Times*, 19 August 1981, 2. A relevant consideration of the changes wrought by revival practice is Louise Creechan, '"Attend the Tale of Sweeney Todd": Adaptation, Revival, and Keeping the Meat Grinder Turning', *Neo-Victorian Studies* 9 (2016): 98–122.
126. Michael Billington, 'A Cut Above the Rest', *Guardian*, 3 July 1980, 11; reprinted in Michael Billington, *One Night Stands* (London: Nick Hern Books, 1993), 155–156.
127. Ned Chaillet, 'Open Blood-Letting in Closed Spaces', *Times*, 30 October 1982, 5; and Martin Cropper, 'Sweeney Todd', *Times*, 2 May 1985, 9.
128. Sheridan Morley, '*Sweeney Todd* on a Small Scale', *International Herald Tribune*, 9 June 1993, 5.
129. Michael Billington, '*Sweeney Todd*', *Guardian*, 7 October 2011, https://www.theguardian.com/stage/2011/oct/07/sweeney-todd-review, accessed 28 June 2020. The production has been recorded: *Sweeney Todd*, London cast album, CD, First Night Records CASTCD113, 2012.
130. Terfel's 'Epiphany' and 'A Little Priest' (with Maria Friedman) from 'Sondheim at 80', BBC Promenade Concert 19, 31 July 2010, Royal Albert Hall, London, is available on YouTube: https://www.youtube.com/watch?v=ba6U4mZpG6Y, accessed 15 March 2020. 'Epiphany' is available on a CD aptly titled *Bad Boys*, Bryn Terfel and Anne Sofie von Otter, Swedish Radio Symphony Orchestra, conducted by Paul Daniel, Deutsche Grammophon, DG 477 8091, 2009.
131. Charles Spencer, 'Love Letter Written in Blood', *Daily Telegraph*, 23 July 2004, 20; and Ben Brantley, 'Grand Guignol, Spare and Stark', *New York Times*, 4 November 2003, E1, 4.
132. Hilary Finch, 'Opera', *Times*, 4 November 1991, 20.
133. Henry Hitchings, 'Chilling and Thrilling', *Evening Standard* (London), 28 October 2014, 34; and Robert Dex, 'Tooting Pie Shop *Sweeney Todd* Is a Meaty Hit for New York Theatre', *Evening Standard*, 24 February 2017, 21.
134. Robert Orr, 'London Loses Appetite for Pie and Mash Shops', *Financial Times*, 7 June 2019, https://www.ft.com/content/8b7e1ac6-765e-11e9-bbad-7c18c0ea0201, accessed 18 May 2020.

## BIBLIOGRAPHY

Banfield, Stephen. *Sondheim's Broadway Musicals*. Ann Arbor: University of Michigan Press, 1993.
Banfield, Stephen. 'Sondheim and the Art That Has No Name', in *Approaches to the American Musical*, ed. Robert Lawson-Peebles, 137–160. Exeter: University of Exeter Press, 1996.

Banfield, Stephen. 'Sondheim's Genius'. In *The Oxford Handbook of Sondheim Studies*, edited by Robert Gordon, 16–19. Oxford and New York: Oxford University Press, 2014.

Billington, Michael. 'A Cut Above the Rest'. *The Guardian*, 3 July 1980, 11.

Bond, C. G. *Sweeney Todd*. London: Samuel French, 1974.

Bond, Christopher. 'The Theater of Pyramids: (And a Camel)'. In *Melodrama*, edited by Daniel Charles Gerould, 15–18. New York: New York Literary Forum, 1980.

Booth, Michael R. *Theatre in the Victorian Age*. Cambridge: Cambridge University Press, 1991.

Brenna, Dwayne. *George Dibdin Pitt: His Life and Work*. PhD diss., Royal Holloway, University of London, 2000.

Brooks, Peter. *The Melodramatic Imagination*. 2nd ed. New Haven, CT: Yale University Press, 1995.

Bruce, Graham. *Bernard Herrmann: Film Music and Narrative*. Ann Arbor: UMI Research Press, 1985.

Burton, Brian J. *Sweeney Todd the Barber: A Melodrama*. 1962. London: French, 1984.

Collins, Dick. 'Introduction'. In *Sweeney Todd*, 2nd ed, vi–xix. Ware: Wordsworth Editions, 2010.

Creechan, Louise. '"Attend the Tale of Sweeney Todd": Adaptation, Revival, and Keeping the Meat Grinder Turning'. *Neo-Victorian Studies* 9 (2016): 98–122.

Crone, Rosalind. *Violent Victorians: Popular Entertainment in Nineteenth-Century London*. Manchester: Manchester University Press, 2012.

Dickens, Charles, Jr. *Dictionary of London*. London: Charles Dickens, 1879.

Dobraszczyk, Paul. *Into the Belly of the Beast: Exploring London's Victorian Sewers*. Reading: Spire Books, 2009.

Erle, Thomas William. *Letters from a Theatrical Scene-Painter*. 2nd ser. London: Printed by J. Chisman, 1862.

Fenton, James. 'The Barberous Crimes of Sondheim and Prince'. *Sunday Times*, 6 July 1980, 40.

Franklin, Peter. *Seeing through Music: Gender and Modernism in Classic Hollywood Film Scores*. Oxford and New York: Oxford University Press, 2011.

Godwin, George. *The Churches of London*. London: C. Tilt, 1838.

Haining, Peter. *Sweeney Todd: The Real Story of the Demon Barber of Fleet Street*. London: Robson, 1998.

Halliday, Stephen. *The Great Stink of London: Sir Joseph Bazalgette and the Cleansing of the Victorian Metropolis*. Stroud: Sutton, 1999.

Hamilton, Patrick. *Hangover Square*. 1941. London: Penguin, 2001.

Hand, Richard J., and Michael Wilson. *Grand-Guignol: The French Theatre of Horror*. Exeter: University of Exeter Press, 2002.

Hand, Richard J. , and Michael Wilson. *London's Grand Guignol and the Theatre of Horror*. Exeter: University of Exeter Press, 2007.

Hazelton, Frederick. *Sweeney Todd: The Barber of Fleet Street; or, The String of Pearls*. London: Samuel French, 1862.

Hepworth Dixon, William. *The London Prisons [. . .]*. London: Jackson & Walford, 1850.

Herrmann, Bernard. 'Music in Films'. *New York Times*, 24 June 1945, 27.

Hirsch, Foster. *Harold Prince and the American Musical Theatre*. Cambridge: Cambridge University Press, 1989.

Holloway, Stanley. *The Stanley Holloway Monologues*. Edited by Michael Marshall. London: Elm Tree Books, 1979.

Kilburn, Matthew. 'Sweeney Todd (*called* the Demon Barber of Fleet Street)'. In *Oxford Dictionary of National Biography*, 54:887–888. Oxford and New York: Oxford University Press, 2003.

Kilgarriff, Michael. *The Golden Age of Melodrama*. London: Wolfe, 1974.

Knapp, Raymond. *The American Musical and the Performance of Personal Identity*. Princeton, NJ: Princeton University Press, 2006.

Lawson-Peebles, Robert. 'The Beggar's Legacy: Playing with Music and Drama, 1920–2003'. In *The Oxford Handbook of the British Musical*, edited by Robert Gordon and Olaf Jubin, 585–611. Oxford and New York: Oxford University Press, 2016.

Lawson-Peebles, Robert. '*Follies*: Musical Pastiche and Cultural Archaeology', in *The Oxford Handbook of Sondheim Studies*, ed. Robert Gordon, 384–403. Oxford and New York: Oxford University Press, 2014.

Lawson-Peebles, Robert. 'From Macheath to Mackie Messer and Mack the Knife: Transatlantic Transformations of *The Beggar's Opera*, 1920–1956', *Symbiosis* 22, no. 1 (2018): 3–28.

Lipton, James. 'Stephen Sondheim: The Art of the Musical'. *Paris Review* 39 (Spring 1997): 264.

Mack, Robert L. *The Wonderful and Surprising History of Sweeney Todd: The Life and Times of an Urban Legend*. London: Continuum, 2007.

McGill, Craig. M. 'Sondheim's Use of the "Herrmann Chord" in *Sweeney Todd*'. *Studies in Musical Theatre* 6, no. 3 (2012): 291–312.

McLaughlin, Robert L. *Stephen Sondheim and the Reinvention of the American Musical*. Jackson: University Press of Mississippi, 2016.

Mollin, Alfred. 'Mayhem and Morality in *Sweeney Todd*'. *American Music* 9 (1991): 410–412.

O'Byrne, Alison. '"Unceasing Bustle and Traffic": Print Culture and Metropolitan Spaces in the 1830s'. *Yearbook of English Studies* 48 (2018): 171–198.

Paulson, Ronald. *Representations of Revolution (1789–1820)*. New Haven, CT: Yale University Press, 1983.

Pitt, George Dibdin. *The String of Pearls*. Edited by Sharon Arononfsky Weltman, *Nineteenth Century Theatre & Film* 38, no. 1 (2011): 1–85.

Powell, Sally. 'Black Markets and Cadaverous Pies: The Corpse, Urban Trade and Industrial Consumption in the Penny Blood'. In *Victorian Crime, Madness and Sensation*, edited by Andrew Maunder and Grace Moore, 45–58. Aldershot: Ashgate, 2004.

Richards, Jeffrey. 'Tod Slaughter and the Cinema of Excess'. In *The Unknown 1930s: An Alternative History of the British Cinema 1929–1939*, edited by Jeffrey Richards, 139–159. London: I. B. Tauris, 1998.

Rosser, Austin. *Sweeney Todd: A Victorian Melodrama*. London: French, 1971.

Ryan, Michael. *Prostitution in London, with a Comparative View of That of Paris and New York*. London: H. Bailliere, 1839.

Secrest, Meryle. *Stephen Sondheim: A Life*. London: Bloomsbury, 1998.

Shelley, Mary. *Frankenstein, or The Modern Prometheus*. Edited by J. Paul Hunter. 1818;. New York: W. W. Norton, 1996.

Sondheim, Stephen. 'Larger than Life: Reflections on Melodrama and *Sweeney Todd*'. In *Melodrama*, edited by Daniel Charles Gerould, 3–14. New York: New York Literary Forum, 1980.

Sondheim, Stephen. *Finishing the Hat: Collected Lyrics (1954–1981), with Attendant Comments, Principles, Heresies, Grudges, Whines and Anecdotes*. New York: Alfred A. Knopf, 2011.

Sondheim, Stephen. *Sweeney Todd: The Demon Barber of Fleet Street*. Vocal score. New York: Rilting Music, 1981.

Sondheim, Stephen, and Hugh Wheeler. *Sweeney Todd: The Demon Barber of Fleet Street.* London: Nick Hern Books, 1991.

Swayne, Steve. *How Sondheim Found His Sound.* Ann Arbor: University of Michigan Press, 2007.

*Sweeney Todd: The Demon Barber of Fleet Street.* Edited By Robert L. Mack. Oxford and New York: Oxford University Press, 2007.

*Sweeney Todd: The Demon Barber of Fleet Street,* directed by George King, George King Productions, 1936. DVD. Odeon Entertainment ODNF127.

*Sweeney Todd: The Demon Barber of Fleet Street,* directed by Terry Hughes, 1982. DVD. Los Angeles: Warner Home Video DVD Z1 T 6750, 1982.

*Sweeney Todd: The Demon Barber of Fleet Street.* 2 CDs. Original Broadway Cast. RCA, , 3379-2-RC, 1979.

Taylor, Millie. '*Sweeney Todd*: From Melodrama to Musical Tragedy'. In *The Oxford Handbook of Sondheim Studies,* edited by Robert Gordon, 335–349. Oxford and New York: Oxford University Press, 2014.

Thornbury, Walter. *Haunted London.* London: Hurst & Blackett, 1865.

Thornbury, Walter. *Old and New London: A Narrative of Its History, Its People and Its Places.* Vol. 2. London: Cassell, Petter & Galpin, 1873–1874.

Walkowitz, Judith R. *City of Dreadful Delight. Narratives of Sexual Danger in Late-Victorian London.* London: Virago Press, 1992.

White, Jerry. *London in the Nineteenth Century: A Human Awful Wonder of God.* London: Jonathan Cape, 2007.

Winter, Sarah A. '"His Knife and Hands Bloody": Sweeney Todd's Journey from Page to Stage—Melodrama, Adaptation and the Original 1847 Manuscript'. *Journal of Adaptation in Film & Performance* 8, no. 3 (2015): 233–247.

# PART IX

## NATIONAL GENRES OF MUSICAL THEATRE IN WESTERN EUROPE

# CHAPTER 25

## THE FRENCH *SPECTACLE MUSICAL*

### LUCA CERCHIARI

## THE BEGINNINGS OF MUSICAL THEATRE IN FRANCE

IF we consider the entire history of the musical, the French contribution seems to be most meaningful and relevant at the very beginning of its development. Jacques Offenbach (a German immigrant of Jewish heritage who arrived in Paris midway through the nineteenth century) became first a French and then an international master of the new genre, influencing both Austrian and English authors and plays with his brilliantly modern concept of modern musical theatre. Nurtured by his long experience at the Comédie Française, Offenbach had the idea not only to criticise contemporary cultural, socio-political, and military values, but also to satirise classical opera stereotypes and recurring topics, as well as contemporary French opera masters.

The success of his compositions and smaller theatrical productions (hence *operetta*, a 'small opera') was also the consequence of a stylistic revolution based on an unprecedented mix of highbrow and lowbrow values, art and new popular culture, ballet and cabaret-style dance as well as untrained approaches to musical and theatrical interpretation. Offenbach was frequently scouting out untrained but exceptionally skilled actors and singers, such as the soprano Hortense Schneider, who would become the beloved star of his unique concept of a *théâtre des bouffes*.

Another French source in the early history of the musical is vaudeville, a non-metropolitan (and to some extent even non-urban) genre based on music, dance, and drama; but we need further research to better trace its dynamics and developments, both in Europe and in the United States, where the shows associated with this name were slightly different. A third French source for the early musical may be identified, in more general terms, in terms of physicality: costumes, bodily freedom, and rhythmic movement, three concepts mostly associated with female images and roles. These features transferred to American serial revues such as the *Follies*, which clearly had their original source of inspiration in the Parisian shows presented at the famed Théâtre des Folies Bergère.

Between 1920 and 1960 the history of international musical theatre was largely American, but European contributions arose once again in the second half of the twentieth century, when the musical became an entirely multi-continental, indeed global, affair, with rock music as one of its new features. Austria, initially a major European source for the development of the American stage and film musical—just consider Viennese operetta and its palingenesis in Hollywood classics—was not part of this late twentieth-century phenomenon, but France and Britain certainly were. Once again, as in the time of Offenbach (with his co-authors Henry Meilhac and Ludovic Halévy) and the British team of W. S. Gilbert and Arthur Sullivan, social ideas and musical creations were closely related. Of course, some important differences existed. Musicals from the time of Offenbach were often small-scale productions,[1] while the French *spectacle musical* from the end of the twentieth century falls almost entirely within the (Anglo-American) category of what has come to be called by journalists and some scholars the megamusical.

The other main difference concerns source material. If Offenbach had started a sort of disintegration of classical dramatic forms in moving towards a new kind of popular musical theatre, contemporary musicals (including megamusicals) often tend to recuperate older literary and theatrical texts, thus moving away from a traditional musical comedy format. Of course, this trend goes back to some post–World War II American shows: Bella and Samuel Spewack adapted William Shakespeare's *The Taming of the Shrew* for Cole Porter's *Kiss Me, Kate* (1946), Alan Jay Lerner and Frederic Loewe transformed George Bernard Shaw's *Pygmalion* into *My Fair Lady* (1956), and Arthur Laurents, Leonard Bernstein, and Jerome Robbins recreated Shakespeare's *Romeo and Juliet* as *West Side Story* (1957).

*Cats* (1981), the first of the megamusicals and one of the longest-running British musicals, is based on the twentieth-century poet T. S. Eliot's *Old Possum's Book of Practical Cats*. Before *Cats*, Andrew Lloyd Webber and Tim Rice's *Jesus Christ Superstar* (1970) had already marked a turning point in the history of the musical. Not only did the New Testament topic represent a wholly new idea, but also their concept of a youth-oriented rock-style celebration of Christ as pop star was unprecedented. Being sung through—that is, telling its story without dialogue—*Jesus Christ Superstar* sounded more like an opera than a musical, hence the label 'rock opera'. Once again the musical returned, albeit unconsciously, to its nineteenth-century 'highbrow' roots, though we might assume that grand opera was initially a cultivated *and* popular genre. As the term was only coined in the following decade, *Jesus Christ Superstar* was yet not labelled a megamusical.

That moniker was first applied to shows of the 1980s, which followed the patterns of the ambitious British producer Cameron Mackintosh's association with Andrew Lloyd Webber (later the founder of his own Really Useful Company). With *Cats*, Mackintosh discovered how to turn certain shows into global hits, reproduced identically wherever they were performed: musicals first staged in one of his own network of West End theatres found huge commercial success on Broadway before being profitably marketed and staged around the world in numerous foreign languages. The megamusical has been defined as a 'through-composed popular opera' where 'set design, choreography and special effects are at least as important as the music', and also as a 'reinvigoration of nineteenth-century French grand opera'.[2] In some ways, the 1980s concept of stage spectacle was also influenced by cinema.[3] Moreover, Paul Prece and William Everett suggest a parallel between Mackintosh and French grand opera's main promoter, Louis Véron, in terms of spectacular stage conceptions.[4]

# *LA RÉVOLUTION FRANÇAISE* (1973): THE FIRST BOUBLIL/SCHÖNBERG SHOW

The Broadway production of *Jesus Christ Superstar* had among its enthusiasts a French lyricist and bookwriter, Alain Boublil, born in 1941 in Tunisia to a Sephardic Jewish family. Some years before he had seen *West Side Story* in Paris and thought he might try a career in musical theatre; he would later be impressed by a revival of *Oliver!*, produced by Mackintosh.[5] Influenced by Lloyd Webber and Rice's work, Boublil spent some time pondering a suitable topic for his own musical and finally decided on the French Revolution. He contacted the French author, pianist, and singer Claude-Michel Schönberg (born in 1944), and a successful partnership began. Both had professional training in record production; Schönberg with the French label Pathé Marconi, where he would record Frank Pourcel, Gilbert Bécaud, and Véronique Sanson, among others, while Boublil had started a publishing company and begun writing songs.[6] Schönberg, like Lloyd Webber, was a young prodigy who began composing music at age six and later developed an extensive knowledge of the European classical and operatic repertoire. Also like Lloyd Webber, the French composer's musical background was both classical and rock oriented. Thus, it is not surprising that *Jesus Christ Superstar* encouraged Schönberg to write his own rock opera.[7]

*La Révolution Française* (1973), the first musical written—with two other authors, Raymond Janneau and Jean-Max Rivière—by Schönberg and Boublil, began life as a concept album, a Vogue double LP (later re-released on CD by First Night Records), which then was staged, just like Lloyd Webber and Rice's *Jesus Christ Superstar*. The album sales rocketed after one song was presented on a Saturday evening television program, and the show itself played successfully for one year at the 4,500-seat Palais des Sports in Paris. Schönberg himself took on the role of Louis XVI, the first and last time he appeared in one of his own shows.

FIG. 25.1 Rehearsals at the Palais des Sports in Paris for the premiere staging of rock opera *La Révolution Française*; the show opened on 2 October 1973. Photo: Alain Dejean/Sygma © Getty Images.

*La Révolution Française* is the fictional story of the impossible love between an aristocrat, Isabelle de Montmorency, and Charles Gauthier, a shopkeeper who becomes a member of the Third Estate (Tiers-État). The show describes the 1789 uprising and overthrow of the Bourbon dynasty, followed by Robespierre's Reign of Terror, set to a catchy rock score. All of the historically important figures are represented: there is also an appearance by a young Napoléon Bonaparte, who sings a comic song with a group of washerwomen. *La Révolution Française* later received a second staging in Paris, at the Théâtre Mogador. But the show was never translated into English—its subject was considered 'too French'—and thus remains relatively unknown to Anglophone audiences.

Ironically, Boublil and Schönberg became world-famous in a genre which is not particularly popular in their country. Owing partly to the fact that musical comedy is an English-language genre, few twentieth-century musicals reached Paris, and even fewer French authors wrote shows of this kind, two exceptions being Guy Bontempelli (*Mayflower*, 1975) and Michel Legrand (*Le Passe-Muraille* [*Amour*], 1997, and *Marguérite*, 2008), both of whom were also very active in film music.[8] As Boublil later remarked, 'In order to be able to have musical theater performed in France, a country where the genre does not exist, you have to touch something that is deep in the heart of the people.'[9] In fact, only a very few Broadway shows were imported to Paris during the 1960s, including *How to Succeed in Business Without Really Trying*, *A Funny*

*Thing Happened on the Way to the Forum, Man of la Mancha, Hair, Sweet Charity*, and *Godspell*.

Therefore, *La Révolution Française*, like the later shows written by the two French authors, took inspiration from both previous rock music recordings and from French literary sources, which had two significant consequences: one, the casts of these *spectacles* tend to be made up of pop singers rather than stage actors; and two, because the story is based on a well-known French literary source, there is little need for a detailed rendition of the original narrative, so the storytelling aspect of the musical is minimal. *La Révolution Française*, inaugurated a new trend in French musical theatre—*spectacles*. According to Rebecca-Anne C. Do Rozario:

> French musicals differ from their contemporary English and German language cousins in that their techniques and artistry came not predominantly from theatre, but from show business. In a culture that has been critically antagonistic to the musical genre over the past decade, *les spectacles musicaux* have nonetheless had extraordinary success in Europe and Canada.[10]

As Olaf Jubin explains, the production circumstances clearly influence both the form and the content of these shows:

> Because [they] are housed in sports palaces or rock arenas, they are usually cast with [ . . . ] performers who have the experience in playing to a huge crowd and can attract enough fans to fill the space. The choice of venue is dictated partly by the fact that neither the subsidized French theatres nor the private companies put on musicals with open-ended runs, which means those established venues are unavailable. Yet if a much larger stage is the only alternative, it affects every detail of the production, not just the casting: the set, the choreography, the costume and lighting design need to go for bold artistic statements instead of subtle indications. In order for the creative decisions and ideas to be picked up by an audience of up to 5,000 people, they have to be big and spectacular, which explains the term *spectacle musical*.[11]

# *Les Misérables* (1): From Paris (1980) to London

For their next collaboration in the late 1970s Boublil chose to recreate for the stage Victor Hugo's classic tale *Les Misérables*. First published in 1862, it is regarded as one of the greatest novels of its century. The story narrates the interrelated lives of several characters, particularly the struggles of Jean Valjean, a former convict, and Javert, a police officer who hunts him down. Hugo's novel elaborates on a wide range of topics, including French history, the architecture and urban design of Paris, the nature of law, and questions of politics, justice, and religion, as well as romantic and familial love. From the outset the novel became a literary phenomenon. Hugo's brilliant self-promotion guaranteed sales of seven thousand copies on the first day of publication, and the novel, translated into many languages, has remained successful ever since. Its popular themes, especially young love in the context of freedom and justice for the poor, made it a popular choice for dramatic adaptations, the first of which appeared in 1863. Silent and sound film versions (more than a dozen in all) followed in France, in other European countries, in North America (the United States and Mexico), and even in Asia (India and Japan). Hugo's monumental novel has spawned numerous television versions, including an Italian one (1964).

Boublil's adaptation focused on the novel's main historic events (running from 1815 to 1832), leaving out some of its philosophical reflections and the family histories of some characters, which, in theatrical terms, would run the risk of boring audiences. Boublil's text matched Schönberg's music, which has been repeatedly labelled 'Gallic' by music critics, but more precisely is built largely on the principle of recurring motifs, not unlike Richard Wagner's use of leitmotifs, to which different lyrics are sometimes set. Another typical feature of Schönberg's music is the use of recitative. (It must be remembered he is also a singer.) When it comes to pitch, one of Schönberg's distinguishing ideas, developed further in later shows with Boublil,[12] was to use the pentatonic scale in order to add an ethnic and romantic flavour to his musical numbers. This technique is evident in *Les Miz* in numbers such as 'Stars'.

The two-year collaboration of Boublil and Schönberg on the project resulted in a demonstration tape featuring Schönberg as singer and pianist. The songs were subsequently orchestrated by John Cameron and finally released as a double album, featuring the nineteenth-century illustrator Émile Bayard's popular image of the young girl Cosette on the cover. It sold over 250,000 copies. The excellent sales helped secure financial support for a staging, which followed in September 1980 at the Palais des Sports in Paris, directed by Robert Hossein. In all, the first French production was seen by half a million people and featured, among others, Maurice Barrier as Jean Valjean, Jean Vallée as Javert, Yvan Dautin as Monsieur Thénardier, Marie-France Roussel as Madame Thénardier, and Fabienne Guyon as Cosette. Most of these performers had been featured on the double album.

But the turning point, both for this work and for its two French authors, would be their meeting with the producer Cameron Mackintosh, who happened to hear their concept album at the end of 1982 and soon began to conceive an English-language stage production of the piece. This was risky. With few exceptions—a famous one being *The Merry Widow*—translating and adapting a work of musical theatre into other languages has often been problematic, which is one of the reasons the musical never became popular in France in the twentieth century.

Besides managing financial matters, Mackintosh was able to bring to the British production of *Les Misérables* two key figures: Herbert Kretzmer, a lyricist whose various credentials included awkward yet popular translations of Charles Aznavour's *chansons*,[13] and Trevor Nunn, an experienced stage director. Nunn had been appointed artistic director of the Royal Shakespeare Company (RSC) in 1968, directing, among many other works, *Macbeth*, creating a musical adaptation of Shakespeare's *The Comedy of Errors*, and directing a nine-hour theatrical version of Charles Dickens's *Nicholas Nickleby*. In 1980 Mackintosh's invitation to direct Lloyd Webber's *Cats* had inaugurated Nunn's parallel career as a director of musicals.

The connection between Lloyd Webber–Rice and Schönberg-Boublil would become even more concrete in the process of staging the English-language version of *Les Misérables*. When casting began, a major problem arose concerning who would play Jean Valjean. Nunn had through the RSC secured actors for other major roles (Javert and Monsieur and Madame Thénardier), but it was Tim Rice who suggested Colm Wilkinson—a very good choice indeed. Wilkinson, not yet well-known (though he had appeared in *Jesus Christ Superstar* and had created the part of Che on the recording of *Evita*), would become one of the main attractions of the show and contribute to its growing success, first in London and then in New York. The British team for *Les Miz* also included the co-director John Caird, the designer John Napier (another key figure of *Cats*), the musical director Martin Koch, and the orchestrator John Cameron (who had orchestrated the French recording of the show).

Boublil and Schönberg, for their part, were more than happy to take an active role in the adaptation, expansion, and translation of their show, finding the Barbican Center—at that time the London home of the RSC—a very sympathetic work environment. The shift from the French original to the English version of the show logically entailed a rather different theatrical rendering of the Hugo novel. As Jessica Sternfeld points out:

> [T]he French version assumed the audience knew the story, and a great deal of action happened offstage; Nunn described it as scenes of impressions from the novel, rather than a full telling of it. The team returned to the novel, pulling from it all the pertinent action, emotions, and plot points, and removing the specifically French colloquialisms and references that did not translate well.[14]

Furthermore, Mackintosh decided to reduce the play from three acts to two so that its overall length was compressed from three and a half hours to three.

One of the most significant features of this show is its songs, which Kretzmer was obliged to both translate from Boublil's French and sometimes to rewrite in English. Among the most famous numbers are 'Do You Hear the People Sing?', almost an anthem; the comic 'Master of the House'; the ensemble numbers 'Look Down' and 'Lovely Ladies'; and the ballads 'On My Own' and 'I Dreamed a Dream'. During the English adaptation of the show, several (now hugely popular) songs were added, including 'Stars', 'One Day More', and 'Empty Chairs at Empty Tables'. Some of these numbers have been used to great effect elsewhere: 'Do You Hear the People Sing?' was heard at both the 2000 Sydney Olympic Games and the 2002 opening of the World Cup, while 'One Day More' was adopted by the American Democratic Party during the 1992 presidential campaign.

The two versions, the French and the English, share the same choral and dance numbers, which are closely interwoven with the dramaturgical structure of the play.

Audiences everywhere can appreciate the social and human messages implied in the text. But the two versions have some obvious differences. The original French version has some explicit pop-video aspects (which relate it more to cinematic than to stage forms) and thus a looser theatrical structure. The British one, mainly because the director Trevor Nunn's extensive Shakespearian experience had made him a master of epic staging, is on the other hand much more skilfully developed in dramaturgical terms and refers more specifically to the original literary text. Nunn combines a close interpretation of the narrative with an alternation of epic and intimate visual moments, both features for which his Shakespearian stagings had been celebrated. Therefore, if Hugo's novel was alluded to implicitly in the French version, reducing storytelling to a minimum, the British one replaces this approach with greater storytelling detail and better-integrated spectacular moments:

> The creative team of *Les Miz* achieved its objective of narrative clarity, which is so important for attracting theatregoers who are unfamiliar with the novel, partly through the musical's staging and stage design. Both were developed based on considerations of how best to present the show's rapidly evolving story: because right from the prologue, the musical's settings change constantly and because Trevor Nunn saw Javert's unremitting pursuit of Valjean as a never-ending chase, he and designer John Napier decided to employ a revolving stage. This allowed for perpetual motion but also gave the production cinematic flair—as did another of the musical's most famous directorial flourishes, the use of slow motion in key moments.[15]

Mackintosh, showing an uncommon ability in putting together different forces and sources, on one hand—through the participation of the co-directors, Nunn and Caird—combined the public funding of the RSC with private investment. He also motivated Schönberg and Boublil, who at first assumed thought the producer would simply buy the rights to their work, instead to take an active part in the process of reconceiving *Les Miz*.

## *LES MISÉRABLES* (2): FROM LONDON (1985) TO AROUND THE WORLD

As Prece and Everett note, '*Les Misérables* epitomises the pan-national production of megamusicals',[16] not least in its global success. What follows is a list of a few landmarks set by the show.[17]

- It transferred to the West End on 8 October 1985, where to this day it continues to draw packed houses.
- On 9 October 2006 *Les Misérables* became London's longest-running musical with its 8,372nd performance.

- The New York production opened on 12 March 1987 and closed on 18 May 2003 after a staggering 6,680 performances.
- Attesting to the show's continued popularity and viability as a New York tourist attraction, a Broadway revival opened at the Broadhurst Theatre on 9 November 2006, just three and a half years after the initial production closed.
- The show has been performed in countries as different as Hungary, Iceland, Norway, Austria, Poland, Sweden, the Netherlands, France, Germany, the Czech Republic, Spain, Israel, Japan, Denmark, and Finland, in each case translated into the native language.
- There are cast recordings in English, Hungarian, German, Swedish, Dutch, French, Czech, Danish, Hebrew, Japanese, and Spanish.
- By May 2017, *Les Misérables* had played in more than 349 cities in forty-four countries in twenty-two languages and has been seen by more than seventy million people worldwide.

In October 1991 the show played in Paris at the Théâtre Mogador, and then transferred to Montreal, Canada. The revised English version was back-translated into French, but after an encouraging beginning the show stopped attracting audiences, and for the first time in its international career it lost money. Ironically, French audiences once again revealed a lack of interest in imported musical productions.

When moving the show to Broadway, Cameron Mackintosh had two clever ideas. The first was to avoid co-producers, a courageous decision during a period when almost all musicals were benefitting from a group of producers. The second was to find just a few large investors—not minor ones, as had happened in the past, but big companies which could provide as much as a million dollars. Mackintosh, with his years of professional experience, was able to circumvent Broadway conventions and reach a successful agreement with Mutual Benefit Life Insurance. In order to ensure strong ticket sales, Mackintosh started an aggressive advertising campaign in all media from newspapers to radio and television and simultaneously released the *Les Miz* London cast album in the United States.

From the beginning, and in each new city, Mackintosh's advertising and marketing machine proved remarkably effective, partly, as Sternfeld underlines, because the tone of the show's publicity was different:

> [It] convinced millions that *Les Miz* was not just a musical, but a moving, powerful, life-changing journey. Promising this sort of atmosphere proved extremely effective in selling tickets, but had the show not delivered on this promise, the long runs in almost all cities around the world would not have happened. [ . . . ] The show proved as powerful as it claimed, judging from the unflagging attendance of audiences, and the idea of *Les Miz* as an event became perpetuating.[18]

Many of the reviews of the London *Les Misérables*; a number of British critics probably disliked the musical adaptation because of its divergence from the typical profile and structure of a traditional West End or Broadway show. One of the few dissenting voices belonged to Sheridan Morley, theatre critic of the *International Herald Tribune*:

> There are songs of love and war and death and restoration: there are patter songs, arias, duets and chorus numbers of dazzling inventiveness and variety. For this is not the French *Oliver!* or even the musical *Nicholas Nickleby*, though it owes a certain debt to both. Rather, it is a brilliantly guided tour of the 1,200-page eternity that is Hugo's text, and indeed there is no way that in three orchestral hours we can ask for more than that.[19]

One of the most enthusiastic American reviews was that of Frank Rich in the *New York Times*. He categorised the musical as a 'gripping pop opera', praising its 'fusion of drama, music, character, design and movement' that 'links this English adaptation of a French show to the highest tradition of modern Broadway musical production.'[20] When discussing the music, besides noticing that 'motifs are recycled with ironic effect throughout, allowing the story's casualties to haunt the grief-stricken survivor long after their deaths,' Rich appreciated various melodies and the show's mixture of rock, Kurt Weill, Georges Bizet, and madrigals, attesting that with this show 'the contemporary musical theater can flex its atrophied muscles and yank an audience out of its seats.'[21]

## *STARMANIA* (1978): AN EARLY
### *SPECTACLE MUSICAL*

The songwriter Luc Plamondon is one of the most important artists in the realm of French musical theatre. Born in Canada in 1942 and raised in Quebec, Plamondon studied piano and developed a lasting interest in painting alongside his first attempts as a poet and lyricist. Professionally, however, he has been based in Paris since the beginning of his career. After seeing *Hair* in New York in the late 1960s, Plamondon decided that, in addition to stand-alone songs, musical theatre would be part of his future; he thus started to compose dramatic songs that would be recorded by a growing number of French, Canadian, and international stars, including Gilbert Bécaud, Petula Clark, Renée Claude, Céline Dion, Diane Dufresne, Emmanuelle, Johnny Halliday, Françoise Hardy, Monique Leyrac, Noa, Bruno Pelletier, Gino Vannelli, and Sylvie Vartan.

A turning point in Plamondon's career was his meeting with the composer Michel Berger (b. 1942). The two conceived a rock opera, which had its first public performance in Paris at the Palais des Congrès on 10 April 1979. *Starmania* would become one of the best-known and longest-running musicals in the French language. Like the other shows mentioned above, it was originally conceived as a concept album that in 1978 sold an impressive 2.2 million copies. Two very famous American jazz musicians, Randy and

Michael Brecker (trumpet and saxophone), can be heard on the recording alongside Michel Bernholc (keyboards), Claude Engel (guitar), André Ceccarelli (drums), and Serge Planchon (piano), among others.

Constructed in two acts, *Starmania* has been described as a 'cyberpunk rock opera'. It tells the story of the struggles of two young lovers—Marie-Jeanne, who works in a bar called Underground Café, and Ziggy (the name is inspired by David Bowie's Ziggy Stardust)—as they fight the tyranny of the star system. Good and evil clash as the inhabitants of the futuristic city of Monopolis, the capital of the Western world, struggle with pervasive corruption, fighting to overcome an oligarchy obsessed by entertainment and media. Other main characters include Johnny Rockfort and his female boss, Sadia, who belong to the Étoiles Noires (Black Stars), and Zéro Janvier, a businessman and politician who wants to be elected president of Monopolis.

The first live production of *Starmania* at the Palais des Congrès starred Daniel Balavoine (Johnny), Fabienne Thibéault (Marie-Jeanne), and Étienne Chicot (Zéro); it also featured forty singers and dancers. Its high-tech staging concept included three giant screens, a laser, and sixty televisions. The creative team consisted of the choreographer Serbe Gubelmann and the director Tom O'Horgan, who had previously staged *Hair* and *Jesus Christ Superstar* in New York. The show was produced by Roland Hubert.

FIG. 25.2 The scenography of the first *Starmania* stage production, which was performed in 1978 at the Palais des Congrès in Paris. Photo: Manuel Litran/Paris Match © Getty Images.

In the following four decades, the musical would be restaged all around the world. In 1980 *Starmania* opened at Montreal's Comédie National, directed by Olivier Reichenbach; it played the city again in 1986–1987 in a reduced version. In 1988 Plamondon and Berger prepared a second version of *Starmania* for the Théâtre de Paris, with a cast including Maurane as Marie-Jeanne, Norman Groulx as Johnny Rockfort, Wenta as Sadia, and Richard Groulx as Zéro Janvier. *Starmania* was translated into German and performed in 1991 at Essen's Aalto-Theater. An operatic version , with the title *Starmania Opéra* played at the Grand Théâtre de Quebec in May 2008. In addition, a DVD version was released in 1989 by Warner Visions.

An English-language version of the show was written by the lyricist Tim Rice. Titled *Tycoon*, it was recorded in 1992 by a star-studded cast made up of international recording artists: Céline Dion, Nina Hagen, Kim Carnes, Cyndi Lauper, Tom Jones, Peter Kingsbery, and Willy DeVille. Dion had already included several songs from the musical on her 1991 album, *Dion chante Plamondon*. Four years later, in 1996, *Tycoon* premiered in El Paso, Texas, at the UTEP Dinner Theatre.

## NOTRE-DAME DE PARIS (1998) AND ROMÉO ET JULIETTE (2001): THE SPECTACLE MUSICAL ABROAD

In spite of the great popularity of *Starmania*, Luc Plamondon is actually better known in musical theatre for another show, this one written with Riccardo 'Richard' Cocciante. The Italian pianist, singer, and author has dual nationality, his mother being French; he works in both Rome and Paris but composed some of his most successful and emotionally touching pop songs ('Bella senz'anima', 'Margherita', and 'L'Alba') in the 1970s and 1980s for the Italian market.

The collaboration between Plamondon and Cocciante proved to be even more successful than *Starmania*, although it is completely different. *Notre-Dame de Paris* is an ambitious rewriting of Victor Hugo's first novel, published in 1831. Directed by Gilles Maheu, with choreography by Martino Muller, décor by Christian Ratz, and costumes by Fred Sathal, it opened at the Palais de Congrès on 16 September 1998 with Hélène Segara as Esmeralda, Garu as Quasimodo (the hunchback), Bruno Pelletier (who appeared in *Starmania* in 1994) as Gringoire, Patrick Fiori as Febo/Phoebus, Luck Marvand as Clopin, and Julie Zenatti as Fleur-de-Lys. The producer was Charles Talar, who, as with many other shows originating in Paris, first promoted the recording and then the stage version.

Part of the appeal of this show lies in Victor Hugo's romantic and melodramatic plot. In Paris, at the end of the fifteenth century, a group of Romani, headed by Clopin Trouillefou, ask to live in the city, but the Notre-Dame Cathedral archdeacon, Claude

Frollo, orders the captain of the guards, Febo (aka Phoebus de Chateaupers), to send them away. Three different men—Febo, who is already engaged, Frollo, and Quasimodo, the hunchbacked bell-ringer of the cathedral—all fall in love with the beautiful young Roma dancer Esmeralda. The book's passions will be propelled to a bitter, violent conclusion: Frollo, refused by the Roma girl, sentences Esmeralda to death on a false charge of murder. Quasimodo helps her escape prison, but Febo arrests her and the other Romani. Esmeralda is executed, and Quasimodo kills Frollo by throwing him off the top of Notre-Dame. The bell-ringer finally embraces Esmeralda's corpse but soon dies a lonely death.

For their stage version, Plamondon and Cocciante were inspired by the 1956 French-Italian screen adaptation of *Notre-Dame de Paris*, which was written by Jacque Prévert and directed by Jean Delannoy. There are of course certain differences between the film and the *spectacle musical*; one of these concerns Esmeralda, who agrees to marry the poet Pierre Gringoire (a secondary character) in order to save him from being killed by Clopin. The creators of the musical retelling also decided to cut the first part of the story, set on 6 January, a specific day in Paris, when French people celebrate both Epiphany and the Feast of Fools. During the latter, Quasimodo is elected the 'pope' of crazy people and is first celebrated before the crowd turns vicious and tortures him. The moment when Esmeralda intervenes and shows him kindness—she gives him water—is the moment when the hunchback becomes obsessed with her.

*Notre-Dame de Paris* would also be performed in many countries, with translations into nine foreign languages (Italian, Spanish, Korean, Dutch, English, Polish, Russian, and Chinese). All in all, it had more than five thousand performances worldwide, with a total viewership of fifteen million people. In 2000, after touring through Switzerland, Belgium and Canada, the show was translated into English by Will Jenkins. This adaptation was first performed in Las Vegas, at the Paris Las Vegas Hotel-Casino, and later in London, at the Dominion Theatre, where it lasted for seven months in spite of having been savaged by the British critics. In contrast to this, Italy truly welcomed *Notre-Dame de Paris*, with two and a half million people attending the local version, produced by David Zard and translated by the lyricist Pasquale Panella. The production toured to more than forty cities, including Milan, Rome (where it played at the Gran Teatro, specifically built for the production), and Verona (at the famous Arena). In 2016 the authors prepared a new version of the show which included several acrobats and has since toured successfully in France and abroad. The show, with lyrics retranslated into English by Jeremy Sams, also returned to London's West End, where in January 2019 it played four performances at the Coliseum, this time getting mixed reviews.

*Notre-Dame de Paris* was well received by the press in France and other European countries, but in Anglophone cultures reviewers have been extremely critical of the work's dramaturgy. Luc Plamondon, in fact, is a lyric writer, rather than a book writer, or dramaturge, which might explain why the show is sung through. In 2000 London critics found Cocciante's music, inspired more by French and Italian opera than by Broadway or West End musicals, the only pleasing element in the show.

FIG. 25.3 A crowd scene from the touring production of *Notre Dame de Paris*, which in January 2009 played with great success in Milan. Photo: Massimo Barbaglia © Alamy Stock Foto.

One reason for the poor reception of *Notre-Dame de Paris* in English-speaking countries is that in theatrical terms, the show is once again not your typical Anglophone musical;[22] for instance, singers perform separately from dancers. Like the other shows discussed so far, the Hugo adaptation is sung through. Yet unlike most American and British rock operas or megamusicals, the music is prerecorded and played through the theatre sound system rather than played live by an orchestra in the pit.

It seems that Cocciante, when asked by Plamondon to write the music for this project, hesitated, since he was worried about treating such a monument of French literature. But then, inspired by the story, he was able to conceive music that has been popular worldwide, especially the songs 'Vivre' (sung by Esmeralda), 'Le temps des cathédrales' (Gringoire), 'Dieu que le monde est injuste' (Quasimodo), and 'Belle' (a trio featuring Quasimodo, Frollo, and Phoebus, the three men enthralled by the Roma dancer). Recordings of the last-named song sold 2.5 million copies. Cocciante composed the music first, which Plamondon adapted to suit the lyrics. The group of musicians working with Cocciante for the album recording and the original stage production included Serge Perathoner (keyboards and arrangements), Jannick Top (bass and arrangements), Claude Engel (guitars), and Marc Chantereau and Claude Salmiéri (percussion). The seven singers and sixteen dancers on-stage were chosen from hundreds after a long and arduous audition process.

Again, it is a tragic love story, Shakespeare's *Romeo and Juliet* (1596), which served as inspiration for another French *spectacle* that became a major hit a few years after *Notre-Dame de Paris*. As in the case of *West Side Story*, the source material is radically transformed; references to the original text are sparing in *Roméo et Juliette: De la haine à l'amour* (2001). The author of both the music and lyrics of this popular show is Gérard Presgurvic (b. 1953), who also, together with Carolin Petit, created the musical arrangements. Presgurvic is said to have been inspired more by Franco Zeffirelli's 1968 film adaptation of *Romeo and Juliet* than by Shakespeare's tragedy.

In fact, there are some drastic alterations to the play, including new characters such as Death and the Poet, while Lady Capulet has a greatly increased role, although otherwise Presgurvic follows Shakespeare's story quite closely. As with the other shows discussed, a CD was recorded before *Roméo et Juliette* premiered on stage. The album was successful, selling half a million copies. After playing for a year in Paris, *Roméo et Juliette* toured to Lille, Amnéville, Brussels, Strasbourg, Orléans, Les Mans, Caen, Rouen, Grenoble, Lyon, Montpellier, Marseille, Nice, Bordeaux, and Geneva in 2002. In 2010 a revival was presented at the Palais des Congrès, with Damien Sargue again as Romeo but featuring Joy Esther as Juliet and a new title, *Roméo et Juliette, les enfants de Vérone*. The piece has been translated into several other languages; as *Romeo and Juliet: The Musical* it played for four months at London's Piccadilly Theatre in a translation by Don Black and with new orchestrations. That production, directed as well as choreographed by David Freeman, once again was widely panned by the British critics. In *Variety*, Matt Wolf accused the show of displaying 'such mind-numbing ineptitude that one only wishes it were that little bit worse so it could qualify as a camp classic.'[23] However, other countries, for instance Italy, Canada, the Netherlands, Hungary, Russia, Austria, South Korea, and Mexico have taken far more enthusiastically to the work; in these countries the musical was quite successful.

## Conclusion: Anyplace but Here?

So why is it that the French variant of the musical, the country's version of a *comédie musicale*, has been embraced by the nations listed above as well as by Germany, Spain, and Japan, but not by English-speaking cultures? Some of these *spectacles musicaux* had no hope of ever being presented on Broadway or even in London. It seems the Anglophone resistance to practically all of these French shows is a consequence of three factors: (1) the traditional difficulties of translating the original text, (2) their limitations in theatrical and dramaturgical terms and (3) the cultural differences between French and Anglophone musical theatre.

## Notes

1. This applies especially to Offenbach's own shows, since he was forced by social and economic circumstances to produce them himself in his own theatres; they were also subject to strict censorship.

2. Paul Prece and William A. Everett, 'The Megamusical: The Creation, Internationalisation and Impact of a Genre', in *The Cambridge Companion to the Musical*, ed. William A. Everett and Paul R. Laird (Cambridge: Cambridge University Press 2017), 281–302; here: 301. Prece and Everett also note how 'aspects of the megamusical demonstrate a reinvigoration of nineteenth-century French grand opera. Where audiences in the late twentieth century were dazzled by stage effects such as the chandelier and underground lake in *The Phantom of the Opera*, the staircase in *Sunset Boulevard*, the barricade in *Les Misérables* and the helicopter in *Miss Saigon*, the nineteenth-century French counterparts saw the eruption of Vesuvius in Daniel-François-Ésprit Auber's *Le muette de Portici* (1828) and the St Bartholomew's Day Massacre in Giacomo Meyerbeer's *Les Huguenots* (1836). In both megamusicals and French grand opera, striking things happen amidst imaginative surroundings' (ibid.).

3. As Elizabeth Wollman points out: 'The term *spectacle* here denotes scenic technology that has, in recent decades, become sophisticated enough to allow the simulation of special effects previously only possible on film [ . . . ] Yet what is perhaps most significant here is the way in which both the mass media and the rock musical have influenced the aural aesthetics of the musical theater in general, and the megamusical in particular.' Elizabeth L. Wollman, *The Theater Will Rock: A History of the Rock Musical, From 'Hair' to 'Hedwig'* (Ann Arbor: University of Michigan Press, 2006), 124.

4. "While it is Mackintosh's vision that defines the genre theatrically, parallels must be drawn between the British producer of three of the longest-running musicals of all time (*Cats*, *Les Misérables* and *The Phantom of the Opera*) and one of his nineteenth-century French predecessors, Louis Véron, director of the Paris Opera and a major force in nineteenth-century French grand opera. By definition, works in this genre related some sort of socio-political message through a grandiose medium that combined music, drama, dance, lavish costume and set designs and special effects. [ . . . ] French grand operas were frequently set against war backgrounds; likewise, the Schönberg-Boublil musicals [ . . . ] all have war settings. Sharing the desire to bring in some sort of social change with their nineteenth-century predecessors, Schönberg and Boublil include some sort of edifying message in their shows, whether it is the power of forgiveness in *Les Misérables*, the hideous personal consequences of war in *Miss Saigon* or the repercussions of deception in *Martin Guerre*'. Prece and Everett, 'The Megamusical: The Creation, Internationalisation and Impact of a Genre', 302.

5. *Les Misérables* took over some of its main features from those two highly successful British musicals. As Olaf Jubin points out, '[Alain Boublil] and his writing partner Claude-Michel Schönberg wanted to follow the path forged by Andrew Lloyd Webber and Tim Rice's *Jesus Christ Superstar* (1970). The two Frenchmen not only modelled their dramaturgical format on the concept album with its innovative approach of telling its story entirely through song, but it [*sic*] also encouraged Schönberg to construct his score in a similar fashion to the earlier musical by using reprises and contrafacta, exactly like the British composer had done. While seeing a revival of Lionel Bart's *Oliver!* (1960), the Artful Dodger, one of its most colourful characters, reminded Boublil of street urchin Gavroche in Hugo's novel, and that was the starting point for the whole project.' Olaf Jubin, 'Narrative and Story-Telling in the British Musical since 1970', in *British Musical Theatre since 1950*, ed. Robert Gordon, Olaf Jubin, and Millie Taylor (London and New York: Bloomsbury, 2016), 141–211; here: 169.)

6. One common problem of rock musicals (as well as megamusicals and French *spectacles musicaux*) is the lack of dramaturgical and theatrical know-how of its lyricist-librettists. Most Broadway writers of lyrics and books have a background in drama and/or theatre. However, it would be difficult to argue that Boublil has a specific knowledge of the stage or the theatre industry. For how this has affected *Les Misérables*, see Edward Behr, *Les Misérables: History in the Making* (London: Pavilion Books, 1996).

7. 'When asked about his influences, Schönberg cites, among others, Offenbach, much admired for his use of recitative. Schönberg describes both Offenbach's and his own recitative in similar terms: they contain little "treasures of melody" that can be developed into whole songs, or may just exist as perfect one-off moments.' Jessica Sternfeld, *The Megamusical* (Bloomington: Indiana University Press, 2006), 422 n. 5.

8. Among Michel Legrand's most famous works are the original film scores for Jacques Demy's *Les Parapluies de Cherbourg* (1964) and *Les Demoiselles de Rochefort* (1967).

9. Quoted in Leslie Bennetts, 'Les Misérables for Its American Debut', *New York Times*, 6 December 1986, https://www.nytimes.com/1986/12/06/theater/les-miserables-ready-for-its-american-debut.html, accessed 15 January 2020.

10. Rebecca-Anne C. Do Rozario, 'The French Musicals: The Dramatic Impulse of Spectacle', *Journal of Dramatic Theory and Criticism* 19, no. 1 (2004): 125–142; here: 125.

11. Jubin, 'Narrative and Story-Telling in the British Musical since 1970', 168.

12. Other works—which met with varying degrees of success—by the two French artists include *Le Premier pas, Elle et moi, Miss Saigon, Martin Guerre, The Pirate Queen, Marguerite,* and *Cleopatra*.

13. In fact, Kretzmer replaced the poet James Fenton as lyricist when Fenton proved to be too slow.

14. Sternfeld, *The Megamusical*, 180.

15. Jubin, 'Narrative and Story-Telling in the British Musical since 1970', 174.

16. Prece and Everett, 'The Megamusical: The Creation, Internationalisation and Impact of a Genre', 304.

17. The data has been taken from Prece and Everett.

18. Sternfeld, *The Megamusical*, 222–223.

19. Sheridan Morley, '*Les Misérables*: Blazing Theatrically', *International Herald Tribune*, 16 October 1985, 7.

20. Frank Rich, 'Stage: *Misérables*, Musical Version Opens on Broadway', *New York Times*, 19 March 1987, https://www.nytimes.com/1987/03/13/theater/stage-miserables-musical-version-opens-on-broadway.html, accessed 14 January 2020.

21. Ibid.

22. In general terms, we must note that since the end of the 1960s, most modern musicals (including *spectacles*) can no longer be related to the traditional form and structure of the American musical; rather, they belong to a broader category of contemporary musical theatre. We also should remember that almost all megamusicals and French *spectacles* are sung through, since, as has already been pointed out, they are modelled after *Jesus Christ Superstar*, a rock opera, not a musical in the format of golden-age Broadway classics.

23. Matt Wolf, 'Review: *Romeo and Juliet: The Musical*', *Variety*, 7 November 2002, https://variety.com/2002/legit/reviews/romeo-and-juliet-the-musical-2-1200544969/, accessed 15 January 2020.

## BIBLIOGRAPHY

Behr, Edward. *Les Misérables: History in the Making*. London: Pavilion Books, 1996.

Bennetts, Leslie. 'Les Misérables for Its American Debut', *New York Times*, 6 December 1986, https://www.nytimes.com/1986/12/06/theater/les-miserables-ready-for-its-american-debut.html, accessed 15 January 2020.

Do Rozario, Rebecca-Anne C. 'The French Musicals: The Dramatic Impulse of Spectacle'. *Journal of Dramatic Theory and Criticism* 19, no. 1 (2004): 125–142.

Jubin, Olaf. 'Narrative and Story-Telling in the British Musical since 1970'. In *British Musical Theatre since 1950*, ed. Robert Gordon, Olaf Jubin, and Millie Taylor, 141–211. London and New York: Bloomsbury, 2016.

Morley, Sheridan. '*Les Misérables*: Blazing Theatrically'. *International Herald Tribune*, 16 October 1985, 7.

Prece, Paul, and William A. Everett. 'The Megamusical: The Creation, Internationalisation and Impact of a Genre'. In *The Cambridge Companion to the Musical*, ed. William A. Everett and Paul R. Laird, 281–302. Cambridge: Cambridge University Press. 2017.

Rich, Frank. 'Stage: *Misérables*, Musical Version Opens on Broadway'. *New York Times*, 19 March 1987, https://www.nytimes.com/1987/03/13/theater/stage-miserables-musical-version-opens-on-broadway.html, accessed 14 January 2020.

Wolf, Matt. 'Review: *Romeo and Juliet: The Musical*'. *Variety*, 7 November 2002, https://variety.com/2002/legit/reviews/romeo-and-juliet-the-musical-2-1200544969/, accessed 15 January 2020.

Wollman, Elizabeth L. *The Theater Will Rock: A History of the Rock Musical, From 'Hair' to 'Hedwig'*. Ann Arbor: University of Michigan Press, 2006.

# CHAPTER 26

························································

# THE GERMAN/AUSTRIAN 'DRAMA MUSICAL', OR 'I SING ALONE'

························································

## OLAF JUBIN

How do you learn to write musicals in a culture where not only is the genre not taken seriously,[1] but where there are to this day no training facilities for composers, lyricists, or librettists who want to work in this highly profitable field of popular entertainment?

The career of Michael Kunze (b. 1943) provides an intriguing answer to this very question; his progress towards conceiving his own shows is as instructive as it is unusual. Kunze started writing songs at the age of fourteen;[2] however, he first attained a law degree before finding great success as a lyricist and creative producer of German Schlager and other forms of popular music.[3] In 1975 the song 'Fly, Robin, Fly' by Silver Convention reached number 1 on the US Billboard charts and won him a Grammy. Kunze then had a seminal encounter with musical theatre when he was commissioned to provide a translation for the 1981 Viennese production of *Evita*[4]—like those in the West End and on Broadway directed by Harold Prince. His celebrated German version of Tim Rice and Andrew Lloyd Webber's show led to an illustrious career as the most in-demand translator of musicals for the German and Austrian markets.

Encouraged by Prince and Lloyd Webber, both of whom Kunze has described as his 'mentors',[5] he started in the 1990s to create his own material with great success. The long-running shows for which he wrote both libretto and lyrics, most of which premiered in Vienna, include *Tanz der Vampire* (*Dance of the Vampires*, 1997; music by Jim Steinman), *Elisabeth* (1992), *Mozart! The Musical* (1999), and *Marie-Antoinette* and *Rebecca: The Musical* (both 2006); the last four were composed by his longtime collaborator Sylvester Levay. All of these musicals, which will serve as case studies,[6] have been produced abroad, to enthusiastic audience responses in Japan, South Korea, Sweden, Hungary, Poland, France, and elsewhere.[7]

Kunze calls his own works 'drama musicals', a form that he has developed since the early 1990s—and one that he devised himself;[8] in this respect, he claims to have invented his own subgenre. This chapter will investigate to what degree the storytelling techniques employed in the five shows listed above differ significantly from those of their British and American counterparts. It will explore how their dramaturgy functions, where influences from the famous musicals that Kunze has translated are detectable, and how he moves beyond these new forms.

## ORIGINS: THE PATH TOWARDS THE DRAMA MUSICAL

Kunze spent a lot of time studying Anglophone musical theatre and related genres before taking the decisive step of creating his own full-length theatrical works, as he explained 2009 during a master class in Hamburg:

> I don't deny that I have talent, but the reason I'm so successful is not so much my talent. A lot of people have talent. I can say, I work a little bit harder than most people, and part of that harder work is getting to know what the musical is all about, and what the art form demands.[9]

Apart from songwriting, the various experiences that infused the drama musical are his work as, in chronological order, a creative producer of popular music (1970–1981), a novelist (1982–1990),[10] a television writer for entertainment shows (ca. 1976–1994), and a translator (1980–2007), in addition to his participation in story seminars. All of these activities would help Kunze forge his own dramaturgical conceits.[11]

*Evita*, the first major show for which Kunze wrote German lyrics, was based on a concept recording, a form of musical storytelling that fascinated the lyricist.[12] Yet his own attempts at devising concept albums failed—most strikingly in 1976, when the Silver Convention release *Madhouse* turned into 'a terrible flop'.[13] In order to learn how to successfully structure a complex narrative using popular song, he would later carefully analyse the shows he was asked to adapt into German. On these occasions he also sought the advice of the shows' creators; when Kunze attests that he 'really learned from the masters',[14] he refers not only to Harold Prince and Andrew Lloyd Webber, but also to Stephen Sondheim, Gillian Lynne, and other pre-eminent artists in the field.[15]

At the same time, Kunze was exploring various forms of long-form storytelling: in addition to historical novels, he also created several ninety-minute programmes for German and Austrian television, which usually employed the format of galas, award shows, or variety specials built around popular entertainers from the world of the German Schlager.[16]

Kunze next tried his hand unsuccessfully at a movie script; it was then that he decided to learn more about structuring plots and began attending story seminars for prospective screenwriters.[17] At one of these he encountered Robert McKee, an expert in film narrative and script construction, who would become a close personal friend,[18] and whose teachings on organising movie scripts would become highly influential. Kunze credits McKee with getting him to 'think about the idea of *telling* a story',[19] that is, of redirecting him from concerns about narrative details to contemplating how to turn a tale into a plot.

As a result, the budding librettist adapted the three-act structure of film screenplays to musical theatre: his shows maintain the traditional division into two acts but are actually constructed like a classic movie around the basic elements of exposition, confrontation, and resolution.[20] The second part, the confrontation, covers the events both before and immediately after the intermission, which Kunze, in sync with the classic book musical, places two-thirds of the way through the evening.[21] The interval marks a point of no return for the protagonist; although the climax (or crisis) occurs early in act 2, at the end of the first half the leading character has reached a stage in her or his development where a major decision marks a moment that has repercussions for everything that follows.

Consequently, the dramaturgical design of shows such as *Elisabeth*, *Mozart!*, and *Rebecca* is rather intricate. Because the individual scenes result in a painstakingly constructed plot line, Kunze has compared his works to a well-built edifice: his shows combine the various 'bricks' of an idea into an artefact that is too solidly assembled to be toppled.[22] Extending this image to his professional understanding of working in musical theatre, the German calls himself a 'story architect', a term he has also chosen as the name for his homepage.[23]

# Impact of Kunze's Work as a Translator of British and American Musicals

In the last forty years Kunze has written the German lyrics for many important shows, including Andrew Lloyd Webber's *Cats* (1981/German version 1983), *The Phantom of the Opera* (1986/1988), *Aspects of Love* (1989/1996), and *Sunset Boulevard* (1993/1995); Stephen Sondheim's *Company* (1970/1987), *Follies* (1971/1991), *Into the Woods* (1987/1990), and *Assassins* (1991/1993); and the jukebox musical *Mamma Mia!* (1999/2002), as well as several Disney productions, such as *The Lion King* (1997/2001), *The Hunchback of Notre-Dame* (Berlin 1999),[24] and *Aida* (2000/2003).[25]

Tellingly, Kunze himself has rejected the term 'translation' as inappropriate,[26] preferring instead 'adaptation'. He argues that in order for the original work to retain its impact, it needs to be modified, in both linguistic and cultural terms, which means that a strictly verbatim rendering of the English lyrics and dialogue in German would not suffice. Although Kunze's argumentation is not entirely plausible—every good translation ensures that idiosyncrasies of both the original language and its cultural framework are rendered faithfully in the new version—[27] there can be no doubt that his adaptations have received a lot of praise, not least from performers who have complimented Kunze on his 'very singable' German lyrics.[28]

Particularly influential for *Elisabeth* was Kunze's translation of *Evita*: the role of Luigi Lucheni, who leads the audience through the life and death of the Austrian empress, is clearly modelled on Che. Just like the revolutionary in the show about Eva Perón, the Italian assassin recaps the life of the eponymous heroine in flashbacks, is present in various guises (waiter, souvenir vendor, and others) at major public and private events and constantly criticises her behaviour. His act 2 opener, 'Kitsch', closely resembles 'And the Money Kept Rolling In' from the 1976 Lloyd Webber–Rice musical, down to a reference to a Swiss bank account.[29] Count Cagliostro, the narrator in *Marie Antoinette*, also occasionally meddles in the events he evokes; in act 2, scene 7 he becomes a member of the Jacobin committee, thus moving from mere observer to active participant. However, Cagliostro's presence and actions in the 2006 musical are both less frequent and less well motivated than Lucheni's in *Elisabeth*. Another key element of *Evita*, the montage preceding her death, found its way into *Mozart!* (act 2, scene 9).

Kunze has incorporated into his own works one more feature regularly used first by the British composer: foreshadowing key songs by introducing parts of them before they are heard in full. This particular Lloyd Webber technique—basically an inverse of the classic reprise—is controversial,[30] yet Kunze obviously agrees with the composer's dictum that '[y]ou never give away a great song before establishing it.'[31]

There are also additional elements in Kunze's five major drama musicals that closely resemble whole numbers or moments in some of the Anglophone works the German has adapted. Just like *The Phantom of the Opera*, with 'Masquerade', several of his shows (*Dance of the Vampires*, *Rebecca*, and *Marie Antoinette*) include a costume ball where people hide their identities and real selves behind masks,[32] a motif that also has made its way into *Mozart!* Moreover, the vampire Graf Krolock's wooing of Sarah in 'Wohl der Nacht' ('Nightly Good') has more than a passing resemblance to the seductive 'Music of the Night', used by the Phantom to lure Christine over to his side. Like Christine,[33] Sarah moves as if in trance after her prolonged encounter with the creature hidden in the shadows.[34] She also vocalises like Rapunzel in *Into the Woods*.[35] Another correspondence to Sondheim's 1987 fairy-tale musical is the long list of infinitive verbs in 'Die fröhliche Apokalypse' ('Happy Apocalypse'; *Elisabeth*, act 1, scene 10),[36] a stylistic device the American songwriter uses in the show's title song and its reprises.

On occasion, one can detect parallels to Broadway musicals that Kunze did not translate himself. The sleazy number 'Eine Hand wäscht die and're Hand' ('You'll Scratch My Back'; *Rebecca*, act 2, scene 8) deploys the same conceit as 'When You're Good to Mama' in *Chicago* (1975). Finally, the protagonist of *Marie Antoinette*, Margrid Arnaud, is first seen selling violets, recalling that other lower-class heroine who dreams of upward social mobility, Eliza Dolittle in *My Fair Lady* (1956).

# DRAMA MUSICAL: DEFINITION AND KEY ELEMENTS

Just like the labels 'concept musical' and 'megamusical',[37] the term 'drama musical' was coined by a journalist.[38] For some time now Kunze has given master classes on his form of musical theatre and thus has spoken on numerous occasions on what characterises it.[39] A detailed definition of the term was provided by Kunze in a short YouTube video, helpfully titled 'What Is a Drama Musical?':

> It is a European form of the musical that is not a copy of the Broadway musical, and it is distinguished by the domination of the story. Everything, every element of the musical—the lyrics, the words, the dialogue, the music, the choreography, the sets, the costume design—everything, even the lighting design, is there to tell the story. And this is the number one purpose of everything we do. And this is why I call it the drama musical, because the drama is the most important part of these shows.[40]

Since all the dramaturgical elements of the drama musical should serve to tell the story,[41] Kunze rejects outright the notion of calling his works 'musical dramas', 'because the drama comes first, *not* the music!'[42]

A drama musical has a single protagonist who clashes with a powerful and equally determined antagonist in the process of solving a problem or achieving a goal.[43] The lyricist-librettist has listed several additional important ingredients that feature in every one of his shows; these include 'the point of no return', the 'climax/crisis', breaking the fourth wall, numerous locations, a romantic interest, a mentor, and a trickster (basically a character who is responsible for providing surprising plot elements and developments).[44] Table 26.1 provides an overview of how these elements are handled in the five musicals under discussion.

However, when trying to identify where and how Kunze employs what he proposes as drama-musical essentials, it turns out that in more than one case a clear designation proves problematic, because all of the shows are ambiguous in one respect or another. For instance, who is the protagonist of *Dance of the Vampires*? While Professor Ambronsius, with his unshakeable trust in the powers of logic and reason, is set in direct opposition to Count Krolock, the representative of everything that defies scientific explanation, it is Alfred who not only pursues the love interest but also serves as the main figure of audience identification, simply through the many instances when his life and his love are in danger.

In *Mozart!* and *Rebecca*, on the other hand, it is the antagonist who is difficult to identify: regarding the 1999 musical about the classical composer, a convincing case can be made that Mozart's real opponent on the artistic level is his father, Leopold, who constantly brags about his own part in creating a 'genius', thereby denigrating his son's talent. Furthermore, he accuses Wolfgang not only of ruining the family financially, but also of causing his mother's death, in a blatant attempt to make him feel guilty. In addition, there is also Amadé, the second incarnation of the composer. That the fabulously talented child genius never stops working and literally kills the adult artist marks him as the truly unsurmountable force set in opposition to Mozart.

Adapted from the perennially popular Daphne du Maurier novel of 1938, *Rebecca* is narrated by a shy young woman who marries a wealthy widower and who, as the new mistress of his vast country estate, Manderley, is confronted by the lingering influence

## Table 26.1 Key Elements of the Drama Musical, According to Michael Kunze

| Drama musical elements | *Elisabeth* (1992) | *Dance of the Vampires* (1996) | *Mozart!* (1999) | *Rebecca* (2006) | *Marie Antoinette* (2006) |
|---|---|---|---|---|---|
| Protagonist(s) | Empress Elisabeth | Professor Ambronsius; his assistant. Alfred | Wolfgang | 'I' | Margrid Arnaud |
| Antagonist | Death | Count Krolock | Count Colloredo; Leopold; Amadé | [Rebecca]; Mrs Danvers | Marie Antoinette |
| Protagonist's goal | Personal freedom | Defeating the vampires | Artistic freedom | Overcoming the stifling influence of the first Mrs de Winter | Social justice |
| Protagonist's problem | Stifling court etiquette | Being rational in an irrational world | Lack of discipline and true friends | Lack of self-esteem | Arrogance |
| Point of no return (end of act 1) | Elisabeth's ultimatum | Professor Ambronsius and Alfred enter Count Krolock's castle | Wolfgang breaks with Count Colloredo | 'I' is tricked into wearing Rebecca's old costume to the masked ball | Marie Antoinette is increasingly under pressure: the necklace affair is uncovered and Margrid accuses her of murder |
| Climax/crisis (in the first third of act 2) | Franz Josef cheats on his wife and then infects her with syphilis (act 2, scenes 5–6) | Alfred cannot kill the vampires in their coffin (act 2, scene 4) | Mozart is tricked into marrying Constanze (act 2, scene 3) | "I" nearly commits suicide (act 2, scene 1c); Maxim's confession (act 2, scene 3b) | The crowd storms Versailles (act 2, scene 4) |
| Breaking the fourth wall | Act 1, scene 3; act 1, scene 9 | Act 2, scenes 9, 10, and 11 | Act 1, scenes 12 and 14 | Act 1, scene 10 | Prologue; act 1, scene 6 |
| Number of locations | 27 | 18 | 28 | 26 | 24 |
| Romantic interest | Franz Josef; Death | Sarah Chagal | Constanze Weber | Maxim de Winter | Count Axel von Fersen |

## Table 26.1 Continued

| Drama musical elements | Elisabeth (1992) | Dance of the Vampires (1996) | Mozart! (1999) | Rebecca (2006) | Marie Antoinette (2006) |
|---|---|---|---|---|---|
| Mentor | Duke Max in Bayern (Elisabeth's father) | Professor Ambronsius | Leopold Mozart; Baronin von Waldstätten; Emanuel Schickaneder | Beatrice (Maxim's sister) | Sister Agnés |
| Trickster | Luigi Lucheni | Herbert Krolock | Emanuel Schikaneder | Jack Favell | Count Cagliostro |

of her husband's previous wife, the first Mrs de Winter. 'I'—the narrator's name is never revealed—has to first become aware of the manipulations and intrigues of the sinister housekeeper Mrs Danvers, who seems to be the obvious antagonist, before finding the inner strength to thwart them; yet the more dangerous adversary is actually Rebecca herself. Her ghostlike presence—although she has died, everyone is still in thrall to her—makes her a much more formidable foe to reckon with and of course also imbues the story with its gothic atmosphere: how can you defeat a woman whose influence extends beyond the grave?

*Rebecca*'s (2006) 'point of no return' is also weak in comparison with those of the other four shows: Mrs Danvers gaslighting of her new mistress, to the point where 'I' is ready to jump out of the window (act 2, scene 1c), would have made a far more effective finale for act 1 than 'I''s misguided choice of costume for the masked ball, which is merely one more public embarrassment in a long line of social missteps. This also affects the understanding of what should count as the real climax of *Rebecca*: is it 'I' nearly committing suicide, or Maxim's confession that he not only never loved his first wife but is actually responsible for her death? After all, it is the second incident that has the more significant repercussions for everything that follows: it directly or indirectly leads to 'I''s newfound confidence, the public inquiry into Rebecca's death, and eventually the destruction of Manderley.

Just as problematic are the romantic interest in *Elisabeth*, the mentor in *Mozart!*, and the trickster in *Dance of the Vampires*. *Elisabeth* (1992) is conceived as a lifelong, passionate love affair between the Austrian empress and Death, which only finds fulfilment with her assassination. Yet where does that leave Elisabeth's husband, Franz Josef? Together with the fact that the show never firmly establishes what exactly draws the young princess to her cousin, the fact that he turns out to be a mere substitute for her real romantic interest further undermines the effectiveness of the character.

As a young composer trying to find his way through the treacherous waters of the European salons and courts, Mozart actually has *three* mentors who point out potential routes to financial success and artistic fulfilment: his father, Leopold, the authorial voice who insists that his son not defy the powers that be; Baronin von Waldstätten, who encourages the budding musician to venture out into the unknown on his own; and Emanuel Schikaneder, with his appealing view that all social interaction is performance and that art needs to be entertaining.

Lastly, according to Kunze,[45] Herbert Krolock functions as the trickster in *Dance of the Vampires*, yet he is not given enough weight to spring any surprises or to wrong-foot the spectators: he features prominently in a mere two out of twenty-one scenes (act 1, scene 10, and act 2, scene 8), and the show would only have taken a startling turn if he had actually succeeded in seducing Alfred, as that would have significantly manipulated both audience expectations and the outcome of the story.

# ADDITIONAL RECURRING FEATURES OF THE DRAMA MUSICAL

A close analysis of Kunze's main works reveals several other elements that appear with a certain frequency. I will discuss them in the order in which they have been listed in Table 26.2.

Occasionally Kunze employs a narrator, who guides the audience through the proceedings. It can easily be surmised why the German writer resorted to this dramaturgical ploy in *Elisabeth*, *Rebecca*, and *Marie Antoinette*: as explained above, Luigi Lucheni in the 1992 show is modelled after Che in *Evita*, while the first-person narrator of du Maurier's novel is one of the author's most famous stylistic devices, so it would be potentially self-defeating and thus unwise to jettison it. The addition of Count Cagliostro to the musical about the French queen is an overt attempt to give shape to what could become a confusingly complex series of historical events. The latter strategy is not entirely successful, considering that Cagliostro disappears for long stretches of the plot and, unlike Lucheni, who has a real investment in the proceedings, does not actually have a reason to be present at some of the famous incidents he observes.

Kunze also has a penchant for characters who can only be described as obvious villains, people without any redeeming qualities. These are not necessarily the same as the antagonists, with the notable exceptions of Count Krolock as leader of the vampires and Count Colloredo as the man who undermines Mozart's chances of finding professional employment outside his own court. Often these wholly unsympathetic figures are ruthless and overbearing parents or parents-at-law, such as Archduchess Sophie and Cäcilie Weber.[46]

While there is a last—and, I would argue, unsuccessful—endeavour to humanise the mother of Emperor Franz Josef in a short scene ('Bellaria') that was added in 2001 for the

## Table 26.2 Additional Recurrent Features of the Drama Musical

| Drama musical elements | Elisabeth (1992) | Dance of the Vampires (1996) | Mozart! (1999) | Rebecca (2006) | Marie Antoinette (2006) |
|---|---|---|---|---|---|
| Framing device? | Yes | No | Yes | Yes | No |
| Narrator? | Luigi Lucheni | – | – | 'I' | Count Cagliostro |
| Villain(s) | Archduchess Sophie | Count Krolock; Chagal | Count Colloredo; Cäcilie Weber | [Mrs van Hopper]; Jack Favell | Duke of Orléans; Robespierre |
| Number of scenes | 29 total: act 1: 14 (+ Prologue); act 2: 13 (+ Epilogue) | 21 total: act 1: 10; act 2: 11 | 28 total: act 1: 14 (+ Prologue); act 2: 13 | 29 total: act 1: 15 (+ Prologue); act 2: 12 (+ Epilogue) | 26 total: act 1: 11 (+ Prologue); act 2: 14 |
| Key scene in the se-cond half of act 2 | Act 2, scene12: Rudolf's suicide | Act 2, scene 6: Sarah opts not to flee with Alfred | Act 2, scene 10: Leopold's death | Act 2, scene 7: Maxim is suspected of killing Rebecca | Act 2, scene 11: Marie Antoinette refuses to escape without her children |
| Dcenes without a clear location | Prologue & Epilogue ('Cemetery of the Past'); act 1, scene 9 ('Stages of a Marriage'); act 2, scene 7 ('Restless Years'); act 2, scene 13 ('Deck of the Sinking World') | – | Act 2, scene 15 (Mozart's death) | – | Prologue |
| Nightmare | Act 2, scene 15 (Franz Josef) | Act 2, scene 2 (Alfred) | Act 2, scene 4 (Wolfgang) | – | – |
| Dance scenes? | [Choreographed movement] | Yes | [Choreographed movement] | [Choreographed movement] | [Choreographed movement] |
| Other notable aspects | In its dramaturgical structure very close to Evita | Could be construed as both sexist and homophobic; slapstick interludes | The score is more rock-orientated | Minor characters sing about the protagonists' problems; comic elements | Puzzling use of French; relies more on dialogue |

first German production of *Elisabeth*, Sophie's harsh treatment of her daughter-in-law and her cruel means of child-rearing mark her as a character audiences are bound to detest.[47] In this context it also doesn't help that the archduchess fails to notice that her drastic methods of turning grandson Rudolf into a 'real man' and suitable future leader of the Habsburg Empire are as pedagogically unsound as they are ineffective: after all, subjecting his father to the same (military) drill merely resulted in reducing him to an indecisive weakling. Cäcilie Weber, on the other hand has absolutely no redeeming features; not above pimping out her own daughters, her parasitical behaviour reaches a new low when she rushes in immediately following Mozart's death to steal money from his still-warm corpse.

The permanently horny Chagal in *Dance of the Vampires* stands out in Kunze's line-up of nasty characters in that the innkeeper, who forces himself on his employee Magda while paranoically guarding his own daughter's chastity, is a hypocrite. Usually the villains in a drama musical do not feel the need to hide their true motives from the audience; on the contrary, they may proudly declare their decadence and viciousness in solo numbers, such as *Rebecca*'s Jack Favell, in 'You'll Scratch My Back', and *Marie Antoinette*'s Duke of Orléans, who extols his determination to move ever closer to the seat of power in the song 'Weil ich besser bin' ('Because I Am Better').

What furthermore characterises every villain in a drama musical is his or her thirst for riches and for domination over others; the latter is a particularly distinctive quality of both the Duke of Orléans and Robespierre in *Marie Antoinette*. That the noble intriguer gets his comeuppance at the end of the show is one of the rare instances when outer forces intervene to mete out a form of justice.[48] Other evildoers die from natural causes (Archduchess Sophie) or by suicide (Mrs Danvers), or simply continue with their nefarious schemes (Count Krolock, Chagal, Cäcilie Weber, and Jack Favell).

Apart from the breaking of the fourth-wall convention and multiple locations, Kunze lists two additional 'special elements' to be found in his shows: dance numbers and dreamlike or irreal scenes.[49] I have not included these in Table 26.1, because they do not recur in all of the five musicals: *Dance of the Vampires* is the only one with extended dance sequences; the other four shows content themselves with choreographed movements,[50] which is not surprising considering that three of them were staged by opera directors (Harry Kupfer and Francesca Zambello, respectively),[51] who are not necessarily interested in the use of dance to convey narrative, given that they predominantly work with performers unskilled in that discipline.[52]

As for scenes not anchored in reality, there are the Prologue and Epilogue of *Elisabeth*, which take place in what the libretto calls 'the Cemetery of the Past',[53] and the nightmare sequences in Kunze's three shows from the 1990s. The first of these, set 'on the deck of the sinking world',[54] sees the Austrian Emperor Franz Josef suffer a horrifying vision of the end of the Habsburg dynasty. Here (act 2, scene 13), *Elisabeth* switches focus from its protagonist to a mere supporting player in order to make a historical point, thereby privileging the show's socio-political dimension over dramaturgical necessity, as the theatre-goers at this point in the musical have no close connection to the emperor so therefore do not care about his fears. In order for the sequence to have an emotional impact, it would have to be something experienced by the eponymous heroine.

In this context, the frightening dreams depicted in *Dance of the Vampires* and *Mozart!* are much more effective, because they are experienced by figures with which the audience identifies—Alfred and the famous composer, respectively. In addition, within the gothic world of Transylvania as depicted in the 1997 musical, with its supernatural creatures and traditional horror genre features, a nightmare seems particularly apt.

Most drama musicals consist of between twenty-six and twenty-nine scenes; the one notable exception is *Dance of the Vampires*, where there are only twenty-one, because the show is adapted from a movie of just 107 minutes. Yet each musical also has notable aspects that are in each case unique. *Elisabeth*'s debt to the dramaturgical tropes of *Evita* has already been considered, while the score for *Mozart!*, the follow-up to Kunze and Levay's 1992 smash hit, contains more rock elements.[55] In contrast, *Marie Antoinette* relies to a larger degree than any of Kunze's other shows on dialogue, although this may be due to its source material. What is otherwise striking about the first Kunze-Levay work to be conceived for the Japanese Takarazuka company is the rather peculiar use of French—at least in the German version.[56]

*Rebecca*, their other musical to première in 2006, is notable in two respects: on the one hand, its comic elements, which are very different from the physical comedy in *Dance of the Vampires*, where the slapstick interludes hark directly back to the 1967 movie. In the du Maurier dramatisation, the humorous elements address national stereotypes; however, in their lack of subtlety, these satirical jibes do not necessarily hit their targets, as will be explained later. On the other hand, *Rebecca* continues a development that started with *Mozart!* regarding the dramaturgical use of numbers allocated to secondary characters. In the 1999 show, Baronin von Waldstätten's 'Gold von den Sternen' ('Gold from the Stars') is a rare example of the musical theatre song as allegory, to be deciphered by the people the ballad is addressed to,[57] but not intended as a means of developing the character singing it. *Rebecca* goes even further in this in that both Beatrice, Maxim de Winter's sister, and Frank Crawley, the agent of Manderley, have been given songs ('Was ist nur los mit ihm' ['What Is the Matter with Him?'] and 'Ehrlichkeit und Vertrauen' ['Honesty and Trust']) that have nothing whatsoever to do with either their character development or their own situation, but that ponder—rather selflessly, in musical-theatre terms—other people's problems.

Lastly, among the recurring themes in Kunze's shows is a disavowal of purely rational thinking. This strand is particularly evident in Kunze's second and third musicals: Professor Ambronsius's stubborn belief in the benefits and achievements of logic, espoused in his act 1, scene 6 solo 'Wahrheit' ('Truth'), at the end proves both naïve and fatal, while Count Colloredo's insistence on the values of the Enlightenment makes him incapable of fully comprehending Mozart's artistic stance and of accepting that European culture has changed.[58]

# Inconsistencies in Concept and Execution

Throughout the years, Kunze's definition of the drama musical has been strictly consistent, with only minimal variations in his choice of words. Nonetheless, he himself has occasionally contributed to potential confusion regarding his preferred terminology—for instance, when he calls *Elisabeth* 'ein musikdramatische[s] Werk' ('a music-dramatical work') in the show's published libretto.[59] On another occasion, during a keynote speech he delivered at the now defunct Stage School Hamburg in 2009, he made the following observation: 'Story is not the most important thing. The story doesn't happen just by chance. It happens to this protagonist to teach him something.'[60] This suggests that Kunze's main focus in his shows is actually the emotional journey of the lead character, and that any plot development merely functions to occasion changes in the protagonist.

In interviews Kunze has declared that certain American and British shows, such as *Wicked* (2003) and *Billy Elliot* (2005), can be categorised as drama musicals.[61] This is rather confounding, since their dramaturgical structure is very different from that of Kunze's own shows, which leads to the question of how they fulfil the requirements of the genre. If all that is needed to qualify as a drama musical is a dramatic story which is well told and has a socio-political dimension, then the category should also extend to classic book musicals such as *South Pacific* (1949), *West Side Story* (1957), and *Fiddler on the Roof* (1964).

Yet the librettist and his collaborators have not always strictly followed their own dictum that '[a]ll elements of the drama musical need to serve the story'. How else explain the comic number 'An American Woman'—tellingly, the title is English even in the original German version—in *Rebecca*? In the one major change to the source material, the authors of the stage adaptation bring back Mrs van Hopper, for whom the heroine works at the beginning of the novel before she marries Maxim de Winter, in order that she may attend the masked ball at Manderley.

This is illogical for several reasons: not only do both 'I' and her husband despise the American socialite, being glad to see the back of her once they leave Monte Carlo, but it also seems unlikely that Mrs van Hopper would travel all the way from New York for a single social occasion. In a musicalisation that otherwise adheres very closely to du Maurier's neo-gothic thriller, this marked departure is rather startling and can only be explained by the desire of the creative team to add a light-hearted number before the dramatic end of act 1. Unfortunately, the supposedly funny 'An American Woman' constitutes a regrettable low in Kunze's lyric writing, a lazy collection of tired clichés about the Unites States and its popular culture:

> I'm an American Woman.
> [...]

I am not discreet
[ ... ]
Besides, I am rich.
I have a swing in my skirt
And Coca-Cola in my throat
And a gospel choir
Sings in my soul.
[ ... ]
I don't care a fig for taste
I like it garish.
[ ... ]
I can do anything, except
Make a mistake.[62]

The intention may have been to expose the character singing these lines as both brash and coarse, but instead it merely underlines the crassness of the songwriters.[63] It is one thing to playfully satirise national stereotypes; it is another to cater to an audience's unconscious prejudice against the 'other'. That the song became a fan favourite in *Rebecca's* German-language productions merely illustrates H. L. Mencken's aphorism that 'no one [ ... ] has ever lost money underestimating the intelligence of the [ ... ] people'.[64]

Kunze has endeavoured to avoid any notion that his shows resemble what is regularly staged on Broadway or in the West End—and not just when talking about his shows in the United States or the United Kingdom: 'You can call it a musical, if you wish to do so, but what I do is not what is commonly understood as a musical'.[65] In what may be the result of a reductive interpretation of (American) musical theatre history, the librettist sets his own creations apart from Anglophone works because, according to Kunze, Broadway shows regularly privilege the music above other creative contributions; he claims that '[o]riginally, as everybody knows, musical is musical comedy'.[66] For him, it is musical comedy, with its roots in vaudeville, its dance numbers and spectacle,[67] which epitomises 'the typical Broadway-type musical'.[68] While a point could be made that classical musical comedy of the 1920s and 1930s prized songs over plot, or at least entertainment over content, nevertheless, when Kunze demands that all parts of the production that do not serve the telling of the story be cut,[69] he actually follows in the wake of prominent American trailblazers: the musical play (or book musical) à la Rodgers and Hammerstein is based on exactly the same principle, namely, that the 'dramatic narration is king. And everything else is servant'.[70] All classic book musicals strive for unity of book, lyrics, music, and choreography and use musical numbers consistently as a means to delineate the characters.[71] As Ethan Mordden has pointed out: 'If the Rodgers & Hammerstein revolution could be boiled down to three words, they would read, Story is Everything'.[72]

In addition, even the most admired of Broadway composers, such as Leonard Bernstein and Stephen Sondheim, agree with Richard Kislan's directive that '[t]he book always comes first. That is a chronological fact, a philosophical imperative, and a practical principle'.[73] While this may not have prevented American artists and producers from occasionally sneaking in a number with hit potential,[74] as has been shown, Kunze and his collaborators themselves sometimes include songs or musical scenes whose dramaturgical necessity is questionable.

There is another parallel to the Broadway musical: all of the drama musicals under consideration are very carefully structured, even if occasionally their exposition is decidedly clumsy.[75] Striving for the utmost efficiency in their storytelling, their scenes move swiftly, thus fulfilling another requirement that US professionals insist on as key to a successful book: 'make your point and move on!'[76]

Finally, it could also be pointed out that Kunze's approach to musical theatre is exactly the same as that of any artist with integrity, since he endeavours to 'write something for the local audience, to write something that really means something for myself and not just for the market.'[77] However, that integrity may be easier to maintain in a subsidised theatre system, such as the one in Germany and Austria, than in strictly commercial environments like those of Broadway or the West End.

# THE DRAMATURGY OF KUNZE'S ORIGINAL DRAMA MUSICALS: *ELISABETH* AND *MOZART!*

Michael Kunze had long wished to write a musical about the fall of the House of Habsburg. When he settled on Empress Elisabeth as the perfect character to illustrate the decline of this dynasty, he was determined to correct the powerful but historically false image of the sweet, nature-loving royal instilled in several generations of audiences by the immensely popular trilogy of *Sissi* films (1955–1957), starring Romy Schneider.[78] He intended to show the truth about the strictly regimented life and political intrigues at the Austrian court in order to portray the empress as 'a woman fighting for her personal freedom, far ahead of her time'.[79] As the show's director, the opera luminary Harry Kupfer, pointed out: '*Elisabeth* is the story of an attempted, but misguided emancipation, that led to its very reverse. Elisabeth freed herself from the restraints of the Viennese court, but did not know what to do with her freedom.'[80]

The musical's depiction of various historical events and private tragedies in the life of the empress—the show covers forty-five years—is given coherence by a dramaturgical trick Kunze would reuse seven years later to similarly striking effect in *Mozart!*: he externalises the inner conflict of his main protagonist and turns *Elisabeth* into a love story between the eponymous character and Death, who strutted the stage in the original production as an androgynous, 'attractive young man with the aura of a pop star'.[81] Death appears early on in Elisabeth's life and remains her constant companion until their passionate affair is finally consummated with her assassination in 1898 by the anarchist Luigi Lucheni.

The musical tries hard to establish Elisabeth's unhappy life and her accidental assassination as symptomatic of her time and the state of the Austro-Hungarian empire. Yet this attempt is thwarted by several factors: for one thing, the empress was not much involved in her country's politics.[82] For another, the authors' determination to stay true to historical facts results in a title character who, in spite of loud protestations about wanting her freedom—the highlight of every *Elisabeth* performance is her power ballad 'Ich gehör' nur mir' ('I Belong to Me')—remains frustratingly opaque. At first Elisabeth does not act, but merely *reacts*—to her governess's rules, to Franz Joseph's proposal, and to her mother-in-law's attempts to re-educate her. Later on the older Elisabeth succeeds in giving the Viennese court the slip, and the character does the same to the musical.

FIG. 26.1 A lifelong love affair, only consummated after the empress's assassination: Death (Florian Silbereisen) carries Elisabeth (Pia Douwes) in the 2006 Stuttgart production of the musical named for her. Douwes here recreated the role which she originated in the 1992 Viennese world première of *Elisabeth*. Photo: Peter Bischoff © Getty Images.

Act 2 announces what Elisabeth does or rather doesn't do in her later years without offering any insight into *why* she fails to find any satisfaction.[83] Surely if she wants to give meaning to her life as the empress of Austria, she is in a much better position to at least try than any of her subjects?

It is also rather telling that the musical never answers the question of why Death is so obsessed with Elisabeth in particular. The reasons behind Death's decades-long campaign to lure the empress to his side seem to be exactly the same attributes that make Elisabeth worthy of our attention in the *Sissi* films: her beauty, her royal status, and her glamorous lifestyle.

While there may be more significant rulers in Austria's history than Empress Elisabeth, there definitely is no Austrian artist more widely admired than Wolfgang Amadeus Mozart. In the roughly 225 years since the composer's death, nothing has done more to mythicise him as a personality than Peter Shaffer's 1979 play *Amadeus* and Milos Forman's subsequent screen adaptation, which won eight Academy Awards.[84] Yet both the play and the movie were highly controversial, mainly because of their portrayal of Mozart as an uncouth, immature man-child and their mystification of his talent as something that defies mortal analysis and comprehension.[85] It is instructive to compare the 1984 movie with the 1999 musical, not least because the Kunze-Levay version of the composer's life has a similar take on these issues.

Just like *Amadeus, Mozart!* uses a framing device and tells the bulk of its story in flashbacks. The film begins and ends with the testimony of the ancient Antonio Salieri, a former court composer, whose confession of killing his rival Mozart out of professional jealousy is ambiguous enough to be doubted. In contrast, the musical begins and ends at the Viennese cemetery St Marx, where Dr Franz Mesmer, with the help of Mozart's widow, Constanze, tries to exhume the composer's skull.

But this is where the apparent similarities end. In Kunze's libretto, Salieri is reduced to a mere bit player who only appears in two of the twenty-nine scenes. Instead, the musical transforms two supporting characters from Shaffer's play into the main villains: Archduke Colloredo and Mozart's mother-in-law, Cäcilie Weber. In both fictitious accounts of the composer's life, Colloredo comes across as haughty, superior, and humourless—true to life, as some historians would note. Cäcilie Weber, on the other hand is turned from a mere irritation in Shaffer's version into a cold-hearted, money-grubbing schemer. In addition, Mozart's wife, Constanze, an airhead in the movie, is shown as loving but lazy, her big solo in act 2 asserting: 'It's unhealthy to get up./I cannot bear the bright light./[ . . . ]/For a housewife, works never stops./It's better if I don't even start'.[86] She is mainly interested in self-preservation.

Once again Kunze makes apparent what ails his protagonist, this time by presenting on-stage two sides of the artist simultaneously: on the one hand, the child Amadé, who looks like a China doll and is always composing; in the words of the authors, he 'represents exactly the image that millions of people have of Mozart: a cute rococo icon of human yearning for angelic innocence and divine genius'.[87] On the other hand, there is the adult and decidedly human Wolfgang, who always seems overshadowed by the *Wunderkind*, the child prodigy he once was, and who is unable to resist the temptations both of Vienna and of false friends.

THE GERMAN/AUSTRIAN 'DRAMA MUSICAL', OR 'I SING ALONE'     735

Wolfgang realises that Amadé's brilliance offers him unique opportunities: 'Because of you I will be free/We only will do what we like./You and I are not afraid of anything or anyone./We don't care about duty.'[88] In the last analysis, however, the genius destroys the human: the prodigy literally starts drawing blood from the grown-up in order to be able to continue notating his compositions before finally stabbing him fatally with his quill. Whatever one's reaction to this interpretation of the demands supreme talent makes upon an artist, the musical ultimately takes the same stance as both the theatrical and cinematic versions of *Amadeus*: by separating the person from his work, it forfeits any exploration of how Mozart's 'human' existence, that is, his emotional experiences, his psychological and physical state, may have affected his art.

The show highlights the cost of being a genius, but Mozart's talent once again remains an enigma—bestowed by God, it cannot be investigated, only acknowledged in awe. The ensemble exults: 'Is he really human like all of us?/[ ... ]/God gave this world/The wonder of Mozart/Star to light up the world/Until the edge of eternity.'[89] It is concluded that '[n]othing on this earth has ever been so perfect.'[90]

Even if the musical in many respects employs a radically different approach to representing Mozart's life and death, its portrayal of the composer itself has a certain affinity with the 'grinning buffoon with a randy turn of mind' in *Amadeus*.[91] Once again the artist is in thrall to sensuality—in his own words, 'I am [ ... ]/Clever and stupid and horny and good'[92]—although his womanising and his colourful language are handled more discreetly. For instance, in the musical, when the composer performs a naughty song ('Ich bin extraordinär' ['I'm Extraordinary'], act 1, scene 12),[93] every single vulgar rhyme is drowned out by a horn. This up-tempo solo number is a reconceived and extended version of 'Sauschwanz von Drecken' ('Pigtail of Muck'),[94] which was used in the 1999 world première, with one crucial difference: whereas the rewritten version shows Mozart purposefully provoking Colloredo's servant, Count Arco, the more playful original—chock-full of puns and neologisms—is much closer to a nonsense song. But the replacement not only paints Mozart as less exalted and more calculating, it also loses two important lines ('I have a dozen faces/And I play thousands of roles'),[95] which highlighted another aspect of the composer Kunze and Levay wished to present: that he adopts Emanuel Schikaneder's view of life as a performance.[96] However, that is not borne out by how the protagonist is portrayed in the libretto.

Adding to the confusion as to how to read the eponymous character are those moments in the show when Mozart falls back into childish behaviour: occasionally he 'giggles without any obvious reason.'[97] At other times his speech pattern becomes breathless with free association or simply incoherent: 'Bad, bad, bad wolves, all. Snakes.'[98] Yet in contrast to Shaffer's *Amadeus*, where the composer's depiction as a kind of *idiot savant* is part of an overall conception, in the musical these spurious episodes never come together into a coherent interpretation of the historical figure.

In *Elisabeth* and *Mozart!*, what unites the two Austrians, the empress and the composer, is their yearning for freedom. The clichéd image of the Gypsy, free to roam, free from suffocating responsibilities, can be found in each show to express the characters' desire to evade their respective constraints.[99] Also to be found in each musical is a

736    OLAF JUBIN

highly critical portrayal of the cultural centres Vienna and, to a lesser degree, Salzburg as duplicitous places of nefarious gossip and barely concealed malice, where people are obsessed with their own advancement and rejoice in the misfortune of others. The two choral numbers to that effect in *Elisabeth*—'Alle Fragen sind gestellt' ('We Have Posed All the Questions', act 1, scene 6) and 'Happy Apocalypse' (act 1, scene 10)[100]—are mirrored by another two in *Mozart!*, 'Halten Sie den Atem an!' ('Hold Your Breath', act 1, scene 12), and the act 2 opener 'Hier in Wien' ('Here in Vienna', act 2, scene 1).[101]

In these major cities, everybody seeks to fleece everybody else while honesty is regarded as weakness. Considering that both shows premiered in the Austrian capital, this is rather surprising; Kunze and Levay clearly do not shy away from attacking their own audience, even if they do so in historical garb.[102]

One might wonder whether the authors were already anticipating the downright vile notices that greeted *Elisabeth* when it opened in the Theater an der Wien in 1992.[103] Undoubtedly they were aware of how poorly the musical as a genre had fared with Austrian reviewers and cultural critics ever since the venue, rich in tradition and thus one of the city's most revered performance spaces, had dedicated itself entirely to musical theatre productions in 1965.[104] Surprisingly, considering how deeply the composer is revered in Austria, *Mozart!*'s critical reception by the local newspapers and magazines was slightly less hostile, even though the reviews were still largely negative.[105]

However, the fact that a similar sentiment of pervasive deceptiveness and malice is articulated in *Marie Antoinette* in respect of the French court ('Nobody means what he says/Every friend/Is secretly an enemy'[106]) indicates Kunze and Levay's general mistrust of the intellectual and social elite. There is in their works a through-line from the blabbing relatives and the decadent intellectuals in *Elisabeth* to the contemporaries revelling in *Mozart*'s misfortunes, the arrogant upper-class twits in *Rebecca*, and the profligate courtiers in *Marie Antoinette*.

## Adapting Source Material into Drama Musicals: The Dramaturgy of *Dance of the Vampires*, *Rebecca*, and *Marie Antoinette*

The 1997 screen-to-stage transfer of *Dance of the Vampires/The Fearless Vampire Killers* (1967) is in many ways an anomaly among Kunze musicals: it is the only one of his shows that is based on a film, and the only one that has a comic tone throughout. Moreover, it has music by Jim Steinman—much of it not composed specifically for the screen-to-stage adaptation[107]—and was directed not by an opera or musical theatre expert, but by a film director, the one responsible for the original movie. Roman Polanski not only co-wrote the screenplay but also starred in the spoof, together with his future wife, Sharon Tate. The film, which mixes a lampoon of the narrative and visual tropes of the horror films from the Hammer studio in the 1960s with silent-movie slapstick, tells the story of Professor Ambronsius and his shy assistant Alfred, who arrive in the Carpathian Mountains to research and to fight supernatural evil. In the end, their attempt at defeating the vampire Count Krolock, leader of the undead, and to save the young Sarah, with whom Alfred has fallen in love, backfires. Unwittingly, they are responsible for spreading vampirism all over the world.

Even if the 2002 Broadway production of the substantially rewritten *Dance of the Vampires* had not been such an unmitigated disaster,[108] it seems questionable whether the show could ever find an audience in the United States. Roman Polanski was already a highly controversial figure before the start of the #MeToo movement; since then every single artistic endeavour in any way related to the Oscar-winning filmmaker has triggered controversy.[109]

In this context it only adds to the polemic that the vampire musical can be accused of displaying both sexist and homophobic attitudes. The former are personified by the lecherous innkeeper Chagal: he not only spanks his adult daughter but also forces himself on the voluptuous barmaid, Magda who—in a not entirely convincing twist—finds his unwanted advances far less objectionable once he has turned her into a vampire. As far as Count Krolock's gay son Herbert is concerned, the character may have been

FIG. 26.2 Professor Ambronsius (Werner Bauer) is left dangling during his hapless attempt to defeat the undead. A comic moment from the 2003 Hamburg production of *Tanz der Vampire* (*Dance of the Vampires*). Photo: dpa © Alamy Stock Photo.

surprising in 1967, but his libidinous harassment and lecherous admiration of Alfred's 'süßen Po' ('sweet tush') amount to the kind of clichéd portrayals of a homosexual which should now be relegated to the trash heap of history.[110] On the whole, the show is anything but subtle in its humour; its double entendres are decidedly crude.[111]

A major alteration in the move from screen to stage is in tone, which is a consequence of the show's choice of composer. Jim Steinman's typically bombastic compositions at times threaten to overwhelm what on-screen is a straightforward parody.[112] In order to accommodate the type of rock music that, in spite of being innately theatrical in its affect, refrains from descending fully into camp, Kunze's lyrics have Count Krolock brooding about the boredom of eternity,[113] which adds an incongruous ingredient to the show. Power ballads are not the most effective way to musicalise *Weltschmerz*, which as an expression of melancholia suggests defeat and feebleness. They also are at odds with the more satirical numbers. Moreover, why should the audience sympathise with the plight of being a vampire,[114] especially when Krolock's army of undead are about to take over the world? However, the show's melodious score does feature two rather unusual numbers: a virtuoso patter song for Professor Ambronsius, 'Wahrheit' ('Truth', act 1, scene 6), and a torch song for a male character, Alfred's ballad 'Für Sarah' ('For Sarah', act 2, scene 3).[115]

In many ways, *Rebecca* is dramaturgically the most satisfying of Kunze's five major shows, partly because it follows its meticulously plotted novelistic source very closely. If the show (which is musically not as rich as Levay's previous two scores) has one major shortcoming, it is that the adaptation is decidedly less ambiguous in its portrayal of Maxim de Winter than Daphne du Maurier's original, which reflects the author's ambivalence about her own marriage, gender, and sexuality.[116] The mysterious death of the dazzling Rebecca can be interpreted as the cautionary tale of a sexually transgressive female who crosses a man obsessed with staying in control. When Maxim cannot contain or silence his wife, he kills the woman who undermines him both socially and sexually.[117] In order to prevent this from happening again, he chooses as his second spouse someone who is significantly younger and so demure that she is unlikely ever to challenge the status quo. Avoiding his previous mistake of taking a wife with excessive charisma and will, Maxim opts for a girl with so little personality that du Maurier doesn't even give her a name. The only identity 'I' has is the one which she acquires through her marriage, and which is completely bound to her husband: Mrs de Winter.

The most famous of the various screen adaptations, Alfred Hitchcock's classic 1940 Oscar-winning film, still permits this reading,[118] despite turning Maxim's cold-blooded murder of Rebecca into a fatal accident—a change enforced by the Hays Production Office, Hollywood's official censor. In contrast, the musical privileges a more traditional romantic interpretation of a devoted girl saving the tortured man she loves, coyly and conveniently having Max suffer from memory loss about how exactly his first wife died.[119] Otherwise, apart from the occasional questionable choice of words for both 'I' and Mrs van Hopper,[120] the only other striking element in the musical's dramaturgical construction is the not-always-successful attempt to inject its dark story with humour.

*Marie Antoinette* (2006) recounts the years before and immediately after the French Revolution through focusing on the intertwined fate of two women who are similar in

FIG. 26.3 The Austrian on the French throne (Roberta Valentini, *centre*) surrounded by her courtiers. Scene from the 2009 European première of *Marie Antoinette* in Bremen. Photo: dpa © Alamy Stock Pictures.

looks but could not be more different in their social background: the eponymous character and the pauper Margrid Arnaud, who will become actively involved in the political uprising. In many ways, this musical is the least successful of the drama musicals: whereas all of Kunze's other major works have been staged and recorded in Europe multiple times, the tragic tale about the French empress has only been performed twice.[121] The very short cast album (thirty-eight minutes) not only abbreviates the score to 'highlights' but hints at a major problem with the musical conception of the show: the three female leads, with their strong pop belt (Margrid, Marie Antoinette, and Sister Agnés), all have a comparable vocal range and sound very much alike.

More important, however, the musical very closely resembles *Elisabeth* in its structure, themes and details as the following chronological list proves.

- Marie Antoinette, another member of the Habsburg dynasty—although on the throne in France—yearns for freedom, just like her relative over a hundred years later.
- Madame Lapin's entrance song 'Gib' ihnen alles, was sie woll'n' ('You've Got to Give Them What They Want', act 1, scene 5) is clearly modelled on the number of that other brothel owner, Frau Wolf, in *Elisabeth* ('Nur kein Genieren' ['Don't Be Shy', act 2, scene 5]).

- Following in Lucheni's footsteps (act 1, scene 13), the playwright Beaumarchais and his actors also incite the citizens of the capital against the decadent woman sitting on the throne (act 1, scene 8).
- As a member of the Habsburg dynasty and to prepare for her future as a royal, Marie Antoinette has been trained not be overly emotional;[122] Archduchess Sophie still practices this kind of education a century later with both her son, Franz Josef, and her grandson, Rudolf.
- In both musicals, the emperor is a weakling, unsuited to lead the nation.
- In the second half, the death of a child is used to gain sympathy for the eponymous character: Marie Antoinette mourns the death of the dauphin (act 2, scene 2), while Elisabeth is devasted by her son's suicide (act 2, scene 13).
- In act 2, scene 3, Count Cagliostro sums up the political events in France in a style closely resembling Lucheni's précis of Elisabeth's restless years (act 2, scene 7).
- Like Elisabeth, Marie Antoinette is imprisoned and forbidden to raise and educate her own children (act 2, scene 11).
- Once again, only death will set the queen/empress free.[123]

The collaborators also borrow freely from their other shows. For instance, Marie Antoinette's assertion 'I want to live/I want to be young/And entertained/I want to laugh,/I want to do stupid things/And I want to dance in the light' echoes those of both Sarah in *Dance of the Vampires* and Constanze in *Mozart!*[124]

The musical has several major deficiencies, which may help explain why European audiences so far have resisted it: as an artist with a keen interest in history, Kunze works very hard not to unduly simplify the events around 1789, and still the plethora of social factors and political intrigues interacting in *Marie Antoinette* results in an overabundance of characters and incidents.

On another level, in her first few scenes the eponymous character behaves so abominably that later attempts to humanise her through her growth in stature in prison may simply arrive too late to be effective.[125] Equally unsatisfying is the show's handling of its protagonist: according to Kunze, Margrid starts her journey as an arrogant young firebrand who over the years learns compassion and forgiveness.[126] Yet most theatre-goers will find her outrage at the poverty and exploitation around her as well as her disgust with the upper classes entirely justified. It also proves unsatisfying that important plot elements, introduced early on, are not followed through,[127] and that the girl throughout seems completely oblivious to how the Duke of Orléans constantly manipulates her for his own ends.

# THE DRAMA MUSICAL AS AN 'EUROPEAN FORM'

One aspect that supposedly distinguishes the drama musical from its American counterparts is its sensibility, which Kunze has characterised as 'something very

European and [ ... ] something very German.'[128] For the librettist, drama is the most important element of the performing arts,[129] and he argues that his kind of musical stands in a continental tradition that favours 'highly dramatic stories',[130] as evidenced by Italian, French, German, and Austrian opera. In Kunze's view, 'our audiences in Europe [ ... ] are more interested in going to theatre and having a real theatrical experience, a genuinely emotional experience, not just an entertaining evening, but something they can discuss after the show.'[131]

This broad generalisation fails to take into consideration the vastly different theatre systems operating on Broadway and in the West End, and in continental Europe. Working in a purely commercial industry, New York and London producers emphasise the values of commercial entertainment as a means of attracting the largest number of spectators, while in Germany, Austria, and Switzerland, where the performing arts, including opera, are heavily subsidised, artists are tasked with educating and challenging the public. Thus Kunze basically blurs the question of cause and effect while also disregarding several generations of Broadway and West End composers, book writers, and lyricists who were determined to engage their audience emotionally as well as on a socio-political level and were highly skilled in doing so.[132]

Yet, in what ways exactly do Kunze's works differ from Broadway shows? On the one hand, all of them have a European setting (the Austro-Hungarian Empire, Transylvania, France, and England). Because they either cover European history, such as the French Revolution and the fall of the Habsburg Empire, or are based on intellectual properties, which are more popular outside North America, like *Tanz der Vampire* and *Rebecca*,[133] the topics of most of his musicals do not immediately appeal to producers on the Great White Way.

While all of the above may be unusual, it is not enough to support Kunze's claim that the drama musical could not have originated in the United States.[134] Perhaps the clue lies in one of the key elements of the drama musical genre, the breaking of the fourth wall. As a theatrical device, the direct address of the audience has been most famously employed by Bertolt Brecht and Erwin Piscator in their epic theatre, and by making use of the same means, Kunze takes up a tradition that to this day remains highly influential in German-language theatre.

It must be emphasised, however, that the drama musical does not incorporate instances of breaking the fourth wall in the didactic sense of the classic *Verfremdungseffekt* (defamiliarization effect). In fact, Kunze has stated repeatedly that he abhors teaching the audience,[135] and that he works very hard to prevent his musicals from becoming 'too intellectual'.[136] For the librettist, musical theatre is all about 'elicit[ing] emotions',[137] and in that respect he could not be further removed from Brecht.

A close look at when exactly Kunze has his actors step out of their roles and acknowledge the spectators offers intriguing insights into the topic(s) so close to the writer that he chooses to communicate them directly to his audience. These moments occur in all of his five major shows: twice in *Elisabeth* (act 1, scene 3; and act 2, scene 9), *Mozart!* (act 1, scenes 12 and 14) and *Marie Antoinette* (Prologue; and act 1, scene 6), and once in *Rebecca* (act 1, scene 10), as well as three times in *Dance of the Vampires* (act 2, scenes 9, 10, and 11).[138] In the last, two of these instances of subverting theatre conventions are in keeping with the show's parodistic spirit, since both Sarah and Professor Ambronsius look into the audience to signal mischief and misplaced optimism, respectively.[139]

In the 1992 musical about the Austrian empress, it is during their cold-blooded manipulation of the emperor that Archduchess Sophie and her advisors, staunchly opposing any socio-political reforms that might undermine their power, address the theatregoers. Later in the show's most controversial scene ('Hass' ['Hate']),[140] a parade of xenophobic and totalitarian demonstrators from various points in Austrian history links the fall of the Habsburg Empire with the rise of 1930s fascism.

*Tanz der Vampire* offers a comparable lesson concerning inhumanity and selfishness, with Count Krolock predicting the arrival of a society without any moral qualms or consideration for others where all are equally doomed: 'Here and now/I prophesy you mortals of tomorrow/As soon as your next millennium begins/The only God whom everybody serves/Will be unquenchable greed.'[141] The undead about to take over the world advise the audience: 'Be a pig/Or they will have your guts for garters/[ ... ]/Show them your fist/Otherwise you'll be beaten/[ ... ]/If you want to decide/Instead of asking others/You have to learn to take no prisoners.'[142] This mirrors the pointed critique of capitalism in the famous song by Brecht and Weill, 'Denn wie man sich bettet' ('Alabama Song'), from *Aufstieg und Fall der Stadt Mahagonny* (*The Rise and Fall of the City of Mahagonny*, 1930).[143]

One could thus argue that a typically Brechtian view of ruthlessness and greed dominating the world imbues the finale of *Tanz der* Vampire, with the undead intoning: 'We drink blood, we have no morals whatsoever./We don't give a fuck about what happens to the world.'[144] Yet, unlike Brecht, Kunze presents this depravity not as an inexorable consequence of capitalism,[145] but as behaviour that characterises all of humankind and, in this case even extends to another kind of bloodsucker.

In *Mozart!* it is in the Prater, Vienna's famous fun fair, that the actors first step out of their roles and address the audience, after they have pointed out that

> The world is full of wonders
> And each and every one is some kind of trick.
> All is humbug!
> All is fraud!
> If today a person is honest,
> He is not clever.
> In talk and in action everybody cheats everybody else
> For their own advantage and because everybody does it.[146]

To prove that point, Mozart has just been 'beheaded' in a fairground illusion in front of the fun fair visitors. Two scenes later the composer himself poses a question to the audience, seemingly asking it for help, in a reprise of his act 1 finale, 'How do you escape your own shadow?'

Perhaps because its source material does not really lend itself to postmodern tropes, *Rebecca* features only one example of breaking the fourth wall, in a scene added for the musical: in the Kerrith country club, male and female golfers assure us that their seemingly vicious gossiping is only a reflection of their attempt to cultivate a certain class, in more ways than one; after all, specific standards need to be maintained: 'We are British, we are noble./We are an exclusive company.'[147] In this case, Kunze and Levay strive for a more satirical edge—the scene ends in a comic tableau[148]—than for dire warnings.

Although it is supposed to be a key feature of the drama musical, acknowledgement of the audience is used least consistently and thus least effectively in *Marie Antoinette*. The musical begins with the narrator figure, Count Cagliostro, introducing the spectators to eighteenth-century France in a direct address, but after the Prologue he never does so again. In act 1, scene 6, both Margrid and the empress look out into the auditorium once, which seems simply another means of twinning them in the mind of the playgoers. This time only, the dramaturgical device is not employed to warn against humanity's cruelty and inherent selfishness, perhaps because these sentiments are already articulated elsewhere in the show.[149]

Yet while the breaking of the fourth wall may be an element that links Kunze with a metatheatrical tradition of European theatre, it is not merely because he doesn't use it for its original political purpose that its usefulness as a distinct element of the drama musical is limited. British theatre has a long tradition of politically engaged musicals that directly address the audience, especially in shows developed by Joan Littlewood, John McGrath, and Peter Nichols, and over the last five decades several important Broadway musicals have done the same, including *Chicago* (1975), *Sweeney Todd* (1979), *Ragtime* (1997), and *Hamilton* (2015).

# Conclusion: The Drama Musical—a New Subgenre?

Considering all the above points, the question is, how far does Kunze's approach to musical theatre really break new ground? Thanks to his close study of the organisational principles of screenplay writing, his shows are distinguished by their intricate plotting. Detailed scrutiny, however, reveals that both his original musicals and those based on source material reveal dramaturgical weaknesses, indicating that the structural spine of Kunze's drama musicals may not be quite as sturdy as he may have intended. They are flawed because, as with other narrative strategies, the execution matters more than the underlying principles.

Still, the drama musical does have at least one unique feature: the way the score depicts the relationship between the protagonist and the ensemble. Whereas most musicals use choral and production numbers to present the leading character as part of a community or to set them apart from the crowd to which they belong, in a drama musical the protagonist is never part of the group. If British musical theatre is particularly interested in community, and the American musical is always intrigued by individuals who stand apart from their fellow human beings as extraordinary, in the drama musical the leading character is separated from the rest of society right from the start by birth, education, talent, or morality, so that she or he can never join in with the others.

In the drama musical, the protagonist stands and sings alone, and the chorus fulfills other functions: it comments—often on the hero and/or heroine—or imparts background information, thus appearing in various guises, such as those of servants, courtiers, crowds, citizens, traders, shoppers, theatre audiences, and party guests. Depending on the musical, the company also takes on more unusual roles, such as the dead (*Elisabeth*), the undead (*Dance of the Vampires*), 'shadows' (*Mozart!* and especially *Rebecca*), and the poor (*Marie Antoinette*).

This is certainly a startling departure from the Anglophone traditions that the drama musical grew out of; though whether it makes the form distinct enough to constitute its own subgenre is debatable.

## NOTES

1. For a historical overview of the reception of the Anglophone musical in Germany and Austria after the end of World War II, see Olaf Jubin, *Entertainment in der Kritik: Eine komparative Analyse von amerikanischen, britischen und deutschsprachigen Rezensionen zu den Musicals von Stephen Sondheim und Andrew Lloyd Webber* (Herbolzheim: Centaurus Verlag, 2005), 172–190.
2. Michael Kunze, 'Musical Master Class 1: Introduction Michael Kunze', https://www.yout ube.com/watch?v=87IrL5_IUQc, accessed 6 August 2019.
3. Kunze has won fifty-six gold and twenty-three platinum records, writing for and producing hits for performers such as Peter Maffay ('Du', 1970), Udo Jürgens ('Griechischer Wein', 1974; 'Ein ehrenwertes Haus', 1975), Penny McLean ('Lady Bump', 1975), Peter Alexander ('Die kleine Kneipe', 1976), Jürgen Drews ('Ein Bett im Kornfeld', 1976), Gitte Hænning ('Ich will alles', 1983), Juliane Werding ('Nacht voll Schatten', 1983; 'Stimmen im Wind', 1985; 'Das Würfelspiel', 1986) and Münchener Freiheit ('Ohne Dich schlaf ich heut' Nacht nicht ein', 1985).
4. Before that, Kunze had already adapted the 1977 Michael Stewart and Cy Coleman musical *I Love My Wife* for its German première at the Stadttheater Oberhausen in North Rhine–Westphalia.
5. Michael Kunze, 'Musical Master Class 3: Adaptions [*sic*]', https://www.youtube.com/watch?v=87IrL5_IUQc, accessed 6 August 2019.
6. There are three additional musicals in Kunze's oeuvre which will not be discussed, either because their reach has been limited or because neither the score nor the libretto is available: his very first show with Sylvester Levay, *Hexen Hexen* (1991), a musical about seventeenth-century witch hunts, has only been staged once, at the Open Air Theatre in Heilbronn, but has never had a cast recording. The duo's show about young English monarch Elizabeth I, *Lady Bess* (2014), which—like *Marie Antoinette*—was commissioned by the Takarazuka theatre company, has not been performed outside Japan (where it has been

recorded on DVD). Kunze's latest musical is *Don Camillo & Peppone* (2016); it has music by Dario Farina and is based on the novel *Il mondo piccolo* by Giovannino Guareschi. The musical was co-produced by the Swiss theatre S. Gallen and the Viennese Ronacher Theater, where it ran for 117 performances. Since then the show's director, Andreas Gergen, has taken the work to the Open Air Festival in Tecklenburg (2019), but on the whole, the response in German-speaking countries so far has been muted.

7. That Kunze's shows have not yet conquered the English-language market is mostly due to the misguided attempts to bring two of them to Broadway: *Dance of the Vampires* was completely rewritten for its US première and then closed quickly in 2002, while a planned 2012 New York production of *Rebecca* was doomed when its US producer was convicted of fraud and sentenced to prison. Justified or not, both shows are now branded 'spoiled goods', and this impression may also extend to the other drama musicals. For more information see Jessie McKinleyjan, '*Dance of the Vampires*, a $12 Million Broadway Failure, Is Closing', *New York Times*, 16 January 2003, https://www.nytimes.com/2003/01/16/theater/dance-of-the-vampi res-a-12-million-broadway-failure-is-closing.html, and Michael Riedel, 'Hate at 1st Bite: How *Vampires* Got Drained of Its Blood', *New York Post*, 13 December 2002, https://nypost. com/2002/12/13/hate-at-1st-bite-how-vampires-got-drained-of-its-blood/, both accessed 15 June 2019, as well as David Kamp, 'The Road to *Rebecca*', *Vanity Fair*, June 2913, 106–118.

8. Angela Reinhardt, 'Im Gespräch mit Michael Kunze', *Musicals: Das Musicalmagazin* 88 (2001): 21.

9. Kunze, 'Musical Master Class 1'.

10. Kunze has written two historical novels: *Straße ins Feuer: Vom Leben und Sterben in der Zeit des Hexenwahns* (Munich: Kindler, 1982), and *Der Freiheit eine Gasse: Traum und Leben eines deutschen Revolutionärs* (Munich: Kindler, 1990). The former has been translated into several languages; the English version was published by University of Chicago Press in 1987 under the title *High Road to the Stake: A Tale of Witchcraft*.

11. Michael Kunze, 'Musical Master Class 5: Developing the Drama Musical *Elisabeth*', https://www.youtube.com/watch?v=87IrL5_IUQc, accessed 6 August 2019.

12. He has stated that *Jesus Christ Superstar* hit him like 'lightning'; Michael Kunze, 'Musical Master Class 2: Discovering Musical Theatre', https://www.youtube.com/watch?v=87IrL5_IUQc, accessed 6 August 2019.)

13. Ibid. According to Kunze, *Madness* only sold 100,00 copies, whereas the previous album by Silver Convention had sales of 2 million (ibid.)

14. Kunze, 'Musical Master Class 5'.

15. Kunze, 'Musical Master Class 3'.

16. These include *Katja & Co.* (1976), featuring Katja Epstein, *Die Peter Alexander Show* (1992), and *Salut für Harald Juhnke* (1994).

17. Kunze, 'Musical Master Class 2'.

18. Jonathon Collis, 'BWW Interviews: Writer and Interpreter Michael Kunze', 2 October 2009, https://www.broadwayworld.com/westend/article/BWW-INTERVIEWS-Writer-And-Interpreter-Michael-Kunze-20091002, accessed 1 May 2019.

19. Kunze, 'Musical Master Class 5'; emphasis suggested by Kunze's intonation.

20. Reinhard, 'Im Gespräch mit Michael Kunze'.

21. Ironically, this division may remain more of an ideal that an actual achievement: the two acts of *Elisabeth* are basically equal in length (sixty-seven and sixty-six minutes, respectively), while the first half of *Mozart!* is only about twelve minutes longer than the

second (seventy-five minutes and sixty-three minutes, respectively). Act 2 of *Dance of the Vampires* is, at eighty-one minutes, actually *longer* than act 1 (seventy-eight minutes).

22. Michael Kunze, 'Wie ein Drama Musical entsteht', https://pagewizz.com/michael-kunze, accessed 8 November 2018.

23. See www.storyarchitekt.com.

24. To this day, *The Hunchback of Notre Dame* remains the only Disney stage adaptation to premiere in continental Europe and in a language other than English. The production closed in 2002 without turning a profit and for a variety of reasons never moved to Broadway. The (rewritten) show finally had its first North American staging in 2014.

25. Among the other Broadway classics Kunze has translated are *A Chorus Line* (1975/German version 1986), *Little Shop of Horrors* (1982/1986), *Kiss of the Spider Woman* (1992/1993), *City of Angels* (1989/1995), and *Wicked* (2003/2007).

26. 'I don't like the word translator, because translating is not really what I do'; Kunze, 'Musical Master Class 3'.

27. For a first foray into the German discourse on translation, see Walter Benjamin, 'Die Aufgabe des Übersetzers', in *Das Problem des Übersetzens*, ed. Hans Joachim Störig (Darmstadt: Goverts, 1963), 182–195; and Otto Hesse-Quack, *Der Übertragungsprozeß bei der Synchronisation von Filmen: Eine interkulturelle Untersuchung* (Munich: E. Reinhardt, 1969).

28. His long experience of writing German lyrics for performers with varying vocal skills clearly has stood him in good stead in this context; Kunze, 'Musical Master Class 3'.

29. 'Sie lebte von der Monarchie/Und richtete sich in der Schweiz/Ein Nummernkonto ein' ('She lived off the monarchy/And opened a bank account/In Switzerland'). These lines, which can be heard on the 1992 Viennese cast recording, were replaced in the 2001 Essen production with a reference to Elisabeth's pride at having been crowned queen of Hungary. Thus they are no longer included in the official libretto, which now reads: 'Jetzt ist sie Ungarns Königin,/Sie trägt den Kopf so hoch wie nie/Und strahlt im Glorienschein' ('Now she is queen of Hungary/She never held her head higher,/Beaming in her halo'); Michael Kunze and Sylvester Levay, *Elisabeth: Libretto der deutschen Erstaufführung* (Grünwald: Edition Butterfly, 2001), 50.

30. Joseph P. Swain argues that the composer's method of foreshadowing as well as repeating key numbers with different lyrics 'risks a fatal weakening of the melody's dramatic function', since it undercuts the dramatic association between the music and the action in the musical. Joseph P. Swain, *The Broadway Musical: A Critical and Musical Survey* (Oxford and New York: Oxford University Press, 1990), 298).

31. Michael Kunze, 'Musical Master Class 6: Basic Drama Musical Structure', https://www.youtube.com/watch?v=87IrL5_IUQc, accessed 6 August 2019.

32. 'But whatever we see/Is just merely/A game of masks' ('Doch was wir seh'n/Ist immer nur/Ein Maskenspiel'); Michael Kunze and Sylvester Levay, *Marie Antoinette: Das Musical; Libretto* (Hamburg: Edition Butterfly, 2009), 33–34.

33. Robert Gordon, Olaf Jubin, and Millie Taylor, *British Musical Theatre since 1950* (London: Bloomsbury, 2016), 183.

34. Michael Kunze and Jim Steinman, *Tanz der Vampire: Das Musical; Libretto* (Hamburg: Edition Butterfly, 2018), 65.

35. Ibid., 88.

36. 'Stieren, schnofeln, plauschen, plaudern, rauchen, pofeln, raunzen, zaubern, lesen, dösen beim Kaffee' ('To stare, to sniff, to chat away, to natter, to smoke, to fume, to grunt, to

THE GERMAN/AUSTRIAN 'DRAMA MUSICAL', OR 'I SING ALONE'    747

hesitate, to read, to snooze while drinking coffee'); Kunze and Levay, *Elisabeth: Libretto der deutschen Erstauffuhrung*, 39.

37. Eugene Robert Huber claims that 'concept musical, was first used by Martin Gottried, who reviewed New York theatre for *Women's Wear Daily*, in his review of Kander and Ebb's *Zorba* (1968), directed by Harold Prince; Eugene Robert Huber, 'Stephen Sondheim and Harold Prince: Collaborative Contributions to the Development of the Modern Concept Musical, 1970–1981' (PhD diss., New York University, 1990), 2. Jessica Sternfeld traces the neologism 'megamusical' to the *New York Times*: in the 1980s, America's newspaper of record was the first to apply it to the blockbuster musicals coming over from London; Jessica Sternfeld, *The Megamusical* (Bloomington: Indiana University Press, 2006), 1.

38. Kunze, 'Musical Master Class 5'.

39. It seems that he stopped when *Rebecca* failed to move to Broadway in 2012. He also no longer regularly updates his website www.storyarchitekt.com. This may be less a reflection of his second major set-back when attempting to conquer the world of English-speaking musical theatre after the disastrous run of *Dance of the Vampires* in New York in 2002, than simply a matter of age: Kunze is now in his mid-seventies.

40. Michael Kunze, 'What is a Drama Musical?', https://www.youtube.com/wathc?v=kakS RwdiWcg, accessed 6 August 2019. Other definitions, which differ from the quote above only marginally, can be found in Reinhardt, 'Im Gespräch mit Michael Kunze'; Kunze, 'Musical Master Class 5'; and Kunze, 'Wie ein Drama Musical entsteht'.

41. Michael Kunze, 'Musical Master Class 8: Serve the Story', https://www.youtube.com/watch?v=87IrL5_IUQc, accessed 6 August 2019.

42. Kunze, 'Musical Master Class 5'; emphasis suggested by Kunze's intonation.

43. One can detect here clearly the influence of Robert McKee, see e.g. his remarks in 'The Protagonist', in McKee, *Story: Substance, Structure, Style, and the Principles of Screenwriting* (New York: itBooks, 1997), 136–141.

44. Michael Kunze, 'Von der Idee zur Premiere: Die Entstehung eines DramaMusicals [*sic*]; Teil 14: Weitere Figuren des Musicals II', http://storyarchitekt.com/workshop/masterclas s14.php, accessed 7 May 2019.

45. Ibid.

46. While Leopold Mozart for a long time is just as domineering as these two women, he is a far more complex character, drawn both in more shades and with deeper understanding.

47. The actress playing the archduchess was often booed by audiences.Birgit Rommel, *Aus der 'Schwarzen Möwe' wird 'Elisabeth': Entstehung und Inszenierungsgeschichte des Musicals über die Kaiserin von Österreich* (Hamburg: Diplomica Verlag GmbH, 2007), 81.

48. Robespierre has him arrested just before the curtain falls; Kunze and Levay, *Marie Antoinette: Das Musical; Libretto*, 107. Of course, anyone versed in European history knows that Robespierre himself later fell victim to the violent events he instigated.

49. Michael Kunze, 'Von der Idee zur Premiere. Die Entstehung eines Drama Musicals. Teil 4: Besondere Elemente des Musiktheaters', http://storyarchitekt.com/workshop/mastercla ss4.php, accessed 7 May 2019.

50. As instructed by the director, Harry Kupfer, the choreographer, Dennis Callahan, devised movement for *Elisabeth* that is 'a little bit unnatural and against the music' ('ein bisschen unnatürlich und gegen die Musik'); quoted in Susanne Haizmann, 'Im Gespräch mit Dennis Callahan', *Musicals: Das Musicalmagazin* 73 (1998): 28.

748   OLAF JUBIN

51. Tamiya Kuriyama, who staged the world première of *Marie Antoinette* 2006 in Japan as well as its first German production three years later, has experience in a broad variety of genres, from straight plays to musicals and opera.

52. As the filmed records of *Elisabeth* and *Mozart!* prove, like many opera directors Harry Kupfer is also very fond of blatant symbolism, especially in his use of stage design. The oversized insignia of the Habsburg Empire (the crown, the eagle, carriages) in the former, and the tilted, looming ceilings of various Viennese and Salzburg residences in the latter threaten to crush the protagonists in both musicals.

53. In German, 'der Friedhof der Vergangenheit'; Kunze and Levay, *Elisabeth: Libretto der deutschen Erstauffuhrung*, 9.

54. In German, 'An Deck der sinkenden Welt'; ibid., 77.

55. This has occasionally encouraged some of the actors in the show to over-do the rock licks in their big solos: Oedo Kuipers (Mozart) and—to a lesser degree—Mark Seibert (Colloredo) in the 2015 Viennese production (available on DVD)—can serve as examples of how quickly seemingly valid performance choices can turn into mannerisms.

56. It is illogical that in a show which otherwise is performed completely in German, the courtiers in Versailles (act 1, scene 10), Cagliostro and a national guard in the Parisian Temple Prison (act 2, scene 9) should occasionally speak French; Kunze and Levay, *Marie Antoinette: Das Musical; Libretto*, 52, 85, and 87.

57. The closest equivalent in an Anglophone musical might be 'Meadowlark' in Stephen Schwartz's *The Baker's Wife* (1976). The main difference is that Geneviève sings the fable to herself; not only is she aware of its allegorical content, she also employs the song to gain new insight and to then reach a decision. Another example from an American show is 'The Schmuel Song' from Jason Robert Brown's 2002 two-hander *The Last Five Years*.

58. 'I thought what would advance us are insight and criticism' ('Ich dachte, was uns weiterbringt, sind Einsicht und Kritik'); Michael Kunze and Sylvester Levay, *Mozart! Ein Musical; Libretto* (Hamburg: Edition Butterfly, 2016), 95.)

59. Kunze and Levay, *Elisabeth: Libretto der deutschen Erstauffuhrung*, 3.

60. Michael Kunze, 'Musical Master Class 9: Drama Musical Structure; The Summary', https://www.youtube.com/watch?v=87IrL5_IUQc, accessed 6 August 2019.

61. Kunze calls *Wicked*, which he translated into German, a 'milestone' in musical theatre history, since he considers it 'the first [show] that really combines the European tradition with the Broadway tradition'; quoted in Collis, 'BWW Interviews: Writer and Interpreter Michael Kunze'. This is another one of his claims that does not withstand scrutiny. I would argue that, among others, *Lady in the Dark* (1941), *My Fair Lady* (1956), *Cabaret* (1966), *A Little Night Music* (1973), and *Sweeney Todd, the Demon Barber of Fleet Street* (1979) got there first.

62. 'I'm an American Woman/[ ... ]/Ich bin nicht diskret/[ ... ]/Ausserdem bin ich reich./Ich hab' Swing im Rock/Und Cola in der Kehle,/Und in meiner Seele/Singt ein Gospelchor/[ ... ]/Ich pfeif' auf Geschmack,/Ich mag es schrill./[ ... ]/Ich kann alles, ausser/Einen Fehler machen'; Michael Kunze and Sylvester Levay, *Rebecca: Das Musical; Libretto* (Hamburg: Edition Butterfly, 2006), 52–53.

63. It also completely contradicts Mrs van Hopper's behaviour earlier in the show (act 1, scene 1) when she insists on class and refinement (ibid., 10).

64. H. L. Mencken, 'Notes on Journalism', *Chicago Tribune*, 19 September 1926, 87.

65. 'Man kann das von mir aus Musical nennen, aber was ich mache, ist nicht was darunter verstanden wird'; Kunze, 'Wie ein Drama Musical entsteht'.

THE GERMAN/AUSTRIAN 'DRAMA MUSICAL', OR 'I SING ALONE'    749

66. Kunze, 'Musical Master Class 5'.

67. Collis, 'BWW Interviews: Writer and Interpreter Michael Kunze'.

68. Quoted in ibid.

69. Kunze, 'Wie ein Drama Musical entsteht'.

70. Kunze, 'Musical Master Class 5'.

71. 'If the characters make sense, the action makes sense. And the characters only make sense if their singing makes sense. A song was a projection of character—socially, psychologically, morally and intellectually'; Gerald Mast, *Can't Help Singin': The American Musical on Stage and Screen* (New York: Overlook Press, 1987), 290.

72. Ethan Mordden, *Rodgers & Hammerstein* (New York: Harry N. Abrams, 1992), 54.

73. Bernstein: '[T]he book is the essential basis of musical comedy'; Leonard Bernstein, 'American Musical Comedy', in Bernstein, *The Joy of Music*, 2nd ed (London: Panther Arts, 1968), 168. Sondheim: 'Books are what musical theatre is about, it's not songs, and I'm not being modest'; Stephen Sondheim, 'Theater Lyrics', in *Playwrights, Lyricists, Composers on Theatre: The Inside Story of a Decade of Theater in Articles and Comments by Its Authors, Selected from Their Own Publication, 'The Dramatist Guild Quarterly'* (New York: Dodd, Mead, 1974), 61–97; here: 91. Kislan: Richard Kislan, *The Musical: A Look at the American Musical Theater*, 2nd, rev. and expanded ed. (New York: Applause, 1995), 171.

74. The most obvious example may be 'Brush Up Your Shakespeare', from Cole Porter's *Kiss Me, Kate* (1948).

75. In *Dance of the Vampires*, Alfred arrives shouting, '[I]t's me, Professor, your ingenious and discretion-resistant assistant' ('ich bin's, Professor, Ihr patenter und dezenter resistenter Assistant'); Kunze and Steinman, *Tanz der Vampire: Das Musical; Libretto*, 13. Marie Antoinette's servant announces a visitor to the empress with the words 'Princesse de Lamballe, Her Majesty's friend' ('Princesse de Lamballe, die Freundin Ihrer Majestät!'); Kunze and Levay, *Marie Antoinette: Das Musical; Libretto*, 20. The chance encounter with Sister Agnés has Margrid wonder: 'How does my favourite teacher come to be in Paris?' ('Wie kommt meine Lieblingslehrerin nach Paris?'); ibid., 23.

76. Kislan, The Musical: A Look at the American Musical Theater, 173.

77. Kunze, 'Musical Master Class 5'.

78. Schneider was just sixteen years old when she first appeared as Empress Elisabeth—commonly called 'Sissi'—in the 1955 costume drama of the same name. The film was so successful that it was immediately followed by two sequels, *Sissi: Die junge Kaiserin* (*Sissi, the Young Empress*) and *Schicksalsjahre einer Kaiser* (*Fateful Years of an Empress*). All three movies were written and directed by Ernst Marischka and co-starred Karlheinz Böhm, Magda Schneider, and Gustav Knuth. The trilogy became one of the biggest box-office sensations of the decade and was seen by approximately twenty-five million people in Germany and Austria alone. It was also a smash hit in France and Italy. To this day, the films remain beloved by moviegoers and television audiences; in Germany, they are broadcast at least once a year, usually on Christmas.

79. '[E]ine um ihre Freiheit ringende Frau, die ihrer Zeit weit voraus ist'; Kunze and Levay, *Elisabeth: Libretto der deutschen Erstauffuhrung*, 5.

80. 'Elisabeth ist die Geschichte einer versuchten, aber fehlgeleiteten Emanzipation, die in ihr Gegenteil umschlug. Elisabeth hat sich von den Zwängen des Wiener Hofes befreit, aber mit ihrer Freiheit wußte sie dann nichts anzufangen'; Harry Kupfer, quoted in Sigrid Löffler, '*Elisabeth*: Ein Totentanz', *Die Zeit*, 28 August 1992, https://www.zeit.de/1992/36/elisabeth-ein-totentanz, accessed 25 May 2019.

# 750    OLAF JUBIN

81. '[E]in attraktiver, junger Mann mit der Ausstrahlung eines Popstars'; Kunze and Levay, *Elisabeth: Libretto der deutschen Erstaufführung*, 5.

82. Rommel, Aus der 'Schwarzen Möwe' wird 'Elisabeth', 68. One potentially powerful scene hinting at social unrest, 'Milch' ('Milk', act 1, scene 13), never seizes its dramatic potential: what is the point of having the anarchist, Lucheni, whip the deprived crowds into a frenzy by needling them with stories of Elisabeth's wasteful beauty regime, when the Austrian empress is never confronted with or by the common people?

83. At the beginning of the show, the young Elisabeth confesses that all she wants to do is 'Dream and write poetry/Or ride with the wind' ('Träumen und Gedichte schreiben/Oder reiten mit dem Wind'); Kunze and Levay, *Elisabeth: Libretto der deutschen Erstaufführung*, 12. The authors seem unaware of the irony that in her restless later years Elisabeth winds up doing exactly what she had once hoped for.

84. A. Peter Brown, '*Amadeus* and Mozart: Setting the Record Straight', *American Scholar* 61, no. 1 (1992): 49–66; here: 49.

85. See e.g. Joseph Horowitz, 'Mozart as Midcult: Mass Snob Appeal', *Musical Quarterly* 76, no. 1 (1992): 1–16; and Guido Heldt, 'Playing Mozart: Biopics and the Musical Reinvention of a Composer', *Music, Sound, and the Moving Image* 3, no. 1 (2009): 21–46.

86. 'Aufsteh'n ist ungesund./Ich halt' das grelle Licht nicht aus./[ . . . ]/Für eine Hausfrau hört Arbeit niemals auf./Am besten, ich fang' gar nicht erst an!'; Kunze and Levay, *Mozart! Das Musical; Libretto*, 91.

87. 'Der kleine Pianist entspricht genau dem Bild, das sich Millionen von Mozart gemacht haben: Eine niedliche Rokoko-Ikone der menschlichen Sehnsucht nach engelhafter Unschuld und göttlichem Genie'; ibid., 9.

88. 'Durch dich werde ich frei sein./Wir tun nur, was uns gefällt./Du und ich haben vor nichts und niemand Angst./Uns kann die Pflicht einerlei sein'; ibid., 20–21.

89. 'Ist er wirklich ein Mensch wie wir alle?/[ . . . ]/Gott gab dieser Welt/Das Wunder Mozart./Stern, der die Welt erhellt/Bis an den Rand der Ewigkeit'; ibid., 116–117.

90. 'Nichts auf der Erde war je so vollkommen'; ibid., 117.

91. Pauline Kael, *State of the Art* (New York: E. P. Dutton, 1995), 251.

92. 'Ich bin [ . . . ]/Klug und dumm und geil und brav'; Kunze and Levay, *Mozart! Das Musical; Libretto*, 22.

93. The German 'extraordinär' has a double meaning: it can be translated as either 'extraordinary' or 'extra-vulgar'.

94. This title is another play on words: it can also mean 'Knobhead of Muck'. The song is included in the original Viennese cast recording.

95. 'Ich habe Dutzende Gesichter/Und spiele tausend Rollen'; *Mozart! Die Höhepunkte der Weltaufführung*, CD, track 12: 'Sauschwanz von Drecken', Universal/Polydor, 1999, 543 107-2.

96. When the impresario espouses that philosophy, the stage directions read: 'Mozart is thrilled' ('Mozart ist begeistert'); Kunze and Levay, *Mozart! Das Musical; Libretto*, 48. '[Mozart] takes on various roles. Increasingly, the world seems to him a stage, where all players wear masks' ('[Mozart] schlüpft in verschiedene Rollen. Die Welt erscheint ihm mehr und mehr als Bühne, auf der alle Spieler Masken tragen'); ibid., 6.

97. 'Er lacht albern und ohne erkennbaren Grund'; ibid., 102.

98. Free association: ibid., 63; incoherent: 'Alle böse, böse. Böse Wölfe. Schlangen!', ibid., 102.

99. As a young princess in Bavaria, Elisabeth tells her father that she longs to '[l]ive free like a Gypsy/With the zither tucked under my arm./To only do what I would like to do'

('Leben, frei wie ein Zigeuner/Mit der Zither unterm Arm/Nur tun was ich will'); Kunze and Levay, *Elisabeth: Libretto der deutschen Erstaufführung*, 13. Mozart, for his part, is accused by Leopold: 'You live like a Gypsy.' The young man's reply is: 'I have to be free' ('Du lebst wie ein Zigeuner.'—'Ich muss frei sein.' Kunze and Levay, *Mozart! Das Musical; Libretto*, 99.)

100. At Elisabeth's wedding the guests sing: 'Because we take delight in all suffering/We love to see you go under/Elisabeth' ('Weil jedes Leid uns delektiert/Seh'n wir dich gerne untergeh'n/Elisabeth'); Kunze and Levay, *Elisabeth: Libretto der deutschen Erstaufführung*, 25–26. In 'Happy Apocalypse', assorted intellectuals—specified in the libretto as journalists, professors, students, poets, and bohemians—profess that neither looming wars nor political stalemate will upset their inertia and boredom.

101. 'Halten Sie den Atem an!' will be discussed in more detail below. 'Hier in Wien': 'Here in Vienna/Where the infants already start to/Weave webs of intrigue because it's entertaining/[ ... ]/Where they can forgive everything/Except being successful/[ ... ]/Vienna stays Vienna/That is a threat' ('Hier in Wien/Wo schon die Kinder beginnen/Intrigen zu spinnen weil es unterhält/[ ... ]/Wo man alles verzeiht/Nur nicht, dass irgendwer erfolgreich ist./[ ... ]/Wien bleibt Wien./Das ist eine Drohung'); Kunze and Levay, *Mozart! Das Musical; Libretto*, 75–76.

102. This criticism of the audience is especially pronounced in 'Kitsch', the opening number of *Elisabeth*'s second act, where the theatregoers are chastised by Luigi Lucheni for favouring the myth above the facts: 'Don't pretend/You are interested in the truth!' ('Tut bloss nicht so,/Als wärt Ihr an der Wahrheit interessiert!'); Kunze and Levay, *Elisabeth: Libretto der deutschen Erstaufführung*, 49–50.

103. In spite of its critical reception—the show was universally panned by the Viennese critics (see Rommel, *Aus der 'Schwarzen Mowe' wird 'Elisabeth'*, 97—100)—*Elisabeth* became a massive hit. It ran for six seasons, until 1998, and had 1,239 performances, selling 1.25 million tickets; Peter Back-Vega, *Theater an der Wien: 40 Jahre Musical* (Vienna: Almathea Signum Verlag, 2008), 149.

104. In his historical overview of the forty years during which the Theater an der Wien only offered musicals, Back-Vega addresses this topic several times; ibid., see e.g. 30, 46, and 150. After the discourse on how to best use the venue was reignited in the early 2000s, the city of Vienna finally gave in to the artistically conservative voices and announced that the famous building from 2006 onwards would once again host only classical performances. Since then, the theatre has acquired a new title: 'the New Opera House'.

105. Rommel, *Aus der 'Schwarzen Mowe' wird 'Elisabeth'*, 98.

106. 'Niemand meint das, was er sagt./Jeder Freund/Ist ein heimlicher Feind'; Kunze and Levay, *Marie Antoinette: Das Musical; Libretto*, 73.

107. See the show's German-language Wikipedia page for a detailed list of which numbers or musical motifs from the score are based on material originally used elsewhere; https://de.wikipedia.org/wiki/Tanz_der_Vampire_(Musical), accessed 5 May 2019.

108. See McKinleyjan, '*Dance of the Vampires*, a \$12 Million Broadway Failure, Is Closing', for more details.

109. See e.g. the debate (predominantly in American media outlets) over whether his 2019 movie, *J'accuse (An Officer and Spy)*, should have been included in the line-up for that year's Venice film festival. A typical broadside would be Scott Roxborough and Tatiana Siegel, ' "Completely Tone-Deaf!": How Venice Became the F-You Film Festival', https://

www.hollywoodreporter.com/news/how-venice-film-fest-became-tone-deaf-metoo-times-up-1233163, accessed 24 August 2019.

110. Kunze and Steinman, *Tanz der Vampire: Musical; Libretto*, 93.

111. Professor Ambronsius, referring to bulbs of garlic, asks Alfred: 'What do you think of these small round things, boy?' His assistant, fascinated by Magda's cleavage, replies: 'Small? They're big!' ('Was hältst du von diesen kleinen runden Dingern, Junge?'—'Klein? Sie sind gross!'); ibid., 17.

112. Other adjectives used by the journalists to describe the songwriter's signature style include 'Wagnerian', 'almost pantomime', 'extravagant', and 'over-the-top'; see James Hall, 'The Best-Selling Album Nobody Wanted to Release: How Jim Steinman and Meat Loaf Made *Bat out of Hell*', *Daily Telegraph*, 20 June 2017, https://www.telegraph.co.uk/music/artists/best-selling-album-nobody-wanted-release-jim-steinman-meat-loaf/, accessed 23 August 2019; and Dave Itzkoff, 'Bursting onto the Stage like a *Bat out of Hell*', *New York Times*, 25 July 2019, https://www.mytimes.om/2019/07/25/arts/meatloaf-bat-out-hell.html, accessed 23 August 2019.

113. '[Count Krolock] realises the misery of his existence. Whenever he grasps for happiness, he destroys it. The more he tries to satisfy his greed, the bigger it becomes' ('Ihm wird das Elend seiner Existenz bewusst. Wann immer er nach dem Glück greift, zerstört er es eben dadurch. Je mehr er seien Gier zu stillen versucht, desto grösser wird sie'); Kunze and Steinman, *Tanz der Vampire: Das Musical; Libretto*, 11.

114. A crucial addition to the stage version is Alfred's realisation that '[vampires] have feelings!/Just as we do' ('Sie haben Gefühle!/Genau wie wir'); ibid., 101.

115. Even before the Gilbert and Sullivan–style tongue-twister was more or less completely replaced in musical theatre by fast-flowing rap cadences, it was rarely employed. The only other major example of this kind of song from the turn of the millennium might be 'Words, Words, Words' from *The Witches of Eastwick* (2000).

116. See Olive Laing, 'Sex, Jealousy and Gender: Daphne du Maurier's *Rebecca* 80 Years On', *Guardian*, 23 February 2018, https://www.theguardian.com/books/2018/feb/23/olivia-laing-on-daphne-du-mauriers-rebecca-80-years-on, accessed 24 August 2019.

117. See Robin Wood, *Hitchcock Revisited* (London and Boston: Faber & Faber, 1989), 231–232.

118. See Robin Wood, 'The Two Mrs de Winters', in *Alfred Hitchcock's Rebecca*, DVD booklet, Criterion Collection #135, CC1576D, 2001, 5-8; here: 6.

119. The second Mrs de Winter asks him 'But it was an accident, wasn't it?' ('Es war doch ein Unfall . . . oder?'), to which Maxim responds: 'Ich weiss es nicht. Ich schwöre, ich weiss es nicht', which can be translated as either 'I don't remember. I swear, I don't remember' or 'I can't tell. I swear, I can't tell'; Kunze and Levay, *Rebecca: Das Musical; Libretto*, 71.

120. In act 1, scene 'I' apologises to her employer using the English (!) expression 'sorry' (ibid., 7), while Mrs van Hopper chides her lady companion for 'gawping' and 'ogling' (8)—the German verbs ('glotzen' and 'begaffen') here are decidedly slangy for a woman who may be crude but is still a member of high society.

121. The German première took place in 2009 in Bremen, where over the course of 120 performances the show accrued a huge deficit; 'Musical *Marie Antoinette* mit Millionverlusten', *Hannoversche Allgemeine*, 2 June 2009, https://www.haz.de/Nachrichten/Kultur/Uebersicht/Musical-Marie-Antoinette-mit-Millionenverlust, accessed 24 August 2019. The only other German-language production was staged three years later in Tecklenburg's open-air theatre.

122. 'My mother taught me/That it is unseemly/For the rulers of the world/To be sentimental' ('Herrschern der Welt/Lehrte mich Mutter,/Ziemt es nicht/Sentimental zu sein'); Kunze and Levay, *Marie Antoinette: Das Musical; Libretto*, 64.

123. After Marie Antoinette's execution, her lover, Axel von Fersen, states: 'And only death/Did free you' ('Und erst der Tod/Hat dich befreit'); ibid., 106.

124. Marie Antoinette: 'Ich will leben,/Ich will jung sein/Und vergnügt./Ich will lachen,/Ich will Dummheiten machen,/Und ich will tanzen im Licht'; ibid., 14. Sarah: 'I want music./I want to dance and float' ('Ich will Musik./Ich will tanzen und schweben'); Kunze and Levay, *Tanz der Vampire: Das Musical; Libretto*, 48. Constanze: 'There's always dancing somewhere/And it would be such a pity/To miss any fun./I like to live, I like to give/I like to float on dreams' ('Irgendwo wird immer getanzt,/Und es wäre do zu schad'/Einen Spass zu versäumen./Ich leb' gern, ich geb' gern,/Ich schweb' gern auf Träumen'); Kunze and Levay, *Mozart! Das Musical; Libretto*, 91.

125. These missteps include her cruel jest of pouring champagne over Margrid's head in front of Parisian society, her financially irresponsible urge to dwell in the utmost luxury, and her infamous utterance 'Let them eat cake', which even the authors themselves judge to be a 'stupid remark'; Kunze and Levay, *Marie Antoinette: Das Musical; Libretto*, 13. The Austrian empress gains insight only during her ordeal: 'Here and now I realise/I am truly myself only in my suffering' ('Jetzt und hier erkenn' ich mich./Erst im Leid bin ich ganz ich'); ibid., 102.

126. Kunze, 'Musical Master Class 9'.

127. The authors never resolve the mystery of who the girl's father is, while the physical resemblance between Margrid Arnaud and Marie Antoinette—the dialogue helpfully points out that they even share the same initials (Kunze and Levay, *Marie Antoinette: Das Musical; Libretto*, 8)—is never properly exploited apart from Margrid's brief involvement in the necklace affair. In addition, her stint as a spy in the employ of the empress turns into a narrative dead end, not least because Marie Antoinette immediately recognises her. Finally, Kunze and Levay skirt over Margrid's descend into prostitution.

128. Kunze, 'Musical Master Class 1'.

129. 'I believe in drama as the key entertainment in theatre'; quoted in Collis, 'BWW Interviews: Writer and Interpreter Michael Kunze'.

130. Quoted in ibid.

131. Quoted in ibid.

132. A list of these artists would include, in vaguely chronological order, Kurt Weill, E. Y. Harburg, Marc Blitzstein, Leonard Bernstein, Arthur Laurents, Harold Prince, Stephen Sondheim, John Weidman, John Kander and Fred Ebb, and Jeanine Tesori in the United States; and Gilbert and Sullivan, Monty Norman, Wolf Mankowitz, Lionel Bart, Joan Littlewood, Peter Nichols, John McGrath, Willy Russell, Lee Hall, and Richard Thomas in the United Kingdom.

133. Roman Polanski has blamed interference by the producer Martin Ransohoff for the fact that his film was a commercial misfire in the United States, yet a huge hit abroad. For its North American release, MGM wanted to make the movie more 'farcical' and thus retitled it *The Fearless Vampire Killers or Pardon Me but Your Teeth Are in My Neck*; the studio partly redubbed it, removed twelve minutes of material, and also added an animated sequence at the beginning, all without consulting the director. American Film Institute, *Dialogue on Film: Roman Polanski*, vol. 3, no. 8 (Beverly Hills: American Film Institute, 1974), 9; Christopher Sandford, *Polanski* (London: Century, 2007), 131; and

754 OLAF JUBIN

Roman Polanski, *Roman Polanski*, trans. Günter Panske (Bern: Scherz Verlag,1984), 233–234. Since then the movie has been restored and is now available only in the form Polanski intended. Hitchcock's *Rebecca* (1940), still the most famous of the novel's adaptations, was decades later followed by two TV miniseries (1979 and 1997) and a 2020 Netflix film. All of these were either made by British companies (the BBC and Carlton Television, respectively) or initiated by British artists, like the latest version, which was written by Jane Goldman and directed by Ben Wheatley; this indicates that over the decades the source material has resonated the strongest in the author's homeland.

134. It should be noted that all of Lerner and Loewe's major works are set in the European past, including *Brigadoon* (1947), *My Fair Lady* (1956), *Gigi* (1958), and *Camelot* (1960).

135. 'I don't want that!'; Kunze, 'Musical Master Class 5'.

136. Ibid.

137. Ibid.

138. In the latter show, the involvement of the theatregoers—some of the action takes place in the auditorium—can partly be explained as a consequence of the musical's overall parodic tone.

139. Kunze and Steinman, *Tanz der Vampire: Das Musical; Libretto*, 108.

140. Rommel, *Aus der 'Schwarzen Mowe' wird 'Elisabeth'*, 67–68.

141. 'Euch Sterblichen von morgen/Prophezeih' ich heut' und hier:/Sobald euer neues nächstes Jahrtausend beginnt,/Ist der einzige Gott/Dem jeder dient,/Die unstillbare Gier'; Kunze and Steinman, *Tanz der Vampire: Das Musical; Libretto*, 101.

142. 'Sei ein Schwein/Oder man macht dich zur Sau./[ ... ]/Zeig' deine Faust,/Denn sonst wirst du geschlagen./[ ... ]/Willst du bestimmen,/Statt and're zu fragen/Musst du lernen über Leichen zu geh'n'; ibid., 110.

143. 'Denn wie man sich bettet, so liegt man/Es deckt einen da keiner zu./Und wenn einer tritt, dann bin ich es./Und wird einer getreten, dann bist's du'; Bertolt Brecht and Kurt Weill, 'Denn wie man sich bettet', https://muzikum.eu/en/123-797-118238/jenny-arean/denn-wie-mann-sich-bettet-lyrics.html, accessed 7 July 2019. The 'Alabama Song' also seems to have coloured Margrid's reaction to seeing Madame Lapin being whipped to death in *Marie Antoinette*: 'Those who are helpless/Get kicked/And nobody takes pity/No matter how loud we scream' ('Wer hilflos ist/Auf den wir eingetreten/Und niemand erbarmt sich,/So laut wir auch schrei'n'); Kunze and Levay, *Marie Antoinette: Das Musical; Libretto*, 39.

144. 'Wir trinken Blut/wir haben null Moral./Was aus dieser Welt wird, ist uns scheissegal'; Kunze and Steinman, *Tanz der Vampire: Das Musical; Libretto*, 114. The vampires then go on in English (!): 'We drink your blood and then we eat your soul./Nothing's gonna stop us, let the bad times roll'; ibid.

145. 'Nothing satisfies our hunger/The greed never stops' ('Nichts macht uns satt./Die Gier kommt nie zur Ruh'); ibid., 103.

146. 'Die Welt ist voll Wunder/Und jedes ist irgendein Trick./Alles Schwindel!/Alles Betrug!/Ist heut einer ehrlich,/Dann ist er nicht klug./Im Handeln und Reden belügt Jeder Jeden/Zum eigenen Vorteil und weil's jeder so macht'; Kunze and Levay, *Mozart! Das Musical; Libretto*, 57.

147. 'Wir sind Britisch, wir sind fein./Wir sind ein exclusiver Verein'; Kunze and Levay, *Rebecca: Das Musical; Libretto*, 42.

148. 'Ein komisches Tableau'; ibid., 43.

149. See e.g. the Prologue and act 1, scenes 1 and 8, and act 2, scenes 1, 6, and 13.

## Bibliography

American Film Institute. *Dialogue on Film: Roman Polanski*, vol. 3, no. 8. Beverly Hills: American Film Institute, 1974.

Back-Vega, Peter. *Theater an der Wien: 40 Jahre Musical*. Vienna: Almathea Signum Verlag, 2008.

Benjamin, Walter. 'Die Aufgabe des Übersetzters'. In *Das Problem des Übersetzens*, edited by Hans Joachim Störig, 182–195. Darmstadt: Goverts, 1963.

Bernstein, Leonard. 'American Musical Comedy'. In Leonard Bernstein, *The Joy of Music*, 2nd ed., 152–179. London: Panther Arts, 1968.

Brown, Peter. '*Amadeus* and Mozart: Setting the Record Straight'. *American Scholar* 61, no. 1 (1992): 49–66.

Collis, Jonathon. 'BWW Interviews: Writer and Interpreter Michael Kunze', 2 October 2009, https://www.broadwayworld.com/westend/article/BWW-INTERVIEWS-Writer-And-Inte rpreter-Michael-Kunze-20091002, accessed 1 May 2019.

du Maurier, Daphne. *Rebecca*. With an afterword by Sally Beauman. 1938; London: Virago, 2003.

*Elisabeth: Live aus dem Theater an der Wien*. DVD. Hit Squad Records 6682527, 2006.

Haizmann, Susanne. 'Im Gespräch mit Dennis Callahan'. *Musicals: Das Musicalmagazin* 73 (1998): 28.

Hall, James. 'The Best-Selling Album Nobody Wanted to Release: How Jim Steinman and Meat Loaf Made *Bat out of Hell*'. *Daily Telegraph*, 20 June 2017, https://www.telegraph. co.uk/music/artists/best-selling-album-nobody-wanted-release-jim-steinman-meat-loaf/, accessed 23 August 2019,

Heldt, Guido. 'Playing Mozart: Biopics and the Musical Reinvention of a Composer'. *Music, Sound, and the Moving Image* 3, no. 1 (2009): 21–46.

Hesse-Quack, Otto. *Der Übertragungsprozeß bei der Synchronisation von Filmen: Eine interkulturelle Untersuchung*. Munich: E. Reinhardt, 1969.

Horowitz, Joseph. 'Mozart as Midcult: Mass Snob Appeal'. *Musical Quarterly* 76, no. 1 (1992): 1–16, https://de.wikipedia.org/wiki/Tanz_der_Vampire_(Musical), accessed 5 May 2019.

Huber, Eugene Robert. 'Stephen Sondheim and Harold Prince: Collaborative Contributions to the Development of the Modern Concept Musical, 1970–1981'. PhD diss., New York University, 1990.

Itzkoff, Dave. 'Bursting onto the Stage like a *Bat out of Hell*'. *New York Times*, 25 July 2019, https://www.mytimes.om/2019/07/25/arts/meatloaf-bat-out-hell.html, accessed 23 August 2019.

Jubin, Olaf. *Entertainment in der Kritik: Eine comparative Analyse von amerikanischen, britischen und deutschsprachigen Rezensionen zu den Musicals von Stephen Sondheim und Andrew Lloyd Webber*. Herbolzheim: Centaurus Verlag, 2005.

Kael, Pauline. *State of the Art*. New York: E. P. Dutton, 1995.

Kamp, David. 'The Road to *Rebecca*'. *Vanity Fair*, June 2013, 106–118.

Katsura, Mana. '*Lady Bess* Set to Make Grand Tokyo Entrance'. *Japan Times*, 9 April 2014, https://www.japantimes.co.jp/tag/lady-bess/, accessed 7 May 2019.

Kislan, Richard. *The Musical: A Look at the American Musical Theater*. 2nd, rev. and expanded ed. New York: Applause, 1995.

Kunze, Michael. 'How to Write a Musical Drama: 9 Essential Drama Elements', https://www.sli deshare.net/chefkeem/how-to-write-a-musical-drama', accessed 4 April 2019.

Kunze, Michael. 'Musical Master Class 1: Introduction, Michael Kunze', 23 March 2011, https://www.youtube.com/watch?v=87IrL5_IUQc, accessed 6 August 2019.

Kunze, Michael. 'Musical Master Class 2: Discovering Musical Theatre', 23 March 2011, https://www.youtube.com/watch?v=87IrL5_IUQc, accessed 6 August 2019.

Kunze, Michael. 'Musical Master Class 3: Adaptions [*sic*]', 23 March 2011, https://www.youtube.com/watch?v=87IrL5_IUQc, accessed 6 August 2019.

Kunze, Michael. 'Musical Master Class 5: Developing the Drama Musical *Elisabeth*', 23 March 2011, https://www.youtube.com/watch?v=87IrL5_IUQc, accessed 6 August 2019.

Kunze, Kunze. 'Musical Master Class 6: Basic Drama Musical Structure', 23 March 2011, https://www.youtube.com/watch?v=87IrL5_IUQc, accessed 6 August 2019.

Kunze, Michael. 'Musical Master Class 8: Serve the Story', 23 March 2011, https://www.youtube.com/watch?v=87IrL5_IUQc, accessed 6 August 2019.

Kunze, Michael. 'Musical Master Class 9: Drama Musical Structure; The Summary', 23 March 2011, https://www.youtube.com/watch?v=87IrL5_IUQc, accessed 6 August 2019.

Kunze, Michael. 'Von der Idee zur Premiere: Die Entstehung eines DramaMusicals. Teil 4: Besondere Elemente des Musiktheaters', http://storyarchitekt.com/workshop/masterclass4.php, accessed 7 May 2019.

Kunze, Michael. 'Von der Idee zur Premiere: Die Entstehung eines DramaMusicals. Teil 14: Weitere Figuren des Musicals II', http://storyarchitekt.com/workshop/masterclass14.php, accessed 7 May 2019.

Kunze, Michael. 'What Is a Drama Musical?', 27 September 2009, https://www.youtube.com/watch?v=kakSRwdiWcg, accessed 6 August 2019.

Kunze, Michael. 'Wie ein Drama Musical entsteht', https://pagewizz.com/michael-kunze, accessed 8 November 2018.

Kunze, Michael, and Sylvester Levay. *Elisabeth: Libretto der deutschen Erstaufführung*. Grünwald: Edition Butterfly, 2001.

Kunze, Michael, and Sylvester Levay. *Marie Antoinette: Das Musical; Libretto*. Hamburg: Edition Butterfly, 2009.

Kunze, Michael, and Sylvester Levay. *Mozart! Das Musical; Libretto*. Hamburg: Edition Butterfly, 2016.

Kunze, Michael, and Sylvester Levay. *Rebecca: Das Musical; Libretto*. Hamburg: Edition Butterfly, 2006.

Kunze, Michael, and Jim Steinman. *Tanz der Vampire: Das Musical; Libretto*. Hamburg: Edition Butterfly, 2018.

Laing, Olive. 'Sex, Jealousy and Gender: Daphne du Maurier's *Rebecca* 80 Years On'. *The Guardian*, 23 February 2018, https://www.theguardian.com/books/2018/feb/23/olivia-laing-on-daphne-du-mauriers-rebecca-80-years-on, accessed 24 August 2019.

Löffler, Sigrid. '*Elisabeth*: Ein Totentanz'. *Die Zeit*, 28 August 1992, https://www.zeit.de/1992/36/elisabeth-ein-totentanz, accessed 25 May 2019.

Mast, Gerald. *Can't Help Singin': The American Musical on Stage and Screen*. New York: Overlook Press, 1987.

McKee, Robert. *Story: Substance, Structure, Style, and the Principles of Screenwriting*. New York: itBooks, 1997.

McKinleyjan, Jessie. '*Dance of the Vampires*, a $12 Million Broadway Failure, Is Closing'. *New York Times*, 16 January 2003, https://www.nytimes.com/2003/01/16/theater/dance-of-the-vampires-a-12-million-broadway-failure-is-closing.html, accessed 15 May 2019.

Mencken, H. L. 'Notes on Journalism'. *Chicago Tribune*, 19 September 1926, 87.

Mordden, Ethan. *Rodgers & Hammerstein*. New York: Harry N. Abrams, 1992.

*Mozart! Die Höhepunkte der Weltaufführung*. CD. Universal/Polydor, 1999, 543 107-2.

*Mozart! Das Musical*. DVD. Hit Squad Records, 2016, 668368.

'Musical *Marie Antoinette* mit Millionverlusten'. *Hannoversche Allgemeine*, 2 June 2009, https://www.haz.de/Nachrichten/Kultur/Uebersicht/Musical-Marie-Antoinette-mit-Millionen verlust, accessed 24 August 2019.

Polanski, Roman. *Roman Polanski*. Translated by Günter Panske. Bern: Scherz Verlag, 1984.

'Review: *Rebecca*'. *Variety*, 8 October 2006, http://variety.com/2006/legit/reviews/rebecca-3-1200512838/, accessed 6 June 2019.

Reichardt, Angela. 'Im Gespräch mit Michael Kunze'. *Musicals: Das Musicalmagazin* 88 (2001): 21.

Riedel, Michael. 'Hate at 1st Bite: How *Vampires* Got Drained of Its Blood'. *New York Post*, 13 December 2002, https://nypost.com/2002/12/13/hate-at-1st-bite-how-vampires-got-drai ned-of-its-blood/, accessed 15 June 2019.

Rommel, Birgit. *Aus der 'Schwarzen Möwe' wird 'Elisabeth': Entstehung und Inszenierungsgeschichte des Musicals über die Kaiserin von Österreich*. Hamburg: Diplomica Verlag Gmbh, 2007.

Roxborough, Scott, and Tatiana Siegel. '"Completely Tone-Deaf!" How Venice Became the F-You Film Festival', *The Hollywood Reporter*, 23 August 2019, https://www.hollywoodrepor ter.com/news/how-venice-film-fest-became-tone-deaf-metoo-times-up-1233163, accessed 24 August 2019.

Sandford, Christopher. *Polanski*. London: Century, 2007.

Sondheim, Stephen. 'Theater Lyrics'. In *Playwrights, Lyricists, Composers on Theatre: The Inside Story of a Decade of Theater in Articles and Comments by Its Authors, Selected from Their Own Publication, the Dramatist Guild Quarterly*, edited by Otis L. Guernsey, 61–97. New York: Dodd, Mead, 1974.

Sternfeld, Jessica. *The Megamusical*. Bloomington: Indiana University Press, 2006.

Swain, Joseph P. *The Broadway Musical: A Critical and Musical Survey*. Oxford and New York: Oxford University Press, 1990.

Wood, Robin. 'The Two Mrs de Winters'. In *Alfred Hitchcock's 'Rebecca'*, DVD booklet, 5–8. Criterion Collection #135, CC1576D, New York: Criterion, 2001.

Wood, Robin. *Hitchcock Revisited*. London and Boston: Faber & Faber, 1989.

Zarges, Torsten. 'Erst Kaiserin Elisabeth, jetzt Mozart: Michael Kunze im Gespräch mit Torsten Zarges'. *Musicals: Das Musicalmagazin* 79 (1999): 14–17.

# CHAPTER 27

---

# THE SWEDISH FOLK MUSICAL

---

## MIKAEL STRÖMBERG

It is difficult not to compare *Kristina från Duvemåla*, first staged in 1995, with the 1999 musical megahit *Mamma Mia!*, since they have the same lyricist and composer—Björn Ulvaeus and Benny Andersson. The two musicals differ in a number of ways. *Kristina* is tragic, with a strong story based on real events from Swedish history. It has an elaborate score with few standout numbers or songs. *Mamma Mia!*, on the other hand, is a romantic comedy whose story is just a vehicle for a long list of ABBA hits. Another thing that sets the two musicals apart is that the former has only been fully staged in Sweden and Finland, while the latter is performed all over the world, having been seen by more than sixty-five million people.[1] Why has *Kristina från Duvemåla* not been able to attract a larger international audience? The answer may be that the extensive use of specific Swedish references, familiar to a Swedish audience, prevents *Kristina* from being successful on global musical stages.

As the idea of the people—in Swedish, *folket* (from the same root as *das Volk* in German)—grew in popularity during the nineteenth century, it was often connected to nationalism.[2] In Sweden, however, it was not that important as a unifying force related to nationality, primarily because Sweden has been a stable nation-state for a very long time.[3] *Folket* was rather connected to a specific cultural heritage. The traditions and customs of the Swedish people living in the countryside became recognised as a valuable heritage that should be cherished and kept alive. This idea is still active in *Kristina från Duvemåla*. By using music inspired by Swedish folk music and adapting a set of popular novels by Vilhelm Moberg—*Utvandrarna* (*The Emigrants*, 1949), *Invandrarna* (*Unto a Good Land*, 1952), *Nybyggarna* (*The Settlers*, 1956), and *Sista brevet hem* (*The Last Letter Home*, 1959)—regarded by many as Swedish classics, the musical glorifies a Swedish cultural heritage through signs associated with the Swedish countryside, making it a Swedish folk musical, or perhaps a Swedish people's opera, rather than a musical destined for an international stage.

FIG. 27.1 The cast and creators of the original 1995 production of *Kristina från Duvemåla*. Back row, from left: Lars Rudolfsson (director), Benny Andersson (composer), and Björn Ulvaeus (lyrics and book). *Front row*: Helen Sjöholm (Kristina), Anders Ekborg (Karl Oskar), Åsa Bergh (Ulrika), and Peter Jöback (Robert). Photo: Brannäs Mikael, provided by the editors.

## Sweden and Emigration

Sweden was fortunate enough not to have been actively involved in either World War I or World War II. The most recent traumatic development for the nation as a whole occurred during the middle and second half of the nineteenth century, when a large number of Swedes left their homes in search of a better life in America. The Swedish population doubled during the nineteenth century from little more than 2.5 million inhabitants to 5 million in 1900. Roughly 80 percent of the population lived in the countryside, and a majority of them worked as farmers or hired hands smaller farms.[4] Starvation was a huge problem. Either too much or too little rain could result in severe consequences, with far-reaching implications for large areas and many, many Swedes.

The peasants were in addition badly affected by a number of agricultural land reforms called partitions (*Skiftesreformer*). These new government regulations amounted to the greatest land reform in Swedish history.[5] They slowly changed the way the countryside and smaller communities had been organised since the Middle Ages. The aim was to increase profits by shifting the land of small village communities and relocating its inhabitants.[6] Some farmers benefited greatly from the reform, while others found themselves unable to earn a living. The result for the poorest among them was devastation. As the number of poor grew, most were forced to leave their homes and live in cottages built for those without land.

As it became more and more difficult to survive in Sweden, dreams of a better future, of better living conditions, began to spread. Reports from America on the prosperous country on the other side of the ocean started to circulate, and more and more people saw emigration as their only viable option.[7] Even though it was only a dream, the uncertain future held more promise than the actual living conditions in Sweden. The hope of something better became so strong that more than a million people decided to leave their homes for the chance of a better future in America.[8]

# Kristina från Duvemåla

A rather serious depiction of demographic changes in Sweden is the starting point for *Kristina från Duvemåla*, one of the most popular Swedish musicals. The musical follows the journey of a group of emigrants—Kristina; her husband, Karl Oskar; his brother, Robert; Ulrika i Västergöhl; and several of their friends and relatives—as they travel across the Atlantic in search of a new home.[9]

Emigration from Sweden to America began around 1840 and increased incrementally during the rest of the century.[10] Act 1 of the musical depicts life in Sweden in 1844, especially the living conditions in and around the small village of Duvemåla in Småland, followed by the journey across the Atlantic Ocean. Act 2 is set in America as the emigrants work on their new home outside Minnesota. After its première in 1995 at the opera house in Malmö, the musical transferred to the Gothenburg Opera (1996) and in 1998 to the Cirkus Arena in Stockholm.[11] Its revival at the Swedish Theatre in Helsinki in 2012 was followed by another Swedish run in Gothenburg and Stockholm. In November 2015 the number of performances since its première twenty years earlier hit one thousand performances. When the run ended in 2016, the musical had been performed 1,037 times and attracted an audience of more than 1.3 million people.[12] Despite its popularity in Sweden, the musical has never managed to appeal to an international audience. Although its creators have made several attempts to secure financing for an English-language staging of *Kristina*,[13] including concert presentations in New York's Carnegie Hall (2009) and London's Royal Albert Hall (2010), there has so far been no full-scale production of the show outside of Sweden and Finland.

# A Swedish Classic

*Kristina från Duvemåla* is an adaptation of Vilhelm Moberg's (1898–1973) epic tale in four parts of a family's struggle to leave Sweden in pursuit of a dream of better prospects in America. Moberg was a Swedish journalist, author, playwright, historian, and debater. He wrote several much-loved novels, including *Raskens* (1927) and *Ride This Night* (*Rid i natt*, 1941). However, he is primarily associated with the *Emigrant* series published between 1949 and 1959.[14] Moberg often turned to the life of the hard-working lower classes of society, their customs and traditions, as inspiration for his novels. A closeness to nature and dependence on the earth for growing crops to support one's family are recurring themes in Moberg's work. His books are seen not only as great literary works, but also as important depictions of Swedish social history.[15] The emigration quartet combines historical details in a fictional narrative, making it a gripping testimony of what life in Sweden might have been like during the mid-nineteenth century. Having seen at first hand how emigration affected not only the emigrants themselves but also the people left behind, Moberg gave a national trauma an artistic form, turning the suffering of the poorest part of the population into a vivid and captivating story.[16]

## THE COUNTRYSIDE

The countryside has been an important political topic in Sweden for more than a hundred years. The division between city and countryside can be traced back to the second half of the nineteenth century. Before that, almost all of Sweden was rural.[17] There were a few larger cities, but since urbanisation was intertwined with industrialisation, most cities were only established in the later part of the century. The late onset of the Industrial Revolution, which did not start in that country until between 1870 and 1890, meant that for the most part Sweden had a rural economy during almost all of the nineteenth century. Following the Industrial Revolution people left the countryside in search of new work opportunities in the growing cities. As Sweden slowly became more and more urbanised, the countryside, both in actuality and as an idea, changed.

The countryside slowly became separated from the city, not just physically but also through what it came to represent. As I explain below, there was a need within certain groups of society to distinguish the city or urban areas from the rest of the country. The city was associated with rapid technological advancements and a new or modern lifestyle, while the countryside was connected to history and tradition, to something stable and old-fashioned. This coincides with a renegotiation of Sweden as a nation-state, where two opposing viewpoints struggled for precedence. One view, primarily represented by the upper classes of society, advocated an idealised image of Sweden connected to its history. This romantic image of the nation and its people gradually changed. The strong emphasis on Sweden's past was replaced by a focus on the future and what the nation could become, primarily advocated by different people's or popular movements (*folkrörelser*).[18]

Consequently, different groups within society as well as different social classes used the countryside in different ways. Organisations among the working classes, for example the temperance movement, actively used the countryside to advocate a healthy lifestyle by arguing for a connection between nature, sobriety, health, and Swedish history through hiking and other outdoor activities. Urban residents started to travel to the countryside to experience not only their historical and cultural heritage, but also the nature and the health and fresh air with which it was associated.

The gap between the city and countryside grew wider as urban residents' romanticised image cultivated the latter as 'harmonious and happy'. The rural landscape became part of a heritage that was to be preserved. During the 1930s and 1940s the ideal of the countryside had another boost and rose in popularity again as urban residents, predominantly from the middle and upper classes, started to buy summer houses there. This strengthened the association of the countryside with recreation and with a place connected to leisure and holidays. As this further developed during the ensuing decades, Swedes became tourists in their own country.

Thus, the idea of the charming countryside has been strong in Sweden from the turn of the nineteenth century until today. However, a competing image—that of an abandoned place—was introduced in newspaper articles and films, and on TV during the last decades of the twentieth century, primarily by debaters, journalists, and organisations actually living or working in the countryside. They believed it was neglected and slowly becoming deserted.

The ongoing process of urbanisation has had severe consequences for rural areas in Sweden, and the government has launched several initiatives to revive them. Huge sums are allocated each year to support these areas and stimulate a reverse movement from the city to the country. One way of stimulating an interest in country life, thereby reducing the steady flow of people leaving in favour of urban life, has been to emphasise the idealised image of the countryside more strongly. The ongoing process of urbanisation, therefore, both undermines the actual countryside and reinforces an idealised image of what it should be.

## CREATING A SWEDISH LOOK: SCENOGRAPHY AND COSTUMES

The concept of the countryside as a place to be proud of and to enjoy lies at the heart of *Kristina från Duvemåla*. Even though only half the musical takes place in Sweden, one of its key aims is the idealisation of the rural Swedish landscape. Strong visual images overpower some of the other historical themes, such as refugees seeking a new home. Regardless of whether hardship or happiness is being depicted, the musical strengthens the belief in the rural environment as a valuable cultural heritage, something important for the Swedish people not just today but throughout history. What the natural environment of Sweden looks like and how it sounds is an integral part of *Kristina från Duvemåla*, making the musical distinctively Swedish. The emphasis on a Swedish look invites the audience to dream about a national heritage, to recognise and be proud of the beauty of nature—an apple tree, or a grassy meadow surrounded by birches. However, the musical does not treat beautiful natural surroundings as something entirely positive. The strong emphasis on nature is also connected to Kristina, the heroine, and her homesickness. Her memories of the pastures surrounding Duvemåla function as both a precious memory and the cause of her uneasy feeling of never being at home. In this context, the stage production's use of clear and distinct images works together with the score and the lyrics to enhance the importance of the countryside.

A substantial part of the success of *Kristina från Duvemåla* resides in its huge stage production.[19] The director, Lars Rudolfsson; the scenographer, Robin Wagner; and the costume designer, Kersti Vitali contributed to a specific visual impression that strengthened the narrative's connection to history and emphasised its uniquely Swedish nature. It is of course difficult to define exactly what constitutes 'Swedish' in this context, but there are certain signs that are familiar to a Swedish audience.

Vitali, who created the costumes for both the original production and the revival, has described their colours and the fabrics as an important part of the scenography, illustrating Kristina's journey through life from Sweden to America. In Sweden Kristina is dressed in dark shades of wool and linen. This gradually changes, and in America she uses lighter materials, such as cotton, together with brighter, warmer colours. All costumes were meant to look handmade: no seams from sewing machines should be visible. The costumes also needed to resemble what people like Kristina wore around 1850.

The lower classes usually wore clothes made from cotton, flax, and wool. Natural colours were common, and a recurring pattern was stripes. The apron was a must for anyone working on a farm or doing any kind of manual labour. It had several different functions and also a variety of forms: it was designed to protect the clothes underneath but was also used as an accessory. There were aprons for rough work on the farm, for indoor use, and for church on Sundays. The appearance could also differ, from aprons with a narrow waist usually topped with pleated fabric, to larger ones that covered most of the skirt. Some aprons had chest flaps, while others had pockets and so on. The aprons came in different colours and patterns depending on what they were used for. Kristina uses several different aprons. Figure 27.2, taken from the revival at the Swedish Theatre in Helsinki in 2012, shows a typical large apron in white with beige stripes.

In Sweden weaving remained a craft until the 1820s. It was mainly a female occupation, done at home during the winter months. The textiles produced were primarily for the weavers' own use, but any surplus was exchanged for food and other necessities. Even after mass production started, weaving in the home continued to play a significant role. This was probably due to the strong traditions of female work and to the fact that there were few other jobs for women at this time. Domestic weaving was mostly seen in a region from Gothenburg to Jönköping, not far from Småland or Duvemåla. Textile production is regarded as a cultural heritage, and many of the factories that started in the middle of the nineteenth century are still producing first-class wool and linen—significant exports from Sweden today. This makes the clothes Kristina wears in the performance a typical sign of Swedish cultural heritage associated with the rural environment. Her clothes represent a tradition of crafting high-quality fabrics that started with women weaving and sewing at home all over Sweden.[20]

FIG. 27.2 Kristina (Maria Ylipää), dressed in a traditional Swedish apron. Scene from *Kristina från Duvemåla*, Svenska Teatern in Helsinki, 2012. Photo: Cata Portin, provided by the author.

The scenic design of the show is simple, yet specific, and particularly effective in evoking powerful associations with typical features of the rural Swedish landscape. One example is the use of the birch tree. In Figure 27.2, Kristina is sitting on a swing, surrounded by tall birch trees. That she is actually in America in this scene is not that important. The trees help her remember how she used to sit in the swing under her apple tree back in Duvemåla. The trunks are an effective way of creating an environment that is familiar and well-known to all Swedes, which highlights Kristina's longing for her home back in Duvemåla. The birch tree is abundant in Sweden. Its green leaves are a certain sign that spring has arrived, and its branches are used to decorate the maypole when celebrating the summer solstice during the midsummer celebration. The use of the birch is emblematic of Swedish nature and emphasises its serene qualities. The use of such iconic images connotes rural Sweden as someplace worth longing for, powerfully invoking a sense of home and thereby connecting the scenography to Kristina's emotions and the homesickness that haunts her. The argument as to how the musical glorifies the countryside through a strategic use of certain images will be developed further later on in relation to Kristina's treasured apple tree.

## THE PRECIOUS COUNTRYSIDE

With this in mind, how the rural is defined, especially in opposition to the urban, is revealing. David L. Brown and Kai A. Schafft write that '[t]he strongest disagreement is between scholars who consider rural to be a type of socio-geographic locality and those who see rural as a social construct.'[21] Brown and Schafft are referring to Keith Halfacree, who distinguishes a more material understanding or interpretation of the rural based on statistics from a 'dematerialized concept that places rural within the realm of imagination.'[22] If the rural is part of a belief system shaped by people's imagination, then the origins of these beliefs are important objects of study. *Kristina från Duvemåla* functions as one such source of the cultural imaginary. The use of the countryside as either a specific environment, a place where certain traditions and customs are practiced and cherished, or an historically important area establishes and reinforces its value as a unique and interesting place. For contemporary audiences, the countryside depicted in *Kristina* no longer exists as an actual place—only in memory or imagination. The spectator is offered the opportunity to envision a stunning natural environment, inhabited by hard-working people who grow their own food and struggle to get by. The starvation that affected so many during the latter half of the nineteenth century is almost inconceivable for a modern Swedish audience. Sweden today is a highly industrialised nation. Farming is no longer a labour-intensive job but has been transformed into an agricultural industry.

Magnus Andersson and André Jansson argue that places tend to be regarded as consumer goods in a post-industrial society.[23] This leads to a commodification of geography where for marketing purposes cities are packaged as tourist destinations. The commodification process turns former sites of production into scenic landscapes for tourists and other visitors. The present-day countryside, where agrarian activities no longer constitute the economic, cultural, and social basis of everyday life, is more and more seen as a picturesque recreational location, perfect for holiday adventures. This image of the countryside as a tourist commodity is emphasised in *Kristina från Duvemåla*. Although it is a drama about a catastrophe in Swedish history, it also represents the countryside of Sweden as an idyllic natural environment, inhabited by authentic individuals who value traditions, love nature, and are faithful to their beliefs.

## ADAPTING MOBERG'S CLASSIC

The assumption that *Kristina från Duvemåla* ought to be successful on an international level is most probably a consequence of the fame of its two main creators, the lyricist Björn Ulvaeus and the composer Benny Andersson. Being well known throughout the world as the two B's in ABBA automatically implies that their work is destined for an international audience. Popularity, that is, the writing of a hugely profitable musical destined to be produced all over the world, does not, however, seem to have been the driving force behind their dramatisation.[24]

Ulvaeus and Andersson's earlier high-profile collaboration with the lyricist Tim Rice on the 1984 concept recording of *Chess* met with very mixed responses once it was transferred to the stage. This convinced them that a strong story was necessary to create a successful musical. A good score made up of several pop songs was not enough: there had to be a strong dramaturgical concept to justify the lyrics. In an interview before *Kristina*'s opening, Ulvaeus commented on why Moberg's four-part emigrant series became the foundation for their project. He described the series as having the exact qualities they were looking for: it provided a universal drama that had a specifically Swedish tone.[25] Refugees fleeing poverty and various social injustices for asylum was as relevant in the 1990s as it had been a hundred years earlier. Being a Swedish classic also meant that most Swedes had a prior relationship to the novel and were familiar with the characters and the story. The specific Swedish tone commented on by Ulvaeus also interested Andersson. After ABBA split up in 1982, Andersson continued to explore his longtime interest in folk music, and in 1987 he formed the group Orsa spelmän together with six folk musicians.[26] Some of the members of Orsa spelmän later became part of Benny Anderssons Orkester (BAO).[27] Andersson's work as a composer covers a variety of music genres from rock 'n' roll, pop, and folk music to classical music, and *Kristina från Duvemåla* is a result of all that.

Adapting a novel into a musical requires new lyrics.[28] It was a daunting task to streamline a musical from Moberg's two-thousand-page opus. An important decision taken by Andersson and Ulvaeus together with director Lars Rudolfsson was to write a musical that related to Moberg's novels rather than following them in detail. Ulvaeus has described the process of transferring Moberg's text into song lyrics as a way of emulating or imitating Moberg's language in another form.[29] Ulvaeus primarily prepared by reading the novels over and over again to emulate Moberg's style of writing, capturing the nineteenth-century idiom employed in the emigration era. This gave the Swedish lyrics a sense of authenticity. An example of the detailed structure of the lyrics, their closeness to the music, and how that can be lost in translation can be found in Kristina's first song.

## 'Duvemåla hage'

The focal point of the musical is Kristina. The audience meet her just after the Prologue, as she awaits Karl Oskar's arrival in Duvemåla. She is seated in a swing hanging from an apple tree and picturing Karl Oskar as he makes his way through the fields surrounding the farm. The places mentioned in the song can be found in Moberg's text, but not as a list, as in the lyrics.[30] Ulvaeus has chosen places close to Duvemåla to dramatise Kristina's narration and to paint an image of the surroundings for the audience. The song is, however, not only a description of Karl Oskar's path towards Duvemåla. It contains several details that illustrate how Ulvaeus and Andersson worked together combining text and music to achieve different dramatic effects.

First, it is a good illustration of the unique sound and musical setting developed from Swedish folk music by Benny Andersson. A group of violins play a typical Swedish *polska* as an interlude. The *polska* is a traditional dance, usually in three-quarter time. It has a long history in Sweden going back several hundred years. Different tunes and styles were usually passed down from one generation to the next within families or local communities, with many regional varieties.[31] The use of the violin, one of the most frequently employed instruments in traditional Swedish folk music, is a significant feature.[32]

Kristina's entrance also introduces two important and dominant themes of the musical: the beauty of the natural environment surrounding Duvemåla and the love between Kristina and Karl Oskar. The Swedish title of the song, 'Duvemåla hage' (literally, 'Duvemåla Pasture'), indicates that it is about the surroundings of Duvemåla. This is not evident in the official English title, 'Path of Leaves and Needles'.[33]

A small detail from the lyrics and the music shows how the song paints a picture of the countryside. This is only part of the Swedish version. When Kristina sings about how Karl Oskar passes the dark water of Lake Kråke ('Kråkesjöns dunkla vatten'), the word 'dunkla' is reflected in the music by a slight ritardando and some light bells, meant to represent ripples on the dark water. This detail adds to the overall emphasis on the beautiful nature that surrounds Duvemåla and helps the audience to envision the magical countryside. There are several differences between the Swedish lyrics and the English translation.[34] The Swedish version of the song is longer and relies on a clear distinction between the different passages or sections of the song, making the original dramaturgically more elaborate.[35] This is a consequence of distinguishing descriptions of Karl Oskar's route from accounts of how he moves. The English translation throughout the song mixes these depictions, although the strong separation in the Swedish version is strategically designed to introduce the love between Kristina and Karl Oskar, which is developed in the following scene.

'Duvemåla hage' is made up of a number of different sections containing four stanzas each. The third of these sections returns again and again, like a refrain.[36] That part is the only one to describe how Karl Oskar moves, as Kristina sings about the ease and lightness with which the young man runs towards her. A flute echoes the girl's singing, rendering the repeated section a joyous illustration of the happiness Kristina feels at Karl Oskar's approach. The poetic language, in combination with the airy music, offers a first glimpse of the strong bond between them. This number also leads directly to 'Min lust till dej' ('Where You Go I Go With You'), in which they sing about their love for one another.

Love is a strong theme both in Moberg's books and in *Kristina från Duvemåla*. The musical differs from the novels, however, in how strongly it emphasises the love between Kristina and Karl Oskar. This emphasis is dramaturgically important and is responsible in part for the success of the musical. The love scenes, for which Andersson has composed a specific melodic theme representing Kristina's and Karl Oskar's feelings for each

FIG. 27.3 A couple very much in love: Kristina (Helen Sjöholm) and Karl Oskar (Anders Ekborg). Photo: Martin Skoog, courtesy of the photographer.

other (first introduced in 'Min lust till dej'), create powerful breaks in the otherwise descriptive narrative. The theme returns every time the two characters express their love for each other, jointly or on their own.[37] The love motif, primarily used in the first act, is heard one last time in the final scene, when Kristina dies, and so the love between Kristina and Karl Oskar is what connects the beginning and the end of *Kristina från Duvemåla*.

## Kristina's Beloved Apple Tree

*Kristina från Duvemåla* is not the first adaptation of Moberg's novels. In 1971–1972 the Swedish filmmaker Jan Troell adapted the books into two films (*Utvandrarna* [*The*

THE SWEDISH FOLK MUSICAL    769

*Emigrants*] and *Nybyggarna* [*The New Land*]), starring Max von Sydow as Karl Oskar and Liv Ullman as Kristina. These became very successful because of the powerful imagery depicting Kristina, Karl Oskar, and their family's harsh living conditions and sparked new interest in Moberg's by then twenty-year-old work.[38] Troell's film version offered a visual illustration of what the endeavours of Karl Oskar and Kristina, their trials and tribulations, would have looked like. An important difference between the film and the musical is that while Troell followed Moberg's novels more closely, Andersson and Ulvaeus selected certain aspects or themes from the novels as the basis for their adaptation. The biggest change in the musical is turning Kristina into the main character, instead of Karl Oskar. The change signifies more than just the depiction of events from Kristina's perspective: Ulvaeus and Andersson also altered her personality, showing a strong, determined woman in contrast to Moberg's Kristina, who is more insecure, unhappy, and anxious about the misfortunes that can befall her and her family. This change is made evident by highlighting a feature associated with nature and the countryside—*Astrakanäpplen* ('Summer Rose' apples). It is interesting to note that an apple tree, something representative of nature and part of most gardens in the Swedish countryside, is emphasised as an image. Apples appear a number of times in the musical. In the final number in act 1, 'Min astrakan' ('Summer Rose'), Kristina tells her newborn son about her much-loved home back in Sweden and about how the apple tree provided them with sweet apples throughout the summer. The song starts with Kristina and a few instruments and then builds to a majestic finale with chorus and full orchestra.[39]

The image is just as important for the end of the musical when Kristina dies.[40] With her last words, Kristina tells Karl Oskar that she will be waiting for him in Duvemåla by the tree, as she used to when they first fell in love. For the 2012 revival of the musical, a new number, 'Kristinas äppelträd', was added to the first act.[41] In it Kristina describes her beloved tree as a friend, turning it into a compelling metaphor for how important the home in Duvemåla is to her.[42] It seems likely that the song is intended to introduce the apple tree to the audience earlier on in order to accentuate the references at the end of each act. The apple tree as a symbol of Duvemåla and as Kristina's special memory of all that was good in Sweden is as dramaturgically significant as it is effective. What caused the emigrants to leave Sweden was the infertile soil and the poor crops. Kristina's vivid memory of home completely edits out her family's struggle to avoid starvation and repurposes the meaning of the tree: as a source of nourishment, of both body and soul. The soul is not only nourished by the memories of the apple tree back home, but of the sense of freedom that the sturdy tree provides. This is visualised in the production, where Kristina swings back and forth on a swing supported by the apple tree.

The apple tree, such a common feature of the Swedish countryside, is what supports Kristina in the musical, literally and figuratively. It gives her energy, and she describes how her dream in life, creating a family of her own, was conceived beside the roots of the tree.[43] The apple tree is thus intertwined with her dream of what her life should be. The close relationship between the tree and her family becomes even more evident in the act 1 finale when she introduces her son to the apple tree. She sings, 'In all my dreams I return/To where my apple tree grows/My precious Summer Rose'.[44] The closest Kristina can come to the original apple tree back home is through the fruit grown from seeds sent by her family. The apple tree as nourishment for her soul, rather than her body, is evident in the death scene, where Kristina is too weak to take a bite from her first American-grown apple. Instead, the apple is what gives her peace to finally embrace death, a death she believes will reunite her with her tree and her home in Duvemåla: 'You remember Duvemåla/Where I waited for you then/[ . . . ]/You'll find the way, I know it in my heart/ And I'll be waiting there.'[45] As used in the musical, the apple tree becomes a dominant and idealised image of the happy and prosperous countryside.

Accompanying Kristina's death is the love motif, primarily used in the score for act 1, which is set in Sweden and during the crossing of the Atlantic. A relevant question is how the music develops once the group of immigrants have left their home country and begun to settle in America, and how that might influence the audience. Overall, the general sound is the same, but there are a lot more American influences in act 2. Examples of this can be found both in the score and in the orchestration. The chorus 'Down to the Sacred Wave' is inspired by gospel music, there are references to Native American music on several occasions, and in the second half banjos are used together with different sets of percussion instruments. This does not diminish the importance of the aural world established in act 1. Rather, the opposite: before the interval, the audience is introduced to a specific musical sound often associated with Swedish folk music which represents a feeling of being at home. In act 2 these familiar motifs (including the love theme) only recur now and again, thereby emphasising a sense of being uprooted or displaced. Whenever the familiar music returns, the audience will remember act 1 and may start to miss some of its soundscape. This mimics Kristina's homesickness, triggering a similar response among the audience. Even though the score does develop in act 2 and incorporates new compositional idioms, the musical cues established in the first half remain the dominant ones.

## KRISTINA'S DOUBT

Besides finding solace in the memories associated with Duvemåla represented by the Summer Rose apple tree, Kristina finds comfort in her faith in God. It hardly ever falters except for a brief moment, when she seems to be surrounded by an endless darkness. Towards the end of act 2, after various kinds of tragic incidents, she finally voices her growing doubt in God in 'Du måste finnas' ('You Have to Be There'), one of the score's most famous songs. Its introduction is dark and solemn, with muffled flute tones creating an eerie atmosphere. For a Swedish listener, the music connotes something close to nature, sorrow, a solemn darkness, but also something mystical connected to the unknown wilderness. Andersson's extensive use of folk harmonies and references attunes the music to a Swedish ear and helps the audience empathise with Kristina's thoughts and feelings. The opening section emphasises nature as another source of faith, imbuing Kristina's surroundings, the forest, and perhaps even trees with a quasi-religious subtext. As the music swells to a majestic electric guitar riff coupled with solemn hints of Swedish folk music, the song proper commences. The gloomy beginning quickly changes into a slow but forward-driving section in which Kristina questions the existence of the God she has relied on for support and solace for such a long time. He is the reason she has had to leave her home: 'You have banished me/From the land where I was born.' She has followed him to this new land in undoubting faith. Now she feels forsaken, because no matter what she does, misfortune follows: 'Should I kneel to you?/When I rise You strike me down/Once again a little one you've taken/Everywhere I turn it's darker still.'[46]

After this angry beginning, the song transforms into a gentler mood as Kristina ponders: 'What is it, Lord, that you want/And that I am not seeing?' Her crisis of faith increases to the point where, for the first time in her life, she doubts that there is a God ('Are you there, after all?'): 'Never before have I questioned/The truth of your being/Never once have I dared/Never until today.' Kristina begs him to be there for her; the thought of all their efforts having been in vain is unbearable. The song develops into a strong anthem that illustrates Kristina's belief that God *has* to be there, and that she is determined to continue living the life she believes is right.

Helen Sjöholm, the first Kristina, played a huge part in the success of the song and of the musical as a whole.[47] She gave Kristina a natural and direct honesty coupled with phenomenal singing. 'Du måste finnas' shows off the impressive range of her voice, while her bright timbre adds a lustre and intensity to the feeling of being deserted or alone. The music, coupled with Sjöholm's excellent singing, convinces not only Kristina herself, but the audience as well, that her doubts about God are a mistake. Sjöholm's strong, beautifully controlled voice exudes confidence and a decisiveness that is a key feature of Kristina's character throughout the musical. She always fights for what she believes is right or best for her and her family. 'Du måste finnas' is the moment when Kristina questions all misfortunes that have happened and reconciles herself with how her life has turned out. She continues to believe—not only in God but also in the idea that everything happens for a purpose, and that her purpose as a wife and mother is to be close to her husband and continue building a family, despite previous miscarriages. The dramatic irony is that Kristina's firm belief, powerfully expressed in the song, will lead to her death after yet another miscarriage.

# Kristina as Refugee

Perhaps part of the reason *Kristina* has never been a success on an American stage is the character of Kristina herself. Her reluctance to feel satisfied in the Midwest of the United States is closely connected to her vivid—and, as explained above, rose-coloured—memories of Duvemåla. In the opening passage of 'Du måste finnas', she describes how God forced her against her will to seek a new home. This feeling of having no choice but to leave haunts her and perhaps even clouds her judgement on her new life. Karl Oskar,

FIG. 27.4 Robert (Peter Jöback) returning to his brother's family after his failed attempt to find gold. Photo: Martin Skoog, courtesy of the photographer.

on the other hand, feels more at ease in Minnesota, seeing it as a promising new beginning for the family. The fate of the characters reflects an ambivalent view of emigration. While Karl Oskar and Ulrika are content in their new home country, Kristina and Robert embody a darker, more discouraging side of settling abroad.

Robert, for example, never finds the gold, nor the happiness, he so desperately seeks. For him and Kristina, life in exile is nothing but a struggle leading ultimately to death. What *Kristina från Duvemåla* offers as a story about emigration is a nuanced and critical discussion of whether the grass really is always greener on the other side. It offers a gripping portrayal of hope as a driving force among emigrants and of what happens when dreams are not fulfilled. This is perhaps not what is expected of a traditional musical in the United States, where the genre so far has portrayed the immigrant experience as mainly positive. This more general theme of emigration could in the current context increase its relevance for a larger international audience.

When she finally expresses her growing doubt in God, Kristina says that she has become a stranger and a refugee. Images of people fleeing their home were a regular part of the daily news coverage when *Kristina* had its première; however, most of the reports at the time were about refugees far from Sweden. When *Kristina* was revived in 2012, all of this had changed. After the civil war in Syria began in 2011, more than 5.6 million Syrians fled the country and became refugees. Footage and photographs of people fighting for their lives as they crossed the Mediterranean to settle in Europe soon became part of almost every news report in Sweden. This gave the story of Kristina and Karl Oskar a new meaning and a contemporary frame of reference.[48]

As the musical was being revived in Gothenburg and in Stockholm, the Red Cross organised specific workshops for newly arrived refugees. One of the organisers, Rita de Castro, described the aim of the workshops as creating personal connections which would enable access to Swedish society.[49] In this context, Ulvaeus argued in an article in one of Sweden's daily newspapers, we should accept all individuals who seek our help. He pointed out that in the novel, Karl Oskar relates that no one contested their arrival or refused them entry into America. Ulvaeus proposed that this should be the way we treat refugees today.[50] He also suggested that when debating the tough questions of who should be allowed to settle in Sweden and of how many refugees there is room for, the musical—especially its powerful score—can help us understand what exiles go through when they are forced, for one reason or another, to leave home. Empathy with their plight is important and something that, according to Ulvaeus, the music in *Kristina från Duvemåla* can reinforce, not least because the musical genre makes this message easier to digest and to identify with.

# CONCLUSION—TOWARDS A MORE PROMISING FUTURE

The reasons *Kristina från Duvemåla* has never managed to be more successful on the international stage are many. The huge original production and the operatic score might not be what a global audience expects of a typical musical, in terms of either music or length.[51] *Kristina från Duvemåla* is almost four and a half hours long, with only a few stand-out songs. Some would argue that at the centre of the show are the historical events anchored in the sweep of Swedish history; for others, the emigrants' gruelling struggle is merely the historical surface, beneath which more general themes, such as sorrow, longing, being uprooted from one's home, and so on, constitute the show's true essence. These two aspects of the show are closely interrelated, yet that the original staging gave more weight to the former while de-emphasising the latter, possibly explains why *Kristina från Duvemåla* has so far failed to attract an audience outside the Nordic countries. Relying on a distinctively Swedish subject, concerning a specific epoch in Sweden's history, and emphasising a number of features primarily related to a glorified image of the Swedish countryside, the authors have created a national or perhaps even local musical. An emphasis on its more general themes that is not so strongly embedded in events from Swedish history might make the musical more global, since it would gain relevance as a portrayal of the struggle and hardships that people forced to leave their home have always faced.

So far, the question of whether *Kristina från Duvemåla* could be reconceived as a musical about refugees today has in all its productions been overshadowed by the combined effect of the script, the music, and the production, which have highlighted those features of the work directly connected to Sweden. *Kristina's* potential as a global musical might have been compromised by its use of so many Swedish references, with music closely modelled on the country's folk music, a script adhering closely to a homegrown novel, and a production heavily relying on domestic visual tropes.

In light of *Kristina från Duvemåla's* reception, it appears that what is needed for a musical to be successful on the international musical stage is a powerful story coupled with a high-quality score. Although *Kristina* has both, in its current form it overemphasises elements that require extensive prior knowledge, including familiarity with specific musical styles and an inside understanding of the local significance of the narrative, which act as obstacles to audiences beyond the country of its origin. What has not yet been found is the perfect balance between the local elements, which set the tone and offer a unique style and sound, and the musical's more general theme, which can immediately chime with the concerns of a broader public.

To complicate things further, the balance between *Kristina's* local and global aspects is not stable but fluctuates over time. New historical contexts might alter the perception of a piece, changing the audience's frame of reference and thereby requiring a different balance between the local and the general. What makes a musical 'global' changes over time in response to its social context and intended audience. For *Kristina från Duvemåla*, this means that her journey to another part of the world in search of a better, more promising future still awaits.[52] In its original production, however, it appears not to be a piece destined for the global musical stage, but rather a Swedish folk musical, primarily popular among a homegrown audience.

## NOTES

1. For more statistics please visit the webpage of one of the producers of *Mamma Mia!*, Judy Craymer: http://www.judycraymer.com/press-centre/facts-and-figures.php, accessed 22 September 2019.
2. Peter Burke, *Popular Culture in Early Modern Europe*. 3rd ed. (Farnham: Ashgate, 2009), 23–48.
3. Neil Kent, *A Concise History of Sweden* (Web version, 2008), 49–60. https://doi.org/10.1017/CBO9781107280205, accessed 1 July 2019.
4. Thomas Lindkvist, Maria Sjöberg, Susanna Hedenborg, and Lars Kvarnström, *A Concise History of Sweden from the Viking Age to the Present* (Lund: Studentlitteratur, 2018), 146–153. See also Lennart Schön, *An Economic History of Modern Sweden* (London: Routledge, 2012), 142.
5. Schon, *An Economic History of Modern Sweden*, 34–35.
6. Before the reforms, people could earn their living using common areas in each village. As the laws changed this community property was removed, and the inhabitants who did not have a piece of land of their own were forced to live on the streets. They moved from village to village and lived in specific cottages scattered all over the countryside.
7. What made letters from America and emigrant guide books so important was the high level of literacy in Sweden. The church had begun emphasising reading as early as the late

fifteenth century, focusing primarily on the Bible and the Lutheran catechism. That most people could read news and letters coming from America was a contributing factor to the widespread interest in emigration. Ulf Beijbom, 'Kristina från Duvemåla' och en miljon andra utvandrare: Om verkligheten bakom Vilhelm Mobergs utvandrarepos (Gothenburg: Forsman & Bodenfors, 1995), 10–11.

8. Most of them ended up in North America, but some set sail for South America. As the living conditions in Sweden improved during the first decades of the twentieth century, emigration decreased.

9. Carl-Johan Seth was initially part of the collaboration.

10. When the United States completed its 1900 census, the city of Chicago claimed a higher number of Swedes than the city of Gothenburg. Ulf Beijbom, *Swedes in Chicago: A Demographic and Social Study of the 1846–1880 Immigration*, PhD diss. Uppsala University (Uppsala: Acta Universitatis Upsaliensis, 1971), 38.

11. Cirkus, with 1,650 seats, is the largest private theatre in the Nordic countries. It was originally built as a circus arena but is today used mostly for concerts and musical shows.

12. For more statistics, see www.charlottateater.se, accessed 15 September 2019.

13. The English version of the musical is called *Kristina*. I use *Kristina från Duvemåla* and the shorter version, *Kristina*, throughout the article. References to the specific English version are indicated in the text.

14. All four novels have been translated into English.

15. Moberg did extensive research on Swedish emigrants over a period of almost twelve years. See e.g. Jens Liljestrand, *Mobergland: Personligt och politiskt i Vilhelm Mobergs utvandrarserie* (Stockholm: Ordfront, 2009); and Jens Liljestrand, *Mannen i skogen: En biografi över Vilhelm Moberg* (Stockholm: Bonniers Förlag, 2018).

16. When Moberg was growing up he saw the consequences of people leaving their farms in search of a more promising future. The Swedish province of Småland is not only the birthplace of Moberg himself, but also the place the emigrants in *Kristina* leave behind. Like the heroine of the musical, Moberg's grandmother was born in Duvemåla. Ulf Beijbom, *Mobergs utvandrarbygd och Amerikas Småland* (Stockholm: Carlssons, 2015), 33–39.

17. Urbanisation occurred in three phases in Sweden: the Middle Ages, 1580–1690, and finally 1800–1900.

18. Examples of these movements of politically involved ordinary people are workers' unions, the temperance movement, and the women's movement.

19. The venues where *Kristina från Duvemåla* has been staged in Sweden are all fairly big stages. The opera houses in Malmö and Gothenburg have 1,500 and 1,200 seats, respectively. As already mentioned, the Cirkus in Stockholm has 1,650 seats. The Swedish Theatre in Helsinki is an exception, being a much smaller theatre with only 700 seats.

20. Schön, An Economic History of Modern Sweden, 49. See also, Lennart Schön, 'Från hantverk till fabriksindustri: Svensk textiltillverkning 1820–1870' (PhD thesis, University of Lund, 1979).

21. David L. Brown and Kai A. Schafft, *Rural People and Communities in the 21st Century: Resilience and Transformation* (Cambridge: Polity Press, 2011), 4.

22. Ibid.

23. Magnus Andersson and André Jansson, *Landsbygdens globalisering: medier, identitet och social förändring i nätverkssamhällets marginaler* (Gothenburg: Daidalos, 2012), 28.

24. The aim was rather to deliver a strong script based on a gripping story and an elaborate score. Lars Ramklint, 'Svenska sångare sökes', interview with Benny Andersson, Björn Ulvaeus, and Lars Rudolfsson, *Dagens Nyheter*, 18 October 1994, B:4.
25. Ibid.
26. The group has released several albums and songs popular among a Swedish audience.
27. The Benny Andersson Orchestra was created in 2001 and is made up of some of Sweden's most experienced contemporary and folk musicians. Helen Sjöholm, the original Kristina, is also a member of the orchestra.
28. *Kristina från Duvemåla* is by no means the first musical to be adapted from a literary work. But it is one of the few epic musicals, i.e. based on an epic story that covers several years or decades.
29. Peter Fröberg Idling, 'Från det ena till det andra', interview with Björn Ulvaeus, *Tidningen Vi* 10 (2015): 44–49.
30. This is an example from the beginning of the song: 'I see him leaving Korpamoen/Run the path down to Olsson's landing./[ . . . ]/I see him crossing Devil's Glade/Where the giant old oak lies dying'. *Kristina*, CD Carnegie Hall recording, booklet with lyrics by Björn Ulvaeus and Herbert Kretzmer, Mono Music AB, 2010, Mono Music – B0014228–02.
31. What characterises a traditional *polska* is its underlying structure of two related eight-measure phrases that are repeated, in various combinations. S.v. 'polska', . https://www.bri tannica.com/art/polska , *Encyclopædia Britannica*, 2019, accessed 11 November 2019.
32. Andersson has also commented on how he perceives Swedish folk music as being built around the violin as a key instrument. Beata Bergström, Jan Mark, Lars Rudolfsson, and Joel Berg, *Bortom en vid ocean: 'Kristina från Duvemåla'* (Lund: LeanderMalmsten, 1996), unpaginated.
33. The English text was written by Björn Ulvaeus and Herbert Kretzmer.
34. For a comparison, please contrast the Swedish studio recording (Mono Music AB, 1996) with the English-language version, recorded live at Carnegie Hall (Mono Music AB, 2010).
35. Only the 1995 production featured the song in its original length. The 2012 version is shorter, more similar to the English version.
36. 'Över grind och stätta/har han svingat sej, nu är han nära/Fötterna är lätta/för han vandrar vägen till sin kära'. Benny Andersson, *'Kristina från Duvemåla' sånger ur 'Kristina från Duvemåla'* (Stockholm: Mono Music 1997). This section begins with 'Path of Leaves and Needles' in the Carnegie Hall recording, but then it is not repeated in the English version.
37. You hear the love theme in the music when Kristina sings 'Min man [ . . . ]' ('My man [ . . . ]').
38. The first of the four novels was published in Sweden in 1949, the last in 1959.
39. The music also resembles the love theme introduced earlier in the act.
40. As Kristina is dying, Karl Oskar offers her the first apple from the Summer Rose apple tree they planted together.
41. In English: 'Kristina's Apple Tree' (my translation). The number is only part of the revised Swedish edition. It is placed quite early in the act, after 'Missväxt' ('Bad Harvest'). Björn Ulvaeus, *'Kristina från Duvemåla': Sångtexterna* (Gothenburg: GöteborgsOperan, 2014), 9.
42. 'Skogen står avog och sträng/runt Korpamoen/Mitt äppelträd är en vän/strax invid knuten/Tungsinta står de där tätt/Furan och granen/Löven rörs lekande lätt/på Astrakanen'; ibid.
43. Her position on the swing is once again emphasised and connected to her love to Karl Oskar and their family: 'Drömmen den liksom tog mark/vid trädets rötter'; ibid.

THE SWEDISH FOLK MUSICAL    777

44. From the finale of act 1, entitled 'Summer Rose'.
45. The final Swedish words are difficult to translate ('Jag är i gott bevar') but emphasise even more strongly that Kristina believes that she will be safe and happy where she is going after death.
46. *Kristina*, CD, Carnegie Hall recording, booklet with lyrics by Björn Ulvaeus and Herbert Kretzmer, Mono Music AB, 2010.
47. She was virtually unknown when she auditioned as one of thousands of singers for the part of Kristina. Only twenty-five years old, she managed to give voice and body to the complex character of Kristina and was praised by critics.
48. This frame of reference continually develops and changes as immigration continues to be a hotly debated topic on an international level. A recent example is the former American president Donald Trump's decision to make immigration a priority of his administration.
49. Matilda Gustavsson, 'Musikalen ska hjälpa nyanlända in i samhället', interview with Björn Ulvaeus and Rita de Castro, *Dagens Nyheter*, 27 May 2015, A:4.
50. Björn Ulvaeus, 'Sverige måste visa värme och tolerans', *Dagens Nyheter*, 22 October 2014, A2:6.
51. Camilla Lundberg, review, *Expressen*, 8 October 1995, 35; Jens Peterson, review, *Aftonbladet*, 8 October 1995, 21.
52. Some members of the creative team behind *Kristina från Duvemåla* have continued to collaborate on other projects. In 2013 Andersson, Ulvaeus, and Rudolfsson worked together with the Swedish poet and dramatist Kristina Lugn on *Hjälp sökes (Help Wanted)*. The play is about a small farm in the Swedish countryside owned by two brothers who decide to advertise for a female farmhand. While there are some similarities, for example regarding their depiction of the Swedish countryside, *Hjälp sökes* differs a lot from *Kristina*, since it is a spoken drama, with music and lyrics being used merely as embellishments and additions.

## BIBLIOGRAPHY

Andersson, Magnus, and André Jansson. *Landsbygdens globalisering: Medier, identitet och social förändring i nätverkssamhällets marginaler*. Gothenburg: Daidalos, 2012.
Beijbom, Ulf. '*Kristina från Duvemåla*' och en miljon andra utvandrare: Om verkligheten bakom Vilhelm Mobergs utvandrarepos. Gothenburg: Forsman & Bodenfors, 1995.
Beijbom, Ulf. *Mobergs utvandrarbygd och Amerikas Småland*. Stockholm: Carlssons, 2015.
Beijbom, Ulf. *Swedes in Chicago: A Demographic and Social Study of the 1846–1880 Immigration*. PhD diss., Uppsala University. Uppsala: Acta Universitatis Upsaliensis, 1971.
Bergström, Beata, Jan Mark, Lars Rudolfsson, and Joel Berg. *Bortom en vid ocean: 'Kristina från Duvemåla'*. Lund: LeanderMalmsten, 1996.
Brown, David L., and Kai A. Schafft. *Rural People and Communities in the 21st Century: Resilience and Transformation*. Cambridge: Polity Press, 2011.
Burke, Peter. *Popular Culture in Early Modern Europe*. 3rd ed. Farnham: Ashgate, 2009.
Kent, Neil. *A Concise History of Sweden*. Cambridge: Cambridge Concise Histories, 2008.
Lindkvist, Thomas, Maria Sjöberg, Susanna Hedenborg, and Lars Kvarnström. *A Concise History of Sweden from the Viking Age to the Present*. Lund: Studentlitteratur, 2018.
Schön, Lennart. *An Economic History of Modern Sweden*. London: Routledge, 2012.
Schön, Lennart. 'Från hantverk till fabriksindustri: Svensk textiltillverkning 1820–1870'. PhD thesis, University of Lund, 1979.

# PART X

## NATIONAL TRADITIONS OF MUSICAL THEATRE IN EASTERN EUROPE

# CHAPTER 28

..............................................................................................

# 'THEY DATED OUT OF PURE LOVE'

## A Brief History of the Czech Infatuation with the Musical

..............................................................................................

JAN ŠOTKOVSKY

TRANSLATED BY SIMON HOOPER AND KAREL M. PALA

Dedicated to the memory of Eva Stehlíková (1941–2019)

This essay about the pre- and postwar Czech musical will concentrate on the years 1945–2000; the preceding period will be tackled only insofar as it concerns the important figures of Oldřich Nový and the trio of Jiří Voskovec, Jan Werich, and Jaroslav Ježek, the first two actors and playwrights and the third a composer; I will attempt to characterise the period after 2000 by sketching the dominant trends.

While fully aware of how hard it is to define the boundaries, I shall concentrate on the history of the Czech musical and not on Czech operetta, which developed in its own distinctive manner from impulses in the world of the Anglo-American musical. Here it should be noted that in the years 1948–1989—under the communist dictatorship, when Czechoslovakia was part of the Eastern bloc—this distinctiveness was to a significant extent the result of the limited information available in Czechoslovakia about the Western musical. The end of private theatre impresarios after 1945 effectively ended the influence of the Broadway and West End models, even at the level of production.[1] In this respect the situation did not change until after 1989. Thus, essentially it can be said that the history of the best of the Czech musicals of the twentieth century is the history of creative deviations from the norms of Broadway and the West End.

In the essay, operetta will offer a consistent background to musical theatre endeavours, forming the expectations of audiences and critics but mainly influencing the staging and production conditions within which original Czech musicals were created. The vast majority of state theatres or companies that specialised in musical theatre (led by Prague's Karlín Musical Theatre) performed mainly operettas.[2] Especially with regard to the professional experience of stage artists, this influenced and limited their achievements in the field of musicals.[3] The situation of these operatic attempts at a musical became more complicated after 1989, when local theatre-goers could compare them with the work of private musical theatres. (As I will demonstrate later on, however, those are themselves in many ways different from private productions of the Anglo-American type.) During the forty years of communist rule, the most interesting Czech musicals came from beyond the specialist state theatres, particularly out of the small theatre movement between the 1960s and the 1980s.

An important guide to the landscape of the Czech musical is the dramaturge, semiotic theorist, and translator Ivo Osolsobě (1928–2012), who spent virtually his whole professional career as dramaturge to the musical theatre company of the State—today, National—Theatre in Brno. His theoretical and musical theatre interests came together in his key publication *Divadlo, které mluví, zpívá a tančí* (*Theatre That Speaks, Sings and Dances*, 1974), an attempt to interpret musical theatre using the terms of the contemporary communication theory of modelling. Aside from theoretical texts about the musical,[4] in his popular book *Muzikál je, když* (*A Musical Is When*, 1967) he attempted a comprehensive history of the Czech musical after 1918. Even if Osolsobě's text reveals a marked one-sidedness (for example, in his distaste for rock and pop operas, which led him to view the international development of the musical from the start of the 1970s with growing displeasure), until Pavel Bár's *Od operety k muzikálu: Zábavněhudební divadlo v Československu po roce 1945* (*From Operetta to Musical: Popular Musical Theatre in Czechoslovakia after 1945*, 2013),[5] this was the only comprehensive attempt to analyse the key trends in the development of the Czech musical.

# The Pre-war Highlights: The Liberated Theatre and Oldřich Nový

As generally agreed by Anglophone historians and critics,[6] the foundational American musical was *Show Boat*, which premièred on 27 December 1927. With a certain degree of exaggeration, it could be said that the Czech musical came into being eight months earlier, on 19 April 1927, in Prague's Artistic Fellowship, with the première of the *Vest Pocket Revue* by Voskovec and Werich. This production quickly made the two young authors and comics (both at that time twenty-two) famous and led to their entry into the experimental avant-garde Osvobozené divadlo (Liberated Theatre), where they quickly took charge and which is today entirely associated with them.

It appears, however, to be one of the laws of theatre history that major new events are not immediately understood and valued as such. In the case of *Vest Pocket Revue* and the recognition of its potential as a musical, this is not necessarily surprising. Even though it was an immediate and unexpected success, with jazz songs as an essential part of the work of V + W (as the duo are referred to in the Czech Republic and Slovakia), it still took several years before its creators' endeavours led to a show that in terms of overall integrity and plot coherence could be called a musical of the same order as *Show Boat*:

During its brief existence their Liberated Theatre presented twenty-five full-length original productions, variations on a basic revue pattern which they developed into a flexible, distinctive form that moved toward musical comedy, or, indeed, drama with musical interludes, with political satire at its core.[7]

The true strength of V + W lay neither in integrity nor coherence. Their talent was far more inclined towards the theatrical than the dramatic: Přemysl Rut, the Czech essayist and historian of song, put it succinctly when comparing their work with the role of the satirical couplet in nineteenth-century drama:

If [ ... ] couplets function like a note in brackets and can be deleted from the play when they no longer seem relevant to the events of the day, the *forbínas* of Voskovec and Werich [ ... ] is already the focus and purpose of the evening,[8] from which the actual play could even be removed as a dramatic excuse for the commentary and songs.[9]

Even in the most successful works of V + W (*Kat a blázen* [*Executioner and Fool*, 1934]; *Balada z hadrů* [*The Rag Ballad*, 1935]; and *Těžká Barbora* [*Big Bertha*, 1937]), we come across operetta-like moments and difficulties of reconciling the plot with making room for an edgy pair of comic authors (who as a duo of timeless clowns had to both take part in the story and at the same time to some extent stand outside it) and of bringing an often highly ambitious tale to an acceptable end. Rather than dramatists, V + W were primarily brilliantly coordinated comic songwriters with exceptional improvisational skills; they were sufficiently sensitive artistically that in their revue and other types of commercial theatre, they employed the top avant-garde artists of their time as directors, choreographers, and stage designers.[10] What at the beginning of their plays looks like a bold satirical parable in the shape of a historical story (V + W draw, for example, from the legend of the Golem, the story of Robin Hood, Wieland's ancient anecdotes of *The Trial of the Donkey's Shadow*, and the biography of François Villon) gradually falls apart: V + W are much better at setting up a story than at developing and closing it. To provide an impressive ending, stories had to be set aside in favour of an appellative: *forbína*, or song.[11]

It is the songs—'Život je jen náhoda' ('Life Is Only Chance'), 'Klobouk ve křoví' ('A Hat in the Bushes'), 'Nebe na zemi' ('Heaven on Earth'), 'Tmavomodrý svět' ('Dark Blue World'), and 'David a Goliáš' ('David and Goliath'), to name just the most popular—that make up the most enduring part of the legacy of Voskovec, Werich, and their composer, Ježek; these are in fact the only true jazz standards that pre-war Czech culture can claim. V + W were the first to manage to capture in Czech the full spirit of jazz, and their linguistic playfulness, rhythmic mastery, thematic inventiveness and in places almost Dada-like creativity established a model, still valid, for all who try to write songs in Czech.

Today the songs of V + W + J function independently, both of the context of the plays from which they came and frequently also of their political intent. From their relaxed parodic playfulness in the years 1931–1934 they moved on to markedly satirical comedies, the targets of which were various contemporary anti-democratic trends, in particular the rise of Nazism in Germany. This effort to 'mobilise' the audience of course sometimes brought V + W + J into the area of direct political agitation and even of naïve and simplistic optimism: verses such as:

> Když nás půjdou milióny, všichni proti větru,
> každý ujde ten svůj metr, dáme metr k metru.
> Kde je síla zpátečníků, kde je síla větru,
> proti větru postoupíme o sta kilometrů.[12]
> When we go in millions, all against the wind,
> each one goes one metre, moving metre by metre.
> Where is the power of diehards, where is the strength of the wind
> we will go a hundred kilometres against the wind.

In their anthemic generality, songs like the one above could bring together an audience with completely different political beliefs to those of the authors. However, it is true that the plays of V + W were even more radical than the engaged American musicals of that period such as *The Cradle Will Rock* or *Pins and Needles*, theatrically more innovative and informed by the non-illusory approach of certain forms of popular theatre (such as *commedia dell'arte*).[13] Ivo Osolsobě also rightly points out how, because of the significant way in which the ballet scenes are integrated into their musicals, V + W + J anticipated the American musical ballet.[14]

Another important personality of the Czech interwar musical was the actor and director Oldřich Nový. In many ways he opposed the efforts of V + W + J, but at the same time his style differed significantly from the operetta mode of that period. The difference was above all in his cautious apolitical position: during his happiest years of artistic direction at the Nové divadlo (New Theatre, 1936–1948), he consistently developed a genre of escapist romantic comedy for the higher social classes, strongly marked by the influence of French culture.[15] These comedies differ from operettas not so much in style, as do the works at the Liberated Theatre, but in their degree of taste and theatrical intelligence. In fact, Nový entered the New Theatre after a successful fifteen-year career as an operetta actor and director: between 1925 and 1935 he was the director of the Brno operetta ensemble. According to the writer Eduard Bass:

> [Nový] cast away all the external and empty visual pomp of operetta productions, concentrating on the discreet effect of good acting, which moves from humour and comedy to singing a part as simply, lightly, and naturally as possible.[16]

Here, the operetta clichés were consistently ousted.[17] In regard to singing technique, Nový systematically suppressed exhibitionistic ostentation and paid attention to the importance of the sung word, precise emotional expression, and contact with the audience, supported by the intimacy of an orchestral quartet. In the New Theatre, Nový reduced sentimentality by using the 'discreet and subtle intimacy' of his staging style as well as conversational irony.[18] At that time, Nový also appeared as the character of the 'elegant lover who stays on top of things' in Czech films. He became one of the main film stars at the end of the 1930s. His role of the timid clerk Alois, who once a month plays the seducer Kristian in a luxury bar, became iconic. The film *Kristian* was directed by Martin Frič and based on a theatre play by Yvan Noé (1939). In its pure form, there were two basic dimensions to the characters Nový created in *Kristian*: the elegant romantic dreamer and its slightly ironic degradation.

## *THE MAGIC CAULDRON*: A COMBINATION OF DAWN AND DUSK

Given their tastes, it is no coincidence that when V + W returned from their American exile after World War II (Ježek had died there),[19] where they had become thoroughly acquainted with the American musical yet were not able to write any new shows, they finally went for a fresh Broadway novelty, *Finian's Rainbow*, by Burton Lane, E. Y. Harburg, and Fred Saidy. The straightforward social and anti-racist critique, delivered in the form of a fairy tale that has a certain simplicity of both characters and message - these are the features of Finian's Rainbow which must have appealed the most to for V+W.[20] Its paradoxical adherence to the original can be seen in the fact that it is more an adaptation than a translation: V + W changed the name of the musical to *Divotvorný hrnec* (literally, *The Magic Cauldron*),[21] the figures of Irish immigrants into Czechs, and the leprechaun Ogg into a typical Czech folk- and fairy-tale being, the *vodyanoy* Čochtan (Jan Werich wrote this part, greatly expanded from the original, for himself). The historian of the Liberated Theatre, Vladimír Just, from a distance of half a century, describes *Finian's Rainbow* as 'naively simple'; the actor saw in the character of Čochtan the core of the production: 'Čochtan gradually became Werich's one great *forbína*,[22] changing daily and with the help of reprises growing into a kind of extra-theatrical being, a grotesque monolith.'[23]

The production of *Finian's Rainbow*, directed by Jiří Voskovec, was apparently the first performance of a Broadway musical in continental Europe. However, in Czechoslovakia it was also the last for fifteen years, even though the production met with exceptional acclaim from audiences; contemporary reviews are testament to the rejection of the musical as a genre as well as all of 'cultural imports' from the United States.[24] Voskovec's second emigration in 1949 placed the two halves of this authorial pair on different sides of the Iron Curtain, unfortunately bringing their collaboration to an end during its most productive period.

However, there was no company capable of responding to the impact of *The Magic Cauldron*. The communist takeover in February 1948 led to the vigorous suppression of entertainment, including musical theatre. The Karlín Musical Theatre became a home for various more or less unwanted top theatre performers, who then had to cope with the absurd demands of the era, including the fact that musical theatre entertainment, a genre inherently cosmopolitan, was criticised for its cosmopolitanism and entertainment values. A combination of these political attacks and various misunderstandings drove the excellent director of the Karlin ensemble, Jiří Frejka, to suicide.

Even the classical operetta disappeared from Karlín for several years, only to return there almost triumphantly after it turned out that the socialist forms of musical theatre did not attract sufficient public interest. This happened in November 1953 with a production of Hervé's *Mam'zelle Nitouche*, directed by Oldřich Nový. In this staging, which he had already tried out in the interwar years, Nový played the central dual role of Célestin/Floridor. The production had a record 354 performances. The programme for *Mam'zelle Nitouche* illustrates the coded newspeak of that period, intended to reinforce the return of the operetta repertoire: 'Basically, the optimistic works of the Offenbach school have nothing to do with the broken salon-bourgeois tunes of most of Kálmán's and Lehár's operettas'.[25]

# ALFRÉD RADOK, THE SECRET MUSICAL INNOVATOR

A separate chapter in the history of Czech musical theatre in the 1950s is represented by the work of one of the most important twentieth-century Czech directors, Alfréd Radok, usually regarded as a director of straight plays. Czech theatrical historiography sharply distinguishes him from directors of 'musical and entertainment theatre'—a specific Czech umbrella term for operetta, revue, and musical, which are genres considered to be lacking in artistic quality. Radok's theatre, however, is unthinkable without his significant employment of music and songs. Two of his productions, traditionally ranked among the highlights of the postwar Czech (drama) theatre, provide particular examples. In John Osborne's *Komik* (*The Entertainer*, National Theatre, 1957, music by Zdeněk Petr), he achieved a sharp contrast between the sparkling entertainment clichés of the comedian Archie Rice and the inexorable deterioration of his own private life by trimming the lyrics and incorporating new music-hall songs in a retro style. In Romain Rolland's *Hra o lásce a smrti* (*The Game of Love and Death*), which premièred at the Městská divadla pražská (Prague City Theatres) in 1964, the additional pathetic musical arias (music by Zdeněk Liška, lyrics by Pavel Kopta) deliberately emphasised the melodramatic atmosphere of Rolland's story. Radok, however, starkly juxtaposed the music with the appended revolutionary utterances of the plebeian crowd. This crowd watched the intimate love story from the galleries of the arena stage in which the protagonists of the story were trapped. The original intimate story, in which the revolutionary era is only an anticipated background, was transformed into essentially political theatre. The staging must undoubtedly have reminded many viewers of the cruelty of the political terror of the 1950s.

During that decade Radok was the only one to contribute to the development of Czech musical aesthetics. He managed to do so firstly by radically musicalising Ferdinand František Šamberk's *Jedenácté přikázání* (*The Eleventh Commandment*, Karlín Musical Theater, 1950). The nostalgic fin-de-siècle atmosphere of the piece was furthered by projections of pre-shot films (stylised as vintage silent movies) which reacted directly to the situations taking place on-stage (and vice versa). This combination of film and theatre foreshadowed the principles Radok would later employ to the full in his celebrated Laterna Magika project. Secondly, he made the first Czech film musical, *Divotvorný klobouk* (*The Miracle Hat*, 1953). Just as in the case of *The Eleventh Commandment*, it was an adaptation of a nineteenth-century Czech dramatic piece by V. K. Klicpera, with music by Jiří Sternwald. Thirdly, Radok staged his own intimate lyrical musical for two actors, *Stalo se v dešti* (*It Happened in the Rain*, 1955).[26]

# The Golden Sixties: Importing the International Musical and the Young Theatre Movement

A symbolic moment in the development of the Czech musical was the year 1958. First, this was because a decade after the performance of *Finian's Rainbow* on a Czech stage, another musical with Western origins appeared. It was the Italian musical comedy *Un paio d'ali* by the famous duo Pietro Garinei and Sandro Giovannini and the composer Gorni Kramer, which was staged at the State Theatre in Karlín; it could be seen in Czechoslovakia just one year after its Italian première. It was followed by the Czech premières of musicals from Germany and the United Kingdom and, after 1963, also from the United States: key events were the Czech premières of *My Fair Lady* (1964) and *Hello, Dolly!* (1966), both at the Karlín Theatre, culminating and also closing with the first performance of *West Side Story* (1970), almost simultaneously in Brno and Prague, after which the political situation significantly restricted—and in a number of cases made impossible—the performance of Anglo-American musicals.

In 1958 also under Darek Vostřel there was a renewal of cabaret activities, which had been extensive in the pre-war period, at the Rococo Theatre, which then in the 1960s gained prominence itself as a theatre for musical productions, including programmes with the top pop vocalists of the time. Finally, in the same year 1958 Ivan Vyskočil and Jiří Suchý opened the smaller—176 seats, including the balcony—Divadlo na Zábradlí (Theatre on the Balustrade) with the revue *Kdyby tisíc klarinetů* (*If a Thousand Clarinets*), the first stage version of one of the key Czech film musicals of the 1960s. Both of the founders of the theatre (which gradually became an important Prague experimental dramatic venue) soon departed, but Suchý, a lyricist, librettist, actor, and singer, set up the Semafor Theatre a year later with the composer (and, later, actor and singer) Jiří Šlitr. Originally a partly amateur ensemble, from its very first production, *Člověk z půdy* (*The Man from the Attic*, 1959), Semafor exerted a major influence on the development of the Czech musical.

Despite Suchý's advanced age (he was born in 1931), he is still active in Semafor as of 2023, participating closely and enthusiastically. However, its peak period is traditionally considered to be its first decade, ending with the societal changes in 1969–1970 resulting from the Soviet occupation and then the death of Jiří Šlitr in December 1969. This perception is to some extent an illusion, resulting from the extraordinary interest in Semafor by audiences and critics in the first years of its existence, when its company included several exceptionally popular singers. However, the fact is that this extraordinary communion with the spirit of the age, which Semafor experienced in 1959–1964, was not to be repeated, just as Suchý was never to find a comparable composer to replace Šlitr.[27]

Like the Liberated Theatre, Semafor won its permanent place in Czech musical theatre culture primarily for its songs.[28] One of the main productions in its first season was *Zuzana je sama doma* (*Zuzana Is Home Alone*), in which the songs of Suchý and Šlitr were framed by the very simple tale of a girl named Zuzana who has been left by her boyfriend and in her loneliness plays songs on tape which are heard live on the stage. (This simple but effective concept was followed up in Semafor in the years after in the form of further Zuzanas) Exceptionally hard work on the parts of Suchý and Šlitr—together they wrote almost three hundred songs—was married to extraordinary creativity and a range of genres, from rock 'n' roll hits through swing comedy songs to chansons and complicated ballads (in which, however, poetry and humour predominated over dramatic pathos). Their uncommon inventiveness disguised from the listeners at the time how strongly retro, in a time of modern pop and rock, the songs of Suchý and Šlitr were: their main inspiration could be found in pre-war and wartime swing music and film musicals and sometimes even in older music cabarets.[29] Finally, Suchý and Šlitr found their most personal theatrical expression in the intimate musical *Jonáš a tingl-tangl* (*Jonáš and Tingl-Tangl*, 1962), a conscious tribute to basic cabaret theatricality,[30] in which Suchý shaped the figure of the mercurial cabaret artist Jonáš, who was to accompany him for a significant part of his theatrical career.[31]

The most emphatic move by Semafor away from the aesthetics of cabaret nostalgia and shows with songs to the form of a coherent musical was the 'comic opera' for five characters *Dobře placená procházka* (*A Worthwhile Walk*, 1965). The word 'opera' in the subtitle is a little bit of an exaggeration—as Ivo Osolsobě convincingly argues, 'The continuous singing in this "opera" is not stylisation or convention but rather a break with convention, a joke'.[32] So it is a musical playing at being an opera, in addition to adopting a deliberately vague tone. Essentially it exposes a dubious morality: a couple, Uli and Vanilka, who are about to get a divorce, and the cunning plebeian lawyer are fighting over an inheritance from the enigmatic Aunt from Liverpool, who is neither dead nor living. To the latter is given the most-performed number from the piece, the complex chanson 'Proč je to tak' ('Why It Is So'). The couple are willing to marry just about anyone to obtain a cheque for several millions. At the end, while they hunt for that cheque, the fifth character in the play, the poetic Postman, a demiurge, symbolically cuts out a heart. The point here is not so much to mock people's greed; rather, the work encourages us to 'perceive other things', of which the Postman sings on his entrance and which for Suchý as a poet is a major theme.[33] Otherwise the glitzy gospel finale of the first half of the play, in which the Aunt, independently of the plot, recounts the story of an angel's apparition on the wings of the plane in which she flew from Liverpool, culminates in the following verse:

| | |
|---|---|
| Andělé budou | Angels will exist |
| I když my tu už nebudem | Even though we'll no longer be around |
| Sedat na kormidla strojů | To sit at the helm |
| Lítat lidem do pokojů | To fly people into rooms |
| Pro poezii dnů | For the poetry |
| Nevšedních[34] | Of remarkable days. |

## *LEMONADE JOE*, VRATISLAV BLAŽEK, AND THE CZECH ECHOES OF *WEST SIDE STORY*

If there was someone who—at least partially—followed up on the tradition of the Liberated Theatre and the unique stature of *The Magic Cauldron* in the decade between 1948 and 1958 it was, rather logically, the ensemble led in 1955–1961 by Werich (returning from a forced six-year period away from the theatre), the Divadlo estrády a satiry (Vaudeville and Satire Theatre), later renamed the ABC Theatre.[35] Aside from works revived with minor revisions from the repertoire of the Liberated Theatre,[36] the venue created several distinctive works, including *Limonádový Joe aneb Koňská opera* (*Lemonade Joe, or The Horse Opera*, 1955; book and lyrics by Jiří Brdečka,[37] music by Jan Rychlík and Vlastimil Hála), the most enduring member of the 'gold ring' of Czech musicals.[38] The show was based on the parody of a cheap western, which was published in serial form in a newspaper in 1940. During World War II there already had been a small-scale dramatisation of the material at the Divadlo Větrník; in 1964 an exceptionally successful film adaptation of the stage musical was released, which—like the theatre version—was directed by Oldřich Lipský.[39]

*Lemonade Joe* is a representative example of how communist Czechoslovakian artists in the 1960s and 1970s responded to products of popular culture from beyond the Iron Curtain: they exploited 'lowbrow genres' typical of Western culture (westerns and spy and horror films) in the form of a parody or a burlesque. With their playful and open-minded spirit, the Czech works thus managed to share both the magic of the chosen genre while at the same time providing the creators with a suitable out when they were criticised for being 'lackeys of the West'. The creators of this distinctive parody had to assume that their audience was not sufficiently acquainted with the given genre that it would be possible to specifically parody its stereotypes: their film did not intend 'to make fun of Western pop culture, or to replace it, and in no way was an imitation, but rather an unusual fantasy playing with its very freely interpreted conventions.'[40] In the case of *Lemonade Joe*, this dual strategy is even more obvious thanks to its form as a musical. While the plot itself, centred on a gunslinger who always hits his target thanks to complete teetotalling and the regular consumption of lemonade, tends towards parody, the songs express genuine enchantment with American popular culture.[41]

The 1960s were not only a golden age for Czechoslovakian artistic films, referred to as the Czechoslovakian New Wave, they were also an exceptionally fertile creative period in the area of comedies, musicals, and film entertainment in general. In the area of the musical, its peak was represented by *Lemonade Joe* and two films by the librettist Vratislav Blažek and the composers Jiří Bažant, Vlastimil Hála, and Jiří Malásek, *Starci na chmelu* (*The Hop Pickers*, 1964) and *Dáma na kolejích* (*The Lady of the Lines*, 1966), both directed by Ladislav Rychman. The exceptional quality of both films resulted from both the thoroughness of the team's preparation and from the films' unusual form as integrated musicals:[42] twentieth-century Czech works were never to come closer to the classical Broadway model than this. At the same time, both films draw on typical local phenomena in their plots: obligatory summer holiday work by school students on the hop harvest (*The Hop Pickers*) and the hard work of women who return home after work to a second shift of housework and caring for their families (*The Lady of the Lines*).

*The Hop Pickers* reveals the film version of *West Side Story* as an influence,[43] which, since the creators of the former did not know that much about Anglo-American stage entertainment, was taken as the model of a 'musical *about* something'. With the passage of time, it is possible to see a rather vague link between the two works in that they are both musicals that treat love between young people under difficult circumstances. While *West Side Story* is about the open hostility between two gangs, so that the relationship between Tony and Maria inevitably leads to several deaths, in *The Hop Pickers* that of Filip and Hanka leads only to the expulsion of both from school and their stigmatisation as nonconformists, which will follow them throughout their lives. In his screenplay, however, Blažek is not elevating or lyricising the feelings of Filip and Hanka, which he tries to depict as healthy and completely normal: when in the final song we hear that 'they dated out of pure love', it is a deliberate cliché, but the sincerity of their feelings allows the author to unmask the prevailing hypocrisy of society.[44] Thus, even in an apparently lyrical tale Blažek comes across more as a satirist and moralist: it is no accident that (as already noted by Ivo Osolsobě[45]) this musical lacks any notable song expressing the protagonists' love but is rather dominated by chorus numbers (with significant appearances by a trio of beat guitarists in black, forming the narrative chorus of the story), which made it possible for Blažek to express the moral commentary of the story in a sarcastic tone.[46]

In *The Lady of the Lines* we can again speak of Blažek as the main author of the musical: the music here does not aim to be distinctive in style or to be the element that holds the work together.[47] To be precise, the screenplay does not leave room for either of these approaches. Its critical reception was much more mixed than that of *The Hop Pickers*, which might be the result of the work's internal contradictions: despite the revue-like spectacle, this is an ironic parable without a happy ending, showing a regime that officially proclaimed the 'liberation of working women' in a harshly satirical light. The tram driver Marie Kučerová reacts to her husband's infidelity by ostentatiously spending the family savings and exhibiting the sort of behaviour which in the eyes of society is permitted only to men; for example, after a rather innocent flirtation in a bar one night she is taken to the police and accused of prostitution. Yet her revolt ends in an apparently romantic confession of love to her unfaithful husband. The conclusion of the film, however, shows that the whole tale of exaggerated revenge took place merely in Marie's imagination, so the reconciliation and forgiveness at which she arrives is actually resignation. Marie's return to her everyday routine as well as her decision to ignore the accidentally revealed infidelity is commented on ironically by the chorus:

| | |
|---|---|
| Tak to na tom světě kráčí | So this is the way of the world |
| Jednou k smíchu—jindy k pláči | Sometimes funny—sometimes sad |
| [ ... ] | [ ... ] |
| Netrapte se nad tím více | Do not worry any more |
| Snad to byla sestřenice[48] | Maybe it was just his cousin. |

Audiences at that time were not, of course, fully prepared for such a resolutely feminist message, which was so radical that Ivo Osolsobě dubbed the film an 'Anti–*My Fair Lady*'.[49]

The ambitious *Hop Pickers* and *Lady of the Lines* were only possible thanks to the resources of state cinematography. Private film studios would clearly not have invested in narrative musicals that were not based on guarantors of success such as successful theatre works, popular books, or singing stars in the main roles. It has to be admitted, however, that at least in the case of *The Hop Pickers* (the theatre version of *The Lady of the Lines* had its première at the same time as the film), no Czechoslovak theatre ensemble in the mid-1960s would have been capable of performing it successfully.[50] This was confirmed by the difficulty that permanent theatre companies (still mainly operetta and musical theatre) had during the production process of the delayed Czech première of *West Side Story* in 1970.[51]

Before *West Side Story* arrived on Czech stages, a local work consciously varied its theme, while acknowledging its inspiration. *Gentlemani* (*Gentlemen*, 1967) was the work of two of the top hit-makers in Czechoslovak pop at that time, the composer Bohuslav Ondráček and the lyricist Jan Schneider, who are connected primarily with the Rococo Theatre. The story of 'troubled youth—uprooted hooligans from boarding schools - belonged thematically and musically (as it used rock) to the environment of small theatres of the 1960s, but it was performed on the stage of the large Karlín Musical Theatre, whose ensemble still more or less specialised in operetta.[52] Ivo Osolsobě admits that in the musical, 'they exploited [ ... ] the exotic appeal of teenage gangs', and that comparison with *West Side Story*, it is 'extremely overdone'; however, he also asserted that *Gentlemani* has 'magic, strength, courage, and poetry', and that 'our Czechoslovak problems are presented here in the form of a musical'.[53] On the other hand, the foremost rock critic at that time, Jiří Černý, sarcastically noted in his article 'Gentlemanství po našem' ('Being a Gentleman Our Way') the schematic nature of Schneider's libretto and concluded that it was a 'series of interviews, allusions, jokes, and effects, which taken together formed not a skeleton but a mess'.[54] With the benefit of half a century of hindsight, it is clear that the main problem with *Gentlemani* was its lack of drama: the sequence of scenes from the lives of—in the words of Černý—'seemingly bad but at their core [ ... ]... decent youngsters'[55]—lacks real conflict, culminating in nothing more than the unmotivated, completely accidental, yet serious injury to the show's most sympathetic character, the naïve outsider Prcek.[56]

The musical that actually was able to fully express 'our Czechoslovak problems' premiered shortly after *Gentlemani* at the Rococo Theatre: an adaptation of a nineteenth-century Czech historical novella by Alois Jirásek, *Filosofská historie* (*The Philosopher's Story*, 1968). It depicts the life of students from a small town who, over the objections of the local people, organise the May Festival and then take part in the revolutionary

FIG. 28.1 The students Márinka (Helena Vondráčková) and Lenka (Marta Kubišová) amongst several of the villagers, including Vavřena (Waldemar Matuška, *above, second from left*), Frýbort (Karel Štědrý, third from the left) and Špína (Václav Neckář, *fourth from left*). Scene from *Filosofská historie* (*The Philosopher's Story*, 1968) at the Rokoko Theatre, Prague. Photo: Vilém Sochůrek, courtesy of the Arts and Theatre Institute Prague. Used by kind permission of Veronika Hypšová.

upheavals of 1848. *Filosofská historie* managed to connect the poetics of 'song theatre', where popular singers performed in compilation programs seemingly for themselves, in the mode of an 'intimate' musical in an almost off-Broadway style. Despite the apparent historical distance, *Filosofská historie* congenially addressed its era. It aptly anticipated the repeat of the events of 1848 in the form of the Prague Spring of 1968, including the subsequent invasion by the Warsaw Pact armies. Thus, even though it was set 120 years in the past, it became the postwar Czech musical to speak most directly to the local audience in its own language, akin to what Leonard Bernstein had termed 'vernacular'.[57]

As for *Filosofská historie*, it should be added that many Czech pop singers were socially and politically engaged at the time—often through performing in the satirical television revue *A Song for Rudolph III* (1967–1968). Its scriptwriter was the author of *Filosofská historie*, Jaroslav Dietl, while the main protagonist was played by the artistic director of the Rococo Theatre, Darek Vostřel. On the television programme, 'A Prayer for Marta' was performed by the famous pop star Marta Kubišová (who also acted in *Filosofská historie*). This song became the unofficial anthem of the Prague Spring of 1968 and turned Marta Kubišová into a political icon of the time. As a result, she was banned from making public appearances between 1970 and 1989.[58]

# UNDER THE SURFACE OF 'NORMALISATION': MOSCOW IS CLOSER THAN BROADWAY

As in almost all sectors of public and cultural life, the occupation of Czechoslovakia by the Warsaw Pact armies, followed by the 'normalisation of the current situation',[59] resulted in stunting the growth of Czech musical theatre. An example of this is the fate of Semafor, where political pressure was compounded by the tragic death of Jiří Šlitr at the end of 1969 at the age of only forty-five.

Jiří Suchý, on the other hand, who had congenially expressed the naïveté and optimism of the 1960s in his lyrics, 'became an orphan with his poetics'[60]: his playful cabaret philosophy did not fully resonate with the restrictive atmosphere of the 1970s. One can, of course, imagine that the constant political pressure on Suchý, as well as a number of censorship constraints, might have led to his stubborn desire to creatively stand firm and refuse to compromise. Throughout the 1970s and 1980s his access to radio and television was severely limited, and he was barely allowed to record new albums. Nevertheless, his choice of a new chief composer (Šlitr's regular music arranger, the swing musician Ferdinand Havlík) seemed to indicate Suchý's reluctance to leave 'the legacy of jazz standards',[61] as the music critic Pavel Klusák wrote years later. He briefly summed up the situation of the normalised Semafor in his description of the finale of *Jonáš, dejme tomu v úterý* (*Jonáš, Shall We Say Tuesday*, 1985):

They are searching for success which Jonáš very well knows is impossible to achieve [ ... ] and yet they are going on, because there is nothing stronger for Jonáš than dreaming about the stage, the lights, the music and the beautiful back-up girls.[62]

Even in its weaker moments, Suchý's production significantly exceeded the quality of those put on by permanent musical ensembles. The latter suffered from a number of problems during that period. The ideological demands of the totalitarian establishment rose sharply, leading to an increased presentation of Soviet musicals as well as to the presentation of domestic musicals on politically engaged topics (e.g. *Cindy*, a 1979 Czech musical staged in Brno linking a traditional Cinderella love story with tendentious anticapitalist satire).[63] A marked decline in creativity and a rise in conformity were also evident in the state-controlled pop music industry, whose status is usually closely tied to that of musical theatre. Contact with the international musical world was severely disrupted. In the late 1960s the Anglo-American musical novelties were introduced to the Czech Republic with a three-year delay. With the exceptions of *Cabaret* (Czech première 1977), *Chicago* (1978), and *Promises, Promises* (1972), Czech theatres in the 1970s and 1980s basically presented only classic musicals of the golden era: 1972 saw the Czech première of *Show Boat, Oklahoma!* was imported in 1976, and *Annie Get Your Gun* reached the country in 1982. However, this situation was a consequence not only of the political constraints and lack of funds but also of the inadequate professional education of performers and other artists. In those theatres, whose dominant expertise remained classical operetta, chamber musical comedies, and plays with singing, specialised training of musical theatre performers was lacking, unsurprisingly. 'A sort of a dead and degraded common [artistic] language—generally comprehensible but incapable of communicating a genuine message—has been left to the contemporary theatre',[64] concluded Josef Herman in his review of the Karlín Theater's repertory in 1986.

Therefore, the most original musical to be set in the past was created in an unexpected place: Husa na provázku (Goose on a String Theatre), a studio theatre where music and songs were usually employed in an experimental way that referenced the avant-garde of the 1920s and 1930s. *Balada pro banditu* (*Ballad for a Bandit*, 1975), written by the classical composer Miloš Štědroň and the satirical playwright Milan Uhde—who had been banned from working[65]—combined the story of the legendary Carpathian Ruthenian outlaw Nikola Šuhaj with classical folk music. Uhde conceived the story of a bandit revolt, which seemed particularly relevant during the period of stagnant normalisation, in a non-romantic way, leading to an ironic climax: 'What is the end? When they get you, or when you have only one way left? I didn't want it like that. God only knows where it screwed up',[66] says Nikola just before his death.

The plot culminates in an ironic climax when, at the very end the chief of the gendarmes, virtually the only positive character in the play (except for Nikola's beloved Eržika), finds out that the corrupt village of Kolochava Lad, in which the plot takes place, has essentially sacrificed Nikola for its own convenience, even though it benefited from his crimes. The conspiring businessman Mageri, who leaves Kolochava Lad because he wants to enjoy a wealthy lifestyle, invites the gendarme: 'I'm moving to Mukachevo.

FIG. 28.2 The Bandit and his beloved: Nikola (Miroslav Donutil) and Eržika (Iva Bittová) in *Balada pro banditu* (*Ballad for a Bandit*, 1975). Scene from the first production of the musical at the Goose on a String Theatre Brno. Photo: Jef Kratochvil, used by kind permission of Tino Kratochvil.

When you pass through, pay a visit. Grand Hotel Polonina. Stylish meals and liveried service'.[67] The irony of the libretto is counterbalanced by the lyricism of the songs, which, with the exception of the central ballad 'Zabili, zabili chlapa z Koločavy' ('They Killed, They Killed the Kolochava Lad'), are Uhde's adaptations of classical folk poetry.[68] The powerful songs with their harmonious and instrumental simplicity became popular as no songs from other Czech musicals had ever been. Although almost none of the musicals created by the larger venues in the 1970s and 1980s are performed (or even remembered) anymore, *Ballad for a Bandit* enjoyed eighteen local stagings after 1989.

## 1990s Musicals: Shots in the Dark

The fall of the communist regime in 1989 did not destroy permanent opera and operetta ensembles, nor did it shake up the extensive network of state and city theatres. Their activity in the musical field, however, was suddenly exposed to competition from private musical productions. The first of these was the production of *Les Misérables* in 1992 at Divadlo na Vinohradech (Vinohrady Theatre) in Prague. The production, by director

Petr Novotný and producer Adam Novák, confirmed that there was enough 'singing power' in the Czech Republic to meet the demands of this type of pop opera. At the time, however, their endeavour had to negotiate the limitations of commercial show business in a country where its traditions had been forgotten. Novák could only rent the playhouse for the theatrical holiday period. Therefore, he had to stop the production after nearly a hundred performances, leaving him unablet to exploit its commercial potential. Despite all his efforts, he was unable to find another suitable venue in Prague. To this day, that situation has not changed: even in 2019, there is not a single suitable commercial West End–style theatre available in Prague for private musical productions.

The first show that broke the bank by successfully responding to the hunger of Czech audiences for an authentic global musical thus another Novotný production, *Jesus Christ Superstar* (JSC), which premièred in 1994 at the Divadlo Spirála (Spirála Theatre). The production, featuring the best Czech rock singers in their thirties, had a total of 1,288 performances over four years, a record so far unsurpassed for a Czech private production. It was seemingly invincible, because it triggered multiple instances of cultural nostalgia: for rock music, whose production and distribution had been limited throughout the twenty years of normalisation; for religious expression, which the communist regime had consistently suppressed and which *JCS* depicted in an attractively open-minded way; and for its idealised hippie image of the 1960s, of which the Czechs had little direct experience.

A similar type of cultural nostalgia infused the last major attempt at an original Czech international-style film musical, *Šakalí léta* (*Jackal Years*, 1993). It depicts the 'rock 'n' roll revolt' against the 'socialist dullness' of the late 1950s in the story of a free-thinking young man nicknamed Bejby. He is part of the musical tradition of 'rainmakers' who use music to activate sleepy environments, like Ren McCormick in *Footloose* (1984) or Dewey Finn in *The School of Rock* (1993). Although the musical's plot, which centres on the love between Eda, the waiter, and Alice, the policeman's daughter, was not very coherent, other ingredients were more impressive: the show's benign mockery of communist officials' dullness, its skilful take on rock 'n' roll by the singer-songwriter Ivan Hlas,[69] and above all its nostalgia for the rock 'n' roll fever of the late 1950s in its idealised form— the euphoric verses of the final song declare: 'Na počest hrdinům, co kdysi zbláznili lidi' ('In honor of the heroes people were once crazy about'). As a result, from today's perspective the film appears to be a typical product of the optimistic atmosphere after the end of the Cold War, when it seemed for a while that the energy of electric guitars had managed to overthrow communism.

An analogous—and typically Czech—manifestation of cultural nostalgia is represented by the work of the director Ondřej Havelka. Since the early 1990s he has been developing a distinctive genre of swing revues. By presenting the smash hits of the period, his shows depict an idealised world of the interwar upper classes in the form of a collectively shared dream about a more decent, more cultivated, more elegant past. Havelka's work is actually an intentional but more theatrically inventive return to the poetics of Oldřich Nový, whose acting and singing style the younger director obviously observed closely. He also shares Nový's slightly ironic and detached attitude to the idyll being created.[70]

*Dracula* (1995) had the kind of initiatory importance for the presentation of domestic musicals that *Jesus Christ Superstar* had for the presentation of foreign ones. For the creation of this pop opera, the producer and choreographer Richard Hes invited two major pop music hit-makers of the normalisation era, the composer Karel Svoboda and the lyricist Zdeněk Borovec.[71] He cast well-known pop singers in the lead roles and attempted to disguise their possible acting and dancing shortcomings (as well as the opera-like stiffness of a number of scenes) by employing his dance group UNO,[72] by avoiding spoken dialogue, and by the dynamic direction of Jozef Bednárik, who was, along with Novotný, one of the most significant directors of the musical theatre scene in Prague in the 1990s.

*Dracula* met a rather negative critical response, especially to Karel Svoboda's music, which was (quite rightly) accused of repeating clichéd patterns and of unimaginative orchestrations. At the same time, the reviews revealed a bias against this type of commercial musical. The only unprejudiced evaluation was by Josef Herman: 'To what extent is the rendering of *Dracula* an artistic setback? And to what extent does the musical represent an accurate reflection of the potential viewer's taste? These are the essential questions.' He further praised 'a technically sophisticated production, generally considered virtually flawless'.[73] Despite being panned by critics, *Dracula* became the most successful indigenous musical of all time, with 916 performances.[74] Its epic portentousness and spectacle remains unsurpassed; it also became the initiatory musical experience for a whole generation of teenagers in the 1990s.

The success of Hes's production seems to have created a paradigm for other private musical productions in Prague. This model usually consists of a romantic story set in the past and based on a well-known literary or cinematic source, the requisite love affair, an emphasis on elaborate costumes, the casting of popular singers or other 'media faces', and so on. *Monte Cristo* (2000), another production from this creative team, seemed determined to diverge from the *Dracula* prototype as little as possible.

In the 1990s most of the stable musical ensembles went through a crisis when the unexpected increase in musicals' popularity caught them off guard. Their expertise in operetta did not prepare them to cope with the requirements of a musical, and there were no sufficiently trained actors or directors. The Karlín Musical Theatre, led by Ladislav Županič, was probably the most successful in coping with the new situation. In Karlín the permanent ensemble performed the operetta repertoire, which was cited as the main reason the subsidised theatre was irreplaceable, since it was obvious that in the Czech Republic classical operettas would not be taken up by any private producer. Classical musicals created between the 1940s and 1960s were staged with guest theatre stars in the lead roles. The Karlín Theatre also distinguished itself by the above-mentioned nostalgic swing revues staged by Ondřej Havelka.

However, Městské divadlo Brno (the Brno City Theatre) unexpectedly entered into competition with musical and operetta companies. Under the leadership of the director and playwright Stanislav Moša, it revealed a desire to become a drama-musical theatre. In doing so, it took advantage of the fact that the theatre faculty of the Janáček Academy of Music and Performing Arts in Brno was the only school in the Czech Republic that

FIG. 28.3 Scene from Stanislav Moša's celebrated 1995 staging of *West Side Story* at the Brno City Theatre featuring Petr Gazdík as Tony and Alena Antalová as Maria. Photo: Jef Kratochvil, used by kind permission of Tino Kratochvil.

had started teaching the specialised skills of musical theatre acting. Unlike Prague productions, the Brno City Theatre was not limited to casting well-known faces. Moša's self-authored musicals, created with his composer-partner Zdenek Merta, have been characterised by apparent philosophical ambitions that have differed sharply from those of commercial productions in the Czech capital. Apart from that, Moša's direction, in particular of *West Side Story* (1995), became a model for a new generation of young musical performers who were not burdened by the old operetta stereotypes.

## The Czech Musical after 2000: Looking for Balance

The high expectations engendered by the presentation of Anglo-American musical hits in private productions, which had led to the success of *Jesus Christ Superstar*, were disappointed by the poorer reception of *Evita* (331 performances) by the same production team. The commercial failure of Prague's première of *Cats* (2004, 164 performances) brought to an end a series of ambitious presentations of international musicals in commercial productions.[75] František Janeček, the impresario of normalised pop music, remained the sole player in this field.[76] His productions emphasise highly sensationalist marketing as well as the casting of media celebrities regardless of their professional training and suitability—for example, the casting of the thirty-eight-year-old 1980s Czech pop star Iveta Bartošová in the role of seventeen-year-old Kim in *Miss Saigon*.

A symbol of the transfer of power in the Czech musical theatre scene was the disbanding of the Národní divadlo Brno (National Theatre Brno) operetta ensemble and its transformation into a component of the Brno City Theatre in 2003. A year later, the Brno City Theatre launched its Hudební scéna (Music Scene) venue, with more than seven hundred seats. Since the premières of the musicals *Oliver!* (2005) and *The Witches of Eastwick* (2007), it has become the centre for the production of top contemporary musicals in the Czech Republic. Apart from the creative duo Merta-Moša and their own self-authored productions, four musicals by the above-mentioned duo Štědroň-Uhde were staged, based chiefly on classic novels. After a time the Brno model was adapted by the operetta ensembles in Pilsen and Ostrava. They gradually abandoned operetta productions and started staging only musicals. In Ostrava they have mainly specialised in musicals by Andrew Lloyd Webber. As a result of the rising demand, since the late 1990s the musical has become a regular feature of the repertoire of the former dramatic regional theatres. At present, all of them offer at least one musical première per year.

Under the leadership of the producer Egon Kulhánek, the Karlín Musical Theatre has also gradually changed its profile and started moving towards the production mode of private commercial theatres. In doing so, it has minimised its permanent ensemble, practically abandoned operettas, and presented the most commercially attractive contemporary Anglo-American musicals.[77] It too began casting celebrity personalities, such as the popular Czech female pop singer Lucie Bílá. She played the lead in the musical *Carmen* (2008), which represents the biggest step for the Karlín Theatre outside its circle of local collaborators. The music was commissioned from the American composer Frank Wildhorn. The Karlín Theatre benefits from the fact that it has the only musical stage in Prague suitable for mounting a truly epic show. Thus, its recent première *Legenda jménem Holmes* (*Holmes, the Legend*, 2018; music and libretto by Ondřej Gregor Brzobohatý) represents an unexpected shift in a new direction. It is a serious attempt at an original musical comedy of the classical Broadway type, one that avoids the portentous stiltedness of historical pop operas. Brzobohatý confirms his awareness of current musical trends in his other works for the Karlín Musical Theatre, but—unlike *Holmes, the Legend*—he ensures their success by adapting successful and popular Czech films.

The Karlín Theatre has also followed the imported trend of jukebox musicals.[78] Since the première of *Dětí ráje* (*Children's Paradise*, 2009; Goja Music Hall), with songs by Michal David, the Czech disco hit-maker of the 1980s, this trend has become a distinct element of the Czech musical scene, though it was anticipated by the nostalgic swing revues of the 1990s. Nevertheless, with a limited number of Czech bands or singers offering songs stored in the collective memory, the trend may soon exhaust itself.

The majority of private producers in Prague have found out that it is better to rely on the work of local artists or on jukebox musicals than to depend on the complicated process of securing a licence for foreign hits.[79] However, the present contact with the international musical world is probably now, in 2023, at its peak in the Czech Republic. More theatres and producers have been competing for the Czech premières of the latest foreign hits. The quality of the performers is reflected in the gradual expansion of training opportunities, in the experience of international engagements, and in the audience's experience of international productions. Currently, the greatest weakness of the Czech musical lies in its lack of local authors, as well as in the absence of a domestic off-Broadway type of scene that would allow artists to workshop drafts of musicals in small-scale performances. The vast majority of composers who shaped the Czech commercial musical scene after 1989 had experience as pop-music songwriters, as well as some knowledge of show business. However, they had little experience of theatre, often resulting in works in which a series of songs was bolted onto a very weak story line. This odd genre might be called 'songical' rather than musical, although in recent years the number of such shows has decreased. Hopefully that change will be permanent.

## Acknowledgements

The author would like to thank David Drozd, Patrick Fridrichovský, and Michal Zahálka for their kind words of advice and assistance, and Radomír D. Kokeš for his help with obtaining secondary literature.

## Notes

1. On those occasions when things went differently it almost always involved the endeavours of individual 'enlightened' theatre directors—see e.g. Ota Ornest, a man with a wealth of experience in how English theatre operated, who as director of the Prague City Theatre (1950–1973) within the given political limitations was essentially an impresario of the Western type.
2. The Czech Republic even today retains that Central European speciality, the multi-company theatre, where together one theatre (and frequently even one stage) is shared by dramatic, musical, operetta, opera, and sometimes even ballet companies, despite all the obvious operational and production disadvantages that this brings. Karlín Musical Theatre maintained its speciality notwithstanding the efforts after 1948 to suppress operetta as a 'bourgeois genre', linked according to party ideologues with that social class, which had been defeated by the communist revolution.
3. The foremost Czech musical theatre critic Josef Herman fittingly speaks of joint playhouses, 'in which the landlady operetta accommodates the musical as a sub-tenant'. Josef Herman, 'Muzikály podobojí', *Divadelní noviny* 10 (2019): 4.
4. The most important of these theoretic texts is *Estetika zábavněhudebního divadla* (*Aesthetics of Popular Musical Theatre*), published in 1979.
5. Pavel Bár, *Od operety k muzikálu: Zábavněhudební divadlo v Československu po roce 1945* (Prague: KANT, 2013). Bár's book—which ends at the start of the 1990s—is more a collection of case studies than a comprehensive history and mainly focuses on the 'specialised stages', especially the Musical (previously State) Theatre in Karlín and the musical theatre

'PURE LOVE': THE CZECH MUSICAL    801

companies of the multi-company theatres in Brno, Pilsen, and Ostrava; his assertion that 'the Karlín Theatre represented the main trends in the domestic development of operetta and the musical' (5) is, to say the least, debatable; but it nonetheless is an indispensable work in any attempt to understand the history of the Czech musical.

6. In the emphatic words of Miles Kreuger: 'The history of the American Musical Theatre, quite simply, is divided into two eras—everything before *Show Boat* and everything after *Show Boat*.' Quoted in Geoffrey Block, *Enchanted Evenings* (Oxford and New York: Oxford University Press 2009), 4.

7. Jarka M. Burian, *Leading Creators of Twentieth-Century Czech Theatre* (London: Routledge, 2002), 20.

8. The term *forbína* (a slang expression for proscenium) is used in the plays of V + W to refer to the dialogue of the two main figures—played by the authors—in front of the curtain, which allowed for an up-to-date, partly improvised politico-satirical commentary or a separate comic study, more or less independent of the events of the play.

9. Přemysl Rut, 'Osobnost a doba', *O divadle* 5 (October 1989): 57.

10. These included the director Jindřich Honzl, the choreographers Joe Jenčík and Saša Machov, and the artists Bedřich Feuerstein, Alois Wachsmann, and František Zelenka.

11. The most successful work by V + W is the last piece they worked on together, *Pěst na oko aneb Caesarovo finale* (*A Fist in the Eye, or Caesar's Finale*, 1938). It involves a return to the format of the revue, but is thematically unified and framed by the principle of a theatre within a theatre, where parodistic sketches on the theme of 'historically significant figures' are performed.

12. This is the finale from the play *Balada z hadrů* (*The Rag Ballad*); Jiří Voskovec and Jan Werich, *Hry* (Prague: Československý spisovatel, 1980), 390.

13. Some of the later plays of the Liberated Theatre sharply attack the problems of the contemporary Czech parliamentary system and a particular political figure. For example, in the 1937 play *Rub a líc* (*Two Sides*), Voskovec and Werich played two unemployed workers who discover a secret store of weapons and grenades belonging to the fascist party. The whole play describes the revolt of the workers' movement against the rise of fascism and is a very clear reference to the situation in Nazi Germany.

14. Ivo Osolsobě, *Muzikál je, když* (Prague: Supraphon, 1967), 152–153.

15. Šárka Gmiterková has written in depth about how Nový shaped his theatrical profile as well as his acting type in her dissertation, '*Kristian v montérkách*': Hvězdná osobnost Oldřicha Nového mezi kulturními průmysly, produkčními systémy a politickými režimy v letech 1936–1969' (PhD diss., Masarykova Univerzita, 2018).

16. Eduard Bass, 'Opereta pro kulturní lidi', *Lidové noviny*, 28 November 1936, 9.

17. 'He replaced the exterior pomp of operetta and revival productions with the suggestive atmosphere of a tastefully furnished modern interior, the impact of operetta acting with a sophisticated social behavior that was a model of contemporaneity and used elegant stage gowns and dresses,' writes Josef Herman; s.v. 'Nové divadlo', in *Česká divadla: Encyklopedie divadelních souborů*, ed. Eva Šormová (Prague: Divadelní ústav, 2000), 369.

18. Bass, 'Opereta pro kulturní lidi'.

19. In 1939 they had to leave the country quickly before it was occupied by Hitler's armies. The Liberated Theatre had already been banned. In order to do this, the regional office had to resort to a theatre law from 1850, which clearly demonstrates the desire of not only

German but also Czech official insitutions to punish the two comics for their political engagement. For further details see Michal Schonberg, *Osvobozené* (Prague: Odeon, 1992), 383–389.

20. V + W returned from the United States evidently very much affected by American theatre; had it not been for the Communist takeover they would undoubtedly have continued performing American plays and musicals on Czech stages.

21. The name of the play seems to refer to the most important Czech playwrights of the 19th century, V. K. Klicpera and J. K. Tyl, who were the chief developers of the genre of satirical fables with supernatural elements.

22. See n. 8.

23. Vladimír Just, 'Peripetie a návraty V + W', in *Hry Osvobozeného divadla*, ed. Jiří Voskovec and Jan Werich (Prague: Karolinum + Progetto, 2000), 18.

24. For further details see Bár, *Od operety k muzikálu*, 88–89.

25. Note, in *Mam'zelle Nitouche*, programme, Karlín Musical Theatre, Prague, 1953, unpaginated.

26. The show was composed by Oldřich Letfus and Jan Kaláb, with lyrics by Jiří Aplt and Mojmír Drvota.

27. When in 2009 Pavel Klusák produced an album of cover versions of Semafor songs on the fiftieth anniversary of this theatre entitled *For Semafor*, it was made up only of hits from the first decade.

28. Vladimír Just, however, correctly points out that while the plays of Voskovec and Werich were frequently performed also in the postwar period without the actual presence of the authors—even if it clearly was because in the period 1948–1989 it provided contact with the interwar culture (idealised owing to the Communist regime)—the production of Semafor titles outside of Semafor was 'the exception that confirmed the rule of its spatial and temporal non-transferrability'. Vladimír Just, 'Mýtus Semafor?', *Divadelní revue* 4 (1999): 4. In short, only the songs from their productions survived outside Semafor.

29. There is a range of testimony to the disdain with which Šlitr viewed the 'noisy' rise of rock music in the second half of the 1960s and how he did not want to adapt to it. See e.g. Jan Kolář, *Jak to bylo v Semaforu* (Prague: SCÉNA, 1991), 44–45.

30. 'Please allow us to show our love for cabaret, music hall and tingl-tangl, which we never visited but the atmosphere of which we can sense, with this performance', wrote S + Š in the programme for the production. For further details on Jonáš and his significance in the history and style of Semafor, see Vladimír Just, *Proměny malých scén* (Prague: Mladá fronta, 1984).

31. Shortly before Šlitr's death S + Š brought back the character in *Jonáš a doktor Matrace* (*Jonáš and Doctor Mattress*, 1969), for a duo between the sprightly Jonáš (in Suchý's iconic straw hat) and his stubborn, pedantic partner at the piano. This production came about partly due to popular demand, as people wanted 'the return of Jonáš'. However, after 242 performances of *Jonáš a tingl-tangl*, S+Š decided to withdraw the production from the repertoire—not because audience interest had waned, but because they were tired of the constant reprises. Later, the aging dreamer Jonáš appeared together with his down-to-earth housekeeper Žofie Melicharová (played by Suchý's key post-Šlitr partner, Jitka Molavcová) in the production *Jonáš, dejme tomu v úterý* (*Jonáš, Shall We Say Tuesday*, 1985) and in several subsequent shows and revues.

32. Ivo Osolsobě, 'Muzikál v Československu', in *Muzikál*, ed. Siegfried Schmidt-Joos (Prague: Editio Supraphon, 1968), 262.

33. This is succinctly expressed in one of his and Šlitr's most popular songs, 'Marnivá sestřenice' ('The Vain Cousin'), the tale of a girl who burns her hair, which was very important to her, ending in the verse: 'O vlasy už nestará se/A diví se světa kráse/Vidí spoustu jiných věcí/A to za to stojí přeci' ('She no longer cares for hair/And wonders at the world of beauty/She sees a lot of other things/And it's worth it after all'). Jiří Suchý, *Trocha poezie* (Prague: Československý spisovatel, 1989), 84.

34. Jiří Suchý, *Encyklopedie Jiřího Suchého*, vol. 10, *Divadlo 1963–1969* (Prague: Karolinum—Pražská imaginace, 2002, 91.

35. Werich was against 'the institutionalisation of satire' in his theatre, well aware that those who were officially requesting satire would not have been happy to actually defend it.

36. All in all, there were three revivals: *Caesar* (1955), *Balada z hadrů* (1957), and *Těžká Barbora* (1958), with Voskovec being replaced as Werich's partner by the gifted comic writer Miroslav Horníček.

37. Aside from Brdečka, Vratislav Blažek, Pavel Kopta, and Jan Rychlík also had a hand in writing the lyrics.

38. In 1989 alone it was performed by a total of twenty-six Czech professional theatres.

39. At a time when the Czechoslovakian population totaled 15 million, it was seen by 4,556,352 people. Václav Březina, *Lexikon českého filmu* (Prague: Cinema, 1996), 20.

40. Petr Szczepanik, *Továrna Barrandov: Svět filmařů a politická moc 1945–1970* (Prague: Národní filmový archív, 2016), 351.

41. For example, the song of the play's main villain, 'Horácovo pohřební blues' ('Horác's Funeral Blues'), is clearly a variation of the 'St. James Infirmary Blues' and its motif of a man who goes to see his woman in hospital, unaware that she is already dead.

42. This is apparent particularly in comparison with the second Czech film musical, which arrived in cinemas only four months after *The Hop Pickers*. *If a Thousand Clarinets* features the songs of Suchý and Šlitr and has a screenplay by Suchý and Ján Roháč. It was co-directed by Roháč and Vladimír Svitáček. The film contains the best songs by the two Semafor artists and stars the best Czech singers of their time, but this anti-war parable suffers from a discrepancy between its thematic ambitions and its loose, revue-like narrative, which clearly shows Semafor's tendency at that time toward shows as mere vehicles for songs.

43. See Martin Šrajer, 'Starci na chmelu [1964]', *Filmový přehled*, https://www.filmovyprehled.cz/cs/film/396586/starci-na-chmelu, accessed 15 September 2019.

44. When the chorus of teachers accuses Filip of taking Hanka to his secret hideaway on the school campus (the other casual workers sleep together, separated by gender in school classrooms), they show their indignation with the words, 'What you think was going on there, what two people could do together at home in a house, or every day in Stromovka [a park in Prague]. And he will say that he was at basketball and she that she went to play the piano.'

45. 'The songs are rather on the margins of the tale than forming its axis'. Osolsobě, *Muzikál je, když*, 187.

46. See the ironically exaggerated song of the three guitarists who sing at the moment the teachers are to vote on Filip's expulsion from school: 'Běda ti chlapče třikrát běda,/běda ti hochu zpozdilý,/sbor zachmuřený k soudu sedá,/co nezná bratra, soudí-li./Soudit tě budou soudci přísní,/co nikdy v tísni nebyli./A jestli někdy byli v tísni,/tak brzy paměť ztratili./Je přece v zájmu společnosti/oddělit plevel od zrna./A tys dělal jen mrzutosti,/toť věc je zjevně patrná' ('Woe be to you and three times woe/woe to him who his own way

will go,/sitting in judgement are judges severe,/knowing no brother but judging here./ In judging you will be so stern,/who never have known sorrow's burn./And if ever they were in distress,/that memory is now much less./After all society must have/the separation of wheat from chaff,/and you have only harmful intent,/a thing that is very evident'). In contrast to the 'rebel' dress of the singers (black short-sleeved T-shirts, black jeans, and sunglasses), the lyrics employ the stylised language of literature as high art with brilliant rhymes, which makes no attempt to imitate the 'language of contemporary youth'.

47. "This does not show the birth of drama 'from the spirit of music'; rather, here the music is always a mere tool for dramatic communication and is used somewhat sparingly." Osolsobě, 'Muzikál v Československu', 255.

48. Vratislav Blažek, *Dáma na kolejích* (Prague: DILIA, 1966), 73.

49. Osolsobě, 'Muzikál v Československu', 263.

50. Blažek himself tried to stage *The Hop Pickers*: 'I gave up in horror at the prospects of the musical in the theatre with actors who could either act but not sing and dance, or could sing but not dance or act, and there was still the third variant.' Quoted in Marie Valtrová, *Vratislav Blažek: Hráč před Bohem a lidmi* (Prague: Achát, 1998), 117.)

51. 'Karlín's *West Side Story* inevitably created controversy with its clash between operetta and musical theatre acting, with the criticism centred on the role of Tony, acted in an operetta style, sharply attacking Karel Fiala (some six years earlier the lauded performer of Lemonade Joe!) and only praising [ ... ] the physically capable actors unburdened by the conventions of operetta.' Josef Herman, 'České muzikálové herectví?', *Divadelní noviny* 2 (1995): 1.

52. However, in the case of *Gentlemani*, the theatre had to at least partly accept 'Western customs' and with the aid of auditions fill certain roles with guests from outside the company. Bár, *Od operety k muzikálu*, 212.

53. Osolsobě, 'Muzikál v Československu', 255.

54. Jiří Černý, ... *na bílém 1: Hudební publicistika 1956–1969* (Prague: Galén, 2014), 240.

55. Ibid.

56. Bár, *Od operety k muzikálu*, 211.

57. I paraphrase here Ivo Osolsobě observations in his study 'Paradox muzikálu', *Svět a divadlo* 5 (1992): 74.

58. For more details, see the chapter 'Life Is Like a Man' in Mariusz Szczygiel, *Gottland: Mostly True Stories from Half of Czechoslovakia* (New York: Melville House, 2014).

59. This cynical term was first used in the so-called Moscow Protocol, which was signed on 21 August 1968, five days after the occupation began, by the Czechoslovak government officials (who were de facto kidnapped and taken to Moscow) under pressure from the Soviet government. It became a slogan defining the country's political direction, as postulated in the official document published by the Czechoslovak Communist Party in December 1970 under the title 'Poučení z krizového vývoje' ('Lessons Drawn from the Crisis Development'). This official position of the Communist Party regarding the events of 1968–1970 constituted a binding interpretation of the occupation as 'international aid'.

60. Přemysl Rut, 'Dvojice osamělých', *O divadle* 3 (November 1987): 148–164.

61. Pavel Klusák, 'Jak přežít horší časy', *Lidové noviny*, 20 October 2012, 28.

62. Ibid.

63. In this area in the 1970s, probably the most diligent musical composer of Czechoslovak 'normalisation', Jindřich Brabec (paradoxically the author of the aforementioned *A Prayer*

## 'PURE LOVE': THE CZECH MUSICAL    805

*for Marta*), dominated with his musicals *The Road to Life* (1973, Makarenko), *Young Guard* (1973, Fadeyev), and *Aristocrats* (1977, Pogodin). See Bár, *Od operety k muzikálu*, 235–236.

64. Josef Herman, 'Nejen karlínské problémy po čtyřiceti letech', *Scéna* 9 (1986): 7.

65. In addition to writing classical music, Štědroň had been the main composer of music for Goose on a String Theatre since its foundation (1968). When he was working on *A Ballad for the Bandit*, he had no idea that Uhde was the author of the libretto. Only the director of the production, Zdeněk Pospíšil, knew.

66. Milan Uhde, *Balada pro banditu a jiné hry na zapřenou* (Brno: Atlantis, 2001), 205.

67. Ibid., 209.

68. Many years later, Uhde admitted that one of his main inspirations had been the productions of E. F. Burian, which were based on classical folk poetry.

69. In *Šakalí léta*, Hlas suppressed his own distinctive style to such an extent that the result is reminiscent of a jukebox musical, similar to David Bryan's songs for the musical *Memphis* (2010).

70. Like Nový, Havelka exploits his high public profile in various art forms: in addition to directing, he is also a bandleader and the frontman of his own retro swing orchestra, Melody Makers.

71. For decades the two of them jointly created the repertoire of Karel Gott, the most popular of Czech singers. Svoboda, however, also composed the music for a successful musical comedy based on an historical subject, *Noc na Karlštejně* (*A Night at Karlstein*, 1974, screenplay and direction by Zdeněk Podskalský).

72. The casting of musical roles with singers who are not trained as actors is a persistent (albeit gradually fading) and often-discussed flaw of the Czech musical; it also affects the creation of new works.

73. Josef Herman, 'Velký trpaslík *Dracula*', *Divadelní noviny* 20 (1995): 1.

74. It should be pointed out that the Congress Center, where *Dracula* was staged, has a total of 1,562 seats—almost twice the capacity of the Spirála Theatre (832 seats), where *Jesus Christ Superstar* was performed.

75. Ironically, the show's producers had been striving to mount a Czech production of *Cats* since the early 1990s. The successful Czech première of *Jesus Christ Superstar* only came about because they could not obtain the rights for *Cats*.

76. Janeček's productions include *Les Misérables* (2003 and 2012), *Miss Saigon* (2004), *The Phantom of the Opera* (2014), and *Tanz der Vampire* (*Dance of the Vampires*, 2017).

77. For instance, *Aida* (2012), *The Addams Family* (2014), *Bonnie and Clyde* (2016), and *Sister Act* (2017).

78. In this context, *Čas růží* (*The Season of the Roses*, 2017), built around the songs of Karel Gott, with an amateurish libretto by Sagvan Tofi, represents one of the weakest offerings of the Karlín Musical Theatre in the new millennium.

79. In many respects they still modify 'the *Dracula* model'. *Mona Lisa*, which opened at Prague's Divadlo Broadway in 2009, epitomises the pursuit of musical properties promising romance: the show does not even rely on a well-known story, just an iconic title.

## BIBLIOGRAPHY

Bár, Pavel. *Od operety k muzikálu: Zábavněhudební divadlo v Československu po roce 1945.* Prague: KANT 2013.

806  JAN ŠOTKOVSKÝ

Bass, Eduard. 'Opereta pro kulturní lidi'. *Lidové noviny*, 28 November 1936, 9.

Bauer, Jan. *Muzikálový triumf*. Prague: Brána, 1999.

Blažek, Vratislav. *Dáma na kolejích*. Prague: DILIA, 1966.

Block, Gregory. *Enchanted Evenings*. Oxford and New York: Oxford University Press, 2009.

Březina, Václav. *Lexikon českého filmu*. Prague: Cinema, 1996.

Burian, Jarka M. *Leading Creators of Twentieth-Century Czech Theatre*. London: Routledge 2002.

Černý, Jindřich. 'Padne mu jak ulitá'. *Divadlo*, 5/1968, 29–34.

Černý, Jiří. . . . *na bílém 1: Hudební publicistika 1956–1969*. Prague: Galén, 2014.

Gmiterková, Šárka. 'Kristian v montérkách: Hvězdná osobnost Oldřicha Nového mezi kulturními průmysly, produkčními systémy a politickými režimy v letech 1936–1969'. PhD diss., Masarykova Univerzita, 2018.

Hedbávný, Zdeněk. *Alfréd Radok: Zpráva o jednom osudu*. Prague: Národní divadlo and Divadelní ústav, 1994.

Herman, Josef. 'Nejen karlínské problémy po čtyřiceti letech'. *Scéna* 9 (1986): 7.

Herman, Josef. 'České muzikálové herectví?' *Divadelní noviny* 2 (1995): 1, 4.

Herman, Josef. 'Velký trpaslík Dracula'. *Divadelní noviny* 20 (1995): 1.

Herman, Josef. 'Opereta versus muzikál'. *Divadelní noviny* 19 (1996): 1, 4.

Herman, Josef. 'Muzikály podobojí'. *Divadelní noviny* 10 (2019): 4.

Just, Vladimír. *Proměny malých scén*. Prague: Mladá fronta, 1984.

Just, Vladimír. 'Mýtus Semafor?' *Divadelní revue* 4 (1999): 3–10.

Just, Vladimír. 'Peripetie a návraty V + W'. In: Voskovec, Jiří/Werich, Jan. *Hry Osvobozeného divadla*, 11–18. Prague: Karolinum + Progetto, 2000.

Just, Vladimír. *Werichovo Divadlo ABC*. Prague: Brána, 2013.

Klusák, Pavel. 'Jak přežít horší časy'. *Lidové noviny*, 20 October 2012, 28.

Kolář, Jan. *Jak to bylo v Semaforu*. Prague: SCÉNA 1991.

Machalická, Jana. 'Potíže se zlatým vejcem'. *DISK* 39 (March 2012): 132–137.

Marklová, Milada. *Nová česká operetní a muzikálová tvorba 1970–1980*. Prague: Divadelní ústav, 1980.

Marklová, Milada. *Nová česká operetní a muzikálová tvorba 1980–1990*. Prague: Divadelní ústav, 1990.

McMillin, Scott. *Musical as Drama*. Princeton, NJ: Princeton University Press, 2006.

Osolsobě, Ivo. *Muzikál je, když*. Prague: Supraphon, 1967.

Osolsobě, Ivo. 'Muzikál v Československu'. In *Muzikál*, edited by Siegfried Schmidt-Joos, 249–266. Prague: Editio Supraphon, 1968.

Osolsobě, Ivo. *Divadlo, které mluví, zpívá a tančí*. Prague: Supraphon, 1974.

Osolsobě, Ivo. 'Paradox muzikálu'. *Svět a divadlo* 5 (1992): 68–76.

Osolsobě, Ivo. *Marsyas: Apollón . . . a Dionýsos: Přibližování k muzikálu*. 2 vols. Brno: Divadelní fakulta Janáčkovy akademie múzických umění, 1996.

Prostějovský, Michael, and Pavel Bár. 'Fenomén "český" muzikál'. *DISK* 39 (March 2012): 120–131.

Rut, Přemysl. 'Dvojice osamělých'. *O divadle* 3 (November 1987): 148–164.

Rut, Přemysl. 'Osobnost a doba'. *O divadle* 5 (October 1989): 45–59.

Rut, Přemysl. *Písničky: Eseje se zpěvy*. Brno: Petrov, 2001.

Sílová, Zuzana, and Pavel Bár, eds. *Frejkovy Schovávané na schodech*. Prague: KANT, 2014.

Sílová, Zuzana, and Jaroslav Vostrý, eds. *Městská divadla pražská v éře Oty Ornesta (1950–1972)*. Prague: KANT, 2014.

Schonberg, Michal. *Osvobozené*. Prague: Odeon, 1992.

Suchý, Jiří. *Trocha poezie*. Prague: Československý spisovatel, 1989.

Suchý, Jiří. *Encyklopedie Jiřího Suchého*. Vol. 10, *Divadlo 1963–1969*. Prague: Karolinum—Pražská imaginace, 2002.

Suchý, Jiří. *Encyklopedie Jiřího Suchého*. Vol. 11, *Divadlo 1970–1974*. Prague: Karolinum—Pražská imaginace, 2002.

Suchý, Jiří. *Encyklopedie Jiřího Suchého*. Vol. 12, *Divadlo 1975–1982*. Prague: Karolinum—Pražská imaginace, 2003.

Szczepanik, Petr. *Továrna Barrandov: Svět filmařů a politická moc 1945–1970*. Prague: Národní filmový archív, 2016.

Szczygiel, Mariusz. *Gottland: Mostly True Stories from Half of Czechoslovakia*. New York: Melville House, 2014.

Šormová Eva, ed. *Česká divadla: Encyklopedie divadelních souborů*. Prague: Divadelní ústav, 2000.

Uhde, Milan. *Balada pro banditu a jiné hry na zapřenou*. Brno: Atlantis, 2001.

Valtrová, Marie. *Vratislav Blažek: Hráč před Bohem a lidmi*. Prague: Achát, 1998.

Vaněk, Jan J. *Muzikál v Čechách*. Prague: Knihcentrum, 1998.

Voskovec, Jiří, and Jan Werich. *Hry*. Prague: Československý spisovatel, 1980.

# CHAPTER 29

........................................................................................................................

# POLISH MUSICAL THEATRE SINCE THE 1960S

........................................................................................................................

## ALEKSANDRA ZAJAC-KIEDYSZ

POPULAR music theater in Poland commonly derives from the activities of state theatres established after 1952: in the period up to 1958, as many as nine theaters were founded. The inauguration of these institutions was a manifestation of changes taking place throughout the country. Operetta became an extremely popular genre in the second half of the 1950s; it turned out to be a great propaganda instrument, and during this period there was a thaw in the official approach to culture so that previously neglected forms of entertainment began to be presented. The authorities suddenly realised that popular musical theater could become a useful art for the 'working masses' while in addition offering employment for many amateur ensembles and a wide group of pre-war artists from operetta and vaudeville theaters.

In the wake of these changes in Poland, nine popular musical theaters were founded—in Gliwice, Warsaw, Wrocław, Łódź, Poznań, Lublin, Szczecin, Kraków, and Gdańsk (later Gdynia). Not for nothing is this phenomenon referred to as the 'operetta epidemic'.[1] It is worth noting, however, that popular musical theater faced enormous obstacles—largely because of the huge resistance of the socialist authorities, who treated it as an anachronistic relic of a previous culture, and a sign of the 'decadent West'. Other barriers were the limited repertoire, because there was virtually no access to Western musicals and no modern Polish scores. A lack of professionally trained actors together with a number of technical difficulties complete the picture of those years.

The majority of theatres exploited the classical canon (like Kálmán, Lehár, Johann Strauss, and Offenbach), but there were also early and very modest endeavours to refresh the repertoire. The first American musical in Poland appeared, surprisingly, in a straight theatre: the première of *Daj Buzi Kate* (*Kiss Me, Kate*), by Cole Porter, was held in 1957 at the Comedy Theatre in Warsaw. It initiated the era of modern musical theatre in Poland, but it should be recognised that this first attempt at the genre was rather weak; the greatest achievements were to come a few decades later. In the first years, beside *Kiss Me, Kate*, one could see *My Fair Lady*, *Can-Can*, and *Fantastyczny rejs* (*Anything Goes*).[2]

It seems that the censors found it easier to accept a work with a European character or style than with an entirely American milieu.

The main part of this essay will focus on the history of musical theatre in Gdynia, as a case study of Polish musical theatre.[3] The local's musical theatre came into existence in 1958 and was almost from the start one of the most interesting examples of its type in Poland, where it was regarded for a long period as the best theatre for musicals. Significantly, unlike other venues of this kind, which were usually called 'operetta theatres', Gdynia's theatre was from the start named 'Musical Theatre'. The new institution was formed in order 'to promote full-length operetta, musical comedy, vaudeville and revue in the province of Gdańsk'.[4] From the very beginning it was intended to constitute the place above all others for the production of a modern rather than merely the classic repertoire. The theatre was originally situated in the Culture House in Gdańsk—Nowy Port.

## Gdynia: The Early Years

The theatre's first management was appointed on 1 January 1958; the post of director was held by Wacław Śniady. The early days of the theatre were extremely difficult; not only did it lack professionally trained actors, but the auditorium of the Culture House did not have good acoustics, and there were no workshop or technical facilities. The first production in the colourful saga of Gdynia's Musical Theatre was a light, humorous, and melodious work, Richard Heuberger's *Bal w operze* (*Der Opernball*, 1876); the inaugural première took place on 18 May 1958. After this first production the theatre moved to Gdynia, to the building at 26 Bema Street, where it remained for the next twenty years.

Śniady, who had built the theatre from nothing, was soon dismissed. Until 1965 the executive directors changed often, and the profile of the theatre was not particularly interesting. All the executive directors had the same problems: a budget that was too small, almost no technical facilities, and a building that, having been damaged in World War II and was in the 1950s only slowly being reconstructed, was in poor condition (and was, moreover, shared by three different theatres and two households). This was typical of the period; many other venues where in the same situation. The repertoire was fairly typical, and no artistic innovations were made.

## Danuta Baduszkowa, First Lady of Polish Musical Theatre

All of this changed in 1965 when one of the founders of the theatre, Danuta Baduszkowa, became its artistic director—and in 1973 its executive director. She was a tireless reformer who at a conference about indigenous operetta in 1958 had noted that 'until now, the genre was being directed in the same old way.... We need to create something new at least.'[5]

The ambitious plans evident in Baduszkowa's new repertoire—based on more modern scores as opposed to the classic operettas of the Lehár or Kálmán style—required professionally trained actors. According to Baduszkowa, the actor is the lifeblood of the theatre: 'Without actors, my musicals are worth nothing. Training should be comprehensive. Unfortunately, most of the students of drama schools aren't prepared to work in the theatre of which I dream.'[6] She rightly regarded musical theatre as the most difficult of the actor's art forms, understanding that without well-prepared artists she could not make the musical theatre she envisaged.

There was no school at the tertiary education level in theatre or music academies that educated actors in popular musical theatre in any communist Eastern bloc country. In Poland there were some courses, mostly in the music academies, that prepared soloists to sing in opera houses. The graduates of these academies, however, were not interested in performing in popular musical theatre: working in this genre was regarded as something of an comedown, because it didn't enjoy the prestige of opera. Baduszkowa therefore chose to make a groundbreaking move: on 4 October 1966 she opened the Vocal Training and Acting Studio at Gdynia's theatre. It was the first institution in Poland that prepared young people to work on musical theatre stages. Worth mentioning is the school's informal status in its early years. Later the minister of culture started using Baduszkowa's school as an example to other theatre managers.

In the early years of its existence there were many compulsory courses at the Studio, such as solo singing, vocal reproduction, music (solfège, theory, and history), elementary acting, interpretation of poetry and prose, and diction, as well as dancing and fencing. The fourth year was focused on preparing for the diploma, the programme concluding with an exam presentation before the State Verification Commission. Upon satisfaction of all the requirements, the certificate for a soloist or actor of musical theatre was awarded, and the graduates were qualified to work in any type of theatre in Poland. It is worth noting that from the beginning Baduszkowa hired outstanding specialists: employing the best possible teachers became a hallmark of the school. Therefore, it is no wonder that student performers attained excellent results and that Baduszkowa, and the directors who followed, were able to convince specialists from various music or drama theatres all over Poland to work there. Students of the Studio participated in performances of the theatre from their first year, in the vocal or dance ensemble: this was a significant aspect of the system of education. Also, from the start, some students were even cast in leading roles. Within the first six years of the school's existence, the programme was finalised, equipping its students to perform modern repertoire and encouraging them in a range of challenges. During this period, there were many interesting premières in the theatre; some of them will be mentioned in the next parts of the essay. The students were involved at various levels in all of them.

After this start, Baduszkowa began to implement her ideas concerning the repertoire. Wanting to break away from staging exclusively classic operettas, yet not having

FIG. 29.1 Danuta Baduszkowa rehearsing with students of the Vocal Training and Acting Studio in Gdynia. Photographer unknown; image courtesy of the archive of the Musical Theatre of Gdynia.

access to the contemporary repertoire from the West End or Broadway, she decided on her next experiment: introducing the theatre to the lesser-known works of Polish composers and to specially commissioned works. The following years witnessed a sequence of premières of Polish musicals and musical comedies, including *Madagaskar* (*Madagascar*, 1968), *Kaper królewski* (*The Royal Privateer*, 1969), *Diabeł nie śpi* (*The Devil Doesn't Sleep*, 1970), *Kariera Nikodema Dyzmy* (*The Career of Nikodem Dyzma*, 1971), *Pan Zagłoba* (*Mr Zagloba*, 1972), *Pancerni i pies* (*Tank Drivers and a Dog*, 1973), and *Szwejk* (*Schweik*, 1977). In addition, this repertoire provided audiences with a musical education: the spectators became acquainted with a modern repertoire rather than an exclusively classical one, an extremely important consequence of Baduszkowa's work.

Her repertoire included *Madagascar*, composed by Ryszard Damrosz, which was based on the history of the romantic and infamous Polish troublemaker Maurycy Beniowski. The book was written by Danuta Baduszkowa and Jacek Korczakowski, and the show opened on 14 December 1968 as the central feature of the celebrations for the tenth anniversary of Gdynia's theatre. It was full of duels and romance and was presented with a large dose of humour: colourfully designed, the show included many wonderful crowd scenes in a melodious musical framework of partly stylised African folk music. Above all, however, the score was based on popular music that reinforced the action.

Another show commissioned by the theatre was *Mr Zagloba*. The music was composed by the famous contemporary Polish composer Augustyn Bloch, and the book, based on the Henryk Sienkiewicz novel *Ogniem i mieczem* (*With Fire and Sword*), the first part of *The Trilogy*, was by Wanda Maciejewska. The main protagonist of the piece is the titular Mr Zagloba, an iconic figure known to every Pole. His sense of humor, wiliness, and cunning, as well as his eloquent tirades, all set against the background of the turbulent history of seventeenth-century Poland, turned out to be excellent source material for a musical. The show's première, on 7 May 1972, inaugurated one of the theatre's greatest successes. It is now considered to be one of the most important artistic events of the period. It is notable that Baduszkowa chose a very specific time for this première: *Pan Wolodyjowski* (*Fire in the Steppe*), the third part of *The Trilogy*, had been filmed a few years earlier in 1969, and the screen adaptation of the second part (*Potop* [*The Deluge*]) was to open in 1974. Baduszkowa cleverly exploited the popularity of the title to promote her own production.

One of the most interesting premières at the time was *Tank Drivers and a Dog*, based on the extremely popular TV series *Czterej pancerni i pies* (*Four Tank Drivers and a Dog*).[7] The show opened on 15 December 1973. Based on the novel by Janusz Przymanowski, who with his wife also wrote the book of the musical, the production captured the attention of the media, as it was rare in those days for a theatre to compete with television. It was well received by both the press and the general public. The canine that played the eponymous dog was called War; it was borrowed from a police station and generated huge interest, receiving a sausage after every performance as well as a special fee for its appearances. Although War was well behaved, it occasionally disappeared behind the scenes during a performance. During this period there were also a few premières of Western musicals, such as *My Fair Lady* (1965), *Anything Goes* (1966), and *Promises, Promises* (1976).

*Noc w San Francisco* (*Night in San Francisco*) was a particularly interesting indigenous show that premiered on 4 November 1969. The operetta, by Giudo Masanetz (music) and Otto Schneidereit (book), was funded by an East German company. However, it ran for only sixteen performances because its translator, Krystyna Żywulska, escaped to the West; once the authorities discovered her flight, they closed the production. Besides the shows listed above, the repertoire still featured classic operettas and musical comedies, from different parts of the world such as Italy (*Rinaldo* [*Rinaldo in campo*], 1966), the USSR (*Sewastopolski walc* [*Sevastopol's Waltz*], 1967), Austria (*Wesoła wojna* [*Der lustige Krieg*], 1967), Great Britain (*Gejsza* [*The Geisha*], 1968), France (*Córka Madame Angot* [*La Fille de Madame Angot*], 1971), Georgia (*Kto się boi starych kapci* [*Babadżane Koszebi*], 1971), and even Cuba (*Cecylia Valdes*, 1973).

As previously mentioned, the theatre building was not technically equipped for modern musical theatre productions. Eventually Baduszkowa succeeded in her attempts to secure the building of a new theatre, and in 1972 a project team managed by Józef Chmiel started to realise her concept. It was intended to have modern technical facilities in addition to being user-friendly for both performers and audiences. After moving to the new building, there were plans to rename the theatre the National Musical Theatre, in order to confirm its renown as one of the most important of its kind. According to the plans, the building was due to be finished by 1975, but in the end the opening was delayed until 1979—a typical example of socialist inefficiency. In the meantime, Baduszkowa had not only already augmented the ensemble for the new, much bigger stage, but she also planned the celebration for the theatre's twentieth anniversary, wishing to revive its first production of *Der Opernball* to inaugurate the new building. When the legendary director died after a long illness in December 1978, the show opened without her. During her last years as executive director, she devoted most of her energy to the development of a repertoire based largely on contemporary Polish works in collaboration with many composers and writers, both nationally known and local. She continuously introduced the public to new titles and genres: of twenty-five productions between 1973 and 1978, twenty-three were premières. In addition to the ones listed above, such as *Tank Drivers and a Dog* and *Schweik*, these included *Prawo pierwszej nocy* (*First Night's Right*, 1974), *Madame Sans-Gêne* (1975), *Pinokio* (*Pinocchio*, 1977), and others.

It is worth pointing out that Baduszkowa not only adopted a fresh approach to the expansion of the musical theatre repertoire, she also had innovative ideas about musical theatre in general. She built up a good relationship with the critics because she was very skilful in her treatment of representatives of the press. She was committed to the attendance of children at theatre performances, seeking the opinions of young audiences who she believed would form an educated theatre audience in the future. Her greatest legacy—and one which affected not only Gdynia's theatre heritage but the growth of popular musical theatre in Poland generally—was the founding of the Vocal Training and Acting Studio in 1966. Up to then no performers had been trained in the skills required by roles in contemporary musicals. Without doubt, professionalism was very important to Baduszkowa. Both the Theatre and the Studio are now named after her to honour her visionary outlook and significant achievements; she is known as the First Lady of Musical Theatre in Poland.

# ANDRZEJ CYBULSKI AND HIS THEATRE OF SOCIAL RESONANCE

Succeeding her at the Gdynia Theatre was Andrzej Cybulski, whose earliest task was overseeing the final stage of its completion. Activity in the new building was inaugurated on 8 December 1979 with the celebrated première of *Krakowiacy i Górale* (*Natives of Cracow and Highlanders*), written by Wojciech Bogusławski. The new manager developed his own concept of the theatre's repertoire and mission. He wanted to react, in artistic ways to significant social and political events, reflecting the turbulence of recent Polish history. It was intended as a theatre of 'social resonance', so Cybulski aimed to continue researching the international repertoire as his predecessor had, but in different

## 814 ALEKSANDRA ZAJAC-KIEDYSZ

fields of theatre. In his opinion, the Viennese operetta convention had to be abandoned, as should the rigid understanding of Polish music theatre imposed by other artistic directors, which limited its activities.[8] Whereas Cybulski wanted to follow his own concept of the musical theatre, the repertoire of practically all other musical theatres in Poland was still based mostly on classic operettas; only occasionally did they create something more modern. Their directors probably were afraid of experiments and thus preferred safer options; they gave their spectators works that were well known and liked, but as a consequence their theatres were stuck in days gone by.

Cybulski was the exception, as he wished to create something new. Thus, for instance, on 28 November 1980, *Piraci* (*The Pirates of Penzance*), by Gilbert and Sullivan, was presented, although (comic) operettas were not performed at all at that time. Thus, the new director found his own artistic approach. Up to then historical events made no serious impact on Gdynia's Musical Theatre; however, as was the case with other such cultural institutions, the socio-political context was obviously a factor in determining the course of the theatre's progress. All Polish theatres of this era struggled against restrictions imposed on their choice of artistic material, with some institutions succeeding better than others in their interactions with the authorities.

Under Cybulski's management the situation changed drastically. The theatre fell on extremely hard times at this juncture of Polish history. The government announced increases in food prices on 1 July 1980. The next day protests began in Ursus, Sanok, and Tarnów, joined by other factories in the days that followed. In the shipyard of Gdańsk, on 14 August the trade union leader Lech Wałęsa ordered a strike. Two days later the August Agreements were signed in Gdańsk, and the Supreme Court registered the labour union NSZZ Solidarność (Solidarity). Quite unexpectedly, these events changed the course of history, including the future of Gdynia's Theatre.[9]

What occurred in Poland in 1980 was the inspiration for an unusual performance: *Kolęda-Nocka* (*Carol-Singing Night*) opened on 20 December 1980, with book and lyrics by Ernest Bryll and music by Wojciech Trzciński. Initially it was intended as a concert, but during the rehearsal its creators, responding to the volatility of the changing context, decided to mount the show as a full-scale production. The directorate of the theatre wanted the show to reflect the atmosphere in households and on the streets in reaction to what was happening. This represented a new approach to popular musical theatre. At this historic moment the Polish theatre found a voice to express the crucial social realities as for a short time artists were allowed relative freedom. While the staging presented a series of poetic impressions, the plot was vague. The lack of a coherent book was one of the reasons *Kolęda-Nocka* has sometimes been compared to the musical *Hair*. The mise-en-scène was saturated with national and religious symbols, with the costumes, set design, various gestures, and entire scenes conceived as iconic images. Huge shipbuilding cranes appeared as an element of the scenography, with references to recent happenings; for example, when the Archangel presented the Star of Bethlehem to the carol singers, it bore the inscription 'Solidarity'.

On the stage was represented the ordinary weekday of Poles in crowded trains, cramped flats, and never-ending queues. The most controversial moment was when

FIG. 29.2 A scene from *Kolęda-Nocka* (*Carol-Singing Night*, 1980), the defining production of the Gdynia Theatre under director Andrzej Cybulski. Photo: Grzegorz Haremza, courtesy of the archive of the Musical Theatre of Gdynia.

the crowd raised the door on which the body of the young man was hanging from his shoulders, passing it from hand to hand before placing it on the top of the scaffolding. This was a reference to the events of December 1970. Between 14 and 19 December strikes and protests took place in many cities in Poland, mostly in Pomerania—in Gdańsk, Gdynia, Szczecin, and Elbląg. Just like ten years later, the immediate cause of the protests was an increase in food prices. The protests were violently suppressed by the army and police—45 people were killed in the streets (16 of them in Gdynia alone), 1,165 were injured, and more than 3,000 were arrested. Many who had not even taken part in the protests died on their way to work or school. The death of a young man became the symbol of these events: during the protest in Gdynia, the crowd carried his body aloft on a door. This was one of the darkest moments in postwar Polish history. Referring to that tragedy in the place where it had occurred in front of many witnesses was overwhelmingly moving in performance.

It is worth pointing out that *Kolęda-Nocka* was the first theatrical response to the birth of the Solidarity movement and soon became legendary. None of the other productions of Gdynia's Theatre was so famous or controversial in Poland. With a single show Cybulski fulfilled his ambitious dreams to provide 'socially resonant' theatre. However, the authorities monitored the performance carefully, and in 1981 it was banned on a

# 816    ALEKSANDRA ZAJAC-KIEDYSZ

number of occasions. Martial law put an end to the show's brief, tumultuous history. Cybulski was fired at the end 1982; the unofficial reason given for his 'resignation' was his decision to produce *Kolęda-Nocka*.

## 'POLISH BROADWAY ON THE BALTIC SEA'

Cybulski's successor was Jerzy Gruza, a popular director of TV series and theatre performances who had organised the Sopot Festival.[10] He completely changed the theatre's approach to repertoire, opting to stage musicals from the West End and Broadway. During the decade of his management, there were premières of shows such as *Skrzypek na dachu* (*Fiddler on the Roof*, 1984), *The Fantasticks* (1984), *Jesus Christ Superstar* (1987), *Les Misérables* (1989), *Oliver!* (1990), and *West Side Story* (1992). This period is commonly known as 'Polish Broadway on the Baltic Sea'.[11] It is worth stressing that the new director was 'encouraged' in his new aims: after the lifting of martial law,[12] the attitude of the authorities towards the modern repertoire from Broadway or West End began to change. Censorship was still in place, but it was less restrictive. Despite this, Polish theatres rarely staged Western musicals for various reasons, among them the lack of an appropriately qualified creative team and of adequate financing and stage facilities. The necessity of purchasing licences for the shows in dollars was probably the greatest barrier. When licences were granted, they specified the time period but were valid for all the theatres in the country, so a single show was often produced by several stages at the same time, with the theatres owning only the rights to the première production.

The performance that opened the sequence of Western musicals in Gdynia's Theatre was *Fiddler on the Roof*. Gruza, the show's director, prepared for this première very carefully. First of all, he invited experts on Jewish folklore and customs as advisors. One of them was Jan Szurmiej, the manager of the Warsaw Jewish Theatre, who was the show's choreographer; the dance in the tavern—the famous bottle dance—honoured the Jewish tradition, enrapturing the audience with its authenticity and charm. There were also deliberate references to the popular film version.[13] The show opened on 24 November 1984. The critics asserted that Gruza was able to bring out all the inherent values of the score. Just as in Jerome Robbins's 1964 Broadway production, the dancers in Gdynia actually balanced bottles on bowler hats (in other theatres they were put into holes cut into the bottom of the hat).[14] This was one of the reasons the media valued the Gdynia production so highly; press interest had been enormous—there were close to sixty reviews. The show provoked great enthusiasm among the spectators: on opening night, the standing ovation lasted half an hour.

The reasons behind such enthusiastic reaction of both the press and the audience are complex. First, after the end of martial law, Polish culture opened up to trends and opportunities from the West, including the repertoire of musical theatres. Censorship had eased greatly. Gruza managed to attract a young public hungry for world-class

FIG. 29.3 Krzysztof Stopa (Fiddler) and Juliusz Berger (Tevye) in a scene from the director Jerzy Gruza's celebrated 1984 production of *Fiddler on the Roof*, the first time the Broadway classic was staged in Poland. Photo: Grzegorz Lewandowski/Tomasz Degórski, courtesy of the archive of the Musical Theatre of Gdynia.

entertainment known only from films watched mostly on smuggled VHS tapes, rarely in the cinema. Secondly, the Gdynia version was the third attempt by Polish theatres to pull off this particular musical: it had already been staged in 1983 in Łódź and at the beginning of 1984 in Poznań, but both productions were rather unsuccessful. The two theatres were simply not prepared to produce musicals of this scale. However, as already mentioned, Gruza prepared very carefully for his own production, scrupulously watching the two earlier Polish premières. In addition, he had many assets the previous two versions did not have—a well-equipped stage, but above all a perfectly prepared acting team. The audience received, probably for the first time in the history of Polish musical theatre, a production of the quality of those on Broadway or in the West End. No wonder it soon became legendary. It is also worth mentioning that *Fiddler* turned into the most popular musical in modern history of Polish musical theatre.[15] There were many productions; almost every theatre had this title in its repertory, and some of the theatres, including the one in Gdynia, have already revived it. In the 2019–2020 season, the Jerry Bock–Sheldon Harnick musical was scheduled in eleven different theatres— not only in those specialising in musicals, but also opera houses. The original Gdynia production stayed popular for many years. Before it closed in 1999, *Fiddler on the Roof* had been performed almost five hundred times; no other show has ever had as many performances in Gdynia.

Almost as successful with the public was *Jesus Christ Superstar*. For its première on 6 June 1987 Gruza deliberately cast rock vocalists in the leading roles: Marek Piekarczyk from the hard rock band TSA as Jesus and Małgorzata Ostrowska from Lombard as Mary Magdalene. Gruza had created a cost-effective, breathtakingly minimalist entertainment which introduced the genre of the rock opera, with its attendant countercultures, to Polish audiences. For young people in particular, this was a momentous event that appealed to them in ways earlier musicals had not. Although it was first seen on stage in 1971, Lloyd Webber and Rice's show constituted something completely new and original to Polish theatre-goers.

Poland's third enormous success with the modern international repertoire was also the first exclusively licensed musical to play in Poland; in fact, *Les Misèrables* on 30 June 1989 was referred to as a 'compact musical'.[16] According to the licensing agreement, the director was not permitted to offer his own interpretation of the work, because the entire production was under the close supervision of both the original artistic and technical teams. The producer Cameron Mackintosh and the composer attended the première in Gdynia and were enraptured by its grand scale and energy, admitting that the London original had an orchestra of only half the size of that in Gdynia and scenery on a much smaller scale.

It is certainly true that Gruza's notion of introducing the modern Western repertoire exploited the circumstances in Poland at precisely the right moment; however, no other Polish theatre rivaled Gdynia Theatre's record of success in this respect. On the other hand, Gruza sought American and British staples of the genre while resolutely facing financial and other difficulties. His staging of a wide repertoire of classic musicals became well-known throughout Poland, attracting large audiences and much press attention, not only locally but nationally, with highlights from premières appearing on TV news programmes.

Gruza's well-trained ensemble, his modern scenography, and his newly obtained access to contemporary Western scores ushered in the greatest period in the history of Gdynia's Theatre. Some productions toured not only through Poland but also to the Soviet Union, the United Kingdom, and the United States. *Fiddler on the Roof* was performed in Plymouth, the UK sister city of Gdynia, in 1989 as a result of cooperation between the theatres of the two cities, garnering extremely positive reviews. The consequence of this was the opening up of more dialogue between Polish communist and English capitalist cultures.

# The Recent History of Gdynia's Theatre

After Poland's political transformation in 1989, successive directors of Gdynia's Theatre tried to balance out the opposing concepts of repertoire as conceived by Baduszkowa

POLISH MUSICAL THEATRE SINCE THE 1960S    819

and Gruza. Well-known Western shows such as *Evita* (1997), *Hair* (1999), *Chicago* (2002), *Piękna i Bestia* (*Beauty and the Beast*, 2008), *Shrek* (2011), *Avenue Q* (2014), *Ghost* (2015), and *Notre-Dame de Paris* (2016) were produced; Maciej Korwin (the Theatre's executive director between 1995 and 2013 and the first one chosen through an open competition) maintained the theatre's unique artistic identity, with a place for original Polish productions chiefly based on literature, such as *Sen nocy letniej* (*A Midsummer Night's Dream*, 2001), by Wojciech Kościelniak (book) and Leszek Możdżer (music); and *Lalka* (*The Doll*, 2010), by Kościelniak (book) and Piotr Dziubek (music).

Political and systemic changes transformed the culture as well. Given the high cost of mounting musicals, functioning under market conditions turned out to be difficult, causing Gdynia's Theatre to be plunged into stagnation and debt in the early 1990s. Under these conditions the new director did surprisingly well. Not only did he get the theatre out of financial trouble, but he also implemented several interesting innovations in the repertoire; he began to co-produce productions with Western agents and producers and tour them throughout Europe. One of the greatest of Korwin's achievements was to give a chance to Wojciech Kościelniak, who had very little experience but soon became one of most the interesting creators in Polish musical theatre. Kościelniak has consistently followed the path he calls a 'third way'.[17] His first show as a director was *Hair*, staged in 1999. After this he started working on a musical adaptation of Shakespeare's *A Midsummer Night's Dream*, premiering in 2001.

With subsequent adaptations, his concept of musical theatre developed:

> I try to move between tradition of opera and operetta and everything connected with the American musical. That doesn't mean I don't value those paths. However, it seems to me that we can look for our own way based on music and literature, and the style in which we perform and stage theatre in European and even Polish traditions.[18].

In his productions he effectively combines elements of dramatic theatre, music, singing, and dancing with acting, scenography, and space into a completely integrated mise-en-scène. It seems that his 'third path' represents the search for a genre between popular music and dramatic theatre, incorporating the rich tradition of Polish theatre. Nowadays Kościelniak is considered a specialist in the adaptation of literature, transferring *Ziemia obiecana* (*Promised Land*, 2011) and *Chłopi* (*The Peasants*, 2013) by Reymont, *Idiota* (*The Idiot*, 2009) by Dostoevsky, *Mistrz i Małgorzata* (*The Master and Margarita*, 2013) by Bulgakov, *Cyberiada* (*Cyberiad*, 2015) by Lem, *Wiedźmin* (*The Witcher*, 2017) by Sapkowski, and *Blaszany bębenek* (*The Tin Drum*, 2018) by Günter Grass. However, he does not confine himself to literary adaptations; Kościelniak is also passionate about film and has produced not only a musical version of *Hallo Szpicbródka* (*Hello, Fred the Beard*, 2012), one of the most popular movies from the Polish People's Republic period, but also the American *Frankenstein* in 2011 (although based on a novel, it was actually the 1931 film adaptation that inspired the director). The company's one of latest première, *Śpiewak jazzbandu* (*The Jazz Singer*), is based on the very first American sound film; it opened on 14 June 2019 at the Jewish Theatre in Warsaw. He also devised performances based on original scripts (such as *Scat, czyli od pucybuta do milionera* (*Scat, from Bootblack to Millionaire*, 2005). Although he got his start at the Musical Theatre in Gdynia, the director now cooperates with many musical theatre companies in Warsaw, Wrocław, and Kraków as well as venues in Gdańsk, Kalisz, and Bielsko-Biala. After Korwin's sudden death in 2013, Kościelniak said: 'Maciej was the most important person in my career. He trusted me as an unknown director. Without him, I probably wouldn't have been able to enter the professional theatre so quickly.'[19]

Korwin's successor, Igor Michalski, has continued with the kind of repertoire conceived by Korwin, staging well-known Western musicals as well as original indigenous scores. It is worth stressing that since the 1960s there have been other notable events in Polish musical theatre, such as Mitch Leigh's *Człowiek z La Manchy* (*Man of La Mancha*), which premiered in 1970 at the Silesian Operetta in Gliwice;[20] *Metro*, by the composer Janusz Stokłosa, in 1991 at Warsaw's Dramatic Theatre;[21] and *Upiór w operze* (*The Phantom of the Opera*) by Lloyd Webber (2008), at the Roma Theatre in Warsaw.

Nowadays popular musical theatre in Poland is undergoing impressive developments. Contemporary scores form the basis of the repertoire in most popular musical theatres, even being staged in opera houses and occasionally in drama theatres. Currently, there are twenty-four 'music theatres' in Poland; ten of these focus on musical theatre. The rest of them produce the occasional musical; for example, the one in Białystok does so almost every season. As mentioned above, some of the straight theatres regularly stage musicals, such as the Warsaw Drama Theatre, which in 2017 staged *Kinky Boots* (2017). In the same city there are also two theatres—Rampa and Syrena—which are not called musical theatres but which schedule musical works almost exclusively. In this context it should be pointed out that almost all of the Polish musical theatres are financed by public funds on the federal or local level. Only one music theatre in Poland (Studio Buffo) works as a private company.

Second decade brought a visible development of the genre, we can call it 'musical epicemic', and the list of titles staged is impressive. It includes *Deszczowa piosenka* (*Singin' in the Rain*, 2012), *Nine* (2014), *Avenue Q* (2014), *Mamma Mia!* (2015), *Rodzina Addamsów* (*The Addams Family*, 2015), *Zakonnica w przebraniu* (*Sister Act*, 2016), *Doktor Żywago* (*Doctor Zhivago*, 2017), *Sunset Boulevard* (2017), *Gorączka Sobotniej nocy* (*Saturday Night Fever*, 2018), *Next to Normal* (2019), and many others. The third decade seems to continue this trend, to mentione only a few premiere: *Waitress* (2021), *Something Rotten* (2022), *Beauty and the Beast* (2023) and many others. There are musical acting and singing classes at theatre and music academies in Gdańsk (opened in 2009), Łódź (2014), Warsaw (2015), and Poznań (2020). The general popularity of musicals can further be grasped by audience figures: in 2016, the Musical Theatre in Gdynia was visited by 212,603 spectators, equating to ticket sales of almost thirteen million Polish zloty. In the following two years the numbers were on a similar level of about fifteen million Polish zloty. The total number of visitors to the Polish music theatres in 2018 was 2.3 million, according to Statistic Poland (which does not compile specific data for musicals). This also attests to the continuingly important role of the Musical Theatre in Gdynia, which is still the market leader: 10 percent of the audience for all of the country's music theatres visited this particular venue.

Over the decades, the contribution of Gdynia's Music Theatre to original native musical theatre has been exceptional. Many theatres, like the ones in Wrocław and Gliwice, followed Gdynia's model to create their own repertoires; others have reproduced some of Gdynia's original works—*Kaper królewski* was also staged in Łódź, Lublin, and Kiev, at the Silesian Operetta, and elsewhere. The Vocal Training and Acting Studio has had a major impact on musical theatre, providing well-trained performers for musical ensembles across Poland. The roster of outstanding graduates of the School is long, and almost the entire team of the Gdynia Theatre has been recruited from the Studio. Moreover, its graduates have joined the teams of many other musical theatres. It is difficult to find a musical theatre in Poland which does not employ alumni of the institution, while in other theatres they constitute the foundation of the team. The Studio might be said to be one of main reasons musical theatre in 1980s Poland and after could develop as extraordinarily as it did. Conversely, it is precisely a consequence of the lack of this kind of school in other countries under socialism that musical theatre was almost nonexistent prior to 1989. In Czechoslovakia the first such school was founded in the 1990s, while in Hungary there were some attempts in the 1970s to establish proper training facilities, but without success. Nowadays in Hungary there is musical actor training faculty on The University of Theatre and Film Arts. It's the only higher education acting school there, from 2020 it's no longer national, but private. There are still no one musical theatre singing class on Hungarian music academies.

Until 1989 most musical theatres in Poland had a very conservative repertoire and rarely staged native works or musicals from the West; they simply eschewed experimentation. The theatre in Gliwice may be an exception to this rule: it had several interesting productions to its credit during this period, such as *Kiss Me, Kate, Man of La Mancha*, and *West Side Story*. The rest of the country staged classic operettas almost exclusively. Not until the twenty-first century did Poznań, Wrocław, or Łódź take a new approach to their repertoire; those cities did not take the drastic step of finally breaking with the tradition of offering nothing but operettas, slowly changing their repertiore profile.. Finally, it could be pointed out that the exceptional development in Gdynia may have been enhanced by the town's reputation as a windy seaside resort which is not merely always open to people but is also always crowded. This is the place, from where, starting in the 1930s, the ocean liner *M. S. Batory* sailed the seas, from where people travelled all over the world. Many historical changes began in Gdańsk. In the gloomy and sobering communist reality, these sort of things might have made a difference.

Currently, musical theatre remains extremely popular in Poland and the country continues to stage both indigenous and international works. In the upcoming season (2023–2024) there will be productions of *Six, Calendar Girls The Musical, School of Rock, Kopernik (Copernicus), Singin' in the Rain* and many others. Other shows that have been announced for the future include Heathers. The Musical, Quo Vadis, Casanova, Chicago and Tick, Tick... Boom.. To the delight of Polish audiences, the creators have not slowed down, Indeed many theatre managers even signal a further expansion of the industry.

## NOTES

1. Witold Andrzejewski, 'W sprawie „epidemii" operetkowej', *Teatr* 22 (1956): 18.
2. It is worth noticing that some of the titles had very unfortunate translations: *Anything Goes* was rendered as *Fantastyczny rejs*, which means 'Fantastic Voyage'. Nowadays many of the Anglophone shows play under their original title; in addition, the title of *Kiss Me, Kate* is no longer translated.
3. Zajac-Kiedysz, Aleksandra. 'Musical Theatre in Gdynia from 1958 to 1989 as an example of modern musical theatre and one of the most important institution in Poland under Socialism'. In Jansen Wolfgang ed. Popular Music Theatre under Socialism. Operettas and Musicals in the Eastern European States 1945 to 1990. Münster-New York, 2020.
4. This is only a small part of the colorful history of musical theatre in Gdynia. For more information, see Aleksandra Zając-Kiedysz, *50 i pięć lat Teatru Muzycznego w Gdyni 1958–2013* (Gdańsk-Gdynia: University of Gdansk, 2015); and 'Teatr w Polsce—Polski wortal teatralny', http://www.e-teatr.pl, accessed 20 July 2019.
5. Małgorzata Komorowska, *Kronika teatrów muzycznych PRL* (Poznań: Poznan Society of the Friends of Science, 2003), 89.
6. Quoted in 'Załącznik do Protokołu Prezydium Wojewódzkiej Rady Narodowej', 28 October 1957.
7. The TV series 'The Four Tank-Drivers and a Dog' was broadcast between 1966 and 1970; there were twenty-one episodes over three seasons.
8. Roman Heising, 'Artystyczny testament Baduszkowej', *Dziennik Baltycki* 17–18 (February 1979): 8.
9. Andrzej Cybulski, 'Teatr Muzyczny w nowym gmachu', in *Program do Koncertu z okazji przekazania nowego gmachu Teatru Muzycznego* (Gdynia: Music Theatre, 1979).
10. The Sopot Festival is an international pop music festiwal and contest, held at the Forest Opera in Sopot since 1961. Among the winners of the competition are Samantha Jones, Ałła Pugaczowa, Kenny James and Mattafix.
11. Glenn Loney introduced this term in the late 1980s; see Glenn Loney, 'Polish Theatre, 1988', *Soviet and East-European Drama, Theatre and Film* 8, nos. 2–3 (December 1988): 39–46.
12. Martial law was declared in Poland on 13 December 1981. It was introduced as a delayed reaction by the authorities to social resistance, strikes and the creation of the first trade union, 'Solidarity'. Officially, the state of emergency was supposed to counteract the worsening economic situation in the country; however, it is also said that the authorities wanted to protect the country from an invasion by the USSR. All trade unions, strikes and social activities were banned, a curfew was introduced, the borders were closed, and the Military National Rescue Council, i.e. the army, took control over the county. Under martial law, all institutions, including cultural venues such as theatres, and the press were subject to state supervision; telephone conversations were wiretapped and private correspondence was intercepted. Over 10,000 Solidarity activists were interned, many people lost their job, while others escaped abroad. Martial law was suspended on 31 December 1982 and fully abolished on 22 July 1983.
13. Norman Jewison's 1971 screen adaptation became available on VHS in Poland only in 1990, but Gruza had a smuggled videotape of the film, which is how it could serve as inspiration for his 1984 staging of *Fiddler on the Roof*.

## POLISH MUSICAL THEATRE SINCE THE 1960S  823

14. Tomasz Raczek, 'Dom dla Albertynki', *Polityka* 12 (1985): 8; Jacek Sieradzki, '*Coctail gdański*', *Teatr* 3 (1985): 28; Marian Fuks, 'Skrzypek na dachu po raz trzeci', *Ruch Muzyczny* 2 (1985): 20.

15. More popular title was only *The Threepenny Opera* Kurt Weil and Bertolt Brecht, but I was staged in the dramma theatre mostly.

16. Aleksandra Zając-Kiedysz, 'Trzecia droga: Rozważania o teatrze Wojciecha Kościelniaka', *Autograf* 3 (2016), http://www.e-teatr.pl/pl/artykuly/226660.html, accessed 30 June 2019.

17. Presently, most of the Western musicals presented in Poland are non-replica shows, i.e. they do not slavishly follow the original productions.

18. Jacek Wester, 'Trzecia droga Kościelniaka i "Lalka" po gdyńsku: Rozmowa z Wojciechem Kościelniakiem', *Polska Dziennik Bałtycki*, 9 November 2009, http://www.e-teatr.pl/pl/artykuly/82097.html, accessed July, 21 2019.

19. Quoted in Katarzyna Fryc, 'Maciej Korwin, dyrektor Teatru Muzycznego w Gdyni, nie żyje', *Gazeta Wyborcza-Trójmiasto*, 11 January 2013, https://trojmiasto.wyborcza.pl/trojmiasto/1,35612,13178896,Maciej_Korwin__dyrektor_Teatru_Muzycznego_w_Gdyni.html, accessed 21 July 2019.

20. Jacek Mikołajczyk, *Musical nad Wisłą: Historia musicalu w Polsce w latach 1957–1989* (Gliwice: Musical Theatre, 2010): 28.

21. To this day, this is the only Polish musical ever to be staged on Broadway; it wasn't a success, but it received a Tony Award nomination for Best Original Score.

## BIBLIOGRAPHY

Andrzejewski, Witold. 'W sprawie "epidemii" operetkowej'. *Teatr* 22 (1956): 53.

Baduszkowa, Danuta, 'Nowoczesny teatr muzyczny'. *Teatr* 7 (1973): 17.

Bielacki, Marek. *Musical. Geneza i rozwój formy dramatyczno – muzycznej*. Łódź: University of Lodz, 1994.

Bieńkowska, Elżbieta (ed.). *Teatr Muzyczny*. Gdynia: Music Theatre, 1980.

Braun, Kazimierz. *Krótka historia teatru amerykańskiego*. Poznań: University of Adam Mickiewicz, 2005.

Chojka, Joanna. 'Trans nocy letniej', *Teatr* 1 (2002): 25.

Cybulski, Andrzej. 'Teatr Muzyczny w nowym gmachu', In *Program do Koncertu z okazji przekazania nowego gmachu Teatru Muzycznego*, 3. Gdynia: Music Theatre, 1979.

Fryc, Katarzyna. 'Maciej Korwin, dyrektor Teatru Muzycznego w Gdyni, nie żyje'. *Gazeta Wyborcza—Trójmiasto*, 11 January 2013, http://trojmiasto.wyborcza.pl/trojmiasto/1,35612,13178896,Maciej_Korwin__dyrektor_Teatru_Muzycznego_w_Gdyni.html, accessed 20 June 2019.

Fuks, Marian. 'Skrzypek na dachu po raz trzeci'. *Ruch Muzyczny* 2 (1985): 20.

Gierjatowicz, Aleksandra, ed. *Teatr Muzyczny w Gdyni im. D. Baduszkowej 1958 – 1998*. Gdynia: Music Theatre, 1998.

Gołębiowski, Marek. *Musical amerykański na tle kultury popularnej*. Warszawa: PWN, 1989.

Grun, Bernard. *Dzieje operetki*. Kraków: PWM, 1974.

Heising, Roman. 'Artystyczny testament Baduszkowej'. *Dziennik Bałtycki*, 17–18 February 1979, 8.

Karwat, Krzysztof. *Stąd do Broadwayu: Historia Teatru Rozrywki*. Chorzów: Rozrywka Theatre, 2011.

Komorowska, Małgorzata. 'Z wizytą w Teatrze Muzycznym w Gdyni'. *Ruch Muzyczny* 2 (1965): 5.

Komorowska. Małgorzata. *Kronika teatrów muzycznych PRL*. Poznań: Poznan Society of the Friends of Science, 2003.

Kydryński, Lucjan. 'Pierwszy polski superstar'. *Przekrój* 2200 (1987): 9.

Kydryński, Lucjan. *Przewodnik operetkowy*. Kraków: PWM, 1977.

Loney, Glenn. 'Polish Theatre, 1988'. *Soviet and East-European Drama, Theatre and Film* 8, nos. 2–3 (December 1988): 39–46.

Marianowicz Antoni, *Przetańczyć całą noc . . . Z dziejów musicalu*. Warszawa: Artistic and Film Publisher, 1979.

Marianowicz, Antoni (et al.). *Cały ten 'jazz'*. Warszawa: Common Knowledge, 1990.

Mikołajczyk, Jacek. *Musical nad Wisłą: Historia musicalu w Polsce w latach 1957–1989*. Gliwice: Music Theatre, 2010.

Mikołajczyk, Jacek. *Operetka przy Nowym Świecie: Historia teatru muzycznego Gliwicach w latach 1952–2015*. Gliwice: Museum of Gliwice, 2016.

Mokrzycki, Ludwik, ed. *W kręgu kultury, muzyki i baletu: Szkice i materiały z dziejów życia muzycznego na Wybrzeżu Gdańskim i pracy kulturowo oświatowej*. Gdańsk: Gdansk Society of the Friends of Science, 1971.

Raczek, Tomasz. 'Poszukiwania dyrektor Baduszkowej'. *Kultura* 41 (1978): 12.

Raczek, Tomasz. 'Dom dla Albertynki'. *Polityka* 12 (1985): 8.

Sieradzki, Jacek. 'Przyczyna wszelkich buntów w tym się kryje'. *Teatr* 13 (1981): 6.

Sieradzki, Jacek. 'Teatr cienkiej kreski'. *Teatr* 5 (1987): 7.

Sieradzki, Jacek. '*Coctail gdański*'. *Teatr* 3 (1985): 28.

Wester, Jacek. 'Trzecia droga Kościelniaka i "Lalka" po gdyńsku: Rozmowa z Wojciechem Kościelniakiem'. *Polska Dziennik Bałtycki*, 9 November 2009, http://www.e-teatr.pl/pl/artyk uly/82097.html, accessed 21 July 2019.

Zajac-Kiedysz, Aleksandra. 'Musical Theatre in Gdynia from 1958 to 1989 as an example of modern musical theatre and one of the most important institution in Poland under Socialism'. In Jansen Wolfgang ed. *Popular Music Theatre under Socialism. Operettas and Musicals in the Eastern European States 1945 to 1990*. Münster-New York, 2020.

Zając-Kiedysz, Aleksandra. *50 i pięć lat Teatru Muzycznego w Gdyni 1958–2013*. Gdańsk-Gdynia: University of Gdańsk, 2015.

Zając-Kiedysz, Aleksandra. 'Trzecia droga. Rozważania o teatrze Wojciecha Kościelniaka'. *Autograf* 3 (2016), http://www.e-teatr.pl/pl/artykuly/226660.html, accessed 30 June 2019.

Zając-Kiedysz, Aleksandra. 'Zaginiony i odnaleziony'. *Autograf* 6 (2017), http://www.e-teatr.pl/pl/artykuly/254762,druk.html, accessed 20 July 2019.

Żurowski, Andrzej. 'Danka'. *Czas* 3 (1979): 28.

Żurowski, Andrzej. 'Śpiewogra czyli western po polsku'. *Teatr* 16 (1972): 8.

# CHAPTER 30

# ENTERTAINMENT, PROPAGANDA, AND/OR RESISTANCE IN STAGING MUSICALS IN HUNGARY AFTER WORLD WAR II—*ISTVÁN, A KIRÁLY* (*STEPHEN, THE KING*, 1983) AND BEYOND

### ZOLTÁN IMRE

> A young intellectual: I must admit, I have a rather negative opinion about *István, a király* as a production. [ ... ] It manipulated a little bit [ ... ], no, not a bit, but hugely, it was often viciously and irresponsibly manipulative. [ ... ] Another young intellectual: Standing on my chair with tears in my eyes, I was singing the *Himnusz* [national anthem] together with others. [ ... ] I loved it, it was so beautiful as it was all about us, Hungarians. It might sound as if I am a nationalist, but it has nothing to do with that. Those who saw it later or earlier, they were also standing on their chairs, and they were also crying, because they were moved, and that was beautiful.[1]

THOUGH their opinions were radically different, these young intellectuals referred to a rock opera that worked in popular registers and dealt with an ancient tale about the establishment of the kingdom of Hungary around 1000. It was in 1983 when *István, a király* was staged at the Városliget, a city park in Budapest. Though originally organised for a one-day film shoot, it ran for seven nights and was seen by thousands of people. In the same year, when the double album came out, it sold over a million copies. And in 1984, when its film version appeared, it was seen by millions in cinemas and on television. Truly, for a Hungarian rock opera it was an amazing success.

Since then *István* has become one of the most often performed musicals in Hungary. Nowadays it is considered a national classic and is often staged at the National Theatre (or, in 2020, at the Hungarian State Opera), on national celebration days, and at various Hungarian open-air theatres and festivals inside and outside of Hungary by both professionals and amateurs. Before analysing *István*, however, I will analyse the various roles and functions art and theatre fulfilled in the socialist period after World War II and then briefly outline the appearance of modern musical as a genre in Hungary. Situating *István* within the Hungarian musical scene of the 1980s, I will also investigate how the rock opera reused an ancient historical tale to reflect the current political and social conflicts of the Kádár regime as well as its journey to national-classical status. Finally, I will outline briefly the current situation of musical theatre in Hungary.

# THE CULTURAL-POLITICAL FRAME AND THE THEATRE STRUCTURE OF THE KÁDÁR REGIME (1957–1989)

Coming to power after the 1956 revolution, the Kádár regime positioned itself still within the dualistic frame of the Cold War as a member of the Soviet-ruled Eastern bloc. Public discourse and official institutions of the regime (such as theatre) were censored and restricted according to a range of temporary and permanent taboos.[2] The price of the social compromise ensuring the country's relative welfare meant partly that 'the survivors had to forget the past',[3] and partly that they had to bypass the regime's systemic problems. As a result, certain elements of the immediate past and the present fell out of the official order, as dictated by the socialist elite. As the cultural historian Péter György pointed out, '[T]he borders were sealed, the past was only partly available, and the norms and the rules of Hungarian-speaking society were cemented into the seemingly still-standing present'.[4]

The Kádár regime's decision to link art to power enabled the regime to use art for overt and covert political propaganda. With the state taking over the theatre system as early as 1949, the theatre policy of the government in principle served democratisation, offering potential access to the theatre for every sector of society. Cultural institutions and official ('stone') theatres in socialist Hungary were promoted and subsidised by the state, so they were spared the laws of the market. In exchange, cultural leaders on both the national and local levels subordinated theatre to politics, as theatre was considered to be ideological propaganda. The regime had total control over programming, repertoire, and even who worked at each theatre company. The state's colonisation of culture introduced the politicisation of art as the norm, resulting in censorship; at the same time, it ensured that (subversive) messages would be sought and found in any artwork no matter what—including music, poetry, and theatrical performance.

Although its censorship was totalitarian, the state pretended to be democratic, populist, and educative: as the music historian Anna Szemere notes, '[I]t presupposed a political logic that preferred less visible, softer forms of oppression to [overt] censorship and exclusion.'[5] The frightening feature of censorship was, however, that there were secret but institutional connections with the State Security Office and the Secret Police. Without a central state office and exact rules, socialist censorship in Hungary was a strange exercise of power and negotiation, combining, in Gramscian terms, domination by force with cultural hegemony. As the sociologist Miklós Haraszti highlighted as early as 1987, '[T]he state represents not a monolithic body of rules but rather a live network of lobbies. We play with it, we know how to use it, and we have allies and enemies at the control.'[6] Like other Eastern European artists, Hungarian theatre groups and companies used various tactics and strategies to negotiate within that live network of lobbies.[7] In the 1980s, as Hungary was seeking international acceptance, censors were more reluctant to ban productions, and they placed more emphasis on the preselection of appropriate texts, pre-performance discussions. and viewing previews.

Parallel to the official theatre system, since the middle of the 1960s there were alternative, unsubsidised theatre groups, officially classified as 'amateur', working in marginalised circumstances in community centres and/or at university campuses.[8] With their minimal infrastructural background, these companies existed as autonomous, independent, civic enterprises, and worked, as one of the participants, Endre Szkárosi, expressed it, having a 'not always conscious [ ... ] resistance towards the existing cultural and theatrical institutional system.'[9] Between the official theatres and the amateurs there was no real connection, as none of the amateur theatrical groups was part of an institution, and their participants were accepted by the official world only on a case-by-case basis, if at all. In any case, thanks to the tours of Western and Eastern theatres to Hungary,[10] Hungarian theatres' participations in festivals outside of Hungary,[11] and the various experiments of the amateurs, theatrical life was forced to partially open its institutional forms, and a certain controlled but still aesthetic pluralism appeared after the early 1970s.[12]

## MUSICALS AND THE KÁDÁR REGIME

In this theatrical structure, musicals appeared as early as the 1960s as a reaction to operetta. During the 1950s the long tradition of Hungarian operetta was banned by the authorities, considering it the 'kitsch' of the previous era, the Horthy regime. The cultural leaders preferred Soviet-style, socia(l-rea)list operettas with working-class characters about building the socialist state and fighting against corruption and/or devilish Western aggressors, as in the two most popular new-style operettas, Iszak Dunajevszkij's *Szabad szél* (*Free Wind*) in 1950 and Tibor Barabás and Béla Gádor's *Állami áruház* (*State Department Store*) in 1952.[13] Owing to the failure of most of the socialist operettas with

## 828 ZOLTÁN IMRE

audiences, some of the earlier successes of the genre, such as Imre Kálmán's *Luxemburg grófja* (*Count of Luxemburg*) and *Csárdáskirálynő*, for instance, in 1952 and 1954 respectively, could return to the repertoire of the Fővárosi Operettszínház (Operetta Theatre of the Capital), though in revised forms dictated by the expectations of the regime.[14] During the Kádár regime, the most successful operettas of the previous eras reappeared on the stages of the main Hungarian theatres, though they were still considered kitsch. In order to compensate for the reappearances of operettas, new musicals, considered modern and progressive by the socialist cultural authorities, were introduced to the Hungarian stage as early as 1960.

# HUNGARIAN MUSICALS STAGED BY PROFESSIONALS AND 'AMATEURS'

Established as a professional musical theatre in 1960, Petőfi Színház (Petőfi Theatre) opened with Bertolt Brecht and Kurt Weill's *Threepenny Opera* (*Háromgarasos opera*), but its first success, and the first Hungarian musical, premièred only a year later: *Egy szerelem három éjszakája* (*Three Nights*).[15] The music was composed by György Ránki, the book was written by Miklós Hubay, the lyrics were by István Vas, and the production was directed by Miklós Szinetár.[16] Subtitled *A Tragic Musical*, its very serious story followed a young couple's struggle to survive the end of World War II. Based on the life of a Hungarian poet with a Jewish background, Miklós Radnóti, who was murdered in a concentration camp near Bori in 1944, the protagonist of the musical, Bálint, and his wife, Júlia, are looking for shelter in a deserted villa with their friends at the end of the war. Júlia survives, but, like Radnóti, Bálint is murdered by Hungarian fascists just before the Allies declare victory.

Although it performed other Hungarian and foreign musicals,[17] the Petőfi Színház could not repeat the success of *Egy szerelem*. Existing between 1960 and 1964, though from early 1962 with a programme more focused on prose drama than musicals, as Luca Varga pointed out, the Petőfi Színház 'experimented with the introduction of the musical genre, declared modern and progressive, into Hungarian theatrical practice'.[18] Audiences, however, were not (yet) enthusiastic about the new genre, and severe financial losses led to the closure of the theatre; its company merged with that of the Fővárosi Operettszínház.

Without a theatre designed solely for them, the experiment with musicals continued at different professional venues, and from the late 1960s to the late 1970s they were staged at the Fővárosi Operettszínház and the Vígszínház (Comedy Theatre), and by some of the amateur theatre groups. With solo singers backed by a choir, a dance ensemble, and a huge orchestra—all professionals—the Operettszínház staged traditional operettas set in modernised circumstances, Western hit musicals, and new Hungarian musicals.[19] Apart from the Operettszínház, one of the leading amateur theatre groups, the Szegedi

FIG. 30.1 Gyula Bodrogi (Bálint) and Ági Margittai (Júlia) in *Egy szerelem három éjszakája* (*Three Nights*, 1961) at the Petőfi Színház, 1961. Photo © Fortpan.

Egyetemi Színpad (University Stage of Szeged), led by the director István Paál, also experimented with the musical format in 1972 when they premièred *Petőfi-rock*.[20] The music was composed by László Vági; the performance was created by the company and directed by Paál. Based on the events of 15 March 1848, the day revolution broke out in Pest-Buda, the script also included reports of the secret police, extracts from the correspondence between the authorities, and three poems by Sándor Petőfi written in the days of the revolution. And then, as Paál explained in an interview, 'came the idea of the music, and the title: *Petőfi-rock*'.[21]

Surrounded by the audience, and besides telling and singing the various historical texts and the poems, the performance, as István Nánay remarked in retrospect, included:

> the continuous movement of the players, the constant transformation of the theatrical space, the striking vision of jumping and falling actors, a pyramid, made of

human bodies like in a circus, and the phalanx of the people clinging together, which all evoked strong emotional and intellectual responses from the spectators.[22]

Based on contemporary beat music, solo and choral singing, dancing, and acrobatics, the performance lasted only half an hour, but at its conclusion they repeated it again, and again until, as Paál explained, 'we managed to move the spectators to the point when they either joined us or made their passivity obvious.'[23]

As the theatre historian Katalin Demcsák explains, Paál's experiment 'attempted to create a public political theatre with avant-garde formulas. One of its characteristics was the elimination of the [fourth] wall, between the stage and the auditorium, by creating physical and emotional unity between players and performers.'[24] By creating an open theatre practice inspired by Jerzy Grotowski and the Living Theatre, *Petőfi-rock* produced a contemporary event out of historical materials that spoke about both the past and contemporary issues—revolution, freedom, police control, and censorship, all of which had relevance in 1972—and invited the audience to become part of the action by asking them to make conscious decisions about their presence and participation.[25] Though the Szegedi Egyetemi Színpad was extremely popular among the students and young people of the city of Szeged and beyond, the authorities, though they refrained from banning it outright, administratively destroyed the group through police investigations of some of the group members and by offering Paál a professional contract at an official theatre, the Pécsi Nemzeti Színház (National Theatre of Pécs).[26]

# MUSICALS AT THE VÍGSZÍNHÁZ, BUDAPEST

The next year the experiment with Hungarian rock music in professional theatrical productions continued at the Vígszínház in Budapest. Though not a musical theatre per se, it staged the most popular Hungarian musicals of the 1970s, starting with *Képzelt riport egy amerikai popfesztiválról* (*Imaginary Report about an American Pop-Festival*) in 1973.[27] Adapted for the stage by Sándor Pós, it was the musical version of Tibor Déry's short novel, published in 1971. Its musical score was composed by a young rock musician, Gábor Presser, and was played live by his band, Locomotive GT, one of the most popular Hungarian bands of the time. The lyrics were written by Anna Adamis. The production was performed by the young members of the company and directed by László Marton.

While based on real events, the story was set in America, and its focus was on a young Hungarian émigré couple who were searching for and hiding from each other in the chaos of a rock festival. Like the novel, the musical focused on the events of the 1969 Altamont Speedway Free Festival, including the stabbing death Meredith Hunter,[28] though it was set in Montana and narrated from the couple's perspective. While József, a 1956 emigrant, is searching for his wife, Eszter is running away from him and the nightmares of her childhood past. In Eszter's drug-influenced imagination, the mass

FIG. 30.2 The company of *Képzelt riport* (*Imaginary Report*, 1973) at the Vígszínház in Budapest. Photo © Fortepan.

violence of the festival, caused by the confrontation of drug users and alcoholics with the authorities, reminds her of the violence done to her and her family by the Hungarian Nazis in Budapest in 1944.

Though presenting important issues such as youth and drug culture, America, Western rock music, emigration, and the Hungarian Holocaust, *Képzelt riport* was attacked even before its première. It was not criticised, however, because it presented some of the taboos of the Kádár regime (such as drugs, homosexuality, the Holocaust, etc.), but because of its inherent contradictions. Though it depicted extremely negative characteristics of American pop and youth cultures—drug use, sexual harassment, violence, and so on—it still fully utilised the music of these cultures. Consequently, the theatrical world opposed the integration of the 'anarchic and rebellious' rock music into theatre, while the music industry dismissed the musical for its stance against youth culture and rock music. Thus, they regarded the participation of a rock group like LGT in such a tendentious theatrical performance as treason.

Despite these problems, *Képzelt riport* became a financial and artistic success, and most of the critics within and outside Hungary welcomed it as well. One of the few exceptions was Bart Mills of *The Times*, who rated the quality of the music very high, but despised the propagandistic story. As he wrote, 'the music [ ... ] shows enough talent', but the story 'reflects only those [negative] images which exist about America in most Eastern Europeans' imagination'.[29] And he was right. Neither Déry nor the director, Marton, had ever been to a rock festival, so in their musical they offered only stereotypically negative representations of the festival and of American popular and youth culture. In *Képzelt riport*, apart from the fact that the crowd of attendees consists only of drug addicts, homosexuals, lesbians, alcoholics, and other outsiders—and therefore, in the context of 1970s Hungary's 'normal' social-realist conventions, a truly frightening horde—the organisation of the festival is represented as awful and dangerous, the sound amplification as horrible, and the security, managed by the motorcycle gang Hell's Angels, as sadistic. This was in fact intentional. In order to receive the necessary permission to open, Zoltán Várkonyi, the general director of the theatre, presented the musical to the Central Committee of the Party (MSZMP) as 'a criticism of Western hippie culture'.[30] As a result, the negative representation was the price the theatre and the authors had to pay if they wanted to produce a musical about a large-scale Western festival with rock music.

The negative images, however, did not bother the spectators. At that time, travelling to the West was beyond the reach of most Hungarians, not only because of lack of financial means but also because such travel was a political instrument used by the state to reward or punish its citizens.[31] As a result, most of the youth of the Kádár regime had no personal experience of the West; what they knew they had learned from Hollywood films, magazines, and most of all the music and songs they listened to. These fragments of information, however, led not to ignorance, but, surprisingly, to exaggerated fantasies. As the cultural historian Zsolt K. Horváth puts it, '[I]n the closed system of state socialism, it is not surprising that the partial and accidental knowledge and the lack of information about the West was compensated for by imagination; the lack of information enhanced people's creativity'.[32]

Apart from the rare and therefore special concerts of Western popular music stars,[33] Hungarian youth interested in contemporary popular music could listen to the music programmes of the supposedly hostile foreign radio stations Radio Free Europe, Voice of America, and Radio Luxembourg, as well as to the albums at first smuggled in but from the 1980s onwards occasionally played by the special music programmes of the three Hungarian radio stations and officially sold in certain music shops. In front of the controlling eyes of the socialist authorities, disc jockeys were also allowed to play foreign, mostly Western, music in local clubs, while the black market flourished with records smuggled in from Western countries as well as from Yugoslavia. Moreover, though, having often and willingly listened to these Western songs, most of the youngsters could not understand their lyrics for want of linguistic competence.

For most Hungarians, the West remained a mediatised image created by films, movies, theatre performances, magazines, and most of all music, by means of which they could satisfy their own dreams and desires. In the Hungarian imagination, the West was considered 'the representation of prosperity, affluence, freedom, tranquillity, and sex, while the East became synonymous with deprivation, incompleteness, dependency, anxiety, and ascetism'.[34] In this context, incorporating Western-style rock, pop, and beat music into a musical about the West, like *Képzelt riport*, 'shows not only the impact and influence of the West, but also a feeling attached to the new music: the freedom of society's outcasts, counter-hegemonic emotional and sexual behaviours, and opposition to the parents' world'.[35] As a result, the songs, the music, even the musical instruments (e.g. electric guitar) created an imaginary world imbued with desires, emotions, and feelings which were automatically built into the music of Hungarian popular music bands, be they rock, hard rock, new wave, or punk, and musicals as well.[36]

In *Képzelt riport*, the audience of 1973 found the music, the Western clothing, the seemingly uncontrollable dance, the freedom associated with drugs, and the atmosphere of a rock concert in an official theatre more powerful than the propaganda. Just as in other areas of everyday life, they used their imagination to supplement the performance with their own desired details. Despite its propagandistic story and its negative representation of the West, the fantasised world of new, Western-style images, and especially the music of *Képzelt riport*, successfully replaced the banned *Jesus Christ Superstar* (which will be discussed in more detail below) and opened the way for pop, rock, new wave, and other musical styles into the theatre and other arts as well. While the production was still running in Budapest and touring in Eastern Europe, the music and the songs were recorded for an album, which began to have a life independent of the propagandistic content of the musical.[37] Hungarian youth renamed the performance *Popfesztivál*, reflecting that they experienced a live mega-event quite distinct from the one intended, and they would indeed desire more events like this. This was unsurprising considering that, although rock concerts were first staged in Hungary in the 1960s, they did not surge until the late 1970s and early 1980s, due to authorities' fears: concerts were live events where a crowd was gathered, and its control was not immediately effective and never total.[38]

All these, of course, influenced the interpretation of *Képzelt riport*. As a contemporary critic, Erika Szántó, pointed out, despite its pejorative images, 'the performance is not the mourning procession of rotten humankind, running irreversibly towards its own destruction. Rather, the movements, the faces, the eyes and even the stage, appear as a kind of electric field, offering special lustre, and altogether they express power'.[39] In this form, *Képzelt riport* remained on the stage of Vígszínház for eight years; including its revival in 1981, it had more than four hundred performances.[40] As Luca Varga has suggested, its propagandistic story notwithstanding, 'the musical has become a classic in Hungarian pop culture, and in a country, where, at that time, there was no other medium with offering a comparable experience, it created a kind of "Hungarian hippie-mythology", serving for generations as an iconic reference point in Hungarian musical and theatrical mass culture'.[41] When the long-haired young people, dressed in ragged jeans and other shabby outfits—'in pretty authentic rock rags', as Mills expressed it[42]—occupied one of the official stages of the Hungarian theatre world, they not only represented generational and cultural change but also offered a desired representation of the West, such as most spectators could seldom if ever experience in their own lives. Apart from the fact that *Képzelt riport* was the first theatrical piece of Presser's long theatrical career, it was the first widely known rock musical, introducing contemporary pop and rock music into the official world of the Hungarian theatre.

Thanks to the nationwide success of *Képzelt riport*, the Vígszínház continued its experiment with Hungarian rock musicals. Two years later, in 1975, *Harmincéves vagyok (I Am Thirty)* premièred; it too built on the positive connotations of rock music. Focusing on Hungarian issues and subtitled 'A Documentary Musical', the text was based on Rezső Szirmai's psychoanalytic conversations with World War II Hungarian war criminals and János Szilágyi's interviews with contemporary Hungarian youth and was intended for the celebration of the thirtieth anniversary of Hungary's so-called 1945 liberation.[43] As a contemporary critic, Tamás Tarján, remarked, '[N]ot only the last and the first few years before and after WWII appear on stage, but also our relationship towards them'.[44] A collage of stories of the Hungarian past with contemporary images, and again utilising the special power of Hungarian rock music, it was composed by Presser, once more working with lyrics by Adamis, and played live by the popular band Apostol. The musical was a reflection on the distant and recent past from the perspective of the present. As the critic Péter Molnár Gál suggested after the première, the work 'investigates the past, but it speaks to and about the present. [ ... ] The young players [ ... ] question yesterday's decency; they also question today's decorum. When they speak about yesterday's ideals, they are searching for today's as well'.[45]

Two years later, in Vígszínház's next musical, the imaginary West once more became the central theme. Based on a 1969 novel by one of the country's most prominent writers, Endre Fejes, the musical version of Jó estét nyár, jó estét szerelem (Good Night Summer, Good Night Love) was staged in 1977, again with music composed by Presser. Based on a real crime story, the musical centred on a young blue-collar labourer. After working for a month as a locksmith in a factory, he loafs around for a few days until his salary runs out, pretending to young and attractive women to be a Greek diplomat called Viktor Edmund. When exposed, he tries to change his life, but then he meets another woman, Zsuzsanna, falls in love with her, and starts to play the diplomat again. He finally reveals himself to her in an effort to make their relationship honest, but Zsuzsanna is furious and wants to report him to the authorities, so he kills her. After murdering her, however, he turns himself in to the police. The musical focused on the contrast between a Hungarian worker's real possibilities and his dream of being a rich Western diplomat. Jó estét explored the contrast between reality and imagination, fact and desire, ordinariness and appearance, and thus offered social criticism: while utilising the images of an imagined Western existence, it severely criticised the socialist reality of the Kádár regime.[46]

A few years later, in 1982, the Vígszínház premièred another musical, Kőműves Kelemen (Kelemen the Mason), by the authors of István, the pop musicians of the legendary late 1960s group Illés.[47] The music of Kőműves was composed by Levente Szörényi and had lyrics by János Bródy; Imre Sarkadi's unfinished drama was adapted for the stage by Csaba Ivánka.[48] It opened at the chamber theatre of the Vígszínház, Pesti Színház (Pest Theatre), again directed by Marton with contributions from the music group Kormorán.

The piece was based on a historical ballad from the Middle Ages that tells of the difficulties of twelve masons who built the fortress of Déva. Their problem is that every night, what they built during the day collapsed. In order to appease the ghosts apparently preventing the construction, they finally come to an agreement that a young woman has to be sacrificed and her body built into the walls before the construction can be settled.

FIG. 30.3 The company of *Kőműves Kelemen (Kelemen, the Mason*, 1982) at Pesti Színház. Photo: Ilovszky Béla © MTVA Archive.

When the wife of their leader, Kelemen, arrives, they murder her and hide her body in the walls, thereby managing to finish the construction. Using contemporary rock music and motifs from folk songs, the historical theme of the musical was utilised as a parable in order to ask topical questions about individual responsibility, the fate of the community, superstition, sacrifice, and creative work. The performance was a success, and its music, recorded as an album in 1982, became nationally known.[49]

## Musicals at the Rock Színház (Rock Theatre)

In the early 1980s, musical as a genre was so popular that a theatre was again dedicated to the sole purpose of staging modern musicals. Compared to the Petőfi Színház of the 1960s, established by official decree, the Rock Színház developed from individual initiatives, its first production being Andrew the Lloyd Webber and Time Rice hit musical *Evita*, in an open-air movie theatre on the Margitsziget (a small island in the centre of Budapest) during the summer of 1980. Although established only in 1980, the history of the theatre goes back to the early 1970s. In 1972 the core members of the future theatre, Tibor Miklós and Mátyás Várkonyi, together with the rock band Korong, staged a concert version of *Jézus Krisztus Szupersztár* (*Jesus Christ Superstar, JSC*) at one of the clubs of the Technical University, Budapest.

They received official permission to perform *JSC*, since the central Party newspaper, the *Népszabadság*, had earlier written approvingly about it. Parts of it had also been been sung on the *Ki mit tud?* show,[50] while Hungarian Radio had often played the most popular numbers from the album. Despite its previous manifestations, after Korong played the musical, the state authorities suddenly reacted. In a report to the Ministry, one of the main socialist bureaucrats, András Rajki, insisted that 'we have to stop the popularisation of the *Szupersztár*'.[51] At the bottom of his memo were a few handwritten lines stating that the regime's cultural leader, György Aczél, already had 'stopped it on the radio, and prevented Korong from performing it at the Fővárosi Operettszínház'.[52] Although *JSC* and even Korong were banned, they had already played some *samizdat* (secretly distributed) performances of the piece.[53]

Having been members of various musical theatre companies (Operettszínház and Bartók Színház) until 1980, Miklós and his companions premièred *Evita* in 1980 with special permission. Without any proper infrastructural and financial background, the seemingly hopeless endeavour eventually succeeded, although many actors and directors quit during rehearsals. The Rock Színház was organised as a musical theatre with its own company, but without a permanent venue. In 1982 they produced their first own work, the rock opera, *Sztárcsinálók* (*Star Makers*), based on the historical theme of Nero's relation to power, the state, his subjects, and of his madness and cruelty. The music was composed by Várkonyi and the book and lyrics were by Miklós. The company toured the play to various community centres in the countryside and in Budapest, at the Vígszínház and other theatrical venues there. Miklós was the artistic director, and Várkonyi was the musical director, and it featured professional musicians and singers as well as a dance ensemble. The Rock Színház premièred major foreign musicals in addition to new Hungarian musicals.[54] In 1995, however, when the Rock Színház still could not get a permanent building and financial support, the company dissolved, and its members transferred to the company of the Fővárosi Operettszínház.

# THE APPEARANCE OF ROCK MUSIC IN HUNGARIAN FILMS

Parallel to the stage, the Hungarian film industry had also utilised the power of rock music since the late 1960s. In 1967, Tamás Banovich directed the first Hungarian film musical, *Ezek a fiatalok* (*These Youngsters*), which used the songs of the three most popular contemporary pop groups, Illés, Metró, and Omega. Dressed in suits and ties with relatively conservative haircuts in the film, the musicians had to police their behaviour and avoid any shocking moves. The songs were also moderate in content, without any political or ideological content, and remaining within the general frame of love, loneliness, longing, and desire. The film, as the popular music historian Ádám Ignácz explained, 'neither really wanted to challenge the general Hungarian public opinion, which was often against rock and pop music, nor to provoke the anger of society towards the various new behavioural patterns of the Hungarian younger generation'.[55]

The film tells the dilemmas and difficulties of eighteen-year-old Laci Koroknai, who is about to choose his professional career. While Laci prepares for his A-levels, he also plays in a rock band made up of the young workers in the nearby factory; the band is supported by the one of most popular rock bands of the time, Illés, (whose members later created *István*). Although Laci argues with his father, their conflict, representing the chasm between the world of adults and that of youth, is finally settled by his father's understanding of his son's choice: Laci wants to be a worker instead of attending university. In the final scene of the film, his parents, who have not supported his rock band until now, give a standing ovation to him as a worker and beat musician at his concert, while Laci's final song, taken from the repertoire of Illés, draws attention to the emerging youth culture.

Despite its didactic story and one-dimensional characters, the film was a huge success, for one reason only: the simplistic narrative gave the most popular bands of the time the opportunity to play their own songs publicly and officially in a new Hungarian film. As with *Popfesztivál*, though more aware of its propaganda function, audiences appreciated the music and the songs, independent of the movie's didacticism. Making the film was the necessary prerequisite for spreading the new style of popular music and proved that pop culture in Hungary could also appear in visual media. In the following years, owing to the influence of Western and Eastern film musicals, there were a number of Hungarian movies in which contemporary pop, rock, and later new wave and even punk groups appeared regularly.[56]

Parallel to these efforts, more and more musicals appeared in Hungary in their film and or theatrical versions, staged by professionals or 'amateurs' in the late 1970s and early 1980s. Apart from the problematic *Jézus Krisztus Szupersztár*, some Hungarian fans could also listen to several numbers from *Hair* when the singer István Tarjányi received special permission in 1971 to present them at the 'Made in Hungary Fortuna Show' at the Fortuna Bar.[57] Though the Fortuna Bar's high cover charge meant that the 'Fortuna Show' was available only to a privileged few, *Hair* became an immediate and nationwide success when Milos Forman's film version reached Hungarian cinemas in 1980. Another Lloyd Webber musical was performed for the first time in Budapest in 1983 when Tamás Szírtes directed *Macskák* (*Cats*) at the Madách Színház (Madách Theatre). In the late 1970s and early 1980s the Operettszínház staged contemporary and classic musicals like *Kabaré* (*Cabaret*, 1977),[58] *Chicago* (1980), and Rodgers and Hammerstein's *Carousel* (1986), while the Operaház premièred *Porgy and Bess* (1980), and the Theatre Academy staged *Olivér* (*Oliver!*, 1983). As a result of the presentation of both foreign and Hungarian works, the musical as a genre was firmly established in the Hungarian theatre, film, and music industries by the time *István, a király* was staged in 1983.

# ISTVÁN, A KIRÁLY (STEPHEN, THE KING, 1983)

Opening on 19 August 1983, *István, a király* was based on Miklós Boldizsár's drama *Ezredforduló* (*Turn of the Millennium*, 1972–1974, published in 1981), its book written by Boldizsár, Levente Szörényi, János Bródy, and Gábor Koltay. Its musical score was composed by Szörényi with lyrics by Bródy, and the work was directed by Koltay. It was originally intended not as a theatrical performance but as a film shoot before a live audience; most of the scenes were meant to be recorded at that one location, with additional scenes shot at various Hungarian historical and natural settings.[59] Therefore, the project was produced under the auspices of the Budapest Filmstúdió. Because film studios were not independent organisations at that time but under the control of the state, the script of *István* had to be submitted to the Filmfőigazgatóság (Central Bureau for Films) of the Cultural Ministry for permission to be granted.[60]

Though the Filmfőigazgatóság refused permission, the leader of the Filmstúdió, István Nemeskürty, gave the project the go-ahead; but as the Filmstúdió had no budget of its own and was dependent on funding from the Ministry, he could only provide minimal financial backing. Out of necessity, the project was finally presented in a single location, Városliget, as a series of open-air performances, with a paying audience of more than ten thousand each night. As a result, the audience members covered the financial shortfall for both theatrical performances and the film while at the same time providing important publicity, as can be seen in the quotations at the beginning of this chapter.

Submitted to the Filmfőigazgatóság in early 1983, the technical script of the film summarised the story as follows:

> [T]he basic conflict of the musical is set in the 10th century, when, after the death of the monarch Géza, István and Koppány are fighting one another for power. While Koppány wants to defend ancient traditions and the country's independence, István recognises that the country needs religion and alliances. In addition to his concern over losing the nation's independence, Koppány also fears that the people would lose their roots and dissolve into the Western states. [ ... ] István, however, recognises that [ ... ] Hungarians need peace and safety to build a country.[61]

Although the subject was an ancient historical tale, the civil war was and still is regarded in the Hungarian imaginary as a turning point in the life of the Hungary as a nation when two equally valid sets of beliefs and traditions clashed. The rock opera focused on the battle between István and Koppány. István, who eventually became king, represented modern Western beliefs and values and was supported by Hungarian tribesmen, German knights, and Roman Christianity. In contrast, Koppány's allies included other Hungarian tribesmen; represented traditional Hungarian values and Eastern roots and stood for both pagan traditions and Eastern Christianity (Constantinople). In the show their conflict was extended to the present day by the songs, the music, the dances, and the production design (discussed in more detail below). At the Városliget, the performance was presented on an artificial hill created by the ruins of World War II, covered in lawn, green grass, and surrounded by the trees of the park.

Before the première, the publicity was well organised, exploiting all possible media including—surprisingly—Hungarian television and radio, which at that time held a monopoly as the only available radio and television channels.[62] The reaction after the show opened was phenomenal. Judit Kabar pointed out in the *Daily News*, a Hungarian weekly published in English: '[T]hese days Budapest celebrates the birth of the "Hungarian Superstar"—a king, who ruled about a thousand years ago, and has been made the central figure of a magnificent new rock opera'.[63] The national newspapers admitted, even in reviews with negative undertones, that the production was, as the critic Tamás Mészáros opined, 'an exceptional success with the spectators',[64] and other articles praised 'the ravingly celebratory audiences', 'the sublime and moving singing between the players and the audience at the end',[65] and 'the cathartic impact'.[66]

The critics called the production 'a mystery play',[67] 'a real two-hour feast',[68] 'a miracle',[69] 'a folk feast',[70] and 'a ceremony' which 'not only recalled, but achieved the direct communion of real ceremonies, their sense of community connecting the eternal with a rock festival'.[71] Highlighting the relation between the performance on 20 August, a national holiday celebrating the Socialist Constitution of 1949, and the ancient St Stephen's Day, the dance historian Anna Poór argued that 'with the new Hungarian rock opera, a celebratory historical folk drama was born on the hills of Városliget, connecting the tradition of St Stephen's Day with the usual spectacle of the fireworks and the water parade'.[72] While for some reviewers it was merely 'an historical revue, a rock show',[73] others

FIG. 30.4 The original open-air production of *István, a király* (*Stephen, the King*, 1983) on an artificial hill at Városliget. Photo © Fortepan.

called the production 'a collective national myth',[74] or—in an attempt to legitimise the genre of the rock opera by association with an elite art form—'an opera'.[75]

The set of *István* combined the natural location and especially designed structures. Situating the elements of the set within their historical context, Poór noted that 'in the middle, on the hill, there is the huge columned gate of István, down on the right, there is the wooden fortress of the rebellious pagan, Koppány; in front on the left, there is a small round altar-like stone wall, a reference to Roman and European influences and representing the location of Christian funeral rites, the wedding, and the coronation, and finally, an enormous, lit/illuminating cross is on the left. These are the main symbols of the set/location where the historical event takes place'.[76] The set did not represent these locations realistically, but, as in *JSC*, only recalled them by evoking their most characteristic fragments. Among these fragments, the historical story emerged from the figures of István, Koppány, their allies, and the ever-present population, all in modern dress and represented by folk dancers.

The music was complex, deriving from various sources and consisting of three different but connected strands. The first layer, as János István Németh explained, 'was the musical style of the Hungarian light rock music, which appeared with Illés and in the songs of Szörényi and Bródy, and can be characterised by its modulated melody, demanding and diverse orchestrations, and harmonic variety, complemented by polyphonic vocality and Hungarian folklore motives'.[77] The second strand is 'hard rock music, characterised by its motoric rhythm, strong singing, [and] large-scale electronic distortion; contrasting with the simple harmony, the emphasis is on the solo instruments and the singers' virtuosity'.[78] The third strand consists of 'the modern adaptation of Transylvanian-Hungarian instrumental folkloric songs'.[79] All these strands were supplemented by 'most of the elements of European music history [ ... ] from the Gregorian through Bach chorales to the Romantic operatic inheritance',[80] which were all synthesised to form the musical texture of the new, sung-through rock opera.

Professional actors played the solo roles of István and his circle, which were musically characterised by the first strand of 'the softer, more melodic beat rhythm' and by the Gregorian songs for the representatives of the Roman Catholic Church.[81] Koppány and his circle were represented by the rebellious Hungarian rock stars of the time, their songs described as 'hard rock tunes'.[82] Represented by folk dancers, the Hungarian folk were characterised by folk music. Szörényi thus created an elaborate, multilayered structure for the music combining ancient and modern, foreign and Hungarian styles, with each of the different groups having its own distinctive musical idiom.[83] *István, a király* was the first grand Hungarian experiment in combining pop, rock, hard rock, folk, Gregorian, choral, and operatic music.

The choreography was also complex, as the singers were surrounded by more than two hundred professional folk dancers. As Poór remarked, the choreography, created by Ferenc Novák, 'effectively applies the inexhaustible motives of East-European folklore, whenever necessary, even to the rock's high-toned, ecstatic rhythms'.[84] Novák's choreography partly combined the various folkloric traditions of the Carpathian Basin, adjusting it to the modern music of the rock opera, which partly 'made it possible

# ENTERTAINMENT, PROPAGANDA, RESISTANCE    841

to it move beyond its traditional content'.[85] As a result, the choreography of the folk, represented by dancers in modern dress, who stayed on stage most of the time, created 'the real context of the performance' and achieved a monumental mass impact,[86] expressing continuity between the traditional and the contemporary and adapting the traditional folkloric display to modern needs.

While most of the critics greatly appreciated *István*, they found some of its symbols, and in particular its final scene, problematic. As Mészáros described it:

> During the musical epilogue, which is the newly orchestrated *Himnusz* [Hungarian national anthem], the newly crowned Hungarian king stands magnificently amidst the splendour of his insignias by the light of fireworks in front of a national flag which stretches over the horizon. Part of this monumental closing scene is also the spectacle of the nearly ten thousand spectators, and with their exhilaration they transform the celebratory performance into a folk festival.[87]

Others called the scene simply 'heroic',[88] while other reviewers interpreted it within the general structure of the performance. A critic writing for *Magyar Ifjúság*, István Feitl, remarked that though the fight between Koppány and István is a massacre where Hungarians kill their fellow countrymen, it can only be resolved by the final scene, which

> elevates us beyond the unbearable. The mundane here is not enough, and that is why they choose such a finale, which unites the pagan sacrifice and the Christian coronation rite, giving the spectators not only the community of musical experience, but also the feeling of belonging to a national community.[89]

To this view another critic, János István Németh, added:

> [A]lthough in the grand finale our eyes could drown in the flashing lights of the fireworks and participate in the powerful parade of national symbols, it escapes from the empty hallucination of the spectacle, because it is constructed as an honest celebration of power.[90]

So, for them, the final scene of the production with the national flag and the national anthem, with the spectators joining in, created a national community based on the unification of the distant past of István and Koppány with the present.

Other critics were less enthusiastic about the ending. Drawing attention to the gratuitous bloodshed, Gábor Bányai remarked that 'out of the historical dilemma [of István and Koppány], Koltay makes a nationalistic parade'.[91] Like one of the interviewees quoted at the beginning of this chapter, his main problem was that with the tricolour and the *Himnusz*, 'Koltay manipulates us until the very end—and we, who are outraged by this, have to sneak out shamefully from the feverish circus-like auditorium. Maybe this is my problem, but I am alarmed by this overdose of nationalism, as it fills me with fear'.[92]

Similarly, Endre Varjas criticised the 'pathetic' final scene, 'when the theatrical performance turns into a celebratory rite. It offends my genre expectations and violates my taste as well':[93]

> ['he] hymnal end, full of nationalistic symbols and fireworks, dissolves the tension, as its impact relies on convention, which has nothing to do with the actual production. Thus, the catharsis fails to materialise, or at least it slips onto another level, from where it should have been realised.[94]

The critic Lajos Tandi drew the conclusion that

> [i]t's a pity that the historically inspired, high-standard enterprise, speaking honestly with its distinct voice to contemporary generations, is transformed into self-serving pretentiousness with its fireworks, rain of sparks, 150-metre long tricolour fence, and its *Himnusz*, adapted for electric guitar.[95]

# READING *ISTVÁN, A KIRÁLY*: VARIOUS INTERPRETATIONS OF A ROCK OPERA

The disagreement about the final scene draws attention to the contemporary political interpretation of this ancient tale. Using historical stories as parables to represent contemporary issues so that one can read between their lines was a very common practice during the Kádár regime, when censorship aimed to control even people's dreams and desires. That the rock opera referred not only to the past but also to the present was hinted at by Koltay several times before the première.[96] It was also implied by the opening song, 'Mondd, te kit választanál?' ('Tell me, who would you choose?'), sung by Bródy himself: this suggested a contemporary reading that there is always a choice to be made—in the past as well as in the present. Moreover, it also hinted that in 1983 Hungarians confronted a similar situation, when they had to once again decide where their allegiances lay. From the opening song, the rock opera was interpreted by experienced spectators as a historical allegory.

Thus it is not surprising that nearly one year after the première, a reporter from Hungarian Radio, Miklós Győrffy, subtly proposed in an interview with one of the scriptwriters, Miklós Boldizsár, that *István* 'seems to be a parable which speaks to the present'.[97] Probably fearing political repercussions, Boldizsár refuted this interpretation publicly, while at the same time admitting that 'this play was not written in 1000, [ ... ] so it is obvious that we could not avoid reflecting our era, although we did not want to'.[98] Thus, what we have here are denial and assertion of the same issue side by side, even in the same sentence. The cultural practice of the Kádár regime often resulted in this strange exercise in negotiation, producing resistance and self-censorship in equal measures.

ENTERTAINMENT, PROPAGANDA, RESISTANCE    843

Győrffy's careful formulation and Boldizsár's careful rebuttal of *István* as parable referred to an earlier article, written by János Emericus, the pen name of János Krasznai,
for the October 1983 issue of *Hírmondó*, a samizdat magazine. For the journalist, the
rock opera represented one of the major but silenced conflicts concerning the origin of
the Kádár regime: the execution of the leader of the 1956 Revolution, Imre Nagy, by János
Kádár, who in 1983 was still the leader of the socialist regime. Emericus pointed out:

> For the intention of its authors and the director, the historical theme, regarded as
> timeless in the performance, is used as an apology for Kádár and the Kádár regime.
> [ ... ] István [ ... ] is depicted by such characteristics through which the Party propa-
> ganda mechanism attempts to clear Kádár's shameful role in 1956. István has no lust
> for power—he is concerned simply about the fate of the country; only his responsi-
> bility and the demands of the situation force him to execute the rebels, because they
> risked the future of the nation with their wanton desire for freedom. He takes re-
> venge unwillingly, only under pressure, but his achievements speak for themselves:
> he creates the condition for peaceful nation-building as well as for the independence
> of the country. [ ... ] These are the exact images with which the Kádár regime wished
> to identify itself, not only because it likes the echoes of its own propaganda, but also
> because it legitimates its claim to protect 'the national interest', thereby creating a
> thousand-year-long continuity for the regime, through which Kádár would attempt
> to march even into the National Pantheon.[99]

Krasznai ended his review by claiming that 'on the 25th anniversary of his execution [ ... ],
Imre Nagy was not legitimised, but his image was at least commemorated';[100] and in a
clear reference to Kádár, he also warned his readers that 'the murderer of Imre Nagy has
no place in the National Pantheon'.[101]

The critic thus interpreted *István, a király* as a historical allegory, explicating the historical István-Koppány conflict of the rock opera as the more recent political conflict
between Imre Nagy and János Kádár. Because this was stated only via samizdat, public
discourse over the interpretation of the rock opera continued without ever directly
mentioning, yet often implying, the Kádár-Nagy interpretation,[102] like Győrffy's, focusing on whether the rock opera—especially its ending—was honestly patriotic or cyn-
ically nationalistic. On the one hand, as Feitl argued, the conclusion 'finally transforms
the entire performance into a myth of creation, illustrating not only how Hungarians became Europeans but also how they created their own nation'.[103] On the other hand, some
called it 'jingoistic',[104] 'an overdose of nationalism',[105] since—as Győrffy recounted—'the
entire atmosphere of the performance is capable of provoking nationalistic exaltation'.[106]

In retrospect, it is difficult to judge the debate; I can only claim, as Szilárd Béla
Jávorszky did in 2002, that 'from the political point of view, *István, a király* in 1983
created controversy. Undoubtedly, in that political climate, *István* as a political parable was brave; but as a production, permitted by the Central Bureau of the Budapest
Communist Party, it also offered opportunities for manipulation'.[107] It is clear that a
really complex interpretative scheme developed around the rock opera, which was
probably one reason for its success. As a result, in 1983 the dominant political logic of

Hungarian culture basically defined the interpretation of the performance, and, since, as Cecília Kovai explained, 'the audience, "reading between the lines", started searching to identify who was in reality being referred to in the performance, a series of inverse references and contradictory associations started to work'.[108] Reading between the lines proved not an obvious but a rather complicated task.

Looking back, it seems that there were at least five interpretative schemes. As Jávorszky summarised it, one group spoke about 'an unwanted nationalist breakthrough, especially the enormous national tricolour, the *Himnusz* and the fireworks of the final scene'. For the second group, 'the production was an obvious statement for Kádár, [... and] it can be interpreted as a proof of Kádár's version of [what happened in] 1956'. The third group stated that 'though it is true that the process of history demands István's triumph, the real hero, artistically and aesthetically, is Koppány; therefore the performance is an obvious statement [in favour of] Imre Nagy'.[109] The fourth group interpreted the performance as 'a reflection of the inner conflict among the Party members over Kádár's succession',[110] and its participants—reform communists, radical communists, national left-wingers—saw the pattern of their struggle in the performance. The fifth group, as Balázs Házi remarked, 'regarded the performance as the representation of national self-esteem'.[111] Though different in their directions and conclusions, these interpretations were connected to the various social-political groupings of Hungarian society, showing exactly what Haraszti referred to as 'a live network of lobbies' within the apparently monolithic regime. As a result, reading *István, a király* as an historical parable raised important questions to which various strata of society would have liked to have different answers.

Nonetheless, we can point out, as Péter G. Tóth remarked, that on a political level *István, a király* 'not only channelled the conflicts induced by national feelings, but [...] was also seen as a kind of mystery play: it prepared the purification from guilt for those who had committed revenge after 1956'.[112] In 1983, on the twenty-fifth anniversary of Imre Nagy's death, the executioners could live through the punishment of the rebel again while experiencing the absolution achieved through their own penitence. As a result, they attempted to reinvent their own power in order to achieve a new social consensus over the issues of 1956. In 1983 *István* was possibly the first public occasion through which the situation of revenge and survival could be relived on a collective level by both the executioners and the survivors. The *Himnusz* and the endless ovations of the spectators at the end of each performance 'was a kind of redemption from the burdens of conscience, repressed for decades, on both sides'.[113] In 1983 the rock opera was thus seen as a kind of ritual; as Kovai notes, '[I]ts power lay in the fact that it represented different sides all at once, because it showed the punishment of the rebel together with the penitence of the oppressor—it became a rite that invoked the collective experience of those who were punished, of the survivors as well as of the executioners'.[114]

The rock opera fused the opposition with those in power for the ostensible survival of the nation. Finally, both groups could assert that 'we had undergone the sacrifice and the nation survived—we have enough to celebrate, and from this point of view, it does not matter who was either victim or perpetrator, as they died or became murderers for the same reason'.[115] In general, the impact of the production was tremendous, as it erupted after such a long hiatus. As the cultural historian András Rényi states, '[A]fter 1956, the Kádár regime kept the use of national symbols under strict control and did not attempt to legitimise itself by symbolic politics. At the beginning of the 1980s, however, it was more and more obvious that the relative affluence of "goulash communism" could not be maintained forever'.[116] That might be the reason cultural leaders became less strict when it came to politicising symbols, allowing their representation and even providing the necessary support for a rock opera such as *István*. Without doubt it was a risky business, as it strengthened anticommunist feeling and reminded the citizens of the socialist state of their lack of personal freedom and national independence.

In 1983 *István* was not a single event: its success was, as planned, extended to different media. While the seven performances in Városliget had already been seen by more than 100,000 people, more than 250,000 copies of a double album were sold between November 1983 and May 1984, while the film version was viewed, even before its official première in March 1984, by more than 100,000 people.[117] By April 1984 it had been seen by more than half a million people,[118] although it played only in small venues all over Hungary. In addition, another open-air version, directed by Koltay, was seen in 1984 by thousands at the Szegedi Nyári Játékok (Summer Fest of Szeged), and when Hungarian Television broadcast its film version, *István* was seen and heard by more than seven million people—more than two-thirds of the Hungarian population.[119]

Having already achieved huge popularity between 1983 and 1984, the next phase of its canonisation occurred when it opened at the Hungarian National Theatre in 1985. It was performed by the members of the National and directed by Imre Kerényi. In Kerényi's version, however, a different *István* appeared. Observed the critic János Péter Sós:

> István's life is a series of failures and unwanted compromises, [ ... ] his coronation represents total subservience to the Church, [and at the end] he remains alone on-stage with his flags and the symbols of his kingdom, while Koppány and his followers look down on him from their statues. And to the sounds of the *Himnusz*, [ ... ] he transforms from [hesitating] monarch into a cruel king.[120]

Contrary to Koltay's, Kerényi's direction did not show national unification, but rather the loss and pain of transition. Despite its new interpretation, Kerényi's version was also successful and remained in the National's repertoire for years, also touring Germany and Italy.[121] Tim Rice saw not only the National's production but the earlier Szeged-version as well. In an interview in 1986, he remarked that 'the story of *István, a király* is clear and obvious to me' but suggested that for its adaptation for the West End, 'it would be a great help if the production were produced only three to four times by a Hungarian company with all the grand visual effects'.[122] Rice probably knew that for financial reasons this was never going to happen, so in the end the planned adaptation never materialised, since Rice even wanted the authors to change the script and some of the music, which they refused to do.[123]

As the critic Péter Molnár Gál emphasised, 'Since the successful première of the operetta, *János vitéz* (*John, the Valiant*) in 1904, *István, a király* has been the biggest Hungarian theatrical hit'.[124] After the versions of Szeged (1984) and the National (1985), *István* soon became one of the most widely performed official pieces on 20 August, the national holiday of King István and the founding of the state, by both professional companies and amateurs. Its success reached its zenith in Erdély (Transylvania, Romania), when, as observed by Molnár Gál, 'at Csíksomlyó, in 2003, in front of three hundred thousand people, members of the Honvéd Táncszínház (Budapest), Hargita Nemzeti Székely Népi Együttes (Csíkszereda), and the Háromszék Állami Együttes (Sepsiszentgyörgy) played it as a theatrical mass spectacle'.[125] In Erdély it was performed during the closing ceremony of the annual Ezer Székely Leány Napja (Day for the One Thousand Transylvanian Girls), at the 'location of the Pentecostal Feast, on the hills of the Somlyó, on the altar stage of Hármashalom',[126] where it attained a quasi-sacred status through being connected to the annual performance of *Csíksomlyói passió* (*The Passion Play of Csíksomlyó*).

Though *István, a király* was expected to provoke a major backlash from the state apparatus, it received official support and recognition as early as the 1980s. Although the Filmfőigazgatóság did not give its permission and there was no formal opening gala for the film première, Béla Köpeczy, the minister of culture, in 1986 called it 'a new endeavour' in his report to the Central Committee.[127] Apart from that, in the words of Tamás Szőnyei, *István, a király* made 'rock music dealing with national issues politically acceptable'.[128] Moreover, as the music journalist János Sebők claimed, '[I]t was the first time, a rock performance received national-political significance, and when it opened we witnessed the rebirth of the collective national myth, despised and suppressed for decades'.[129]

As a result, the national sentiment exploded its confines, and the newer interpretations of the work, as Tibor Miklós remarked, 'showed with remarkable power the huge need in the Hungarian public for the expression of national communion, deliberately suppressed during the Kádár regime, as well as the ritual reimagining of the historical past'.[130] At the Városliget, *István* was a local event, though publicity for it had already appeared in various media in the capital as well as the rest of the country. With its album, cassette, and film versions, however, *István* stepped out of the local frame of theatrical performance to become a national event, and with its performances outside of Hungary it went on and still continues to unite Hungarians beyond the country's borders.

## AFTER *ISTVÁN, THE KING*

In retrospect, there is no doubt that *István* was a turning point in the history of musical theatre in Hungary. Though there had been earlier attempts, *István* made it possible to use a previously despised genre of popular entertainment to stage politically, socially, and aesthetically relevant issues like the operettas of the 1910s and 1920s did,[131] and also to create a situation in which a theatrical genre once again became a popular medium, cutting across different strata of society and as a result being financially rewarding as well. Consequently, it paved the way for other Hungarian and foreign musicals on the Hungarian stage. Thanks to its success, Koltay, Szörényi, and Bródy went on to experiment with different historical themes. In 1985 Koltay staged *Itt élned, halnod kell* (*You Are to Live and Die Here*), a 'historical musical play' at a historical location, Hősök tere (Heroes' Square) in Budapest, which recounted the major historical events of Hungary from the settlements of the Hungarians in the Carpathian Basin to the so-called liberation of 1945 with the rock singers he employed in *István*. With them, Koltay also staged *Atilla, Isten kardja* (*Atilla, the Sword of God*) in 1993, dealing with the famous Hun emperor and his supposed relationship with Hungarian tribes.

Szörényi and Bródy continued the historical themes with the musical *Veled, Uram!* (*With You, My God!*), which was staged at Esztergom in 2000.[132] Thanks to the earlier success, historical themes for musicals have become popular in Hungary: the Rock Színház staged *A krónikás* (*The Chronicler*) as early as 1984, and 1997 saw the première of *Egri csillagok* (*The Stars of Eger*) at Margitsziget, which musicalised the successful 1552 war against the Turks. In 2016 Koltay modernised and restaged *Itt élned, halnod kell*, its new story spanning the ancient times of Árpád, the conqueror of the Carpathian Basin for the Hungarians, to 1989 and presented as a sequence of historical tableaus, and in 2018 he premièred another 'historical tale with music', *Trianon*, with strong governmental support, again at Hősök tere.[133] Like *Itt élned, halnod kell*, *Trianon* consisted of historical tableaus from the 'great days' of the late nineteenth-century Austro-Hungarian Empire to the present, focusing on Hungary's 'Trianon trauma', caused by the 1920 Trianon Treaty, which cost Hungary 71 percent of its historical territory and 64 percent of its population.[134]

Apart from historical shows, other musicals with contemporary themes have also appeared on the stages of Hungary's theatres. As early as 1985, the Rock Színház staged *A bábjátékos* (*The Puppeteer*), while in 1988 the Vígszínház premièred Presser's fairy-tale musical *A padlás* (*The Attic*), dealing with lost fairy-tale characters who, caught between two worlds, want to go to their final resting place with the help of a young man living in the present and his computer.[135] At the same time, Madách Színház presented *Doctor Herz*, with book by Péter Müller, score by László Tolcsvay, and lyrics by János Bródy, and directed by Viktor Nagy. The musical was also set in an attic, where the Nobel Prize winner Doctor Herz lives and invents a machine, the WIM, with which he is able to embody persons living in our memory and imagination. Apart from his friends and relatives, the army shows also great interest in the invention. Finally, when the army invades his attic to get the machine, he destroys it.

Since then Hungarian musicals, historical and contemporary, have featured from time to time in Hungarian theatrical repertoires: *Légy jó mindhalálig* (*Be Good till Death*, 1991); *Anna Karenina* (1994); *A vörös malom* (*The Red Mill*, 1994); *Valahol Európában* (*Somewhere in Europe*, 1995); *Utazás* (*Journey*, 1996); *Dzsungel könyve* (*The Jungle Book*, 1996); *Made in Hungária* (2001); *56 csepp vér* (*56 Drops of Blood*, 2006); *Abigél* (2008); *Nem tudok élni nélküled* (*I Can't Live Without You*, 2010); *Én, József Attila* (*I'm*

848 ZOLTÁN IMRE

*Attila József*, 2012), *A Pál utcai fiúk* (*The Paul Street Boys*, 2016), *Nikola Tesla: Végtelen energia* (*Nikola Tesla: Infinite Energy*, 2020), *Puskás –: a musical* (*Puskas: the Musical*, 2020), *Kőszívű –: A Baradlay-legenda* (*Stoneheart – The Legend of Baradlay*, 2022), *A tizenötödik* (*The Fifteenth*, 2022), *Monte Cristo grófja* (*The Count of Monte Cristo*, 2023) and many others. Unfortunately, though some of them have been successful, none has achieved the complex iconicity of *István* or its status as a classic.

At the same time, Hungarian theatres have staged nearly all the major contemporary musicals from Broadway and the West End. As early as 1987, *Nyomorultak* (*Les Misérables*) opened at the Rock Színház, and since then dozens of musicals have been imported to Hungary, including *Sakk* (*Chess*, 1992), *Elisabeth* (1996), *Az operaház fantomja* (*The Phantom of the Opera*, 2003), *Mozart!* (2003), *Romeó és Júlia* (*Roméo et Juliette*, 2004), *A szépség és a szörnyeteg* (*Beauty and the Beast*, 2005), *Producerek* (*The Producers*, 2006), *Aida* (2007), *József és a szélesvásznú álomkabát* (*Joseph and the Amazing Technicolor Dreamcoat*, 2008), *Mi jöhet még?* (*Anything Goes*, 2008), *Monty Python's Spamalot* (2009), *Avenue Q* (2009), *Mamma Mia!* (2014), *Billy Elliot* (2016), *We Will Rock You – Queen Musical* (2017), *Apáca Show* (*Sister Act*, 2018), *Aranyoskám* (*Tootsie*, 2022)[136] and many others. It seems that the Hungarian theatrical scene is once again part of the international musical theatre circuit. Unfortunately, however, the flow goes only one way: it is very rare that a Hungarian or any other Eastern European musical reaches Western musical centres, the West End, or the Broadway.

Apart from the frequent restagings of pieces from the classical operetta canon such as Kálmán's *Csárdásfürstin* (1915) as *Csárdáskirálynő, 1916* in 1993,[137] there have been only a few attempts to revitalise the genre of operetta: *Virágos Magyarország* (*Flowery Hungary*) was presented by the Katona József Színház in 2012, and *Röpülj, lelkem!* (*Fly, My Soul!*) was staged by an alternative company, K2 Színház, in 2016. Nonetheless, thanks to the enormous achievement of *István*, as well as other Hungarian and foreign musicals, the musical as a genre has reached a stable position in the repertoires of Hungarian theatres. The popularity of the current musical theatre scene in Hungary is evidenced by the fact that in Budapest two theatres, the Madách Színház and Budapesti Operettszínház, are dedicated to the production of musicals, both foreign and Hungarian, and that occasionally the Vígszínház and other theatres in Budapest present musicals too. For instance, Tom Waits and Kathleen Brennan's *Woyzeck* could be seen at the Katona József Színház in 2011, and *Vámpírok bálja* (*Tanz der Vampire*) had its first Hungarian production at the Pesti Magyar Színház in 2007. Around the country, each major theatre at the regional centres offers musicals and plays with music as part of their repertory, and touring companies of artistic quality also help meet the demand for musicals.

Nowadays, however, though still popular and successful, the musical is commonly regarded as simply a form of popular entertainment, without any of the serious social, political, and cultural complexity it had when *István* premièred in 1983. The changing function of musical theatre is connected to the changed function of art and theatre since the 1990s. Previously, as exemplified by *Képzelt riport*, *Kőműves Kelemen*, and *István*, art and theatre had a special role: they functioned as a substitute which also enabled the expression of prohibited views. In the 1990s, when the political system changed from socialist to capitalist, the public channels of everyday life—media, public and political institutions, and the like—opened up, and through them Hungarians could express themselves freely. As a result, though art and theatre regained their freedom and independency, they lost their special social function. This led to the social devaluation of theatre and to a crisis of the creators, as the previous double code no longer worked.

Throughout the years, theatre became less and less engaged in the public discussion of important social, political, and economic issues, and at the time of this writing socially engaged theatre—that is, theatre as public forum for society—has nearly disappeared from Hungary. There still are exceptions, such as Katona József Színház, and parts of the independent theatre sector, such as Pintér Béla Társulata, PanoDráma, K2 Színház, Stúdió K, and others, but in general theatre has been reduced to popular (or less popular) entertainment. Musicals and operettas, which in Hungary have recently focused on staging escapist stories, always with a happy ending, light music, and flashy sets and costumes, have played and continue to play a crucial role in that change. As for the future, who knows what it will bring for musical theatre in the 2020s in a Hungary that is ruled by a right-wing government?

# NOTES

1. The title of the chapter in the book is 'Young People about *István, a király*'; then comes a subchapter, titled 'Young Intellectuals'. They do not give their names, so I did not quote them by name. Quoted in Gábor Koltay, *István, a király* (Budapest: Ifjúsági, 1984), 144–146. This and the following translations by the author.
2. Permanent taboos included references to the 1956 Revolution, the Soviet Army in Hungary, the role of the Soviet Union in Eastern Europe and in Hungary, and the integral problems and debates within the leadership. Temporary taboos were the ethnic, economic, moral and cultural problems, poverty, national identity, and nationalism.
3. Péter György, *Kádár köpönyege/Kádár's Mantle* (Budapest, Magvető, 2005), 45.
4. Ibid., 54.
5. Anna Szemere, *Up from the Underground: The Culture of Rock Music in Postsocialist Hungary* (University Park, PA: Penn State University Press, 2001), 12.
6. Miklós Haraszti, *The Velvet Prison: Artists under State Socialism* (New York: Basic Books, 1987), 78–79.
7. See e.g. Seth Baumrin, 'Ketmanship in Opole: Jerzy Grotowski and the Price of Artistic Freedom', *TDR: The Drama Review* 53, no. 4 (2009): 49–77; Margaret Setje-Eilers, '"Wochenend und Sonnenschein": In the Blind Spots of Censorship at the GDR's Cultural Authorities and the Berliner Ensemble', *Theatre Journal* 61, no. 3 (2009): 363–386; and Dennis C. Beck, 'Divadlo Husa na Provázku and the "Absence" of Czech Community', *Theatre Journal* 4 (1996): 419–441.
8. These companies included Universitas, Kassák Ház Stúdió [Kassák House Studio], Orfeo, Stúdió K [Studio K], Kovács István Stúdió [István Kovács Studio], Manézs Színház [Manege Theatre], Bányász Színház [Miners Theatre], Szegedi Egyetemi Színház [Szeged University Theatre], Brobo Társulat [Brobo Company], and others.

850 ZOLTÁN IMRE

9. Endre Szkárosi, 'A tér mint művészetszervező erő: Experimentális színház, hangköltészet, plurilingvizmus', in *Né/ma? Tanulmányok a magyar neoavantgárd köréből*, ed. Pál Deréky and András Müllner (Budapest: Ráció, 2004), 149–150.

10. See e.g. Ágnes Alpár, *Harminc év vendégjátékai, 1945–1975* (Budapest: OSZMI, 1977); and Zoltán Imre, 'Theatre, Propaganda and the Cold War', in *Theatre, Globalization and the Cold War*, ed. Christopher B. Balme and Berenika Szymanski-Dül (London and New York: Palgrave Macmillan, 2017), 107–130.

11. Zoltán Imre, ed., *Alternativ színháztörténetek: Alternatívok és alternatívák* (Budapest: Balassi Kiadó, 2008).

12. Tibor Várszegi, ed., *Felütés: Írások a magyar alternatív színházról* (Budapest: W. P., 1990); Tibor Várszegi and István Sándor L., eds., *Fordulatok* (Budapest: W. P., 1993); and Imre, *Alternativ színháztörténetek*.

13. Dániel Molnár, *Vörös csillagok: A Rákosi-korszak szórakoztatóipara és a szocialista revük* (Budapest: Ráció, 2019).

14. Gyöngyi Heltai, *Az operett metamorfózisai: A 'kapitalista giccs'-től a 'haladó mímusjáték'-ig, 1945–1956* (Budapest: Eötvös, 2012), esp. 39–69 and 145–252.

15. See its music and the songs at https://www.discogs.com/Gy%C3%B6rgy-R%C3%A1nki-Mikl%C3%B3s-Hubay-Istv%C3%A1n-Vas-Egy-Szerelem-H%C3%A1rom-%C3%89js zak%C3%A1ja-Three-Nights-Musical-Traged/release/8060379, accessed 26 June 2023.

16. See the contemporary TV news about the 1961 première at https://www.youtube.com/watch?v=WvUs4DS3BYM, accessed 26 June 2023.

17. In 1961: *Tüzijáték (Fireworks)*, *Mélyvíz (Deep Water)*, and *Üvegcipő (Glass Shoes)*; in 1962: *Hét pofon (Seven Snaps)* and *Légy szíves Jeromos (Please Jeromos)*; and in 1963: *Írma, te édes (Irma la Douce)*, for instance.

18. Luca Varga, 'A *Képzelt riport egy amerikai popfesztiválról* vígszínházi előadásának recepciója a Kádár-korszak kultúrpolitikájának tükrében', *Korall* 39 (2010): 67.

19. The operettas included e.g. Ferenc (Franz) Lehár's *Víg özvegy (Die lustige Witwe*, dir. László Seregi) in 1968 and *Cigányszerelem (Zigeunerliebe*, dir. András Békés) in 1976; Viktor Jacobi's *Sybill* (dir. Seregi) in 1972; Albert Szirmai's *Mágnás Miska (Miska the Magnet*, dir. Imre Kerényi) in 1972; and Kálmán's *Cirkuszhercegnő (Die Zirkusprinzessin*, dir. Seregi) in 1978. Among the Western musicals were *West Side Story* (1965), *Hello, Dolly!* (1968), *La Mancha lovagja (Man of La Mancha*, 1971), *Hegedűs a háztetőn (Fiddler on the Roof*, 1973), and *Kabaré (Cabaret*, 1977). Examples of original Hungarian musicals are the first Roma (Gypsy) musical, *Piros karaván (Red Caravan*, 1974), and *A kutya, akit Bozzi úrnak hívtak (The Dog, Called Mr. Bozzi*, 1976).

20. See its short television version from 1973 at https://www.youtube.com/watch?v=zgfb qHCnf2o&t=5s , accessed 26 June 2023.

21. László Bérczes, 'Volt egyszer egy *Petőfi-rock*: Beszélgetés Árkosi Árpáddal, Dózsa Erzsébettel, Paál Istvánnal és Vági Lászlóval', *Film, színház, muzsika*, 11 March 1989, 6. Its première was at the Community Centre, Bordány, Hungary, on 12 November 1972.

22. István Nánay, 'Partizánattitűd', *Színház* 8 (2003): 3.

23. Bérczes, 'Volt egyszer egy *Petőfi-rock*', 6.

24. Katalin Demcsák, 'A Paál István vezette Szegedi Egyetemi Színpad', in *Alternatív színháztörténetek: Alternatívok és alternatívák*, ed. Zoltán Imre (Budapest: Balassi Kíado, 2008), 257.

25. In its use of music and the crowd and its manner of organising the theatre space, *Petőfi-rock* belongs to a trend characterised by such productions as Peter Brook's *US* (1966) and Arianne Mnouchkine's *1798* (1970).

ENTERTAINMENT, PROPAGANDA, RESISTANCE    851

26. See also István Nánay, 'Elkötelezett amatőrök és az új színpadi nyelv', *Színház* 10 (1973): 31–34. See also the detailed documentation of *Petőfi-rock*: https://hiaszt.hu/petofi-rock/, accessed 26 June 2023.

27. Its première was on 2 March 1972.

28. 'The Rolling Stones Disaster at Altamont: Let It Bleed', *Rolling Stone*, 21 January 1970, https://www.rollingstone.com/music/music-news/the-rolling-stones-disaster-at-altamont-let-it-bleed-71299/, accessed 26 June 2023.

29. Bart Mills, 'Altamont or Montana', *Times*, 28 July 1973, 12. The quoted passage is my own back-translation, as unfortunately I did not have access to the English version, only its Hungarian translation. It would have been nice to have the original here.

30. Művelődési Minisztérium tájékoztató jelentés, 18 July 1972, National Archive, Budapest, MNL OL M-Ks 288.f.41/1972, 85.ö.e., pp. 6–29.

31. Hungarian citizens were only allowed to travel to the West every third year, but this permission was not automatic. Before the journey, they had to apply for a so-called Western passport, and they either got it or not depending on what the authorities decided.

32. Zsolt K. Horváth, 'Vágyakba fojtott Nyugat: Az occidentalizmus formái a magyar popzenében az 1960-as és az 1970-es évek között', 68, https://www.academia.edu/39176980/V%C3%A1gyakba_fojtott_Nyugat._Az_occidentalizmus_form%C3%A1i_a_magyar_pop zen%C3%A9ben_az_1960-as_%C3%A9s_1980-as_%C3%A9vek_k%C3%B6z%C3%B6tt, accessed 26 June 2023.

33. The first beat group from the West to perform in Hungary was the Spenser Davis Group in 1966, then came the Nashville Teens in 1968; Duke Ellington in 1971; the Free, Oscar Peterson, and Rhoda Scott in 1972; and many more. At the same time, Hungarian bands and singers went to Western countries and to the Eastern 'friendly' countries of the Warsaw Pact: Bergendy (Denmark, 1962); Illés (Graz and Vienna, 1967; London, 1970); Omega (London, 1968, 1973); Syrius (Australia, 1970); Kati Kovács (Tokyo, 1972); Sarolta Zalatnay (Cannes, 1972); LGT (Tokyo, 1971; London, 1973, US tour, 1974); and many more.

34. K. Horváth, 'Vágyakba fojtott Nyugat', 64.

35. Ibid., 65.

36. On the contemporary music scene, see Bence Csatári, *Az ész a fontos, nem a haj: A Kádár-rendszer könnyűzenei politikája* (Budapest: Jaffa, 2015); Szemere, *Up from the Underground*; Tamás Szőnyei, *Nyilván tartottak: Titkos szolgák a magyar rock körül* (Budapest: Magyar Narancs, 2005); János Sebők, *Rock a vasfüggöny mögött: Hatalom és ifjúsági zene a Kádár-korszakban* (Budapest: GM & Társa, 2002); and László Kürti, 'Rocking the State: Youth and Rock Music Culture in Hungary, 1976–1990', *East European Politics and Societies* 3 (1991): 483–513.

37. Its tour included the Nationaltheater Weimar, 1974; Schauspielhaus Leipzig, 1977; Volksbühne East-Berlin, 1978; Bulandra, Bucharest, and the BITEF, Belgrade, 1973; and National Theatre, Prague, 1974. The album was recorded on Qualiton, cat. no. SLPX 16579, https://www.youtube.com/watch?v=nP3xlduwISw, accessed 26 June 2023.

38. On the popular music concert boom in Hungary in the 1980s, see József G. Rácz and Zolt Zétényi, 'Rock Concerts in Hungary in the 1980s', *International Sociology*, 1994(1): 43–53.

39. Erika Szántó, '*Képzelt riport*: A Vígszínházban', *Színház* 6 (1973): 16.

40. Martin P. Kelly, 'Hungarian-American Rock Play Depends on Pessimism to Work,' *Times Union*, 16 March 1986, https://archive.is/20130222000744/http://albarchive.merlinone.net/mweb/wmsql.wm.request?oneimage&imageid=5466651, accessed 26 June 2023.After the Vígszínház première it soon was staged all over Hungary: Szeged and Kecskemét,

852   ZOLTÁN IMRE

1974; Pécs, Miskolc, and Szolnok, 1975; Győr, 1979; Veszprém, 1986; and Eger, 1988. It was performed in New York at the Egg and at the Empire State Institute for the Performing Arts, Albany, in 1986; see https://en.wikipedia.org/wiki/An_Imaginary_Report_on_an_American_Rock_Festival. It remained popular even after the 1989 change of the political system, with eighteen productions in the Hungarian-speaking theatre world since then.

41. Varga, 'A *Képzelt riport egy amerikai popfesztiválról* vígszínházi előadásának recepciója a Kádár-korszak kultúrpolitikájának tükrében', 85.

42. Mills, 'Altamont or Montana', 12. Again, the passage as rendered is my own back-translation, since I did not have access to the original, only to a Hungarian translation.

43. At the time it was officially called 'liberation from the Wehrmacht', but actually it was the start of another occupation by the Soviet Red Army—one that lasted for more than forty years.

44. Tamás Tarján, 'Boldog születésnapot! A *Harmincéves vagyok* a Vígszínházban', *Színház* 6 (1975): 1.

45. Péter Molnár Gál, 'Harmincéves vagyok: Bemutató a Vígszínházban', *Népszabadság*, 23 March 1973, 6. See also Pál Geszti, 'Harmincéves vagyok: Színpadi kollázs a Vígszínházban', *Magyar Hírlap*, 23 March 1973, 10; and Ottó Major, 'Fiatal Magyarország', *Tükör*, 25 March 1975, 13. The piece was never again performed in Hungary.

46. Until 1989 it was performed only at Szeged, where it played in 1984; since then, it has had ten other productions all over the country.

47. Illés was one of the first bands to play Western-style music with Hungarian lyrics. They were extremely popular with the bands Metró and Omega until they broke up in 1973.

48. The theme of the ballad was very popular in the Kádár regime. In 1973 the Szegedi Egyetemi Színpad, for instance, also adapted it for the stage, though in a prose version; see Győző Dúró, 'Az életmű csúcsai', *Színház* 8 (2003): 6–7, and István Nánay, 'Partizánattitűd', *Színház* 8 (2003): 4–5.

49. See the production at https://www.youtube.com/watch?v=alPglaX7DBk, accessed 26 June 2023.

50. *Ki mit tud?* (lit. 'Who knows what?') was a multi-genre talent show on Hungarian National Television that ran for ten seasons between 1962 and 1996. Greatly popular in the 1960s, it helped to launch the career of many artists who later became household names in Hungary. It was originally conceived as a national talent search, with contestants coming from city-, county-, and finally country-wide finals, which were televised live. A vast array of genres covering nearly all fields of the performing arts were judged separately: vocal music (including pop, rock, opera, and folk), instrumental music (including classical, jazz, dance, pop, and rock), poetry reading, folk and contemporary dance, and 'other' (such as circus productions, magic shows, stand-up comedy, pantomime, and puppetry). The 1988 contest also welcomed amateur film submissions. The jury usually included a number of celebrities from the country's theatre, music, and art scenes. Prizes ranged from common household goods to a trip to the next World Festival of Youth, and even, after the 1980s, luxury trips to foreign countries.

51. Jelentés a Tudományos, Közoktatási és Kulturális Osztálynak, National Archive of Hungary, MNL OL M-KS 288.f.36/1972, 18.ő.e. 85.

52. Ibid.

53. These unofficial performances were organised secretly in private flats and advertised only by word of mouth among friends and other trusted individuals.

54. The foreign musicals included *West Side Story* (*Lázadók*, lit.: *Rebels*, 1982); *Hair*, 1985; *Jézus Krisztus Szupersztár*, 1986; *Les Misérables* (*Nyomorultak*, 1987); and *Chess*, 1992. The

ENTERTAINMENT, PROPAGANDA, RESISTANCE    853

Hungarian ones were *Sztrácsinálók* (*Star Makers*, 1981); *Üvöltés* (*Howl*, 1983); *Farkasok* (*Wolves*, 1983); *A krónikás* (*The Chronicler*, 1984); *A bábjátékos* (*The Puppeteer*, 1985); *Café Rock*, 1985; *Csillag Nápoly egén* (*Star in the Sky of Naples*, 1987); *Dorian Gray*, 1990; and *Anna Karenina*, 1994, among others.

55. Ádám Ignácz, *Ezek a fiatalok* (1967): Az első magyar beatfilm szerepe a szocialista Magyarország könnyűzenei életében, *2000*, http://ketezer.hu/2013/10/ezek-a-fiatalok-1967/, accessed 26 June 2023.

56. Among the imports were *Slágerrevű* (*Pop Gear*, 1966); *Big Beat* (*Mocne Uderzennie*, 1968); *A Hard Day's Night*, 1968; and, later, *Hair*, 1979; and *Üvegtörők* (*Breaking Glass*, 1981). The Hungarian films included *Az éltebe táncoltatott lány* (*A Girl Danced into Life*, 1964); *Extázis 7-től 10-ig* (*Ecstasy from 7 to 10*, 1969); *Válogatás* (*Selection*, 1969); *Szép lányok, ne sírjatok* (*Pretty Girls, Don't Cry*, 1971); *Ballagás* (*Farewell*, 1980); *A koncert* (*The Concert*, 1981); *Városbujócska* (*Playing Hide-and-Seek in the City*, 1985); and *Rocktérítő*, 1988.

57. The permission indicated when exactly these songs were to be performed, since Tarjányi was allowed to sing them only between midnight and one o'clock in the morning.

58. It premièred at the Theatre Academy in 1976, directed by Miklós Szinetár. Its success led to his being asked to stage it at the Operettszínház.

59. According to the script, the outside locations were supposed to include Hungarian historical and natural sites: 'somewhere in Hungary, Hősök tere [Heroes' Square] in Budapest, a mountain path, a lawn, and a mountain chapel near Balaton, the inner castle of Esztergom, somewhere in the *puszta*, the inside of a church in Kollósd, the baronal castle and the *puszta* in Somogy, Margaret Island'. 'István, a király', forgatókönyv [script], 5–89, MNL OL XXIX-I-1-a, 89. doboz/box.

60. Previously Koltay had made a film title *A koncert* (*The Concert*) under similar circumstances. For the film, the legendary rock-pop band Illés, which had broken up in 1973, was reunited for a single concert, in which Koltay and his team recorded the songs as a live event, together with the spectators' reactions and some backstage scenes. Premièring in 1981, it was the first concert film in Hungarian history and a phenomenal success.

61. 'István, a király', technikai forgatókönyv [technical script], 3–4; see also 'István, a király', dialóglista [list of dialogues], 1983, 1–2. MNL OL XXIX-I-1-a, 89. doboz/box.

62. Although the film did not receive general permission or support, the state-controlled radio and TV still agreed to promote an event that another government organisation had classified as 'problematic'. Because there was no central bureau nor any formal rules for censorship, the different institutions and their leaders could make different decisions regarding the same issue: what one institution did not allow might be permissible in another. It required special negotiations; see the quote cited at note callout 6.

63. Judit Kabar, 'Hungarian Superstar: *Stephen, the King*', *Daily News*, 21 August 1983, 7.

64. Tamás Mészáros, 'István, a király: Rockopera a Városligetben', *Magyar Hírlap*, 27 August, 1983, 5; see also György Petrus, 'Rockopera: Nemcsak fiataloknak', *Ország-Világ*, 31 August 1983, 10–11.

65. Tamás Ligeti Nagy, 'István, a király', *Képes Újság*, 10 September 1983, 3.

66. - Sági, 'István, a király', *Esti Hírlap*, 13 September 1983, 7.

67. Kabar, 'Hungarian Superstar', 7.

68. Lajos Tandi, 'István, a király: Avagy történelmi lecke rockzenére', *Dél-Magyarország*, 31 August 1983, 6, see also András Pályi, 'Dráma vagy apoteózis? István, a király a Városligetben', *Színház* 11 (1983): 1–3.

69. János István Németh, 'István, a király', *Alföld* 10 (1984): 92.

854    ZOLTÁN IMRE

70. Mészáros, 'István, a király: Rockopera a Városligetben', 5.
71. István Feitl, 'Sztár lett István király?', *Magyar Ifjúság*, 21 October 1983, 41.
72. Anna Poór, 'Az *István, a király* táncos kórusa', *Színház* 12 (1983): 20.
73. Gábor Kapuvári, 'István, a király: Rockopera a Városligetben', *Magyar Nemzet*, 31 August 1983, 8.
74. Mészáros, 'István, a király: Rockopera a Városligetben', 5.
75. Ligeti Nagy, '*István, a király*', 3.
76. Poór, 'Az *István, a király* táncos kórusa', 21.
77. Németh, '*István, a király*', 93.
78. Ibid.
79. Ibid.
80. Ibid. For instance, the rock opera starts 'with Beethoven's romantic *István király* overture' (Pályi, 'Dráma vagy apoteózis?', 3.), which was composed for the opening of the Deutsches Theatre of Pest in 1812 and on that occasion was conducted by the composer himself.
81. Endre Varjas, 'Jancsó keze nyomán', *Élet és irodalom*, 26 August 1983, 11.
82. Ibid. Koppány was played by Gyula Vikidál, an ex-member of P. Mobile, Laborc by Ferenc 'Feró' Nagy, the founder and the lead singer of Beatrice, and Torda by Gyula 'Bill' Deák, the soloist of the Hobó Blues Band. All these bands were considered outcasts by the establishment and played at the Black Lambs Festival in 1980.
83. See Tandi, '*István, a király*: Avagy történelmi lecke rockzenére', 6; Pályi, 'Dráma vagy apoteózis?' 3; Ligeti Nagy, '*István, a király*', 3; and D. L., 'Gregorián már volt, Rékáét most írta: Interjú Szörényi Leventével' *Hétfői Hírek*, 22 August 1983, 6.
84. Poór, 'Az *István, a király* táncos kórusa', 21.
85. Ibid.
86. Varjas, 'Jancsó keze nyomán', 11.
87. Mészáros, 'István, a király: Rockopera a Városligetben', 5.
88. Ligeti Nagy, '*István, a király*', 3.
89. Feitl, 'Sztár lett István király?', 41.
90. Németh, '*István, a király*', 93.
91. Gábor Bányai, 'Minek tapsolunk?', *Népszava*, 10 September 1983, 7.
92. Ibid.
93. Varjas, 'Jancsó keze nyomán', 11.
94. Ibid.
95. Tandi, '*István, a király*: Avagy történelmi lecke rockzenére', 6; see also Kapuvári, '*István, a király*: Rockopera a Városligetben', 8.
96. See *Esti Magazin*, Kossuth Rádió, 18:30, 7 July 1983, gépirat [transcription], OSZMI; and Éva Bársony, 'István, a király a Királydombon', *Esti Hírlap*, 4 August 1983, 6.
97. Miklós Győrffy, interview with Miklós Boldizsár and Péter Hanák, 168 óra in italian, Kossuth Rádió, 4 August,1984, gépirat [transcription].
98. Ibid.
99. János Emericus [János Krasznai], 'István, a király: Avagy árad a kegyelem fénye ránk (gondolatok egy áltörténelmi misztériumjáték margójára)', *Hírmondó*, 23 October 1983, 16.
100. And he was not the only one as one of the daily operative reports of the secret police drew the attention to the fact that 'at Koppány's funeral, imitating the supers, the ELTE-students, probably without tickets, lighted their own candles. At the end of the production, approximately 150–200 persons went to the front of the stage, where they were

singing Himnusz for 15–20 minutes with the lighted candles in their hands'. Napi operatív információs jelentés, Budapest, 22 August 1983, 119, ABTL 2.7.1..

101. Emericus, 'Stefan, a király: Avagy árad a kegyelem fénye ránk', 17.

102. Győrffy, interview with Boldizsár and Hanák.

103. Feitl, 'Sztár lett István király?', 41.

104. Teljesítmények nyomában, szerk. [ed.], műsorvezető [speaker], Gábor Bányai, vendég [guest], Ferenc Kőhalmi, Kossuth, 18 October 1983, gépirat [script].

105. Bányai, 'Minek tapsolunk?', 7.

106. Győrffy, interview with Boldizsár and Hanák.

107. Szilárd Béla Jávorszky, 'István, a király: Koppány, a szupersztár', Népszabadság, 18 August 2002, 9.

108. Cecília Kovai, 'Oly nehéz a választás! Az István, a király és az értelmezés kényszerei', AnBlokk 1 (2008): 68.

109. Jávorszky, 'István, a király: Koppány, a szupersztár', 9.

110. Ibid.

111. Balázs Házi, '"Mondd, te kit választanál?" Narratívák az István, a király bemutatója kapcsán', Rendszerváltó Archívum 2 (2017): 86.

112. Péter G. Tóth, 'Lázadók idézőjelben: Koppányok és Laborcok a nem underground zenében,' in Avantgárd, underground, alternatív: Popzene, művészet és szubkulturális nyilvánosság Magyarországon, ed. József Havasréti and Zsolt K. Horváth (Budapest: Artpool Művészetkutató Központ, Kijarat, and PTE Kommunikációs, 2003), 70.

113. Ibid.

114. Kovai, 'Oly nehéz a választás!, 71.

115. Ibid.

116. 'András Rényi in Megérteni a konfliktust: Rényi András és Sándor Erzsi beszélgetése az István, a királyról', http://epa.oszk.hu/01300/01326/00154/pdf/EPA01326_mozgo _vilag_2013_10_6752.pdf, accessed 26 June 2023; see also Péter Molnár Gál, 'Sikerrel nem vitatkozunk!', Népszabadság, 2008, http://epa.oszk.hu/01300/01326/00101/MV_2 008_07_14_4.htm, accessed 26 June 2023.

117. See the 1984 film version with English subtitles at, https://www.televizio.sk/2022/08/ist van-a-kiraly-teljes-film/ accessed 23 June 2023.

118. Molnár Gál, 'Sikerrel nem vitatkozunk!'

119. The film version received a special invitation as the opening programme to the Semaine Internationale de la Critique Françoise of the 1984 Cannes Festival, where it received international acclaim.

120. János Péter Sós, 'Szobrok: Tojások a szerzőknek', Magyarország 40 (1985): 13.

121. In Germany it played in Baden-Baden, Cologne, and Berlin; on the reception in Berlin, see Christine Schulz, 'Eine alte Geschichte spannend aufbereitet', Neue Zeit, 15 April 1989, 5. In Italy, it played in Peregine; see G. Cs., 'István napja leáldozott,' Film, színház, muzsika, 4 August 1990, 26.

122. 'ades', 'Mi lesz veled, István?', Magyar Hírlap, 17 February 1986, 7.

123. Gábor Koltay, conversation with the author, 12 July 2019.

124. Molnár Gál, 'Sikerrel nem vitatkozunk!'

125. Ibid.

126. Ibid. After the political system changed in 1989, there were additional productions of István: Népstadion, 1990; Seville, 1992; Margitsziget, 1995; Nemzeti Színház, 2000; Esztergom, 2002; Csíksomlyó, 2003; Budapest Sportcsarnok, 2008; Szeged, 2013;

856    ZOLTÁN IMRE

Kolozsvár, 2013; Városliget, 2015; Nemzeti Színház, Győr; Fővárosi Operettszínház, 2018; and Operaház, 2020.

127. Béla Köpeczi's jelentése [report], National Archives of Hungary, MNL OL M-KS 288-41/ 469.ö.e.15.

128. Szőnyei, *Nyilván tartottak*, 435. The LP *Honfoglalás* by the rock group P. Mobil was only allowed to be released in 1984, after *István*, although the group had played its concert version since 1978.

129. Ibid., 368.

130. Tibor Miklós, *MUSICAL! Egy műfaj és egy szerelem története* (Budapest: Novella, 2002), 370.

131. See my article about the preimiéres of Kálmán's *Die Czárdásfürstin* in Vienna in 1915 and in Budapest in 1916 and the social, political and cultural problems articulated by the two stagings: Zoltan Imre, 'Operetta beyond Borders: The Different Version of *Die Csárdásfürstin* in Europe and in the United States (1915–1921)', *Studies in Musical Theatre* 2 (2013): 175–205.

132. See Balázs Perényi, 'Turáni átok', *Zsöllye* 6-7 (2001): 40–41.

133. The main patron of the performance was Zsolt Semjén, the deputy prime minister of the right-wing Orban government.

134. The critic István Pion remarked: '[M]any of you will not like this, but the spectators with critical thinking probably will have problems with this overly nationalistic kitsch, with the overemphasised sorrow and with the fact that the piece nourishes such hopes in vain, to which we have not had any remedy for the past 98 years. Instead of helping to deal somehow with the trauma, it pulls its spectators again into the pain Hungarians suffered due to the consequence of the 1920 Trianon Treaty'. István Pion, 'Kétórányi tömény szomorúságnak álcázta a *Trianon* rockoperát Koltay Gábor', https://zoom.hu/hir/2018/ 06/22/ketoranyi-tomeny-szomorusagnak-alcazta-a-trianon-rockoperat-koltay-gabor/, accessed 24 January 2020.

135. At the time of writing, *Padlás* (*The Attic*) is being adapted by a New York musical agency for a planned Broadway opening.

136. It was staged by the company of the Magyar Állami Operaház (Hungarian State Opera) at the Erkel Színház (Erkel Theatre), causing a huge controversy. On 21 June 2019 Szilveszter Ókovács, the general director of the Operaház and the Erkel Színház, announced that he was cancelling fifteen performances of the musical *Billy Elliot* (see András Király, 'Az Opera lemondta a *Billy Eliot* [*sic*] 15 előadását', https://444.hu/2018/06/21/az-opera-lemondta-a-billy-eliot-15-eloadasat, accessed 24 January 2023). His reason was that due to the negative media campaign, public interest in the musical had severely decreased. A right-wing media campaign had started a few weeks before, when an article titled 'Botrányos előadás az Erkel Színházban' ('Scandalous Performance at the Erkel Theatre') appeared in the government-influenced right-wing newspaper *Magyar Nemzet*. Zsófia N. Horváth accused the production of 'homosexual propaganda' and asked 'how it happens that such a prestigious institution as the Opera goes directly against the aims of the government, and uses the production made for youngsters in their most fragile age to such a penetrant, boisterous gay propaganda.' Zsófia N. Horváth, 'Botrányos előadás az Erkel Színházban', https://www.magyaridok.hu/velemeny/botranyos-eloadas-az-erkel-szinhazban-3146662/, accessed 24 January 2023. A few days later Ókovács responded that the première of the production had been nearly two years earlier, in July 2016, and that they had created a new version. In their version, 'Billy is not gay, [ ... ] his friend, [ ... ]

Michael might later become a homosexual, but that is not confirmed in the performance'. Nonetheless, 'in our version, we have cut down Michael's role and significance and elevated Billy's role'. Szilveszter Ókovács, 'Meleg helyzet, avagy kiborul a Billy', https://www.origo.hu/kultura/20180604-okovacs-szerint-az-opera.html, accessed 24 January 2023. N. Horváth's article was part of a right-wing media campaign in which conservative leaders of prestigious cultural institutions were attacked by extremist journalists in a culture war for not being right-wing enough. After a while, however, the right-wing hysteria over the production died down, and the production remained part of the Opera's repertory until the end of September 2019.

137. It was played by the Csíky Gergely Színház, Kaposvár, and directed by János Mohácsi; see https://www.youtube.com/watch?v=5w14EJD032A, accessed 26 June 2023.

## BIBLIOGRAPHY

'ades'. 'Mi lesz veled, István?' *Magyar Hírlap*, 17 February 1986, 7.

Alpár, Ágnes. *Harminc év vendégjátékai, 1945–1975*. Budapest: OSZMI, 1977.

Bányai, Gábor. 'Minek tapsolunk?' *Népszava*, 10 September 1983, 7.

Bársony, Éva. '*István, a király* a Királydombon'. *Esti Hírlap*, 04 August 1983, 6.

Baumrin, Seth. 'Ketmanship in Opole: Jerzy Grotowski and the Price of Artistic Freedom'. *TDR: The Drama Review* 53, no. 4 (2009): 49–77.

Beck, Dennis C. 'Divadlo Husa na Provázku and the "Absence" of Czech Community'. *Theatre Journal* 4 (1996): 419–41.

Bérczes, László. 'Volt egyszer egy *Petőfi-rock*: Beszélgetés Árkosi Árpáddal, Dózsa Erzsébettel, Paál Istvánnal és Vági Lászlóval'. *Film, színház, muzsika*, 11 March 1989, 6–7.

Csatári, Bence. *Az ész a fontos, nem a haj: A Kádár-rendszer könnyűzenei politikája*. Budapest: Jaffa, 2015.

Demcsák, Katalin. 'A Paál István vezette Szegedi Egyetemi Színpad'. In *Alternatív színháztörténetek: Alternatívok és alternatívák*, edited by Zoltán Imre, 242–264. Budapest: Balassi Kíado, 2008.

Dúró, Győző. 'Az életmű csúcsai'. *Színház* 8 (2003): 6–7.

Emericus, János [János Krasznai]. '*István, a király*: Avagy árad a kegyelem fénye ránk (Gondolatok egy áltörténelmi misztériumjáték margójára)'. *Hírmondó*, 23 October 1983, 10–21.

*Esti Magazin*. Kossuth Rádió, 18:30, 7 July 1983, gépirat [transcription], OSZMI, File of *István, a király*.

Feitl, István. 'Sztár lett István király?' *Magyar Ifjúság*, 21 October 1983, 41.

G. Cs. 'István napja leáldozott'. *Film, színház, muzsika*, 4 August 1990, 26.

Geszti, Pál. 'Harmincéves vagyok: Színpadi kollázs a Vígszínházban'. *Magyar Hírlap*, 23 March 1973, 10.

'Gregorián már volt, Rékáét most írta: Interjú Szörényi Leventével'. *Hétfői Hírek*, 22 August 1983, 6.

Győrffy, Miklós. Interview with Miklós Boldizsár and Péter Hanák, *168 óra*, Kossuth Rádió, 4 August 1984, gépirat [transcription].

György, Péter. *Kádár köpönyege*. Budapest: Magvető, 2005.

Haraszti, Miklós. *The Velvet Prison: Artists under State Socialism*. New York: Basic Books, 1987.

## 858 ZOLTÁN IMRE

Házi, Balázs. 'Mondd, te kit választanál? Narratívák az István, a király bemutatója kapcsán'. *Rendszerváltó Archívum* 2 (2017): 80–93.

Heltai, Gyöngyi. *Az operett metamorfózisai: A 'kapitalista giccs'-től a 'haladó mímusjáték'-ig, 1945–1956.* Budapest: Eötvös, 2012.

Horváth, Zsolt K. 'Vágyakba fojtott Nyugat: Az occidentalizmus formái a magyar popzenében az 1960-as és az 1970-es évek között', 68. https://www.academia.edu/39176980/ V%C3%A1gyakba_fojtott_Nyugat._Az_occidentalizmus_form%C3%A1i_a_magyar_pop zen%C3%A9ben_az_1960-as_%C3%A9s_1980-as_%C3%A9vek_k%C3%B6z%C3%B6tt, accessed 26 June 2023.

Ignácz, Ádám. 'Ezek a fiatalok (1967): Az első magyar beatfilm szerepe a szocialista Magyarország könnyűzenei életében', 2000, http://ketezer.hu/2013/10/ezek-a-fiatalok-1967/ , accessed 23 June 2023.

Imre, Zoltán, ed. *Alternatív színháztörténetek: Alternatívok és alternatívák.* Budapest: Balassi Kiadó, 2008.

Imre, Zoltán. 'Operetta beyond Borders: The Different Versions of *Die Csárdásfürstin* in Europe and in the United States (1915–1921)'. *Studies in Musical Theatre* 2 (2013): 175–205.

Imre, Zoltán. 'Theatre, Propaganda and the Cold War'. In *Theatre, Globalization and the Cold War*, edited by Christopher B. Balme and Berenika Szymanski-Dül, 107–130. London and New York: Palgrave Macmillan, 2017.

*István, a király*, dialóglista [list of dialogues], 1983, 1–2. National Archive of Hungary, MNL OL XXIX-I-1-a, Box 89.

*István, a király, forgatókönyv* [script], 5–89. National Archive of Hungary, MNL OL XXIX-I-1-a, Box 89.

*István, a király, technikai forgatókönyv* [technical script], 3–4. National Archive of Hungary , MNL OL XXIX-I-1-a, Box 89.

Jávorszky, Szilárd Béla. 'István, a király: Koppány, a szupersztár'. *Népszabadság*, 18 August 2002, 9.

'Jelentés a Tudományos, Közoktatási és Kulturális Osztálynak'. National Archive of Hungary. MNL OL M-KS 288.f.36/1972, 18.ő.e. 85.

Kabar, Judit. 'Hungarian Superstar: *Stephen, the King*'. *Daily News*, 21 August 1983, 7.

Kapuvári, Gábor. 'István, a király: Rockopera a Várossligetben'. *Magyar Nemzet*, 31 August 1983, 8.

Kelly, Martin P. 'Hungarian-American Rock Play Depends on Pessimism to Work'. *Times Union*, 16 March, 1986. https://archive.is/20130222000744/http://albarchive.merlinone.net/ mweb/wmsql.wm.request?oneimage&imageid=5466651, accessed 23 June 2023.

Király, Andras. 'Az Opera lemondta a *Billy Eliot* [sic] 15 előadását', https://444.hu/2018/06/21/ az-opera-lemondta-a-billy-eliot-15-eloadasat, accessed 23 June 2023.

Koltay, Gábor. Conversation with the author, 12 July 2019.

Koltay, Gábor. *István, a király.* Budapest: Ifjúsági, 1984.

Köpeczi Béla's jelentése [report]. National Archives of Hungary. MNL OL M-KS 288-41/ 469.ö.e.15.

Kovai, Cecília. 'Oly nehéz a választás! Az István, a király és az értelmezés kényszerei'. *AnBlokk* 1 (2008): 63–70.

Kürti, László. 'Rocking the State: Youth and Rock Music Culture in Hungary, 1976–1990'. *East European Politics and Societies* 3 (1991): 483–513.

Ligeti Nagy, Tamás. 'Tamás, *István, a király*'. *Képes Újság*, 10 September 1983, 3.

Major, Ottó. 'Fiatal Magyarország'. *Tükör*, 25 March 1975, 13–14.

ENTERTAINMENT, PROPAGANDA, RESISTANCE    859

Mészáros, Tamás. 'István, a király: Rockopera a Városligetben'. *Magyar Hírlap*, 27 August 1983, 5.

Miklós, Tibor. *MUSICAL! Egy műfaj és egy szerelem története*. Budapest: Novella, 2002.

Mills, Bart. 'Altamont or Montana'. *Times*, 28 July 1973, 12.

Molnár Gál, Péter. 'Harmincéves vagyok: Bemutató a Vígszínházban'. *Népszabadság*, 23 March 1973, 6.

Molnár Gál, Péter. 'Sikerrel nem vitatkozunk!' *Népszabadság*, 2008, http://epa.oszk.hu/01300/01326/00101/MV_2008_07_14_4.htm, accessed 26 June 2023.

Molnár, Dániel. *Vörös csillagok: A Rákosi-korszak szórakoztatóipara és a szocialista revük*. Budapest: Ráció, 2019.

Művelődési Minisztérium tájékoztató jelentés. 18 July 1972. National Archives of Hungary, . MNL OL M-Ks 288.f.41/1972, 85.ö.e., 6–29.

N. Horváth, Zsófia. 'Botrányos előadás az Erkel Színházban', https://www.magyaridok.hu/velemeny/botranyos-eloadas-az-erkel-szinhazban-3146662/, accessed 23 June 2023.

Nánay, István. 'Elkötelezett amatőrök és az új színpadi nyelv'. *Színház* 10 (1973): 31–34.

Nánay, István. 'Partizánattitűd'. *Színház* 8 (2003): 3–6.

'Napi operatív információs jelentés'. Historical Archives of Hungarian State Security, Budapest, 22 August 1983, 119. ABTL 2.7.1.

Németh, János István. 'István, a király'. *Alföld* 10 (1984): 90–94.

Ókovács, Szilveszter. 'Meleg helyzet, avagy kiborul a Billy'. https://www.origo.hu/kultura/20180604-okovacs-szerint-az-opera.html, accessed 26 June 2023.

Pályi, András. 'Dráma vagy apoteózis? *István, a király* a Városligetben'. *Színház* 11 (1983): 1–3.

Perényi, Balázs. 'Turáni átok'. *Zsöllye* 6–7 (2001): 40–41.

Petrus, György. 'Rockopera: Nemcsak fiataloknak'. *Ország-Világ*, 31 August 1983, 10–11.

Pion, István. 'Kétórányi tömény szomorúságnak álcázta a *Trianon* rockoperát Koltay Gábor'. https://zoom.hu/hir/2018/06/22/ketoranyi-tomeny-szomorusagnak-alcazta-a-trianon-roc koperat-koltay-gabor/, accessed 24 January 2020.

Poór, Anna. 'Az *István, a király* táncos kórusa'. *Színház* 12 (1983): 19–21.

Rácz, József G., and Zoltán Zétényi. 'Rock Concerts in Hungary in the 1980s'. *International Sociology* 1 (1994): 43–53.

Rényi, András, and Erzsi Sándor. 'Beszélgetése az *István, a királyról*', http://epa.oszk.hu/01300/01326/00154/pdf/EPA01326_mozgo_vilag_2013_10_6752.pdf, accessed 26 June 2023.

'The Rolling Stones Disaster at Altamont: Let It Bleed'. *Rolling Stone*, 21 January 1970, https://www.rollingstone.com/music/music-news/the-rolling-stones-disaster-at-altamont-let-it-bleed-71299/, accessed 23 June 2023.

'Sági'. 'István, a király'. *Esti Hírlap*, 13 September 1983, 7.

Schulz, Christine. 'Eine alte Geschichte spannend aufbereitet'. *Neue Zeit*, 15 April 1989, 5.

Sebők, János. *Rock a vasfüggöny mögött: Hatalom és ifjúsági zene a Kádár-korszakban*. Budapest: GM & Társa, 2002.

Setje-Eilers, Margaret. '"Wochenend und Sonnenschein": In the Blind Spots of Censorship at the GDR's Cultural Authorities and the Berliner Ensemble'. *Theatre Journal* 61, no. 3 (2009): 363–386.

Sós, János Péter. 'Szobrok: Tojások a szerzőknek'. *Magyarország* 40 (1985): 13.

Szántó, Erika. 'Képzelt riport: A Vígszínházban'. *Színház* 6 (1973): 13–16.

Szemere, Anna. *Up from the Underground: The Culture of Rock Music in Postsocialist Hungary*. University Park, PA: Penn State University Press, 2001.

860 ZOLTÁN IMRE

Szkárosi, Endre. 'A tér mint művészetszervező erő. Experimentális színház, hangköltészet, plurilingvizmus'. In *Né/ma? Tanulmányok a magyar neoavantgárd köréből*, edited by Pál Deréky and András Müllner, 146–172. Budapest: Ráció, 2004.

Szőnyei, Tamás. *Nyilván tartottak: Titkos szolgák a magyar rock körül*. Budapest: Magyar Narancs, 2005.

Tandi, Lajos. '*István, a király*: Avagy történelmi lecke rockzenére'. *Dél-Magyarország*, 31 August 1983, 6.

Tarján, Tamás. 'Boldog születésnapot! A *Harmincéves vagyok* a Vígszínházban'. *Színház* 6 (1975): 1–4.

Teljesítmények nyomában, szerk. [ed.], műsorvezető [speaker] Gábor Bányai, vendég [guest] Ferenc Kőhalmi, Kossuth, 18 October 1983, gépirat [transcription]. Archives of the Hungarian Theatre Institute, File of István, a király.

Várszegi, Tibor, and István Sándor L., eds. *Fordulatok*. Budapest: W. P., 1993.

Tóth, Péter G. 'Lázadók idézőjelben: Koppányok és Laborcok a nem underground zenében'. In *Avantgárd, underground, alternatív: Popzene, művészet és szubkulturális nyilvánosság Magyarországon*, edited by József Havasréti and Zsolt K. Horváth, 61–84. Budapest: Artpool Művészetkutató Központ, Kijarat, and PTE Kommunikációs, 2003.

Varga, Luca. 'A *Képzelt riport egy amerikai popfesztiválról* vígszínházi előadásának recepciója a Kádár-korszak kultúrpolitikájának tükrében'. *Korall* 39 (2010): 58–88.

Varjas, Endre. 'Jancsó keze nyomán'. *Élet és irodalom*, 26 August 1983, 11.

Vászegi, Tibor, ed. *Felütés: Írások a magyar alternatív színházról*. Budapest: W. P., 1990.

# PART XI

## OUTLOOK, OR THE ROAD AHEAD

# CHAPTER 31

......................................................................................................

# A *BRAN NUE DAE*? DECOLONISING THE MUSICAL THEATRE CURRICULUM

......................................................................................................

## PAMELA KARANTONIS

IN declaring a 'brand new day' for the decolonisation of musical theatre, the title of this chapter indicates a focus on the Indigenous Australian musical *Bran Nue Dae* (Jimmy Chi and Kuckles 1990) and its subsequent film adaptation (2009)[1] and stage revivals (2020–2021). The aims of creating the show are, on the surface, common to a range of decolonised musical stage works, with a focus on revealing the unsung true stories—the honest (political) telling of fictionalised works that touch upon the lived experiences of Indigenous people: while *Bran Nue Dae* was multi-authored, it was led by Jimmy Chi, who saw it as a parable for his life, if not strictly autobiographical.

More broadly, the chapter will consider how a very grounded story about a very particular set of lived circumstances is instructive for how we begin to decolonise our understanding of commercial musical theatre globally and the university sector's growing deference to commercialised cultural industries since around 2000. Universities and conservatories are increasingly identified by government as places that find their graduates employment. The challenge for academic leaders in musical theatre is that they are preparing students for an industry which does not see decolonisation as one of its main objectives, so students will need to be coached into navigating systems that have other priorities or may even be hostile, in terms of racial and other micro-aggressions. Students are taught in an academic environment to question everything, but will then need to anticipate an employment culture where it may be advantageous to keep quiet on certain issues and 'just take the note'. Decolonising the curriculum is much more radical and comprehensive than simply exposing students to a greater volume of commercially celebrated work featuring Black and Asian artists. Entailed in this process are matters of who curates and theorises this material, who performs it as part of an educational curriculum, how teachers decolonise the training of skills in both analysing and performing the genre, and the productions we stage: 'When universities do accommodate decolonial demands, they frequently do so in a way that ensures that they remain marginal and do not bring about structural change in the institution as a whole'.[2] The process of decolonisation begins by understanding how we could make universities accountable to the circumstances of the real artists who create the work.

# 'A Truly Indigenous Musical'

Jimmy Chi was born in 1948 in the West Australian pearl-diving port town of Broome to a Bardi Indigenous and Scottish mother and a father of Chinese and Japanese heritage. In 1981 Chi and other musicians from his hometown travelled to Adelaide to join a one-year foundation degree course in music at the Centre for Aboriginal Studies in Music (CASM) at the University of Adelaide—a course made available exclusively to Indigenous Australians with the aim of celebrating Indigenous music-making. This point is crucial to the relevance of universities as a decolonising influence: that they make inclusive choices and offer a space to nurture opportunity and mentorship for new popular music. As a result of his studies there, Chi and friends formed the band Kuckles. According to one of the show's writers, Peter Bibby, the idea for *Bran Nue Dae* then began with a few new songs in 1986 and the subsequent mentorship of the Aboriginal Writers Oral Literature and Dramatists Association (AWOLDA). AWOLDA encouraged staging a workshop of the show materials in the city of Perth, with Marita Darcy contributing to script development and the acclaimed playwright and poet Jack Davis also advising on the libretto. At the same time, the new Indigenous publishing house Magabala Books, which had opened in Broome, offered to publish the book and score.[3]

The work had its stage première at the Perth Festival in 1990, followed by Australian tours from 1991 to 1995 and a major revival in 2020, produced by Opera Australia, the nation's flagship opera company. In sum, the way in which this musical took shape was very much from the grass roots and not an 'intercultural' commission. Emerging from the students' own initiative in an academic setting that nurtured Indigenous talent, it progressed to a structure that maintained the authenticity of music-making and storytelling. Its success was in avoiding the shoehorning of creative content into preconceived models of how an integrated commercial musical book should be structured, produced, and marketed.

Paul Makeham observed that *Bran Nue Dae* heralded a new chapter in Australian popular musical theatre by, for the first time, placing Indigenous voices at the centre of the story. His analysis of the book and score is a reliable and enduring study of the many decolonising practices embedded in the work, with an emphasis on oral storytelling focused through a 'hero's quest' but with deference to a traditional respect for nomadic identities—a balance within the dramaturgical structure to draw audiences in. The narrative is a coming-of-age chronology presented through the eyes of the protagonist, Willie. He is joined by Uncle Tadpole on a road trip that becomes a homecoming, referencing the material history of violent colonial institutions: 'Willie's journey traces a transition from Edenic innocence to worldly experience [which] is compromised by the fact that the "Eden" from which he is expelled (Rossmoyne), like that to which he returns (Lombadina), is a mission, a site of oppression as well as of protection'.[4] The creators of the show kept control of its intention to function as parody and socio-political critique by rewriting popular theatrical languages, appropriating and then subverting 'white discourses [and] cultural forms'.[5]

Crucially, the production and process were by Indigenous artists and creators, so that key creative input and content were underpinned by lived experience and not compromised by the limitations inherent in an 'intercultural' project or one predicated upon cultural appropriation. It was performed mainly in Broome *kriol*, and on this point it is important to acknowledge that there are over two hundred and fifty Indigenous language groups in Australia, so there is no homogeneous 'Indigenous' identity that *Bran Nue Dae* speaks for, although politically the show does achieve a unified sense of Indigenous visibility to Australian and global audiences. Makeham observes that the work 'celebrates this cultural diversity, but also the sense of racial solidarity which characterises contemporary Aboriginality'.[6]

The musical is presented in two acts with twenty-one songs, the majority of which are original and written in popular genres and styles that borrow from many global musics of Black origin, such as reggae, spirituals or church song, and jazz and its

FIG. 31.1 John Moore (Willie) in the 1991 TV documentary about the creation of *Bran Nue Dae*. Photo: Kylie Anee Picket © Getty Images.

associated dance forms such as the Charleston. The musical eclecticism is a strong signifier of the work's commitment to seeing Indigenous Australians as having agency in a contemporary, cultural, urban worldview (especially if that does mean the borrowing of musics from many global Black cultures) and not limiting a view of the key players as subject to a salvage ethnography, where a homecoming is stereotyped as a finite return to ancient forms and places. Equally, Jimmy Chi had a personal affection for Broadway musicals such as *West Side Story* (1957) and *The Sound of Music* (1959).[7] So there is a musico-dramatic hybridity in that 'the structural motif of the journey in *Bran Nue Dae* is overlaid onto the specifically Aboriginal form of the song cycle, a type of ritual journey of re-enactment which, like Chi's play, is also "a musical journey" and a renewal of origins'.[8]

In 2009 the film adaptation of *Bran Nue Dae*, directed by the Indigenous Australian filmmaker Rachel Perkins, enjoyed a major global theatrical release. The comedy-drama film musical had a unity of form but a lightness of comedic approach that entertained but also bemused international audiences: 'Perkins saw the play at the time (along with 200,000 others), in her early twenties, and describes it as "one of the most iconic Australian theatre works", a "life-affirming piece of creation".[9] International audiences and university students may not have an opportunity to see the live stage work as part of learning, so a film adaptation is an important and more permanent point of access. Yet it is crucial to be able to explain to students how a work might change in adaptation, in this case from a 'life-affirming' piece for the film's director in the 1990s to an over-the-top comedy almost two decades later.

In her sociological study about the reception of the film by international students based in Tokyo, Catriona Elder reflected the expectation that

> films about Aboriginal people [had] to be serious. Other students agreed [ ... ] and though they had watched the film and understood the underlying stories of child removal and broken families and comprehended the impact of assimilation policies, they did not expect to see them packaged as comedy. The students were also surprised by what many others who had seen the film were surprised by: its 'unashamedly populist' approach.[10]

On one level, the criticism of the film involved acting and characterisations that relied on stock comedic types. While the film does not depict Black characters as 'happy' within the context of racist treatment and oppression, it may nevertheless appear to minimise the political issues. For some, it may repeat a trope of the extracted labour of Black artists in popular and comic but discredited performance genres. However, to Australian viewers it represents a determination to be authentic in showing a 'true' history that any viewer might find distressing, while at the same time engaging those troubling experiences with particular kinds of agency through humour. Coming from an Indigenous viewpoint too, the aesthetic intervenes by exploiting historical trauma as a spectacle because it achieves an alienation effect in the act of viewing, allowing the Indigenous creators to up-end the narrative.

FIG. 31.2 Difficult to cast outside its intrinsic setting of Australia, the film version of *Bran Nue Dae* (Rachel Perkins, 2009) may be the best way for international students and scholars to get acquainted with the Indigenous musical. The film, about an Indigenous teenager on a road trip in the late 1960s, stars Rocky McKenzie (*centre*). Photo Allstar Picture Library Ltd. © Alamy Stock Photo.

## A 'Bran Nue Dae' for the Opera Company

Going back to its roots as a life-affirming stage show, especially for Indigenous Australian audiences, we might now consider *Bran Nue Dae*'s impact on the positioning of musical theatre as a platform for cultural commentary. It needs to be noted that the twenty-first-century stage revival of *Bran Nue Dae* was produced by Opera Australia, which superficially seems a world away from the grass roots of AWOLDA's mentorship of the early workshops of the musical. However, this opportunity is a strategic one for a work that has now seen many seasons; *Bran Nue Dae*'s endurance can be credited to its adherence to the truth of many Indigenous Australian experiences, which has built community and wider recognition over a number of decades. Its promotion by an opera company suggests an ambition for inclusivity in programming and an embrace of more popular forms of music theatre. Politically, this indicates progress from the situation in which European opera was complicit with colonialism, wherein First Nations and Indigenous peoples may have been depicted visually in mythic and fictional works but their voices were not raised in song, nor were their real stories told. The cultural and ideological power of opera in the colonial setting of nineteenth-century Australia included its capacity as a genre to sublimate and even obfuscate racial tensions in the country by displacing the depiction of exotic stories as naturally consistent with a Eurocentric worldview.

When producers and impresarios sought to stage opera in nineteenth-century Australia, they aimed to reconfigure the burgeoning cities through the lens of the imagined metropolitan centres of Europe. Helen J. English, Stephanie Rocke, and Michael Williams account for the Australian colonial performance histories of the subsequent popular forms of nineteenth-century minstrelsy, music hall, and imported dramatic and musical forms, which include, respectively, 'Ethiopian operas' or blackface performance, burlesque, pastiche, and Chinese opera.[11] That these works were imported is significant in accounting for what can be seen as their artistic and cultural inferiority to the other great import—European opera.

Popular genres such as minstrelsy, burlesque, and music hall brought to the fore the racial and economic tensions of global matters such as the Opium Wars, colonisation, immigration, and the gold rushes, even through the veil of humour—but never once dealing with the local reality of the violence perpetrated against Indigenous Australians. There was a specific anti-theatrical prejudice operating against popular forms of entertainment in the nineteenth century that could be seen in Australia's relationship to twentieth-century musical theatre as an imported and in many ways inferior tradition. This was evident in the business strategy of the 'the largest theatrical firm in the world': Australia's J. C. Williamson, which deliberately neglected the development of Australian musical theatre at key points in the twentieth century in favour of producing opera.[12]

That *Bran Nue Dae* should have assisted the musical in coming full circle, in the sense that it engaged audiences with a story developed via a grassroots process, now very much part of an Australian performing-arts methodology, suggests that decolonising practices can be very powerful. The work also achieved this notable status while avoiding engagement with nation-building narratives for the very obvious reason that it charts the journey of groups institutionalised and oppressed. Anthony Wyllie Johnston's contextual study of Australian musical theatre reveals the artifice and self-consciousness of staging and talking about 'Australian' identities. The introduction of *Bran Nue Dae* to the global musical theatre stage was the first gesture in which Indigenous Australians were 'expressing themselves in their own musicals',[13] although not as a nation-building exercise. *Bran Nue Dae* was a new type of Australian musical, but it drew upon the multi-arts contexts of performances maintained by Indigenous cultures, where singing, dancing, and storytelling are always already intrinsically at the centre of cultural life and community.

# THE UNIVERSITY AS A VENUE FOR DECOLONISATION

For the globalised musical, the nexus of Broadway and the West End is the cornerstone of an unyielding power structure that relies upon multiple canons of work enabled by a network of capitalist-colonialist nation-states whose social, economic, and cultural structures depend upon the centrality of these canons. When musical theatre entered the university curriculum as a subject of study, spreading beyond the remit of conservatories and vocational training colleges, all the texts that underpinned these structures came under increasing scrutiny. By the early twenty-first century that scrutiny increased with the move to decolonise Western academia's monopoly on culture and politics. According to Julie Cupples, '[T]he westernized university is a site where learning and the production, acquisition, and dissemination of knowledge are embedded in Eurocentric epistemologies that are posited as object, disembodied and universal.'[14]

For musical theatre scholars and students, the relevant disciplines of study include musicology, theatre studies, dance studies, acting, singing, voice studies, and even the 'transferrable' skills of industry-facing exercises, which underline the importance of labour and productivity to students of the discipline. Much of this is at odds with liberatory pedagogies, as Cupples elaborates: 'The westernized university, like colonial conquest and slavery, is then a globalized phenomenon' where 'for certain kinds of people, especially women, people of colour and Indigenous people [ ... ] both the pre-and-post-neoliberal university is a site of elitism, pain, exclusion, coloniality and Eurocentric thinking,'[15] and 'it is not uncommon for students to complete an entire degree and not read a single Black or Indigenous scholar.'[16]

In postcolonial or post-invasion societies, there has been more evidence of decolonisation than in UK universities. Most specifically, we can see programmes of study that overhaul political structures in the institutions. This goes beyond being tokenistic by 'adding' Indigenous content excised from multiple theoretical frameworks into a course of study. More specific to musical theatre in Australia, the Eora College of Performing Arts (part of an umbrella of Further Education colleges) ran a 'Music Theatre' course for Indigenous-identified students which integrated skills into studies of culture and history, plus Indigenous values and knowledge systems. 'Indigenous-identified training schools' in Australia have been seen as a place that is 'safe' for Indigenous students to train. Sometimes shorter or foundational courses can be offered within a mainstream actor-training school. Many of these arrangements pre-date a wider move to decolonise the academy, so that all courses are 'safe' (culturally) for all students.[17] These issues of safety suggest a musical theatre curriculum that has a capacity to cause unintentional harm and that therefore we should seek types of pedagogy that are more affirming.

To prevent harm, we must look at the intersectional issues that surround the need to decolonise, which also concern gender, class, sexuality, and even the connection between the colonial and the ableist in musical theatre education:

> Book writers, librettists, composers, choreographers, directors, critics, and fans imagine actors in musical theatre to be exceptionally able-bodied. [ ... ] This constellation of excellence in acting, dancing, and music—commonly referred to as a 'triple-threat'—while invested in the historical expression of the musical theatre art form that emerged from vaudeville variety shows in the early twentieth century,

is predicated on expectations of the performer's bodily congruity with a kind of exceptionalism or athletic productivity.[18]

Such an emphasis on martial levels of rigour renders musical theatre training unsustainable for students with any kind of disability as well as an unsuitable environment in which to create and analyse performance work in ways that address colonial legacies appropriately. The term 'triple threat' in relation to the bodies on stage suggests an atmosphere that is competitive, military, and even potentially violent. This is why we must explore the decolonising potential of the skills-based elements of musical theatre curricula.

A decolonised methodology is that exemplified by Wiradjuri scholars and Elders in their approach to 'groundwork' in the physicalised training of actors:

> In order to 'play', actors need to be fully aware of themselves and know who and where they are, to tell stories that have foundations, and have meaning in relationship to the country in which they live and perform. We do not live in isolation and we certainly do not share stories without permission and an understanding of this connection.[19]

A sense of place for the student is much more central to the process of learning than the global metropolis of their university campus. Indigenous use of the word 'country' (no article) in Australia 'acknowledges Aboriginal and Torres Strait Islander ownership and custodianship of the land, their ancestors and traditions'.[20] This means that '[g]roundwork is about where you are in country, doing things the right way, in order to be in the right place at the right time with the right people to understand the significance of that country; the Wiradjuri name for this is *Yindyamarra*'.[21] By recognising their physical situation in training, students are also comfortable articulating other levels of awareness: 'Grounding is achieved by having an open, honest conversation between the conscious, the subconscious, the body and the environment with a strong emphasis on connection to the ground'.[22] While this might seem to be relevant only to one cultural group, there are parallels to this approach in broader approaches to decolonised performance training methods, to be described later in this chapter. I undertake this with a critical view to the past limitations of the 'intercultural'.

The interest in 'intercultural' performance theory (the label that emerged in the 1990s) would pre-date the expansion of academic interest in musical theatre degree courses in the early twenty-first century by more than a decade. Musical theatre works which seem to celebrate a cultural hybridity might occasionally be appraised as 'intercultural', but more often they are now themselves subject to decolonising or antiracist scrutiny of how the musical was created and which voices are represented: 'The politics of interculturalism are a distant, almost invisible second to the social and economic impact of the work on the lived experience. [ ... ]'[23]. Writing in 2019, Guillermo Verdecchia cites his own students on a welcoming of the '*next-level* intercultural performance scholarship' that moves on from 'Patrice Pavis's highly influential hourglass formulation of intercultural theatre, in which (decontextualized) elements of a source culture are filtered, made legible, and presented to a (presumably homogeneous) recipient culture. [ ... ]'[24] The examples given below will expand on this development when considering which works a decolonised music curriculum should cover.

University students approach musical theatre curricula with a great deal of enthusiasm for the discipline, given its performative and culturally engaging nature. Many will have had exposure to, and usually some identification with, commercial musical theatre works and some belief in the myths of the athletic 'triple-threat' artist who delivers the work. Therefore, decolonising the musical theatre curriculum is a comprehensive process, one that begins much earlier than when students learn to read or manage other academic skills. The use of animated film musicals has had an impact on early childhood learning, as children learn about archetypal characters, dramatic narratives, and heightened emotions of very limited or fantastical kinds of lived experiences before they are exposed to the kinds of critical thinking that aid decolonisation.

# Disney and Pre-University Education: A Case Study

From the late twentieth century into the twenty-first, the US-based Disney corporation produced animated film musicals that appropriated and to varying extents mythologised Black, Asian, and First Nations geolocations, stories, and cultures in films including *Aladdin* (1992), *The Lion King* (1994), *Pocahontas* (1995), *Mulan* (1998), and *Moana* (2016). As many Black, Asian, and First Nations scholars have had the opportunity to theorise and critique these works, their voices are an important first step in helping university musical theatre students to revise any assumptions about musical theatre's capacity to fully speak for all lived experiences.

Because its target audience was children, Disney's *Pocahontas* could not have reasonably depicted the full truth of colonial violence, thereby obfuscating the historical reality; thus, the process of its creation would be viewed with suspicion in a decolonised reading, and questions would be raised as to how an animated musical might affirmatively educate and entertain children about First Nations culture, given the right protocols.[25] Very often this is about choices that move beyond the heroic, singular individual and looking at the wider communities being depicted.

The same process is questioned in the creation of *Mulan*, which is based upon a more complex historical work, *The Ballad of Mulan*.[26] Rather than these being perceived as minor inaccuracies, choices in adaptation can serve to maximise colonial tropes: 'Disney's iteration perpetuates Orientalized stereotypes by conflating racial and gender perceptions, where the Oriental other is both effeminate and irrational, and this depiction serves to motivate the conflict.'[27] This relies upon a harmful binary of othering colonised peoples in ways that imply that difference is a character flaw, thereby drawing on other forms of prejudice, including gender and sexuality. In animation work for children, this message is received at a very early age. By ascribing individual, fictional examples with personality traits that are rigid and stereotyped, writers are likely to significantly inhibit the young viewer's taste for nuanced cultural readings later in the educational process.

Almost twenty years later, the Samoan filmmaker and visual anthropologist Dionne Fonoti worked on *Moana* with the Disney team, in addition to Pacific artists and scholars who formed a group named the Oceanic Stories Trust. There was definitely a sense of shifting protocols concerning the way cultural materials were cited and depicted; however, Disney's *Moana* was not a grassroots production process, even though key Pacific Islander stakeholders were engaged and some First Nations audiences were moved by the work. According to A Mārata Ketekiri Tamaira:

> *Moana* offers a useful case study for thinking about strategic collaborative engagements between Native communities and global corporate enterprises like Disney in ways that can be productive and that acknowledge and affirm Indigenous agency while remaining attentive to the potential tensions and risks of such undertakings.[28]

Such tensions included the stereotyping of deities in the animation and subsequent merchandising of products based on the characters, which were withdrawn after complaints. The issues remain as to whether 'consultation' is a performative exercise, a tokenistic gesture, or, at worst, an opportunity for extracting surplus labour—for instance, potentially asking First Nations artists to improve or rewrite the script or score:

> Samoan artist Yuki Kihara cleverly offered the term 'Pasifikation' (in contrast to Disneyfication) to describe the way Pacific people co-opt what is foreign and make it their own. Indeed, the notion of Islanders making *Moana* their own has found expression in a way that has for decades been fundamental to building cultural resilience and self-empowerment in the Pacific—language revitalization.[29]

Such audience adaptations should be factored into any study of the work's reception.

The enthusiasm that young children have for these animated films is capitalised upon by educational settings and companies that trademark the experience of staging the show. Music Theatre International (MTI) offers the rights in Europe for primary-school-age children to stage *Moana JR*, even though the population of Pacific Islanders in the United Kingdom and the European Union is less than several thousand. The sensitivity of the language on this issue is evident, and it is important that MTI encourage community consultation, in addition to respectful representation:

> [A]lthough fictional, the island of Motunui is an amalgamation of many real Oceanic cultures. So, unlike the stories of some musicals, *Moana JR.* is based on the beliefs and customs of real people. Before casting, consider how this cultural representation intersects with your potential cast members and greater audience:

are there students with ties to Oceanic cultures in your theater program? Is there a Pacific Islander population in your area?[30]

These kinds of questions invoke the discipline of applied and community theatre, which is the best way to go in decolonising an approach to this kind of activity. A decolonised approach would necessitate conversations with the local Pacific Islander community and diaspora about the work and may lead to more creative options in adding to the existing book or score, though performers would then encounter the limitations imposed by copyright law.

## The Study of Music and Scores

Some attention has been directed towards musicology, especially music theory, in the musical theatre curriculum, wherein students are expected to engage with sheet music and analyse scores. Darren Hamilton's work on embedding anti-racist practice into music education points to a 'deficit' model of Western classical music education, where students are expected to 'acquire' musicality through literacies that are lacking, and this can impact upon students of colour:

> The traditional Western classical music program can be an alienating space for Black students as it demands the development and use of musical literacies such as the sight reading of music notation. The Western classical music program also ignores the aural musicianship skills—the community cultural wealth—that many Black students do possess.[31]

Christopher Small once opined that 'musicking' is a verb and an action;[32] subsequently, Burke Stanton proposed viewing Small's provocation as a much broader means to the end of decolonising the 'musics' we are producing, and not just to see 'musicking' as something actor-musicians and musical theatre songwriters might do within popular, commercial, or Western classical traditions. In this context, Chela Sandoval's *Methodology of the Oppressed* offers the opportunity to decolonise an episteme itself by building on the abundance of skills that students bring to the act of making music—and this would change the relationship between Western classical music and its relationship to musical theatre education.[33] For instance, learning by ear is not only the most historically enduring and reliable way of learning a song, but it is a much more profound way of embodying the demands of a song and committing it to muscle memory. When we link this approach with the Black acting methods considered below, it produces a joined-up and decolonised approach to training that can be more inclusive for many students. In this way, a physical score is a marginal artefact, but the essence of understanding comes through a living score, enacted in the studio.

## Voice Training: Singing and Speech

Musical theatre singing is synonymous with the demand to belt, balanced with the pedagogy of more classically centred 'legit' singing. In many instances, students aspire to styles of singing that are represented by Black artists and popular music traditions. This is not only an embodied type of cultural appropriation; it also creates stereotypes for Black performing artists too. Masi Asare interviewed the Black New York–based creative and performing artists John Bronson, Jamal James, Dionne McClain-Freeney, Khiyon Hursey, Rheaume Crenshaw, Elijah Caldwell, and Zonya Love Johnson on the myths around Black vocality in theatre:

> [T]here does seem to be a default or expected 'Broadway voice' (high [ ... ] a bright-sweet Disney sound) and that although some Black performers are able to create such a sound, it is generally understood to be a marker of whiteness. [In contrast,] the standards of [the] Black Broadway voice to which this group of performers often feel they are held is a discrete, different sound. Unspoken industry expectations about such a 'Black Broadway voice' mistakenly assume that Black singers [ ... ] sing only in a heavy, (power) sound virtuosically ornamented with riffs that evokes for (white) listeners a misleadingly monolithic idea of 'the Black church'.[34]

A decolonised approach would be to train each voice to its unique strengths and best-matched (or most comfortable) repertoire, as well as to make an effort to avoid these types of vocal stereotyping. However, vocal categorisation has a complex history in Western culture, remnants of which persist in musical theatre practice. Rather than identifying the 'Disney' vocality as racialised, as it is in Asare's interview, it could also be read as infantilised and resisting the full-throated singing of mature adult 'legit' singing. The *Fach* system of classical voice categorisation deployed in opera is arguably an influence: where the vocal timbre, range, weight, and associated repertoire also call upon stock character traits in casting, though this is most evident in the repertoire of the eighteenth- and nineteenth-century operatic canon. The process of undermining these categories is also parallel to decolonising other music-dramatic genres like musical theatre, because we merge the lived experiences of artists with new stories rather than relying on a prescribed vocality indexical to a stock character.

Musical theatre students will be expected to deliver spoken dialogue if they are engaging in production work. Given the Broadway–West End model, many will aim in speech training for either a standard Midwestern American accent or the Received Pronunciation of British English. However, this kind of training can come with some risks. Amy Mihyang Ginther studied the way that the UK conservatoire (drama school) system may have historically seeded 'dysconscious racism' in the practice of spoken voice training. Dysconscious racism is a type of racism that owns its level of harmful discrimination but considers that harm incidental to a greater purpose (for example, the erasure of regional and ethnic difference in the promotion of a common speech accent for performers). According to Joyce E. King, 'Dysconscious racism is a form of racism that tacitly accepts dominating White norms and privileges. It is not the absence of consciousness [ ... ] but an impaired consciousness or distorted way of thinking about race'.[35] By reading embodied socio-cultural trauma as a tension that needs to be 'trained' out of Black and Asian students in the spoken voice, the purpose of training that worked towards a standardised British accent became problematic. This is because students will be trained to have more confidence in projecting their voice, and the previously diagnosed lack of confidence may be perceived as an embodied effect of racial trauma that is not openly disclosed. So when the goal is to get the student to speak with a standardised accent, the means of undoing that trauma is undermined by the end. At best, these embodied traumas were worked through as physical 'tensions' to be released in the pursuit of 'neutrality', but there is the possibility that drama schools themselves create a sociocultural space in which these tensions increase because of an unintentional shaming about individual accents.[36]

## DANCE TRAINING AND EMBODIMENT

Dance training is an aspect of the musical theatre curriculum that retains the most harshly prescriptive and authoritarian vestiges of a colonial education in the notion of a 'mastery' (colonial language in itself) of a variety of dance styles, without regard for the process of liberation in the enhancement of somatic empowerment, kinaesthetic experience, and psychophysical creativity that derives from a grounded, cultural response to each dance tradition. Tamara Thomas observes that 'a prevailing colonial mentality in higher education dance spaces, as it relates to jazz dance, is responsible for the lack of serious engagement and appropriate regard'. She suggests the following alternative:

> [T]hrough their exploration of jazz dance, students can gain from the form's historic, cognitive, and somatic information while also being exposed to qualities of an African aesthetic. The experience can shape and develop body, mind, and spirit while facilitating the development of students' dynamic range.[37]

In the context of decolonising dance programmes at UK and US universities, we need to break the link between learning and the marketisation of dance traditions by opening Westernised universities to many global cultures and theoretical frames.[38] This would begin with a study of the cultural context of each dance style and an appraisal of leading Black, Asian, and Indigenous artists who are creators and practitioners in the field. Learning a dance style is more than pursuing a gymnastic delivery of gestures, with the aim of imitation and standardisation. The work would start with somatic liberation, each participant standing in her own power politically, growing in awareness and creativity, to contribute choreographically to a shared expressive discourse: a somatographia (writing with the body) enabled by global dance traditions.

## 876 PAMELA KARANTONIS

# ACTOR TRAINING

The benchmark of authentic characterisation in musical theatre curricula is very high, or, more accurately, quite prescriptive, compared to the experimental licence in performer-training systems explored in wider university drama education. Musical theatre usually emphasises realistic acting that relies upon negotiated standards of emotional 'truth' in order for students to account for the artifice of bursting into song and making the transition from song to scene and then to song again. Sometimes this is taught in a white monoculture, as if realistic acting came from a base of a neutrality that is 'white'. On this point Kaja Dunn argues:

> [W]hat becomes more damaging for people of colour is when cultural nuances get trained out of them. In acting class, we tell people to bring who they are. So, teachers should first do no harm to their students of colour. If you don't understand it, ask questions, get help, hire more people who do.[39]

Some cultural nuances could include postural or physical habits that are completely natural but read as racialised and therefore as 'breaking character' or a 'barrier' to truthful characterisation, because such gestures, posture, or habits might be read by the teacher as extraneous to dramatic texts that suggest the (white) 'character must be brought to the student', rather than the student bringing who they are to the rehearsal room. A much more profound and proactive approach can be found in Sharrell D. Luckett and Tia M. Shaffer's work *Black Acting Methods*:

> Black acting methods are defined as rituals, processes, and techniques rooted in an Afrocentric centripetal paradigm where Black theory and Black modes of expression are the nucleus that informs how one interacts with various texts, literary and embodied, and how one interprets and (re)presents imaginary circumstances.[40]

Within this approach the Hendricks method, named after Freddie Hendricks, the founder of the Youth Ensemble of Atlanta (YEA), makes a significant contribution to global performer training and an alternative curriculum in musical theatre–making. Relying on a triad of devising, spirituality, and the 'hyper-ego', his system of learning succeeds on the basis of creating work from either the direct lived experience or identified socio-political struggles and sympathies of the group; an ancestral lineage, with spiritual connectedness to creative gifts (regardless of whether the individuals identify with a major religious faith); and the embedding of positive affirmations as a way of joining the subject formation of the student-in-training with personal development.[41] Some of this approach may correlate to the Indigenous Australian approach of groundwork, though due respect is needed for each cultural context:

Hendricks's devising process is unique to Afrocentric values that signify the importance of orality and memory in Black communities. Thus, Hendricks has an 'on your feet' approach where one takes notes in their mind, keeping the material fully embodied from conception to presentation. To that effect, full scripts for the majority of YEA's devised musicals have never existed. The ensemble members and design teams worked primarily off of embodied scripts, memory, and repetition.[42]

Once again, the idea of the living score and the kinaesthetic approach to learning could be an extra benefit of decolonising and emancipating curricula on a number of fronts.

# CHOOSING WHICH WORKS TO STUDY

In decolonising musical theatre curricula, the works explored will also change once skills education and the nature of productions are decolonised. Sean Mayes issues a powerful call to action in his preface to *An Inconvenient Black History of British Musical Theatre 1900–1950*: 'How quickly through time erasure becomes *passive*—an act of not *actively* knowing a name, or not *actively* knowing whose land you stand on, or not *actively* knowing a true history turns into an actively *passive* form of erasure.'[43] His and Sarah Whitfield's study considers Black artists in Britain in the early twentieth century, pointing out that traditional definitions of musical theatre are destabilised by the professional versatility and skills of named Black artists in a number of genres. The gatekeeping of predominant definitions of what constitutes 'musical theatre' in our academic discourses, particularly the commercially successful examples documented in scores and books. many of which are influenced by music of Black origin that is never properly recognised, is something that needs to be decolonised.

There is an entanglement of the artistic content of what we study with racial capitalism—the confluence of two forces whose powers are often unseen in the enjoyment and appraisal of artworks. Racial capitalism is categorised by Gargi Bhattacharyya as the phenomenon whereby

> contemporary capitalism continues to operate through and alongside processes of racialised expropriation and that challenging these more recent technologies of dehumanisation requires a renewed attention to the manner in which economic exploitation and racist othering reinforce and sometimes amplify each other.[44]

This is why it is important to examine works such as *Bran Nue Dae* in a decolonised musical theatre discourse, especially when they seem to be genre-subversive. Thus, there needs to be a constant reckoning of the shortcomings of musical theatre scholarship as we update or radically question our canon.

# INTERSECTIONALITY

*Bran Nue Dae* serves as an example of how songs of many popular origins can form the score of a work because it is refracted through the narrative point of view of the male protagonist/narrator on a very personal journey. It illustrates how the dramaturgy of decolonised musicals follows less prescriptive standards than purely commercial works. It is also important to balance this example with representations of Black women—and a notable example is the Australian stage musical *The Sapphires*. With a book by Tony Briggs, *The Sapphires* (2004) is based on the real-life events of his mother and aunt, as well as other women close to him, recounting how Indigenous Australian women travelled to Vietnam in the 1960s to sing to the soldiers on active duty in the Vietnam War. Its adaptation to the screen placed it on the global stage when the film premiered at the Cannes Film Festival in 2012 and later won eleven out of its twelve nominations at the Australian Academy for Cinema and Television Arts (AACTA) awards in 2013. It was also honoured at the Thirty-fifth Denver Film Festival, where it was given the People's Choice Award for Best Narrative Feature.[45]

The screenplay addresses the issue of the gap between Indigeneity and global Black identity politics: '[I]n *The Sapphires*, "black" is represented not as an imposed racial identity, but rather, as a mobile signifier—a chosen social and political identity, which expresses a will to fight oppression, and a commitment to a black aesthetic marked by creativity and innovation.'[46] However, there are subtleties missed by conflating local identities and global politics. In the narrative, the Sapphires are pressured into being 'the Australian version of The Supremes' because of audience prejudices about Indigenous Australian women; they were viewed with the same colonial gaze as Black entertainers in the United States and thus 'were sometimes introduced as American or Tahitian, because that went across better; "As soon as the word Aboriginal came up, no one was interested." [ ... ] Tahitians were exotic, [while] African Americans were acceptable as entertainers'.[47]

This resistance to an internal colonisation was magnified when the stage musical was turned into a movie:

> [D]irector Wayne Blair's film adaptation applies all the imaginative liberties of fiction while keeping the story rooted in reality and history. Based in 1968, the Sapphires are first introduced as the Cummeragunja Songbirds, [which] carries the undercurrents of the racial differences between white country and black soul music. [ ... ] It showcases their talent, their ironic adulation for Nashville country and western music.[48]

The intersectional aspects of this work show that there is specificity to the Indigenous status of the women of Cummeragunja, that their femininity was at stake in certain colonial ideas of 'Blackness', and that Indigenous Australian contemporary artists magnified the message about community underpinning individual achievement in a text for global audiences:

> The strong sense of belonging is expressed through the film's non-representational qualities such as the vibrant saturated colour of Warwick Thornton's cinematography, the 'up-beat' energy of the musical performance and the spontaneity of Stephen Page's choreography. As that which brings the community back together, musical performance is shown and heard here as a form of community strengthening. Moreover, there is a lovely irony in that the film's Indigenous 'mutation' of the musical [ ... ] includes an ending in which the performers turn their back on globalized showbiz.[49]

## SUBVERSIONS: *THE BIG LIFE* AND *SOFT POWER*

New musicals that subvert the power structures of the coloniser by appropriating Western texts and performance traditions also reflect the parodic and satirical power exemplified in *Bran Nue Dae*. Shakespeare was the target for *The Big Life: The Ska Musical*, with book and lyrics by Paul Sirett and music by Paul Joseph. It premièred at the Theatre Royal Stratford East in London in May 2004, with a short West End transfer a year later. Lesley Ferris indicates that it was 'the first Black British [ ... ] musical to ever be performed in the commercial sector of London theatre'.[50]

The work uses the Shakespearean allegory of *Love's Labour's Lost*, in which a group of men forsake the distractions of romantic (heteronormative) love in the pursuit of self-improvement. By indicating its style of music in the title of the show, in this case the mid-twentieth century Jamaican music tradition of ska, Sirrett and Joseph use the sensibilities of a culturally popular commercial style as musical metonymy for audiences who are being drawn in by that title; it was a celebration of the Windrush generation of Caribbean people who arrived in the United Kingdom on the *SS Empire Windrush* from the late 1940s throughout the following decades. Ultimately the Shakespearean comic theme of self-improvement could be seen as correlating with the repressive and colonial narratives that impede people as immigrants in colonial centres, whereby 'assimilation' or the achievement of 'respectability' is often characterised by unreasonable (in this case farcical) self-denial as a way of gaining respect within a structurally racist society. The use of ska and popular musical forms is a powerful way of reappropriating that narrative by grounding performers in their own musical traditions.

*Soft Power*, with book and lyrics by David Henry Hwang and music by Jeanine Tesori, premièred in Los Angeles and San Francisco in 2018 before moving to off-Broadway. Rather than reappropriating a fictional text, it references Joseph Nye's concept of the seductive 'soft power' that large nations have in influencing the world through cultural commodities such as film, television, sports, music, and performance as a proxy for other modes of international diplomacy or in preference to direct coercion or conflict.[51]

Performed by an Asian American cast, this work positions Chinese characters at the centre of the world order. Its staging deploys theatrical spectacle and large musical forces, allowing the audience to see the medium as the metaphor. The work critiques liberal democracy by positioning the action in many ways as a counterfactual history (in which China is the traditional creator of the commercial musical, for one thing), but in which Asian American actors appear in 'whiteface', and by exposing the weaknesses of the US electoral system.

## BRITISH ASIAN MUSICALS

Globalisation and the aspirational lifestyle that it promised around the beginning of the new millennium for many industrialised communities in the Global South was also championed in the West via a cultural appraisal of 'hybridity'—the idea that two cultures could share a mutually beneficial vision of what we see now as a neoliberal story of self-realisation and material success. In this context, the phenomenon of British Asian musicals provides a useful case study in issues confronting the attempt to decolonise the curriculum.

However, it should be noted that in regarding this body of work as a decolonising canon of sorts, the issue of documentation and archival materials forms part of the politics and material challenge for educators. Apart from CDs of the songs, there are no permanent teaching materials for many of the musicals mentioned here. It is a challenge for students and academics to discuss the musical *Bend It like Beckham,* for instance, without a published libretto, video clips, or filmed performances. This curriculum-building work involves dedicated research commitment and the fostering of personal, professional, and community connections to find appropriate sources. Ideally, a network of musical theatre academics should liaise with the creators and casts of these shows to secure teaching packages that would include documentation and workshop teaching opportunities. Consideration should also be given to institutions located remotely. More often than not, adaptation helps when the musical begins or ends its creative life cycle as a major feature film, thereby providing students with an accessible platform—as long as the film version is the product of a thoughtful enough process.

The multiple award–winning *Hum Aapke Hain Kaun (Can You Name Our Relationship?)* by Sudha Bhuchar and Kristine Landon-Smith was a stage adaptation by London's Tamasha Theatre Company of the 1995 Hindi film with the same title by Sooraj Barjatya; its working title translates as *Fourteen Songs, Two Weddings, and a Funeral* (Tamasha). Rather than presenting a decolonising message per se, the work celebrated the fraught nature of relationships that collided with expectations of marriage. According to the film scholar Jyotsna Kapur, *Hum Aapke Hain Kaun* 'locates the big wedding as a product of the emerging Bollywood culture industry and its ideological redefinition of nationalism/citizenship as both acts of consumption and the re-enactment of patriarchal and caste-based identities'.[52] Arguably the Bollywood identity is safely housed within late twentieth-century, middle-class-family-centred dramas that translate well to an era of globalisation and capitalist markets of domestic consumption, symbolised by dowries and wedding gifts:

> In *Hum Aapke Hain Kaun*, when the protagonist is asked what kind of marriage he would like—an arranged or a love marriage—he replies, without a moment of hesitation, an 'arranged love marriage' [ ... ] a match between families of equal social status where sexuality is sublimated in the acquisition of goods and the maintenance of traditional hierarchies; where free market meets the hierarchies of caste, class, and gender; and all contradictions of capital are happily resolved by a voluntary return to patriarchal tradition.[53]

In contrast, the 2002 musical *Bombay Dreams* was received more critically. On the one hand, the global labour law historian Neilesh Bose's review of the show's 2004 Broadway production expressed hopes of 'inclusivity' for Asian performers in the early part of the twenty-first century and pointed quite crucially to issues of employment and opportunity:

> In *Bombay Dreams*, over thirty South Asian performers (mostly American and Canadian trained) were able to find gainful employment in a venue where brown skin and Hindi film songs are the centrepiece. [ ... ] Yes, this is not the work of Utpall Dutt or Alyque Padamsee, stalwarts of today's Indian theater. [ ... ] It simply does what Broadway usually tries to do: entertain. And if brownness and brown people happen to be 'in' right now, more power to the performers who are initiating and just possibly transforming what entertainment and real inclusiveness on Broadway and America could one day mean.[54]

Looking back to this period now, the hope was not just for the industry, but in the optimistic cultural theory of the new millennium, which included terms such as 'hybridity' and 'interculturalism', as ways in which new theatre voices could be heard within the prevailing (white) commercial models of production. Consequently, the theatre scholar Jerry Daboo placed her analysis of *Bombay Dreams* within the framework of John Tomlinson, Richard Dyer, and Erika Fischer-Lichte's respective versions of utopia:

> If theatre can resist a Lloyd Webber style of cultural commodification and instead reveal the contemporary world of deterritorialization, diaspora and the challenge to nation-state identity as creating a new sense of cultural awareness as Tomlinson suggests, then perhaps Fischer-Lichte's version of utopia may become more than a future possibility.[55]

The revision of these kinds of projects within the terms of racial capitalism may see such theatre works as being dependent on the market-driven *what happens to be in right now* (to paraphrase Bose's review), rather than promoting permanent structural change of the way musical theatre production and audience-building works.

# 882    PAMELA KARANTONIS

In a much more provocative frame, Rifco Theatre's *The Deranged Marriage* (2005–2006/2015) touched upon cultural taboos,

> in particular about those marginalised by the process of arranged marriages such as older women, in this instance the widowed mother, women who are not conventionally attractive, Asian women who have been dumped by white boyfriends, and gays. In a carnivalesque reversal of the marriage convention, some of those usually marginalised become the centre of the wedding feast in *The Deranged Marriage*, and the gay groom manages to leave his closet without being alienated from his family.[56]

To get its point across, the work used comedy and a citation of rituals:

> It's got music, dance, audience participation and broad humour. An over-protective mother-in-law, autocratic aunties, drunken uncles, a confused bride and a reluctant groom all turn the arranged marriage of Rishi and Sona, the wedding of the year in Slough, into disaster.[57]

Such musicals give students the opportunity to explore intersectional identity politics within a process of decolonisation. Another production from Rifco Theatre was *Laila: The Musical*, with a residency at Watford Palace in April 2016. It featured music by Sumeet Chopra, lyrics by Dougal Irvine, and book by Pravesh Kumar. Rather than 'a more earnest re-telling of an ancient Persian story',[58] in this case the Laila and Qays allegory, it was a more contemporary setting of a North of England romance-drama about star-crossed young lovers. Chopra and Kumar are also the creative team behind *Britain's Got Bhangra* (2010), a dance-led musical, celebrating the fusion of styles that is bhangra dance music. Set against the austerity of Thatcherite Britain, the narrative presents the answer to escaping a socio-economic rut as the creation of a commercial hit, monetising a dance style in the popular crossover achieved by bhangra. There is a theme in many British Asian musicals whereby the protagonist seeks individual fame, riches, and acclaim but is grounded by community values and a critique of the systems that promise success.

In the early twenty-first century, the issue of racism in sport is an important context for the British Asian musical *Bend It like Beckham*. It concerns the rise of a female Asian protagonist as a football prodigy who must overcome racism and sexism on the path to success and self-realisation. It should be noted that the work includes a non-Asian composer who co-orchestrated with Kuljit Bhamra, and this process of orchestration should be analysed within a decolonising framework:

> Howard Goodall's gorgeous score, which he has co-orchestrated with Bhangra maestro Kuljit Bhamra, ranges from an exquisite traditional pre-wedding lament for the loss of a daughter (hauntingly sung by Rekha Sawney) to mainstream musical-theatre fare where you can still hear Indian inflections. [ ... ] You also get to hear how it looks from the parents' point of view. Lovely Tony Jayawardena sings of his

own youthful dreams [in cricket], dashed by racism and of his desire to protect his daughter from similar disappointment.[59]

The broader theories of community-based decolonised practice could be useful in appraising this work, including the attendant issues of racism in commercial sport.

# CURRICULUM-BASED PRODUCTIONS

The variety of works available for study in a decolonised musical theatre curriculum could give voice to a genuine and wonderful diversity of lived experiences. However, we must confront the reasons it would be inappropriate for many degree programmes to cast and stage these works as large-scale productions if the students to be cast are not appropriately diverse. If musical theatre programmes take the approach of decolonising all elements of skills training, their case studies and critical perspective, then the final step involves addressing the production elements of the curriculum. Universities could seek to decolonise the musicals they stage by commissioning new works that respond to unsung stories of the oppressed and uphold the individualities of students. However, commercial bidding processes and private endowments could be subject to terms and conditions that do not prioritise decolonisation. Ultimately, commissions are expensive, and it would be necessary to decolonise the labour relations of this process as a priority in engaging Black, Asian, and Indigenous artists to create new works.

Ultimately, the most thorough form of decolonised production work in musical theatre would be the collaborative approach of Freddie Hendricks. It is similar to applied and community theatre methods, where students and staff consult and dedicate a period of discussion to identify a story, share lived experiences, commit music to muscle memory, and embody choreography so that production work is continuous, with a lived experience of liberatory skills education and the affirmation of those skills through audience-building events in sharing meaningful stories that identify and specify voices which have been silent.

# *HANGING ROCK* (2021): A CASE STUDY

To illustrate both the potential and limitations of practical work featuring musical theatre students, this essay will end with a closer look at a recent production staged by Goldsmiths, University of London. In the summer of 2021 the university commissioned a new musical with the title *Hanging Rock*, to be adapted from Joan Lindsay's 1967 Australian novel *Picnic at Hanging Rock*. The musical was commissioned because

FIG. 31.3 A scene from the musical version of *Picnic at Hanging Rock*, performed at Goldsmiths, University of London, in 2021. Photo provided by the author.

the source material offered so many quality ensemble roles for those identifying as women. This is where the realities of performing arts degree courses intersect, and perhaps sometimes are in tension with, attempts at decolonisation. The production at Goldsmiths highlighted the gender- and class-related aspects of the story and even had a female creative team writing the songs.[60] Thus, with its feminist slant, it would be seen in the United Kingdom as a progressive, worthy endeavour, though it must be considered that the work would need a different process, especially with regard to casting, staging, and locally sourced decolonised education packs were it to be staged in Australia. This will be explained in more detail below.

The source material is a novel that concerns itself with a cautionary tale of the fault line in colonial education systems. In the plot, students at an Australian boarding school for girls and their mathematics tutor disappear without explanation after straying too far on a walk at the Hanging Rock Reserve, a real Indigenous site sacred to the Gunung Willam Baluk clan in the Macedon ranges of southeast Australia. The implication that the fiction was partly based on the fact of an historical disappearance contributed to an enormous mythology surrounding the book. International audiences may be familiar with the classic film adaptation of 1975, which put the Australian director Peter Weir and a cast of relatively unknown Australian schoolgirls under a global spotlight and scored a BAFTA win for cinematography. In recent years a revival of curiosity in the work led to a stage adaptation by Tom Wright from 2016 and the BBC Drama miniseries of 2018.

FIG. 31.4 The students and teaching staff pose for a school photo before they embark on their fateful excursion. The women of the predominantly female cast, including Rachel Roberts (*second row from the bottom, second from the right*), featured in Peter Weir's famous 1975 movie version of *Picnic at Hanging Rock*. Production still provided by the editors.

The success of this specific musical adaptation relies upon the historical status of homosocial bonds evident in colonial boarding schools, which provocatively mirrors the demographic of many performing arts degree courses and the damage in not being connected to decolonising voices. Invoking a genre of Australian gothic horror that concerns itself with the institutionalisation of gender, race, and class in educational settings, as well as the suppressed sexuality of the late Victorian era, some of the tensions in this work mapped across to other popular cultural references, such as films dealing with cloistered, homosocial residential settings and female sexuality in *Black Narcissus* (1947), *The Children's Hour* (1961), and *The Beguiled* (1971; remade in 2017).

Recent critics in Australia see the persistent obsession with the story of *Picnic at Hanging Rock* as an enduring colonial fixation with 'white vanishing', particularly in Indigenous territories, that obscures the real vanishing of Indigenous and First Nations children; it is the latter who never (dis-)appear in these colonial narratives. However, in the most recent small-screen adaptation of *Picnic at Hanging Rock*, one of the actors cast as a student protagonist, is the Indigenous Australian Madeleine Madden, granddaughter of the noted Indigenous rights activist Charles Perkins. Nonetheless, the narrative of that adaptation does not update itself to convey the historical truth of Indigenous Australians. Madden's character, Marion, is still encased in the politics of class, race, and gender that see her disappearing at the rock along with the protagonist, Miranda—both outcasts of the school because of their independent spirits. In a subplot, the fatal mistreatment of another character from the novel, Sara Waybourne, who was housed in an orphanage for much of her life, is more likely to resemble what we know in the twenty-first century as the tragedies of Indigenous and First Nations students in residential schools. These latter revelations were highlighted in Canada in 2021, where 751 unmarked graves of Cowessess First Nation children were discovered at the Marieval Indian residential school in the province of Saskatchewan.

In Australia there is a call for the novel's protagonist to disappear again with the campaign 'Miranda Must Go', led by the artist and scholar Amy Spiers, who advocates that Indigenous voices must now be centred at the site, which has a disproportionate amount of tourist interest triggered by the novel and film:

> The Hanging Rock's interpretive 'Discovery Centre' dedicates the majority of display space to the *Picnic at Hanging Rock* story. [ . . . ] In contrast, just two panels are dedicated to describing the continuing significance of Hanging Rock for Aboriginal people, their prior ownership and dispossession. It is also outdated and incorrect, attributing the site to the 'land of the Wurundjeri' and not also 'the Taungurong and Djadja Wurrung'.[61]

This intersection of production practice and theory, in exposing students to a case study of a colonial narrative and some attendant theory, could create the experience of allowing students to embody the coloniser in a staged work, but it would need to be done with the appropriate protocols of contextual study and reading materials to effect a decolonising gesture within the curriculum. Due attention would also need to be paid to students who identify as Black, Asian, and/or Indigenous, as well as the intersectional issues surrounding gender, sexuality, and/or religious identity, so that narratives and depictions did not repeat colonial hierarchies and harm. This is why academic settings where reflective write-ups and research portfolios that accompany production work are so important in decolonising the curriculum. Ultimately, the pedagogic structures of embodiment and intellectual reflection are the measures of effective decolonising aims.

## NOTES

1. Rachel Perkins, dir., *Bran Nue Dae*, Robyn Kershaw Productions, Mayfan, Film Victoria, Melbourne International Film Festival (Omnilab Media and Screen Australia, 2009). The spelling of 'Indigenous' will be capitalised throughout to reflect the political specificity of a named group of people.

2. Julie Cupples, 'Introduction: Coloniality Resurgent, Coloniality Interrupted', in *Unsettling Eurocentrism in the Westernized University*, ed. Julie Cupples and Ramón Grosfoguel (London: Routledge, 2018), 12.

3. Peter Bibby, 'Introduction', in Jimmy Chi and Kuckles, *'Bran Nue Dae': A Musical Journey* (Broome and Sydney: Magabala Books and Currency Press, 1991), vii.

4. Paul Makeham, 'Singing the Landscape: *Bran Nue Dae*', *Australasian Drama Studies* 28 (April 1996): 117–132; here: 118.

5. Ibid., 117.

6. Ibid.

7. Ibid., n. 2.

8. Ibid., 120.

9. Kirsten Krauth, 'The Frangipani Is Starting to Bloom: A New Brand of Musical in *Bran Nue Dae*', *Metro Magazine: Music and Education Magazine* 164 (2010): 10–15; here: 12.

10. Catriona Elder, 'Watching *Bran Nue Dae* in Japan', *Journal of Australian Studies* 40, no. 1 (2016): 109–117; here: 111.

11. Jane W. Davidson, Michael Halliwell, and Stephanie Rocke, eds., *Opera, Emotion, and the Antipodes*, vol. 1, *Historical Perspectives: Creating the Metropolis; Delineating the Other* (Abingdon: Routledge, 2021).

12. Peter Wyllie Johnston, '"Australian-ness" in Musical Theatre: A Bran Nue Dae for Australia?', *Australasian Drama Studies* 45 (2004): 157–179; here: 158 n. 7.

13. Ibid., 157.

14. Cupples, 'Introduction', 2.

15. Ibid., 3.

16. Ibid., 10.

17. Geoffrey Milne and Liza-Mare Syron, 'Indigenous Performing Arts Training in Australia', *Australasian Drama Studies* 57 (October 2010): 148–162; here: 148.

18. Samuel Yates, 'Disability and the American Musical Stage', in *The Routledge Companion to Literature and Disability*, ed. Alice Hall (Abingdon: Routledge, 2020), 265–277; here: 266.

19. Robert Lewis, Letetia Harris, Stan Grant, Dominique Sweeney, and Samantha Dowdeswell, 'Groundwork: Place-Based Integrative Actor Training in a Fluctuating World', *Theatre, Dance and Performance Training* 12, no. 3 (2021): 358–369; here: 360.

20. Australian Institute of Aboriginal and Torres Strait Islander Studies (AIATSIS), https://aiatsis.gov.au/explore/welcome-country, accessed 6 Feb 2022.

21. Lewis, Harris, Grant, Sweeney, and Dowdeswell, 359.

22. Ibid., 363.

23. Glenn Odom, 'Asking the Wrong Questions: Musings on a Conversation with Gakire Katese Odile about "Intercultural Theatre"', *Studies in Theatre and Performance* 41, no. 1 (2021): 50–67; here: 62.

24. Guillermo Verdecchia, 'Exploding the Hourglass: Next-Level Intercultural Theatre Research', *Canadian Theatre Review* 178 (2019): 83–85; here: 83.

25. Mary J. Couzelis, 'Generic Pocahontas: Reinforcing and Subverting the Whiteness of Mythohistory', *Children's Literature* 43 (2015): 139–160. Cornel Pewewardy (Comanche-Kiowa) asserts that the now heavily critiqued *Pocahontas* 'can be easily caricatured as politically correct yet historically incorrect, sexist yet feminist, and both ethnographically sensitive and ethnographically suspect' (quoted in ibid., 139–140). Consequently, the Disney film ultimately 'reasserted the racist and sexist Pocahontas mythohistory in children's consciousness' (ibid.), even though it tried to be culturally respectful.

26. Jing Yin, reflecting on the process of adapting *Mulan*, observes 'how such a cultural artifact can be abstracted, westernised, and then supplant the original, culturally authoritative narrative. For context, briefly, the ballad itself depicts a well-known story of which there are multiple iterations, with the earliest recording dating from approximately 568 A.D., and the oldest currently available iteration of the text dating from the Song dynasty (12th century). In this narrative, a young woman disguises herself to take her father's place in the army out of a sense of filial duty—and this is the key part—with her parents' blessing. The secret of her sex is kept for twelve years after which she retires, refusing any reward'. Quoted in Michelle Anya Anjirbag, '*Mulan* and Moana: Embedded Coloniality and the Search for Authenticity in Disney Animated Film', *Social Sciences* 7, no. 11 (2018): 1–15; here: 7.
27. Ibid., 5.
28. A Mārata Ketekiri Tamaira and Dionne Fonoti, 'Beyond Paradise? Retelling Pacific Stories in Disney's *Moana*', *Contemporary Pacific* 30, no. 2 (2018): 297–327; here: 298.
29. Ibid., 319.
30. https://www.mtishows.co.uk/disneys-moana-jr, accessed 10 December 2021.
31. Darren Hamilton, '#BlackMusicMatters: Dismantling Anti-Black Racism in Music Education', *Canadian Music Educator* 62, no. 2 (2021): 16–28; here: 20.
32. Christopher Small's concept of 'musicking' is the foregrounding of the verb of participation in any aspect of music-making, which could be producing the sound or listening to it. It privileges the act of doing over and above analysing and therefore has the power to connect to many students drawn to participate in musical theatre performance.
33. Burke Stanton, 'Musicking in the Borders: Toward Decolonizing Methodologies', *Philosophy of Music Education Review* 6, no. 1 (2018): 4–23.
34. Masi Asare. 'The Black Broadway Voice: Calls and Responses', *Studies in Musical Theatre* 14, no. 3 (2020): 343–359; here: 358.
35. Amy Mihyang Ginther, 'Dysconscious Racism in Mainstream British Voice Pedagogy and Its Potential Effects on Students from Pluralistic Backgrounds in UK Drama Conservatoires', *Voice and Speech Review* 9, no. 1 (2015): 41–60; here: 45.
36. Ibid., 43. Furthermore, this shaming of accents can also see an intersection with the identity markers of class, as working-class accents and speech idioms may be seen as less desirable in vocational training when placed against an impossible ideal of standardised speech.
37. Tamara Thomas, 'Making the Case for True Engagement with Jazz Dance', *Journal of Dance Education* 19, no. 3 (2019): 98–107; here: 98.
38. Janet O'Shea, 'Decolonizing the Curriculum? Unsettling Possibilities for Performance Training', *Brazilian Journal of Presence Studies* 8, no. 4 (2018): 750–762; here:758.
39. Kaja Dunn, Sharrell D. Luckett, and Daphnie Sicre, 'Training Theatre Students of Colour in the United States', in 'Against the Canon', ed. Mark Evans, Cass Fleming, and Sara Reed, special issue, *Theatre, Dance and Performance Training* 11, no. 3 (2020): 274–282; here: 280.
40. Sharrell D. Luckett and Tia M. Shaffer, *Black Acting Methods: Critical Approaches* (Abingdon: Routledge, 2017), 2.
41. Ibid., 19–36.
42. Ibid., 24.
43. Sean Mayes and Sarah K. Whitfield, *An Inconvenient Black History of British Musical Theatre: 1900–1950* (London: Methuen Drama, 2022), xvi.

44. Gargi Bhattacharyya, *Rethinking Racial Capitalism: Questions of Reproduction and Survival* (London and New York: Rowman & Littlefield, 2018), 102.

45. Lynn Griffin, Steven Griffin, and Michelle Trudget, 'At the Movies: Contemporary Australian Indigenous Cultural Expressions—Transforming the Australian Story', *Australian Journal of Indigenous Education* 47, no. 2 (2017): 134.

46. Rosanne Kennedy, 'Soul Music Dreaming: *The Sapphires*, the 1960s and Transnational Memory', *Memory* Studies 6, no. 3 (2013): 331–344; here: 338.

47. Jon Stratton, citing Philippa Hawker, in 'The Sapphires Were Not the Australian Supremes: Neoliberalism, History and Pleasure in *The Sapphires*', *Continuum* 29, no. 1 (2015): 27.

48. Mabel Ho, Review of *The Sapphires*, *Alternative Law Journal* 37, no. 4 (2012): 293–297; here: 295.

49. Terese Davis, 'Locating *The Sapphires*: Transnational and Cross-Cultural Dimensions of an Australian Indigenous Musical Film', *Continuum: Journal of Media and Cultural Studies* 28, no. 5 (2014): 594–604; here: 602.

50. Lesley Ferris, Review, *The Big Life: The Ska Musical*, *Theatre Journal* 57, no. 1 (2005): 110–112; here: 110.

51. Dorinne Kondo, 'Soft Power: (Auto)ethnography, Racial Affect, and Dramaturgical Critique', *American Quarterly* 71, no. 1 (2019): 265–285; here: 265.

52. Jyotsna Kapur, 'An "Arranged Love" Marriage: India's Neoliberal Turn and the Bollywood Wedding Culture Industry', *Communication, Culture and Critique* 2 (2009): 221–233; here: 221.

53. Ibid., 228.

54. Neilesh Bose, Review, *Bombay Dreams*, by A. R. Rahman, Meera Syal, Thomas Meehan, Anthony Van Laast, Farah Khan and Stephen Pimlott, *Theatre Journal* 56, no. 4 (December 2004): 703–705; here: 705.

55. Jerri Daboo, 'One under the Sun: Globalization, Culture and Utopia in *Bombay Dreams*', *Contemporary Theatre Review* 15, no. 3 (2005): 330–337; here: 337.

56. Gabriele Griffin, 'Gagging: Gender, Performance and the Politics of Intervention', *Contemporary Theatre Review* 17, no. 4 (2008): 541–549; here: 547–548.

57. Ian Johns, *The Deranged Marriage* (Review), *Theatre Record* 25, no. 24 (2005): 1583.

58. Mark Shenton, *Laila: The Musical* (Review), *Theatre Record* 36, no. 7 (25 March–7 April 2016): 391.

59. Paul Taylor, *Bend It like Beckham* (Review), *Theatre Record* 35, no. 13 (18 June–1 July 2015): 641.

60. Rebecca Applin and Susannah Pearse were creators of the show. The production was licensed by arrangement with The Agency (London) and Micheline Steinberg Associates and permissions from the Joan Lindsay estate granted by Jane Novak, Sydney.

61. Amy Spiers, 'Miranda Must Go: Rethinking the Generative Capacities of Critique, Discomfort and Dissensus in Socially Engaged and Site Responsive Art' (PhD diss., University of Melbourne, 2018), 105.

## BIBLIOGRAPHY

Australian Institute of Aboriginal and Torres Strait Islander Studies. https://aiatsis.gov.au/expl ore/welcome-country, accessed 6 Feb 2022.

Anjirbag, Michelle Anya. '*Mulan* and *Moana*: Embedded Coloniality and the Search for Authenticity in Disney Animated Film'. *Social Sciences* 7, no. 11 (2018): 1–15.

Applin, Rebecca, and Susannah Pearse. *Hanging Rock*. A Musical. Adapted from Joan Lindsay's 1967 Australian novel *Picnic at Hanging Rock*, 2021.

Asare, Masi 'The Black Broadway Voice: Calls and Responses'. *Studies in Musical Theatre* 14, no. 3 (2020): 343–359.

BBC British Broadcasting Corporation. https://www.bbc.co.uk/sport/cricket/59166142, accessed 6 Jan 2022.

Bibby, Peter. "Introduction'. In Jimmy Chi and Kuckles, *Bran Nue Dae: A Musical Journey*. Broome and Sydney: Magabala Books and Currency Press, 1991.

Billington, Michael. 'Britain's Got Bhangra'. *Guardian*, 29 April 2010, https://www.theguardian.com/stage/2010/apr/29/britains-got-bhangra-review, accessed 6 January 2022.

Bhattacharyya, Gargi. *Rethinking Racial Capitalism: Questions of Reproduction and Survival*. London and New York: Rowman & Littlefield, 2018.

Bose, Neilesh. Review of *Bombay Dreams*, by A. R. Rahman, Meera Syal, Thomas Meehan, Anthony Van Laast, Farah Khan, and Stephen Pimlott. *Theatre Journal: Theorizing the Performer* 56, no. 4 (2004): 703–705.

Chi, Jimmy, and Kuckles. *Bran Nue Dae: A Musical Journey*. Broome and Sydney: Magabala Books and Currency Press, 1991.

Couzelis, Mary J. 'Generic Pocahontas: Reinforcing and Subverting the Whiteness of Mythohistory'. *Children's Literature* 43 (2015): 139–160.

Cupples, Julie. 'Introduction: Coloniality Resurgent, Coloniality Interrupted'. In *Unsettling Eurocentrism in the Westernized University*, edited by Julie Cupples and Ramón Grosfoguel, 1–22. London: Routledge, 2018.

Daboo, Jerri. 'One under the Sun: Globalization, Culture and Utopia in *Bombay Dreams*'. *Contemporary Theatre Review* 15, no. 3 (2005): 330–337.

Davis, Terese. 'Locating *The Sapphires*: Transnational and Cross-Cultural Dimensions of an Australian Indigenous Musical Film'. *Continuum: Journal of Media and Cultural Studies* 28, no. 5 (2014): 594–604.

Dunn, Kaja, Sharrell D. Luckett, and Daphnie Sicre. 'Training Theatre Students of Colour in the United States'. In 'Against the Canon', edited by Mark Evans, Cass Fleming, and Sara Reed. Special issue, *Theatre, Dance and Performance Training* 11, no. 3 (2020): 274–282.

Elder, Catriona. 'Watching *Bran Nue Dae* in Japan'. *Journal of Australian Studies* 40, no. 1 (2016): 109–117.

English, Helen J. 'Ethiopian Entertainers and Opera Burlesque: Blackface Parodies in Colonial Australia'. In *Opera, Emotion, and the Antipodes*, vol. 1, *Historical Perspectives: Creating the Metropolis; Delineating the Other*, edited by Jane W. Davidson, Michael Halliwell, and Stephanie Rocke, 137–165. Abingdon: Routledge, 2021.

Ferris, Lesley. *The Big Life: The Ska Musical* (Review). *Theatre Journal* 57, no. 1 (2005): 110–112.

Galella, Donatella. *Soft Power* by David Henry Hwang (Review). *Theatre Journal* 71, no. 2 (2019): 211–213.

Ginther, Amy Mihyang. 'Dysconscious Racism in Mainstream British Voice Pedagogy and Its Potential Effects on Students from Pluralistic Backgrounds in UK Drama Conservatoires'. *Voice and Speech Review* 9, no. 1 (2015): 41–60.

Griffin, Gabriele. 'Gagging: Gender, Performance and the Politics of Intervention'. *Contemporary Theatre Review* 17, no. 4 (2008): 541–549.

Griffin, Lynn, Steven Griffin, and Michelle Trudget. 'At the Movies: Contemporary Australian Indigenous Cultural Expressions; Transforming the Australian Story'. *Australian Journal of Indigenous Education* 47, no. 2 (2017): 131–138.

Hamilton, Darren. '#BlackMusicMatters: Dismantling Anti-Black Racism in Music Education'. *Canadian Music Educator* 62 (2021): 16–28.

Ho, Mabel. Review of *The Sapphires*. *Alternative Law Journal* 37, no. 4 (2012): 293–297.

Johns, Ian. *The Deranged Marriage* (Review). *Theatre Record* 25, no. 24 (2005): 1583.

Johnston, Peter Wyllie. '"Australian-ness" in Musical Theatre: A *Bran Nue Dae* for Australia?' *Australasian Drama Studies* 45 (2004): 157–179.

Kapur, Jyotsna. 'An "Arranged Love" Marriage: India's Neoliberal Turn and the Bollywood Wedding Culture Industry'. *Communication, Culture and Critique* 2 (2009): 221–233.

Karantonis, Pamela. '"They Were Dancing": Re-Membering Vanished Voices through the Separation of Voice and Body in a Post-Covid-19 Musical Staging'. Unpublished plenary paper presented at 'Vicarious Vocalities', online conference hosted by Interdisciplinary Voice Centre and Oxford University, 27 September 2021.

Kennedy, Rosanne. 'Soul Music Dreaming: *The Sapphires*, the 1960s and Transnational Memory'. *Memory Studies* 6, no. 3 (2013): 331–344.

Kondo, Dorinne. 'Soft Power: (Auto)ethnography, Racial Affect, and Dramaturgical Critique'. *American Quarterly* 71, no. 1 (2019): 265–285.

Krauth, Kirsten. 'The Frangipani Is Starting to Bloom: A New Brand of Musical in *Bran Nue Dae*'. *Metro Magazine: Music and Education Magazine* 164 (2010): 10–15.

Lewis, Robert, Letetia Harris, Stan Grant, Dominique Sweeney, and Samantha Dowdeswell. 'Groundwork: Place-Based Integrative Actor Training in a Fluctuating World'. *Theatre, Dance and Performance Training* 12, no. 3 (2021): 358–369.

Luckett, Sharrell D., and Tia M. Shaffer. *Black Acting Methods: Critical Approaches*. Abingdon: Routledge, 2017.

Makeham, Paul. 'Singing the Landscape. *Bran Nue Dae*'. *Australasian Drama Studies* 28 (April 1996): 117–132.

Mayes, Sean, and Sarah K. Whitfield. *An Inconvenient Black History of British Musical Theatre, 1900–1950*. London: Methuen Drama, 2022.

McCallum, John. 'Studying Australian Drama'. *Australasian Drama Studies* 12–13 (1988): 150.

Milne, Geoffrey, and Liza-Mare Syron. 'Indigenous Performing Arts Training in Australia'. *Australasian Drama Studies* 57 (October 2010): 148–162. https://www.mtishows.co.uk/disn eys-moana-jr, accessed 10th December 2021.

Odom, Glenn. 'Asking the Wrong Questions: Musings on a Conversation with Gakire Katese Odile about "Intercultural Theatre"'. *Studies in Theatre and Performance* 41, no. 1 (2021): 50–67.

O'Shea, Janet. 'Decolonizing the Curriculum? Unsettling Possibilities for Performance Training'. *Brazilian Journal of Presence Studies* 8, no. 4 (2018): 750–762.

Perkins, Rachel, dir. *Bran Nue Dae*. Robyn Kershaw Productions, Mayfan, Film Victoria, Melbourne International Film Festival, Omnilab Media and Screen Australia, 2009.

Phillips, Sandra R., and Clare Archer-Lean. 'Decolonising the Reading of Aboriginal and Torres Strait Islander Writing: Reflection as Transformative Practice'. *Higher Education Research and Development* 38, no. 1 (2019): 24–37.

Rifco Theatre. *The Deranged Marriage*. 2005–2006. Revival 2015, Riverside Theatre, London, 1–24 December 2015.

Rocke, Stephanie. 'Chinese Opera and Racism in Colonial Victoria 1853-1870'. In *Opera, Emotion, and the Antipodes*, vol. 1, *Historical Perspectives: Creating the Metropolis; Delineating the Other*, edited by Jane W. Davidson, Michael Halliwell, and Stephanie Rocke, 209–231. Abingdon: Routledge, 2021.

Shenton, Mark. *Laila: The Musical* (Review). *Theatre Record* 36, no. 7 (25 March–7 April 2016): 391.

Spiers, Amy. 'Miranda Must Go: Rethinking the Generative Capacities of Critique, Discomfort and Dissensus in Socially Engaged and Site Responsive Art'. PhD diss., University of Melbourne, 2018.

Srinivasan, Priya. 'Decolonising Moves: Gestures of Reciprocity as Feminist Intercultural Performance'. *South Asian Diaspora* 11, no. 2 (2019): 209–222.

Stanton, Burke. 'Musicking in the Borders: Toward Decolonizing Methodologies'. *Philosophy of Music Education Review* 6, no. 1 (2018): 4–23.

Stratton, Jon. 'The Sapphires Were Not the Australian Supremes: Neoliberalism, History and Pleasure in *The Sapphires*'. *Continuum* 29, no. 1 (2015): 17–31.

Strube, Helen. 'White Crocodile, Black Skirt: Theatre for Young People and Cultural Memory'. *Australasian Drama Studies* 47 (October 2005): 56–73.

Suri, Sanjay. '*14 Songs* Returning to London after Tour: Co-director Suman Bhuchar Describes Play as a True Representation of Bollywood on Stage'. *News India Times*, 3 May 2002, 33.

Synot, Edward, Mary Graham, John Graham, Faith Valencia-Forrester, Catherine Longworth, and Bridget Backhaus. 'Weaving First Peoples' Knowledge into a University Course'. *Australian Journal of Indigenous Education* 49 (2019): 222–228.

Tamaira, A Mārata Ketekiri, and Dionne Fonoti. 'Beyond Paradise? Retelling Pacific Stories in Disney's *Moana*'. *Contemporary Pacific* 30, no. 2 (2018): 297–327, https://tamasha.org.uk/projects/fourteen-songs-two-weddings-and-a-funeral/, accessed 6 January 2022.,

Taylor, Kerry. '"Arlathirnda Ngurkarnda Ityirnda": Being-Knowing-Doing; De-colonising Indigenous Tertiary Education (Book Review).' *Health Sociology Review* 20, no. 1 (2011): 111–112.

Taylor, Paul. *Bend It like Beckham* (Review). *Theatre Record* 35, no. 13 (18 June–1 July 2015): 641.

Thomas, Tamara. 'Making the Case for True Engagement with Jazz Dance'. *Journal of Dance Education* 19, no. 3 (2019): 98–107.

Verdecchia, Guillermo. 'Exploding the Hourglass: Next-Level Intercultural Theatre Research'. *Canadian Theatre Review* 178 (2019): 83–85.

Williams, Michael. 'Smoking Opium, Puffing Cigars, and Drinking Gingerbeer: Chinese Opera in Australia'. In *Opera, Emotion, and the Antipodes*, Vol. 1, *Historical Perspectives: Creating the Metropolis; Delineating the Other*, edited by Jane W. Davidson, Michael Halliwell, and Stephanie Rocke, 166–208. Abingdon: Routledge, 2021.

Yates, Samuel. 'Disability and the American Musical Stage'. In *The Routledge Companion to Literature and Disability*, edited by Alice Hall, 265–277. Routledge: Abingdon, 2020.

CHAPTER 32

# 'WHO TELLS YOUR STORY'

## A Reflection on Race-Conscious Casting and the Musical

### HANNAH THURAISINGAM ROBBINS

*THIS chapter was developed as a personal reflection from my position as a mixed-race person of Black heritage in the United Kingdom. My conceptualisation of the state of casting in the global musical is situated in this context. It is important to recognise that our conversations about casting, belonging, and representation vary in different cultures and countries, and in the local politics of expression through writing and developing work for stage and screen. This chapter is presented as a snapshot of the discussions around equitable casting where I am: one of the conspicuously few queer people of colour researching identity and musicals in the UK and US context.*

## WHO TELLS YOUR STORY

Whenever I am asked to comment on questions of representation or diversity in musical theatre, I begin with this lyric from Lin-Manuel Miranda's megamusical *Hamilton* (2015):

> Let me tell you what I wish I'd known
>  When I was young and dreamed of glory
> You have no control
> Who lives, who dies, who tells your story.[1]

In this scene, George Washington warns the protagonist, Alexander Hamilton, that it is fruitless to attempt to control how we are remembered or how our legacies will be maintained. Simultaneously, the content and casting of *Hamilton* challenge us to consider whose histories are preserved in music, in education, and in popular consciousness. There is something exciting and ironic in the textual layers of this musical. The plot shows Hamilton attempting to control his narrative and to create a new history for an independent America, while others (e.g. Thomas Jefferson and Aaron Burr) are represented as attempting to interrupt and undo his work. This musical has skyrocketed an already popular musical theatre creative, Lin-Manuel Miranda, to superstardom, with *Hamilton* regularly bookmarked by critics and creatives as form-changing. Many of the accolades attributed to *Hamilton* include the visibility of a cast predominantly made up of actors of colour. The musical shows us the possibility of representation while highlighting the historical absence of people of colour in accounts of American history *and* in the leading casts of American musicals.

The irony I allude to comes in several forms. Miranda has become the leading voice for 'diverse' representation on stage and screen, even though *Hamilton* does not foreground the people of colour alive when the history took place. Both *Hamilton* and the screen adaptation of *In the Heights* (2021) have been criticised for 'colourism', including erasing and mistreating Black actors involved in telling the stories.[2] In a coauthored think piece on *In The Heights*, *New York Times* reviewers reflected on how the film uses 'language of community celebration and the cultural history of the actual neighborhood of Washington Heights [also known as Little Dominican Republic] to market the film' while erasing dark-skinned Afro-Latinx people from the main cast.[3] This connection is significant because most Dominicans are descended from Africans, and this community is not represented in the named cast of the film. When the director, Jon M. Chu, was challenged about the lack of dark-skinned actors, he responded: 'In the end, you know, when we were looking at the cast, we tried to get the people who were best for those roles.'[4] Chu and Miranda's casting choices were initially defended by the Puerto Rican musical theatre star Rita Moreno, most famous for her portrayal of Anita in *West Side Story* (1961). On *The Late Show with Stephen Colbert* on 16 June 2021, Moreno asked Colbert if they could discuss the criticisms of Miranda and *In the Heights*, arguing:

> You can never do right, it seems. This is the man who has literally brought Latinoness and Puerto Rican-ness to America. I couldn't do it! I mean I would love to say I did but I couldn't. Lin-Manuel has done that, really, singlehandedly and I am thrilled to pieces. [ ... ]
>
> I'm simply saying can't you just wait a while and leave it alone? There's a lot of people who are *puertorriqueño* who are also from, uh, Guatemala, who are dark and who are also fair. We are all colours in Puerto Rico, and this is how it is. And I just—it would be so nice if they hadn't come up with that and left it alone, just for now. I mean, they are really attacking the wrong person.[5]

After her comments, Colbert quickly changes the subject, and the following day Moreno took to Twitter following the public backlash to her comments to say that she was 'disappointed' with herself for being 'clearly dismissive of Black lives that matter in our Latin community.'[6] She continues with the particularly insightful words, 'It is so easy to forget how celebration for some is lament for others.'

FIG. 32.1 Rita Moreno discussing and defending the casting of *In the Heights* (2021) on *The Late Show with Stephen Colbert* in June 2021. Photo: Scott Kowalchyk/CBS © Getty Images.

Across the two musicals, we are forced to wrestle with artistic license, fantasy, and new ways of seeing the world while knowing that the creatives involved repeatedly perpetuate anti-Blackness in their work. This can be seen in the *In the Heights* film where anti-Black racism is removed from the plot of the stage musical to add to the utopian feel of the screen adaptation. Meanwhile, there is something undeniably uncomfortable about watching the Disney+ recording of *Hamilton* or listening to the original Broadway cast album and hearing Miranda spit out the line 'We know who's really doing the planting' in 'Cabinet Battle #1' to Daveed Diggs's Thomas Jefferson.[7] Diggs (African American) is known for his creative work, including the track 'The Deep' critiquing anti-Blackness in America.

There are similar criticisms of the score for Disney's *Moana* (2016), for which Miranda co-wrote most of the songs. In this film based on a Polynesian myth, indigenous performers are present only when voicing ancestors or talking about tradition. Moana's 'princess song' ('How Far I'll Go') is completely detached from these performers and from the tonality, language, and performance styles they bring to the film. In the number 'We Know the Way' (a song about the seafaring background of Moana's people), the lyrics—in English—are performed by Miranda himself, moving the translated text away from the actors of indigenous heritage who had been cast. (It is interesting that, in the sing-along versions of *Moana*, the lyrics in Samoan and Tokelauan are neither transcribed nor offered in translation.)

Our conversation about who gets to be in musicals must always revolve around who is granted power and agency. In the song 'History Has Its Eyes on You', from which Washington's warning (quoted above) is taken, we learn about the massacre that preceded his military fame. There is an uncomfortable parallel between this violence in the song and the burgeoning changes in American and British musical theatre casting practices. Our 'progress' sits against many structural racisms which retain and enforce derogatory racial coding in characters of colour while also allowing productions to erase 'non-whiteness' altogether. In *Buy Black: How Black Women Transformed US Popular Culture*, Aria S. Halliday explains that

> [t]he argument that marginalized people make for greater inclusion as a response to historical erasure is usually made at the level of visibility, partially because finally seeing ourselves communicates some level of inclusion in the mainstream. We recognize the process of interpolation that happens through language and images daily and, therefore, argue that seeing ourselves is important to societal acceptance.[8]

Therefore, our discussions about representation in casting are defined by previous violence against performers of colour in musical theatre productions gone by. There is a tension for those of us seeking (and evaluating) change: in order to be seen we must belong, yet belonging to a majority group often requires us to modify who we are or to embrace a kind of cultural absenteeism where the person we are 'at home' is not who we are 'in public'. This morphing of self is intersectional. It can have manifold repercussions for LGBTQIA+ individuals, especially for those members of our communities who present as overtly queer or can be read as presenting in specific ways.

I have deliberately begun with examples from *Hamilton*, *In the Heights*, and *Moana* to remind us that three widely celebrated examples of 'inclusive' work continue to provoke the same questions as are being asked about the 'classic' musical. How do people of colour become visible in works that are not created to include us or are produced to represent majority white communities first? If musicals are fantasies, does this mean that our lived experiences are irrelevant or that we simply do not exist in an ideal world? Does this utopia require that an inclusive Latinx community not include dark-skinned, African-descended people? That princesses only communicate in American pop ballad songs? That our historical connections to our nationalities are rendered invisible to the extent that we no longer exist? Performers and audiences of colour are caught in a conundrum: wishing to be seen, to be represented, in positive and aspirational ways (addressing other underlying historical misrepresentations of our communities), and to also exist as holistically and messily as white performers. What is appropriate, 'believable', or in fact *authentic* is seldom determined by creative teams who have shared characteristics with their cast members of colour; therefore, on some level, we are still grappling for the right to be seen on any terms.

It is important to note that this discussion of musical theatre is situated in the wider context, in which opera—musical theatre's cognate form—continues to embrace 'historically informed' or 'prestige' performance practices, including casting white actors as

Black, Brown, and Asian characters. For example, the world-renowned soprano Anna Nebtreko has continued to perform the eponymous role of Aida, an Ethiopian princess captured and enslaved by the king of Egypt, in blackface; Nebtreko describes her critics as 'low class'.[9] Similarly, the world-renowned Bolshoi Theatre has said that it will not ban or remove racialised make-up from its productions.[10] Indeed, in 2015 there was surprise that a new production of *Otello* at the Metropolitan Opera in New York elected *not* to have the Latvian tenor Aleksandrs Antonenko wear dark make-up to play the Black main character.[11] However, this decision by the Met was itself framed as 'color-blind' casting, which allows the best singers to perform any role, regardless of their racial background.'[12] While the conditions of musicals are different, it's important to recognise that in a major opera house, 'color-blind' casting is being used to justify traditional casting methods rather than to engage representative or diverse communities of singers on their stage.

There are similar social complexities for productions of musicals in European countries beyond the United Kingdom, which have their own thorny histories of racism. For example, blackface is not uncommon in European theatres, where Black performers are deemed to be 'less available'. This strikes me as especially ironic given that the original migration of American musicals to European opera houses, instigated by Marcel Prawy at the Vienna Volksoper in 1956, relied on bringing in local swing and dance bands to train the orchestras and on flying in African American singers, including Olive Moorefield and William Warfield, to lead transfer productions. Even while Anglophone musical theatre has contrived to mask the threads of minstrelsy in its development (e.g. music written for 'coon shouting' predates the 'Broadway belt' as we know it now), it has also erased the presence of artists of colour in securing its global popularity.

Because of my unique situation, my eyes turn first to the conditions faced by Black people and nomadic communities. However, these trends of invisibility and stereotyping apply widely to the representation of Jewish and Asian characters, who are all too often depicted negatively in musicals that have survived through absent race consciousness, apologies for outdated content that is now 'canonical', and a lack of empowering material available for performers from marginalised backgrounds in Europe and America. However, many of these questions are challenged when we displace the Global North from the centre of the musical theatre universe. For example, we do not see the name of the producer Bolanle Austen-Peters represented broadly in conversations on the contemporary musical at our conferences in the Global North, and yet her production company has staged five original musicals centring Nigerian stories and performers. Meanwhile, the Abuja Metropolitan Music Society (AMEMUSO) presented the first Nigerian-produced performance of *Les Misérables* during their annual festival, Operabuja, in November 2021. Hosted in an events room at a Hilton hotel, this production transcends some of the limits we place on representative or 'landmark' performances when monumentalising particularly successful works. Meanwhile, the musical director Ayo Ajayi has been at the heart of numerous Nigerian Broadway-style musicals, including *Saro the Musical* (2014), *Wakaa the Musical* (2016), and *OMG the Musical* (2021). These Nigerian productions feature entirely or predominantly Black performers and creative teams. In a global majority country, musical theatre belongs to the creatives and cast that make it. However, we are confronted with very different conditions in the Global North, and especially in the United Kingdom and United States. The myth that we have no control over who tells our story is broadly disproven. Yet the dominant ideology that allows white performers to access almost any role in the repertoire is in stark contrast with the experience of performers of colour, who must fight for lead roles or even to be present in performance without having their race noted in the marketing and publicity for productions.

# Visibility in Absence

Phenotypic or biological constructs of race have been fundamentally disproven, and yet, it is impossible not to recognise that musicals deploy superficial understandings of racial identity in all contexts. Confused and uncomfortable challenges about authenticity arise. In some ways, colour-blind casting was introduced to overcome these difficulties, removing the conversation entirely and assuming that an actor of any background can inhabit any role if they are the most able. Disney's 1997 film adaptation of Rodgers and Hammerstein's *Cinderella* remains a best-practice example of this system in action. The king and queen (Victor Garber and Whoopi Goldberg) are of different races to each other, as well as to Paolo Montalban, who plays their son. The fantasy is not disrupted through this casting because it is precisely that: a total fantasy. Meanwhile, colour-conscious casting—where the race of the actor is featured in the work's narrative—has also allowed several experimental ways of embodying identity. *Hamilton*, often wrongly labelled 'colour-blind', deliberately focuses on the personal characteristics of the actors who personify the roles. This can be hugely empowering (and one may laud *Hamilton* for allowing actors to feel seen), but we can also see how it embodies the same principles as traditional casting when characters of colour are played by performers with similar characteristics in every production. We must be careful not to confuse works that deliberately explore or consider a performer's or character's identity to make a show communicate its content sensitively with material in which a character is merely designated a race. Where *Hamilton* initially cast people of similar racial backgrounds in the same roles (e.g. Eliza was of Asian heritage, Angelica was a Black woman, and Peggy/Maria was of Black or mixed Black heritage), the characteristics of those roles also had, and encouraged, racial coding.

The broader conversation about who gets to play what roles resonates throughout the performing arts. For example, there has been debate about the trend of casting Black British actors, including Kingsley Ben-Adir, Cynthia Erivo, Daniel Kaluuya, and David Oyelowo as prominent African American icons, including Malcolm X and Harriet Tubman, on film.[13] In an article defending Kaluuya's casting as the Black Panther leader Fred Hampton in *Judas and the Black Messiah*, Silva Chege reflects:

To limit actors to playing roles that match their birth certificates disadvantages both audiences and performers. It denies us the magic of seeing on-screen transformations take place. While it is natural for tension to rise over who gets what of the few prestigious roles on offer, considering how rare it is for Black people— British and American—to be given the space to tell their stories, divisions and fractures in the diaspora only serve to minimise the collective voice and make it easier to ignore. The reality is that a win for one group of Black people is a win for all its diverse communities across the globe.[14]

I can imagine that critics of diverse casting will make a direct comparison between Chege's words and Moreno's. ? How is Moreno's call for pan-ethnic support of Puerto Rican representation different to Chege's defense of Black diasporic solidarity? [15] In this instance, films about Black icons are few and far between, and there are stark contrasts in industry attitudes to films such as the Black-produced *Judas and the Black Messiah* (2021) and the Oscar-winning *Green Book*, which includes a white saviour figure who continues to be racist despite the friendship he develops with his Black client. In *Green Book*, we access the white spectator who perceives racial difference rather than following the life of the world-renowned pianist Don Shirley (a Black, queer man). Musicals such as *The King and I* and *Hairspray* (2002) (among others) use a similar device. Meanwhile the actors named in Chege's paragraph are all darker-skinned Black actors who are seldom offered romantic and/or heroic leads in multiracial films. Moreno's comments on *In The Heights* respond to the erasure of extant communities, whereas Chege is reflecting on the paucity of roles for dark-skinned Black actors across the whole repertoire.

In a group interview about the film *Fences* (2016), based on August Wilson's Pulitzer Prize–winning play, Denzel Washington responded to a question about 'needing a Black director' by highlighting the power of shared cultural experience: 'It's not color, it's *culture*.'[16] He continued: 'I know, you know, we all know what it is when a hot comb hits your hair on Sunday morning. What it smells like. That's a cultural difference, not just a colour difference.' The group he is addressing continues to laugh about the distinctive hiss of the comb, and he highlights how there's an immediate commonality between him and the other cast members present because this is something recognisable and resonant to most people who grew up with and around Afro-textured hair. In musicals, traces of this cultural bond are exceptionally hard to find and make utopian imaginings such as *In the Heights*, Disney's *The Princess and the Frog* (2009), and Disney/Pixar's *Soul* (2020), in which the Black heroes are dehumanised as a frog and the lost soul of a dead pianist, more bittersweet.

In the UK context, cultural bonding is essential to musical theatre representation because we are so limited in our understanding of community. While a Black British or Asian British actor is judged on their appearance before their nationality, regardless of how many generations their ancestors have lived in the United Kingdom, colour-blind casting is not only out of reach, it is also dangerous. Television series such as *The Crown* and Andrew Garfield's appearance as the musical theatre composer Jonathan Larson in the Netflix film *Tick Tick . . . Boom!* perpetuate the need for physical approximation when playing a historical figure. Meanwhile, this pressure to mimic physical appearances insidiously requires racial authenticity that facilitates ahistorical fictionalisations of British society. Therefore, only musicals such as *& Juliet* and Moss and Harlow's *SIX* allow people of colour to be consistently seen and heard in a historicised setting. Yet, these shows are unified by representing mock-Tudor settings through spectres of contemporary pop icons such as Beyoncé, Adele, and Ariana Grande, or by using a jukebox score of music by other pop artists, including Britney Spears and Katy Perry. As such, people of colour can only be seen in musicals set 'then' if presented through 'now' (a bastardisation of Lin-Manuel Miranda's 'America then through America now' description of *Hamilton*). I highlight that while *Hamilton* erases almost all indigenous, enslaved, and freed persons of colour, British musical theatre conceptions of the historical past assume there were no people of colour whatsoever. Miranda chooses not to deal with these themes. Most British musicals pretend they don't exist.

This erasure of living people of colour is not historical: the fantasy vehicle *Wicked* (2003) brings this reality to the fore. The musical, drawn from Gregory Maguire's 1995 novel, reimagines the life of the Wicked Witch of the West Elphaba, originally from Frank L. Baum's *The Wonderful Wizard of Oz* (1900) and immortalised by Margaret Hamilton in MGM's film musical *The Wizard of Oz* (1939). In the musical, Elphaba is a social outcast amongst her peers for having been born with green skin. For the early scenes of the musical, she is presented as 'different' until she is revealed to have coveted magical powers, which bring her to the attention of the Wizard and his aides, who have nefarious political ambitions for her. Elphaba's oddness is set in contrast to her enemy/best friend counterpart G(a)linda. Glinda is represented (and almost exclusively cast) as a stereotypical white socialite in a bright blonde wig. Her class and social status are connected to her embodiment of a coveted 'ideal' appearance. As a result, Elphaba's otherness, which is framed through her greenness (and not her ability to use magic), has led to an allegorical approach to *Wicked*: Elphaba represents a person of colour.

This rationale has been amplified by the casting of Cynthia Erivo as Elphaba in the forthcoming film adaptation. For some, then, the casting of a Black actor in the film adaptation finally confirms that Elphaba's struggle is connected to inhabiting a racialised body. Indeed, many people rejoiced that Erivo and Ariana Grande (cast as Glinda) will provide racial diversity in the inevitably more high-profile screen production than in those seen on European and American stages. And yet, many mistook Grande (who is Italian American) for a woman of colour because of her use of fake tan and subtle cultural appropriations of Blackness in her performance. However, the notion that Elphaba's green skin is a representation of racialised otherness erases all other non-whiteness present in the stage and screen worlds. In fact, it assumes default whiteness—a 'non-racialised' experience—as the marker of contrast. While fantastical, *Wicked*, like *The Wizard of Oz*, is consciously and conceptually American, and yet, any visible performers of colour in *Wicked* are assumed to be absent or subsumed into this imagined racial neutrality against Elphaba as the marginalised, fantastical other.

This is also a window into the wider traditions of derogatory impersonations (including those from minstrelsy and orientalist fantasies) that have shaped musicals from *Show Boat* (1927) to *Miss Saigon* (1989). *Wicked* regularly reminds me of the limitations of our imagination in fantasy on the musical theatre stage. While there has been pioneering world-building in literature and film (including Afro-futurism and African futurism), stage musicals continue to generate superficial conflicts. For example, there was speculation about how a Black British actress might embody a blonde character, Elle Woods, in a new production of *Legally Blonde: The Musical* at London's Open Air Theatre. Similarly, in 2018 a production of the musical in Seattle shared a video announcing a Black Elle Woods, and the comments are littered with conversations about whether it is appropriation for a Black woman to wear a blonde wig in the role,[17] overlooking the fact that Reese Witherspoon (who originated Woods's character and is known for her glowing blonde bob) is a natural brunette. Here we enter the true challenge in our conversations about representation and embodiment on-stage. Musicals *about* Black, Brown, Asian, Indigenous, Roma, Polynesian, and other races *by* creators from our communities have not been funded or allowed to thrive. Therefore, our presence on-stage perpetuates disruption in musicals that are written according to assumptions of whiteness unless there are characters coded as 'other'. Performers of colour are repeatedly forced to interact with the perception of 'difference' to their white counterparts.

## Somewhere, a Place for Us

As I write in early 2022, *West Side Story* has returned squarely to the mainstream with the release of Stephen Spielberg's 2021 film remake. Historically and concurrently, *West Side Story* provides a challenge to the notions of race-conscious and colour-blind casting, as its finished story polarises two different ethnic groups—the reimagined Montagues and Capulets. The knowledge, then, that the creatives of the first production of *West Side Story* originally envisaged the Puerto Rican Sharks as Jewish shows that the specificity of identity was not itself crucial. Only the collision of difference was dramaturgically significant, and it is more intrusive as a modern viewer to realise how racialised exoticism was added to make this conflict more pronounced. This is especially problematic when viewing stills or film of the Puerto Rican characters, darkened with boot polish to embody the racial other. Moreno's comment 'we are all colours in Puerto Rico' feels even more churlish when considering that, in the 1961 Robert Wise film adaptation, everyone is made up to be the same artificial shade of non-white.

Spielberg and Kushner's reimagining of *West Side Story* provides some answers to this with changes to the script, song use, and casting. With more believable writing, the Puerto Rican dialogue flip-flops between languages, as many polylingual migrant households do. The film also has a diverse representation of Latinx performers who inhabit the Puerto Rican characters while acknowledging Rita Moreno as a community elder. In the 2021 film Moreno plays an updated version of the shopkeeper, Doc, who is familiar with all the youth on both sides and is wise concerning their conflicts. By having Moreno there, a person who has really stood next to white actors in brownface pretending to share her heritage, we are reminded of the past and of what *West Side Story* has been. There is a different gravitas to her spectatorship of the musical's violence because many audience members know that Moreno has actually seen it all before. It is therefore all the more joyful to see her in company with the film's cast at the Sitzprobe of the song 'America', for which she is perhaps best known.[18]

Nevertheless Moreno's amplification of Ariana DeBose, a Black queer Latinx actor who picked up almost every Best Supporting Actress award for her interpretation of Anita, contrasts with her spontaneous choice to criticise Black people who saw colourism in *In the Heights*. This essay does not intend to make Moreno the villain of the piece. She is a complicated figure who is in no way responsible for the conditions of the global entertainment industry. However, she highlights the challenge that no person of colour (myself included) can represent everyone else. The contrast in her attitudes to the celebrating of Ariana DeBose and her insistence that Black Latinx critics should wait their turn to be represented reminds us of the multifaceted problems we face in discussions about casting and 'belonging' in the stage and screen musical. Moreno is comfortable referring to *In the Heights* critics as 'them' (not a part of her community) while also saying that light-skinned Puerto Ricans are part of the fabric of representation too. This is true, but her open disdain for colourist critique in the original interview

FIG. 32.2 Ariana DeBose (Anita) and David Alvarez (Bernardo) lead the Latinx performers of Steven Spielberg's 2021 *West Side Story* remake in the number 'America'. Photo © Alamy Stock Photo.

reminds us that figures such as Moreno and Miranda occupy space as the only visible exemplars of a marginalised community, saying, 'Look, some of us are here and you should be happy for us.' This implicit attitude constitutes internalised racism that leaves the burden of correction and patience in the hands of the most marginalised while ignoring the privileges that lighter-skinned, 'white-proximate' people of colour enjoy as a result of their superior status in a system of racial distinction determined by darkness of skin tone.

## On Belonging

One of the challenges we face in discussions about progressive casting in musicals is the lack of reflection on what it means to belong. It is possible to enjoy and to participate in a culture without feeling a part of it, so the quest for representation, led by those already represented, continues to ignore what this belonging might mean. Speaking personally, the musical *Been So Long* (especially the 2018 film adaptation) could be described as representing me. It is set minutes away from where I grew up and explores stories about Black British life that echo the experiences of many of the people I love. However, *Been So Long* provides representation at its most superficial, because the script leans into stereotypes of toxic masculinity and 'strong Black women'. At the same time, storytelling through music styles like reggae or hip-hop does not truly find its home in musical theatre as I know it. Lee Hall's jukebox musical *Get Up, Stand Up* (2021), about the life of Bob Marley, is yet another reminder that Black musicians are almost only welcome in biographical settings or film adaptations featuring already-famous popular music. The form does not allow shows by us, for us, to survive, and therefore, when we circle back to who is 'seen' in musicals, we confront a conflict.

Until the musical theatre community at large has acknowledged that American and British musicals are steeped in colonial and racist understandings of 'non-white' people and communities (I include anti-Semitic content here), representation in its most ideal form cannot be made good. Ultimately, scholars like me, based in Europe or America, are likely to have internalised Broadway as the basis from which most other musical theatre is derived. Frequently cited examples such as Harold Arlen and Truman Capote's *House of Flowers* (1954), which is an obscure work to most people anyway, do not count. This musical (based on a Capote novella) continues the fractured representation of Blackness of *Porgy and Bess*, with Arlen, like Gershwin, venerating music rooted in experience other than his own. What might the prolific dancer, choreographer, and director Alvin Ailey and/or Geoffrey Holder have achieved in staging a musical that does not fetishise Black Haitians? With the performing talents of Pearl Bailey, Diahann Carrol, and Juanita Hall, where is the landmark musical drama about African American life that we have seen so many times when centred on white American experience? Why was Juanita Hall cast as characters from different racial backgrounds more often than she was offered material where she inhabits her Blackness? The question of who is appropriate to cast in anything is centred in who wrote the material and who it is for. I do not have an 'own voice' position on the original London cast of *Miss Saigon*, but in the casting of the white British actor Jonathan Pryce as the Eurasian character the Engineer, I recognise the same insidiousness that positions Juanita Hall (who was African American and Irish American) in the roles of the 'Tonkinese' Bloody Mary in *South Pacific* (1949) and Madam Liang in *Flower Drum Song* (1958).

Hall inhabits a generalised racial other because those were the only parts available to her. The Engineer has a French father, allowing the casting of a white actor instead of a person of mixed heritage. The point here is not about racial authenticity (which trades in white supremacism) but to focus on who is and is not permitted access to whiteness. Therefore, the first Asian actor to play Christine in *The Phantom of the Opera* (1986) or the first Black actor to play Jean Valjean in *Les Misérables* is neither my concern nor a valuable yardstick in this conversation. While I would love any actor of colour to inhabit roles traditionally interpreted as white, their casting does not change the conditions in

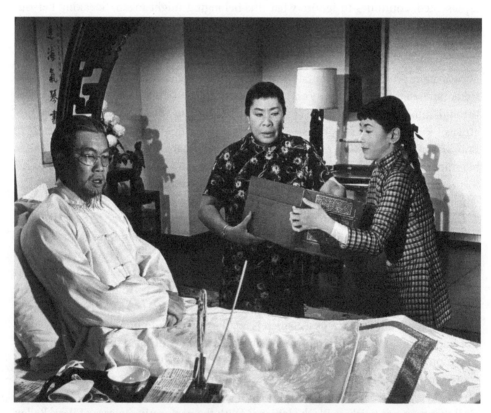

FIG. 32.3 Scene from Henry Koster's 1961 screen adaptation of *Flower Drum Song*. The film is set among the Chinese American community of San Francisco's Chinatown, but features actors of various ethnic backgrounds and nationalities: Kam Tong (*left*, as Doctor Li) is Chinese American, Juanita Hall (*centre*, as Madame Liang) is of African American and Irish American descent, and Miyoshi Umeki (*right*, as Mei Ling) is Japanese. Photo © Alamy Stock Photo.

which our heroes are never given the lead or presented through our eyes. And the rot goes deeper.

A further challenge to this discussion of casting in the West is our persistent belief that all global stories are legitimate subjects for our entertainment. This continues to manifest in musicals about struggle, discrimination, and brutality seen through our cultural lenses. In *Reframing the Musical*, Broderick Chow reflects on the announcement of *Here Lies Love*, a musical about Imelda Marcos: 'The idea of white British audiences happily dancing along to such a recent story of corruption, violence, and brutality was an unbearable prospect. After all, what did they know about Philippine history? Or Filipinos?'[19] Chow encapsulates the weariness and scepticism that we feel when we anticipate one-dimensional representation of our cultures. Musicals in Britain and America continue to rely on the distance of othering to create exotic spectacles out of histories the audience need never properly understand.

This reality is made more difficult when we recognise that our most celebrated composers, lyricists, and book writers have repeatedly mangled the stories of people of colour, and that these wrecks of representation have become the templates for the form. I can see the clumsy (if well-meaning) tussles with colonialism in *The King and I* (1951) alongside Yul Brynner's impersonation of a Thai monarch and trace those efforts to modern attempts to grapple with systemic racism in John Kander and Fred Ebb's *The Scottsboro Boys* (2010). One of my most formative memories as a musical theatre fan and researcher was sitting in the middle of the stalls before and during a performance of the West End revival of *Scottsboro*. I had already experienced a micro-aggression: two well-spoken white people behind me had tapped my shoulder to ask if I would tie my hair up or they wouldn't be able to see. The fact that the floor of the stage was above my seated head was irrelevant to them.

Like the community Chow highlights, I was one of the people in the London audience who had never heard of the landmark miscarriages of justice that the real Scottsboro Boys were subjected to. I came to the performance knowing it had a majority Black cast and rave reviews. *The Scottsboro Boys* has an experimental format using the structure and styles of vaudeville—a minstrel show—to document the repeated mistrial of nine Black youths who were falsely accused of raping two white women in 1932. Through the show the drama uses cakewalks, blackface, and brazen comedy to repeatedly collide the historical racism the nine experienced with the racist roots of musical theatre spectacles. In the songs, Kander and Ebb explore the abuse, fear, and resilience the boys experienced. They also musicalise their trauma. I can never forget nor forgive sitting in that performance during the song 'Electric Chair'. In accounts of the tortures the boys experienced, it has been reported that the youngest defendant, Leroy Wright, who was thirteen years old, was forced to sleep in the electric chair he was slated to die in. Kander and Ebb construct the horror of this through a nightmare ditty performed by the prison guards, which leads to an 'electrifying' tap dance. A fourteen-year-old actor is forced to sit through lyrics like 'your hair fizzles out and your eyes disappear' before dancing a short tap spectacle accented by 'shocks'.[20] The audience laughed around me. It was not uncomfortable laughter. It was mirth. They acknowledged how 'clever' the material is and applauded it. The disconnect between laughing at gallows humour and the real danger our legal and policing structures continue to pose to Black people in both the United Kingdom and the United States weighed heavily on my mind. It still does, many years on. This audience, almost entirely white presenting, had access to social agency that allowed 'Electric Chair' to be funny, rather than a grotesque misjudgement of the very real consequences that Black people face in our criminal justice systems today.

While it might feel easy to absolve Kander and Ebb, and along with the director, Susan Stroman, of the conditions of the audience experience, they chose to create an environment in which a young dancer is given the spotlight through appalling circumstances. Stroman writes on her website:

> *The Scottsboro Boys* still resonates today as we struggle to give voice to those who are marginalized. For all of us who created the show, it remains the most rewarding musical experience of our lifetime. We know this musical starts a necessary conversation with each audience member and, more importantly, every time it plays, it brings the Scottsboro Boys back to life.[21]

I am yet to be convinced that 'Electric Chair' achieves a balance between communicating the fear and horror of the conditions that Black youth experience in the American (and British) carceral systems and employing the spectacle of musical theatre to shock. This is important, because the 'shock' and discomfort are felt differently by spectators for whom these lived realities are distant and impersonal. The collision of genre, impact, and intention suggest, as does Stroman's reflection, that this is a musical written to remind those who are able to ignore and forget.

Looking beyond this specific example, there is a broader conversation to be had about what is written and produced in musical theatre that enables inequality. If we accept that, for musical theatre to be a form, it must have recognisable conventions and rules, then we must look at why these qualities have enabled so many white fantasies, including stereotypes and grotesques of non-white lives. While there are some modest explorations of Jewish stories, there is almost no place for 'own voice' musical theatre in the history of its most popular shows around the world. Even *The Lion King*, which might be written up as a triumph for Black representation in a different context, does not offer much to inspire in terms of creative voice or Black capitalism. It is not Black people or even Black Africans that profit from the global franchise of the *Lion King* stage musical. By acknowledging that there are expectations of dramaturgy and storytelling that we compare work against,[22] we can unpack how roles (and works) are situated. For example, where the Broadway musical is our foundation, we have conceptualisations of an establishing song that introduces all the characters (e.g. 'Another Op'nin', Another Show' from *Kiss Me, Kate* [1948] and 'In the Heights' from *In the Heights* [2008]) or the gendered ballad of unrequited love (e.g. 'Losing My Mind' from *Follies* [1971], 'On My Own' from *Les Misérables* [1985], and 'I'm Not That Girl', from *Wicked*). With that understanding, we can then reflect on who is introduced: if Black and brown actors are in the chorus but do not carry named roles, are they recognised in the establishing song, or do they remain in servile-proximate roles to be seen and support anonymously? Where we see an up-tempo love song like 'Love You I Do' inhabited by a fat Black woman in the film adaptation of *Dreamgirls* (2006), it is striking that Effie White is not permitted this joy on-stage. With the exception of 'I Enjoy Being a Girl' from *Flower Drum Song* and to a much lesser extent 'I Feel Pretty' from *West Side Story*, we do not have historical precedents that allow women of colour to perform empowered romantic and sensual expression in stage musicals.

Songs like 'Helpless' and 'Satisfied' in *Hamilton* seem to provide an antidote to this concern, giving the two female leads, Angelica and Eliza Schuyler, their own musical turns. These heroines (always performed by women of colour) are lively and vivacious, and yet, these songs (two angles on Hamilton's courtship and marriage to Eliza) also highlight their limited interventions in *Hamilton* more generally. Angelica and Eliza's commanding musical presences in *Hamilton* have almost no relevance to the main plot or themes of the show. The single 'First Burn', released as part of the 2018 'Hamilton's Hamildrops', is a first draft of Eliza's broken-hearted ballad 'Burn' after Hamilton publishes the details of his affair to avoid being falsely accused of fraud. In 'First Burn', Eliza is allowed a more fiery, feisty representation of the pain and rage she feels; she is afforded greater insight into her husband's character.[23] Sadly, this thread is diluted in the musical, so that Eliza and Angelica are defined by their love for Hamilton and their role in continuing his legacy. With Effie White in *Dreamgirls*, we see independent and emotional growth through the fall and rise of her career. Eliza and Angelica have no space to develop even though they provide brief moments of on-stage euphoria.

## How Can We Act?

This chapter can only touch on a handful of approaches to representation in musicals presented around the world. However, I hope to encourage all interested parties to pay attention to who is around you and which musicals are repeatedly given space and glory. We can no longer accept that fetishising Global South, non-white, and/or non-Anglophone communities is acceptable in the works we stage, and we must consider thoughtfully the power of revival in musical theatre hubs in different regions. Where Broadway and West End musicals become international sensations, we should learn from staging practices in different locations. We must also look out for musicals like *The Wiz* (1975), which enable empowered performance, but note that transfers to major cities are in conflict with the licences given to small venues. Meanwhile, corporate strategies of organisations like Disney, which regularly remove 'locally sensitive' material from their films, have provided a subconscious filter of bigotry about which audiences will accept musicals on certain themes, which is then reflected back in casting biases. For example, sensitivities about distributing queer scenes in Asia are completely contradicted by domestic productions of *Everybody's Talking about Jamie* (2017) and *Kinky Boots* (2013) in South Korea and Japan. Here we are reminded that blanket labels obscure the nuances of local environments. We are also reminded that the racial biases of our societies do not translate beyond our supposed borders. This means that a production of *Everybody's Talking about Jamie* that only stars Asian British performers would have different significance to a UK audience to having an all-Korean cast in the original South Korean production. In Britain, we continue to talk about adapting musicals like *Jamie* and *Billy Elliot* to allow performers of colour to inhabit roles that were originally conceived as white. Yet, it seems only logical that when a work transfers to a location with different majority groups, the identities of these same characters are changed by default. The uncomfortable truth is that in the Global North, it is still common to perceive white characters as *without* race, and therefore to be challenged by performers of colour inhabiting roles without signifiers of race. These signifiers are important because they are used to define characterisation (signposted in lyrics and dialogue) and are often present in the musical, lighting, and costume choices that fix racialised bodies in place while the 'non-racialised' characters can be mobile.

I began with a quote from *Hamilton*, 'You have no control/Who lives, who dies, who tells your story,' because it simultaneously highlights the way the passing of time changes history and gives weight to the lie that we have no control over what is said and remembered about us. As the earlier examples from Nigeria show, it is completely possible to write popular and commercial musicals with creative teams entirely from the community they centre. In countries where colonialism has been central to the development of our performing arts, this elicits a pressing question: *who is community?* While anti-Semitism abounds in the UK political system and continues to appear in stereotyped representations of Jewishness on-stage, we can and should hand over control of musicals such as *Fiddler on the Roof* and *Falsettos* to creative teams who know and understand the cultures they are presenting. This does not mean that racial and ethnic communities are monolithic. It simply acknowledges that our society is not in a post-racial state where it might be easy to imagine or inhabit the lived experiences of people from different backgrounds to our own.

I use the British context to problematise a universal approach to casting and representation in musicals. In the United Kingdom we are unravelling questions about who is allowed to represent Britishness on-stage in a very different climate to other colonial states in the Global North. For example, there was a transitory moment from the mid-1950s to the 1970s in which African American musical theatre stars were able to develop major careers in Europe. Where did the performers who followed these artists go, and why are they not represented in new musicals coming from countries including France and Germany? Meanwhile, we have to acknowledge that our discourse on casting is never far from the personalities involved. For example, the effervescent cast album of *Wakaa, the Musical* was made more complex by the allegations of sexual abuse directed at the producer and recording artist Brymo (also known by his name, Ọláwálé Ọlọ́fọ̀ọ̀rọ̀) in 2020.[24] In this case, Global North scholars might resist discussing the project at all without recognising how many unsavoury truths are hidden in the musical theatre histories of our countries. Casting is informed by who is seen performing. If we do not recognise the musical works developed outside of Europe and the United States, then we underpin what a musical is with this absence. You may feel inspired to chant 'we cannot be what we cannot see', and I hope you understand this expression in its fullness.

Inclusive casting does not mean 'racially accurate' casting. We do not demand that only Vietnamese actors should play Vietnamese characters in *Miss Saigon*. Instead, we argue that the Chinese and Filipino and Asian British and American actors who are pushed into largely sexualised or villainous roles have a right to play the American GI Chris and his wife, Ellen, as well. I can imagine some recoiling from that last sentence, thinking, 'But *Miss Saigon* revolves around racial difference.' *Miss Saigon* recreates the conditions of *Madama Butterfly* and assumes its audience recognises the Americans as 'non-racialised'; they are the neutral that provides contrast with the other. However, inclusive casting demands something more than this superficial transaction. It requires that there be roles that allow all communities to be seen as they are rather than through historical, fictionalised stereotypes. It requires producers, directors, marketing specialists, composers, lyricists, script writers, costume designers, lighting designers, choreographers, critics, *and audiences* to accept that multiracial communities are, in fact, multiracial. In this way, Black, brown, and other communities that are racially othered in the Global North both belong and are recognzed within the visual and social tapestries of our countries on-stage. Meanwhile, works that are consciously about a specific group should be allowed to continue. This means that an all-white cast cannot stage *Hairspray* because the story revolves around visible and engaged members of a Black community who are subjected to racist oppression. It is not for white actors to imagine or inhabit stories about oppressions that their community has never been subjected to. This is doubly significant when (in this instance) Black actors are not able to inhabit roles that have not been defined as racialised.

The argument that we must centre 'historically accurate' race representation in musicals tends to come to the fore when a person of colour is given space in a story dominated by whiteness, and yet, there is no reciprocal outrage when white children are cast, for example, as the 'Siamese children' in *The King and I*. In the Global North, we have not begun to reach a post-racial society where power is uncoupled from identity characteristics, including gender, sexuality, able-bodiedness, and race. Therefore, it is necessary to demand space where our identities and histories have been commodified and restricted for the sake of another community's entertainment. These are the same relics of colonialism that allows 'This Is Me' from *The Greatest Showman* to be an anthem for the oppressed in a film musical that removes almost all the bitter and grim violations P. T. Barnum inflicted on the people he used in his career. Our empowerment can only be enabled in deference to a white saviour, and, should that saviour have unsavoury practices, those should be minimised.

It strikes me as a great irony that part of the success of Lin-Manuel Miranda's musicals hinges on the premise that people who are marginalised (or are often unheard and/or unseen) are given voice. In the Global North, we are so starved of stories centred on people of colour in families and wider community that we are almost uncritical about their content. I wonder what the enslaved and indigenous people who suffered at the hands of the founding fathers might feel about their erasure in *Hamilton*. What does it mean for diverse casting if actual people of colour no longer exist in the narrative being presented? To what extent does *Hamilton*'s aspiration to flip the power balance and 'put [ourselves] back in the narrative' enable the ambition to make musical theatre more inclusive? Does it not present this intention by rendering the past ahistorically? I remember the glow of happiness I felt sitting in the audience of the West End production because I felt in company for the first time; and yet, I grew increasingly worried about the extent to which one musical can be understood as a solution for all problems. We certainly need these bridging works that remind the Global North that our narratives can be as entertaining and even as commercial as yours. But we are still in a place where musicals written in languages other than English are seldom transferred or adapted while works such as *Phantom, Wicked*, and *Sweeney Todd* (1997) are transferred around the world. I believe that opening our imaginations about who is in community with us is foundational to changing which stories are given space. Casting is important in this task because it challenges audiences and markets. We crave belonging, and we crave new understanding. While musicals remain a form of escapism, we cannot allow this to mask the harm they may do to people whom we are not used to seeing. Empowered representation does not dismantle such masking unless you aspire to a society of people who are in no way different from you.

## Notes

1. Lin-Manuel Miranda, 'History Has Its Eyes On You', from *Hamilton: Original Broadway Cast Album*, performed by Alex Lacamoire, Christopher Jackson, Lin-Manuel Miranda, and original Broadway cast, 2015, streaming audio, Spotify, accessed 1 February 2022.
2. Examples include AnaSofia Villanueva, '*Hamilton*: Anti-Blackness, Indigenous Erasure, and Whitewashing Latinxs', *Minnesota Playlist*, 6 July 2020, https://minnesotaplaylist.com/magazine/article/2020/hamilton-anti-blackness-indigenous-erasure-and-whitewashing-latinxs; Daniel James Belnavis, 'The Unvravelling of a Dream: My Life in the Cast of Hamilton; An American Musical', *An Injustice*, 11 March 2021, https://aninjusticemag.com/the-unraveling-of-a-dream-6824c652c013; and Aja Romano, 'The Backlash against *In the Heights*, Explained', *Vox*, 15 June 2021, https://www.vox.com/culture/22535040/in-the-heights-casting-backlash-colorism-representation; all accessed 20 March 2022.
3. Isabella Herrera, quoted in Maira Garcia, Sandra E. Garcia, Isabelia Herrera, Concepción de León, Maya Phillips, and A. O. Scott, '*In the Heights* and Colorism: What Is Lost When Afro-Latinos Are Erased', *New York Times*, 21 June 2021, https://www.nytimes.com/2021/06/21/movies/in-the-heights-colorism.html, accessed 20 March 2022.
4. Micha Frazer-Carroll, '*In the Heights*: Why the Film's Lack of Dark-Skinned Black People Looks a Lot like Colourism', *Independent*, 16 June 2021, https://www.independent.co.uk/arts-entertainment/films/features/in-the-heights-colourism-latinx-representation-b1868384.html; accessed 20 March 2022.
5. Transcription of Rita Moreno's comments on *The Late Show with Stephen Colbert*, aired 15 June 2021. The section edited out is a comment about Miranda producing her documentary (*Rita Moreno: Just a Girl Who Decided to Go for It*, 2021) and then Colbert's lead-in to the rest of her remark. 'Rita Moreno Defends Her Friend Lin Manuel Miranda over *In The*

*Heights* Controversy', *The Late Show with Stephen Colbert*, 16 June 2021, https://www.yout ube.com/watch?v=CrM5M1ZK1JU, accessed 28 March 2022.

6.  Rita Moreno, 'I'm Incredibly Disappointed with Myself', tweet, 17 June 2021, https://twitter. com/TheRitaMoreno/status/1405322954062376964?s=20&t=BDrox_QSHCCCMX_C237 vBg, accessed 28 March 2022.

7.  Miranda, 'History Has Its Eyes On You'.

8.  Aria S. Halliday, *Buy Black: How Black Women Transformed US Popular Culture* (Urbana: University of Illinois Press, 2022), 17–18.

9.  Nebtreko has faced criticism for her close relationship with the Russian leader Vladimir Putin and has locked her Instagram (on private settings). Therefore, this chapter does not provide a link to the post (still live) on her page. Her words in the comments have been widely reported, including in Helen Holmes, 'The Met Casts Anna Nebtreko as *Aida* Despite Her Past Controversy in the Role', *Observer*, 13 February 2020, https://obser ver.com/2020/02/anna-netrebko-aida-met-opera-casting-2020-2021-season-details/, accessed 22 March 2022.

10. BBC News, 'Russia's Bolshoi Rejects Misty Copeland's "Blackface'" Criticism' *BBC*, 16 December 2019, https://www.bbc.co.uk/news/world-europe-50807742, accessed 22March 2022.

11. Michael Cooper, 'An *Otello* without Blackface Highlights an Enduring Tradition in Opera', *New York Times*, 17 September 2015, https://www.nytimes.com/2015/09/20/arts/music/ an-otello-without-the-blackface-nods-to-modern-tastes.html, accessed 22 March 2022.

12. Brakkton Booker, 'Metropolitan Opera to Drop Use of Blackface-Style Make-Up', *NPR*, 4 August 2015, https://www.npr.org/sections/thetwo-way/2015/08/04/429366961/metropoli tan-opera-to-drop-use-of-blackface-style-makeup-in-otello?t=1652969155364, accessed 22 March 2022.

13. Andreas Wiseman, 'Regina King on Brit Actors Playing U.S. Characters: "If I Was Moved, I Don't Care Where a Person's From'", *Deadline*, 13 January 2021, https://deadline.com/ 2021/01/regina-king-british-actors-playing-us-characters-one-night-miami-1234672664/ , accessed 22 March 2022.

14. Silva Chege, 'Why Shouldn't Black British Actors Play Americans?', *Little White Lies*, 11 April 2021, https://lwlies.com/articles/daniel-kaluuya-judas-and-the-black-messiah-brit ish-actors-american-roles/, accessed 22 March 2022.

15. It is important to acknowledge that the criticism of *In the Heights* was about Dominican representation and that Moreno is specifically commenting as a Puerto Rican.

16. SiriusXM, 'Denzel Washington: "It's Not Color, It's Culture"; Urban View', 20 December 2016, https://www.youtube.com/watch?v=9Ayf8Iny9Eg, accessed 22 March 2022.

17. SBS Australia, 'African-American Woman Cast in Legally Blonde', Facebook, https://www. facebook.com/watch/?v=512924062486247, accessed 31 March 2022.

18. WhatsOnStage, '*West Side Story* Movie: "America" Sitzprobe Performance with Ariana DeBose', https://www.youtube.com/watch?v=-g5X8SA6p1o, accessed 22 March 2022.

19. Broderick Chow, 'Seeing as a Filipino: *Here Lies Love* (2014) at the National Theatre', in *Reframing the Musical: Race Culture, and Identity*, ed. Sarah Whitfield (London: Red Globe Press, 2019), 17–34; here: 19.

20. John Kander and Fred Ebb, 'Electric Chair', *The Scottsboro Boys: Original Off-Broadway Cast*, CD, Jay Records, 2010, CDJAY 1421.

21. Susan Stroman, 'Note from Stro', *Susan Stroman*, [n.d.], https://www.susanstroman.com/ productions/the-scottsboro-boys, accessed 16 May 2022.

22. The musical *Hamilton* is a great example of this: the show's conventional structure is interwoven with innovative use of music and casting. However, the vehicle for innovation is familiar and provides a language of songs and dramatic axes that we understand.
23. Lin-Manuel Miranda, 'First Burn', digital single, performed by Ari Afsar, Julia Harriman, Lexi Lawson, Rachelle Ann Go, and Shoba Narayan, 2018, streaming audio, Spotify, accessed 1 February 2022.
24. The allegations were made via an anonymous Twitter account during a wider exposé of sexual abuse in the Nigerian performing arts scene. Brymo denies all wrongdoing.

## BIBLIOGRAPHY

BBC News. 'Russia's Bolshoi Rejects Misty Copeland's "Blackface" Criticism'. BBC, 16 December 2019, https://www.bbc.co.uk/news/world-europe-50807742, accessed 22 March 2022.

Belnavis, Daniel James. 'The Unvravelling of a Dream: My Life in the Cast of *Hamilton*; An American Musical'. *An Injustice* , 11 March 2021. https://aninjusticemag.com/the-unraveling-of-a-dream-6824c652c013, accessed 20 March 2022.

Booker, Brakkton. 'Metropolitan Opera to Drop Use of Blackface-Style Make-Up'. NPR, 4 August 2015, https://www.npr.org/sections/thetwo-way/2015/08/04/429366961/metropolitan-opera-to-drop-use-of-blackface-style-makeup-in-otello?t=1652969155364, accessed 22 March 2022.

Chege, Silva. 'Why Shouldn't Black British Actors Play Americans?' Little White Lies, 11 April 2021, https://lwlies.com/articles/daniel-kaluuya-judas-and-the-black-messiah-british-actors-american-roles/, accessed 22 March 2022.

Chow, Broderick. 'Seeing as a Filipino: *Here Lies Love* (2014) at the National Theatre'. In *Reframing the Musical: Race Culture, and Identity*, ed. Sarah Whitfield, 17–34. London: Red Globe Press, 2019.

Cooper, Michael. 'An *Otello* without Blackface Highlights an Enduring Tradition in Opera'. *New York Times*, 17 September 2015, https://www.nytimes.com/2015/09/20/arts/music/an-otello-without-the-blackface-nods-to-modern-tastes.html, accessed 22 March 2022.

Frazer-Carroll, Micha. '*In the Heights*: Why the Film's Lack of Dark-Skinned Black People Looks a Lot like Colourism'. *Independent*, 16 June 2021, https://www.independent.co.uk/arts-entertainment/films/features/in-the-heights-colourism-latinx-representation-b1868384.html, accessed 20 March 2022.

Garcia, Maira, Sandra E. Garcia, Isabelia Herrera, Concepción de León, Maya Phillips, and A. O. Scott. '*In the Heights* and Colorism: What Is Lost When Afro-Latinos Are Erased'. *New York Times*, 21 June 2021, Section C, 1. https://www.nytimes.com/2021/06/21/movies/in-the-heights-colorism.html, accessed 20 March 2022.

Halliday, Aria S. *Buy Black: How Black Women Transformed US Popular Culture*. Urbana: University of Illinois Press, 2022.

Holmes, Helen. 'The Met Casts Anna Nebtreko as "Aida" Despite Her Past Controversy in the Role'. *Observer*, 13 February 2020, https://observer.com/2020/02/anna-netrebko-aida-met-opera-casting-2020-2021-season-details/, accessed 22 March 2022.

Kander, John, and Fred Ebb. *The Scottsboro Boys: Original Off-Broadway Cast*. CD. Jay Records, 2010, CDJAY 1421.

Miranda, Lin-Manuel. 'First Burn'. Digital single. Performed by Ari Afsar, Julia Harriman, Lexi Lawson, Rachelle Ann Go, and Shoba Narayan, 2018. Streaming audio, Spotify, accessed 1 February 2022.

Miranda, Lin-Manuel. *Hamilton: Original Broadway Cast Album*. Performed by Alex Lacamoire, Christopher Jackson, Lin-Manuel Miranda, and original Broadway cast, 2015. Streaming audio, Spotify, accessed 1 February 2022.

Moreno, Rita. 'Rita Moreno Defends Her Friend Lin Manuel Miranda over *In The Heights* Controversy'. *The Late Show with Stephen Colbert*, 16 June 2021, https://www.youtube.com/watch?v=CrM5M1ZK1JU, accessed 28 March 2022.

Moreno, Rita. 'I'm Incredibly Disappointed with Myself'. Tweet. 17 June 2021, https://twitter.com/TheRitaMoreno/status/1405322954062376964?s=20&t=BDrox_QSHCCCMX_C237vBg, accessed 28 March 2022.

Romano, Aja. 'The Backlash against *In the Heights*, Explained'. *Vox*, 15 June 2021, https://www.vox.com/culture/22535040/in-the-heights-casting-backlash-colorism-representation; accessed 20 March 2022.

SBS Australia. 'African-American Woman cast in Legally Blonde'. Facebook, https://www.facebook.com/watch/?v=512924062486247, accessed 31 March 2022.

SiriusXM. 'Denzel Washington: "It's Not Color, It's Culture"; Urban View', 20 December 2016, https://www.youtube.com/watch?v=9Ayf8Iny9Eg, accessed 22 March 2022.

Stroman, Susan. 'Note from Stro'. Susan Stroman, n.d., https://www.susanstroman.com/productions/the-scottsboro-boys, accessed 16 March 2022.

Villanueva, AnaSofia. '*Hamilton*: Anti-Blackness, Indigenous Erasure, and Whitewashing Latinxs'. *Minnesota Playlist*, 6 July 2020, https://minnesotaplaylist.com/magazine/article/2020/hamilton-anti-blackness-indigenous-erasure-and-whitewashing-latinxs, accessed 20 March 2022.

WhatsOnStage. '*West Side Story* Movie: "America" Sitzprobe Performance with Ariana DeBose', 2022, tps://www.youtube.com/watch?v=-g5X8SA6p1o, accessed 22 March 2022.

Wiseman, Andreas. 'Regina King on Brit Actors Playing U.S. Characters: "If I Was Moved, I Don't Care Where a Person's From"'. *Deadline*, 13 January 2021, https://deadline.com/2021/01/regina-king-british-actors-playing-us-characters-one-night-miami-1234672664/, accessed 22 March 2022.

# CHAPTER 33

## 'SUPERBOY AND THE INVISIBLE GIRL'

### The Exclusion of the Female Voice from Global Musical Theatre

#### GRACE BARNES

In 1998 the audience at the annual Tony Awards ceremony stood and cheered Julie Taymor when she became the first woman to win the award for Best Direction of a Musical for *The Lion King*. But any observers who saw this as a transformative moment in the history of musical theatre, one which signified the dawn of a new era wherein female directors would be regarded as the equals of their male colleagues, were to be sadly disappointed. In 2019 Rachel Chavkin was only the third woman after Taymor to win the Tony for Best Direction of a Musical for her work on *Hadestown*.[1] In her acceptance speech, Chavkin noted the dearth of opportunities for women: 'I wish I wasn't the only woman directing a musical on Broadway this season. There are so many women who are ready to go. It is a failure of imagination by a field whose job it is to imagine the way the world could be.'[2]

This failure of imagination is doubly frustrating given the heightened consciousness of inclusion and diversity brought about by the advent of the Black Lives Matter and #MeToo movements. The new awareness of difference has made its mark on the global arts sector, provoking challenges to accepted presumptions concerning who makes theatre, and for whom. Long-overdue discussions are currently addressing ways of establishing an industry which is more inclusive on-stage and more accessible to a wider audience demographic. In addition, a re-evaluation of working practices within an industry that is perceived as exclusive and/or hostile to certain groups is aiming to transform the way in which the production of theatre takes place worldwide. In the United States, for example, the testimonial letter 'Dear White American Theatre' (weseeyouwat. com) demanded lasting change via a series of initiatives, including the adoption of an anti-racist code of conduct throughout American theatres, protocols to disrupt racist

FIG. 33.1 Rachel Chavkin accepting the Tony Award for Best Direction of a Musical for *Hadestown* in June 2019. Photo: Brendan McDermid © Alamy Stock Photo.

incidents, and respect for non-white bodies, knowledge, and practices. In the United Kingdom, repertory theatres have actively headhunted non-white artistic staff, included physically disabled performers in productions, and reprogrammed seasons to include narratives by gender-queer practitioners.

These changes are vital to making theatre an art form which is accessible to anyone who wishes to participate, and yet in all of this belated reappraisal, the under-representation of women in musical theatre is still not regarded as an urgent issue. To be more accurate, women are included in the discourse in a tokenistic fashion but excluded from the practice. The lack of any significant challenge to this state of affairs may be a result of feminism fatigue and a view that gender equality is yesterday's battle, but it is an indisputable fact that contemporary musical theatre is the one area of the performing arts which remains almost exclusively under the control of (white) men.

Musicals are more popular today than they have been for decades thanks to the increased accessibility resulting from touring companies, internet marketing which enables online participation in chat rooms and forums, and the streaming of work developed specifically for platforms such as TikTok. The increased accessibility means that musical theatre is now engaging with a broader demographic in terms of age, race, and class than ever before: indeed, for many audience members, a musical is the only experience of live theatre they will ever have. This makes it imperative to examine the wider meanings produced by a popular cultural product aimed primarily at women but created by men owing to the fact that global audiences of women are absorbing values concerning their own behaviour and position in society which emanate from a male perspective. When viewed against moves to manage the inclusion of minority groups within a broader theatrical landscape, the ongoing systemic prejudice against women in musical theatre appears to render their exclusion a calculated act by men determined to retain their grip on the industry.

This chapter will consider how the worldwide preoccupation with diversity and minority voices is being manipulated by those in control of musical theatre either to eliminate women from on-stage narratives or to divert attention away from deeply problematic depictions of female characters. Whilst the spotlight currently illuminating issues concerning race and gender identity has enabled a huge step forward in terms of visibility and validation, it is a leap which has been achieved at the expense of women. As it currently stands, diversity in musical theatre translates as stories about men who are not white and/or straight. What it categorically does *not* mean is stories about women, created and directed by other women.

## Implications of the Missing Female Voice

The exclusion of women from the production of musical theatre has a long history, and it is a practice which remains unchallenged, unnoticed even, by the same critics and arts commentators who should be holding the global industry to account. A myriad of interrelated practices and belief systems have enabled this long-standing prejudice against female practitioners, and the continuing exclusion of women from the creative teams (i.e. director, composer, lyricist, and book writer) of new shows results in men controlling not only female-led narratives, but the depiction of women on-stage. An ingrained, possibly historical opinion that women are not capable of producing and creating hit musicals is soundly refuted by *Mamma Mia!*, and it should be regarded as extraordinary that a show which has played in over fifty countries on six continents, spawned two enormously popular films,[3] and owes its success to the female voice driving the narrative failed to open any doors for women in musical theatre.

While the number of musicals created by women and with narratives concerning the female experience, such as *The Color Purple* (2005), *Fun Home* (2015), and *Waitress* (2016), can be counted on one hand, in the last two decades alone musicals which are ostensibly about women but have male creative teams include (but are not limited to) *The Witches of Eastwick* (2000), *Hairspray* (2002), *Mary Poppins* (2004), *Next to Normal* (2009), *Matilda* (2011), *Beautiful* (2014), *Made in Dagenham* (2014), *Mrs Henderson*

*Presents* (2016), *Calendar Girls* (2017), *Cilla the Musical* (2017), *The Prom* (2018), *Pretty Woman* (2018),*Diana* (2021) and *Tammy Faye* (2022).

The absence of female creative practitioners from the genre enables a male viewpoint which privileges men and ignores women to prevail. The recent British musicals *Everybody's Talking about Jamie* (2017) and *The Boy in the Dress* (2019) effectively wrote women and girls off the stage via an agenda which conferred higher status onto boys who are 'different'. In Australia, *Priscilla, Queen of the Desert* (2006), *Shane Warne: The Musical* (2008), and *King Kong* (2013) quite blatantly reproduced the misogynistic tendencies which the former prime minister, Julia Gilliard, noted as a national issue beyond the political arena.[4] Bio-musicals of female artists such as *Tina – the Tina Turner Musical* (2018), *Beautiful* (2013), which revisited the career of Carole King, and *Dusty: The Original Pop Diva* (2006) tend to focus on the negative aspects of the subject's life and frequently frame the star within a victim narrative. A post-feminist directive which requires women to be silent in the face of discrimination in order to retain the few strides towards equality that have been achieved is visible in the abundance of passive (or irrelevant) female characters inhabiting musicals such as *Kinky Boots* (2012), *Hamilton* (2015), and *Everybody's Talking about Jamie*.

As a genre, musical theatre has traditionally been regarded as 'less than' (particularly in the United Kingdom and Australia) when considered in relation to drama. The intimation that musicals are neither as artistically sophisticated nor as intellectually demanding as drama can be linked to a view of the genre as holding greater appeal to women, and the frequent framing of narratives within a romantic framework consolidates this view. The ability of the so-called megamusicals to attract huge audiences worldwide has resulted in the reappraisal of the art form as mass entertainment, and this association of musical theatre with profit further accounts for the ongoing male domination of the genre. A successful commercial musical can generate staggering worldwide profits: according to the financial magazine *Forbes*, the stage production of *The Lion King* has made over $8 billion.[5] When royalties are introduced into the equation, it quickly becomes apparent why male directors of drama, many of whom roll their eyes at the mention of *Wicked* or *Mamma Mia!*, ferociously canvass to be at the helm of the next jukebox tour or regional theatre musical. Patriarchal power is intrinsically tied to financial power, and any invitation to women to share the spoils of musical theatre thus has the potential to destabilise structures beyond the genre itself.

This reframing of musicals as a profitable brand rather than legitimate theatre has resulted in critics' not applying the same level of intellectual rigour to analysis of a work of musical theatre that they apply to drama. This consequently enables the prejudice against female practitioners to continue unchecked, as no commentator appears to regard the genre seriously enough to question its methods and practice of production. When the musical adaptation of David Walliams's *The Boy in the Dress* premièred at the Royal Shakespeare Company in 2019, for example, it was the fourth commercial musical the RSC had produced without a single woman on the key creative team.[6] And yet, no British critic regarded this habitual exclusion and prejudice against female practitioners by a national subsidised company as something worth noting.

The fact that the absence of women from one of the most popular strands of the performing arts goes unchallenged in the United Kingdom, the United States, Canada, Australia—any nation in fact, which produces new musicals—suggests a global status quo that is so entrenched as to be unremarkable. The lack of a female voice in musical theatre is, in fact, highly notable within the context of a field of the performing arts which is marketed to and consumed primarily by women. Whether the venue is in Sydney, New York, London, or a city on a national tour, coach parties of women on a girls' night out are a defining characteristic of *Mamma Mia!*, *Legally Blonde*, *Wicked*, *Dirty Dancing*, *Waitress*, and *SIX*.[7] And yet, no commercial producer or artistic director has deemed it necessary to cultivate authentic female voices to create the shows which other women support. On the contrary, in fact—and Cameron Mackintosh is not the only producer who returns again and again to the same handful of men to stage his productions. Nor are female producers entirely blameless: Judy Craymer hired a male director on the 'girl power' Spice Girls musical, *Viva Forever* (2012), and Carmen Pavlovich at Global Creatures in Australia—producers of *King Kong* (2013), *Strictly Ballroom* (2014), *Muriel's Wedding* (2017), and *Moulin Rouge* (2018)—has never hired a female director or scriptwriter. Whether this is an example of women in power aping entrenched male behaviour or a result of the invisible barricades preventing female producers from offering support to female colleagues is impossible to know. What is certain is that this practice results in highly talented female practitioners' being denied opportunities to develop a significant body of work, thereby ensuring that the pool of creative talent which is considered when a new show is put together remains a pool of men.

The lack of any significant female contribution to the creation of new musicals enables the reproduction on-stage of patriarchal hierarchies which designate women as the enablers of men and undeserving of the same level of adulation. For all the leaps made by *Hamilton* in relation to racial diversity and visibility, the female characters are one-dimensional clichés, either helpless in the face of the charismatic, powerful male or engineering his downfall through seduction.[8] The positive critical focus on the racially inclusive sensibility of the show successfully diverted attention away from the fact that the sole function of the women within the narrative is to enhance the status of the title character, a criticism which can also be levelled at the 2021 British musical *Get Up, Stand Up! The Bob Marley Musical*. The male protagonists of the British musicals *The Boy in the Dress* and *Everybody's Talking about Jamie* have female 'best friends' whose function is to enable the boys to dress in women's clothes, even to the point of supplying the make-up both boys require. In the latter show, the titular Jamie displays the brash entitlement which often goes hand in hand with teenage masculinity, and he rarely questions that he will not be allowed to do what he wants to do: as a boy, that is his right. His best friend, Pritti, however, has no corresponding freedoms; her life is controlled by her domineering father and a teacher who dismisses her aspirations to be a doctor simply because she is a girl. Lisa James, the best friend in *The Boy in the Dress*, effectively holds Dennis's hand at every step of his cross-dressing journey, even giving him her favourite dress. In doing so, she demonstrates her cognizance of the fact that Dennis's needs are more important than her own—because he is a boy.

FIG. 33.2 The female 'best friend' designed to enhance the status of the male protagonist: the cross-dressing Jamie (John McCrea) with his confidante Pritti (Lucy Shorthouse). Scene from the 2017 London production of *Everybody's Talking about Jamie* Photo: Johan Persson © ArenaPal.

The easiest and most effective way of reaffirming the lower status of women, both in society and on-stage, is to simply write them out of the narrative, as the male creative team did to the key character of Marina in the 2019 musical adaptation of Bill Forsythe's 1983 Scottish film *Local Hero*.[9] A second option is to have the character behave in ways that men would prefer women to behave, thereby utilising the musical theatre form to consolidate patriarchal directives concerning women's place in society. At some point during the process of adapting the 1994 Australian film *Muriel's Wedding* into a stage musical (2017), the director, Simon Phillips, and/or the book writer, P. J. Hogan, decided that the character of Alexander Shkuratov, the Olympic swimmer whom Muriel marries to facilitate his Australian citizenship, should be a gay man. If Muriel's husband is gay, then the magnitude of her decision to walk away from the marriage is significantly diminished, and the audience is subsequently denied the joy of seeing Muriel mature and grow into an empowered woman. Muriel's power to act is thus effectively disabled by the men in charge of the narrative, who seem to favour a version where she dutifully returns to an insipid boyfriend (whom the audience has not seen her with since act 1) than gain any form of independence.

The male creative team presiding over the British musical *Made in Dagenham* (2014),[10] which revisited the 1968 strike by women machinists at the Ford manufacturing plant in East London, also told an inherently female story with a distinctive male voice. Despite a narrative which frames the female protagonists primarily as workers contributing to the national tradition of industrial production, the show opens with a number ('Busy Woman') outlining the importance of work provided by women inside the home, thereby reaffirming the alignment of 'real' work with men and women's natural place as in the kitchen. The message of female empowerment on show in the numbers 'Connie's Song', 'Ideal World' and 'Stand Up' are eradicated by a script laden with misogynistic jokes, and the undercurrent of lewdness which permeated the show (the number 'Cortina' would not be out of place in a Benny Hill sketch) successfully undermined any attempt to position the feminist narrative centre stage.

That is not to say that men cannot write strong and empowered women in musicals—John Kander and Fred Ebb consistently did so in shows such as *Flora the Red Menace* (1965), *Cabaret* (1966), *Chicago* (1975), and *The Rink* (1984). In the United Kingdom, Willy Russell gave us Mrs Johnstone in *Blood Brothers* in 1984, and in 1987 Howard Goodall created an entire show, *Girlfriends*, around the experiences of a group of women serving in the Women's Auxiliary Air Force in 1941. Goodall's characters are independent and resilient; they are active participants in the national war effort and proud of their ability to perform tasks usually defined as 'men's work'. But *Girlfriends* and *Blood Brothers* are now over three decades old, and the Kander and Ebb shows even older—which has to raise questions concerning what has happened in the interim to discourage even the most empathetic male writers from creating three-dimensional and empowered female characters.

# Cross-Dressing as Cultural Appropriation?

Since the 1991 demonstrations on Broadway against the casting of white actor, Jonathan Pryce, as the Eurasian Engineer in *Miss Saigon*, commercial producers have been careful to demonstrate cultural sensitivity where race is concerned, employing non-white creatives on shows with non-white narratives and striving to ensure racial authenticity in casting. This heightened awareness has rendered revivals of classic musicals such as *Finian's Rainbow* (1947), *South Pacific* (1949), *The King and I* (1951), and even *Anything Goes* (1934) problematic due to the portrayal of Black, Asian, and minority ethnic (BAME) characters. The reason 'I'm an Indian Too' is frequently removed from revivals of *Annie Get Your Gun* (1946) is due to the fact that the song parodies Native American culture, reducing it to a series of names that ridicule objects representing historical and cultural affiliations. This throws up associations with the performance practice of black- and yellowface, in which white performers controlled the depiction of ethnic minorities on-stage. Blackface and yellowface were designed to ridicule the ethnicity being parodied and to reassure white audiences of their superior position in the social and racial hierarchies.[11]

The increase in consciousness of what is now denounced as cultural appropriation has rendered it unthinkable to have a white creative team in charge of a revival of *Once* on *This Island* (1990), or of the creation of show with a non-white sensibility, such as *Get Up, Stand Up! The Bob Marley Musical*. Indeed, in London in August 2019, a group of Jewish actors and playwrights signed an open letter accusing the producers of a new production of *Falsettos* of 'a startling lack of cultural sensitivity' and 'overt appropriation and erasure of a culture and religion' owing to the absence of Jewish practitioners from the creative team and the casting of non-Jewish actors in Jewish roles.[12] Yet male directors control female narratives in musicals, male writers create female roles, male actors even play those female roles, and it is not condemned as either culturally insensitive or appropriation.

*Made in Dagenham* recounted a seminal moment in the history of British working women—the passage of the Equal Pay Act—and yet the absence of female practitioners from the creative team was not flagged by commentators as either problematic or insensitive in the way a (hypothetical) musical with a narrative focusing on the 'Strike for Black Lives' protest in 2020 would be if created by white practitioners. This points towards an attitude which deems a non-white voice compulsory for a non-white narrative but regards a female voice as unnecessary to a story concerning women. Female characters subsequently exist in a state of inauthenticity, having been created from the limited male understanding of women: the women on-stage speak to the women in the audience, and for them, but not as *one of* them.[13] That is not to say that feminism is valid only when it originates from lived experience, or that only women can write female stories; but in the Interests of authenticity alone, it would be good practice to have at least one woman on the creative team of a show recreating an intrinsically female experience and/or history. Failure to do so implies that women are incapable of telling their own stories.

A worrying trend in recent British musicals is the hijacking of the diversity/inclusion debate surrounding gender identity to enable a sexist bias which renders women invisible and/or irrelevant to the male-driven narrative. The 2017 musical, *Everybody's Talking about Jamie* was inspired by a 2011 documentary, *Jamie: Drag Queen at 16*, which focused on an English schoolboy who wanted to attend the school prom in drag.[14] When the musical transferred from the Sheffield Crucible to London's Apollo Theatre, it quickly amassed a cult-like following among a predominantly female, teenage fan base who refashioned Jamie into a heroine/diva and bestowed upon him the kind of adulation they formerly reserved for Elphaba in *Wicked*.[15] This transfer of allegiance is partly due to Jamie's drag persona reproducing a traditional reading of the diva as empowering, and partly a consequence of the lack of any strong female characters in the show with whom young women in the audience could better identify. So convinced are the teenage fans that Jamie's conflict with male authority reflects their own experience that they (metaphorically) empower him to speak on their behalf. And it is their enthusiasm for the male/female diva which blinds them to the misogyny embedded in the show and a perspective which automatically confers higher status on boys and men than on girls and women. The female characters are moths fluttering around Jamie's flame, and although Jamie is emboldened by his drag performance in a local club, his mother remains a dependent victim whose lack of glamour serves only to affirm her inadequacies as a woman. 'He looks better in a dress than I do', she remarks, thereby affirming Jamie's inevitable superiority in everything he does, purely because he is man. He is even better at being a woman.

Gregory Doran, artistic director of the RSC and of the company's 2019 musical *The Boy in the Dress*, maintains that his show, about a schoolboy with a desire to wear girls' clothes, is 'celebrating individuality'.[16] While this may be the case where the protagonist, Dennis, is concerned, it categorically does not apply to Lisa James, the enabling best friend who is the only female role model in the show. As with *Everybody's Talking about Jamie*, the girls in the audience at *The Boy in the Dress* are left with no option but to regard Dennis as their substitute spokeswoman due to the passivity of Lisa James and the absence of any strong or relatable women on-stage. The show frames Dennis's gender disruption as emblematic of the power of being true to oneself, but his 'bravery' in putting on a dress is never identified as being associated with his willingness to humiliate himself by pretending to be an inferior girl. Dennis's assertion at the end of the show that wearing a dress is no different to dressing up as Spiderman (or a pirate or a clown) contains the suggestion that the female state is little more than a costume that boys can try on and discard whenever they choose. The resulting message—that gender is fixed for girls and something that they *have*, but malleable for boys and something that they *do*—further enables the sexist ideology which infuses the show.[17]

The intimation that cross-dressing boys are more valid and interesting than girls does not, unfortunately, end there. The British writing team of George Stiles and Anthony Drewe premièred *Becoming Nancy* at the Alliance Theatre in Atlanta in 2019 with aspirations towards a Broadway transfer. This time the variation on the theme concerns protagonist, David, who is cast as Nancy in the school production of *Oliver!* No one on-stage questions the ethics behind giving the only female role in an already boy-heavy musical to a male student (regardless of how well he sings), while the by-now tedious adulation bestowed upon a boy who demonstrates his individuality by performing a version of femininity is given yet another outing. All three cross-dressing musicals lay claim to raising awareness of diversity with a lesson in acceptance of difference, but the shared message is that the casual appropriation of femininity is an entitlement of masculinity, and it is the role of girls and women to display unconditional support. *Hamilton* has been credited with enabling BAME members of the American population to include themselves in a nationhood discourse, but these shows, which deify boys for their 'difference', do the opposite: they consciously exclude girls from any concept of citizenship by rendering them irrelevant to national narratives.[18] In focusing on the necessity for the inclusion of the nonconforming boy within hetero-normative structures, attention is again successfully diverted away from the secondary position of women and girls within the same hierarchies.

No one would deny that musicals from *Hedwig and the Angry Inch* (1998), through *Billy Elliot* (2005) to *The Boy in the Dress* all offer welcome challenges to traditional masculinity, but the fact that there are no shows offering a corresponding message of empowerment to girls or women reflects the consequences of the exclusion of women from the industry. The liberation of masculinity on display in *Everybody's Talking about Jamie*, *The Boy in the Dress*, and *Becoming Nancy* is made possible by the appropriation of femininity, which is, in turn, enabled by the exclusion of women from the discourse. But if 'I'm an Indian Too' is regarded as unacceptable owing to the reduction of cultural heritage to a joke, why are the same standards not given equivalent relevance when applied to sex? that is, why is the grotesque parody of femininity enacted by the drag queen Loco Chanelle in *Everybody's Talking about Jamie* or the headmaster in *The Boy in the Dress* not correspondingly decried as offensive to women due to the reduction of femaleness to objects utilised to ridicule women in order to consolidate the superior status of men?

Blackface and yellowface were performance tools which knowingly reinforced power structures within a societal racial hierarchy. It is therefore unsurprising that in the years immediately preceding and following the American Civil War, theatrical performances which incorporated blackface reached the height of their popularity in the southern states.[19] It is not a stretch to draw a line from the Harvey Weinstein revelations which prompted the advent of the #MeToo movement in 2017 to the disproportionate number of recent shows silencing women through narratives which elevate the status of boys and men for assuming female identities. Add into the equation the musical adaptations of *Tootsie* (2019) and *Mrs Doubtfire* (2020)—two more shows featuring men masquerading as women—and it becomes impossible not to argue that a point is being made regarding the greater relevance to society of men and male stories. . Women, and an authentic female voice, which had only a tenuous presence on the contemporary musical theatre stage to begin with, are now being consciously elbowed aside with the justification of the higher imperative of inclusive practices for more deserving under-represented groups.

The fact that the stories from under-represented groups almost exclusively reproduce the male experience has not been recognised as a reflection of deeply ingrained systemic prejudice. That in itself is a clear indication of just how thoroughly the notion of musical theatre as a male preserve—prerogative, even—permeates the industry and its commentators. The irony is that far from disrupting accepted notions of gender, *Jamie*, *Nancy* and *The Boy in the Dress*, with their all-male creative teams and outmoded assumptions concerning the experience of being female, serve only to reinforce the narrowest definition of femininity. More pertinently, the shows reiterate who holds power within in the genre as the wider meanings circulated by these musicals tacitly reinforce a belief that women are irrelevant to the global production of musical theatre, on-stage and off.

## Post-Feminist Influences in New Musicals

The first new musical presented after the COVID-19 global lockdowns was Andrew Lloyd Webber's *Cinderella*, which premièred in London in August 2021. In the months leading up to the opening, much was made in the media (and in Lloyd Webber's Instagram and TikTok posts) of the empowered and empowering female voice at the heart of this show. Lloyd Webber devotees were assured that this 'bad' Cinderella was a modern, independent woman who had better things to do than dream of lavish gowns, glass slippers, and princes. In fact, she does exactly that, undergoing a beauty makeover ('I want to be hot, toenail to lash') to attend the ball, then running off to a church to stop the prince from marrying someone else. The fact that the show had a female book writer in Emerald Fennell (a family friend with no experience writing for musical theatre) was taken as proof that Lloyd Webber was now leading the charge for gender equality in British musical theatre. It did not, however, open up a conversation as to why Fennell was an anomaly in British musicals. The numerous claims of inclusion and equality conveniently overlooked the fact that Lloyd Webber hired a male lyricist and director to mansplain the perils of the beauty construct to contemporary women.

Following the highly publicised première, it became apparent that *Cinderella* is a series of set pieces on which tired clichés regarding bitchy middle-aged women and appearance-obsessed teens are played out by fairly unpleasant female characters, some of whom spend entire scenes dressed in lingerie. The narrative proves to be more focused on Prince Sebastian than Cinderella, and despite the promise of a female individual asserting her 'difference' in the opening scenes, Cinderella's rebellion consists of little more than a refusal to wear mascara or deodorant. Other than that, she conforms to the dependent, love-struck female stereotype, even spouting the line 'there's a boy I've set my heart on', thereby reinforcing the central theme that, even in 2021, every young woman is desirous of marriage to a man. *Cinderella* is another show subscribing to the fallacy that diversity means men who are not white and/or straight, and the triumphant entrance of Prince Charming with his husband prompts the queen to shriek ecstatically, 'What could be better than one handsome Prince, than two?' The response 'one intelligent woman' obviously never crossed the minds of the creators.

*Cinderella* is clearly intended to appeal to a young audience politically motivated by the Black Lives Matter and #MeToo movements, and Lloyd Webber has been quick to reference the racially inclusive casting as proof of his commitment to the diversity-and-inclusion debate within musical theatre. There is, however, no discernible female voice to back up the claims of empowerment, and slotting in a handful of non-white performers on-stage (via a white creative team) does not an interracial musical make. The eleven o'clock number, 'Marry for Love', is suitably worthy of the 'woke' credentials trumpeted in the programme, but it would be more authentic if a lesbian couple was included in the on-stage partnering to complement the gay male duo. The response of the critics, however, is evidence of the reluctance of contemporary commentators to critique shows which demonstrate diversity credentials (however spurious) with anything other than a positive review in fear of a righteous social media backlash. Only Mark Shenton queried *Cinderella*'s claims to feminism and noted that the brand of female empowerment on display in the musical was the same version that infuses *SIX*.[20]

While it seems incongruous to refer to anything in musical theatre as post-feminist, given that post-feminism necessarily follows a period that is recognisably feminist, what Mark Shenton is referring to is a contemporary assertion that female power is inexorably linked with a woman's ability to attract a man—a position wholeheartedly endorsed by

FIG. 33.3 Feminism filtered through the male gaze: the 'hot', glamorous six wives of Henry VIII after their costume makeover. Scene from the 2020 UK tour of *SIX*. *Left to right*: Jodie Steele, Maddison Bulleyment, Lauren Byrne (*at the back*), Shekinah McFarlane, Lauren Drew, and Althena Collins. Photo: Johan Persson © ArenaPal.

*SIX*. In the original 2017 production of the show at the Edinburgh Fringe, the six wives of Henry VIII were dressed in sneakers, long trousers, and baggy tops—a defiant challenge to the beauty construct. But somewhere in between Edinburgh and the transfer to London, a decision was made to glamourise the wives, presumably because 'hot' women are more marketable than androgynous ones. The glittering and revealing confections which resulted from the costume makeover leave the viewer in no doubt that these women are to be regarded through a lens of sexual availability and that their currency resides solely in their physical attributes. While this is feminism filtered through the lens of the male gaze, it is important to note that many young women do indeed equate the confident display of sexuality with agency. That said, the reworked costumes produce very different meanings within the empowerment framework than the androgynous outfits did. The makeover outfits reframe the exploitation of the male gaze as a choice, one made freely by women who are fully cognizant of both its implications and its ramifications.

The wives in the show are in agreement that being sexually attractive is more important than being clever and that the two are mutually exclusive. Concepts of the beauty ideal are employed to set the women against each other, and the entire plot hinges on which wife suffered the most through her association with the adulterous, controlling and, let's not forget, murderous Henry. Add to that the fact that the women define themselves purely in relation to men and spend their days sexting and swooning over various unsavoury male suitors, and it is difficult to pinpoint exactly how this show produces meanings which empower women.

The critics, however, have fallen over themselves to douse the show in superlatives, driven by a desperate need to reframe *SIX* as proof of gender-inclusive practices in British musical theatre. Almost as one, they have failed to point out the myriad ways in which the show reproduces patriarchal ideals relating to control over women's behaviour and appearance. Nor have they commented on the ethics of reducing six highly educated and sophisticated women of history into semi-literate Barbie dolls. Because, regardless of what is presented on-stage, *SIX* ticks the crucial inclusion box. And these are the same critics who habitually overlook the fact that the co-writer and co-director, Lucy Moss, is outnumbered by men on the creative team, which does raise questions regarding the authenticity of the female voice allegedly at the heart of the show.[21]

The Sara Bareilles musical *Waitress*, with a book by Jessie Nelson and direction by Diane Paulus, which opened on Broadway in 2016, could also be classed as post-feminist but in a more positive way than either *SIX* or *Cinderella*. The narrative of *Waitress* celebrates a domestic burden—baking—and reclaims it as a means of creative expression. Through baking, the female protagonist, Jenna, finds the strength to emancipate herself from unworthy men and gain self-fulfilment from engaging with a skill she loves and is good at. The all-too-rare authentic female voice permeates every song in *Waitress*, and every scene; it results in a narrative and characters which women can recognise and empathise with in a more genuine way than is possible with the shallow and unexamined 'girl power' message of *SIX*.

The musical celebrates sisterhood through friendship and in the passing down of female knowledge through Jenna to her young daughter, whom she teaches to bake. Domestic skills here embody female wisdom, creativity, and strength, and Jenna ultimately rejects male control and her own dependence on men in favour of female friendship. Far from undoing the gains of feminism, as *SIX* and *Cinderella* do with female characters who are disabled by their total dependence on men, *Waitress* values and elevates the status of skills traditionally assigned to women and infuses the show with the authentic feminist sensibility so palpably missing from the two British shows. In a sense, then, *Waitress* reclaims post-feminism and suggests that Jenna embodies post-post-feminism—a fluid state somewhere in between 'What's the Use of Wond'rin'' (*Carousel*) and 'All You Wanna Do' (*SIX*)—where baking and being a single mother are empowered choices and every bit as valid as sexual power over men. The tragedy of *Waitress* is that, other than *Mamma Mia!*, which is now over twenty years old, it is a lone voice in a post-feminist choir of faux women and female characters who willingly accede to every male demand.

## New Ways To Dream: Looking Forward

In January 2020 Rupert Goold, artistic director of the acclaimed Almeida Theatre in London, made a call in the British press for greater government subsidy to develop British musicals with under-represented voices.[22] Unsurprisingly, for the man who worked with all-male creative teams on his musical productions of *American Psycho* (2013) and *Made in Dagenham*, and, most recently, *Tammy Faye* (2022), Goold's understanding of 'under-represented' did not include women. Goold's citing of the British rapper Stormzy and of *Hamilton* as representative of 'where the exciting music is' makes it clear that for him, the term is racially determined. He is, however, conflating the terms 'under-represented' and 'minority', and the meaning implicit in each. Does he know for a fact that women's music is not exciting? Women are not a minority. They make up 49.6 percent of the global population,[23] but they are, without a doubt, under-represented in the industry to which Goold refers. Yet by regarding this fact as irrelevant, he excludes women from a discourse concerning representation.

The Black Lives Matter movement has been enormously successful in compelling the theatre community to examine methods of production and performance practices which privilege certain voices over others. Following the COVID-19 global shutdown, a number of Broadway musicals seized the opportunity to re-examine the meanings produced by shows within the context of race and to accommodate the new ways of seeing and knowing resulting from heightened awareness following the death of George Floyd in 2020. Since *Hamilton* premièred in 2015, for example, the show has fielded accusations of whitewashing the issue of slavery. Prior to the post-pandemic reopening, subtle modifications were made to the production to acknowledge the slavery embedded in the historical narrative, thus enabling the performers to gain a sense of control over the portrayal of the issue.[24] In consultation with cast members, *The Book of Mormon* and *The Lion King* also incorporated revisions which may not have been immediately apparent to the audience but were hugely significant to the BAME performers in the shows.

But while the issues concerning racial (mis)representation and the negative meanings subsequently produced on-stage are now regarded as a priority in Broadway musicals, the same consideration is still not accorded to women. As welcome as this new appraisal undoubtedly is, the steps forward to include and acknowledge racial diversity are happening within an industry which continues doggedly to discriminate against women. *Hamilton* may have incorporated revisions to the text to signal respect for racial identity and history, but the one-dimensional depiction of the female characters remains unchanged. And Broadway is not unique in this: it is exasperating that in all the four-star reviews and breathless adulation for the inclusive and diverse credentials of *The Boy in the Dress* and *Everybody's Talking about Jamie*, not one British critic commented on the all-white, all-male creative teams.

What makes all of this so disheartening is that this is a conversation which has been going on since the orchestrator Trude Rittmann (1908–2005), the woman responsible for the incidental music in almost all of the shows of Rodgers and Hammerstein (including the 'Small House of Uncle Thomas' ballet in *The King and I*, the second-act ballet in *Carousel*, and the vocal arrangements for *The Sound of Music*, including the now-iconic 'do mi mi, mi so so …' section of 'Do Re Mi') was refused a shared credit by Richard Rodgers.[25] It has been going on since the choreographer Gillian Lynne was denied the title of co-director for her work on *Cats* in 1981, and since Julie Taymor became the first woman to win the Tony for directing a musical in 1997. And, as embodied by Rachel Chavkin's award some twenty years later, it is a conversation that is endlessly recycled with no discernible change. Vocational institutions and universities frequently have more female students in directing and creative writing courses than male, and it is the persistent refusal to grant these young women graduates the same opportunities that are granted to men which is responsible for the absence of women from musical theatre. If there is any truth in the excuse that there are no female practitioners in the industry to include, then questions should be raised as to why artistic directors and commercial producers are not actively going into communities and educational establishments to support women at the start of their careers via initiatives similar to those being mobilised to enable the development of minority voices.

Enabling the representation of women on- and offstage in musical theatre should not be part of a wider conversation concerning the inclusion of minority voices. Women are not a minority and therefore should not require special measures to facilitate their accommodation: they should have equal standing as a matter of course. The fact that they do not comes down to nothing more than the resolute refusal of the men in charge of the global industry to cede even a modicum of control to women. It is both depressing and discouraging that no critic has found fault with the duplicitous grandstanding which parades woke credentials via the inclusion of diverse practitioners whilst at the same time pushing women even further out of the industry. Theatre desperately needs a more diverse and accommodating perspective, both with regard to the work that is created and in the audience that the work plays to. But diversity in musical theatre should not be gained at the expense of women, particularly as they have so little space to concede in the first place.

The crux of this entire discussion comes back time and again to a prevailing position that does not acknowledge or notice the chronic under-representation of women and the absence of an authentic female voice throughout the profession. Why, for example, were the ethical implications of the casual appropriation (by the entirely male creative team[26]) of Miss Trunchbull in *Matilda: The Musical*—a character quite clearly written as a woman in the original source material, but played on-stage by a man in drag—not interrogated by commentators?[27] To acknowledge it would necessitate action.

What it all comes down to is the kind of industry we want musical theatre to be in a post-COVID landscape. If the answer is couched in a commitment to inclusion and diversity that goes beyond words, then an intersectional conversation has to begin with regard to what needs to be done by producers, theatre boards, artistic directors, and training institutions to ensure that the global musical theatre industry is a space which can, and does, respectfully make room for women. Such a conversation has to acknowledge that it is not appropriate to have men speaking for women and telling their stories; nor is it appropriate to deluge the genre with stories about boys and men without offering an equal platform for narratives concerning girls and women. Because, as proven unequivocally by *Mamma Mia!*, the female voice is a voice that other women—who buy the majority of tickets to musical theatre—want to hear. As the global industry appears to close ranks around the metaphorical 'men only' directive looming over the creation of new musicals, it becomes apparent that the only place women are welcome within the industry is at the box office, credit card in hand. It is subsequently this 'failure of imagination' cited by Tony winner Rachel Chavkin which will prevent the genre from developing its enormous potential to be a real and lasting instrument of change—one which imagines the world as it could be and contains, at its core, a message of hope.

## NOTES

1. Susan Stroman won for *The Producers* in 2001, and Diana Paulus for *Pippin* in 2013.
2. 'Rachel Chavkin Tony Speech for Best Direction (*Hadestown*)', https://www.youtube.com/watch?v=hoQI88q39aE, accessed 10 November 2021.
3. Despite lukewarm reviews, *Mamma Mia! The Movie* took in $611 million at the box office worldwide, making it the fifth highest-grossing movie of 2008. '*Mamma Mia!*', https://www.boxofficemojo.com/title/tt0795421/?ref_=bo_se_r_1, accessed 29 November 2021.
4. 'Transcript of Julia Gillard's Speech', *Sydney Morning Herald*, 10 October 2012, https://www.smh.com.au/politics/federal/transcript-of-julia-gillards-speech-20121010-27c36.html, accessed 22 August 2021.
5. Lee Seymour, 'Over the Last 20 Years, Broadway's *Lion King* Has Made More Money for Disney than *Star Wars*', *Forbes*, 18 December 2017, https://www.forbes.com/sites/leeseymour/2017/12/18/the-lion-king-is-making-more-money-for-disney-than-star-wars/?sh=1063baf31ffo, accessed 10 November 2021.
6. *The Boy in the Dress* was put together by Gregory Doran (director), Mark Ravenhill (book), and Robbie Williams and Guy Chambers (music and lyrics). Before that, the RSC had (co-)created *Les Misérables* (1985), *Carrie* (1988), and *Matilda* (2011).
7. For more on the topic of stage entertainment aimed at and consumed by women, see Geraldine Harris, Geraldine Harris and Elaine Ashton, *A Good Night Out for the Girls: Popular Feminisms in Contemporary Theatre and Performance* (London: Palgrave Macmillan, 2012).
8. For a critical evaluation of how the women in *Hamilton* are portrayed, see James McMaster, 'Why *Hamilton* Is Not the Revolution You Think It Is', www.HowlRound.com, 23 February 2016, https://howlround.com/why-hamilton-not-revolution-you-think-it, accessed 12 July 2019; and Stacy Wolf, 'Hamilton's Women', *Studies in Musical Theatre* 12, no. 2 (2018): 167–180.
9. The creative team of the show consisted of director John Crowley, librettists David Grieg and Bill Forsyth, and composer and lyricist Mark Knopfler.
10. The musical was directed by Rupert Goold and had a book by Richard Bean, music by David Arnold, and lyrics by Richard Thomas.

11. See Krystyn Moon, *Yellowface: Creating the Chinese in American Popular Music and Performance, 1850s–1920s.* (New Brunswick, NJ: Rutgers University Press, 2005).
12. Lanre Bakare,"'Jewface' Row: West End Musical Accused of Cultural Appropriation", *Guardian*, 23 August 2019, https://www.theguardian.com/stage/2019/aug/23/jewface-row-west-end-musical-falsettos-decried-for-cultural-appropriation, accessed 29 November 2021.
13. For more on this issue, see Trevor Boffone, 'Whitewashed Usnavi: Race, Power and Representation in *In the Heights*', *Studies in Musical Theatre* 13, no. 3 (2019): 235–250.
14. The musical was created by director Jonathan Butterell and features a book and lyrics by Tom MacRae and music by Dan Gillespie Sells.
15. Stacy Wolf, *Changed for Good: A Feminist History of the Broadway Musical* (Oxford and New York: Oxford University Press, 2011). See e.g. the show's official Twitter account (https://twitter.com/jamiemusical), which features a large number of enthusiastic comments by its ardent female fan base.
16. Quoted in Mark Brown, "'It's about Celebrating Difference": *The Boy in the Dress* arrives at the RSC', *Guardian*, 28 November 2019, https://www.theguardian.com/tv-and-radio/2019/nov/28/musical-of-david-walliams-the-boy-in-the-dress-opens-at-rsc, accessed 29 November 2021.
17. Judith Butler exposed this ideology a decade ago, and her attack has lost none of its force. See Judith Butler, *Gender Trouble: Feminism and the Subversion of Identity* (New York: Taylor & Francis, 2011).
18. For how this works in *Hamilton*, see Elissa Harbert, 'Embodying History: Casting and Cultural Memory in *1776* and *Hamilton*', *Studies in Musical Theatre* 13, no. 3 (2019): 251–267.
19. See the discussion of the tradition of blackface in discusses the practice of blackface in Michael Rogin, *Blackface, White Noise: Jewish Immigrants in the Hollywood Melting Pot* (Oakland: University of California Press, 1996).
20. Mark Shenton, '*Cinderella* Review', www.shentonstage.com, 19 August 2021, http://shentonstage.com/review-cinderella/, accessed 2 October 2021.
21. SIX was co-directed by Jamie Armitage and co-written by Toby Moss who, at the time of SIX's premiere, identified as male..
22. Lanre Bakare and Catherine Shoard, 'British Musicals "at Risk without Subsidies like Other Theatre"', *Guardian*, 22 January 2020, https://www.theguardian.com/stage/2020/jan/22/british-musicals-at-risk-without-subsidies-like-other-theatre, accessed 29 November 2021.
23. These are the figures for 2017. Hannah Richie and Max Roser, 'Gender Ratio', www.ourworldindata.org, https://ourworldindata.org/gender-ratio, accessed 10 November 2021.
24. Michael Paulson, 'As Broadway Returns, Shows Rethink and Restage Depictions of Race', *New York Times*, 23 October 2021, https://www.nytimes.com/2021/10/23/theater/broadway-race-depictions.html, accessed 29 November 2021.
25. Recounted on the podcast *David Armstrong's Broadway Nation*, episode 15, 'Trude Rittman and The Women That Invented Broadway', https://broadwaypodcastnetwork.com/broadway-nation/episode-15-trude-rittman-the-women-that-invented-broadway/, accessed 2 September 2021.
26. *Matilda: The Musical* was created by director Matthew Warchus, book writerDennis Kelly, composer-lyricist Tim Minchin, choreographer Peter Darling, set and costume designer Rob Howell, orchestrator and composer of additional music Christopher Nightingale, lighting designer Hugh Vanstone, and sound designer Simon Baker.

27. Sony Pictures version of *Matilda: The Musical*, Miss Trunchbull was played by Emma Thompson (London, October 2022).

## BIBLIOGRAPHY

Bakare, Lanre. '"Jewface" Row: West End Musical Accused of Cultural Appropriation'. *Guardian*, 23 August 2019, https://www.theguardian.com/stage/2019/aug/23/jewface-row-west-end-musical-falsettos-decried-for-cultural-appropriation, accessed 29 November 2021.

Bakare, Lanre, and Catherine Shoard. 'British Musicals "at Risk without Subsidies like Other Theatre"'. *Guardian*, 22 January 2020. https://www.theguardian.com/stage/2020/jan/22/british-musicals-at-risk-without-subsidies-like-other-theatre, accessed 29 November 2021.

Boffone, Trevor. 'Whitewashed Usnavi: Race, Power and Representation in *In the Heights*'. *Studies in Musical Theatre* 13, no. 3 (2019): 235–250.

Brown, Mark. '"It's about Celebrating Difference": *The Boy in the Dress* arrives at the RSC'. *Guardian*, 28 November 2019, https://www.theguardian.com/tv-and-radio/2019/nov/28/musical-of-david-walliams-the-boy-in-the-dress-opens-at-rsc, accessed 29 November 2021.

Butler, Judith. *Gender Trouble: Feminism and the Subversion of Identity*. New York: Taylor & Francis, 2011.

Cavendish, Dominic. '*SIX* Review, Arts Theatre: Glorious Musical Meeting with All Henry VIII's Wives'. *(Daily) Telegraph*, 28 August 2018, https://www.telegraph.co.uk/theatre/what-to-see/six-review-arts-theatre-gloriously-musical-meeting-henry-viiis/, accessed 29 November 2021.

*David Armstrong's Broadway Nation*. Podcast. Episode 15: 'Trude Rittman and the Women That Invented Broadway', https://broadwaypodcastnetwork.com/broadway-nation/episode-15-trude-rittman-the-women-that-invented-broadway/, accessed 2 September 2021.

Harbert, Elissa. 'Embodying History: Casting and Cultural Memory in *1776* and *Hamilton*'. *Studies in Musical Theatre* 13, no. 3 (2019): 251–267.

Harris, Geraldine, and Elaine Ashton. *A Good Night Out for the Girls: Popular Feminisms in Contemporary Theatre and Performance*. London: Palgrave Macmillan, 2012.

Knapp, Raymond. *The American Musical and the Performance of Personal Identity*. Princeton, NJ: Princeton University Press, 2010.

'*Mamma Mia! Here We Go Again*'. https://www.boxofficemojo.com/title/tt6911608/?ref_=bo_se_r_2, accessed 29 November 2021.

'*Mamma Mia!*' https://www.boxofficemojo.com/title/tt0795421/?ref_=bo_se_r_1, accessed 29 November 2021.

McMaster, James. 'Why *Hamilton* Is Not the Revolution You Think It Is'. www.HowlRound.com, 23 February 2016, https://howlround.com/why-hamilton-not-revolution-you-think-it, accessed 12 July 2019.

McRobbie, Angela. 'Postfeminism and Popular Culture: Bridget Jones and the New Gender Regime'. In *Interrogating Postfeminism: Gender and the Politics of Popular Culture*, ed. Yvonne Tasker and Diane Negra. Durham, NC: Duke University Press, 2007.

Moon, Krystyn R. *Yellowface: Creating the Chinese in American Popular Music and Performance, 1850s–1920s*. New Brunswick, NJ: Rutgers University Press, 2005.

Paulson, Michael. 'As Broadway Returns, Shows Rethink and Restage Depictions of Race'. *New York Times*, 23 October 2021, https://www.nytimes.com/2021/10/23/theater/broadway-race-depictions.html, accessed 11 November 2021.

'Rachel Chavkin Tony Speech for Best Direction (*Hadestown*)'. https://www.youtube.com/watch?v=hoQI88q39aE, accessed 10 November 2021.

Rebellato, Dan. *Theatre and Globalization*. London: Palgrave Macmillan, 2009.

Richie, Hannah, and Max Roser. 'Gender Ratio'. www.ourworldindata.org https://ourworldindata.org/gender-ratio, accessed 10 November 2021.

Rogin, Michael. *Blackface, White Noise: Jewish Immigrants in the Hollywood Melting Pot*. Berkeley and Los Angeles: University of California Press, 1996.

Seymour, Lee. 'Over the Last 20 Years, Broadway's *Lion King* Has Made More Money for Disney than *Star Wars*'. *Forbes*, 18 December 2017, https://www.forbes.com/sites/leeseymour/2017/12/18/the-lion-king-is-making-more-money-for-disney-than-star-wars/?sh=1063baf31ffo, accessed 10 November 2021.

Shenton, Mark. 'Cinderella Review'. www.shentonstage.com, 19 August 2021, http://shentonstage.com/review-cinderella/, accessed 2 October 2021.

'Transcript of Julia Gillard's Speech'. *Sydney Morning Herald*, 10 October 2012, https://www.smh.com.au/politics/federal/transcript-of-julia-gillards-speech-20121010-27c36.html, accessed 22 August 2021,

Wolf, Stacy. 'Hamilton's Women'. *Studies in Musical Theatre* 12, no. 2 (2018): 167–180.

Wolf, Stacy. *Changed for Good: A Feminist History of the Broadway Musical*. Oxford and New York: Oxford University Press, 2011.

# INDEX

*For the benefit of digital users, indexed terms that span two pages (e.g., 52–53) may, on occasion, appear on only one of those pages.*

Tables and figures are indicated by *t* and *f* following the page number

## A

Aage, Sven, 206–7
ABBA, 220–21, 226, 438, 629, 758, 765–66
*Abbacadabra,* 220–21, 238n.33
ABC Theatre, 789
Abenius, Folke, 617, 619
Åberg, Magdalena, 633
*Abigél,* 847–48
Aboriginal Writers Oral Literature and
    Dramatists Association (AWOLDA), 864
Abuja Metropolitan Music Society
    (AMEMUSO), 897–98
*Accident of Love, An,* 599, 601
'Accident Waiting to Happen, An,' 304
*Ace of Clubs,* 411, 423–24nn.68–69
Acosta, Marco Antonio, 330
ACT. *See* African Consolidated Theatres
Aczél, György, 836
*Addams Family, The,* 71, 80, 85n.95, 519–20,
    623, 820
Adorno, Theodor, 3, 13, 226, 452–54, 455–56,
    457–58, 533
Aesaert, Yoshi, 258
African Consolidated Theatres (ACT), 158,
    159–60
*African Footprint,* 173
*Agreste,* 361–62, 362f
Åhlén, Carl-Gunnar, 624
Ahlsell, Herman, 618–19, 621
*Aida,* 10, 249, 251, 257, 584, 721, 896–97. *See*
    also *Disney's Aida*
Ainsworth, W. H., 669
Ajayi, Ayo, 897–98
*akgeuk,* 571–72

*Aladdin,* 871
Alba, Octavio, 324–25
'L'Alba,' 712
Alcaraz, José Antonio, 324–25
'Aldolpho,' 304
*Alice in Wonderland,* 160
*Állami áruház,* 827–28
'Alle Fragen sind gestellt,' 735–36
Allen, Lewis, 301–2
Allen, Peter, 178–79
Allott, Nick, 220, 231, 232
*All Shook Up,* 249
'All You Wanna Do,' 926
Alvarez, David, 902f
*Amadeus* (film), 734, 735
*Amadeus* (play), 734, 735
Amberg, Gustav, 131
*Amélie,* 276
AMEMUSO. *See* Abuja Metropolitan Music
    Society
'America,' 902f
*American Idiot,* 443
*American in Paris, An,* 682
*American Psycho,* 927
American Society of Composers, Authors, and
    Publishers (ASCAP), 103
'American Woman, An,' 730–31
Ameye, Christophe, 258
*Anastasia,* 249, 257, 560–62
Anderson, Maxwell, 456
Andersson, Benny, 28, 629, 758, 759f, 765–69,
    770–71, 777n.52
Andersson, Magnus, 765
Andersson, Nils, 619

934   INDEX

*& Juliet*, 632, 899–900
Andras, Gun, 618
'And the Money Kept Rolling In,' 721–22
Anglès, Daniel, 68, 76–77
Anmar, Berit, 629
*Anna Karenina*, 847–48
*Anne*, 478–79
*Anne of Green Gables*, 294–98, 297f, 310
*Annie*, 4, 10, 301–2, 329–30, 347, 355
*Annie Get Your Gun*, 91, 160–61, 920, 922–23
   Czech production of, 794
   Swedish productions of, 191, 192, 195–96,
      197, 204–5, 617, 621
   on West End, 372, 373–74, 375–79, 382–83
*año que nos volvimos todos un poco locos, El*,
   348
'Another Op'nin', Another Show', 906–7
Anselmo, Reynold 'Rene,' 324, 330
Antalová, Alena, 798f
*Antes tarde do que nunca*, 357
anti-Black racism, 895
anti-Semitism, 487, 489–90, 908
Antonenko, Aleksandrs, 896–97
*Anyone Can Whistle*, 510
*Anything Goes*, 219, 272–74, 808–9, 812, 920
*Aparecida: Um musical*, 355
apartheid, 159, 161–62, 163–64, 174–75
Appadurai, Arjun, 47
Archer, William, 91
Archie, Terence, 278f
Arden, Leslie, 295
Armstrong, Alun, 681f
Arnold, Malcolm, 674
Arnold, P. P., 430
Aronson, Boris, 11, 489–90, 653–54
*Arsenic and Old Lace*, 193
Asare, Masi, 874
Asari, Keita, 603, 605
ASCAP. *See* American Society of Composers,
   Authors, and Publishers
Asian British actors, 899–900, 907–8
*Asinamali!*, 170
*Aspects of Love*, 429, 510, 721
*Assassins*, 4, 527, 613, 721
Astaire, Fred and Adele, 371
*Atilla, Isten kardja*, 846–47
Atkey, Mel, 18

*L'Attaché d'ambassade*, 120–21
Auden, W. H., 684
*Aufstieg und Fall der Stadt Mahagonny, Der*, 22,
   454, 464–65, 482–84, 742
Austen-Peters, Bolanle, 897–98
Australian musical theatre, 16, 102–3, 867–68,
   917, 918. *See also* Indigenous Australian
   musical theatre
   *Bran Nue Dae*, 103, 180–81, 183
   British exports to colonial Australia, 160–61
   homosexuality in, 178–80
   *King Kong*, 182–83, 917, 918
   masculinities in, 175–81, 183
   South African musical theatre and, 158–59,
      175, 183
Aventura Entretenimento, 358
*Avenue Q*, 818–19, 820
AWOLDA. *See* Aboriginal Writers Oral
   Literature and Dramatists Association
*Ayrton Senna: O musical*, 354–55

**B**

*Baal*, 436
*Babadżane Koszebi*, 812
Babbitt, Milton, 677, 678, 681–82
*bábjátékos, A*, 847
*Backanterna*, 628
*Bada*, 584, 595f
*Badayeo Malhara*, 572
Baduszkowa, Danuta, 809–13, 811f
*Bagatelle ohne Tonart*, 678
Baguer, François, 328
BA Hons Musical Theatre at Leeds
   Conservatoire, 105
'Bailando el twist,' 80
Baker, George Pierce, 91
*Baker Street*, 294
*Balada pro banditu*, 794–95, 795f
*Balada z hadrů*, 783
Balanchine, George, 94
Balavoine, Daniel, 711
*Balcony, The*, 436
Ball, Benny, 298
Ball, Michael, 683f, 686
'Ballad of Sweeney Todd, The,' 665, 680, 685
Balme, Christopher, 2, 14, 131
*Bal w operze*, 809

## INDEX 935

Bandmann, Maurice E., 53–54, 131–33, 132*t*
Banfield, Stephen, 680–81, 684–85
Bányai, Gábor, 841
BAO. *See* Benny Anderssons Orkester
Bár, Pavel, 782, 800–1n.5
Baranello, Michaela, 123, 124
*Bare: A Pop Opera*, 354–55
Barlach, Björn, 618, 623
Barnes, Clive, 299, 302
Barnes, Grace, 31
*Barnum*, 218, 219, 267
Barnum, P. T., 909
Bart, Lionel, 412, 716n.5
Bartels, Bianca, 256
Bartók, Béla, 142
Bartošová, Iveta, 798–99
Bartram, Neil, 307–8
Barz, Meret, 488, 490
Bass, Eduard, 784
Batalla, Roser, 78
Bauer, Werner, 737*f*
Baumann, Helmut, 492–93
Baxter, Beverly, 404–5
Bažant, Jiří, 790
Beatles, the, 442
Beaton, Cecil, 205–6
*Beautiful*, 916–17
*Beautiful Game, The*, 438
'Beautiful Girls,' 494–95
*Beauty and the Beast*, 17, 77, 235–36, 247, 249,
  251, 253–55, 260–61
   Brazilian production of, 357
   Korean production of, 574
   Marmalade production of, 258, 259*f*, 260
   Mexican production of, 316–17, 320, 331
   Polish production of, 818–19, 820
   Stage Entertainment production of, 270
Becker, Peter L., 14, 45–46
Becker, Tobias, 120, 124, 131–32
*Becoming Nancy*, 922–23
Bednárik, Jozef, 797
*Been So Long*, 903
*Beggar's Opera, The*, 7, 409–10, 669, 675
*Beguiled, The*, 885
Behrent, Megan, 218
Beijing Dance Academy, 606
Belgium, Disney musicals in, 258–59

'Bella senz'anima,' 712
'Belle,' 714
*Bells Are Ringing*, 323, 325, 327, 329–30
*Bem sertanejo: O musical*, 355
Benchley, Nathaniel, 384
*Bend It like Beckham*, 880, 882–83
Benjamin, Walter, 13
Bennett, Michael, 6, 91–92, 95–96
Bennetto, Casey, 103
Benny Anderssons Orkester (BAO), 766
Bentley, Eric, 12–13, 39n.32
'Be Our Guest,' 259*f*
Berg, Alban, 677
Bergen, Ronald, 375–76
Berger, Juliusz, 817*f*
Berger, Michel, 710–11, 712
Berger, Peter L., 50–51, 54, 56, 58–59
Bergh, Åsa, 759*f*
Bergman, Ingmar, 26, 622, 626, 628, 630, 635,
  637
   *A Little Night Music* and, 615–17, 639
   *The Merry Widow* and, 615, 616–17, 621, 639
   *Smiles of a Summer Night* and, 25–26, 614–
    15, 616, 616*f*, 619–20, 621, 622, 623, 624–25,
    626, 627–28, 634–35, 637, 638–39
   Sweden and, 633, 634–35, 644–45n.126
Bergman, Ingrid, 194–95, 199, 206, 207*f*
Berg Ortman, Lisa, 635
Bergström, Lasse, 627
Bering, Rüdiger, 463–64
Berlin, Zeke, 557–58
*Berliner Varieté*, 8
Bernard Shaw, George, 39n.32
Berne Convention, 134–35, 573
Bernstein, Leonard, 480, 525, 702, 731–32,
  792–93
*Best Little Whorehouse in Texas, The*, 316
*Bethune*, 102–3
Bettison, Rob, 226
Beyer, Nils, 202–3
Bhamra, Kuljit, 882–83
Bhattacharyya, Gargi, 877
Bibby, Peter, 864
*Bibi: Uma vida em musical*, 354–55
Bieito, Calixto, 76
Bieri, Tobias, 528*f*
*Biff! Bing! Bang!*, 292–93

# INDEX

Big Bang, 584–85
*Big Fish,* 249
*Big Life, The,* 879
Bijl, Martine, 245, 251, 256, 260–61
Bílá, Lucie, 799
Billington, Michael, 179, 429, 686
*Billy,* 316–17
*Billy Bishop Goes to War,* 292, 300–3, 303*f*
*Billy Elliot,* 85n.95, 98, 347, 355, 362, 730, 856–
    57n.136, 907–8, 922–23
Bing, Herman, 483
*Bite of the Big Apple, A,* 299–300
Bittová, Iva, 795*f*
Black, Don, 715
Black acting methods, 876–77
Black actors, 894, 895, 897–901, 903–5, 906–7,
    909
blackface, 896–97, 905–6, 920, 923
Black Lives Matter movement, 914–15, 924, 927
Black music and theatre students, 873
*Black Narcissus,* 885
Blackness, 878–79, 900, 903–4
*Black Rider, The,* 537
Black vocality, in theatre, 874–75
Black women, 878–79, 903
Bladh, Curt, 635
Blair, Wayne, 878
Blankenbuehler, Andy, 94
*Blaszany bębenek,* 819–20
blaxploitation, 166–67, 173
Blažek, Vratislav, 790–91, 804n.50
*Bleak House* (Dickens), 674–75
Bloch, Felix, 125
*Blood Brothers,* 316, 331, 920
Bloom, Harry, 162
BMI Lehman Engel Musical Theatre
    Workshop, 91, 92*f,* 100–1
Bodrogi, Gyula, 829*f*
*Bohème, La,* 71
*Bohemian Girl, The,* 319
'Bohemian Rhapsody', 438, 440–41, 442
Böhmer, Wolfgang, 466–67
*Bo Jungle,* 160
Boldizsár, Miklós, 838, 842–43
Bollen, Jonathan, 176
Bollywood, 880–81
Bolsonaro, Jair, 362–63

*Bombay Dreams,* 881
Bond, Christopher, 25, 674–76, 682, 684, 686
Bontempelli, Guy, 704–5
*Book of Mormon, The,* 7–8, 927
Boosey, William, 125
Borovec, Zdeněk, 797
Bose, Neilesh, 881
Botelho, Claudio, 353–54
Boublil, Alain, 27, 429, 703–8, 716n.4, 716n.5,
    717n.6
*Bouquet d'Amour,* 556–57
Bourne, Matthew, 219, 397n.34
*Bowery Touch, The,* 407
Bowie, David, 436, 440, 711
'Bowler Hat, A', 654, 657–58, 659, 661–62
*Boy Friend, The,* 299–300, 305, 324–25, 327,
    337–38n.57
*Boy from Oz, The,* 178–79
*Boy in the Dress, The,* 31, 917, 918, 922–23, 927
Bracho, Castillón, 320–21
Bradesco Seguros, 352–53
Bradshaw, Peter, 226
Brahm, John, 678, 679, 681–82
Brandel, Åke, 624
Brando, Marlon, 560*f*
*Bran Nue Dae,* 30, 103, 180–81, 183, 864–66, 865*f*
    decolonised musical theatre and, 863, 877–
        78, 879
    Opera Australia production of, 867–68
*Bran Nue Dae* (2009), 866, 867*f*
Brantley, Ben, 248, 256, 277–78, 306, 307–8, 309
Bratton, Jacky, 339–40n.84, 666
Brau, Lorie, 565
Brazilian musical theatre, 345, 350–55, 361*f,*
    362–63
    federal tax incentives for sponsorship, 356–58,
        359
    Lei Rouanet in industry, 356, 357–58, 359,
        362–63
    local tax incentives, 359–62
    *Les Misérables* production, 352, 353*f,* 357, 358
Brecht, Bertolt, 6–7, 479–81, 483, 488, 489–90,
    683–84
    direct address device of, 741
    Kunze and, 741, 742
    Weill and, 22, 454, 456–57, 464–65, 481–83,
        484, 486, 538, 675, 742, 828

*bribonas, Las,* 133–34
*Brigadoon,* 160–61, 325
Briggs, Tony, 878
*Britain's Got Bhangra,* 882
British Asian musicals, 880–83
British colonialism, 158–60, 161–62, 175, 183
British musical theatre. *See also* West End
    American stars in, 371–74, 375–83, 384–93, 394
    postwar musicals, women and gender roles
        in, 374–78, 381–83, 384–86, 394
British National Theatre: NT Live, 57, 60
British New Dance movement, 95–96
Britten, Benjamin, 677, 680
Britten, Tony, 417
Brno City Theatre, 797–98, 798f, 799
Broadway
    Black Lives Matter movement and, 927
    Black vocality and, 874
    *Cabaret* on, 489–90
    Canadian musical theatre and, 291, 292–93,
        294–95, 296–300, 304, 305–6, 307–9, 310
    *Cats* on, 221–22, 222f
    dance training, 95–96
    deterritorialisation of musicals, 7–8
    drama musicals and, 731–32, 741, 745n.7
    exports, 17, 18
    German-language domestic musicals and,
        533–34
    German reception of musicals from, 459–
        60, 472n.67
    *Guys and Dolls* on, 403–4, 405, 409–10
    imports to Mexico, 318
    *Jesus Christ Superstar* on, 429, 703
    *A Little Night Music* on, 619, 621
    *Mexicana* on, 343–44n.123
    *Les Misérables* on, 227, 709, 710
    *Pacific Overtures* on, 660
    Schmidt on, 193–94, 208
    shows as middlebrow, 12–13
    Soho and, 407–13
    *Starlight Express* on, 429–30, 434–35
    *Sweeney Todd* on, 666, 678–79, 684–85
    van den Ende on, 271, 275
    West End and, 7, 19, 89, 90, 97, 371, 372,
        403–4, 429–30, 444, 533–34, 702–3, 781,
        868–69
Bródy, János, 834, 838, 840, 842, 846–47

Brolly, Brian, 434
Brook, Peter, 227
Brooks, Mel, 493, 494–95, 497
Brown, David L., 765
Brug, Manuel, 472n.77
Bruinier, Bettina, 465
Brymo, 908–9
Brynner, Yul, 905
Buck, Chris, 248
Buckley, Betty, 222f
*Buddy: The Buddy Holly Story,* 226, 269, 520
*Bürgschaft, Die,* 456–57, 482–83
'Burn,' 907
Burroughs, Edgar Rice, 254
Burston, Jonathan, 5, 6, 38n.13, 62n.26, 245–46
Burton, Tim, 686–87
Bus, George Abufhele, 349
*Bus Stop,* 388–89
'Busy Woman,' 919–20
'By Strauss,' 682–83
'By the Sea,' 685

## C

*Cabaret,* 4, 7–8, 160, 267, 269–70, 358, 487–93,
    617, 623
    Czech production of, 794
    at Düsseldorfer Schauspielhaus, 492–93,
        492f
    empowered female characters in, 920
    German-language productions of, 490–93,
        516, 519–20, 525
    Hungarian production of, 837
    on Nazis and Nazi Germany, 479, 483, 484,
        486–88, 490–93
    original Broadway run, 489–90
    original West End run, 490
    *The Producers* and, 493, 496, 497
    *The Sound of Music* and, 487–89, 490, 491,
        493
    Stage Entertainment production of, 269–70
*Cabaret* (film), 493–94, 496
'Cabaret,' 489, 491
'Cabinet Battle #1,' 895
CAEG. *See* China Arts and Entertainment
    Group
*Cage aux Folles, La,* 68, 70–71, 77, 78, 84–
    85nn.94–95, 510, 519–21

938  INDEX

Cai Fangtian, 25
Caird, John, 229–30, 707, 708
Calainho, Luiz, 352–53
*Calendar Girls,* 916–17
*Call Me Madam,* 374, 404
*Camera: The Ingrid Bergman Musical,* 632
Cameron, John, 706, 707
Cameron Mackintosh Organisation, 230, 231, 233
Campbell, Norman, 295
camp sensibility and aesthetics, 443, 495–96, 497
'Canada for Canadians,' 292–93
Canadian musical theatre, 18, 291–92
   *Anne of Green Gables,* 294–98, 310
   *Billy Bishop Goes to War,* 300–3, 310
   Broadway and, 291, 292–93, 294–95, 296–300, 304, 305–6, 307–9, 310
   *Come from Away,* 102–3, 292, 302, 308–10
   *The Drowsy Chaperone,* 292, 304–7, 310
   *The Dumbells,* 292–93, 306–7
   *Les Fridolinades* and *Spring Thaw,* 293–94, 295–96, 304, 306–7
   *Rockabye Hamlet,* 292, 298–300
   *The Story of My Life,* 292, 307–8
Canadian Music Theatre Project, 102–3, 105–6, 308
*Can-Can,* 324, 808–9
Cantoral, Itati, 317*f*
*Cao Xueqin,* 600
*Cape Fear,* 692–93n.86
capitalism, 3–4, 52, 319–20, 357, 456, 573–74
   racial, 877, 881
*Cargas d'água,* 363
Cariou, Len, 685–86
Carlberg, Eva, 630
Carlyle, Thomas, 670–71
*Carmen,* 799
*Carmen, a grande pequena notável,* 355
*Carnival in Flanders,* 373–74
*Caroline, or Change,* 527, 537
*Carousel,* 91, 560–62, 837, 926, 928
Carter, James, 480*f*
Carter, Jim, 414*f*
Casado Trigo, Alfonso, 230
Castillón Bracho, Mario, 320–22

casting
   belonging and, 903–7
   celebrity, in Korean musical theatre industry, 576, 583–89, 591n.21
   colour-blind, 896–97, 898
   cross-gender, 24
   *Hamilton,* 893–94, 895, 896, 898, 909–10
   *In the Heights* film, 894–95, 899
   inclusive, 31, 909, 924
   *Miss Saigon,* 903–4, 909, 920
   progressive, 903
   representation in, 893–96, 898–901, 908–9
   *Tarzan,* 254–56
   *West Side Story* film remake, 2021, 901–3
Castro, Rita de, 773
Catani, Alberto, 324
*Cat on a Hot Tin Roof,* 190, 191, 194
*Cats,* 7–8, 9*f*, 91–92, 98, 270, 928
   on Broadway, 221–22, 222*f*
   Canadian production of, 300–1
   Chinese production of, 594, 596–97
   Czech production of, 798–99
   German-speaking productions of, 507, 515, 520, 522, 525–28, 538
   global market for, 221–22
   Hungarian production of, 837
   Korean production of, 574, 584–85
   logo and branding, 223–24, 225*f*
   Mackintosh production of, 217–18, 219, 220, 221–22, 223–24, 225*f*, 235, 702–3, 706–7
   as megamusical, 5, 7, 8–10, 13–14, 16–17, 702–3
   Mexican production of, 316, 317–18, 331–32, 342n.114
   musical training for, 91–92, 96–97, 98
   Stage Entertainment production of, 269–70
   *Starlight Express* and, 430, 431, 434–35
   Stella AG production of, 269
   Swedish production of, 629
   translations of, 70, 233, 721
Cavett, Dick, 391–92
*Cazuza: Pro dia nascer feliz,* 354
*Cecylia Valdes,* 812
*Celebration,* 617
Central Academy of Drama, 604–5, 606
Cerchiari, Luca, 27
Cerniglia, Ken, 251, 257–58

# INDEX 939

Černý, Jiří, 791–92
Cerveris, Michael, 686–87
Chaim, Sandro, 358
Chaim Produções, 354
Champion, Gower, 298–99
*changgeuk*, 571
Channing, Carol, 373
Chavkin, Rachel, 914, 915f, 928–29
Chege, Silva, 898–99
*Chess*, 10, 28, 766
Chi, Jimmy, 103, 180, 863, 864, 865–66
*Chicago*, 7–8, 11–12, 26, 91–92, 95, 267–68, 532, 533–34, 594, 623, 722, 743, 794, 818–19, 837, 920
Chicot, Étienne, 711
*Chien andalou, Un*, 676
*Children's Hour, The*, 885
Chilean musical theatre, 346–50, 348f, 362
China Arts and Entertainment Group (CAEG), 597
Chinese musical theatre
　industry, 25, 53, 103, 110n.46
　localisation in, 602–4, 605–6
　*The Merry Widow* in, 132–33
　*Les Misérables* in, 233, 594, 596
　musical education in, 604–7
　musicals in translation in, 78, 98, 233
　original musicals, 594, 598–604, 607–8
　Stanislavsky and, 49, 50f
　Western musicals in Chinese language, 594, 596, 605–6
　Western musicals in original languages, 594, 595f
　Western musicals since 1980s, 595–97
*Chłopi*, 819–20
Chmiel, Józef, 812–13
Cho, Kangjoo, 24–25
Chopra, Sumeet, 882
*Chorus Line, A*, 6, 7–8, 26, 91–92, 94, 95–96, 331, 538
Chow, Broderick, 905–6
'Chrysanthemum Tea', 658, 661–62
Chu, Jon M., 894
Churchill, Winston, 371–72
CIE, 352
CIE Stage Holding, 269–70
*Cilla the Musical*, 916–17

Cima, Gibson, 170
*Cinderella*, 160, 594, 923–24, 926
*Cinderella* (film), 898
*Cindy*, 794
*Cindy Reller*, 534–35
Circustheater, 246, 250–51, 252f, 267
*Ciske de Rat*, 266
CJ E&M, 582–83
CJeS Culture, 587–88
Clarke, Kevin, 462–63
Clarke, Sharon D., 430, 439f
*Člověk z půdy*, 787–88
Cocciante, Riccardo 'Richard', 712, 713, 714
Cohen, Allen, 76, 77
Cohen, Malka, 299–300
Cohen, Nathan, 296
Colbert, Stephen, 894, 895f
Cold War, 384, 394
Coleman, Bud, 24, 332
*Cole Porter: Ele nunca disse que me amava*, 354
Collins, Phil, 245, 247, 249, 251, 255
colonialism, 159, 163, 170, 867, 868–69, 875, 878–79, 903–4, 905, 908, 909
　British, 158–60, 161–62, 175, 183
Color, Fernando, 356
*Color Purple, The*, 355, 527, 916
colour-blind casting, 896–97, 898
colourism, 894, 902–3
*Comedy of Errors, The*, 706–7
*Come from Away*, 102–3, 292, 302, 308–10, 623, 644n.122
'Come to Your Senses', 76–77
commodification, of triple threat performers, 94–100
Compañia Mexicana de Operetas, 136
*Company*, 71, 76, 91–92, 391, 525, 527, 537, 613, 615, 617–18, 621, 652, 721
'Concerto Macabre', 678
*Condicional*, 348
'conga, La', 80
'Connie's Song', 919–20
Constable, Paule, 219–20
Constanti, Sophie, 173
*Contigo pan y cebolla*, 330
Cookman, Anthony, 405
*Correndo atrás*, 360
*corrido*, 325–26, 338n.72

940    INDEX

Cortés Camarillo, Félix, 319–20
'Cortina', 919–20
Cottis, David, 21
Coveney, Michael, 302–3, 441
COVID-19 pandemic, 1, 89, 107n.1, 507–8, 579, 923–24, 927
Coward, Noël, 378–79, 381–82, 383f, 388–91, 390f, 393–94, 397–98n.48, 411, 423n.65, 423n.68, 436–37, 680–81
Cradle Will Rock, The, 784
Cranko, John, 674
Craymer, Judy, 220–21, 228, 231, 918
Crazy for You, 254–55, 300–1, 358, 605
Crazy Gang, The, 405, 420n.15
Cregar, Laird, 678, 679
Crooked Mile, The, 411, 412, 420n.19
cross-dressing, 918, 919f, 920–23
Crouse, Russel, 484, 485
Crowley, Bob, 219, 247–48, 251
Crown, The, 899–900
Csárdásfürstin, 848
Csárdáskirálynő, 827–28
Csárdáskirálynő, 1916, 848
Csíksomlyói passió, 846
cultural appropriation, 920–23
cultural globalisation, 3, 4, 5, 14, 50–51, 124, 572–73
cultural institutions, 48–49
cultural translation, 191–92, 198, 371–72, 464–65
Cupples, Julie, 868–69
Curtis, James, 408
Curtis, Richard, 441, 446n.40
Cushman, Robert, 307–8
Cyberiada, 819–20
Cybulski, Andrzej, 813–16, 815f
Cyrano de Musical, 267, 271, 276–77
Czardasfurstinnan, 621
Czech, Stephan, 123
Czech musical theatre, 29
    Karlín Musical Theatre in, 781–82, 785–86, 787, 791–92, 794, 797, 799, 800n.2, 800–1n.5, 804n.51
    in 1990s, 795–98
    in 1960s, 787–93
    under normalisation, 793–95
    Nový in, 781, 784–85, 786, 796

operetta and, 781–82, 783, 784–85, 786, 791–92, 799
Osolsobě and, 782, 788–89, 790, 791–92
pre-WWII, 782–85
Radok and, 786–87
Show Boat and, 782–83, 794
after 2000, 798–800
V + W in, 782–85

D

Daboo, Jerry, 881
Dae Chunhyang-Jeon, 572
Dafeng Musical Theatre, 98–99
'Da geh' ich zu Maxim', 142
Dagoll Dagom, 68
Dáma na kolejích, 790–91
Dance of Death, The, 626
Dance of the Vampires, 270
Dance of the Vampires (film), 736–37
Dance of the Vampires (musical). See Tanz der Vampire
'Dancing Queen', 78
Darcy, Marita, 864
Darlington, Jonathan, 460
Darwin, John, 46
Daubeny, Peter, 164
David, Michal, 799
'David a Goliáš', 783
Davids, Matthias, 465
Davis, Jack, 864
Davis, Tracy C., 54
Deacon, Charles, 223
Deacon, John, 436–37
Dear Evan Hansen, 12, 527
'Dear White American Theatre', 914–15
Death Note, 528–31, 587–88
Death of a Salesman, 80
DeBose, Ariana, 902–3, 902f
decolonisation
    of musical theatre, 863, 877–78, 879
    of musical theatre curriculum, 863–64, 869–71, 874, 875, 876–77, 880–86
    of musics and musicking, 873
    through subversion, 879–80
    university as venue for, 868–71
'Deep, The', 895
Degrande, Magali, 258–59

del Campo, Marina, 331–32
de Llano Palmer, Luis, 324, 330
del Río, Marcela, 326–27, 339n.76
Demcsák, Katalin, 830
'Denn wie man sich bettet,' 742
Dent, Alan, 411
*Deranged Marriage, The*, 882
Desblache, Lucile, 66–67, 72
*Desert Song, The*, 160
'Deshollinador, El,' 322
*Designing Woman*, 378
*Dětí ráje*, 799
Dewhurst, Colleen, 298
*Diabeł nie śpi*, 810–11
Diamond, Dick, 175–76
*Diana*, 916–17
*diario de Ana Frank, El*, 478
*Diary of Anne Frank, The*, 190, 194
Dickens, Charles, 410, 668–69, 673, 674–75,
    706–7
Dicks, John, 672, 673, 674–75, 676
*Dick Whittington*, 160
Dietl, Jaroslav, 793
'Dieu que le monde est injuste,' 714
Diggs, Daveed, 895
Dion, Céline, 712
*Dirty Dancing*, 918
Disney animated film musicals, 871–73, 907–8
Disney musicals, 7–8, 12, 54, 72, 98–99
    in Europe, non-replica, 257–60
    Mackintosh and, 217–18, 220, 224, 226–27,
        228, 233, 235–36, 247
    Marmalade producing, 258–59, 260
    McTheatre and, 245–46, 257–58, 260–61
    Stage Entertainment producing, 233, 246,
        249, 250–57, 252f, 258, 260, 275
    translation of, 245, 251–53
    van den Ende producing, 249–50, 256–57
*Disney's Aida*, 10, 584
Disney Theatrical Productions, 17, 246–47,
    249, 253, 255, 256–58, 259, 260–61
*District Six*, 169
'Dîtes-moi,' 385–86
*Divotvorný hrnec*, 785–86, 789
*Divotvorný klobouk*, 787
Dixon, William Hepworth, 668–69, 672–73
*Dobře placená procházka*, 788–89

*Doctor Herz*, 847
*Doctor Zhivago*, 820
Döhl, Frédéric, 23, 281
*Do I Hear a Waltz?*, 652
*Domingo no parque*, 360, 361f
*Don Camillo & Peppone*, 744–45n.6
Donnellan, Declan, 681f, 686
'Don't Tell Mama!', 489, 492f
Donutil, Miroslav, 795f
Doran, Gregory, 922
'Do Re Mi,' 928
Do Rozario, Rebecca-Anne C., 233–34, 705
Douwes, Pia, 733f
Dow, Steve, 181
*Down in the Valley*, 451
'Down to the Sacred Wave,' 770
'Do You Hear the People Sing,' 232, 707
*Dracula*, 271, 317–18, 527–28, 797
drama musicals, 27–28, 719–21
    adaptation of source material into, 736–40
    breaking of the fourth wall in, 741–43
    Broadway musicals and, 731–32, 741, 745n.7
    definition and key elements, 722–26, 724t
    dramaturgy of, 732–40
    as European form, 740–43
    inconsistencies in concept and execution
        of, 730–32
    Kunze and, 719–21, 722–29, 724t, 730–44
    as new subgenre, 743–44
    origins of, 720–21
    recurring features of, 726–29, 727t
*Dreamgirls*, 246, 429
*Dreamgirls* (film), 906–7
*Dreigroschenoper, Die*, 22, 675
Drew, David, 452–54
*Drowsy Chaperone, The*, 292, 304–7, 307f, 310
*Duddy*, 292
Dueñas, Pablo, 321
Düffel, John von, 466–67
'Du måste finnas,' 770–72
du Maurier, Daphne, 723–25, 726, 729, 730, 738
*Dumbells, The*, 292–93, 306–7
Dunbar, Zachary, 15
Dunn, Kaja, 876
Dunne, Michael, 387–88
*Durante*, 292
Durham, Christian, 228

942  INDEX

*Dusty: The Original Pop Diva*, 917
'Duvemåla hage,' 766–68
Dvořák, Antonín, 121
Dyer, Richard, 12
Dymling, Carl Anders, 614–15
dysconscious racism, 874–75
*Dzsungel könyve*, 847–48

**E**
'Easy Street,' 10
Ebb, Fred, 489, 905–6, 920
Ebsen, Buddy and Vilma, 90–91
Eco, Umberto, 439, 446n.40
*Ecstasy of Rita Joe, The*, 294
Edberg, Ulla-Britt, 620
'Edelweiss,' 486, 488
Eduardo Migliaccio Company, 136
Edwardes, George, 53–54, 125–27
*Egri csillagok*, 847
*Egy szerelem három éjszakája*, 828, 829f
'Ehrlichkeit und Vertrauen,' 729
*Eighteen Springs*, 601
*Eighteen Wheels*, 301
'Eine Hand wäscht die and're Hand', 722, 728
Eisenstadt, S. N., 48–49
Eisler, Hanns, 482–83, 484
Ekborg, Anders, 759f, 768f
*Elaine Stritch at Liberty*, 393
Elder, Catriona, 866
'Electric Chair,' 905–6
Elias, Buddy, 478
Eliot, T. S., 702
*Elisabeth*, 269, 513, 521–22, 533–34, 535, 536,
    537–38, 560–62, 561f, 719, 721–22, 733f
    direct address device in, 741–42
    as drama musical, 725, 726–29, 730, 732–34
    dramaturgy of, 732–34, 735–36
    *Marie Antoinette* and, 739–40
    *Mozart!* and, 735–36
Elizondo, Rafael, 328–29
Elsaesser, Thomas, 679
Elton, Ben, 438, 440, 441
Emericus, János, 843
EMK, 101–2, 582–83
'Empty Chairs at Empty Tables,' 707
*Én, József Attila*, 847–48
*Encounter, The*, 57–58

Endemol, 267
Engel, Lehmann, 91, 92f
Engel, Lya, 327, 328
English, Helen J., 868
*Entre sonhos e sonhos*, 360, 361–62
'Epiphany,' 676–77, 681–82, 683f
Erivo, Cynthia, 900
Erle, Thomas, 672
*Erwartung*, 677
Espasa, Eva, 14–15
*Esta Señorita Trini*, 346
*Eternal Road, The*, 451, 463
ETMB, 360–62
Everett, William, 702–3, 708, 716n.2
*Everybody's Talking about Jamie*, 907–8, 917,
    918, 919f, 921–23, 927
'Every Day a Little Death,' 619
'Everyone's a Little Bit like Shane', 177–78
'Everything's Comin' Up Roses', 379
*Evil Dead: The Musical*, 292
*Evita*, 13, 317, 330–31, 429, 519–20, 522, 572,
    798–99, 818–19
    Hungarian production of, 835–36
    Kunze and, 719, 720, 721–22, 726, 729
*Expresso Bongo*, 411, 413
'Eye of the Tiger,' 277
Eyre, Richard, 218, 219, 223–24, 228, 235, 236,
    413–14, 414f, 416, 425n.85, 480f
*Ezek a fiatalok*, 836–37
*Ezredforduló*, 838

**F**
Fábregas, Manolo, 329–30
FAC. *See* Fundo de Apoio à Cultura
*Fack ju Göhte—Se mjusicäl*, 276, 513
Fägerborn, Erik, 636, 637
Fagerström, Allan, 627
Faiers, Meryl, 231–32
Falla, Manuel de, 661
*Falling in Love with Teresa Teng*, 600, 603f
*Falsettos*, 908, 920–21
*Fame*, 331, 605–6, 629
*Family, The*, 606
*Fanny och Alexander*, 628
*Fantasticks, The*, 319–20, 325, 595–96, 598, 816
*fascinadoras, Las*, 325, 327–28, 333–34
Fasting, Kåre, 203

*Fausto-rock*, 317–18
Fei, Richard, 103
Feingold, Michael, 165–66
Feitl, István, 841
Fejes, Endre, 834
Felix Block Erben, 125–27
*Fences*, 899
Fenton, James, 686
Ferguson, Niall, 46
Ferris, Lesley, 879
Festival de Teatro de las Naciones, 346–47
festivalisation, 55–57
*Fiddler on the Roof*, 6, 7–8, 91–92, 94–95, 160, 316–17, 329–30, 572, 617, 662, 730, 908
   German-language production of, 511–12, 516, 519–20, 525
   Polish production of, 816–18, 817f
Fielding, Harold, 218, 226
Fields, Gracie, 376–77
Fierro, Luis, 347, 348
*56 csepp vér*, 847–48
Filichia, Peter, 308
*Fille de Madame Angot, La*, 812
*Filosofská historie*, 792–93, 792f
*Fings Ain't Wot They Used t'Be*, 412, 413
*Finian's Rainbow*, 785, 787, 920
Fink, Henry T., 119
Fin.K.L, 584
*Firebrand of Florence, The*, 451, 454, 461, 463–64, 465–66
'First Burn,' 907
First Nations culture, Disney animated musicals and, 871, 872–73
Fischer-Lichte, Erika, 881
*Fledermaus, Die*, 145
Fleet Street, 665–71, 672–73, 674–76, 680, 687–88
Flores y Escalante, Jesús, 321
*Flower Drum Song*, 560–62, 903–4, 906–7
*Flower Drum Song* (film), 904f
'Flower Garden of My Heart, The,' 411
Floyd, George, 927
'Fly, Robin, Fly,' 27–28, 719
Flynn, Denny Martin, 9–10
FNC. *See* Fundo Nacional de Cultura
*Folies Bergère*, 160, 557
folk musical, 28

*Follies*, 380–81, 494–95, 613, 615, 683–84, 721, 906–7
Fonoti, Dionne, 872
*Forever Plaid*, 307–8
Forman, Milos, 734, 837
*42nd Street*, 254–55, 271, 597
Fosse, Bob, 91–92, 95, 496
'Four Black Dragons,' 654, 655f, 658
Fővárosi Operettszínház, 828–29, 836
Frank, Anne, 478–79
*Frankenstein*, 819–20
*Frankenstein* (Shelley), 670–71
Fransson, Nina, 636–37
Frederiksen, Jens, 464–65
Fredriksson, Benny, 629, 630, 631, 635–36
Freedman, Bill, 296
Freeman, Ethan, 532f
'Freight,' 431
*Freischütz, Der*, 537
Frejka, Jiří, 785–86
French grand opera, 702–3, 716n.2, 716n.4
French musical theatre, 27
   beginnings of, 701–3
   megamusicals and, 233–34, 702–3, 716nn.2–4
   *Les Misérables*, 705–8
   *Notre-Dame de Paris*, 596–97, 712–14
   *La Révolution Française*, 703–5
   *Roméo et Juliette: De la haine à l'amour*, 714–15
   spectacle musicals in, 233–34, 702, 705, 710–15
   *Starmania*, 710–12
French Revolution, 670–71, 703, 704
*Freudiana*, 513
Friberger, Ulrika, 623, 624
*Frida*, 317, 317f
*Fridolinades, Les*, 293
Friedman, Thomas, 47–48
*Friedrich: Mythos und Tragödie*, 535
*Frogs, The*, 537
'fröhliche Apokalypse, Die,' 722, 735–36
*Frozen*, 247
*Fuehrer's Face, Der*, 481
Fuentes, Carlos, 318
*Full Monty, The*, 511–12
Fundo de Apoio à Cultura (FAC), 359, 360–63

## 944 INDEX

Fundo Nacional de Cultura (FNC), 356, 359
*Fun Home*, 68, 71, 76–77, 79, 79*f*, 527, 537, 916
*Funny Girl*, 511–12
*Funny Thing Happened on the Way to the Forum, A*, 316–17, 325, 330, 331, 525, 613, 645n.139, 704–5
'Für Sarah', 738
'Future of Opera in America, The' (Weill), 454–55

**G**

Gambatese, Jennifer, 249
Gänzl, Kurt, 125
García, Ricardo, 346
Gardner, Lyn, 230
Garebian, Keith, 411–12
Garfield, Andrew, 899–900
Garland, Judy, 496
*Gasping*, 438
Gavilán, Jimmy, 346
Gazdík, Petr, 798*f*
Gdynia's Music Theatre, 809, 810, 811–12, 813, 814, 816–21
*Geisha, The*, 812
Gélinas, Gratien, 293
Gennaro, Liza, 94
*Gentlemani*, 791–93
*Gentle Sex, The*, 374–75, 396nn.19–20
Geo Eventos, 358
Gerard, Jeremy, 436
German-language musical theatre, 8, 21–23, 27–28. See also *Merry Widow, The*
    *Cabaret* in, 490–93, 516, 519–20, 525
    *Cats* in, 507, 515, 520, 522, 525–28, 538
    Deutscher Bühnenverein statistics on, 507, 510, 512–13, 514, 522, 525, 527
    domestic production, 531–38
    *Fiddler on the Roof* in, 511–12, 516, 519–20, 525
    imported repertoire, 514–31
    *Jekyll and Hyde* in, 511–12, 515–16, 527–31, 532*f*
    Lingnau productions in, 522, 534–37
    *The Lion King* in, 516–19, 520, 521–22, 525
    most-produced musicals, 2016-2018, 519*t*
    most-produced musicals since mid-1990s, 509*t*, 517*t*

*My Fair Lady* in, 510, 511*f*, 512–13, 514, 516, 519–20, 521–22, 525
*The Producers* in, 496–98
reception of Broadway musicals in Germany and, 459–60, 472n.67
reception of Weill's American works in, 451, 452–54, 457–62, 458*t*, 463–68
role of musicals in contemporary German theatre, 507–14
Sondheim productions in, 515, 522–27, 524*t*, 526*t*, 528*f*, 537
*The Sound of Music* in, 486–87
*Starlight Express* in, 512, 514, 515, 516–19, 520, 521–22, 525, 541–42n.26
*Sunset Boulevard* in, 511–12, 515–16, 519–20, 522, 523*t*, 528–31
*Sweeney Todd* in, 525–27, 526*t*, 528–31
*West Side Story* in, 511–12, 515–16, 519–20, 525, 535
Wildhorn productions in, 522, 527–31, 529*t*, 532*f*, 535, 536
German opera industry, 456–58, 460–62, 468
German *schlager*, 27–28, 534, 719, 720
German *Sprechtheater*, 461
German *Stadttheater*, 452, 456, 461, 472n.77
Gershwin, George, 455–56, 682
Gershwin, Ira, 682–84
*Get Up, Stand Up*, 903, 918, 920–21
*Ghetto*, 478–79
*Ghost*, 515–16, 818–19
'Gib' ihnen alles, was sie woll'n', 739
Gil, Gilberto, 360
Gilbert, John, 7, 142*f*, 319–20, 324–25, 702
Gilliard, Julia, 917
*Gilt Kid, The* (Curtis), 408
Gilvey, John Anthony, 300
Gindt, Dirk, 16
*Gingerbread Lady, The*, 391
*Girlfriends*, 920
*glade Enke, Den*, 138
*Glass Menagerie, The*, 190, 193
Global Creatures, 918
globalisation, 2–4, 7, 14, 36n.3, 37n.5, 37n.7, 45–46
    capitalism and, 3–4, 52
    cultural, 3, 4, 5, 14, 50–51, 124, 572–73
    first phase of, 319

hybridity and, 880
standardisation and, 48–49, 50–51, 53, 54–55, 60
theatrical, 46–48, 50–60, 234–35, 280, 319–20, 333–34
glocalisation, 47–48, 100–3, 246
*Glöckner von Notre Dame, Der*, 249
'God, That's Good', 684, 685
*Godspell*, 625, 704–5
Gold, Edward Michael, 121–22
Goldberg, Whoopi, 271–72
*Goldilocks*, 388–89
'Gold von den Sternen', 729
Golomb, Harai, 67
Gómez, Marc, 76–77, 78–79
*Gone with the Wind*, 594, 595*f*
Goodall, Howard, 920
'Goodbye Broadway, Hello Montréal', 292–93
'Good Neighbor' policy, 19, 345
*Good Vibrations*, 271
Goold, Rupert, 927
Gordon, Robert, 19–21, 686
Göthe, Staffan, 634–35
Grady, Chris, 228, 230, 232, 233
Graells, Guillem-Jordi, 71, 76
*Graf von Luxemburg, Der*, 123
Gramsci, Antonio, 171, 827
Granados, Luis, 324
Grande, Ariana, 900
Grand Guignol, 676, 682
*Grand Hotel*, 560–62
Gray, Dolores, 19–21, 371–72, 373–74, 375–81, 377*f*, 381*f*, 394
Gray, John MacLachlan, 293, 301, 302, 303*f*
*Grease*, 71, 316, 319–20, 330, 340–41n.102, 629
*Greatest Showman, The*, 909
*Great Expectations* (Dickens), 674–75
Greenberg, Clement, 12
*Green Book*, 899
Greene, Robert, 557–58
Grewal, David Singh, 48–49, 60
Grey, Joel, 489, 490
*gringada* discourse, 318–19, 320, 323, 326–27
Grosch, Nils, 22–23, 454–55
Grotowski, Jerzy, 830
Grudeff, Marian, 304
Grun, Bernard, 121–22, 123

Gruza, Jerzy, 816–18, 817*f*
Gubelmann, Serbe, 711
Guétary, Georges, 682, 683–84
Gunter, John, 414–15
Guo, Annie, 233
Gurrola, Juan José, 328–29
'Guten Tag Hop-Clop, Der', 493–94
Gutiérrez Nájera, Manuel, 319–20
*Guys and Dolls*, 21, 70, 71, 195–97, 204–5, 372, 560–62
    *Ace of Clubs* and, 411, 423–24nn.68–69
    on Broadway, 403–4, 405, 409–10
    London premiere, 404–7
    National Theatre productions of, 409–10, 413–15, 414*f*, 416, 425n.85
    *Pal Joey* and, 411, 423n.65
    as performance of show business, 413–19
    Soho and, 407–13
    on West End, 403–7, 409–10, 413–19, 414*f*, 415*f*
*Guys and Dolls* (film), 409–10, 418–19
Győrffy, Miklós, 842–43
György, Péter, 826
*Gypsy*, 91, 94–95, 160, 373–74, 378–79, 397n.34, 438

## H

'Haben Sie Gehört das Deutsche Band?', 494
*Hadestown*, 527, 914, 915*f*
*Hadrian the Seventh*, 296
Haining, Peter, 665, 667
*Hair*, 7–8, 234, 291–92, 629, 704–5, 710, 814, 818–19, 837
*Hairspray*, 249, 271, 272–74, 511–12, 596–97, 899, 909, 916–17
Hála, Vlastimil, 790
Halévy, Ludovic, 702
Halfacree, Keith, 765
*Half a Lifelong Romance*, 601–2
*Half a Sixpence*, 218, 226
Halfen, Josef, 622
Hall, Adelaide, 371, 904*f*
Hall, Bengt, 637
Hall, Juanita, 903–5, 904*f*
Hall, Stuart, 159, 163, 168, 171
Halliday, Aria S., 896
*Hallo Szpicbródka*, 819–20

946 INDEX

*Hallyu*, 586–88, 589, 591n.25
'Halten Sie den Atem an!', 735–36
*Hamilton*, 12, 31, 508, 527, 535, 538, 653, 743, 908, 922, 927
  casting, 893–94, 895, 896, 898, 909–10
  female characters in, 907, 917, 918, 927
  Stage Entertainment production of, 276
  women of colour in, 907
Hamilton, Darren, 873
*Hamlet*, 317–18
*Hamlet: The Musical*, 298
Hammerstein, Oscar, 6–7, 91, 195–96, 386, 485–87, 489, 731, 928
Hammerstein, Oscar, II, 195–96
Hamou, Ish Ait, 258
Hana, Ranno, 561f
Hanák, Péter, 149n.28
Hancock, Sheila, 686, 687f
*Hangover Square*, 678, 679–80, 681–82
Haraszti, Miklós, 827, 844
*Harmincéves vagyok*, 833–34
Harron, Don, 294–95, 298
Hart, Charles, 7
Hart, Lorenz, 138–42
Hashimoto, Kuni, 661–62
'Hass', 742
Haudenhuyse, Stefaan, 258
Hauff, Andreas, 464–65, 468
Havelka, Ondřej, 796, 797
Havlík, Ferdinand, 793
Hayes, Walter, 405
Hazelton, Frederick, 672, 674–75
Házi, Balázs, 844
Head, Edith, 399n.62
*Heart of Scent*, 598, 599f, 601
*Hedda Gabler*, 194–95
*Hedwig and the Angry Inch*, 591n.28, 922–23
Heed, Sven Åke, 192, 202
'He Got It in the Ear', 299
'Heil Myself', 496
Hein, David, 309
Heinemann, Michael, 149n.29
'Heinrich schlief bei seiner Neuvermählten', 482
*Heiße Ecke*, 512, 520, 521–22, 534–35, 537–38, 540n.13
*Hello, Dolly!*, 4, 160, 329, 374, 386–87, 387f, 478, 787

'Helpless', 907
Hendricks, Freddie, 876–77, 883
Hendriks, Lieve, 259–60
*Here Lies Love*, 99–100, 905
Herman, Jerry, 78
Herman, Josef, 794, 797, 804n.51
Herrmann, Bernard, 678, 680, 681–82, 692–93n.86
Hersey, David, 433
Hertz, Nils A., 624
Hes, Richard, 797
*Heute Abend: Lola Blau*, 519–20, 521–22, 536, 537
*Hexen Hexen*, 744–45n.6
Heymann, Birger, 536
Heyward, DuBose, 680
'Hier in Wien', 735–36
highbrow, middlebrow, and lowbrow culture, 12–14
*High School Musical*, 98–99, 249, 596–97
Hill, Brian, 307–8
*Hinterm Horizont*, 266, 513, 520, 535
Hinton, Stephen, 454
Hinze, Roman, 463–64
Hirschhorn, Clive, 380
'History Has Its Eyes on You', 896
Hitchcock, Alfred, 678, 679, 738, 753–54n.133
Hitler, Adolf, 479, 480f, 481, 493–98
*Hjälp sökes*, 777n.52
Hjertén, Hanserik, 615
Hlas, Ivan, 796
Hlongwane, Gugu, 168
*H.M.S. Parliament*, 291
*H.M.S. Pinafore*, 319
Hoberstorfer, Gerhard, 630
Hobson, Harold, 296, 404–5, 675–76
Hofmannsthal, Hugo von, 55, 56f
Hofsten, Sune, 620
Hogan, P. J., 919
Holden, Stephen, 181
*Holiday on Ice*, 275–76
Holloway, Stanley, 673–74
Holmes, James, 462
Holocaust, 478–79, 484, 485
*homem para chamar de Sir, Um*, 360
'Honey Bun', 385
Hongmei, Liu, 604–5, 606

Hood, Basil, 125
Horkheimer, Max, 3, 533
Hörmann, Veronika, 528f
'Horst-Wessel-Lied,' 482
Hoskins, Bob, 414f, 418–19
Hossein, Robert, 706
*Houdini, la magia del amor,* 317–18
*House of Flowers,* 903–4
Höving, Elisabeth, 460
'How Far I'll Go', 895
*How to Succeed in Business Without Really Trying,* 704–5
*Hoy no me puedo levantar,* 68, 98
*Hra o lásce a smrti,* 786–87
Hubert, Roland, 711
Hughes, Langston, 458–59
Hugo, Victor, 705–6, 707–8, 710, 712–13, 714
*Hum Aapke Hain Kaun,* 880–81
*Hunchback of Notre-Dame, The,* 721
Hungarian films, rock music in, 836–37
Hungarian musical theatre
 *István, a király,* 29–30, 825–26, 837, 838–49, 839f
 *Jesus Christ Superstar* in, 833, 835–36, 840
 Kádár Regime and, 827–28
 musicals staged by professionals and amateurs, 828–30
 from 1984 to present, 846–49
 rock music in, 828–36, 838–46
 at Vígszínház in Budapest, 830–35
Hungary, under Kádár regime, 826–28, 842, 843, 844–45
*Hwaryeohan Sanha,* 572
Hyeyoung Ra, 24–25
Hytner, Nicholas, 219
Hyundai Theatre Company, 572

# I

*I Am from Austria,* 513, 560–62
'I Am the Starlight,' 431
'I Am What I Am,' 78
Ibáñez, José Luis, 329–30
*I Can't Sing! The X-Factor Musical,* 272–74
'Ich bin extraordinär,' 735
'Ich gehör' nur mir', 732–34
*Ich war noch niemals in New York,* 266, 277, 513
*Ich will Spass!,* 513

'Ideal World,' 919–20
*Idiota,* 819–20
'I Dreamed a Dream,' 707
*Idyll of Miss Sarah Brown, The,* 407–8
'I Enjoy Being a Girl,' 906–7
*If a Thousand Clarinets,* 803n.42
'I Feel Pretty,' 906–7
'If I Were a Bell,' 417
'If You Could See Her,' 489–90
Ignácz, Ádám, 836–37
Illés, 834, 837, 840, 853n.60
*I Love My Wife,* 160
*Imagine This,* 478–79
'I'm an Indian Too', 920, 922–23
'I'm Not That Girl', 906–7
*Impempe Yomlingo,* 173–74
Imre, Zoltán, 29–30
'I'm Still Here', 380–81
inclusive casting, 31, 909, 924
Indigenous Australian musical theatre, 863, 864–66, 867–68. See also *Bran Nue Dae*
 decolonised education and training for, 869–71, 876–77
 *The Sapphires,* 878–79
Indigenous South African musical theatre, 159, 161–70
'Inferiority Complex, The,' 320, 321–23
'In Praise of Women,' 619, 630
institutionalised racism, 159
intangible cultural heritage, 58–60, 59f
integrated book musicals, 91
intercultural performance theory, 870–71
intersectionality, 869–70, 878–79, 896
intertheatrical analysis, 666
*In the Heights,* 31, 527, 894, 896, 906–7
*In the Heights* (film), 894–95, 895f, 899, 902–3
'In the Heights,' 906–7
*Into the Woods,* 271, 525, 527, 613, 628, 645n.139, 679, 721, 722
*Iolanthe,* 319
*Ipi Tombi,* 166–67
'I Really Need This Job,' 94
'I Remember,' 634
*István, a király,* 29–30, 825–26, 837, 838–49, 839f
'It Couldn't Please Me More', 489
*It's Always Fair Weather,* 378

948 INDEX

*Itt élned, halnod kell*, 846–47
'I've Never Been in Love Before', 416–17
'I Want It Now', 438
'I Want to Break Free', 438

## J

*Jack Sheppard* (Ainsworth), 669
Jackson, Andrew, 388
Jack the Ripper, 679
*Jack the Ripper*, 586–87
Jahnsson, Bengt, 621, 624
*Jamie: Drag Queen at 16*, 921–22
Janeček, František, 798–99
Jangfeldt, Sara, 635
Janneau, Raymond, 703
*János vitéz*, 846
Jansson, André, 765
Janzen, Chantal, 250, 254–55, 256
Japanese musical theatre. *See also* Takarazuka
  Kabuki and, 558–59, 653, 654–55, 658
  *Pacific Overtures* and, 648–58, 662–63
'Jasmine Flower', 597
Jávorszky, Szilárd Béla, 843–44
*Jaws*, 680
jazz, 455–56, 460, 783
jazz dance, 875
J. C. Williamson Management, 158, 160–61
*Jedenácté přikázání*, 787
*Jedermann*, 56f
*Jekyll and Hyde*, 511–12, 515–16, 527–31, 532f
Jenkins, Henry, 564
Jenkins, Will, 713
*Jesus Christ Superstar*, 7–8, 77–78, 190, 317–18,
    319–20, 357, 511–12, 519–20, 522, 572,
    716n.5
  on Broadway, 429, 703
  Czech production of, 796, 797, 798–99, 837
  Hungarian musical theatre and, 833, 835–36,
    840
  Mackintosh production of, 217, 223
  Polish production of, 816, 818
  *La Révolution Française* and, 703
  as rock opera, 702, 703
  *Starlight Express* and, 431
Ježek, Jaroslav, 781, 783–84, 785
Jöback, Peter, 759f, 772f
*Jó estét nyár, jó estét szerelem*, 834

'Johanna', 685
*John: El último día de Lennon*, 348
*Johnny Johnson*, 451
Johnson, Bill, 378
Johnson, Catherine, 275
Johnston, Anthony Wyllie, 868
*Jonáš, dejme tomu v úterý*, 793–94
*Jonáš a doktor Matrace*, 802n.31
*Jonáš a tingl-tangl*, 788
Jones, Cliff, 298, 299–300
*Jongiyeo Ullyeora*, 572
Joo-hyun, Ock, 584
Joop van den Ende Theaterproducties, 267
*Josefa*, 317
Joseph, Paul, 879
*Joseph and the Amazing Technicolor
    Dreamcoat*, 316–17, 330, 331–32, 334–35n.3,
    430
*Journey under the Midnight Sun*, 594
Joyce, James, 676–77
Jubin, Olaf, 28, 705, 716n.5
*Judas and the Black Messiah*, 898–99
*Jump*, 575–76
Jun-su, Kim, 585–88, 586f, 591n.24
Just, Vladimír, 785, 802n.28

## K

Kabar, Judit, 839
Kabuki, 558–59, 653, 654–56, 658, 661
Kache, Imme, 462
Kádár, János, 826–28, 842, 843, 844–45
Kaiser, Joachim, 479
'Kälbermarsch', 482
KAMS. *See* Korea Arts Management Service
*Kanadehon Chūshingura*, 59f
Kander, John, 488, 489, 905–6, 920
*Kaper królewski*, 810–11, 821
Kaplan, Tony, 620
Kapur, Jyotsna, 880–81
Karantonis, Pamela, 30
Kareda, Urjo, 299
*Kariera Nikodema Dyzmy*, 810–11
Karlín Musical Theatre, 781–82, 785–86, 787,
    791–92, 794, 797, 799, 800n.2, 800–1n.5,
    804n.51
*Kat a blázen*, 783
*Kat and the Kings*, 171–72

Kaufman, George S., 404
*Kdyby tisíc klarinetů*, 787–88
Keane, Glen, 248
*Keating!*, 103
'Keep It Gay!', 496
'Keep On Standing', 277
Kellow, Brian, 385
Kelly, Gene, 90–91, 682
Kemp, Lindsay, 436
Kenrick, John, 8
Kent, Jonathan, 686
Keown, Eric, 404–5
*Képzelt riport egy amerikai popfesztiválról*, 830–34, 831f, 837, 848–49
Kerényi, Imre, 845
Kerr, Walter, 296–97, 302
Kersh, Gerald, 409, 421–22n.47
Kidd, Michael, 404
Kiernander, Adrian, 176
Kihara, Yuki, 872
'Killer Queen', 436–37, 441
Kinch, Olle, 625–26, 628
King, Joyce E., 874–75
*King and I, The*, 899, 905, 909, 920, 928
*King Kong* (Australian version), 182–83, 917, 918
*King Kong* (South African version), 16, 161–63, 170
*King of Jazz*, 455–56
*Kinky Boots*, 12, 520–21, 594, 820, 907–8, 917
Kirby, Blaik, 299–300
Kirk, Sung Hee, 70, 76
Kishida, Tatsuya, 556
Kislan, Richard, 731–32
*Kismet*, 378
Kissel, Howard, 306
*Kiss Me, Kate*, 160–61, 195–97, 478, 511–12, 519–20, 617, 621, 702, 808–9, 906–7
*Kiss of the Spider Woman*, 331
kitsch, 4, 12–13, 39n.32, 479, 827–28
'Kitsch', 721–22, 751n.102
*Kkonnimi Kkonnimi*, 572
*kleine Störtebeker, Der*, 534–35
'Klobouk ve křoví', 783
Klusák, Pavel, 793
*Knickerbocker Holiday*, 451, 464–65
Kobayashi, Ichizo, 553–57

Koch, Martin, 707
Koegel, John, 15–16
*Kolęda-Nocka*, 814–16, 815f
Kollen, Ron, 250–51, 252–54, 257–58
Koltay, Gábor, 838, 841, 842, 845, 846–47, 853n.60
*Komik*, 786–87
*Kőműves Kelemen*, 834–35, 835f, 848–49
*Königs vom Kiez, Die*, 534–35
Köpeczy, Béla, 846
KOPIS. *See* Korea Performing Arts Box Office Information System
Korea Arts Management Service (KAMS), 577, 577t, 578t, 581t, 582t
Korean musical theatre, 55, 101–2, 570–77, 580–83
Korean musical theatre industry, 24–25, 69–70, 98, 105–6
  attributes and prospects, 580–88
  celebrity casting and marketing in, 576, 583–89, 591n.21
  growth of market, 570, 571, 573–77, 588–89
  production system of independent production companies, 583
  SM Entertainment revenue structure, 587t
  status and size of market, 577–80, 577t, 578t, 579t, 580t
  superfans in, 576
  ticket sales, 580, 581t, 582t
Korea Performing Arts Box Office Information System (KOPIS), 578t, 579, 579t, 581t
Korong, 835–36
Korwin, Maciej, 818–20
Kościelniak, Wojciech, 819–20
Kosky, Barrie, 468
*Kőszívű – A Baradlay-legenda*, 847–48
Kovai, Cecília, 843–44
Kowalke, Kim, 452–54
K-pop and idol groups, 24–25, 570–71, 576, 583–87
Kracauer, Siegfried, 124
'Kråkesjöns dunkla vatten', 767
*Krakowiacy i Górale*, 813–14
Krehbiel, Henry, 125–27
Kretzmer, Herbert, 706–7
*Kristian*, 784–85

950 INDEX

*Kristina från Duvemåla*, 28, 629, 768f, 772f
    cast and creators of original production,
        759f
    countryside in, 765, 768–70
    'Du måste finnas' in, 770–72
    'Duvemåla hage' in, 766–68
    emigration and demographics in, 760
    on international stage, 773–74
    Kristina's apple tree in, 768–70
    *Mamma Mia!* and, 758
    Moberg adaptation, 758, 760–61, 765–68
    refugee status in, 771–74
    Swedish folk music and, 758
    Swedish look of, scenography and costumes
        in, 762–64, 764f
'Kristinas äppelträd,' 769–70
*Kronborg 1582*, 298–99
*krónikás, A*, 847
Kruger, Loren, 168
Kubišová, Marta, 793
Kuchwara, Michael, 306, 308
Kuckles, 864
Kulle, Jarl, 198, 200–1, 202–3, 635, 636
*Kumán*, 330
Kumar, Pravesh, 882
Kunimoto, Takeharu, 654
*Kunt u mij de weg naar Hamelen vertellen,*
    *Mijnheer?*, 254–55
Kunze, Michael, 27–28, 719–20
    Brecht and, 741, 742
    drama musicals and, 719–21, 722–29, 724t,
        730–44
    Levay and, 719, 729, 735, 736, 738, 743,
        744–45n.6
    Lloyd Webber and, 719, 720, 722
    Prince and, 719, 720
    Sondheim and, 720, 721, 722
    as translator of British and American
        musicals, 719, 720, 721–22
Kupfer, Harry, 533, 732
Kürten, Peter, 679
Kurt Weill Foundation (KWF), 463–65,
    466–67
Kushner, Tony, 901–2
Kutschera, Rolf, 490, 491
*Kwa Zulu*, 166, 180–81
KWF. *See* Kurt Weill Foundation

L
'Ladies Who Lunch, The,' 391
*Lady Be Good*, 371
*Lady Bess*, 717n.6
*Lady In the Dark*, 440, 451, 459–60, 461, 463–
    65, 480
Lagercrantz, Olof, 615
*Laila*, 882
*Lalka*, 818–19
Lambert, Lisa, 304–5, 306–7
'Lambeth Walk, The,' 372
Lan Creators, 98–99
*Landrú*, 328–29
Lane, Lupino, 372
Lang, Fritz, 679, 686–87
Lansbury, Angela, 373–74, 378–79, 380,
    397n.34, 685–86
Larios, Juan Jaime, 319–20
Larraín, Javiera, 346
Larsén, Carlhåkan, 622, 637
Larsen, Jonathan, 520–21
Larsen, Sven Aage, 197, 206–7
Larson, Jonathan, 899–900
Lars Schmidt & Co., 192–93
Lars Schmidt Productions Société Anonyme, 194
*Last Empress, The*, 575
*Last Five Years, The*, 354–55, 520
*Last Ship, The*, 535
Laurence, Margaret, 293–94
Laurents, Arthur, 702
Lawrence, Stephanie, 432f
Lawson-Peebles, Robert, 26–27
Leander, Zarah, 625–26, 627, 628, 634
*Leave It to Me!*, 382
Lee, Jeff, 250–51, 255
Lefévere, André, 66
*Legally Blonde*, 901, 918
*Legenda jménem Holmes*, 799
Legrand, Michel, 704–5
*Légy jó mindhalálig*, 847–48
Lehár, Franz, 15–16, 119, 120–23, 122f, 124–27,
    133, 136–38, 145
Lei Rouanet, 356, 357–58, 359, 362–63
Lei Sarney, 356
Lemper, Ute, 492–93, 492f
Leñero, Estela, 317, 319–20
Lenya, Lotte, 461

Léon, Viktor, 15–16, 120–21, 122f, 125
Lepage, Robert, 57
Lerner, Alan Jay, 196–97, 200–1, 463–64, 702
Lerner, Robert W., 329–31
Lesley, Cole, 382
Lester, Adrian, 681f
'Let Me Entertain You,' 379
Levant, Oscar, 682
Levay, Sylvester, 719, 729, 735, 736, 738, 743, 744–45n.6
LGBTQIA+ individuals, 896
'Liaisons,' 619, 634
Liang Mang, 103
*Liao Zhai Rocks*, 102
licensing musical productions, 69–71, 72
'Lied vom Soldatenweib, Das,' 483
'Lied von der Moldau, Das,' 483
Liera, Óscar, 330
*Light in the Piazza, The*, 527
*Like Father, Like Fun*, 291
*Lilac Time*, 160
*Limonádový Joe aneb Koňská opera*, 789–90
Lin Chia-yi, 98–99
Lind, Dagny, 622
Lindsay, Howard, 484, 485
Lindsay, Joan, 883–84, 886
Lingnau, Martin, 23, 522, 534–37
*Linie 1*, 511–12, 533–34, 536, 537–38
Link, Ron, 250, 255
*Lion King, The*, 17, 224, 233, 236, 247, 249, 251, 269
  Black representation and, 906–7
  Brazilian production of, 352–53, 357
  Chinese production of, 594, 596–97
  Dutch translation of, 251
  German-language productions of, 516–19, 520, 521–22, 525
  revisions during Black Lives Matter movement, 927
  Shiki production of, 563
  Stage Entertainment productions of, 257, 270, 275
  *Tarzan versus*, 253–54
  Taymor directing, 914
  translation by Kunze, 721
  worldwide profits of, 917
*Lion King, The* (film), 871

Lipský, Oldřich, 789
Liszt, Franz, 678, 680–81
'Little Grass,' 598
*Little Mermaid, The*, 228, 232–33, 246, 253, 256–57, 258–59, 260–61, 270
*Little Night Music, A*, 25–26, 91–92, 525, 613
  on Broadway, 619, 621
  in Gothenburg at Stora Teatern, 617–21, 618f, 622
  in Malmö, 621–22, 636–37
  in Norrköping-Linköping at Stadsteatern, 623–25
  *Smiles of a Summer Night* and, 25–26, 614–15, 616, 619–20, 621, 622, 623, 624–25, 626, 627–28, 634–36, 637, 638–39
  Sondheim, Prince, and Bergman, Ingmar, in creation of, 615–17
  in Stockholm, 625–26, 627–28, 633–36, 634f
  in Sweden, 613, 614, 617–22, 623–26, 627–28, 629–31, 630f, 633–39, 645n.139
  Swedish national tour, 1997-1998, 629–31, 630f, 631f
'Little Priest, A,' 682–84, 685
Littler, Emile, 378
Littler, William, 293, 299
*Little Shop of Horrors*, 519–20
Littlestar Services, 275
Littlewood, Joan, 743
Liu, Rene, 601–2
*llamada, La*, 348
Llano, Bill, 324
Lloyd, Phyllida, 226
Lloyd Webber, Andrew, 5, 6–7, 21, 96
  on *Cinderella* and female empowerment, 923–24
  in creation of *Starlight Express*, 430, 431, 433–34
  critical response to, 13, 40nn.41–42
  Czech productions of, 799
  in German-language market, 522, 527–28
  Kunze and, 719, 720, 722
  Mackintosh and, 218–19, 702–3
  postmodern theatre of, 13–14
  Prince and, 429
  Really Useful Group, 5, 218, 274, 430, 702–3
  Rice and, 7–8, 40n.42, 702, 703, 707, 716n.5
  Schönberg and, 703
  Wildhorn and, 527–31

952  INDEX

*Local Hero,* 919
*Lodger, The* (1927), 679
*Lodger, The* (1944), 679
Loesser, Frank, 21, 403
Loewe, Frederic, 702
Löfvendahl, Bo, 635, 637
'London Pride,' 680–81
*Long Day's Journey into Night,* 191
'Look Down,' 707
López Velarde, José Manuel, 332–33
'Lorelei,' 488
Lorre, Peter, 679
'Losing My Mind,' 906–7
*Lost in the Stars,* 451
'Lotta Locomotion, A,' 430
*Love Life,* 451, 454, 459–60, 463–64, 466–68, 467f, 480
'Lovely Ladies,' 707
*Love of the White Snake,* 594
*Love's Labour's Lost,* 879
'Love You I Do,' 906–7
Low, Peter, 67, 75–76, 77, 80
Lubitsch, Ernst, 138–42
Luckett, Sharrell D., 876
Ludwig, Volker, 536
Lugn, Kristina, 777n.52
Luhrmann, Baz, 179–80
Luis Fierro Producciones, 347
Luitingh Alexander Musical Theatre Academy, 97
'Lullaby,' 684
Lund, Alan, 295–96, 298, 299
Lundskaer-Nielsen, Miranda, 69–70
LuPone, Patti, 686–87
*lustige Krieg, Der,* 812
*lustige Witwe, Die.* See *Merry Widow, The*
*Luther: Rebell Gottes,* 535
*Luxemburg grófja,* 827–28
Lynes, Russell, 12
Lynne, Gillian, 96, 221, 720, 928

**M**

*M,* 679, 680–81
*Macbeth,* 164–66, 706–7
Macdonald, Dwight, 12–13
Mack, Robert, 665
*Mack and Mabel,* 298–99

Mackintosh, Cameron, 6–8, 54, 229f, 296, 433, 918
  brand of, protecting, 223
  *Cats* production by, 217–18, 219, 221–22, 223–24, 225f, 235, 702–3, 706–7
  Chinese productions by, 597
  Disney musicals and, 217–18, 220, 224, 226–27, 228, 233, 235–36, 247
  global branding, 223–27, 225f
  in globalisation of musical theatre, 234–35
  global reproduction, quality control and, 227–29
  *Jesus Christ Superstar* production by, 217, 223
  Lloyd Webber and, 218–19, 702–3
  megamusicals and, 5, 7, 16–17, 69, 233–34, 702–3, 716n.4
  *Les Misèrables* production by, 27, 217, 218, 220–21, 224, 225f, 226, 227, 228, 229–31, 232, 235, 706–7, 708, 709
  *Miss Saigon* production by, 217, 219, 224, 225f, 227, 228–29, 231, 235, 236f
  at Music Theatre International, 69–70
  *Oliver!* production by, 703
  *The Phantom of the Opera* production by, 217, 218–19, 224, 225f, 231, 234, 235
  role of producer and, 218–21
  RSC and, 231
  on Salonga, 99
  as standard setter, 234–37
  theatre infrastructure and, 233–34
  tourism, ticket sales and, 234
  translation and, 232–33
*Macunaíma: Uma rapsódia musical,* 355
*Madagaskar,* 810–12
*Madame Sans-Gêne,* 812–13
*Mädchen Rosemarie, Das,* 532
Madden, Madeleine, 885–86
*Made in Dagenham,* 916–17, 919–20, 921, 927
*Made in Hungária,* 847–48
Magaña, Sergio, 320, 321–23, 325–27
Magaña Esquivel, Antonio, 328
Mago, 622, 625, 627–28
Maheu, Gilles, 712
Mahler, Gustav, 123
*Maiden's Prayer, A,* 483–84
Makeham, Paul, 864–65
Malásek, Jiří, 790

*Malinche,* 317
Malm, Sven, 622
Malmberg, Arne, 624
Malmsjö, Jan, 626
*malvadas, As,* 353
*Mame,* 160, 330–31, 341n.106
*Mamma Mia!,* 5, 7–8, 68, 78, 98, 220–21, 231,
    520, 632, 820
  Chilean production of, 347, 348
  Chinese production of, 594, 596–97
  *Kristina från Duvemåla* and, 758
  Littlestar Services production of, 275
  logo for, 226
  *Mentiras* and, 317–18
  Stage Holding and Stage Entertainment
    productions of, 269–70, 275
  translation by Kunze, 721
  *We Will Rock You* and, 436, 438
  women as consumers of, 918
  women producing and creating, 916, 926,
    928–29
Mandela, Nelson, 162, 167–68, 171, 172, 174–75
*Mandela Trilogy, The,* 174–75, 180–81
*Man of La Mancha,* 329, 572, 704–5, 820
*Man Who Laughs, The,* 528–31, 589
Marcus, George, 47–48
'Margherita,' 712
Margittai, Ági, 829f
*Marguérite,* 704–5
María, Angélica, 330
Maria y Campos, Armando de, 321, 324, 327–
    28, 332
*Mar i cel,* 68
*Marie Antoinette,* 719, 721–22, 739f
  direct address device in, 741–42, 743
  as drama musical, 726, 728, 729, 736, 738–40
  dramaturgy of, 738–40
  *Elisabeth* and, 739–40
*Maritana,* 319
marketisation, 51–53
*Markisinnan de Sade,* 628
Marmalade, 258–59, 259f, 260
'Married Man,' 218–19
'Marry for Love,' 924
*Marry Me a Little,* 76
Marsh, Dave, 442–43
Martin, Bob, 304–5

Martin, Mary, 19–21, 371–72, 373, 374, 376,
    378, 380, 381–83, 383f, 384–87, 387f, 393,
    397–98n.48, 398n.56, 399nn.62–63,
    399nn.64–65
Martin, Tyr, 624
*Martin Guerre,* 218, 224, 225f
Marton, László, 830, 831–32
*Mary Poppins,* 76, 219, 220, 228, 233, 236, 247,
    249, 516–19, 916–17
Masakazu, Yamazaki, 565
Maslen, T. J., 668–69
'Masquerade,' 722
Masteroff, Joe, 487, 489
'Master of the House,' 707
*Mata Hari,* 101–2, 528–31
*Matilda,* 535–36, 538, 916–17, 928
Matshikiza, Todd, 162
Matsuda, Kazuhiko, 232–33
*Má vlast,* 482
May, Brian, 436–37
Mayes, Sean, 877
*Mayflower,* 704–5
McBurney, Simon, 57–58
McCabe, Michael, 234–35
McDonaldisation, 5, 37n.9
McGrath, John, 743
McKee, Robert, 720–21
McKellar, Don, 304–5, 306
McKenzie, Julia, 414–16, 681f
McLaren, Robert Malcolm, 164–65
McTheatre, 4–7, 62n.26, 96–97, 245–46, 257–
    58, 260–61
  megamusicals and, 5, 54, 69, 245–46
McWorld culture, 47–48, 51, 54
Mda, Zakes, 170
*Me and My Girl,* 372, 560–62
Mear, Stephen, 219
mediatisation, 57–58
Meehan, Thomas, 493
'Meeskite,' 487–88
megamusicals, 917
  for American and British audiences, 429
  *Cats,* 5, 7, 8–10, 13–14, 16–17, 702–3
  French musical theatre and, 233–34, 702–3,
    716nn.2–4
  Mackintosh in rise of, 5, 7, 16–17, 69, 233–34,
    702–3, 716n.4

954 INDEX

megamusicals (*cont.*)
McTheatre and, 5, 54, 69, 245–46
*Les Misérables,* 708–10
problems of categorisation, 8–12
spectacle musicals and, 716nn.2–3
training for, 93
translation of, 69
Mehmert, Gil, 465
Mehr-BB Entertainment, 512
Meilhac, Henri, 120–21
Meilhac, Henry, 702
'Me in the Sky,' 309
Meisel, Myron, 442
Melo, Juan Vicente, 328–29
Mencken, H. L., 731
Méndez, Emilio, 18–19
Méndez, Guillermo, 331–32
Mendoza, Edmundo, 320–23, 327,
339–40n.84
*Mentiras,* 317–18, 332–33, 333*f,* 342n.113
Menze, Jonas, 17–18
Mercury, Freddie, 436–38, 437*f,* 440, 443
*Mercury, la leyenda,* 348–49
Mercury Musical Developments, 91, 100–1
Merman, Ethel, 20*f,* 373–74, 376–77, 378, 382–
83, 393
*Meropa,* 160, 166–67
Merrick, David, 218
*Merrily We Roll Along,* 510, 527, 613
*Merry Widow, The,* 7, 34*f,* 119–20, 126*f,* 143*f*
Bandmann Company productions of, 131–
33, 132*t*
Bergman, Ingmar, and, 615, 616–17, 621, 639
countries producing versions of, 129*t*
film and television adaptations, 138–42, 139*f,*
142*f*
in immigrant North America, 134–36
in Latin America, 133–34
Lehár, Stein, and Léon at five hundredth
performance of, 122*f*
Norwegian version of, 128*f*
opera house productions of, 144*f,* 145
parodies of, 136–38, 137*t,* 142
premières, 1905-1909, 128*t*
Savage producing and promoting, 125–29,
130*f,* 134–35
status of operetta and, 124–25

translations and international productions
of, 125–29, 131–36, 706
work and composer, 120–23
*Merry Widow Burlesque,* 136–38
'Merry Widow Waltz, The,' 119, 142
Merta, Zdenek, 797–98, 799
Mészáros, Tamás, 839, 841
#MeToo movement, 737, 914–15, 923, 924
*Metro,* 820
*Metropolis,* 10, 11*f*
Metropolitan Opera, 145
Metropolitan Opera: Live in HD, 57, 60
*Mexicana,* 343–44n.123
Mexican musical theatre, 18–19
*Beauty and the Beast* production, 316–17,
320, 331
*The Boy Friend* production, 324–25, 327,
337–38n.57
*Cats* production, 316, 317–18, 331–32,
342n.114
*Las fascinadoras,* 325, 327–28, 333–34
*gringada* discourse on, 318–19, 320, 323,
326–27
importation of musicals, 316–17, 318–20, 323
integrated musicals in, 325–29
*Landrú,* 328–29
*Mentiras,* 317–18, 332–33, 342n.113
*Les Misérables* in, 316–17, 320, 331
*Ni fu ni fa,* 320–23, 325–26, 327–28, 332,
336n.26
original musicals, 317–18, 320
*The Phantom of the Opera* in, 317–18, 320,
331, 341–42n.108
*¡Qué plantón!,* 317–18, 331–32, 333–34
*Rentas congeladas,* 325–28, 326*f,* 333–34
revivals in, 330–31
successful musicals in Mexico City, 329–31
*teatro de revista* in, 317, 321–22, 323, 324–25,
326–27, 332–34, 335n.4, 337–38n.57
Televisa and Televiteatros in, 316–17, 330–31
translations for, 316, 332–33,
342–43nn.114–15
Meza, Ana María, 349
Michalski, Igor, 820
*Midsummer Night's Dream, A,* 164, 227, 818–19
Mielziner, Jo, 404
Mihyang Ginther, Amy, 874–75

INDEX 955

*Mikado, The,* 68
Miklós, Tibor, 835–36, 846
Mille, Agnes de, 94–95
Miller, Patina, 272, 273f
Mills, Bart, 831–32, 833
*Milton Nascimento: Nada será como antes,* 354
'Min astrakan,' 768–69
Ming, Wei, 601
'Min lust till dej,' 767–68
Minnelli, Liza, 436–38
Minnelli, Vincente, 682
*Minor Adjustment, A,* 291
*Minstrel Scandals, The,* 160
Miranda, Lin-Manuel, 893–94, 895, 899–900,
    902–3, 909–10
*Misantropen,* 628
*Misérables, Les,* 5, 7–8, 10, 429, 572, 716n.5,
    906–7
    Boublil and Schönberg and, 705–8
    Brazilian production of, 352, 353f, 357, 358
    on Broadway, 227, 709, 710
    Canadian production of, 300–1, 309
    Chinese production of, 233, 594, 596
    cultural sensitivity and taste in producing,
        232
    Czech production of, 795–96
    logo and branding, 224, 225f, 226
    Mackintosh production of, 27, 217, 218, 220–
        21, 224, 225f, 226, 227, 228, 229–31, 232,
        235, 706–7, 708, 709
    as megamusical, 708–10
    Mexican production of, 316–17, 320, 331
    musical training for, 96–97, 98
    Nigerian production of, 897–98
    Polish production of, 816, 818
    Swedish production of, 629
    translations of, 67, 232–33, 707
    van den Ende producing, 267
*Misérables, Les* (Hugo), 705–6, 707–8, 710
*Miss Julie,* 621
*Miss Saigon,* 96–97, 99–100, 100f, 232, 520, 605,
    798–99
    Canadian production of, 300–1
    casting, 903–4, 909, 920
    Mackintosh production of, 217, 219, 224,
        225f, 227, 228–29, 231, 235, 236f
    orientalism in, 901

*Mistrz i Małgorzata,* 819–20
*Mitislaw der Moderne,* 136–38
Miyamoto, Amon, 26, 306, 648–49, 651, 653,
    654–56, 655f, 656f, 657f, 658–61, 662
Miyuki, Tsuugi, 564
*Moana,* 31, 871, 872, 895, 896
*Moana JR,* 872–73
Moberg, Vilhelm, 28, 758, 760–61, 765–69
Mock-O'Hara, Johannes, 279
Möeller, Charles, 353–54
Mofokeng, Jerry, 170
Mol, John de, 267
'Moldova Song,' 482
Molnár Gál, Péter, 833–34, 846
'Mondd, te kit választanál?,' 842
'Money Song, The,' 489
*Mon Paris,* 556, 560–62
Monsiváis, Carlos, 318, 320, 338n.72
Montanaro, Anna, 532
*Monte Cristo,* 797
*Monte Cristo grófja,* 847–48
*Moon for the Misbegotten, A,* 298
Moore, John, 865f
Moore, Mavor, 293, 295–96, 301
Moorhouse, Ward, 391
Mordden, Ethan, 435, 731
Moreno, Rita, 894, 895f, 899, 901–3
'morgige Tag ist mein, Der,' 488
*Morir de amor,* 347–48, 348f, 362
Morley, Sheridan, 709–10
Morrison, Greg, 304
Morton, Edward, 125
Moša, Stanislav, 797–98, 798f, 799
Moss, Lucy, 926
Mota, Fernando, 326–27, 339n.79
Mottl, Bernd, 465
*Moulin Rouge,* 918
*Mozart!,* 533, 560–62, 585–87, 586f, 591n.24,
    719, 721–22
    direct address device in, 741–42
    as drama musical, 723, 725–26, 729, 732,
        734–36
    dramaturgy of, 732, 734–36
    *Elisabeth* and, 735–36
    *Marie Antoinette* and, 740
Mozart, Wolfgang Amadeus, 173–74, 734
*MPB: Musical popular brasileiro,* 354–55

956 INDEX

*Mrs Doubtfire*, 923
*Mrs Henderson Presents*, 916–17
Msomi, Welcome, 164–65
MTI. *See* Music Theatre International
*Mudança de hábito*, 357
*Mulan*, 871–72, 888n.26
*Mula sa Buwan*, 102
Muller, Martino, 712
Mundim, Tiago, 19
*Murder for Two*, 348
*Muriel's Wedding*, 226, 918, 919
musealisation, 58–60
musicalisation, 53–55
musical theatre training, 15, 89–90, 93,
    287n.103, 321–22, 536
  for acting, 876–77
  in Brazil, 350, 361–62
  in Chile, 349–50
  in China, 604–7
  choice of works to study in, 877
  for dance and embodiment, 875
  decolonisation of musical theatre
    curriculum, 863–64, 869–71, 874, 875,
    876–77, 880–86
  global transmission of, 93
  glocalisation of musical theatre writing and,
    100–3
  history of, 90–92
  integration and collaboration in, 90, 93, 104
  multidisciplinary, 89, 101, 104, 105
  in Poland, 810–11, 811f, 813, 821
  race, ethnicity, and gender in, 105–6
  for singing and speech, 874–75
  for Sondheim, 91–92, 93
  in Sweden, 613, 629
  for triple threat performers, 94–100, 104–5
musicking, 873, 888n.32
*Music Man, The*, 25, 595–96, 598
'Music of the Night,' 218–19, 722
musicology and music theory, 873
Music Theatre International (MTI), 69–70, 72,
    347, 872–73
*My Fair Lady*, 7–8, 16, 160–61, 191, 325, 329–30,
    510, 650, 722
  Czech première of, 787
  German productions of, 510, 511f, 512–13,
    514, 516, 519–20, 521–22, 525

Polish production of, 808–9, 812
*Pygmalion* and, 702
Schmidt production of, 190, 191, 196–207,
    200f, 208
at Shanghai Theatre Academy, 605
Swedish productions of, 621, 626
translation of, 196–97, 199, 200–1, 206–7
'My Friends,' 681–82, 684
'My Heart Belongs to Daddy,' 382
'My Husband the Pig,' 630
*My Mother's Lesbian Jewish Wiccan Wedding*, 309
*My School Rocks!*, 98–99
'My Ship,' 440
'My Time of Day,' 417

**N**

Nagy, Imre, 843, 844
Naiming, Lou, 595
*Nana*, 330
Nánay, István, 829–30
*Nanta*, 575–76
*NANTA*, 101–2
Napier, John, 9–10, 219, 224, 229–30, 433, 707, 708
*Napoleon*, 300–1
Naughtie, James, 674
Nazis and Nazism, 22–23, 451, 456–57, 478–88,
    490–98, 625–26, 783–84, 830–31
NCCh. *See* Nueva Canción Chilena
'Nebe na zemi,' 783
Nebtreko, Anna, 896–97
Nederlander, Jimmy, 434
*negra Ester, La*, 348–49
Nelson, Stig, 622
*Nelson Gonçalves: O amor e o tempo*, 355
Németh, János István, 840, 841
*Nem tudok élni nélküled*, 847–48
Netherlands, *Tarzan* in, 246, 249, 250–57, 252f
network power, 48–49
*Newsies*, 72, 247
'Next,' 654–55, 660, 661
*Next to Normal*, 520, 527, 820, 916–17
*Nicholas Nickleby*, 706–7, 710
Nicholaw, Casey, 305
Nichols, Mike, 301–2
Nichols, Peter, 743
Nicol, Eric, 291
*Ni fu ni fa*, 320–23, 325–26, 327–28, 332, 336n.26

*Night and the City* (film), 416–17
*Night and the City* (Kersh), 409
*Night at the Opera, A,* 438, 443–44
'Nightwaltz (The Sun Won't Set)', 638
*Nikola Tesla: Végtelen energia,* 847–48
Nilsson, Ola, 617, 618
*Nine,* 820
Nitouche, Mam'zelle, 786
*No, No Nanette,* 319–20, 329–30
*Noc w San Francisco,* 812
'No Place like London', 680–81, 685
*Notre-Dame de Paris* (film), 713
*Notre-Dame de Paris* (Hugo), 712–13, 714
*Notre-Dame de Paris* (musical), 596–97, 712–
    14, 714f, 818–19
Novák, Adam, 795–96
Novák, Ferenc, 840–41
Nové divadlo, 784–85
Novick, Julius, 294
Novo, Salvador, 322, 329, 339n.76
Novotný, Petr, 795–96, 797
Nový, Oldřich, 781, 784–85, 786, 796
'No Way to Stop It', 485
'Now/Later/Soon', 619
Nueva Canción Chilena (NCCh), 346
Nunn, Trevor, 10, 39n.28, 221, 229–30, 433,
    706–8
*Nunsense,* 519–20
'Nur kein Genieren', 739
*Nybyggarna,* 768–69
Nye, Joseph, 879–80

## O

Obama, Barack, 272
Obiera, Pedro, 457–58
O'Brien, Richard, 223
OCESA Entretenimiento, 318, 319–20, 331
off-Broadway, 164, 165f, 292, 301, 303, 308, 649f
Offenbach, Jacques, 7, 27, 701, 702, 703
*Oh, Calcutta!,* 625
O'Horgan, Tom, 711
*Oklahoma!,* 91, 94–95, 160–61, 190, 191, 489,
    560–62
    Czech production of, 794
    Swedish productions of, 190, 191, 192, 195–
        96, 197
    on West End, 372, 376, 382, 404

*Old Possum's Book of Practical Cats* (Eliot), 702
Olin, Stig, 625, 627–28
*Oliver!,* 4, 98, 208, 220, 572, 703, 710, 716n.5,
    799, 816, 837, 922
*Oliver Twist* (Dickens), 669, 673
Olivier, Laurence, 409–10
*OMG the Musical,* 897–98
*Once,* 93
*Once on This Island,* 920–21
*ONDB. See Oxford Dictionary of National
    Biography*
Ondráček, Bohuslav, 791–92
'One Day More', 707
*One Touch of Venus,* 381–82, 451, 452–54, 459–
    60, 461, 462–65, 480, 560–62
'Only You', 432
'On My Own', 707, 906–7
*onnagata,* 558–59
*On the Town,* 94–95, 560–62
'Open the Window', 297f
opera, 53–54, 456–58, 460–62, 677, 788–89,
    896–97
*Ópera do malandro,* 353
operetta, 124–25, 149nn.28–29, 701
    Czech musical theatre and, 781–82, 783,
        784–85, 786, 791–92, 799
    Hungarian, 827–28, 848
    Polish musical theatre and, 808, 809–10, 812
*Opernball, Der,* 812–13
*Opposite Sex, The,* 378
*Ordo Virtutum,* 486
orientalism, 901
Ortiz, Angélica, 330
Osatinski, Amy, 247–48
Oscars Teatern, 195–96, 197, 198–99, 201,
    204–5
Osolsobě, Ivo, 782, 788–89, 790, 791–92
Osterhammel, Jürgen, 53–54
Osterman, Lester, 298–99
Ostrowska, Małgorzata, 818
Osvobozené divadlo, 29, 782–83, 784, 788, 789,
    801n.13, 801–2n.19
*Otello,* 896–97
*otokoyaku,* 24, 554, 555, 556–59, 563–64, 565–67
'Over the Rainbow', 496
*Oxford Dictionary of National Biography
    (ONDB),* 665–66

## P

Paál, István, 828–29, 830
*Pacific 1860*, 374, 376, 381–82, 383*f*
*Pacific Overtures*, 25, 26, 527, 613, 649*f*, 662–63
  gestation and original reception of, 649–51
  Japanese musical theatre and, 648–58,
    662–63
    Miyamoto production of, 648–49, 651, 653,
     654–56, 655*f*, 656*f*, 657*f*, 658–61, 662
    Tokyo production of, 648–49, 651–58, 655*f*,
     656*f*, 657*f*, 661–62
*padlás, A*, 847
Page, Stephen, 879
Paige, Elaine, 306
*paio d'ali, Un*, 787
*Pajama Game, The*, 160–61
Palillo, 321, 324–25
*Pal Joey*, 411, 423n.65
*Pál utcai fiúk, A*, 847–48
*Pancerni i pies*, 810–11, 812–13
Panella, Pasquale, 713
*pansori*, 571
*Pan Wolodyjowski*, 812
*Pan Zagłoba*, 810–11, 812
*Papa, Can You Hear Me Sing?*, 599
*Papacito piernas largas*, 330
*Parade*, 510, 527
*Paramour*, 275–76
Parr, Bruce, 176
*Passe-Muraille, Le*, 704–5
*Passion*, 510, 527, 537, 613
'Path of Leaves and Needles,' 767
*Patience*, 160–61
patriarchy, 385–86, 394, 465, 880–81, 917, 918,
  919, 926
Patterson, Bill, 480*f*
Paulsson, Johanna, 637
Pavis, Patrice, 870–71
*Pearl Harbor Memories*, 648
Peimer, David, 16
Peña, Roger, 78
*Peppermint*, 584
Perfect, Eddie, 177–78
'Perfectly Marvellous,' 489
performance studies, 47–48, 112n.77
performers of colour, 31, 896, 897–98, 900–1,
  902–3, 906–8

*pérgola de las flores, La*, 346, 348–49
Perkins, Rachel, 866
Perlman, Gary, 26
Perlström, Åke, 620
Peroti, Clayton, 252*f*
'Perpetual Anticipation,' 630
*Pěst na oko aneb Caesarovo finale*, 801n.11
PETA. *See* Philippine Educational Theater
  Association
*Peter Grimes*, 677, 680
*Peter Pan*, 355, 572
Peters, Bernadette, 90–91
Peterson, Eric, 301, 302, 303*f*
Petit, Carolin, 714–15
*Petőfi-rock*, 828–30
Petőfi Színház, 828, 829*f*, 835–36
*Phantom of the Opera, The*, 5, 7–8, 96–97, 120,
  217, 520, 820
  Brazilian production of, 355
  Chinese production, 596–97
  at Circustheater, 267
  Korean production of, 69, 571, 574, 575–76,
   584–85
  Kunze and, 721, 722
  Mackintosh production of, 217, 218–19, 224,
   225*f*, 231, 234, 235
  Mexican production of, 317–18, 320, 331,
   341–42n.108
  Stage Entertainment production of, 270
  Stella AG production of, 269
  Swedish production of, 629
Philippine Educational Theater Association
  (PETA), 102
Phillips, Arlene, 430
Phillips, Simon, 919
*Piaf*, 572
*Piano in the Factory, The*, 602–3
*Picnic at Hanging Rock* (film), 884, 885*f*, 886
*Picnic at Hanging Rock* (Lindsay, J.), 883–84,
  886
*Picnic at Hanging Rock* (musical), 883–85, 884*f*,
  886
*Picnic at Hanging Rock* (television series), 884,
  885–86
Piekarczyk, Marek, 818
*Pierrot Players*, 291
'Pigtail of Muck,' 735

Pinal, Silvia, 329–31, 341n.106
Pinochet, Augusto, 346
*Pinokio*, 812–13
*Pins and Needles*, 784
Pion, István, 856n.134
*Pippin*, 329–30
*Pirates of Penzance, The*, 319, 814
Piscator, Erwin, 741
Pitt, George Dibdin, 671–72, 674–75
Plamondon, Luc, 710–11, 712, 713, 714
Planer, Nigel, 430
Platen, Gustaf von, 204–5
'Please Hello,' 653–54, 656–57, 657*f*, 662
Plunkett, Merton, 292
*Pocahontas*, 871
Poe, Edgar Allan, 681–82
Poiret, Jean, 68, 70–71
Polanski, Roman, 736–37, 753–54n.133
Polish musical theatre, 29
    Baduszkowa in, 809–13, 811*f*
    Cybulski in, 813–16
    *Fiddler on the Roof* in, 816–18, 817*f*
    in Gdynia, 809, 810, 811–12, 813, 814, 816–21
    Gruza in, 816–18
    operetta and, 808, 809–10, 812
'Poor Thing,' 684, 685
'Poppa's Blues,' 430–31
*Porgy and Bess*, 98, 510, 572, 680, 837, 903–4
Porter, Cole, 452–54, 455–56, 702
post-feminism, 923–26, 925*f*
postmodern condition, 439
postmodern musical theatre, 3, 5, 10, 11–12, 13–14
*Potop*, 812
*Prawo pierwszej nocy*, 812–13
Prawy, Marcel, 897
'Prayer for Marta, A,' 793
Prece, Paul, 702–3, 708, 716n.2
Presgurvic, Gérard, 714–15
Presser, Gábor, 830, 833–34, 847
'Pretty Lady,' 654–55, 658, 661
*Pretty Woman*, 916–17
Prince, Harold, 94, 527
    *Cabaret* production, 487, 489, 492–93, 497
    Kunze and, 719, 720
    *A Little Night Music* production, 615–17, 620, 630–31, 635, 638

Lloyd Webber and, 429
    *Pacific Overtures* production, 648–49, 650, 654, 662
    Sondheim and, 26, 527, 615–17, 620, 630–31, 635, 638, 648–49, 650, 654, 662, 685
    *Sweeney Todd* production, 685
*Prince of Broadway*, 246
*Princess and the Frog, The*, 899
*Priscilla, Queen of the Desert*, 179, 186n.55, 358, 917
'Proč je to tak,' 788–89
*Producers, The*, 7–8, 319–20, 479, 489, 493–98, 495*f*
*Producers, The* (film), 494–95, 496
Programa Nacional de Apoio à Cultura (PRONAC), 356, 359
Projazz Instituto Profesional, 349–50
*Prom, The*, 916–17
*Promises, Promises*, 794, 812
PRONAC. *See* Programa Nacional de Apoio à Cultura
Pryce, Jonathan, 903–4, 920
*Ptarmigan*, 291
*Puskás*, 847–48
*Pygmalion*, 198–99, 702

**Q**

Queen, 436–38, 440, 441, 442, 443
*Quem um dia irá dizer*, 360–61, 362
*¡Qué plantón!*, 317–18, 331–32, 333–34
'Quiero pedir perdón,' 331–32
Quilley, Denis, 686, 687*f*

**R**

race and racial identity, 898, 907–8, 920, 927
Rachmaninoff, Sergei, 680–81
racial capitalism, 877, 881
racism, 159, 874–75, 882–83, 895, 896, 897, 899, 903–4, 905, 909
RADA. *See* Royal Academy of Dramatic Art
'Radio Ga Ga,' 440
Radok, Alfréd, 786–87
*Ragtime*, 10, 527, 743
Raia, Claudia, 358
*Rainbow of Time, The*, 594
*Rain Shower*, 584–85
*Raise the Red Lantern*, 600

960   INDEX

Rajki, András, 836
*Rak of Aegis*, 102
Ramsberg, Calvin E., 9*f*
*Rastelbinder, Der*, 121
Ratz, Christian, 712
*Räuber Hotzenplotz, Der*, 534–35
Ravel, Maurice, 683–84, 685
Really Useful Group, 5, 218, 274, 430, 702–3
*Rebecca* (du Maurier), 723–25, 726, 729, 730, 738
*Rebecca* (film), 738, 753–54n.133
*Rebecca* (musical), 584, 585*f*, 719, 721, 722, 745n.7
  direct address device in, 741–42, 743
  as drama musical, 723–25, 726, 728, 729, 730–31, 736, 738
  dramaturgy of, 738
Rebellato, Dan, 3, 5–6, 54, 245–46
*Red Book*, 589
*Redhead*, 325
*Reedy River*, 175–76, 177*f*
Reign of Terror, The, 670–71, 684, 704
Reinhardt, Max, 55
'Remember America!', 656
*Rent*, 7–8, 67, 71, 72*f*, 76–77, 331, 352, 515, 520–21
*Rentas congeladas*, 325–28, 326*f*, 333–34
Renton, Ken, 302–3
Rényi, András, 844–45
*revista de 1874, A*, 351
*Revolução na América do Sul*, 351
*Révolution Française, La*, 27, 703–5, 704*f*
Reyes, Alfonso, 328–29
Reyes, Mara, 328
*Rhapsody in Blue*, 455–56
Rice, Elmer, 456, 458–59
Rice, Tim, 7–8, 28, 40n.42, 77–78, 702, 703, 707, 712, 716n.5, 719, 766, 845
Rich, Frank, 170, 222, 223–24, 317, 434–35, 710
*Richard O'Brien's Rocky Horror Show*, 223
Richter, Jan, 622
Riemer, Maja-Rosewith, 491–92
'Right Place, Right Time', 432–33
Riksteatern, 629–30, 630*f*
Riley, Lew, 329
*Rinaldo in campo*, 812
'Ring of Keys', 79
*Rink, The*, 920

Rio, Asumi, 561*f*
*Rite of Spring, The*, 682
Rittmann, Trude, 928
Ritzer, George, 37n.9
Rivera, Chita, 95*f*
Rivière, Jean-Max, 703
Robbins, Hannah Marie, 31
Robbins, Jerome, 6, 91–92, 94–95, 702, 816
*Robert and Elizabeth*, 163–64
Robertson, Jennifer, 554, 558–59
Robertson, Roland, 47–48
Robeson, Paul, 371
*Rockabye Hamlet*, 292, 298–300
Rocke, Stephanie, 868
rock music, 828–37, 838–46
rock opera, 27, 29–30, 233–34, 702, 703, 704*f*, 705, 710–12, 717n.6, 836, 839–40, 842–46
Rock Színház, 835–36, 847, 848
*Rocky*, 246, 277–78, 278*f*
*Rocky Horror Show, The*, 223, 231–32, 519–20
Rodgers, Richard, 6, 91, 138–42, 195–96, 386, 484–87, 489, 731, 928
Roháč, Ján, 803n.42
*Romeo and Juliet*, 594, 702
*Romeo and Juliet* (film), 714–15
*Roméo et Juliette: De la haine à l'amour*, 560–62, 714–15
Rooney, David, 307–8
Roosevelt, Franklin, 19, 345
*Röpülj, lelkem!*, 848
Rosenberg, Justin, 4
Rosenhaus, Steven L., 76, 77
Rosenthal, Jean, 489
*Rose of Versailles, The*, 562
*Rose Paris*, 556–57
'Rose's Turn', 379, 438
Ross, Adrian, 125
Rouanet, Sergio Paulo, 356
Royal Academy of Dramatic Art (RADA), 377–78, 377*f*
Royal Shakespeare Company (RSC), 10, 39n.28, 231, 436, 706–7, 708, 917
*Rub a líc*, 801n.13
Rubinoff, Michael, 102–3, 308–9
Rudolfsson, Lars, 629, 759*f*, 763, 766, 777n.52
Ruffelle, Frances, 432*f*

Runyon, Damon, 21, 403–4, 405–8, 406f, 409, 410–15, 416–17, 419, 421–22n.47
Runyon, Damon, Jr., 405–6
'Ruritania,' 376
Rush, 443–44
Russell, Willy, 920
Rut, Přemysl, 783
Rybrant, Gösta, 196–97, 199, 200–1
Rychman, Ladislav, 790

**S**

'Sad Times, Bad Times,' 162
*Sail Away*, 374, 388–91, 390f
*Šakalí léta*, 796
*Salad Days*, 21, 429–30
Sallert, Ulla, 198, 626, 627
Salonga, Lea, 99–100, 100f
Salzburg Festival, 55, 56f
Sams, Jeremy, 74–75, 713
Sandin, Dennis, 636–37
Sandor, Gluck, 94–95
Sandoval, Chela, 873
Sankoff, Irene, 309
Santander, Felipe, 327–28, 340n.92
Santos, Aicelle, 99–100
*Sapphires, The*, 878–79
*Sapphires, The* (film), 878
*Sarafina!*, 168–70, 171f, 181
Sarich, Drew, 278f
Sarney, José, 356
*Saro the Musical*, 897–98
*Så som i himmelen*, 632
Sathal, Fred, 712
'Satisfied,' 907
*Saturday Night Fever*, 254–55, 820
Savage, Henry W., 125–29, 130f, 134–35
Savary, Jérôme, 11f, 492f, 492–93
Savran, David, 7, 8, 55, 246
Sáyago, Raúl, 327–28
*Sayonara*, 559–60, 560f
*Scarlet Pimpernel, The*, 527–28, 623
*Scat, czyli od pucybuta do milionera*, 819–20
Schafft, Kai A., 765
Scheiblhofer, Susanne, 22–23
*Schikaneder*, 513, 535
Schildt, Jurgen, 621
Schmidl, Jens, 488

Schmidl, Stefan, 124
Schmidt, Lars, 16, 190–91
    Bergman, Ingrid, and, 194–95, 199, 206, 207f
    on Broadway, 193–94, 208
    *Cat on a Hot Tin Roof* production, 190, 191, 194–95, 195f
    early career, 192–95
    *My Fair Lady* production of, 190, 191, 196–207, 200f, 208
Schmiedel, Gottfried, 491–92
Schneider, Hortense, 701
Schneider, Jan, 791–92
Schneider, Peter, 272
Schoenberg, Arnold, 456–57, 677
Schoenfeld, Gerry, 221–22
Schönberg, Claude-Michel, 27, 230, 429, 703–8, 716n.4, 716n.5
*School of Rock*, 355, 796
*School of Rock* (film), 441
Schubert, Gisela Maria, 458–59
Schubert, Giselher, 459–60
Schubring, Marc, 537
*Schuh des Manitu, Der*, 277, 513, 534–35
Schulman, Susan H., 486–87
Schumacher, Thomas, 217–18, 220, 235, 236, 247–48, 250, 251
Schwarz, David R., 405
Schwenkow, Peter, 269
*Schweyk im Zweiten Weltkrieg*, 479–84, 480f, 486, 489
Scott, Derek, 124
*Scottsboro Boys, The*, 527, 905–6
'Screech In,' 309
'Searching,' 684
Seiffert, Klaus, 462
*Sekretärinnen*, 511–12, 519–20, 536, 537–38
Semafor Theatre, 787–89, 793–94, 802n.28
'Send in the Clowns,' 26, 614, 637–38
Senelick, Laurence, 124–25
*Sen nocy letniej*, 818–19
*Señoritas garantizadas*, 322
*Sentimental Bloke, The*, 176–77
S.E.S., 584
Seung-woo, Cho, 585–86
*Sevastopol's Waltz*, 812
*7: O musical*, 353
Shaffer, Peter, 734, 735

962    INDEX

Shaffer, Tia M., 876
Shakespeare, William, 164–66, 173–74, 533, 702, 706–7, 714–15, 818–19, 879
*Shane Warne*, 177–78, 178*f*, 917
Shanghai Theatre Academy, 605
Shannon, Richard M., 16–17
Shaw, George Bernard, 39n.32, 198–99, 200–2, 206–7, 702
Sheader, Timothy, 219
Shell, Ray, 432*f*
Shelley, Mary, 670–71
Shenton, Mark, 230, 924–25
*Shi Jing Cai Wei*, 103
Shiki theatre company, 228, 563
*Shimmer*, 103
Shirley, Don, 899
*Shockheaded Peter*, 535–36
Shostakovich, Dimitri, 142
*Show Boat*, 11, 192, 195–97, 371, 617, 782–83, 794, 901
*Shrek*, 537, 818–19
Shubert Brothers, 131
Shulman, Milton, 433
Sigfridsson, Emil, 257
Silbereisen, Florian, 733*f*
*Silk Stockings*, 324
'Silly People,' 630, 634
Silver Convention, 719, 720
Simon, John, 650
Simon, Neil, 138–42
Sinden, Donald, 391, 392, 392*f*
singable translation, 14–15, 66–67, 74–75, 77, 80
*Singin' in the Rain*, 560–62, 587–88, 820
Sirett, Paul, 879
Siropoulos, Vagelis, 13–14
Sischy, Ingrid, 562–63, 565
*Sissi* films, 732, 734, 749n.78
*Sister Act*, 249, 270, 271–74, 273*f*, 276–77, 820
'Sit Down You're Rockin' the Boat', 416–17
*SIX*, 31, 899–900, 918, 924–26, 925*f*
'Sixteen, Going on Seventeen,' 486
Sjöholm, Helen, 759*f*, 768*f*, 771
Sjöholm, Torsten, 623, 624
Sjöman, Vilgot, 204
ska, 879
Slaughter, Tod, 673, 674
*Sleeping Beauty, The*, 160

Šlitr, Jiří, 787–88, 793, 802n.31, 803n.42
Sliwinski, Adolf, 125
Small, Christopher, 873, 888n.32
*Small Craft Warnings*, 391
'Small House of Uncle Thomas,' 928
'Small World,' 379
SM Entertainment, 583, 584–85, 587–88, 587*t*
*Smiles of a Summer Night*, 25–26, 614–15, 616, 616*f*, 619–20, 621, 622, 623, 624–25, 626, 627–28, 634–36, 637, 638–39
Smith, Loring, 387*f*
Smith, Marlene, 300–1
Smith, Oliver, 205–6
Sneddon, Elizabeth, 164
Snelson, John, 21, 372, 376–77
Śniady, Wacław, 809
*Snow White and the Seven Dwarfs*, 572
*Soft Power*, 537, 879–80
Solana, Rafael, 319–20, 322, 326–27, 328
*Soldier of Orange*, 103, 246
'So Long, Farewell,' 486
'Somebody to Love,' 438
'Someone in a Tree,' 654, 662–63
'Some People,' 379
*Something Rotten*, 820
*Something's Rockin' in Denmark*, 300
*Somewhere in the World*, 307–8
Sommerfield, John, 415
Sondheim, Stephen, 12, 23, 533, 649*f*, 731–32
    Babbitt and, 677, 681–82
    bells in arrangements by, 680–81, 684
    Bergman and, 639
    Bond and, 684, 686
    foreign source material for, 25–27
    in German-language productions of, 515, 522–28, 524*t*, 526*t*, 528*f*, 537
    Grand Guignal and, 682
    Herrmann and, 678, 680, 681–82
    Heyward and, 680
    Japanese production of *Pacific Overtures* and, 648–49, 651–52, 658, 660, 661–62
    Kunze and, 720, 721, 722
    Mack and, 665
    musical training for, 91–92, 93
    origins of *Pacific Overtures*, 649–50
    Prince, Bergman, Ingmar, and, 615–17, 638

Prince and, 26, 527, 615–17, 620, 630–31, 635, 638, 648–49, 650, 654, 662, 685
Ravel and, 683–84, 685
songs and lyrics of *Sweeney Todd*, 680–85, 686
in Sweden, 613, 628, 645n.139
Swedish production of *A Little Night Music* and, 619–21, 622, 624, 625, 626, 627, 630–31, 635–36, 637–39
Sweeney Todd character and, 665–66, 674–75, 676, 678–79
in translation, 76, 77–78, 613, 626, 630, 634, 636, 637
*West Side Story* and, 527–28, 615, 652
*Song and Dance*, 218–19
*Song for Rudolph III, A*, 793
'Song of the Rhineland, The,' 483
*Sonnenallee*, 535
Sontag, Susan, 443, 495–96
*Sophiatown*, 167–69
Sós, János Péter, 845
Šotkovsky, Jan, 29
*Soul*, 899
*Sound of Music, The*, 4, 98, 160, 347, 348, 362, 386, 479, 572, 928
*Cabaret* and, 487–89, 490, 491, 493
Chinese production of, 594, 596–97
on Nazism and Holocaust, 484–88, 493
South African musical theatre, 158–59
ACT in, 158, 159–60
Australian musical theatre and, 158–59, 175, 183
British and Broadway exports to colonial South Africa, 159–60
*Impempe Yomlingo*, 173–74
Indigenous, 159, 161–70
*Ipi Tombi*, 166–67
*King Kong*, 16, 161–63
*The Mandela Trilogy*, 174–75
in Rainbow Nation era, 171–73
*Sarafina!*, 168–70
*Sophiatown*, 167–69
*uMabatha*, 164–66, 165f
*Umoja*, 172–73
*Wait a Minim!*, 163–64
*South Pacific*, 160–61, 195–96, 372, 374, 382–83, 384–86, 560–62, 730, 903–4, 920

'So What,' 489
Spain
*Hoy no me puedo levantar* in, 68, 98
musicals in translation in, 67–68, 70, 71, 72f, 76–80, 79f
*Spamalot*, 7–8, 305, 519–20
spectacle musicals, 233–34, 702, 705, 710–15, 716nn.2–3
Spencer, Charles, 441
Spewack, Bella and Samuel, 702
Spielberg, Stephen, 901–2, 902f
Spiers, Amy, 886
*Śpiewak jazzbandu*, 819–20
*Spring Awakening*, 520, 527
*Spring Thaw*, 293–94, 295–96, 304, 306–7
'Springtime for Hitler,' 489, 493–96, 495f
Stadius, Adam, 112n.77
Stage Entertainment, 70, 250, 285n.86
creative development, 276–78
current business strategy, 274
CVC Capital Partners and, 279–80
Disney musicals produced by, 233, 246, 249, 250–57, 252f, 258, 260, 275
expansion into English-language market, 271–74
German-language productions, 510, 512–13, 515–16, 520, 521
*Hamilton* production by, 276
history of, 267–68
international expansion, 268–70, 280–81
licensed productions, 275–76
*The Lion King* production by, 257, 270, 275
reorganisation and improvement, 278–80
*Rocky* production by, 277–78, 278f
*Sister Act* production by, 271–74, 273f, 276–77
*Tarzan* production by, 250–57, 252f, 260, 275
theatres controlled by, 276
in theatrical globalisation, 280
van den Ende at, 17–18, 233, 246, 249–50, 253–54, 255, 256–57, 266, 268f, 279–80
Stage Holding, 267, 268–70, 275, 280
stage musical, as global phenomenon, 1–2
*Stalo se v dešti*, 787
'Stand Up,' 919–20
Stanislavsky, Konstantin, 48–49, 50f, 60, 191, 560–62

964 INDEX

Stanton, Burke, 873
*Starci na chmelu,* 790–91, 803–4n.46, 804n.50
*Starlight Express,* 10, 13, 21, 96, 97, 269, 316,
    317–18, 331–32
  on Broadway, 429–30, 434–35
  *Cats* and, 430, 431, 434–35
  German-language productions of, 512, 514,
    515, 516–19, 520, 521–22, 525, 541–42n.26
  *Jesus Christ Superstar* and, 431
  in Las Vegas, 436
  lyrics from, 430–33
  original London cast, 432*f*
  revised version of, 433–34, 434*f*
  on self-belief, 430–34
  on West End, 429–30, 433
  *We Will Rock You* and, 441
'Starlight Express,' 431
*Starlight Tours,* 105–6
*Starmania,* 710–12, 711*f*
'Stars,' 706, 707
Staunton, Imelda, 683*f,* 686
Štědroň, Miloš, 794, 799
Steed, Maggie, 416
Stein, Leo, 15–16, 120–21, 122*f,* 125
Steiner, Fritz, 491–92
Steinman, Jim, 719, 736–37, 738
Stella AG, 249, 269
*Stella: Das Gespenst vom Kurfürstendamm,* 535
Sternfeld, Jessica, 10, 707, 709
Stevens, Clifford, 298
Steyn, Mark, 380, 436–38
Stickley, Gustav, 134–35
Stigwood, Robert, 217, 223, 434
Stilgoe, Richard, 431
Stopa, Krzysztof, 817*f*
*Stories from Norway,* 103
*Story of My Life, The,* 292, 307–8
Strauss, Johann, 682
*Streetcar Named Desire, A,* 194
Street-Porter, Janet, 441
*Street Scene,* 451, 454–55, 457–60, 461, 462,
    464–65, 466*f,* 483–84
Streisand, Barbra, 684
Strickland, Josh, 248–49, 255
*Strictly Ballroom, the Musical,* 179–80, 918
Stridh, Renate, 26
*String of Pearls, The* (play), 671–72

*String of Pearls, The* (serial), 26–27, 666–68,
    669–70, 671–72
Stritch, Elaine, 19–21, 371–72, 373, 374, 387–93,
    392*f,* 394
Stroheim, Erich von, 138–42, 142*f*
Stroman, Susan, 906
Strömberg, Mikael, 28
structural racisms, 896
*Struwwelpeter, Der,* 535–36
Stuart, Ross, 293
Stuckenschmidt, Hans Heinz, 457–58
Styne, Jule, 434–35
Suchý, Jiří, 787–89, 793–94, 802n.31, 803n.42
*Sugar,* 316–17
'Sugar,' 78–79
Šuhaj, Nikola, 794
Sullivan, Arthur, 7, 142*f,* 319–20, 324–25, 702
*Sunday in the Park with George,* 525, 527, 528*f,*
    538, 613
Sungmin, 586–87
*Sunset Boulevard,* 10, 511–12, 515–16, 519–20,
    522, 523*t,* 528–31, 721, 820
'Supercalifragilisticexpialidocious,' 236
Super Junior, 584–85
*surpresas do Senhor José da Piedade, As,* 350–51
Sutherland, Joan, 143*f*
Svendal, Sigrid Øvreås, 197, 204
Svoboda, Karel, 797
Swayne, Steve, 676
Sweden
  Bergman, Ingmar, and, 633, 634–35,
    644–45n.126
  countryside and urbanisation in, 761–63,
    765, 768–69
  cultural translation of theatre in, 191–92
  development and status of musical theatre
    in, 1998-2023, 632–33
  development of musical theatre, 1978-1997,
    628–29
  emigration and, 759–60
  folk music of, 758, 767, 770–71, 773–74
  *A Little Night Music* in, 613, 614, 617–22,
    623–26, 627–28, 629–31, 630*f,* 631*f,* 633–
    39, 645n.139
  refugees in, 772–73
  Sondheim in, 613, 628, 645n.139
  Swedish *folket,* 758

INDEX    965

*Sweeney Todd* productions in, 613, 628,
  645n.139
*Tarzan* in, 257
Sweeney Todd (fictional character)
  British popular stage and, 1847-1969, 671–74
  global ambitions of, 1973-1979, 674–76
  origins and history, 665–71
  Sondheim and, 665–66, 674–75, 676,
    678–79
*Sweeney Todd* (film) (2007), 525, 686–87
*Sweeney Todd* (musical), 11, 25, 26–27, 416, 478,
    681*f*, 683*f*, 687*f*, 743
  on Broadway, 666, 678–79, 684–85
  Fleet Street and, 665–66, 674
  German-language productions of, 525–27,
    526*t*, 528–31
  *Hangover Square* and, 678, 679–80, 681–82
  Japanese productions of, 652
  journey from 1979 to present, 685–88
  modern psychology, modernist music and,
    676–79
  opera and, 677
  origins and history of Sweeney Todd
    character, 665–66
  social geography of, 679–85
  Swedish productions of, 613, 628, 645n.139
*Sweeney Todd: The Barber of Fleet Street* (play),
    672–73
*Sweeney Todd: The Demon Barber of Fleet
    Street* (film) (1936), 673
*Sweeney Todd: The Demon Barber of Fleet
    Street* (play), 674–76
*Sweet, Come to Me Stealthily,* 572, 573*f*
*Sweet Charity,* 267, 373, 704–5
*Sweet Smell of Success, The,* 416–17
*Swinging St. Pauli,* 534, 537
Swyngedouw, Eric, 3–4, 37n.7
systemic racism, 905
*Szabad szél,* 827–28
Szántó, Erika, 833
Szegedi Egyetemi Színpad, 828–29, 830
Szilágyi, János, 833–34
Szirmai, Rezső, 833–34
Szkárosi, Endre, 827
Szőnyei, Tamás, 846
Szörényi, Levente, 834, 838, 840, 846–47
*Sztárcsinálók,* 836

Szurmiej, Jan, 816
*Szwejk,* 810–11, 812–13

T
T4F, 357
Takarasiennes, 556, 558–59, 564–65
Takarazuka, 729, 744–45n.6
  *Elisabeth* production by, 561*f*
  fan culture, 562–65
  gender and gender performance in, 557–59,
    564
  Kobayashi at, 553–57
  in 1920s and 1930s, 555–57
  *otokoyaku,* 24, 554, 555, 556–59, 563–64,
    565–67
  post-Kobayashi, 557–59
  repertoire, 560–62
  *The Rose of Versailles* production by, 562
  in *Sayonara,* 559–60, 560*f*
  troupes, 556, 558*f*
Takarazuka Girls' Opera Company, 557
Takarazuka Girls' Opera Training Association,
    553–54
Takarazuka Music School, 554–56, 563
Takarazuka Revue, 24, 565–67, 566*f*
Takarazuka Singing Corps, 554
'Take Back Your Mink,' 416–17
Talar, Charles, 712
Tamaira, A Mārata Ketekiri, 872
Tamasaburō, Bandō, 558–59
*Taming of the Shrew, The,* 702
*Tammy Faye,* 916–17, 927
Tandi, Lajos, 842
'Tango Angèle,' 483–84
Tankard, Meryl, 247–48, 251
*Tanz der Vampire,* 521–22, 525, 533–34, 719, 722,
    737*f*
  as *Dance of the Vampires* on Broadway,
    745n.7
  direct address device in, 741–42
  as drama musical, 723, 725, 726, 728, 729,
    736–38
  dramaturgy of, 736–38
  *Marie Antoinette* and, 740
Tarján, Tamás, 833–34
Tarjányi, István, 837
Taruskin, Richard, 142

## 966  INDEX

*Tarzan*, 245–46, 247–50, 260–61, 520, 525
  casting, 254–56
  marketing, 253–54, 255–56
  Stage Entertainment's Dutch production of,
    250–57, 252f, 260, 275
  translation of, 245, 251, 256
*Tarzan* (film), 248, 249, 253
Taviani, Ferdinando, 51
Tavira, Luis de, 324–25
Taya, Miiko, 560f
Taylor, Bill, 271
Taylor, Roger, 436–37
Taylor, Ronald, 452–54
Taymor, Julie, 914, 928
*Tea and Sympathy*, 194–95
*teatro de revista*, 317, 321–22, 323, 324–25, 326–
    27, 332–34, 335n.4, 337–38n.57
'Telephone Song, The,' 489
'Telephone Wire,' 79
*Tell*, 535
'Tell-Tale Heart, The' (Poe), 681–82
*Tempest, The*, 192–93
'temps des cathédrales, Le,' 714
Terfel, Bryn, 686–87
Tesori, Jeanine, 93, 537
*Těžká Barbora*, 783
Thang Ngyuen, Viet, 231
theatre and music festivals, 55–57, 56f
theatrical globalisation, 46–48, 50–60, 234–35,
    280, 319–20, 333–34
Theorell, Tobias, 633
'There Is No Other Way,' 654, 661–62
'These Wild, Wild Women Are Making a Wild
    Man out of Me,' 292
'They Say It's Wonderful', 378
Thibéault, Fabienne, 711
Thielman, Hans, 13
Thierens, Sanne, 17
Third Reich, 22
*13½ Leben des Käpt'n Blaubär, Die*, 534–35
Thomas, Tamara, 875
Thomas, Virgil, 452–54
Thompson, Emma, 686–87
Thoor, Alf, 620, 623
Thornbury, Walter, 667–68, 669, 672–73
Thornton, Warwick, 879
*Thoroughly Modern Millie*, 395n.10, 537

*3 Musketiers*, 266
*Three Musketeers, The*, 586–87
*Threepenny Opera, The*, 452, 454–55, 457–58,
    459–60, 464–65, 468, 482–83, 531–32,
    537–38, 828
*Tick, Tick . . . Boom*, 76–77, 78–79, 354–55,
    899–900
*Time*, 10
'Time for Baby's Bottle', 411
'Time Marches On,' 494–95
*Tim Maia: Vale tudo; O musical*, 354
*Tina: The Tina Turner Musical*, 272–74, 276–77,
    917
Tinker, Jack, 433
Tirado, Romualdo, 136
Tisch School of the Arts, 100–1
*Titanic*, 10, 271, 516–19, 527
*tizenötödik, A*, 847–48
'Tmavomodrý svět,' 783
*Todos os musicais de Chico Buarque em 90
    minutos*, 354
'Together, Wherever We Go,' 379
Tomoff, Kiril, 124
'Tomorrow Belongs to Me,' 487–88
*Tom Sawyer and Huckleberry Finn*, 451,
    466–67
Tong, Kam, 904f
*Tootsie*, 923
*Top Hat*, 560–62
TopTicketLine, 274
Toshihiro, Tsuganezawa, 557
Tóth, Péter G., 844
translation, 66, 98, 260–61
  adaptation and, 245–46
  of *Cats*, 70, 233, 721
  in Chinese musical theatre, 78, 98, 233
  commercial challenges of, 69–72
  cultural, 191–92, 198, 371–72, 464–65
  cultural challenges of, 67–69
  glocalisation and, 246
  by Kunze, 719, 720, 721–22
  linguistic challenges of, 77–80
  of *A Little Night Music* by Fägerborn, 636,
    637
  of *A Little Night Music* by Wolgers, 626, 630,
    634
  of Mackintosh productions, 232–33

of *The Merry Widow*, 125–29, 706
for Mexican productions, 316, 332–33, 342–43nn.114–15
of *Les Misérables*, 67, 232–33, 707
of *My Fair Lady*, 196–97, 199, 200–1, 206–7
of *Notre-Dame de Paris*, 713
of *Pacific Overtures*, 661–62
singable, 14–15, 66–67, 74–75, 77, 80
of Sondheim, 76, 77–78, 613, 626, 630, 634, 636, 637
in Spanish musical theatre, 67–68, 70, 71, 72*f*, 76–80, 79*f*
of *Tarzan*, 245, 251, 256
theatrical challenges of, 72–74
of Weill, 463–65
transnational musicals, 246, 256
Traubner, Richard, 124
Travers, P. L., 220
Trewin, J. C., 405
*Trial of the Donkey's Shadow, The*, 783
*Trianon*, 847
triple threat performers, 94–100, 95*f*, 104–5, 869–70
*Tristan und Isolde*, 482–83, 677, 678
Troell, Jan, 768–69
Troßbach, Stefan, 463–64
*True Feeling and False Intention*, 598
Trujillo, Sergio, 251
Tunick, Jonathan, 682, 683–84
*2112*, 443–44
*2 Pianos, 4 Hands*, 292
'Two Ladies,' 489
*Two on the Aisle*, 378–79
*Two's Company*, 391, 392–93, 392*f*
'Two's Company', 392–93
'Two Worlds,' 247, 253, 257
*Tycoon*, 712
Tynan, Kenneth, 372, 375–76, 384–85, 404–5, 407, 409–10, 420n.15

## U

UALE. *See* United Asia Live Entertainment
Uhde, Milan, 794–95, 799
*último teatro del mundo, El*, 333
Ulvaeus, Björn, 28, 629, 758, 759*f*, 765–67, 768–69, 773, 777n.52
*uMabatha*, 164–66, 165*f*, 167, 180–81

Umeki, Miyoshi, 904*f*
*Umoja*, 172–73
'U.N.C.O.U.P.L.E.D,' 430
'Under Pressure,' 440
UNESCO, 58–59, 346–47
United Asia Live Entertainment (UALE), 98
Universal Copyright Convention, 572–73, 583
*Urinetown*, 271
Uruchurtu, Ernesto, 323–24
Usigli, Rodolfo, 321–22
*Utazás*, 847–48
*Utvandrarna*, 768–69

## V

*Valahol Európában*, 847–48
Valdés Medellín, Gonzalo, 331
Valentini, Roberta, 739*f*
*Valse, La*, 683–84
*Vámpírok bálja*, 848
van den Ende, Joop, 17–233, 245, 246, 253–54, 255, 267, 272. *See also* Stage Entertainment
on Broadway, 271, 275
Disney musicals produced by, 249–50, 256–57
TopTicketLine founded by, 274
van den Hanenberg, Patrick, 256
van Gelder, Henk, 256
van Laecke, Frank, 259
van Lambaart, Erwin, 256–57
'Van zo ver,' 254–55
Varga, Luca, 828, 833
Varjas, Endre, 842
Várkonyi, Mátyás, 835–36
Várkonyi, Zoltán, 831–32
vaudeville, 701–2
Vega, Ricardo de la, 136
*Veled, Uram!*, 847
Verdecchia, Guillermo, 870–71
Verdon, Gwen, 373
Vereinigte Bühnen Wien, 512–13, 535, 538
*Verfremdungseffekt*, 741
Véron, Louis, 702–3, 716n.4
*Vertigo*, 678
*Vest Pocket Revue*, 782
Vicent, Luis, 325
*viejo del saco, El*, 347
Vígszínház, 828–29, 830–35, 831*f*, 847, 848

968  INDEX

Vilar, Jean, 52
'Vilia,' 122–23
*Villa Sonnenschein,* 534
*Violet,* 537
*Virágos Magyarország,* 848
*Visitors on the Icy Mountain,* 600
Vitali, Kersti, 763
*viúva alegre, A,* 138
*Viva Forever,* 918
'Vivre,' 714
Vocal Training and Acting Studio, at Gdynia's
    Musical Theatre, 810, 811*f,* 813, 821
*vörös malom, A,* 847–48
Voskovec, Jiří, 781, 782–85, 801n.11, 801n.13,
    802n.28
Voskovec and Werich (V + W), 782–85,
    801n.11, 801n.13, 802n.28
Vostřel, Darek, 787–88, 793
V + W. *See* Voskovec and Werich
Vyskočil, Ivan, 787–88

**W**

Waaranperä, Ingegärd, 635
Wada, Emi, 657–58
Wagner, Richard, 482–83, 677, 678, 706
Wagner, Robin, 763
'Wahrheit,' 729, 738
*Wait a Minim!,* 163–64
'Waiting for This Moment,' 254–55
*Waitress,* 644n.122, 820, 916, 918, 926
*Wakaa the Musical,* 897–98, 908–9
Wałęsa, Lech, 814
Walker, Rob, 416
Walkowitz, Judith, 672–73
Walsh, Anne Marie, 235
Wardle, Irving, 675
*War Horse,* 275–76
Warne, Shane, 177–78
Warsaw Pact, 792–93
Washington, Denzel, 899
'Was ist nur los mit ihm,' 729
Watt, Doug, 299
Watts, Richard, 296–97
Waxman, Franz, 416–17
'We Are the Champions,' 438, 443
Webb, Lizbeth, 404
Weber, Joe, 136–38

Weidman, John, 648–49, 649*f,* 650, 652, 658,
    661
Weihe, Richard, 464–65
'Weil ich besser bin,' 728
Weill, Kurt, 451, 452–54, 453*f,* 480, 483–84
    American and European works, perceived
        dichotomy of, 452–54, 459–60, 468
    Americanisation and, 455–57
    Brecht and, 22, 454, 456–57, 464–65, 481–83,
        484, 486, 538, 675, 742, 828
    German opera industry and, 456–58,
        460–62
    German reception of American works, 451,
        452–54, 457–62, 458*t,* 463–68
    jazz and, 455–56, 460
    KWF and, 463–65, 466–67
    popular appeal of, 454–55
    problem with genre and, 458–60
    *Schwejk* projects and, 480–82, 486
    staging trends, 464–68
    translation of, 463–65
Weinstein, Harvey, 923
Weir, Peter, 884, 885*f*
*weißen Rößl, Im,* 8
'We Know the Way,' 895
Welch, Elisabeth, 371
'Welcome to Kanagawa,' 654–55, 661–62
Werich, Jan, 781, 782–85, 789, 801n.11, 801n.13,
    802n.28
West End
    American stars on, 371–72, 373–74, 376
    *Annie Get Your Gun* on, 372, 373–74, 375–79,
        382–83
    Broadway and, 7, 19, 89, 90, 97, 371, 372, 403–
        4, 407–10, 429–30, 444, 533–34, 702–3,
        781, 868–69
    *Cabaret* on, 490
    *Guys and Dolls* on, 403–7, 409–10, 413–19,
        414*f,* 415*f*
    *Oklahoma!* on, 372, 376, 382, 404
    Soho, 407–13
    *Starlight Express* on, 429–30, 433
    *We Will Rock You* on, 429–30, 441, 442
*West End People* (Wildeblood), 411
Westerby, Robert, 408–9
*West Side Story,* 30–31, 91–92, 94–95, 95*f,* 96,
    97, 98, 195–97, 232, 478, 480, 572

in Central Academy of Drama education, 604–5
Czech musical theatre and, 787, 790, 791–92, 797–98, 798f, 804n.51
drama musical and, 730
French production of, 703
German-language productions of, 511–12, 515–16, 519–20, 525, 535
Polish production of, 816
*Romeo and Juliet* and, 702
Sondheim and, 527–28, 615, 652
Swedish production of, 615, 629, 645n.139
Takarazuka production of, 558–59
women of colour in, 906–7
*West Side Story* (film) (1961), 901
*West Side Story* (film) (2021), 901–3, 902f
*We Will Rock You*, 21, 439f, 520, 525
    at Dominion Theatre, 436, 437f
    intertextuality of, 436–41
    in Las Vegas, 436
    in US *versus* UK, 442–44
    on West End, 429–30, 441, 442
'We Will Rock You,' 443
*We Young People Nowadays*, 598
'What Is Musical Theatre?' (Weill), 454–55
'What's the Buzz', 77–78
'What's the Use of Wond'rin', 926
'What Would You Do?,' 489, 490–91
Wheeler, Hugh, 26–27, 616–17, 619–20, 624, 626, 630–31, 634, 638, 676
'When You're an Addams', 80
'When You're Good to Mama', 722
*Where Do We Go from Here?*, 481, 483
*Where's Charley?*, 325
White, George, 595–96
White, Jerry, 668
*White-Haired Girl, The*, 603
*White Horse Inn*, 493–94, 511–12, 537–38
Whiteman, Paul, 455–56
Whitfield, Sarah, 877
'Who Better than Me,' 251
'Why Do the Wrong People Travel?,' 389–90
*Wicked*, 12, 96–97, 516–19, 520–21, 535–36, 644n.122, 730, 906–7, 918
    as allegory of erasure of people of colour, 900–1
*Wicked* (film), 900

*Wide Boys Never Work* (Westerby), 408–9
*Wiedźmin*, 819–20
Wiemers, Judith, 22
*Wie Wordt Tarzan?*, 250, 255–56
Wijhe, Jeroen van, 17
Wikham, Chrissy, 432f
Wild, Jonathan, 668, 669
Wildeblood, Peter, 411
Wildhorn, Frank, 23, 101–2, 522, 527–31, 529t, 532f, 535, 536, 799
Wild Rice, 102
Wilkinson, Colm, 707
Williams, John, 680
Williams, Michael, 868
Williams, Tennessee, 194
Williamson, J. C., 868
'Willkommen,' 489
Wilson, Rebel, 418–19
Wilson, Sandy, 299–300
*Witches of Eastwick, The*, 799, 916–17
Witherspoon, Reese, 901
Wittenbrink, Franz, 536
*Wiz, The*, 907–8
*Wizard of Oz, The* (film), 900
'Wohl der Nacht,' 722
Wolf, Matt, 715
Wolf, Stacy, 382–83, 485
Wolgers, Beppe, 625, 626, 630, 634
Wollman, Elizabeth, 716n.3
*Woman of the Year*, 331
women
    Black, 878–79, 903
    cross-dressing, cultural appropriation and, 920–23
    exclusion of, missing female voice and, 916–20, 927
    inclusion as minority voices, 928–29
    as musical theatre consumers, 918
    post-feminism in new musicals and, 923–26, 925f
    in post-war British theatre, gender roles and, 374–78, 381–83, 384–86, 394
    systemic prejudice against, 915–16
    theatre directors, 914, 916, 918, 926, 928
Wood, David, 221, 235
Woolf, Virginia, 676–77
Woolford, Julian, 327

970 INDEX

'World Is Waiting for the Sunrise, The,' 291
World War II, 372–73, 374–76, 384, 403–4, 461, 555–56, 625–26, 809
'Worst Pies in London, The,' 681–82
*Woyzeck*, 848
*Woza Albert!*, 169, 170
*Wozzeck*, 677, 679
Wright, Adrian, 386
Wright, Laurence, 164–65
*Wunder von Bern, Das*, 513, 534–35

**X**

*Xanadu*, 584–85
*Xcalibur*, 589
Xiaozhong, Xu, 607
Xueqin, Cao, 600

**Y**

YEA. *See* Youth Ensemble of Atlanta
Yegrin Musical Theatre, 572
yellowface, 920, 923
'yenka, La,' 80
YG Entertainment, 584–85
Yin, Jing, 888n.26
Yingchen, Zhou, 599–600
Yi Wang, 3, 4, 36–37n.4

Ylipää, Maria, 764f
Ylvisåker, Vegard and Bård, 103
Yongmin Kwon, 24–25
'You'll Be in My Heart', 253
Young, Toby, 441
'You're a Long, Long Way from America', 389
Youth Ensemble of Atlanta (YEA), 876–77

**Z**

'Zabili, zabili chlapa z Koločavy,' 794–95
Zajac-Kiedysz, Aleksandra, 29
Zard, David, 713
*Zar lässt sich photographieren, Der*, 483–84
Zern, Leif, 627–28, 631, 633
*Zhou Xuan*, 600
Ziegfeld, Florenz, 11, 218
*Ziemia obiecana*, 819–20
Zimmermann, Christoph, 455–56
'Život je jen náhoda,' 783
*Zorba*, 617, 618
*Zorro*, 270
Zou Hang, 103
Županič, Ladislav, 797
*Zuzana je sama doma*, 788
Żywulska, Krystyna, 812